AF605831

Art through a Lifetime

The Mary Griggs Burke Collection

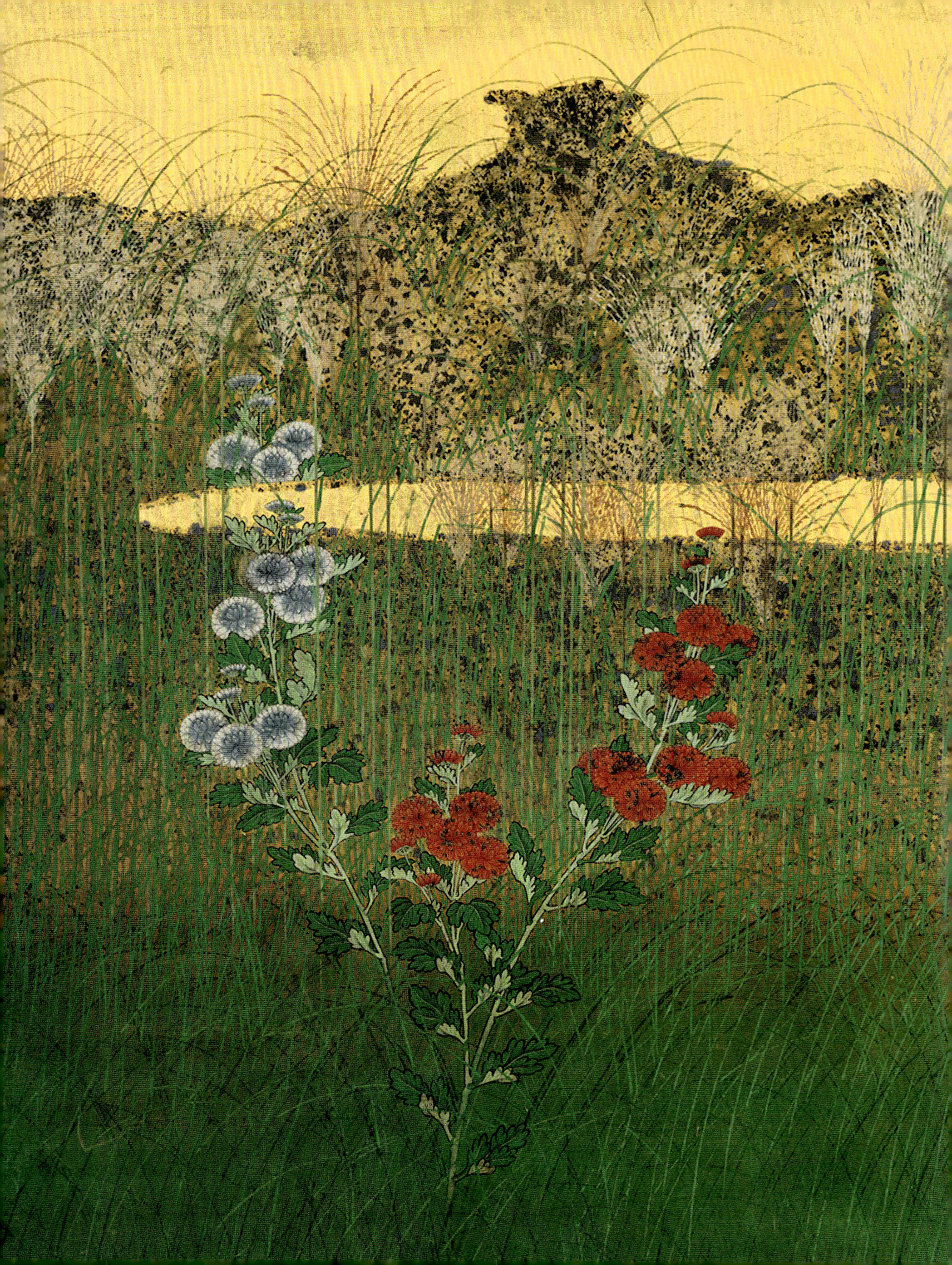

Art through a Lifetime

The Mary Griggs Burke Collection

Volume 1: Japanese Paintings, Printed Works, Calligraphy

Miyeko Murase

Il Kim, Shi-yee Liu, Gratia Williams Nakahashi, Stephanie Wada

MARY AND JACKSON BURKE FOUNDATION

Distributed by University of Washington Press, Seattle

Gratia Williams Nakahashi, Curator
Stephanie Wada, Associate Curator

Mary Gladue, Project Manager
Bruce Campbell, Designer
Amanda Freymann, Production Manager
Aardvark Type, Desktop Publishing
Mary Cason, Bibliography Editor / Proofreader
Il Kim, Special Consultant

Color separations by Professional Graphics, Inc., Rockford, IL
Printed and bound by Conti Tipocolor, Calenzano, Italy

"History of the Collection" by Mary Griggs Burke, is reprinted, in modified form, from *A Selection of Japanese Art from the Mary and Jackson Burke Collection* (New York, 1985) with the kind permission of the Chunichi Shimbun, Nagoya, Japan.

Distributed by:
University of Washington Press
P.O. Box 50096
Seattle, Washington 98145-5096
USA
www.washington.edu/uwpress/

Library of Congress Control Number: 2013949640
ISBN 978-0-295-99268-6

Cover: Flowers of the Four Seasons, Momoyama period, late 16th century
Pair of six-panel screens; ink and color on gilded paper
Detail from No. 136

Frontispiece: Musashino (武蔵野), Edo period, early 17th century
Pair of six-panel folding screens; ink, color, gold and silver on paper
Detail from No. 211

Page ix: Mary Griggs Burke as a young woman
Undated photograph from the collection of Jane Paetzold Matteson, courtesy of Fredric Matteson

Contents

Dedication to Mary Griggs Burke

These volumes are a testament to the late Mary Griggs Burke. During her career, Mary inspired, encouraged, and promoted countless individuals here and abroad—myself included—who are involved in the appreciation and study of the arts of Japan. She, along with the foundation she established, assembled one of the finest private collections of Japanese art, renowned for its broad scope and encompassing remarkable objects from Japan's prehistoric era to the present day. Among its holdings are Buddhist and Shinto art, early narrative painting, ink monochrome painting, works by artists of various Edo-period schools, calligraphy, sculpture, ceramics, lacquer, metalwork, and printed material. Mary's interests also extended to the art of China and Korea, some fine examples of which are in her collection.

Recalling her own childhood, Mary Burke described her fascination with a kimono her mother brought back from a trip to Japan in 1902: a black silk garment whose simple but dramatic decoration consisted of a pine tree covered with snow. There is a striking resonance between her recollection and an episode involving the great Rinpa-school artist Ogata Kōrin (1658–1716), who was asked by one of his patrons, the powerful government official Nakamura Kuranosuke (d. 1730), to design a kimono for his wife to wear to a fashion "contest." The participants in this event were the wealthiest women in Kyoto, and they arrived dressed in the most sumptuous and brightly colored kimonos imaginable. Nakamura's wife made her appearance in the garment designed by Kōrin: a raven-black kimono over an immaculate white robe, which stood out against the riot of colors displayed by other ladies. What was particularly noteworthy about Mary as a collector was her natural appreciation for Japanese aesthetics, and these anecdotes remind me of how she frequently joked that she must have been Japanese in a previous life. She was at ease with scholars, dealers, and other individuals active in the Japanese art world, and they accepted her into their unique circles.

My first collaboration with Mary Burke was in 1965, when she asked me to accompany her to Japan and introduce her to art dealers there. Among her first purchases during that short trip was *Seiryū Gongen* (No. 36), a rare painting of a female Shinto deity; I was truly impressed by her choice. Rather than a pretty rendering of flowers or an *ukiyo-e* beauty, she chose a Kamakura-period Shinto painting, a selection indicative of the serious collector she would become. I might add that a Buddhist mandala she wished to purchase at the same time was denied an export permit by the Bunkachō, Japan's Agency for Cultural Affairs, because it was considered a painting of such importance that it should not be taken out of the country. During this brief stay in Japan, dealers in both Tokyo and Kyoto gave her the nickname "Princess." They were impressed by her genuine modesty, gracious enthusiasm, and intellectual curiosity, attributes they associated with the aristocracy.

Art historians and curators, especially in Japan, assisted Mary in finding objects that might be appropriate for her collection. Especially helpful to her tireless search for important or rare objects were many prominent scholars, among them the late professors Matsushita Takaaki, Akiyama Terukazu, Tanaka Ichimatsu, and Tayama Hōnan. Among the younger generation of scholars were Hashimoto Sumiko, Hayashiya Seizō, Kawai Masatomo, Nakano Masaki, Nishida Hiroko, Shimbo Tōru, and Tsuji Nobuo, whose expertise covered a wide range of genres and periods of Japanese art. All enabled her to expand and enrich her collection. She also enjoyed warm friendships with museum directors, including Hatakeyama Hisako of the Hatakeyama Museum, the late Miho Koyama of the Miho Museum, the late Sugahara Hisao of the Nezu Institute of Art, and the late Yoshioka Yōji of the MOA Museum of Art in Atami and the Hakone Museum of Art in Gōra. In the United States, museum directors—among them the late Gordon Washburn of the Asia Society; the late Harold P. Stern of the Freer Gallery of Art; and Evan Mauer, former director of the Minneapolis Institute of Arts—as well as scholars, including Cornelius Chang, Louise Cort, Wen Fong, Barbara Brennan Ford, Laura Kaufman, Thomas Lawton, Julia Meech, and William Rathbun, aided her in her quest for knowledge.

In the early years of Mary Burke's career as a collector, her husband, Jackson, a noted designer of typefaces, supported her with his keen sensibility, his astute eye, and the intelligent insight of an experienced artist. She treasured and depended on Jackson's help, and was devastated when he passed away in 1975, weeks before the opening of the first exhibition of the Burke Collection at The Metropolitan Museum of Art, New York. A few of us who worked closely with Mary were concerned that she might lose enthusiasm for collecting after this sad event; fortunately, she eventually regained her strength and continued with renewed passion and energy.

Mary impressed a number of art dealers, some of whom expressed a special interest in helping her. The assistance and encouragement of the late Hosomi Minoru, Mayuyama Junkichi, Muraguchi Shirō, Setsu Iwao, Takahashi Tarō, Yabumoto Sōshirō, and the staff of Kochūkyo in Tokyo will always be remembered. Among the next generation of dealers and scholars, Tajima Mitsuru of London Gallery, Tokyo, and, in New York, Frederick Baekeland, Leighton Longhi, Kōichi Yanagi, Sebastian Izzard, and Keum Ja Kang were unstintingly helpful in expanding Mary's knowledge of and appreciation for various aspects of Japanese and Korean art.

Mary's acquisitions increased exponentially, so much so that in 1975 the Metropolitan Museum hosted an exhibition of her collection. In 1985 the Tokyo National Museum also presented an exhibition of the collection—it was, at the time, the museum's only exhibit of a private collection of Japanese art from abroad. Mary continued to make her collected works available to the public through various exhibitions, which culminated in 2000 with a second exhibition at the Metropolitan Museum.

Needless to say, working with Mary also expanded my friendships with collectors, scholars, and dealers, and enriched my career in the field of Japanese art history. The most rewarding experience for me was to watch her respond to objects with genuine appreciation; an example was her instant attraction to the Iga-ware water jar (No. 608) that is one of the gems of her collection. While I understood its unique quality from reading about and studying such pieces, she responded to this object with spontaneous intuition. No explanation was necessary for her to appreciate the peculiar beauty of the vessel, which epitomizes the aesthetics of the tea ceremony.

Not only did Mary make her treasures accessible to students, she was also a devoted patron of my graduate teaching program at Columbia University, New York. As a result, many students received financial support for their study and the opportunity to travel to Japan for research. Once a year, she held a "seminar" at her home in Oyster Bay, Long Island, where my students, and sometimes visiting scholars from Japan, assembled for a weekend of examining works of art in beautiful surroundings. These gatherings remain a cherished memory.

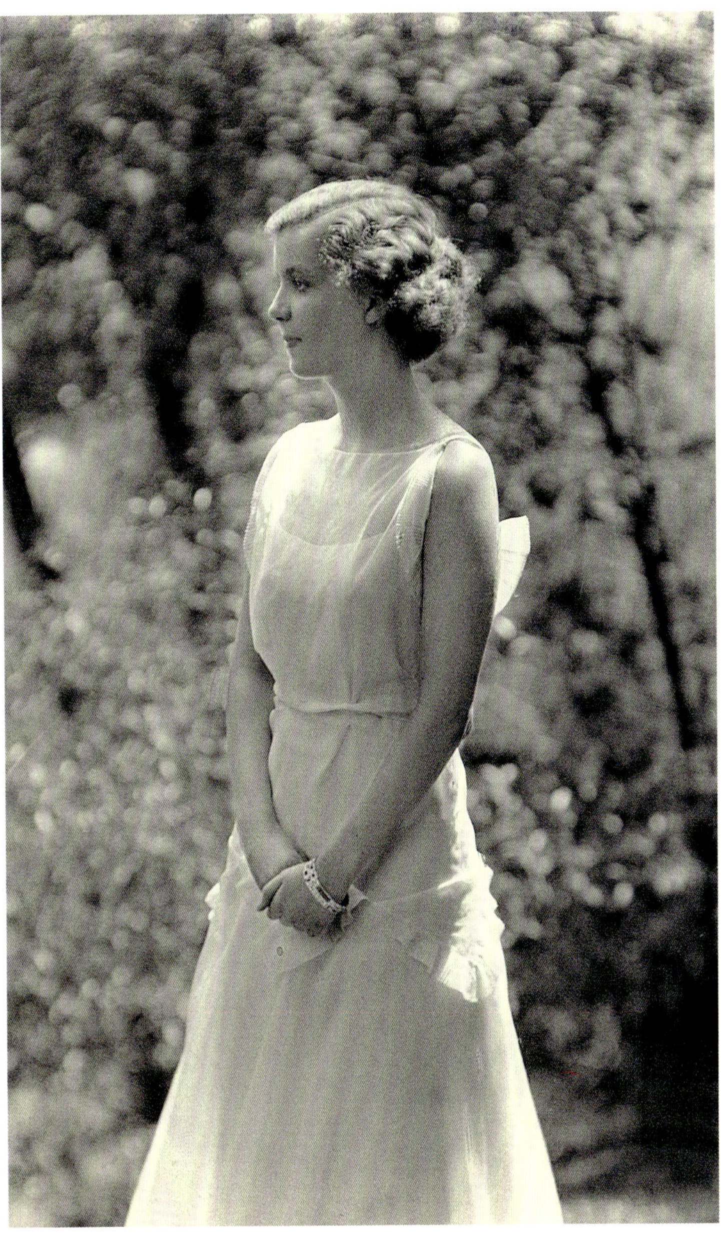

Looking back on the career of Mary Burke, it is truly fitting for her to have been known to the Japanese as "the Mother of Japanese Art in America," and to have been awarded the Order of the Sacred Treasure, Gold and Silver Star, by the Japanese government in 1987. Indeed, she traveled a splendid, treasure-filled road, evolving, over time, from a "Princess" to a "Mother." It has been a rare honor and a most rewarding experience to have collaborated with Mary Burke for more than forty years. I am, as so many are, indebted to her for her tireless devotion to the arts of Japan, and for her outstanding and far-reaching legacy.

Miyeko Murase
Professor Emerita, Columbia University
Former Special Consultant, Department of Asian Art, The Metropolitan Museum of Art

Preface

Mary and Jackson Burke began collecting Japanese art in the 1960s. The number of artworks they acquired quickly grew, but the Burkes soon realized that if their dream to create an outstanding collection was to come to fruition, an additional entity for supporting this goal should be established. In 1972, the Mary and Jackson Burke Foundation was incorporated; its principal purposes, which still govern, are to "operate in the areas of the arts, including the collection of works of art, the exhibition of the same by itself or other organizations... by making the same available for inspection and study to educational organizations, the students thereof, and to other organizations...and to members of the general public."

The Foundation's first board of directors consisted of Mr. and Mrs. Burke; Richard A. Moore and myself, their attorneys; and Orley R. Taylor, their accountant. Mary Griggs Burke served as President of the Foundation from its inception through December 4, 2008. She was then elected Honorary President and served until her death on December 8, 2012; Jackson Burke was Vice President until his death in 1975. C. E. Bayliss Griggs succeeded Mary Burke as President. Current officers, in addition to the undersigned, are Eleanor Briggs, President, and Gale L. Davis, Vice President. The collecting begun by Mr. and Mrs. Burke was continued by the Foundation under the succeeding directors.

Over the years, Mary Burke donated many works of art from her collection to the Foundation. Additional objects were acquired through grants from the Mary Livingston Griggs and Mary Griggs Burke Foundation, and as gifts from others. Most of the objects still owned by Mrs. Burke at her death were bequeathed to the Foundation. Those works, along with those owned by the Foundation, comprise what is now referred to as the Mary Griggs Burke Collection. This assemblage of art objects, which exceeds 1,000 in number, is highlighted in the catalogue and will be distributed to several major museums in the United States.

The Foundation made its first purchase on May 10, 1973: a pair of six-panel folding screens by Kano Sanraku (1559–1635) entitled *View of West Lake* (No. 42). The last work of art acquired, following the death of Mary Griggs Burke, is a magnificent pair of early seventeenth-century six-panel folding screens depicting cherry and willow trees against a background of gold leaf. Both works exemplify the quality of the acquisitions aspired to by the Foundation.

The Burke Collection is generally recognized as one of the most important collections of Japanese art in private hands outside of Japan. Through the generosity of Mary Burke, it has been accessible for study by scholars, students, and specialists in the field, as well as to the general public through loans and exhibitions held at museums here and abroad. With the knowledge that the collection would be dispersed in the near future, it was decided that a catalogue should be compiled to illustrate its scope and richness. The current officers and directors of the Foundation wish to honor the leadership of Mary Burke by creating a lasting record of the collection, and this publication is dedicated to her.

This catalogue, which we hope will benefit scholars, students, and collectors alike, would not have been possible without the efforts of Miyeko Murase, who, throughout the years of collecting, worked so closely with Mary Burke. The assistance of her curators, Gratia Williams Nakahashi and Stephanie Wada and their predecessor Andrew Pekarik, has been outstanding and has enabled the collection to thrive.

We want to thank all who were involved in the preparation of these volumes, as it was a time-consuming, arduous process requiring strong scholarship and dedication. We are honored and proud to present this publication reflecting the career of a remarkable and dedicated collector.

Marvin J. Pertzik
Executive Director, Secretary, and Treasurer
Mary and Jackson Burke Foundation

Acknowledgments

This publication was undertaken to document the outstanding career of Mary Griggs Burke as a collector and connoisseur of Asian Art, in particular the art of Japan. It also marks the closure of a collaboration among Mary Burke, Marvin J. Pertzik, Miyeko Murase, and the curators of the Burke Foundation—Gratia Williams Nakahashi, Stephanie Wada, and, formerly, Andrew Pekarik. This rewarding and fruitful collaboration has spanned nearly fifty years. We must mention that numerous art history scholars in America, Japan, and elsewhere, as well as countless art dealers in America and abroad, have strengthened the collection by offering their unstinting assistance to Mary Burke as her collecting career evolved.

Compiling a record of this magnitude required the efforts of a large number of dedicated individuals. Our deepest gratitude goes to Marvin Pertzik, who, as the Secretary and Treasurer of the Mary and Jackson Burke Foundation, understands the importance of the collection and realized the need to create a record of the outstanding objects acquired by Mary Burke in the tangible form of a book. In addition, we wish to thank the other members of the Burke Foundation board of directors—Eleanor Briggs, President, and Gale Davis, Vice President—for their staunch support of our work.

Indispensable assistance was rendered by Soyoung Lee, Associate Curator of Korean Art, The Metropolitan Museum of Art, New York, and David Ake Sensabaugh, Ruth and Bruce Dayton Curator of Asian Art, Yale University Art Museum, New Haven, Connecticut, who examined and compiled the catalogue of the Korean and Chinese art objects, respectively. Kōichi Yanagi of Kōichi Yanagi Oriental Fine Arts, New York, generously offered his time, knowledge, and expertise in evaluating certain atypical and uncommon pieces. His work was facilitated by his devoted staff members Yoshinori Munemura and Masaki Naitō.

As some objects required conservation treatment before they were photographed, this critical work was carried out with great expertise by two veteran conservators: Mitsuhiro Abe, formerly of The Metropolitan Museum of Art, New York, and The British Museum, London, who worked on paintings, calligraphy, and screens; and Shinichi Doi, formerly of the Metropolitan Museum, who dealt with three-dimensional objects. Their sincere concern for the conservation and preservation of artworks is deeply appreciated. Moreover, we are most grateful to the Sumitomo Foundation in Tokyo for bestowing over a four-year period grant funds to the Burke Foundation for the delicate work of conserving two sets of highly important handscrolls, a *Genji monogatari emaki* (No. 82) and a *Kumano no honji emaki* (No. 41), that were in serious need of repair.

Our special admiration and gratitude go to two scholars in the Department of Asian Art at The Metropolitan Museum of Art: Wei Zheng, Research Consultant, who deciphered many of the artists' seals; and Shi-yee Liu, Assistant Research Curator of Chinese Art, who translated with precision and clarity most of the inscriptions and colophons in Chinese into English. We regret that it was not possible to include here all of Dr. Liu's relevant research, which reflects her considerable scholarship and knowledge of Chinese history and literature; it is hoped that this information will be included in the digital version of the catalogue.

Our most sincere appreciation goes to Dr. Il Kim, Assistant Professor, Department of History of Art and Design, Pratt Institute, Brooklyn, New York. Given his deep knowledge of art history and his thorough understanding of Japanese culture and art in particular, Dr. Kim was invited to act as a special consultant in the preparation of the Japanese art sections. His commitment to scholarship, his meticulous attention to the myriad details required, and his infinite patience were indispensable in the completion of this work.

We are deeply indebted to the following staff members of the Department of Asian Art at the Metropolitan Museum: James C. Y. Watt, Brooke Russell Astor Chairman Curator Emeritus; Maxwell K. Hearn, Douglas Dillon Curator in Charge; Judith G. Smith, Senior Administrator; and Hwai-ling Yeh-Lewis, Senior Collections Manager. These individuals expedited the use of the department's facilities and resources, and thereby greatly aided our research for this publication. In this regard we thank Joan Mirviss of the Mirviss Gallery, who shared with us her knowledge of woodblock prints and made her precious library available for research in the field of contemporary ceramics. We also appreciate the assistance of Matthew Welch, Deputy Director and Chief Curator, The Minneapolis Institute of Arts, regarding technical questions related to the Japanese ceramics section. We also extend our appreciation to Gen P. Sakamoto and Noelle King O'Connor, Burke Foundation gallery and research assistants, for their help over the years.

On numerous occasions there was an urgent need to consult various specialists in Japan, and a number of our close friends and colleagues were generous in their assistance. Those who deserve special mention are Kawai Masatomo, Professor Emeritus, Keio University, Tokyo; Shimbo Tōru, Professor Emeritus, Tsukuba University; Nishida Hiroko, Executive Trustee and Deputy Director of the Nezu Institute of Art, Tokyo, and Matsumura Makiko; the late Nakano Masaki, Professor, Tokyo Art University; and Tajima Mitsuru, London Gallery, Tokyo.

The exquisite design of this catalogue is the work of Bruce Campbell, with whom we have collaborated on a number of occasions. His design sensitivity ingeniously met the needs of the project.

The publication is greatly enhanced by the images produced by a team of renowned veteran photographers under the supervision of Stephanie Wada. Christopher Burke, Sheldan C. Collins, Bruce Schwarz, and Bruce White faithfully captured the integrity and beauty of more than one thousand works of art in the collection.

Amanda Freymann, the Production Manager, expertly fulfilled her role, so demanding with a publication of this size, in assuring the quality of the color reproductions and overseeing prepress and printing. Patrick Goley, CEO of Professional Graphics, Inc., was invaluable in lending his eye for color to the proofing process, and Jane Messenger had the unenviable task of tracking the thousands of images as they went through the color separation and proofing process. The intelligence and care with which their coworker Bob Rubey made endless corrections has served this volume well.

It was an unimaginably complex job that fell on the shoulders of Project Manager Mary Gladue, who tirelessly guided the catalogue through the various phases of publication and also was responsible for copyediting and typesetting the manuscripts. She extends heartfelt gratitude to Mary Cason, who edited the bibliography and proofread both volumes; Sarah Jean Dupont, who helped with fact-checking, word processing, and the initial organization; Melanie B. D. Klein, who proofread portions of the galleys; and Dr. Kim, for being such an effective liaison.

We are deeply grateful to all those who have been involved with this project and who dedicated their energy, time, and talent to this monumental endeavor. While these participants are not responsible for any of the unfortunate yet inevitable errors and omissions, the credit for bringing these volumes to fruition belongs to them.

Miyeko Murase
Gratia Williams Nakahashi
Stephanie Wada

An Appreciation

BY JAMES T. ULAK

This publication marks a moment of transition, closure, and generational shift. It signals the end of a significant episode in the history of Japanese-American cultural exchange. For Mary Griggs Burke, these volumes constitute a summary statement of achievement and draw a gentle line indicating that a deeply consuming personal activity has come to an end. They represent the best available perspectives and research on a splendid range of art—diverse in media and chronology—produced across the history of Japanese visual expression. Scholarly commentary about the collection has emerged in incremental elaborations over many years, often the result of an exhibition project or a discrete research project. The nature of the Burke Collection, in its diversity and depth, is that it bears continued scrutiny and continues to yield surprise and reward.

For more than forty years the Burke Collection has stood as the first among equals: a private Western collection of Japanese art, which both in its scope and in its sense of stewardship has been a benchmark endeavor for like-minded collectors. Now, in that same position of leadership, the Collection, along with several others in that rarefied postwar collectors' fraternity, is poised to come to terms with its own definition of "the fullness of time."

Mary Burke has elsewhere described in the most charming and particular detail the evolution of her interest in Japanese art—tracing early, inchoate exposure that only in a later light indicated influence and direction, extended family interests in Japan, work with Walter Gropius, the essential partnership with Jackson Burke, and the long period after Mr. Burke's passing when, in life radically altered, Mrs. Burke embraced more vigorously than ever the consolations and delights of Japanese art.

Indeed it is from that time through the past forty years that most of us now active in the field of Japanese art came to know Mrs. Burke. She has narrated the details of her collecting experience, the combined moments of rational choice and wild serendipity that bring about a collection of this scale. Although with characteristic modesty she refrains from situating her vocation in historical terms, in reality Mary Burke was in the vanguard of collectors, scholars, and museum professionals who oversaw one of the most important cultural rapprochements in modern times—when the cultural patrimony of a recently vilified enemy became a standard of aesthetic refinement and intense scholarly interest. From the vantage point of nearly seventy years, we can see that Mary and Jackson Burke and their confreres built a welcoming haven of excellence for several generations of scholars, museum professionals, and connoisseurs.

The Burke Collection welcomed all comers but was particularly attentive in encouraging the professional training of academics and museum curators. The Burke Collection has, as well, been a particularly helpful and cordial colleague with museums seeking a collaborative partner or, indeed, assistance in enhancing their collections of Japanese art. Whether by supporting growth in the appreciation of Japanese art through use of the art resources of the Collection, or through the generosity of the Mary and Jackson Burke Foundation, Mary Burke has served as a primary force in creating in the United States what is surely the most vital cadre of Japanese art specialists found anywhere outside of Japan itself.

For many of us, particularly at the graduate-student level, the first visit to the Burke Collection was an important rite of passage. In most circumstances, this visit involved a greeting from Mrs. Burke and her questions about our particular interests. Never pro forma courtesies, her queries were sharp and she listened carefully. Even the most junior among us felt elevated by her attention, taken seriously. Some of us had the privilege of many visits and associations well beyond the student years. Even after the transition from neophyte to good-natured competitor in the market for beautiful things, the gracious, collegial welcome into this rarefied world never changed.

With the initiation came exposure to extraordinary art. Not art as seen in photographs or slides, not art observed in hushed museum galleries or stark storage rooms, but art loved and lived with in an intimate context. This, we learned, was something beyond the level of a convenient repository of extraordinary documentary information that could be used in support of this project or that research. It was a world in which acquisitive passion was endorsed and idiosyncratic perspectives were welcomed. A place where "encounter" trumped "inspection." It was an invitation to look close, to touch, to handle, and to gain confidence in one's unformed but immediate reactions.

Many of us hold particular works in the Burke Collection in the special affection accorded to formative encounters. Over the years, those works have beckoned again and continue to reveal new facets. Or rather, they reveal the maturation of our tastes and understandings.

In her generosity and intelligence, and with her twinkling eyes and gracious, diminutive presence, Mary Burke has orchestrated the essential encounters and enriched us all.

James T. Ulak
Senior Curator of Japanese Art
The Freer Gallery and the Arthur Sackler Gallery
Smithsonian Institution

History of the Collection

BY MARY GRIGGS BURKE

Japanese style and beauty first struck me when I saw my mother's kimono, a padded winter one of black silk displaying at the knee a bold design of twisted pine branches covered with snow. She had gotten it in Japan as a young woman, just after the turn of the century. She wore it with the slim grace of the princess in James Abbott McNeill Whistler's painting *Princess from the Land of Porcelain* (1836–65), which hangs in the famous Peacock Room at the Freer Gallery of Art in Washington, D.C. Mother's taste in clothes was elegant, and the kimono attained its striking effect not through brilliant color or intricate pattern, but by its dramatic white-on-black design. I can remember putting it on and letting it trail behind me; I believe a future collector of Japanese art was born then.

In considering this vivid memory of childhood, I realize that my taste has been influenced by a series of such family experiences associated with travel to and ideas from other countries. Cross-cultural currents shape the lives of many Americans. We look back to Europe, whence many of us came, but we also turn with great expectation and interest toward the Orient. In contemplating the activities of my immediate forebears, I have a sense of the movement, drive, and curiosity that linked them with cultures other than our own.

My maternal grandfather, Crawford Livingston, came from an old New York family.[1] The founder of the Livingston family in America, Robert, was a Scotsman who arrived in this country in the early seventeenth century. He received a large land grant and the title Lord of the Manor from the British crown. Four generations later the American Revolution put an end to the title. Livingstons served in that war and helped draft and sign the Declaration of Independence and the Constitution. They produced several eminent men in the fields of government, law, and commerce in the new United States of America.

Although he grew up in New York, Grandfather Livingston did not remain in the east. He went to Saint Paul, Minnesota, in 1870, fourteen years after my paternal grandfather, Colonel Chauncy Griggs, had moved there from Connecticut. The Colonel had fought in the War Between the States on the Union side. The Griggs family, like the Livingstons, traced its roots in American history to the early seventeenth century. Both of my grandfathers were men of their time. Ambitious and in search of promising business opportunities, each one left the east coast where he was born in order to travel throughout the United States. They both married and raised large families in Saint Paul and established themselves in a variety of successful ventures, including lumber, railroading, and public utilities. Grandfather Livingston eventually returned to New York to help his only surviving son form a banking firm; Grandfather Griggs pressed on to the west coast to extend his lumbering interests in Tacoma, Washington.

While Grandfather Griggs attended to business, his wife and some of his children traveled abroad. Martha Ann Gallop Griggs, my grandmother, took two of her children—my father, Theodore, and a younger sister—to Germany. It was there that Father first studied art. He later learned to express himself in skillful black-and-white ink sketches of landscapes, animals, and people, delighting in caricatures of friends and relatives. His drawings helped sensitize me to the world of the great ink painters of Japan.

His mother—an active, cultured person and a good amateur painter —was a woman of independent mind. She is purported to have made a number of trips to the Orient, including Japan, in the late nineteenth and early twentieth centuries. Unfortunately, I know little of these adventures except for a possibly apocryphal but evidently typical story concerning one of her departures from Tacoma. She was about to board ship when her houseman rushed onto the dock with the news that the house was on fire. She calmly told him to return immediately and put out the fire, while she continued on her journey to Japan with a single-mindedness worthy of a Zen priest.

One of her four sons, my uncle Everett Griggs—who succeeded his father, the Colonel, as head of the Saint Paul and Tacoma Lumber Company—did visit Japan on a business trip after the destructive 1923 earthquake there. While at Yale, Everett had befriended two Japanese classmates. He and his wife, Grace, evidently stayed with these gentlemen and their families in Japan. These friendships must have grown closer during the visit, because soon after their return, the daughter of one Japanese friend came to visit them. She

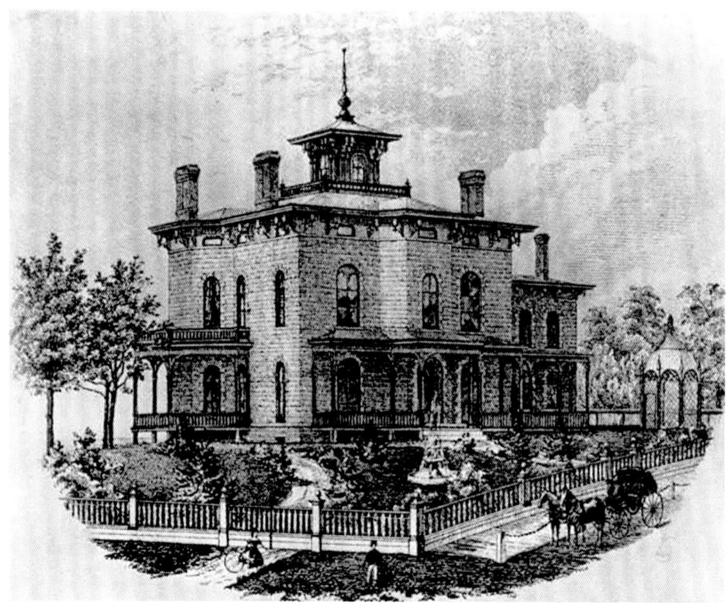

Figure 1. Crawford Livingston residence, Saint Paul, Minnesota. Engraving, 1867

stayed, it is said, for two years and attended school in Tacoma. She brought with her a splendid fourteenth-century painting of a white-robed Kannon [No. 93] as a gift to my aunt and uncle. I have recently acquired this painting, which I had long admired, from the cousin to whom my aunt bequeathed it.

My mother, Mary Livingston Griggs, was not the only member of her family to visit Japan. Accompanied by her mother, a sister, a brother, and two cousins, she went around the world in 1902. In Japan they stopped at Tokyo, Nikkō, and Kyoto, which she especially enjoyed. She went down the Kamo River to shoot the Hozu rapids. She watched cormorant fishing and attended a Noh play. Unfortunately, only her kimono remains to commemorate this early trip to Japan. I believe, however, that the beauty of the country and the spirit of its people affected her deeply. Certainly she loved its gardens. Many years later she built a rock garden with streams, rustic bridges, ferns, moss, and wild flowers in northern Wisconsin at the summer house inherited from her father, Crawford Livingston. This place in turn has meant much to me. Its tall, green pines and sparkling lakes instilled in me a deep love for nature. This feeling helped draw me in my collecting to Zen Buddhist landscape paintings of the Muromachi period that express the essence of natural things and man's close harmony with them. These "landscapes of the soul," which illustrate the quiet seclusion of a mountain retreat, were often used by Zen priests as aids in meditation [No. 104].

Both of my grandfathers acquired large Victorian houses in Saint Paul that were situated on a hilltop boulevard with a commanding view of a magnificent bend in the Mississippi River. There exists a quaint 1867 print of Grandfather Livingston's house, built in 1862–63 by an entrepreneur of the transportation (both riverboat and stagecoach) industry (fig. 1). The print shows the house as a three-story gray-limestone mansion crowned by a low-pitched roof and wooden cupola. The bracketed cornice, round arched windows, and handsomely proportioned belvedere are typical of the villa style so popular in America between 1850 and 1870. Mother, the only one of Grandfather's children to remain in Saint Paul, eventually took it over. My parents were married in this house and I grew up there.

Throughout Mother's life she found much pleasure in collecting antiques, including complete, paneled eighteenth-century European rooms, which were installed cleverly and amazingly in this Victorian house. By the time my mother finished redoing it, the mid-nineteenth-century house contained such a variety of styles and objects from different cultures, including a few Chinese ceramics, that it was like living in a museum. It undoubtedly helped me to develop a respect for old, rare, and carefully crafted objects, and being surrounded by such a variety of interesting things probably gave me an eclectic taste. Collecting was in my blood.

Like Father, Mother was artistically oriented. Late in life she took up painting. She greatly admired the work of the American painter Georgia O'Keeffe, and some of her own pictures resembled that artist's flower paintings. Miss O'Keeffe's exposure to oriental art has manifested itself in her working process of executing a series of paintings on a single theme. Her deep awareness of the forces underlying nature and her adoption of a flat, decorative composition in strong colors also reflected this influence.

Mother was greatly attracted to Miss O'Keeffe's paintings, and in the 1940s she gave me one called *Black Place No. 1* (fig. 2). I believe this painting, more than any other single work of art, has influenced the formation of my own taste.

Another painter who also had a profound influence on my growing aesthetic appreciation was Bradley Walker Tomlin. I studied with him at Sarah Lawrence College. He was an abstract expressionist of the New York School. Tomlin taught me how to look at and really understand a picture. He rejected stereotypes and could grasp the meaning of all true artists. He is purported to have studied Zen ink painting. He introduced me to the calligraphic line of the American action painters, whose brushstrokes resemble oriental calligraphy.

Tomlin inspired me to do some collecting in modern Western art. I acquired a few works by such artists as Maurice Utrillo and Aristide Maillol, as well as a fine example of a surrealist-cubist painting by Tomlin himself.

I studied art history at home and abroad and became more appreciative of modernism in art. The use of shadowless space and unrealistic but strong, clear color had become familiar to me through my acquaintance with the works of both O'Keeffe and Tomlin, as well as through the other modern painters I had collected. When I eventually did go to Japan, I was struck by certain similarities of approach in some traditional schools of Japanese art and some of contemporary Western art, but what impressed me most in Japanese painting was the use of line. In the Ukiyo-e prints and paintings it serves as a strong, black outline for the areas of color, while in ink painting it becomes an extremely sensitive and suggestive shorthand way of presenting both form and content.

It was not until 1954, about thirty years after I coveted my mother's splendid kimono, that I made my first trip to Japan, at the suggestion of the architect Walter Gropius. Becoming more and more involved with the modern movement in painting and architecture, I had decided to build a contemporary open-plan house on the north shore of Long Island near Oyster Bay, New York (fig. 3). For the job I had chosen The Architects Collaborative, or TAC, in Cambridge, Massachusetts, of which Gropius was the head at that time.

He had just returned from a lecture tour in Japan and was full of enthusiasm for things Japanese. The kind of modernism he stood for had much in common with traditional Japanese architecture, epitomized by the Katsura Imperial Villa. Both he and Ben Thompson, the architect of TAC principally responsible for designing my house and its landscaping, thought that visiting the gardens of Japan would give me insight that might help them to create a perfect environment for my house.

Through the International House of Japan, I met the architect Junzō Yoshimura and in his company visited most of the important gardens of the time—both private and public. Mr. Yoshimura was of tremendous help to me in understanding Japanese aesthetics and architecture. We visited many of his buildings and those of other architects of the time, as well as old temples and palaces. We sat on the bamboo moon-viewing platform of the Katsura Imperial Villa and enjoyed looking out over the stroll garden with its lakes, winding paths, and teahouses. From this and other gardens I brought back not only ideas that helped capture some of the spirit of Japan for my own garden but also a profound interest in the entire approach to the arts in that country.

In 1954 the countryside of Japan was still strikingly beautiful. Patterned rice paddies and neat tea plantations surrounded the villages on the plains, covered the low hills, and even reached up to the craggy mountains. The old, dark,

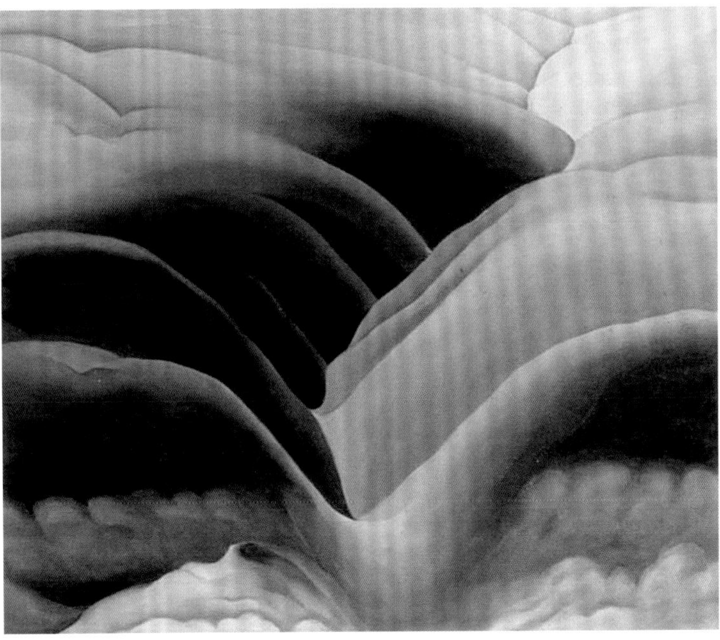

Figure 2. Georgia O'Keeffe (1887–1986), *Black Place No. 1*, 1945. Oil on canvas, 76 x 91 cm (29⅞ x 35⅞ in.). The Mary Griggs Burke Collection

beautifully shaped farmhouses appeared to grow from the green fields, and the people who worked these fields in their dark-blue clothes and broad straw hats evoked a sense of belonging and harmony with the scene. Art played a large part in the daily lives of the people. The distinction between high art and craft was not so sharply drawn as in the West. Art seemed an indivisible whole embracing lacquer, ceramics, paintings, textiles, and much more. This aesthetic sensitivity showed in what the people wore, in the utensils they used for eating, and even in the arrangement of food on a plate, as well as in their architecture and masterpieces of sculpture and painting. Although modern development has done away with much of the picturesque quality of the scenery that I saw in '54, this attitude toward art as a total way of life still prevails in Japan to the present day.

During that trip I fell in love with Japan, and I have continued to admire this country, its people, and its art. Although I was profoundly moved by the beauty of the paintings and the sculptures that I saw in museums and temples, unfortunately I acquired only a few attractive souvenirs—some modern ceramics—including a large plate by Hamada, which I gave away as a present, and a number of Meiji prints.

It was in the United States that I found my first important Japanese art object. In 1956 I bought at auction an Edo-period screen that had once belonged to Frank Lloyd Wright. It depicts six episodes from the early part of *The Tale of Genji* focusing on the Dance of the Blue Waves in chapter seven, "The Autumn Excursion." Although my interest in Japanese

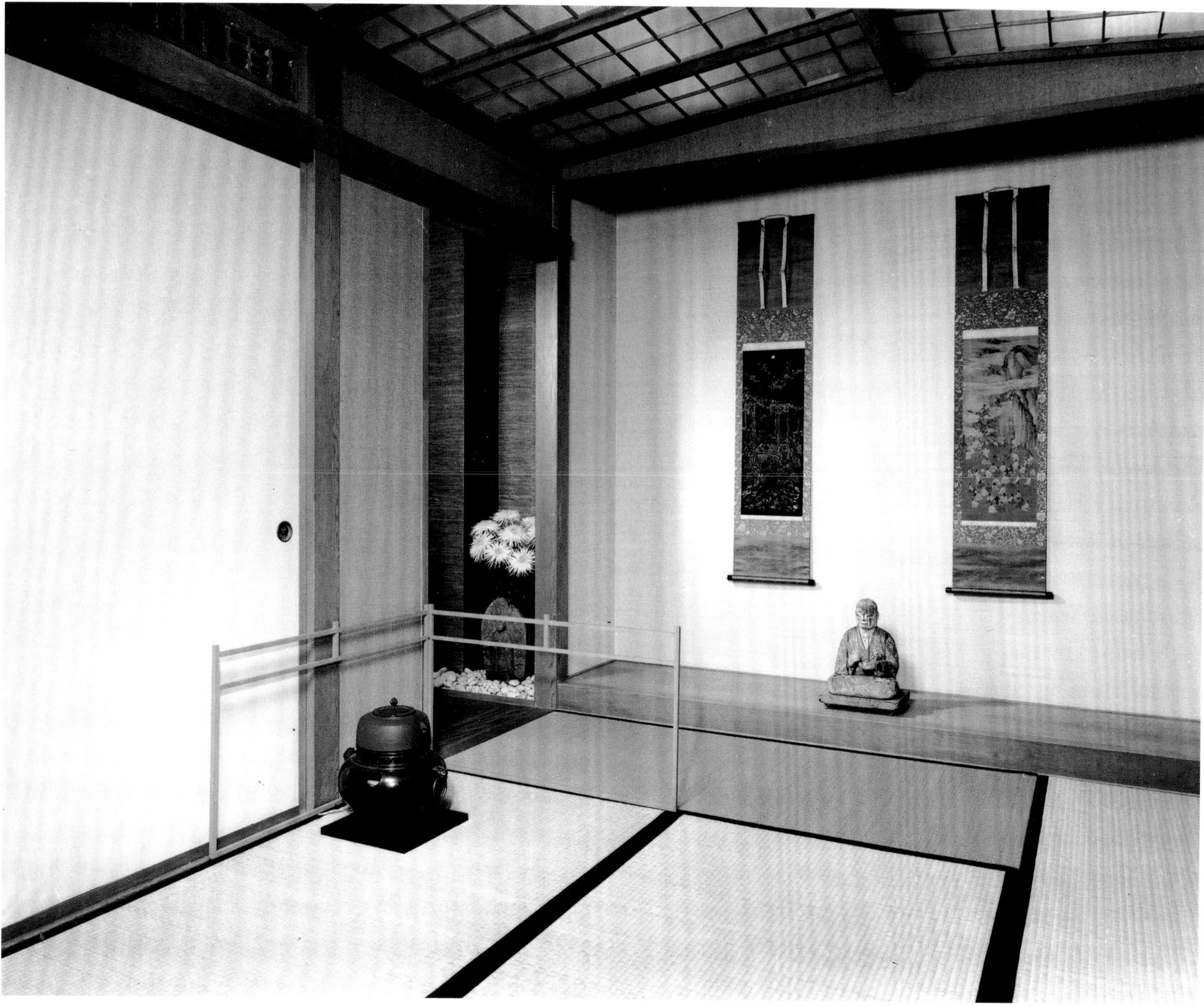

Figure 5. Tea room designed by Yasuhide Kobashi (1931–2003)

also acquired ceramics, lacquer, and metal objects from all periods. I cannot say that we consciously made a decision to amass examples from every area of Japanese art; certain categories of items popular with many collectors, such as prints, inrō, haniwa, and decorative porcelains, are either completely lacking or represented by only a few examples.

As I learned more about Japanese art and its variety, I not only developed more definite preferences for certain areas, but also became more discriminating and able to choose the best from among the paintings and objects available to me. Although I was and still am most deeply moved by Muromachi ink paintings, which I started to collect in 1967 under the guidance of Professor Murase, their number in the collection is small because of their rarity and their value to the Japanese.

The factor of luck—being in the right place at the right time—accounts to some degree for the fact that thirty percent of the collection consists of works from two Edo-period schools, Ukiyo-e and Nanga. We had acquired the entire Hart Collection of Ukiyo-e in 1963 and a large number of Nanga paintings in 1967 and 1968. Those two categories of paintings make good foils for each other. The robust, colorful, town-oriented Ukiyo-e we first admired found their complement in the Chinese-inspired, literary, and nature-celebrating Nanga works. The collection possesses screens by two of the most famous Nanga artists—*The Gathering at the Orchid Pavilion* and *Autumn Festival* by Taiga [No. 323], and *Travels through Mountains and Fields* by Buson [No. 312].

During the 1960s and early 1970s I was able to pick up bargains in both the United States and Japan, because at that time only a few serious collectors of Japanese art existed in America and there was a lull in the art market in Japan. I believe that if we had not built the special gallery to display our treasures, the collection would not have grown so rapidly and successfully during these years of golden opportunity. It was a wonderfully happy and fruitful period of my life for which I shall always remain grateful.

When my husband died in 1975, I did not stop collecting. Although I missed both his good taste and his capacity for organization, there was something still within me that found release only through continuing to seek out the beautiful and enjoy it with others. Perhaps that need to collect and share my treasures became even stronger after I lost him.

My husband and I had always possessed religious works, but after his death I bought more of them. In 1979 it became necessary for the designer Kobashi to add another small gallery to the mini-museum in order to display religious objects, sculpture, and painting—both Shinto and Buddhist. Again the aim was not to produce an authentic setting. Instead of a temple, Kobashi created an atmosphere of calm simplicity in which religious icons would look at home.

The largest statue in the collection—which occupies a special niche in my New York gallery for religious objects—depicts the deity Fudō Myōō [No. 553]. This figure has helped me to gain some insight into the rituals of Shingon, the esoteric sect of Buddhism. The disparity between his fierce face and gentle, childlike body underscores the mystic nature of his power. I know he is a force for good, not evil.

Two depictions of the bodhisattva Jizō also increased my appreciation and understanding of certain aspects of Japanese Buddhism. The small Kamakura-period icon, which I found in Paris in 1970 [No. 549], presents Jizō as a sympathetic and accessible deity as well as a beautiful one. The Edo painting of Jizō by Kano Tan'yū [No. 147] acquired in 1981 is a delightful and humorous version. In this painting Jizō sails along on a cloud wearing a charming floppy lotus hat and playing a flute. In spite of a certain lack of dignity, I find this image very moving in its fluidity of line and lightness of spirit. It fills me with joy and hope.

Extra space was needed to accommodate not only the religious art, but also the significant growth in other categories of the collection. Fine Momoyama tea ceramics were being acquired and in 1980 a more serious attempt to collect both calligraphy and lacquer was fostered by our curator, Andrew Pekarik, who had taken over the care of the collection in 1973, two years before my husband died. Mr. Pekarik helped me maintain and expand the collection for ten years, until he became the director of the Asia Society Galleries in 1984. (Since that time, the collection has been cared for by Gratia Williams Nakahashi, Curator, and Stephanie Wada, Associate Curator, who keep the collection in pristine condition, set up small exhibitions for visiting scholars and friends, and serve as registrars for objects on loan. They are invaluable.)

As a student of Heian literature, Mr. Pekarik has knowledge of and a deep interest in calligraphy. He is also a scholar of lacquer ware. Because of this expertise, he advised me on several collection trips to Japan. As a tea master, he made good use of

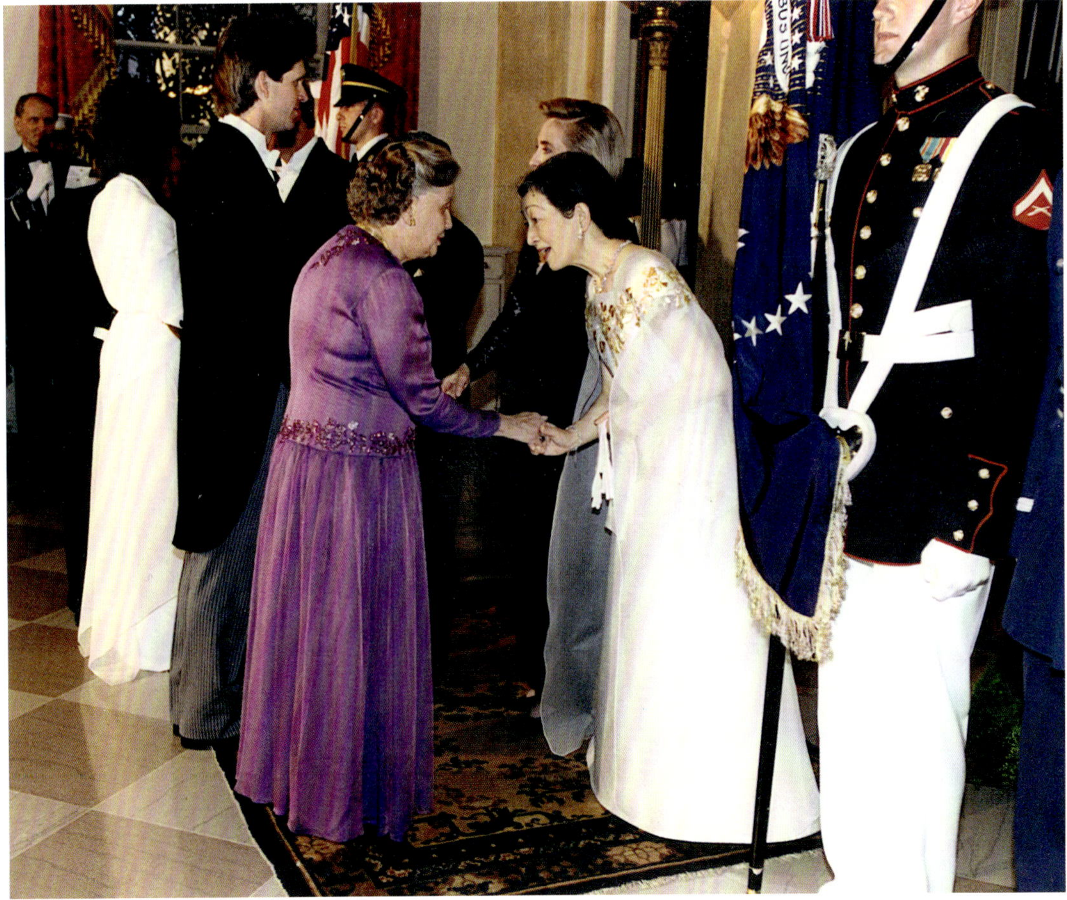

Figure 6. Empress Michiko, wife of Emperor Akihito of Japan, greets Mary Griggs Burke at a White House State Dinner given by President and Mrs. Clinton in honor of the emperor and his wife, June 13, 1994.

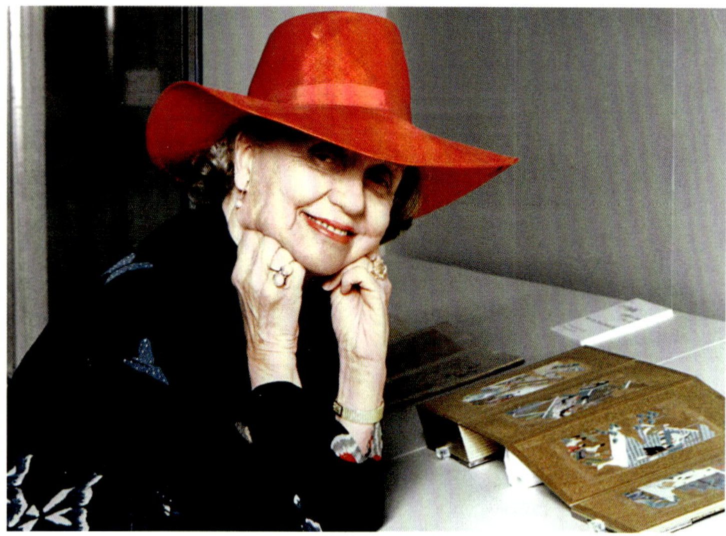

Figure 7. Mary Griggs Burke, 1985

the collection's fine tea ceramics in the tea room that Kobashi had also designed. From 1979 until May 1984 Andrew Pekarik performed 167 tea ceremonies, including the occasional serving of a complete tea meal.

In keeping with its museum function, this tea room could not be completely orthodox. Instead of the usual single one, it possesses two tokonomas, in which attractive groupings of scrolls, objects, and flower arrangements can be made. The fact that Mr. Pekarik held many tea ceremonies in this room for a variety of students and devotees of Japanese art has added a new dimension to the showing of the collection. It demonstrates the way the Japanese share their pleasure in many of the beautiful objects that they collect—flower vases, scrolls of calligraphy and painting, fine ceramics, and lacquer ware—by using them in the tea ceremony. The Japanese are great collectors, and they have a long history of enjoying their collections with others in an intimate and personal way.

The success of this tea room in New York in helping people to appreciate Japanese art has made me think seriously about the future home of these works of art. There are many fine museums in the United States that could care for them properly, but I keep thinking back to my first visit to Japan. I became aware then of the similarity between the Bauhaus theory that inspired my country house and the traditional Japanese approach to art, in which all types of aesthetic manifestations are considered as a creative whole. The traditional Japanese buildings that I visited with the architect Junzō Yoshimura so many years ago had simple, restful interior spaces containing a minimum of carefully crafted furniture and objets d'art. These buildings were set in beautifully and appropriately designed gardens. I have often discussed with Mr. Yoshimura the fact that Japanese art deserves—in fact needs—to be shown in a sympathetic ambience in order to reveal all the nuances of its beauty. This ambience establishes a completeness and wholeness of design in which all of the components, from the smallest to the largest, fit perfectly together. Such a concept exists at the present time as it has in the past. Fortunately, it is seen in Japan not only in the fast-disappearing traditional Japanese buildings but also in a number of fine modern ones, including museums.

Mr. Yoshimura recently made a plan of a museum to house the collection that exemplifies this concept. He combined the best of traditional Japanese architectural ideas with modern technique to create an open, low building that incorporates a garden and a teahouse. This plan includes all the practical modern assets that such a museum must have to protect and display fragile artworks, but it also provides a way to experience and interact with these objects that conveys a sense of their past cultural context. If such a plan were to be realized in a garden near an urban center in the United States, it would have great impact on the way in which Americans perceive Japanese art. It would certainly make a stronger statement than a Japanese setting implanted in a larger, completely Western-style museum. A freestanding museum dedicated entirely to Japanese art and designed by a Japanese architect does not exist in America at the present time. It is still only a dream but perhaps not an impossible one.

1. For additional information on Crawford Livingston, see John M. Lindley, "'No time or sympathy for one who wouldn't work': Crawford Livingston, Colonel Chauncey W. Griggs, and Their Roles in St. Paul History," *Ramsey County History* 34, no. 3 (Fall 1999): 4–29.
2. This essay was slightly modified to conform to the spelling and titles used in the current publication.

Chronology

Protoliterate Era	ca. 12,500 B.C.–A.D. 538
Jōmon period, ca. 12,500–ca. 300 B.C.	
Yayoi period, ca. 300 B.C.–ca. A.D. 300	
Kofun period, ca. A.D. 300–538	
Asuka Period	538–710
Nara Period	710–794
Heian Period	794–1185
Early Heian period, 794–ca. 900	
Late Heian period, ca. 900–1185	
Kamakura Period	1185–1333
Nanbokuchō Period	1333–1392
Muromachi Period	1392–1573
Momoyama Period	1573–1615
Edo Period	1615–1868
Meiji Era	1868–1912
Taishō Era	1912–1926
Shōwa Era	1926–1989
Heisei Era	1989–

Note to the Reader

This two-volume publication offers a visual presentation of the works of art collected by Mary Griggs Burke and the Mary and Jackson Burke Foundation. Included are many of the inscriptions that are visible in the photographs, as well as most of the signatures and seals on the objects themselves. Many of these so-called details are reproduced in close-up and translated at the end of each section.

A number of artworks in volume 1 are related in some way:

- Nos. 161, 305, and 482 have the same subject and closely related compositions;
- Nos. 202 and 494 have the same subject and closely related compositions, including identical figure groupings;
- No. 377 is a sketch of No. 314;
- Nos. 390 and 393 share subject and composition originated by Ōkyo;
- No. 488 is a copy of No. 325;
- No. 501, which bears visual evidence of fire damage to the handscroll, is a record of No. 263;
- No. 503 is a printed record of the pair of screens illustrated in No. 184;
- No. 504 might have been based on No. 288, as they share subject and composition.

All translations of inscriptions, signatures, and seals are by Miyeko Murase and Shi-yee Liu (Japanese art) and David Ake Sensabaugh (Chinese art), unless otherwise noted in Translation Sources, located at the end of volume 2.

Japanese, Korean, and Chinese names appear in traditional style, with family names preceding given names. The Revised Romanization is used for romanization of Korean words. The Pinyin system is used for romanization of Chinese words.

The current owner of each object and a photography credit for its overall image are given at the end of the relevant volume. An index of artists represented in the collection, the bibliography, and acknowledgments of translation sources appear at the end of volume 2.

Following publication of this catalogue raisonné, the Mary and Jackson Burke Foundation intends to sponsor a website (www.burkecollection.org) to greatly expand visual access to the collection. Included will be information that did not fit the format of these volumes, along with comments regarding specific inscriptions, more of the original Chinese characters, and other relevant material.

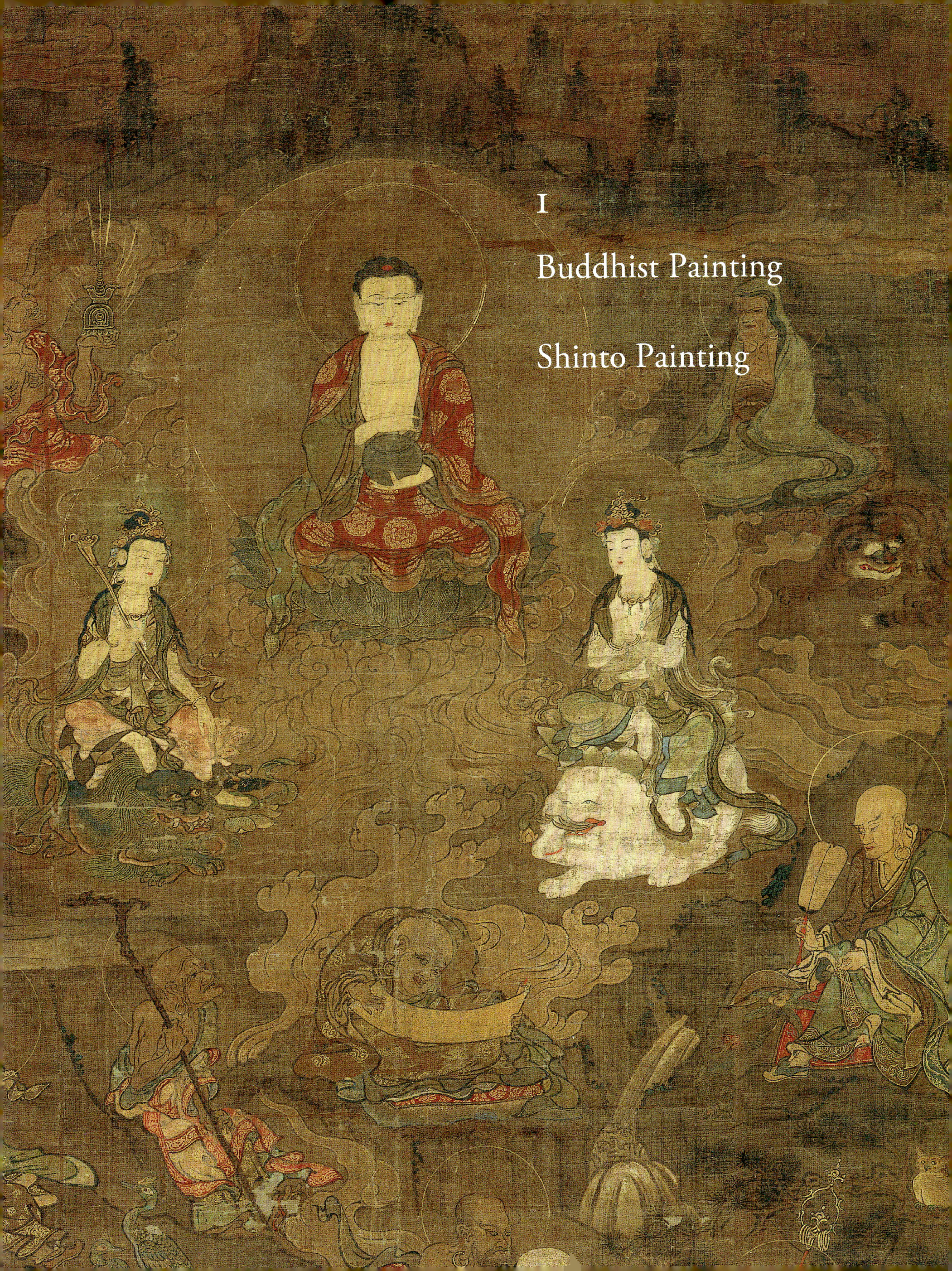

I

Buddhist Painting

Shinto Painting

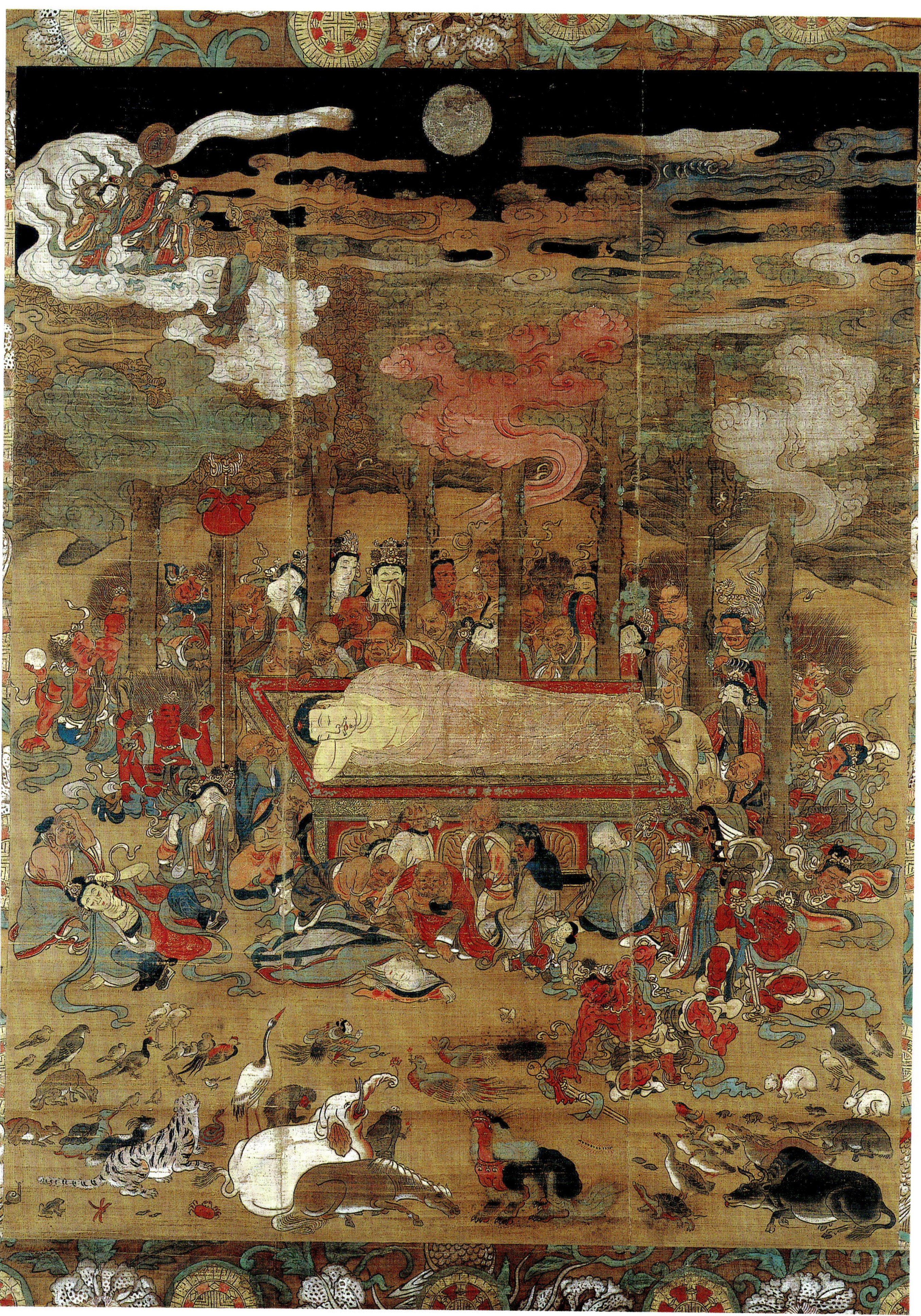

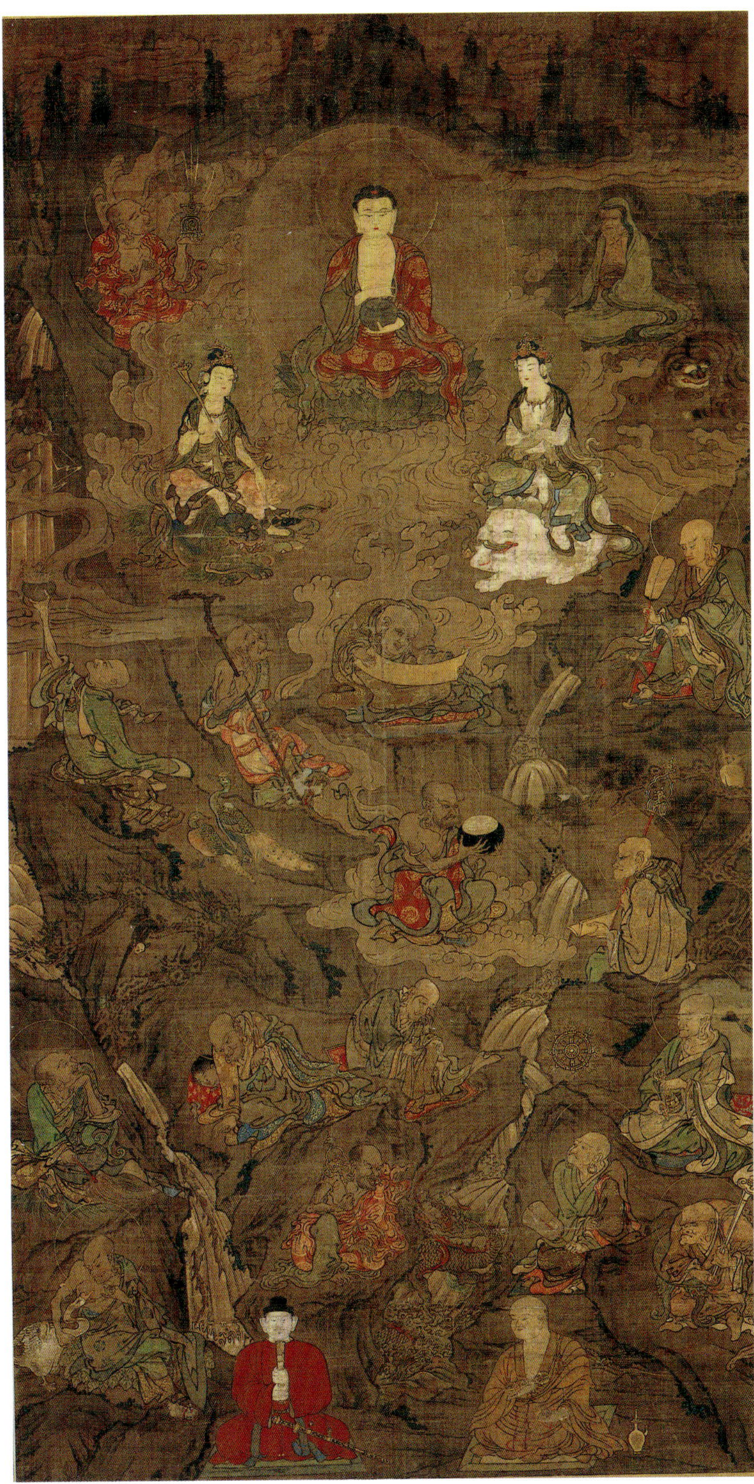

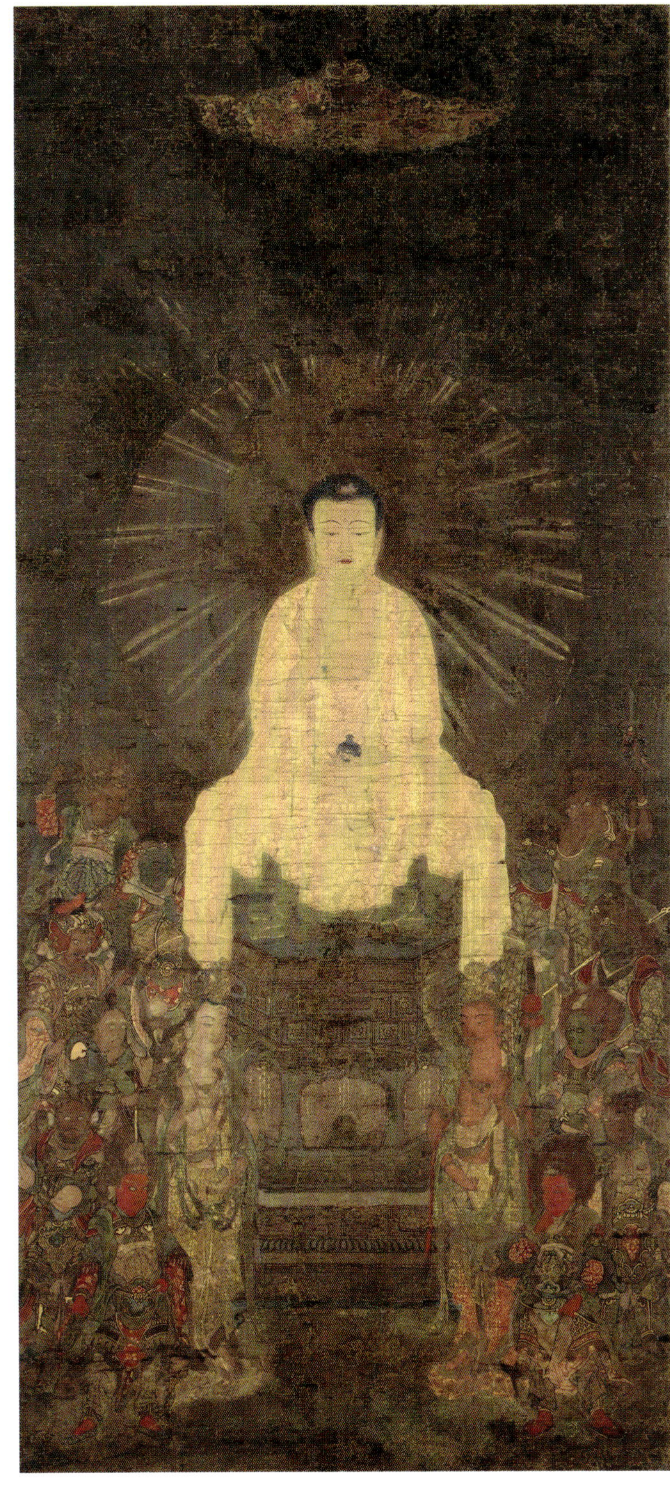

1. Nehan (仏涅槃)

Nanbokuchō period
Hanging scroll; ink, color, and gold on silk
154.9 x 106.4 cm (61 x 41⅞ in.)
Minneapolis Institute of Arts (94.85)

Literature: Murase 1975, no. 17; Kaufman 1985, pp. 92–93, fig. 3; Avitabile 1990, no. 8.

2. Shaka Triad and the Sixteen Rakan (釈迦三尊十六羅漢)

Late Kamakura–early Nanbokuchō period
Hanging scroll; ink, color, and gold on silk
143 x 75.5 cm (56¼ x 29¾ in.)

Literature: Miyama Susumu 1988, fig. 69; Avitabile 1990, no. 7; Murase 1993, no. 6; Murase 2000, no. 25; Tsuji Nobuo et al. 2005, no. 29.

3. Yakushi and Twelve Guardians (薬師十二神将)

Nanbokuchō period
Hanging scroll; ink, color, gold, and cut gold leaf (*kirikane*) on silk
111.5 x 51.1 cm (43⅞ x 20⅛ in.)

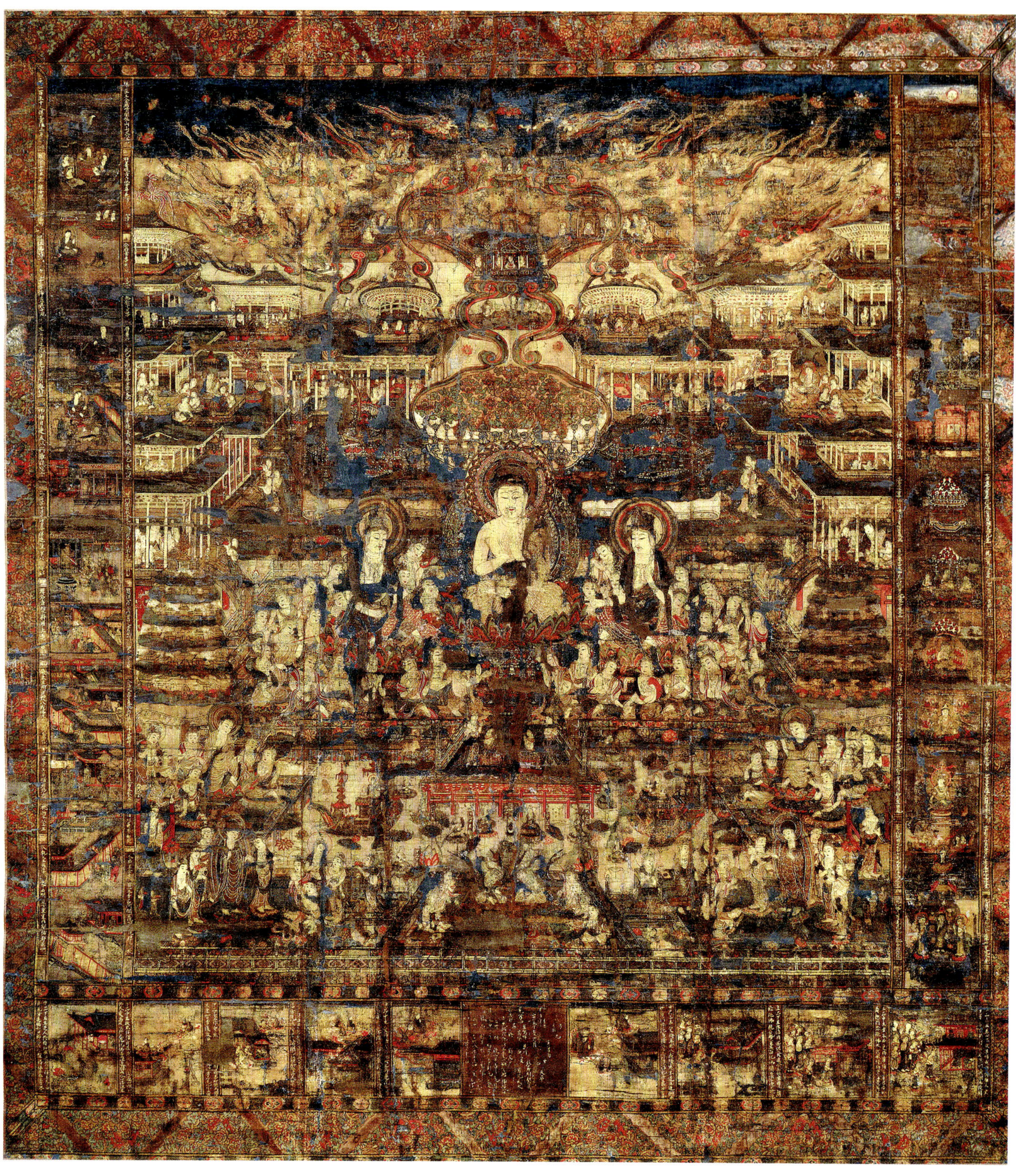

4. Taima Mandala (当麻曼荼羅)

Kamakura period, early 14th century
Hanging scroll; ink, color, gold, and cut gold leaf (*kirikane*) on silk
128.5 x 117 cm (50 5/8 x 46 1/8 in.)
Minneapolis Institute of Arts (85.9)

Literature: Murase 1975, addenda, no. 108.

5. Raigō of the Amida Triad (阿弥陀三尊来迎)

Kamakura period, early 14th century
Hanging scroll; ink, color, gold, and cut gold leaf (*kirikane*) on silk
102 x 40.1 cm (40 1/8 x 15 3/4 in.)

Literature: Murase 1975, no. 15; Kaufman 1985, pp. 91, 92, fig. 2; Avitabile 1990, no. 12; Murase 1992, p. 90; Poster et al. 1999, no. 3; Tsuji Nobuo et al. 2005, no. 30.

6. Thirteen Buddhas and Bodhisattvas

Muromachi period, 16th century
Framed picture; ink and color on paper
51.2 x 24.8 cm (20 1/8 x 9 3/4 in.)

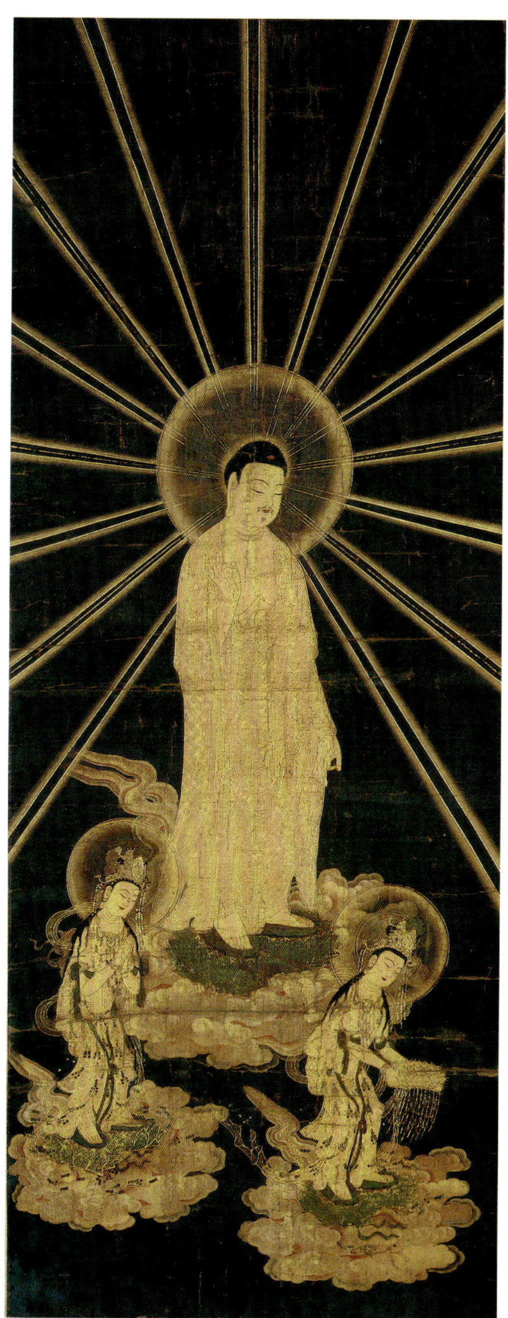

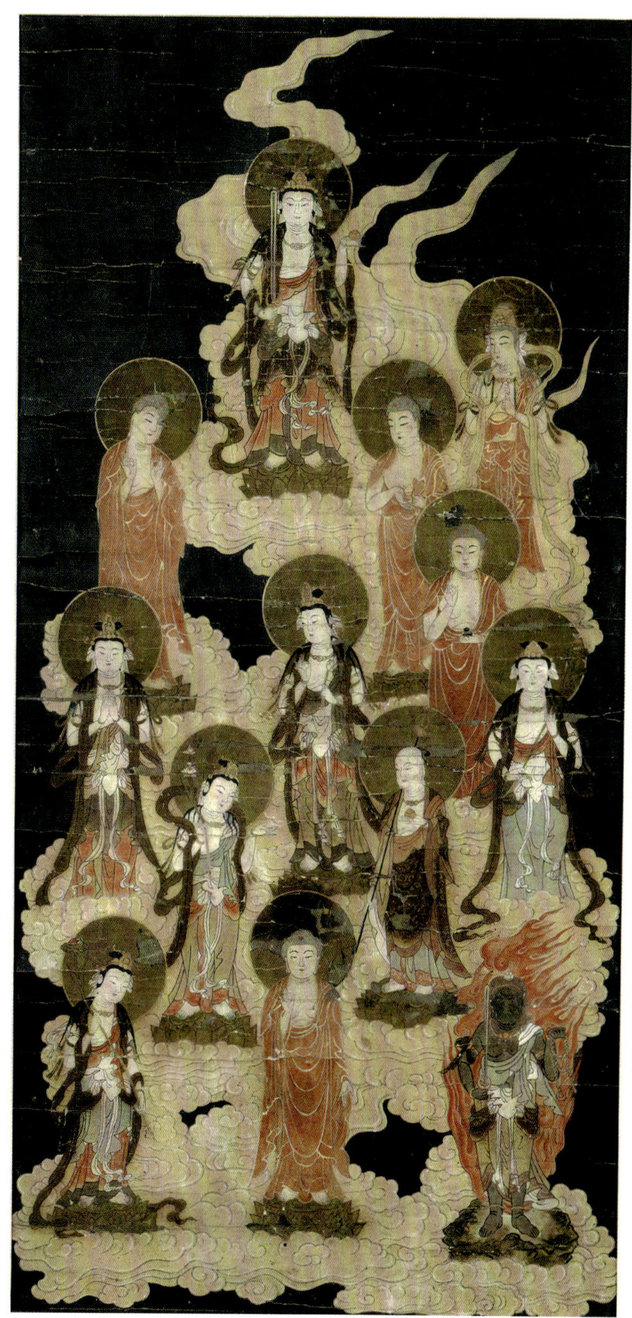

7. Hōshō Nyorai (宝生如来)

Kamakura period, 13th century
Handscroll fragment, mounted as hanging scroll; ink and light color on paper
30.2 x 69 cm (11⅞ x 27⅛ in.)

Gift from Sugahara Hisao, 1967

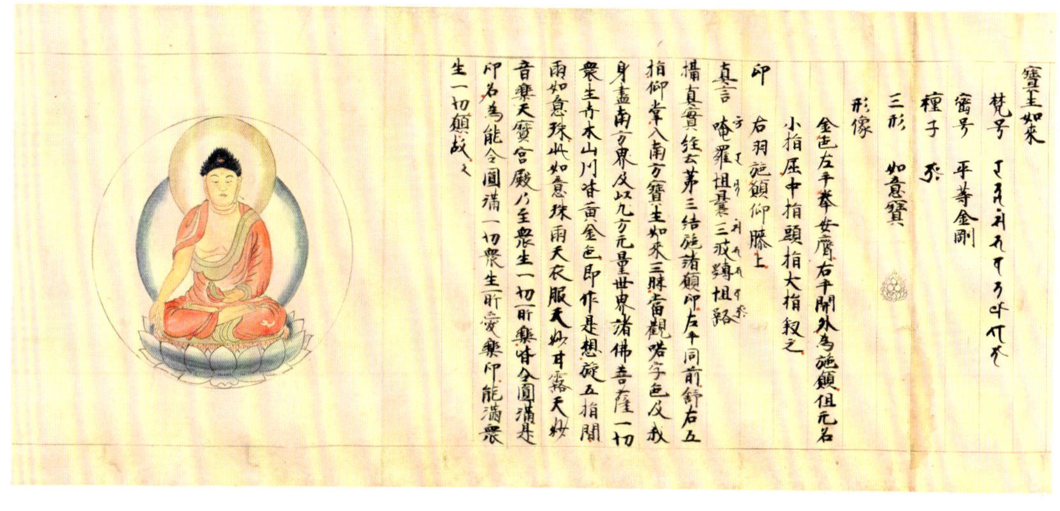

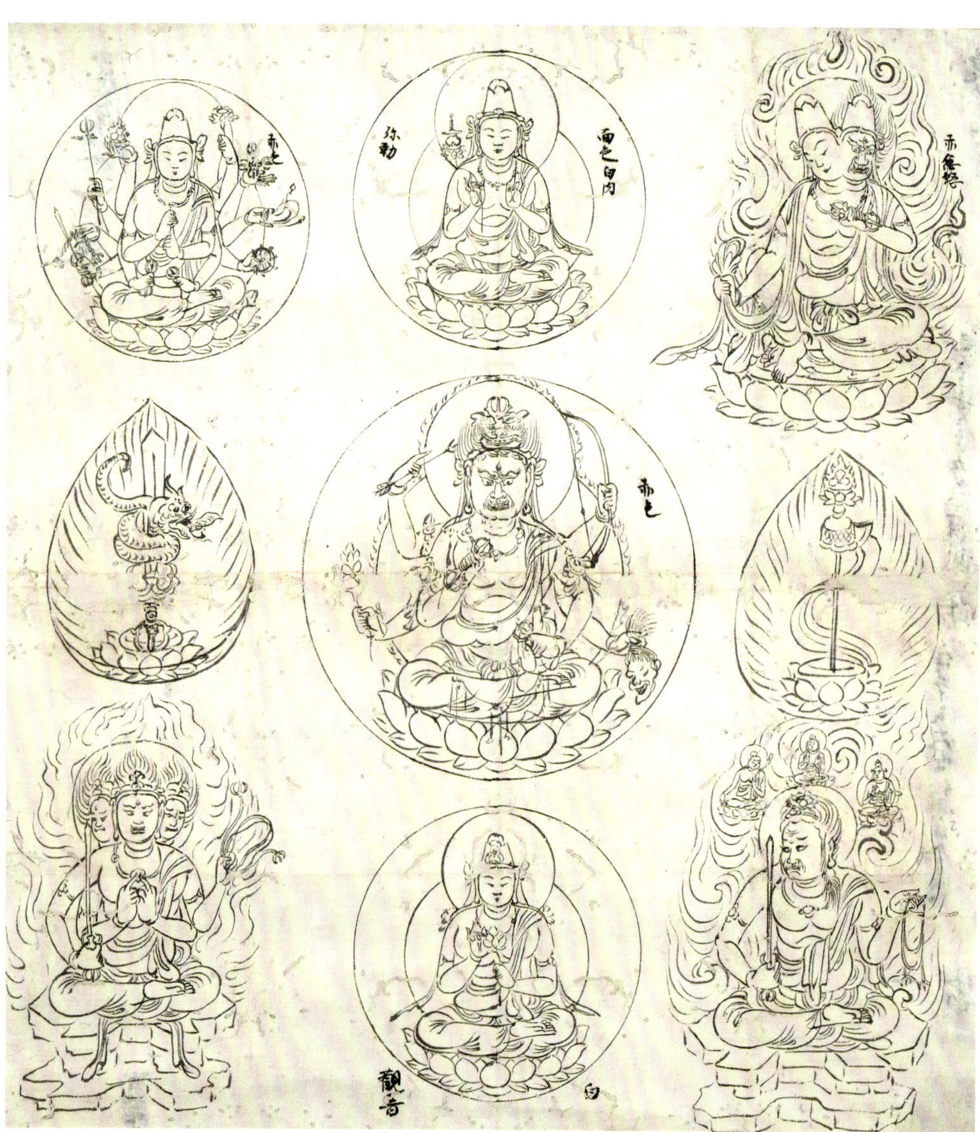

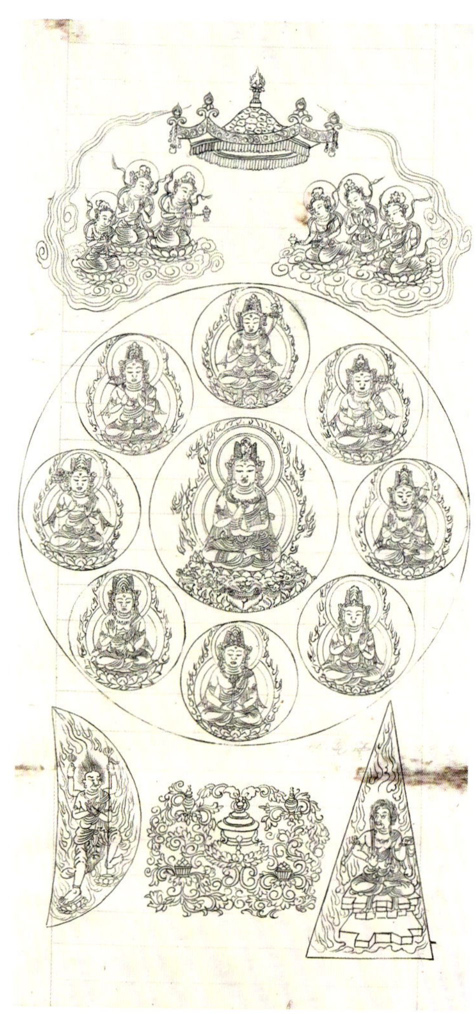

17. Aizen Mandala (愛染曼荼羅)

Late Heian period, 1107
Hanging scroll; ink on paper
58.4 x 53.4 cm (23 x 21 in.)
Text

Ex coll.: Shōren-in, Kyoto

Literature: Yanagisawa Taka 1965, pt. 1, fig. 3 (detail); Rosenfield and ten Grotenhuis 1979, no. 19; Yanagisawa Taka 1980, no. 90; Shinbo Tōru 1985, pls. 130–32; Tokyo National Museum 1985a, no. 1; Avitabile 1990, no. 10; Murase 1992, p. 71; Goepper 1993, pp. 71–72; Nedachi Kensuke 1997, figs. 32 (detail), 118; ten Grotenhuis 1999, fig. 71; Murase 2000, no. 10.

18. Sonshō Mandala (尊勝曼荼羅)

Kamakura period, early 14th century
Framed picture; ink on paper
43.2 x 29.8 cm (17 x 11¾ in.)

19. Mandala of Han'nya Bosatsu (般若曼荼羅)

Muromachi period, 15th century
Hanging scroll, ink, color, and gold on silk, with painted mounting
Overall 211.4 x 146.6 cm (83¼ x 57¾ in.); image 163.9 x 123.6 cm (64½ x 48⅝ in.)
The Metropolitan Museum of Art, New York (2000.289)

Literature: Murase 2000, no. 48.

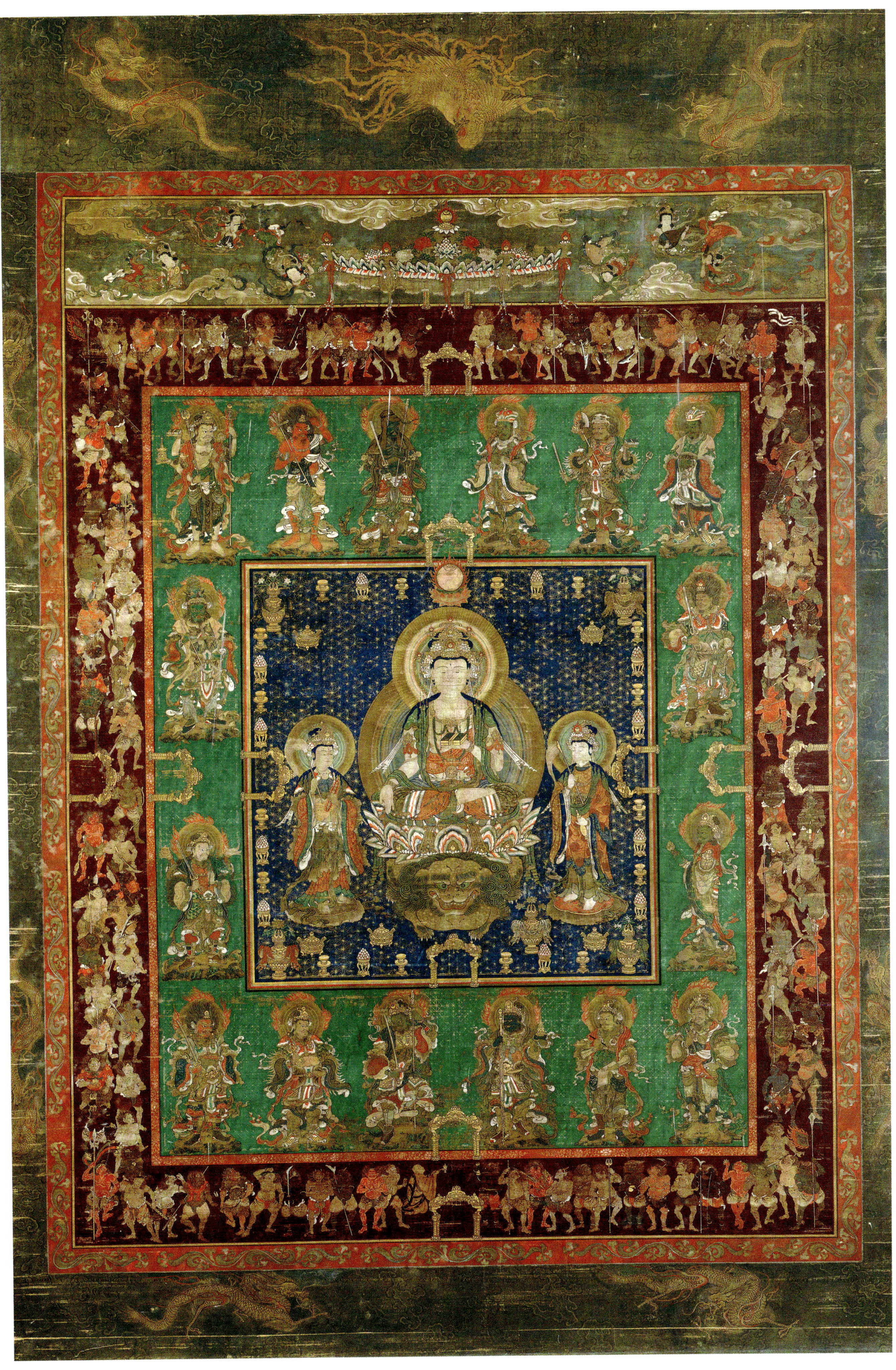

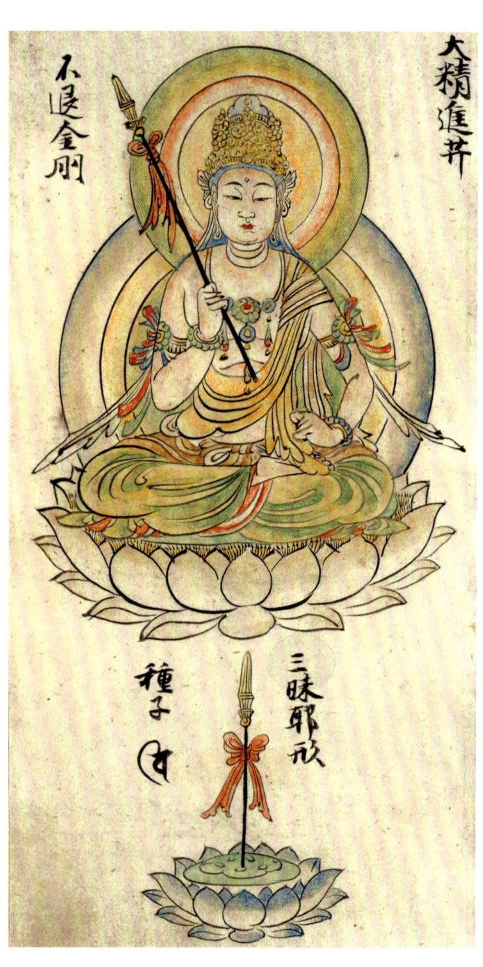

ATTRIBUTED TO TAKUMA TAMETŌ
(宅間為遠; fl. ca. 1132–74)

20. Dai Shōjin Bosatsu (大精進菩薩), from *Kontai butsugajō* (金胎仏画帖)

Late Heian period, mid-12th century
Page from book, mounted as hanging scroll; ink and color on paper
25 x 12.8 cm (9 7/8 x 5 in.)
Text

LITERATURE: Ōmura Seigai 1919–22, no. 11; Murase 1975, no. 14; Yanagisawa Taka 1980, no. 86; Kaufman 1985, fig. 4; Tokyo National Museum 1985a, no. 2; Avitabile 1990, no. 11; Murase 2000, no. 11.

SHINKEN
(深賢; fl. 13th century)

21. Iconographic Drawings (図像抄)

Kamakura period, fifth month of 1230
Two handscrolls; ink on paper
Scroll I (*detail, at right*): Eleven fierce deities
25.3 x 1287 cm (10 in. x 42 ft. 2 3/4 in.)
Scroll II (*detail, below*): Seven Kannon
25.1 x 1193.4 cm (9 7/8 in. x 39 ft. 1 7/8 in.)
Text, signature

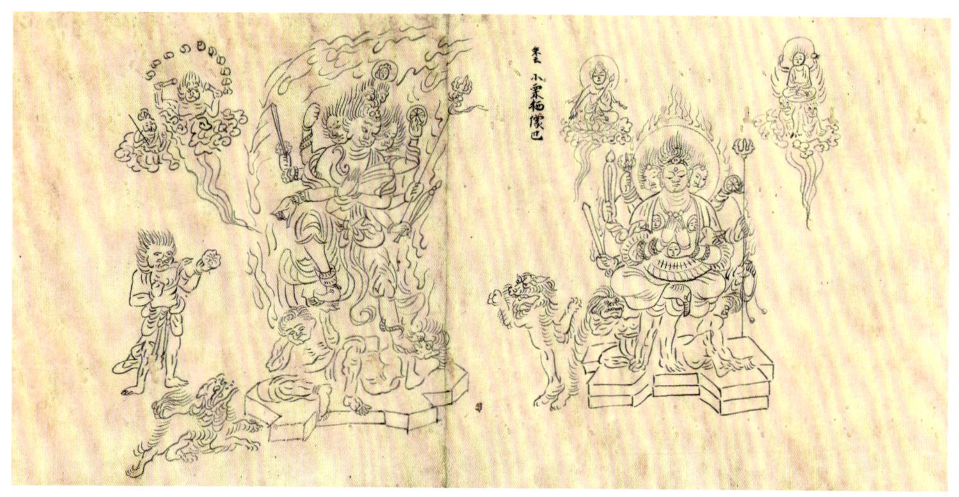

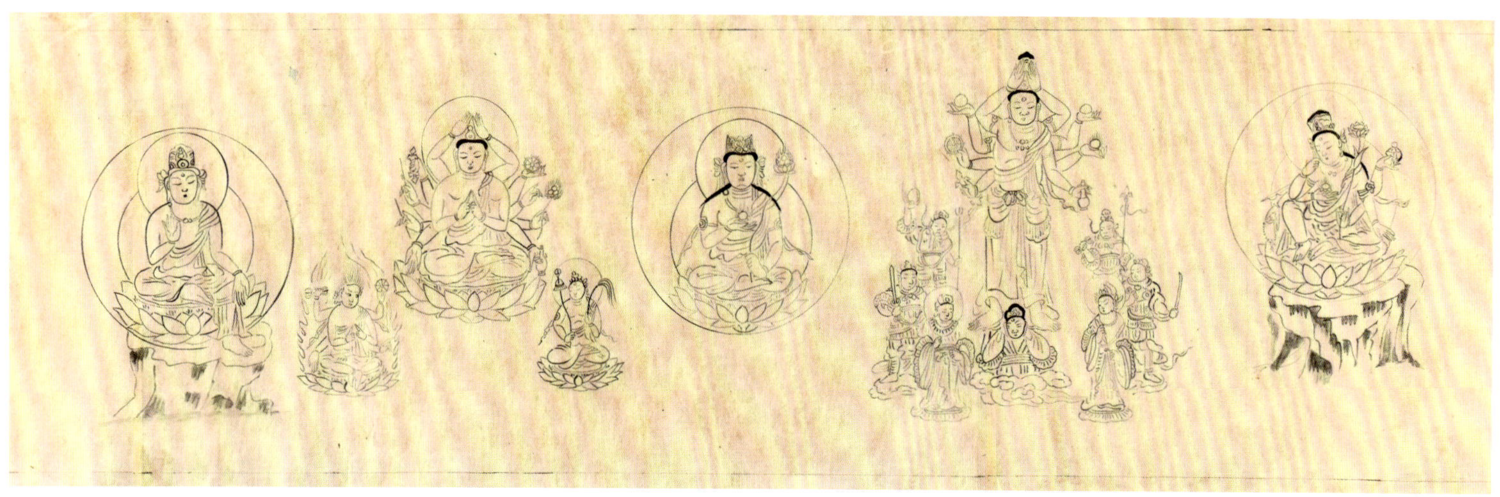

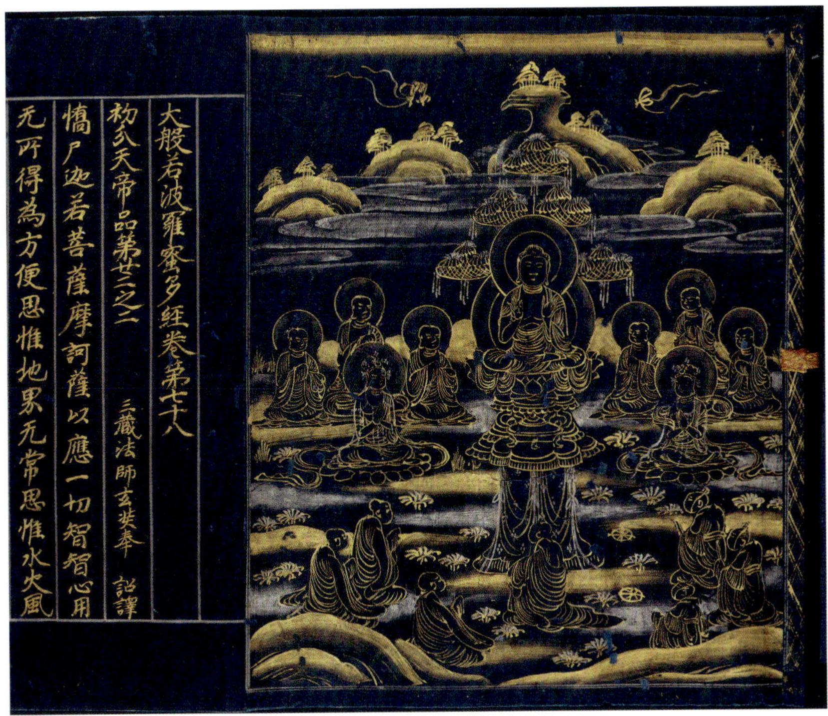

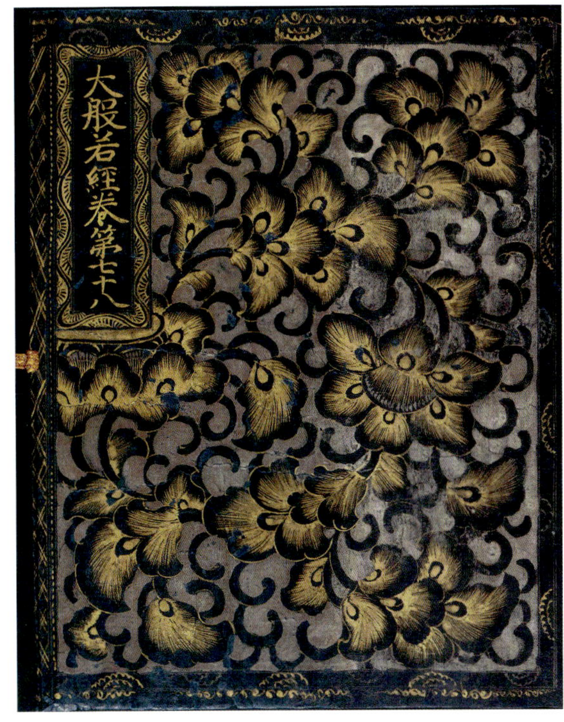

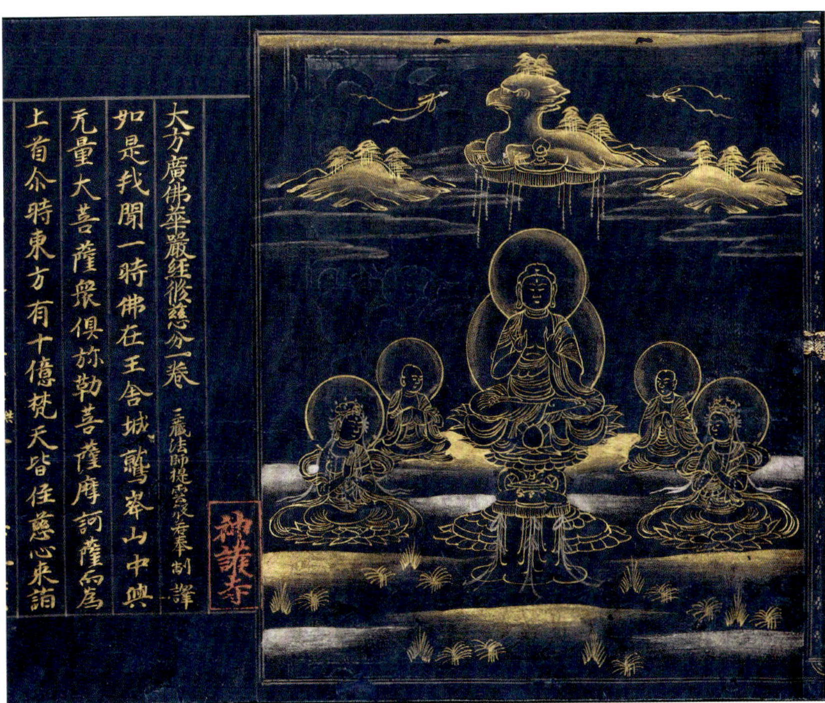

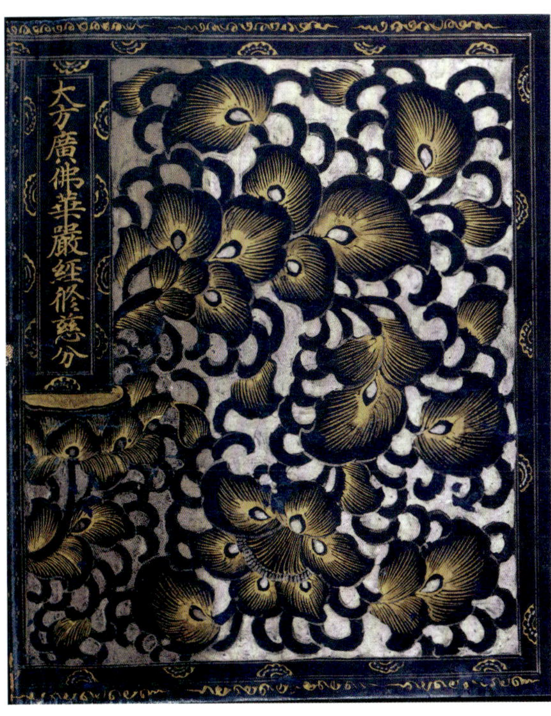

22. Chapter 78 of *Daihan'nya haramitakyō* (大般若波羅密多経)

Late Heian period, 12th century
Handscroll cover and frontispiece; gold and silver ink on indigo paper
25.9 x 21.3 cm (10¼ x 8⅜ in.)

LITERATURE: Murase 1975, no. 10; Murase 2000, no. 15.

23. *Daihōkōbutsu kegonkyō shūjibun* (大方廣佛華厳経修慈分), the so-called *Jingojikyō* (神護寺経)

Late Heian period, before 1156–85
Handscroll cover and frontispiece; gold and silver ink on indigo paper
25.6 x 21.8 cm (10⅛ x 8⅝ in.)
Seal

EX COLL.: Jingoji, Kyoto

LITERATURE: Murase 1975, no. 11; Kaufman 1985, fig. 11; Tokyo National Museum 1985a, no. 68; Pal and Meech-Pekarik 1988, pl. 82; Avitabile 1990, no. 15; Kim 1991, no. 46; Murase 2000, no. 16.

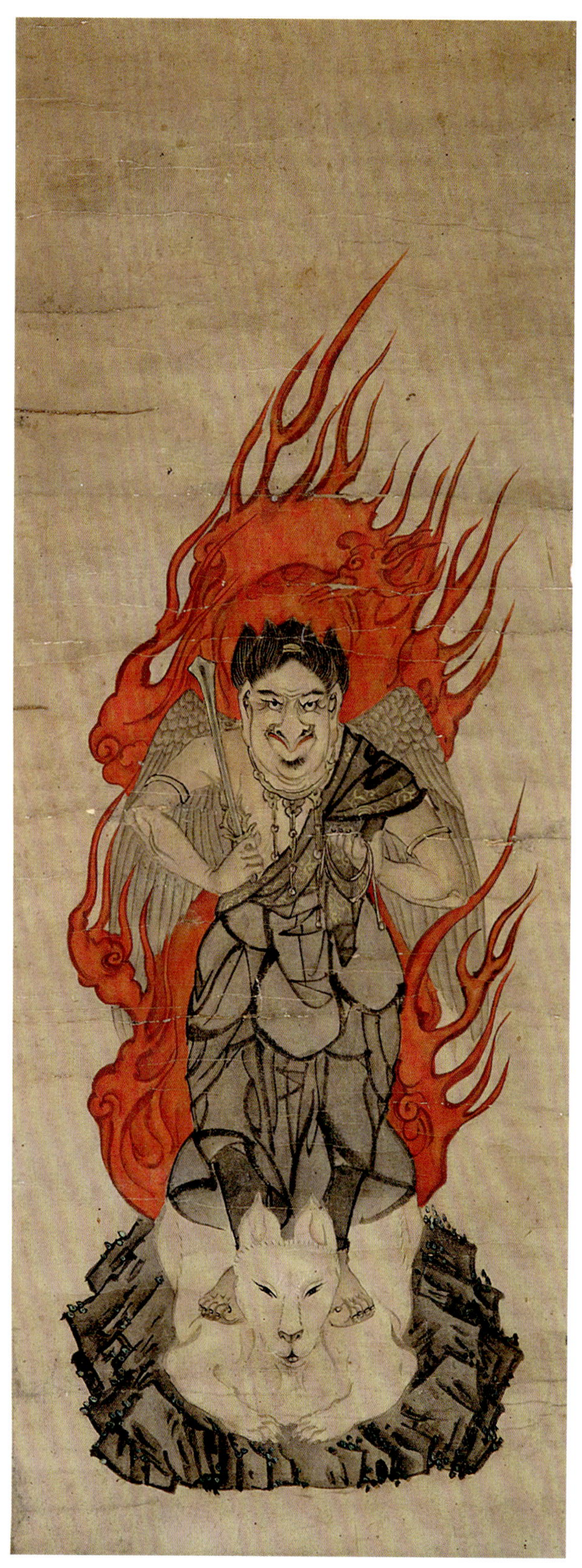

26. Dakiniten (荼枳尼天)

Edo period, 18th century
Hanging scroll; ink and color on paper
72.1 x 37.2 cm (28 3/8 x 14 5/8 in.)

Gift from Jean Archbold, 1989

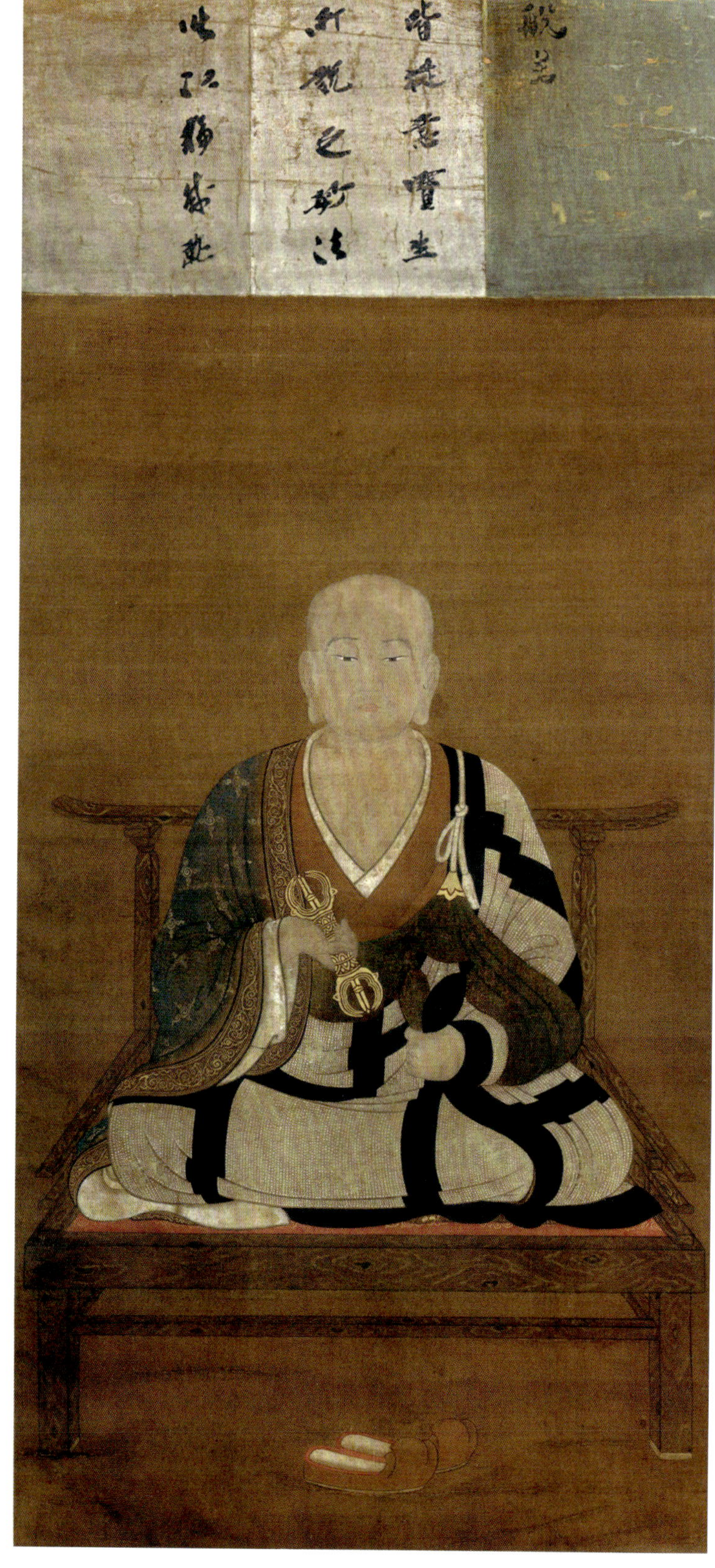

27. Portrait of Monk Rigen (?)
(理源大師?)

Muromachi period, 16th century
Hanging scroll; ink, color, and gold on silk
90.5 x 41.9 cm (35 5/8 x 16 1/2 in.)
Text

LITERATURE: Burke 1993, pp. 6–8, fig. 2, no. 1.

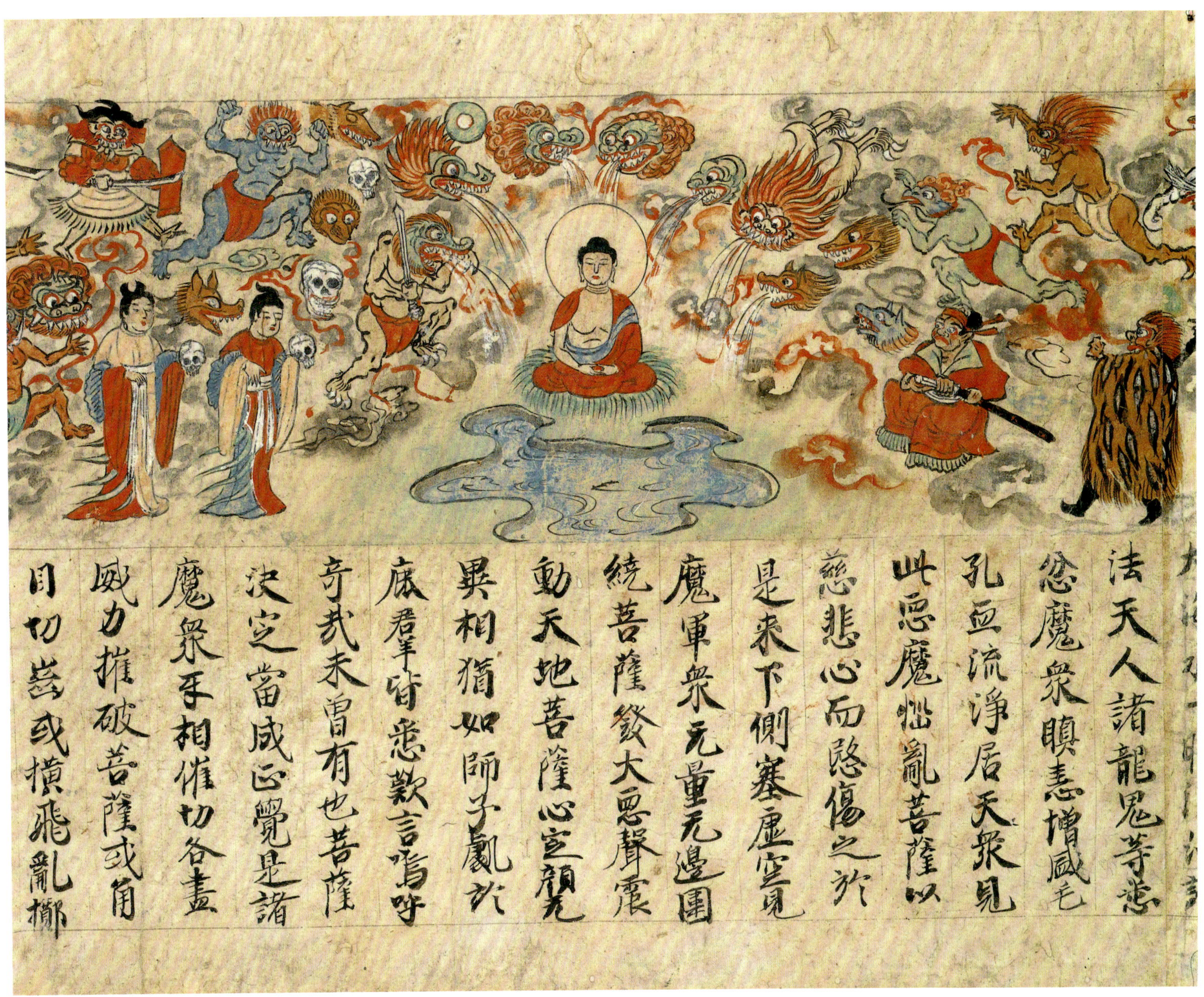

28. From *Kako genzai e-ingakyō*
(過去現在絵因果経)

Kamakura period, late 13th century
Handscroll fragment (*detail*); ink and color on paper
27.7 x 156.4 cm (10 7/8 x 61 5/8 in.)

Ex coll.: Shōriji, Wakayama; Setsuda; Matsunaga Yasuzaemon, Tokyo

Literature: Maruyama Masatake 1963, pp. 144–47; Tanaka Ichimatsu 1965a; Murase 1975, no. 12; Pal and Brown 1984, no. 47; Murase 2000, no. 24; Tsuji Nobuo et al. 2005, no. 23.

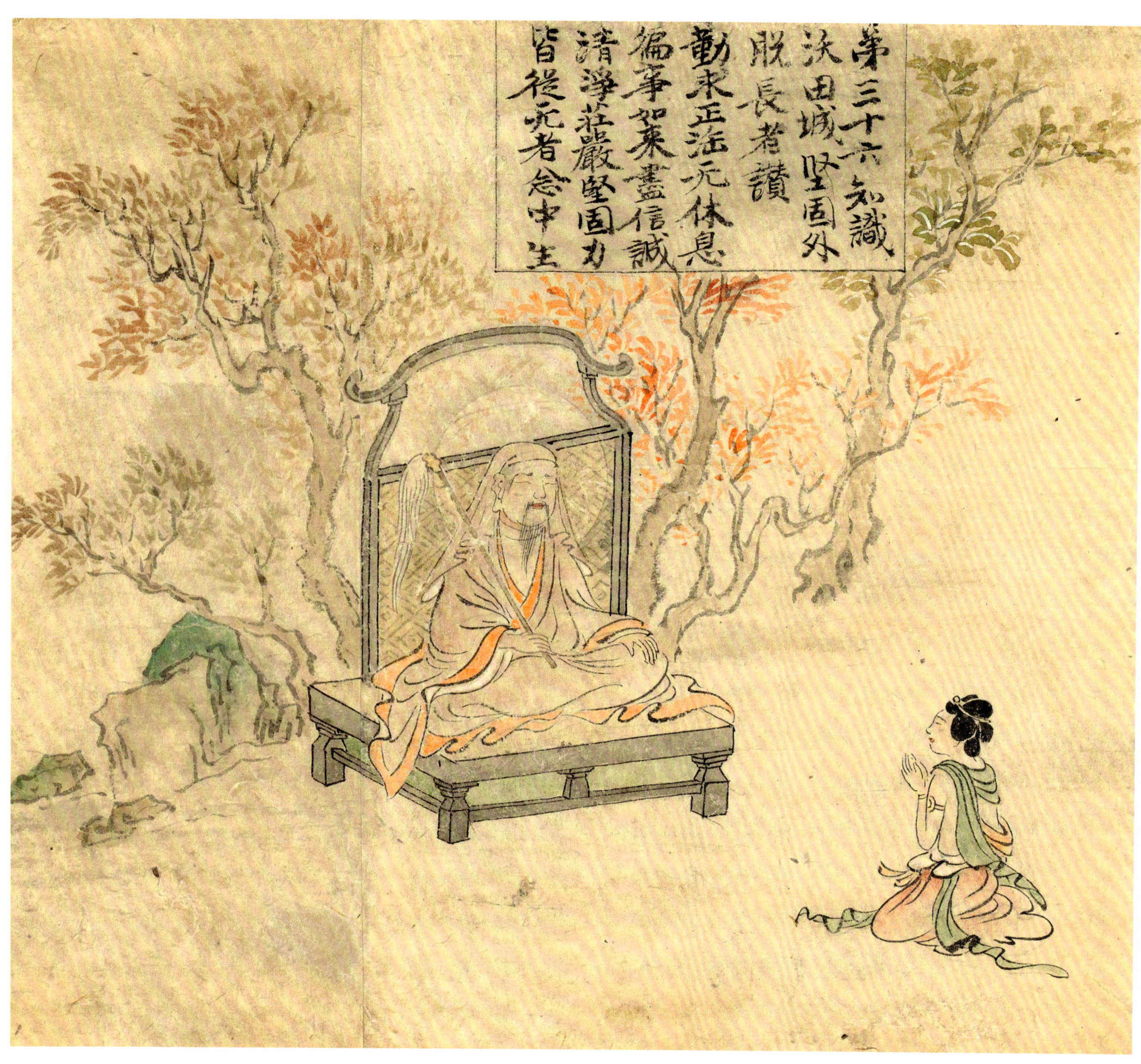

29. The Thirty-sixth Stage, from *Zenzai Dōji's Fifty-five Pilgrimages* (華厳五十五所絵巻), also known as *Zenzai Dōji emaki* (善財童子絵巻)

Kamakura period, early 14th century
Handscroll fragment, mounted as hanging scroll; ink and light color on paper
32.3 x 36.5 cm (12 3/4 x 14 3/8 in.)
Text

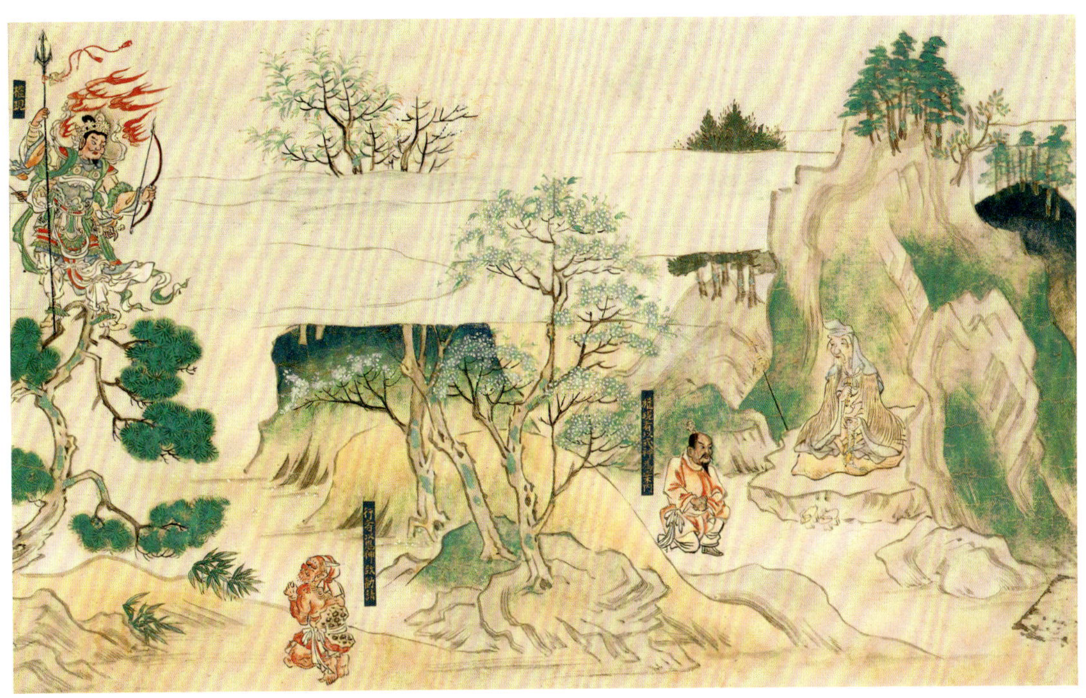

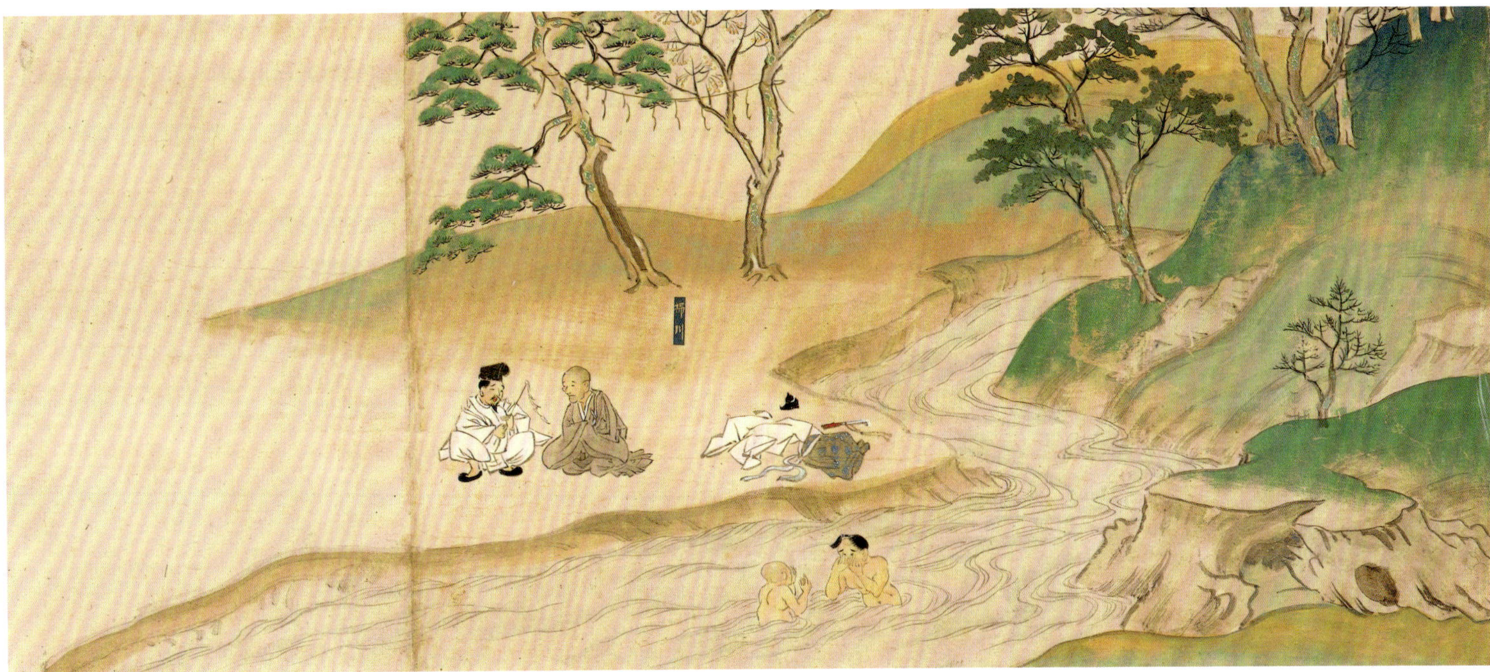

30a, b. From *Jin'ōji engi emaki* (神於寺縁起絵巻)

Kamakura period, early 14th century
Handscroll fragments, mounted as two hanging scrolls; ink and color on paper
(a) 34.4 x 55.8 cm (13½ x 22 in.); (b) 33.5 x 78 cm (13⅛ x 30¾ in.)
Text

Literature: (a): Shimada Shūjirō 1969, vol. 1, p. 88; Murase 1975, no. 24; Rosenfield and ten Grotenhuis 1979, no. 42; Akiyama Terukazu 1980a, no. 87. (b): Akiyama Terukazu 1980b, p. 108; Kaufman 1985, fig. 10; Tokyo National Museum 1985a, no. 8; Avitabile 1990, no. 22; Murase 2000, no. 27; Proser 2010, no. 44.

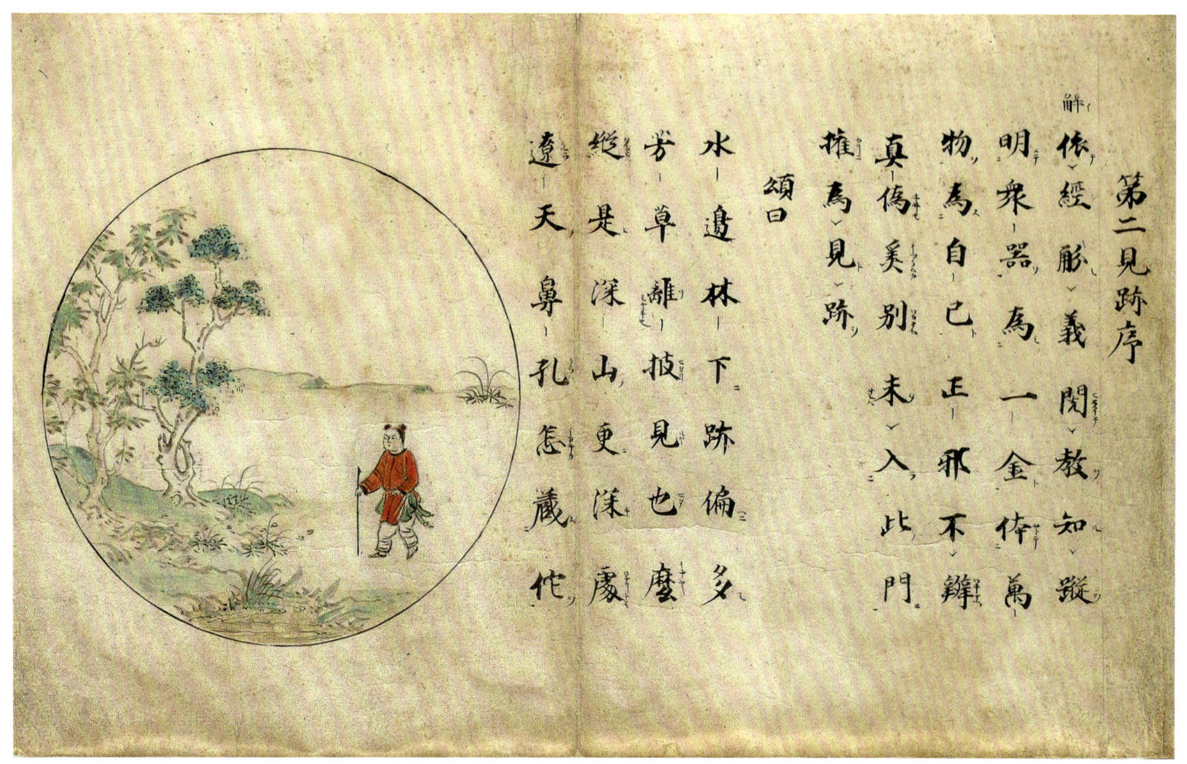

Second song: "Seeing the Footprints of the Ox"

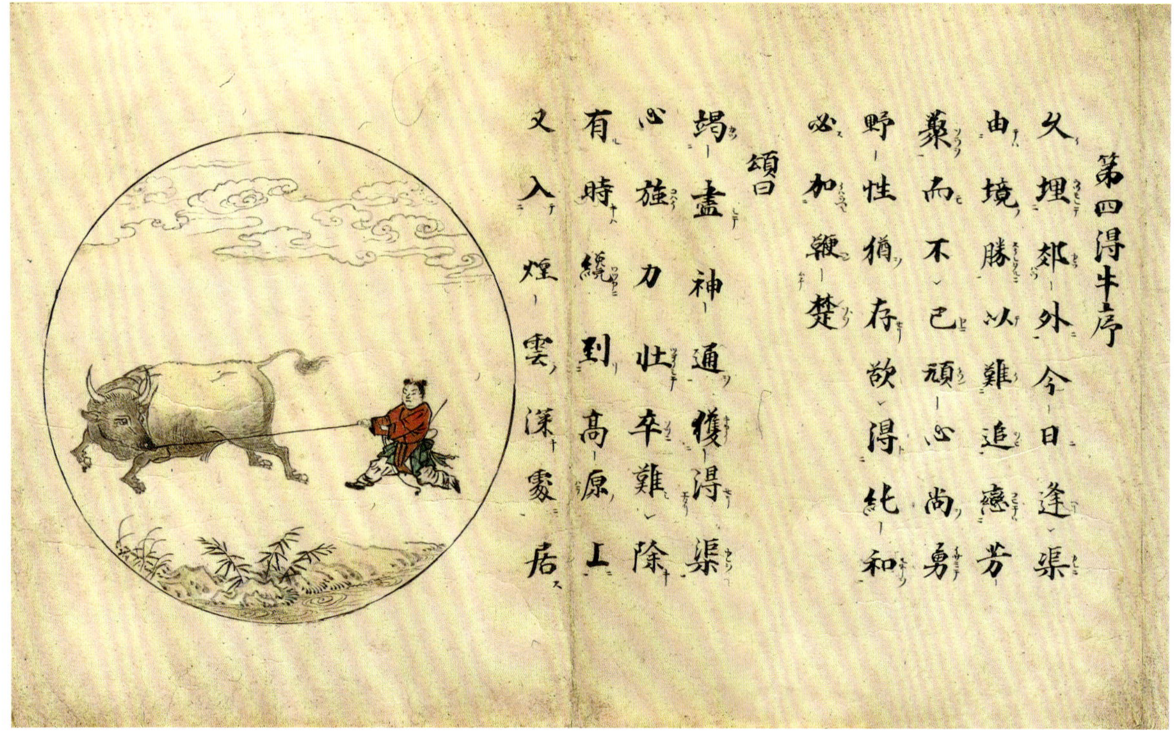

Fourth song: "Catching the Ox"

31. The Ten Ox-Herding Songs (十牛図巻) by the Monk Kakuan (Ch. Guoan, 廓庵; fl. ca. 1150) of Teishū Ryōzan (Ch. Dingzhou Liangshan, 鼎州梁山)

Kamakura period, 1278
Handscroll (*details, above*); ink and color on paper
31 x 624.6 cm (12 1/4 in. x 20 ft. 5 7/8 in.)
Text, signature, seal

Ex coll.: Sorimachi Jūrō, Tokyo

Literature: Shinbo Tōru 1974, pp. 77–79; Murase 1992, p. 71; Ebine Toshio 1994, fig. 31; Murase 2000, no. 42; Wada 2002; Tsuji Nobuo et al. 2005, no. 33.

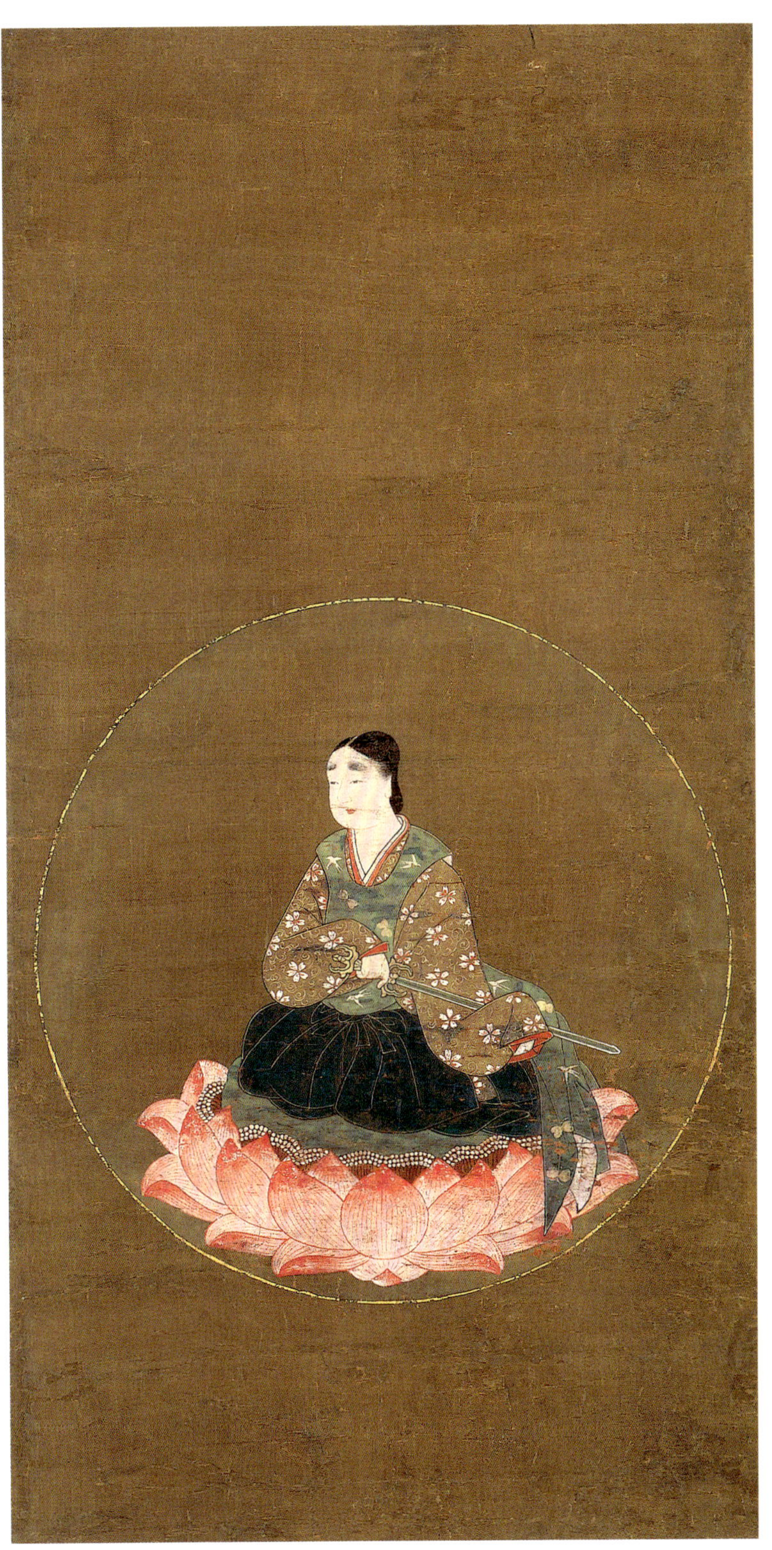

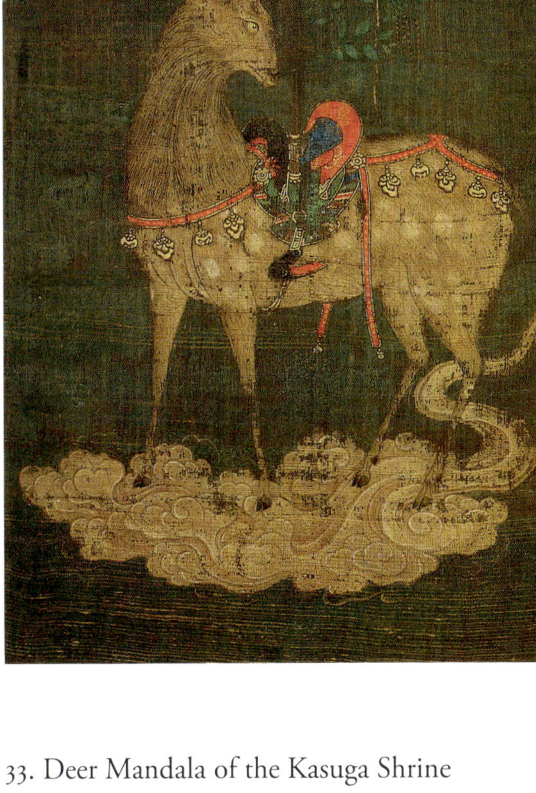

32. Wakamiya of the Kasuga Shrine (春日若宮)

Kamakura period, early 14th century
Hanging scroll; ink, color, gold, and cut gold leaf (*kirikane*) on silk
76.1 x 48.4 cm (30 x 19 in.)
Partial purchase by Lila Acheson Wallace Gift, The Metropolitan Museum of Art, New York (1997.113)

Literature: Murase 1997, p. 91; Fukui Rikichirō 1999, fig. 38; Murase 2000, no. 32; Ōkura Shūkokan 2000, no. 113; Tsuji Nobuo et al. 2005, no. 27.

33. Deer Mandala of the Kasuga Shrine (春日鹿曼荼羅)

Nanbokuchō period, late 14th century
Hanging scroll; ink, color, and gold on silk
85.7 x 35.6 cm (33¾ x 14 in.)

Literature: Murasc 2000, no. 33; Tsuji Nobuo et al. 2005, no. 25; Barnet and Burto 2011, p. 69, fig. 7.

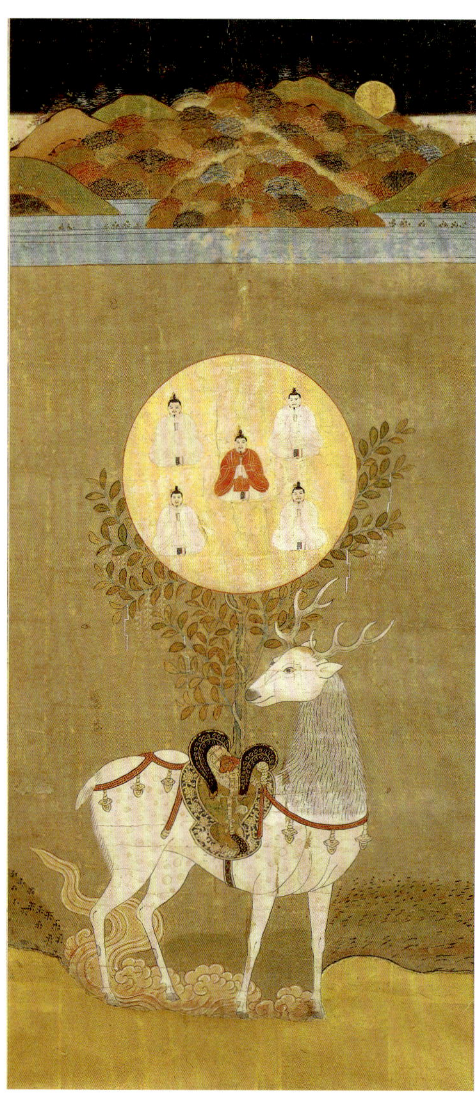

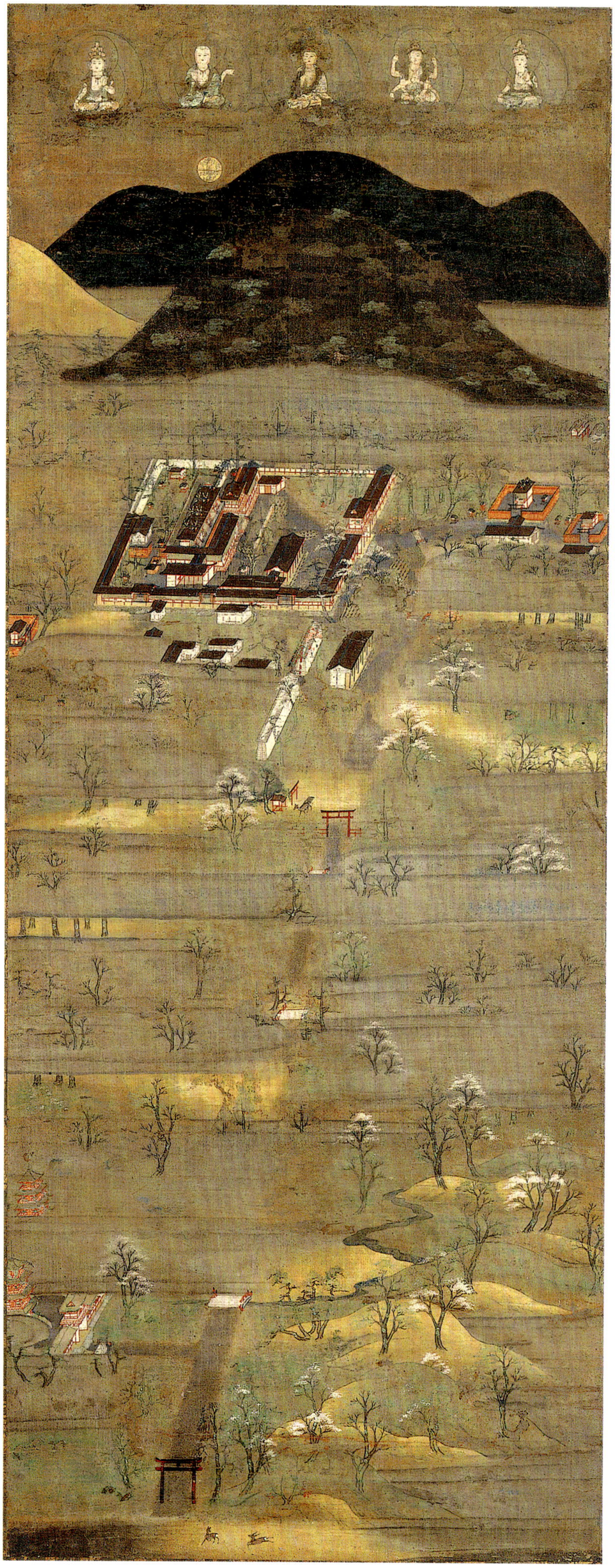

34. Deer Mandala of the Kasuga Shrine (春日鹿曼荼羅)

Muromachi period, first half of 15th century
Hanging scroll; ink, color, and gold on silk
88.9 x 40 cm (35 x $15\frac{3}{4}$ in.)

Literature: Burke 1993, pl. 1, no. 2; Tsuji Nobuo et al. 2005, no. 26; Barnet and Burto 2011, p. 70, fig. 8.

35. Kasuga Shrine Mandala (春日宮曼荼羅)

Kamakura period, late 13th century
Hanging scroll; ink, color, and gold on silk
100.3 x 39.8 cm ($39\frac{1}{2}$ x $15\frac{5}{8}$ in.)

Literature: Sasaki Kōzō and Okumura Hideo 1979, no. 149; Yanagisawa Taka 1980, no. 98; Tokyo National Museum 1985a, no. 3; Avitabile 1990, no. 13; Amino Yoshihiko et al. 1993, p. 161; Gyōtoku Shin'ichirō 1994, fig. 17; Gyōtoku Shin'ichirō 1996, fig. 25 (detail); Murase 2000, no. 31; Tsuji Nobuo et al. 2005, no. 24; Proser 2010, no. 71.

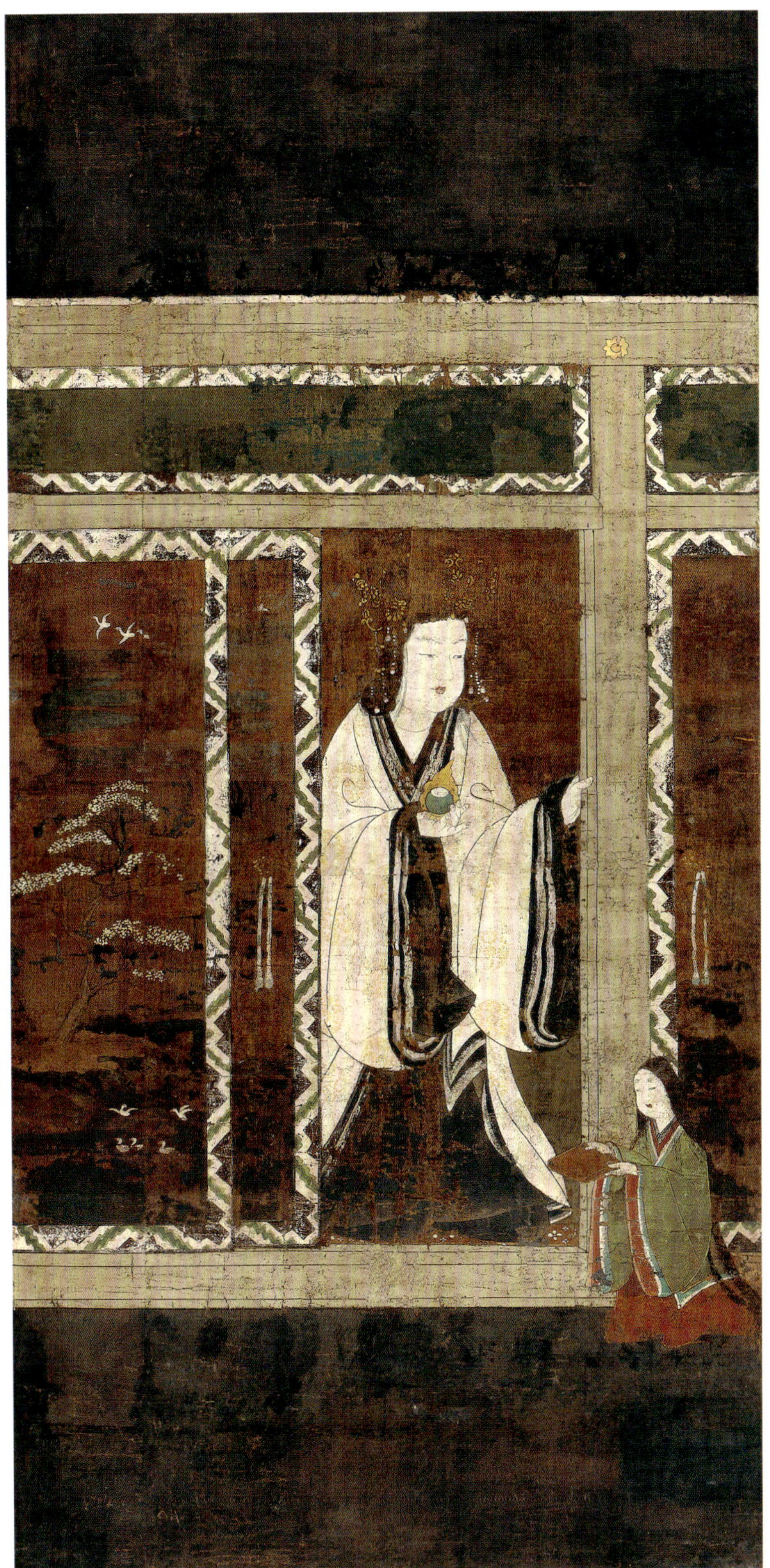

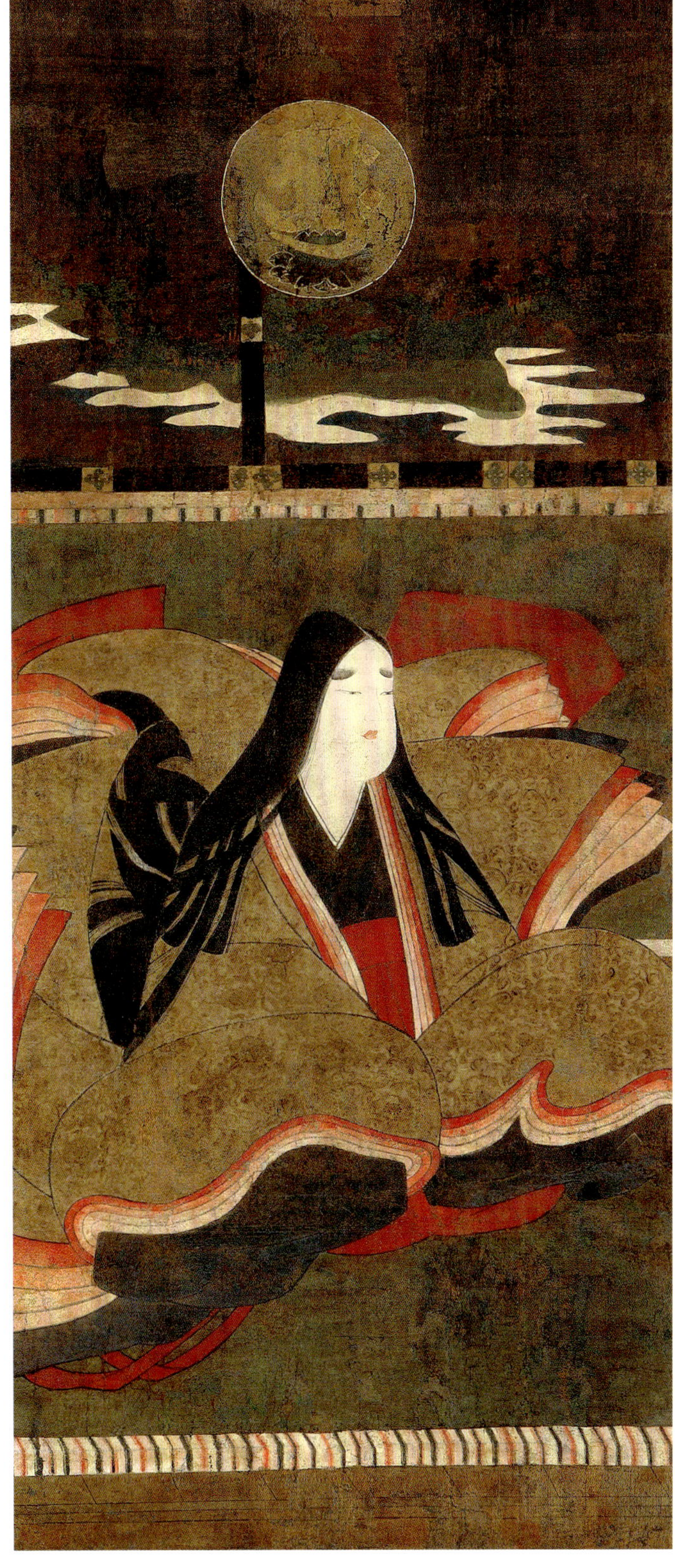

36. Seiryū Gongen (清滝権現)

Kamakura–Nanbokuchō period, first half of 14th century
Hanging scroll; ink, color, and gold on silk
91 x 44.7 cm (35⅞ x 17⅝ in.)

Ex coll.: Maeyama Hisakichi

Literature: Museum of Fine Arts, Boston 1936, no. 45; Kyoto National Museum 1974a, pl. 69; Murase 1975, no. 18; Tokyo National Museum 1985a, no. 4; Murase 2000, no. 35; Tsuji Nobuo et al. 2005, no. 28.

37. Niu Myōjin (丹生明神)

Nanbokuchō period
Hanging scroll; ink, color, and gold on silk
82.8 x 37 cm (32⅝ x 14⅝ in.)

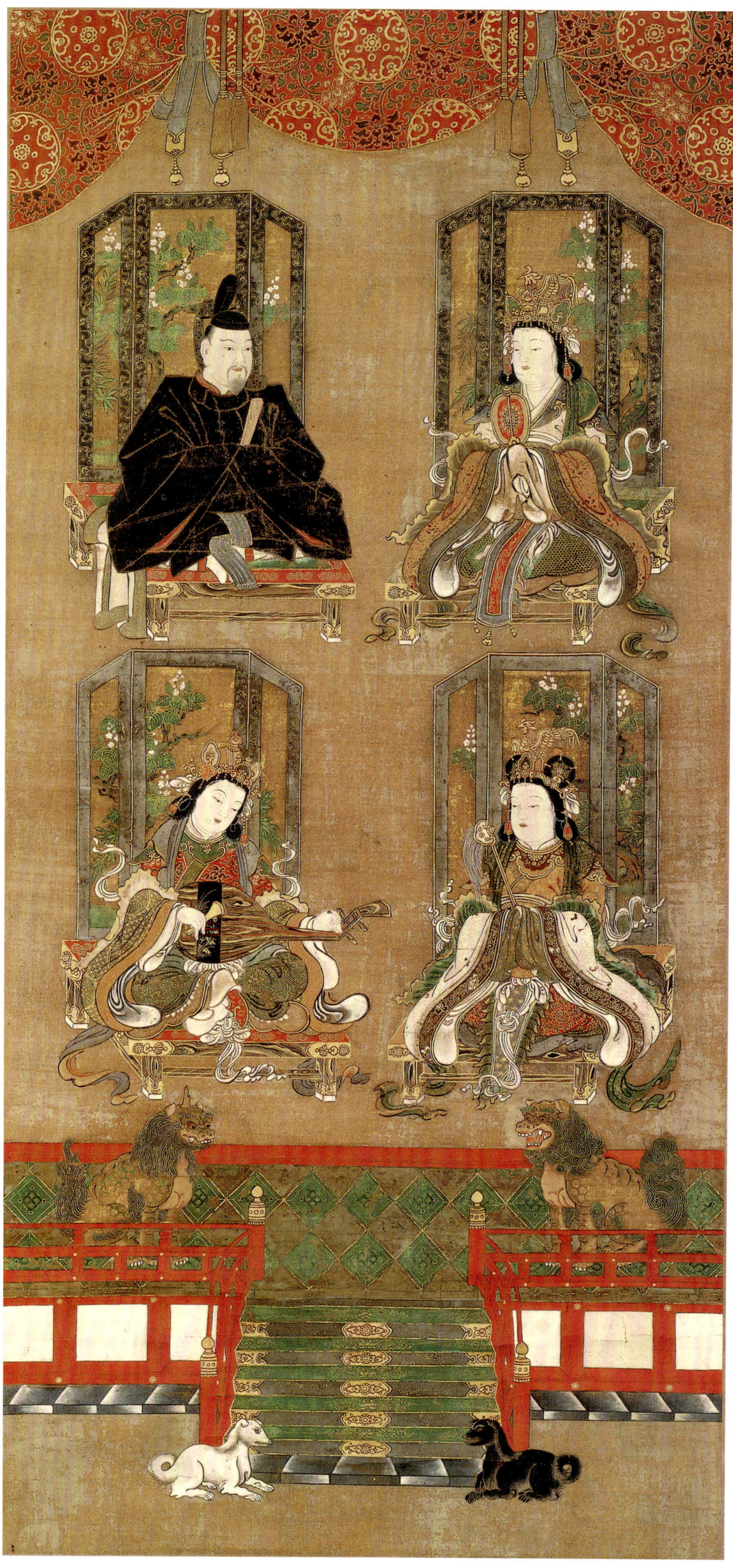

38. Mandala of the Four Deities of Mount Kōya (高野四所明神)

Muromachi period, 16th century
Hanging scroll; ink, color, and gold on silk
103.7 x 50.9 cm (40 7/8 x 20 in.)

LITERATURE: Little 1991, p. 128; Murase 1993, no. 5; Leidy and Thurman 1997, no. 46.

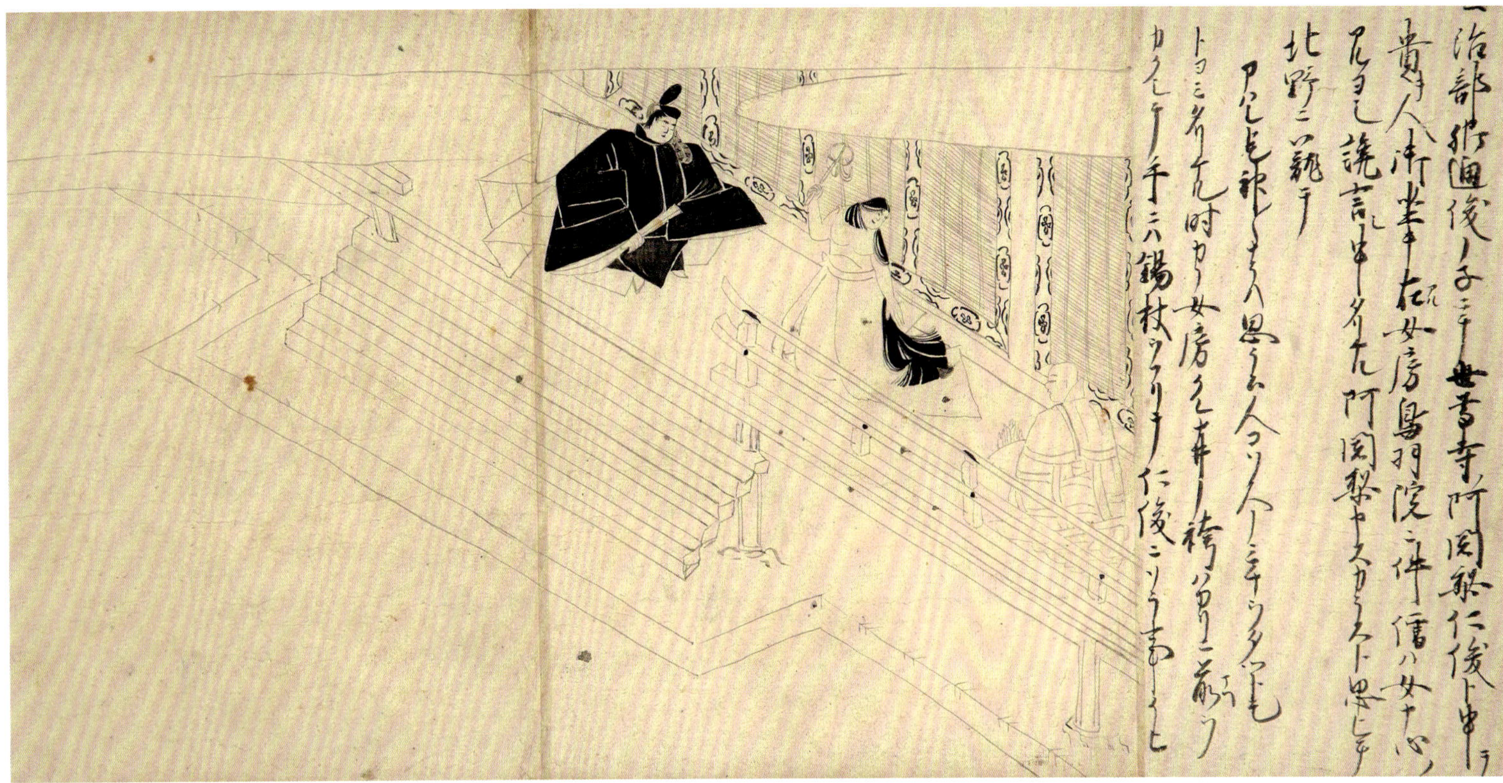

39

39. From *Kitano Tenjin engi emaki*
(北野天神縁起絵巻)

Kamakura period, ca. 1300
Section of handscroll mounted as hanging scroll; ink on paper
28.1 x 58 cm (11 x 22 7/8 in.)

Ex coll.: Yamaoka Teppei; Kishi Kōkei

Literature: Mizoguchi Teijirō et al. 1942, pp. 92–93; Umezu Jirō 1970a, p. 150; Shinbo Tōru 1990, fig. 7 (detail).

40. From *Kitano Tenjin engi emaki*
(北野天神縁起絵巻)

Kamakura period, ca. 1300
Section of handscroll; ink on paper
28.1 x 117.9 cm (11 x 46 3/8 in.)

Ex coll.: Matsumi Tatsuo; Kimura Teizō, Nagoya; Kishi Kōkei

Literature: Mizoguchi Teijirō et al. 1942, pp. 87–89, 105–6; Shimada Shūjirō 1969, vol. 1, p. 79; Umezu Jirō 1970a, p. 149; Murase 1975, no. 22; Akiyama Terukazu 1980a, no. 68; Tokyo National Museum 1985a, no. 7; Avitabile 1990, no. 21; Shinbo Tōru 1990, fig. 1 (detail), pl. 9; Murase 2000, no. 34.

40

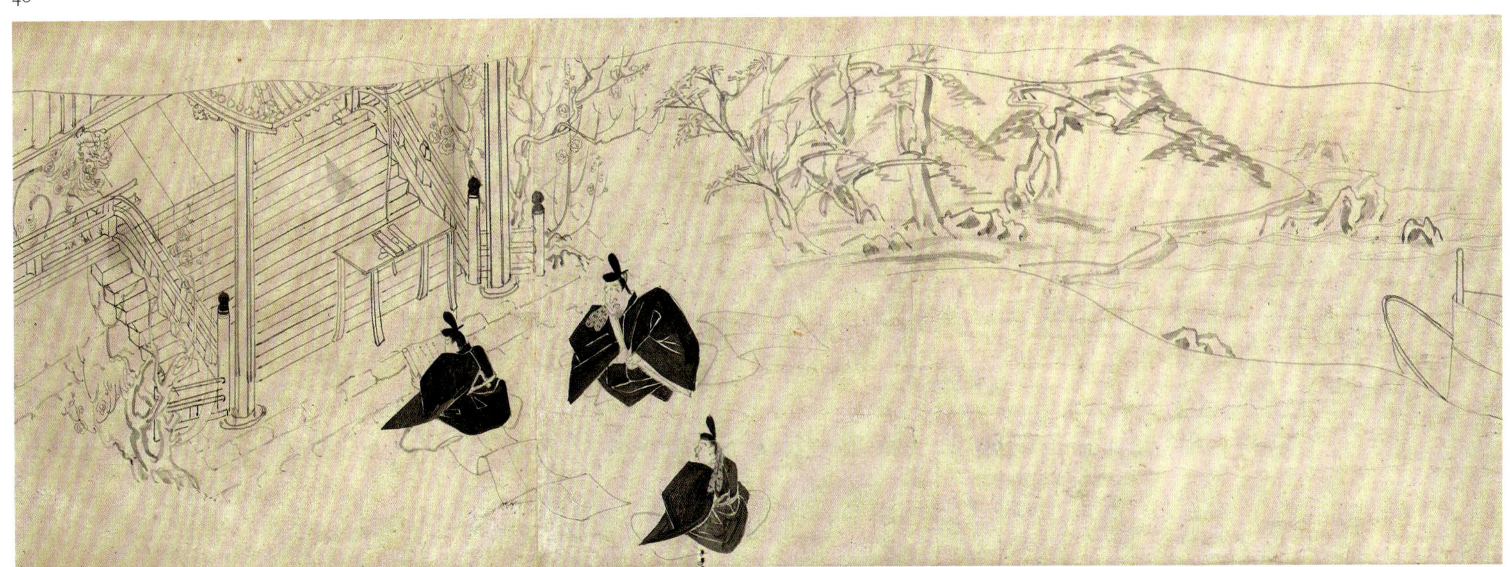

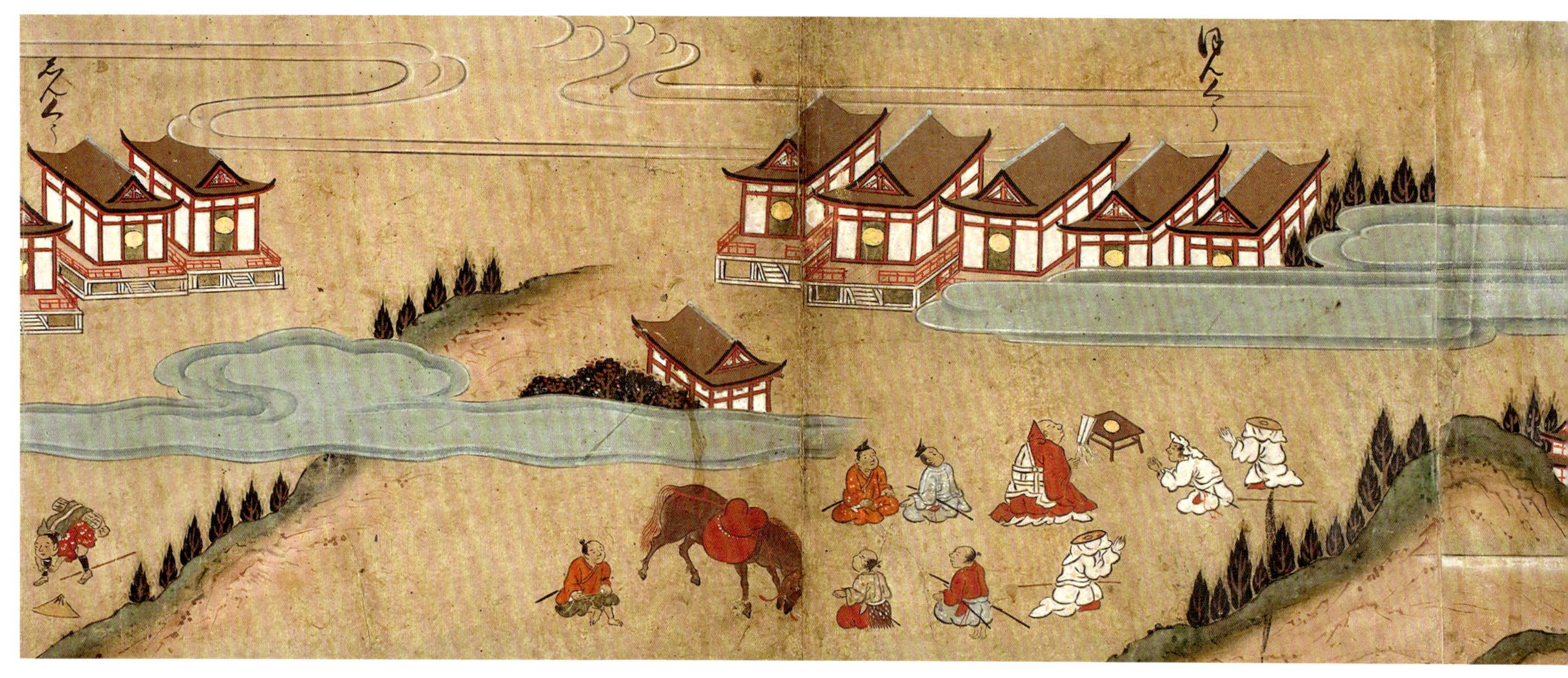

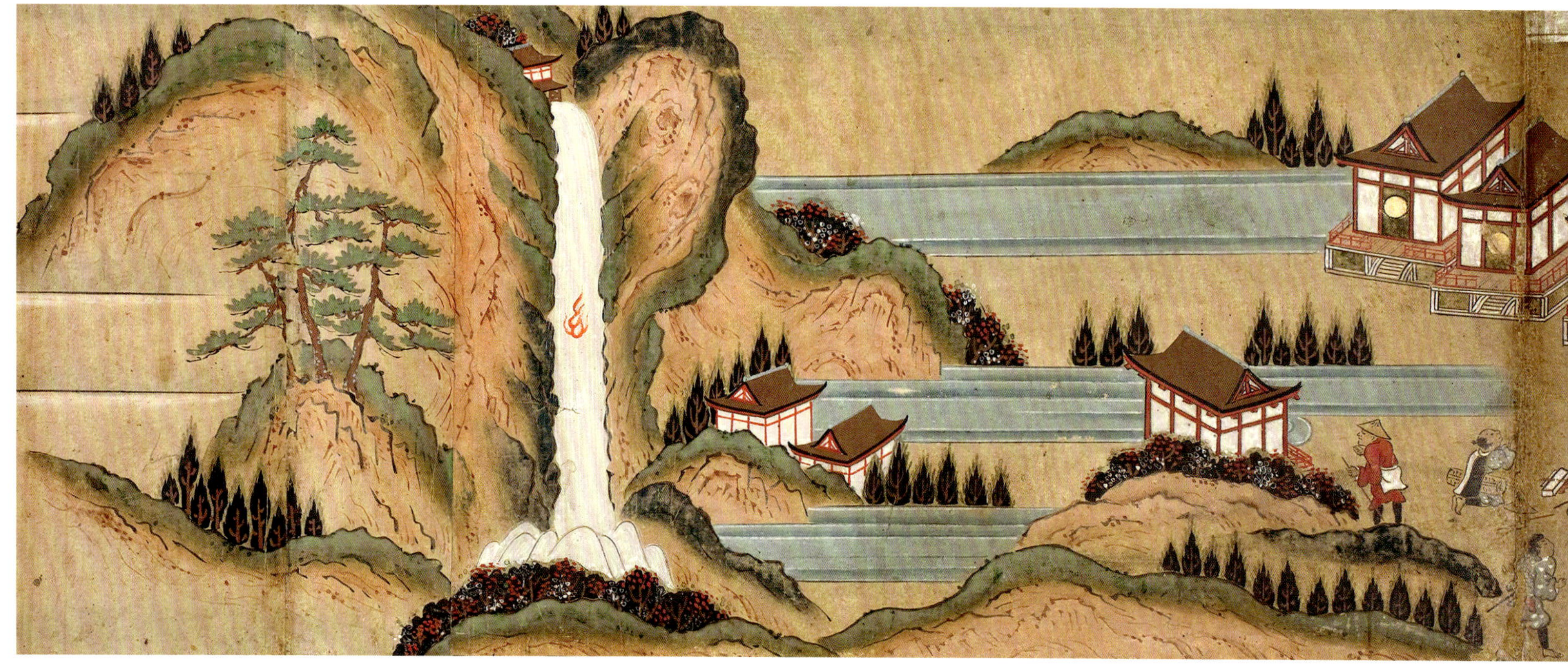

41. *Kumano engi emaki* (熊野縁起絵巻)

Momoyama period, early 17th century
Three handscrolls; ink and color on paper
Scroll I: 24 x 1020.2 cm (9 1/2 in. x 33 ft. 5 5/8 in.)
Scroll II: 24 x 615.5 cm (9 1/2 in. x 20 ft. 2 3/8 in.)
Scroll III (*detail, above*) 24 x 421 cm
(9 1/2 in. x 13 ft. 9 3/4 in.)
Text

Literature: Ruch 1979, nos. 6–8; *Zaigai Nara Ehon* 1981, no. 25; Miya Tsugio et al. 1995, pp. 111–13; Proser 2010, no. 68.

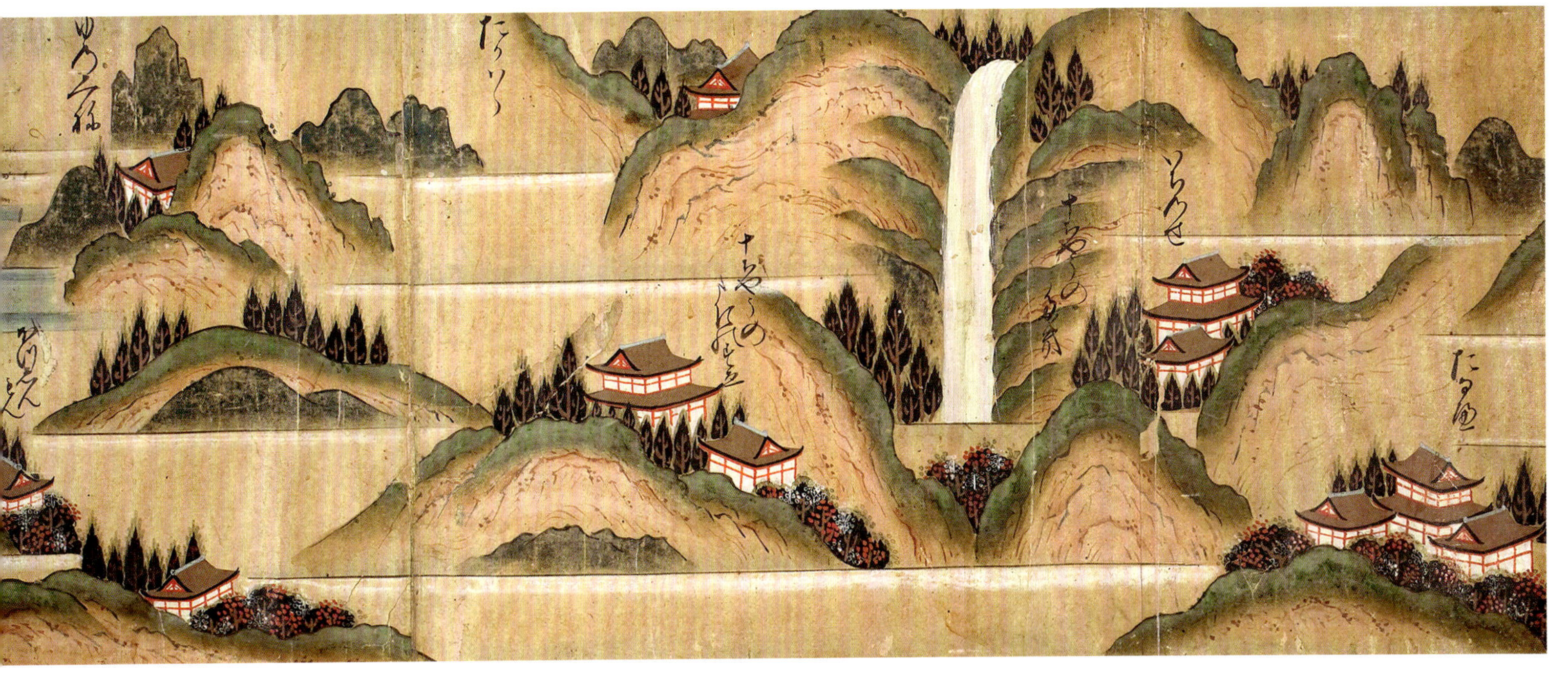

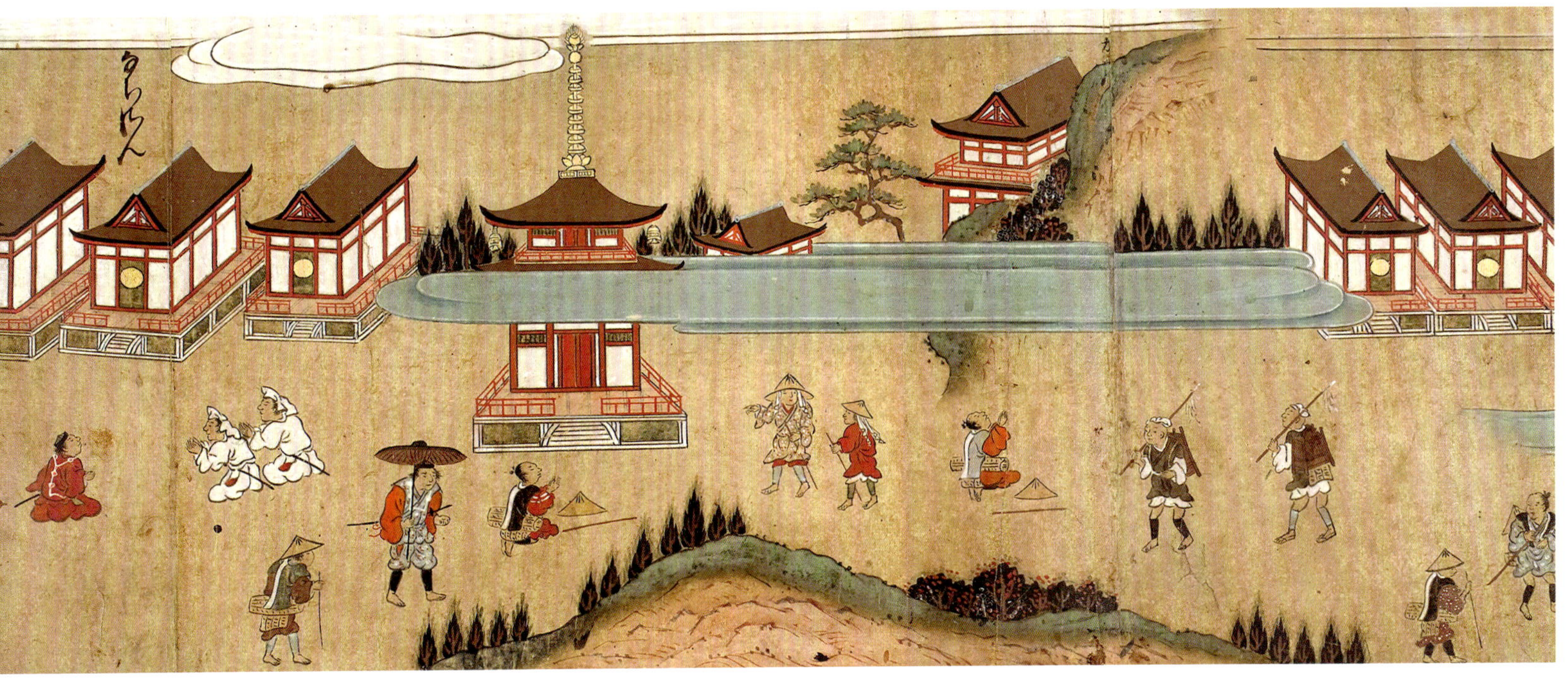

Chapter 1 Details

† *denotes illustrated items*

---

8. Fugen Enmei Bosatsu

Text

I note here: this is according to the description given in the Fugen Enmei Sutra, *translated by Fu Kū* [Ch. Bu Kong], *whitish flesh color.*

---

10. Memyō Bosatsu

Text

Mandala / Memyō Bosatsu, with six arms and in pale flesh color, rides on a white horse. Near the horse's mouth are two figures: one of them named Sanshitsu. At the back are three figures: Sanbo, Sanmyō, and San'in, all stepping on clouds. In front of the horse is a worshipping disciple. / Eulogy: Memyō Bosatsu, incarnating himself in the cosmos, / turns into a silkworm that spits out silk flosses. / Flying around the world, it is heralded by a suffusion of music, / responsive to people's offerings, it brings them boundless good fortune.

[Figures, from right to left]: *Sanmyō, San'in, Sanbo, Sanshitsu; Worshipping disciple making an offering*

---

† 12. Fudō Myōō with Four Attendants

Signature

Seed syllables followed by *Chikai* and *kaō*

---

† 17. Aizen Mandala

Text

[upper right of scroll] *red, wrathful*; [top center]: *face color, flesh white*; *Miroku*; [middle center] *red*; [lower center] *white, Kannon*; [top left] *red*

[on reverse, from upper right to lower left] *Daishō kongō*: *first time this is found in a scripture*; *Kusari*; *Is it Enma?*; *This is a so-called Ten* [*Deva*]; *Aizen Ō Mandala*; *Copied on the fifth day of the third month of 1107 from a model owned by Sanmai Ajari Ryōyū, who had inherited it from his teacher, Ōhara Sōzu Chōen* [1016–1081]; *kaō*

---

20. Dai Shōjin Bosatsu from *Kontai butsugajō*

Text

Dai Shōjin Bosatsu, Sanmaiyagyō, Futaikongō, shuji, followed by a seed syllable for *Naraenten*

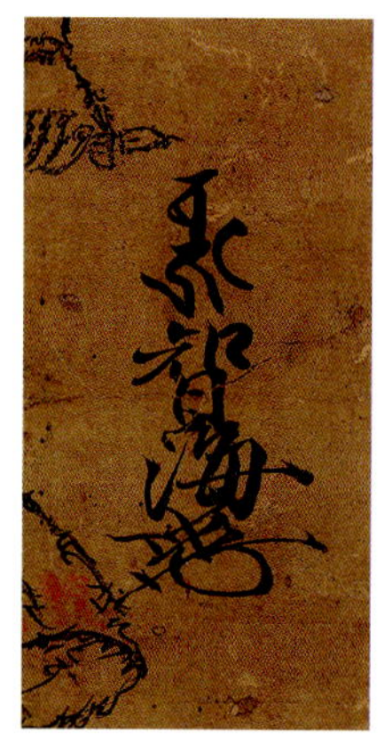

12

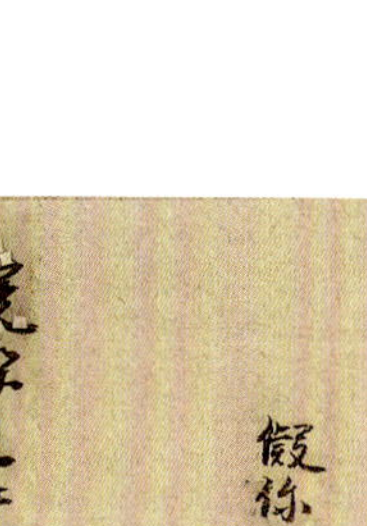

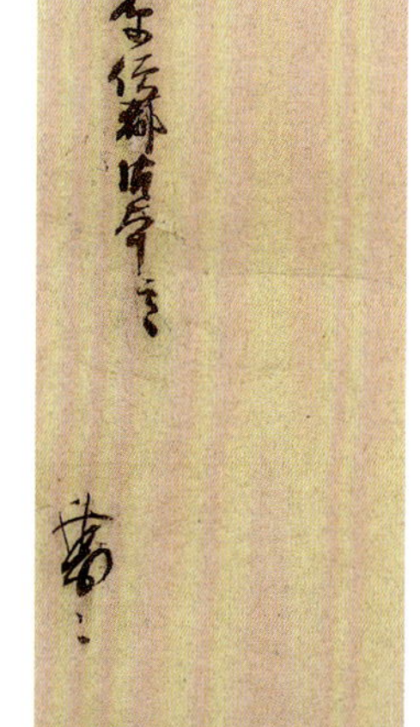

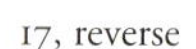

17, reverse

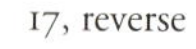

17, reverse

---

† 21. Iconographic Drawings

Text

[at end of scroll I] *Copying of the iconographic drawings completed on the twenty-second day of the fourth month. Shinken completed copying at Jizōin, Daigoji, on the twentieth day of the fourth month of 1230.*

[at end of scroll II] *Completed checking against the Tsūchiin version, in the fifth month of 1230, at Jizōin of Saienji. However, . . .* [illegible]

Signature

[at end of each scroll] *Shinken*

---

23. *Daihōkōbutsu kegonkyō shūjibun*, the so-called *Jingojikyō*

Seal

Jingoji

---

† 25. Satsubari, the Second of the Sixteen Rakan

Text

The second of the Sixteen Rakan, Satsubari [partially illegible]

---

27. Portrait of Monk Rigen (?)

Text

Prajñā Wisdom: / All things are formed by the mind. / The path to wisdom that is spoken of comes entirely from quietude.

---

29. The Thirty-sixth Stage from *Zenzai Dōji's Fifty-five Pilgrimages*

Text

The Thirty-sixth Wise One / The Elder of Firm Deliverance professed at the Fertile Town. / Diligently seeking the orthodox dharma with no respite; / serving the Buddha in all capacities with thorough trust and devotion. / Purity, solemn sanctity, and firmness of will / all emerge from the mind that clings to nothing.

---

† 30a, b. From *Jin'ōji engi emaki*

Text

[30a, right to left] *Gongen takes Shikigami as a guide*; *Gongen invokes a medium and makes a request*; *Gongen*

[30b] *Haraigawa*

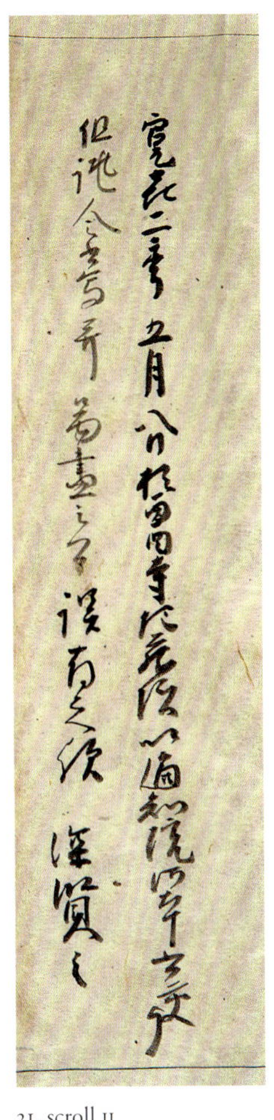

21, scroll II

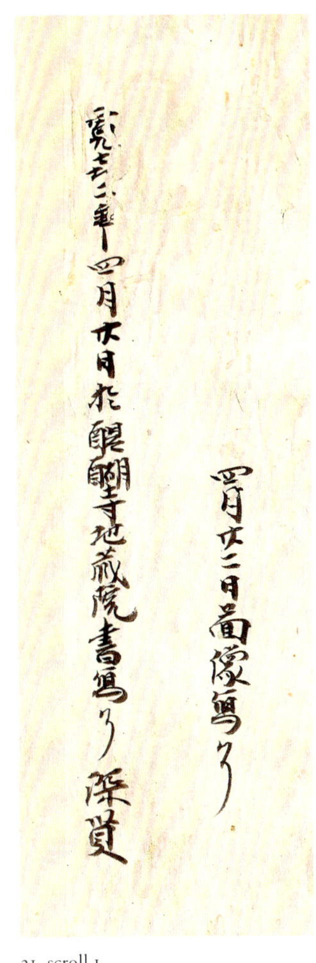

21, scroll I

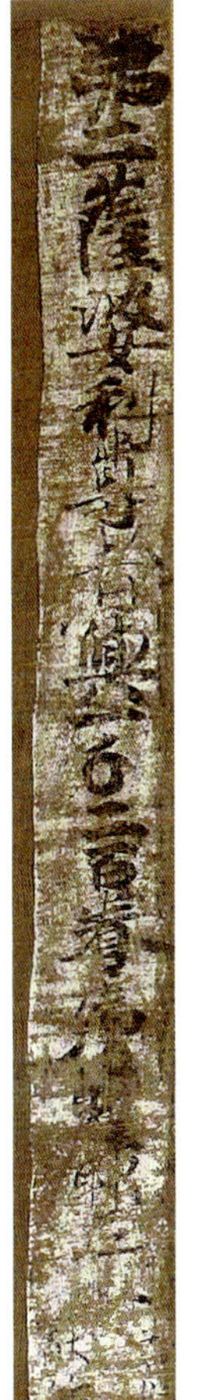

25

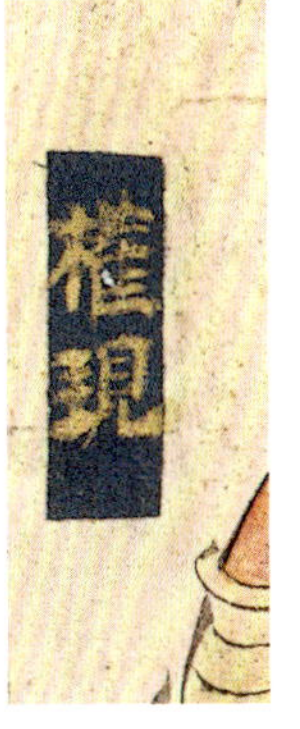

30a

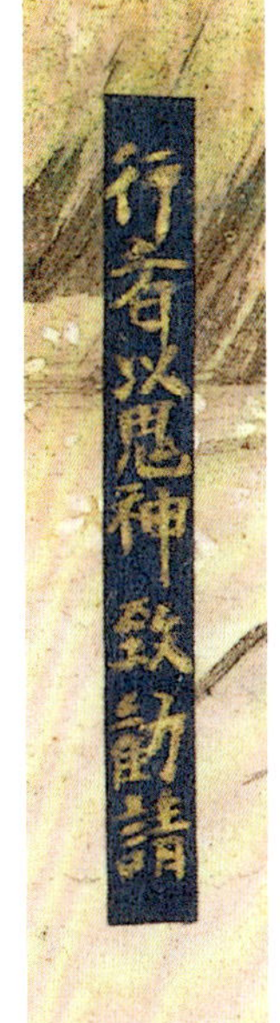

30a

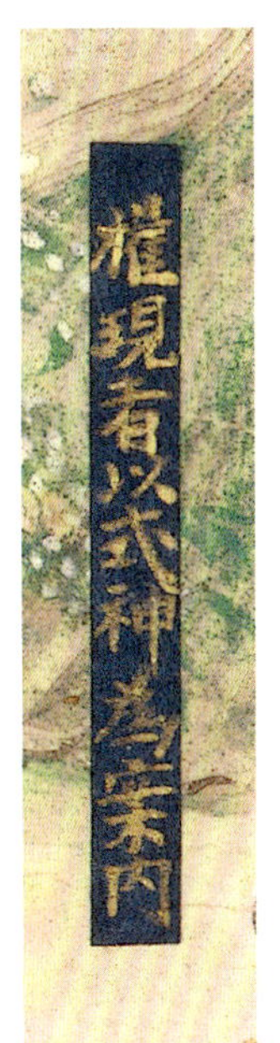

30a

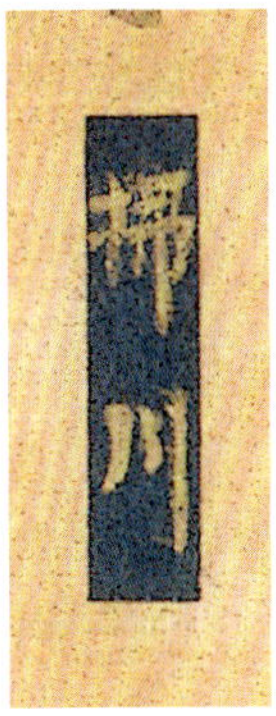

30b

† 31. The Ten Ox-Herding Songs

Text

Song 2. Seeing the Footprints of the Ox
Commentary / Relying on sutras, one comprehends the meaning, / and studying the doctrines, one finds some traces. / As it becomes clear that differently shaped metal vessels / are all made from the same piece of metal, / one realizes that the myriad entities [one thinks one sees] / are formulated by oneself. / Unless one can separate the orthodox from the heretics, / how can one distinguish the true from the untrue? / Not having entered the gate as yet, / at least one has noticed the traces.

Poem / By the water, and under the trees, / there are numerous traces. / Fragrant grasses grow thickly, / did you see the ox? / Even in the depths of the distant mountain forest, / how could the upturned nostrils of the ox be concealed?

Song 4. Catching the Ox
Commentary / The ox lived in obscurity in the field for so long, / but I found him today. // While I am distracted by the beautiful scenery, / and the difficult chase, / the ox is longing for fragrant grass. // His mind is still stubborn. / And his wild nature yet remains. // If I wish him tamed, I must whip him.

Poem / With all my energy, I seize the ox. // His will is strong, and his power inexhaustible. / He cannot be tamed easily. // Sometimes he charges to the high plateau, // and there he stays, deep in the mist.

Signature

In the Year of the Fifth Tiger of the Kōan Era [1278], *on the sixteenth day of the eighth month, I am inscribing the postscript of the Ten Pictures of the Ox*; [illegible] *gi*

Seal

[at end of scroll] *kaō*

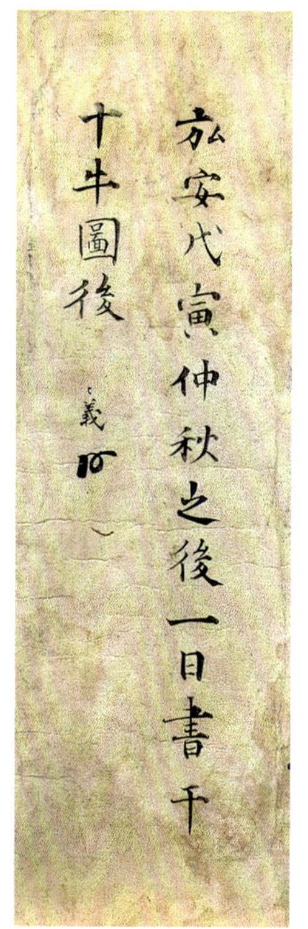

31

41. *Kumano engi emaki*

Text

Minabe; *Tanabe*; *Ichinose*; *Jūjō no Taki*; *Jūjō no Taki no sue*; *Takahara*; *Yu no Mine*; *Busshin mon*; *Hongū*; *Shingū*; *Nachisan*

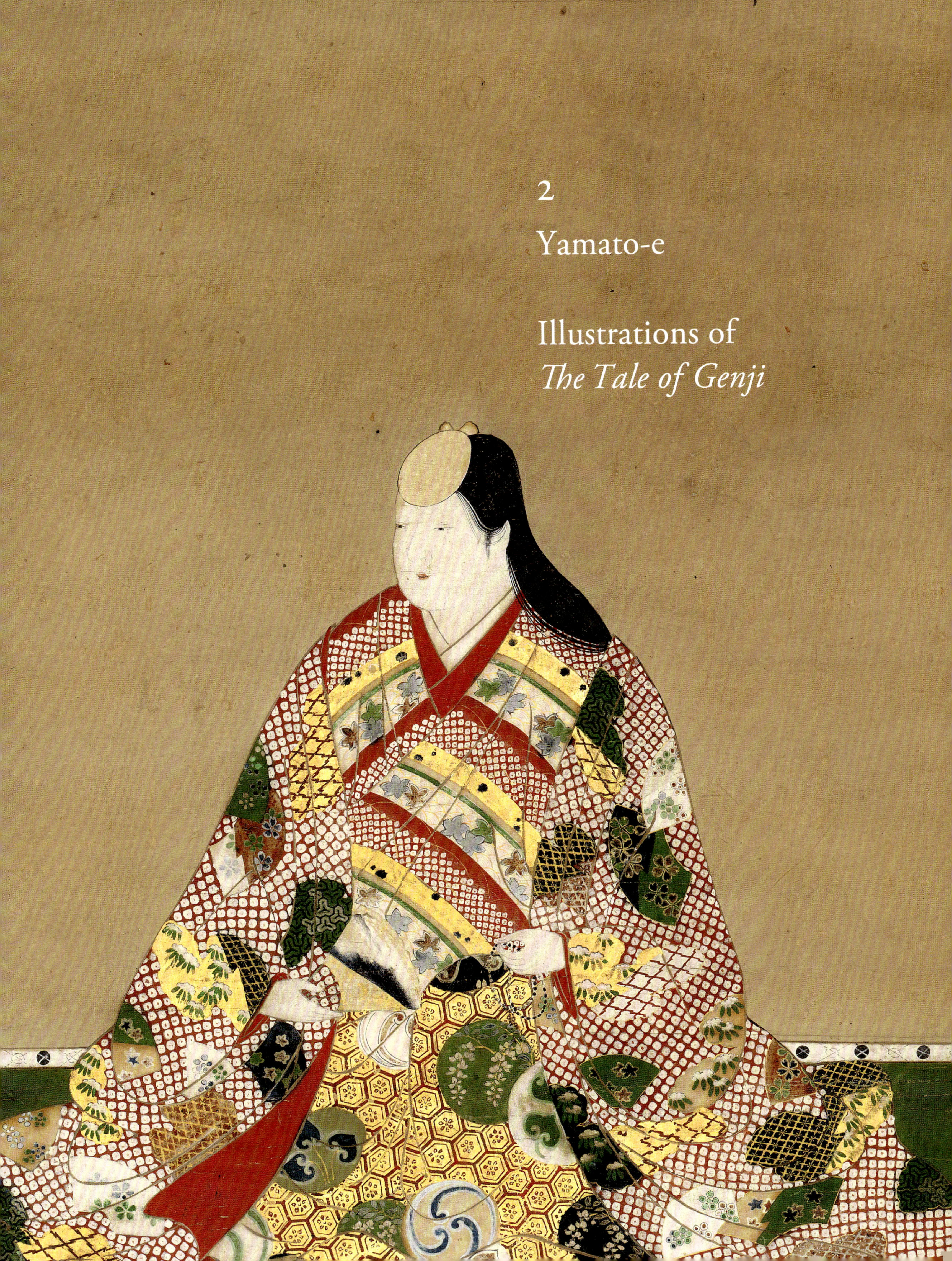

2

Yamato-e

Illustrations of *The Tale of Genji*

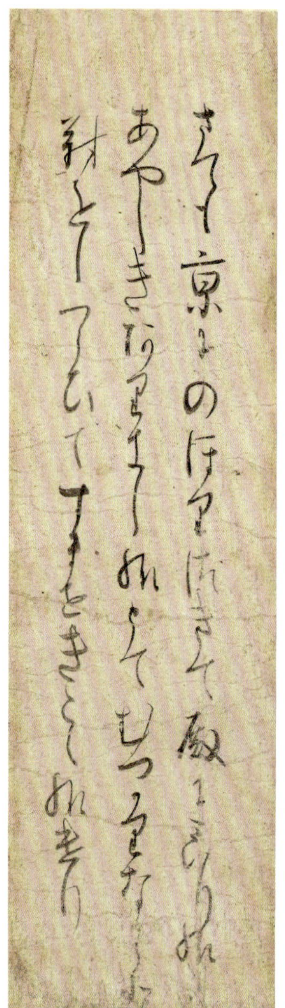

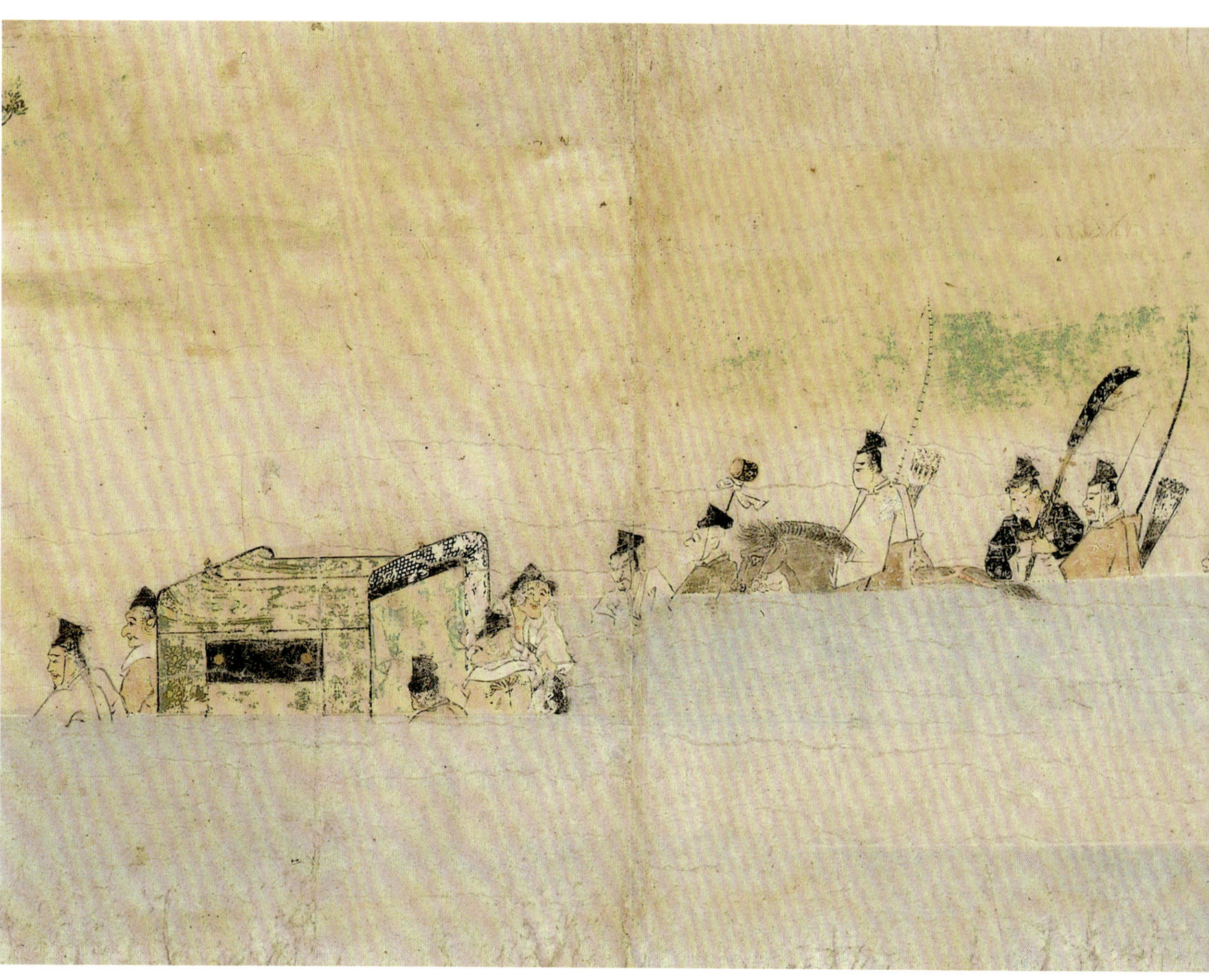

42. From *Sumiyoshi monogatari emaki* (住吉物語絵巻)

Kamakura period, late 13th century
Fragments of handscroll, mounted as two hanging scrolls
Scroll I: ink and color on paper; 31.1 x 71.5 cm ($12\frac{1}{4}$ x $28\frac{1}{8}$ in.)
Scroll II: ink on paper; 30.5 x 8.4 cm (12 x $3\frac{1}{4}$ in.)
Text

Ex coll.: Masuda Tarō, Kanagawa Prefecture; Momiyama Hanzaburō; Yoshida Tanzaemon

Literature: Hirata Hisashi 1912, pl. 30; Murase 1975, no. 21; Tokyo National Museum 1985a, no. 5; Avitabile 1990, no. 20; Tokyo National Museum 1993, no. 19; Murase 2000, no. 37; Tsuji Nobuo et al. 2005, no. 21.

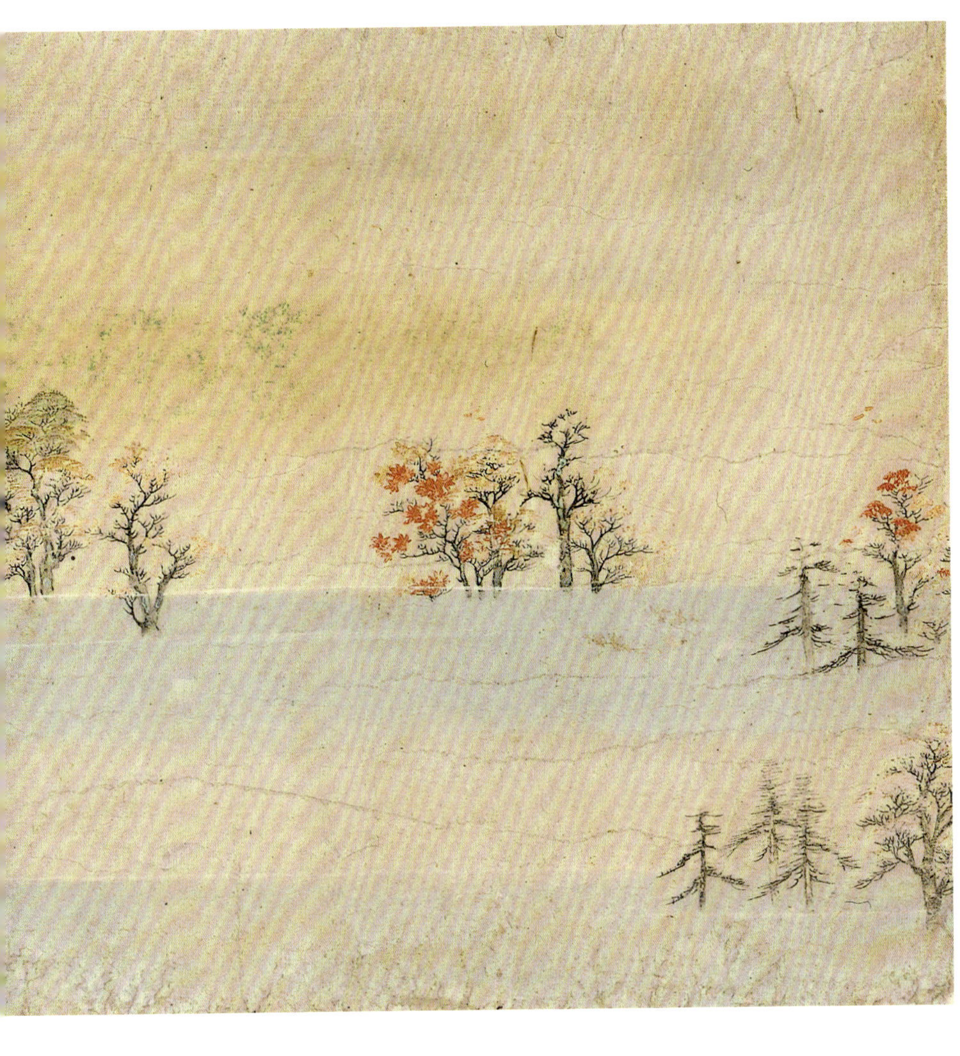

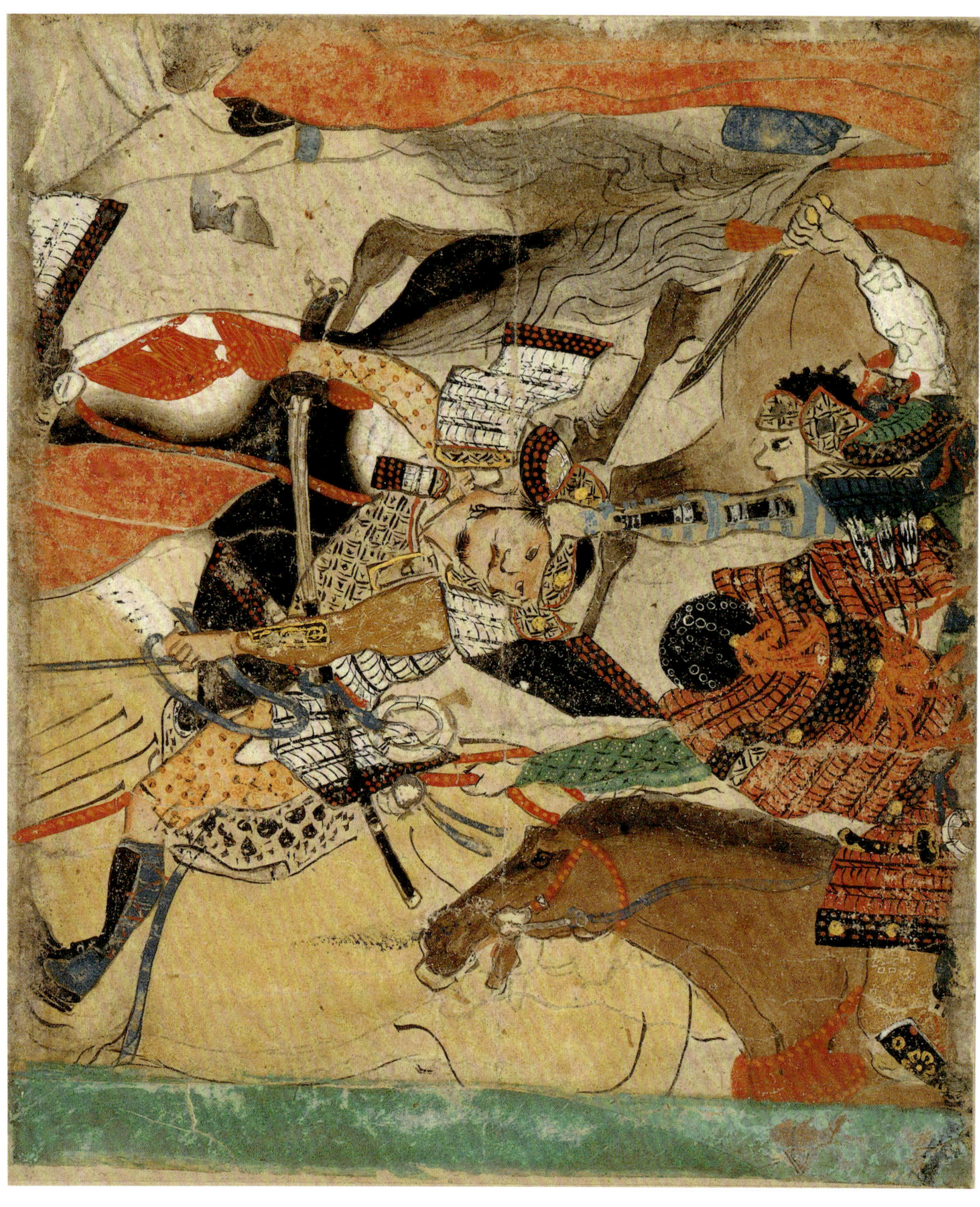

43. Battle at Rokuhara (六波羅合戦), from *Heiji monogatari emaki* (平治物語絵巻)

Kamakura period, first quarter of 14th century
Handscroll fragment, mounted as hanging scroll; ink and color on paper
17.4 x 14.8 cm (6⅞ x 5⅞ in.)

Ex coll.: Okamoto Ryōhei

Literature: Akiyama Terukazu 1952, pl. 9, fig. 10; Murase 1967, fig. 13; Weber 1968, p. 193; Shimada Shūjirō 1969, vol. 1, pl. 14; Matsushita Takaaki 1975, pl. 43; Murase 1975, no. 23; Komatsu Shigemi 1977b, fig. 10; Akiyama Terukazu 1980a, no. 9; Meech-Pekarik 1985, pl. VI; Tokyo National Museum 1985a, no. 6; Avitabile 1990, no. 19; Murase 2000, no. 38; Tsuji Nobuo et al. 2005, no. 22.

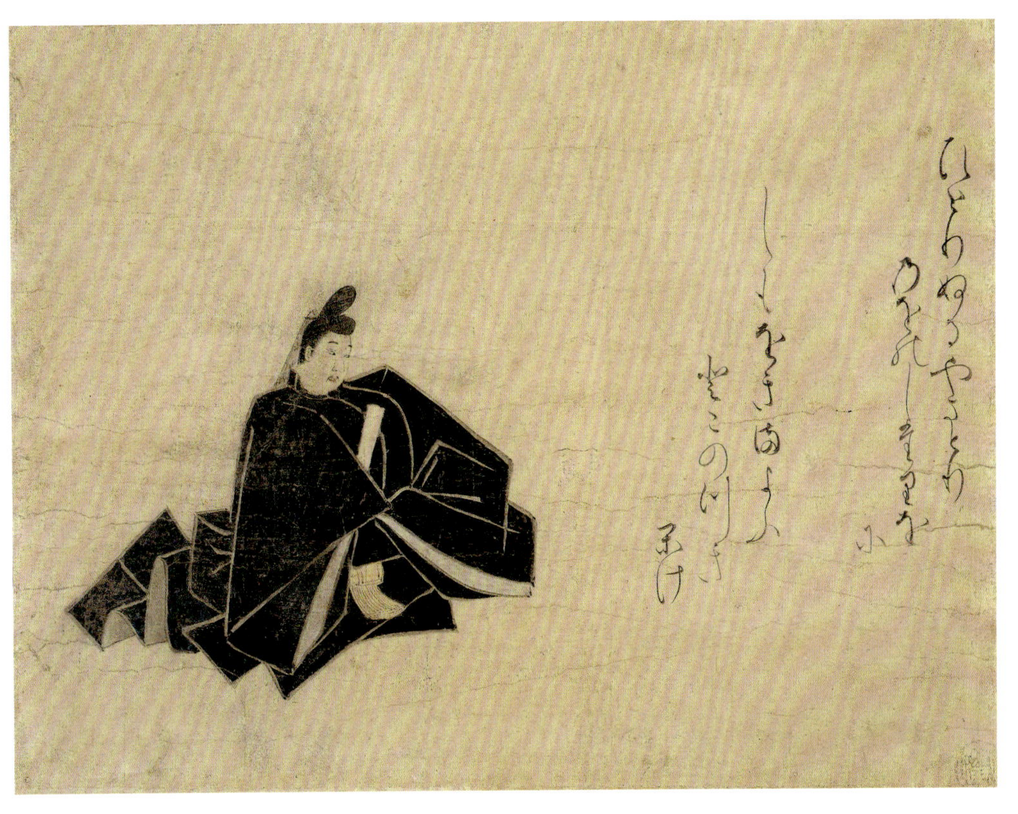

44. Fujiwara Teika (藤原定家), from *Ikkasen isshubon* (一歌仙一首本)

Kamakura period, early 14th century
Handscroll fragment, mounted as hanging scroll; ink and color on paper
28.7 x 37.5 cm (11¼ x 14¾ in.)
Text

Ex coll.: Sekido Akihiko, Nagoya

Literature: Shimonaka Kunihiko 1954–68, vol. 19 (1965), fig. 20; Mori Tōru 1965, fig. 8; Murase 1975, no. 20; Mori Tōru 1978, p. 99, fig. 7; Tokyo National Museum 1985a, no. 9; Wheelwright 1989, no. 3; Avitabile 1990, no. 23; Murase 2000, no. 39.

45. The Poets Henjō (遍昭) and Jichin (慈鎮), from *Mokuhitsu jidai fudō uta awase-e* (木筆時代不同歌合絵)

Nanbokuchō period, mid-14th century
Handscroll fragment, mounted as hanging scroll; ink on paper
31.2 x 52.8 cm (12¼ x 20¾ in.)
Text

Ex coll.: Mori Collection

Literature: Mori Tōru 1965, fig. 6; Mori Tōru 1978, pl. 32; Murase 1993, no. 34; Murase 2000, no. 40.

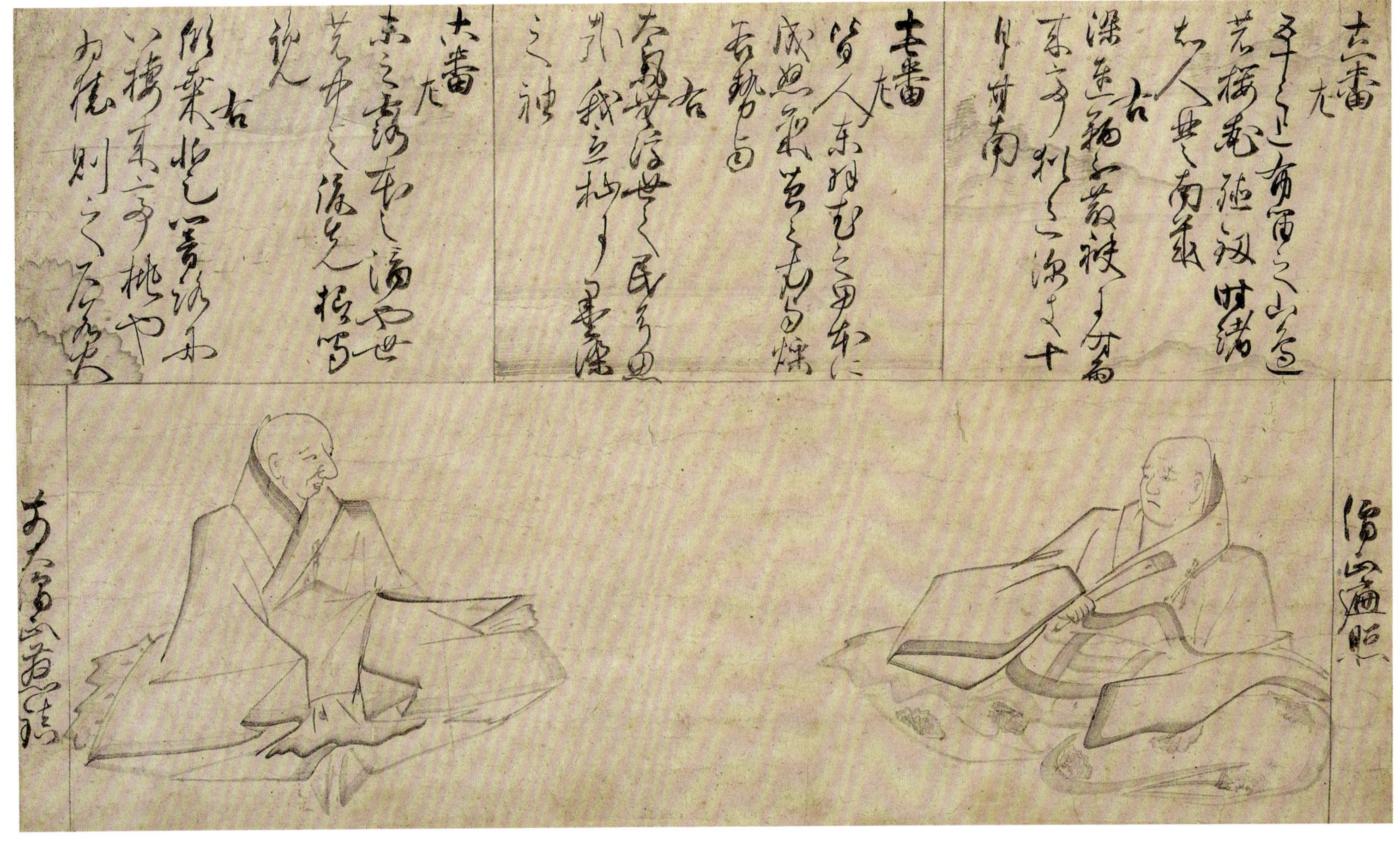

46. Koōgimi (小大君), from Fujifusa version of *Thirty-six Immortal Poets* (藤房本三十六歌仙絵)

Muromachi period, first half of 15th century
Handscroll fragment, mounted as hanging scroll; ink and color on paper
29 x 41.2 cm (11 3/8 x 16 1/4 in.)
Text

Ex coll.: Mrs. John D. Rockefeller III

Literature: Mori Tōru 1978, pl. 11-3; Mori Tōru 1979, pl. 100; Murase 2000, no. 41.

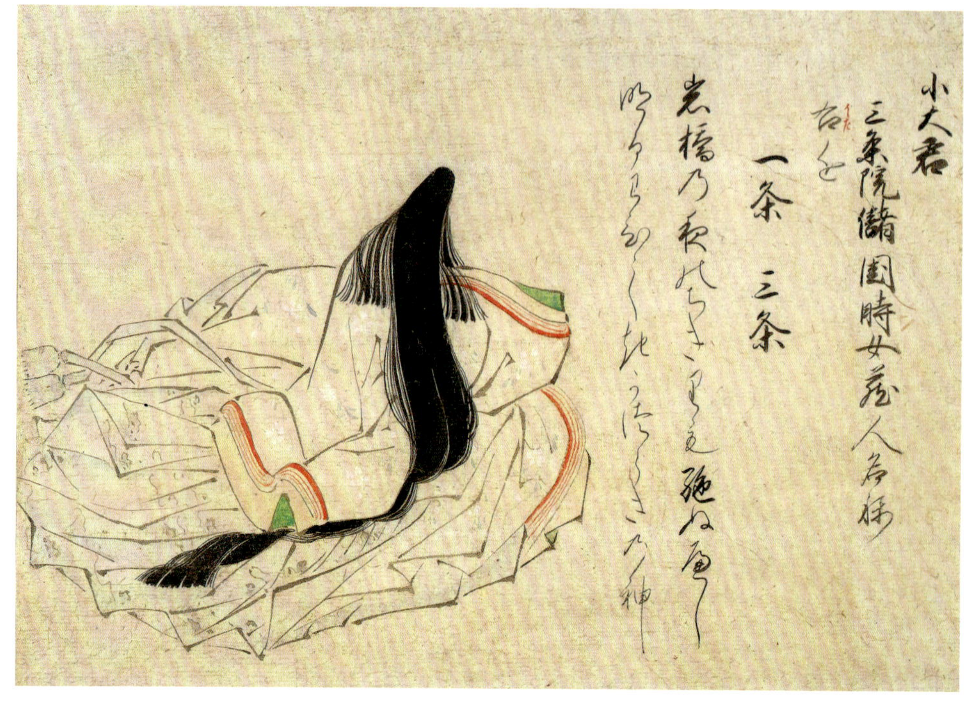

47. Ariwara Narihira (在原業平, 825–880), from Fujifusa version of *Thirty-six Immortal Poets* (藤房本三十六歌仙絵)

Muromachi period, first half of 15th century
Handscroll fragment, mounted as hanging scroll; ink and color on paper
25.2 x 45.7 cm (9 7/8 x 18 in.)
Text

Literature: Mori Tōru 1978, p. 31 (ill.); Mori Tōru 1979, p. 70 (ill.).

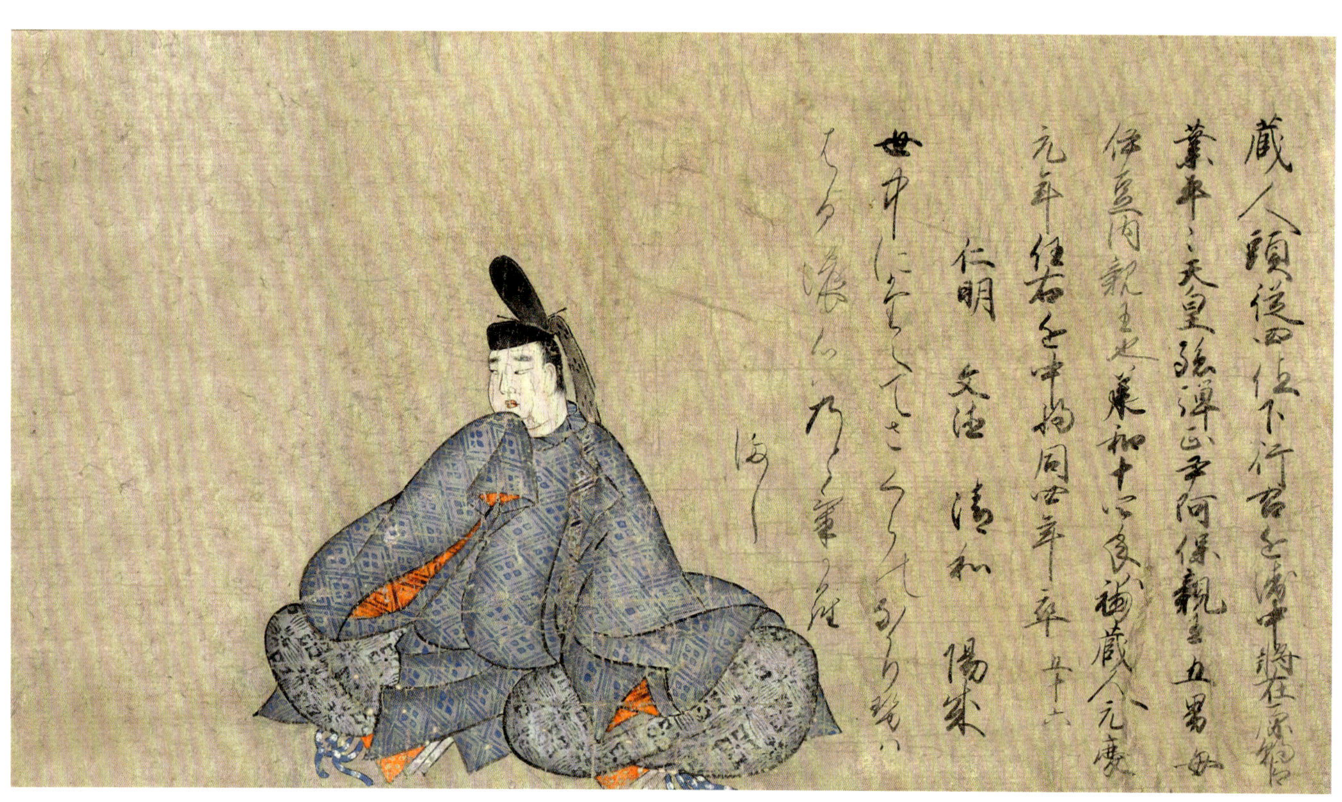

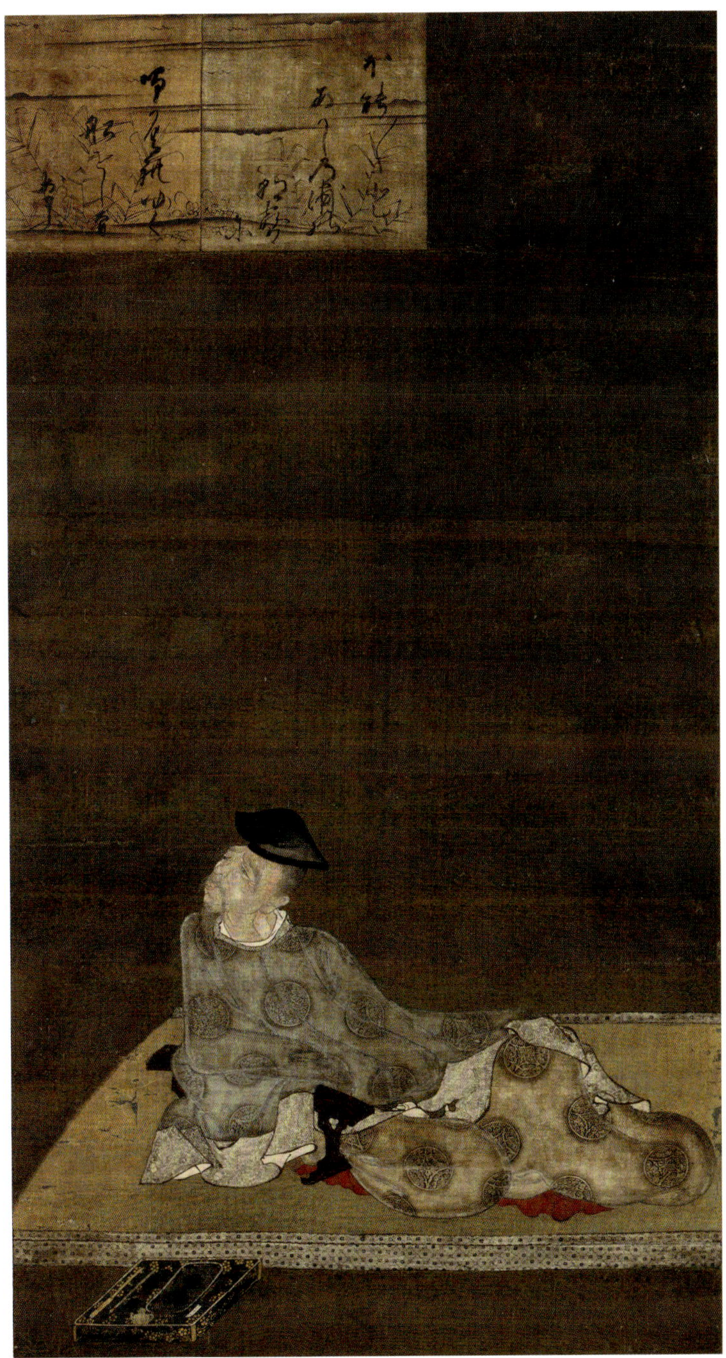

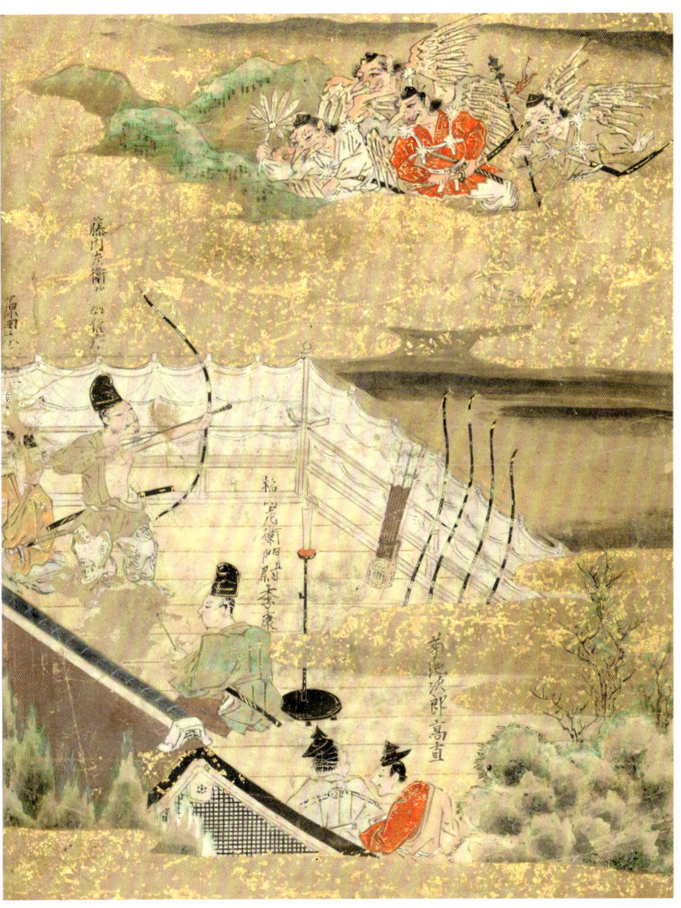

49. From *Tengu zōshi emaki* (?)
(天狗草紙絵巻)

Muromachi period, 16th century
Handscroll fragment, mounted as hanging scroll;
ink, color, and gold on paper
33.3 x 27.1 cm ($13^1/_8$ x $10^5/_8$ in.)
Text

48. Kakinomoto no Hitomaro
(柿本人麻呂)

Muromachi period, 16th century
Hanging scroll; ink, color, and gold on silk
71.1 x 38.2 cm (28 x 15 in.)
Text

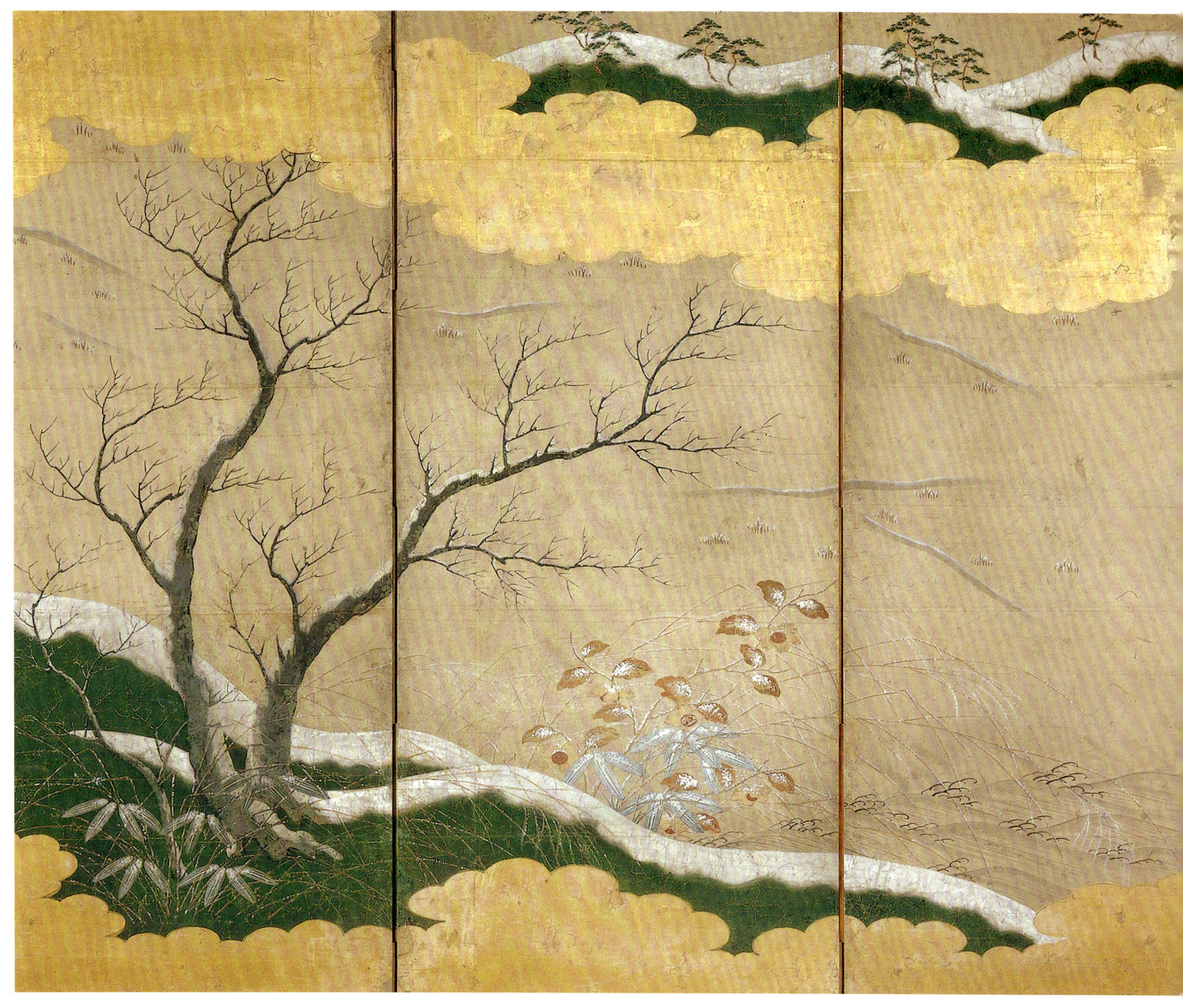

50. Mountains and Streams in Autumn and Winter

Muromachi period, 16th century
Six-panel folding screen; ink, color, and gold on paper
148.6 x 347.3 cm (58 1/2 in. x 11 ft. 4 3/4 in.)

LITERATURE: Tsuji Nobuo et al. 2005, no. 32.

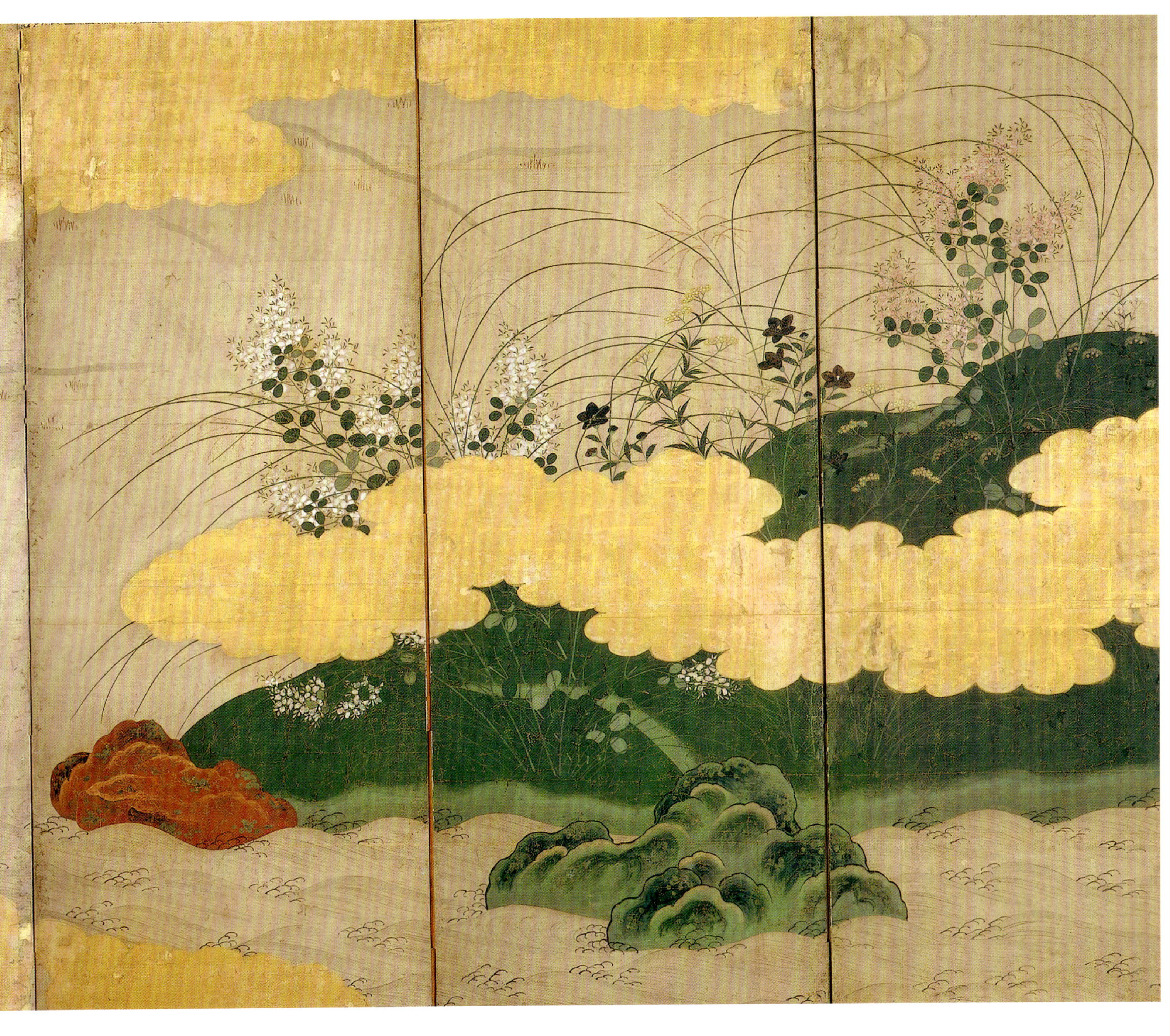

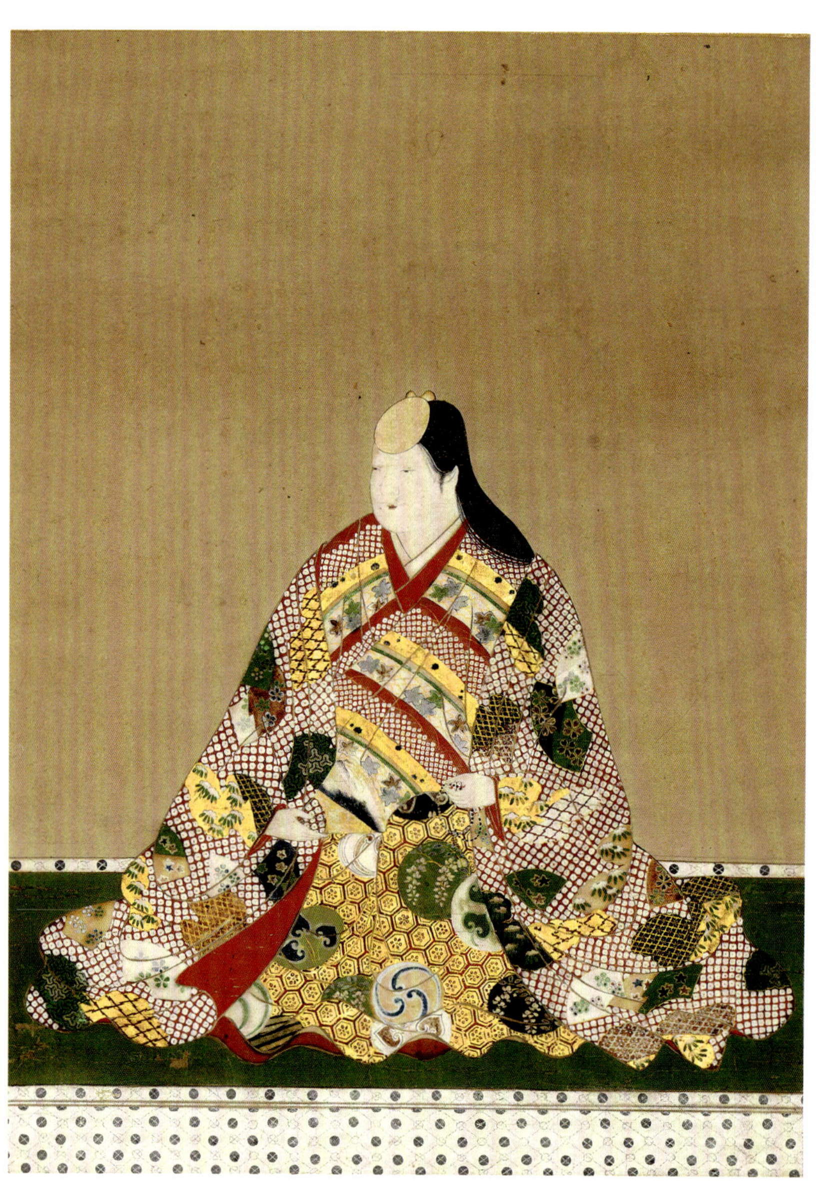

51. Portrait of a Lady

Edo period, early 17th century
Hanging scroll; ink, color, and gold on silk
50.7 x 35.1 cm (20 x 13 7/8 in.)

52. From *Saigyō monogatari emaki* (西行物語絵巻)

Edo period, 17th century
Section of handscroll, mounted as hanging scroll; ink and color on paper
30.6 x 67 cm (12 x 26 3/8 in.)
Text

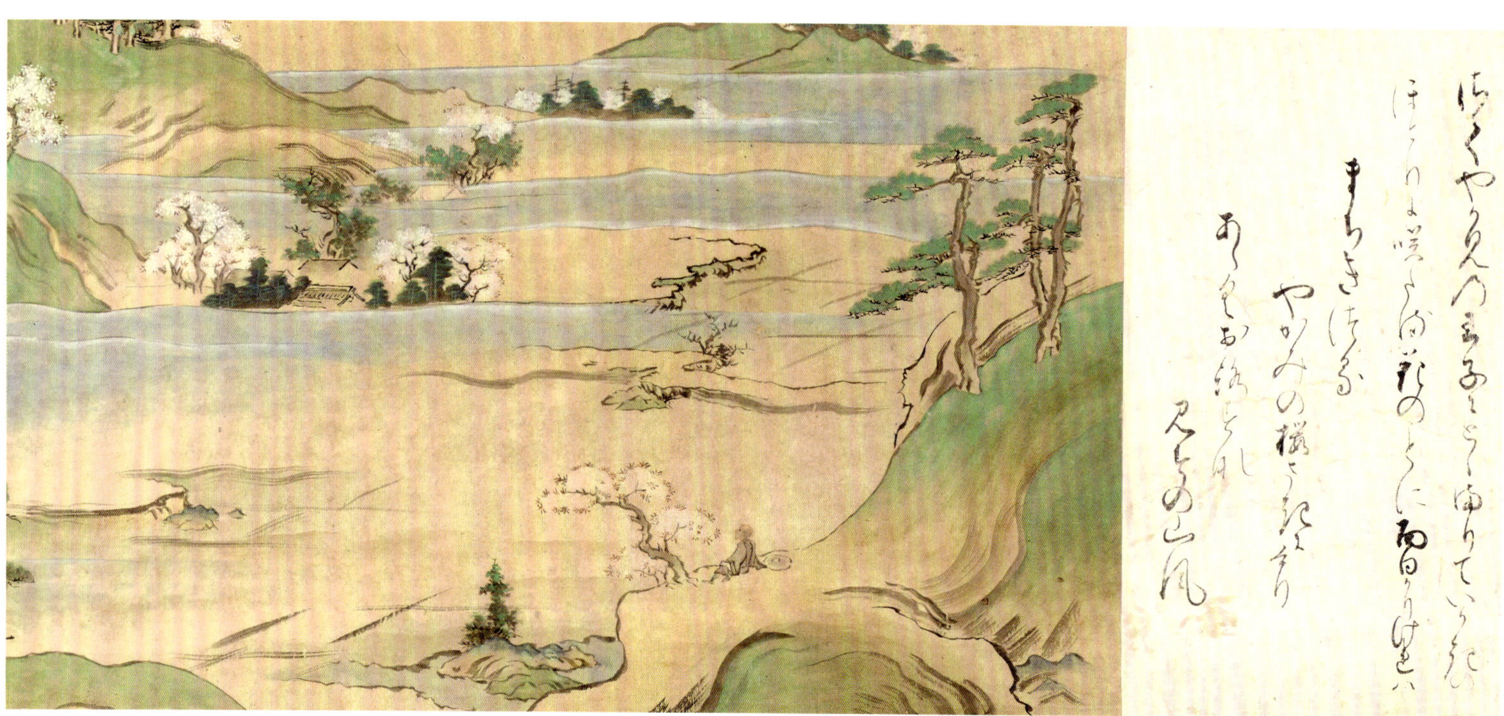

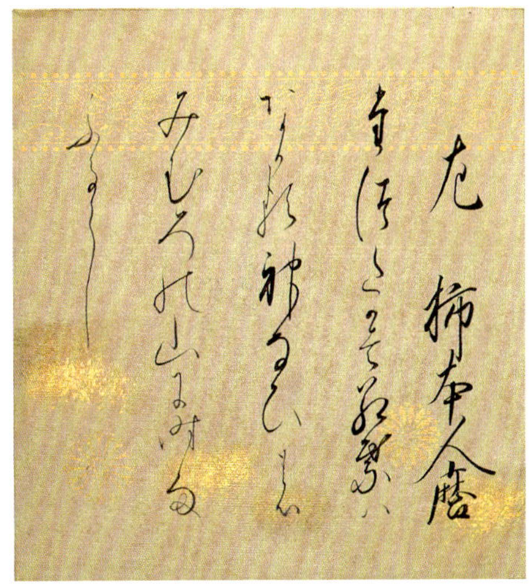

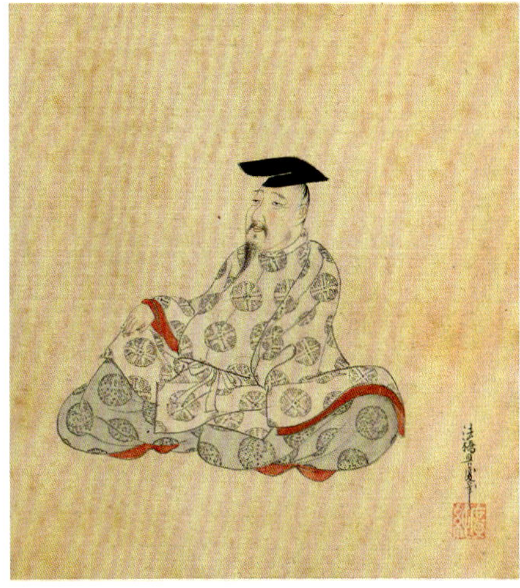

Sumiyoshi Gukei
(住吉具慶; 1631–1705)

53. Kakinomoto no Hitomaro (柿本人麻呂), from *Thirty-six Immortal Poets* (三十六歌仙)

Edo period, 1674–92
Album with thirty-six paintings and thirty-six poems; ink, color, and gold on silk (paintings); ink and gold on paper (poems)
Each leaf 17.5 x 16 cm (6⅞ x 6¼ in.)
Text, signature, seals

Literature: Tokyo National Museum 1985a, no. 41; Avitabile 1990, pp. 122–23, no. 72; Tokyo National Museum 1993, pp. 214, 278, no. 113; Matsubara Shigeru 1996, pp. 58–72.

54. Minamoto Shunrai (or Toshiyori, 源俊頼; 1057?–1129)

Edo period, 17th century
Hanging scroll; ink and light color on silk
99.1 x 36.7 cm (39 x 14½ in.)
Text, seal

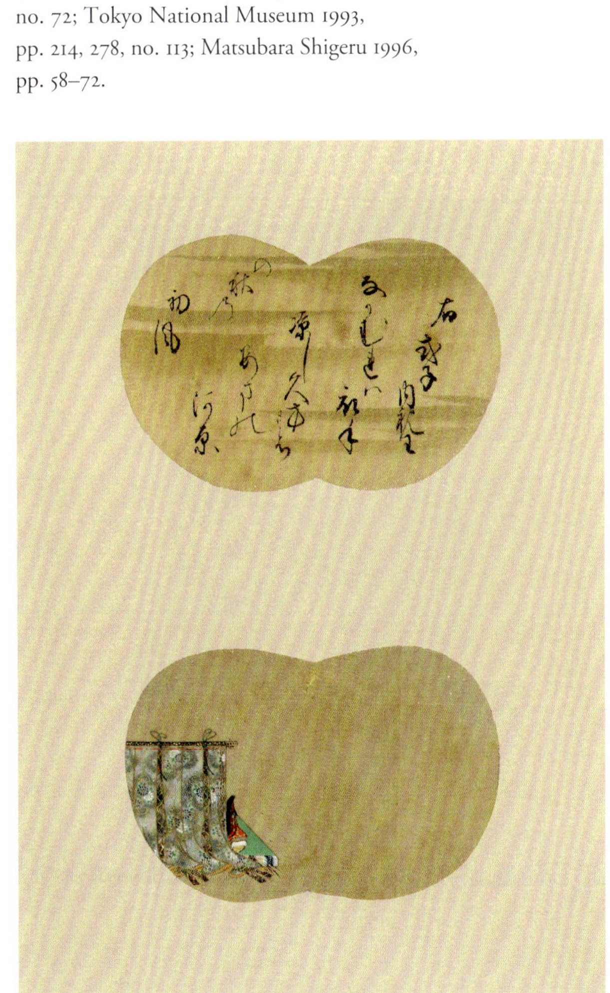

55. Princess Shikishi (式子内親王), from *Thirty-six Immortal Poets* (三十六歌仙)

Edo period, 17th century
Album with thirty-six poems and thirty-six paintings pasted in; ink, color, and gold on fan-shaped silk pieces
Each piece 24.2 x 15.9 cm (9½ x 6¼ in.)
Text

Literature: Burke 1993, fig. 3, pl. 2/no. 20.

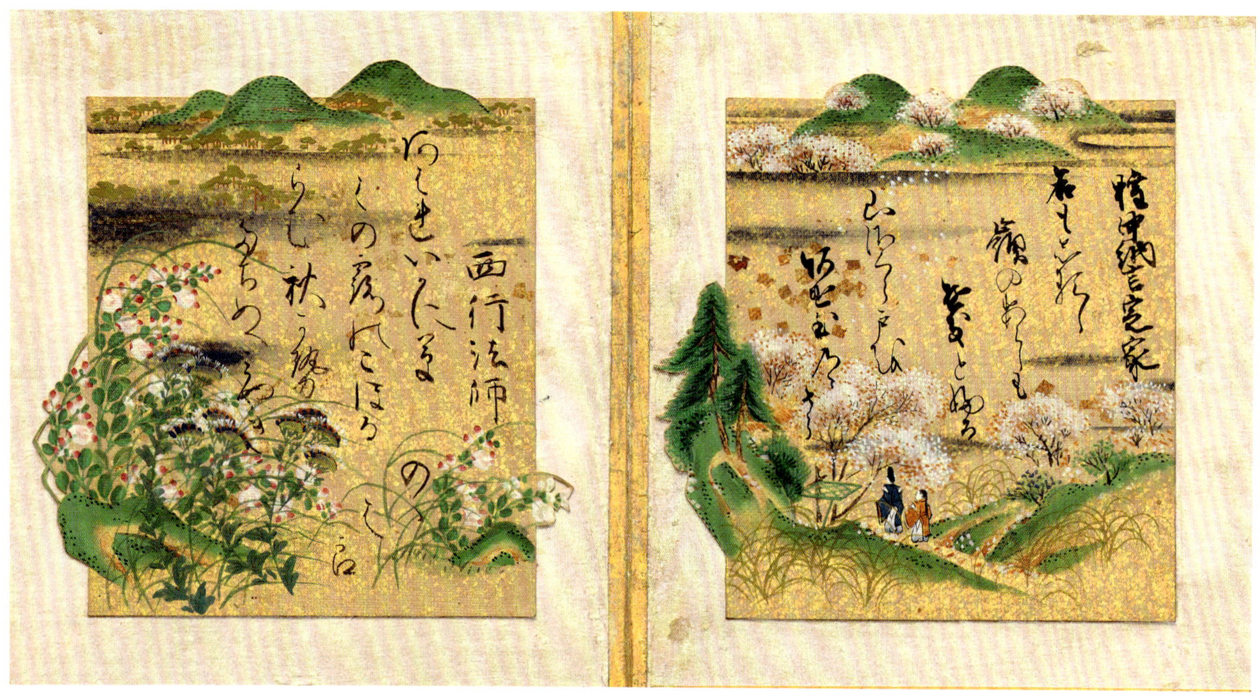

56. "Saigyō"

"Teika"

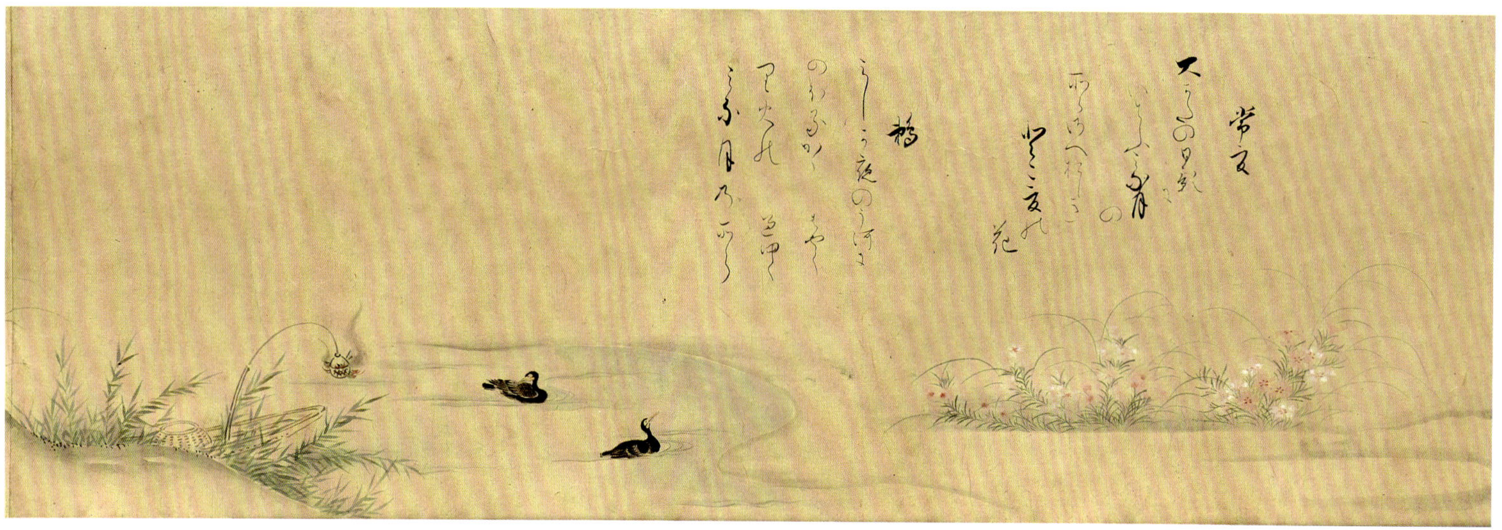

57

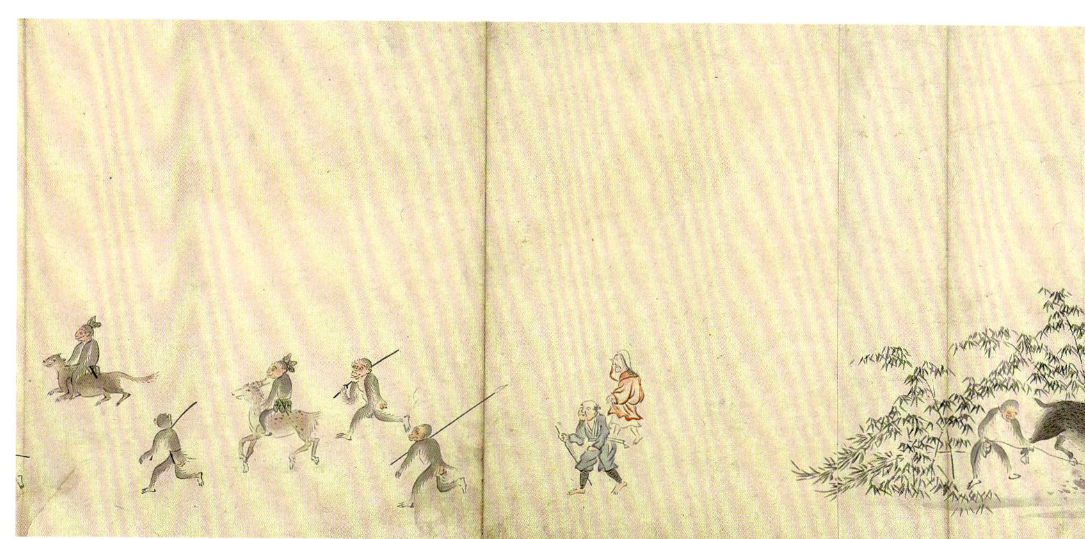

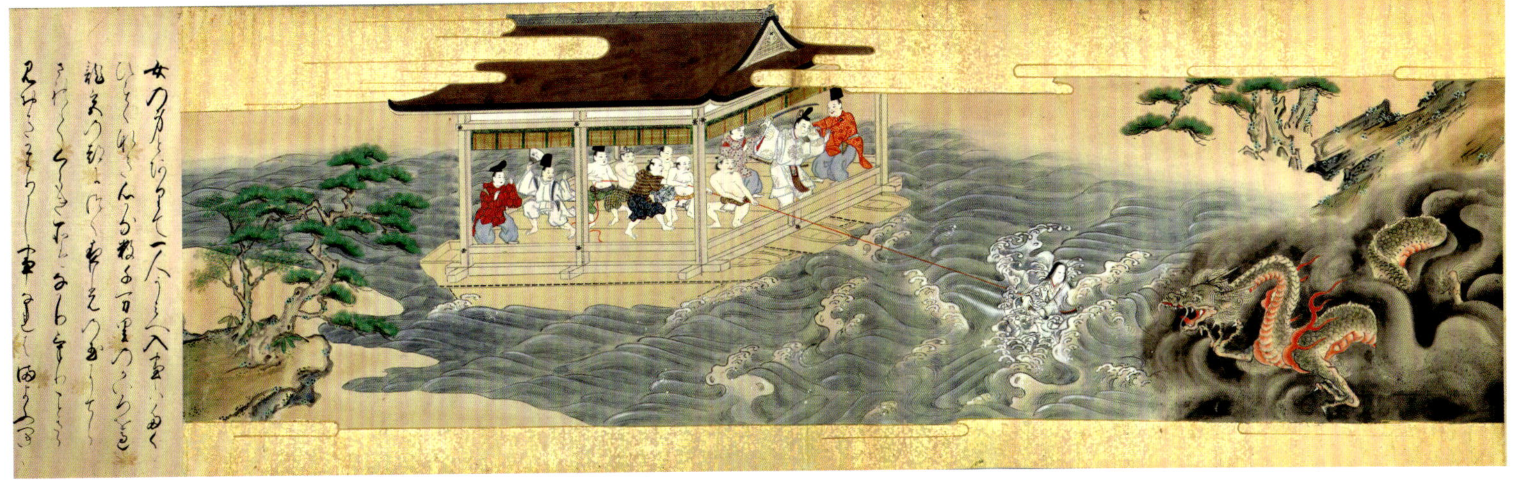

58

56. Poems from *Shūi gusō* (拾遺愚草) and *Shin kokin wakashū* (新古今和歌集)

Edo period, 18th century (before 1719)
Small album with six paintings and poems; ink, color, and gold on paper
Each painting 15.9 x 14.8 cm (6¼ x 5⅞ in.)
Text

57. The Sixth Month of *Teika's Poems on Flowers and Birds of the Twelve Months* (定家詠十二ヶ月花鳥図のうち六月)

Edo period, 18th century
Handscroll; ink and color on paper
18.3 x 567 cm (7¼ in. x 18 ft. 7¼ in.)
Text

Literature: Kasanoin and Heinrich 1998, p. 61.

58. *Taishokkan* (大織冠)

Edo period, 17th century
Three handscrolls; ink, color, and gold on paper
Scroll I: six sections of text and five paintings
42.1 x 1034.1 cm (16½ in. x 33 ft. 11⅛ in.)
Scroll II: four sections of text and paintings
42.1 x 1165.5 cm (16½ x 38 ft. 2⅞ in.)
Scroll III (*detail, above*): five sections of painting and text
42.1 x 1057.8 cm (16⅝ in. x 34 ft. 8½ in.)

Literature: Tsuji Eiko 1999.

59. *Saru no monogatari emaki* (猿の物語絵巻)

Edo period, 17th century
Handscroll; ink and light color on paper
23.8 x 894 cm (9⅜ in. x 29 ft. 4 in.)
Seal

59

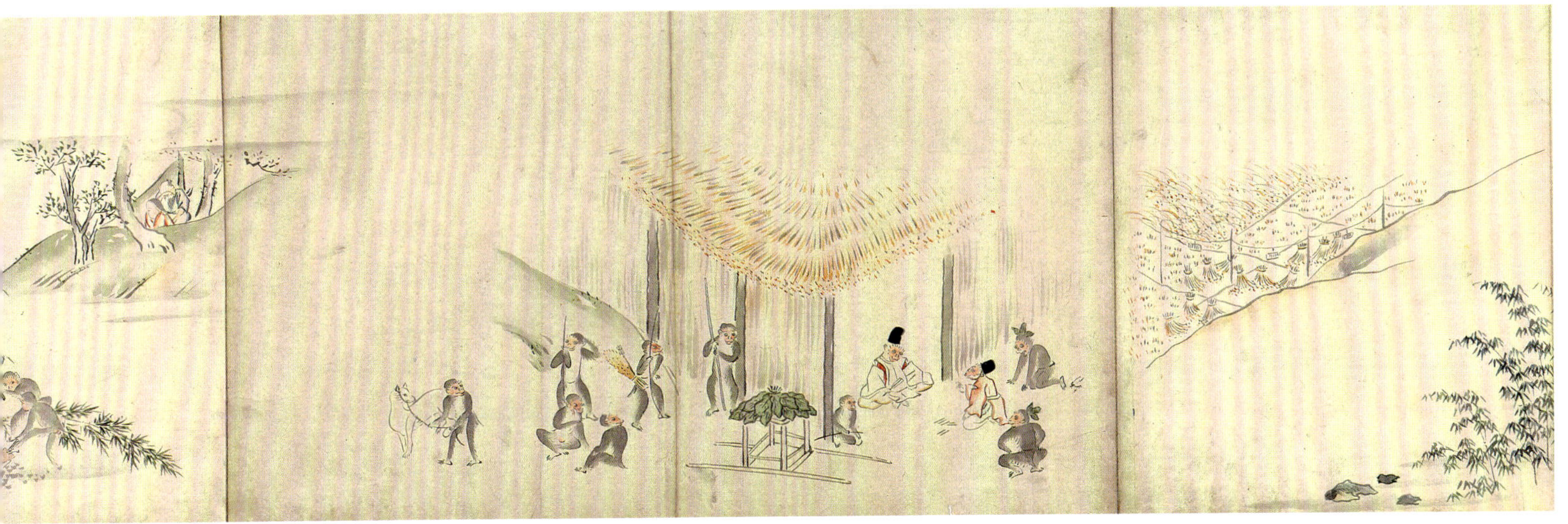

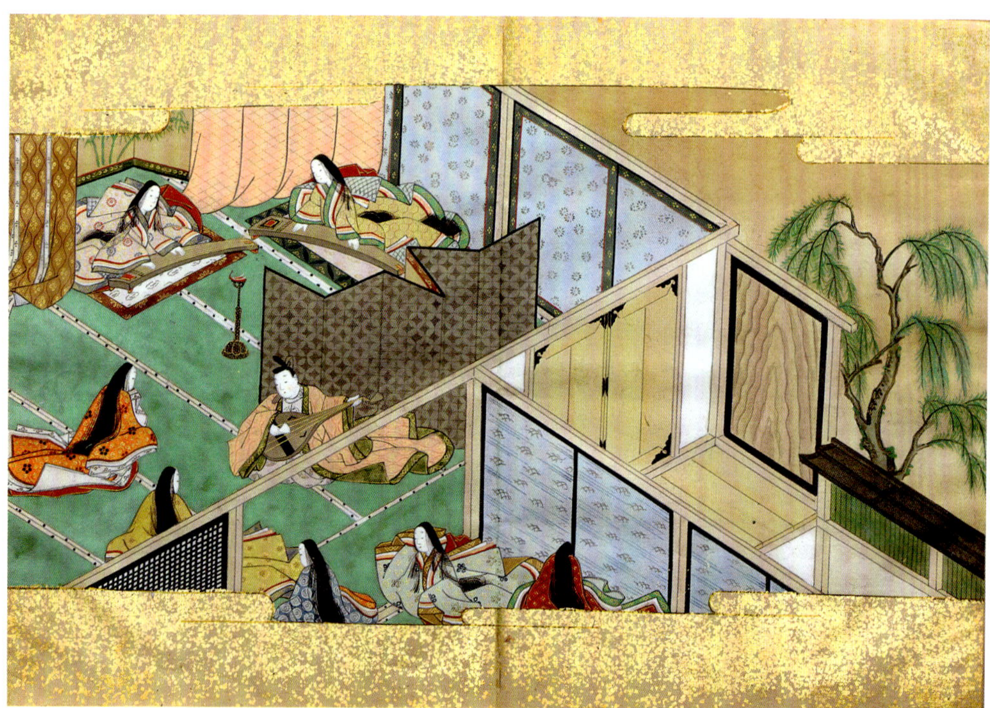

60. *Akizuki monogatari* (秋月物語)

Edo period, 17th century
Nine books (*detail, left, from book 1*); ink, color, and gold on paper
Each book 23.6 x 17.1 cm (9¼ x 6¾ in.)

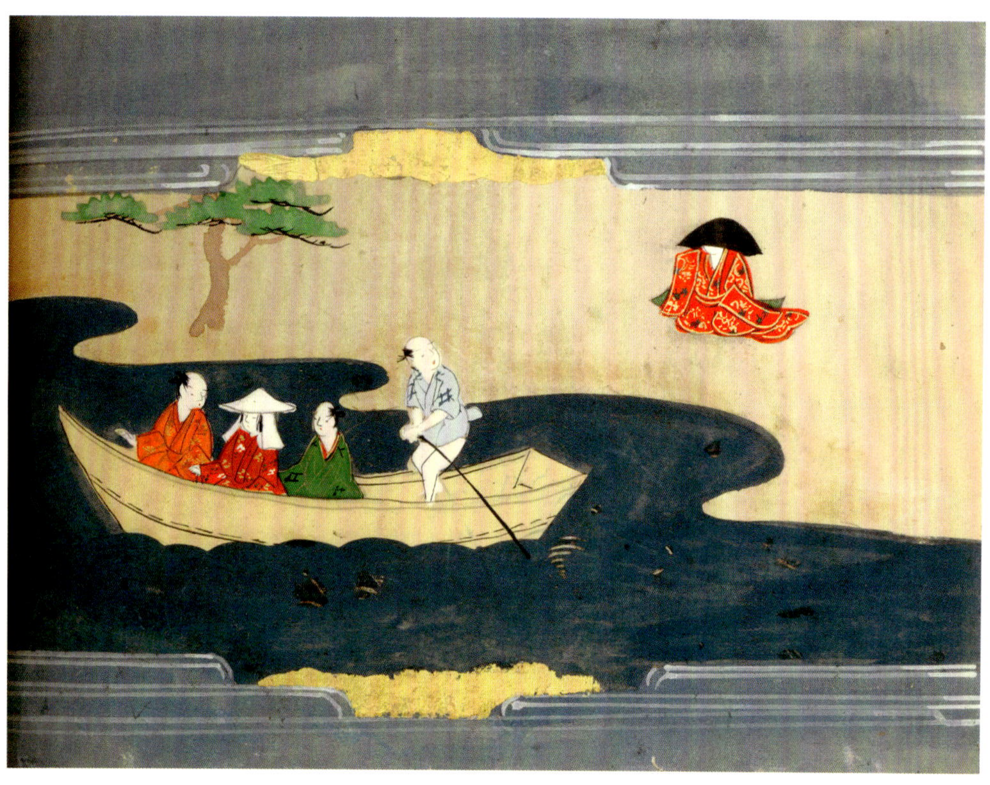

61. *Hachikazuki monogatari* (はちかづき物語)

Edo period, 17th century
Two books (*detail, left, from book 2*), with seven paintings in each; ink, color, gold, and gold leaf on paper
Each book 16 x 32.7 cm (6¼ x 12⅞ in.)

LITERATURE: Kobayashi Kenji 2010.

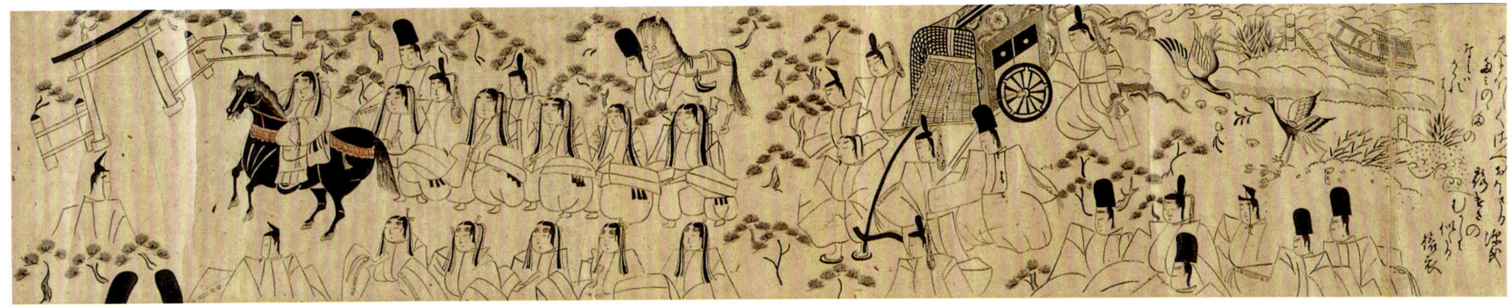

"Miotsukushi"

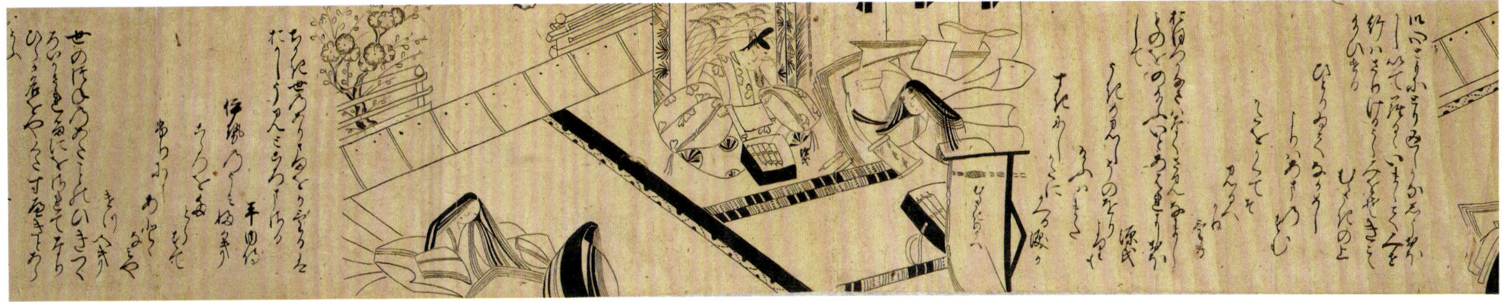

"E-awase"

62. "Akashi," "Miotsukushi," "Yomogiu," "Sekiya," and "E-awase" (明石、澪標、蓬生、関屋、絵合) chapters of *Genji monogatari* (源氏物語)

Muromachi period, 16th century
Handscroll; ink on paper
15 x 1051.5 cm (5⁷/₈ in. x 34 ft. 6 in.)

LITERATURE: Tokyo National Museum 1985a, no. 10; Avitabile 1990, no. 63; Katagiri Yayoi 1996, pp. 69–86; Tsuji Nobuo et al. 2005, no. 31.

63. "Aoi" (葵) chapter of *Genji monogatari* (源氏物語)

Muromachi period, 16th century
Handscroll; ink on paper
12 x 572 cm (4³/₄ in. x 18 ft. 9¹/₈ in.)
Seal

LITERATURE: Burke 1993, fig. 7, p. 24; Katagiri Yayoi 1996, pp. 69–86.

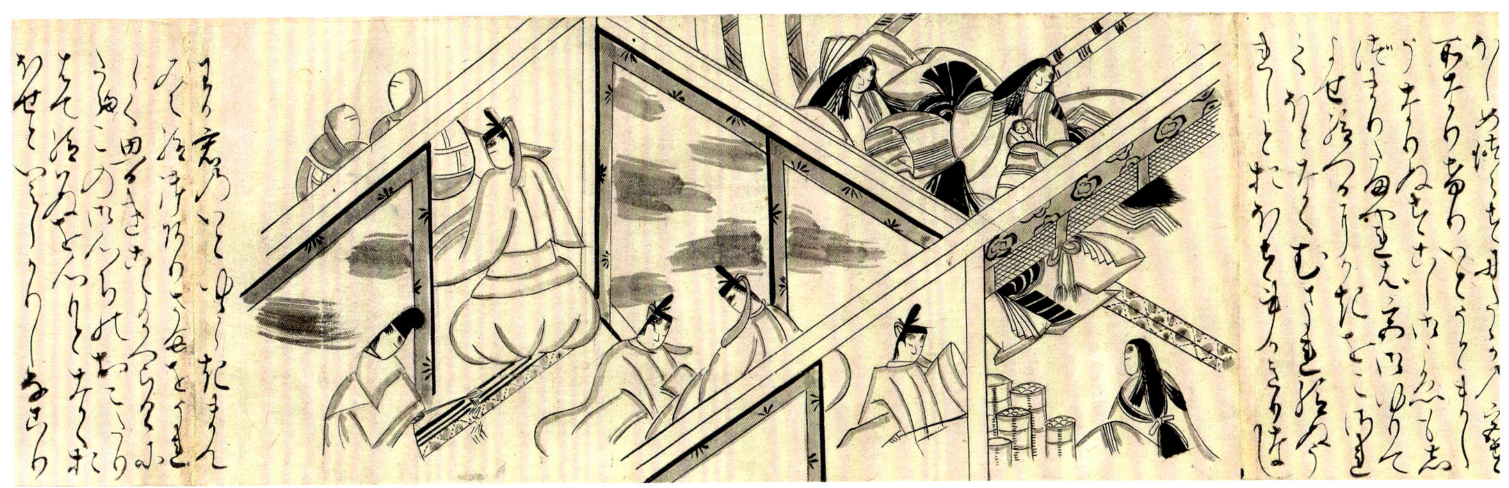

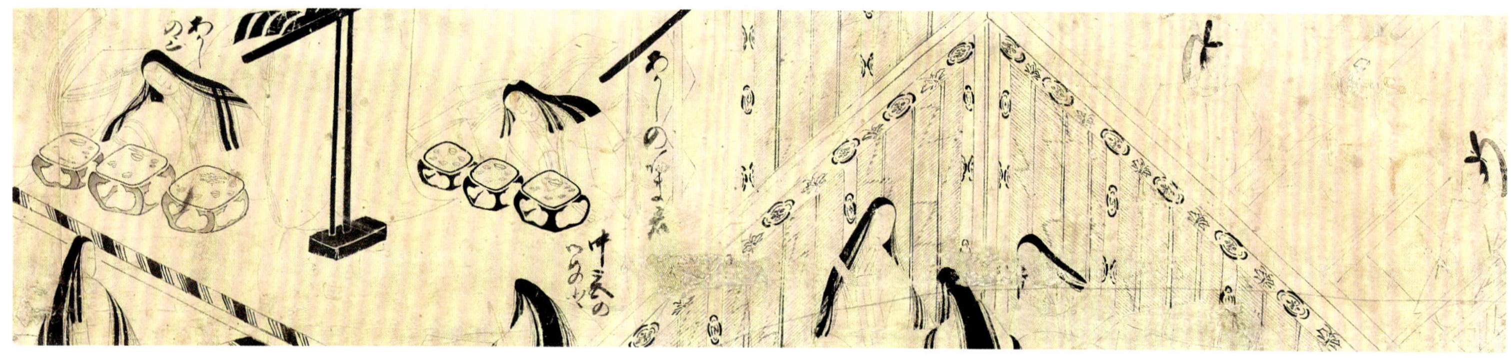

64. "Wakana II" (若菜下) chapter of *Genji monogatari* (源氏物語)

Muromachi period, 16th century
Handscroll fragment; ink on paper
11.3 x 50.5 cm ($4^{1}/_{2}$ x $19^{7}/_{8}$ in.)
Text

65. "Miotsukushi" (澪標) chapter of *Genji monogatari* (源氏物語)

Momoyama period, late 16th century
Folding fan, mounted as hanging scroll; ink, color, and gold on paper
18 x 55.7 cm ($7^{1}/_{8}$ x $21^{7}/_{8}$ in.)
Seal

Literature: Murase 1993, no. 37.

66. "Kochō" (胡蝶) chapter of *Genji monogatari* (源氏物語)

Momoyama period, late 16th century
Folding fan, mounted as hanging scroll; ink, color, and gold on paper
25.2 x 54.6 cm ($9^{7}/_{8}$ x $21^{1}/_{2}$ in.)
Seal

Literature: Murase 1993, no. 36.

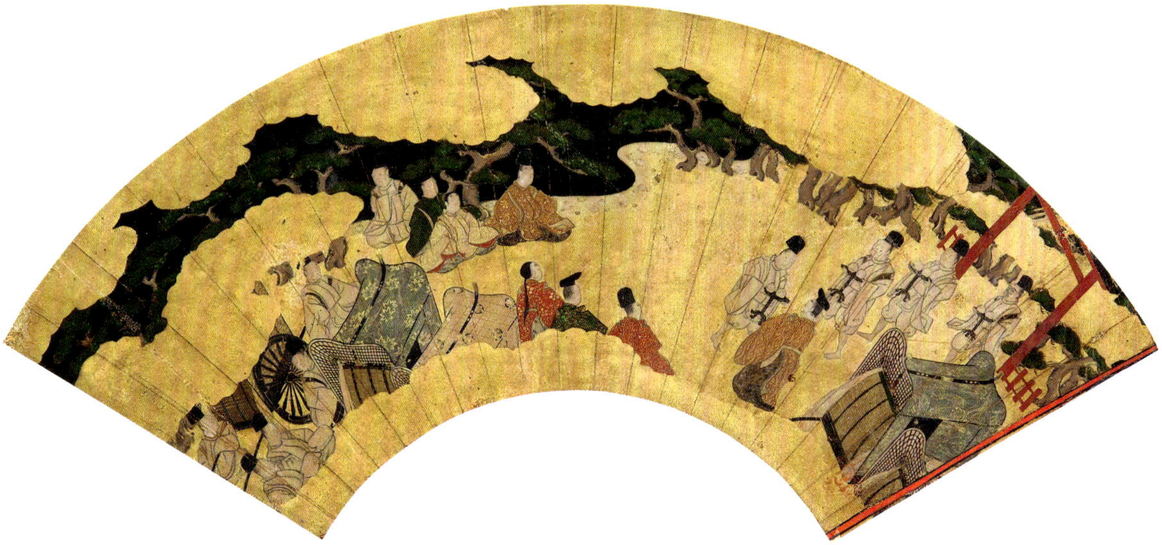

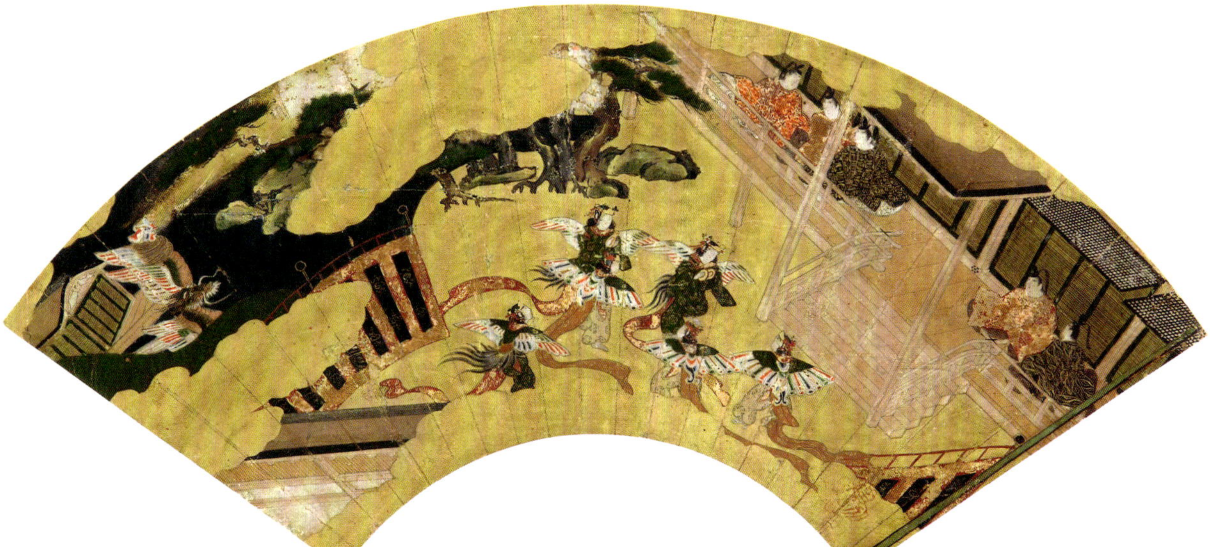

Tosa Mitsuyoshi
(土佐光吉; 1539–1613)

67. "Fujibakama" (藤袴) chapter of *Genji monogatari* (源氏物語)

Momoyama period
Shikishi mounted as hanging scroll; ink, color, and gold on paper
25.9 x 21.3 cm (10¼ x 8⅜ in.)
Seal

Literature: Tokyo National Museum 1985a, no. 37; Avitabile 1990, no. 66.

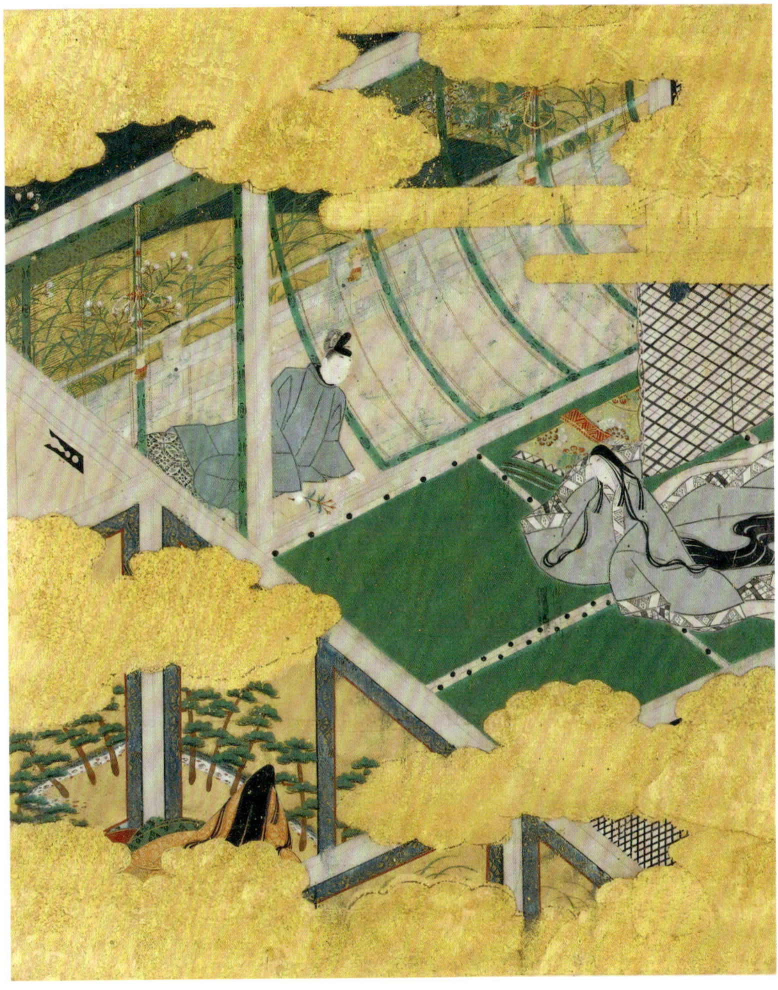

Tosa Mitsuyoshi
(土佐光吉; 1539–1613)

68. "Kashiwagi" (柏木) chapter of *Genji monogatari* (源氏物語)

Momoyama period
Shikishi mounted as hanging scroll; ink, color, and gold on paper
24.6 x 20.8 cm (9⅝ x 8⅛ in.)
Seal

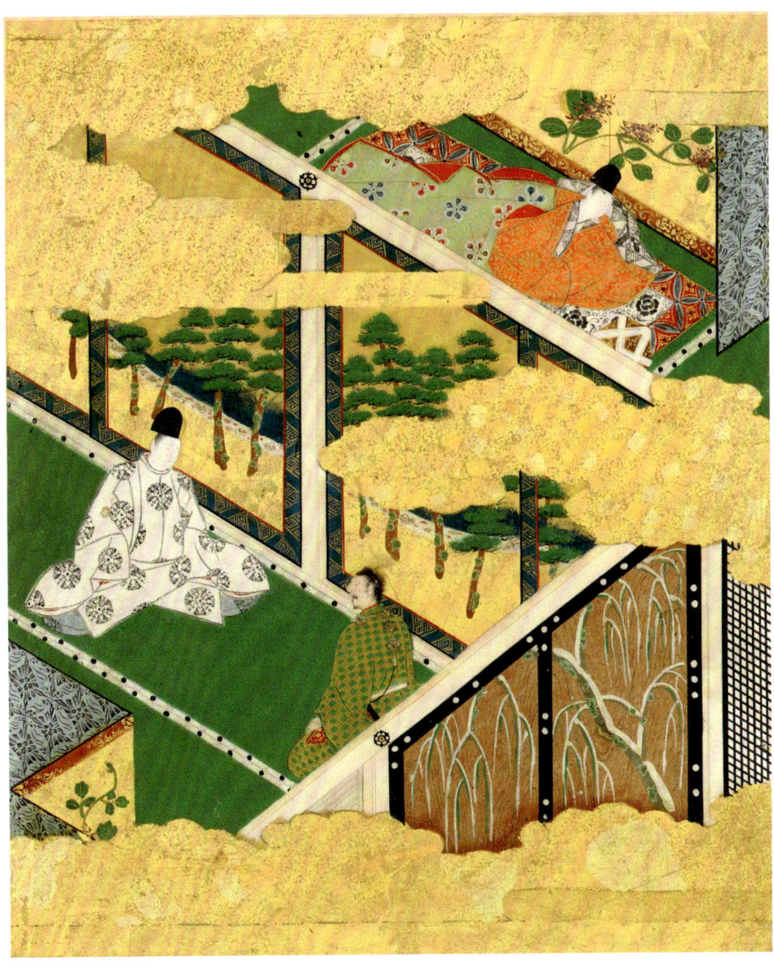

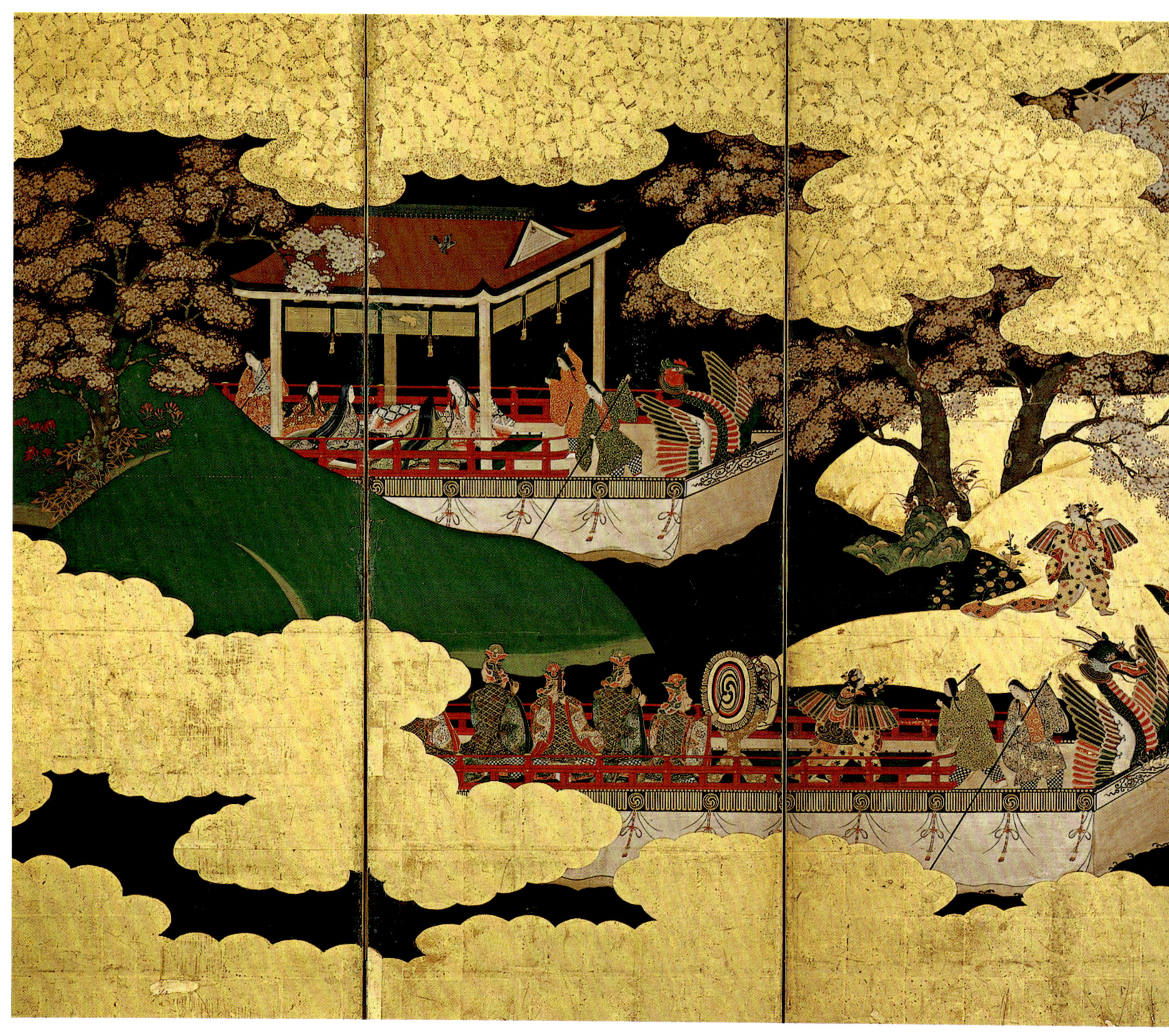

ATTRIBUTED TO TOSA MITSUYOSHI
(土佐光吉; 1539–1613)

69. "Kochō" (胡蝶) chapter of *Genji monogatari* (源氏物語)

Momoyama period
Six-panel folding screen; ink, color, and gold on gilded paper
148 x 359 cm (58 1/4 in. x 11 ft. 9 3/8 in.)

LITERATURE: Tokyo National Museum 1985a, no. 30; Miyajima Shin'ichi 1986, fig. 63 (detail); Akiyama Ken and Taguchi Eiichi 1988, pp. 122–27; Avitabile 1990, no. 65; Akiyima Ken 1998, pp. 56–57; Murase 2000, no. 81; Tsuji Nobuo et al. 2005, no. 72; Suzuki Hideo and Kitani Mariko 2006, pp. 112–13, no. 140; Shirane 2008b, fig. 1, pp. 32–33; Emura Tomoko 2011, pls. 5, 81.

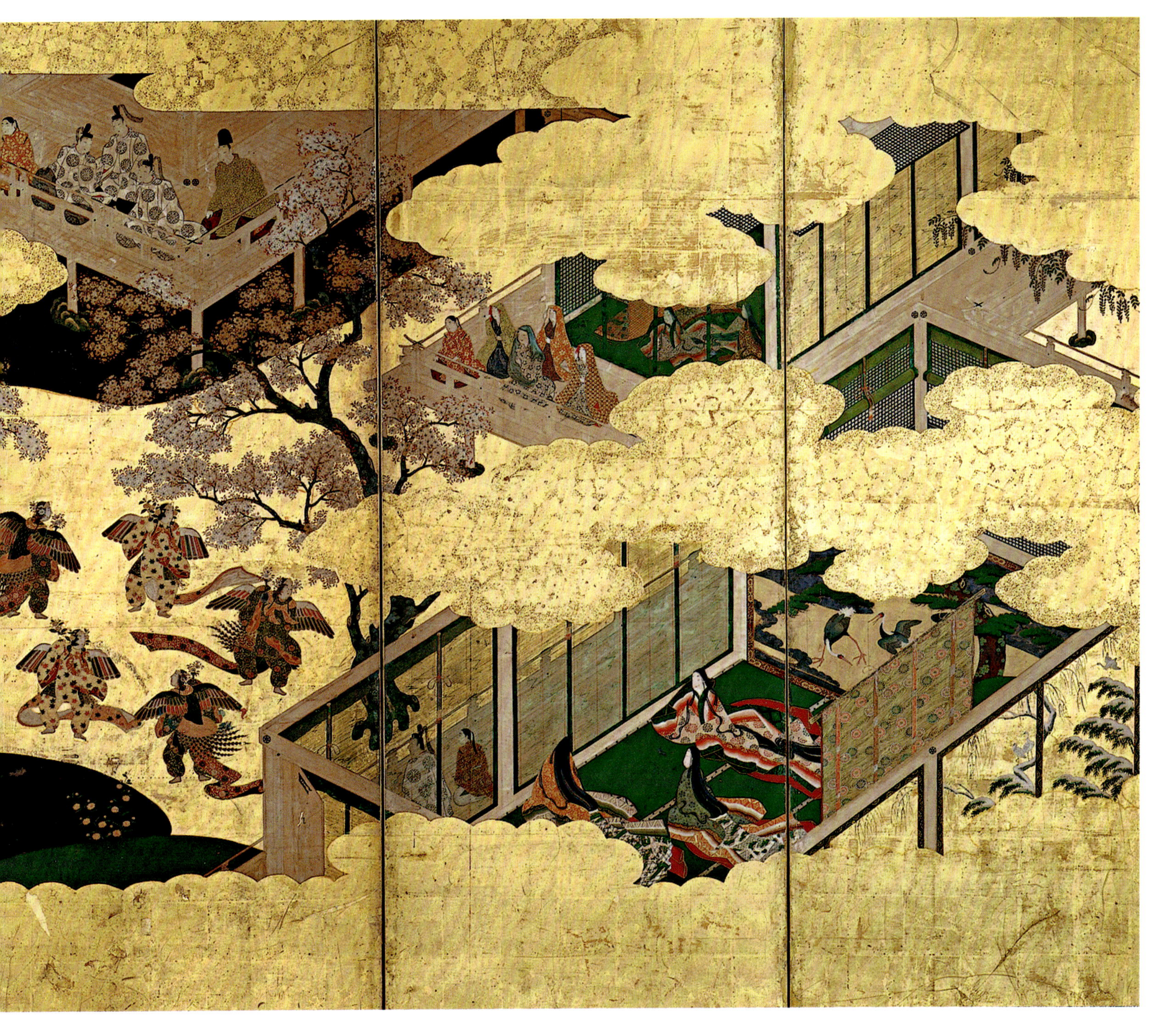

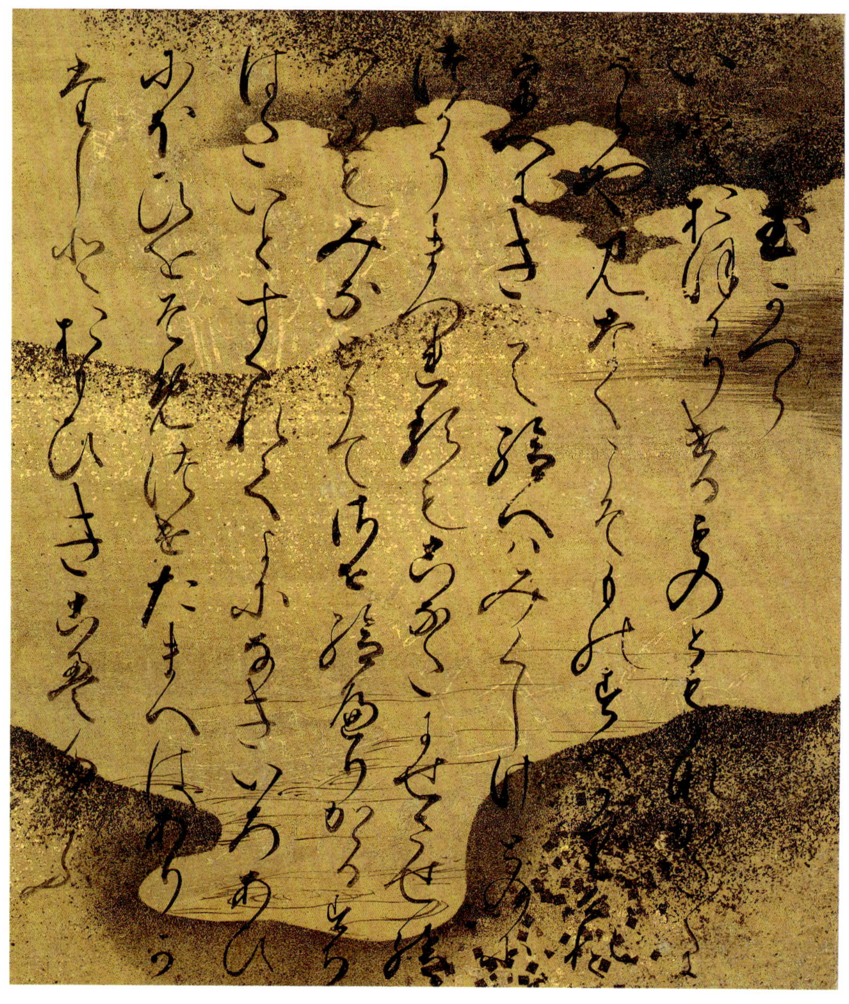

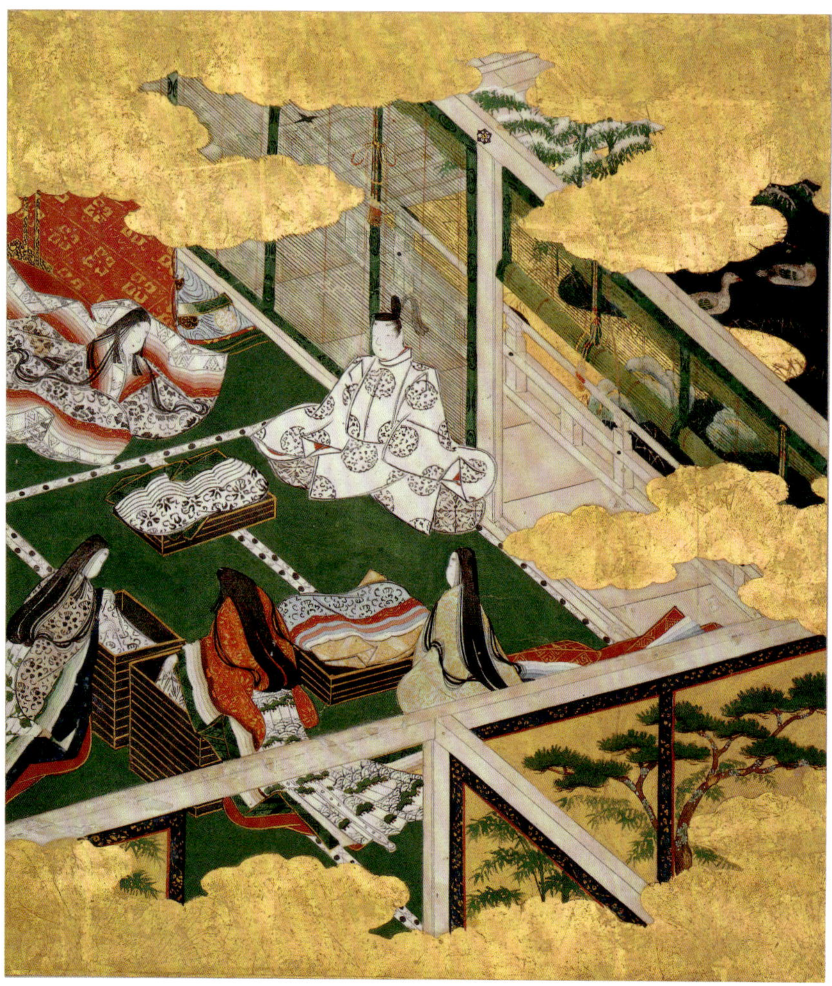

Chōjirō
(長次郎; fl. early 17th century)

70. "Tamakazura" (玉鬘) chapter of *Genji monogatari* (源氏物語)

Momoyama period
Album leaves, mounted as pair of hanging scrolls
Painting: ink, color, and gold on paper; text: ink, gold, and silver on paper
Each leaf 24.1 x 21.4 cm (9½ x 8⅜ in.)
Text

Literature: Tokyo National Museum 1985a, no. 38; Avitabile 1990, no. 67; Murase 2000, no. 82.

Tosa Mitsunori
(土佐光則; 1583–1638)

71. "Yūgao" (夕顔) and "Suzumushi" (鈴虫) chapters of *Genji monogatari* (源氏物語)

Edo period, early 17th century
Two albums of thirty leaves each, with sixty scenes; ink, red pigment, and gold on paper
Each album leaf 13.4 x 12.9 cm ($5^{1}/_{4}$ x $5^{1}/_{8}$ in.)
Seal

Literature: Murase 1975, no. 59; Murase 1983b; Tokyo National Museum 1985a, no. 39; Akiyama Ken and Taguchi Eiichi 1988, pp. 256–63; Avitabile 1990, no. 68; Murase 1992, p. 181; Guth 1996, fig. 16; Murase 2000, no. 109; McCormick 2008, p. 120 and pl. 10; Emura Tomoko 2011, pl. 13.

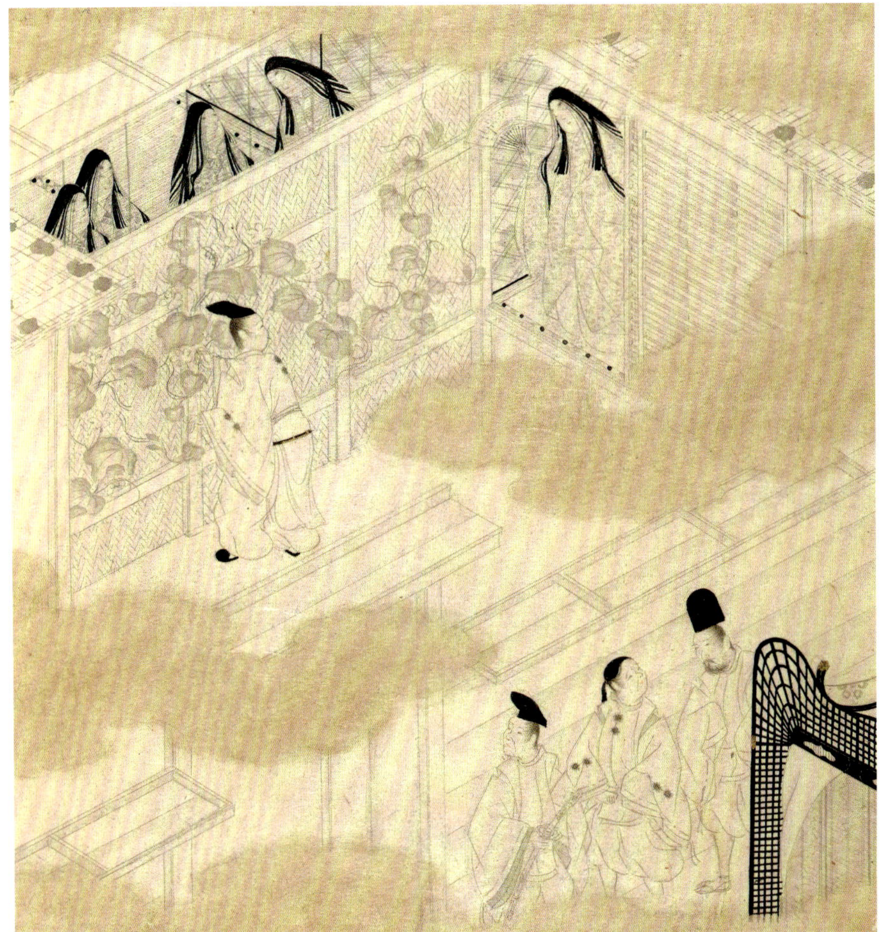

"Yūgao"

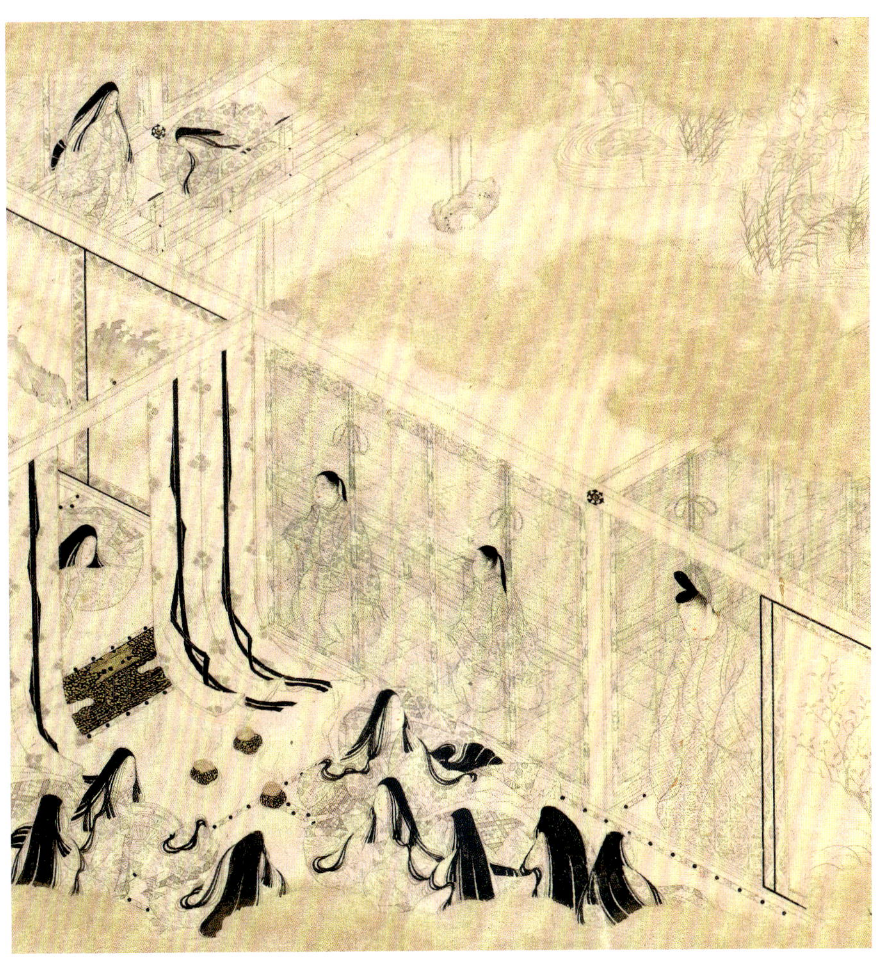

"Suzumushi"

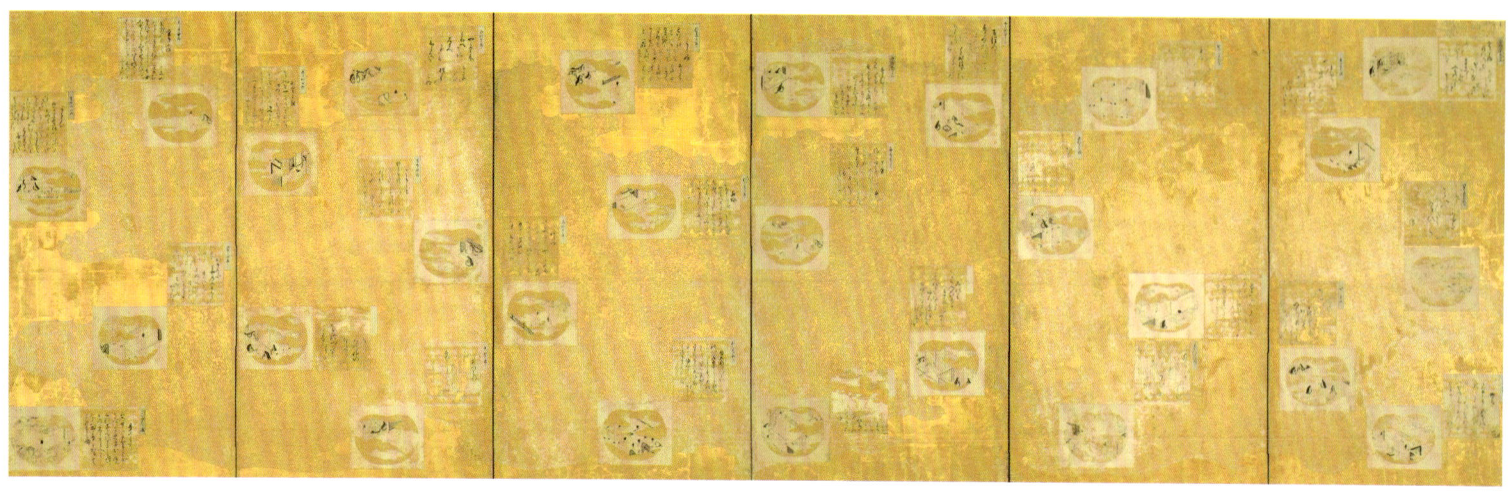

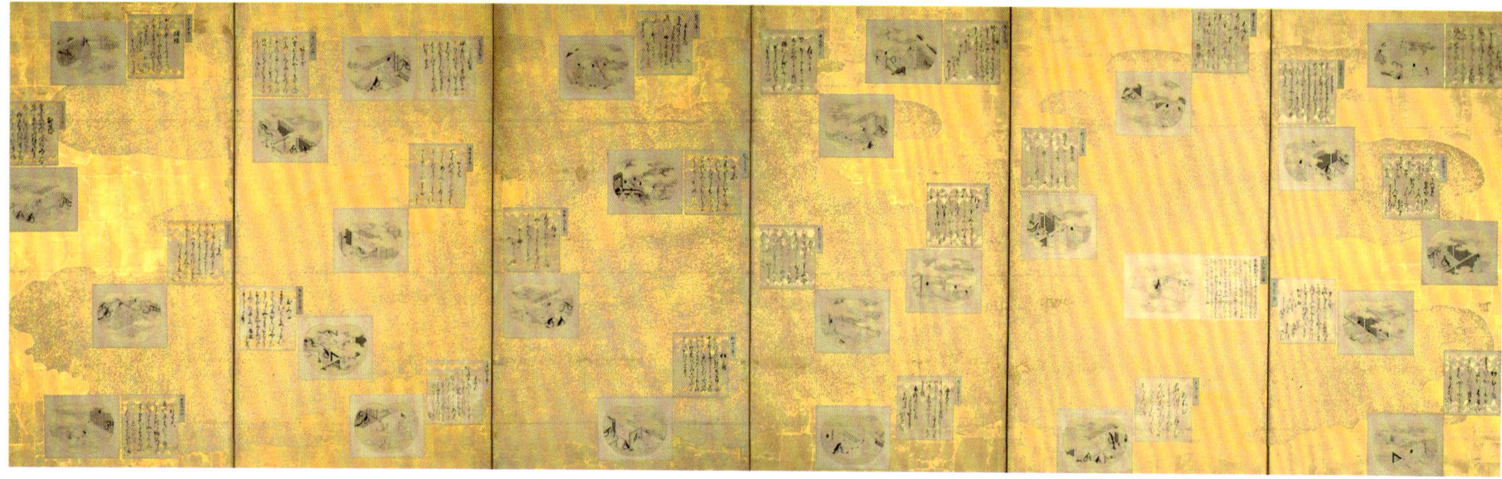

ATTRIBUTED TO TOSA MITSUOKI
(土佐光起; 1617–1691)

72. Fifty-four scenes from *Genji monogatari* (源氏物語)

Edo period, late 17th century
Pair of six-panel folding screens, with fifty-four *shikishi* of painting and fifty-four *shikishi* of text, pasted on gilded paper
Painting: ink and color on paper;
text: ink on paper
Each screen 124.4 x 356.8 cm
(49 in. x 11 ft. 8½ in.)
Text

LITERATURE: Avitabile 1990, no. 64 (right screen only).

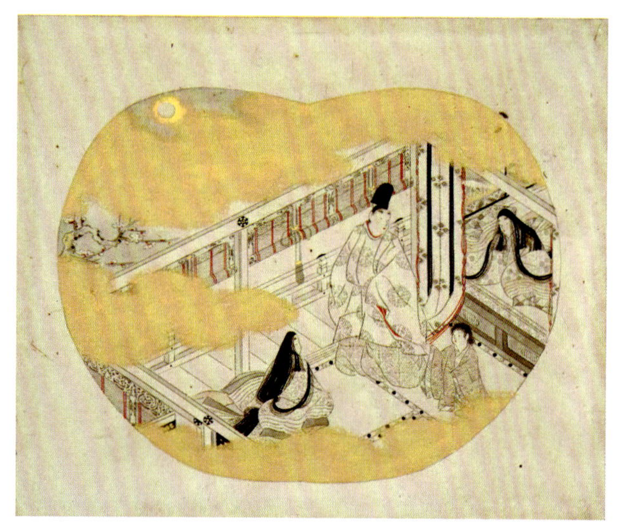

"Usugumo" (from left screen)

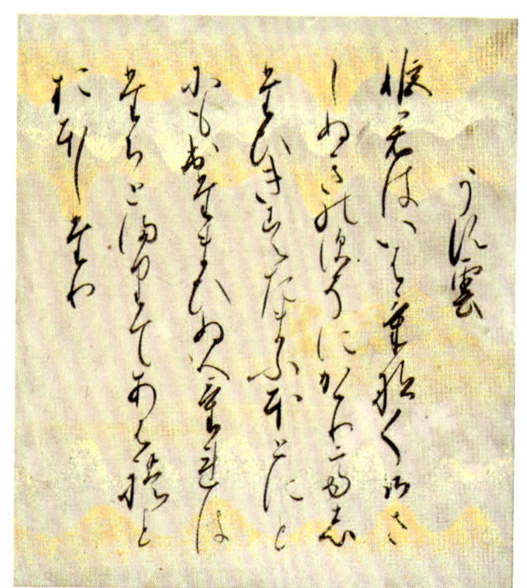

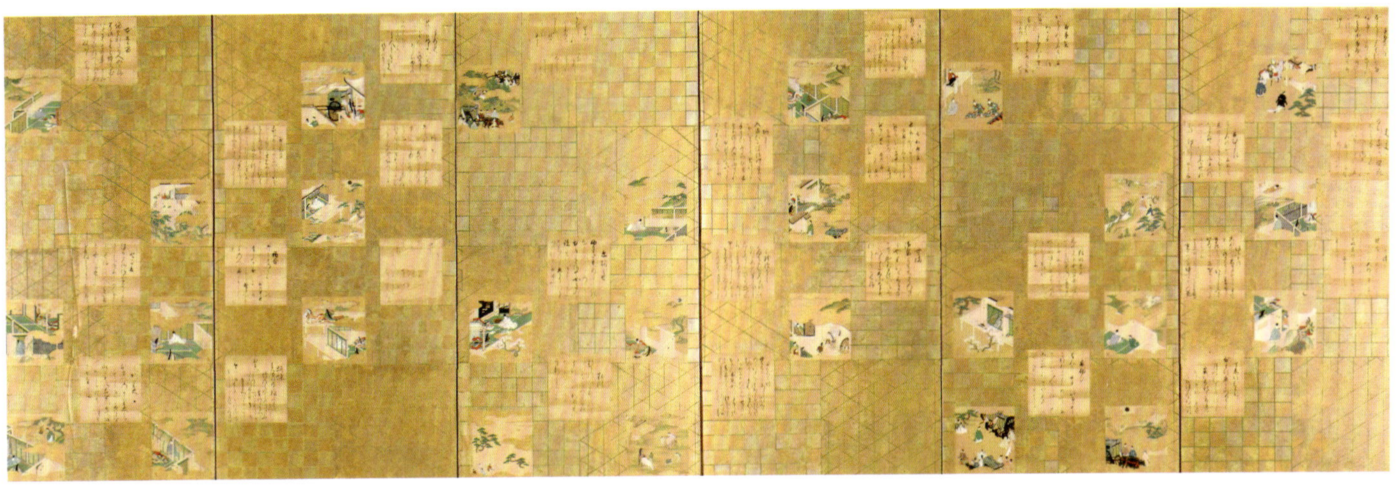

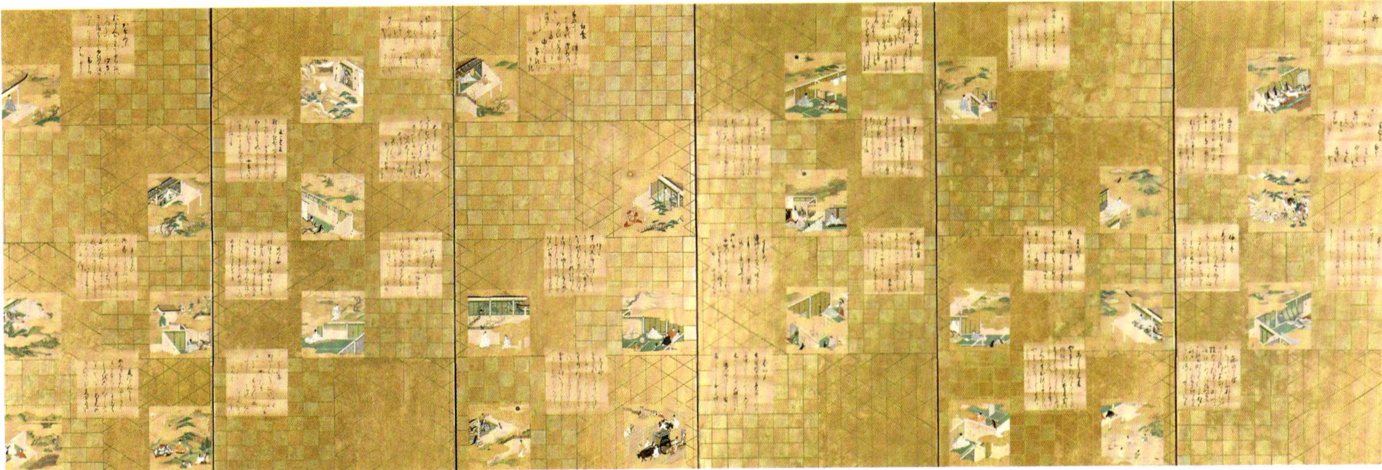

Tosa Mitsunari
(or Mitsushige)
(土佐光成; 1646–1710)

73. Fifty-four scenes from *Genji monogatari* (源氏物語)

Edo period, late 17th century
Pair of six-panel folding screens, with fifty-four *shikishi* of painting and fifty-four *shikishi* of text
Paintings: ink, color, and gold on silver-covered paper; text: ink on paper
Each screen 155.9 (116.8 without silver) x 354.6 cm (61 3/8 [46 without silver] x 11 ft. 7 5/8 in.)
Text, signature, seal

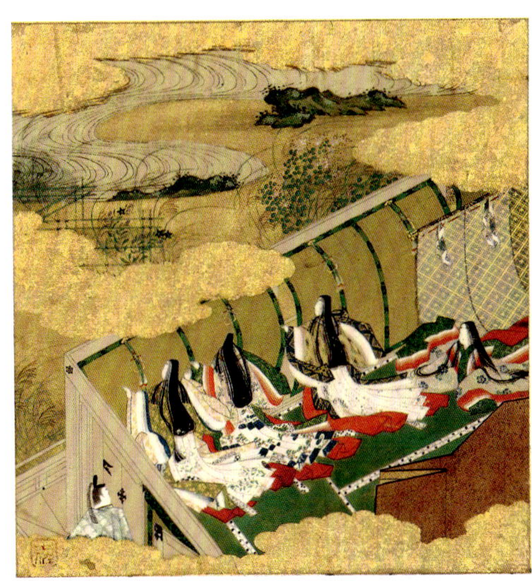

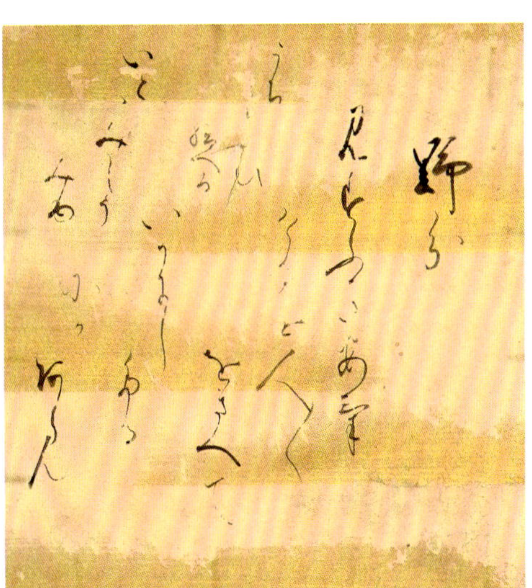

"Nowaki" (from left screen)

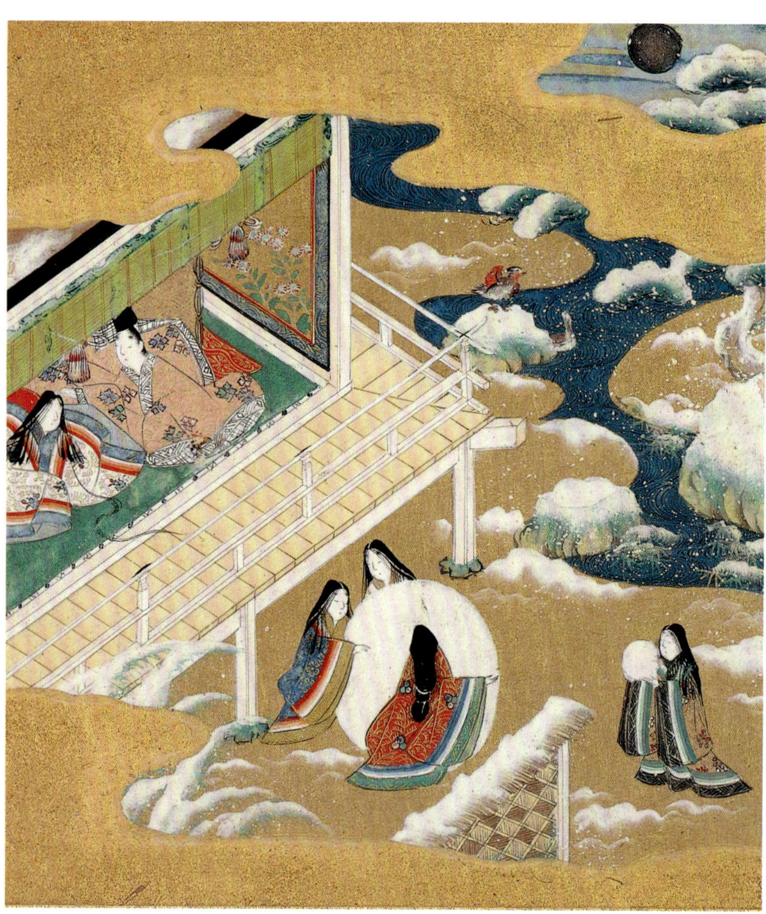

74. "Asagao" (朝顔) chapter of *Genji monogatari* (源氏物語)

Edo period, 17th century
Two albums of painting; ink, color, and gold on paper
Each album 14.7 x 13.1 cm ($5^{3}/_{4}$ x $5^{1}/_{8}$ in.)

Literature: Tokyo National Museum 1985a, no. 40; Avitabile 1990, no. 69; Murase 2001; Mackenzie and Finkel 2004, pp. 206–7, no. 16.6.

75. "Utsusemi" (空蟬) and "Yadorigi" (宿木) chapters of *Genji monogatari* (源氏物語)

Edo period, 17th century
Album with 20 leaves; ink, color, and gold on paper
16.4 x 21.8 cm ($6^{1}/_{2}$ x $8^{5}/_{8}$ in.)

Literature: Burke 1993, fig. 6/no. 22.

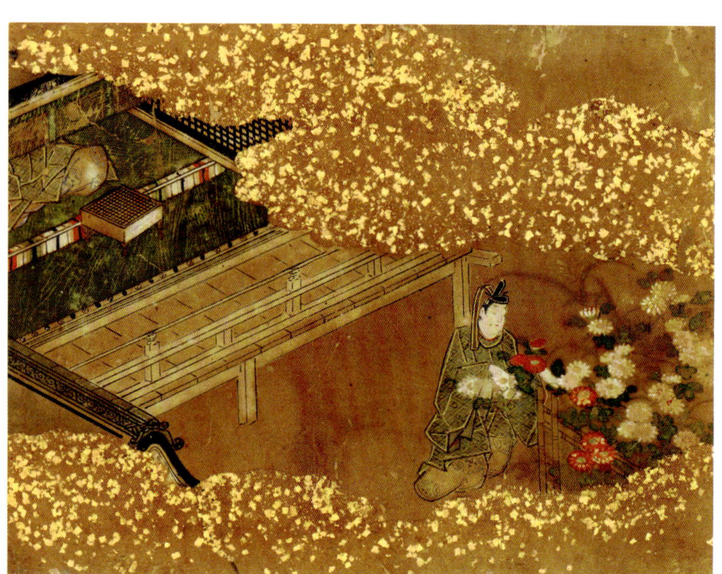

"Yadorigi"

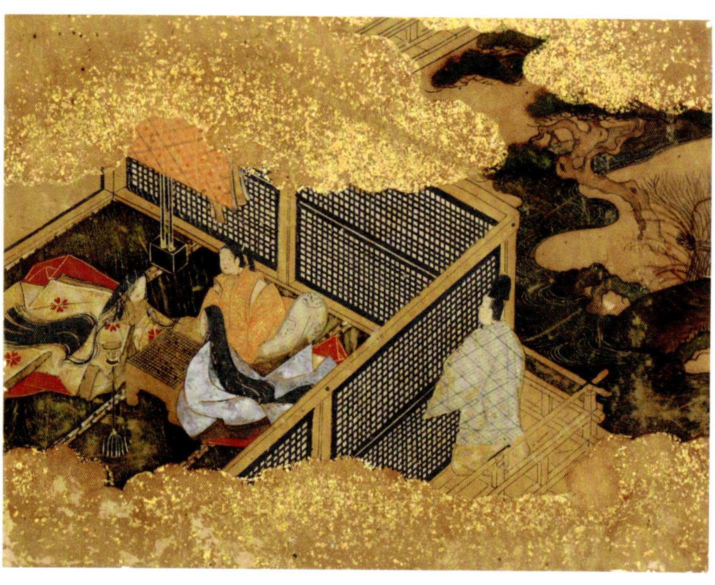

"Utsusemi"

76. "Kiritsubo" (桐壺) and "Utsusemi" (空蝉) chapters of *Genji monogatari* (源氏物語)

Edo period, 18th century
Pair of six-panel screens; ink, color, and gold on gilded paper
Each screen 30.3 x 75.6 cm ($11^7/_8$ x $29^3/_4$ in.)

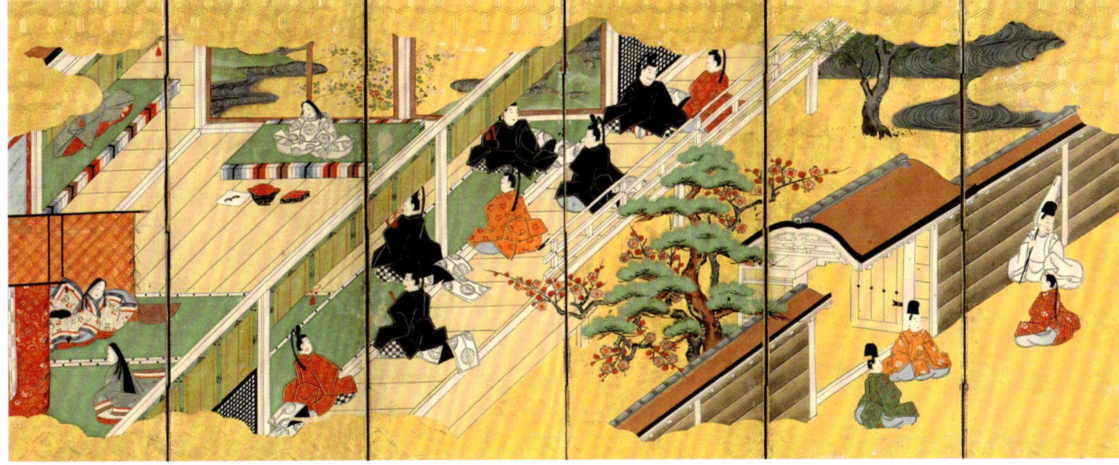

"Kiritsubo"

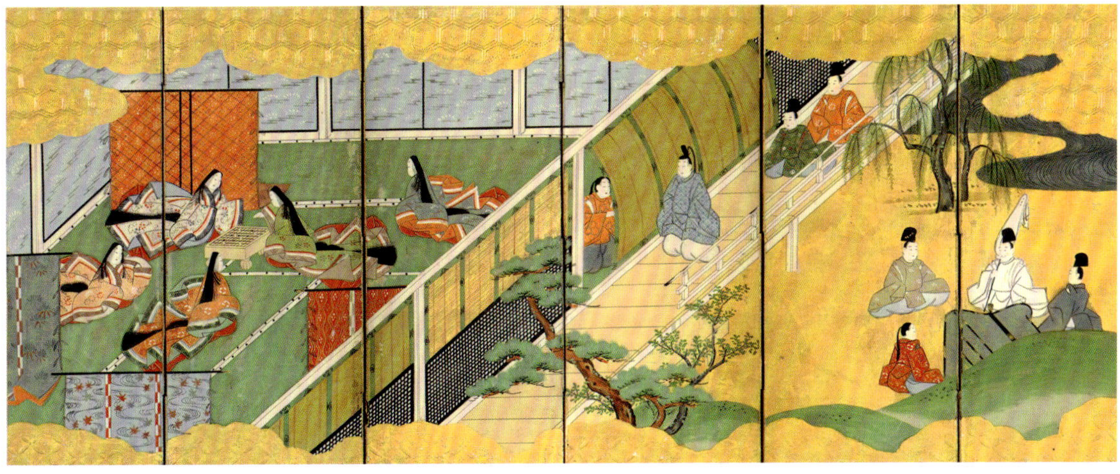

"Utsusemi"

77. "Kiritsubo," "Utsusemi," "Wakana," "Momiji no ga," "Miotsukushi," and "Hatsune" (桐壺、空蝉、若菜、紅葉賀、澪標、初音) chapters of *Genji monogatari* (源氏物語)

Edo period, 18th century
Six-panel folding screen; ink, color, and gold on gilded paper
153.8 x 358.2 cm ($60^1/_2$ in. x 11 ft. 9 in.)

Literature: Burke 1993, pl. 3/no. 26.

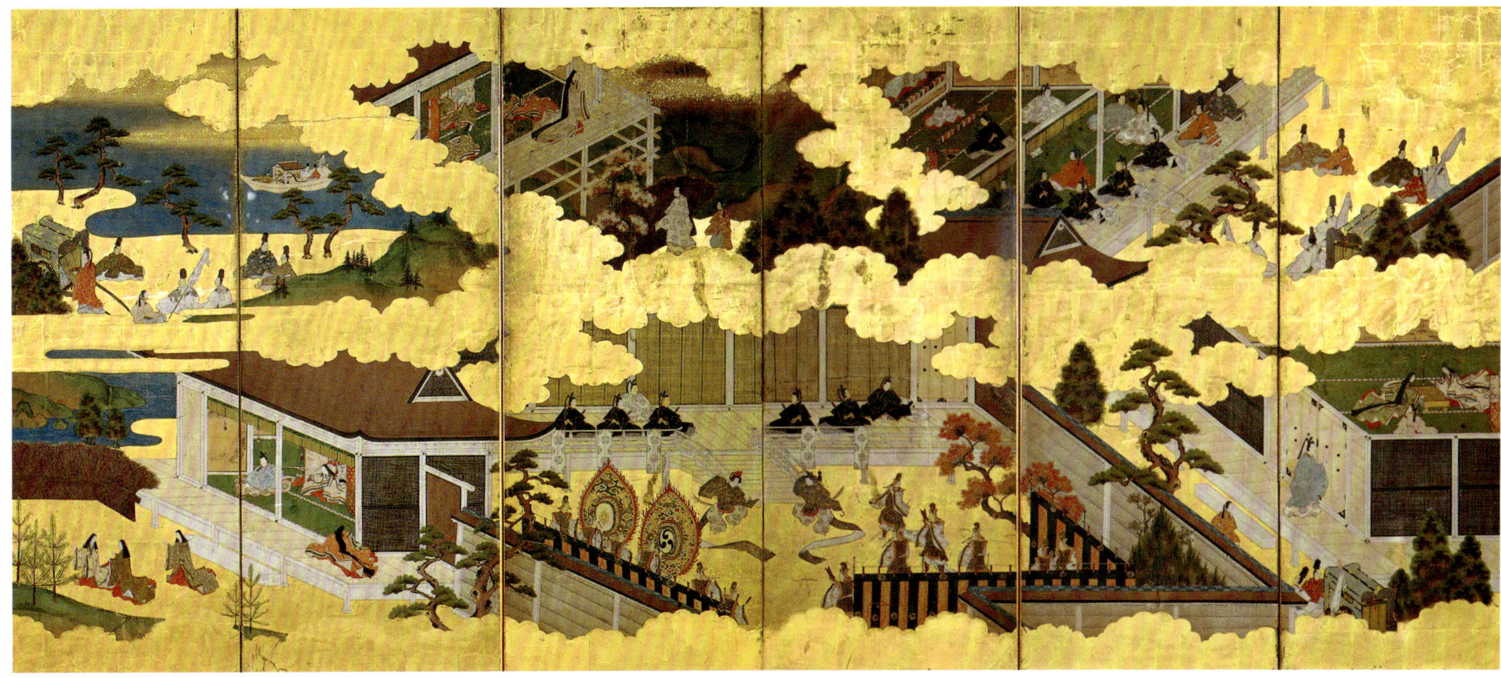

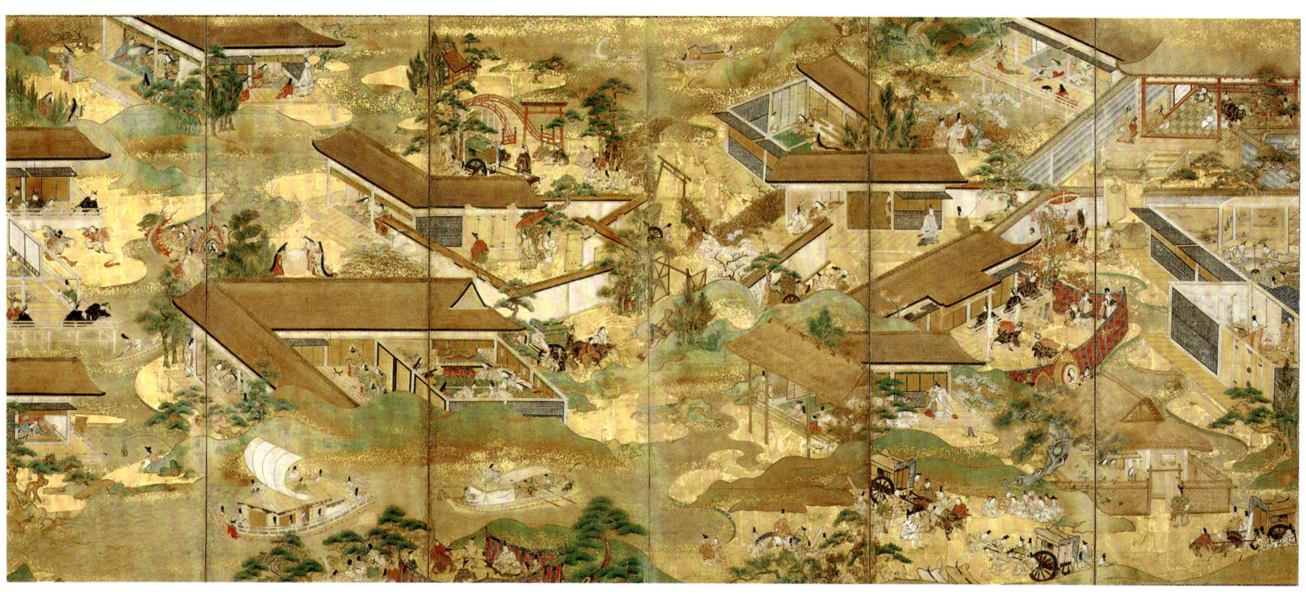

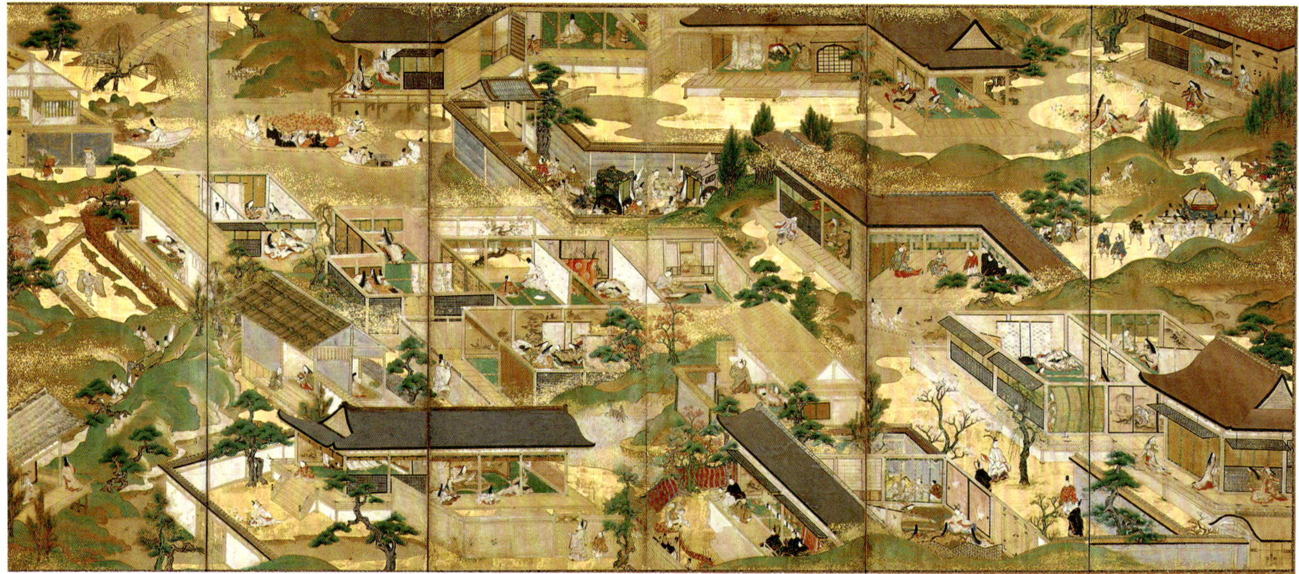

79. Fifty-four scenes from *Genji monogatari* (源氏物語)

Edo period, late 17th century
Pair of six-panel folding screens; ink, color, and gold on gilded paper
Each screen 170 x 379 cm (66⅞ in. x 12 ft. 5¼ in.)

LITERATURE: Murase 1975, no. 58; Tokyo National Museum 1985a, no. 31; Buckland 2004, no. 2.

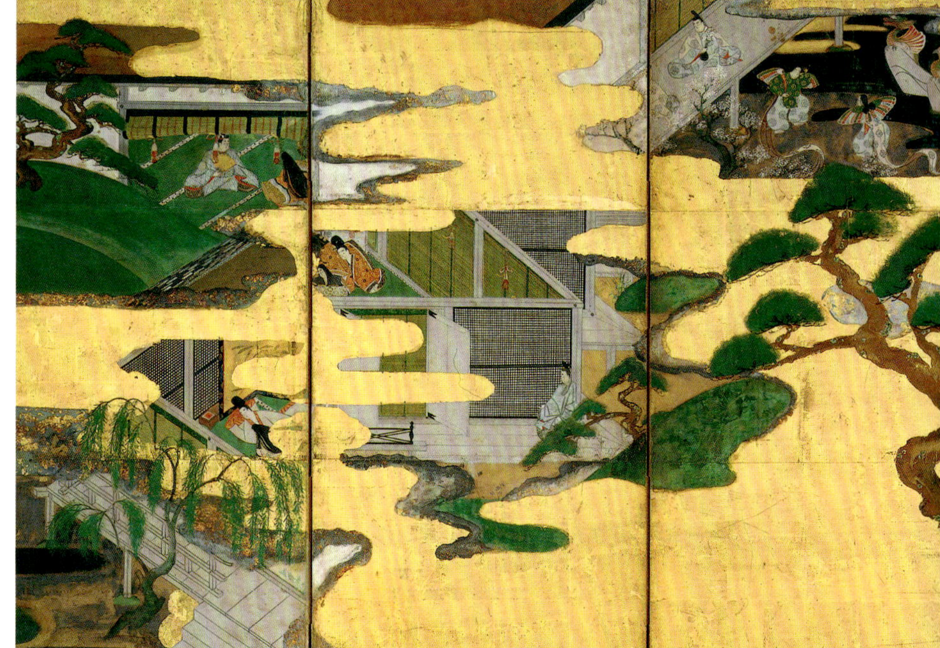

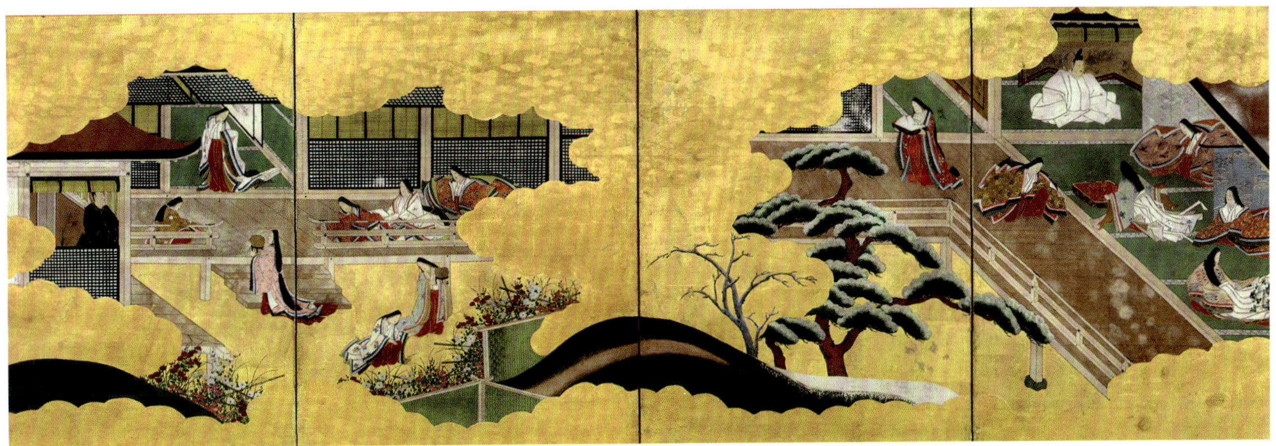

80. "Tamakazura" (玉鬘) and "Nowaki" (野分) chapters of *Genji monogatari* (源氏物語)

Edo period, 18th century
Four-panel folding screen; ink, color, and gold on gilded paper
78 x 247 cm (30¾ in. x 8 ft. 1¼ in.)

Tawaraya Sōtatsu
(俵屋宗達; d. ca. 1640)

81. "Usugumo," "Asagao," "Otome," "Tamakazura," "Hatsune," "Kochō," "Hotaru," and "Tokonatsu" (薄雲、朝顔、少女、玉鬘、初音、胡蝶、蛍、常夏) chapters of *Genji monogatari* (源氏物語)

Edo period, early 17th century
Eight-panel folding screen; ink, color, and gold on gilded paper
81 x 327 cm (31⅞ in. x 10 ft. 8¾ in.)
Signature, seal

Ex coll.: Yoshioka Tajūrō, Kanazawa Prefecture

Literature: Tanaka Kisaku 1933, pp. 366–67, 369–70; Yamane Yūzō 1962b, pls. 42, 43; Murase 1971, no. 1; Murase 1975, no. 51; Yamane Yūzō 1975, fig. 71; Akiyama Terukazu 1976, figs. 14, 141; Yamane Yūzō 1977–80, vol. 1 (1977), pls. 17–19; Akiyama Ken et al. 1978, no. 129; Yamane Yūzō 1979, no. 51; Yamane Yūzō et al. 1979, pl. 12; Murase 1985, pp. 102–3, figs. 4, 5, 7 (detail); Akiyama Ken and Taguchi Eiichi 1988, pp. 160–68; Murase 2000, no. 87; Tsuji Nobuo et al. 2005, no. 89; Carpenter 2012, no. 3.

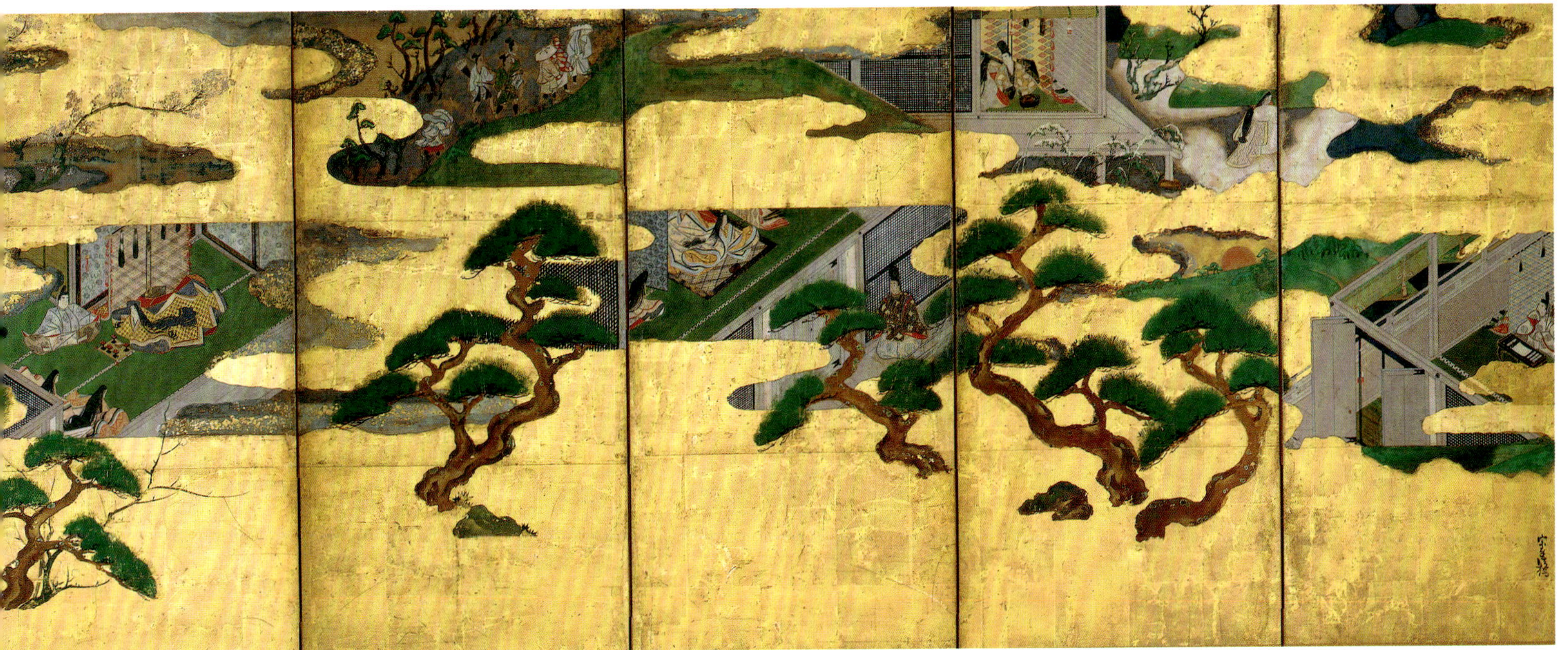

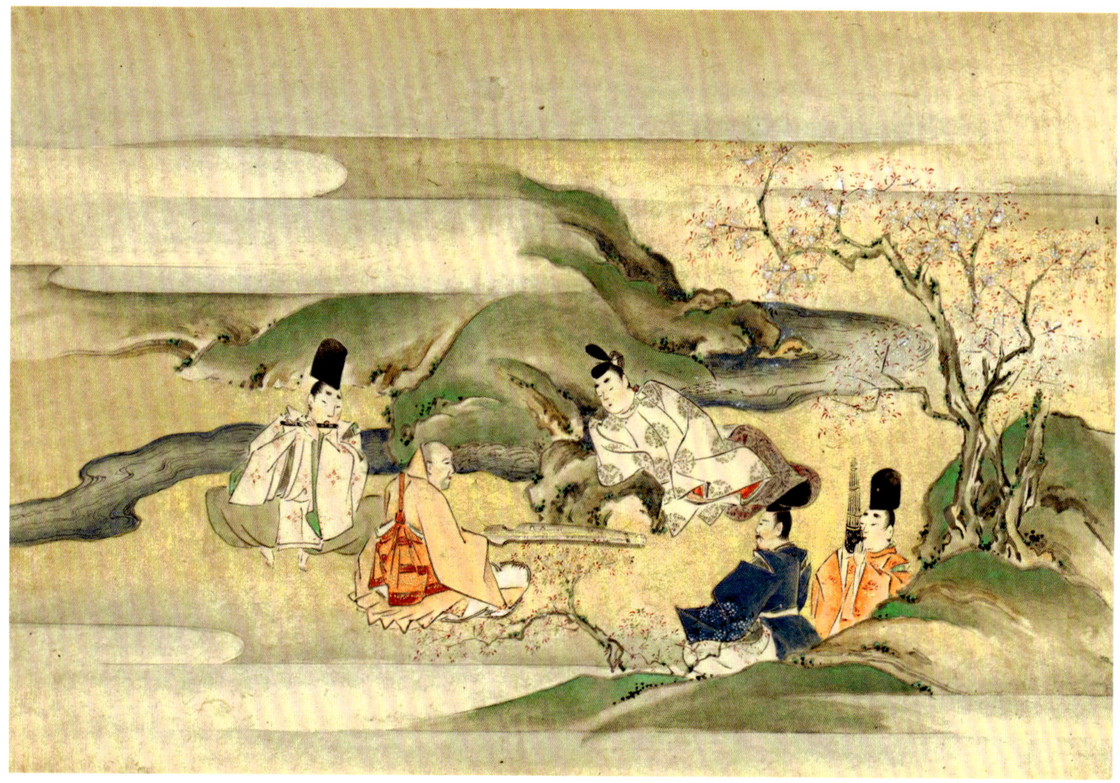

"Wakamurasaki"

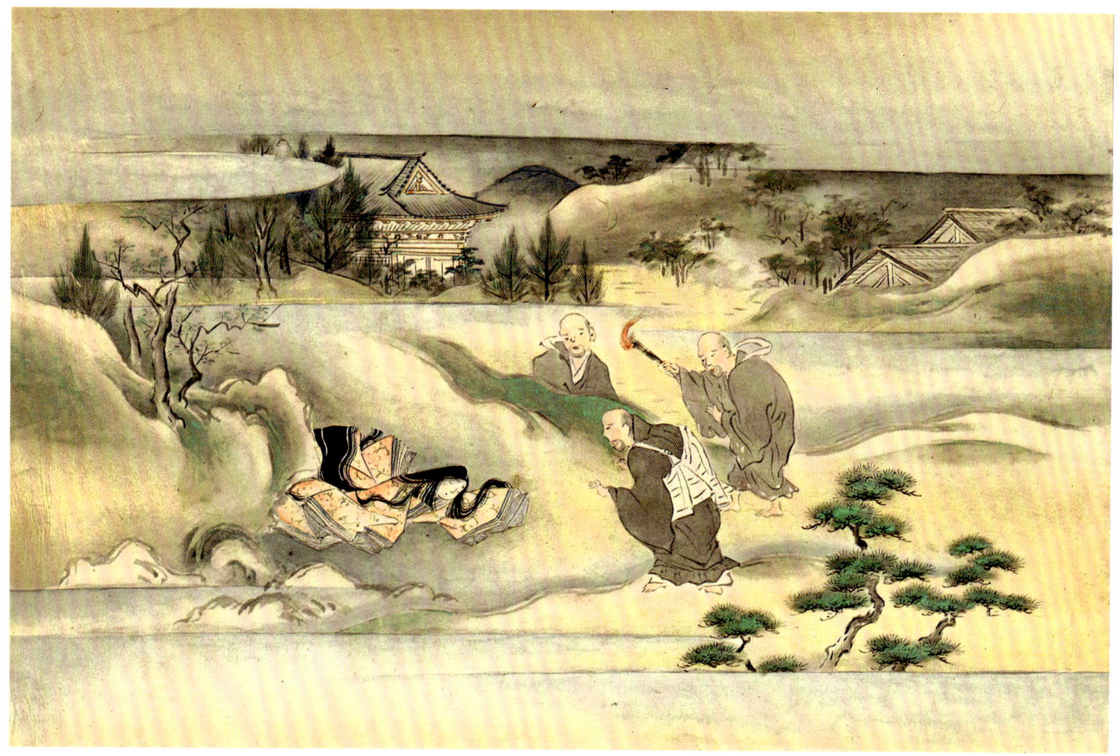

"Ukifune"

ATTRIBUTED TO KAIHŌ YŪSETSU
(海北友雪; 1598–1677)
AND 27 UNNAMED CALLIGRAPHERS

82. "Wakamurasaki" (若紫) and "Ukifune" (浮舟) chapters of *Genji monogatari* (源氏物語)

Edo period, 17th century
Two handscrolls, twenty-seven paintings and texts on each scroll; ink and color on paper
Scroll I (*detail, top*): 23.7 x 1938.3 cm
(9 3/8 in. x 63 ft. 7 1/8 in.)
Scroll II (*detail, bottom*): 23.7 x 1914.6 cm
(9 3/8 in. x 62 ft. 9 3/4 in.)

LITERATURE: Murase 1975, no. 57; Murase 1983b, pp. 333–34; Murase 1985, p. 105, fig. 8; Avitabile 1990, no. 62; Bargen 1997, pl. 2.12; Addiss 1999, pp. 94–95, no. 19; Murase 2008, pp. 39–41.

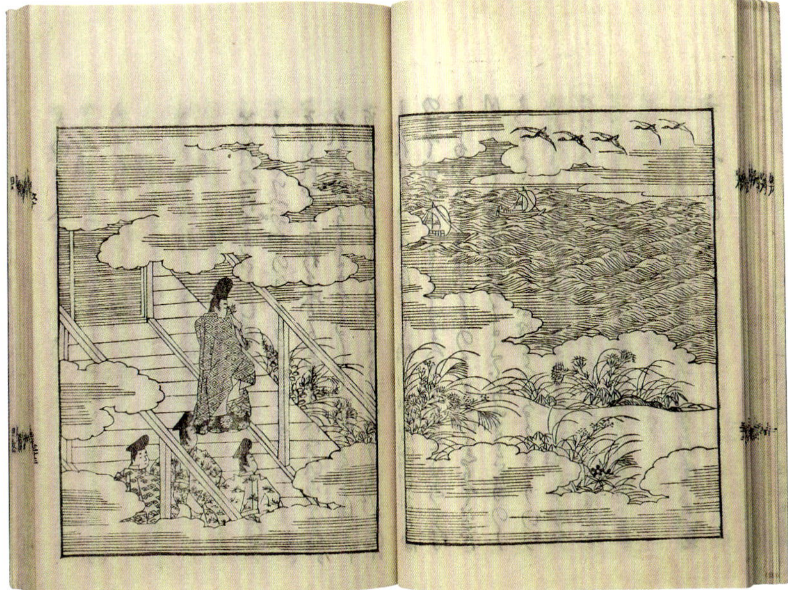

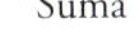

"Suma"

YAMAMOTO SHUNSHŌ
(山本春正; 1610–1682)

83. "Suma" (須磨) and "Asagao" (朝顔) chapters of *Genji monogatari* (源氏物語)

Edo period, 1650
Book in 24 volumes with printed text and illustrations in black ink
26.5–26.7 x 18.7–18.8 cm (approx. 10 1/2 x 7 3/8 in.)
Text

LITERATURE: Bargen 1997, pls. 1.2, 1.9.

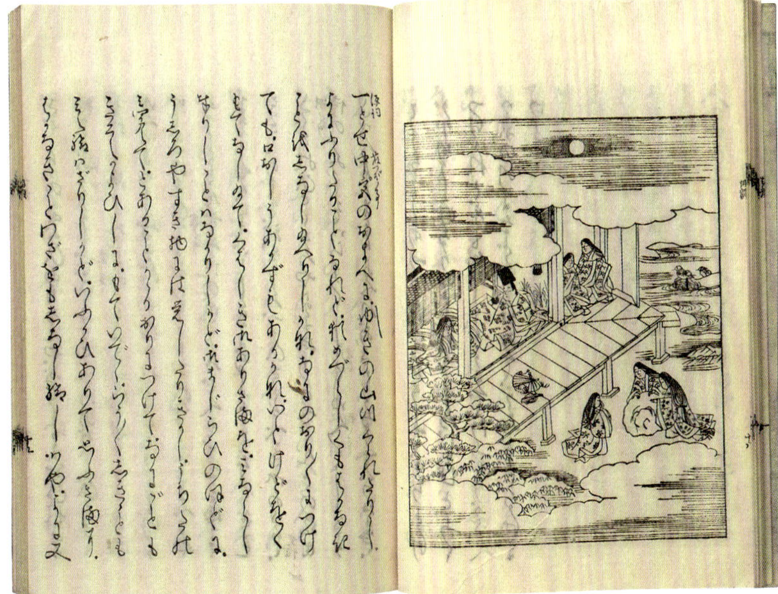

"Asagao"

84. "Hana no en" (花宴) and "Momiji no ga" (紅葉賀) chapters of *Genji monogatari* (源氏物語)

Edo period, ca. 1727
"Hana no en" (one volume), "Momiji no ga" (three volumes) (*detail from vol. 1, below*); illustrations in ink on paper
26.7 x 17.8 cm (10 1/2 x 7 in.)

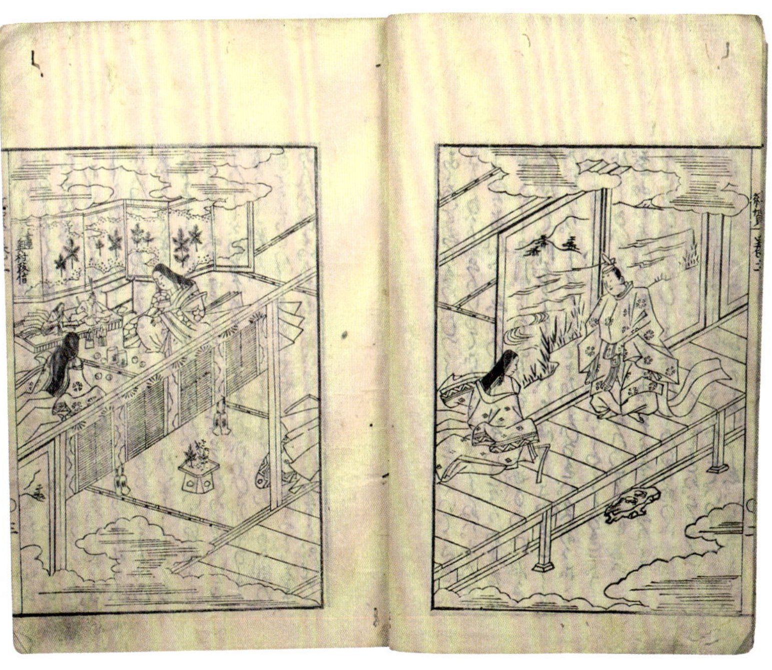

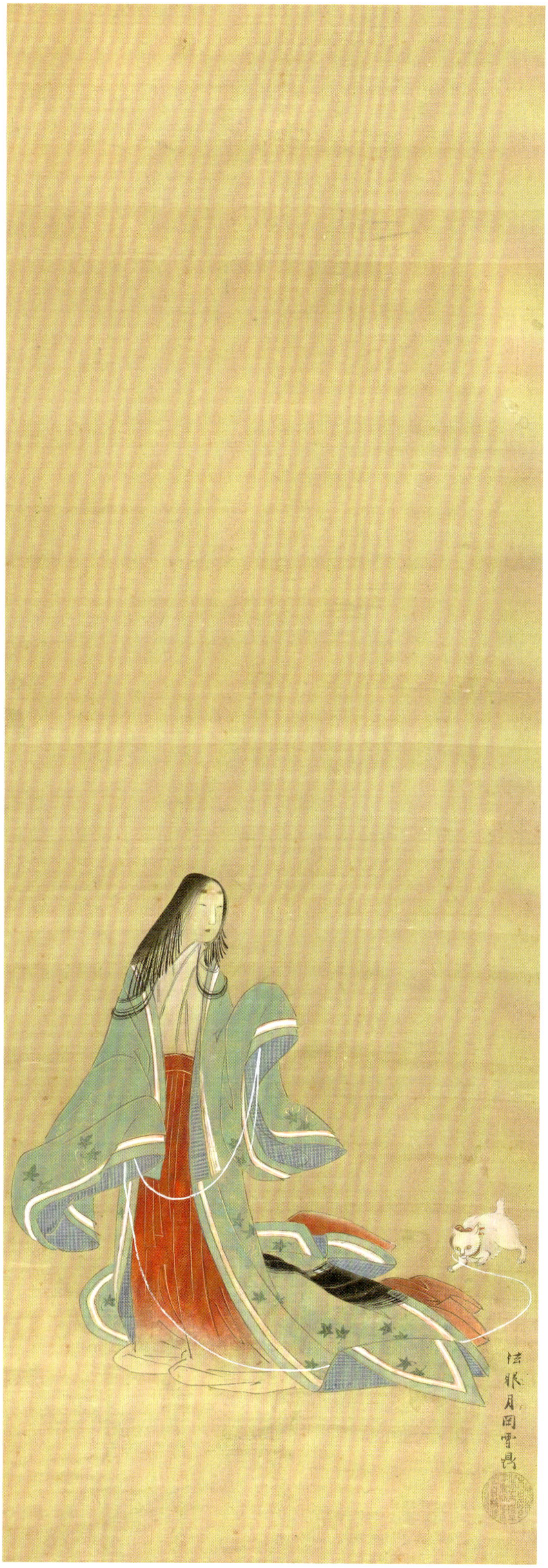

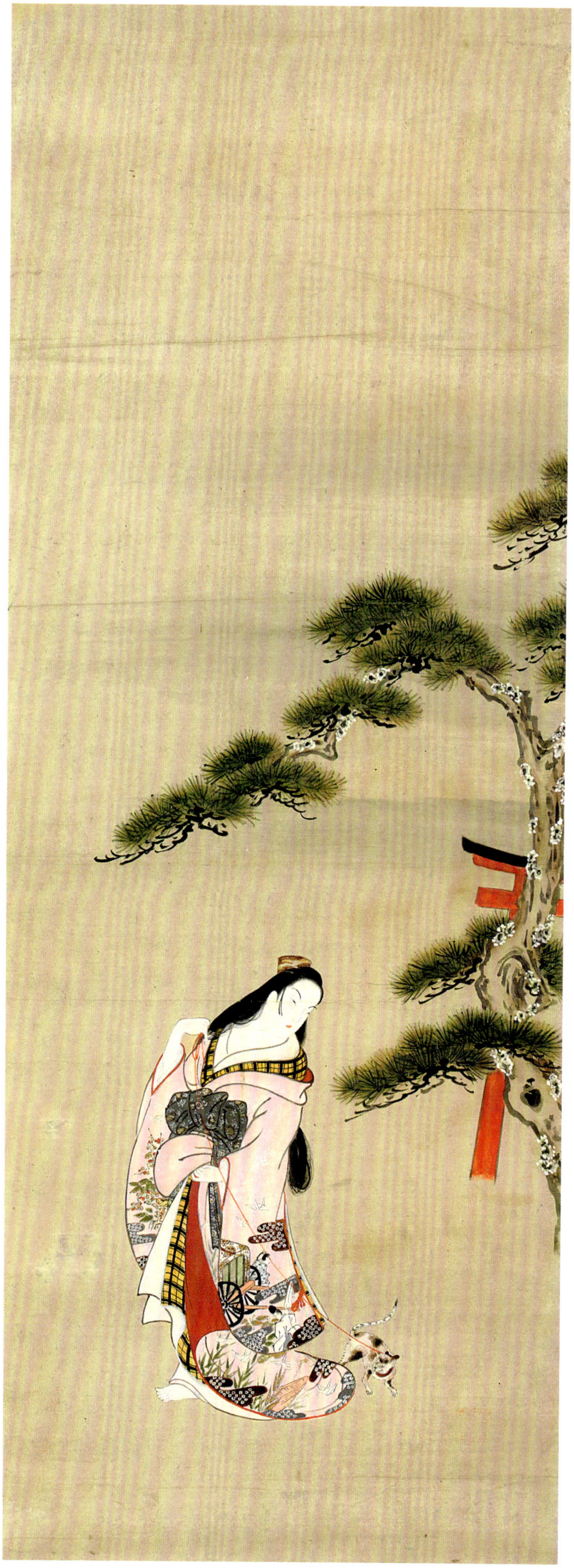

Tsukioka Settei
(月岡雪鼎; 1710–1786)

85. The Third Princess (女三宮) with a Cat, from "Wakana I" (若菜上) chapter of *Genji monogatari* (源氏物語)

Edo period, 18th century
Hanging scroll; ink and color on silk
88.5 x 31.6 cm (34 7/8 x 12 1/2 in.)
Signature, seal

Literature: Murase 1985, p. 105, fig. 9.

attributed to Matsuno Chikanobu
(松野親信; fl. 1716–1735)

86. The Third Princess (女三宮) with a Cat, from "Wakana I" (若菜上) chapter of *Genji monogatari* (源氏物語)

Edo period, 18th century
Hanging scroll; ink and color on paper
79.9 x 29.6 cm (31 1/2 x 11 5/8 in.)

Ex coll.: Frank E. Hart

Kawamata Tsunemasa
(川又常正; fl. mid-18th century)

87. "Yūgao" (夕顔) chapter of *Genji monogatari* (源氏物語)

Edo period, 18th century
Hanging scroll; ink and color on paper
33.4 x 55 cm (13 1/8 x 21 5/8 in.)
Signature, seal

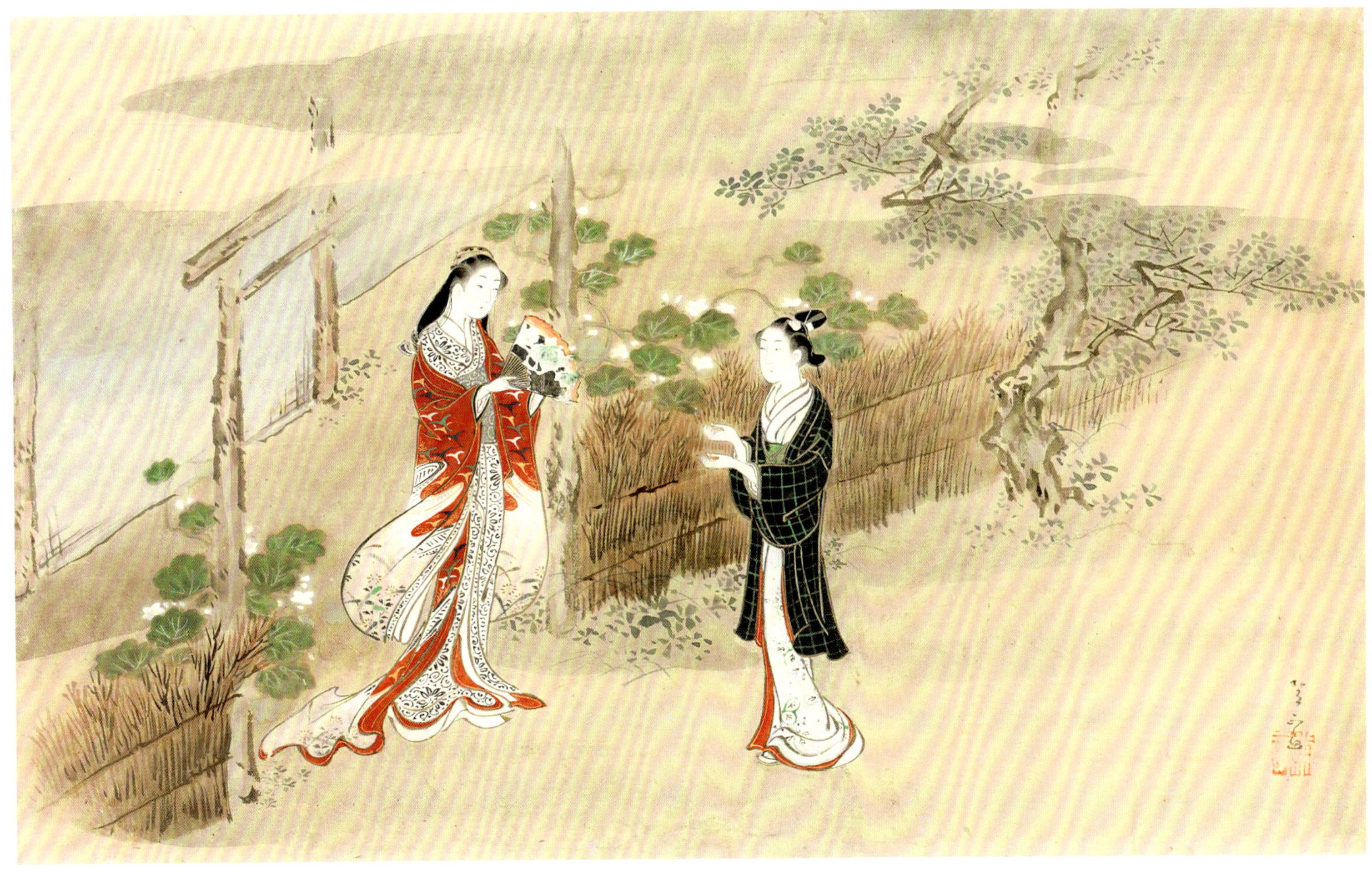

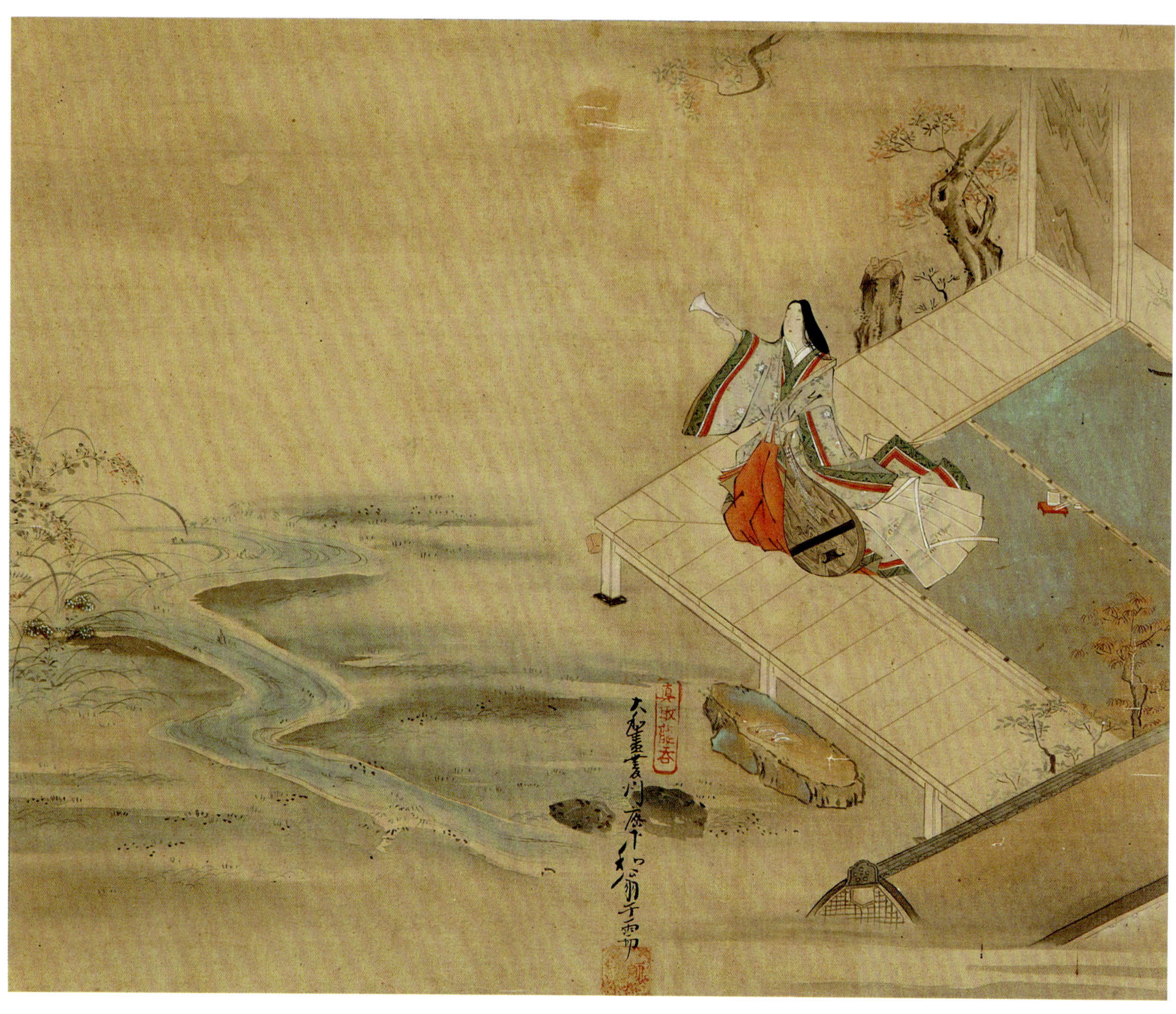

Hishikawa Wāō
(菱川和翁; fl. early 18th century)

88. Princess Ōigimi (大君), from "Hashihime" (橋姫) chapter of *Genji monogatari* (源氏物語)

Edo period, 18th century
Hanging scroll; ink, color, and gold on silk
37.1 x 45.6 cm ($14\frac{5}{8}$ x 18 in.)
Signature, seals

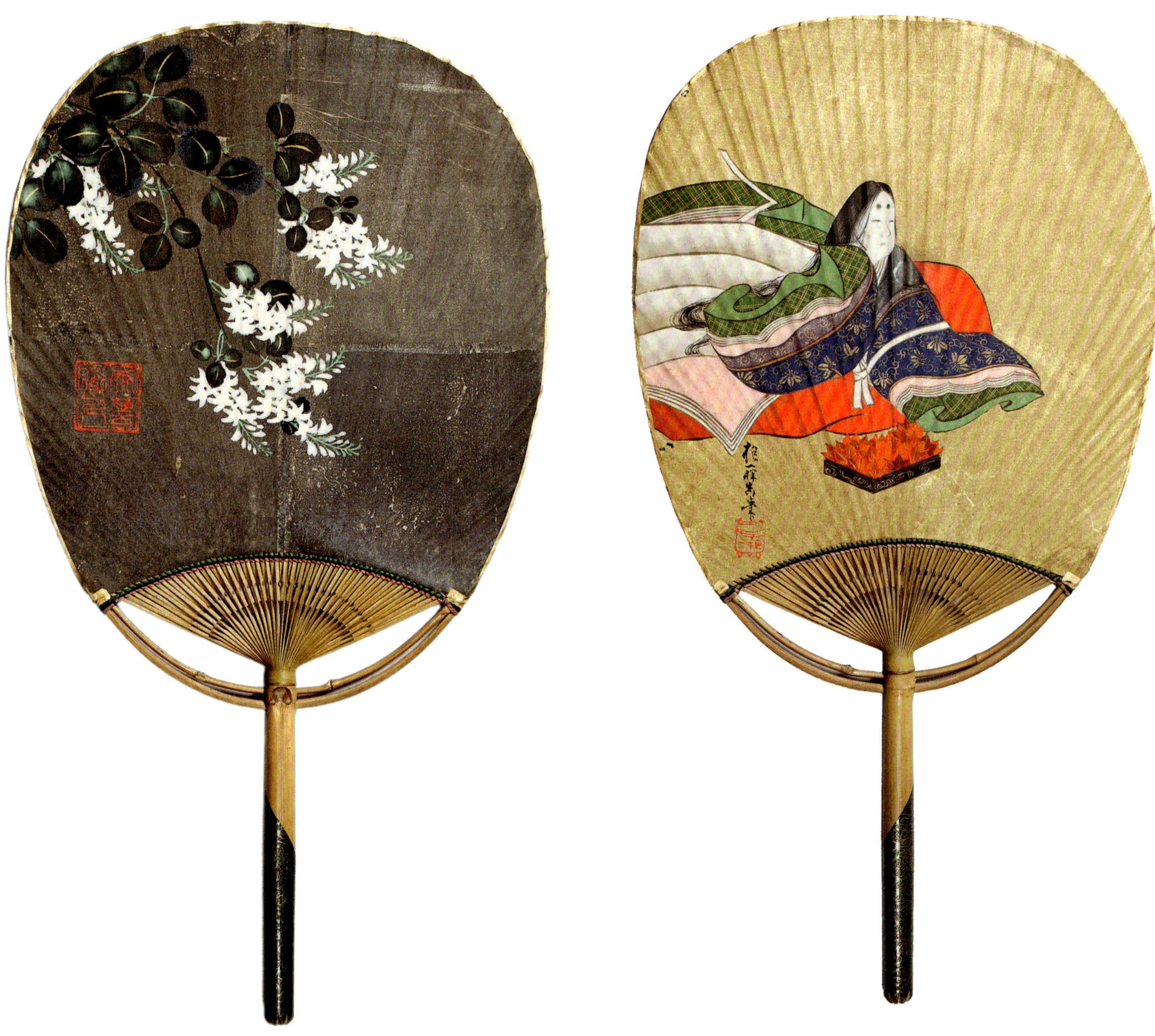

Sakai Hōitsu
(酒井抱一; 1761–1828)

89. (obverse) Princess Akikonomu (秋好中宮), from "Otome" (少女) chapter of *Genji monogatari* (源氏物語); (reverse) Bush clover

Edo period, 18th century
Fan; (*obverse*) ink, color, and gold on gilded silk; (*reverse*) ink, color, and gold on silvered silk
24 x 22 cm (9 1/2 x 8 5/8 in.)
Signature, seals

Literature: Yamane Yūzō 1977–80, vol. 2 (1977), no. 123; Yamane Yūzō 1989, no. 71; Kobayashi Tadashi 1990, p. 282, no. 287; Murashige Yasushi 1991, p. 58, no. 50; Asahi Shinbusha 1994–95, no. 93; McKelway 2012, pp. 122–23, no. 34.

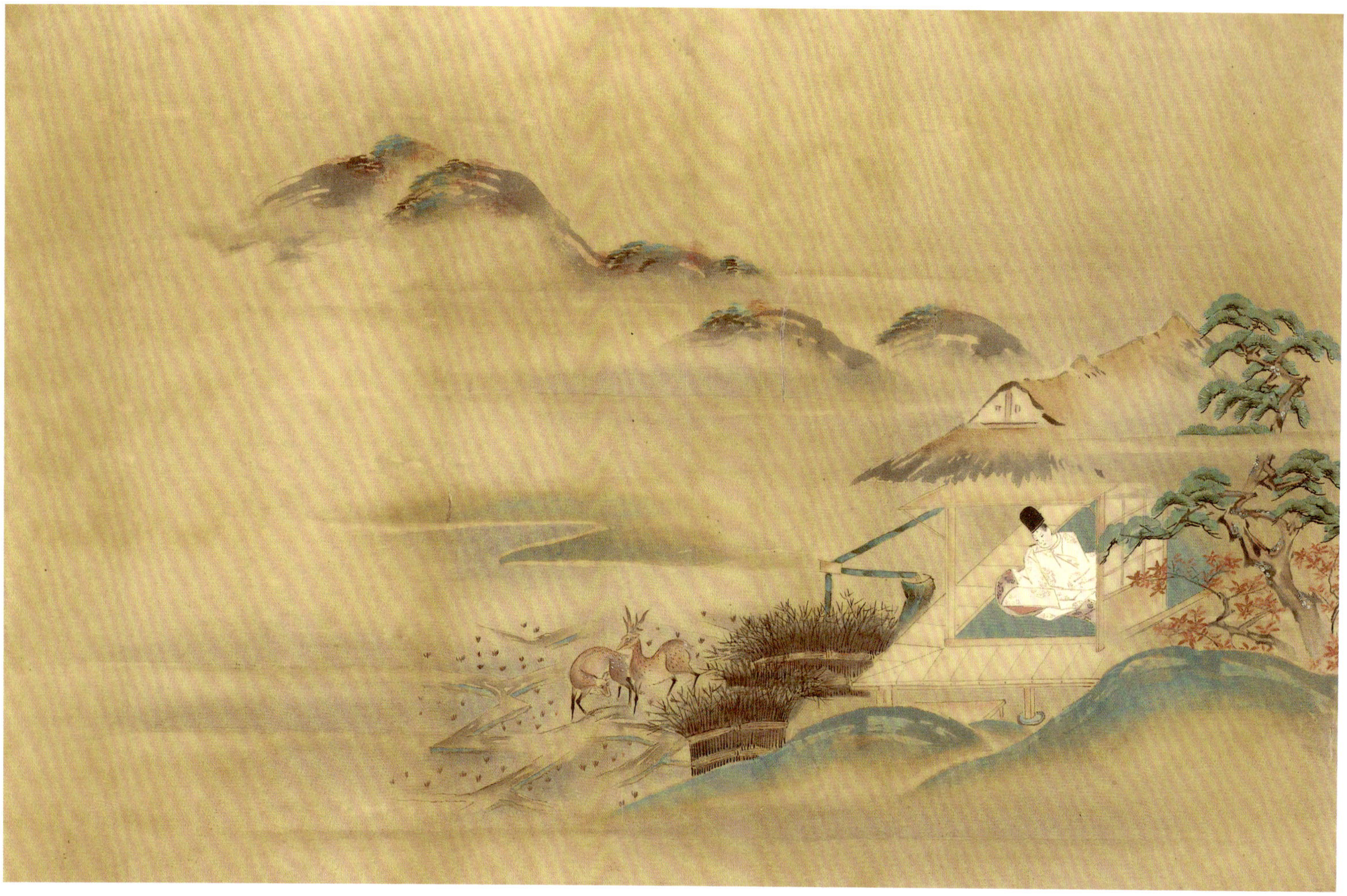

"Yūgiri"

Ishiyama Moroka
(石山師香; 1669–1734)

90. *Genji monogatari hakkei*
(源氏物語八景)

Edo period, 17th–18th century
Handscroll; ink, color, and gold on silk
33 x 768 cm (13 in. x 25 ft. $2\frac{3}{8}$ in.)
Signature, seal

Literature: Murase 2000, no. 110.

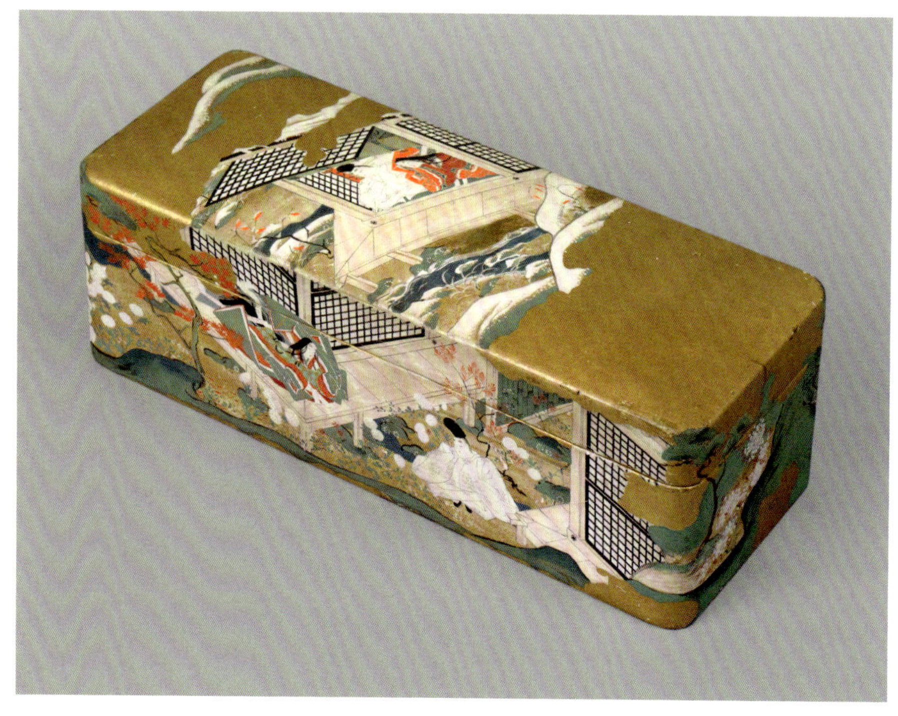

91. "Asagao," "E-awase," and "Yadorigi" (朝顔、絵合、宿木) chapters of *Genji monogatari* (源氏物語)

Edo period, 18th century
Painted wood box; ink and color on gilded wood
8.3 x 25.1 x 9.5 cm ($3\frac{1}{4}$ x $9\frac{7}{8}$ x $3\frac{3}{4}$ in.)

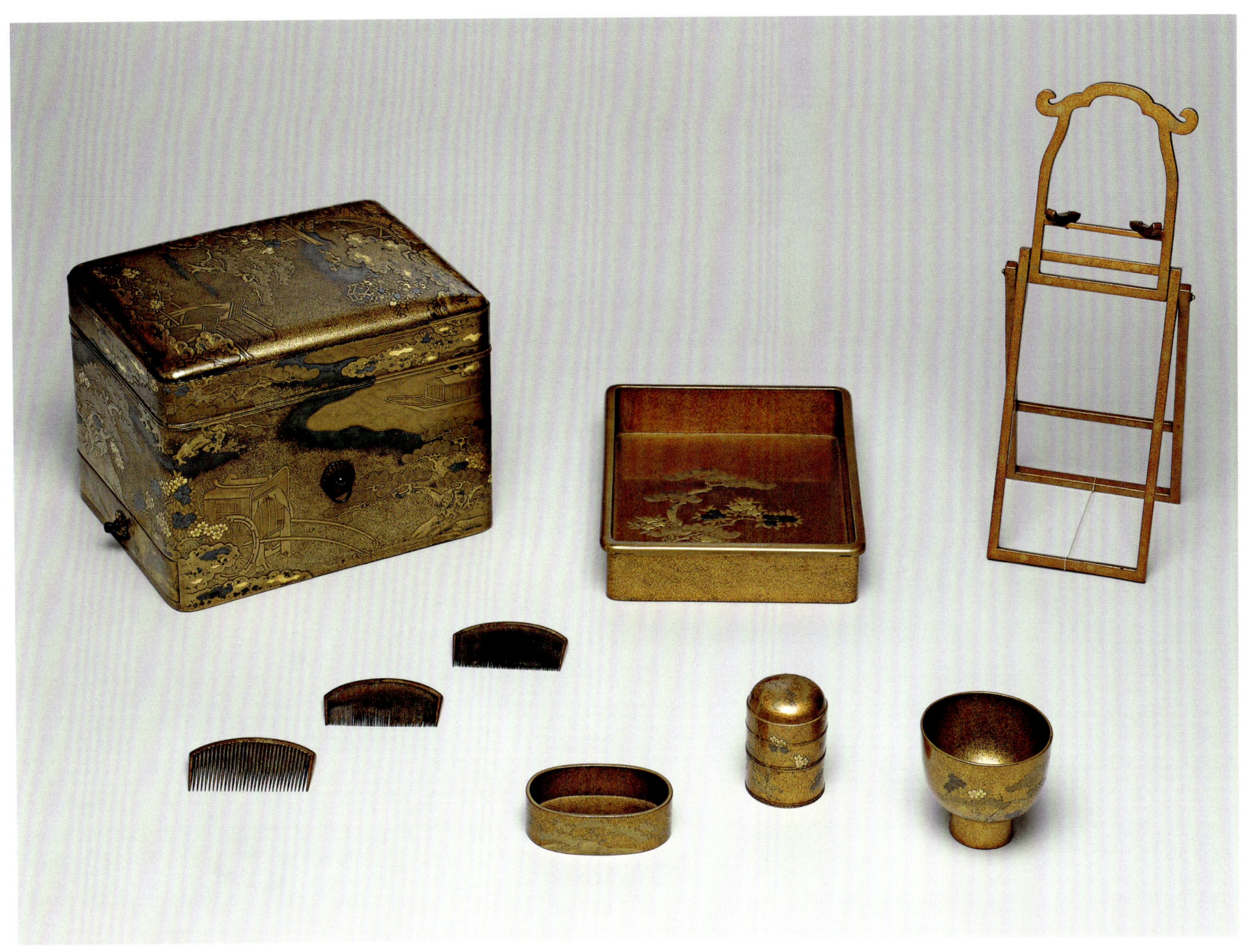

92. Accessories box (*tebako,* 手箱) with scenes from *Genji monogatari* (源氏物語)
Edo period, 17th–18th century
Box with drawer and accessories; gold *maki-e*, silver flakes, and metal inlay on black lacquer
19.1 x 19.9 x 25.2 cm (7 1/2 x 7 7/8 x 9 7/8 in.)

Literature: Murase 1993, no. 69.

Chapter 2 Details

† *denotes illustrated items*

---

42. From *Sumiyoshi monogatari emaki*

Text

Then they arrived in the capital and went to the mansion of Chūjō's father, who was upset about his son's secret marriage to an unknown country girl. Nevertheless, he built a special wing of the house for them and there established the newlyweds.

---

44. Fujiwara Teika from *Ikkasen isshubon*

Text

Frost has formed / on the trailing tail / of a solitary sleeping pheasant, / its bed illuminated / by a cold autumn moon.

---

45. The Poets Henjō and Jichin from *Mokuhitsu jidai fudō uta awase-e*

Text

[right] *Sōjō Henjō* [816–890]

[left] *former Daisōjō Jichin* [1155–1225]

(16th Round, left)

Cherry trees on Mount Furu at Iso no Kami / are as old as the mountain. / No one knows who planted them there.

(16th Round, right)

The leaves have turned, yet linger / still in the valley. / Autumn showers deepen their colors— / the tenth month of the year.

(17th Round, left)

Everyone again is garbed / in hues of springtime blossoms. / Oh, tear-stained sleeves / will you now become dry?

(17th Round, right)

Vainglorious though I may be, / I yearn to protect, under my priestly sleeves, / the people of this woeful world.

(18th Round, left)

Mist on the tips of the leaves, / dew at the roots of the tree, / sooner or later all will vanish.

(18th Round, right)

Oh, that I may linger / on the darkened path, / that it may brighten with / the Buddha's Law.

---

46. Koōgimi from Fujifusa version of *Thirty-six Immortal Poets*

Text

Koōgimi

Held the title of Nyo Kurōdo during the time of the ex-Emperor Sanjō, also known as Sakon. Active during the reigns of Emperors Ichijō [r. 986–1010] *and Sanjō* [r. 1011–15].

Nightly visits across Iwabashi stopped. / When morning came, / sadness surrounded Mount Katsuragi.

---

47. Ariwara Narihira, from Fujifusa version of *Thirty-six Immortal Poets*

Text

Ariwara Narihira: head of Chamberlain's Office in 847; Junior fourth rank lower; Imperial Guard with the rank of lieutenant general in 877; grandson of Emperor Heijō, fifth son of Prince Abo; head of Judiciary Office; mother, Princess Izu; died in 880, aged 56; served under Emperors Ninmei, Montoku, Seiwa, Yōzei.

If this world had never known the ephemeral charm of cherry blossoms, / then our hearts in spring / might match nature's deep tranquility.

---

† 48. Kakinomoto no Hitomaro

Text

Poem by Hitomaro (fl. 8th century), number 409 in *Kokin wakashū*

Dimly, dimly / in the morning mist that lies over Akashi Bay, / my longings follow with the ship / that vanishes behind the distant isle.

---

49. From *Tengu zōshi emaki*

Text

Kikuchi Jirō Takanao; [illegible] *Toraemon no jō Sueyasu*; *Fujiuchi Sae* [illegible]; [illegible] *Harada* [illegible]

---

52. From *Saigyō monogatari emaki*

Text

[*Saigyō*] *composes a poem as he happens upon beautiful cherry trees at the shrine of Yagami Ōji: Long-awaited cherries of Yagami are in bloom, / winds waft over the mountains and pines, / do not disturb these fragile flowers.*

---

† 53. Kakinomoto no Hitomaro from *Thirty-six Immortal Poets*

Text

Poem by Kakinomoto no Hitomaro (fl. 8th century)

Left / Kakinomoto no Hitomaro [Poem 284, *Kokin wakashū*] // *Red leaves float by / on Tatsuta River. / Freezing rains must already be falling / on Mount Mimuro / this autumn day.*

[on back of each text] *Attribution of the text to 36 calligraphers, including Takatsukasa Fusasuke* [1637–1700]

Signature

[on Kakinomoto no Hitomaro, Taira Kanemori, Ki no Tsurayuki, and Nakatsukasa] *Painted by Hokkyō Gukei*

Seals

[on each painting] *Hirozumi*

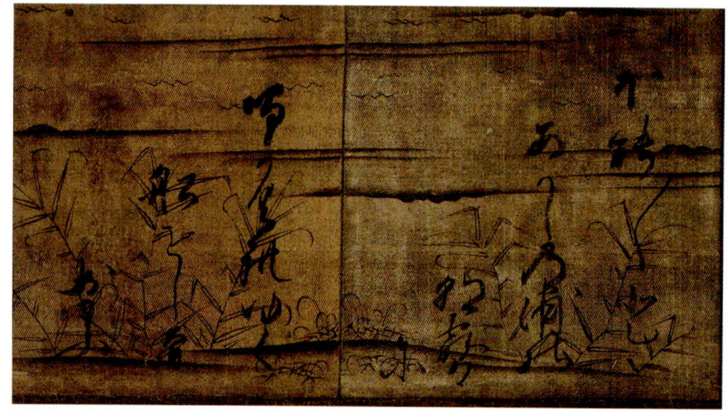

48

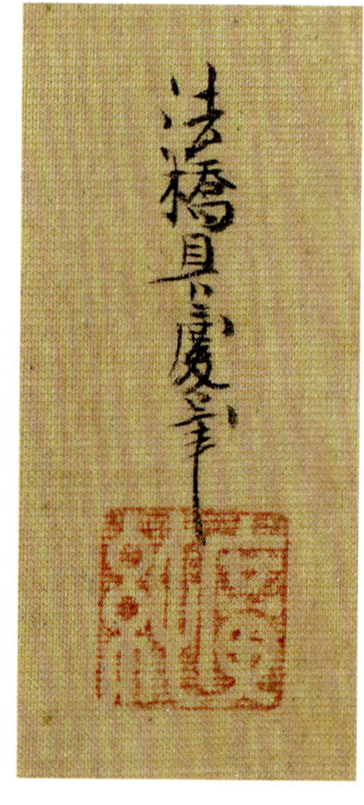

53

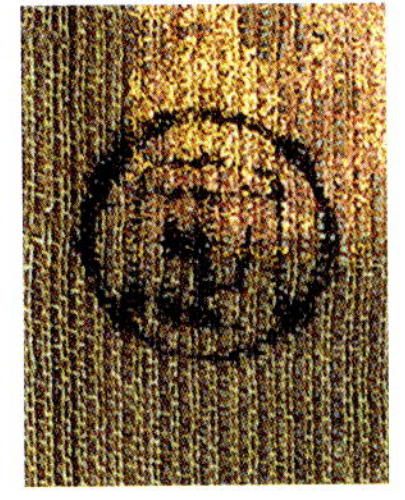

54

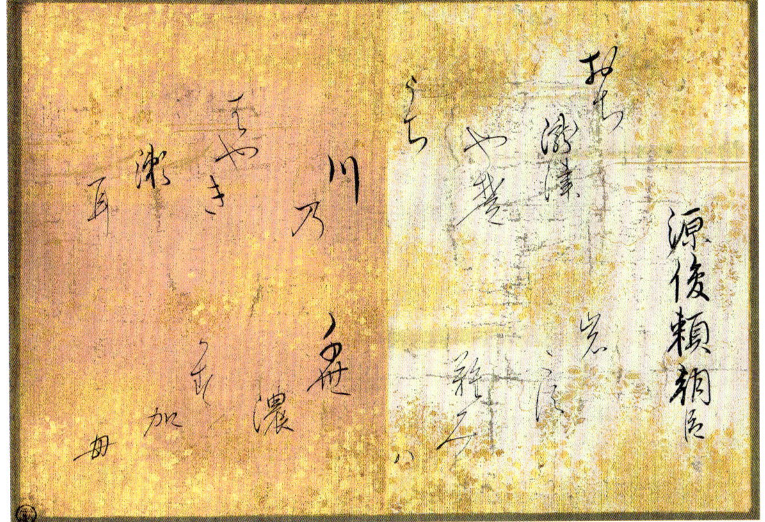

54

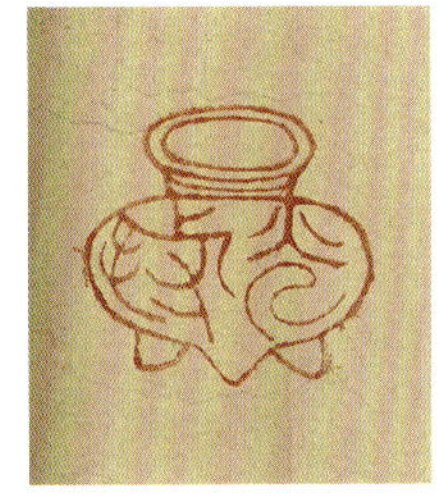

59

65

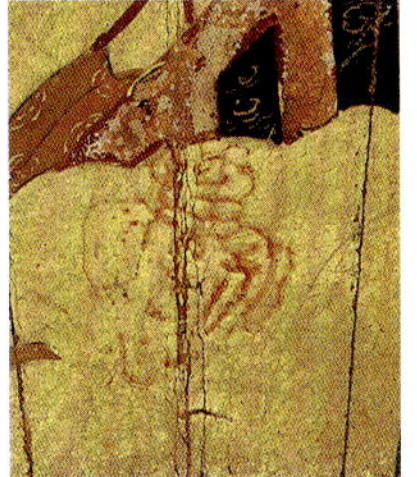

66

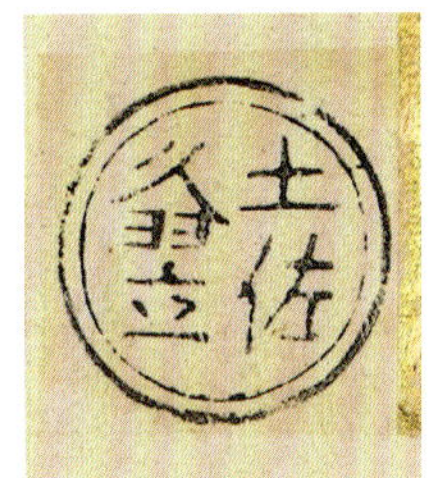

67

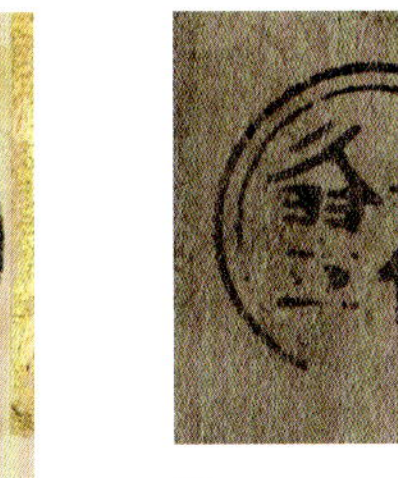

68

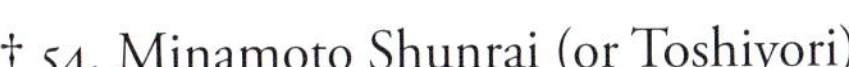

† 54. Minamoto Shunrai (or Toshiyori)

Text

Minamoto Shunrai Ason // Many currents branch out from / a tumbling cascade of a waterfall. / Rocks stand in the midst of waves / formed by rapid flows, / which become an eternal river.

Seal

[lower left corner of poem card] Illegible

55. Princess Shikishi from *Thirty-six Immortal Poets*

Text

Right / Princess Shikishi // When I gaze at the Milky Way, / my sleeves become cooled by / early autumn wind.

56. Poems from *Shūi gusō* and *Shin kokin wakashū*

Text

Poem by Fujiwara Teika (藤原定家; 1162–1241), from his *Shūi gusō*

Mountain cherries fall / from the sky at dawn, / like a snowstorm / over the unknown mountains.

Poem by Priest Saigyō (西行; 1118–1190)

Ah, how many drops of dew / will spill / from leaves of grass— / fall winds are rising / on Miyagino plain.

57. The Sixth Month of *Teika's Poems on Flowers and Birds of the Twelve Months*

Text

For the flower and bird representing the sixth month: *Tokonatsu* [Chinese Pink]

I even miss the weather of this parched month, usually spurned for / its hot sun, because it is the month when the Chinese pink of "everlasting summer" / comes into bloom.

U [Cormorant]

As swiftly as the flares disappear upstream in the river / where the cormorants fish on this short summer night, / this month of parched weather, too, / will soon be gone.

† 59. *Saru no monogatari emaki*

Seal

[at end of scroll] *Mitsutora* [?]

63. "Aoi" chapter of *Genji monogatari*

Seal

Tōkan Family Collection

64. "Wakana II" chapter of *Genji monogatari*

Text

Nun Akashi; Chūgū's nurse, Princess Akashi

† 65. "Miotsukushi" chapter of *Genji monogatari*

Seal

Illegible

† 66. "Kochō" chapter of *Genji monogatari*

Seal

Illegible

† 67. "Fujibakama" chapter of *Genji monogatari*

Seal

[attached to lower left side] *Tosa Kyūyoku*

† 68. "Kashiwagi" chapter of *Genji monogatari*

Seal

[on reverse] *Tosa Kyūyoku*

70. "Tamakazura" chapter of *Genji monogatari*

Text

"Vast numbers of things," he [Genji] said to Murasaki. "We must see that they are divided so that no one has a right to feel slighted." He had everything spread before him, the products of the offices and of Murasaki's personal endeavors as well. Such sheens and hues as she had wrought, displaying yet another of her talents!

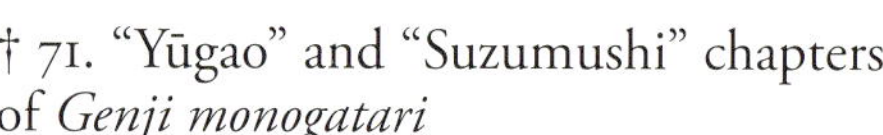

† 71. "Yūgao" and "Suzumushi" chapters of *Genji monogatari*

Seal

Tosa Mitsunori

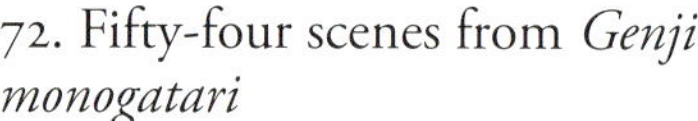

72. Fifty-four scenes from *Genji monogatari*

Text

[on left screen] *Usugumo* [chapter] // *The little girl clung to his trousers and seemed prepared to go with him. . . . [He looked] down at her with fondness.*

† 73. Fifty-four scenes from *Genji monogatari*

Text

[on left screen] *Nowaki* [chapter] // *The screens having been folded and put away, the view was unobstructed . . . She laughed as her women fought with the unruly blinds.*

Signature

[on 54th sheet] *Painted by Tosa Mitsunari*

Seal

[on each sheet] *Tosa*

† 81. "Usugumo," "Asagao," "Otome," "Tamakazura," "Hatsune," "Kochō," "Hotaru," and "Tokonatsu" chapters of *Genji monogatari*

Signature

Sōtatsu Hokkyō

Seal

Taiseiken

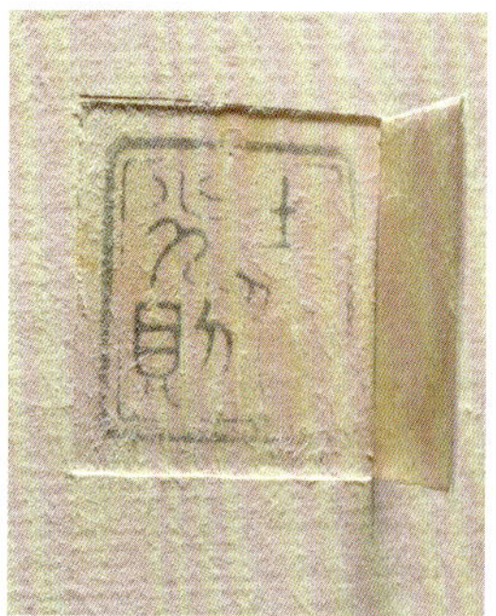

71

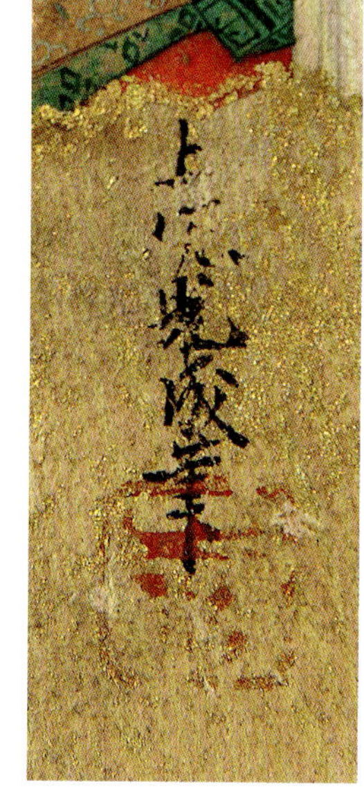

73

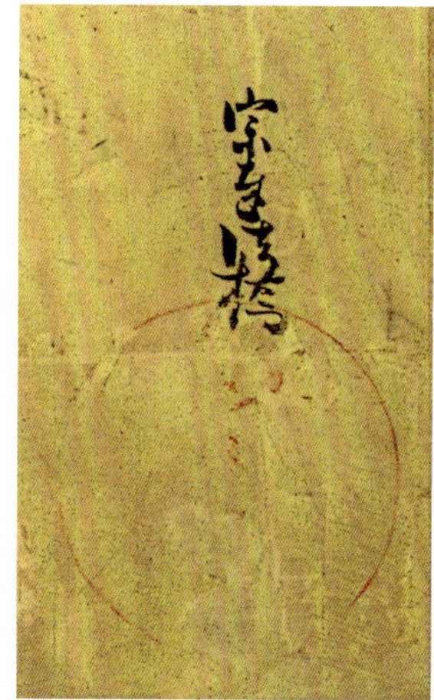

81

† 83. "Suma" and "Asagao" chapters of *Genji monogatari*

Text

[in last volume] *Reverently inscribed by Shunshō of the humble-rank Yama[moto] family in the eleventh month of 1650.*

† 85. The Third Princess with a Cat, from "Wakana I" chapter of *Genji monogatari*

Signature

Hōgen Tsukioka Settei

Seal

Sei Genji Kida na Akinobu aza Taikei gō Settei betsugō Tsukioka jishō Shinten'ō

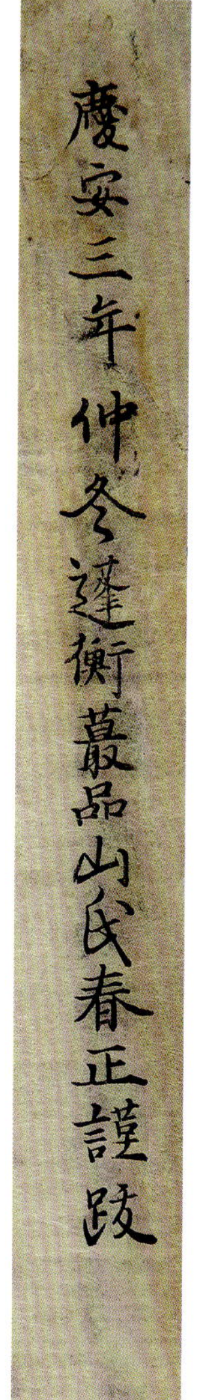

83

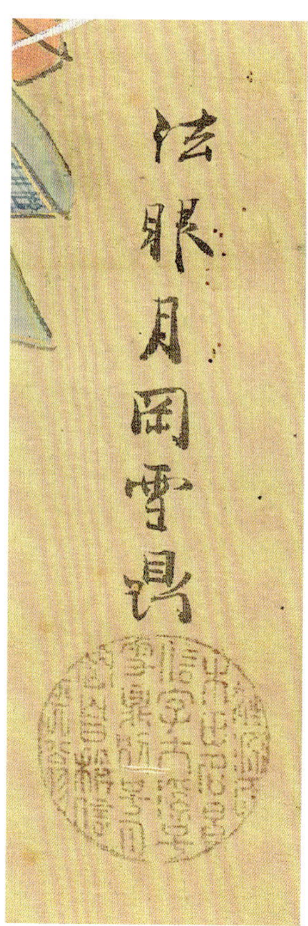

85

† 87. "Yūgao" chapter of *Genji monogatari*

Signature

Painted by Tsunemasa

Seal

Tsunemasa

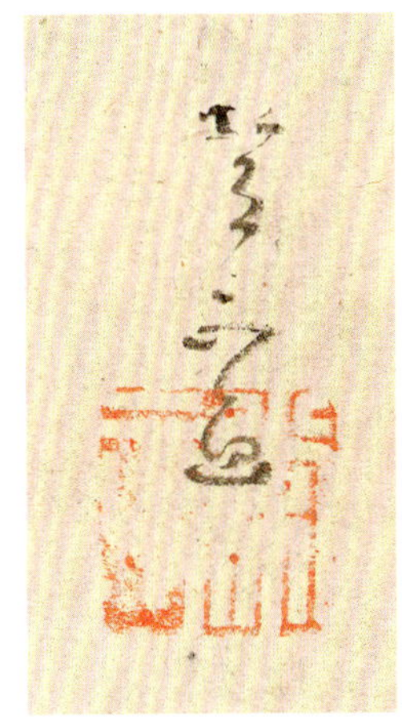

87

† 88. Princess Ōigimi, from "Hashihime" chapter of *Genji monogatari*

Signature

Waō of the Hishikawa Yamato-e School, upon request

Seals

[to right of signature] *Shinju Ryūdon*; [below signature] illegible

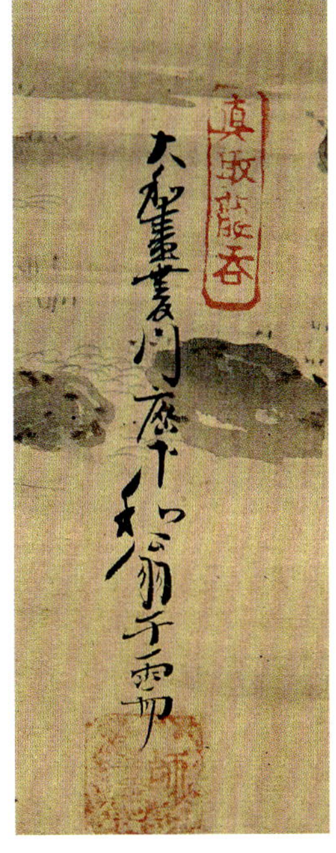

88

† 89. (obverse) Princess Akikonomu, from "Otome" chapter of *Genji monogatari*; (reverse) Bush clover

[obverse]

Signature

Painted by Hōitsu Kishin

Seal

Hōitsu

[reverse]

Seal

Uka Dōjin

89 (reverse)

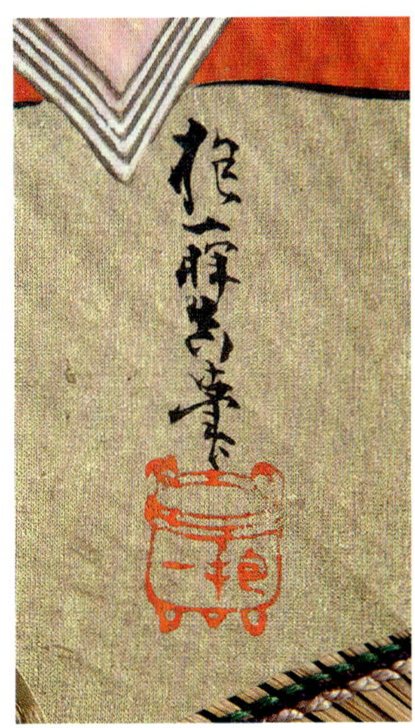

89 (obverse)

† 90. *Genji monogatari hakkei*

Signature

[at end of scroll] *Sahyōe no Kami Mototada*

Seal

[at end of scroll] *Mototada*

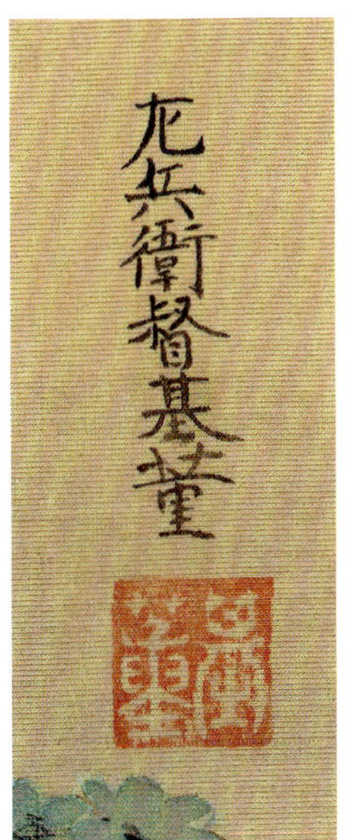

90

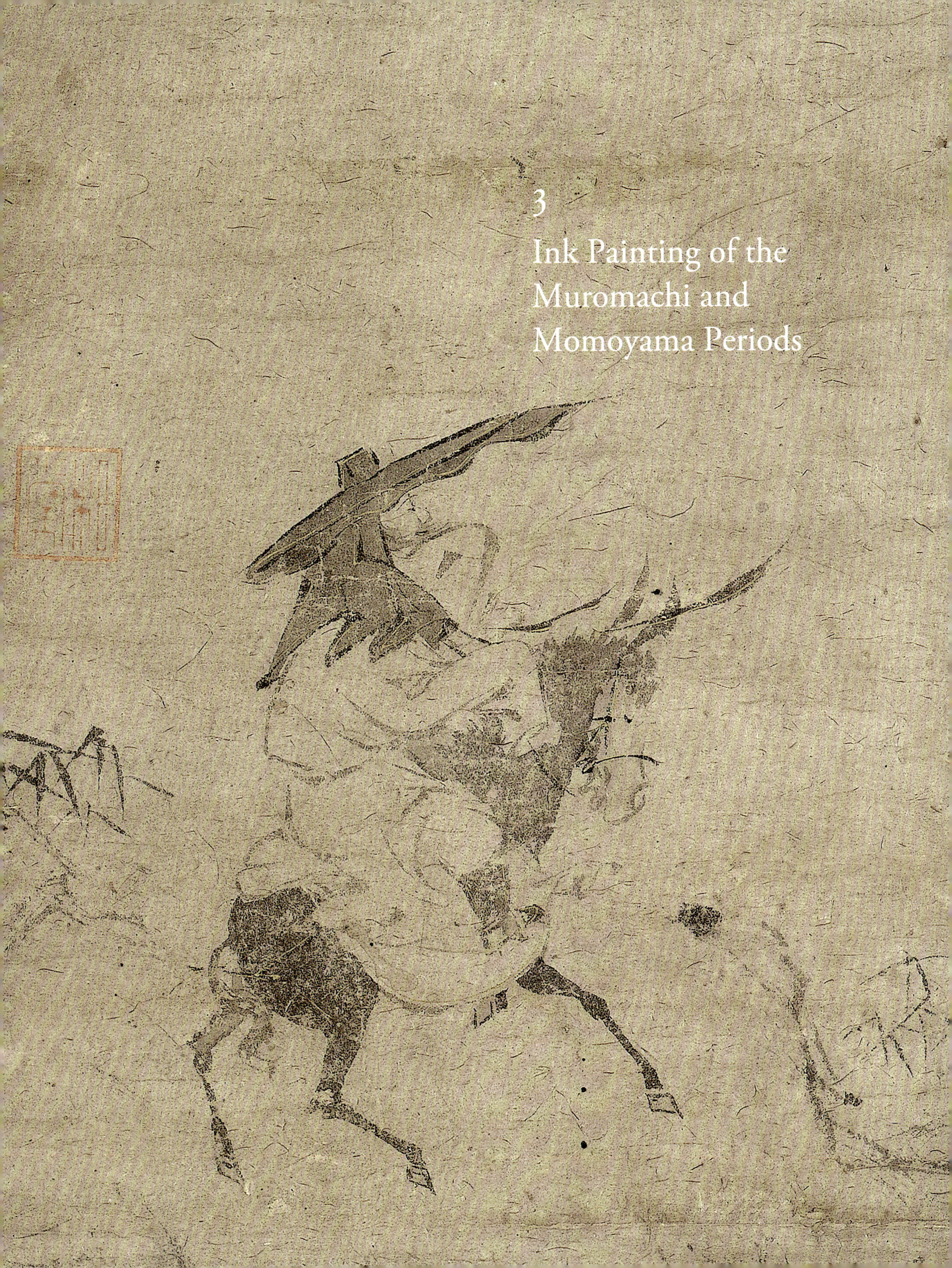

3
Ink Painting of the Muromachi and Momoyama Periods

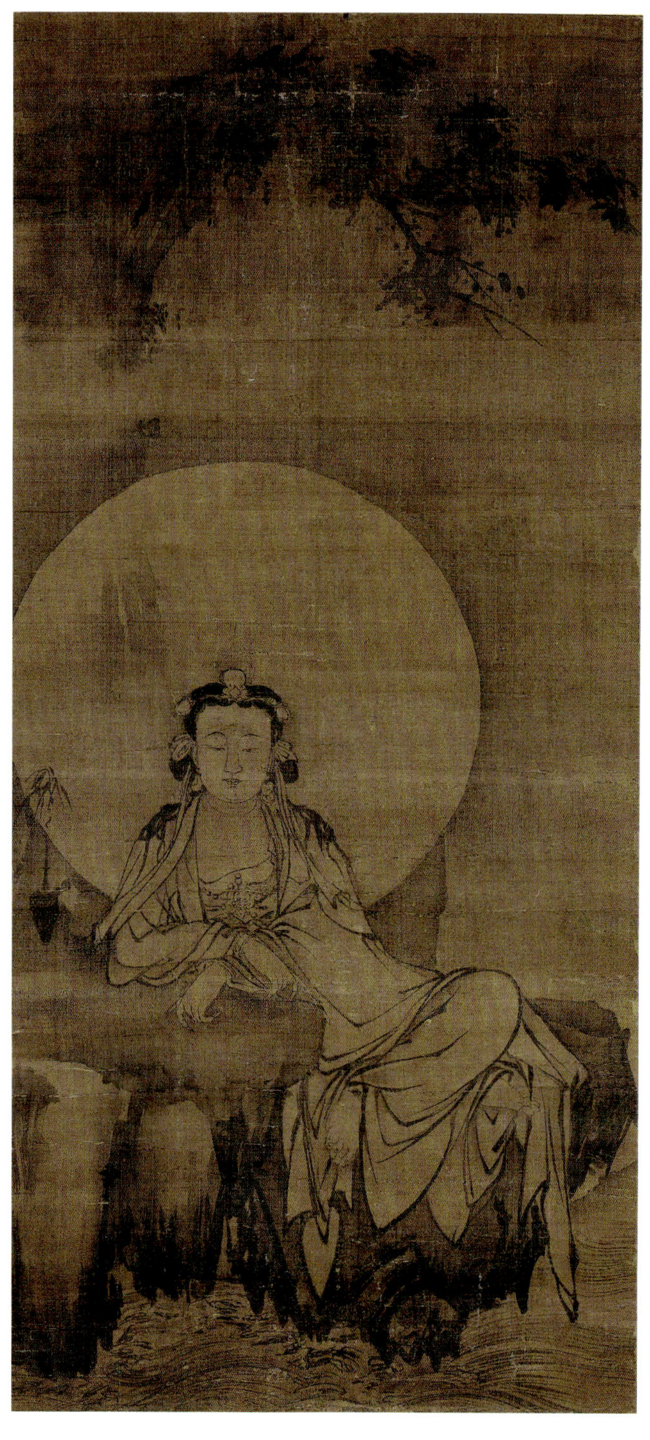

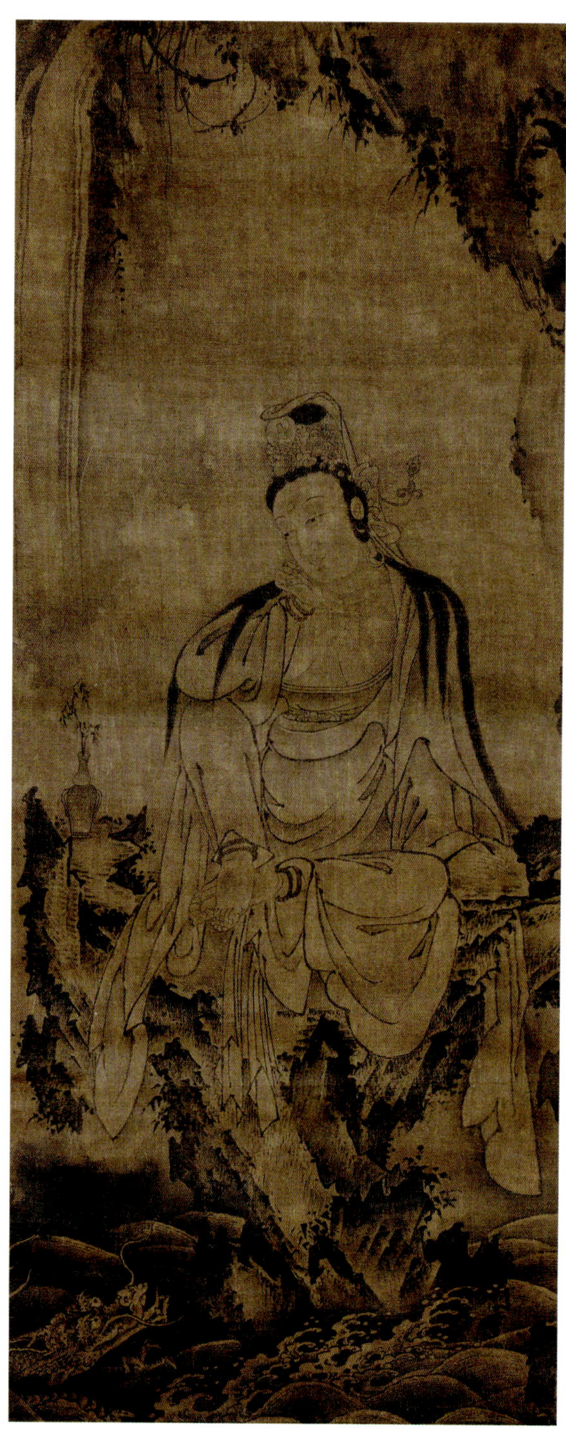

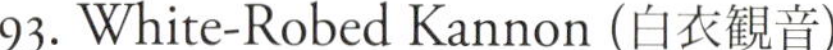

93. White-Robed Kannon (白衣観音)

Muromachi period, early 15th century
Hanging scroll; ink on silk
114.6 x 53.2 cm (45 1/8 x 21 in.)

Ex coll.: Chauncy Griggs, Tacoma, Washington

Literature: Ford 1985, fig. 1; Tokyo National Museum 1985a, no. 19; Avitabile 1990, no. 35; Murase 2000, no. 49; Tsuji Nobuo et al. 2005, no. 36.

94. White-Robed Kannon (白衣観音)

Muromachi period, 16th century
Hanging scroll; ink on silk
97.2 x 39.5 cm (38 1/4 x 15 1/2 in.)

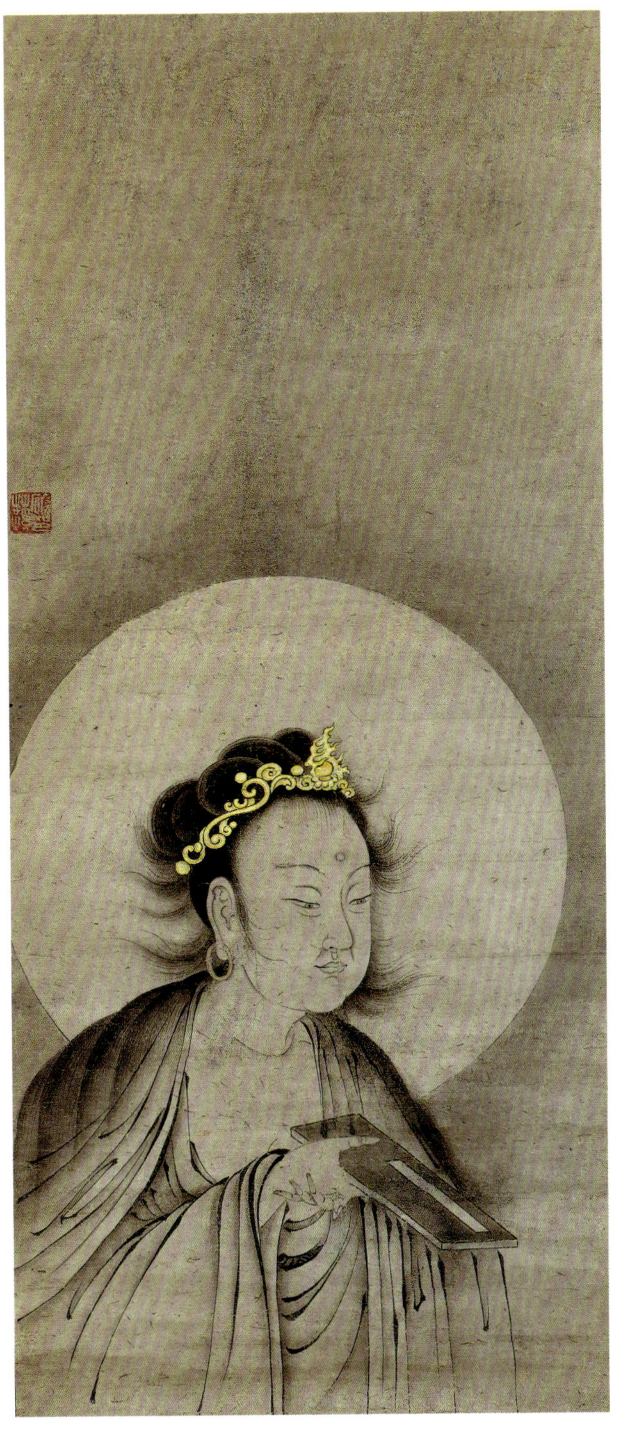

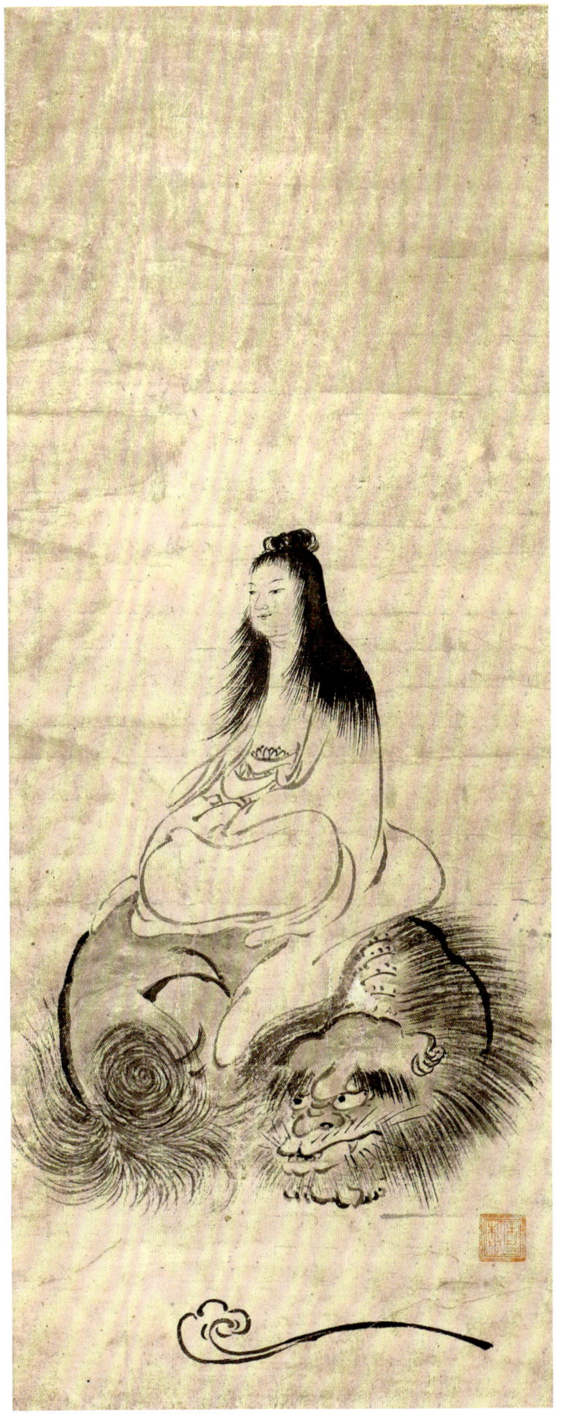

Kichizan Minchō
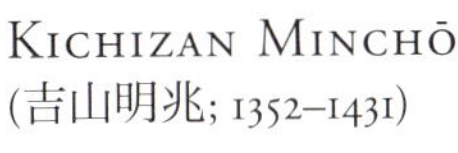
(吉山明兆; 1352–1431)

95. Monju Bosatsu (文殊菩薩)

Muromachi period, 15th century
Hanging scroll; ink and gold on paper
82 x 35.6 cm (32¼ x 14 in.)
Seal

Ex coll.: Nozaki Hirota; Inoue Kaoru

Literature: Murase 1975, no. 29; Avitabile 1990, no. 36; Yamaguchi Prefectural Museum of Art 1998, no. 39.

Shūsei
(秀製?; fl. late 15th century)

96. Monju on a Lion (騎獅文殊)

Muromachi period
Hanging scroll; ink on paper
81.9 x 33.1 cm (32¼ x 13 in.)
Seal

Literature: Murase 1993, no. 8.

Reisai
(霊彩; fl. 1430–50)

97. Bukan; Kanzan, Jittoku
(豊干；寒山、拾得)

Muromachi period
Pair of hanging scrolls; ink and light color on paper
Each scroll 96.5 x 34.6 cm (38 x 13 5/8 in.)

Ex coll.: Satsuma Jihei

Literature: Shimada Shūjirō 1969, vol. 1, pls. 8, 9; Tanaka Ichimatsu 1974, pl. 39; Murase 1975, no. 31; Shimizu and Wheelwright 1976, no. 5; Shimada Shūjirō 1979, nos. 21, 22; Tokyo National Museum 1980, no. 106; Tokyo National Museum 1985a, no. 15; Avitabile 1990, no. 38; Murase 1992, pp. 152–53; Yamaguchi Prefectural Museum of Art 1998, p. 178, no. 8; Murase 2000, no. 54; Tsuji Nobuo et al. 2005, no. 38; Levine and Lippit 2007, no. 17.

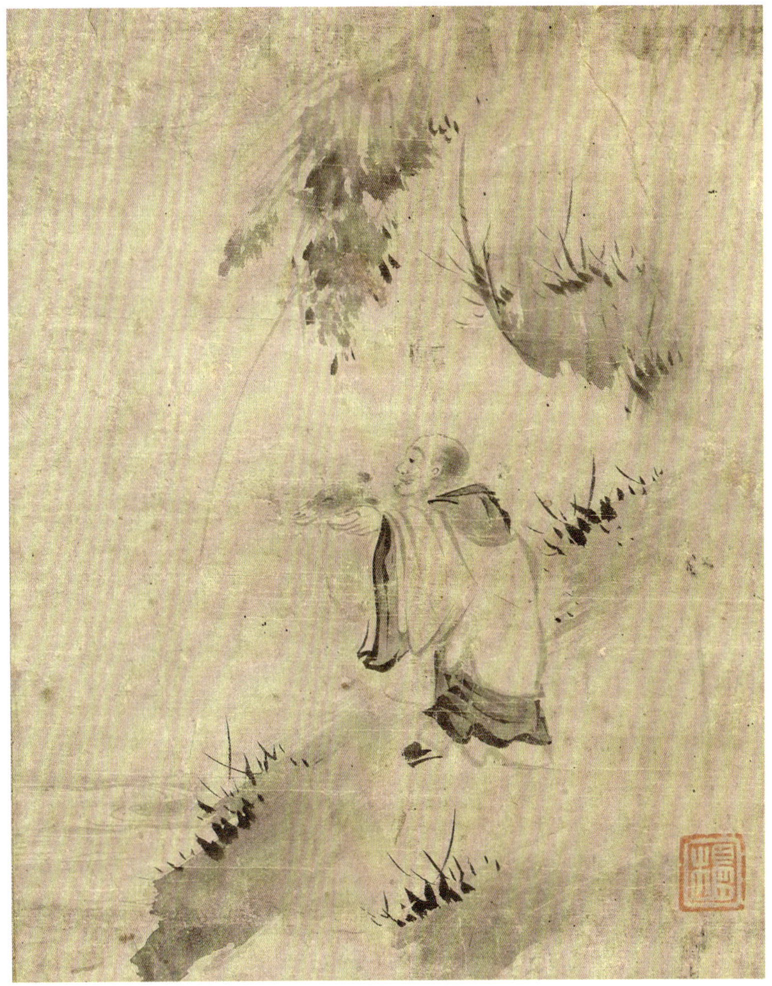

98. Chotō

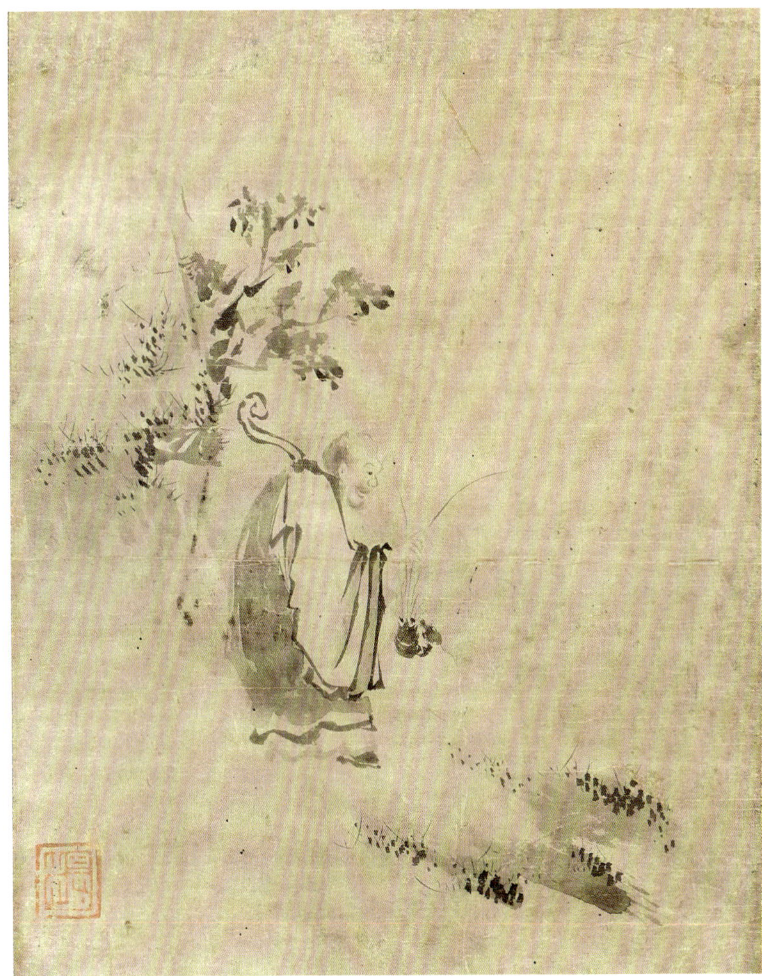

98. Kensu

Yōgetsu
(楊月; fl. late 15th–early 16th century)

98. Chotō (猪頭); Kensu (蜆子)

Muromachi period
Pair of hanging scrolls; ink on paper
Each scroll 28.5 x 22.8 cm (11 1/4 x 9 in.)
Seals

Literature: Matsushita Takaaki 1960, no. 55; Murase 1993, no. 9.

Sekkyakushi
(赤脚子; fl. first half of 15th century)

99. Ox and Herdsman

Muromachi period
Hanging scroll; ink on paper
53.6 x 29.6 cm (21 1/8 x 11 5/8 in.)
Seal

Ex coll.: Nakamura Tanio, Kanagawa Prefecture

Literature: Nakamura Tanio 1959a, pl. 42; Yonezawa Yoshiho 1959, pp. 17–19; Shimada Shūjirō 1969, vol. 1, p. 103; Fontein and Hickman 1970, no. 45; Nakamura Tanio 1970; Tanaka Ichimatsu and Yonezawa Yoshiho 1970, pl. 40; Tanaka Ichimatsu 1974, pl. 106; Murase 1975, no. 30; Shimizu and Wheelwright 1976, no. 4; Kanazawa Hiroshi 1977, pl. 50; Kinoshita Masao 1979, fig. 175; Shimada Shūjirō 1979, no. 18; Tokyo National Museum 1985a, no. 13; Avitabile 1990, no. 37; Yamaguchi Prefectural Museum of Art 1998, no. 9; Murase 2000, no. 53; Wada 2002, p. 24, fig. 4.

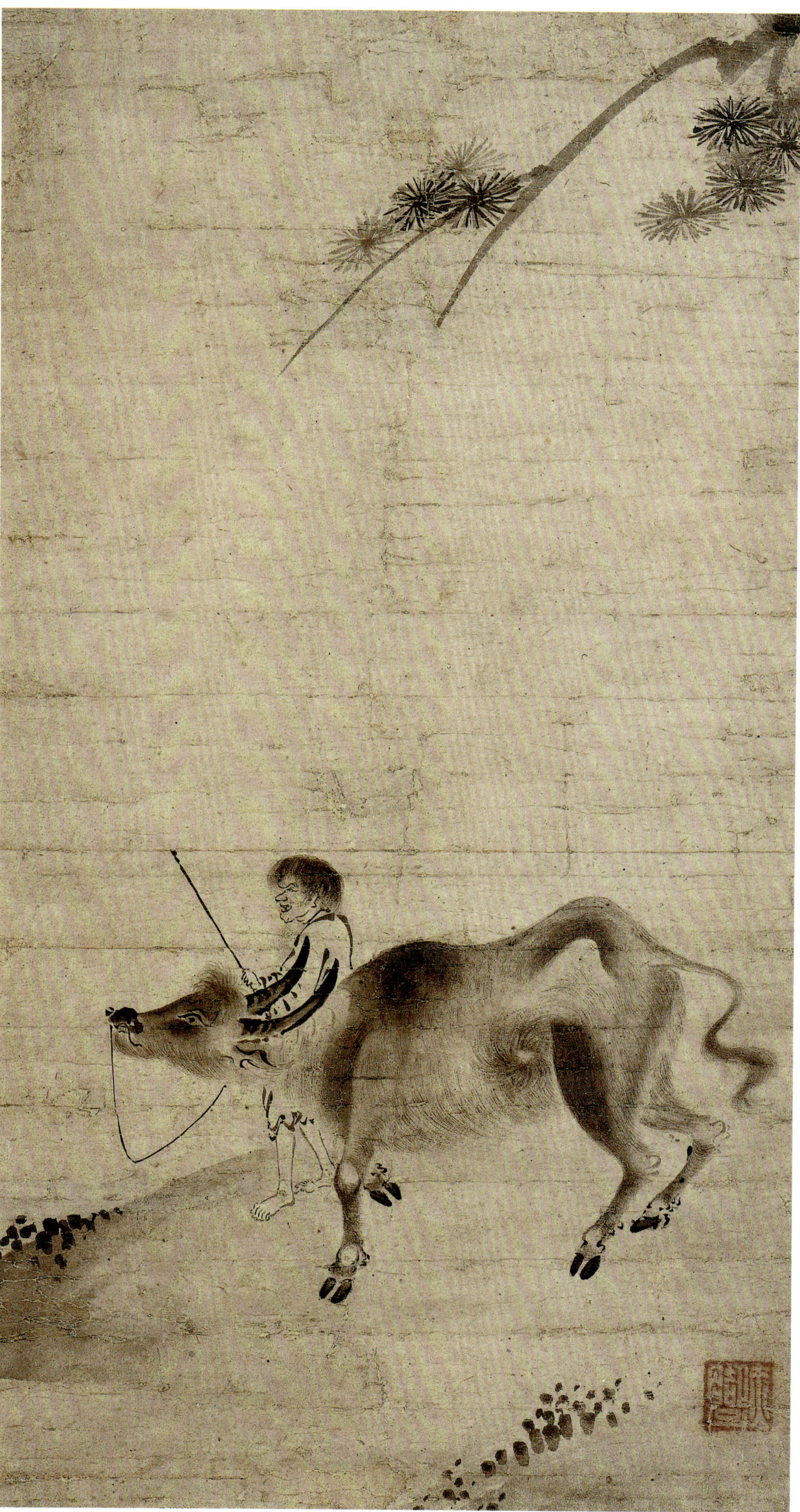

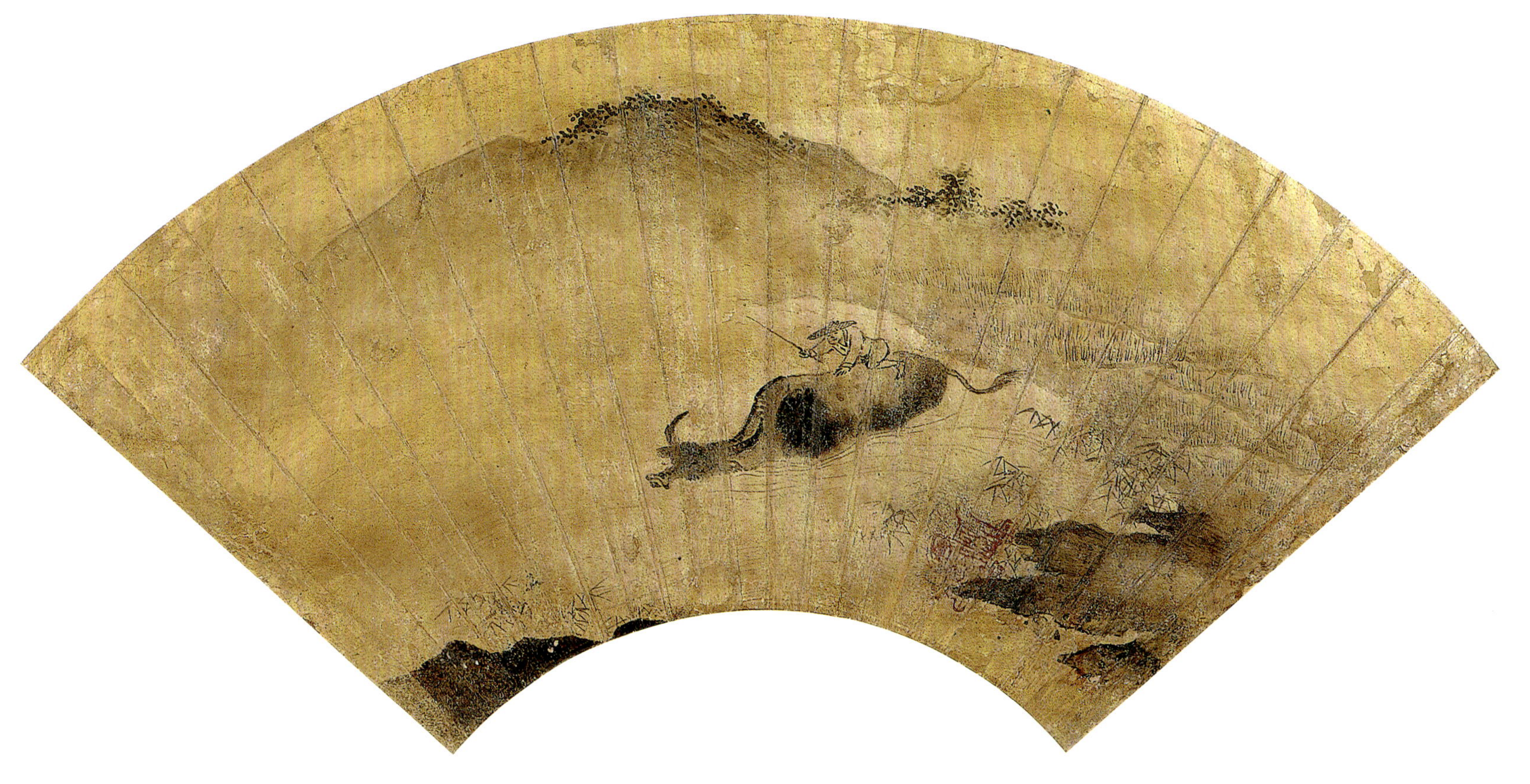

100. Water Buffalo and Herdboy

Muromachi period, late 15th century
Folding fan mounted on hanging scroll; ink on gilded paper
18.2 x 47.1 cm (7 1/8 x 18 1/2 in.)
Seal

LITERATURE: Murase 1993, no. 12; Kyoto National Museum 1996, no. 17; Murase 2000, no. 56.

Bokudō Sojun
(朴堂祖淳; 1373–1459)

101. Soshoku (Ch. Su Shi) on a Donkey
(蘇軾騎驢)

Muromachi period
Hanging scroll; ink and gold on paper
57 x 26 cm (22 1/2 x 10 1/4 in.)
Seal

Literature: Murase 1993, no. 11; Murase 2000, no. 55.

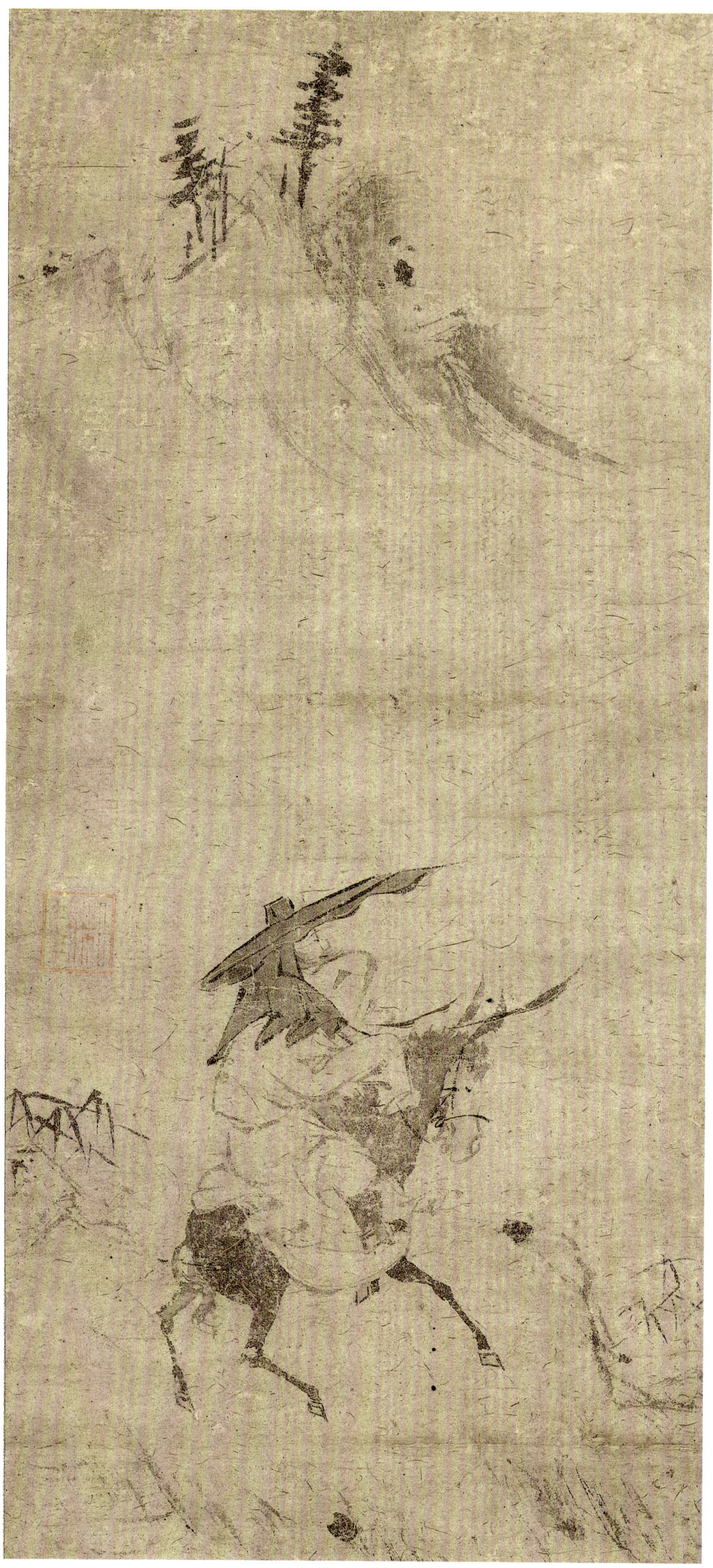

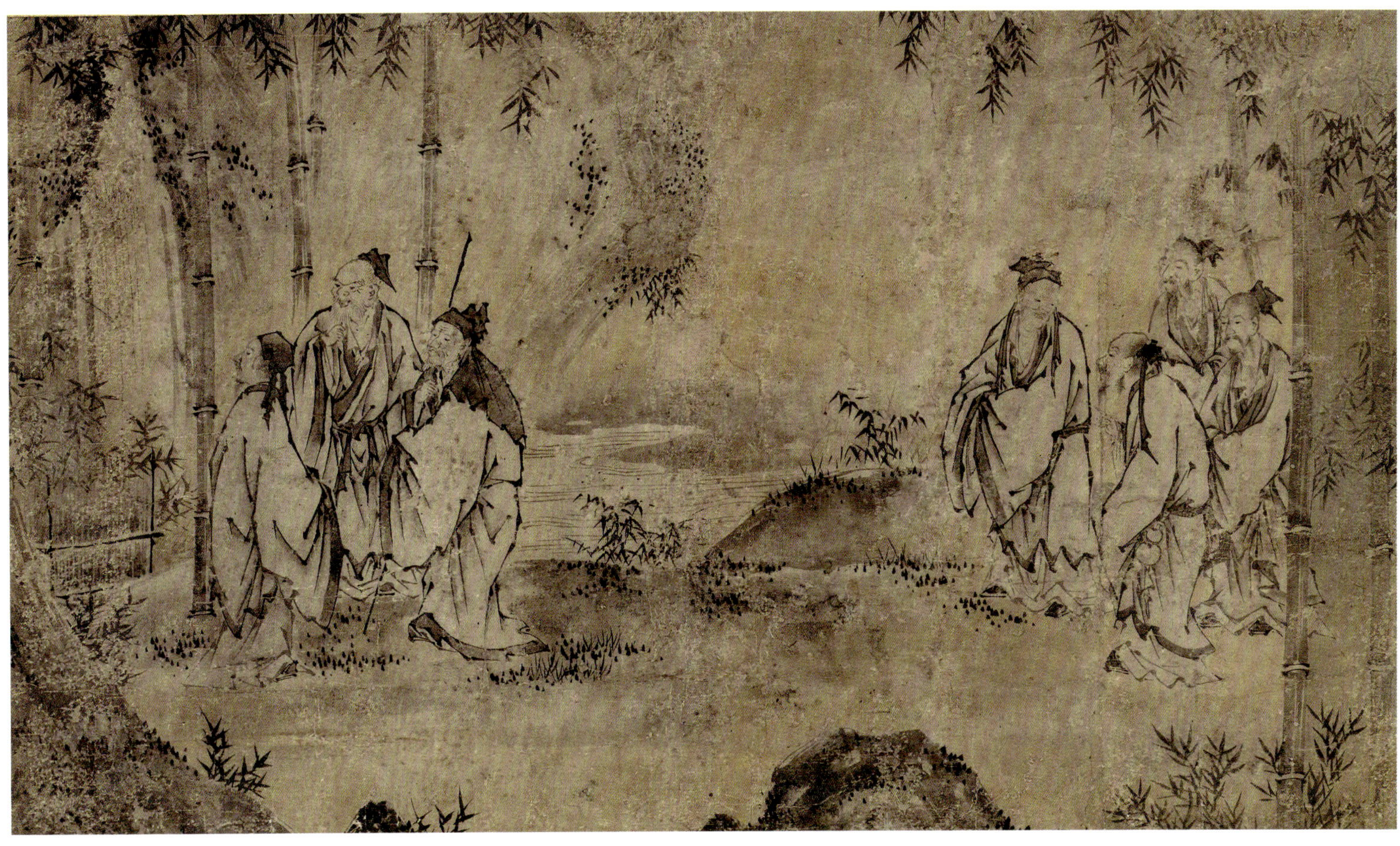

ATTRIBUTED TO SEIKŌ
(制光, also known as Rikō [利光];
fl. second half of 16th century)

102. The Seven Sages of the Bamboo Grove (竹林七賢)

Muromachi period
Hanging scroll; ink on paper
31.2 x 53.7 cm (12¼ x 21⅛ in.)

LITERATURE: Tochigi Prefectural Museum and Kanagawa Prefectural Museum of Cultural History 1998, p. 170, fig. 6; Murase 2000, no. 70; Chiu and Tezuka 2009, p. 28, fig. 14.

Sesson Shūkei
(雪村周継; ca. 1504–ca. 1589)

103. The Seven Sages of the Bamboo Grove (竹林七賢)

Muromachi period
Hanging scroll; ink and light color on paper
102.6 x 51.8 cm (40 3/8 x 20 3/8 in.)
Seals

Ex coll.: Sakata Yasorō; Fukuoka Kōtei; Count Hijikata

Literature: "Sesson hitsu Shichiken suibu zu" 1940, p. 40; Nakamura Tanio 1971, fig. 59; Murase 1975, no. 41; Shimada Shūjirō 1979, no. 91; Akazawa Eiji 1980, fig. 92; Kameda Tsutomu 1980, pl. 23; Etō Shun 1982, pl. 219; Hayashi Susumu 1980, fig. 1; Ford 1985, fig. 11; Tokyo National Museum 1985a, no. 25; Avitabile 1990, no. 45; Nakajima Junji 1994, no. 110; Brown 1997, pp. 80, 201, fig. 8; Murase 2000, no. 69; Yamashita Yūji and Asano Shūgō 2002, p. 52, no. 10; Tsuji Nobuo et al. 2005, no. 44; Chiu and Tezuka 2009, p. 32, fig. 17.

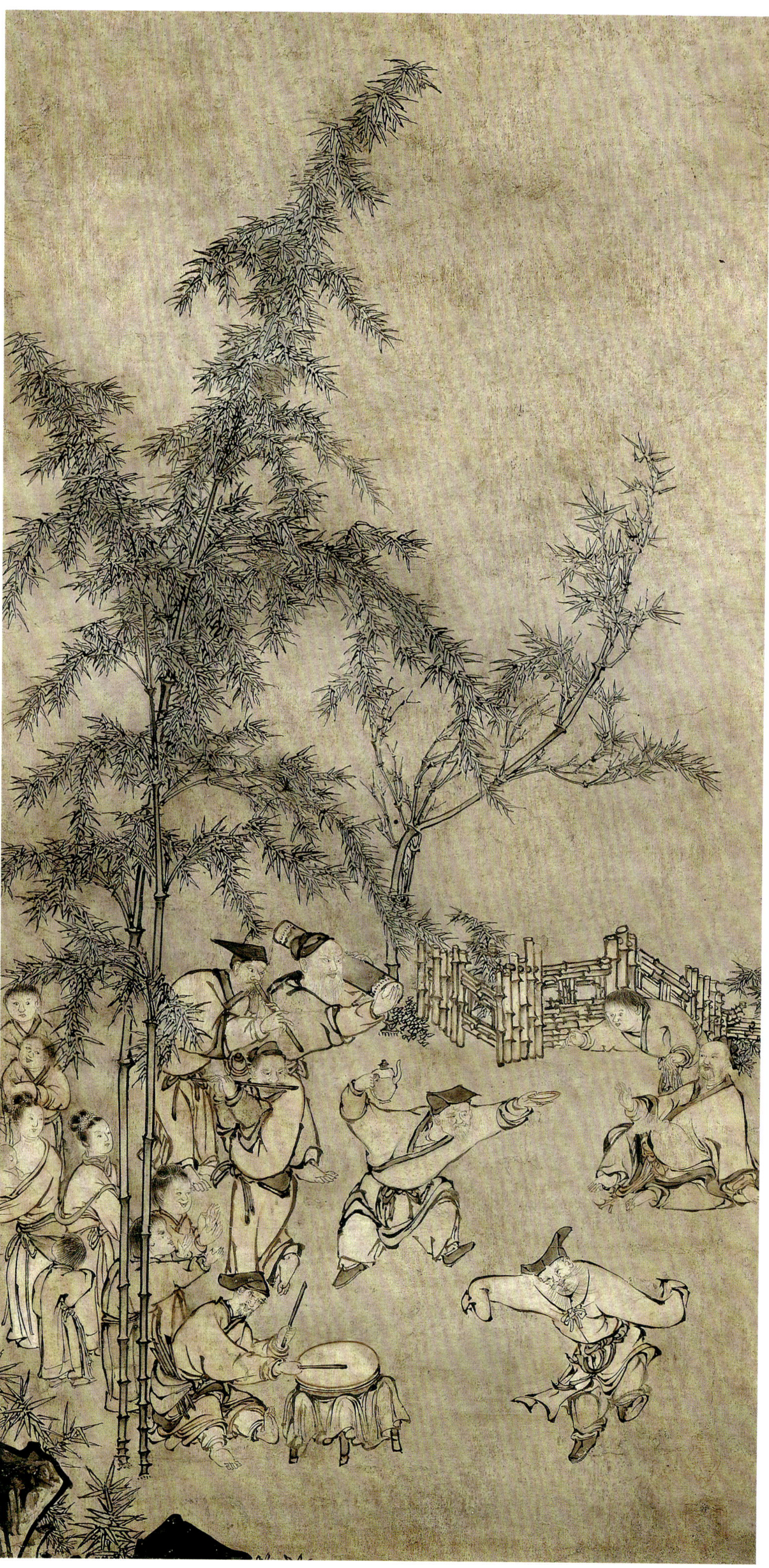

Hidemori
(also known as Shūsei [秀盛]; fl. first half of 15th century)

104. Early Spring Landscape

Muromachi period
Hanging scroll; ink and light color on paper
74.5 x 27.7 cm (29 3/8 x 10 7/8 in.)
Text, signature, seals

Literature: Matsushita Takaaki 1960, no. 29; Matsushita Takaaki 1968, ill.; Matsushita Takaaki and Tamamura Takeji 1974, pl. 64; Murase 1975, no. 33; Matsushita Takaaki 1978, fig. 78; Shimada Shūjirō 1979, no. 62; Ford 1985, fig. 8; Tokyo National Museum 1985a, no. 14; Avitabile 1990, no. 40; Kanazawa Hiroshi 1994, fig. 69; Murase 2000, no. 62.

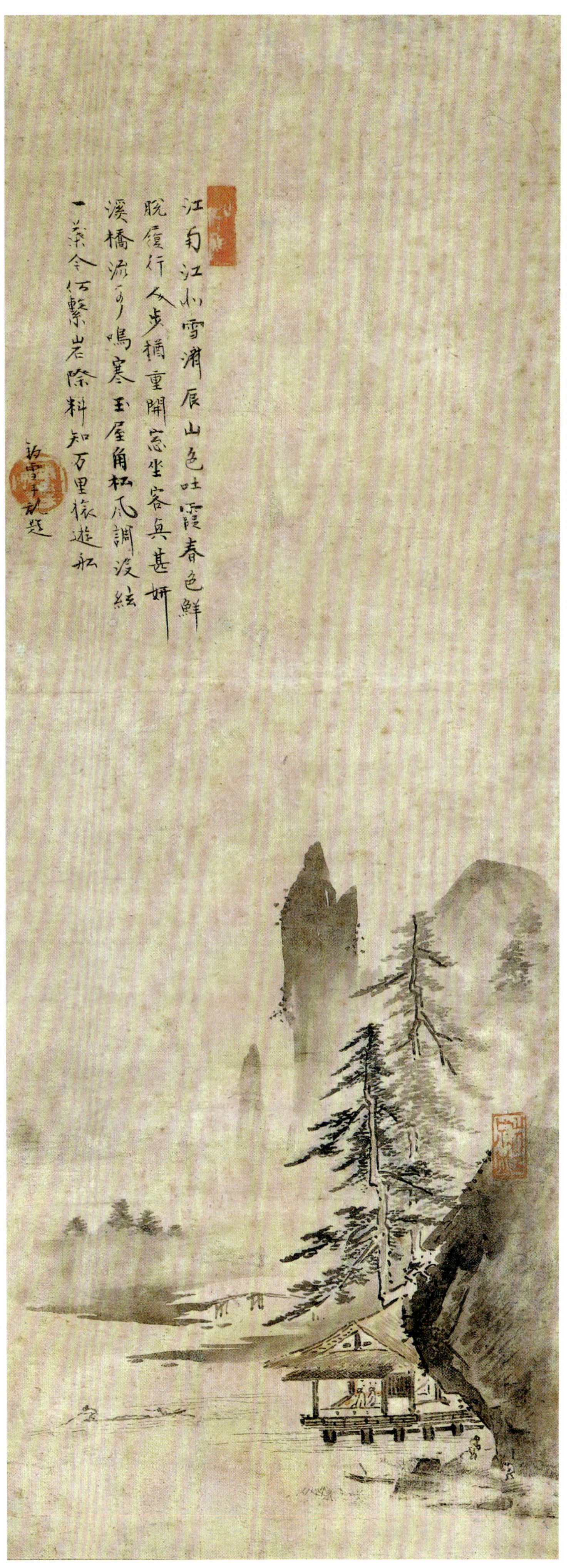

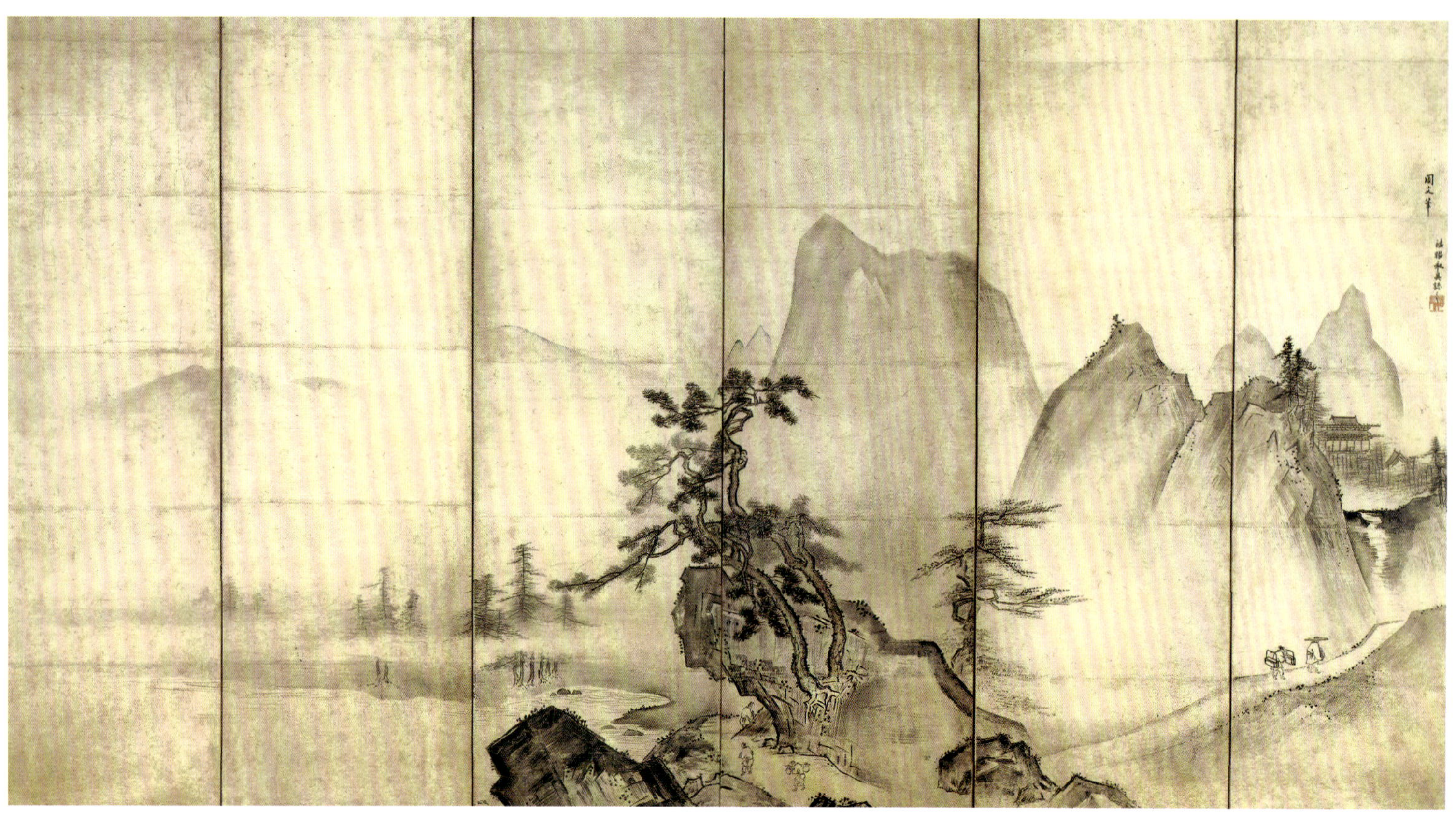

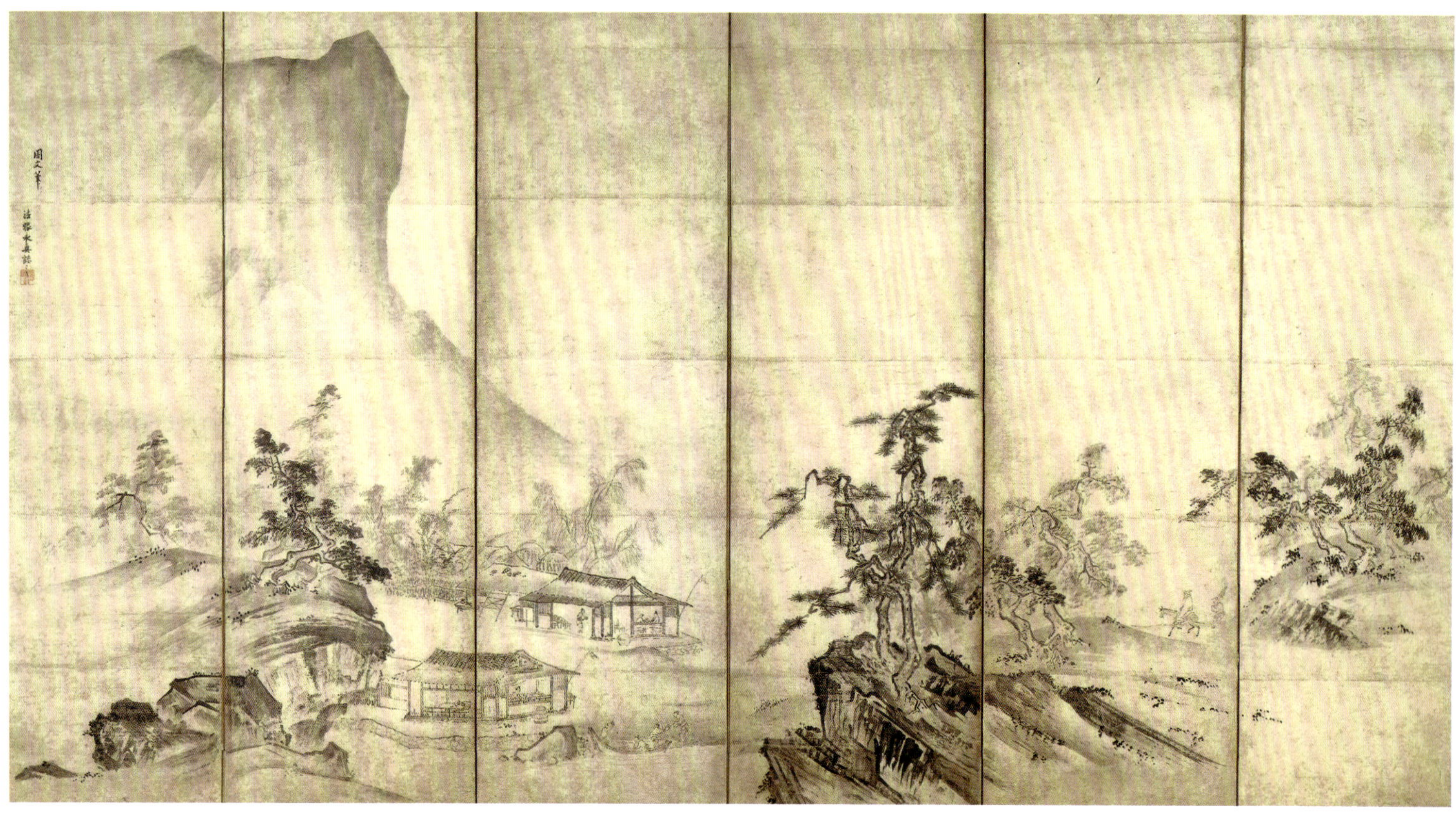

ATTRIBUTED TO
TENSHŌ SHŪBUN
(天章周文; fl. 1414–before 1463)

105. Landscape after Ka Kei (Ch. Xia Gui, 夏珪; fl. ca. 1195–1230)

Muromachi period, first half of 15th century
Pair of six-panel folding screens; ink and light color on paper
Each screen 153.9 x 274.8 cm ($60^{5}/_{8}$ in. x 9 ft. $^{1}/_{8}$ in.)
Signatures, seals

LITERATURE: Tanaka Ichimatsu and Nakamura Tanio 1973, fig. 6; Murase 1975, no. 32; Takeda Tsuneo 1979, no. 31; Ford 1985, fig. 9; Shimao Arata 1989, fig. 16 (detail); Yamashita Yūji 1993, p. 814, fig. 10; Murase 2000, no. 61; Tsuji Nobuo et al. 2005, no. 40.

SHŪTOKU
(周徳; fl. first half of 16th century)

106. Early Spring Landscape

Muromachi period
Hanging scroll; ink and light color on paper
71.1 x 40.6 cm (28 x 16 in.)
Text, signatures, seals

LITERATURE: Matsushita Takaaki 1967, fig. 88; Tanaka Ichimatsu and Nakamura Tanio 1973, pl. 80; Murase 1975, no. 39; Shimizu and Wheelwright 1976, no. 21; Kawai Masatomo 1978, fig. 31; Shimada Shūjirō 1979, no. 60; Akazawa Eiji 1980, fig. 46; Kanazawa Hiroshi 1983, fig. 54; Tokyo National Museum 1985a, no. 22; Shimada Shūjirō and Iriya Yoshitaka 1987, no. 126; Avitabile 1990, no. 43; Fukushima Tsunenori 1993a, fig. 31; Murase 2000, no. 63; Tsuji Nobuo et al. 2005, no. 41.

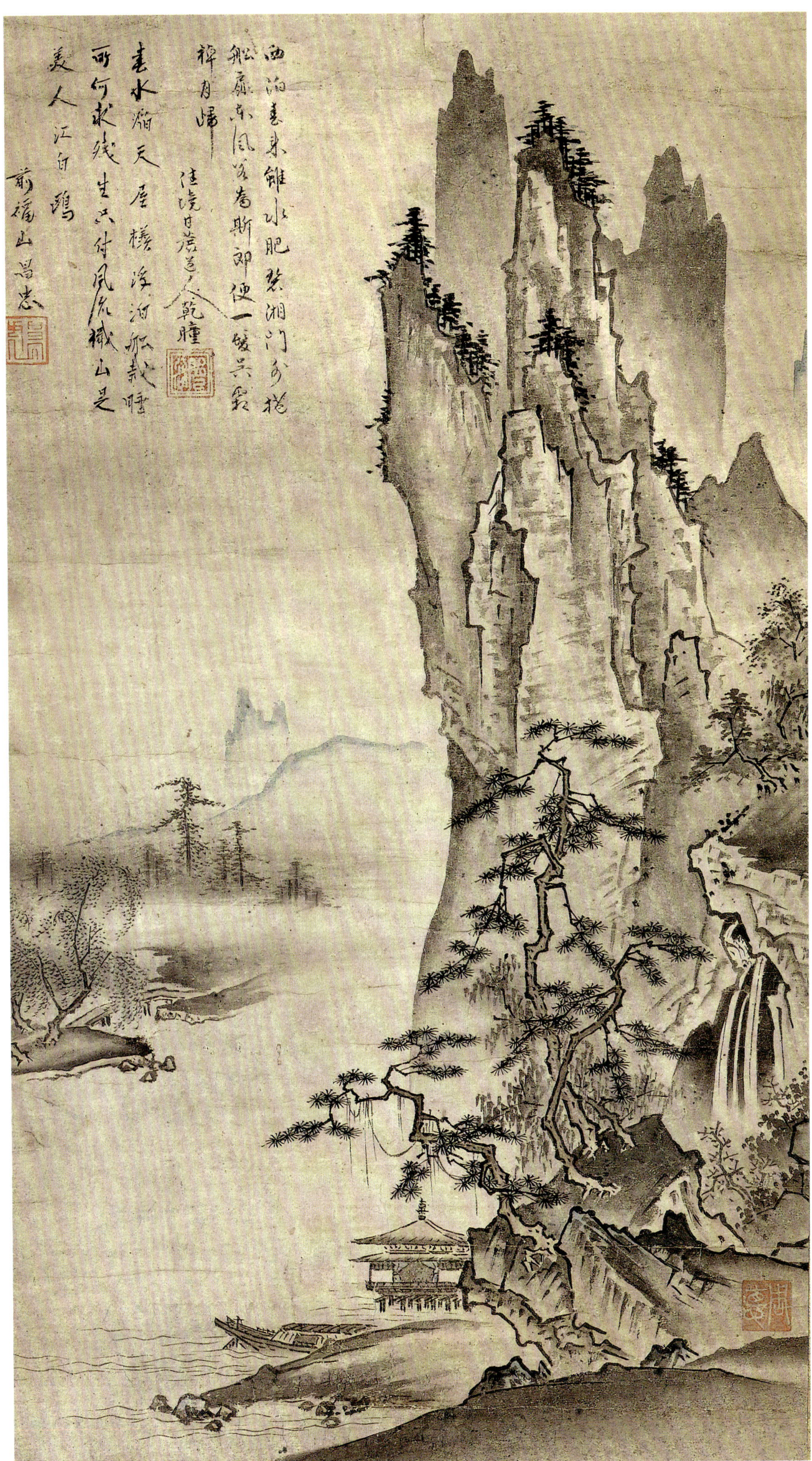

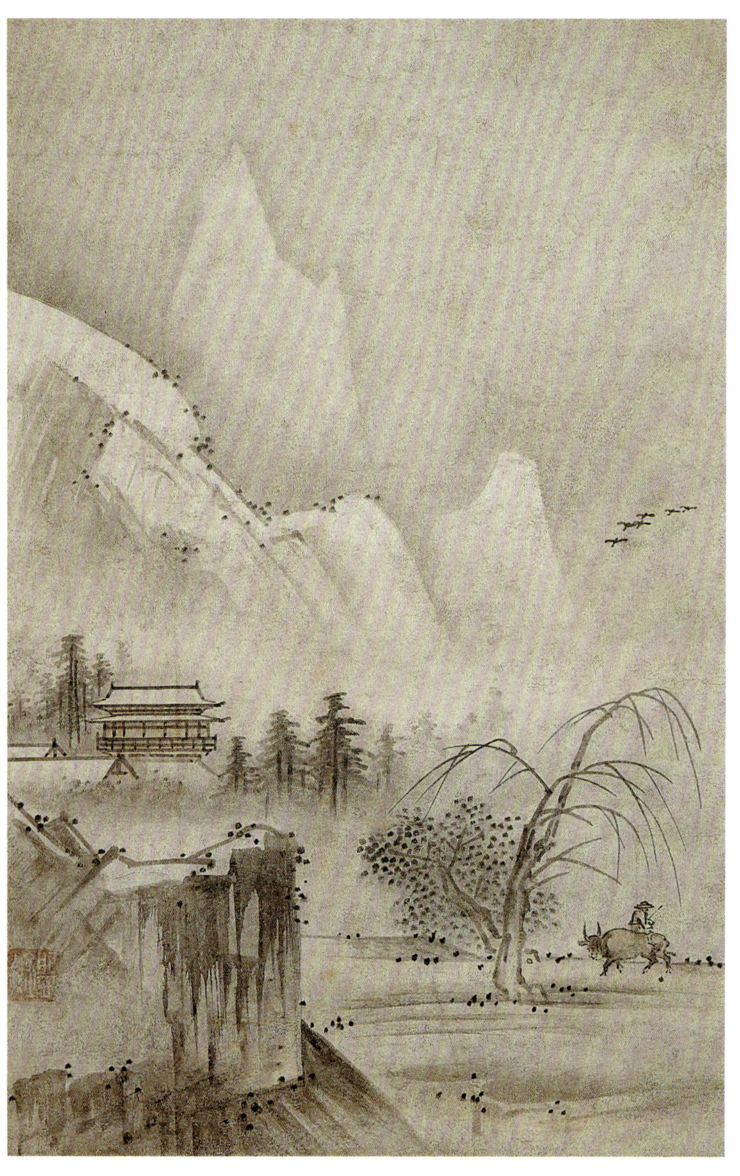
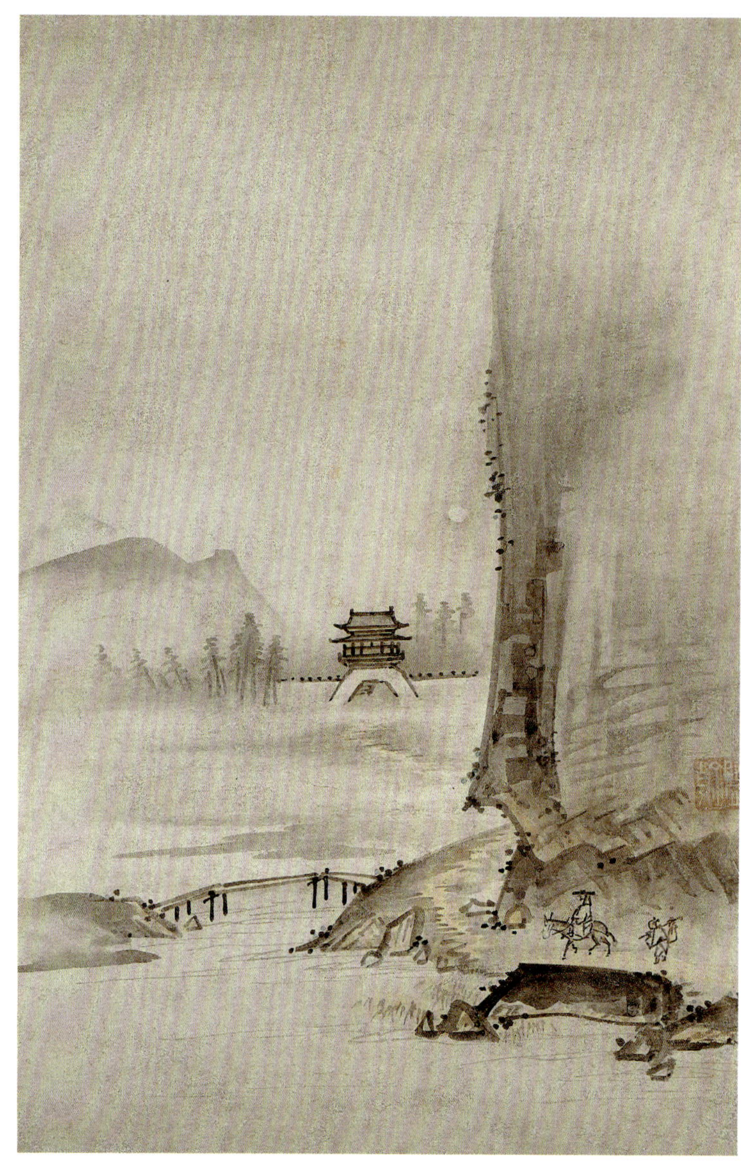

Kantei
(鑑貞; fl. second half of 15th century)

107. Two Views from *Eight Views of the Xiao and Xiang Rivers* (瀟湘八景)

Muromachi period
Pair of hanging scrolls; ink and light color on paper
Scroll I (*left*): 47.6 x 30.1 cm (18 3/4 x 11 7/8 in.)
Scroll II (*right*): 46 x 30.1 cm (18 1/8 x 11 7/8 in.)
Seals

Ex coll.: Kusaba Akira, Tokyo; Hachisuka Yoshiaki, Tokyo

Literature: "Kantei hitsu Sansui zu" 1898, pp. 167, 169; Hasumi Shigeyasu 1935; Matsushita Takaaki 1960, no. 35; Muraki Chii 1960, fig. 4; Matsushita Takaaki 1967, fig. 121; Shimada Shūjirō 1969, vol. 1, p. 121; Stanley-Baker 1974, fig. 17; Murase 1975, no. 34; Shimizu and Wheelwright 1976, no. 15; Shimada Shūjirō 1979, no. 63; Tokyo National Museum 1985a, no. 16; Avitabile 1990, no. 39; Murase 2000, no. 64; Tsuji Nobuo et al. 2005, no. 42.

Keison
(啓孫; fl. late 15th–early 16th century)

108. Landscape of the Four Seasons

Muromachi period
Pair of hanging scrolls; ink on paper
Each scroll 97.5 x 50 cm (38³/₈ x 19⁵/₈ in.)
Seals

Literature: Murase 1975, no. 38; Etō Shun 1979, pl. 71; Tokyo National Museum 1985a, no. 21; Tokyo Metropolitan Teien Art Museum 1986, p. 112; Avitabile 1990, no. 42; Tochigi Prefectural Museum and Kanagawa Prefectural Museum of Cultural History 1998, p. 175, fig. 2; Murase 2000, no. 65.

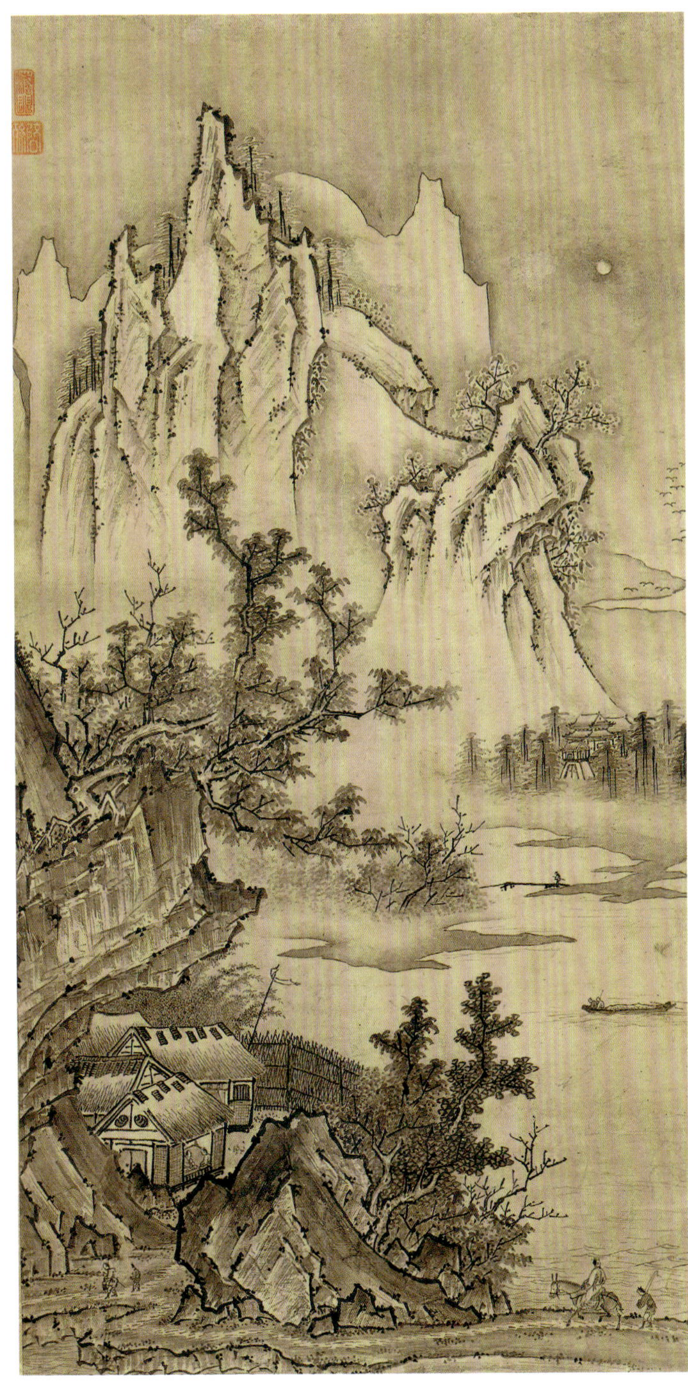

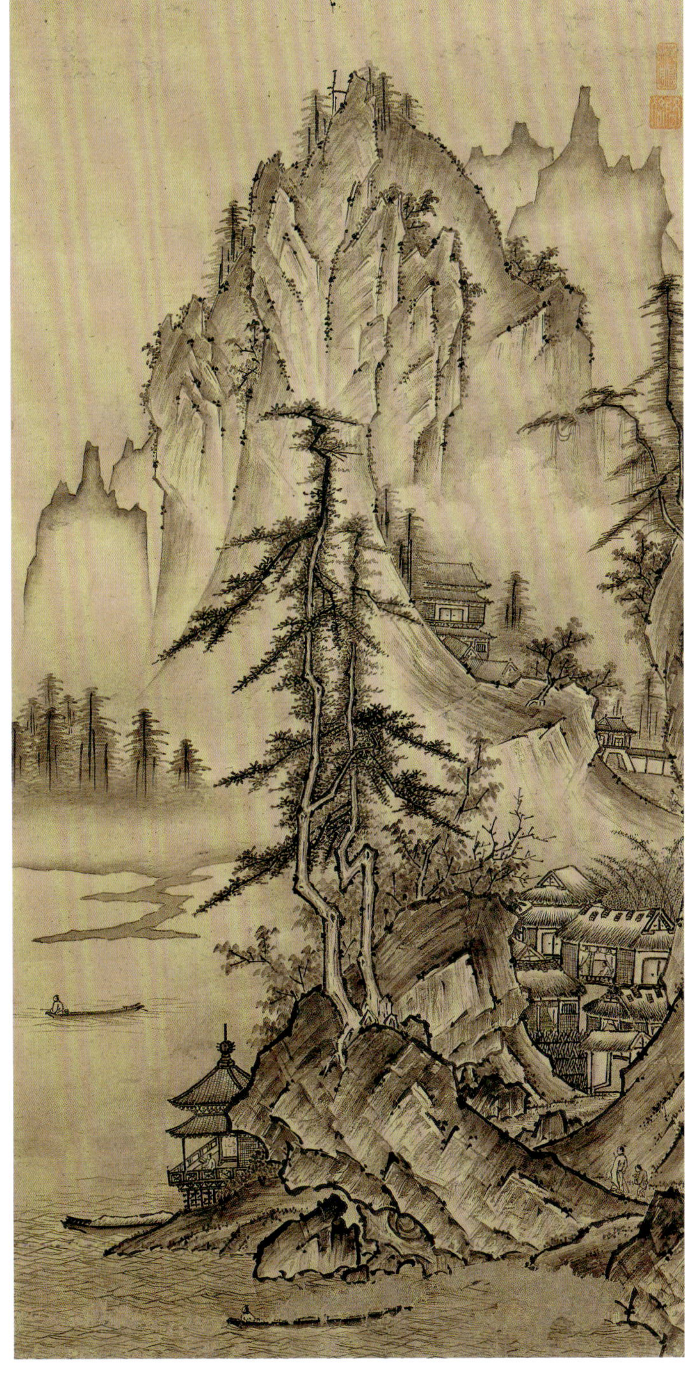

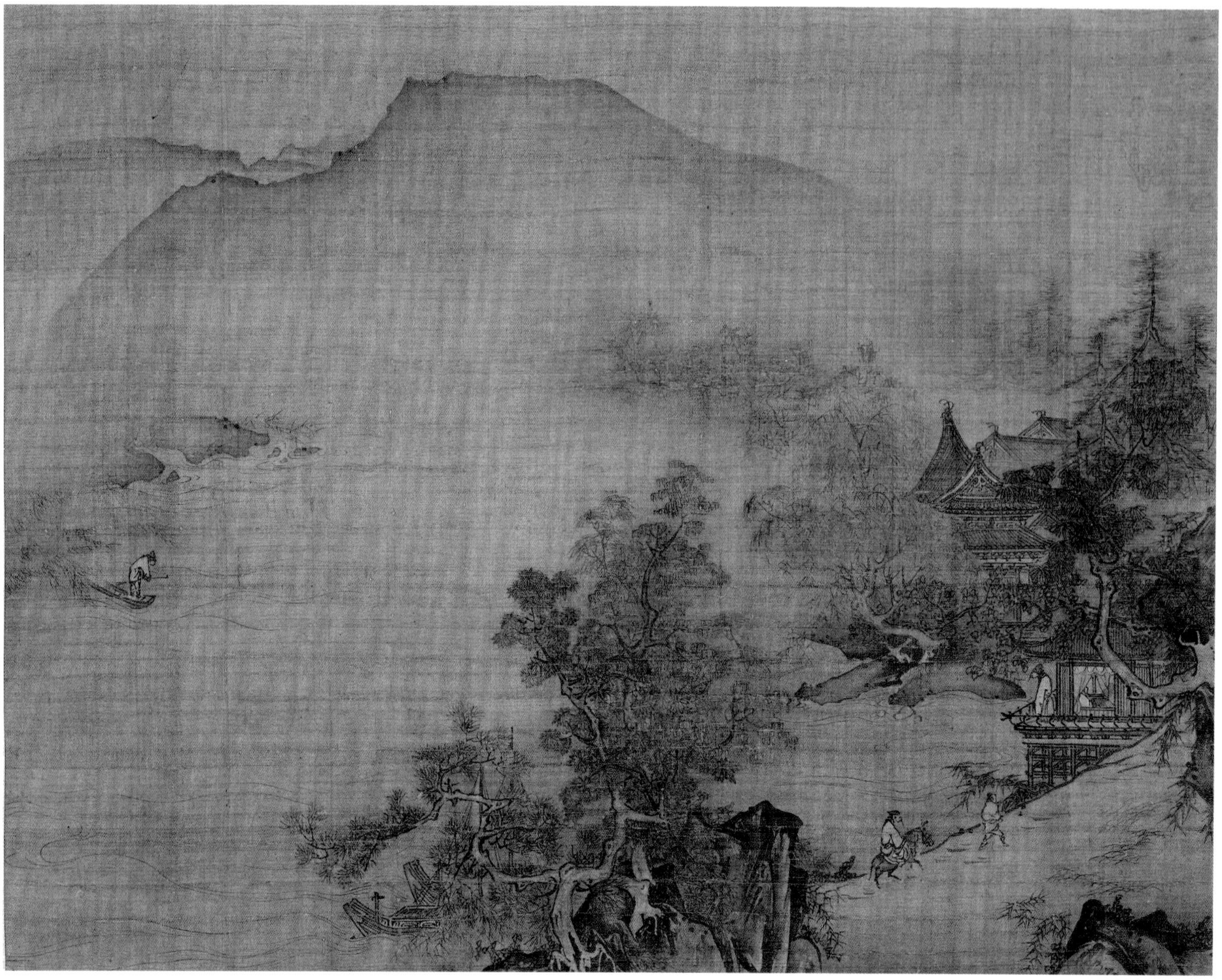

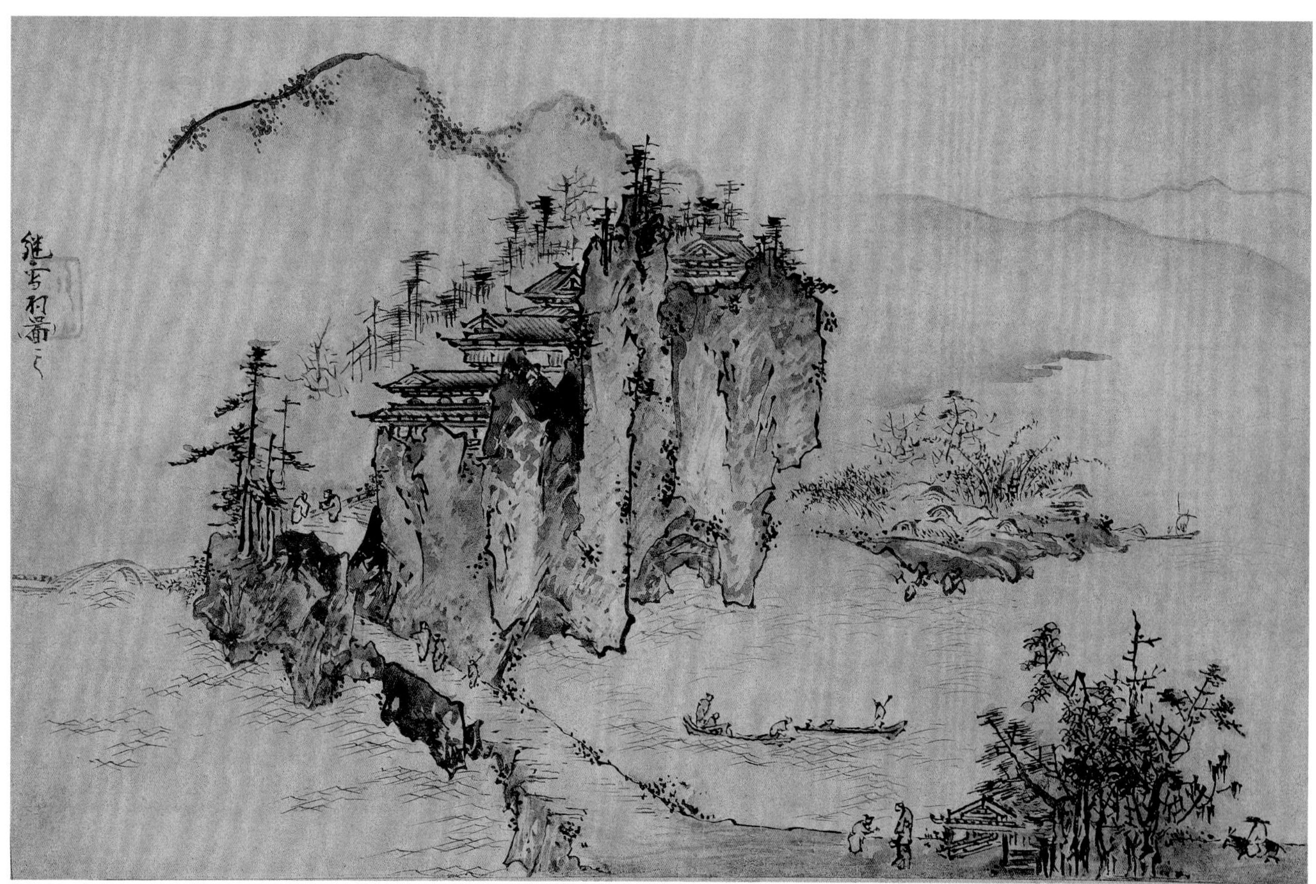

Sesson Shūkei
(雪村周継; ca. 1504–ca. 1589)

109. Landscape with Pavilion

Muromachi period
Hanging scroll; ink and light color on silk
39.8 x 51.3 cm (15 5/8 x 20 1/4 in.)
Seals

Literature: Matsushita Takaaki 1960, no. 70; Nakamura Tanio 1971, fig. 24; Murase 1975, no. 40; Shimada Shūjirō 1979, no. 88; Akazawa Eiji 1980, fig. 68; Etō Shun 1982, pl. 6; Tokyo National Museum 1985a, no. 23; Avitabile 1990, no. 44; Nakajima Junji 1994, fig. 69; Murase 2000, no. 67; Yamashita Yūji and Asano Shūgō 2002, no. 58, p. 113; Tsuji Nobuo et al. 2005, no. 43.

Sesson Shūkei
(雪村周継; ca. 1504–ca. 1589)

110. Landscape with Rocky Precipice

Muromachi period
Hanging scroll; ink and color on paper
30.3 x 46.8 cm (11 7/8 x 18 3/8 in.)
Signature, seal

Ex coll.: Kumita Shōhei, Tokyo

Literature: Etō Shun 1969a, pp. 69–70; Nakamura Tanio 1971, fig. 1; Tanaka Ichimatsu and Nakamura Tanio 1973, pl. 102; Murase 1975, no. 42; Kameda Tsutomu 1980, pl. 10; Etō Shun 1982, pl. 13; Tokyo National Museum 1985a, no. 24; Avitabile 1990, no. 46; Nakajima Junji 1994, fig. 111; Murase 2000, no. 68; Yamashita Yūji and Asano Shūgō 2002, no. 59, p. 114; Tsuji Nobuo et al. 2005, no. 45.

Bokushō Shūshō
(牧松周省; fl. late 15th–early 16th century)

111. Splashed-Ink Landscape

Muromachi period
Hanging scroll; ink on paper
80 x 33.9 cm (31 1/2 x 13 3/8 in.)
Seal

Ex coll.: Umezawa Kinenkan Museum, Tokyo; Moriya Kōzō, Kyoto

Literature: "Bokushō hitsu Sansui zu" 1942, pl. 7; Matsushita Takaaki 1960, no. 43; Murase 1975, no. 35; Shimizu and Wheelwright 1976, no. 19; Shimada Shūjirō 1979, no. 56; Akazawa Eiji 1980, fig. 45; Tokyo National Museum 1985a, no. 20; Avitabile 1990, no. 41; Murase 2000, no. 66.

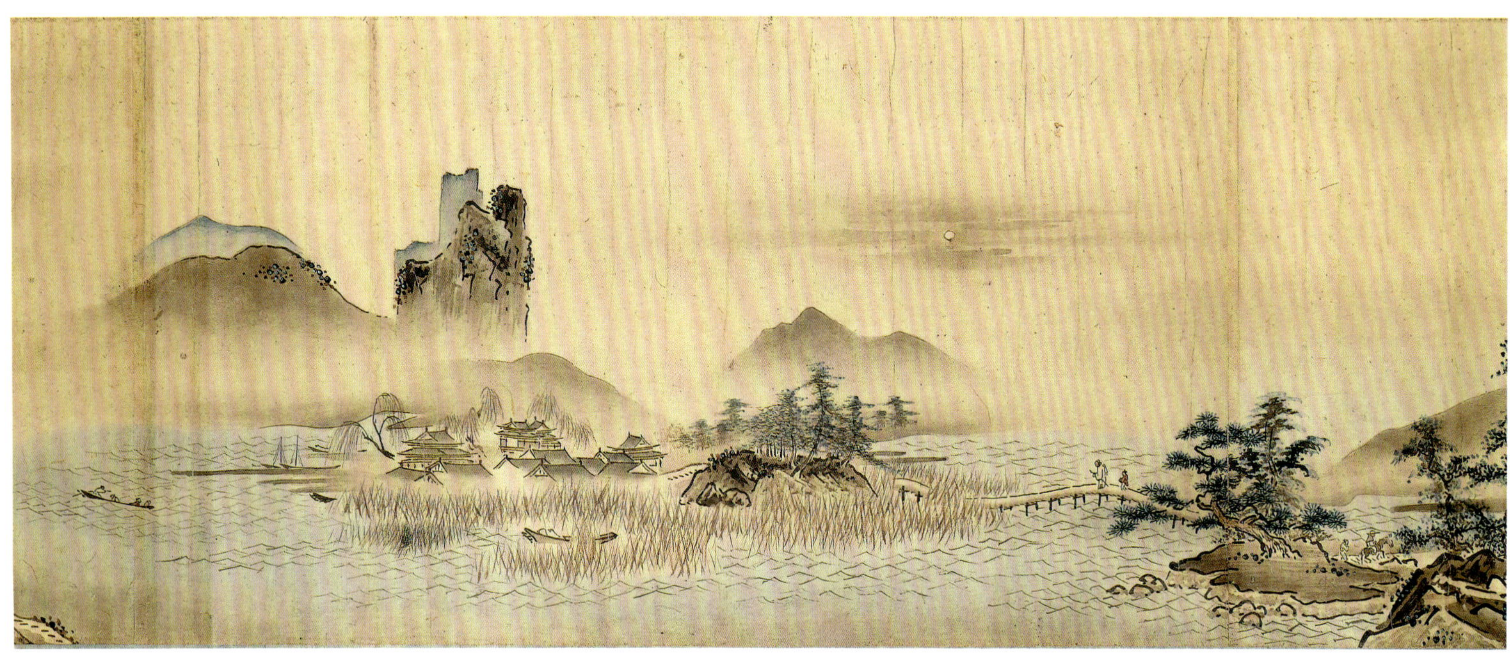

112. Landscape

Muromachi period, 16th century
Handscroll; ink and light color on paper
28.5 x 289.6 cm (11¼ in. x 9 ft. 6 in.)

Attributed to Taikyo Genju
(太虚元寿; fl. second half of 14th century)

113. Wagtail on a Rock

Nanbokuchō period
Hanging scroll; ink on silk
83.1 x 35 cm (32¾ x 13¾ in.)
Text, signature, seals

Literature: Matsushita Takaaki 1960, no. 14; Shibue Jirō 1962, fig. 2; Matsushita Takaaki 1967, fig. 136; Kanagawa Prefectural Museum of Cultural History 1972, fig. 16; Murase 1975, no. 26; Shimada Shūjirō 1979, no. 12; Tokyo National Museum 1980, fig. 100; Ford 1985, fig. 3; Tokyo National Museum 1985a, no. 11; Shimada Shūjirō and Iriya Yoshitaka 1987, no. 148; Avitabile 1990, no. 30; Murase 1992, p. 155, fig. 2; Brinker and Kanazawa 1996, fig. 29; Murase 2000, no. 43; Ohki 2007, p. 76, fig. 8.

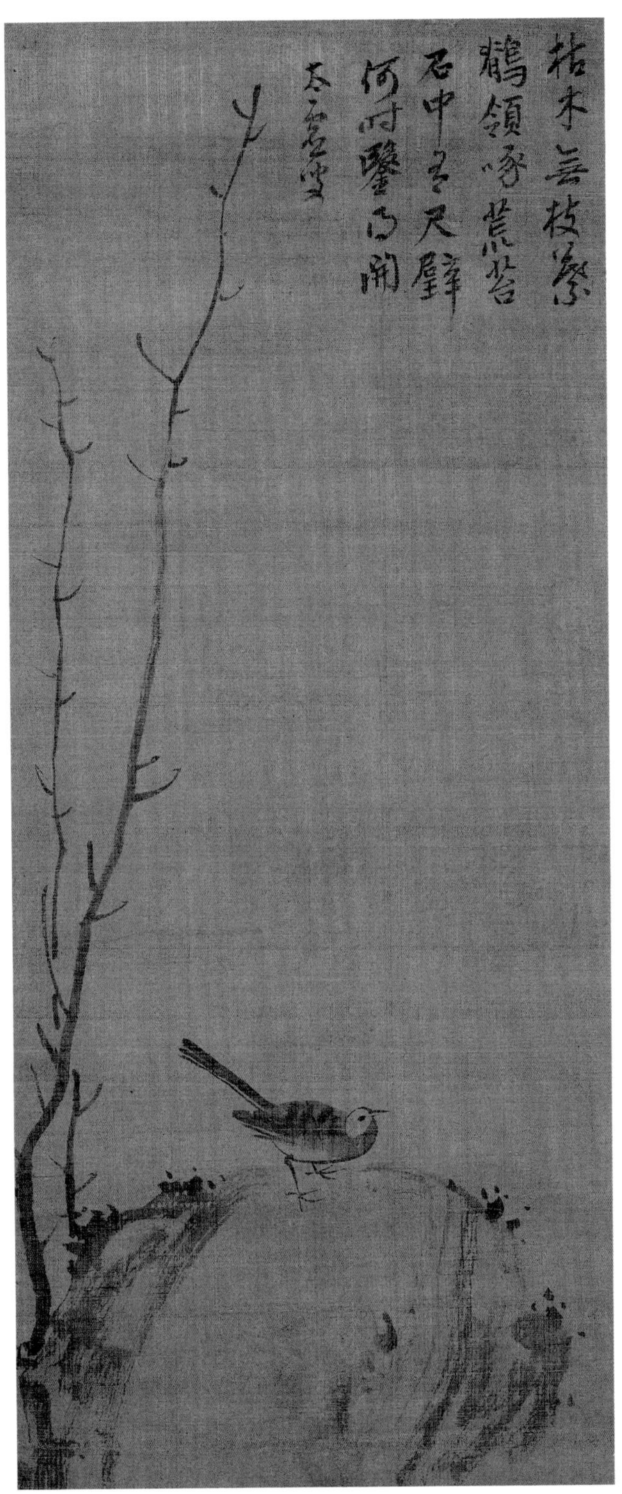

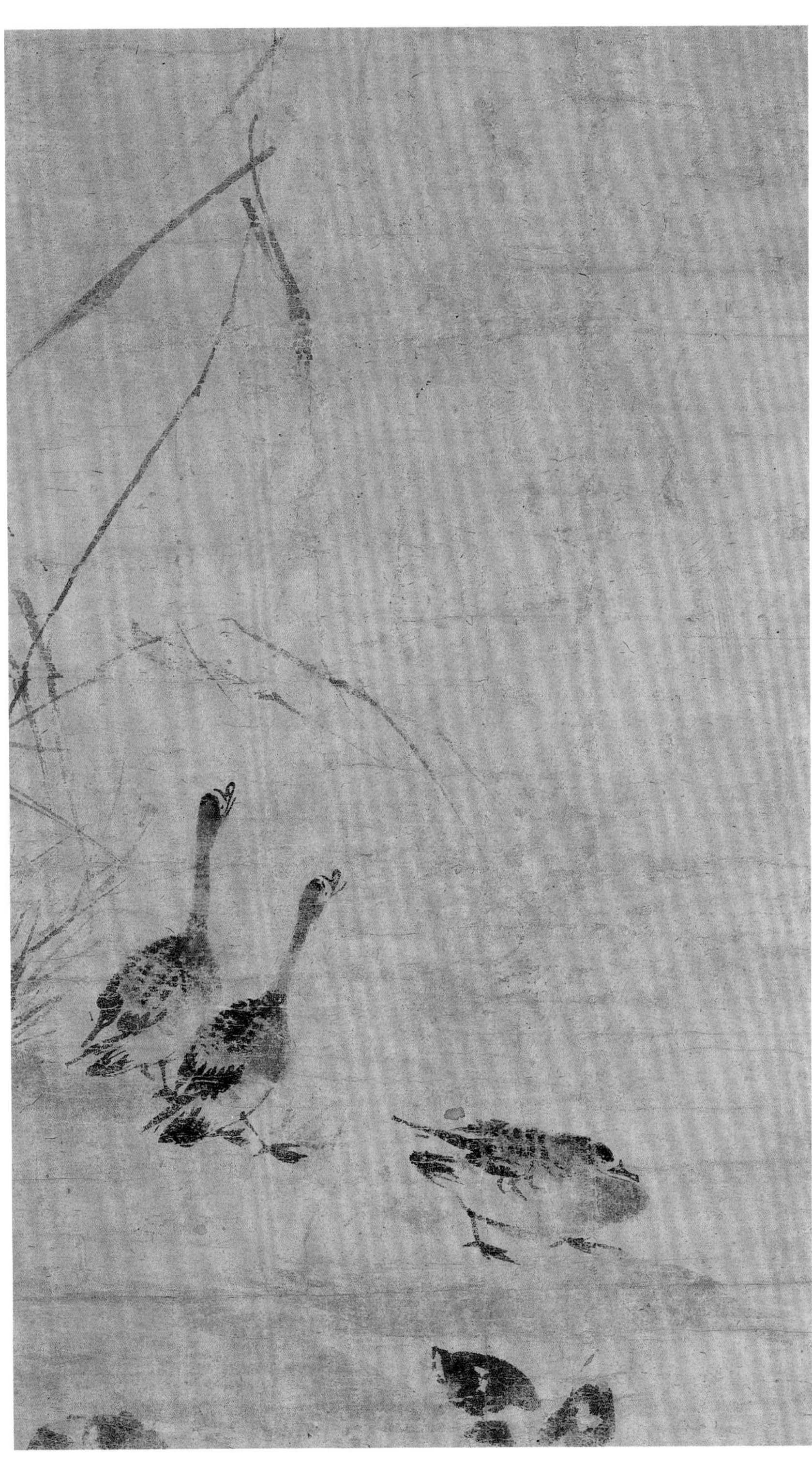

114. Geese and Reeds

Muromachi period, late 14th century
Hanging scroll; ink on paper
49.9 x 29 cm (19 5/8 x 11 3/8 in.)

LITERATURE: Etō Shun 1969b, pp. 83–84; Murase 1975, no. 25; Shimizu and Wheelwright 1976, no. 29; Brinker and Kanazawa 1996, fig. 124; Murase 2000, no. 50; Tsuji Nobuo et al. 2005, no. 35.

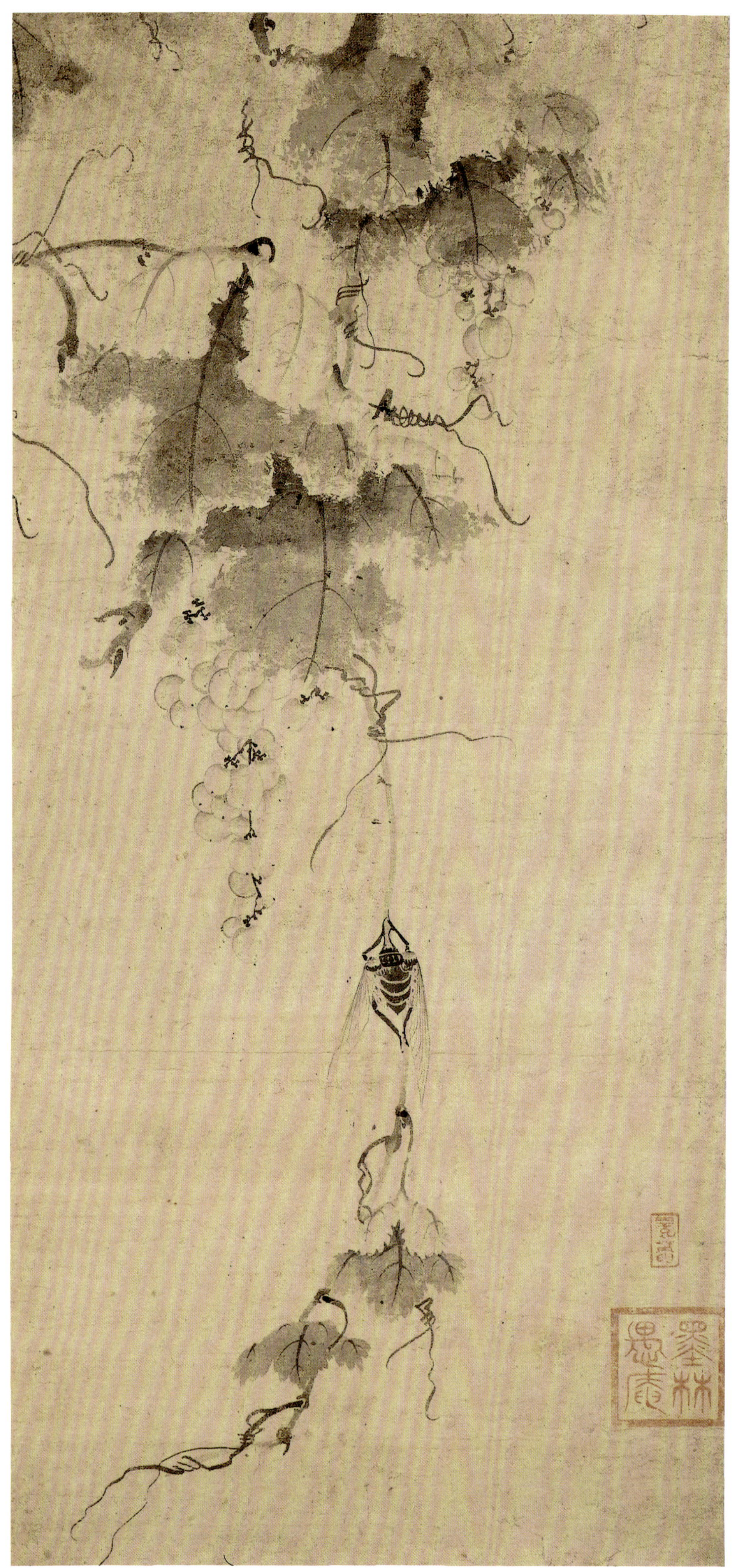

BOKURIN GUAN
(墨林愚庵; fl. 15th century)

115. Cicada on a Grapevine

Muromachi period
Hanging scroll; ink on paper
64.4 x 30.8 cm (25 3/8 x 12 1/8 in.)
Seals

EX COLL.: Watanabe Kazan

LITERATURE: Matsushita Takaaki 1960, no. 101; Murase 1975, addendum no. 107; Shimada Shūjirō 1979, no. 14; Ford 1985, fig. 5; Tokyo National Museum 1985a, no. 17; Avitabile 1990, no. 33; Brinker and Kanazawa 1996, fig. 128; Murase 2000, no. 57; Tsuji Nobuo et al. 2005, no. 39.

KENKŌ SHŌKEI
(賢江祥啓; fl. ca. 1470–ca. 1518)

116. Pair of Wagtails

Muromachi period
Pair of hanging scrolls; ink on paper
Each scroll 38.5 x 58 cm (15 1/8 x 22 7/8 in.)
Seals

LITERATURE: Kanagawa Prefectural Museum of Cultural History 1972, fig. 62; Murase 1975, no. 37; Etō Shun 1979, no. 67; Nakamura Tanio 1985, p. 131; Tochigi Prefectural Museum and Kanagawa Prefectural Museum of Cultural History 1998, p. 181, fig. 20; Murase 2000, no. 52.

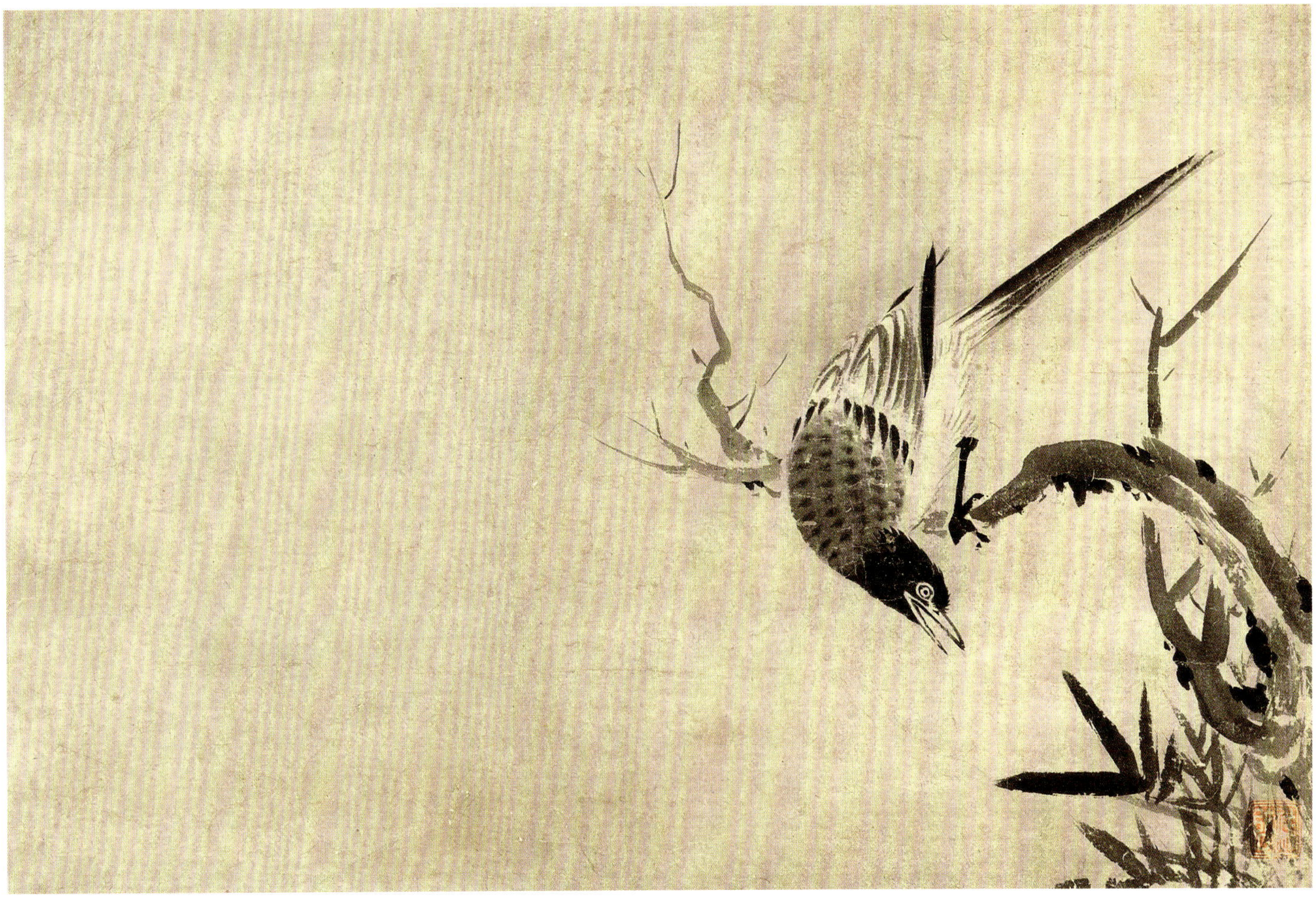

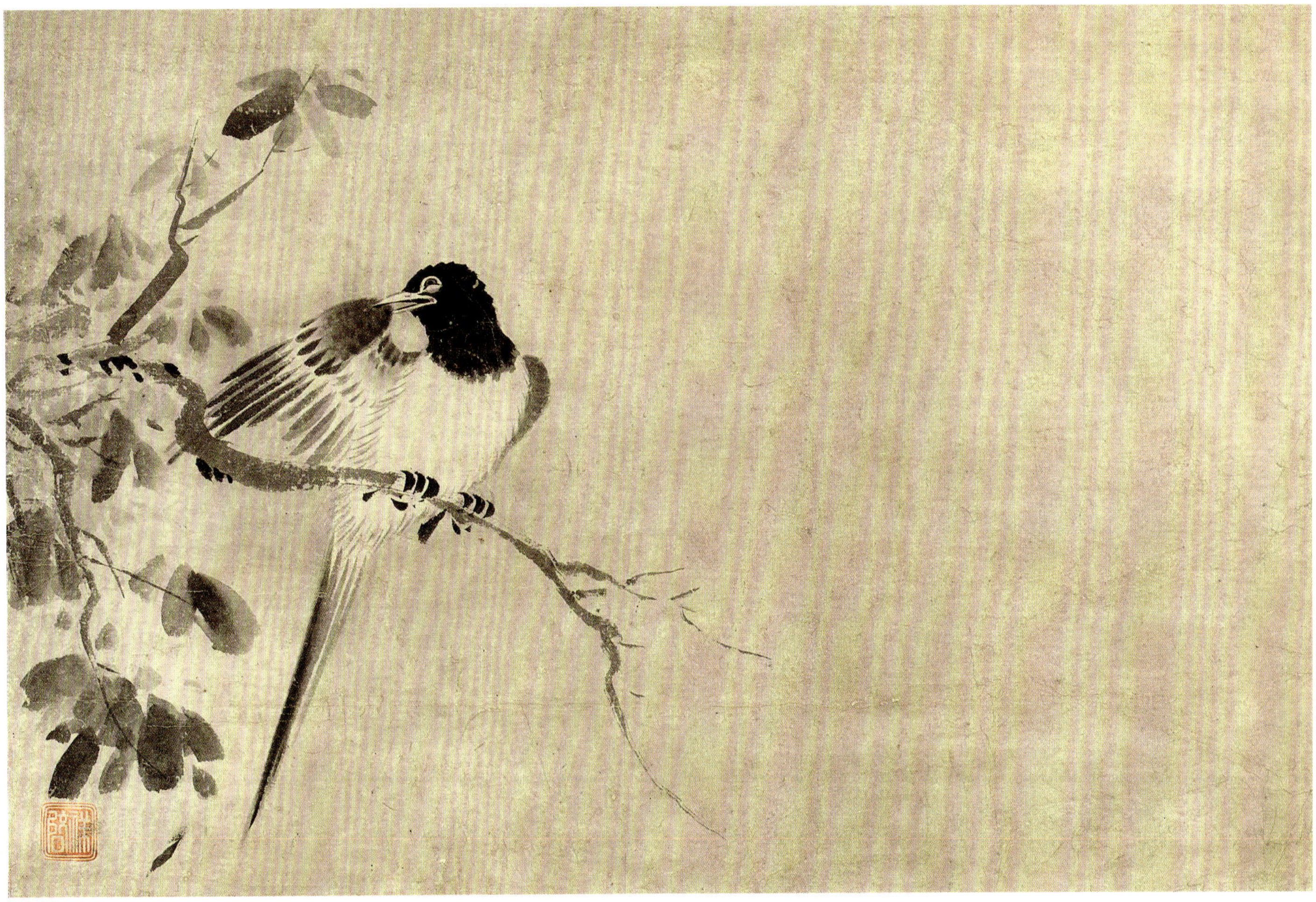

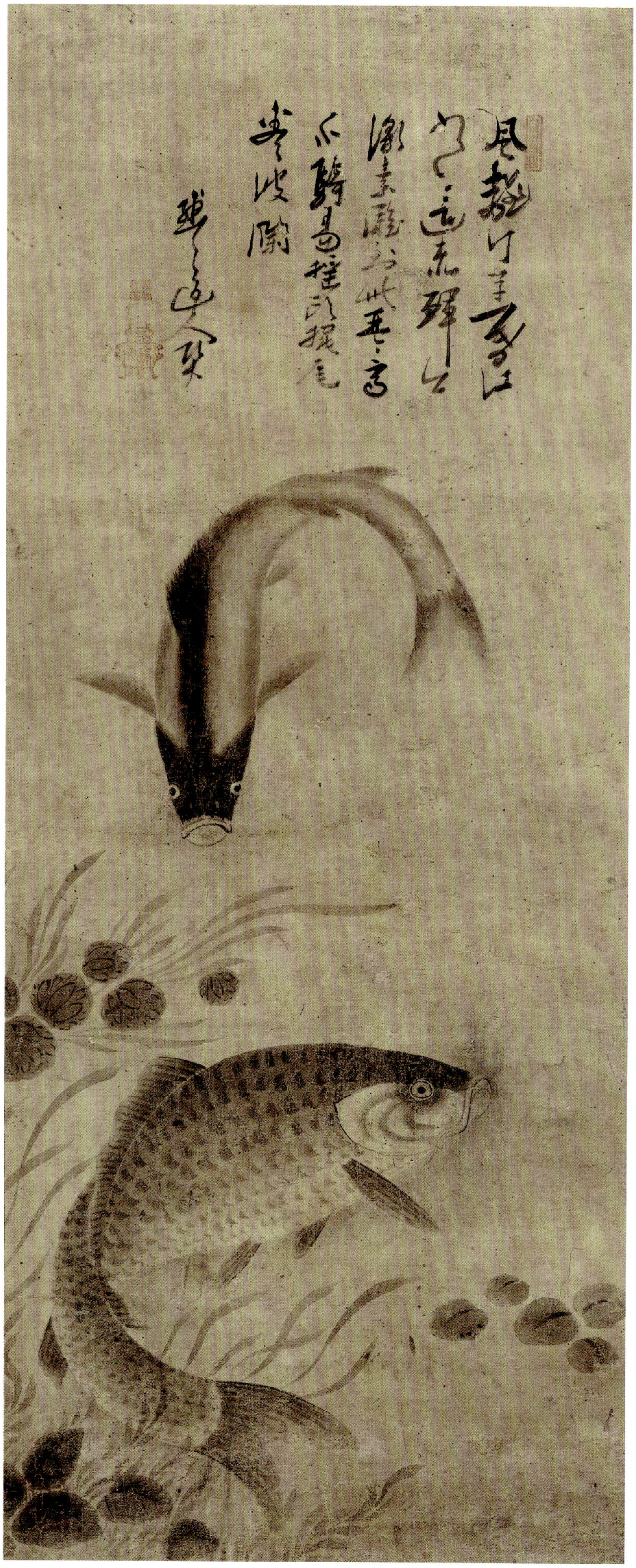

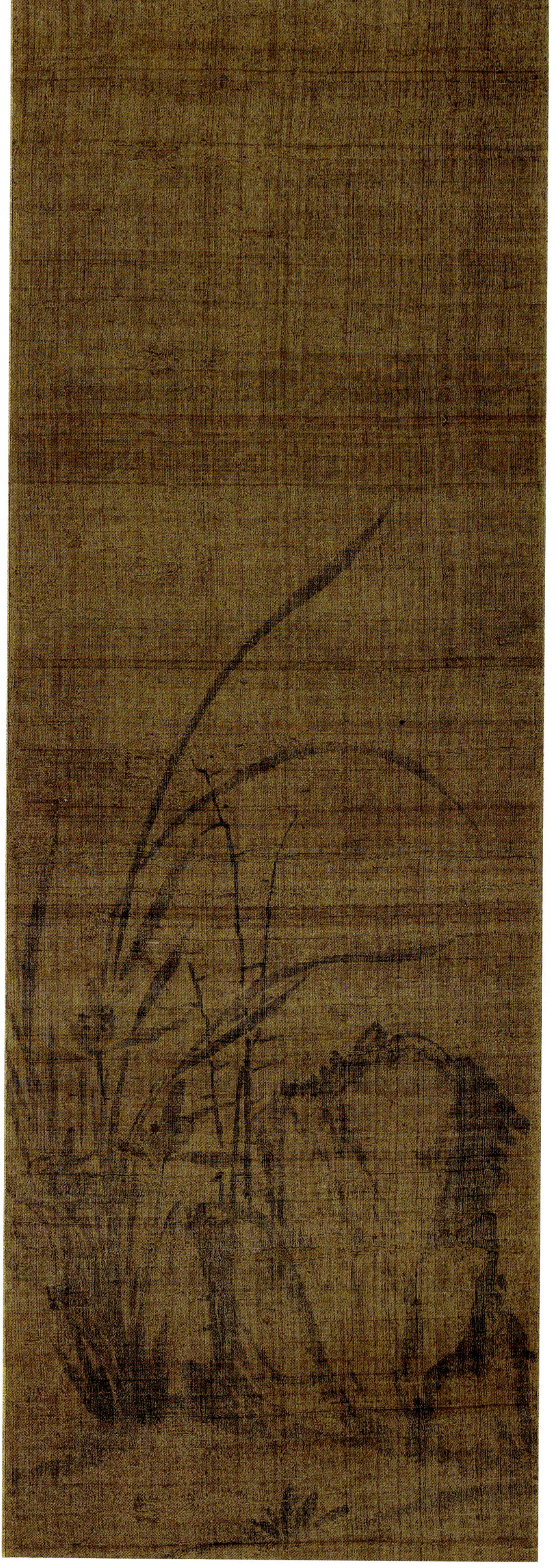

Yōgetsu
(楊月; fl. late 15th century)

120. Two Fish in a Pond

Muromachi period, late 15th century
Hanging scroll; ink on paper
84.9 x 35.4 cm (33 3/8 x 13 7/8 in.)
Text, seals

Literature: Tokyo National Museum 1985a, no. 18; Avitabile 1990, no. 34.

attributed to Tesshū Tokusai
(鉄舟徳濟; d. 1366)

121. Orchids, Bamboo, Brambles, and Rocks

Nanbokuchō period
Hanging scroll; ink on silk
71.3 x 24.9 cm (28 1/8 x 9 3/4 in.)

Tesshū Tokusai
(鉄舟徳済; d. 1366)

122. Orchids, Bamboo, Brambles, and Rocks

Nanbokuchō period
Hanging scroll; ink on paper
72.2 x 37 cm (28 3/8 x 14 5/8 in.)
Text, signature, seal

Ex coll.: Fukuoka Kōtei

Literature: Nakamura Tanio 1973, pp. 65–66; Tanaka Ichimatsu 1974, pl. 16; Murase 1975, no. 27; Shimada Shūjirō 1979, p. 113; Ford 1985, fig. 4; Tokyo National Museum 1985a, no. 12; Avitabile 1990, no. 31; Murase 2000, no. 44; Tsuji Nobuo et al. 2005, no. 34.

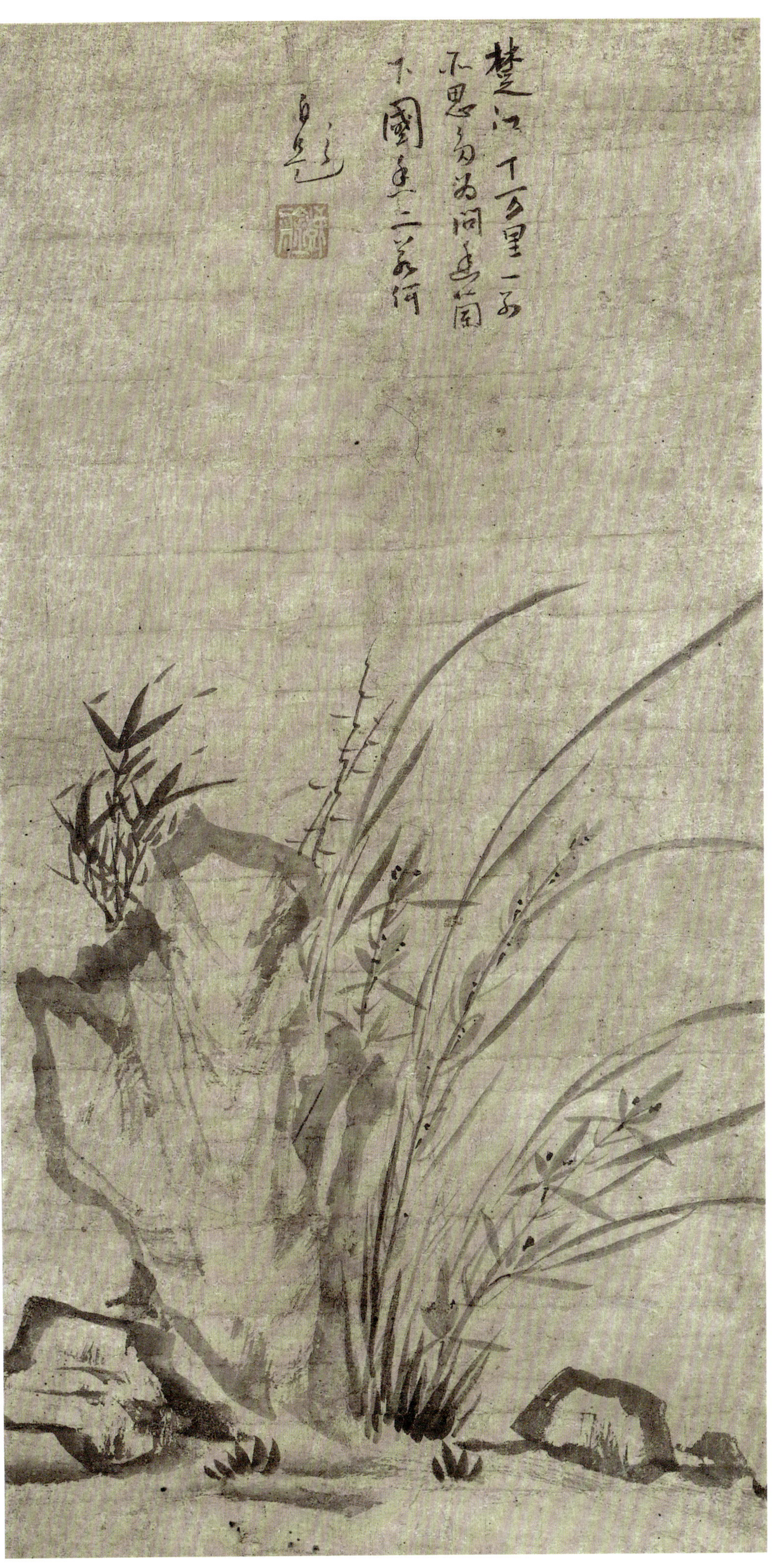

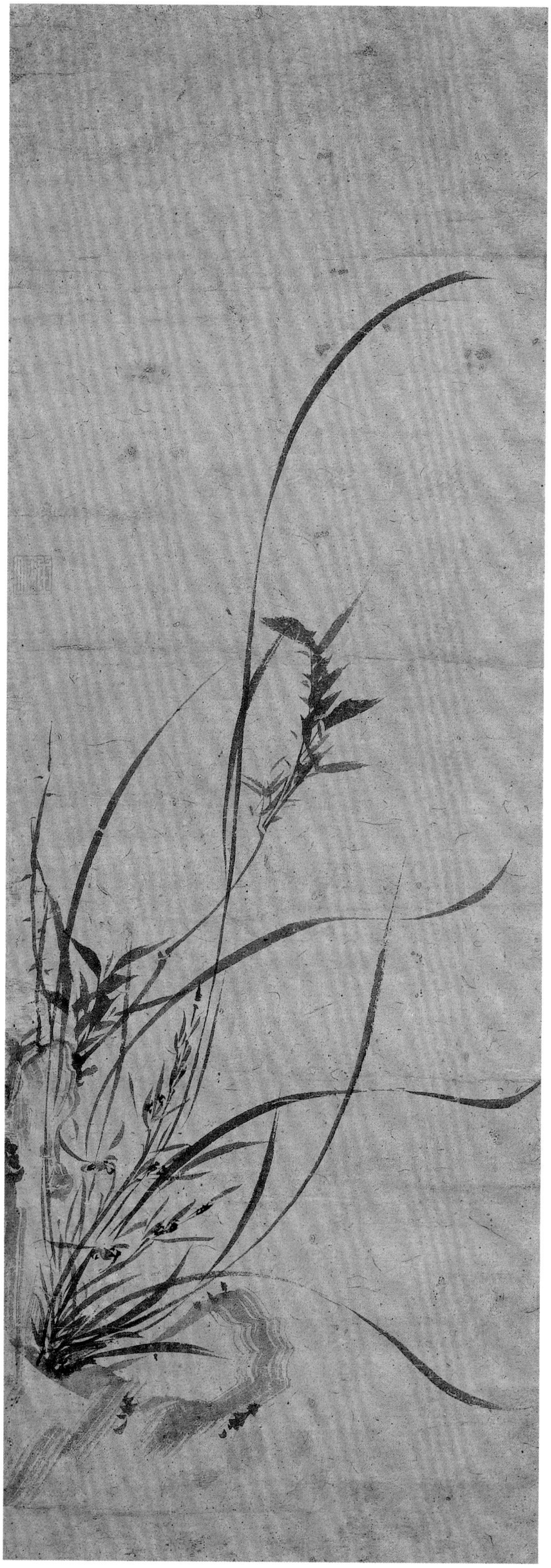

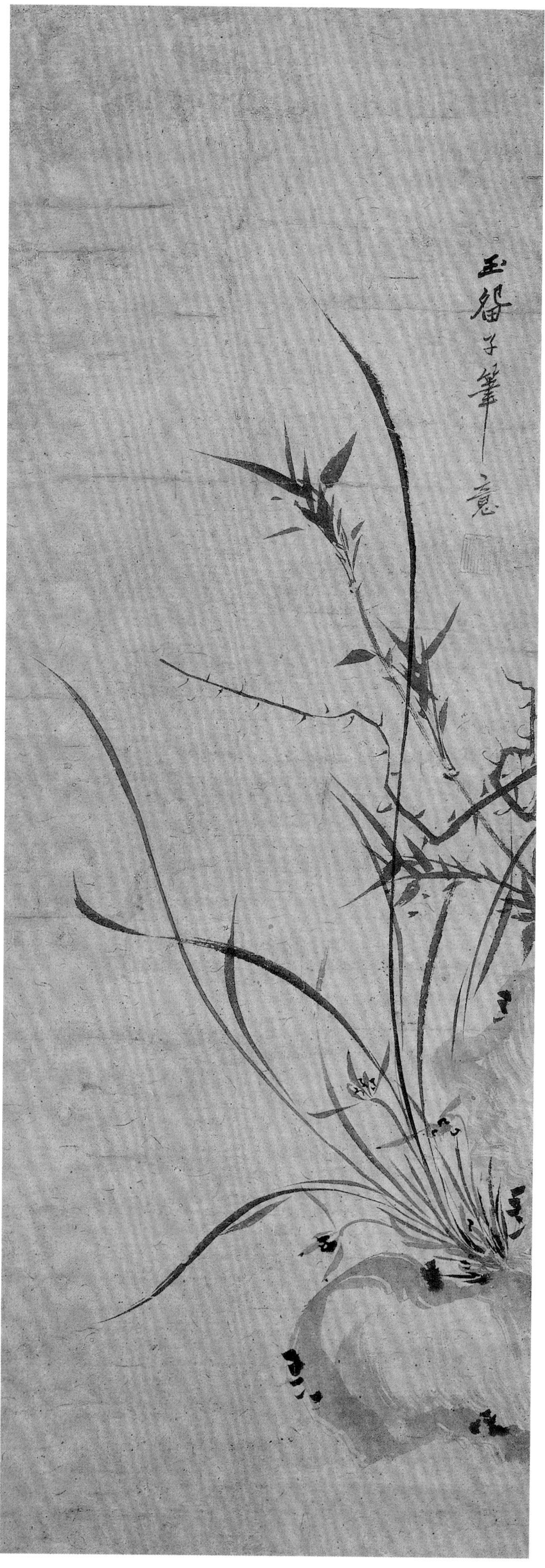

Gyokuen Bonpō
(玉畹梵芳; ca. 1348–ca. 1420)

123. Orchids, Bamboo, and Brambles

Muromachi period, after 1413
Pair of hanging scrolls; ink on paper
Each scroll 89.4 x 31.9 cm (35¼ x 12½ in.)
Signature, seals

Literature: Nakamura Tanio 1966, pp. 105–8; Shimada Shūjirō 1969, vol. 1, p. 102; Asia Society 1970, pp. 128–29; Murase 1975, no. 28; Kinoshita Masao 1979, figs. 163, 164; Ford 1985, fig. 6; Avitabile 1990, no. 32; Murase 2000, no. 51; Tsuji Nobuo et al. 2005, no. 37.

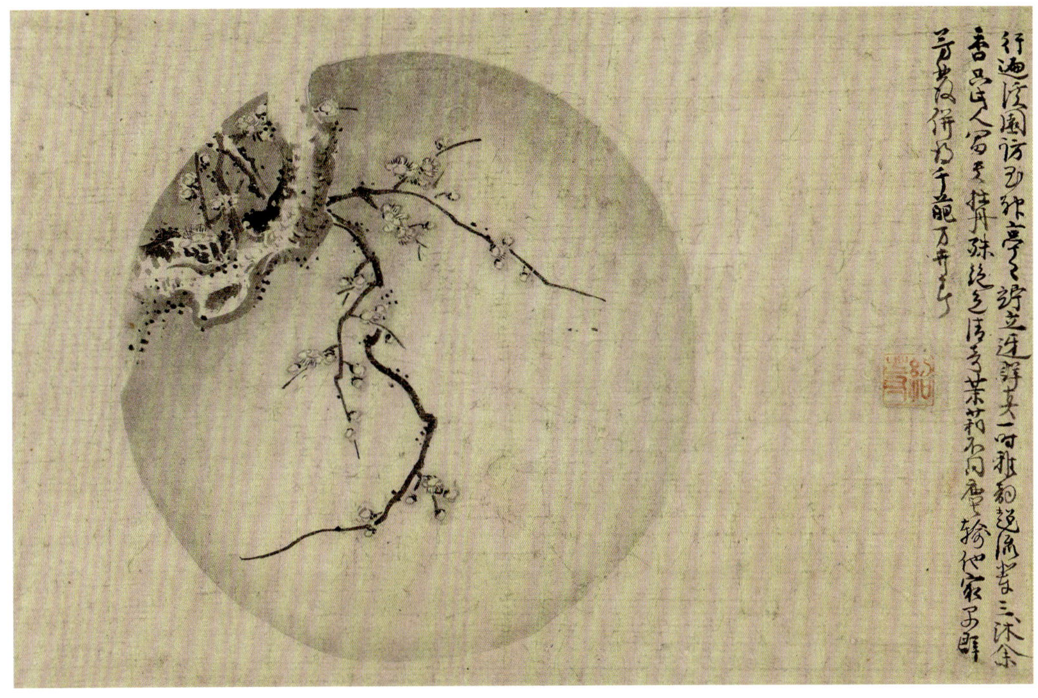

Motsurin (or Botsurin) Shōtō (or Jōtō)
(没倫紹等, also known as Bokusai [墨斎]; d. 1491)

124. Plum Blossoms

Muromachi period
Hanging scroll; ink on paper
27.3 x 42.4 cm (10¾ x 16¾ in.)
Text, seal

Literature: Murase 1975, no. 36; Miyajima Shin'ichi 1994, fig. 60.

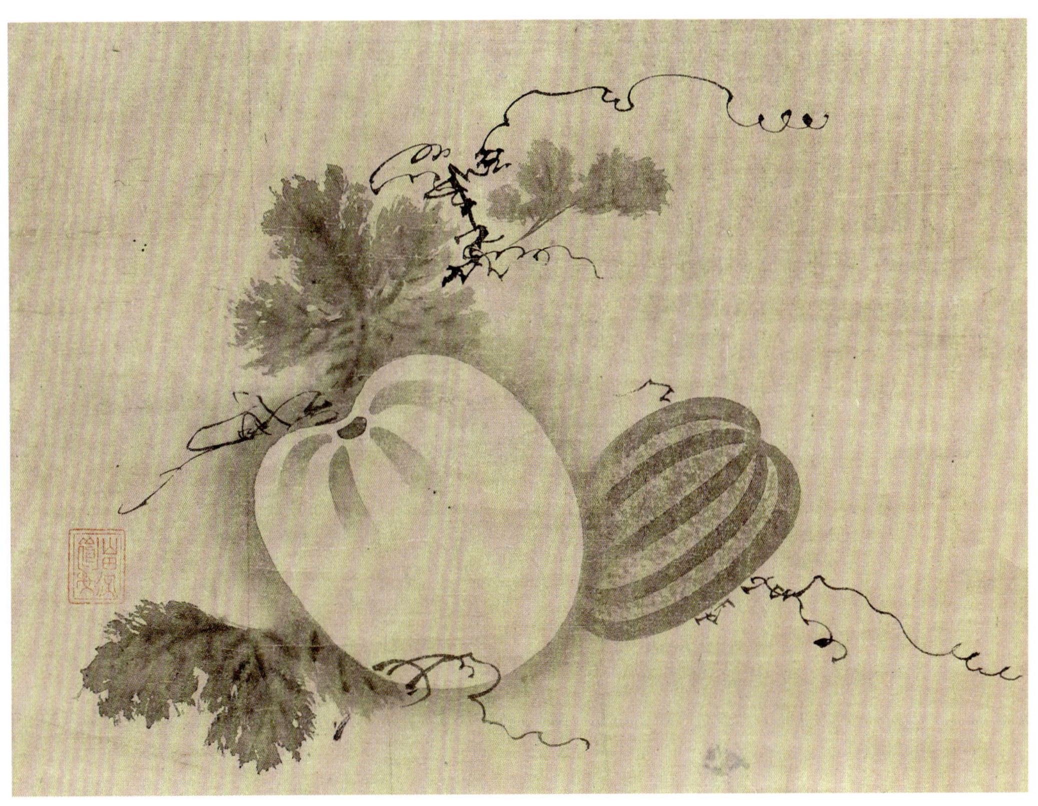

Yamada Dōan
(山田道安; second half of 16th century)

125. Melons

Muromachi period
Hanging scroll; ink on paper
33.7 x 46.3 cm (13¼ x 18¼ in.)
Seal

Literature: Murase 1993, no. 20.

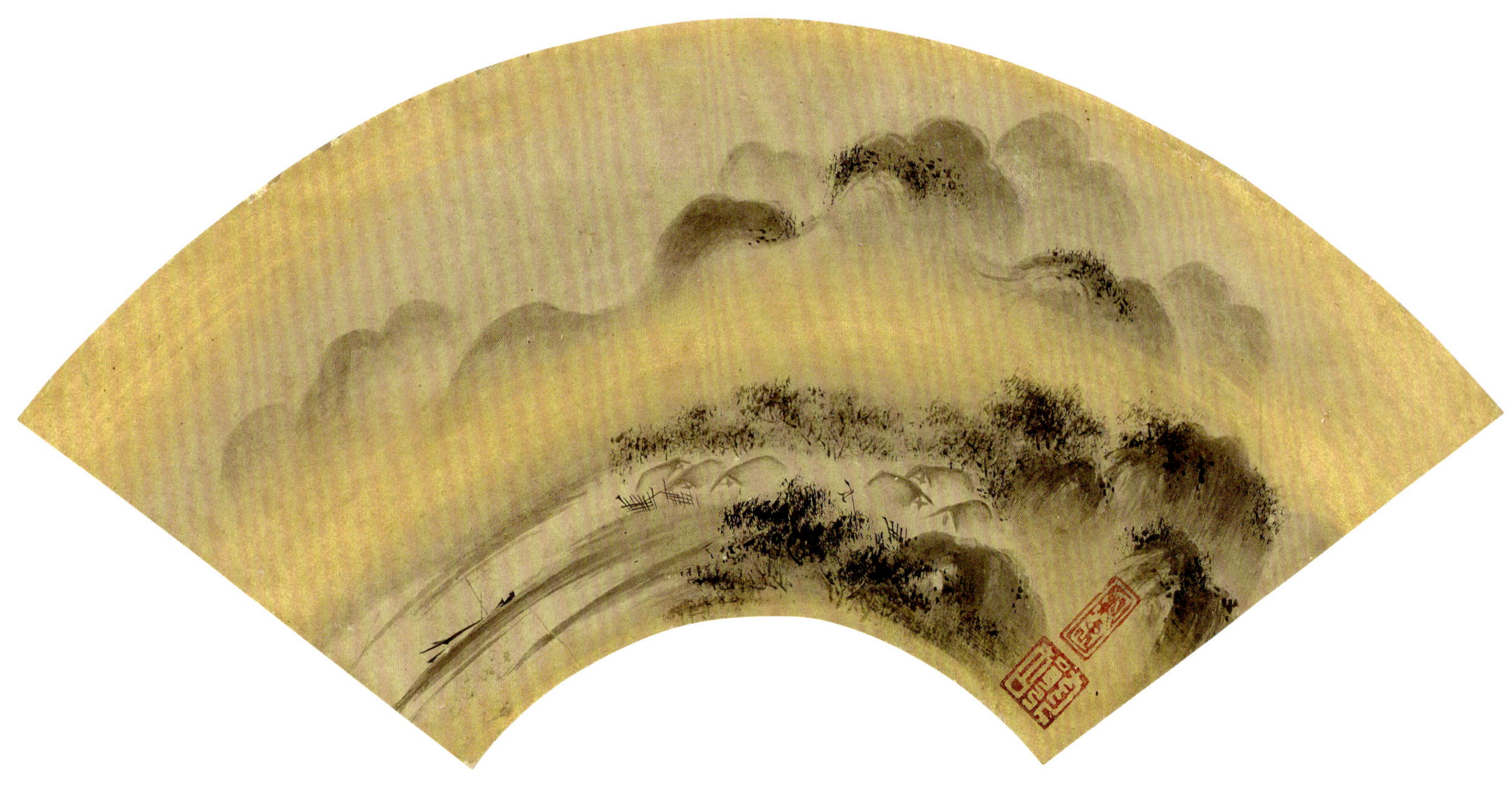

Shikibu Terutada
(式部輝忠, also known as Ryūkyō [竜杏];
fl. mid-16th century)

126. Landscape

Muromachi period
Painting on fan-shaped paper, mounted as hanging scroll; ink and gold on paper
20.7 x 53 cm ($8^{1}/_{8}$ x $20^{7}/_{8}$ in.)
Seals

Ex coll.: Inoue

Literature: Murase 1993, no. 18.

Shikibu Terutada
(式部輝忠, also known as Ryūkyō [竜杏];
fl. mid-16th century)

127. Birds and Flowers of Summer and Autumn

Muromachi period
Pair of hanging scrolls; ink and color on paper
Each scroll 95.6 x 44.8 cm ($37^{5}/_{8}$ x $17^{5}/_{8}$ in.)
Seals

Ex coll.: Maruyama Ryūhei, Kobe

Literature: "Ryūkyō hitsu Kachō zu kai" 1929, pp. 95, 100–105; Nakajima Junji 1968, fig. 23 (left scroll only); Kanazawa Hiroshi and Kawai Masatomo 1982, p. 145; Yamashita Yūji 1985, fig. 11; Tokyo Metropolitan Teien Art Museum 1986, pl. 44; Murase 1993, no. 17; Murase 2000, no. 59; Tsuji Nobuo et al. 2005, no. 47.

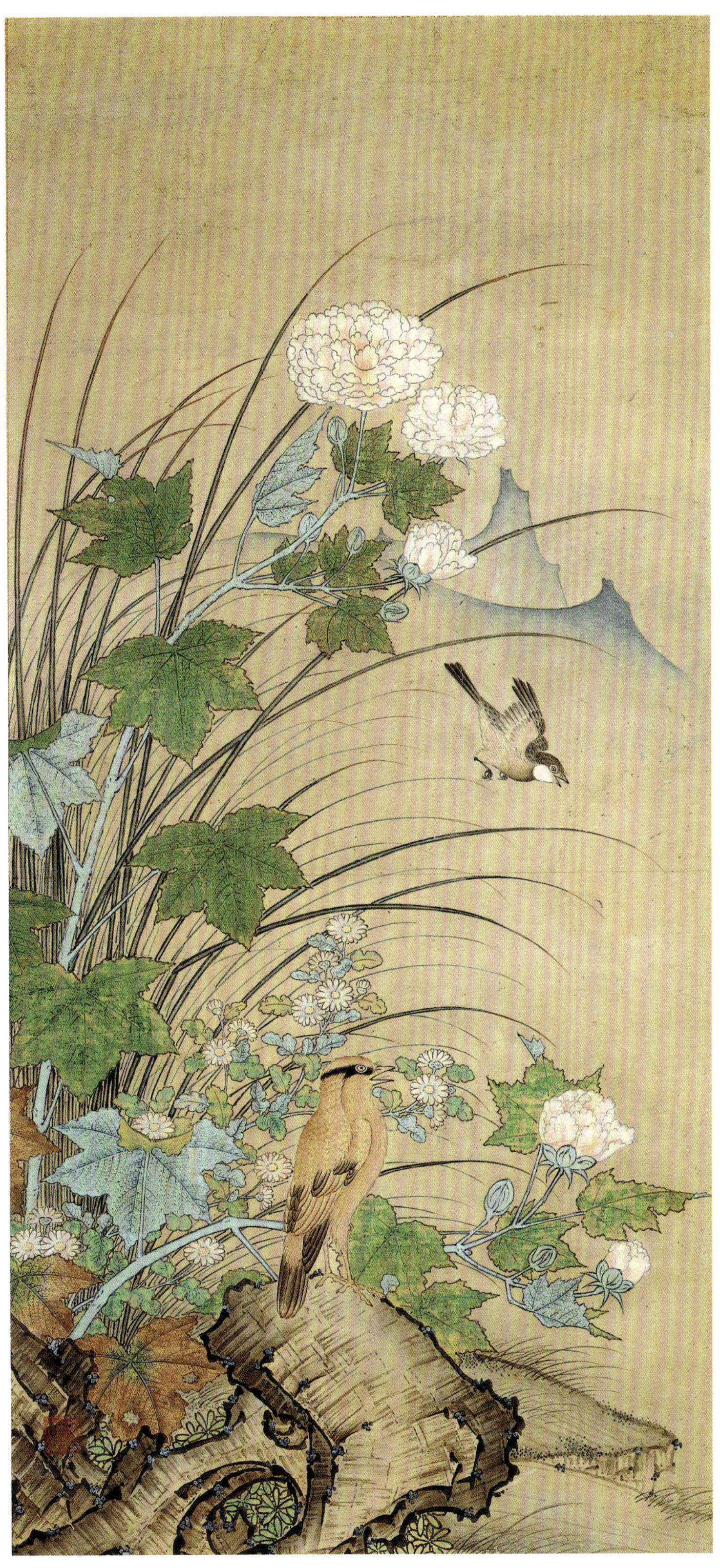

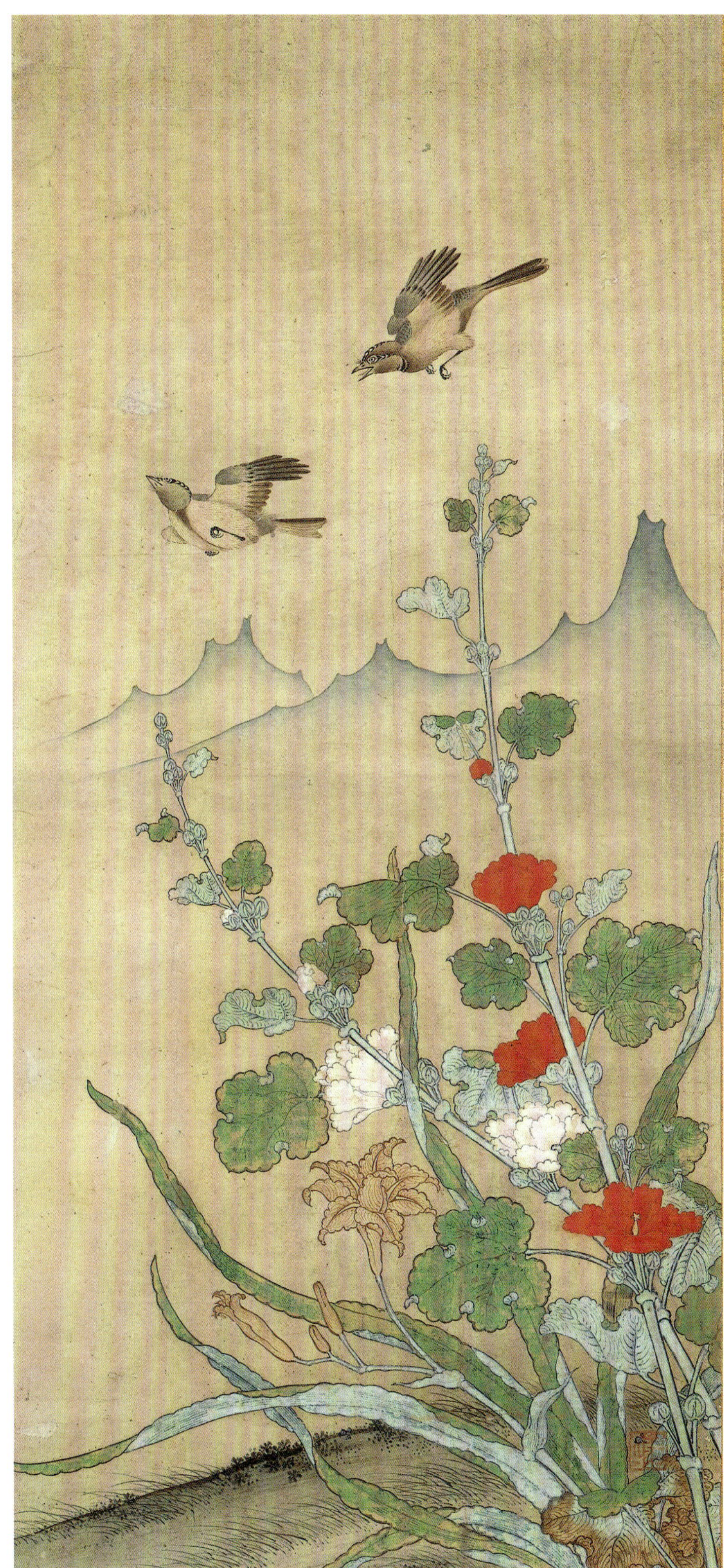

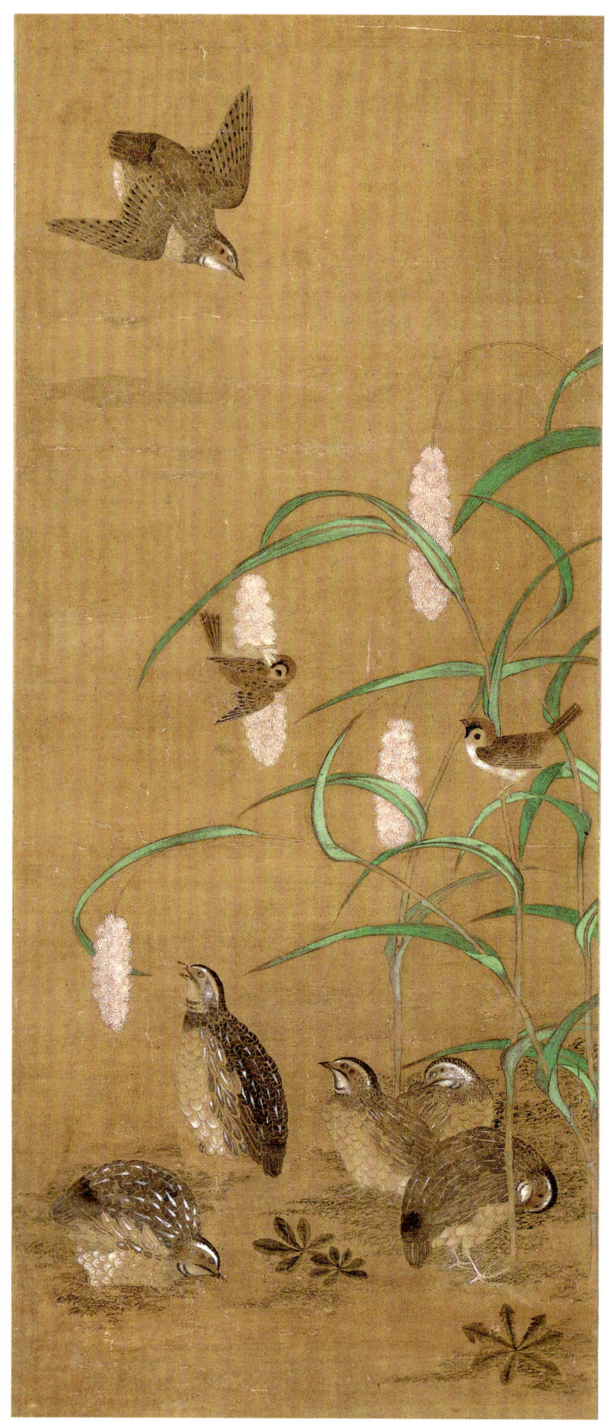

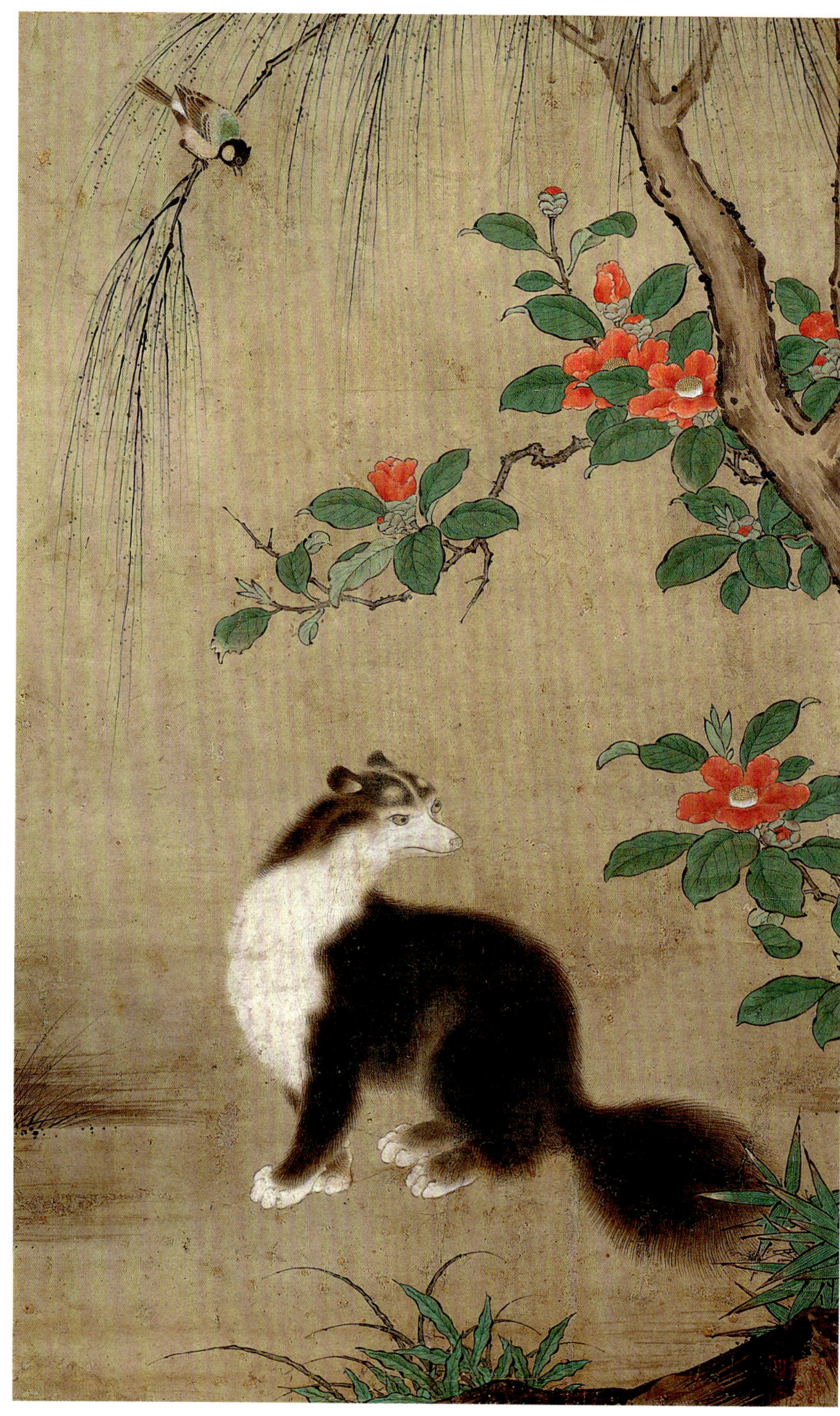

128. Quail, Sparrows, and Millet

Muromachi period, early 16th century
Hanging scroll; ink and color on silk
82.2 x 34.7 cm (32 3/8 x 13 5/8 in.)

LITERATURE: Murase 1993, no. 14.

UTO GYOSHI
(右都御史; fl. second half of 16th century)

129. Jakōneko (麝香猫)

Muromachi period
Hanging scroll; ink and color on paper
76.1 x 46.5 cm (30 x 18 1/4 in.)
Seal

LITERATURE: Murase 1993, no. 16; Kyoto National Museum 1996, no. 119; Sakamoto 1997, figs. 1, 2; Tochigi Prefectural Museum and Kanagawa Prefectural Museum of Cultural History 1998, p. 167, fig. 3; Murase 2000, no. 60.

CIRCLE OF KANO MOTONOBU
(狩野元信; 1476–1559)

130. Bo Ya Plays the Qin as Zhong Ziqi Listens (伯牙弾琴)

Muromachi period
Hanging scroll; ink and light color on paper
165.8 x 87.2 cm (65 1/4 x 34 3/8 in.)

EX COLL.: Hara Tomitarō, Kanagawa; Date Munemoto, Tokyo

LITERATURE: "Ko Kano hitsu Hakuga dankin zu kai" 1937, p. 74; Takeuchi Shōji 1972, pls. 81, 82; Murase 1975, no. 43; Shimizu and Wheelwright 1976, no. 28; Shimada Shūjirō 1979, no. 98; Ford 1985, fig. 10; Tokyo National Museum 1985a, no. 26; Avitabile 1990, no. 47; Tsuji Nobuo 1994, fig. 104; Kyoto National Museum 1996, fig. 16; Murase 2000, no. 71; Tokyo National Museum 2003, p. 11, fig. 6; Tsuji Nobuo et al. 2005, no. 46.

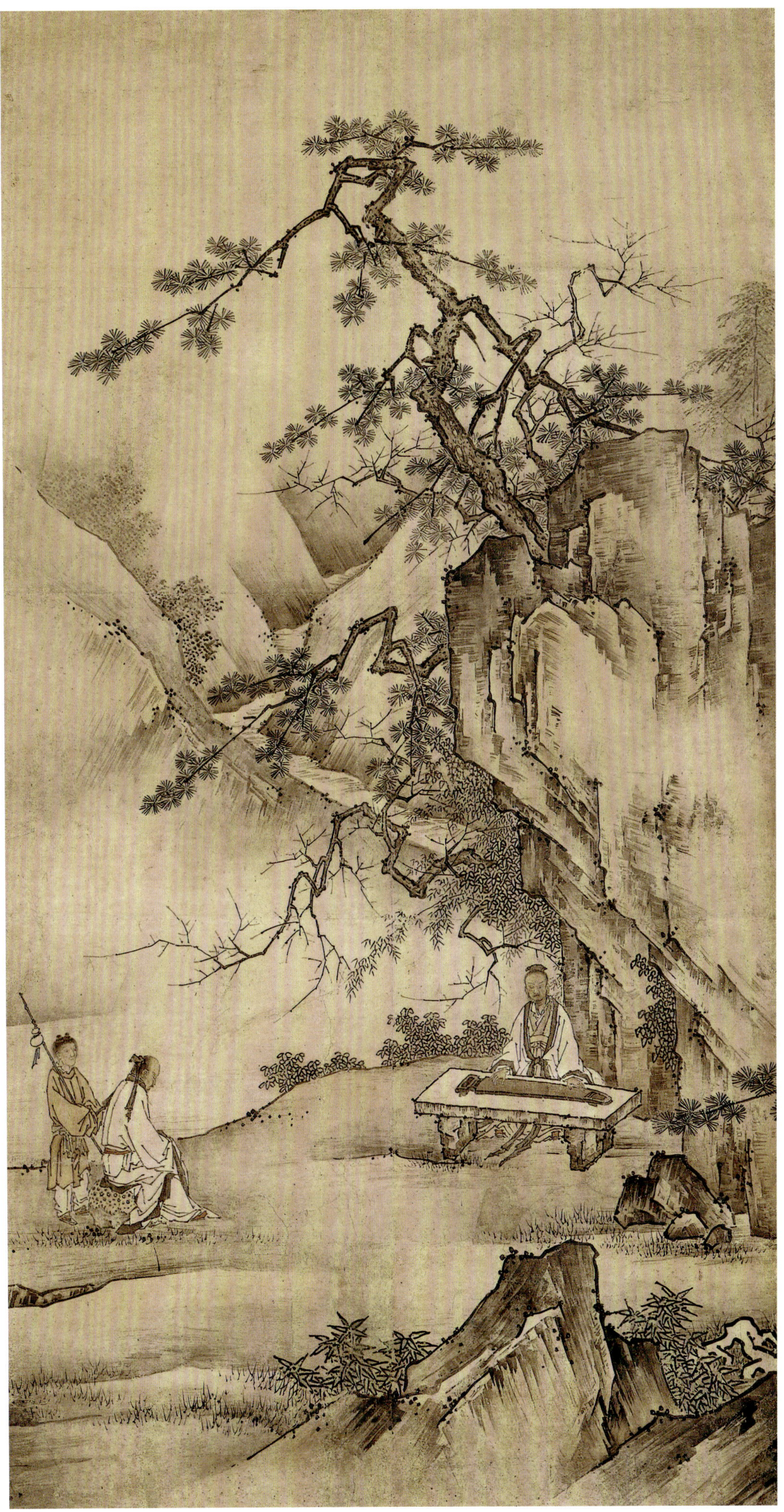

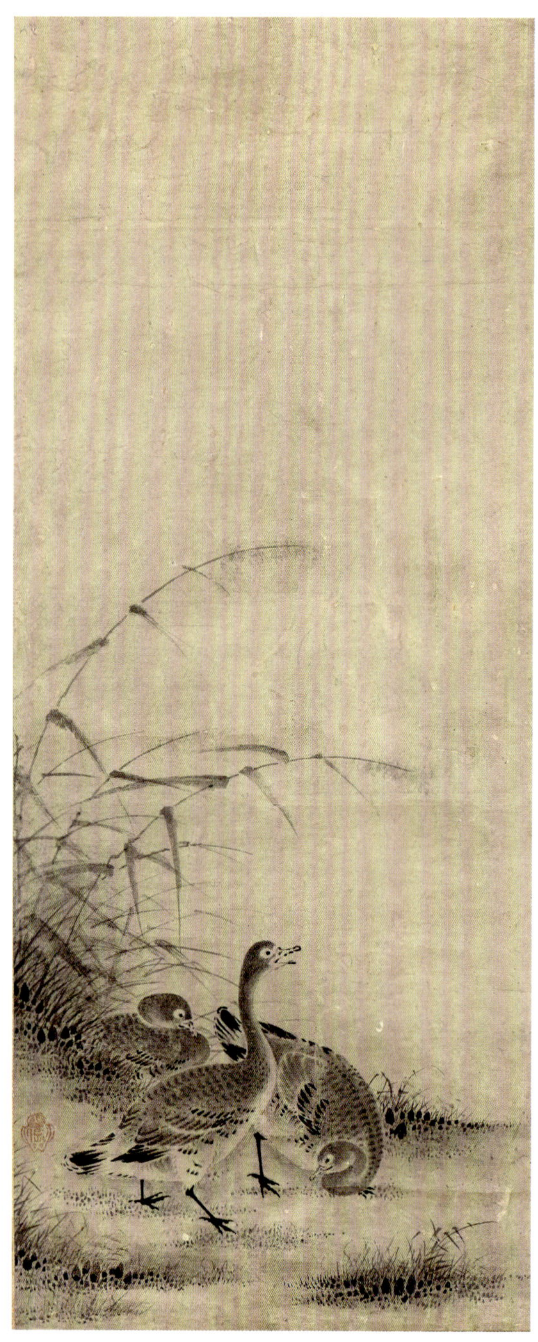

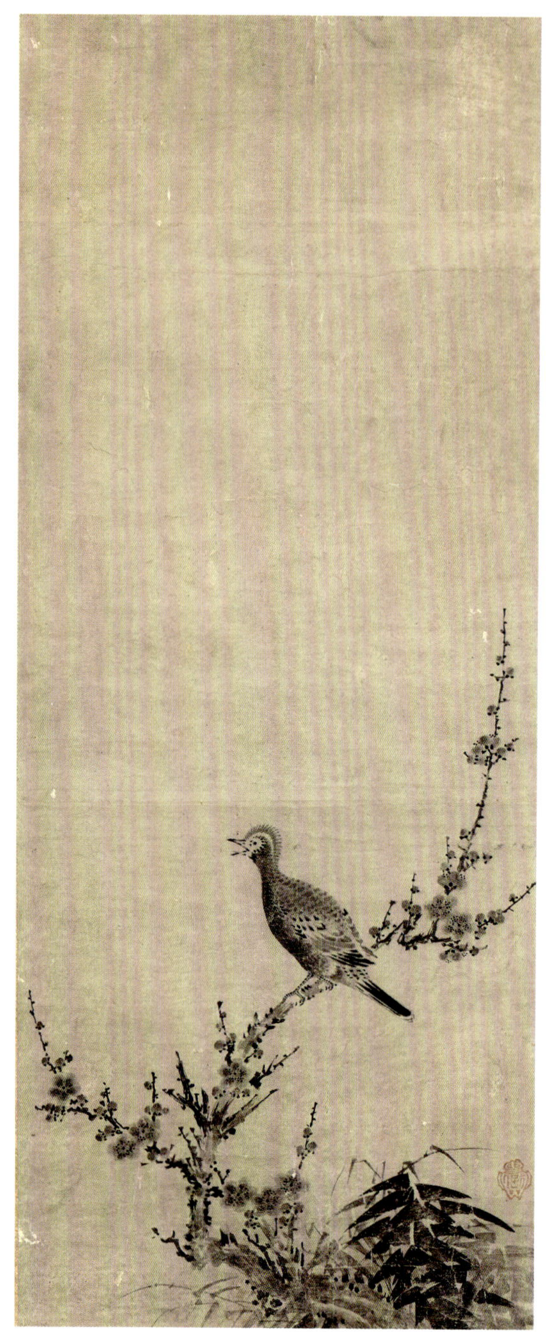

131. Bulbul on a Plum Tree; Geese and Reeds

Momoyama period, 16th century
Pair of hanging scrolls; ink on paper
Each scroll 83.6 x 34.4 cm (32 7/8 x 13 1/2 in.)
Seals

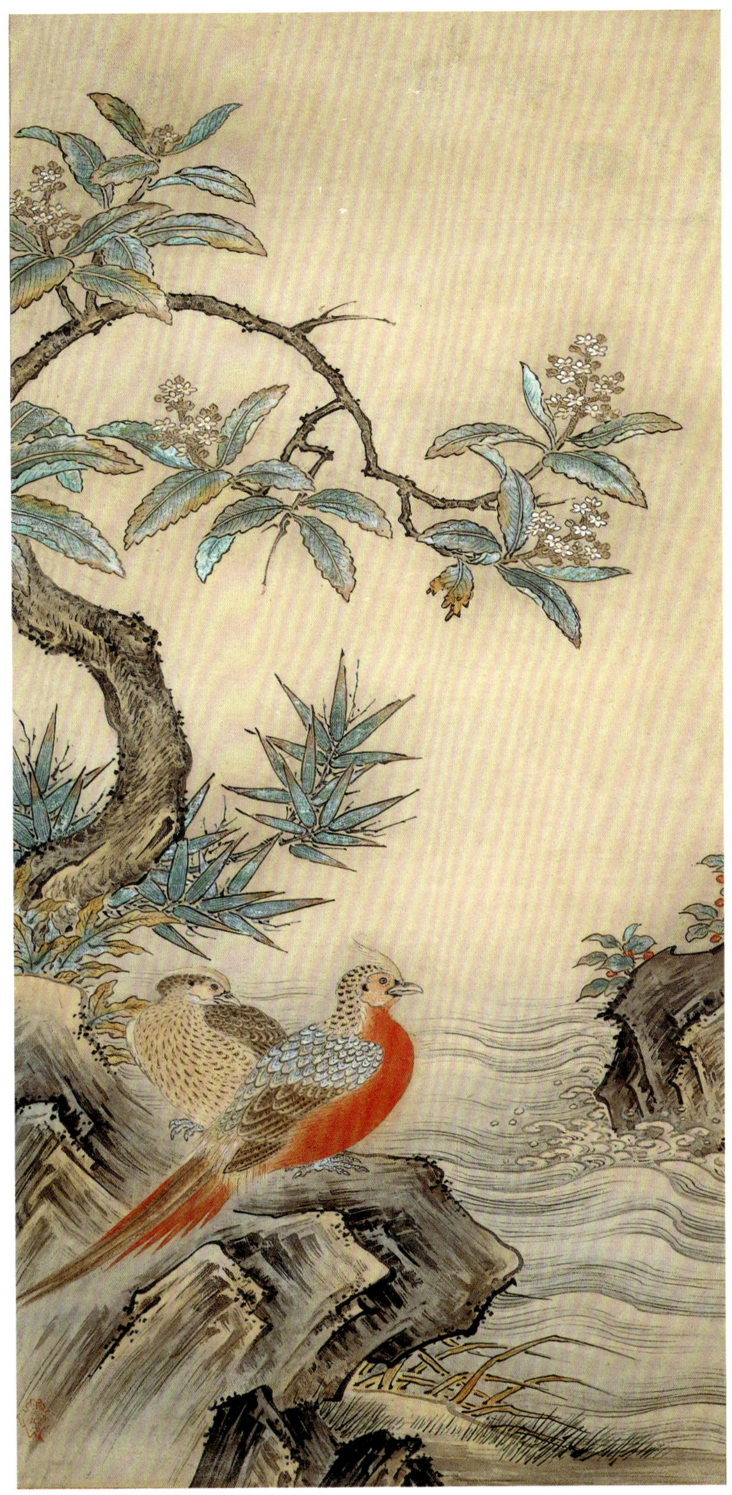

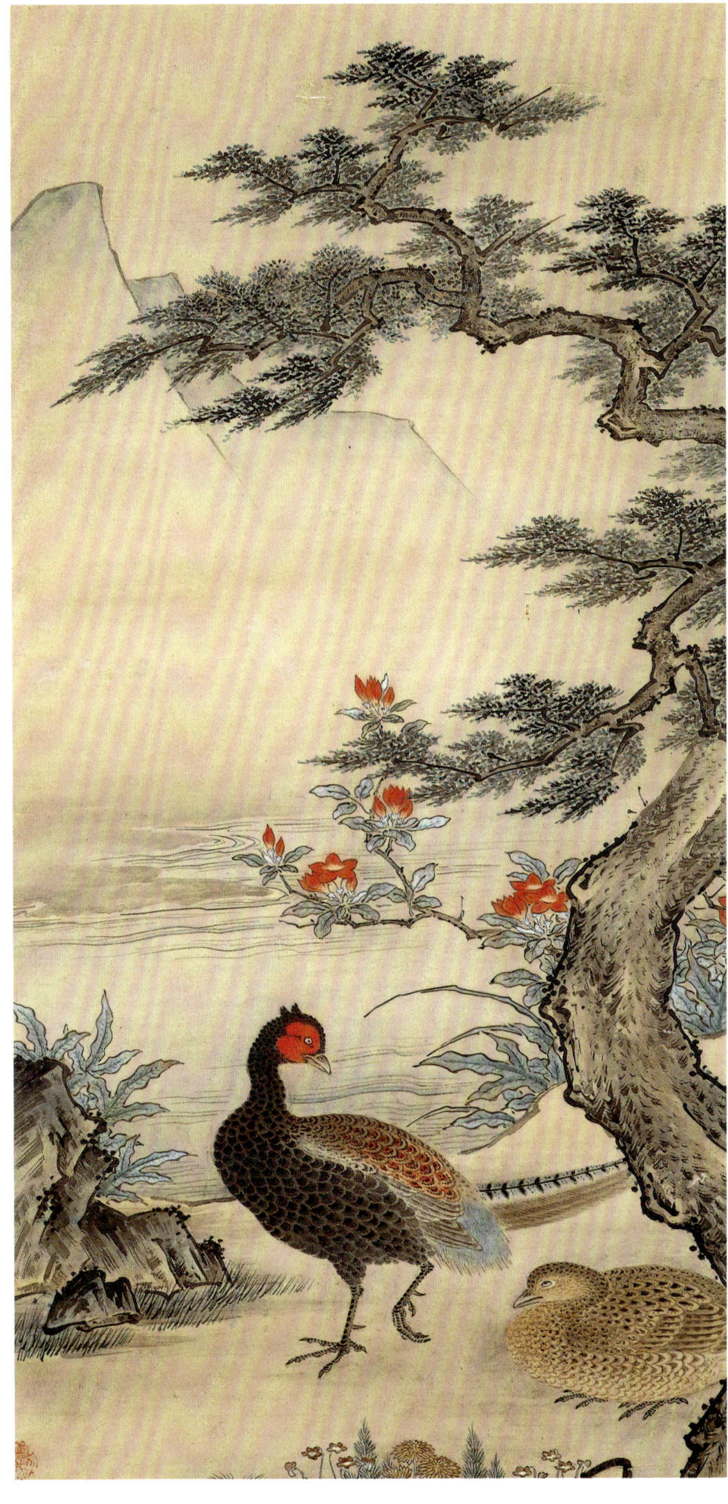

Kano Shōei
(狩野松栄; 1519–1592)

132. Pheasants and Azaleas; Golden Pheasants and a Loquat Tree

Muromachi period, 1560s
Pair of hanging scrolls; ink, color, and gold on paper
Each scroll 101 x 49 cm (39 3/4 x 19 1/4 in.)
Seals

Literature: Takeda Tsuneo 1974, fig. 49; Takeda Tsuneo 1977a, pls. 43, 44; Murase 1993, no. 19; Murase 2000, no. 75; Tsuji Nobuo et al. 2005, no. 48.

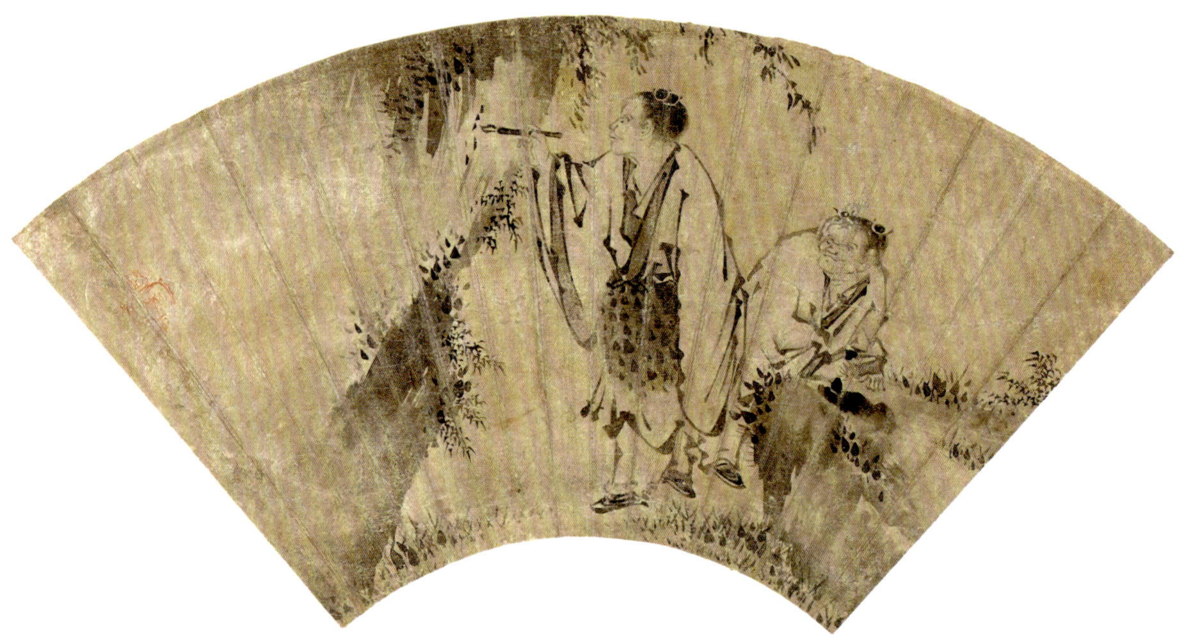

Attributed to Kano Yukinobu
(狩野之信; ca. 1513–1575)

133. Kanzan (寒山) and Jittoku (拾得)

Momoyama period
Folding fan mounted on hanging scroll; ink and gold on paper
18.9 x 43.3 cm (7½ x 17 in.)

134. Cranes under Pine Trees

Muromachi period, 16th century
Six-panel folding screen; ink and color on paper
159 x 346.5 cm (62⅝ in. x 11 ft. 4⅜ in.)

Gift from Leighton Longhi to the Mary and Jackson Burke Foundation, 2001

Kano Naizen
(狩野内膳; 1570–1616)

135. Seiōgyū (Ch. Zhenghuangniu, 政黄牛); Ikuzanshu (Ch. Yushanzhu, 郁山主)

Momoyama period
Pair of hanging scrolls; ink on paper
Each scroll 111.8 x 47.4 cm (44 x 18⅝ in.)
Text, signatures, seals

Ex coll.: Nijō

Literature: Tsuji Nobuo 1980, nos. 97, 98; Narusawa Katsutsugu 1985, fig. 20 (Seiōgyū); Tokyo National Museum 1985a, no. 32; Avitabile 1990, no. 74; Murase 2000, no. 76; Tsuji Nobuo et al. 2005, no. 63.

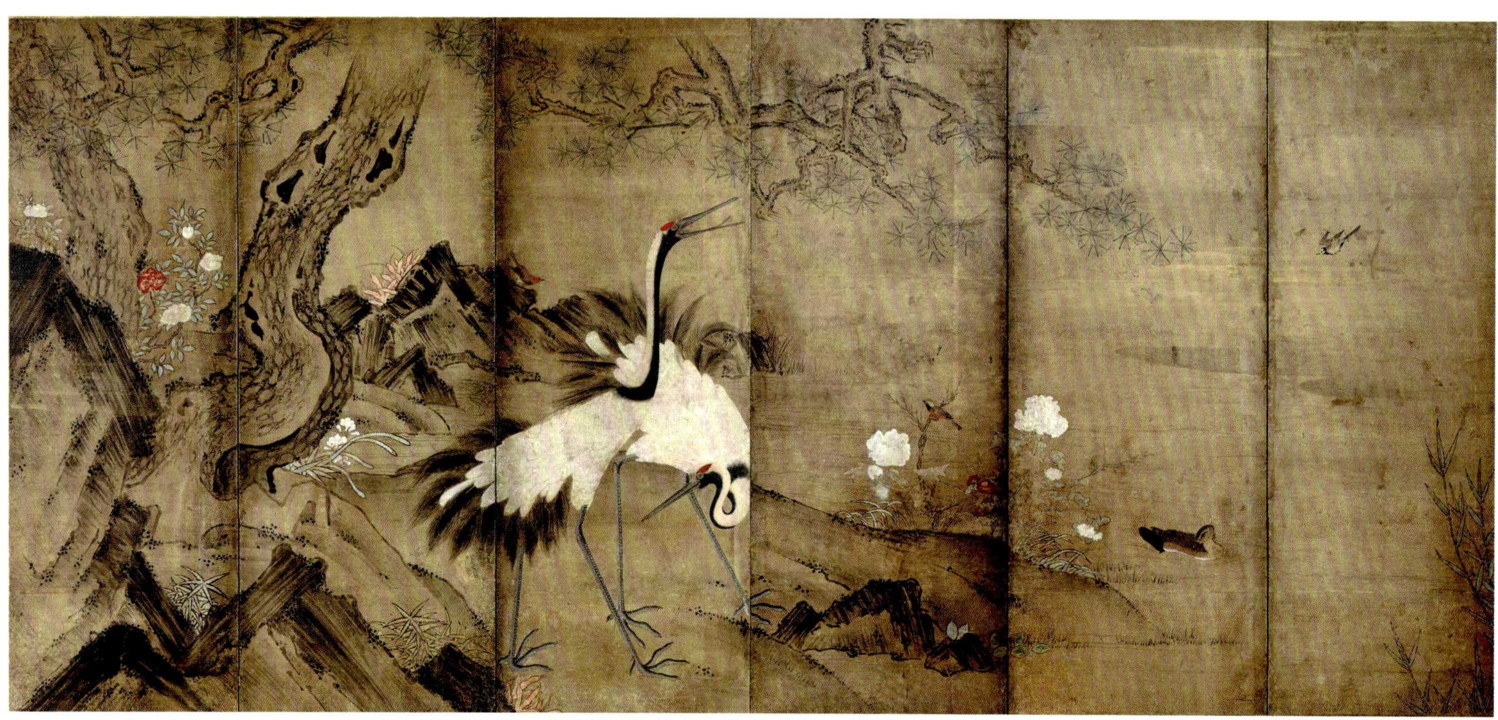

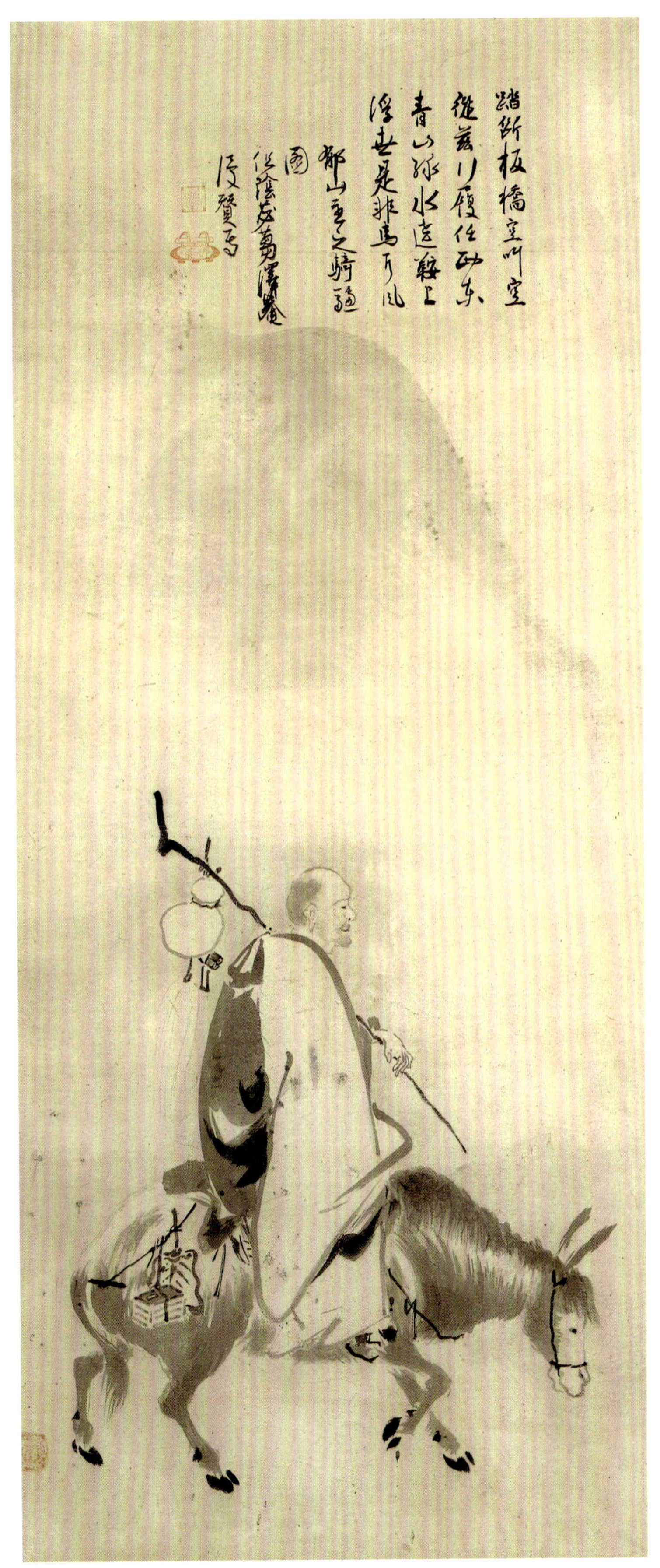

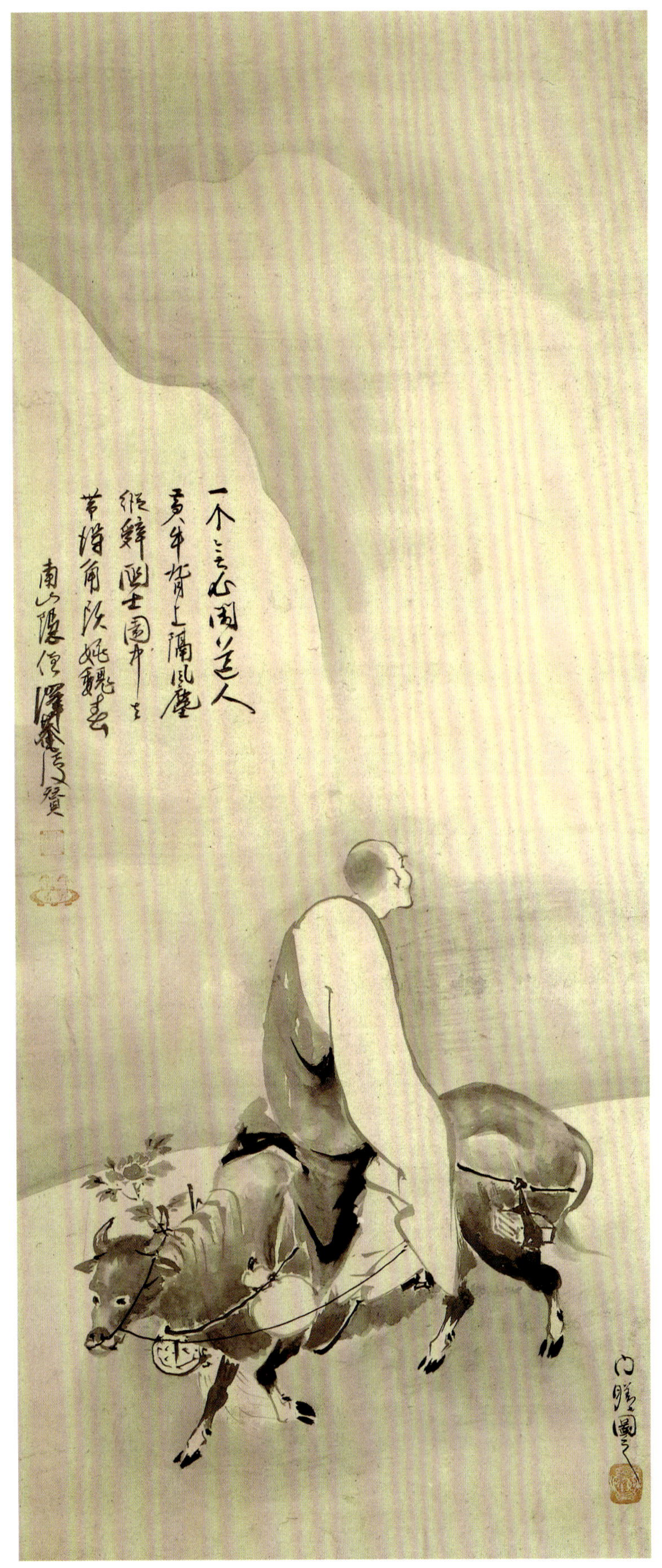

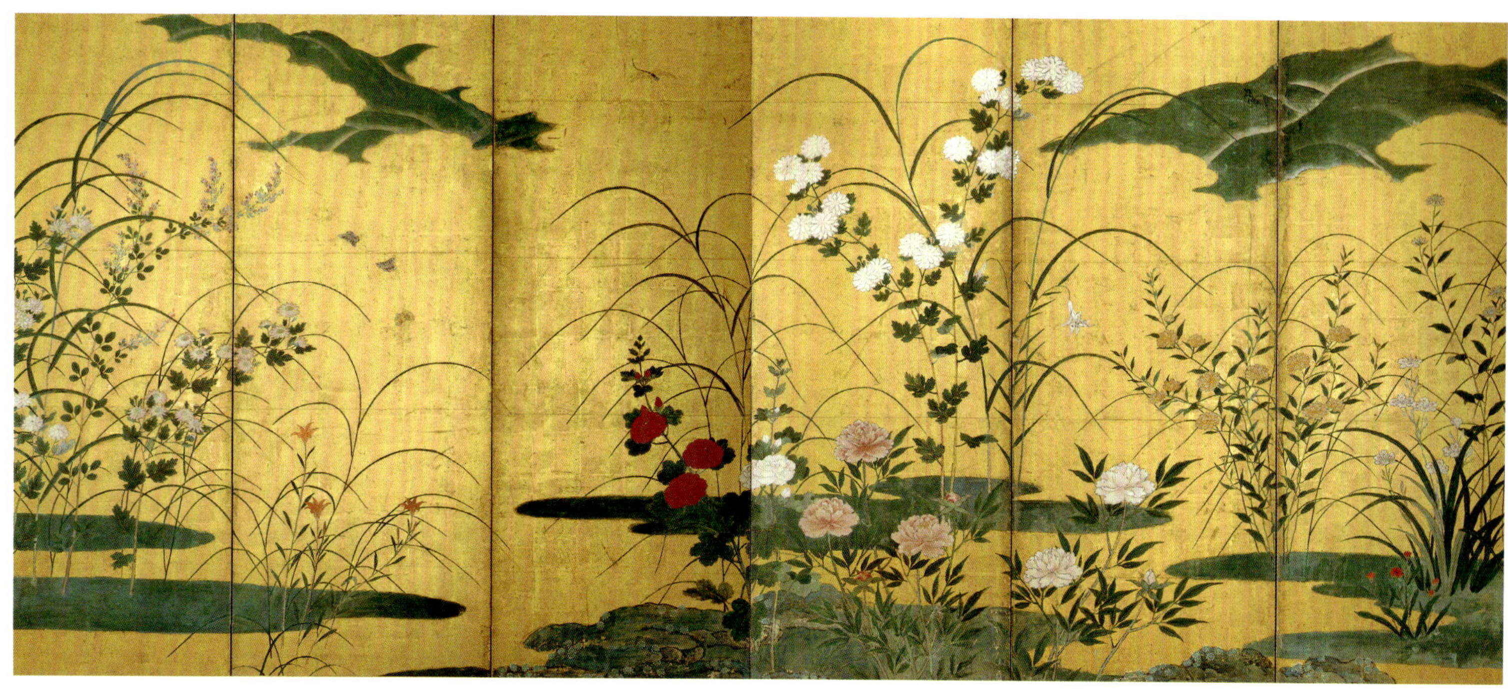

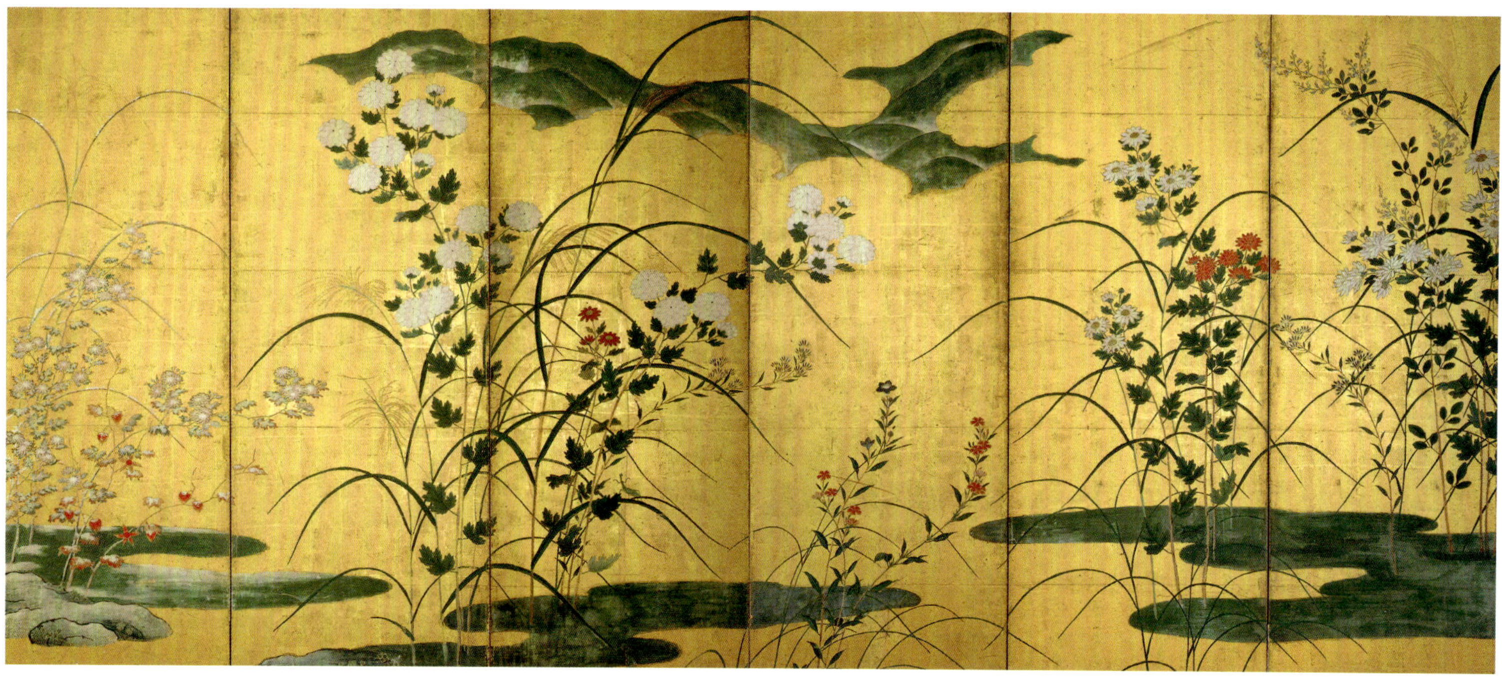

136. Flowers of the Four Seasons

Momoyama period, late 16th century
Pair of six-panel screens; ink and color on gilded paper
Each screen 152.3 x 354.2 cm (60 in. x 11 ft. 7½ in.)

EX COLL.: Idemitsu Museum of Arts

LITERATURE: Idemitsu Museum of Arts 1991, no. 24; Tsuji Nobuo et al. 2005, no. 70.

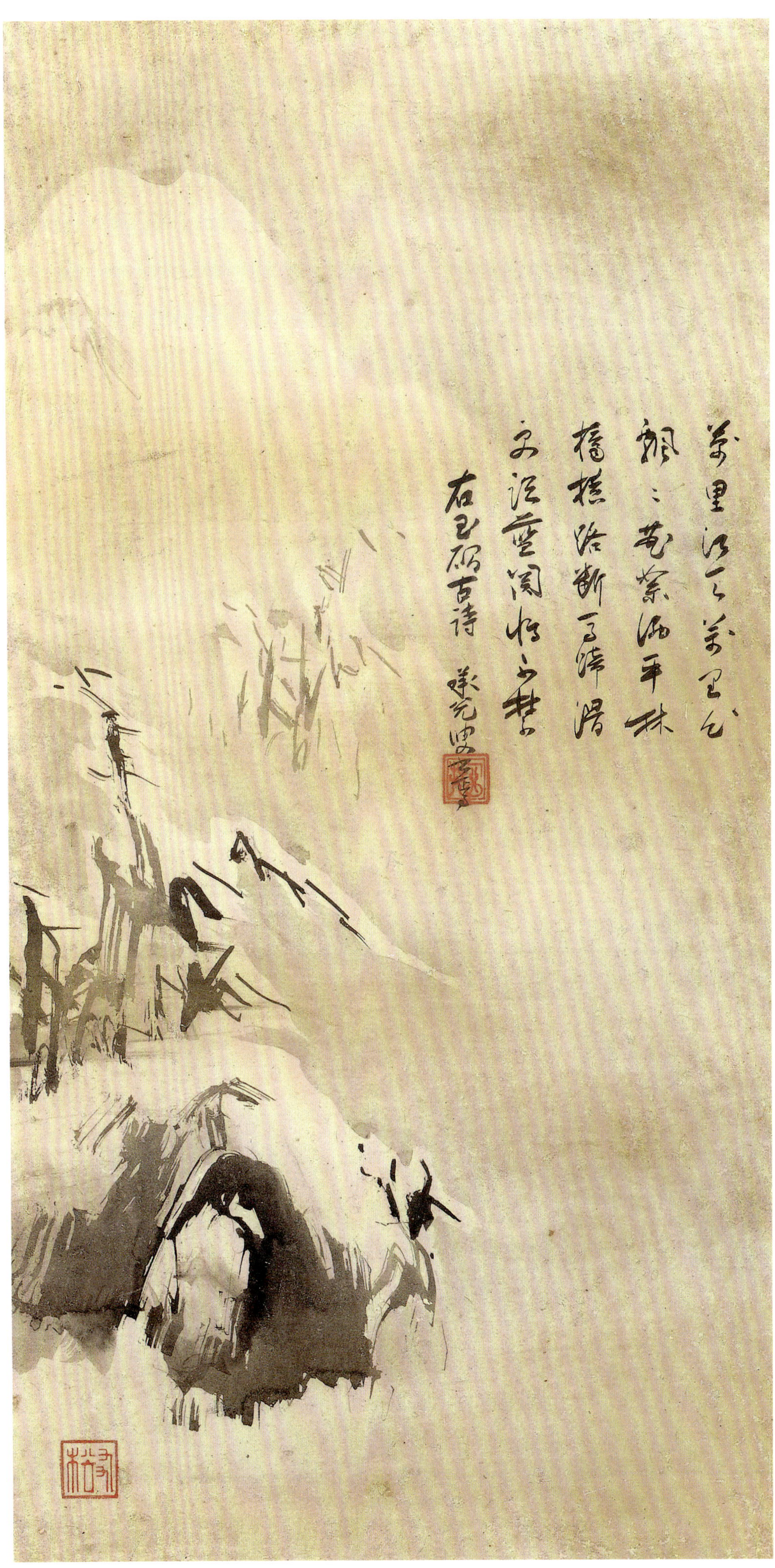

Kaihō Yūshō
(海北友松; 1533–1615)

137. River and Sky in Evening Snow, from *Eight Views of the Xiao and Xiang Rivers* (瀟湘八景 江天暮雪)

Momoyama period, ca. 1602–3
Panel of a folding screen, mounted as a hanging scroll; ink and gold on paper
71.5 x 37.8 cm (28 1/8 x 14 7/8 in.)
Text, signature, seals

Literature: Kawai Masatomo 1966, fig. 4; Kawai Masatomo 1978, p. 108, fig. 19; Ōta Hirotarō et al. 1990, pl. 23; Kawamoto Keiko 1991, pl. 30; Murase 1993, no. 21; Sugimoto Sonoko and Kawai Masatomo 1994, pl. 23; Burke 1996a, fig. 2; Ōtsu City Museum of History 1997, p. 93, no. 12; Murase 2000, no. 77; Tsuji Nobuo et al. 2005, no. 64.

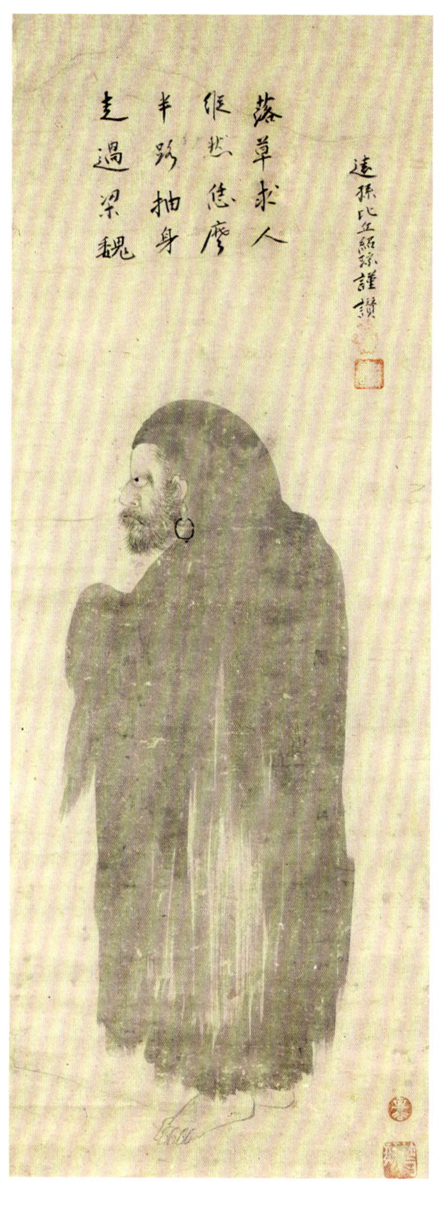

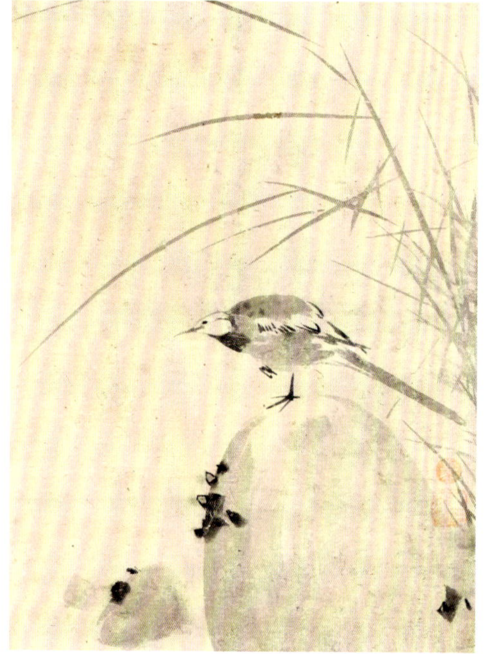

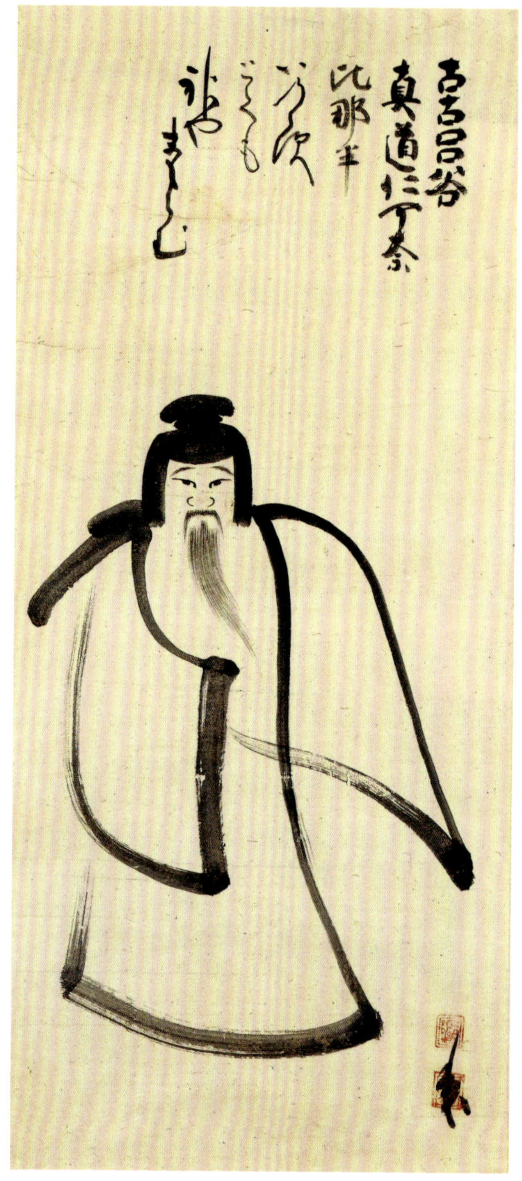

Unkoku Tōgan
(雲谷等顔; 1547–1618)

138. Daruma (達磨)

Momoyama period
Hanging scroll; ink on paper
89.6 x 33.4 cm (35¼ x 13⅛ in.)
Text, signature, seals

Unkoku Tōgan
(雲谷等顔; 1547–1618)

139. Wagtail on a Rock

Momoyama period
Hanging scroll; ink on paper
50 x 37.1 cm (19⅝ x 14⅝ in.)
Seals

Literature: Yamamoto Hideo 2000, p. 46, fig. 3.

Konoe Nobutada
(近衛信尹; 1565–1614)

140. Tenjin Traveling to China (渡唐天神)

Momoyama period, 16th century
Hanging scroll; ink on paper
98 x 42.9 cm (38⅝ x 16⅞ in.)
Text, signature, seals

Literature: Tokyo National Museum 1985a, no. 78; Avitabile 1990, no. 48.

Unkoku Tōgan
(雲谷等顔; 1547–1618)

141. Landscape of the Four Seasons

Momoyama period
Pair of six-panel folding screens; ink, color, and gold dust on paper
Each screen 175.1 x 375.6 cm (68⅞ in. x 12 ft. 3⅞ in.)
Seals

Literature: Murase 1971, no. 10; Murase 2000, no. 78.

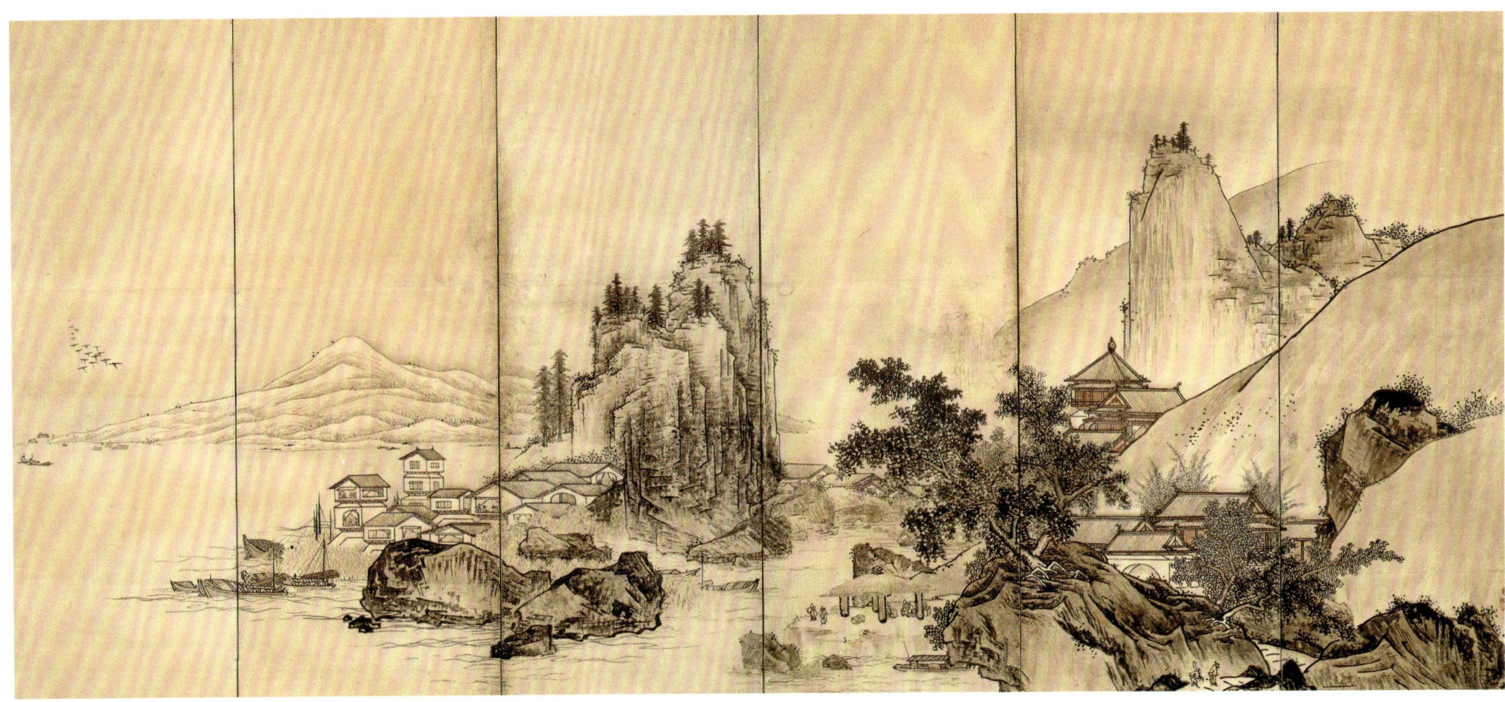

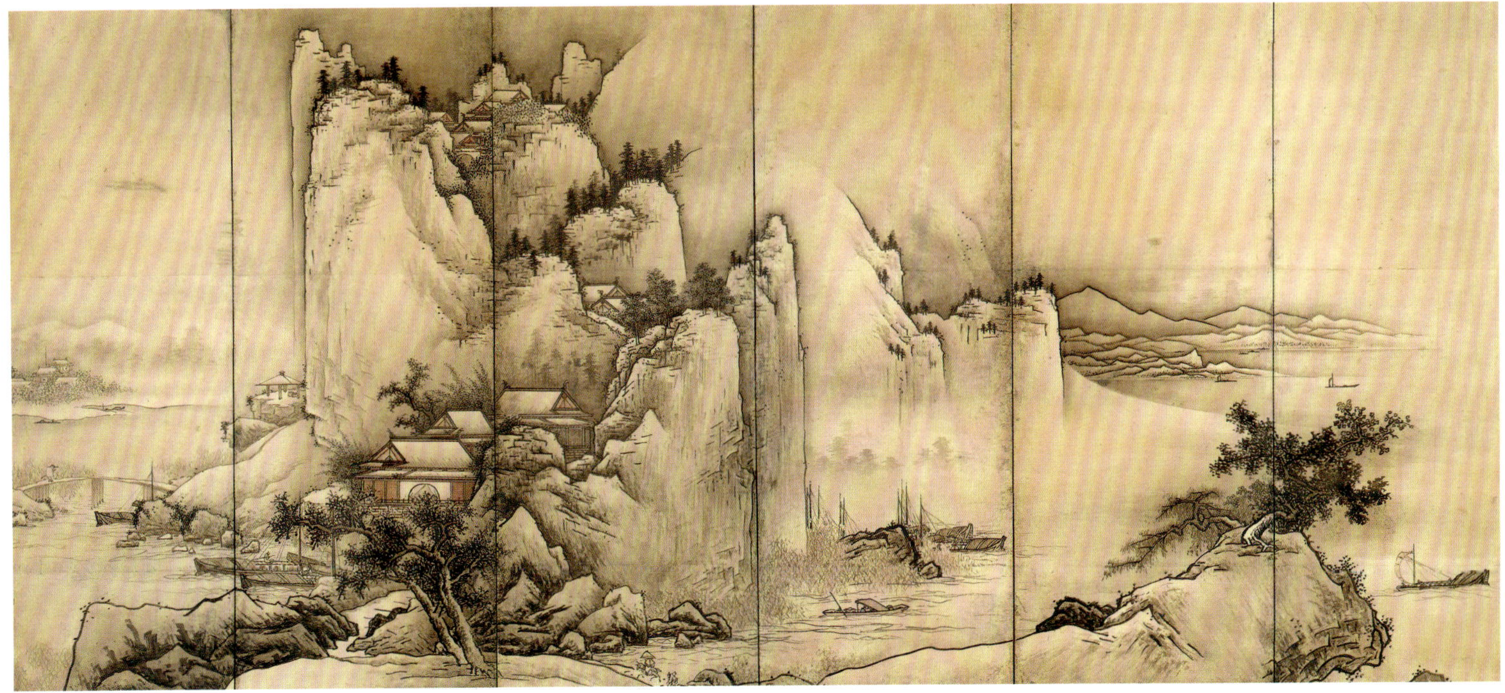

Chapter 3 Details

† denotes illustrated items

---

† 95. Monju Bosatsu

Seal

Hasōai in

---

† 96. Monju on a Lion

Seal

Shūsei (?)

---

98. Chotō; Kensu

Seals

[on each scroll] *Yōgetsu*

---

99. Ox and Herdsman

Seal

Sekkyakushi

---

† 100. Water Buffalo and Herdboy

Seal

Masanobu (?)

---

† 101. Soshoku (Ch. Su Shi) on a Donkey

Seal

Bokudō

---

† 103. The Seven Sages of the Bamboo Grove

Seals

[lower right] *Sesson* (cauldron shaped); *Shūkei* (square)

---

† 104. Early Spring Landscape

Text

by Sesshin Tōhaku (d. 1459)

95

96

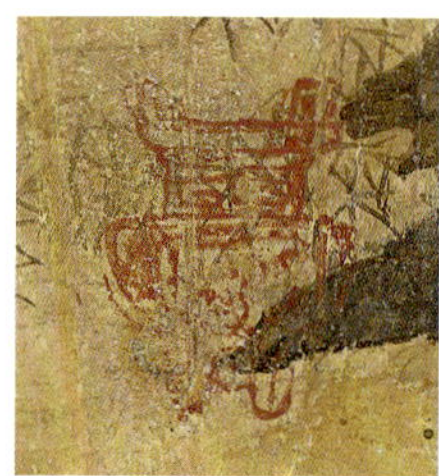

100

101

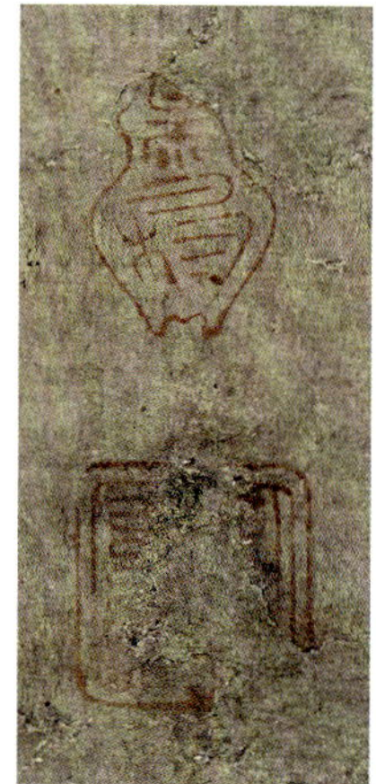

103

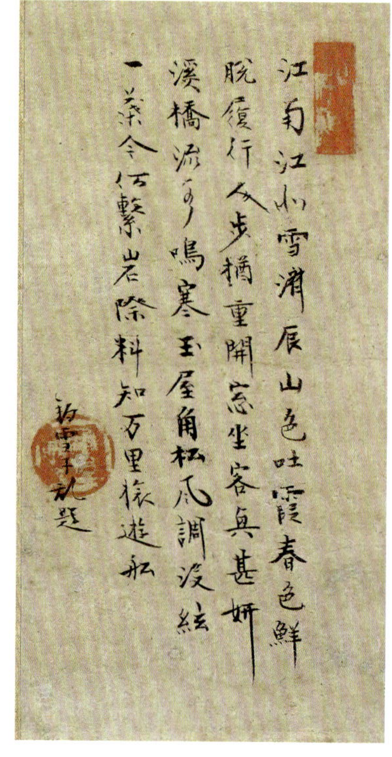

104

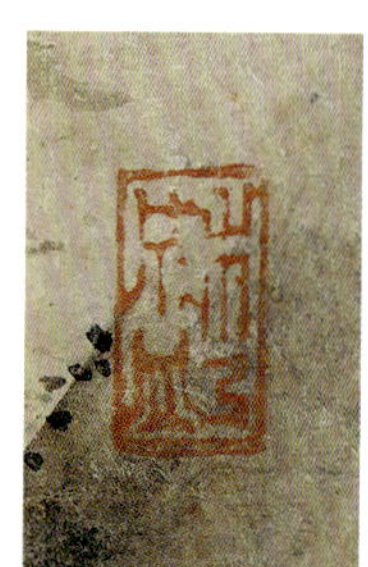

104

South of the river, north of the river, the snow is clearing. / Mountains spew forth rosy clouds, springtime colors are fresh. / Travelers remove their shoes, though the going still is rough. / Opening the window, seated guests enjoy the splendid view. / Water flowing beneath the bridge rings like chimes of jade. / At the eaves, the wind in the pines tunes its stringless lute. / But why is that leaf of a boat moored beside the cliff? / It must be a craft for roving ten thousand miles away.

Signature

Composed at random by Chōsetsushi

Seals

[lower right of scroll] *Hidemori*; [upper right of inscription] illegible; [lower left of inscription] *Sesshin*

---

† 105. Landscape after Ka Kei (Ch. Xia Gui)

Signatures

[on each screen] *Painted by Shūbun; inscribed by Hōgen Eishin* [Kano Yasunobu (1613–1685)]

Seals

[on each screen] *Hōgen*

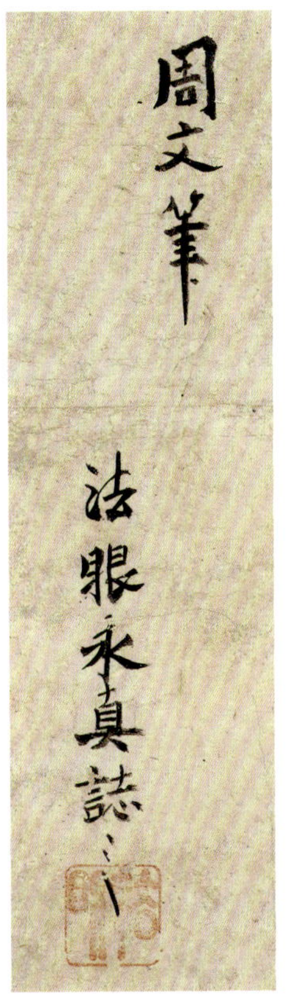

105

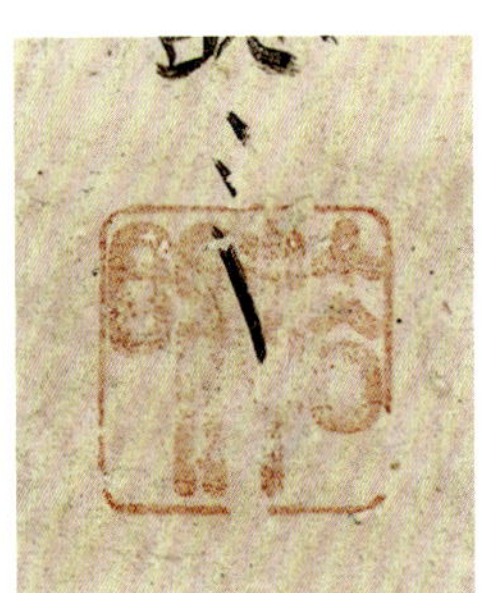

105

108

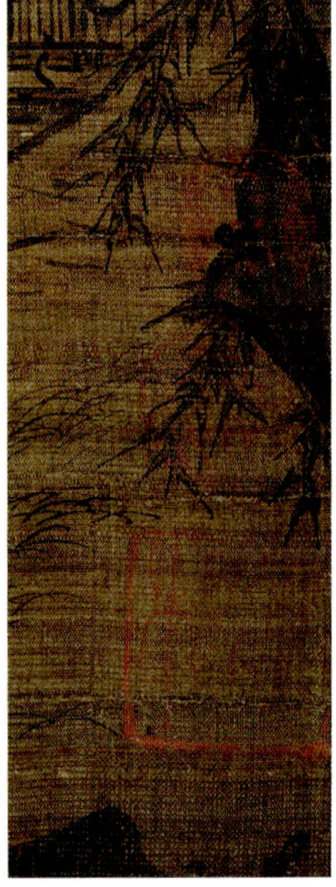

109

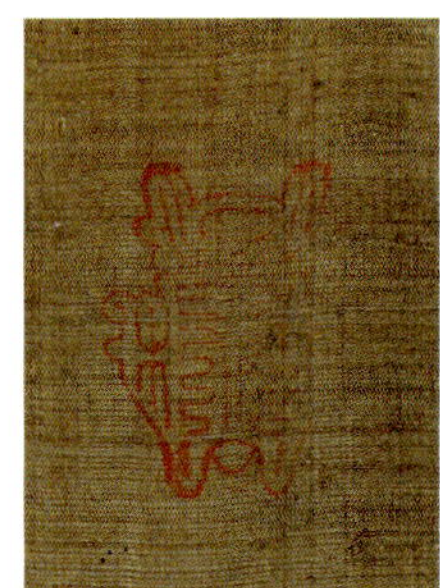

109

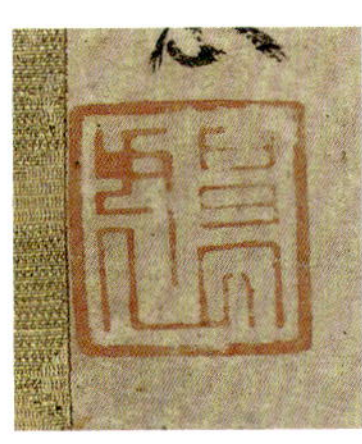

106

106

106

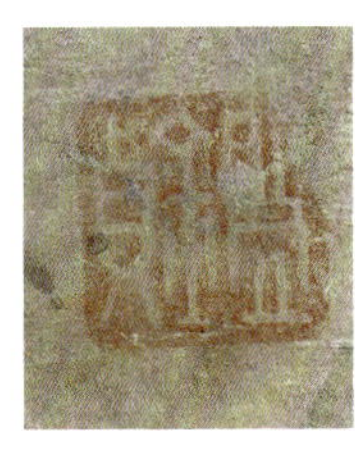

107

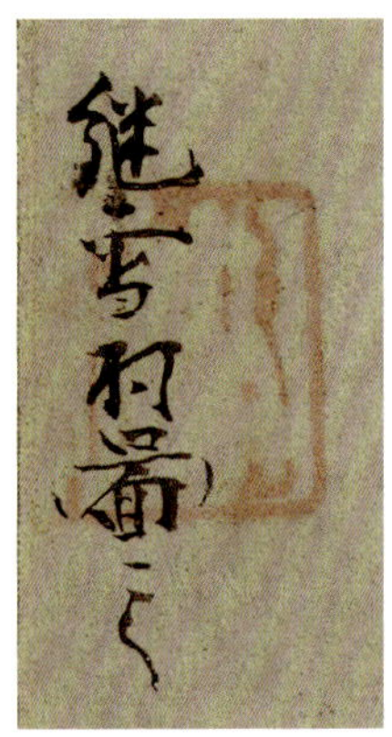

110

† 106. Early Spring Landscape

Seal

[lower right] *Shūtoku*

Text

by Yōkoku Kentō (d. 1533)

Though the west lake swells with water as spring arrives, / the emerald bamboo outdoors blocks the sight of boats. / Had the east wind facilitated his quest, / he would have returned by boat in moonlight to the frosted land of Wu faraway.

Signature

Kakyō Kansho Dōjin Kentō

Seal

[upper left, right-hand seal] *Yōkoku*

Text

by Teihō Shōchū (fl. ca. 1538)

Floating in a boathouse on the brimming spring river, / what could one desire in a sound sleep after mooring? / In nothing but insouciant boating would I spend the rest of my life, / with mountains along the white gull-dotted stream as my beauties.

Signature

[upper left, above left-hand seal] *Shōchū, formerly of Kenchōji*

Seal

[upper left, left-hand seal] *Shōchū*

† 107. Two Views from *Eight Views of the Xiao and Xiang Rivers*

Seals

[on each scroll] *Kantei*

† 108. Landscape of the Four Seasons

Seals

[on each scroll] *Hōgen*; *Keison*

† 109. Landscape with Pavilion

Seals

Sesson (cauldron shaped); illegible; illegible; *Sesson* (square)

† 110. Landscape with Rocky Precipice

Signature

Painted by Kei Sesson

Seal

Shūkei

† 111. Splashed-Ink Landscape

Seal

Bokushō

111

113. Wagtail on a Rock

Text

by Taikyo Genju (fl. second half of 14th c.)

The withered tree has no twigs or leaves; / a wagtail pecks at wild mosses. / Inside the rock is a precious foot-long jade, / but when can it be chiseled out?

Signature

Taikyosō

Seals

Two illegible seals

† 115. Cicada on a Grapevine

Seals

Guan; *Bokurin Guan*

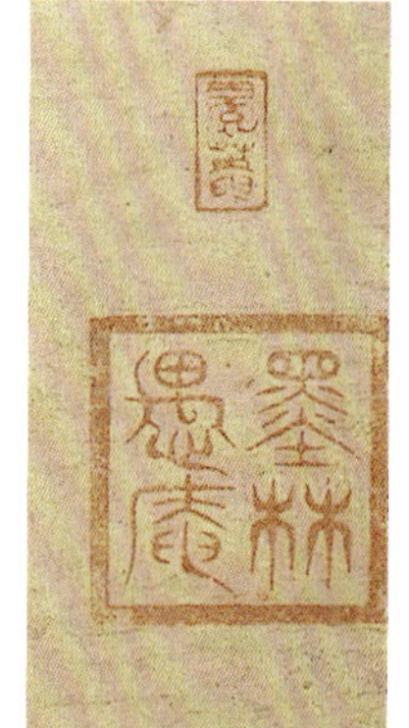

115

† 116. Pair of Wagtails

Seals

[on each scroll] *Shōkei*

116

† 117. Sparrows among Millet and Asters

Seal

Geiai

117

† 118. Sparrow on Bamboo in Rain

Seals

[upper right] *Muqi*; [lower right] two illegible seals

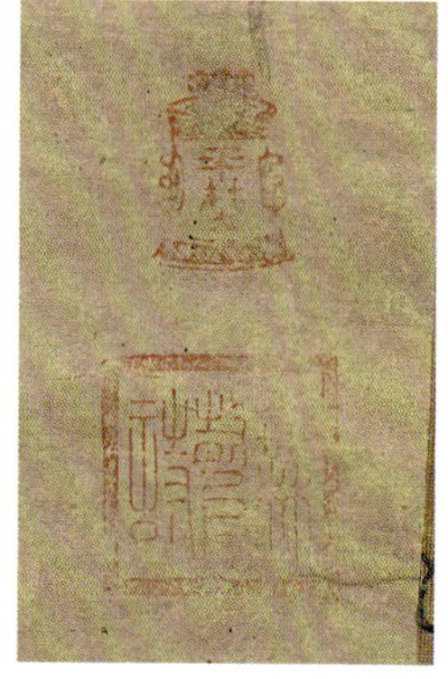

118

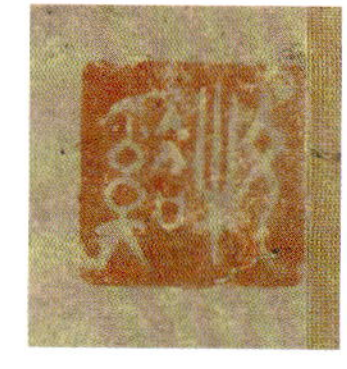

118

119. Bird Resting on a Tree

Seal

Eii

Text

by Daiko Shōkaku (d. 1535)

To the lush woods, good for nesting, birds return. / Reposing on a branch, they cuddle through the night. / The phoenix remains above the blue clouds. / Feathery wings take it to great heights which, however, are not fit for dwelling.

Signature

Composed by Son'an

Seals

Daiko; Shōkaku

† 120. Two Fish in a Pond

Text

by Mokumoku Dōjin

Isle grasses fluttering in the wind, a chilly river at dusk, / a shaft of red glow cast on the whitish bank. / Were Qingao [active ca. 300 B.C.E.] *here, he would not ride a crane, / but would have his mount shake its head and wag its tail to make waves.*

Seals

Shoga tōitsu; *Kin*[illegible]; *Taikyo*; *Shinsō Yōgetsu*

120

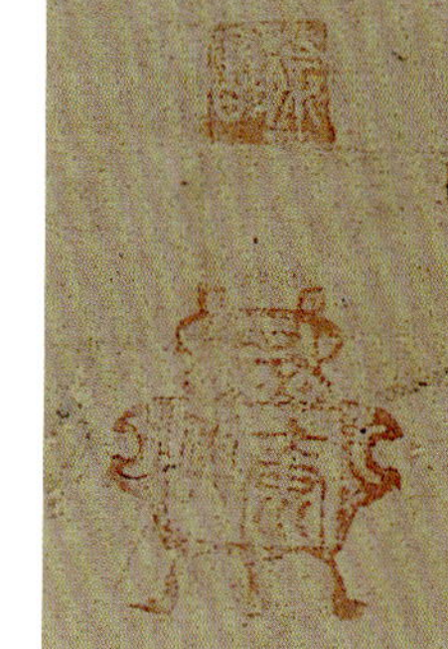

120

120

† 122. Orchids, Bamboo, Brambles, and Rocks

Text

by Tesshū Tokusai (d. 1366)

The Chu River runs a hundred thousand miles. / I think of you every now and then after our parting. / I wonder under the aloof orchids / how the two comparable to the national fragrance are faring.

Signature

An inscription for my own painting.

Seal

Tesshū

122

123

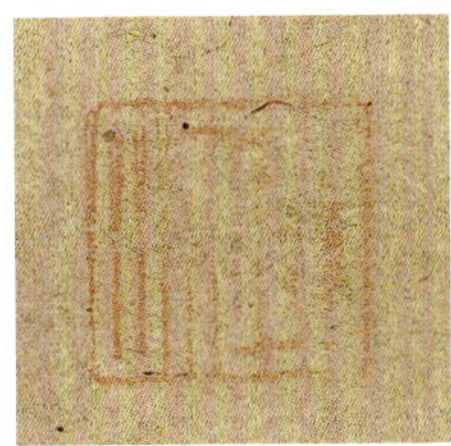

123

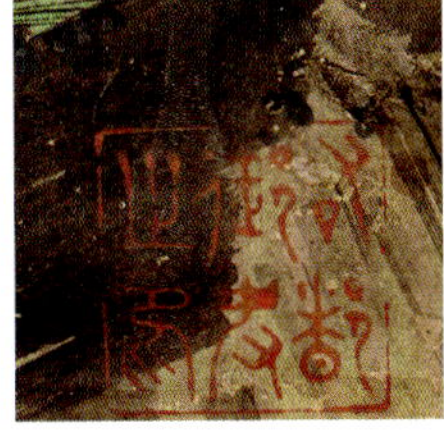

129

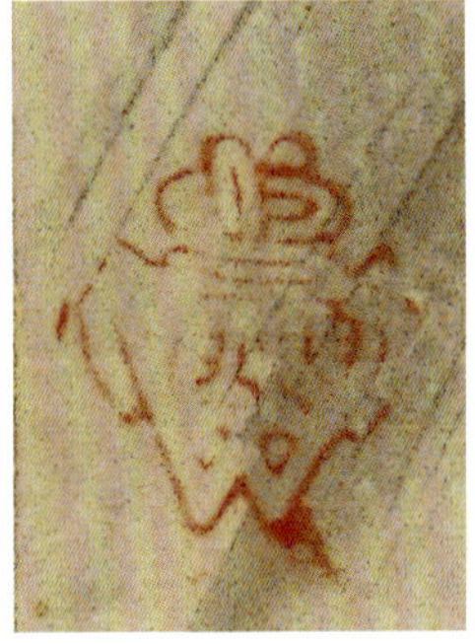

132

124

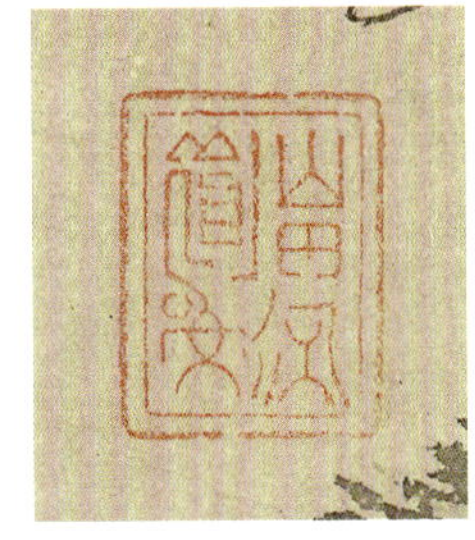

125

131

127

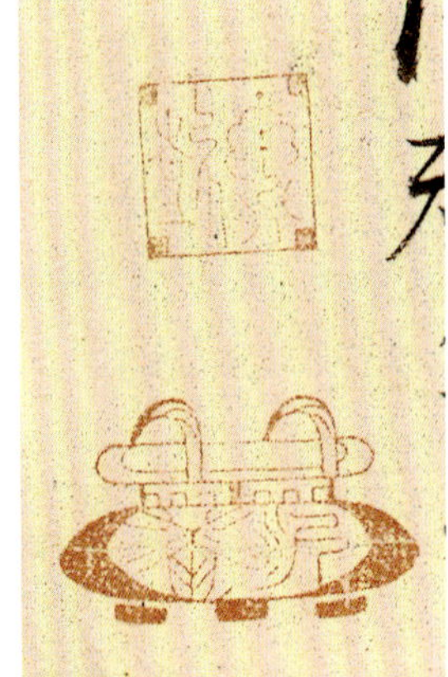

135

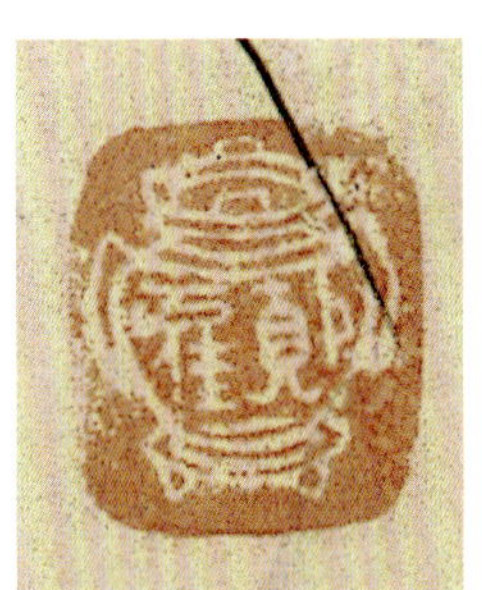

135

† 123. Orchids, Bamboo, and Brambles

Signature

[on right scroll] *Gyokuenshi painted the spirit*

Seals

[on each scroll] *Gyokuen*

† 124. Plum Blossoms

Text

by Motsurin Shōtō (d. 1491)

I walk over the stream and garden in search of flowers. / The plum tree stands tall and welcomes the immortals. / Its elegant appearance in winter surpasses its peers. / Fragrance that lingers even after three bathings is unique to this flower. / Peonies are supreme as the flowers of the rich, / jasmine is superior as the flower of purity. / But these are inferior to this earliest one of flowers, / for it captures the spring of myriad blossoms.

Seal

Shōtō

† 125. Melons

Seal

Yamada-shi Dōan

126. Landscape

Seals

Terutada; Ryūkyō

† 127. Birds and Flowers of Summer and Autumn

Seals

[on each scroll] *Ryūkyō*

† 129. Jakōneko

Seal

Uto Gyoshi no in

† 131. Bulbul on a Plum Tree; Geese and Reeds

Seals

[on each scroll] *Motonobu*

† 132. Pheasants and Azaleas; Golden Pheasants and a Loquat Tree

Seals

[on each scroll] *Naonobu*

† 135. Seiōgyū (Ch. Zhenghuangniu); Ikuzanshu (Ch. Yushanzhu)

Signature

[on right scroll] *Naizen painted this*

Seals

[on each scroll] *Ko*

Text

by Takuan Sōhō (1573–1645)

[right]

A man of the Way sits leisurely without a concern / astride a yellow ox, separated from the wind and dust [of this world]. / He has left the hermitage of his garden, / and from the ox's horn hangs a sprig of peony from the Yao or Wei.

Signature

Casually inscribed by the recluse monk Nanzan Takuan

Seals

Senhō; Gin'an

[left]

Having crossed the plank bridge over and again seeking emptiness in vain, / I embark on a journey with no destination in mind. / Blue mountains and green waters surround the equestrian; / the rights and wrongs in the transient world breeze past the horse's ears.

Signature

Painting of the Master of Mount Yu Riding a Donkey, casually inscribed by Sokuin Hissū Takuan

Seals

Senhō; Gin'an

---

† 137. River and Sky in Evening Snow, from *Eight Views of the Xiao and Xiang Rivers*

Seal

[lower left] *Yūshō*

Text

by Saishō Shōtai (1548–1607)

Ten thousand miles of river and sky send thoughts ten thousand miles away. / Blowy snowflakes fall like catkins over stretches of woods. / The bridge lay sideways; the road was blocked; the horse slipped. / Think further why he felt like turning around at the Lan Pass.

Signature

To the right is an old poem by Gyokukan [Ch. Yujian; fl. mid-13th c.] *transcribed by Shōtai.*

Seal

Saishō

---

† 138. Daruma

Seals

[lower right] *Unkoku; Tōgan*

Text

by Monk Shōsō

Though he grudgingly settled down under patronage, so what? / Taking his leave halfway, he traveled through Liang and Wei. /

Signature

Respectfully inscribed by Enson Biku Shōsō

Seals

Unkoku; Tōgan

---

† 139. Wagtail on a Rock

Seals

Unkoku; Tōgan

---

† 140. Tenjin Traveling to China

Text

by Nobutada

If just the heart is set on the path of truth, / even without prayers, will not gods protect me?

Signature

kaō

Seals

Two illegible seals

---

† 141. Landscape of the Four Seasons

Seals

[on each screen] *Unkoku; Tōgan*

137

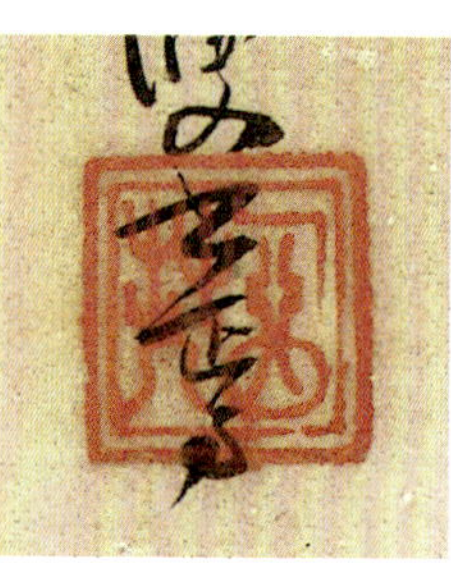

137

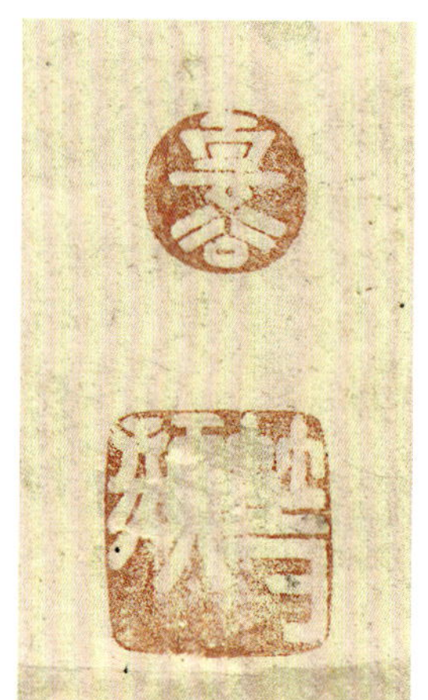

138

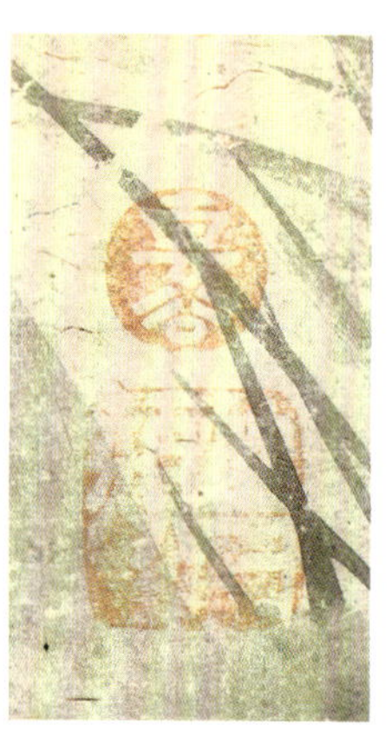

139

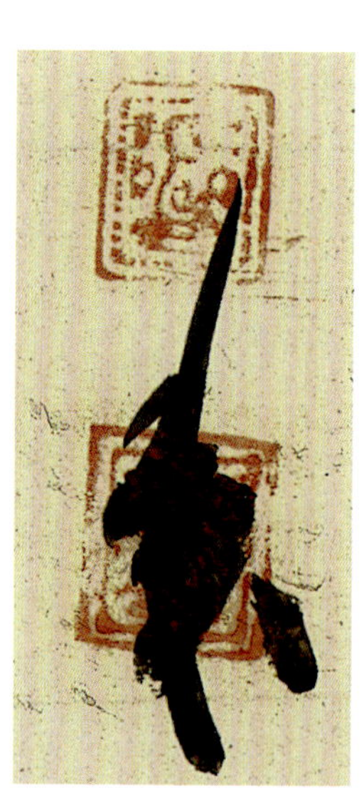

140

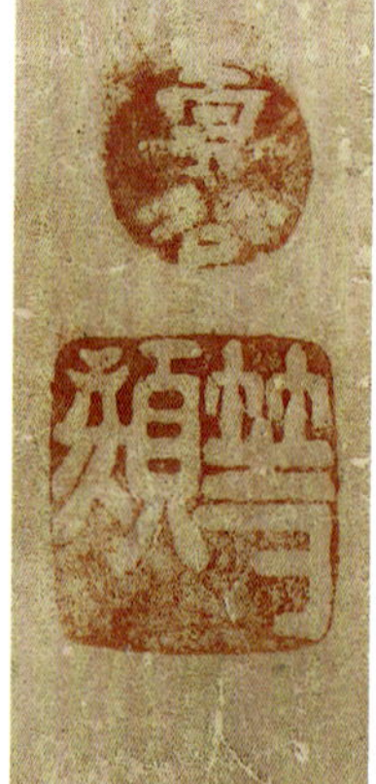

141

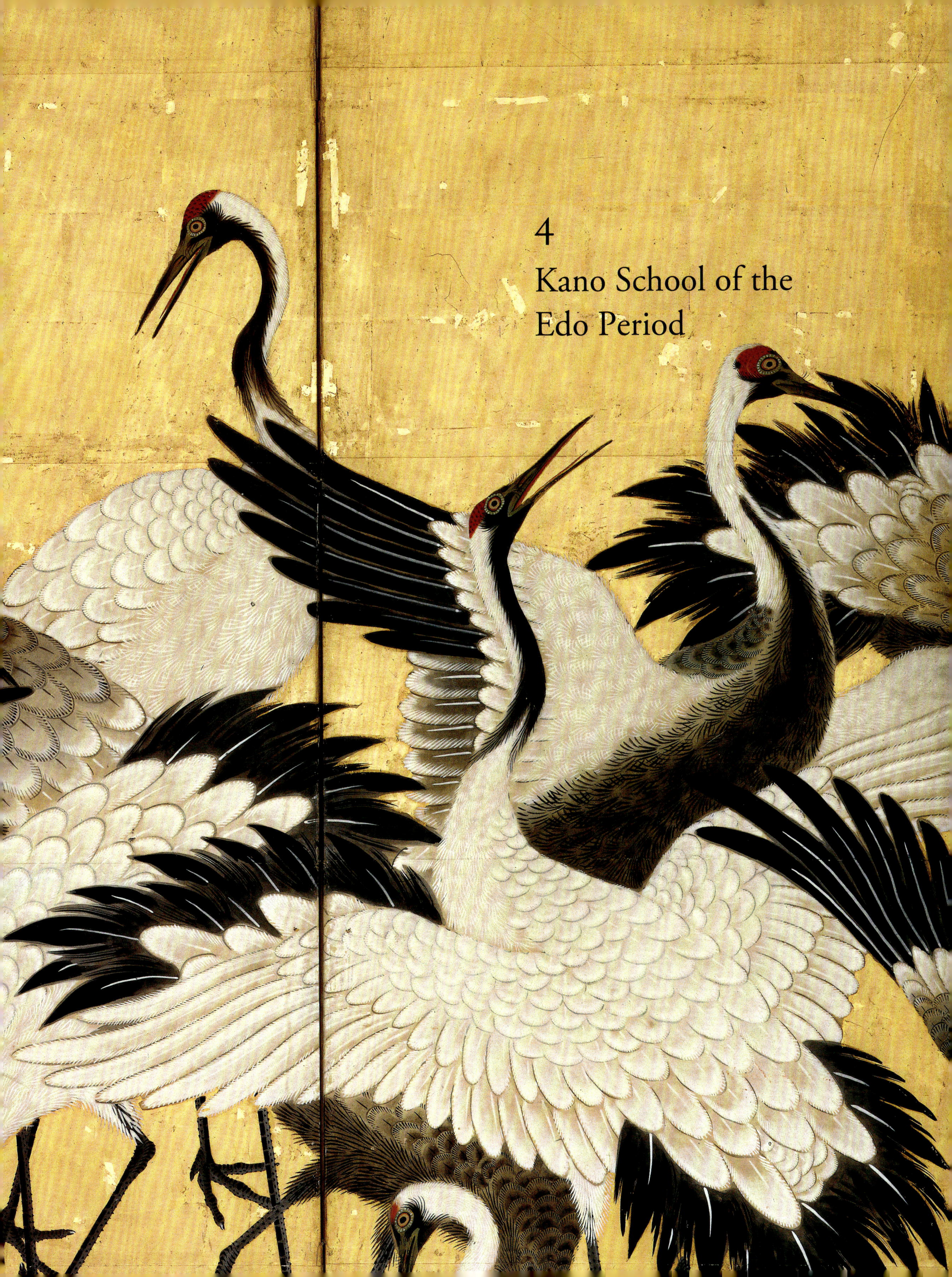

4
Kano School of the Edo Period

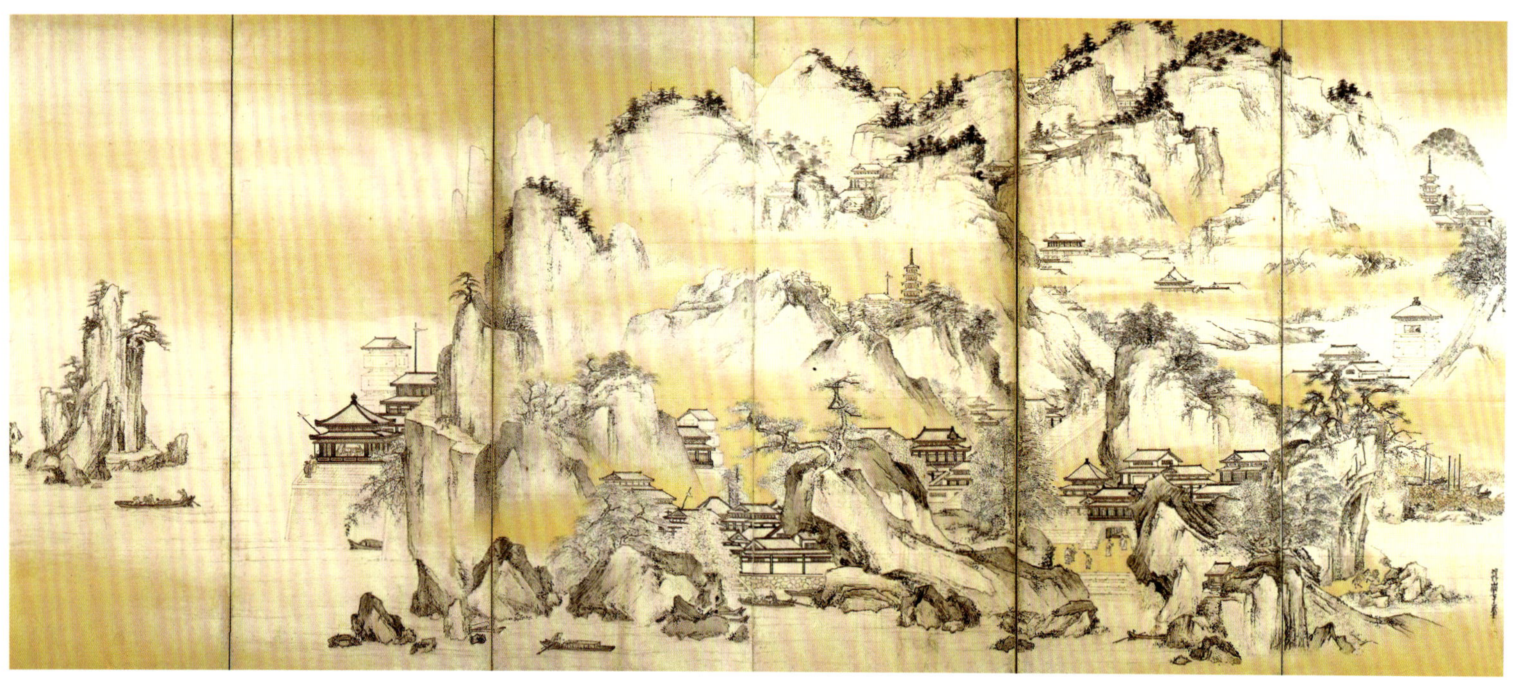

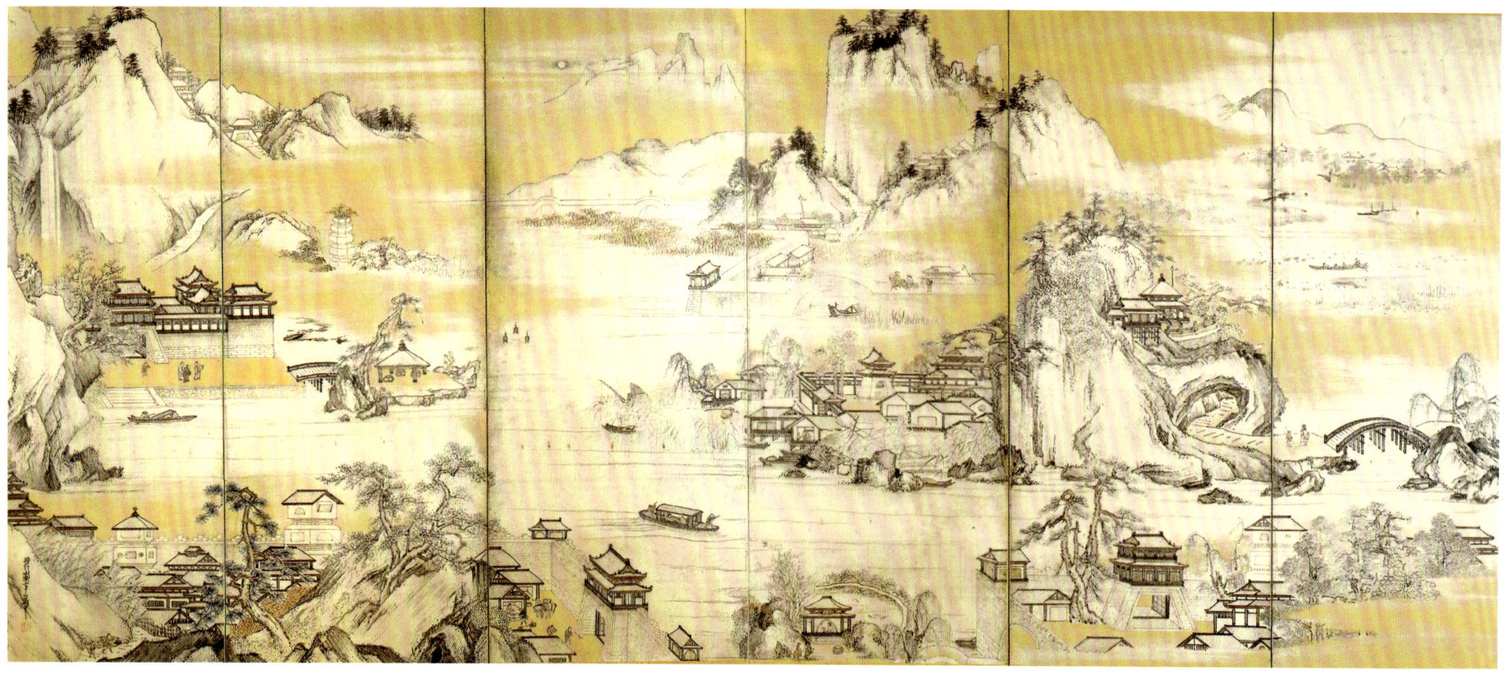

Kano Sanraku
(狩野山楽; 1559–1635)

142. View of West Lake (西湖)

Edo period, 17th century
Pair of six-panel screens; ink, light color, and gold on paper
Each screen 151.6 x 358.2 cm (59 5/8 in. x 11 ft. 9 in.)
Signatures, seals

Literature: Murase 1975, no. 44; Poster et al. 1999, no. 50; McKelway 2002, pp. 39–43; Tsuji Nobuo et al. 2005, no. 62.

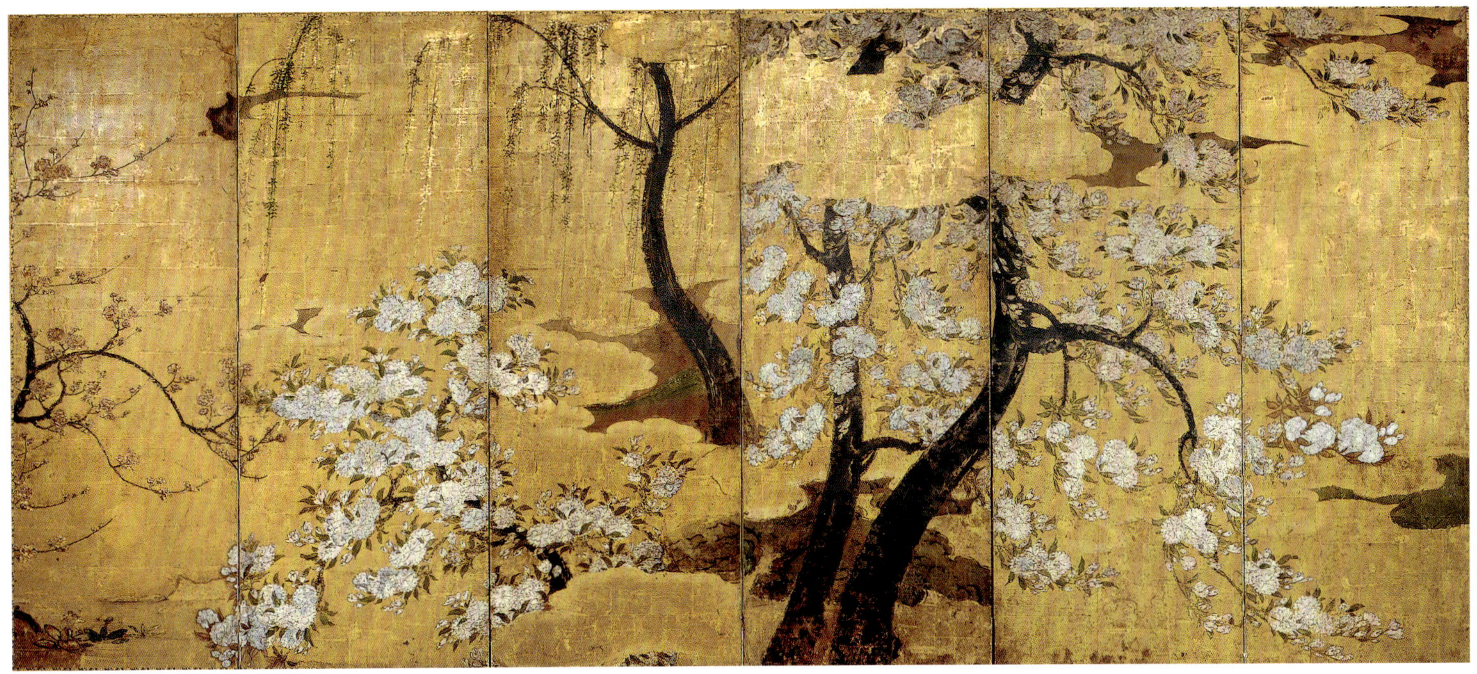

143. Cherry, Plum, and Willow Trees

Edo period, early 17th century
Six-panel folding screen; ink and color on gilded paper
153.4 x 349.4 cm (60 3/8 in. x 11 ft. 5 1/2 in.)
The Metropolitan Museum of Art, New York (2003.334)

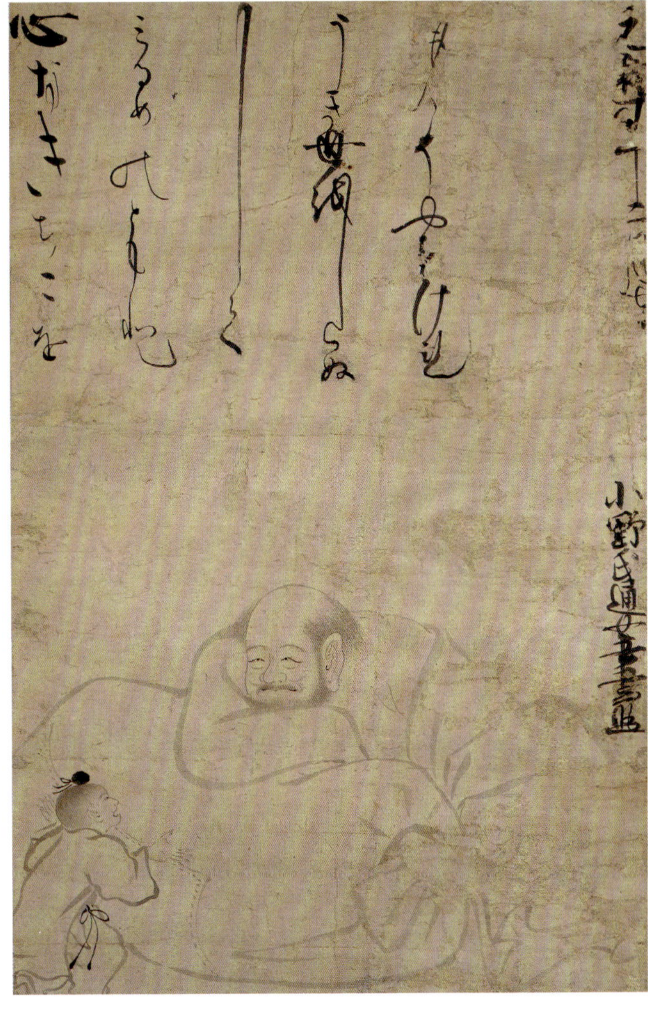

Ono Otsū
(小野お通; 1568–ca. 1631)

144. Hotei (布袋) with a Child

Edo period, 1624
Hanging scroll; ink on paper
63 x 41 cm (24 3/4 x 16 1/8 in.)
Text, signature, seal

Literature: Tokyo National Museum 1985a, no. 75; Avitabile 1990, no. 80; Tsuji Nobuo et al. 2005, no. 65.

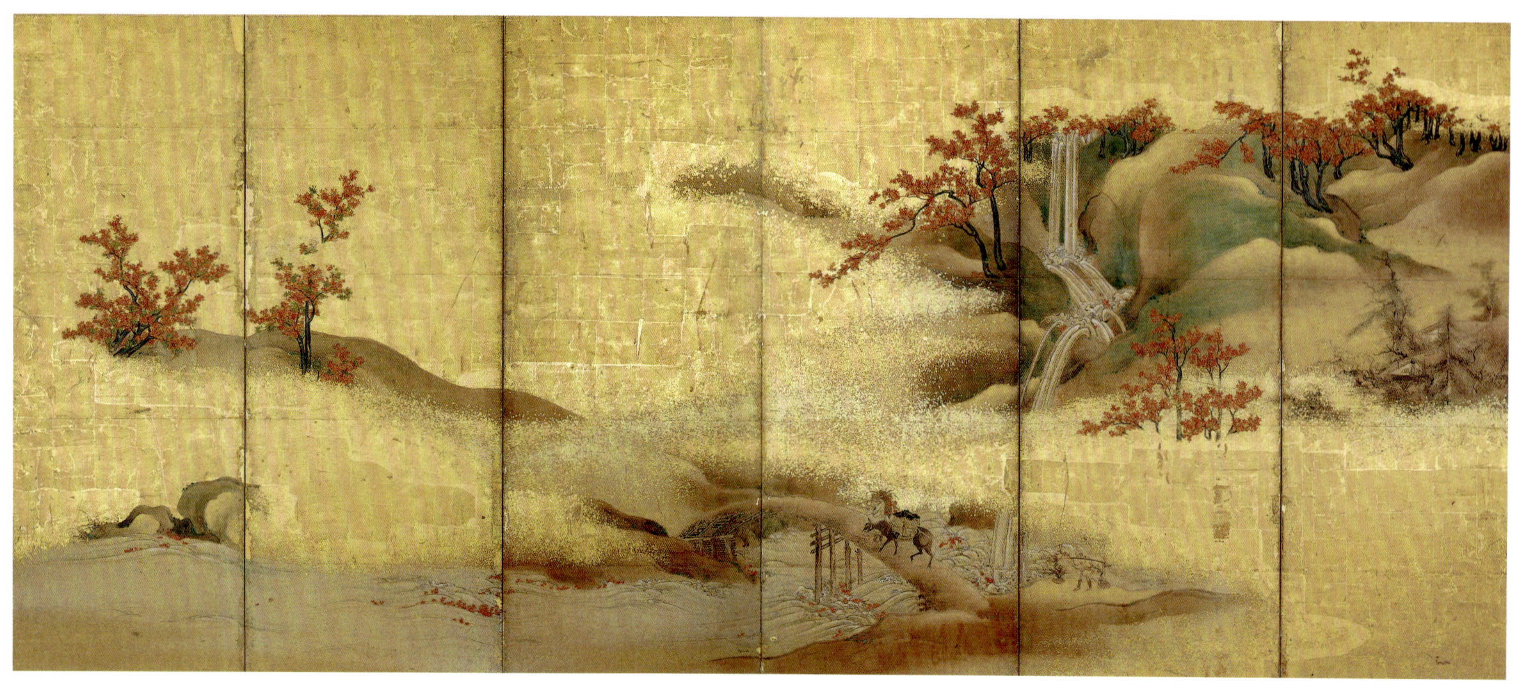

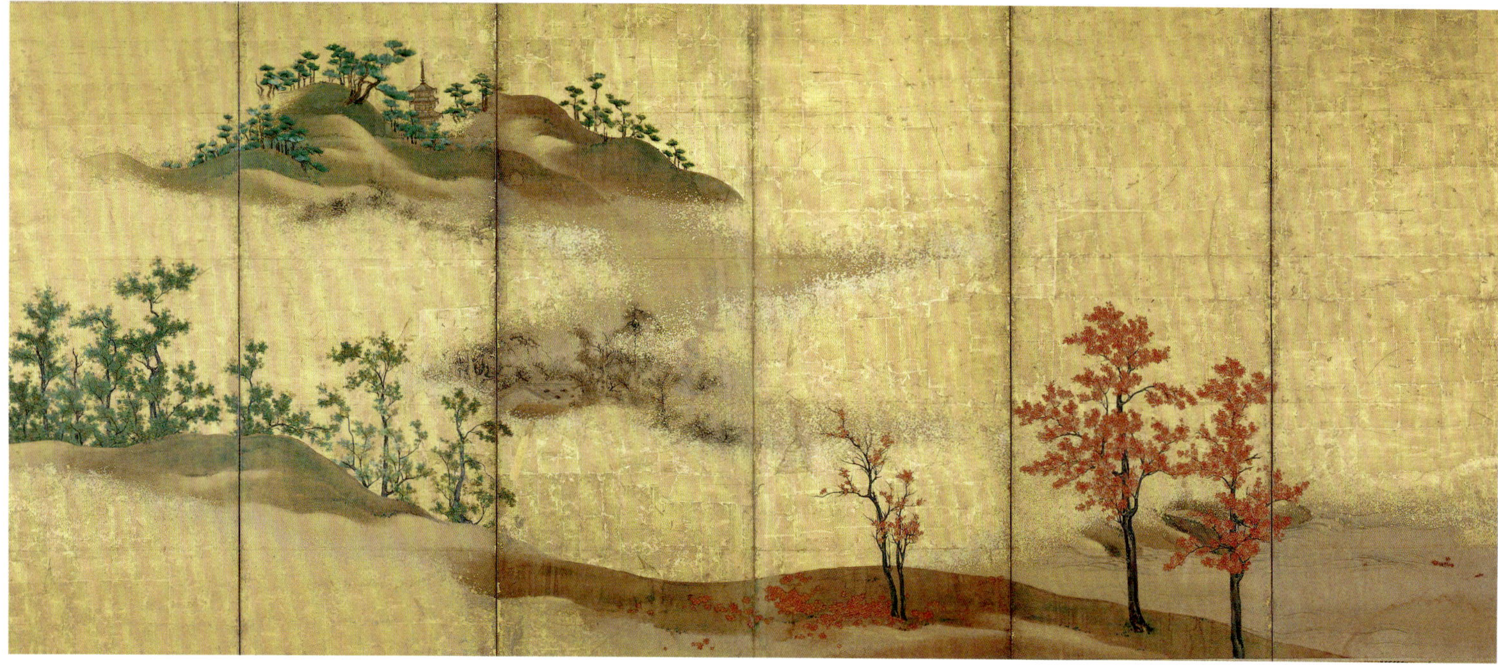

145. Mountains and River in Autumn

Edo period, first half of 17th century
Pair of six-panel folding screens; ink and color on gilded paper
Each screen 172.7 x 381 cm (68 in. x 12 ft. 6 in.)

LITERATURE: Avitabile 1990, no. 51; Murase 1993, no. 51.

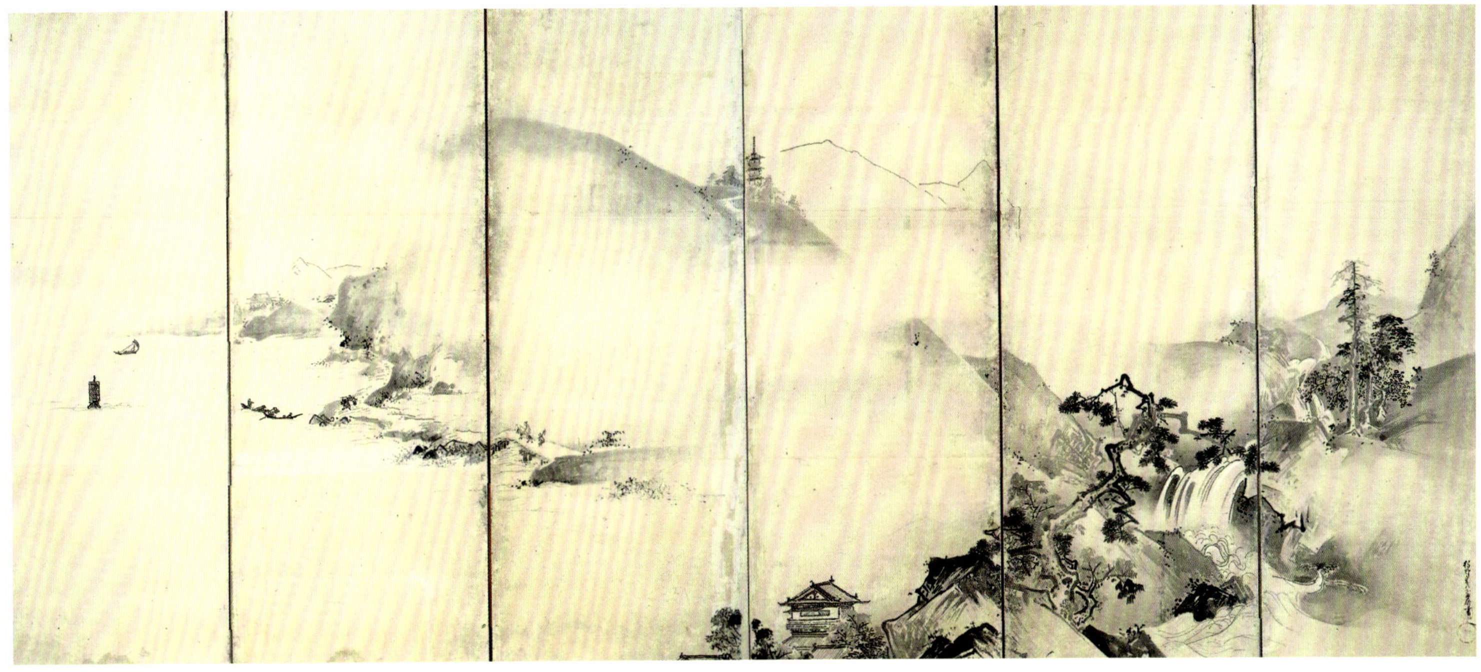

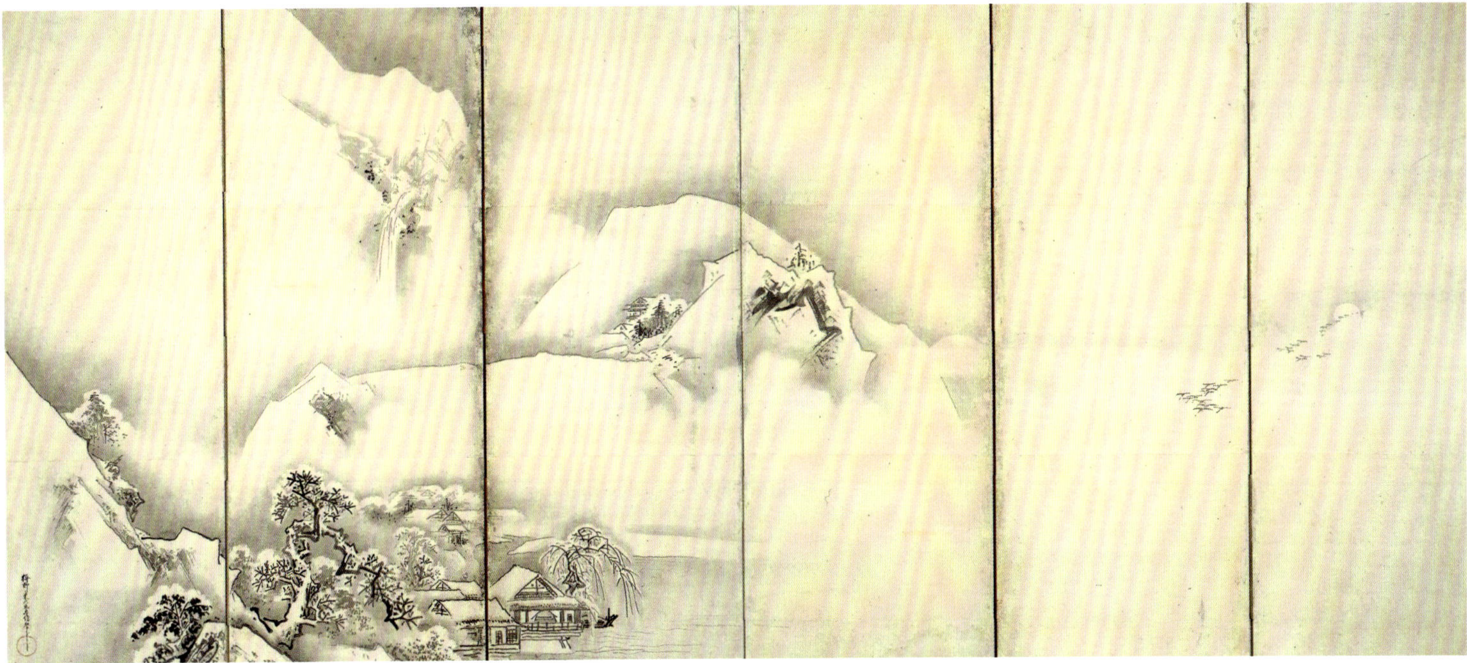

Kano Tan'yū
(狩野探幽; 1602–1674)

146. Landscapes of the Four Seasons

Edo period, 1630s
Pair of six-panel folding screens; ink and light color on paper
Each screen 153.5 x 352.6 cm (60³/₈ in. x 11 ft. 6⁷/₈ in.)
Signatures, seals

Ex coll.: Myōkakuji, Kyoto; Matsukata Iwao, Tokyo

Literature: "Sansui zu byōbu" 1910; Kihara Toshie 1995, fig. 6; Kihara Toshie 1998, pp. 97, 132, fig. 11; Murase 2000, no. 107.

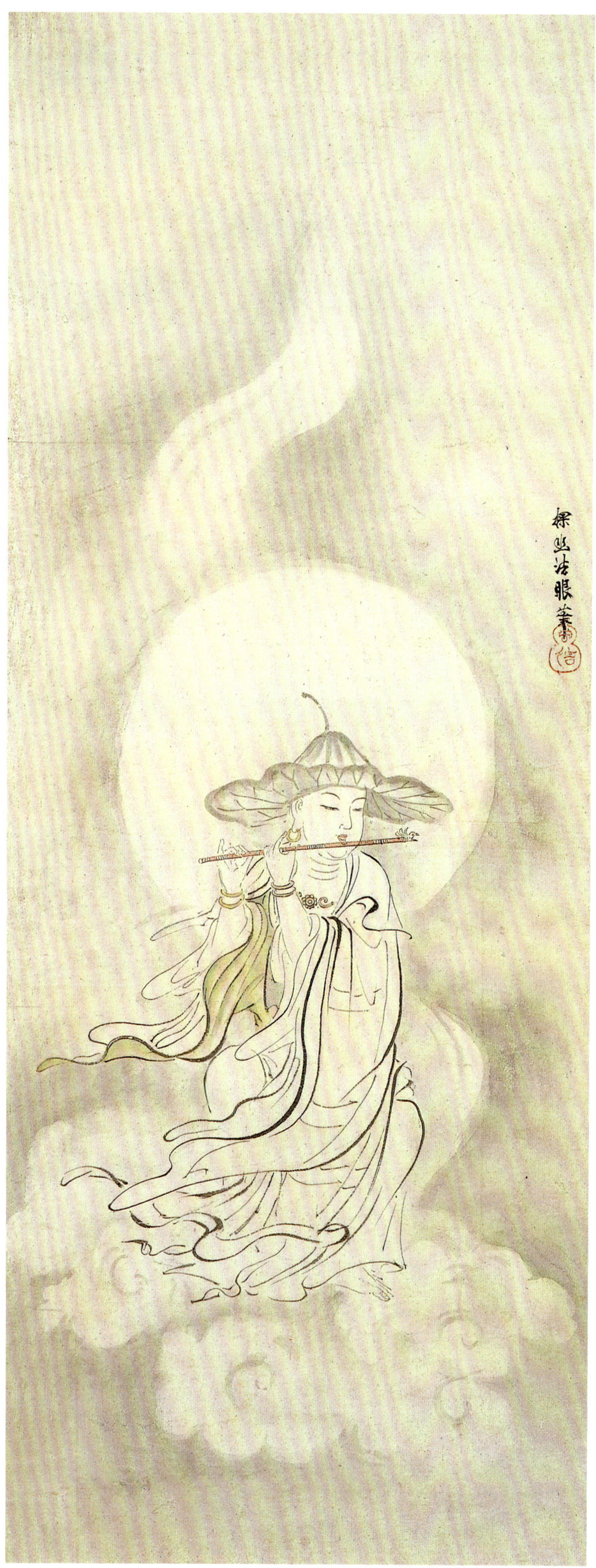

Kano Tan'yū
(狩野探幽; 1602–1674)

147. Jizō Playing a Flute (笛吹地蔵)

Edo period, 1639–62
Hanging scroll; ink and light color on paper
99 x 38.9 cm (39 x $15\frac{3}{8}$ in.)
Signature, seal

Ex coll.: Matsukata Iwao

Literature: Iizuka Beiu 1932a, pl. 58; Takeda Tsuneo 1978b, no. 21; Kōno Motoaki 1982b, fig. 72; Burke 1985, fig. 7; Tokyo National Museum 1985a, no. 33; Japan Society Gallery 1989, no. 11; Avitabile 1990, no. 75; Nakahashi 1990, fig. 1; Kobayashi Tadashi and Kano Hiroyuki 1992, no. 9; Kōno Motoaki 1993, no. 24; Yasumura Toshinobu 1998, no. 24; Kobayashi Tadashi 2000, p. 29; Murase 2000, no. 108; Nakahashi 2002, pp. 37–42, no. 1286; Tsuji Nobuo et al. 2005, no. 66; Nishigōri Ryōsuke 2006.

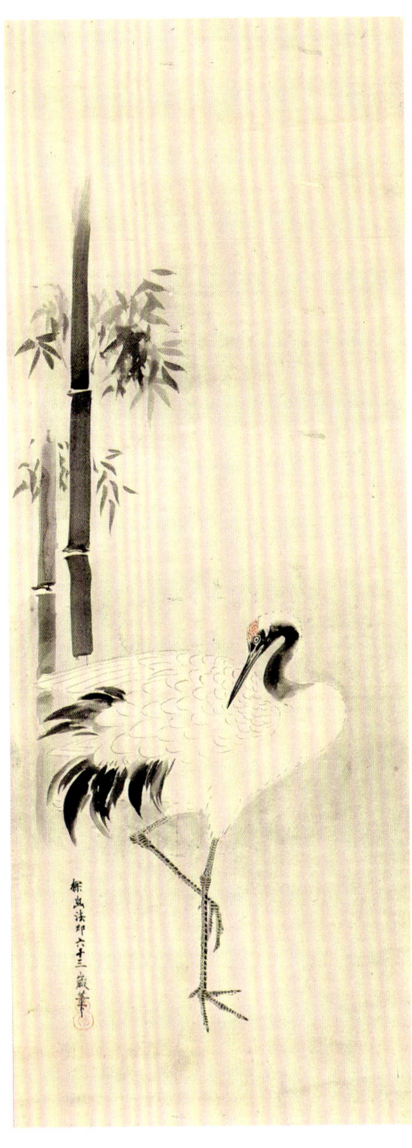

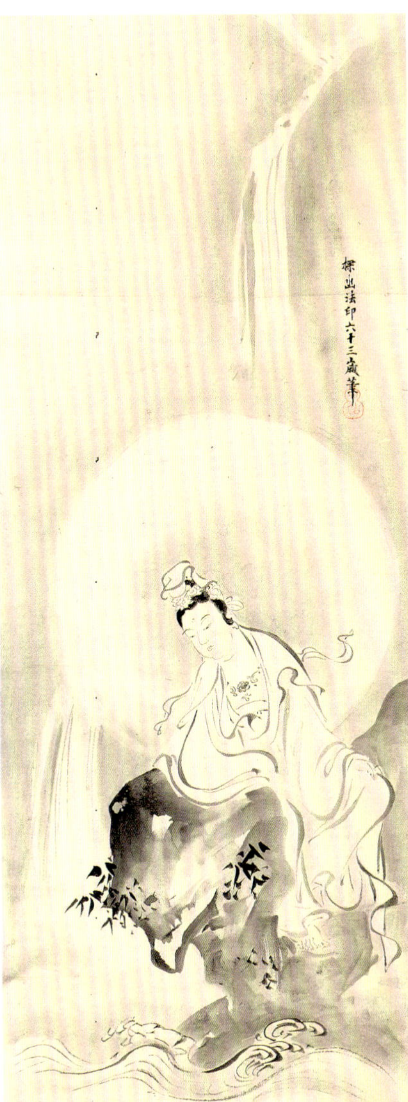

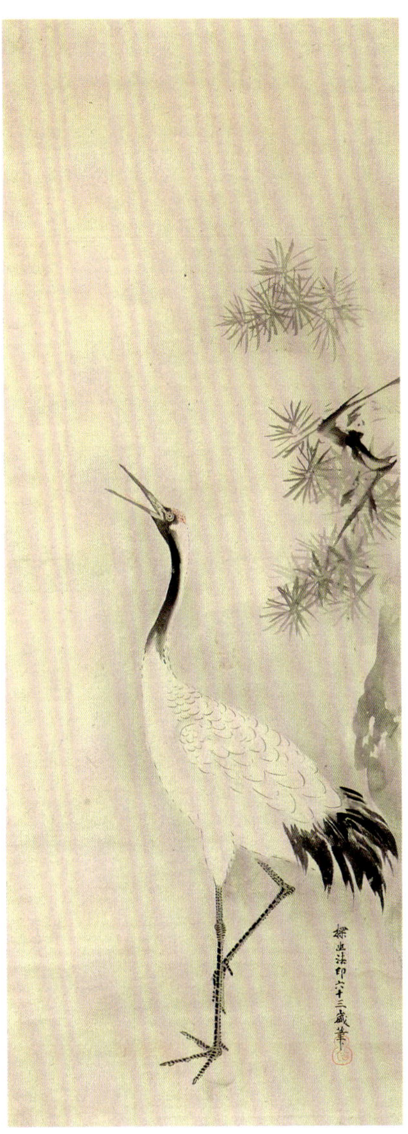

Kano Tan'yū
(狩野探幽; 1602–1674)

148. Triptych of White-Robed Kannon (白衣観音) and Cranes (鶴)

Edo period, 1664
Triptych of hanging scrolls; ink on paper (Kannon), ink and light color on paper (cranes)
112.8 x 42.3 cm ($44^{3}/_{8}$ x $16^{5}/_{8}$ in.)
Signatures, seals

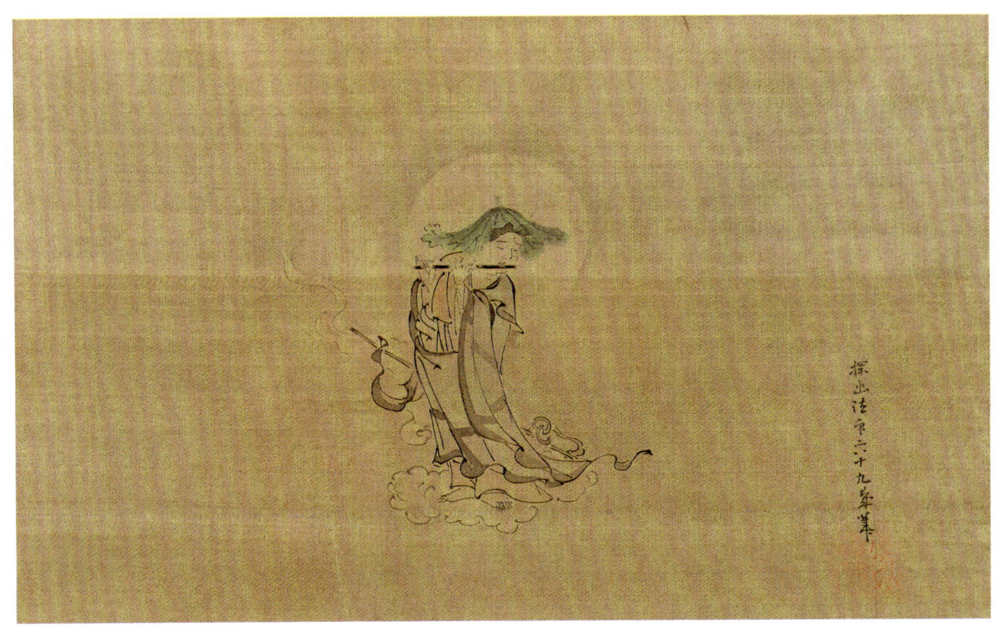

Kano Tan'yū
(狩野探幽; 1602–1674)

149. Jizō Playing a Flute (笛吹地蔵)

Edo period, 1670
Hanging scroll; ink and light color on silk
21.4 x 36 cm ($8^{3}/_{8}$ x $14^{1}/_{8}$ in.)
Signature, seal

Literature: Tsuji Nobuo et al. 2005, no. 67.

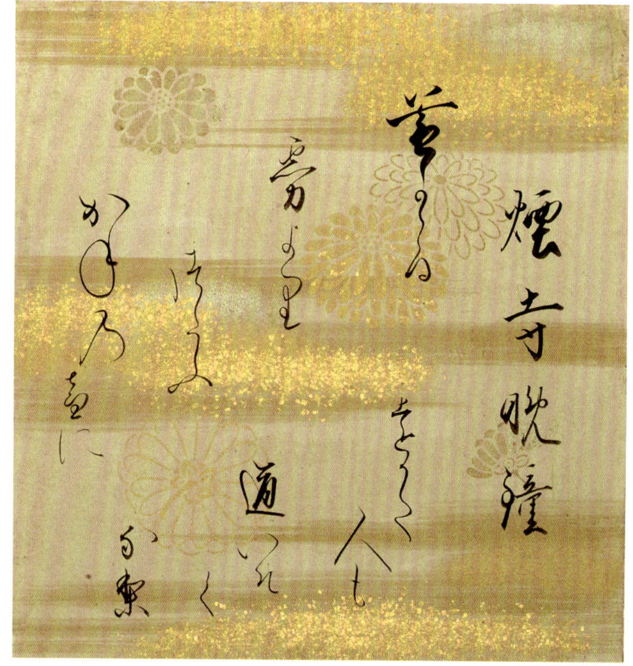

Kano Tan'yū
(狩野探幽; 1602–1674)

150. Evening Bell at the Temple in Smoky Mist, from *Eight Views of the Xiao and Xiang Rivers* (瀟湘八景)

Edo period
Album with eight leaves of painting and eight leaves of calligraphy
Painting: ink on silk
17.8 x 17.4 cm (7 x $6\frac{7}{8}$ in.)
Calligraphy: ink on decorated paper
19.5 x 18.5 cm ($7\frac{5}{8}$ x $7\frac{1}{4}$ in.)
Text, seals

Literature: Burke 1993, pp. 32–35, fig. 9/no. 21.

attributed to Kano Tan'yū
(狩野探幽; 1602–1674)

151. Kensu (蜆子)

Edo period
Hanging scroll; ink on paper
28.2 x 51.3 cm ($11\frac{1}{8}$ x $20\frac{1}{4}$ in.)
Signature, seal

Literature: Tsuji Nobuo et al. 2005, no. 68.

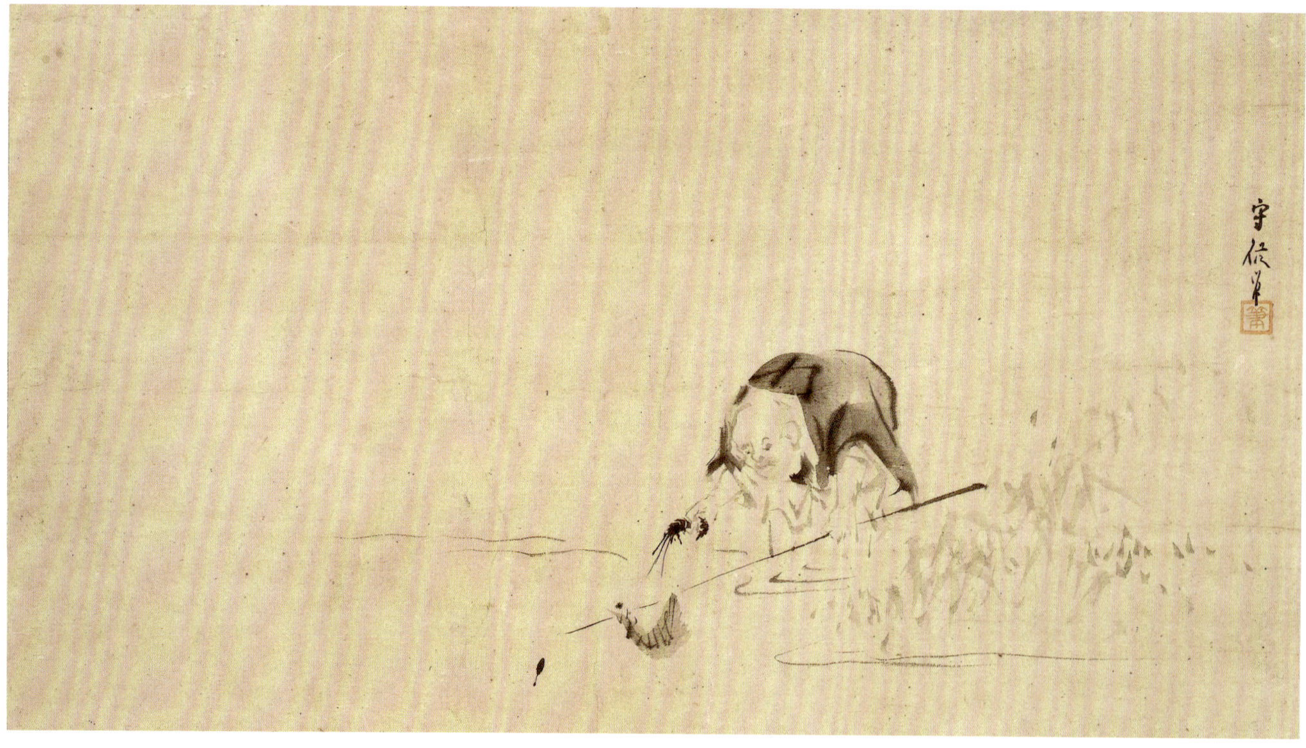

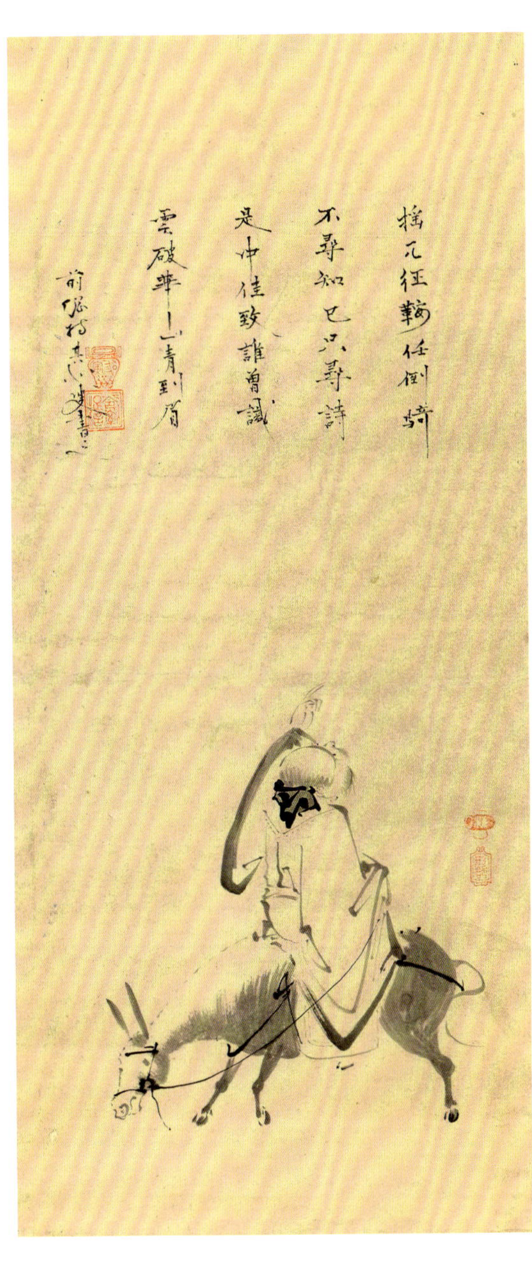

Kano Kōya
(狩野興也; d. 1673)

152. Hanrō (Ch. Fan Lang, 潘閬)

Edo period
Hanging scroll; ink on paper
91.3 x 40.8 cm (36 x 16 1/8 in.)
Text, signature, seals

Kano Tōun
(狩野洞雲; 1625–1694)

153. Autumn Moon over Lake Dongting, from *Eight Views of the Xiao and Xiang Rivers* (瀟湘八景)

Edo period, 1675
Handscroll; ink and light color on paper
27 x 513.3 cm (10 5/8 in. x 16 ft. 10 1/8 in.)
Text, signature, seal

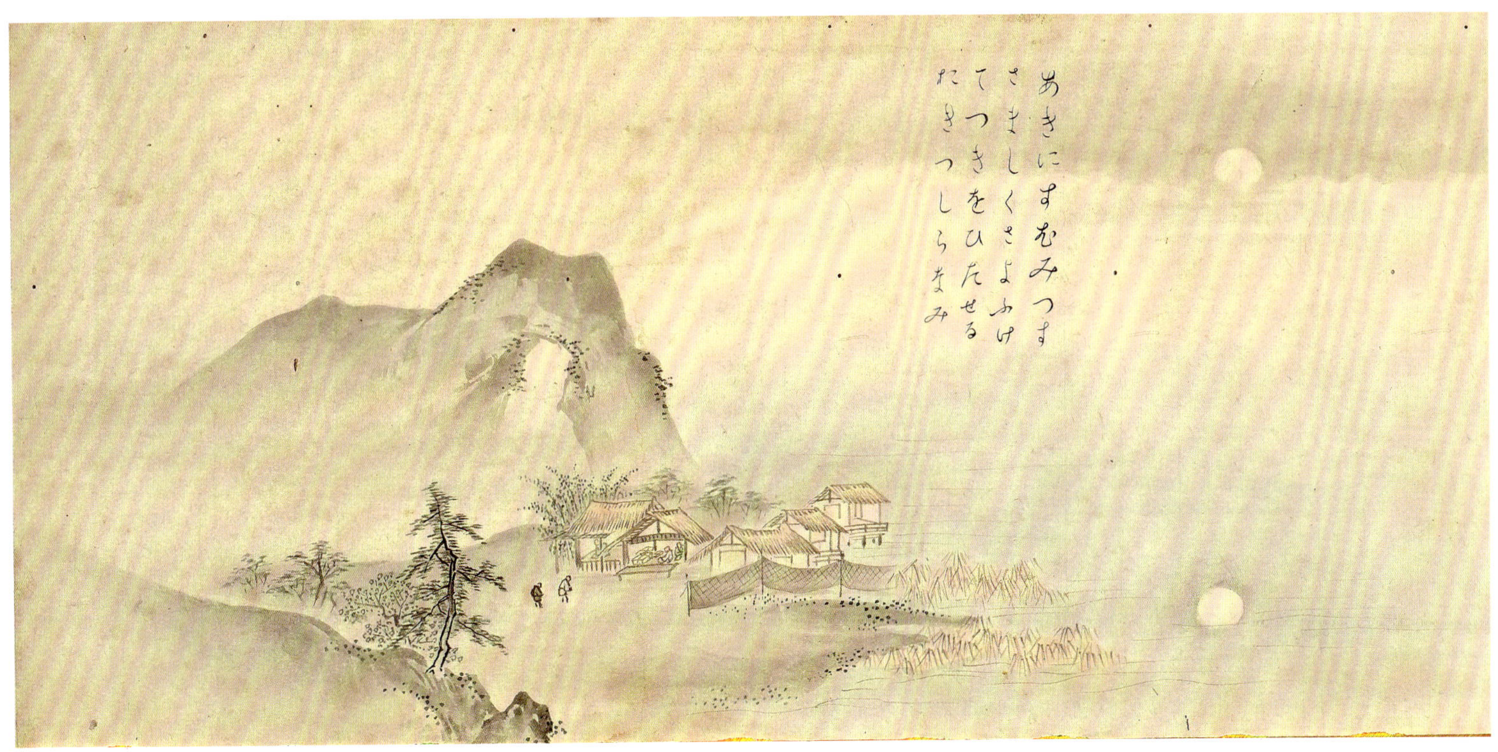

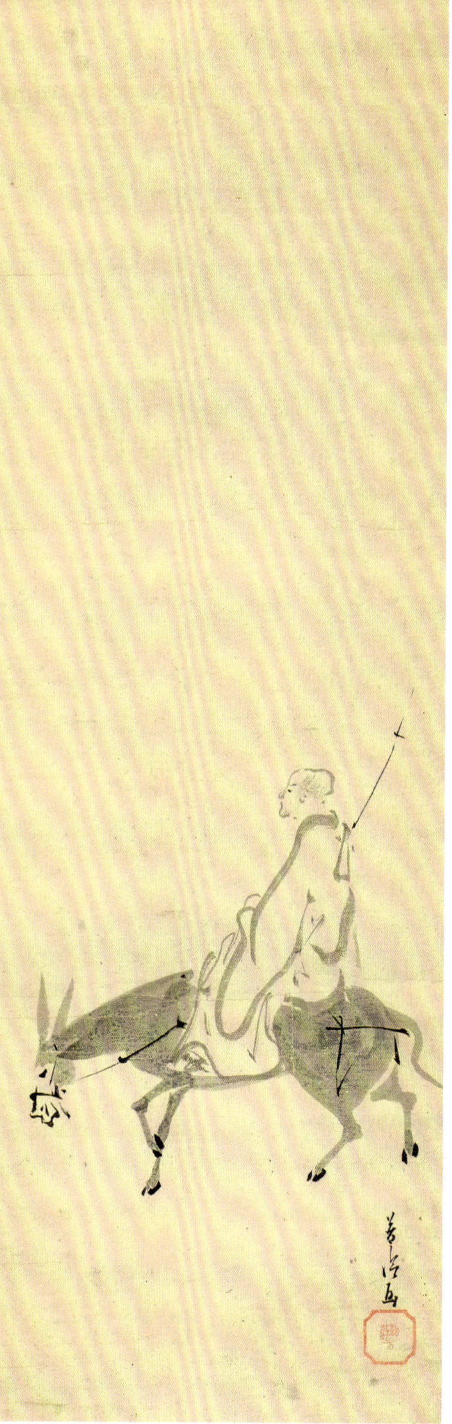

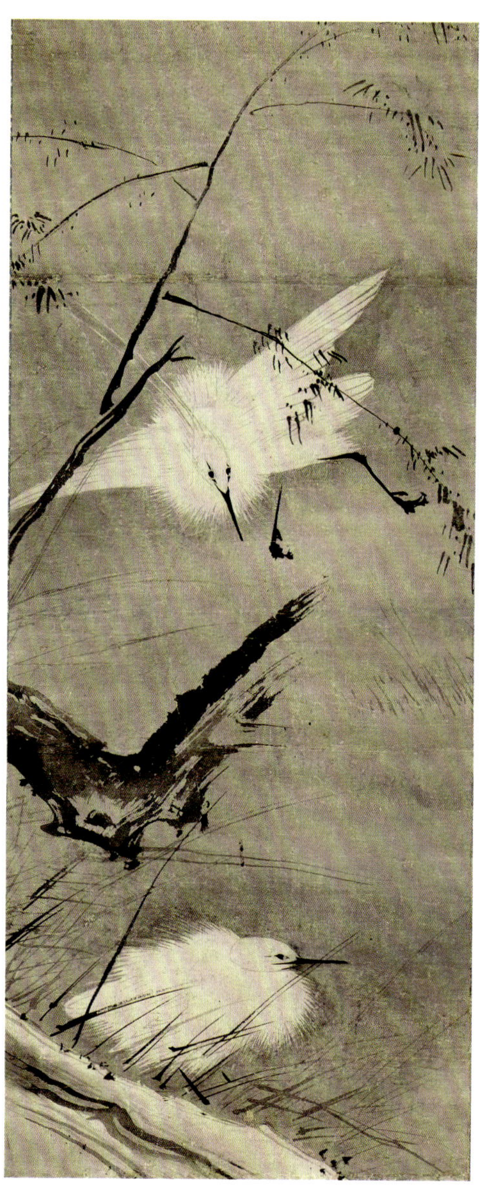

Kano Tōun
(狩野洞雲; 1625–1694)

154. Ikuzanshu (Ch. Yushanzhu, 郁山主);
Seiōgyū (Ch. Zhenghuangniu, 政黄牛)

Edo period
Diptych of hanging scrolls; ink on paper
Each scroll 87 x 26.8 cm (34 1/4 x 10 1/2 in.)
Signatures, seals

155. Herons

Edo period, 17th century
Hanging scroll; ink on paper
83.3 x 34.6 cm (32 3/4 x 13 5/8 in.)

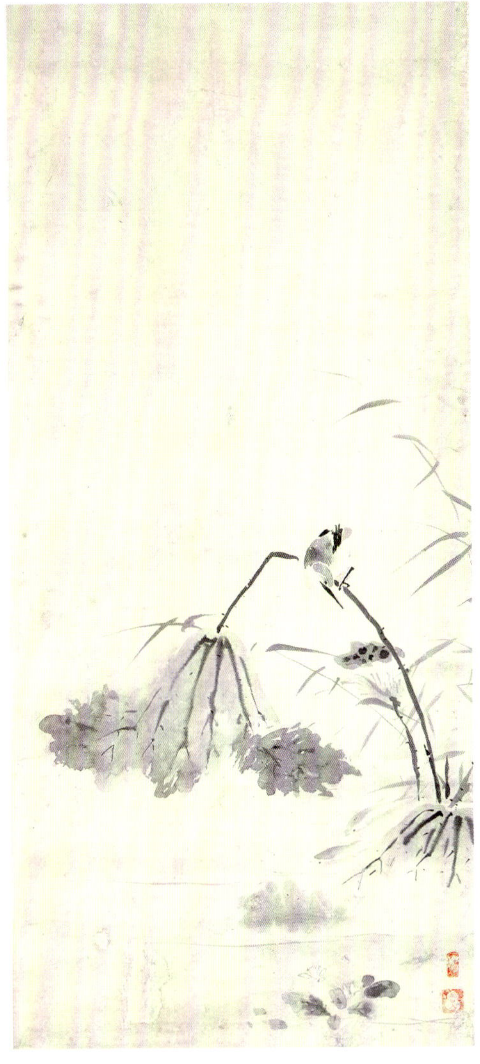

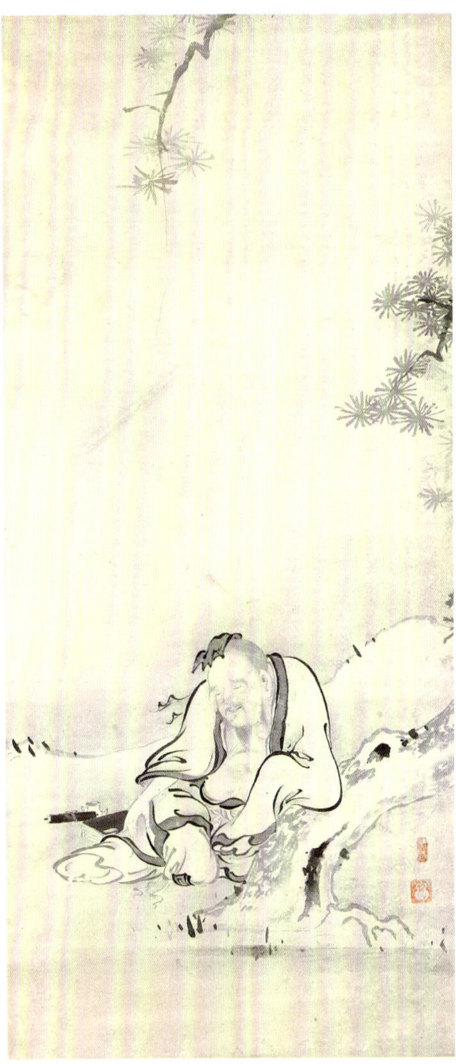

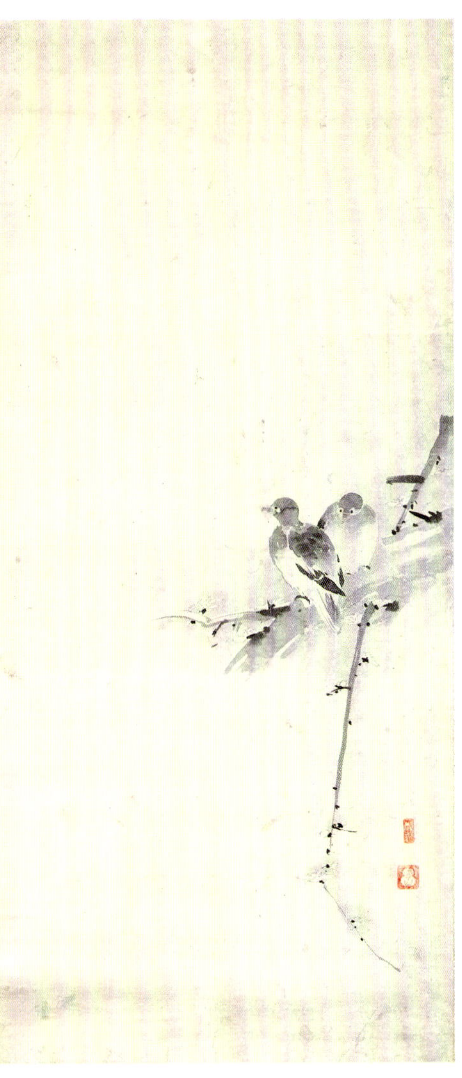

SETSUZAN
(雪山; fl. 17th century)

156. Hermit; Doves on a Plum Tree; Kingfisher with Lotus

Edo period
Triptych of hanging scrolls; ink on paper
Each scroll 111.7 x 50.4 cm (44 x 19 7/8 in.)
Seals

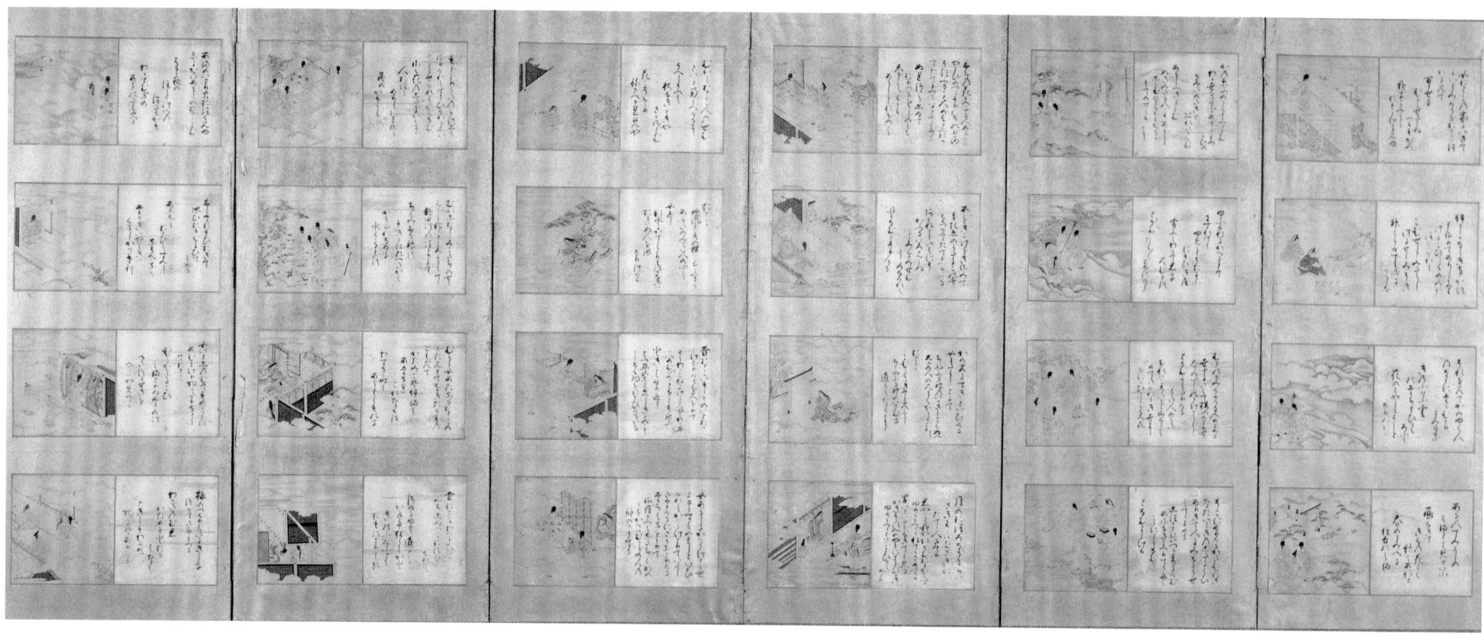

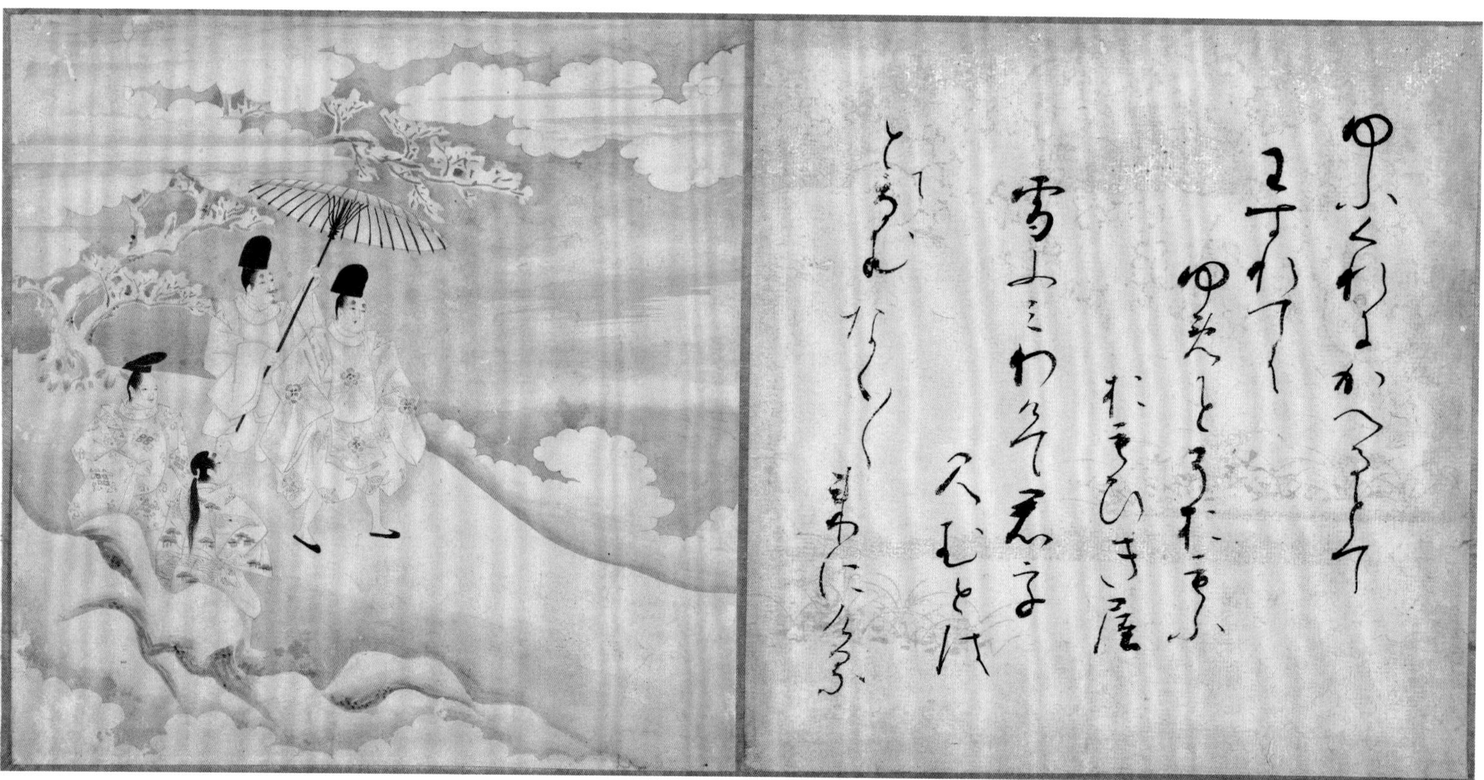

Episode 83

157. Forty-nine scenes from *Ise monogatari* (伊勢物語), with calligraphy attributed to Satomura Genchin (里村玄陳; 1591–1665)

Edo period, mid-17th century
Pair of six-panel folding screens, with 98 *shikishi* of paintings and text; ink and red ink on paper (paintings); ink on paper (text)
Each screen 107.2 x 269 cm (42¼ in. x 8 ft. 9⅞ in.)
Text

LITERATURE: Avitabile 1990, no. 70.

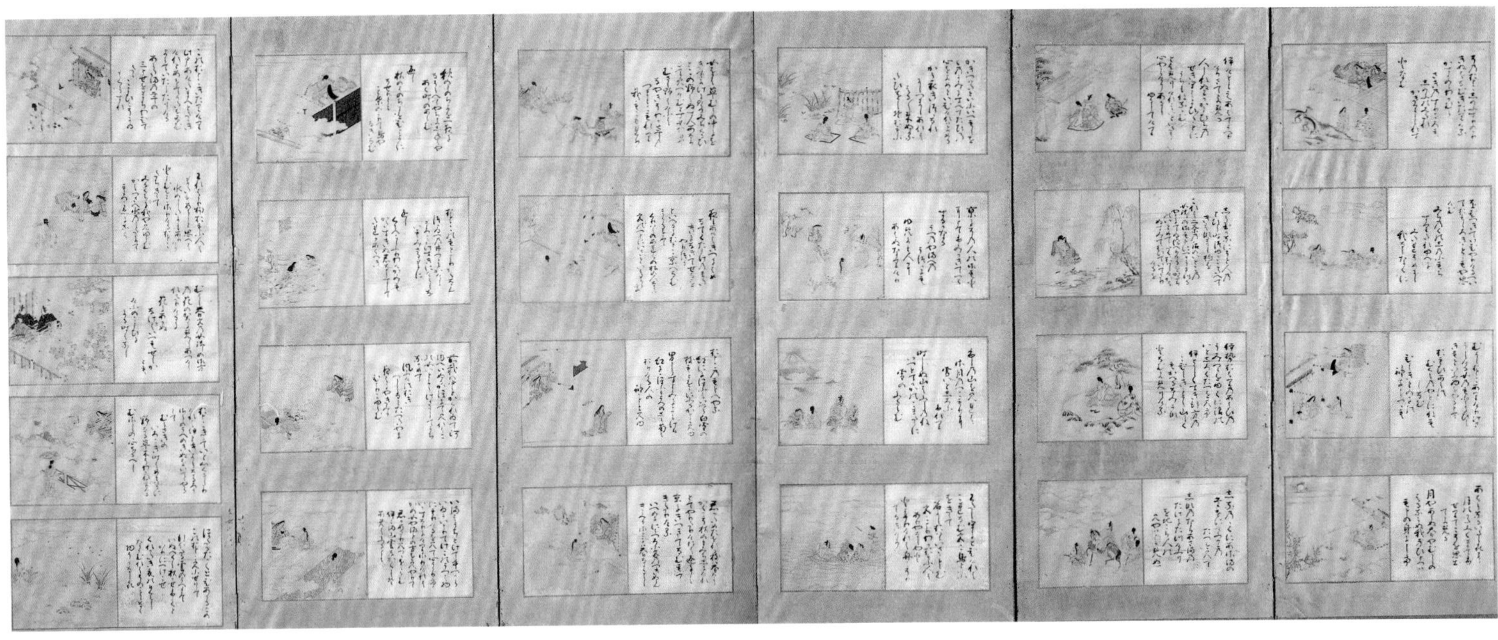

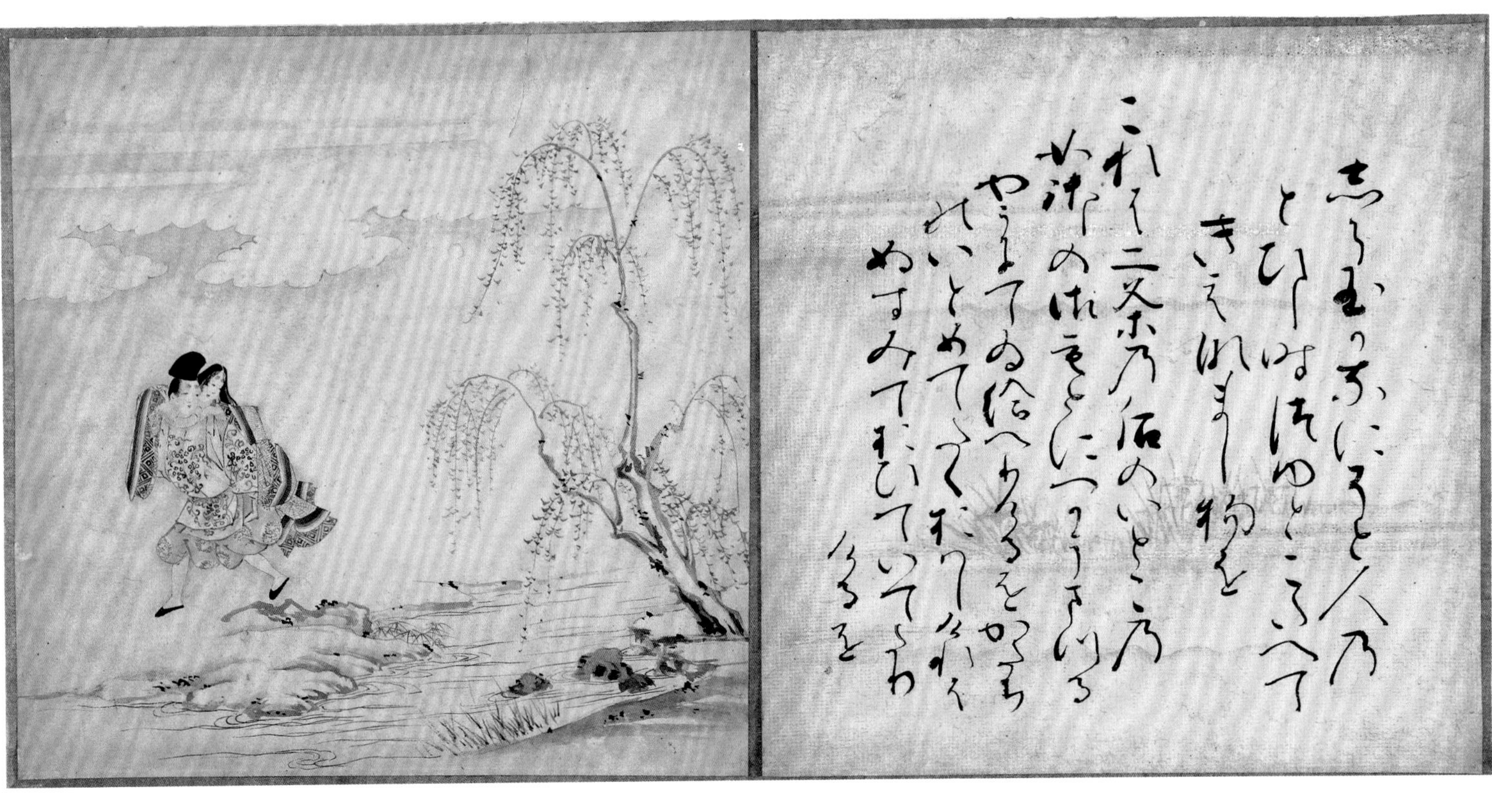

Episode 6

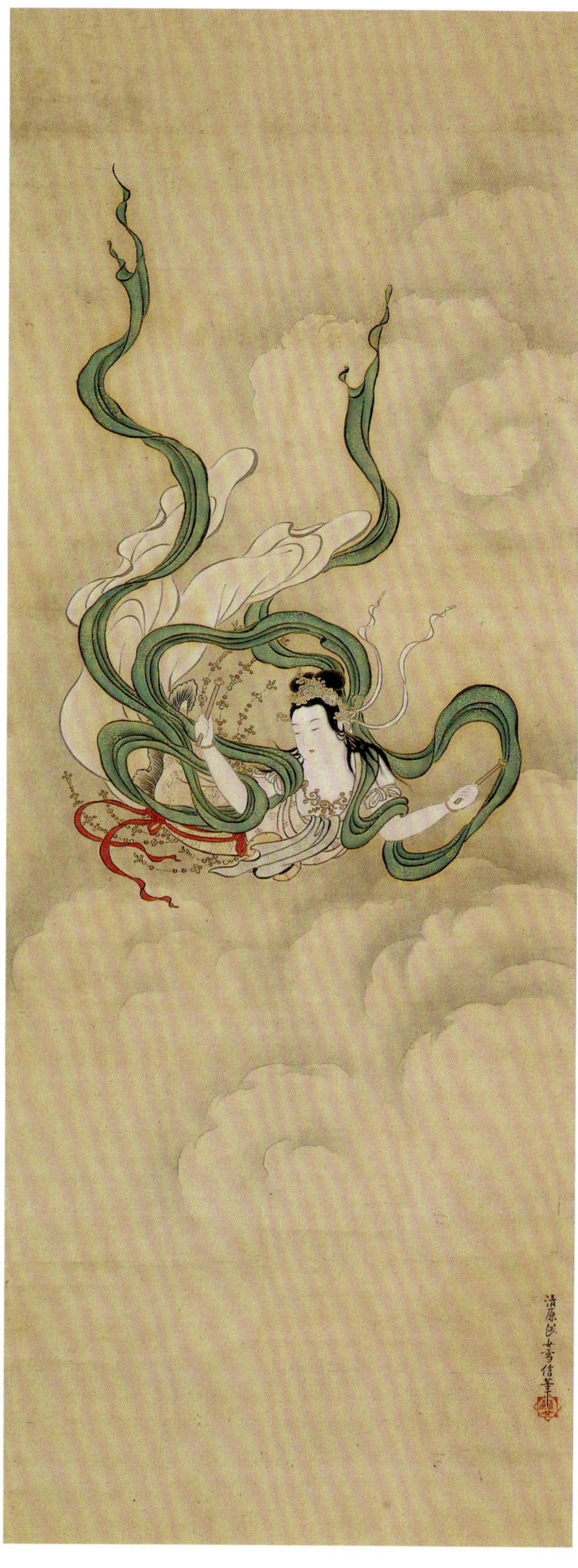

Kiyohara Yukinobu
(清原雪信; 1643–1682)

158. Apsaras (飛天)

Edo period
Hanging scroll; ink and color on silk
116.8 x 44.8 cm (46 x 17⅝ in.)
Signature, seal

Literature: Fister 1988, p. 38, no. 5.

Kiyohara Yukinobu
(清原雪信; 1643–1682)

159. Monju on a Lion (騎獅文殊)

Edo period
Hanging scroll; ink and color on silk
60.9 x 36 cm (24 x 14⅛ in.)
Signature, seal

Literature: Avitabile 1990, no. 76; Burke 1993, fig. 5/no. 4.

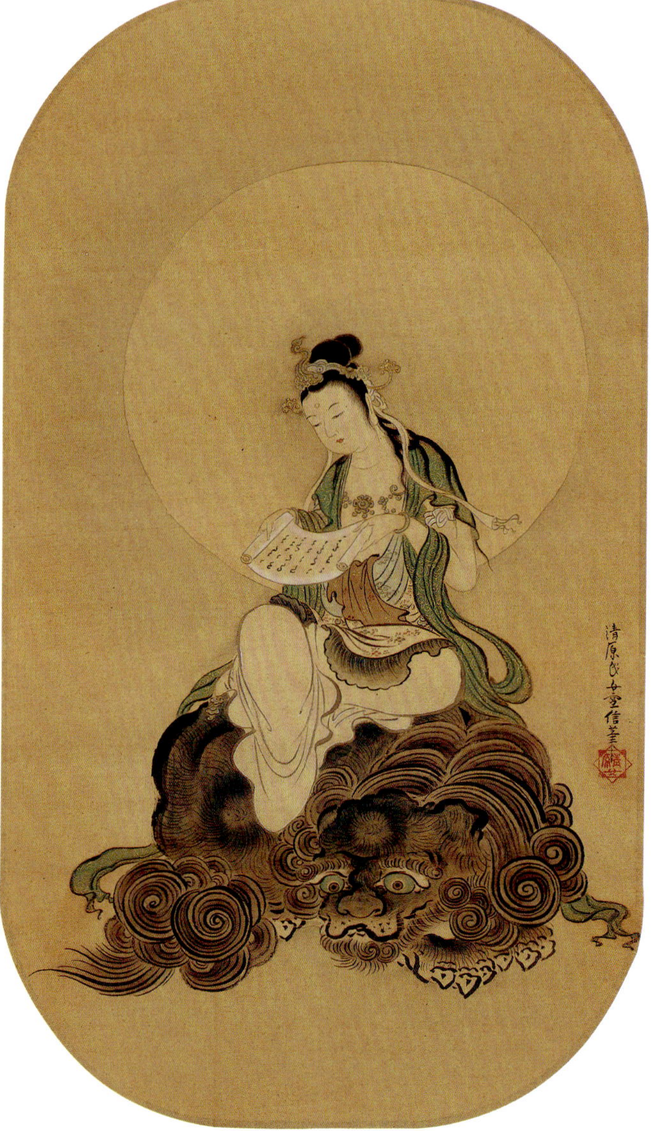

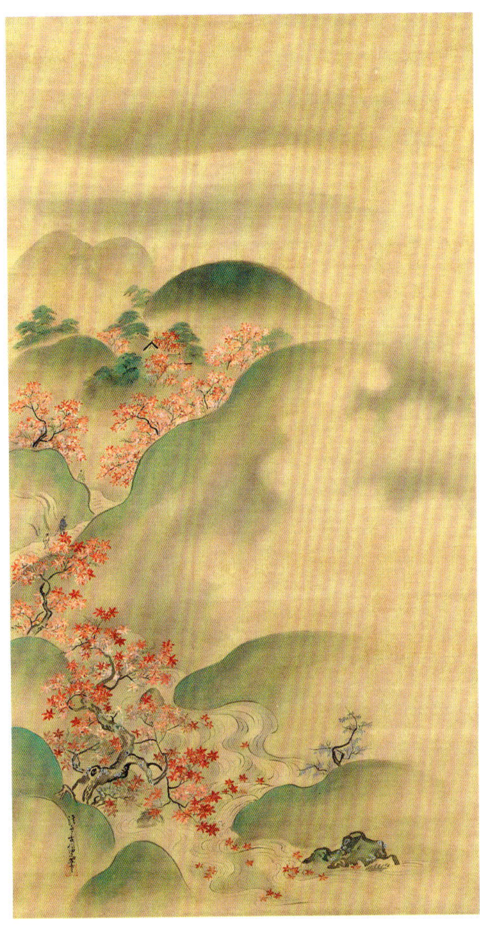
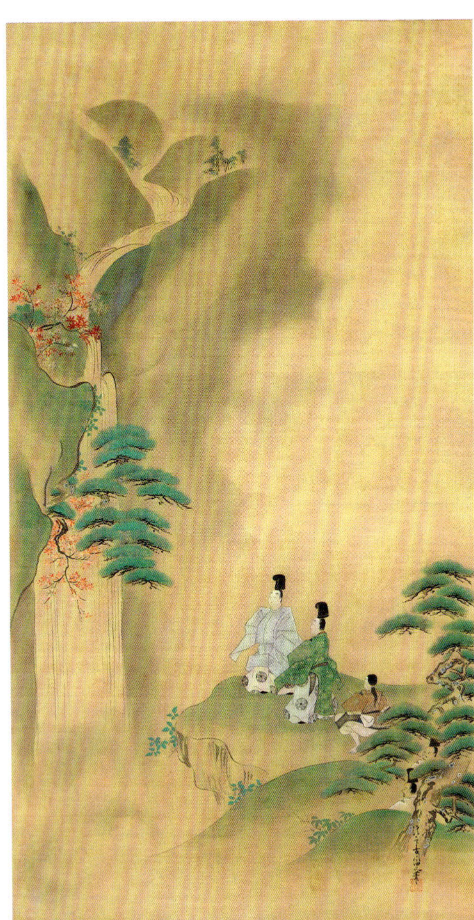
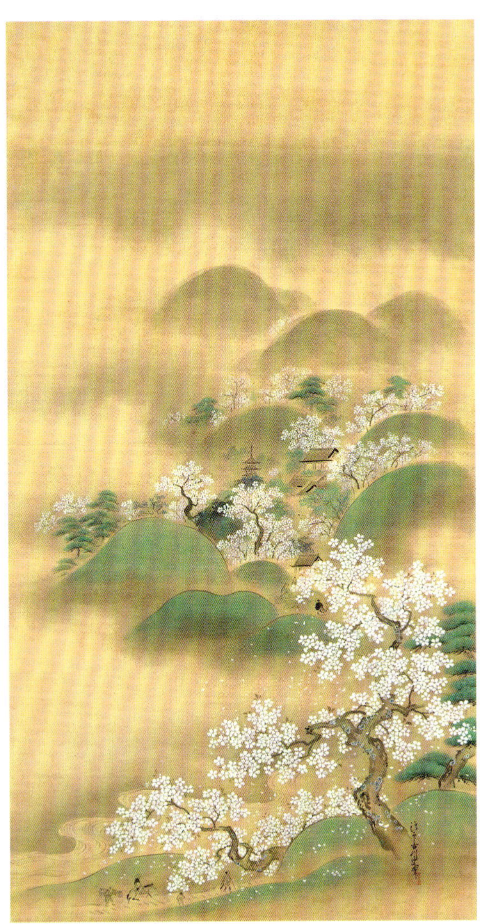

Kano Tsunenobu
(狩野常信; 1636–1713)

160. "Cherry Blossoms at Katano" (交野), "Nunobiki Waterfall"(布引), and "Maples at Tatsutagawa" (竜田川) episodes of *Ise monogatari* (伊勢物語)

Edo period, after 1709
Triptych of hanging scrolls; ink and color on silk
Each scroll 149.3 x 79.8 cm (58 3/4 x 31 3/8 in.)
Signatures, seals

Ex coll.: Frank E. Hart

Literature: Tokyo National Museum 1985a, no. 34; Wheelwright 1986, p. 21, fig. 2; Avitabile 1990, no. 77; Kaneko Nobuhisa 2010, pp. 92–94, no. 12.

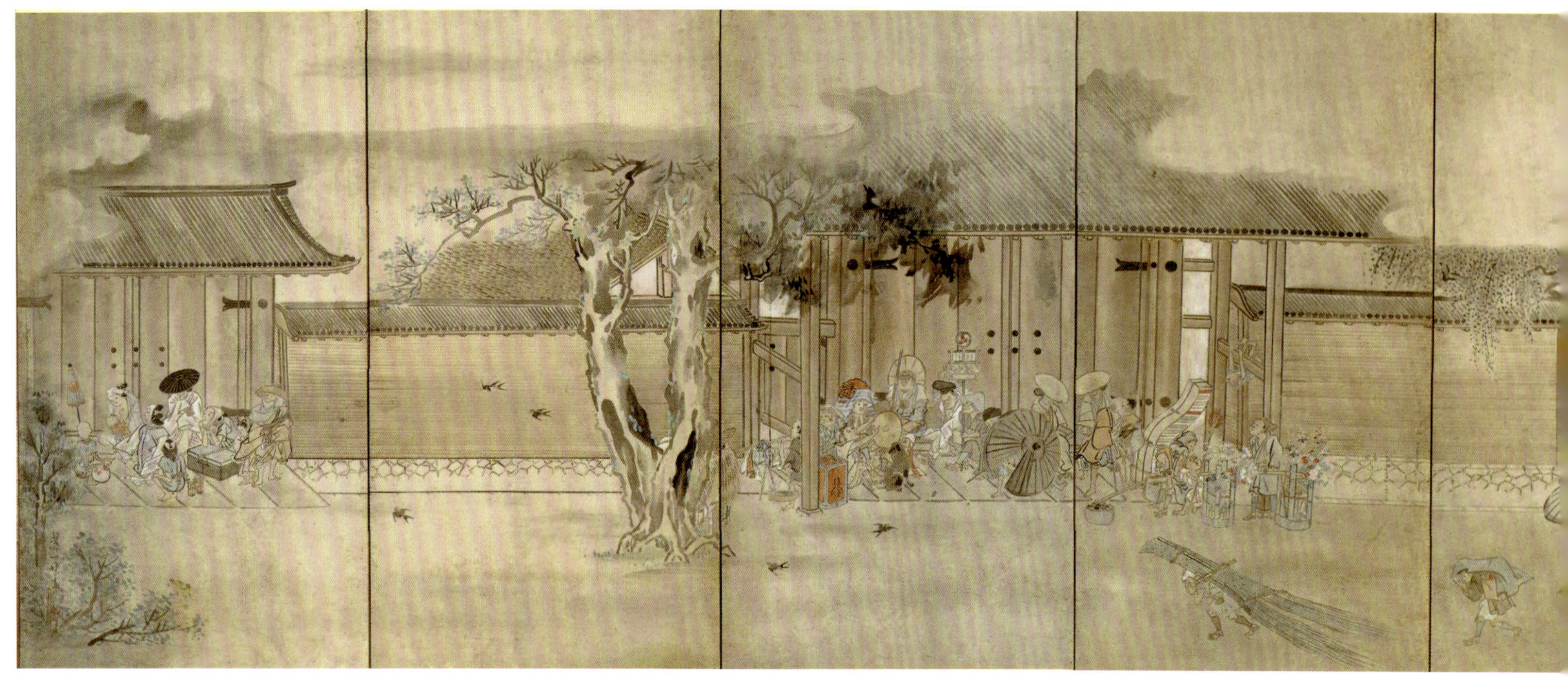

Hanabusa Itchō
(英一蝶; 1652–1724)

161. Taking Shelter from the Rain
(雨宿り)

Edo period, after 1709
Six-panel folding screen; ink and color on paper
121.3 x 316.2 cm (47 3/4 in. x 10 ft. 4 1/2 in.)
Signature, seals

Literature: Kobayashi Tadashi 1968, pp. 28, 29, and 31; Tsuji Nobuo 1968a, p. 35; Murase 1971, no. 26; Murase 1975, no. 89; Takeda Tsuneo 1977b, no. 98; Kobayashi Tadashi and Sakakibara Satoru 1978, no. 48; Tsuji Nobuo 1980, no. 105; Tokyo National Museum 1985a, no. 36; Kobayashi Tadashi 1988, fig. 10; Avitabile 1990, no. 78; Murase 1990, no. 27; Kobayashi Tadashi and Kano Hiroyuki 1992, no. 39; Meech 1993, no. 15; Screech 1995, fig. 1; Chiba Municipal Museum 1996b, pp. 174–75, no. 99; Murase 2000, no. 112; Ruch 2002, pp. 549, 556, fig. 20-10; Tsuji Nobuo et al. 2005, no. 83.

Tsuruzawa Tangei
(鶴沢探鯨; 1688–1769)

162. Landscape

Edo period, 18th century
Hanging scroll; ink on silk
38.2 x 48.2 cm (15 x 19 in.)
Signature, seal

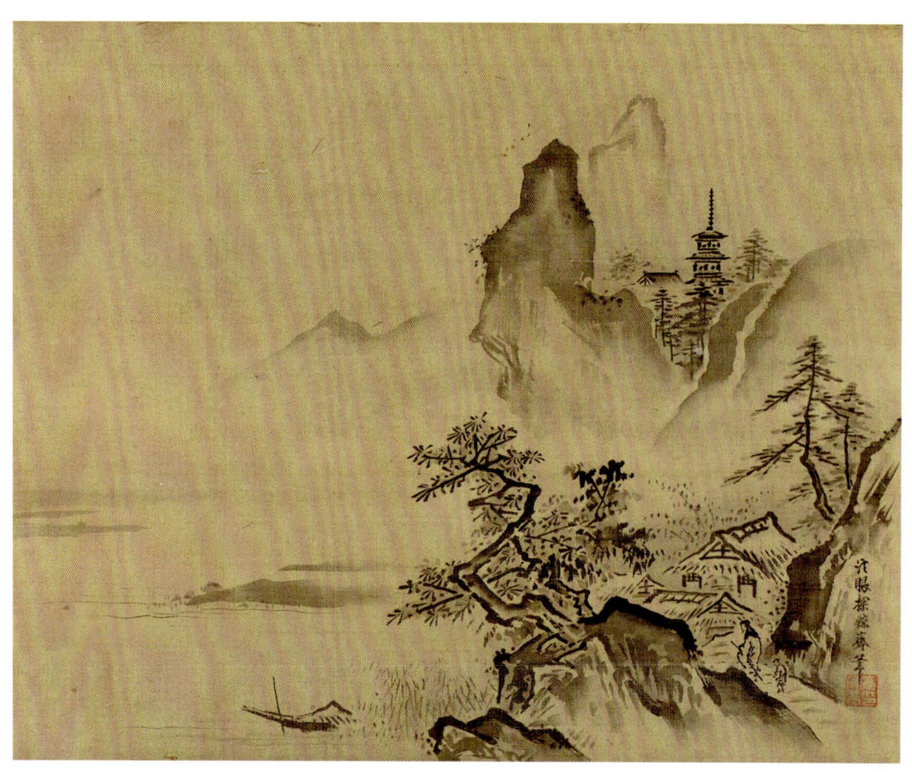

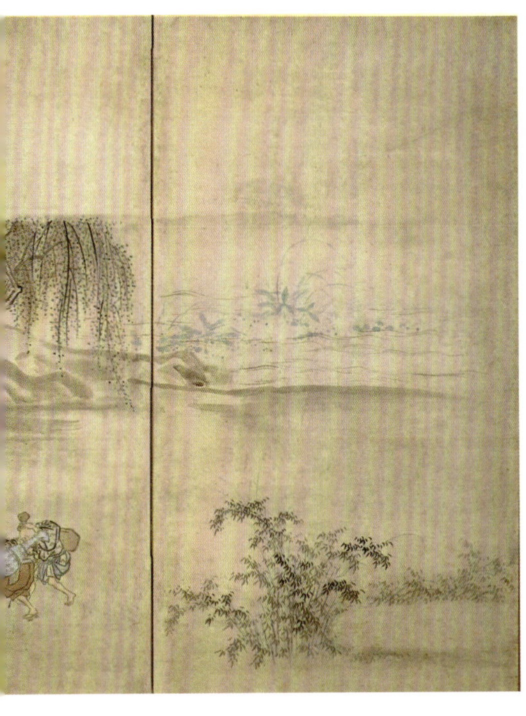

Ishida Yūtei
(石田幽汀; 1721–1786)

163. Flock of Cranes

Edo period
Pair of six-panel folding screens; ink, color, and gold on gilded paper
Each screen 156.5 x 355 cm (61 5/8 in. x 11 ft. 7 3/4 in.)
Signatures, seals

Literature: Sasaki Jōhei 1996a, fig. 4; Sasaki Jōhei 1996b, no. 3; Murase 2000, no. 114.

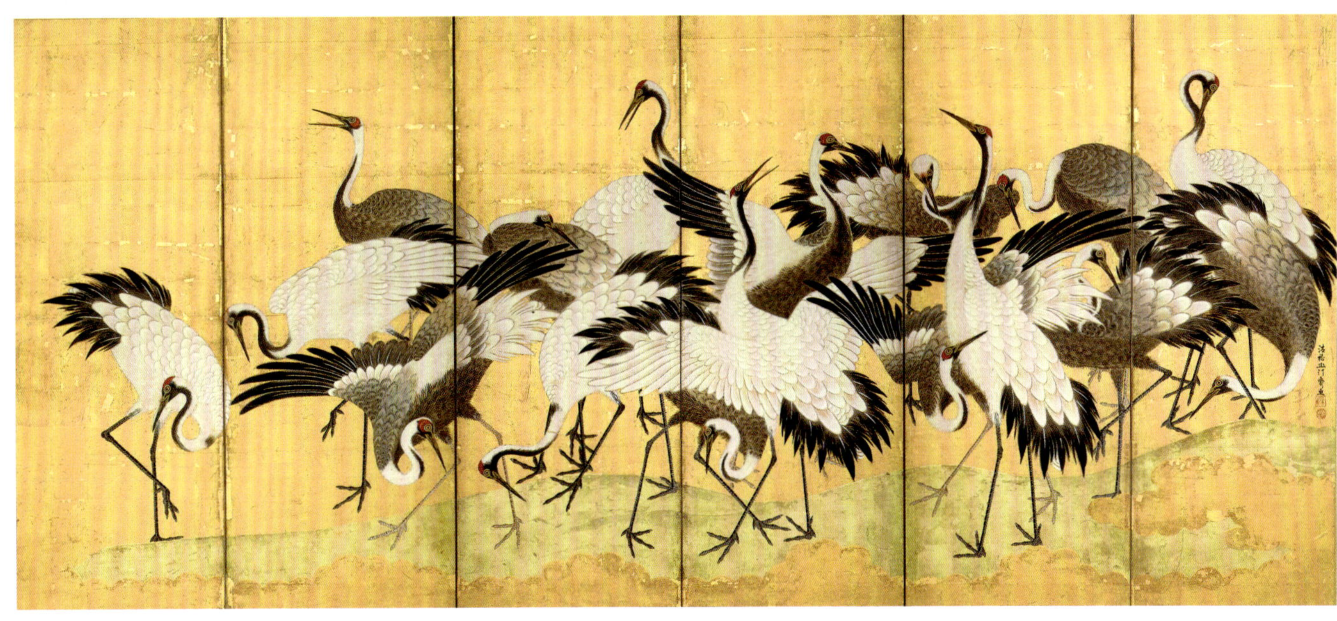

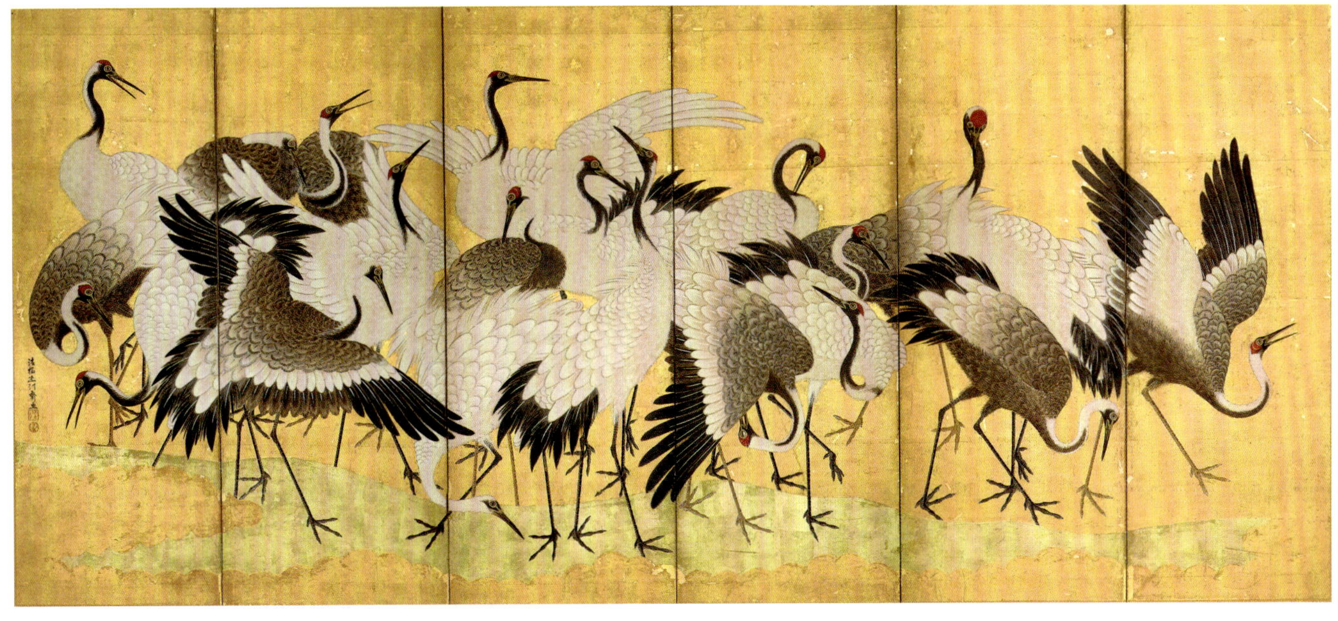

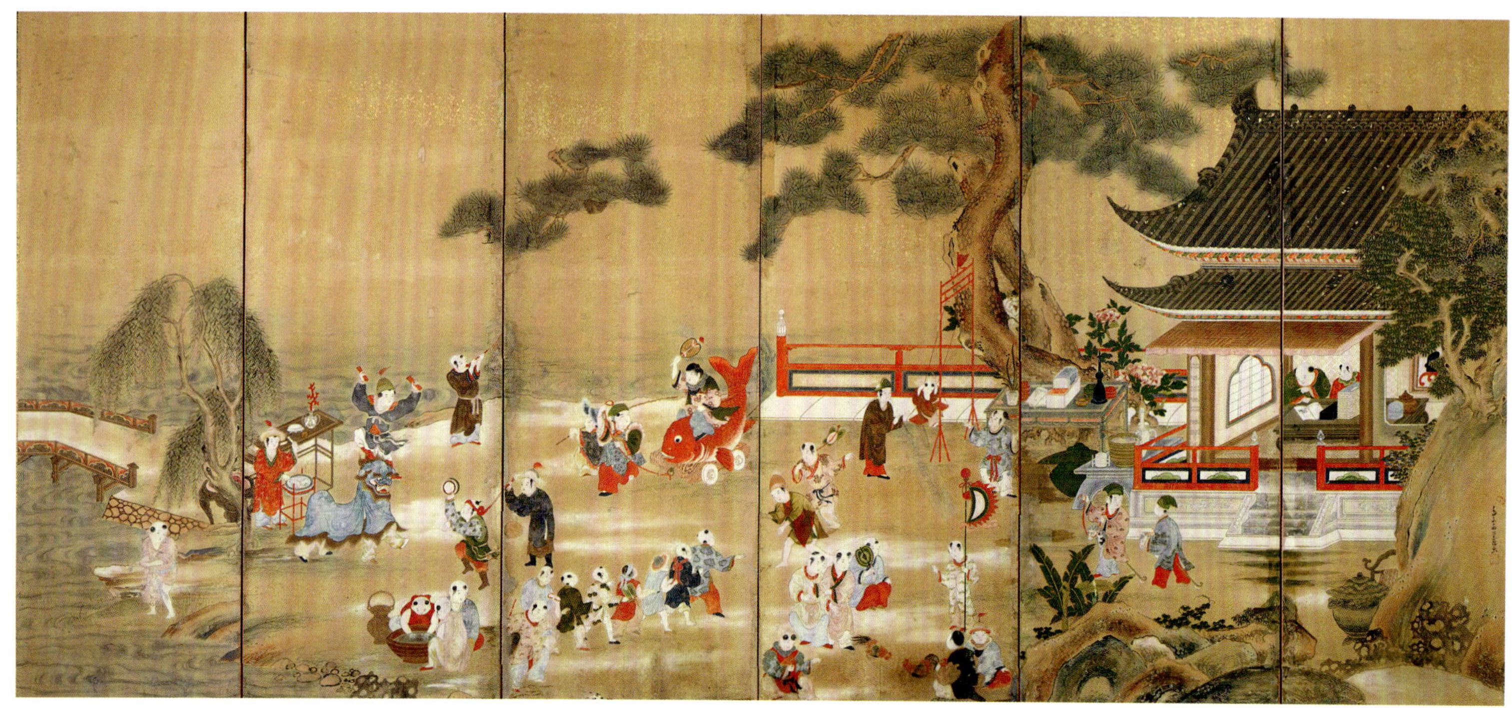

Chōbunsai Eishin
(鳥文斎栄信; fl. 18th century)

164. Chinese Children at Play

Edo period
Six-panel folding screen; ink, color, and gold on paper
127.4 x 279.9 cm (50 1/8 in. x 9 ft. 2 1/4 in.)
Signature, seals

Ex coll.: Frank E. Hart

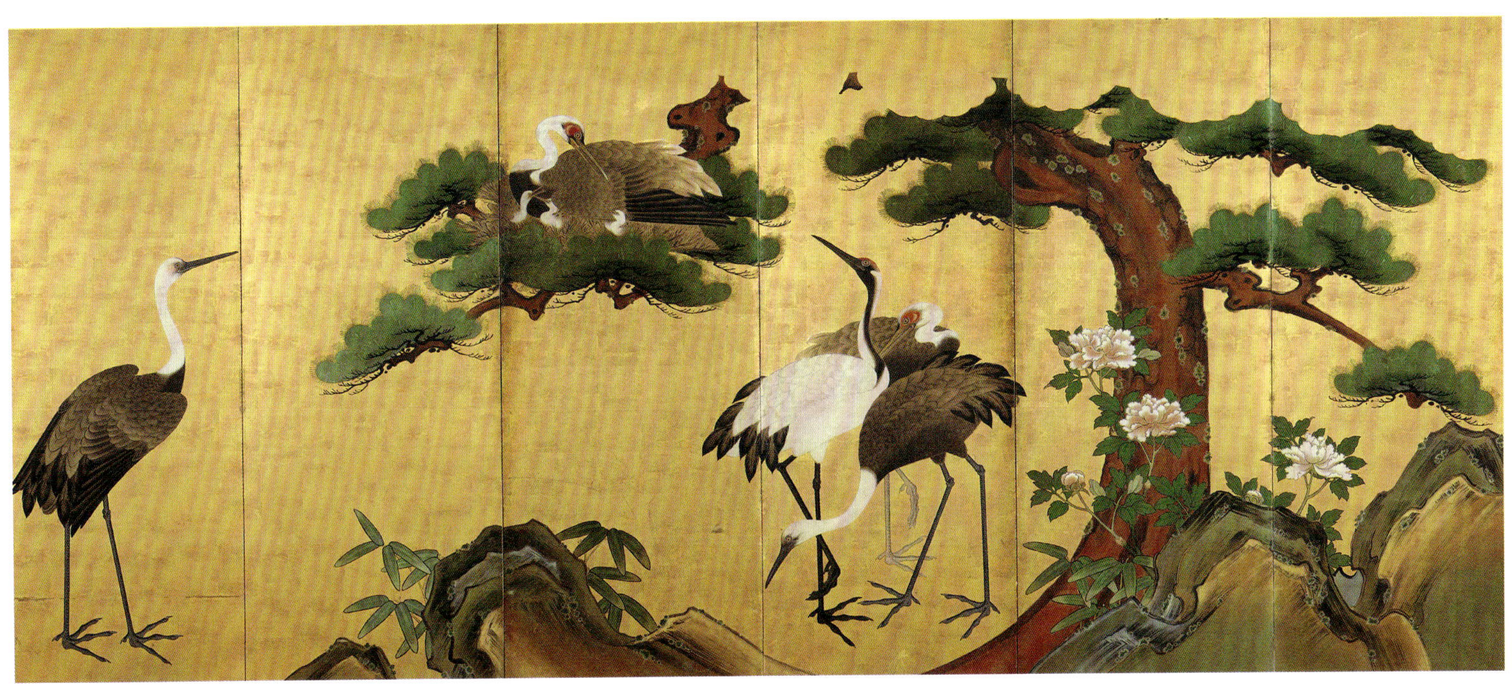

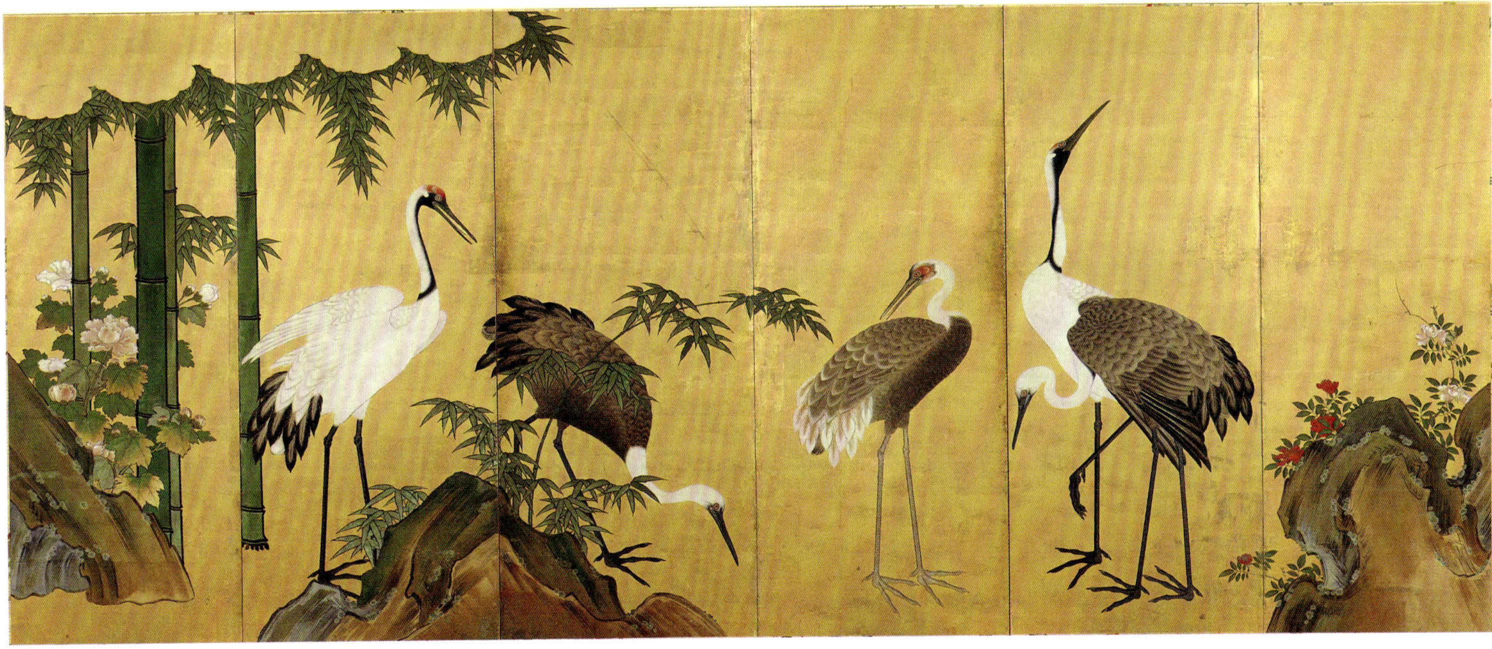

165. Cranes and Pines; Cranes and Bamboo

Edo period, 18th–19th century
Pair of six-panel folding screens; ink and color on gilded paper
Each screen 153.5 x 354.6 cm (60 3/8 in. x 11 ft. 7 5/8 in.)

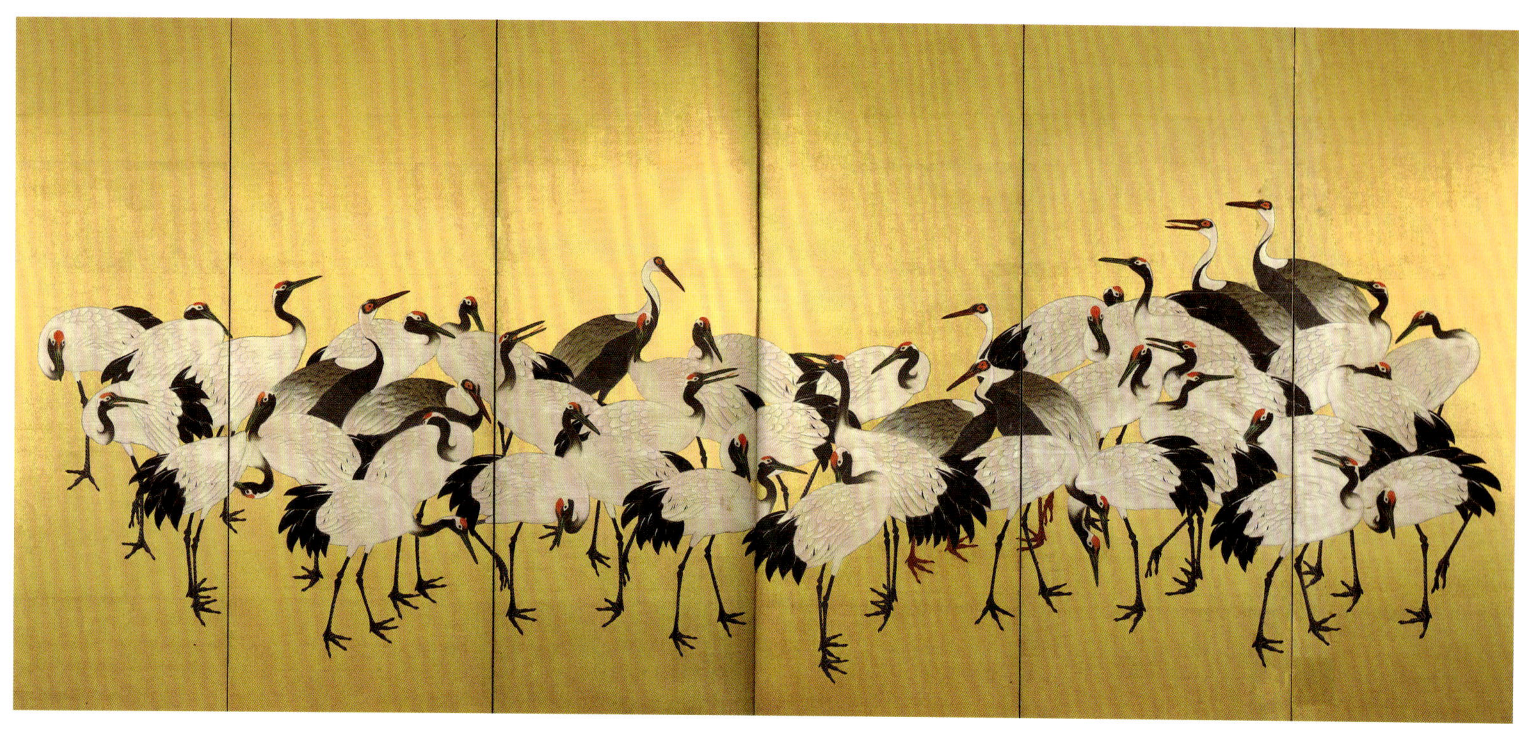

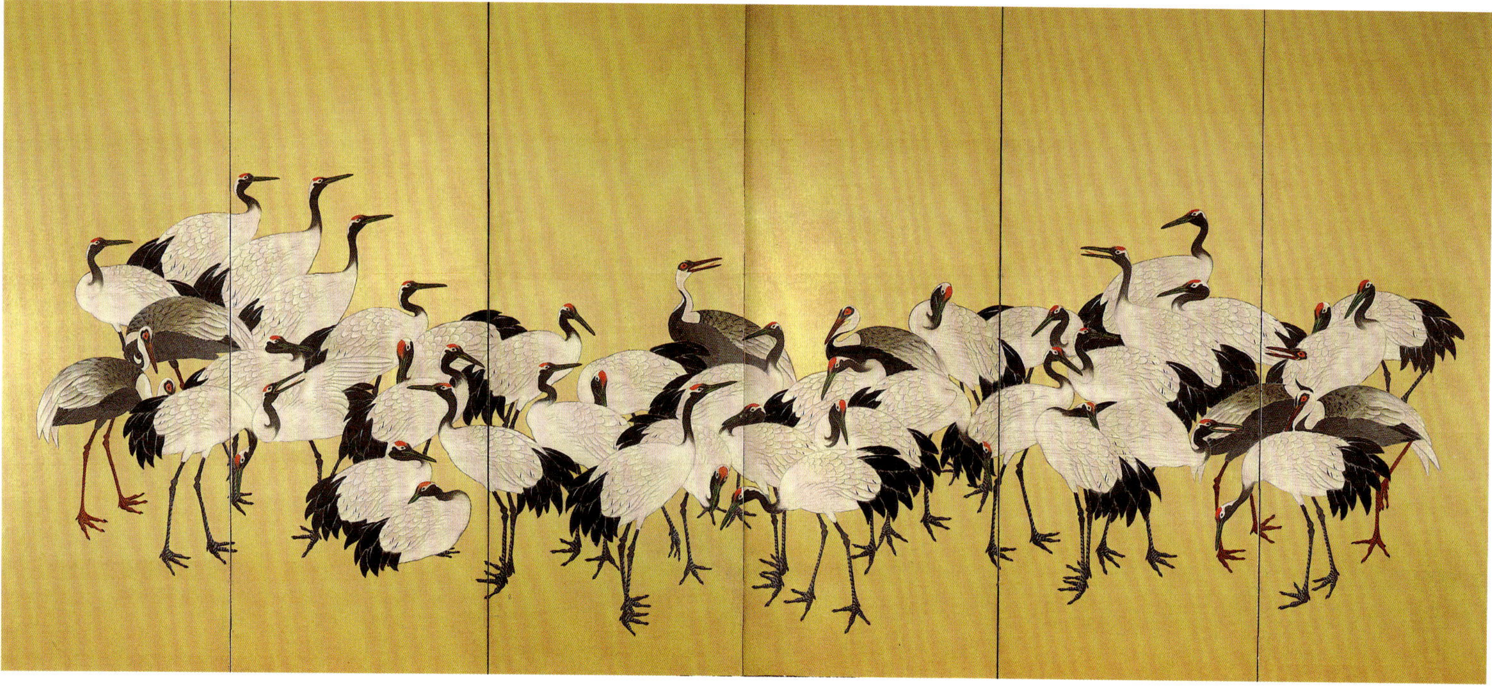

166. Cranes

Edo period, 18th century
Pair of six-panel folding screens; ink and color on gilded paper
Each screen 154.7 x 350.6 cm (60⅞ in. x 11 ft. 6 in.)

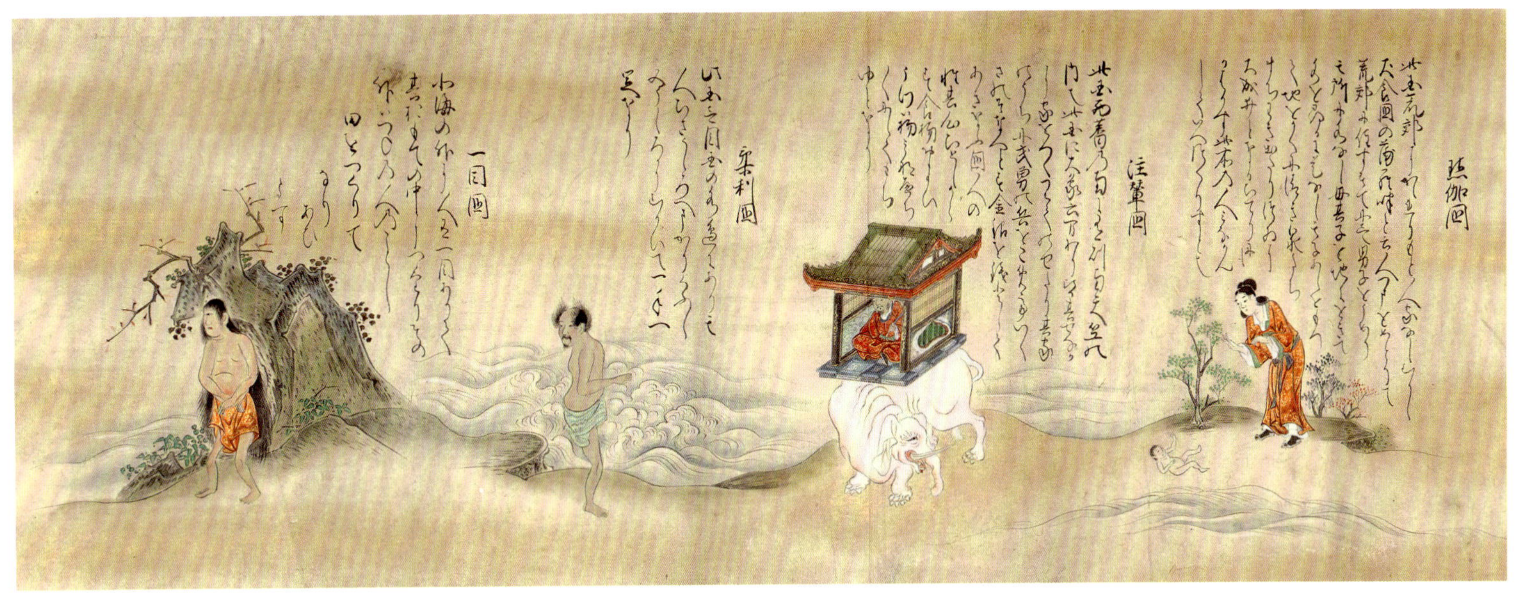

167. Inhabitants of Fourteen Strange Lands

Edo period, 18th century
Handscroll; ink, color, and gold on paper
30 x 392.8 cm ($11\frac{3}{4}$ in. x 12 ft. $10\frac{5}{8}$ in.)

Nonoyama Kōzan
(野々山緱山; 1780–1847)

168. Kabuki Theater

Edo period, 1822
Handscroll; ink, color, and gold on paper
34.6 x 149.6 cm ($13\frac{5}{8}$ x $58\frac{7}{8}$ in.)
Signature, seal

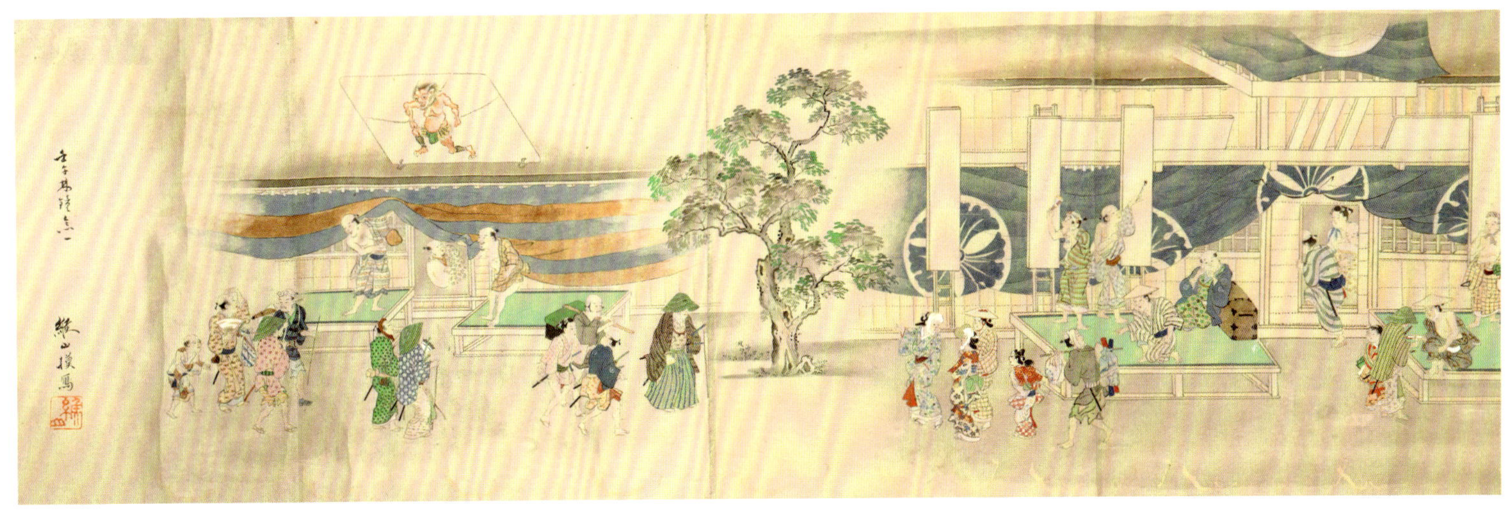

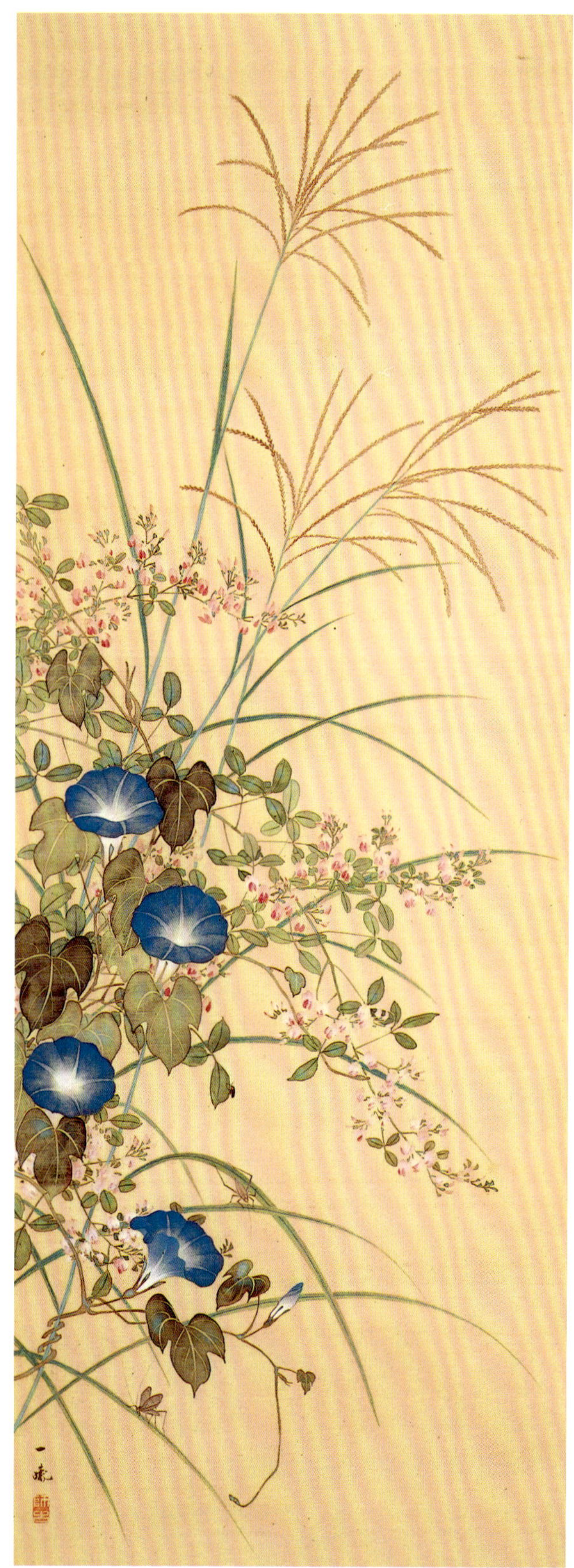

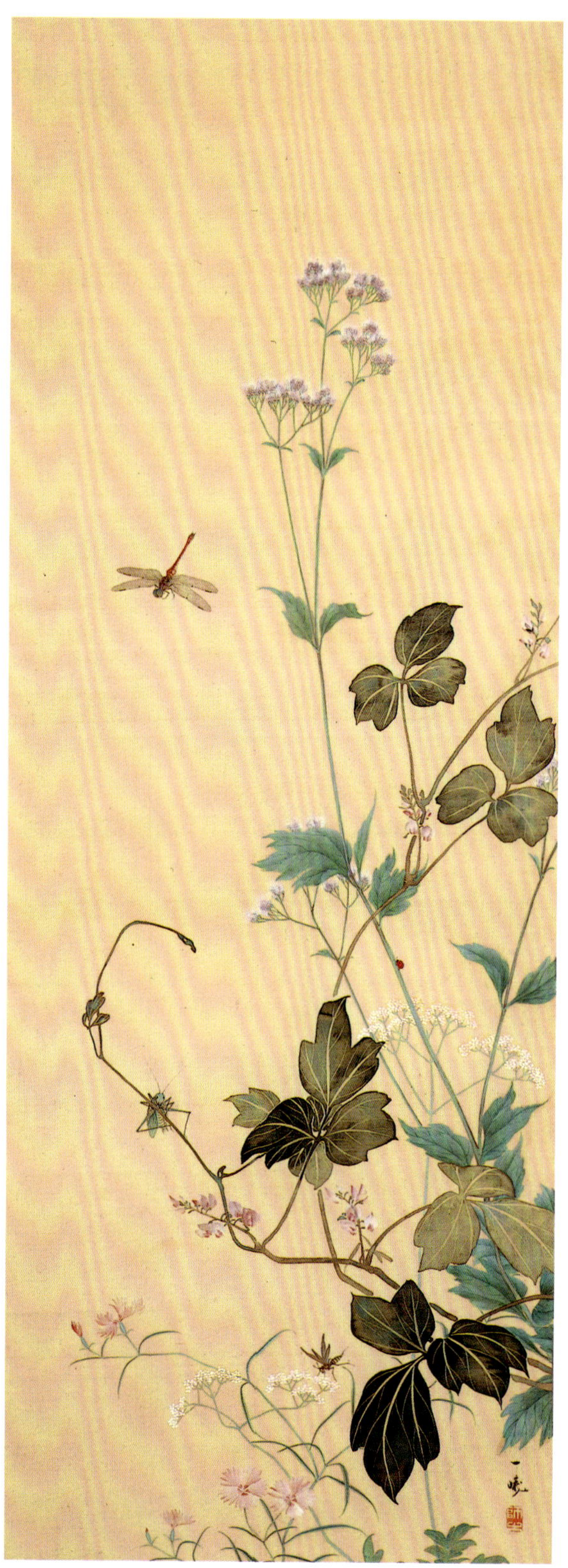

Oki Ichiga
(沖一峨; 1796–1855)

169. Autumn Flowers

Edo period
Diptych of hanging scrolls; ink and color on silk
Each scroll 115.9 x 41.6 cm ($45^{5}/_{8}$ x $16^{3}/_{8}$ in.)
Signatures, seals

Literature: Tottori Prefectural Museum 2006, p. 43.

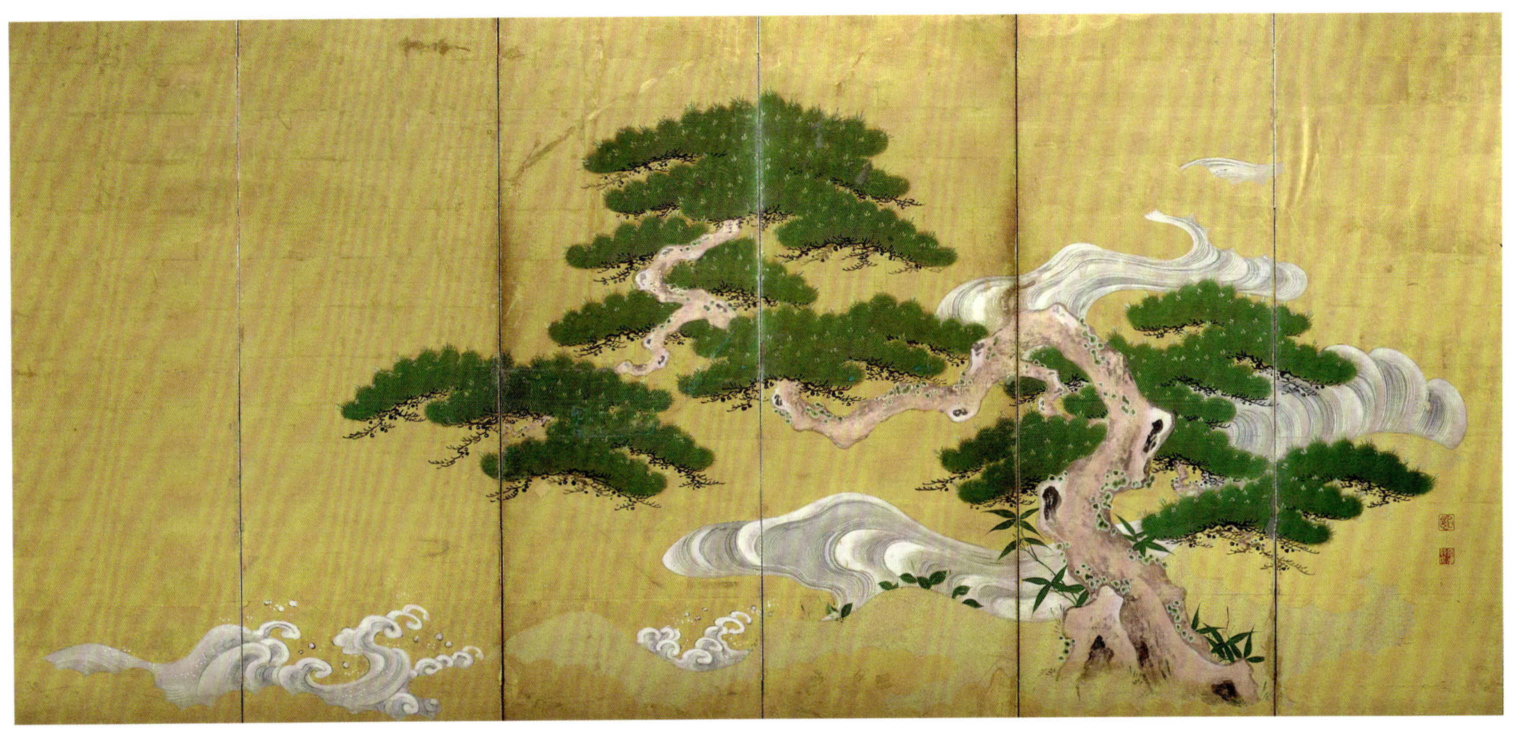

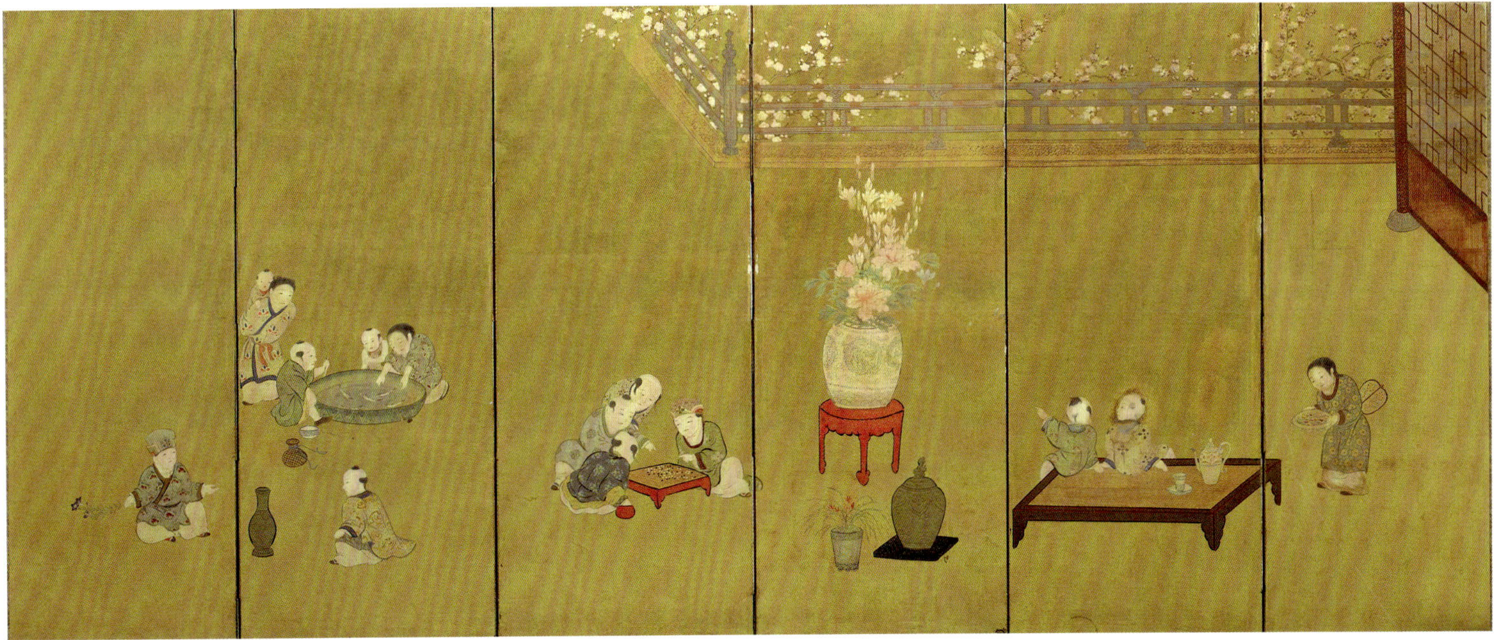

170. Pine Tree by a Stream

Edo period, 19th century
Six-panel folding screen; ink and color on gilded paper
156.6 x 337.2 cm (61⅝ in. x 11 ft. ¾ in.)
Seals
Minneapolis Institute of Arts (2004.245)

171. Chinese Children at Play

Edo period, 19th century
Six-panel folding screen; ink and color on gilded paper
107.8 x 260.6 cm (42½ in. x 8 ft. 6⅝ in.)
Minneapolis Institute of Arts (2004.244)

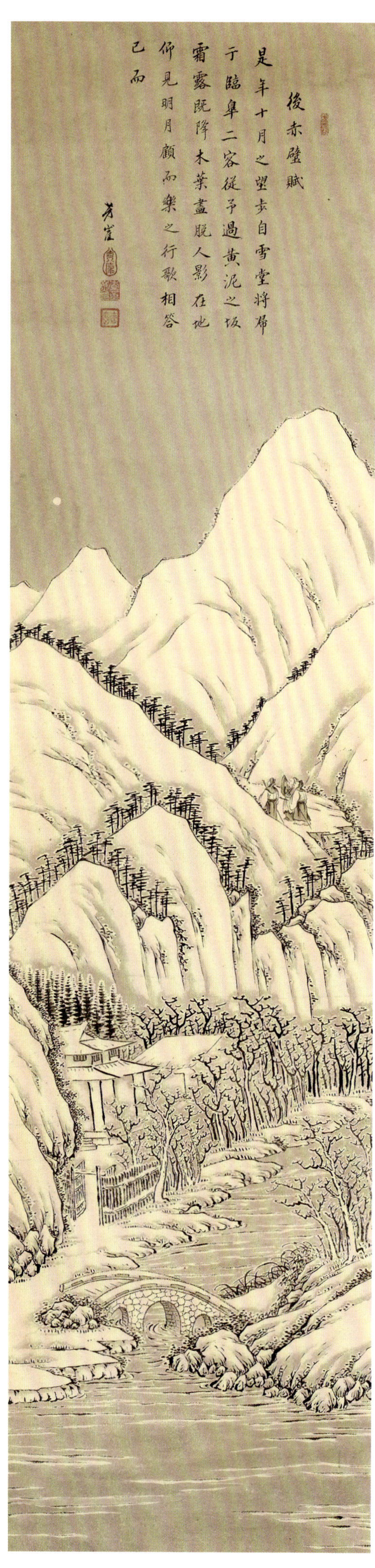

Kano Hōgai
(狩野芳崖; 1828–1888)

172. Soshoku's (Ch. Su Shi, 蘇軾) "Ode to His Second Visit to the Red Cliff" (後赤壁賦)

Edo period–Meiji era
Hanging scroll; ink on paper
129.2 x 32.2 cm ($50^{7}/_{8}$ x $12^{5}/_{8}$ in.)
Text, signature, seals

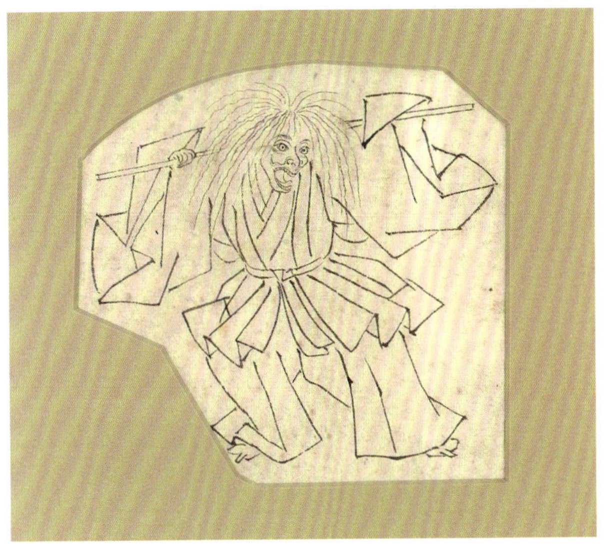
a

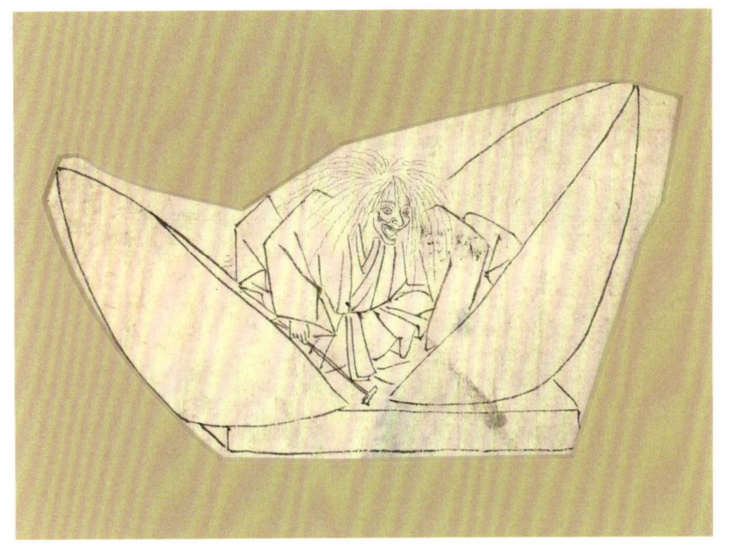
b

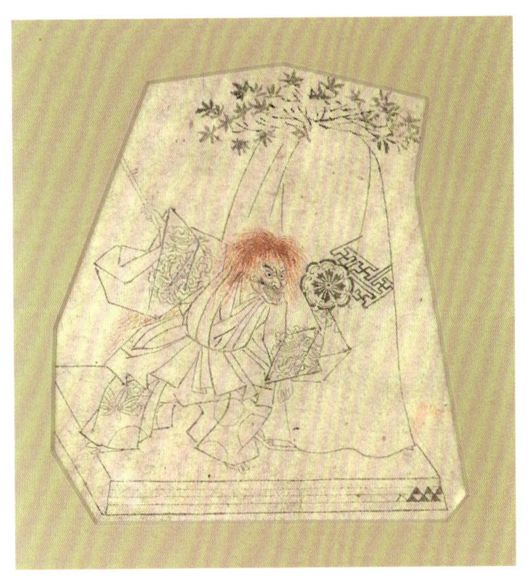
c

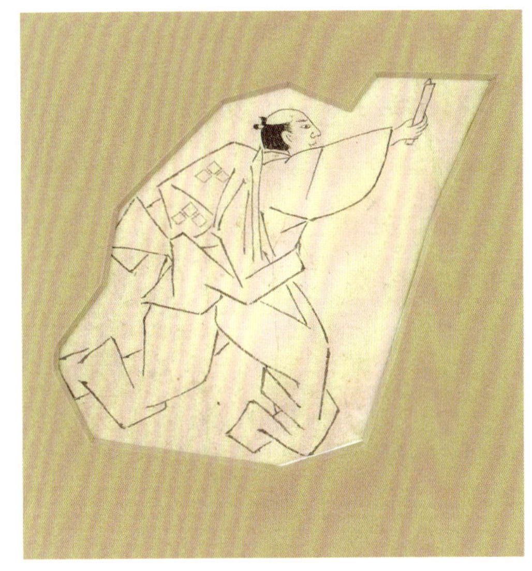
d

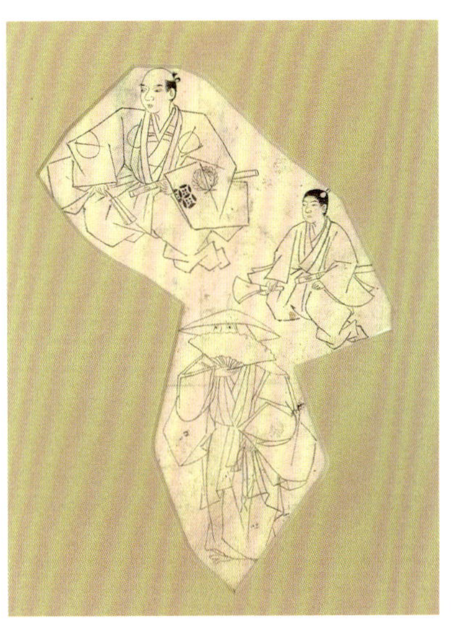
e

Kawanabe Kyōsai (or Gyōsai)
(河鍋暁斎; 1831–1889)

173a–f. Sketches

Edo period–Meiji era
Six matted sketches; ink on paper
Varying sizes

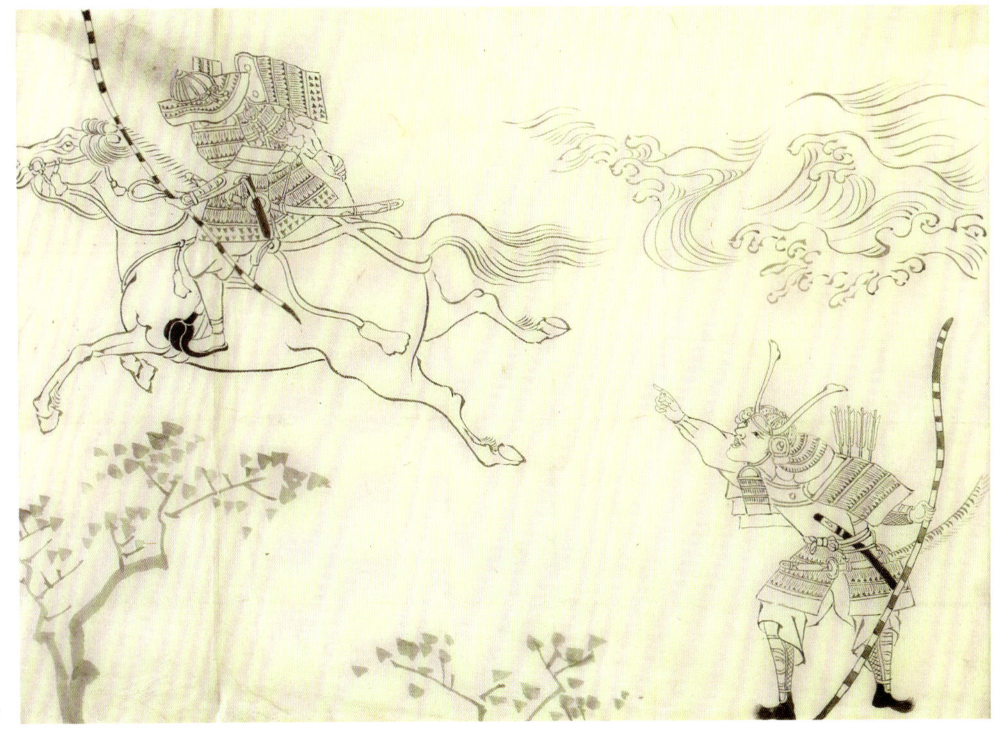
f

Chapter 4 Details

† *denotes illustrated items*

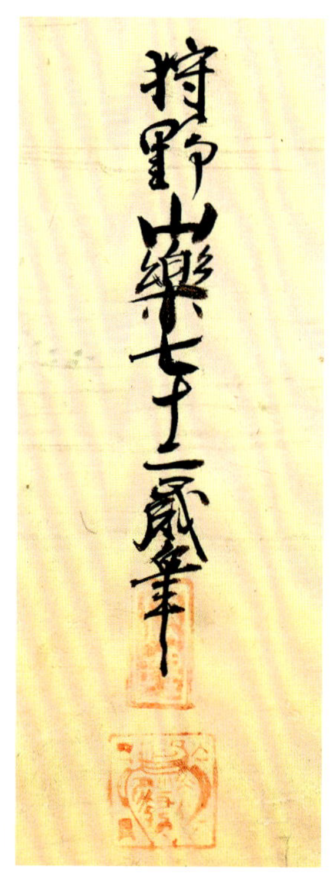

142

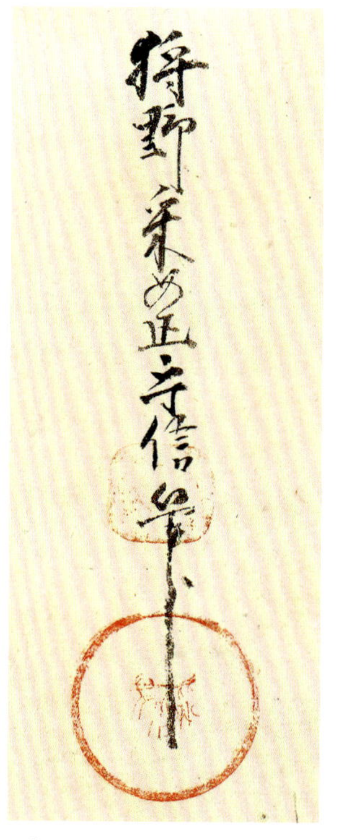

146

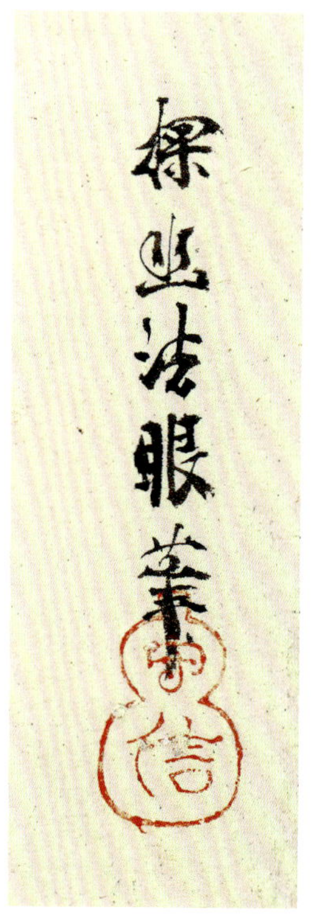

147

† 142. View of West Lake

Signatures

[on each screen] *Painted by Kano Sanraku at age 72*

Seals

[on each screen] *Shuri*; *Mitsuyori*

144. Hotei with a Child

Text

by Otsū

The eye that regards the guileless child / is a friendly soul who is outside this soiled world. / Seventh day of the second month, 1624

Signature

Painted and inscribed by Tsūjo of the Ono Clan

Seal

Kaō

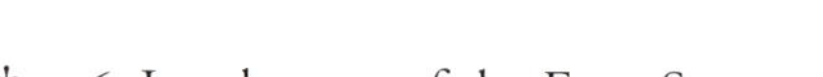

† 146. Landscapes of the Four Seasons

Signatures

[on each screen] *Painted by Kano Uneme no shō Morinobu*

Seals

Illegible; *Uneme*

† 147. Jizō Playing a Flute

Signature

Painted by Tan'yū hōgen

Seal

Morinobu

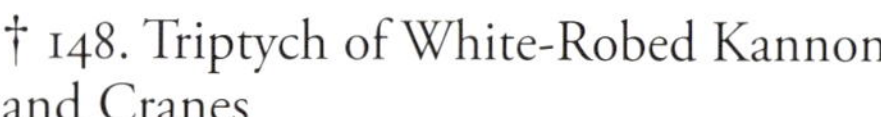

† 148. Triptych of White-Robed Kannon and Cranes

Signatures

[on each scroll] *Painted by Tan'yū hōin at age 63*

Seals

[on each scroll] *Morinobu*

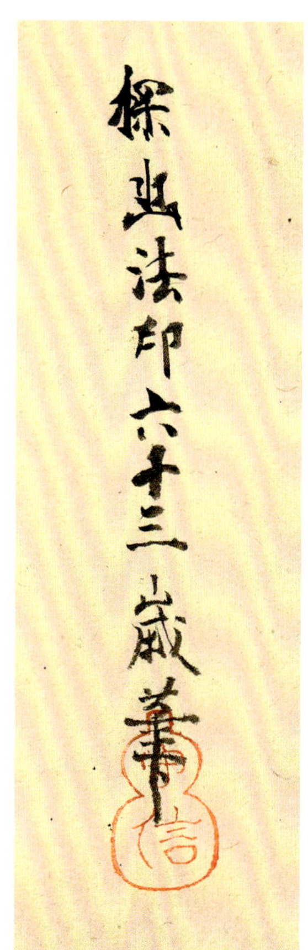

148

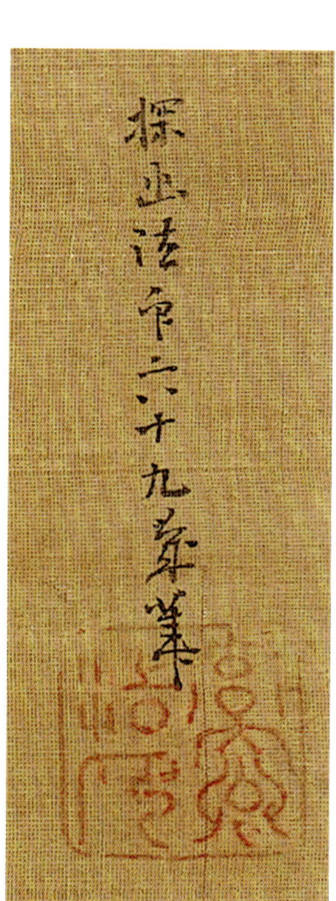

149

† 149. Jizō Playing a Flute

Signature

Painted by Tan'yū hōin at age 69

Seal

Kunaikyō hōin

150

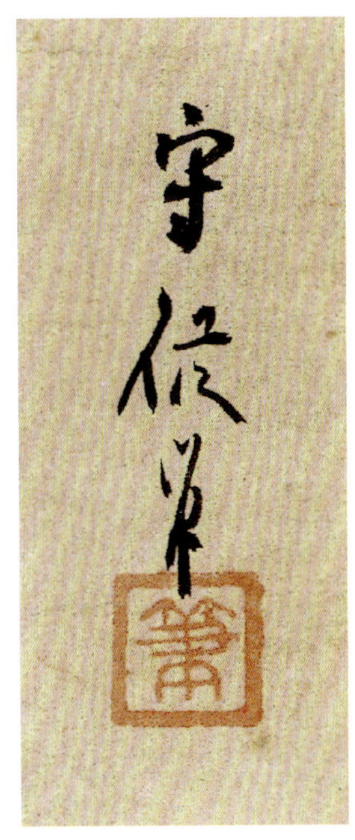

151

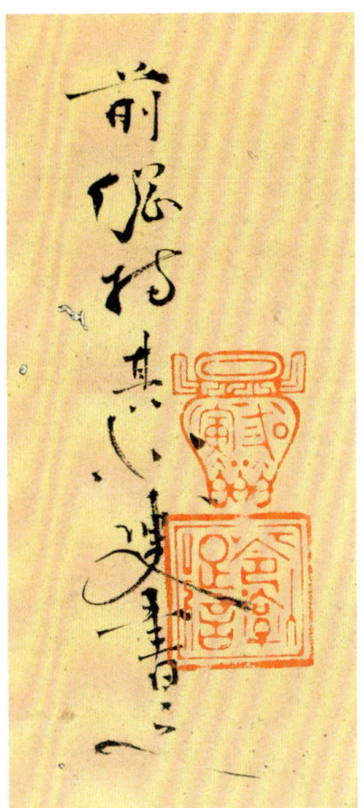

152

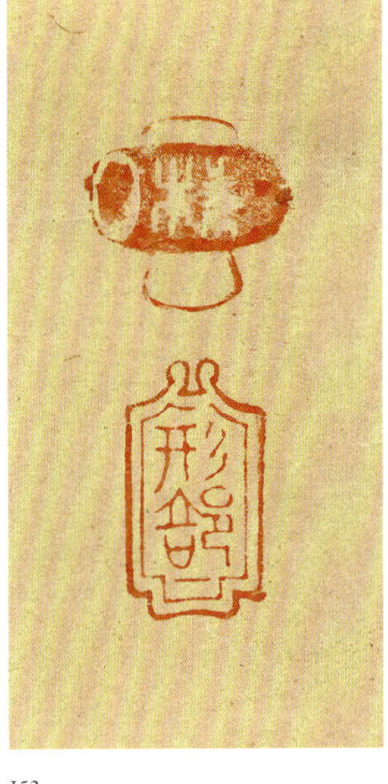

152

† 150. Evening Bell at the Temple in Smoky Mist, from *Eight Views of the Xiao and Xiang Rivers*

Text

Evening Bell at the Temple in Smoky Mist. // At sunset the temple bell sounds through the fog. / People in distant places, too, hurry on their way.

Seals

[on each leaf] *Tan'yū*

† 151. Kensu

Signature

Painted by Morinobu

Seal

Hitsu

† 152. Hanrō (Ch. Fan Lang)

Seals

[lower right] *Sei*; *Gyōbu*

Text

by Kishinsō

Teetering on horseback, idly riding backward, / I seek no bosom friends but poetry on my journey. / Who has ever recognized the beauty / of the cloud-piercing Mount Hua, whose blue hue tinges my brows?

Signature

Written by Kishinsō, formerly of Sōjiji

Seals

Sanshin; *Reijun Sokushin*

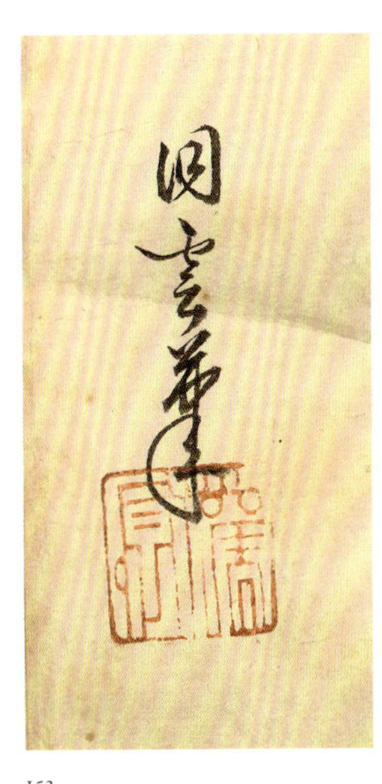

153

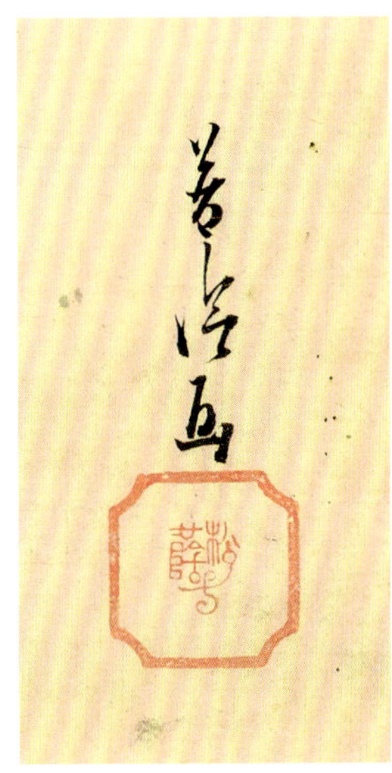

154

† 153. Autumn Moon over Lake Dongting from *Eight Views of the Xiao and Xiang Rivers*

Text

Poem by Ichiki Konzan

Autumn water is very clear, / late at night the moon is dipped / in the white caps of waves.

Signature

[at end of scroll] *Painted by Tōun*

Seal

[at end of scroll] *Kanbara*

† 154. Ikuzanshu (Ch. Yushanzhu); Seiōgyū (Ch. Zhenghuangniu)

Signatures

[on each scroll] *Painted by Masunobu*

Seals

[on each scroll] *Shōinshi*

† 156. Hermit; Doves on a Plum Tree; Kingfisher with Lotus

Seals

[on each scroll] *Unzen*; *Setsuzan*

157. Forty-nine scenes from *Ise monogatari*

[right screen] Episode 6

When my beloved asked, / "Is it a clear gem or / what might it be?" / would that I had replied, / "A dewdrop!" and [it] perished. // It is said that while the future Empress from the Second Ward was in attendance upon her cousin, the imperial consort, someone was fascinated by her beauty and carried her off on his back.

[left screen] Episode 83

. . . at nightfall. As he set out he recited. // When for an instant I forget, / how like a dream it seems . . . / never could I have imagined / that I would plod through snowdrifts / to see my lord. // He went back to the capital in tears.

† 158. Apsaras

Signature

Painted by the Woman of the Kiyohara Clan, Yukinobu

Seal

Kiyoharajo

† 159. Monju on a Lion

Signature

Painted by the Woman of the Kiyohara Clan, Yukinobu

Seal

Kiyoharajo

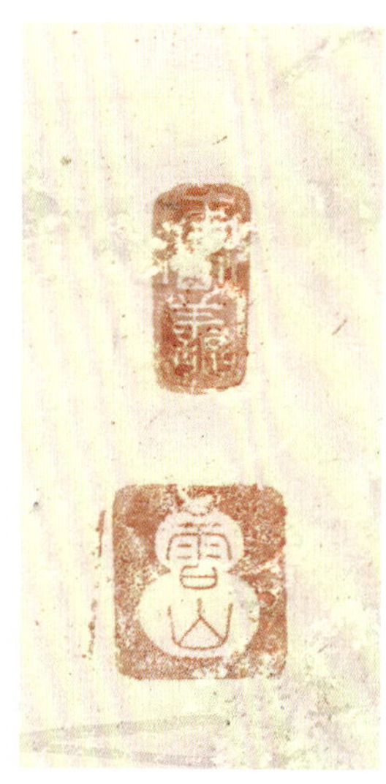

156

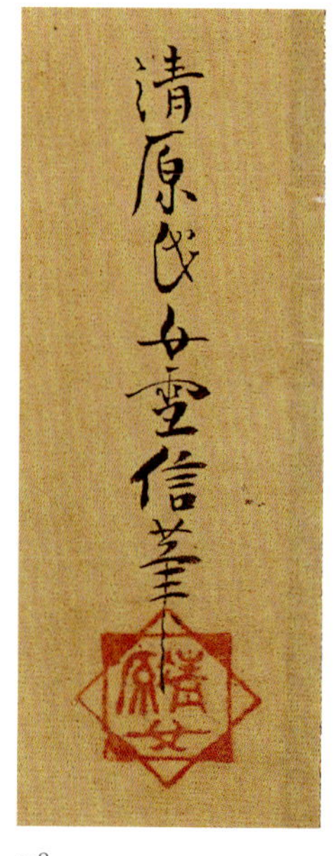

158

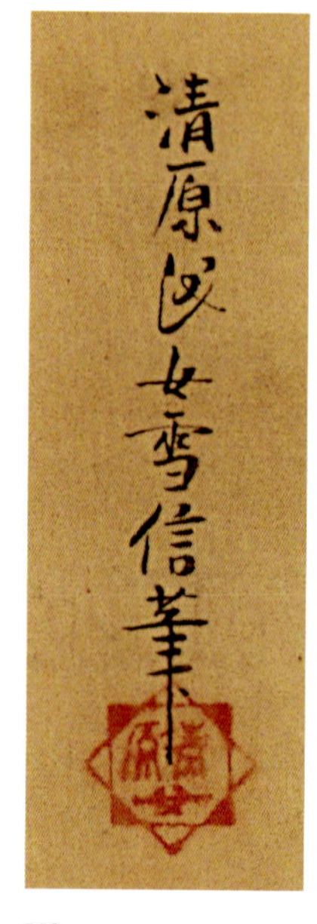

159

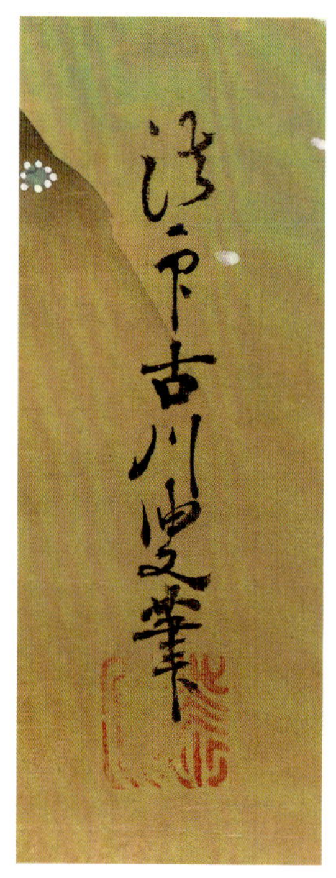

160

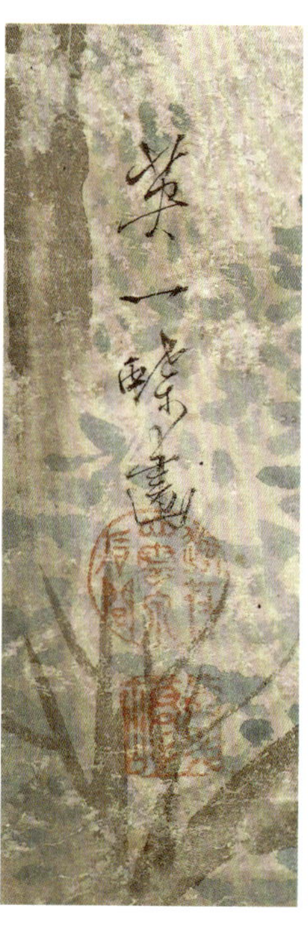

161

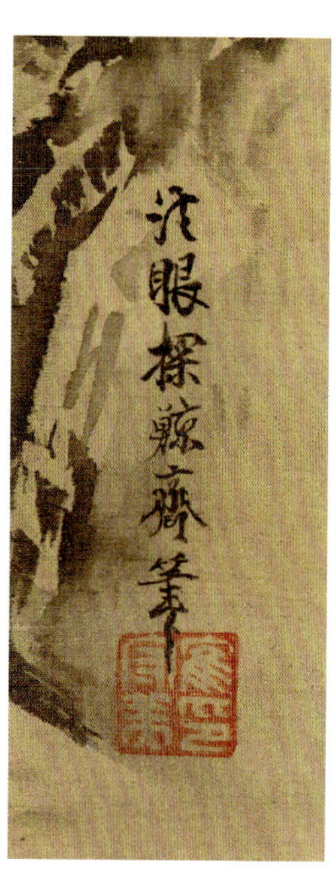

162

† 160. "Cherry Blossoms at Katano," "Nunobiki Waterfall," and "Maples at Tatsutagawa" episodes of *Ise monogatari*

Signatures

[on each scroll] *Painted by Hōin Kosensō*

Seals

[on each scroll] *Fujiwara*

† 161. Taking Shelter from the Rain

Signature

Painted by Hanabusa Itchō

Seals

Shuzai San'un Senseki kan; *Ai Moko*

† 162. Landscape

Signature

Painted by Hōgen Tangeisai

Seal

Tsuru Moriyoshi in

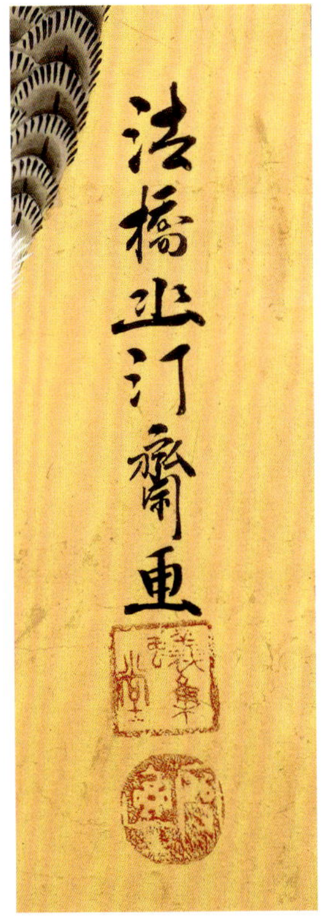
163

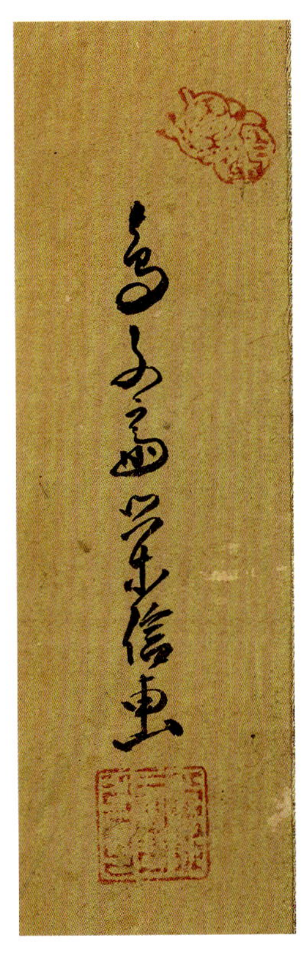
164

168

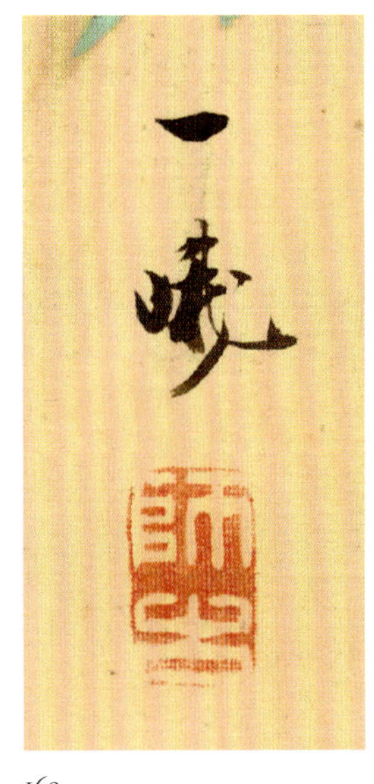

169

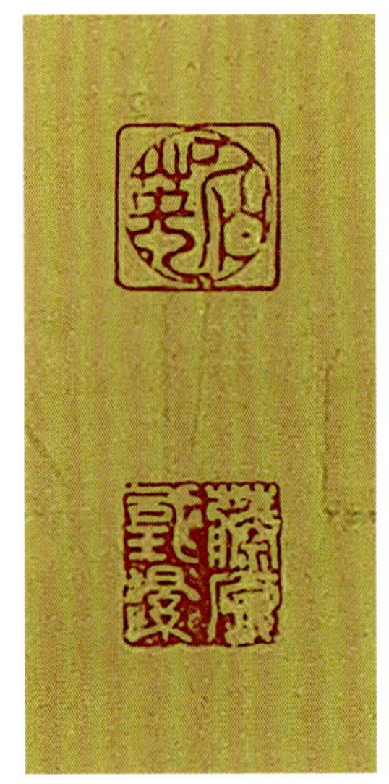
170

† 163. Flock of Cranes

Signatures

[on each screen] *Painted by Hokkyō Yūteisai*

Seals

[on each screen] *Gishūdō*; *Morinao*

† 164. Chinese Children at Play

Signature

Painted by Chōbunsai Eishin

Seals

Two illegible seals

† 168. Kabuki Theater

Signature

Kōzan copied this on the second day of the sixth month of 1822.

Seal

Kōzan

† 169. Autumn Flowers

Signatures

[on each scroll] *Ichiga*

Seals

[on each scroll] *Shiko*

† 170. Pine Tree by a Stream

Seals

Hakuei; *Fujiwara Tetsukage*

† 172. Soshoku's (Ch. Su Shi) "Ode to His Second Visit to the Red Cliff"

Text

by Hōgai

Ode to the Second Visit to the Red Cliff // On the fifteenth of the tenth month of the same year (1082) I set out on foot from Snow Hall, intending to return to Lin'gao. / Two guests accompanied me as we passed Yellow Dirt Hill. / Dew had fallen and the trees had shed all their leaves. / Our shadows lay on the ground, and we gazed up at the bright moon. / Delighted by our surroundings, we sang back and forth to each other as we walked.

Signature

Hōgai

Seals

Shōzan Nōtan; Sōkō; Sa Furetsu in; Shōzan

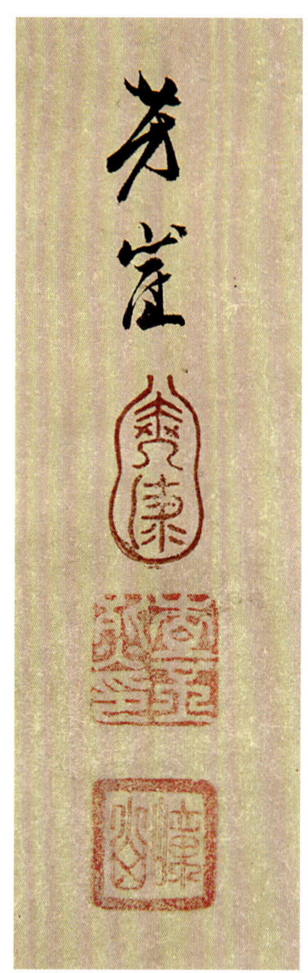

172

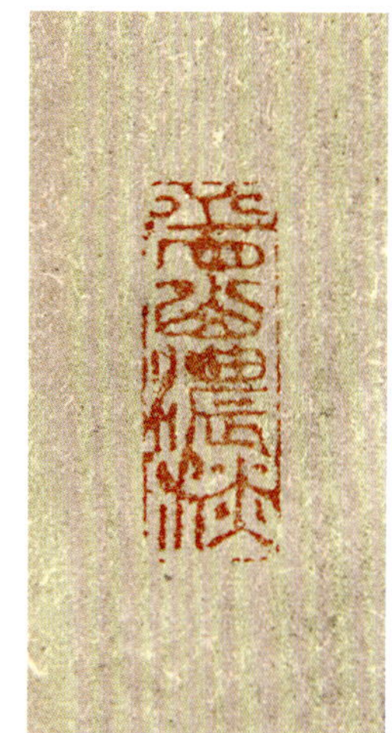

172

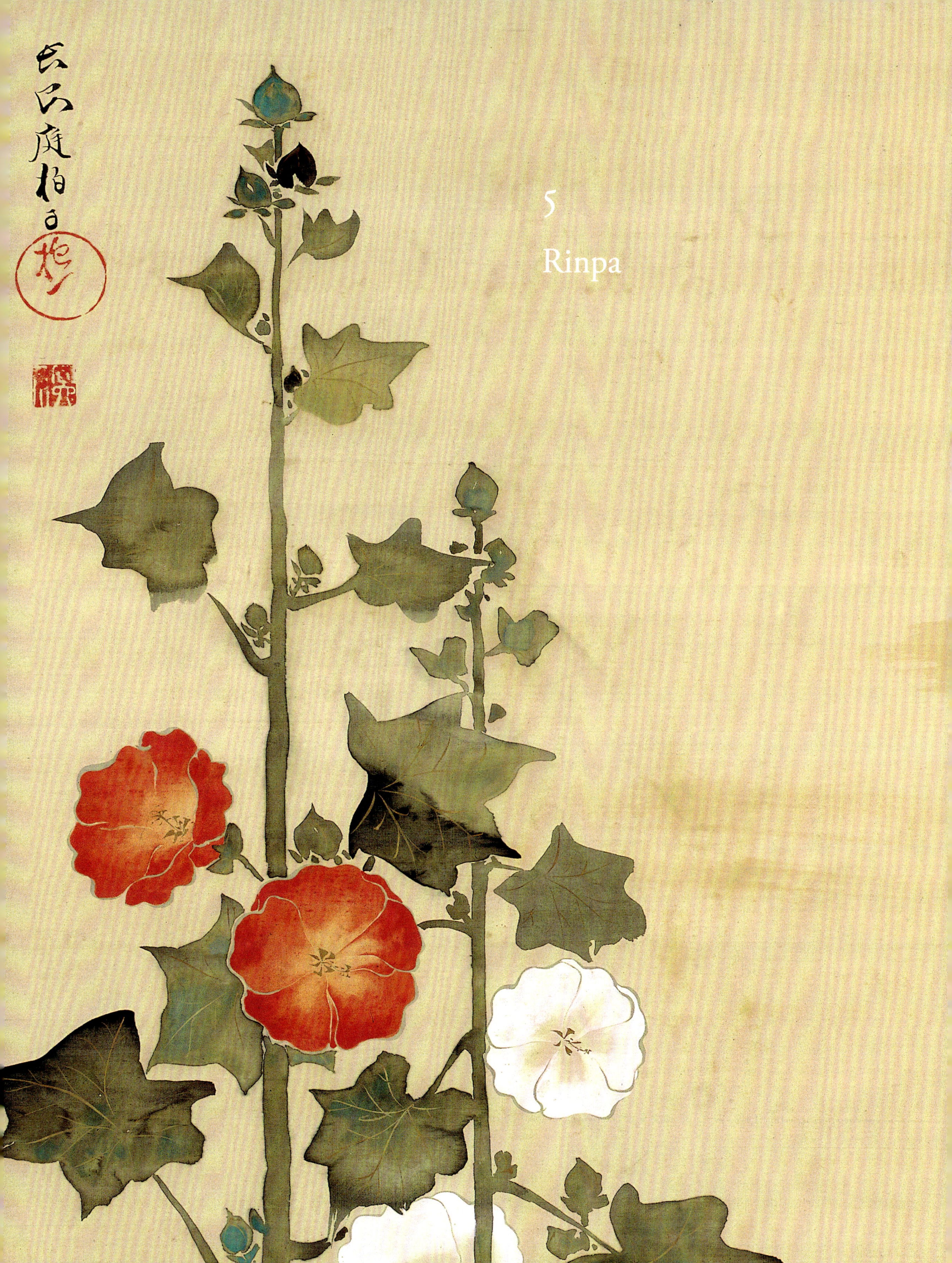

5

Rinpa

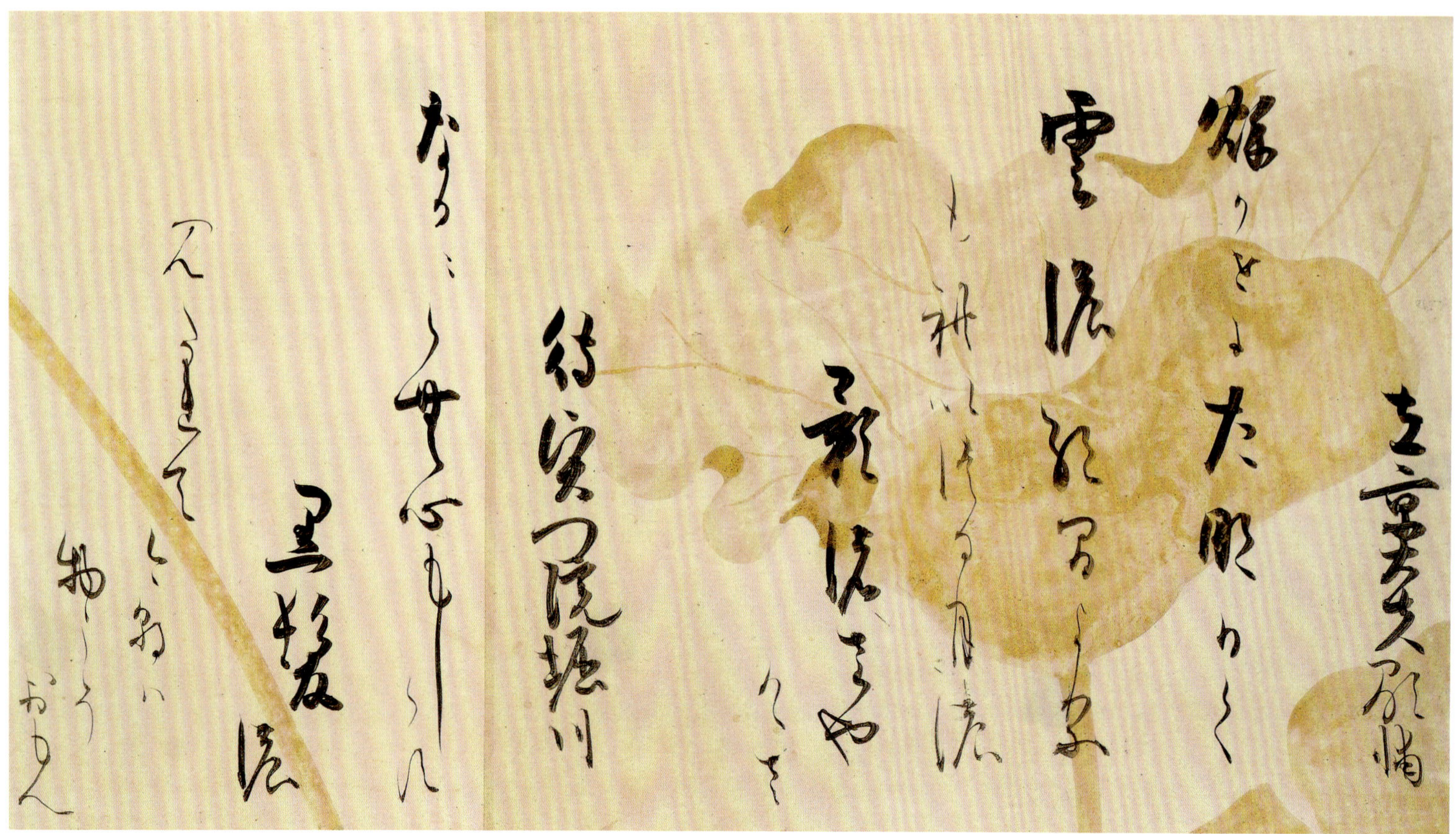

Hon'ami Kōetsu
(本阿弥光悦; 1558–1637)
Tawaraya Sōtatsu
(俵屋宗達; d. ca. 1640)

174. Two poems from *Ogura hyakunin isshu* (小倉百人一首)

Momoyama period, early 17th century
Fragment of a handscroll, mounted as hanging scroll; ink, silver, and gold on paper
32.8 x 60.3 cm (12⅞ x 23¾ in.)
Text

Ex coll.: Asada

Literature: Hayashiya Tatsusaburō et al. 1964, p. 21; Mizuo Hiroshi 1965–66, vol. 2, p. 83; Murase 1975, no. 49; Tokyo National Museum 1978, no. 244; Yamane Yūzō 1979, no. 11; Komatsu Shigemi 1981, pl. 13; Pekarik 1985a, fig. 8; Tokyo National Museum 1985a, no. 76; Kobayashi Tadashi 1990, no. 84; Avitabile 1990, no. 54; Fischer 2000, pp. 197–98, no. 63; Murase 2000, no. 84; Tsuji Nobuo et al. 2005, no. 91; Graham 2007, no. 6.10.

Hon'ami Kōetsu
(本阿弥光悦; 1558–1637)
Tawaraya Sōtatsu
(俵屋宗達; d. ca. 1640)

175. Poem from *Kokin wakashū* (古今和歌集)

Momoyama period, early 17th century
Album leaf, mounted as hanging scroll; ink and gold on paper
18.3 x 16.3 cm (7¼ x 6⅜ in.)
Text

Ex coll.: Ōkura

Literature: Murase 1975, no. 48; Avitabile 1990, no. 52; Murase 2000, no. 83.

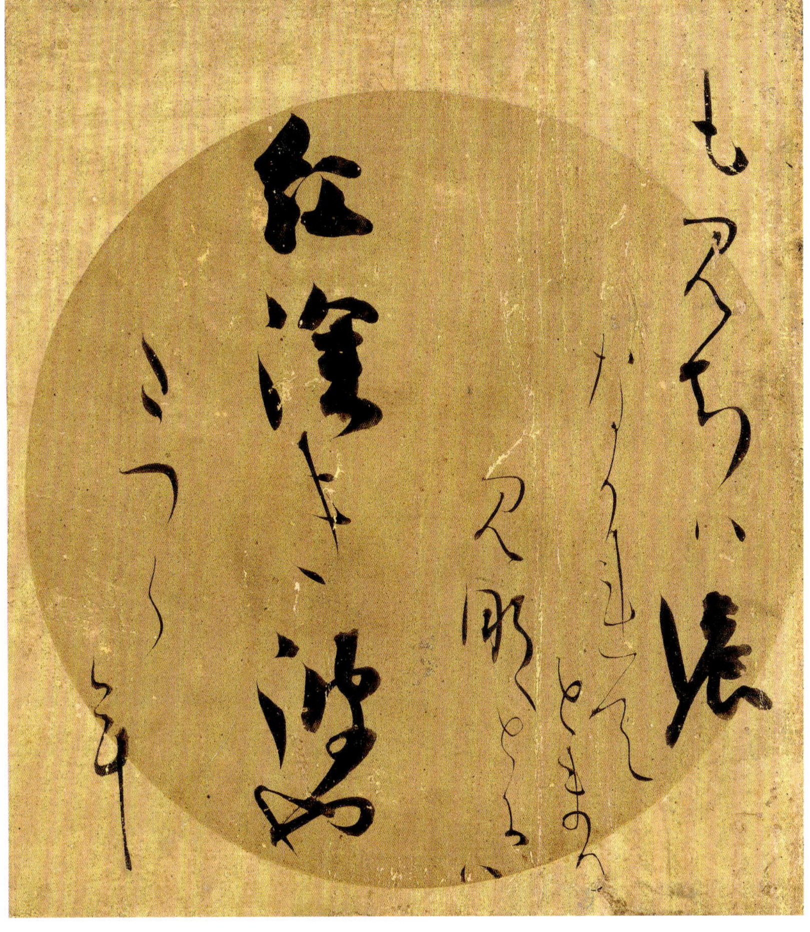

Hon'ami Kōetsu
(本阿弥光悦; 1558–1637)
Tawaraya Sōtatsu
(俵屋宗達; d. ca. 1640)

176. Poem from *Kokin wakashū* (古今和歌集)

Momoyama period, early 17th century
Album leaf, mounted as hanging scroll; ink and gold on paper
18.3 x 16.3 cm (7¼ x 6⅜ in.)
Text

Ex coll.: Ōkura

Literature: Murase 1975, no. 48; Avitabile 1990, no. 52; Murase 2000, no. 83; Tamamushi Satoko 2004, p. 67.

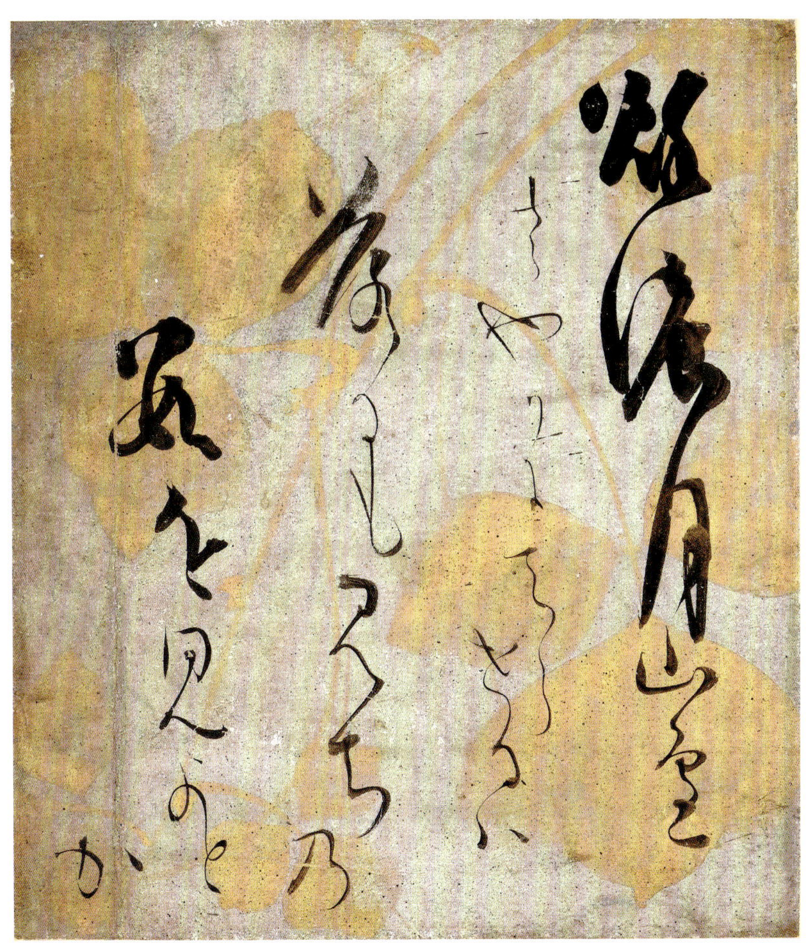

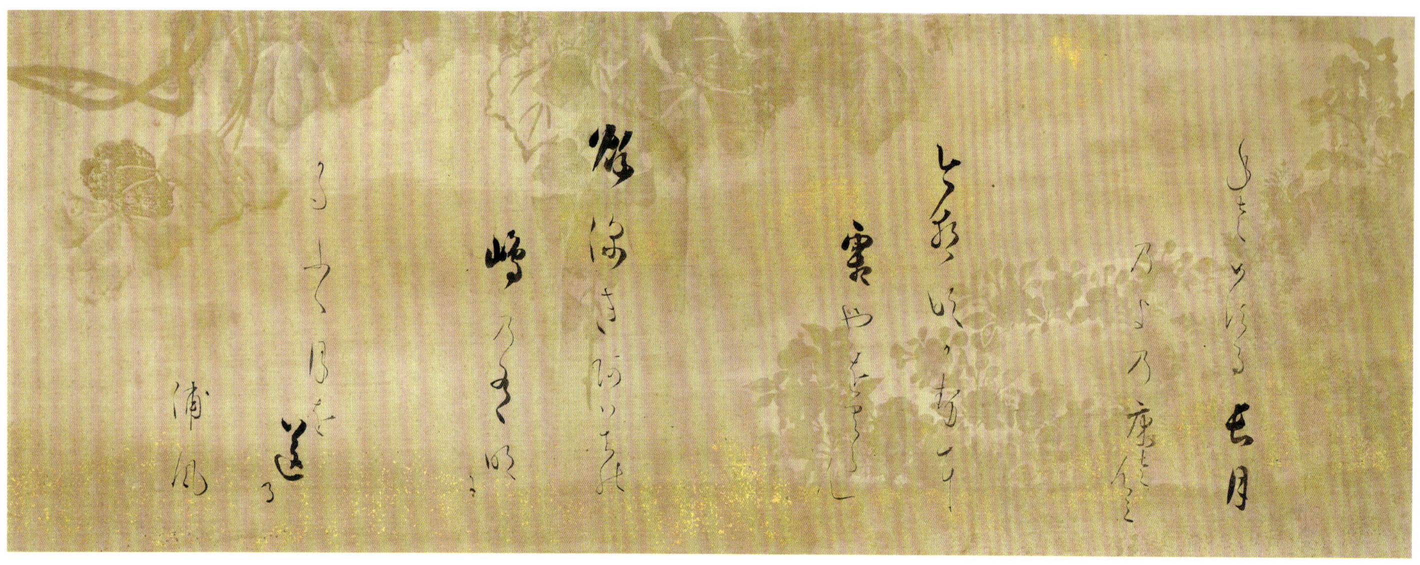

Hon'ami Kōetsu
(本阿弥光悦; 1558–1637)
follower of Tawaraya Sōtatsu
(俵屋宗達; d. ca. 1640)

177. Twelve poems from *Shin kokin wakashū* (新古今和歌集)

Edo period
Handscroll (*detail*); ink and printed with gold on silk
33.7 x 489.8 cm (13¼ in. x 16 ft. ⅞ in.)
Text, signature, seals

Ex coll.: Marquis Asano, Tokyo

Literature: Murase 1975, no. 50; Yamane Yūzō et al. 1978, pp. 82–83, fig. 50; Tokyo National Museum 1978, no. 265; Yamane Yūzō 1977–80, vol. 5 (1978), pp. 82–83, fig. 50; Tokyo National Museum 1985a, no. 77; Avitabile 1990, no. 53; Murase 2000, no. 85.

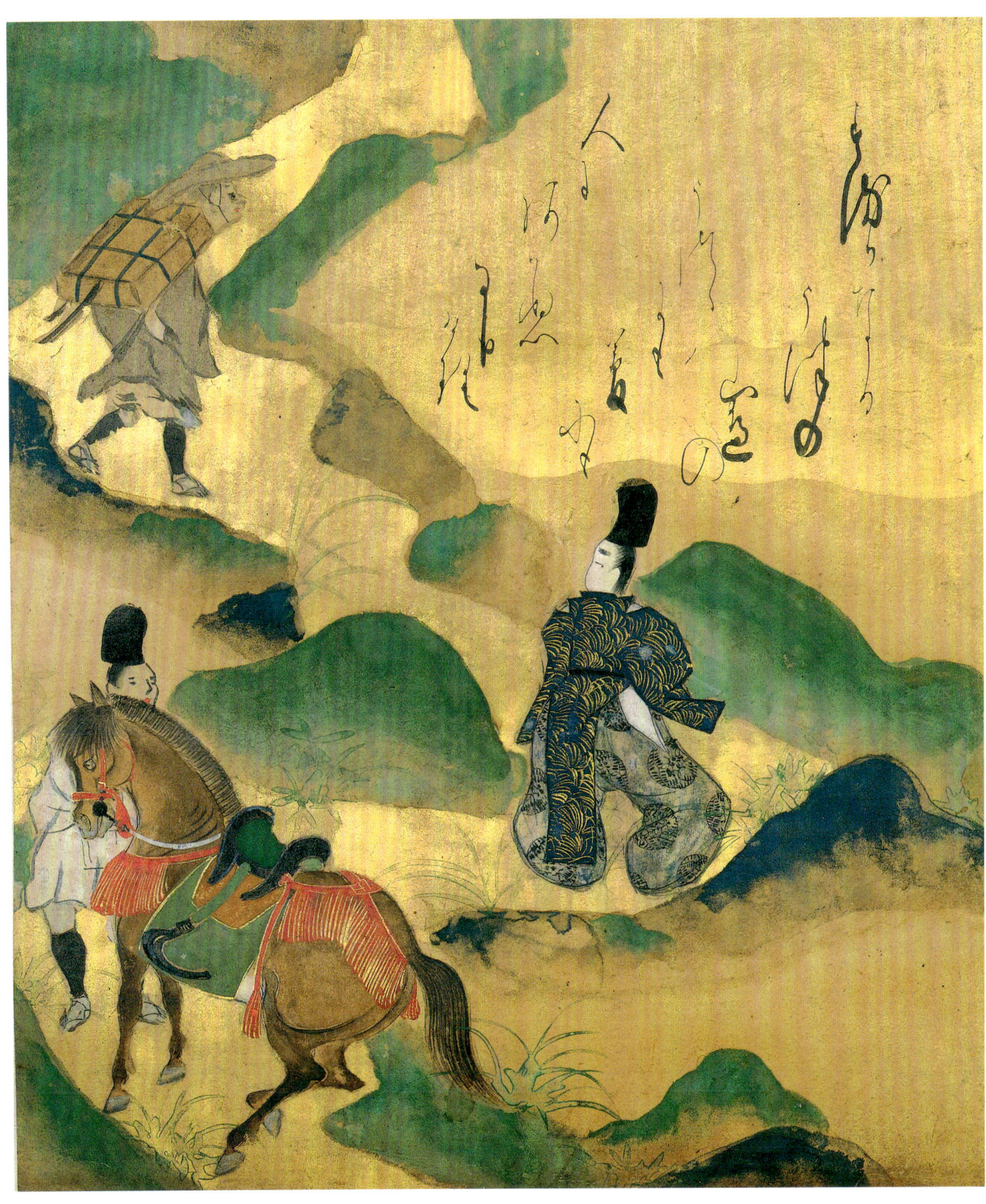

Tawaraya Sōtatsu
(俵屋宗達; d. ca. 1640)
Takeuchi Toshiharu (calligrapher)
(竹内俊治; 1611–1647)

178. "Utsu no yama" (宇津の山), from episode 9 of *Ise monogatari* (伊勢物語)

Edo period
Album leaf, mounted as hanging scroll; ink, color, and gold on paper
24.4 x 20.8 cm (9 5/8 x 8 1/8 in.)
Text

Ex coll.: Masuda Takashi

Literature: Tanaka Shinbi 1932, pl. 10; Tanaka Kisaku 1941, pl. 23; Tokyo National Museum 1952, no. 59; Yamane Yūzō 1962b, pl. 174; Tokyo National Museum 1972, pl. 99; Yamane Yūzō 1974, fig. 14; Murase 1975, no. 52; Shirahata Yoshi 1975, vol. 1, pl. 28; Yamane Yūzō 1975, p. 19; Yamane Yūzō 1977–80, vol. 1 (1977), pl. 56; Yamane Yūzō 1979, no. 1; Kita Haruchiyo 1985, p. 81; Murase 1985, pl. v; Tokyo National Museum 1985a, no. 42; Kobayashi Tadashi et al. 1990, p. 152, fig. 14; Avitabile 1990, no. 55; Murashige Yasushi 1991, pl. 1-4; Murashige Yasushi 1993, pl. 63; Murase 2000, no. 86; Tsuji Nobuo et al. 2005, no. 90; Carpenter 2012, no. 1; Institute of Japanese Culture 2013, p. 41

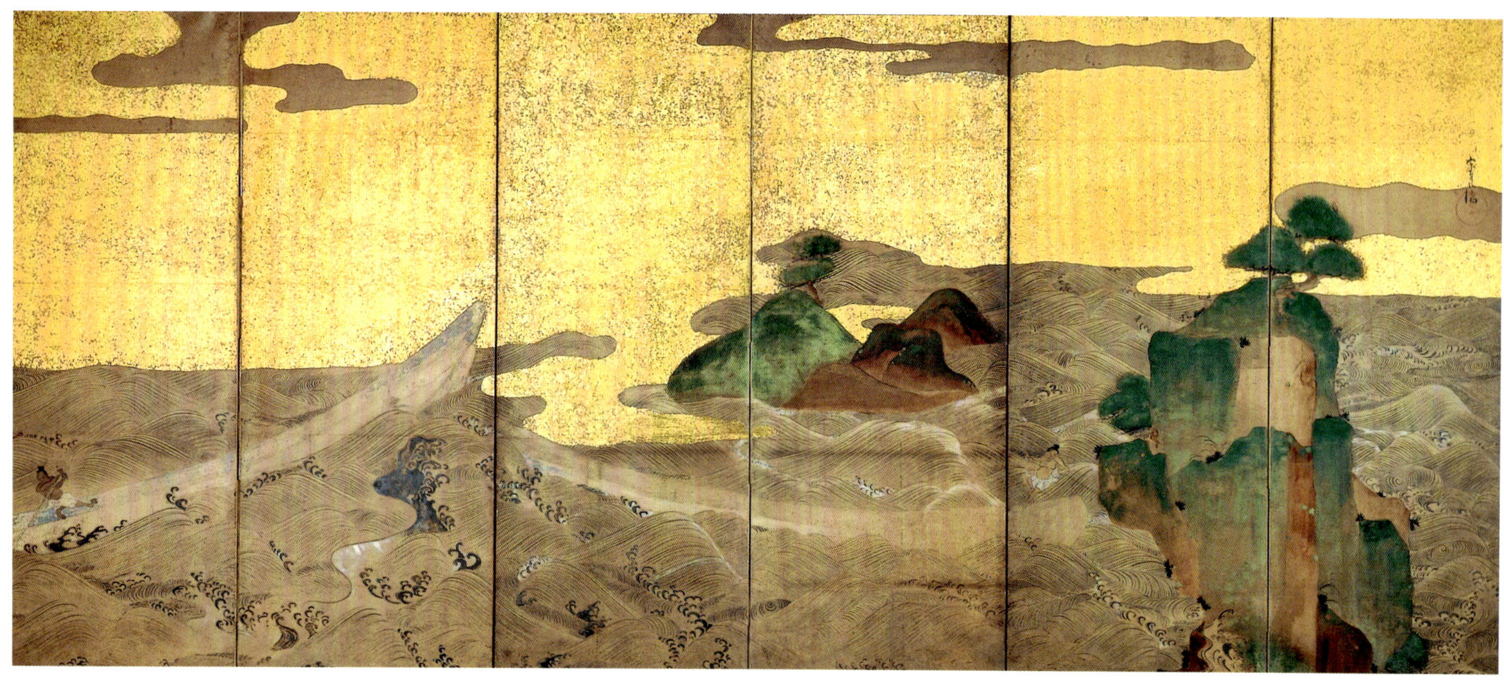

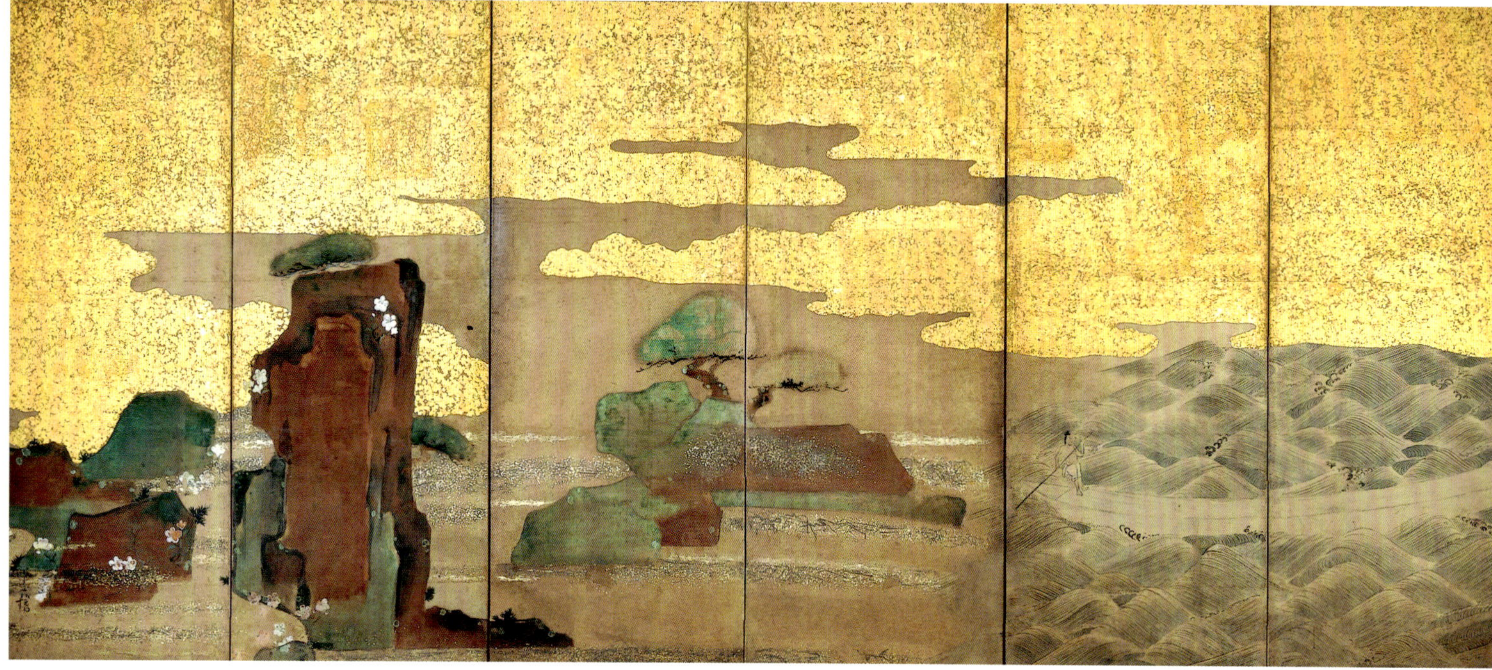

STUDIO OF TAWARAYA SŌTATSU
(俵屋宗達工房)

179. Boats on the Sea

Edo period, 17th century
Pair of six-panel folding screens; ink, color, gold, and silver on paper
Each screen 154.5 x 357.8 cm (60⅞ in. x 11 ft. 8⅞ in.)
Signatures, seals

LITERATURE: Burke 1993, pp. 40–41, no. 25; Hiroshima Prefectural Museum of Art et al. 2005, no. 133.

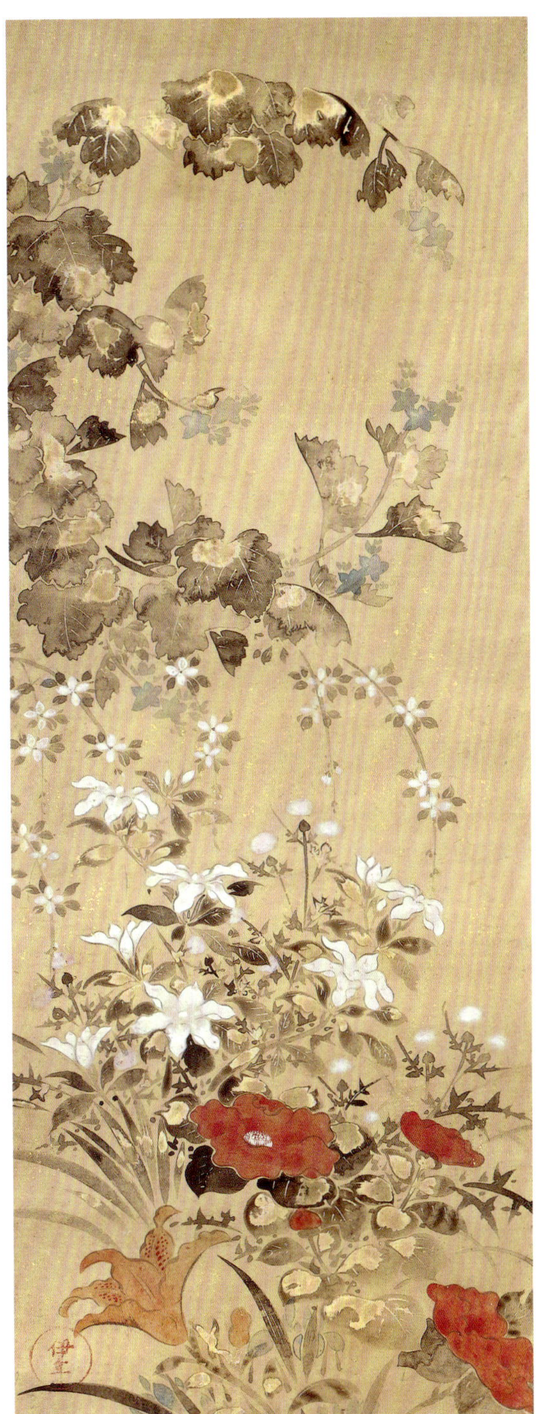

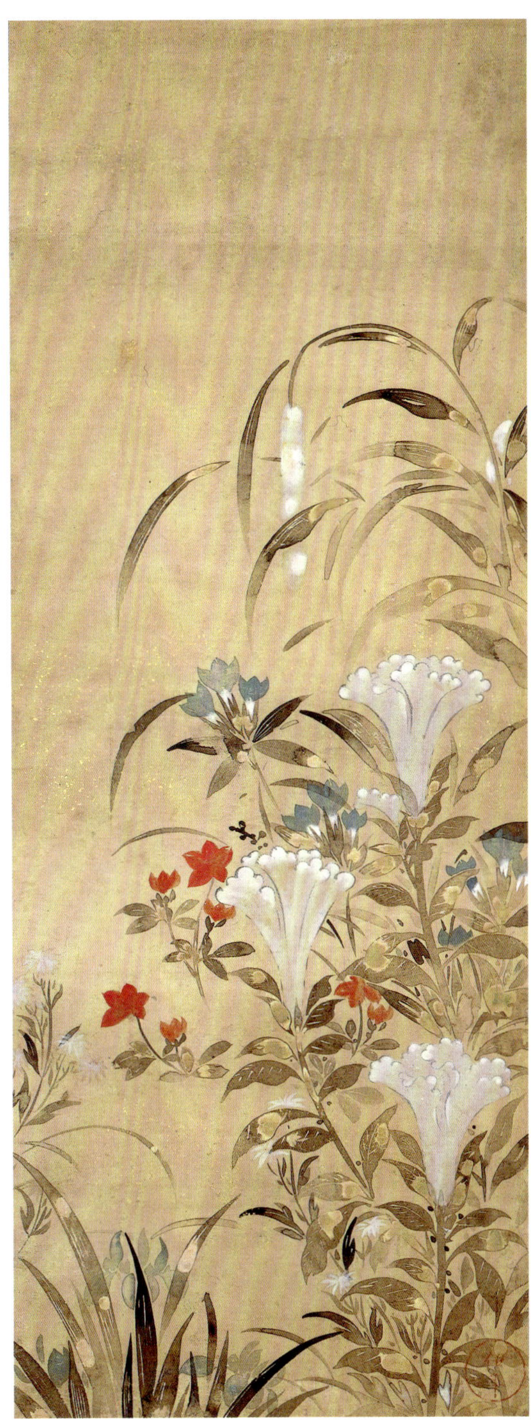

Tawaraya Sōsetsu
(俵屋宗雪; fl. 17th century)

180. Flowers of Summer; Flowers of Autumn

Edo period, first half of the 17th century
Pair of hanging scrolls; ink, color, and gold on paper
Each scroll 130.9 x 49.5 cm (51 1/2 x 19 1/2 in.)
Seals

Literature: Murase 1975, no. 53; Avitabile 1990, no. 56.

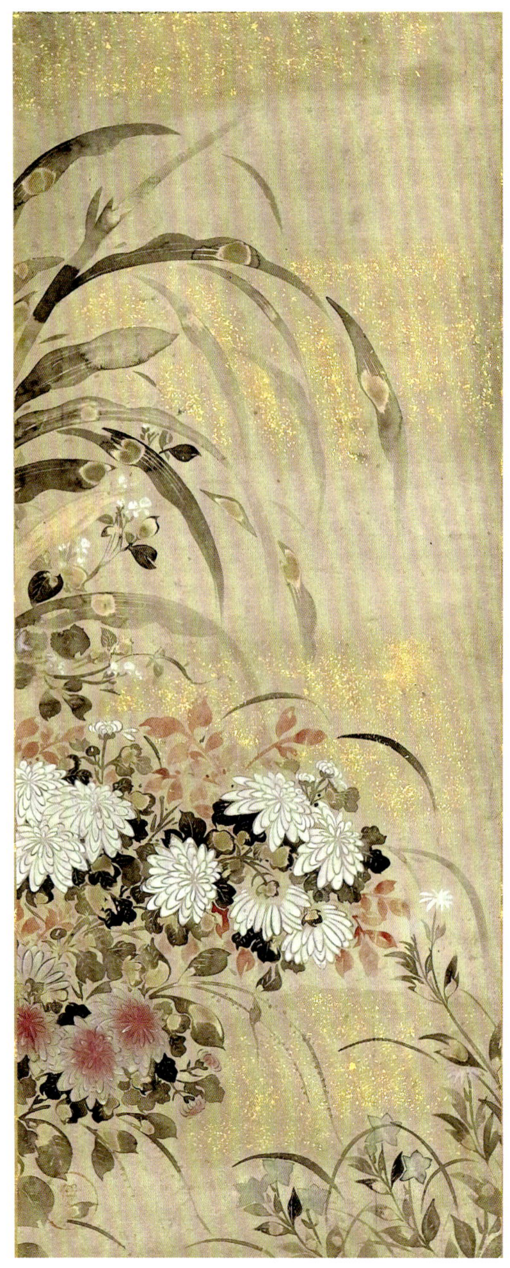

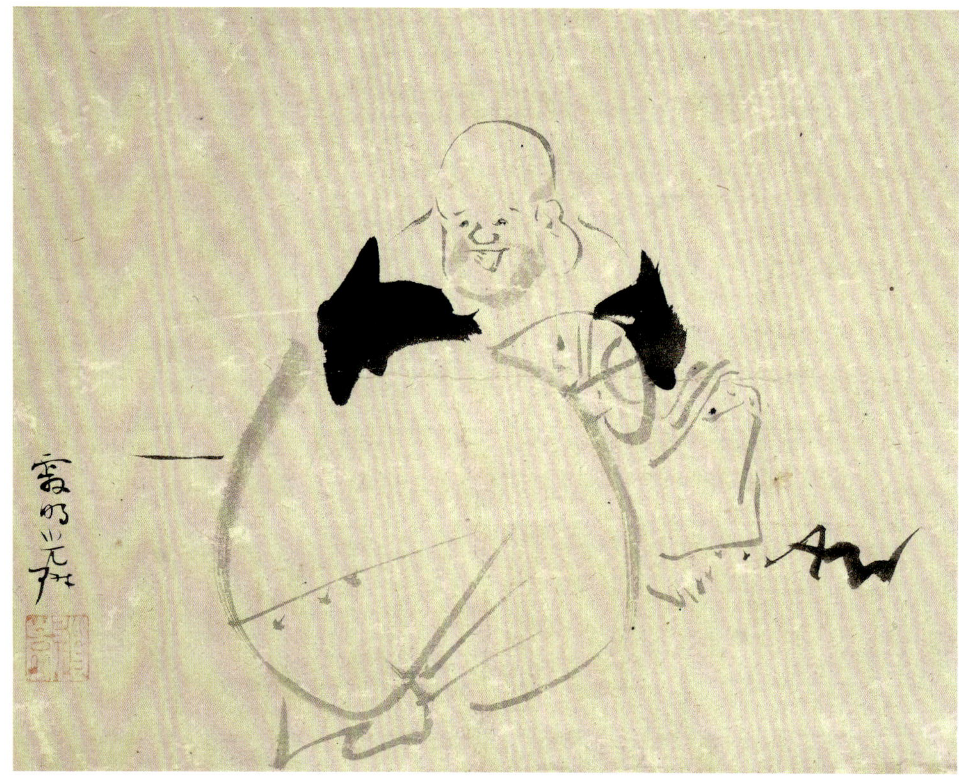

Tawaraya Sōsetsu
(俵屋宗雪; fl. 17th century)

181. Flowers of Autumn

Edo period, first half of the 17th century
Hanging scroll; ink, color, and gold on paper
123.9 x 49.8 cm (48 3/4 x 19 5/8 in.)
Seal

Literature: Burke 1993, fig. 10/no. 3.

Ogata Kōrin
(尾形光琳; 1658–1716)

182. Hotei (布袋)

Edo period
Hanging scroll; ink on paper
28.5 x 36.9 cm (11 1/4 x 14 1/2 in.)
Signature, seal

Ex coll.: Hara Tomitarō, Kanagawa Prefecture

Literature: Uemura Masurō 1940, fig. 110; Tanaka Ichimatsu 1965b, fig. 42; Shimada Shūjirō 1969, vol. 2, p. 81; Murase 1975, no. 55; Tokyo National Museum 1985a, no. 44; Avitabile 1990, no. 58; Murashige Yasushi 1991, fig. 162; Murase 2000, no. 133; Tsuji Nobuo et al. 2005, no. 92; Carpenter 2012, no. 26.

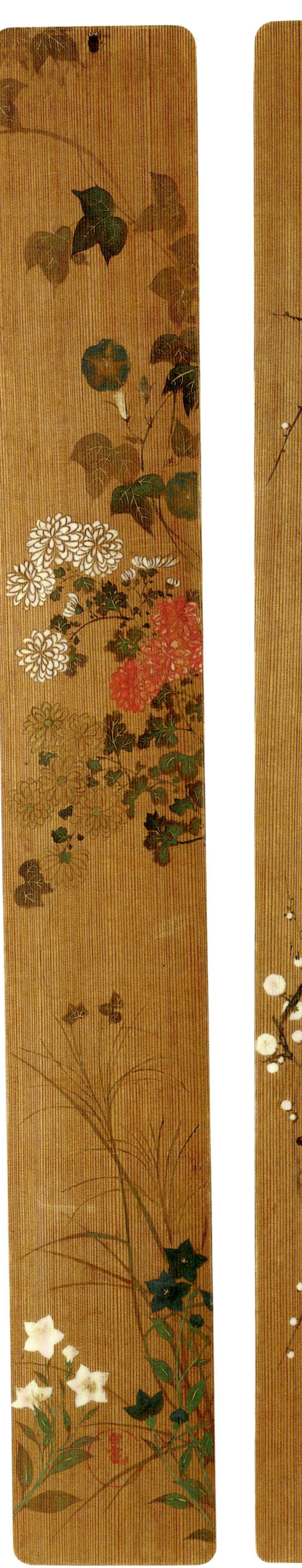

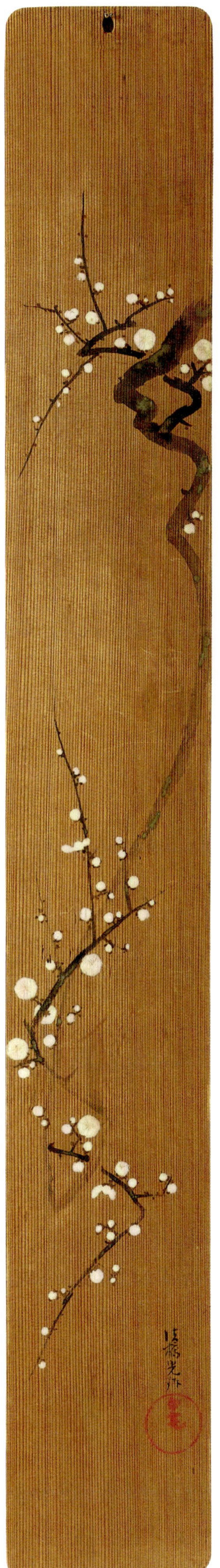

Ogata Kōrin
(尾形光琳; 1658–1716)

183. Flowers of Spring; Flowers of Autumn

Edo period, shortly after 1701
Pair of panels; ink and color on cryptomeria wood
Each panel 137.2 x 19.9 cm (54 x 7 7/8 in.)
Signature, seals

Ex coll.: Hosomi Ryō, Osaka; Inoue Tatsukurō

Literature: Tanaka Ichimatsu 1965b, fig. 1; Mizuo Hiroshi 1965–66, vol. 3, pl. 68; Stern 1971, no. 18; Murase 1975, no. 54; Tokyo National Museum 1985a, no. 43; Avitabile 1990, no. 57; Murase 2000, no. 132.

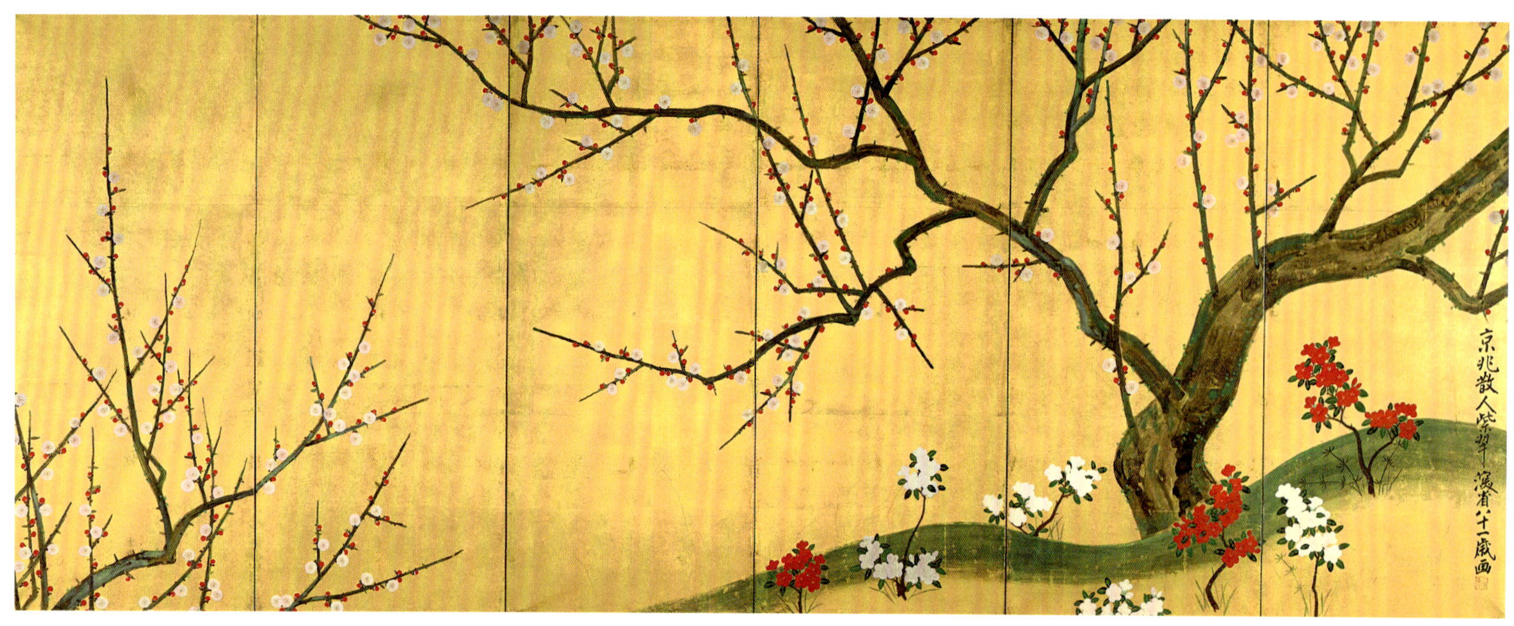

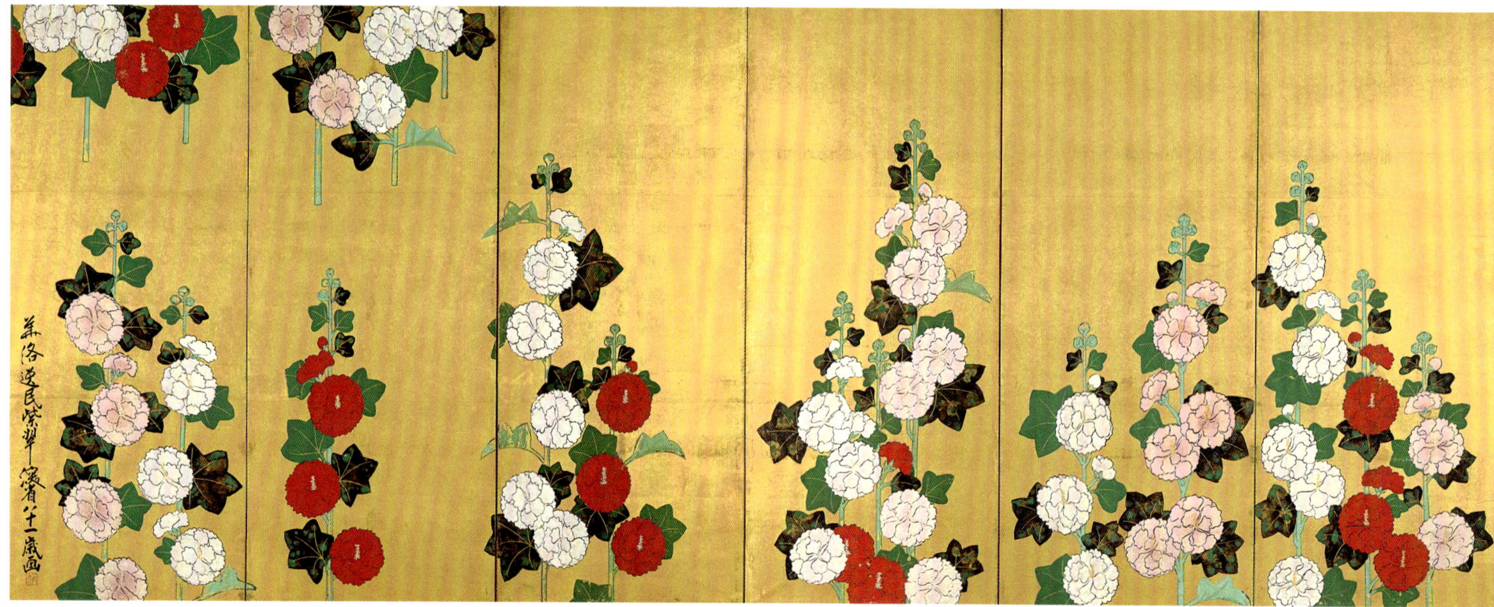

Ogata Kenzan
(尾形乾山; 1663–1743)

184. Plum Trees; Hollyhocks

Edo period
Pair of six-panel folding screens; ink and color on gilded paper
Each screen 110.8 x 286 cm ($43\frac{5}{8}$ in. x 9 ft. $4\frac{5}{8}$ in.)
Signatures, seals

Ex coll.: Prince Komatsu

Literature: S.E. Lee 1961, pls. 82, 83; Tokugawa Art Museum 1966, unnumbered; Nakamura Tanio 1967a, pp. 89–90; Stern 1971, no. 30; Murase 1975, no. 56; Carpenter 2012, no. 61.

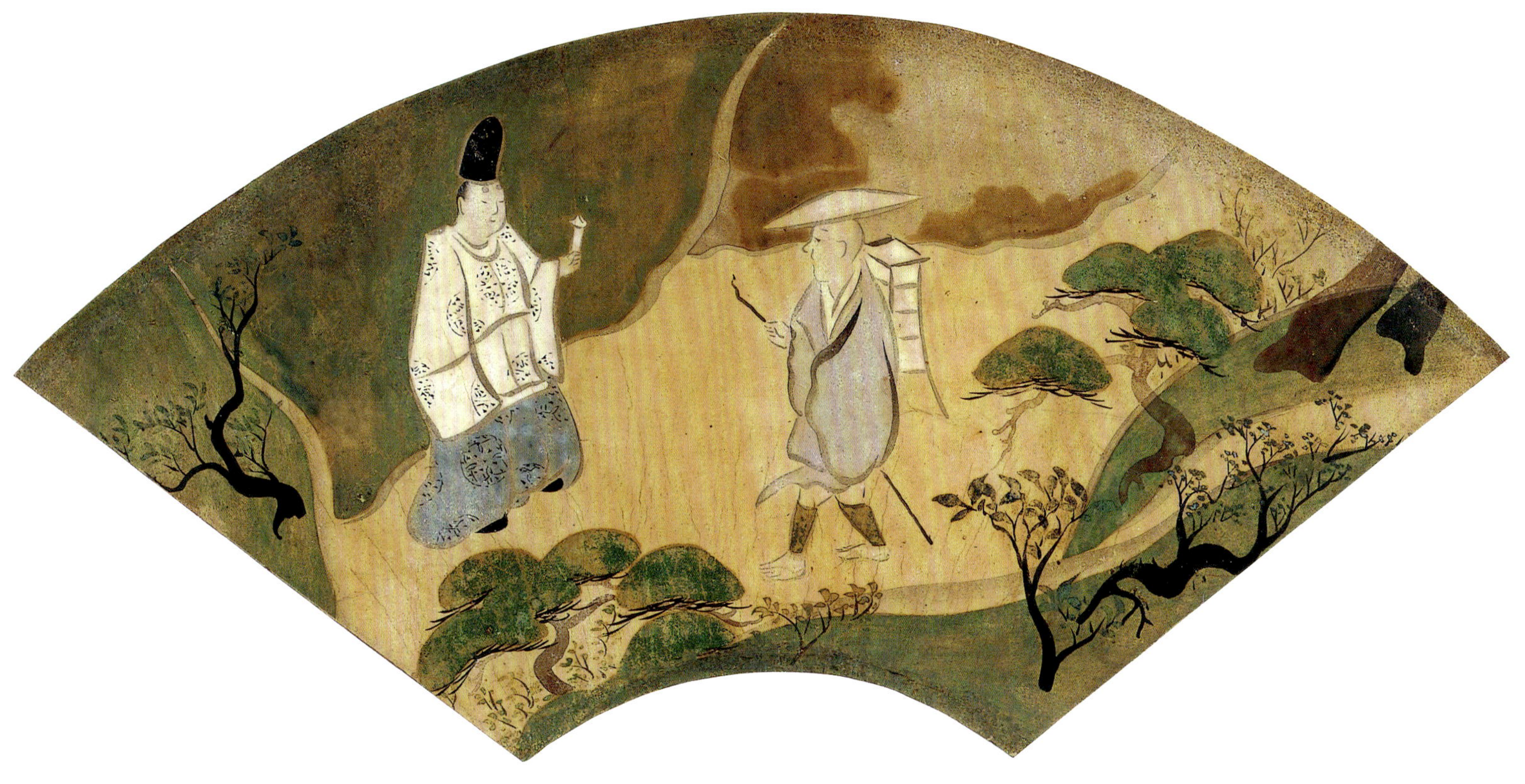

attributed to Fukae Roshū
(深江蘆舟; 1699–1757)

185. "Utsu no yama" (宇津の山), from episode 9 of *Ise monogatari* (伊勢物語)

Edo period
Fan-shaped painting, mounted on hanging scroll; ink and color on paper
22.2 x 46.2 cm (8 3/4 x 18 1/4 in.)

Literature: Stern 1971, p. 75, no. 44; Burke 1993, fig. 11, no. 5; Carpenter 2012, no. 2.

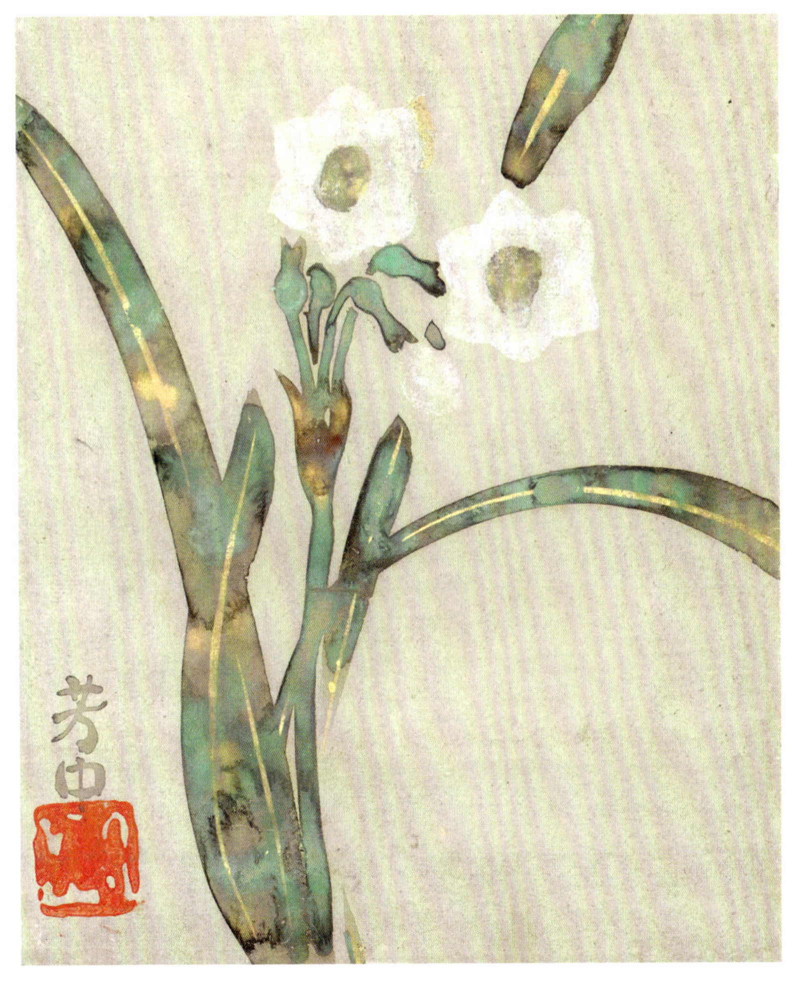

Nakamura Hōchū
(中村芳中; d. 1819)

186. Narcissus

Edo period
Hanging scroll; ink and color on paper
20.7 x 17.3 cm (8 1/8 x 6 3/4 in.)
Signature, seal

Literature: Burke 1993, p. 45, no. 12.

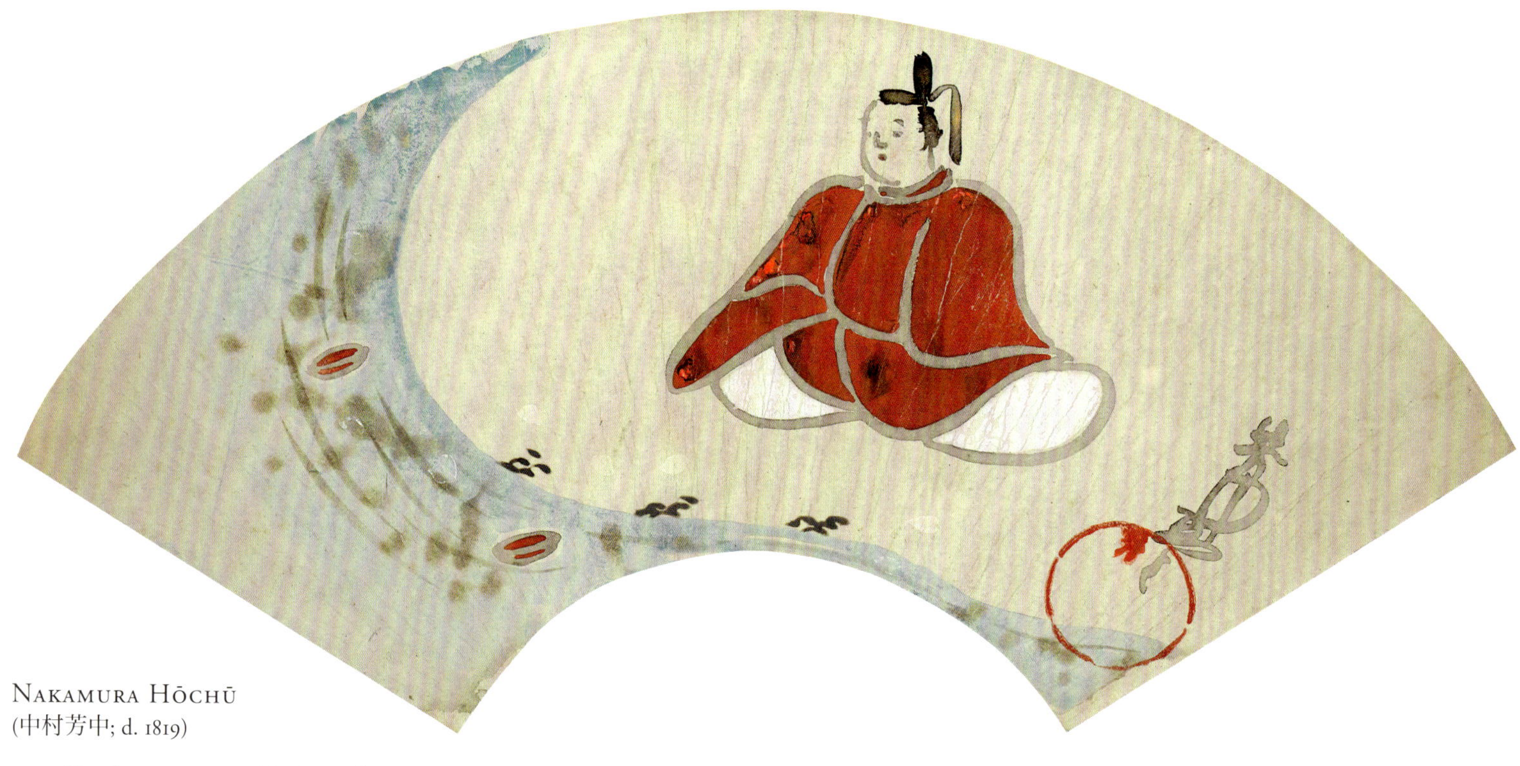

Nakamura Hōchū
(中村芳中; d. 1819)

187. Kyokusui no en (曲水の宴)

Edo period
Fan-shaped painting mounted on hanging scroll; ink and color on paper
20.8 x 59.7 cm ($8^{1}/_{8}$ x $23^{1}/_{2}$ in.)
Signature, seal

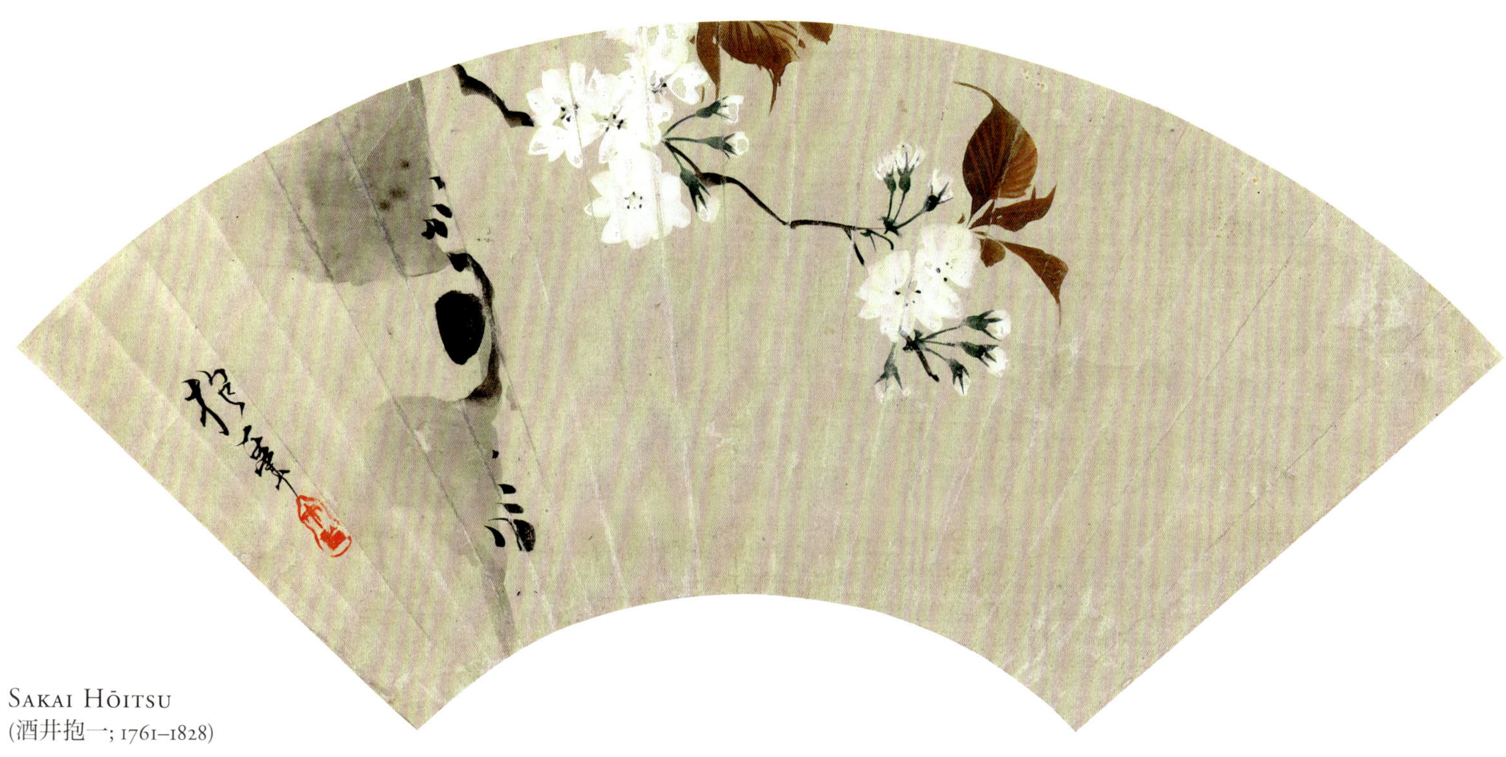

Sakai Hōitsu
(酒井抱一; 1761–1828)

188. Cherry Blossoms

Edo period, 18th century
Folding fan, mounted on hanging scroll; ink and color on paper
16.8 x 44.9 cm ($6^{5}/_{8}$ x $17^{5}/_{8}$ in.)
Signature, seal

Gift from Setsu Iwao, 1974

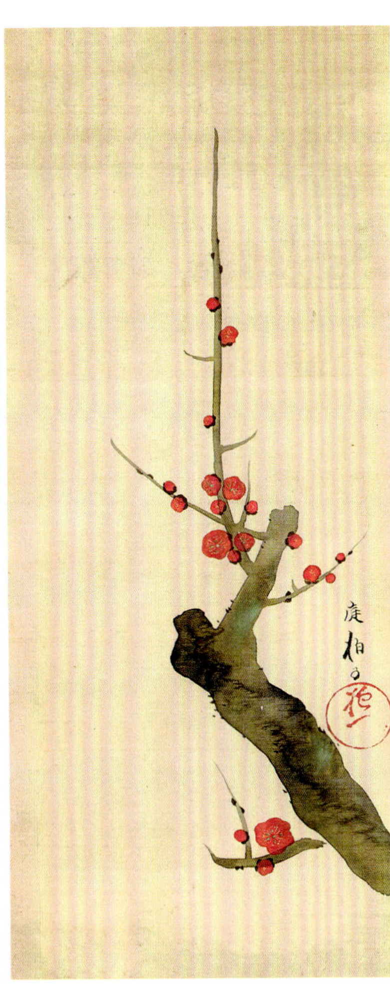

Sakai Hōitsu
(酒井抱一; 1761–1828)

189. Red Plum Blossoms

Edo period, 18th century
Hanging scroll; ink and color on silk
69.7 x 29 cm ($27\frac{1}{2}$ x $11\frac{3}{8}$ in.)
Signature, seal

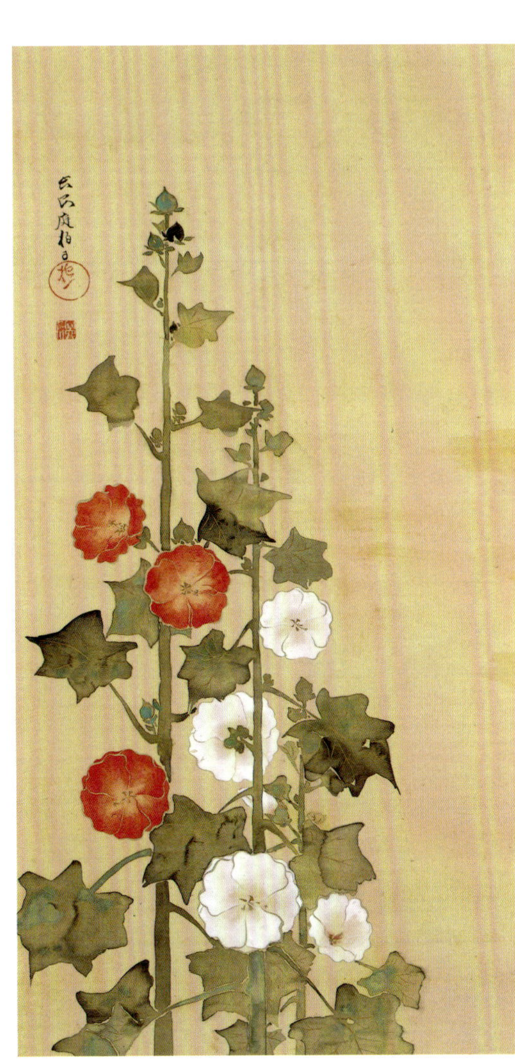

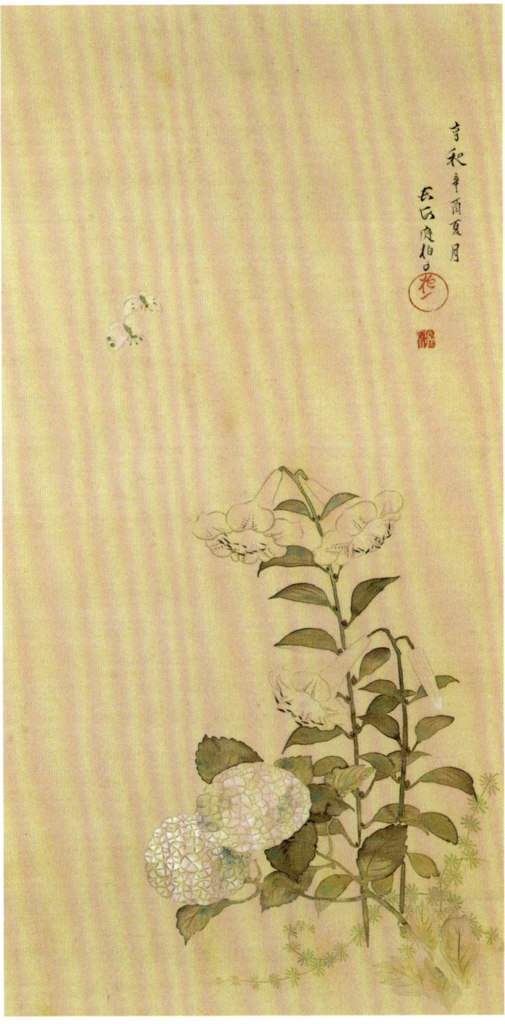

Sakai Hōitsu
(酒井抱一; 1761–1828)

190. Lilies and Hydrangeas; Hollyhocks

Edo period, 1801
Two-panel folding screen; ink, color, and gold on silk
Each panel 124.4 x 63.5 cm (49 x 25 in.)
Signatures, seals

Literature: Kōno Motoaki 1978, pp. 33–34, fig. 5; Tamamushi Satoko 1997, pl. 6; Tamamushi Satoko 2008, p. 19; Nakamachi Keiko 2010, p. 36; McKelway 2012, pp. 56–57, no. 6.

Sakai Hōitsu
(酒井抱一; 1761–1828)

191. Blossoming Cherry Trees

Edo period, ca. 1805
Pair of six-panel folding screens; ink, color, and gold on gilded paper
Each screen 96.5 x 208.8 cm (38 in. x 6 ft. 10¼ in.)
Signatures, seals

Ex coll.: Iwasaki, Tokyo

Literature: Honma Art Museum 1969, no. 18; Yamane Yūzō 1977–80, vol. 5 (1978), pls. 10, 23, 24; Chizawa Teiji 1981, fig. 40; Tokyo National Museum 1985a, no. 45; Kobayashi Tadashi 1990, pl. 57; Avitabile 1990, no. 59; Nakamachi Keiko 1992a, pp. 1032–33; Tamamushi Satoko 1997, pl. 10; Murase 2000, no. 134; Tsuji Nobuo et al. 2005, no. 93; Tamamushi Satoko 2008, p. 25; Nakamachi Keiko 2010, pp. 64–67; McKelway 2012, p. 43 (detail), no. 7.

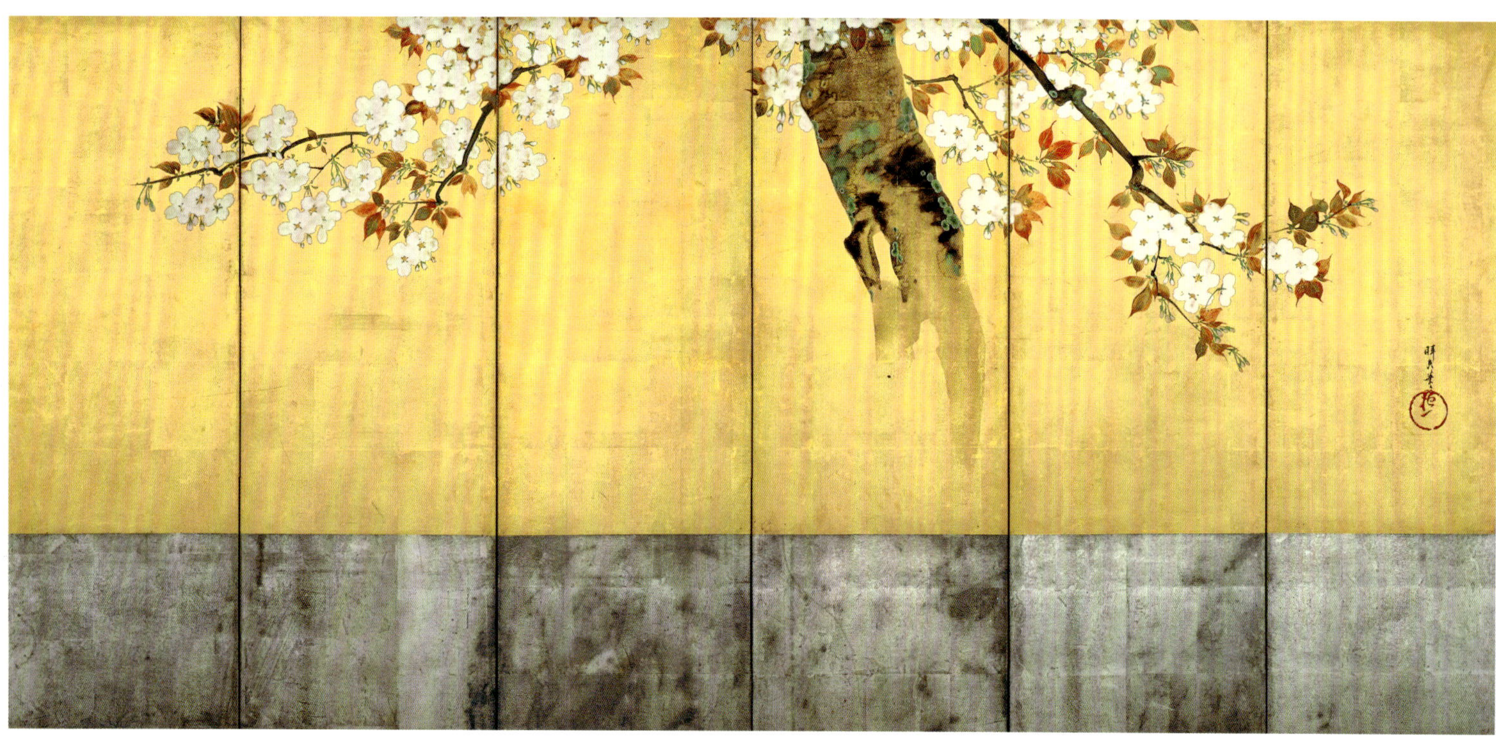

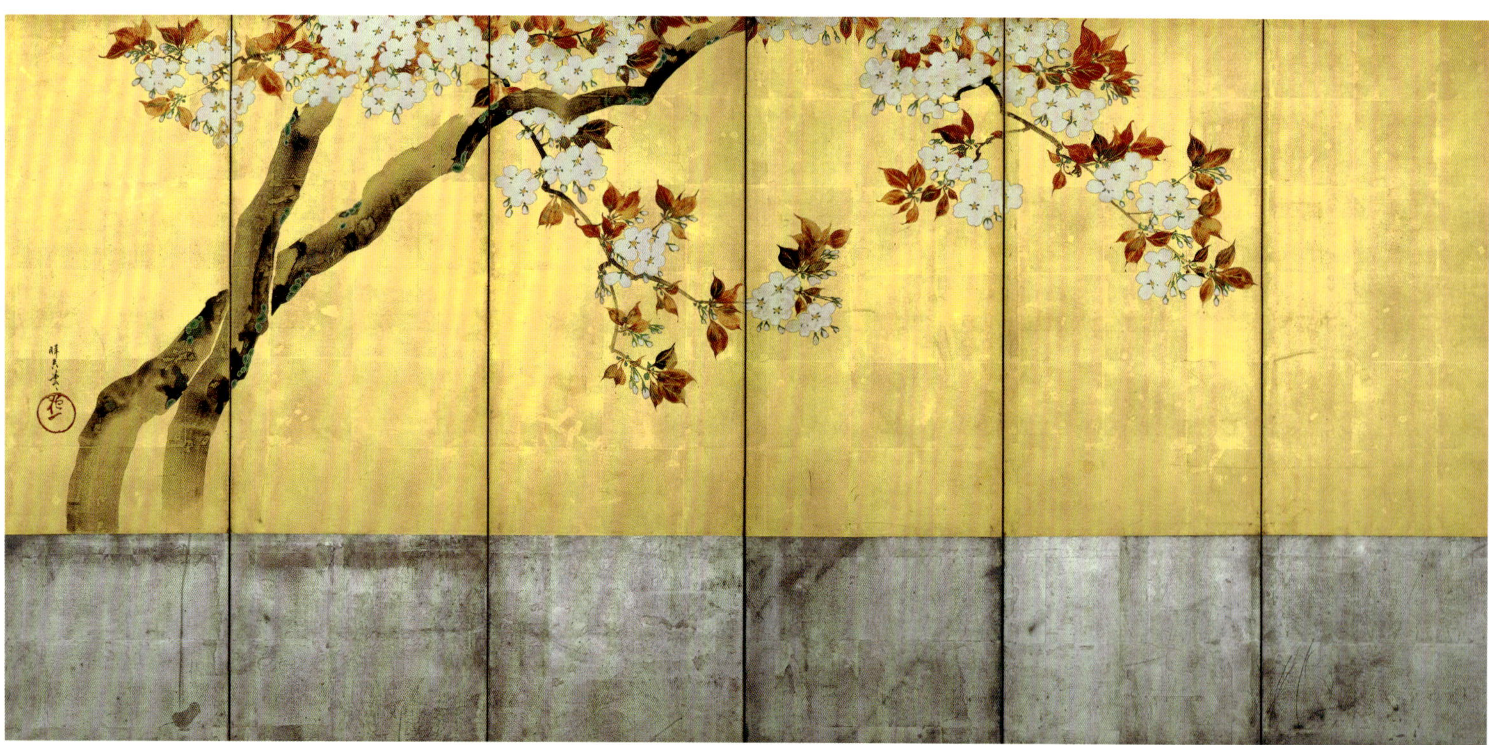

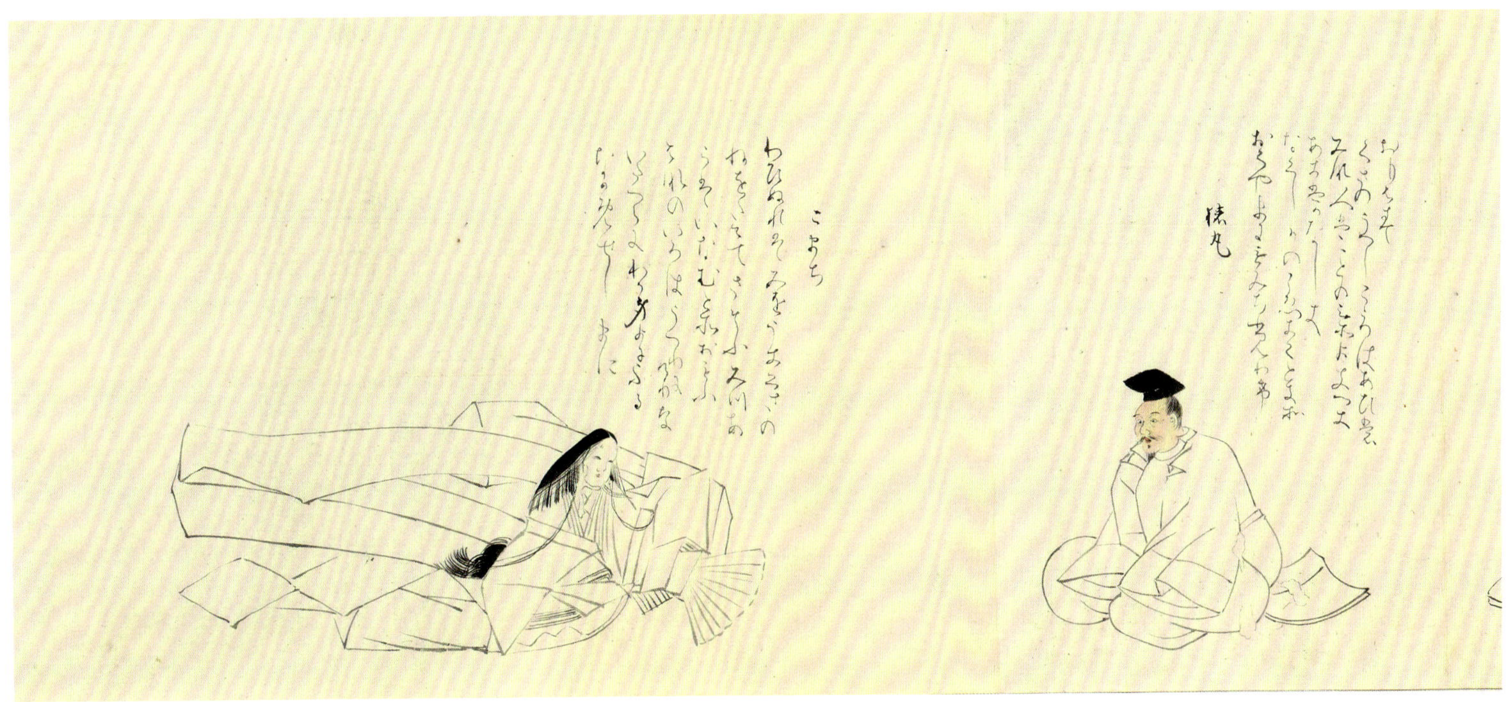

Sakai Hōitsu
(酒井抱一; 1761–1828)

192. Thirty-six Immortal Poets
(三十六歌仙)

Edo period, 1824
Handscroll; ink and light color on paper
29.5 x 827.6 cm (11 5/8 in. x 27 ft. 1 7/8 in.)
Text, signature, seal

Literature: McKelway 2012, pp. 126–27, no. 36

193. Chrysanthemums

Edo period, 18th century
Six-panel folding screen, ink and color on gilded paper
153.1 x 399.8 cm (60 1/4 in. x 13 ft. 1 3/8 in.)

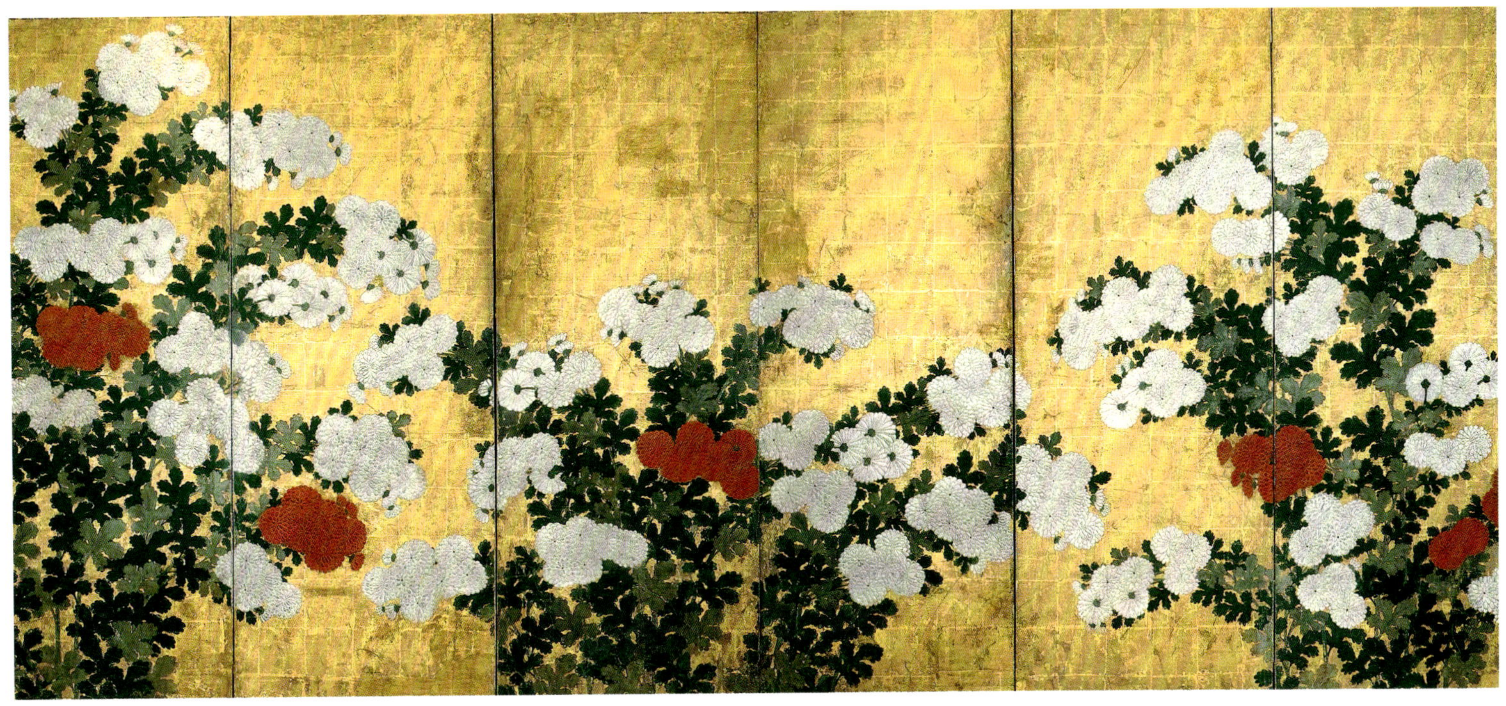

Suzuki Kiitsu
(鈴木其一; 1796–1858)

194. Hollyhock and Lilies

Edo period
Hanging scroll; ink and color on silk
110 x 35.8 cm (43 1/4 x 14 1/8 in.)
Signature, seal

Literature: Burke 1993, p. 83, no. 14.

Suzuki Kiitsu
(鈴木其一; 1796–1858)

195. Bird and Flowers

Edo period
Hanging scroll; ink and color on silk
96.4 x 30.8 cm (38 x 12 1/8 in.)
Signature, seal

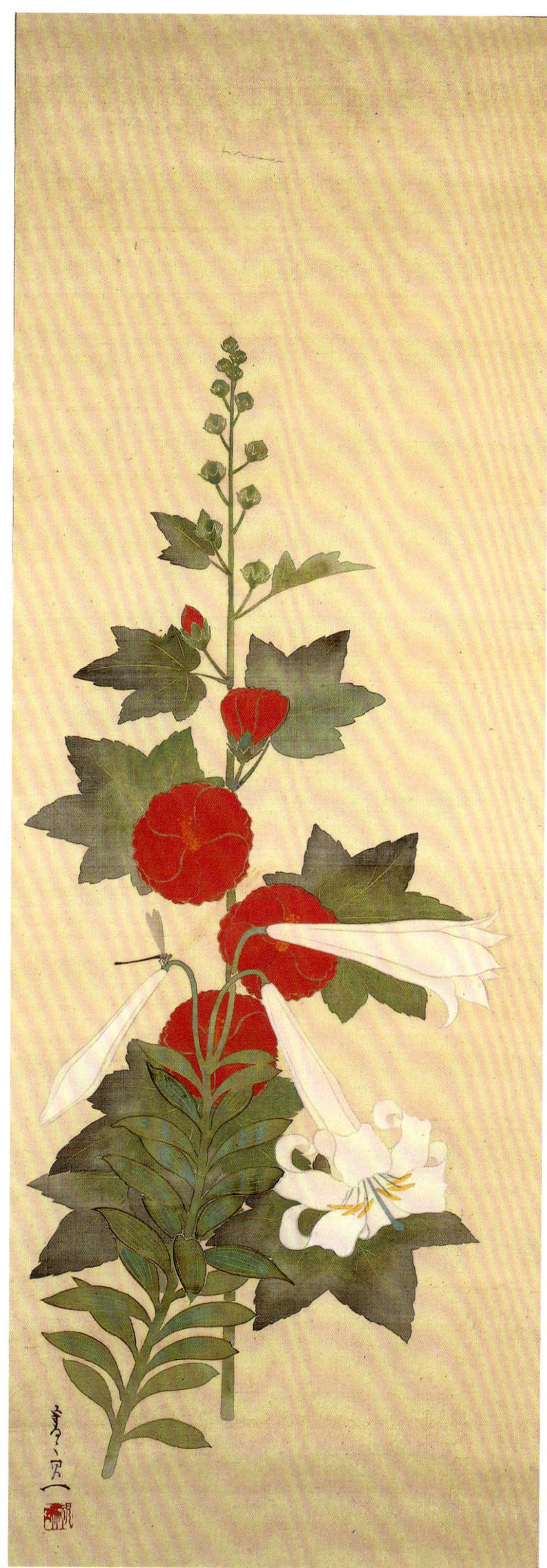

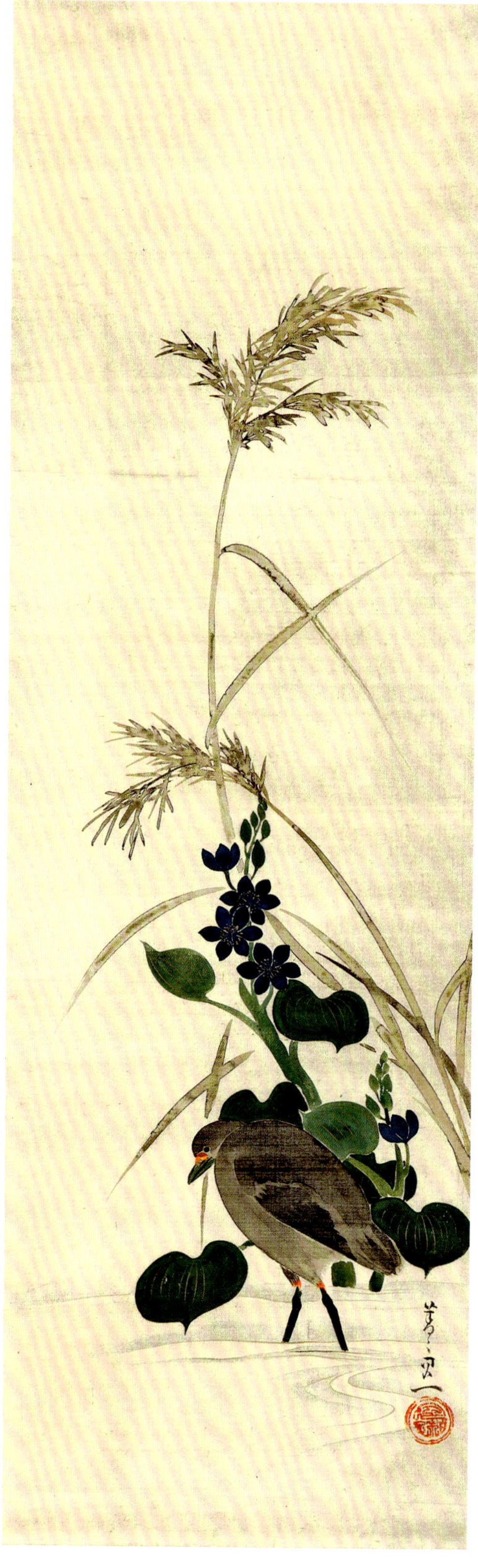

Suzuki Kiitsu
(鈴木其一; 1796–1858)

196. Irises and Moth

Edo period
Hanging scroll; ink, color, and gold on silk
101.6 x 33 cm (40 x 13 in.)
Signature, seal

Literature: Murase 1975, addendum, no. 109; Shirahata Yoshi 1975, vol. 3, pl. 54; Yamane Yūzō 1977–80, vol. 5 (1978), pls. 156, 182; Hosono Masanobu 1979, pl. 53; Nakamura Tanio 1979, vol. 5, pl. 73; Kōno Motoaki 1982a, fig. 25; Tokyo National Museum 1985a, no. 46; Kobayashi Tadashi 1990, pl. 132; Avitabile 1990, no. 60; Murase 2000, no. 135; Tsuji Nobuo et al. 2005, no. 94; Tamamushi Satoko 2008, p. 68; McKelway 2012, p. 159, no. 48.

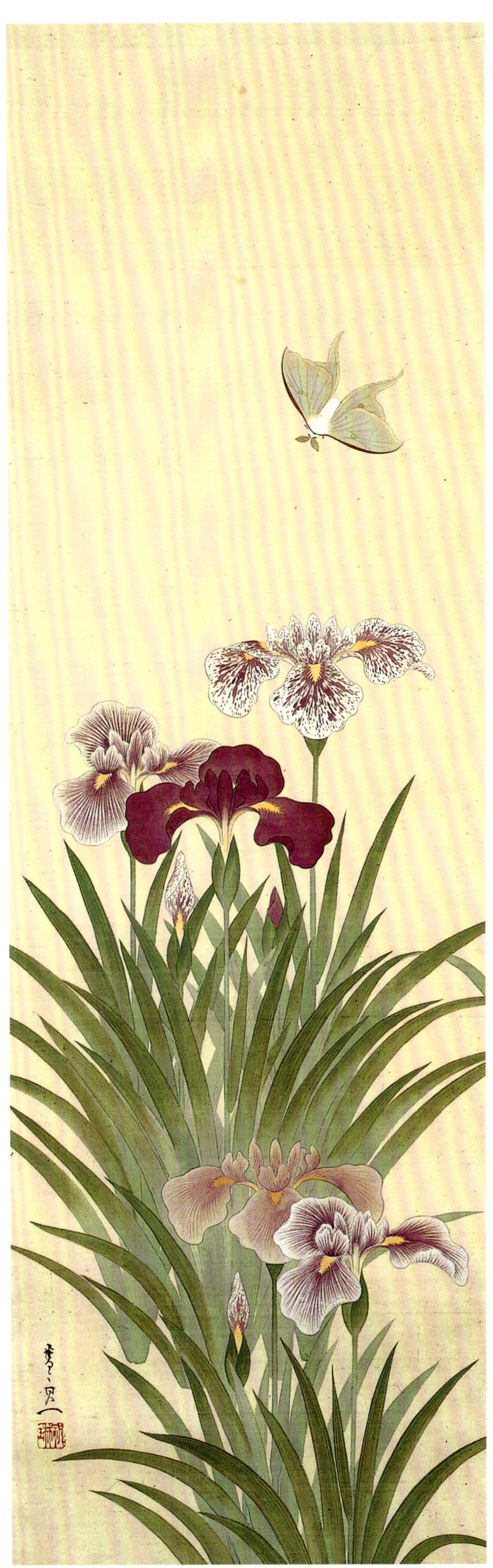

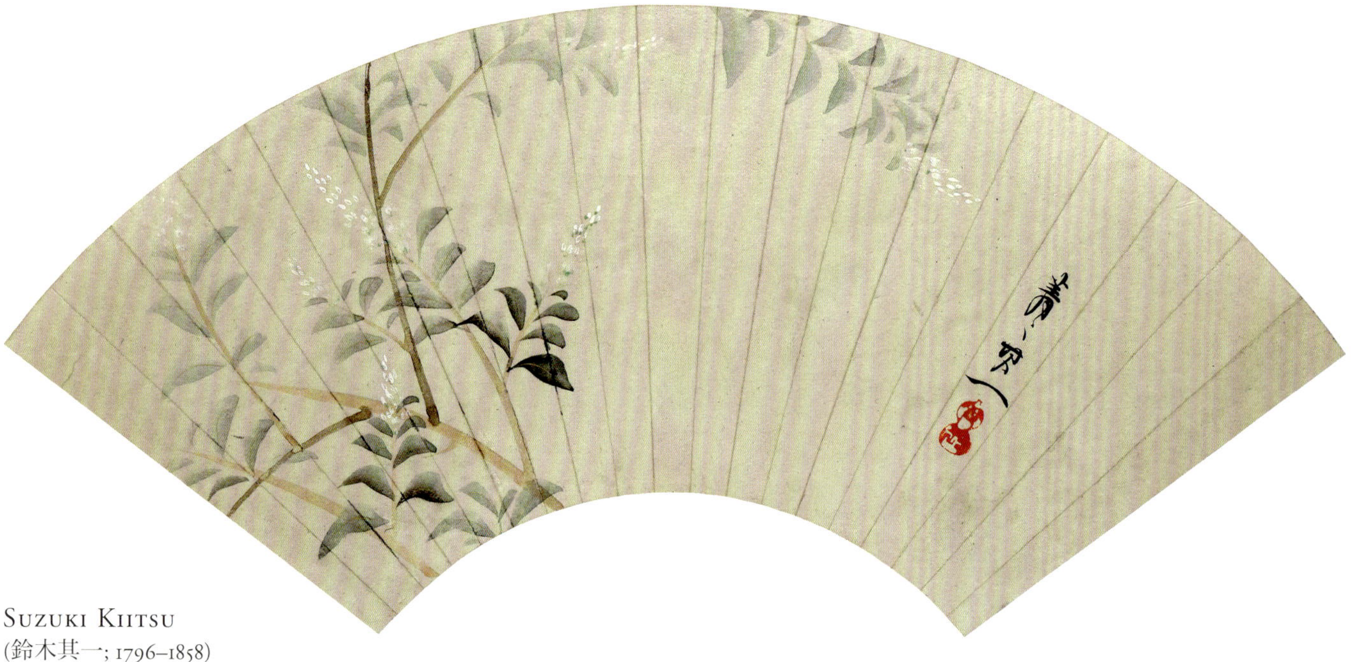

Suzuki Kiitsu
(鈴木其一; 1796–1858)

197. Bush Clover

Edo period
Folding fan mounted on hanging scroll; ink and color on paper
18.2 x 52 cm (7 1/8 x 20 1/2 in.)
Signature, seal

Literature: Moes 1975, pp. 63, 68, no. 15.

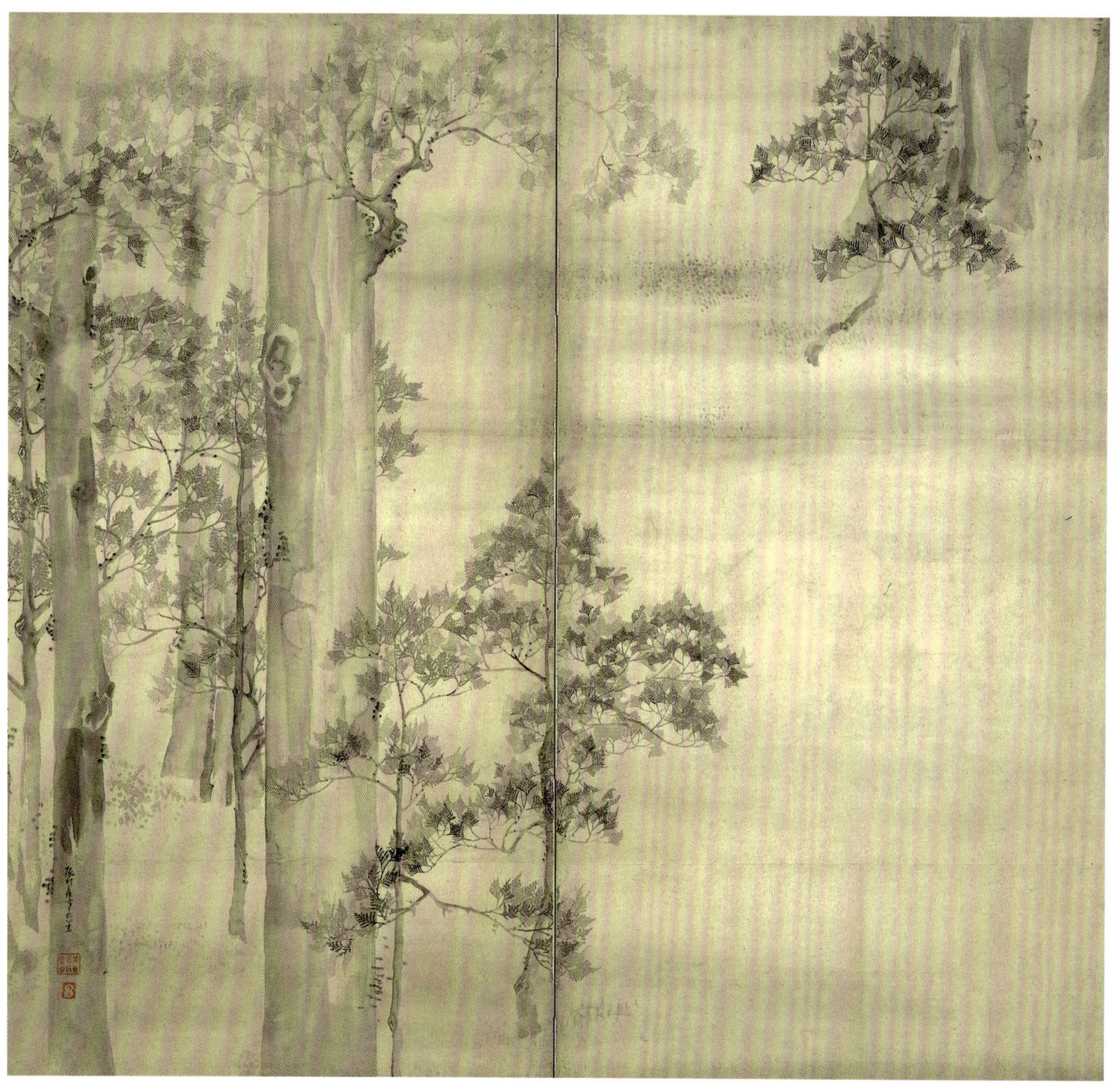

Ikeda Koson
(池田孤邨; 1802–1867)

198. Cypress Trees

Edo period
Two-panel folding screen; ink on paper
150.6 x 160.2 cm (59 1/4 x 63 1/8 in.)
Signature, seals

Literature: Murase 1971, no. 7; Yamane Yūzō 1977–80, vol. 5 (1978), pl. 213; Tokyo National Museum 1985a, no. 47; Murase 1990, no. 9; Avitabile 1990, no. 61; Kobayashi Tadashi 1991, pl. 92; Murase 1992, p. 214; Kōno Motoaki 1993, pp. 176–77, no. 57; Yasumura Toshinobu 1993, p. 81, no. 80; Murase 2000, no. 136; Furuta Ryō and Nakamura Reiko 2004, pp. 104–5, no. 35; Carpenter 2012, no. 19.

Suzuki Kiitsu
(鈴木其一; 1796–1858)

199. Setsubun Festival at Sensōji
(浅草寺節分)

Edo period, 1857
Hanging scroll; ink and light color on paper
99.6 x 28.9 cm (39 1/4 x 11 3/8 in.)
Text, signature, seal

Literature: Murashige Yasushi 1991, pp. 342–43, no. 297, ill. p. 209.

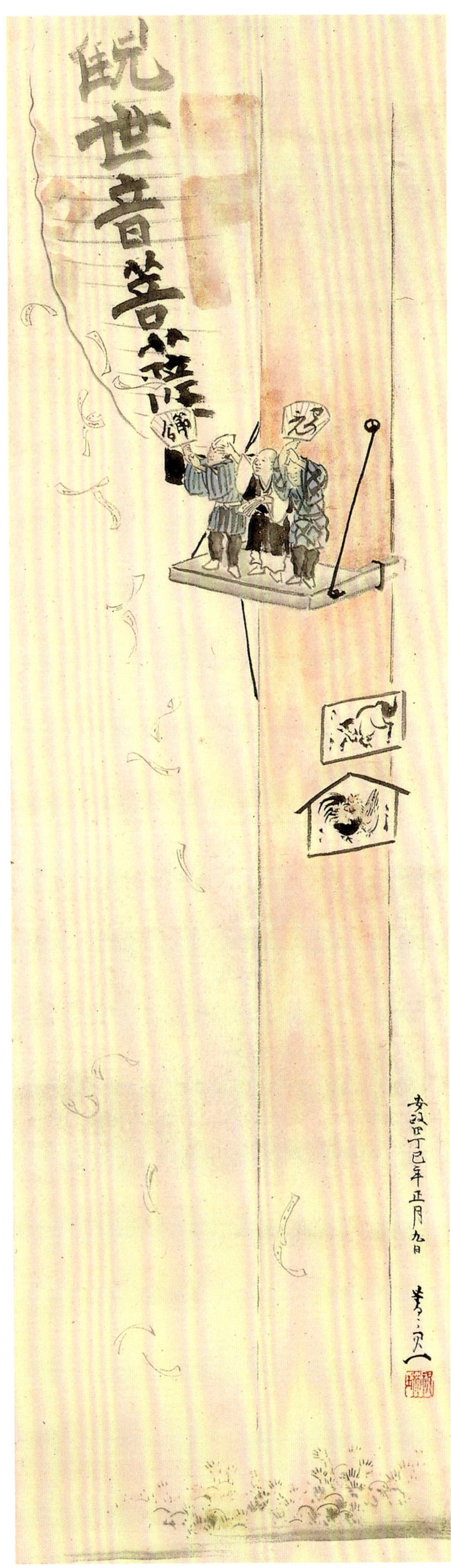

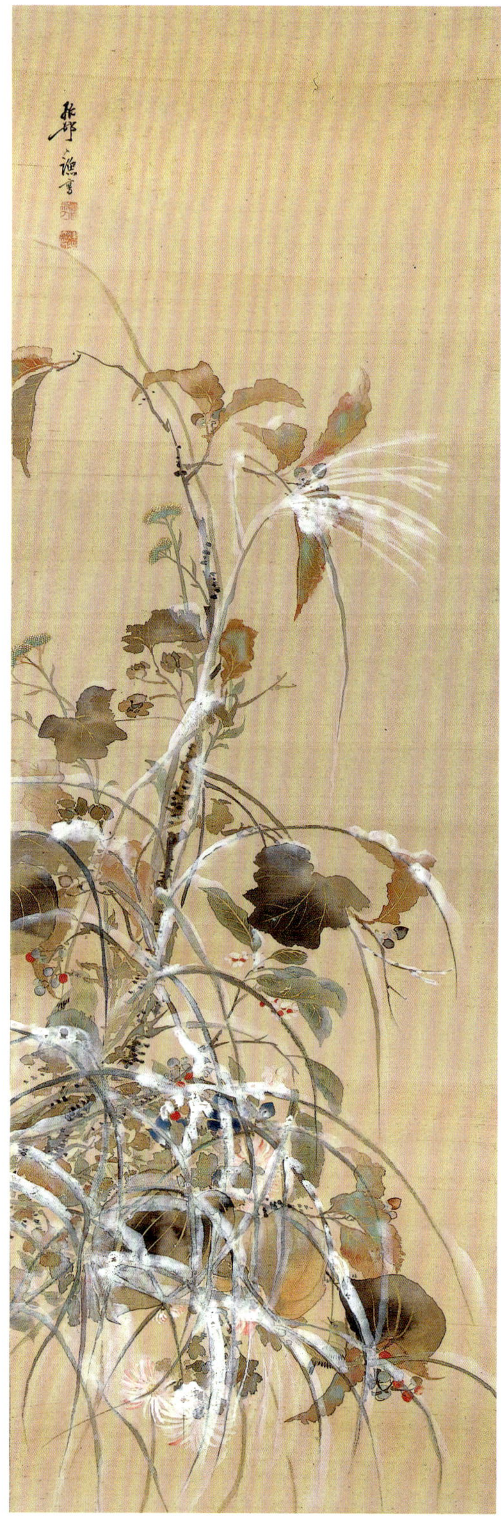

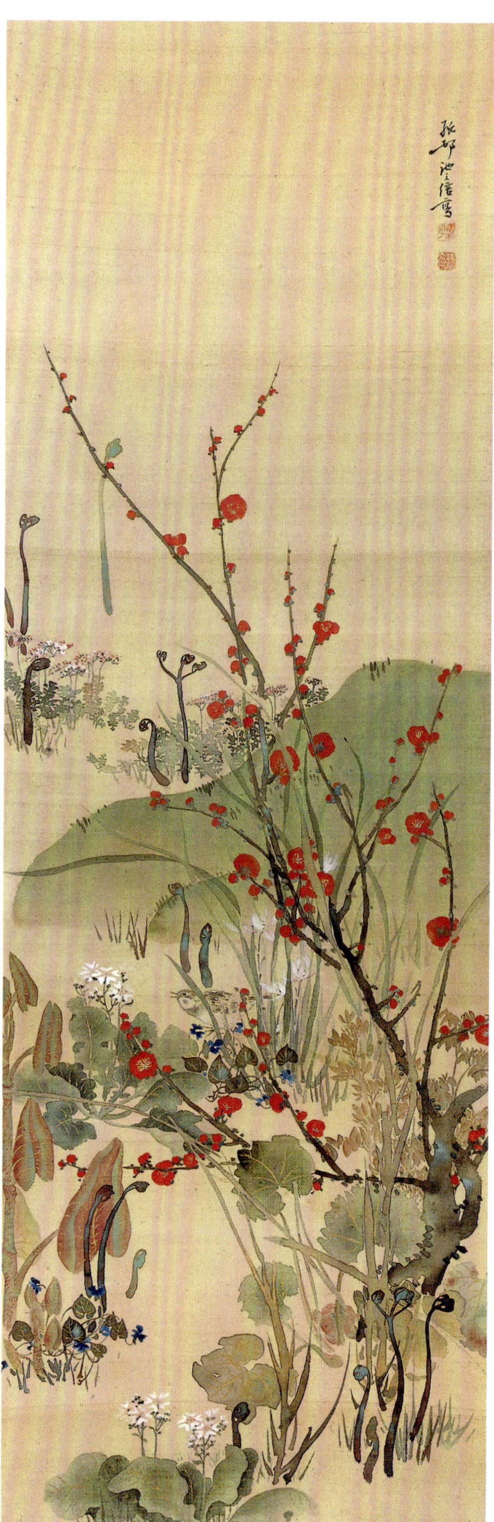

Ikeda Koson
(池田孤邨; 1801–1866)

200. Flowers and Birds of the Four Seasons

Edo period
Pair of hanging scrolls; ink, color, and gold on silk
Each scroll 109 x 36.4 cm (42 7/8 x 14 3/8 in.)
Signatures, seals

Literature: Nakamura Tanio 1979, vol. 5, pls. 115-1, 115-2; Suntory Museum of Art 1982, pp. 60, 78, no. 77; Murashige Yasushi 1989, pl. 84; Murase 1993, no. 41.

Ikeda Koson
(池田孤邨; 1802–1867)

201. Thirty-six Immortal Poets (三十六歌仙)

Edo period
Two-panel folding screen; ink and color on silk
172.8 x 174.6 cm (68 x 68 3/4 in.)
Signature, seals

Literature: Yamane Yūzō 1977–80, vol. 5 (1978), pl. 214; Takeda Tsuneo et al. 1982, p. 47; Murashige Yasushi 1991, pl. 74; Kano Hiroyuki et al. 1993, p. 116, no. 130; Yamane Yūzō et al. 1994, no. 13; Murase 2000, no. 137; Tsuji Nobuo et al. 2005, no. 95; Carpenter 2012, no. 65.

Overleaf:

Sakai Ōho
(酒井鶯蒲; 1808–1841)

202. Mu Tamagawa (六玉川)

Edo period, ca. 1839
Six handscrolls; ink, color and gold on silk
Each handscroll approx. 9 x 119.6 cm (3 1/2 x 47 1/8 in.)
Signatures, seals

Literature: Murashige Yasushi and Kobayashi Tadashi 1992, suppl. 3, no. 111; Murase 1993, no. 39; Yasumura Toshinobu 1993, nos. 94–101; Murase 1995, pp. 94–97; Murase 2000, no. 138; Tsuji Nobuo et al. 2005, no. 96; Nakamachi Keiko 2010, pp. 156–57; Carpenter 2012, no. 38 (Kinuta no Tamagawa).

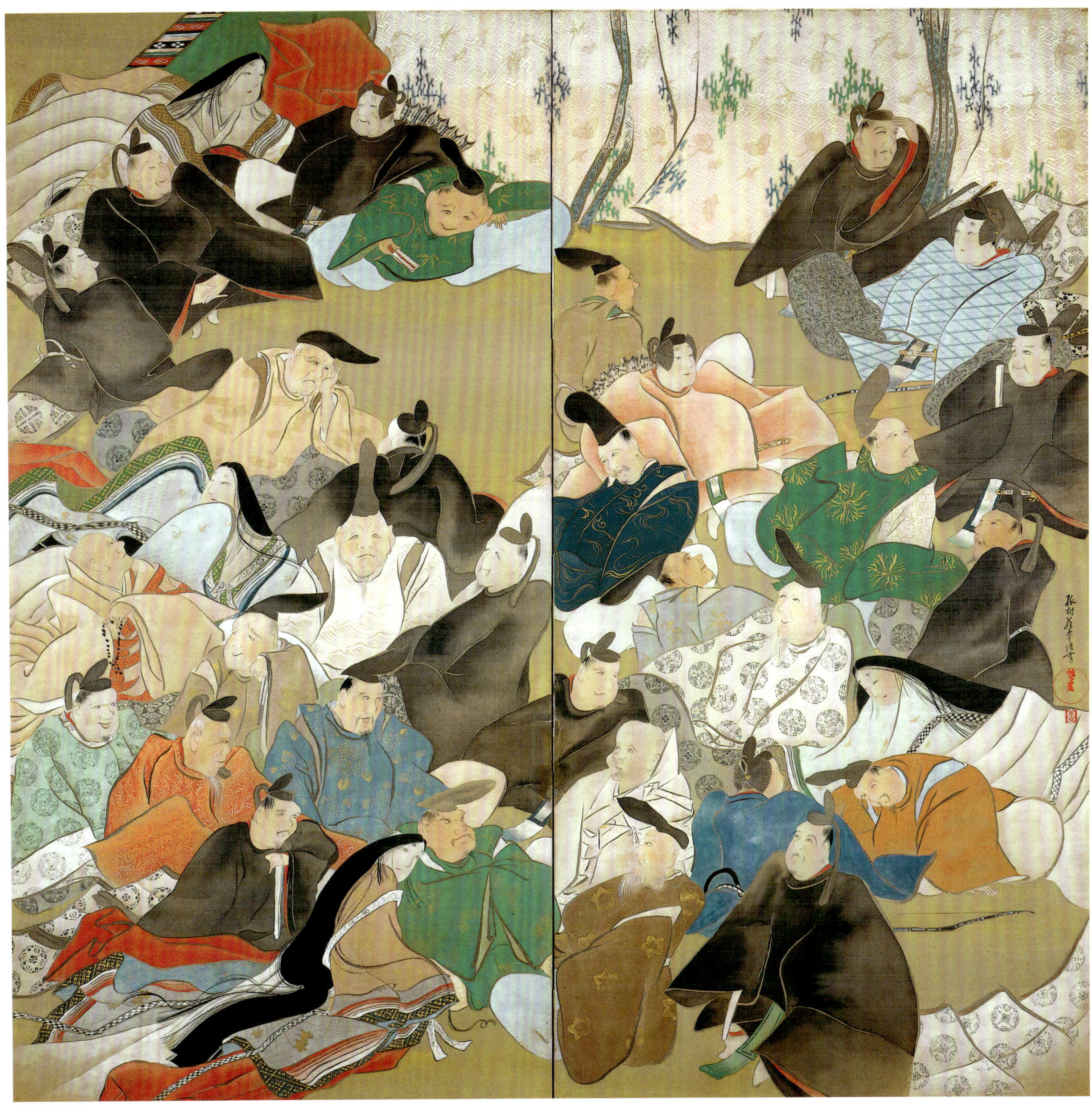

201

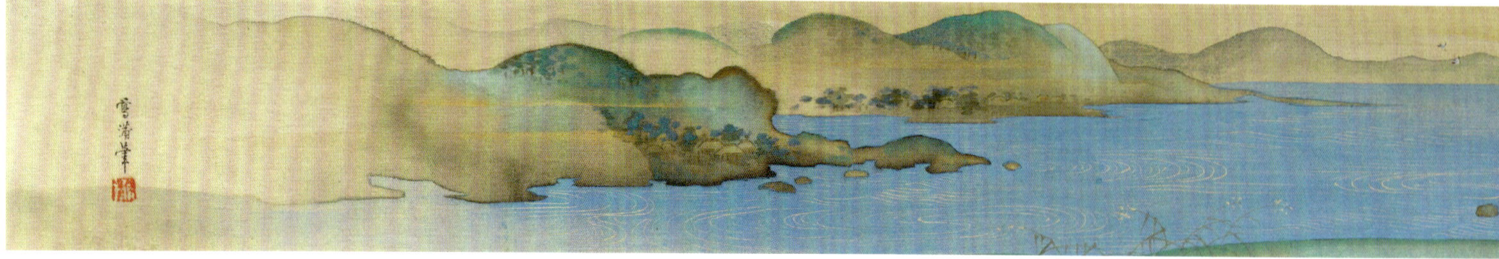

Noda no Tamagawa

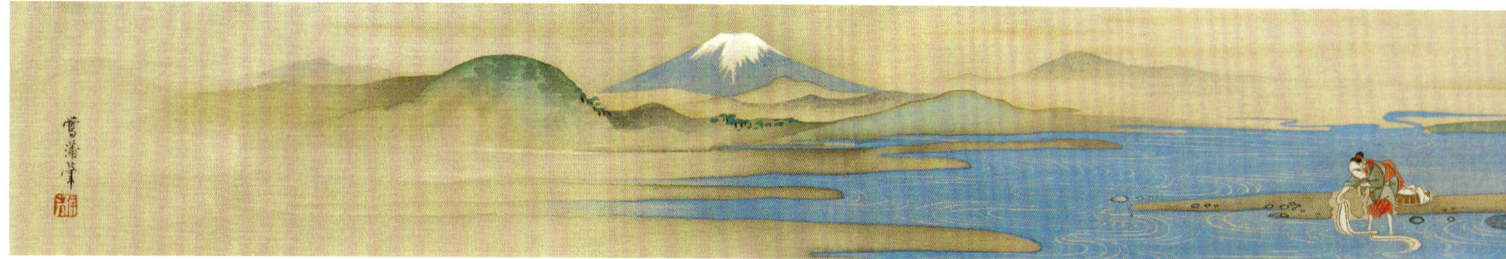

Tetsukuri no Tamagawa

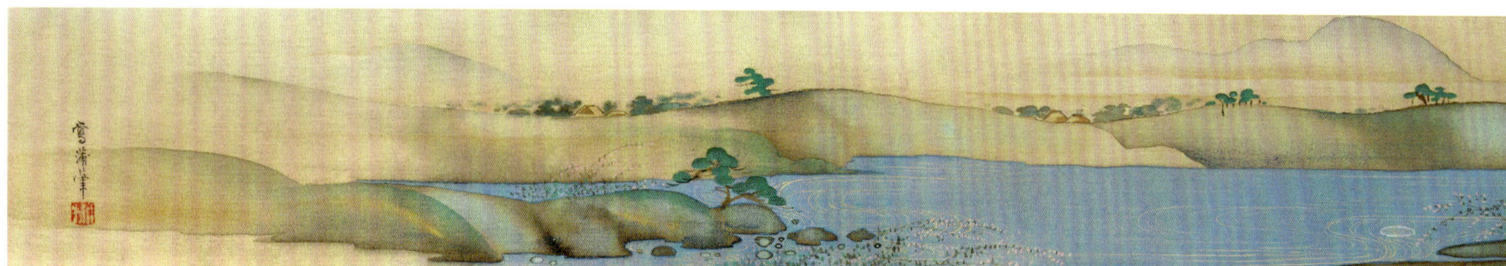

Noji no Tamagawa

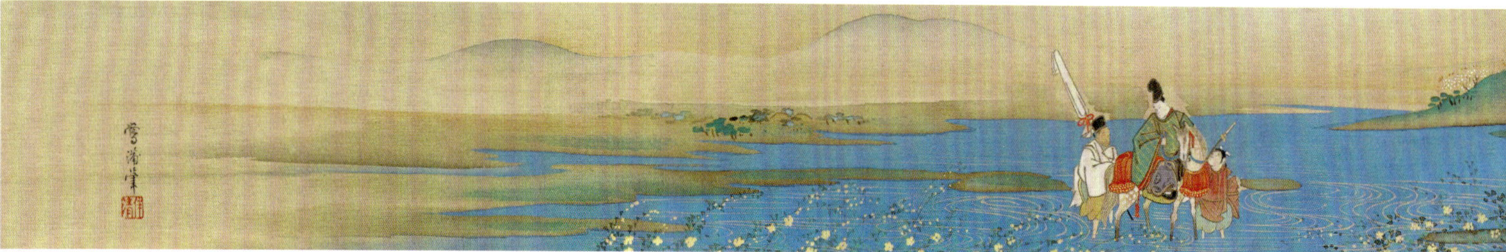

Ide no Tamagawa

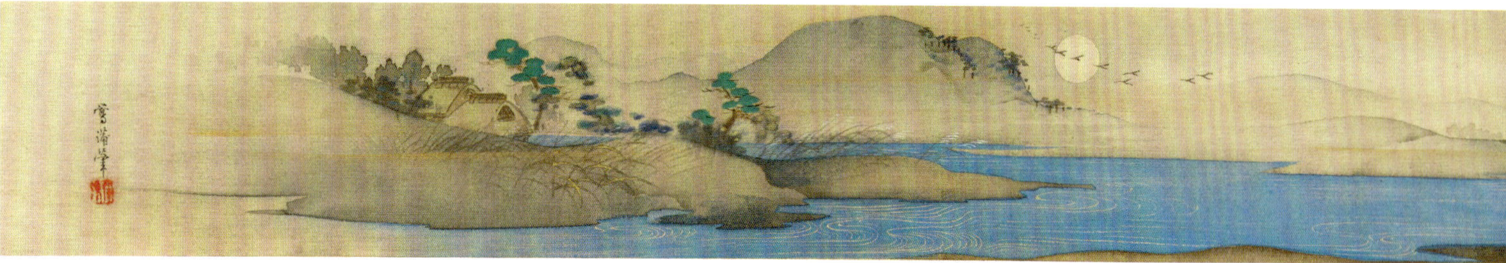

Kinuta no Tamagawa

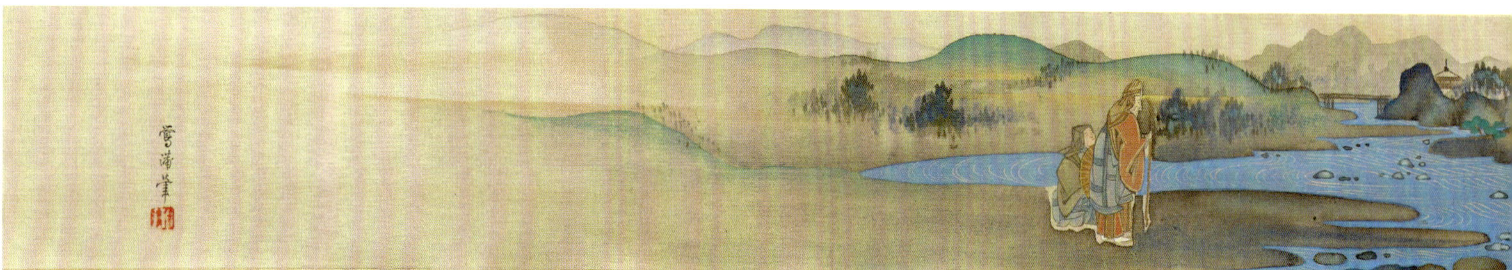

Kōya no Tamagawa

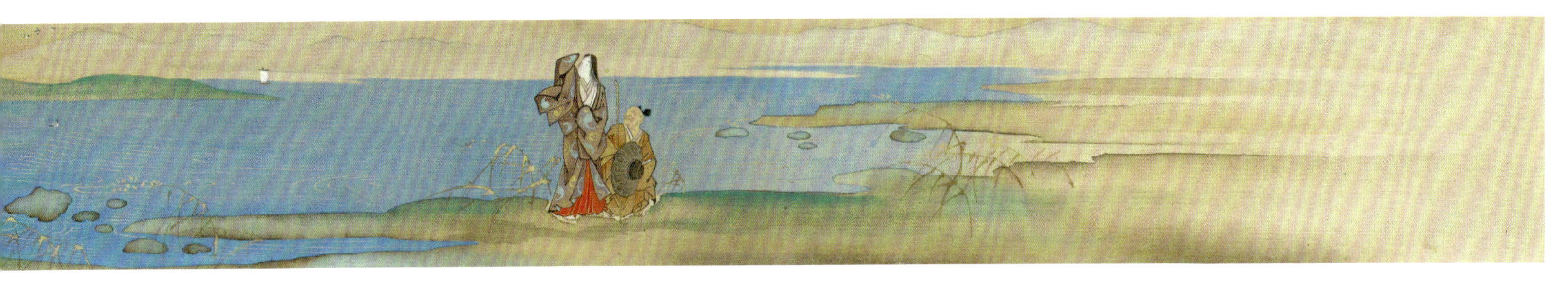

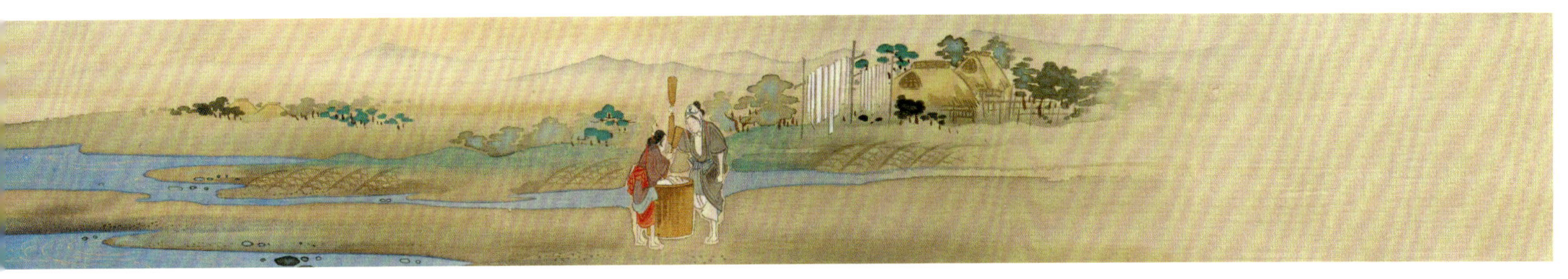

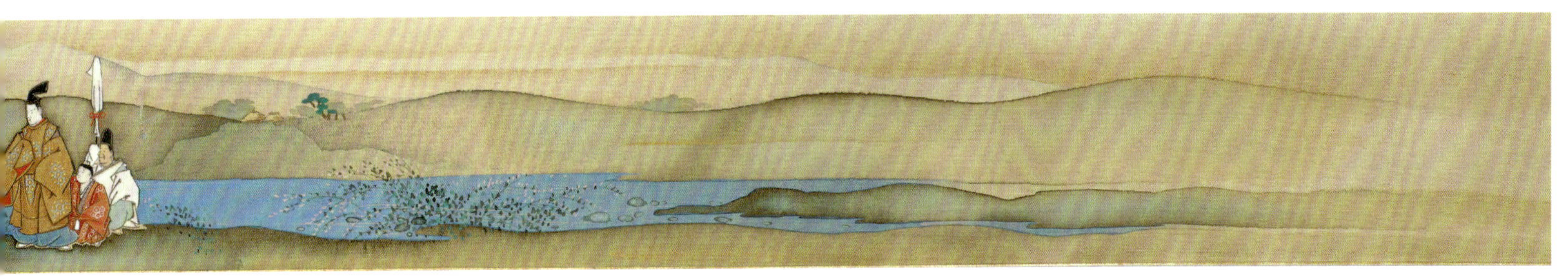

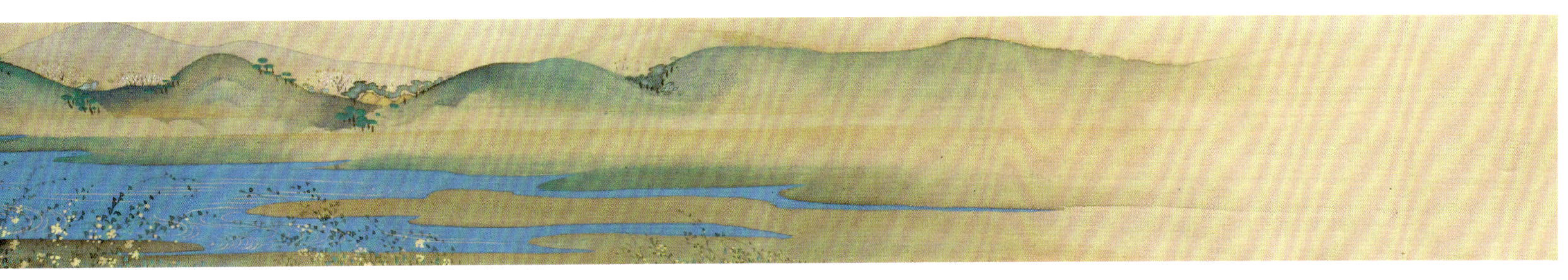

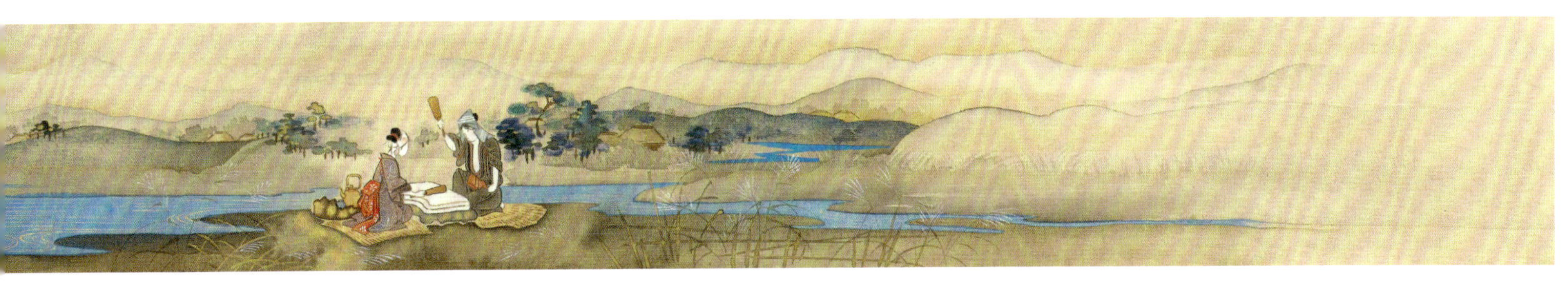

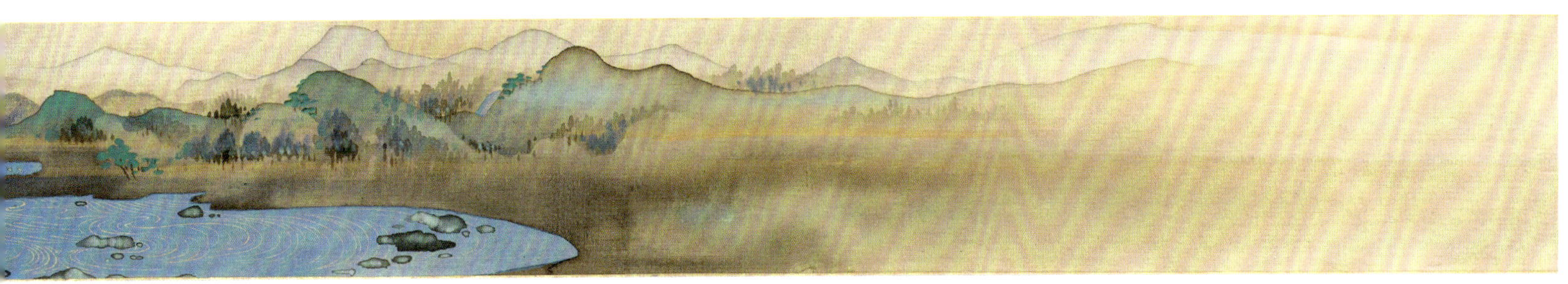

Sakai Ōho
(酒井鶯蒲; 1808–1841)

203. Hollyhocks

Edo period
Hanging scroll; ink and color on silk
103 x 35.7 cm (40 1/2 x 14 in.)
Signature, seal

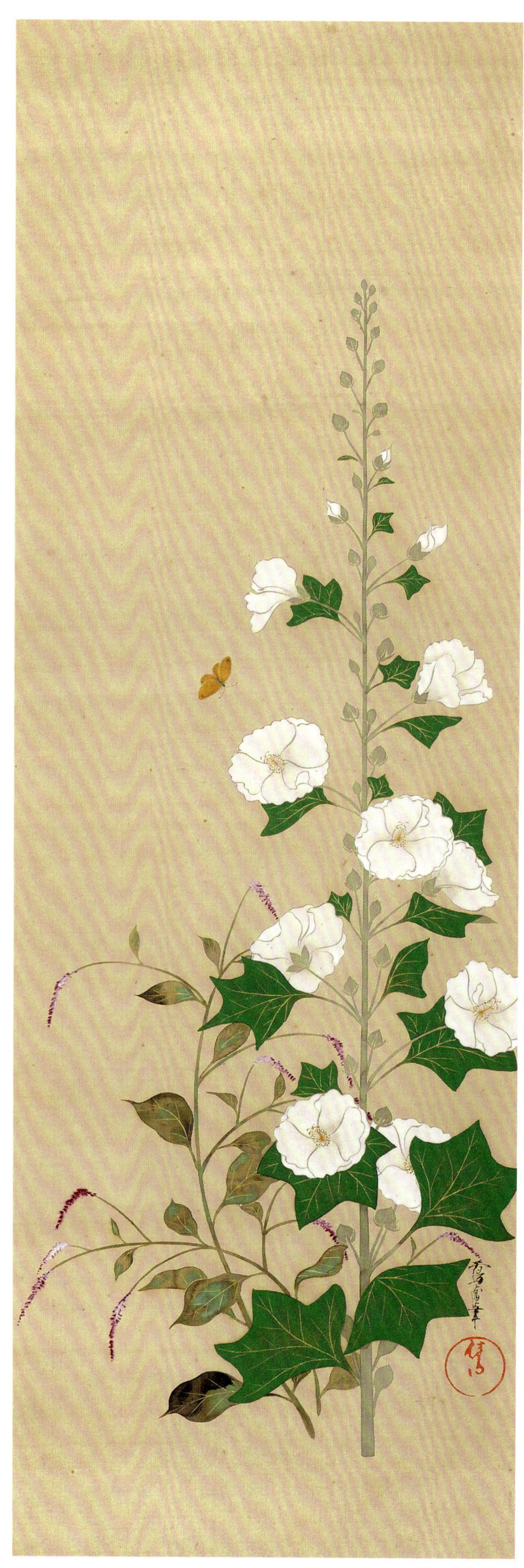

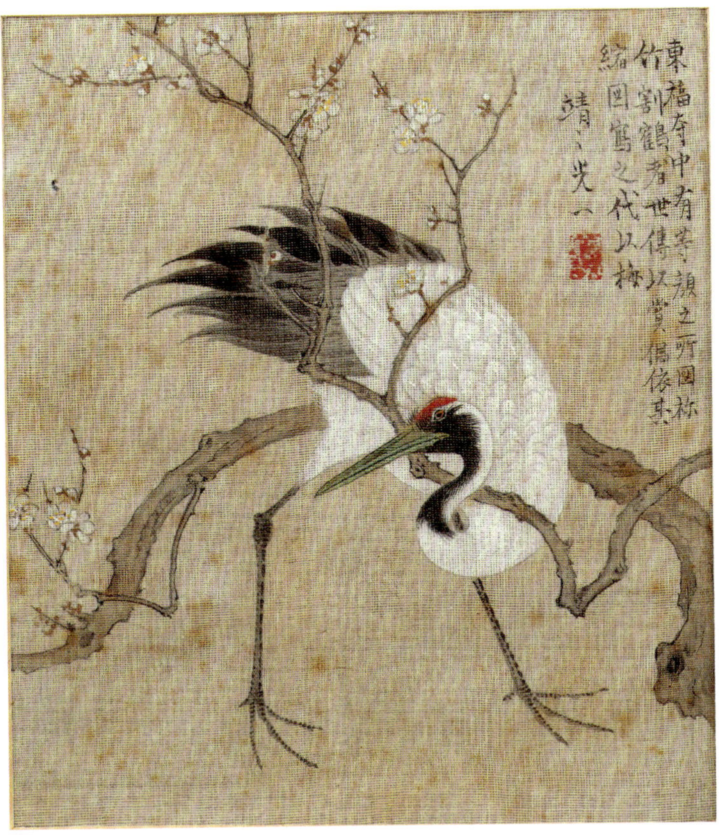

Yamamoto Kōitsu
(山本光一; fl. late 19th century)

204. Crane in a Plum Grove

Meiji period
Framed album piece; ink and color on silk
11.7 x 10.3 cm (4 5/8 x 4 in.)
Text, signature, seal

Gift from Kōichi Yanagi, 2003

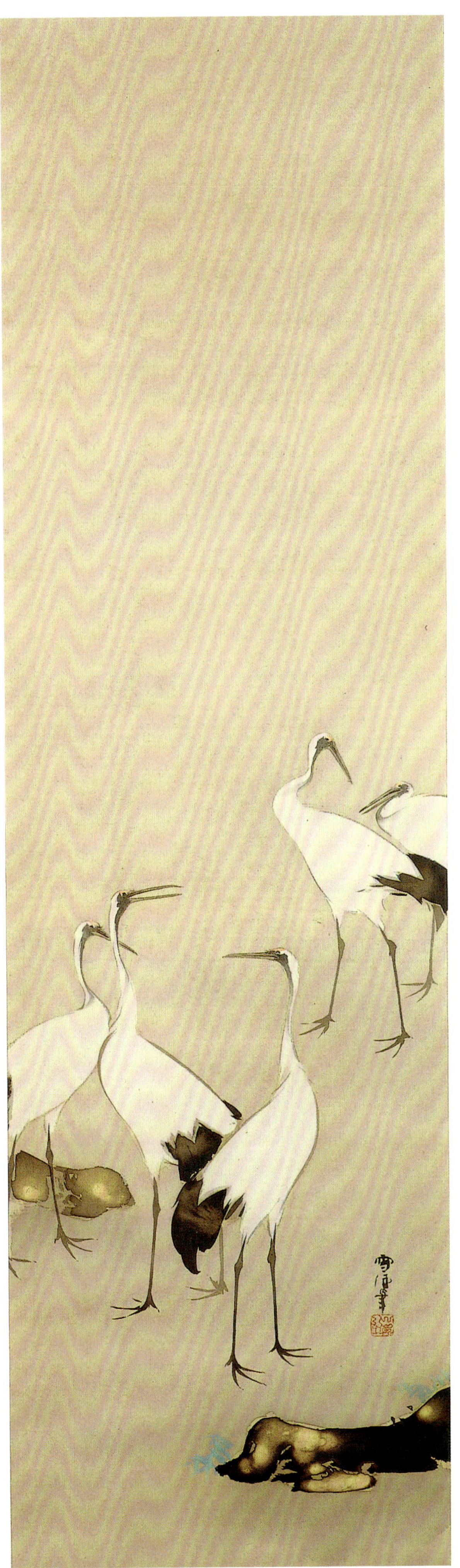

Kamisaka Sekka
(神坂雪佳; 1866–1942)

205. Family of Cranes

20th century
Hanging scroll; ink and color on silk
92 x 26.9 cm (36 1/4 x 10 5/8 in.)
Signature, seal

Literature: Wood and Ikeda 2003, pl. 136.

Chapter 5 Details

† *denotes illustrated items*

174. Two poems from *Ogura hyakunin isshu*

Text

Sakyō Dayū Akisuke // Breezes blow long / trailing clouds / across the sky / on this dark / autumn night. / Through breaks / the moon / so clear, so bright!

Taikenmon'in Horikawa // I do not know if you / will always be true. / This morning after you left, / I recalled your vows to me / looking at my long black hair / so disheveled— / like the tangles in my heart.

175. Poem from *Kokin wakashū*

Text

[Poem 293] *In the harbor where the waters converge, / the waves are deep red / as the floating autumn leaves swirl and eddy.*

176. Poem from *Kokin wakashū*

Text

[Poem 289] *The autumn moon shines brightly / upon the mountains, / illuminating every fallen colored leaf.*

† 177. Four poems from *Shin kokin wakashū*

Text

[Poem 519]
Cold wakens me / this dawn in the ninth month. / Chill winds have beckoned forth the frost.

[Poem 520]
The color of autumn deepens on the Isle of Awaji. / The salty breeze over the ocean fans away / the fading glow of the morning moon.

[Poem 525]
Showers on the mountains in these autumn days. / How are the trees at Mount Mimuro, / where the ancient gods have resided so long?

[Poem 526]
Fallen leaves crowd the waters of the Suzuka River. / I count the days and listen to the sleet / as it falls on the fields of Yamada.

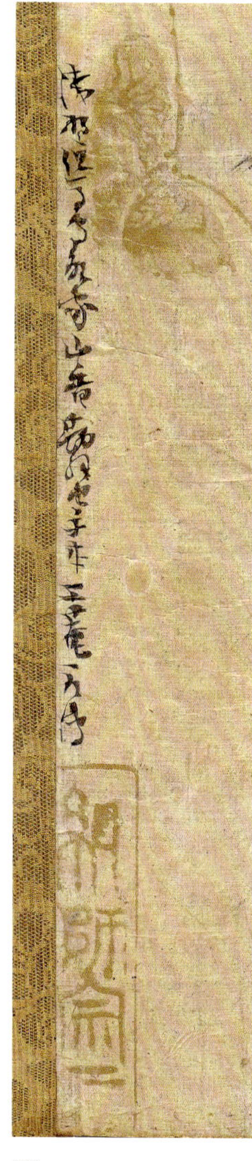

177

[on reverse] inscribed by Akiba Kōan
A handscroll, formerly owned by Kōan, was used as a model by Yamaga Kageyu, who was in the service of the Lord Asano Tajima no kami.

Signature

Kōetsu, 1616

Seals

Kōetsu; [on reverse] *Kamishi Sōji*

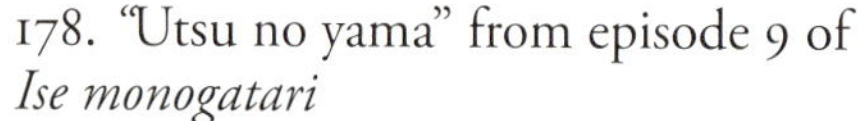

178. "Utsu no yama" from episode 9 of *Ise monogatari*

Text

by Takeuchi Toshiharu

Beside Mount Utsu in Suruga, / I can see you neither in waking nor, / alas, even in my dreams.

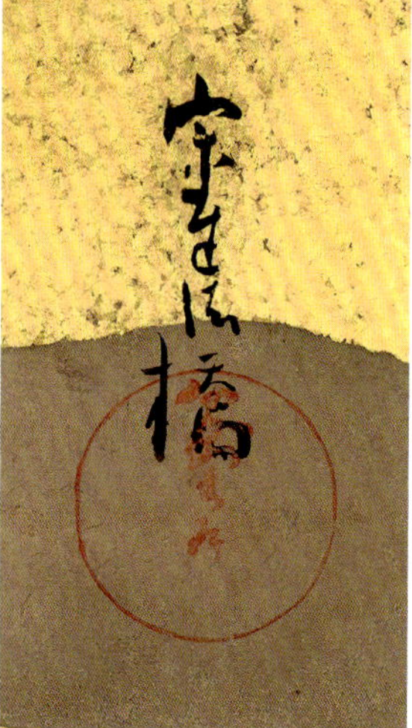

179

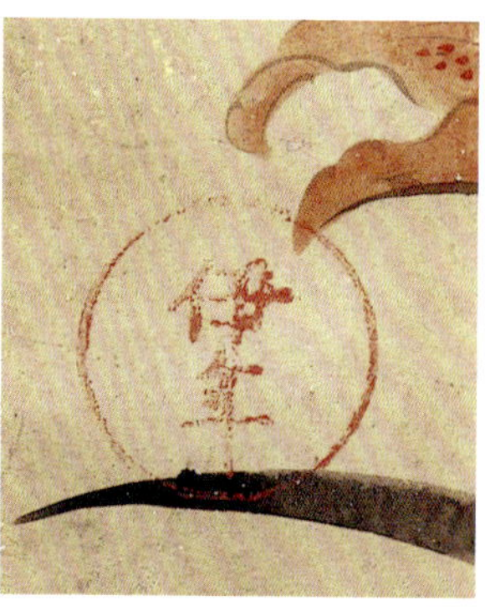

180

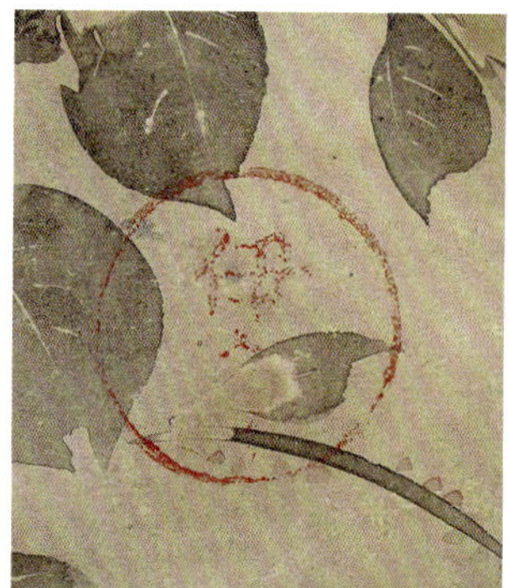

181

† 179. Boats on the Sea

Signatures

[on each screen] *Sōtatsu hokkyō*

Seals

[on each screen] *Taiseiken*

† 180. Flowers of Summer; Flowers of Autumn

Seals

[on each scroll] *Inen*

† 181. Flowers of Autumn

Seal

Inen

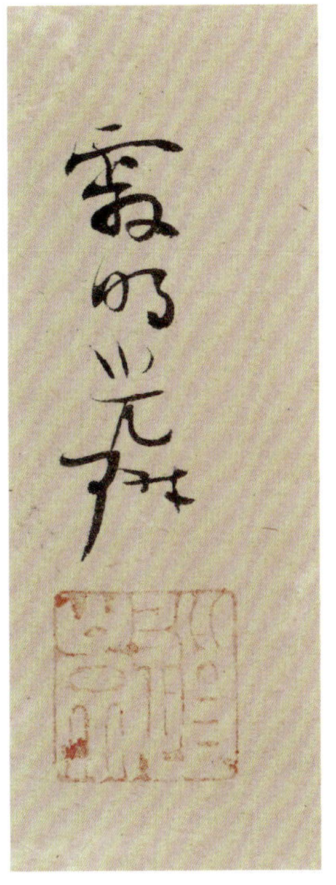

182

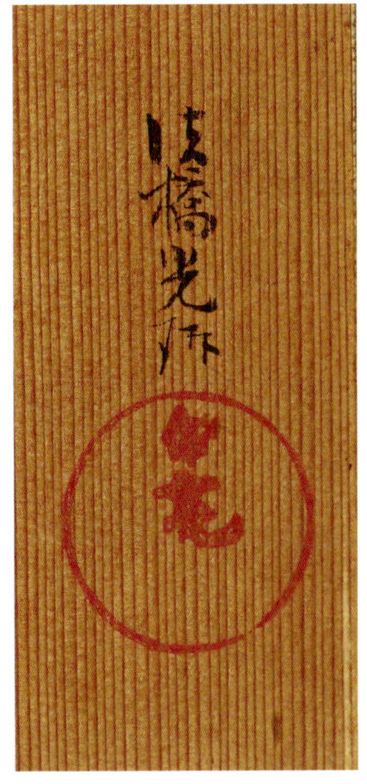

183

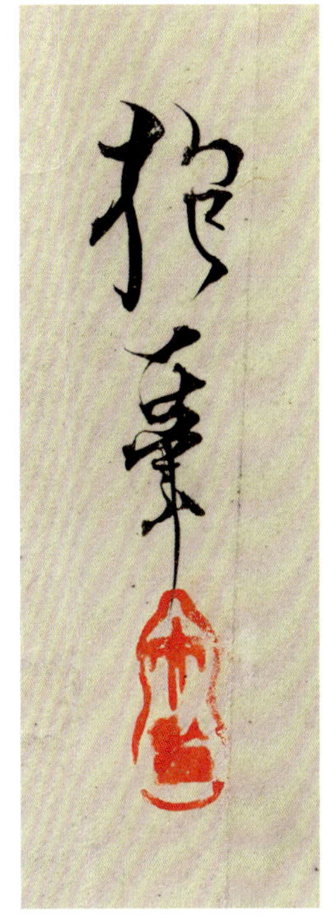

188

† 188. Cherry Blossoms

Signature

Painted by Hōitsu

Seal

Monsen

189. Red Plum Blossoms

Signature

Teihakushi

Seal

Hōitsu

† 190. Lilies and Hydrangeas; Hollyhocks

Signatures

[on right screen] *Summer month, 1801, Chōan Teihakushi*
[on left screen] *Chōan Teihakushi*

Seals

[on each panel] *Hōitsu; Meimeikyo*

† 182. Hotei

Signature

Jakumei Kōrin

Seal

Dōsū

† 183. Flowers of Spring; Flowers of Autumn

Signature

[right panel] *Hokkyō Kōrin*

Seals

[on each panel] *Koresuke*

† 184. Plum Trees; Hollyhocks

Signatures

[on right screen] *Painted by the Recluse from the capital Kyoto Shisui Shinsei at age 81*
[on left screen] *Painted by the Eremite from the Flowering Capital Shisui Shinsei at age 81*

Seals

[on each screen] *Reikai*

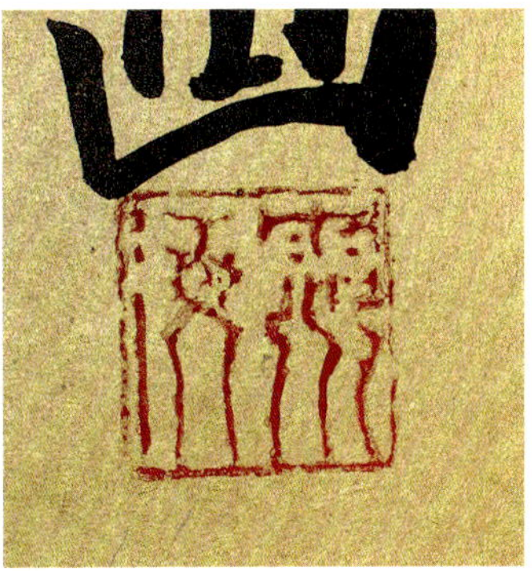

184

186. Narcissus

Signature

Hōchū

Seal

Illegible

187. Kyokusui no en

Signature

Painted by Hōchū

Seal

Hō

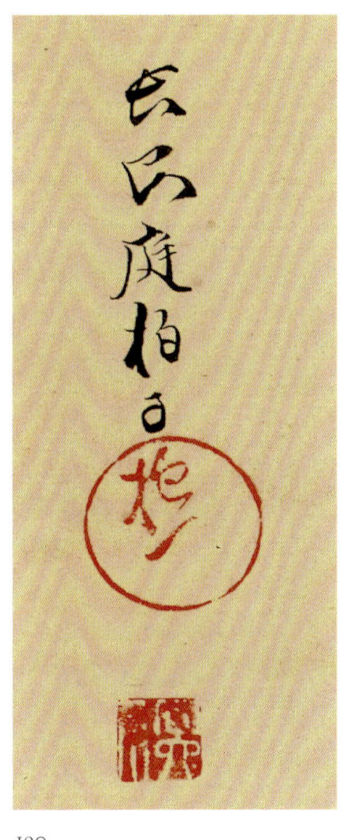

190

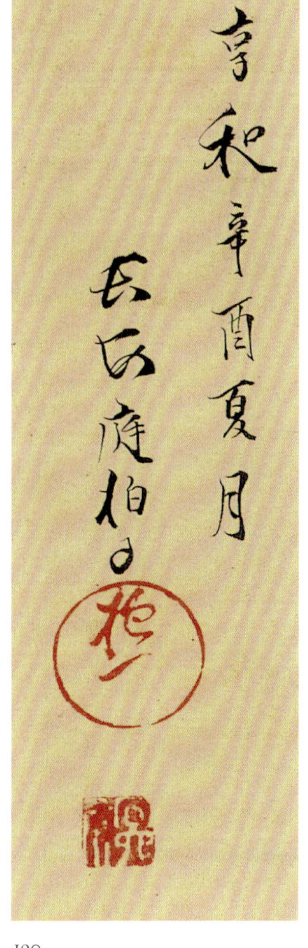

190

† 191. Blossoming Cherry Trees

Signatures

[on each screen] *Painted by Kishin*

Seals

[on each screen] *Hōitsu*

† 192. Thirty-six Immortal Poets

Text

by Hōitsu

[at right, poems by Sarumaru Dayū]
[*Sarumarushū* 3] *Sarumaru // Everyone has reasons / to change his heart / like Tsukikusa grass shifts its colors.*

[*Kokin wakashū* 215] *Treading through the autumn leaves in the deepest mountains, / I hear the belling of the lonely deer— / then it is that autumn is sad.*

[at left, poems by Ono no Komachi]
[*Kokin wakashū* 938] *I have sunk to the / bottom, / and like the rootless / shifting water weeds / should the currents summon me / I too would drift away.*

[*Kokin wakashū* 113] *A life in vain. / My looks, talents faded / like these cherry blossoms / paling in the endless rains / that I gaze out upon, alone.*

Signature

[at end of scroll] *Recorded by Uge-an [Ukaan] Hōitsu, tenth month, winter of 1824*

Seal

[at end of scroll] *Monsen*

† 194. Hollyhock and Lilies

Signature

Seisei Kiitsu

Seal

Shukurin

† 195. Bird and Flowers

Signature

Seisei Kiitsu

Seal

Teihakushi

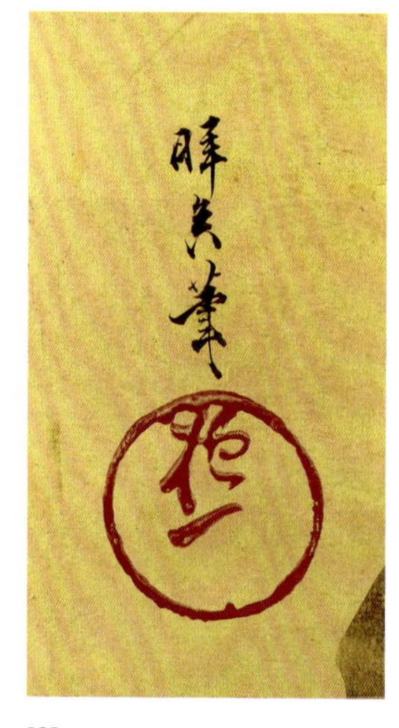

191

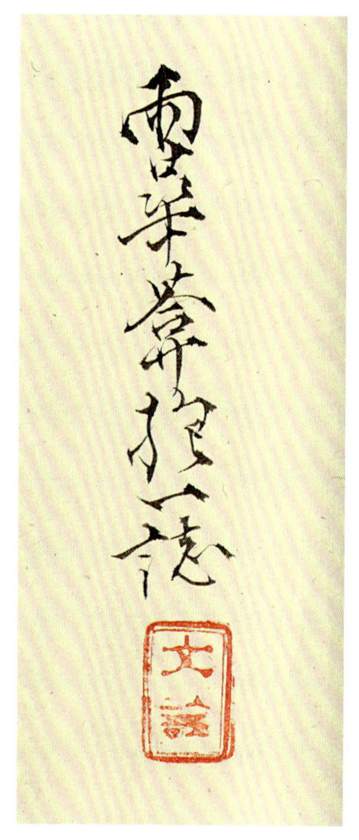

192

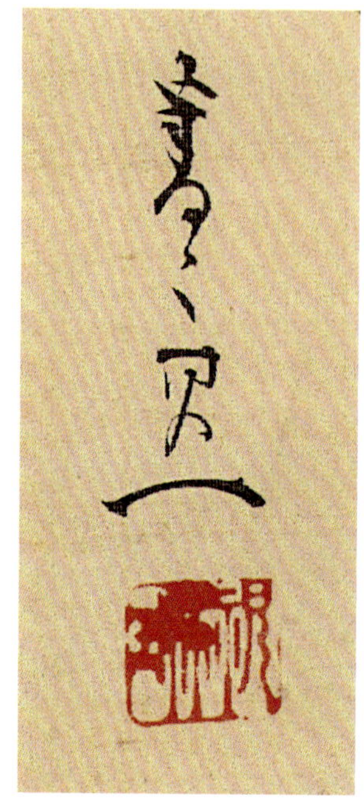

194

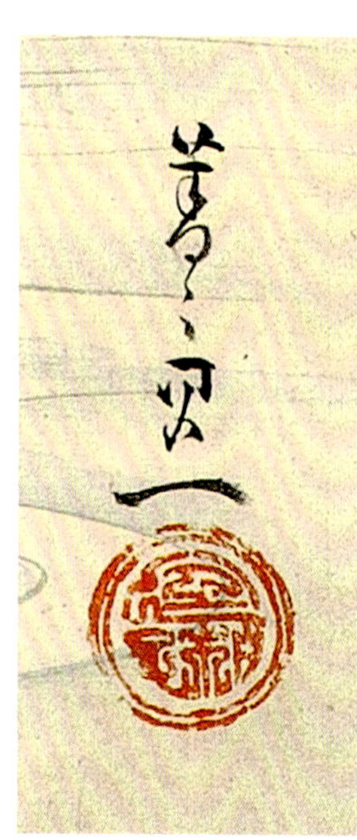

195

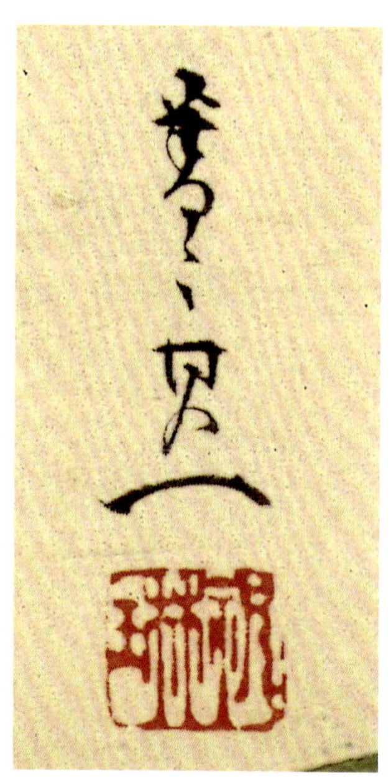

196

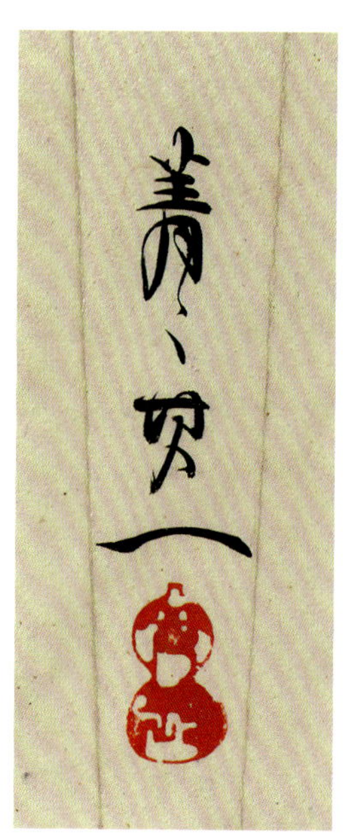

197

† 196. Irises and Moth

Signature

Seisei Kiitsu

Seal

Shukurin

† 197. Bush Clover

Signature

Seisei Kiitsu

Seal

Kiitsu

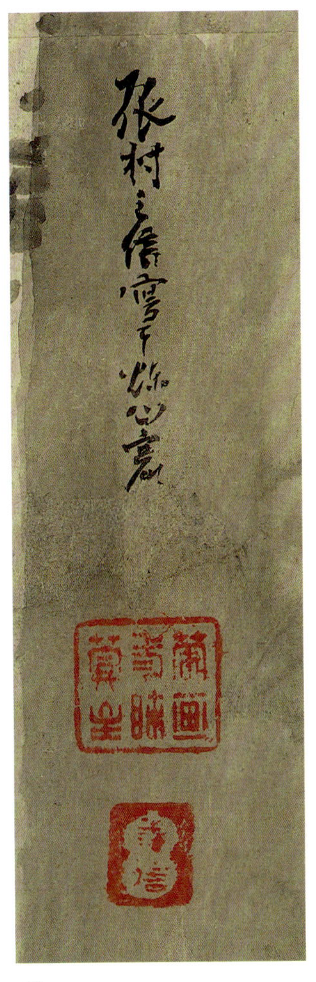

198

199

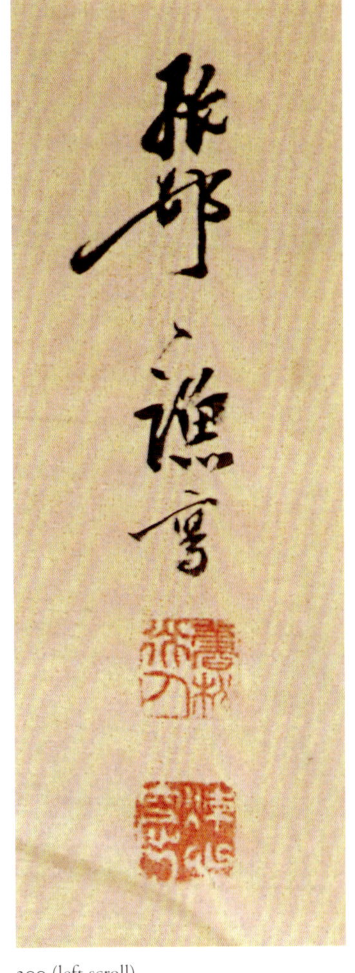

200 (left scroll)

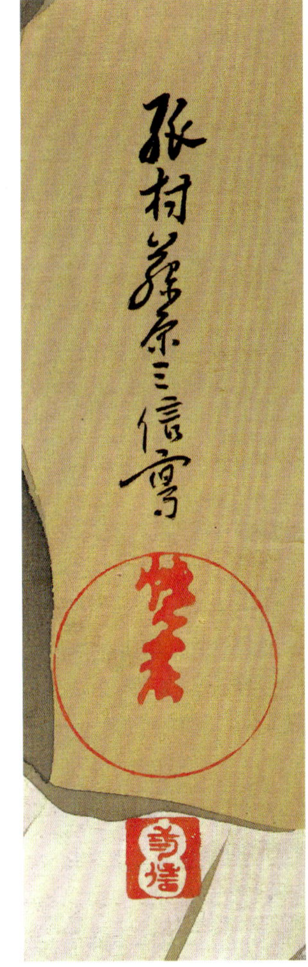

201

† 198. Cypress Trees

Signature

Painted by Koson Sanshin at Renshinkutsu

Seals

Chaga zanmaian shu; *Sanshin*

† 199. Setsubun Festival at Sensōji

Text

by Kiitsu

Kanzeon Bosatsu; *Setsubun*; *Setsubun*

Signature

First month, ninth day of 1857, Seisei Kiitsu

Seal

Shukurin

† 200. Flowers and Birds of the Four Seasons

Signatures

[right scroll] *Painted by Koson Ike Sanshin*
[left scroll] *Painted by Koson Songyo*

Seals

[on each scroll] *Kyūshō Dōjin*; *Renshinkutsu*

† 201. Thirty-six Immortal Poets

Signature

Painted by Koson Fujiwara Sanshin

Seals

Renshinkutsu; *Sanshin*

† 202. Mu Tamagawa

Signatures

[on each scroll] *By Ōho*

Seals

[on each scroll] *Hansei*

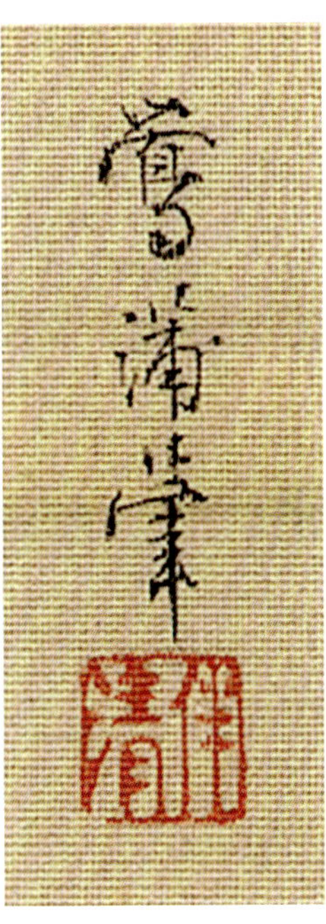

202

† 203. Hollyhocks

Signature

Painted by Ōho

Seal

Bansei

† 204. Crane in a Plum Grove

Text

by Kōitsu

In the temple Tōfukuji is a painting by Tōgan entitled Bamboo and Crane, which has been widely admired. I happened to have a chance to make a sketch of it, substituting plum branches [for bamboo].

Signature

Seisei Kōitsu

Seal

Illegible

† 205. Family of Cranes

Signature

Painted by Sekka

Seal

Sekka

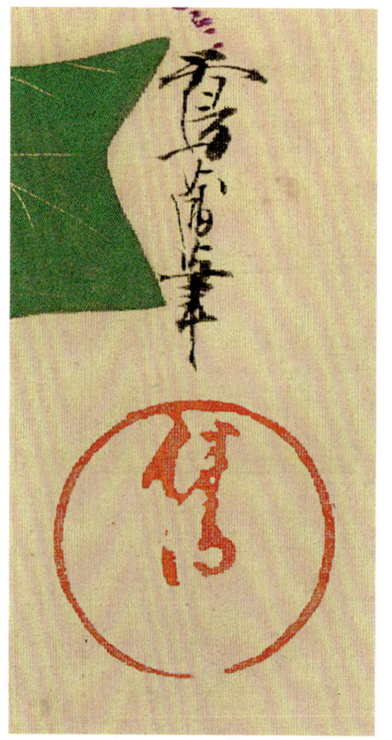

203

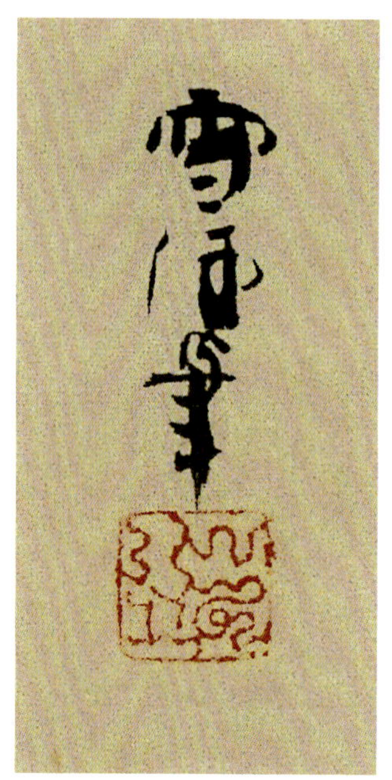

205

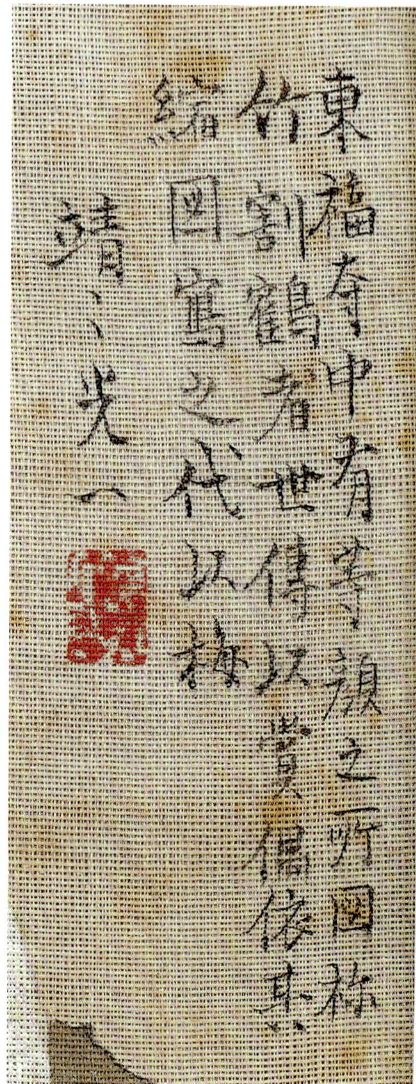

204

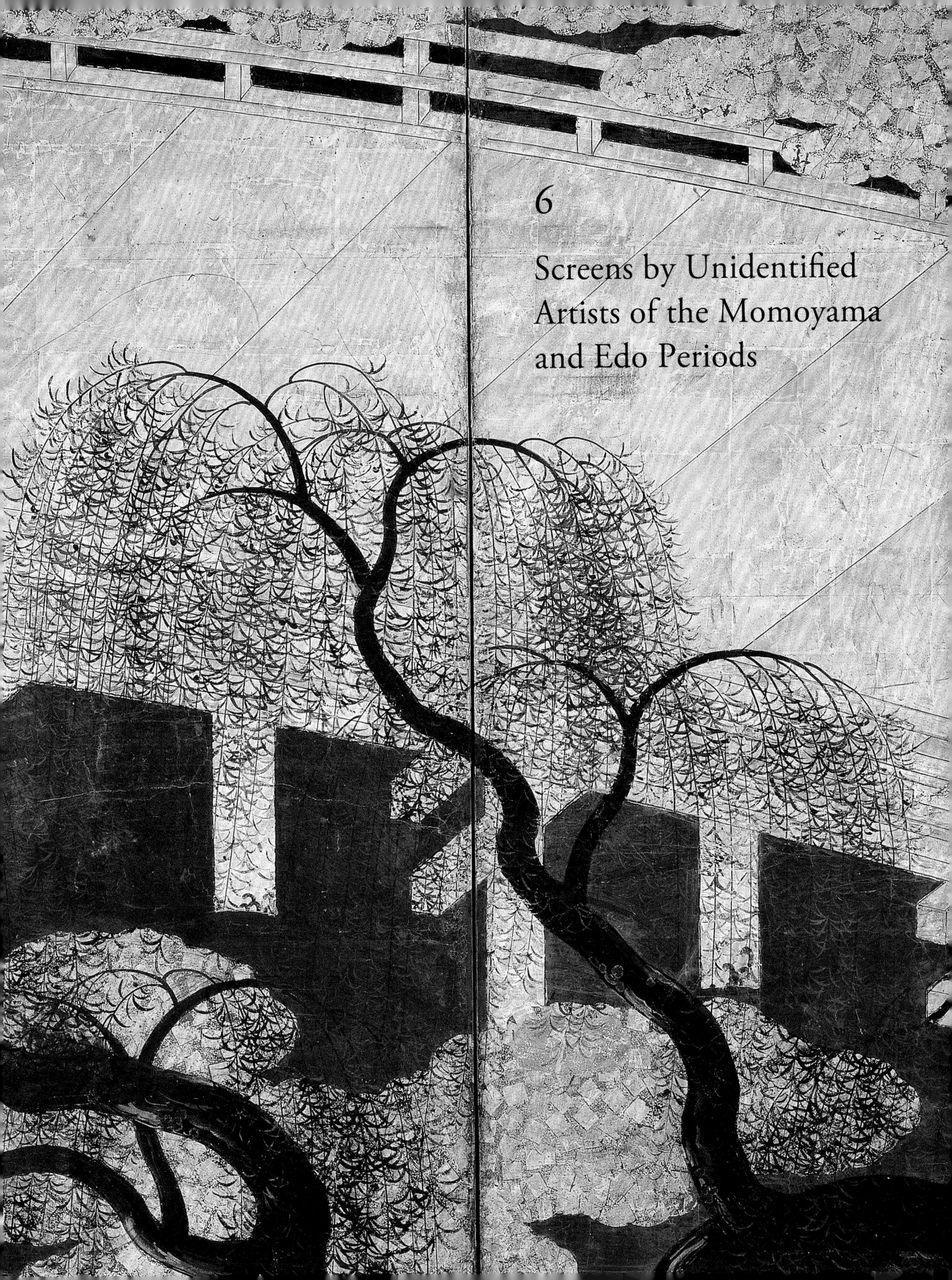

6

Screens by Unidentified Artists of the Momoyama and Edo Periods

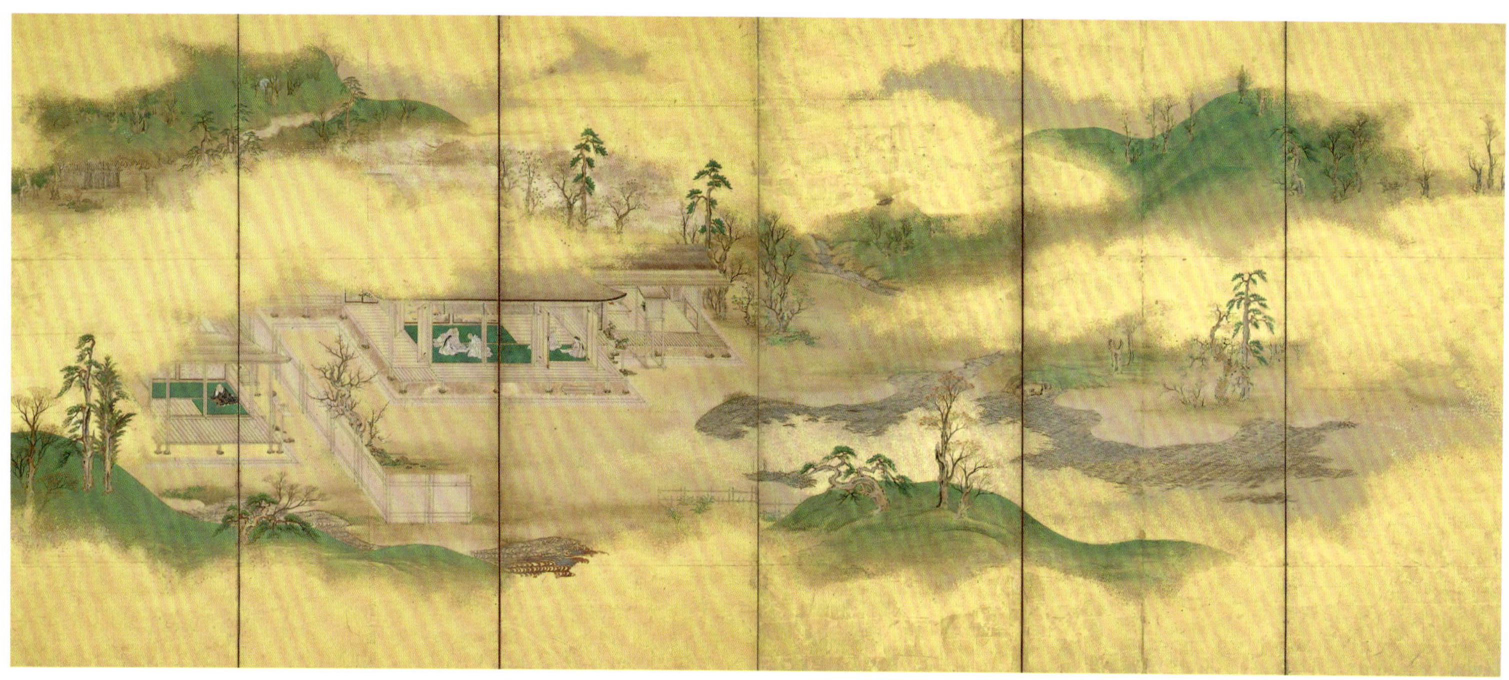

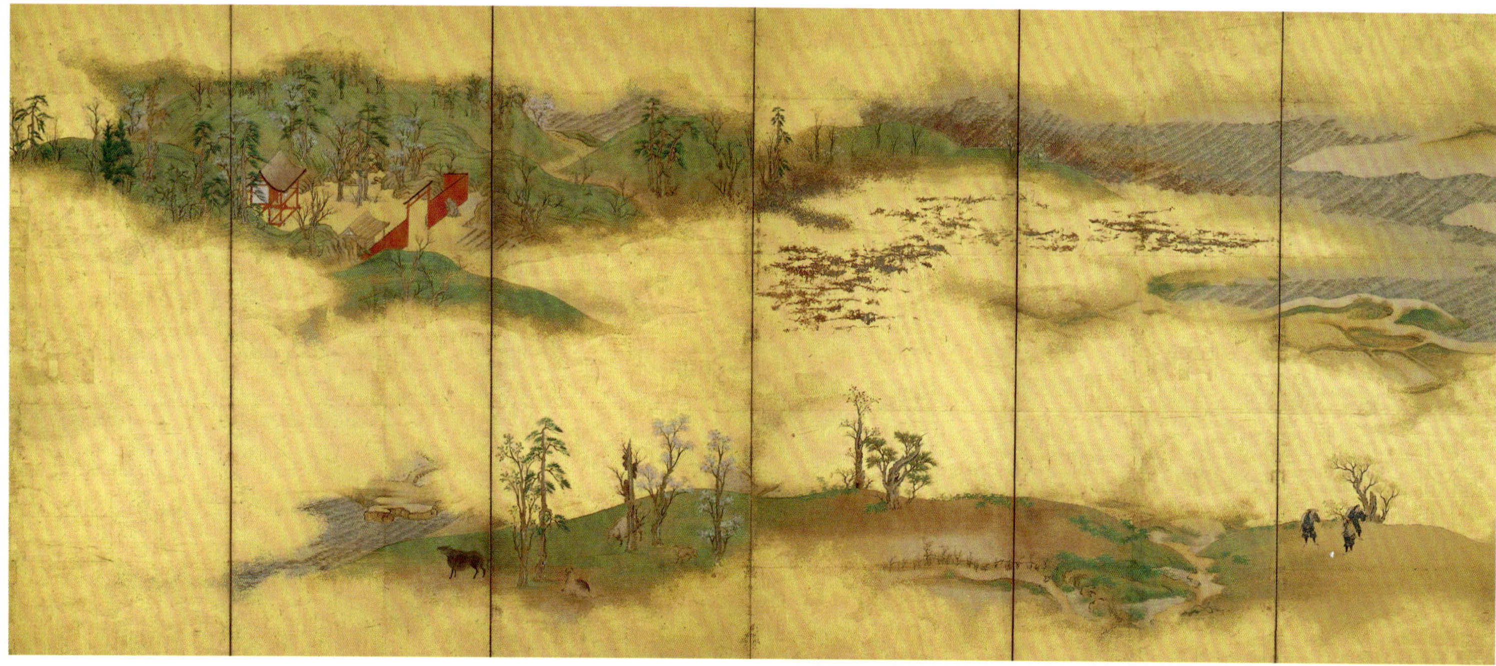

206. *Saigyō monogatari*
(西行物語)

Momoyama period, 16th century
Pair of six-panel folding screens; ink, color, gold, and silver on gilded paper
Each screen 152 x 353.8 cm (59⅞ in. x 11 ft. 7¼ in.)

LITERATURE: Shirahata Yoshi 1964, pp. 103–7; Murase 1971, no. 21; Yamane Yūzō et al. 1979, pls. 73, 74; Takeda Tsuneo 1980, no. 95; L. Cunningham 1984, no. 2; Tokyo National Museum 1985a, no. 28; Murase 2000, no. 79; Tsuji Nobuo et al. 2005, no. 74; Proser 2010, no. 26.

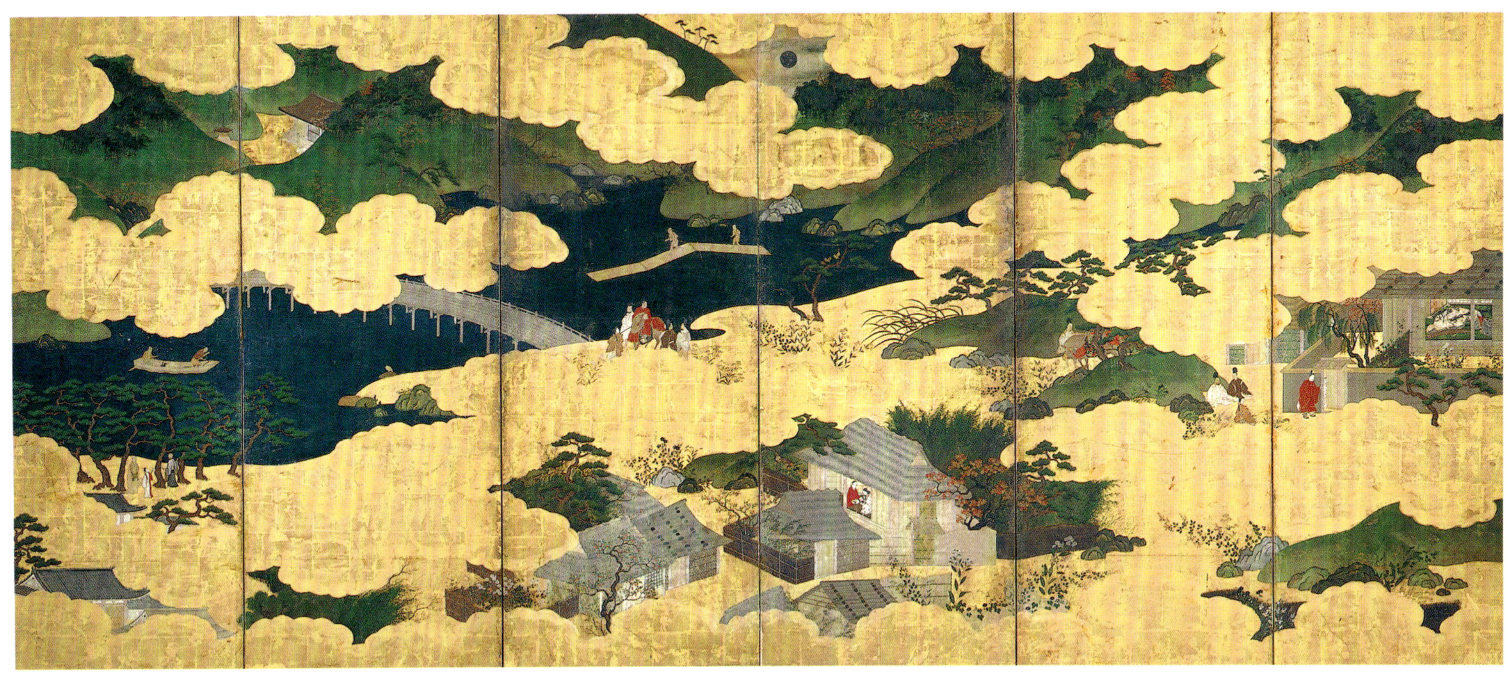

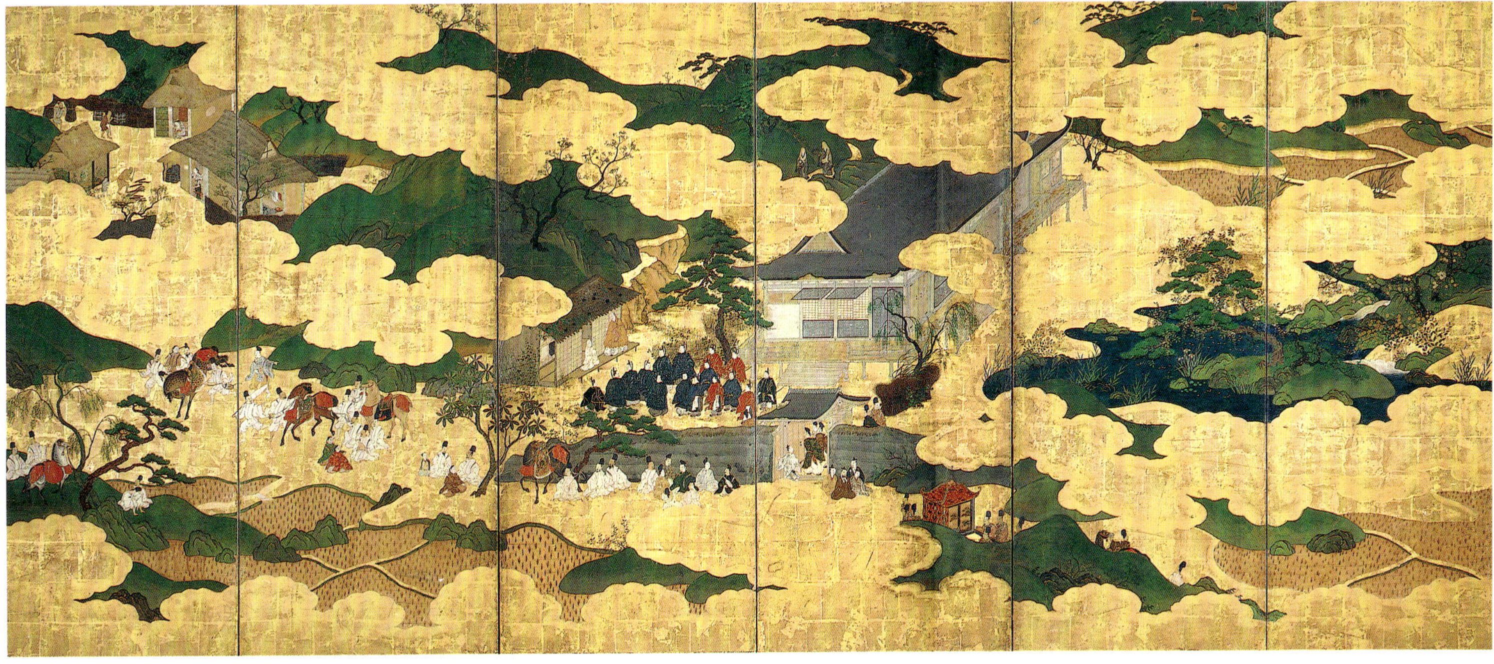

207. "Kogō" (小督) and "Goshirakawa's Visit to Ōhara" (大原御幸) episodes of *Heike monogatari* (平家物語)

Edo period, first half of 17th century
Pair of six-panel folding screens; ink, color, and gold on gilded paper
Each screen 154.7 x 360.4 cm (60 7/8 in. x 11 ft. 9 7/8 in.)

Literature: Takeda Tsuneo 1980, nos. 84, 85 ("Goshirakawa's Visit to Ōhara"); Tokyo National Museum 1985a, no. 29; Ford 1997, pp. 41–45; Murase 2000, no. 111; Tsuji Nobuo et al. 2005, no. 73.

208. Seventeen scenes and poems from *Ise monogatari* (伊勢物語)

Edo period, 17th century
Pair of six-panel folding screens; ink, color, and gold on gilded paper
Each screen 93.2 x 262.2 cm (36¾ in. x 8 ft. 7¼ in.)
Text

LITERATURE: Itō Toshiko 1984, pp. 162–63; Murase 1985, pp. 102–4; Avitabile 1990, no. 71; Buckland 2004, no. 1.

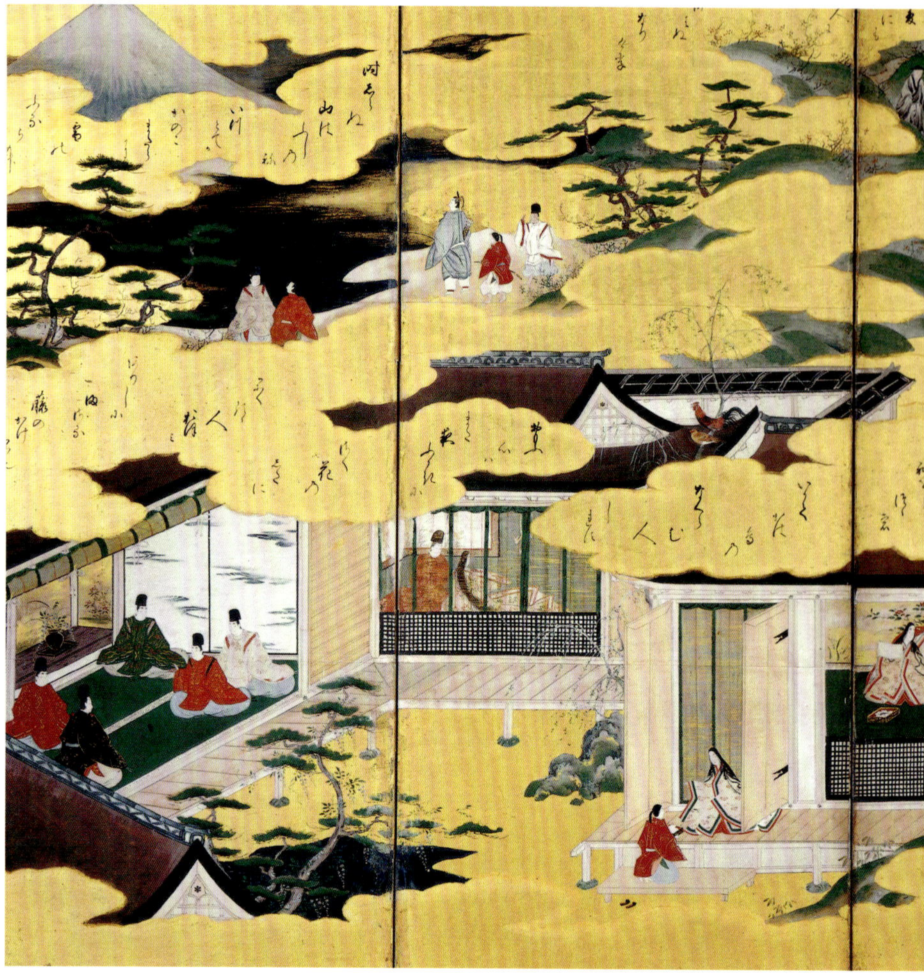

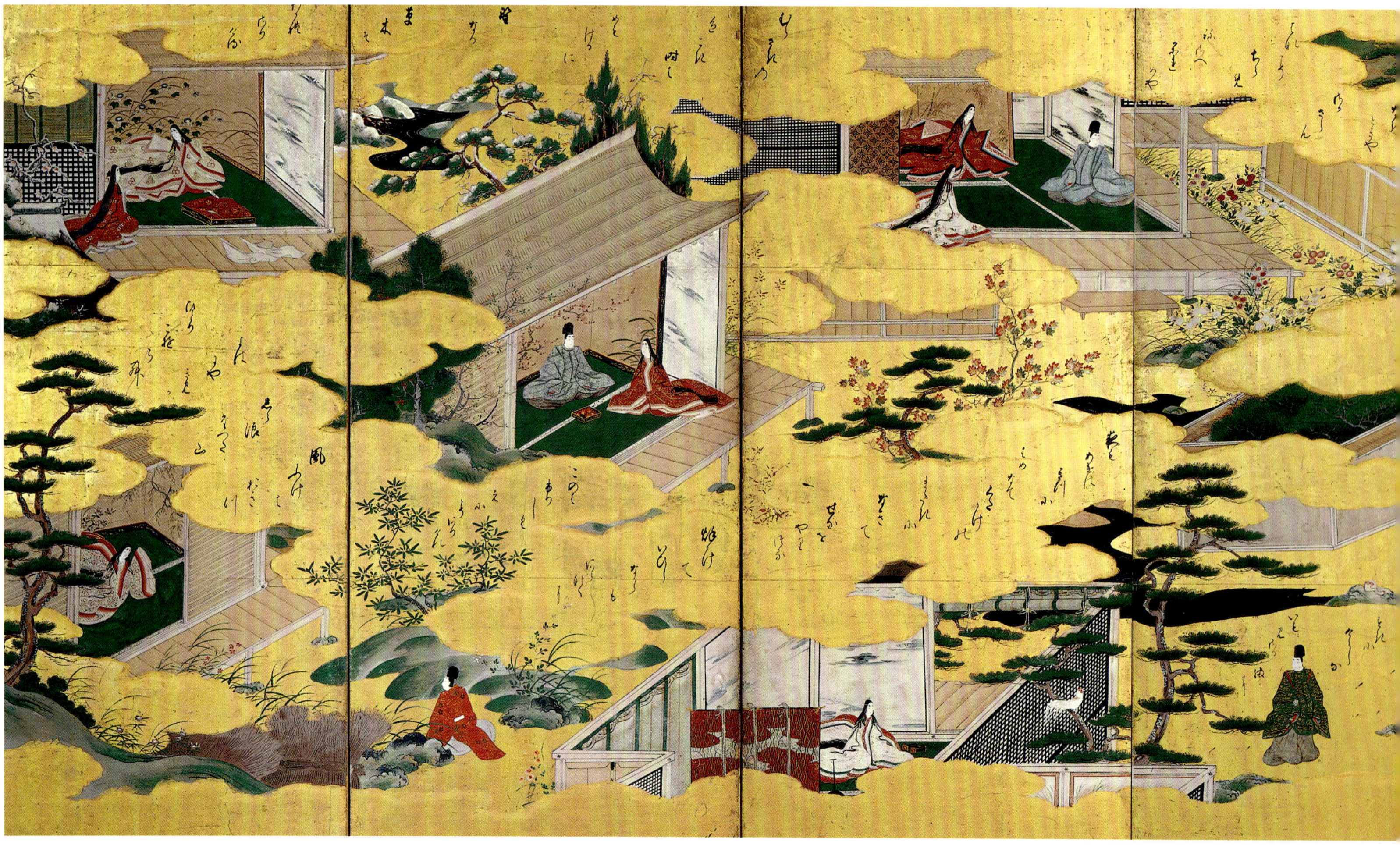

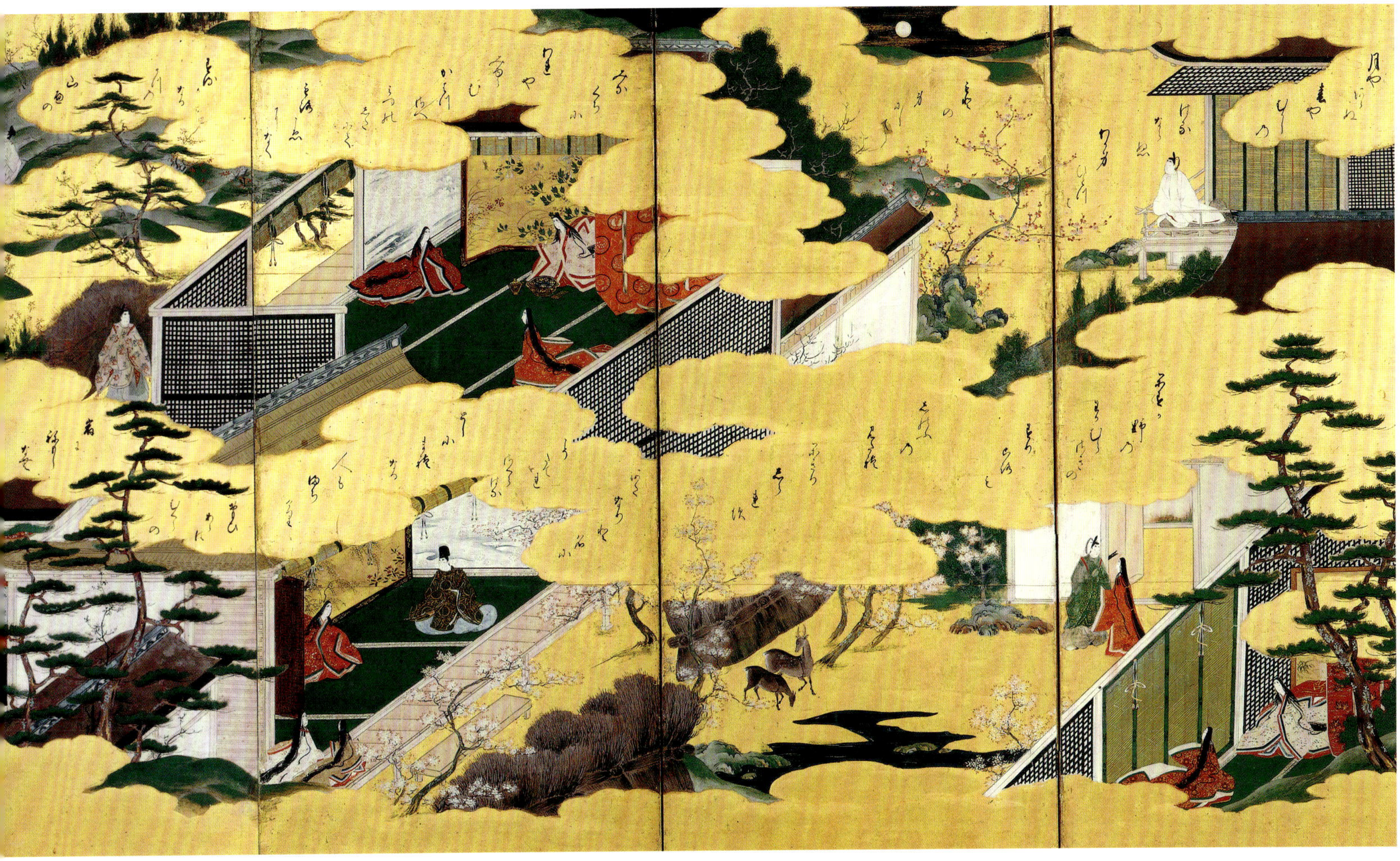

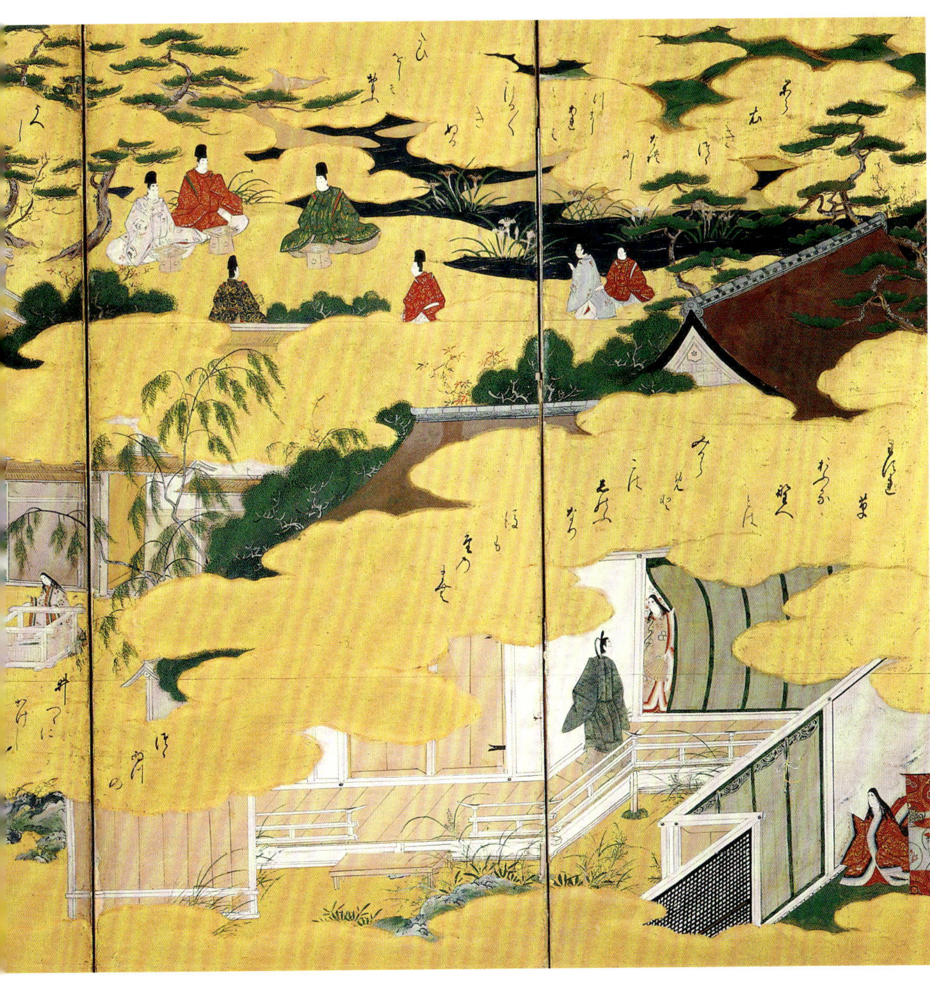

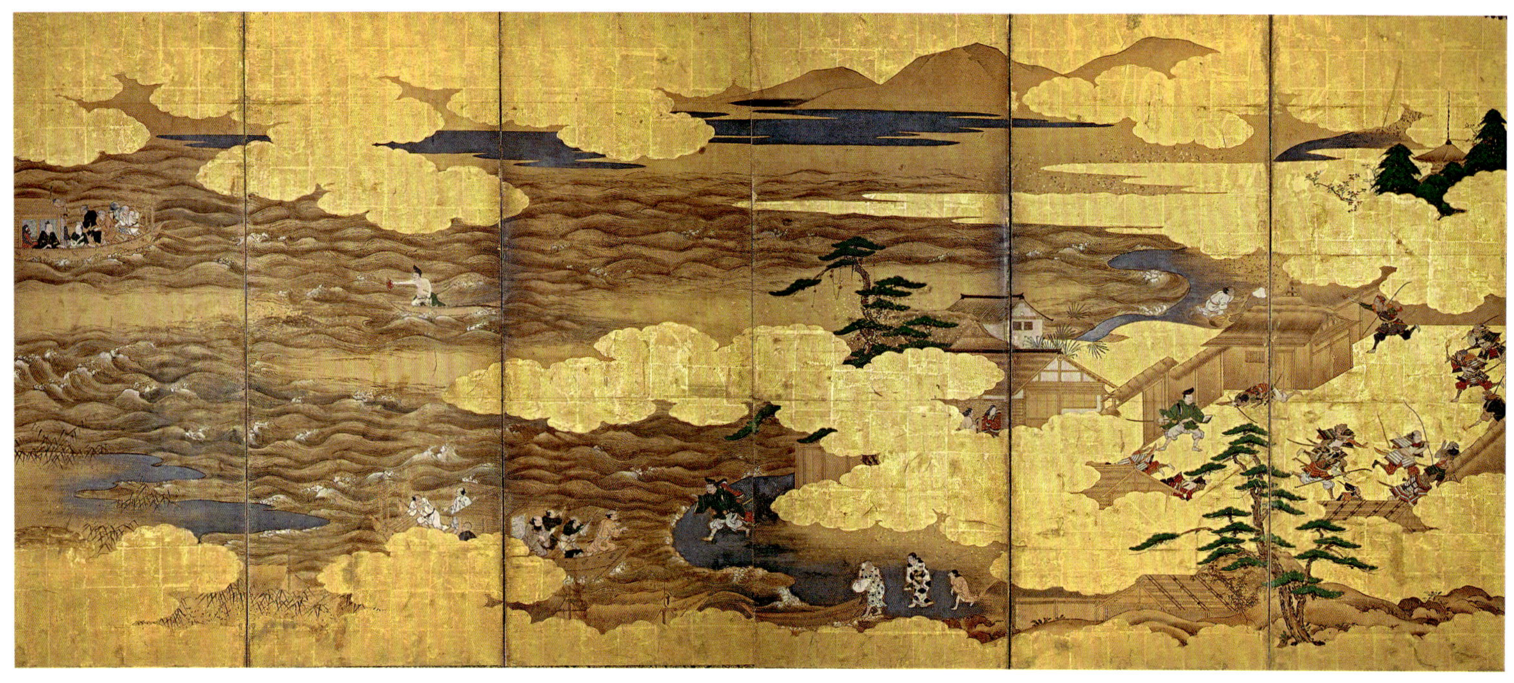

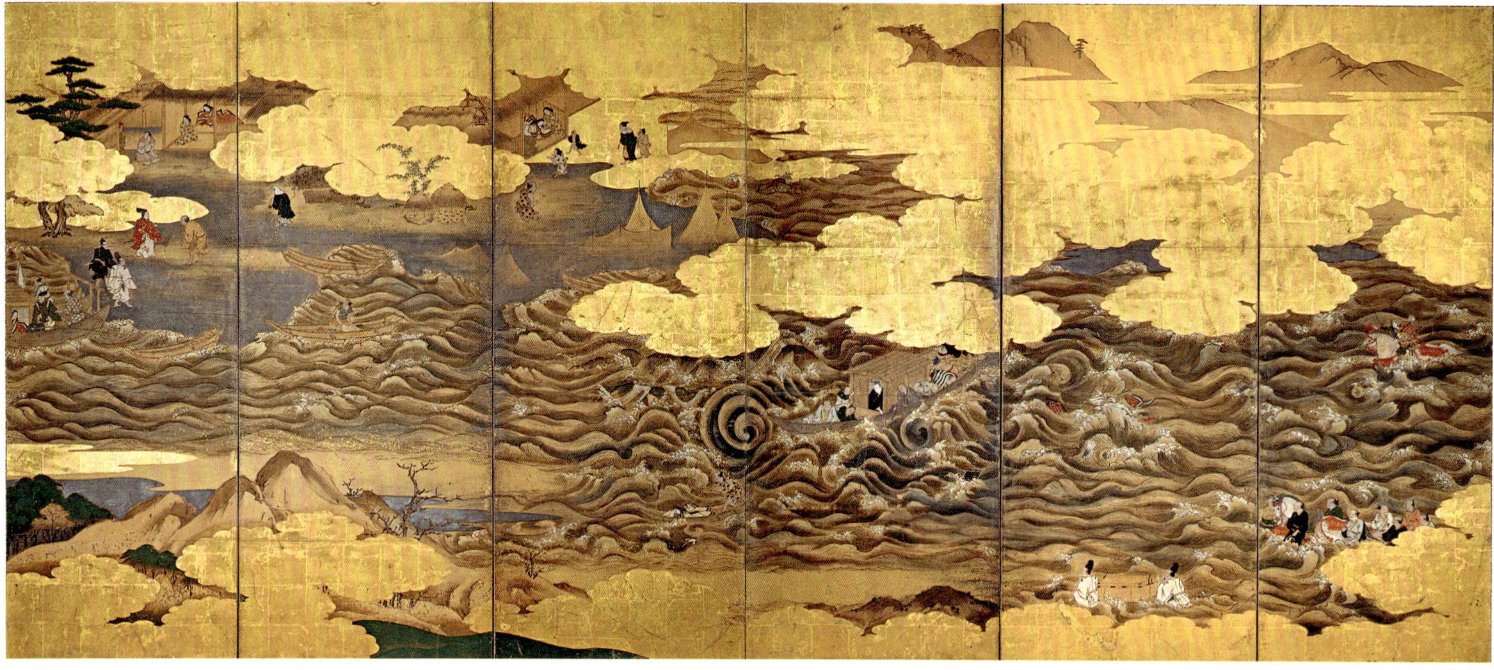

209. Scenes from *Kōwakamai, New Piece, Takebun* (幸若舞 新曲 武文)

Edo period, early 18th century
Pair of six-panel folding screens; ink, color, gold, and silver on gilded paper
Each screen 156 x 362 cm (61 3/8 in. x 11 ft. 10 1/2 in.)

LITERATURE: Ōta Shōko 1993, pp. 22–23; Murase 1993, no. 52; Buckland 2004, no. 5; Tsuji Nobuo et al. 2005, no. 75.

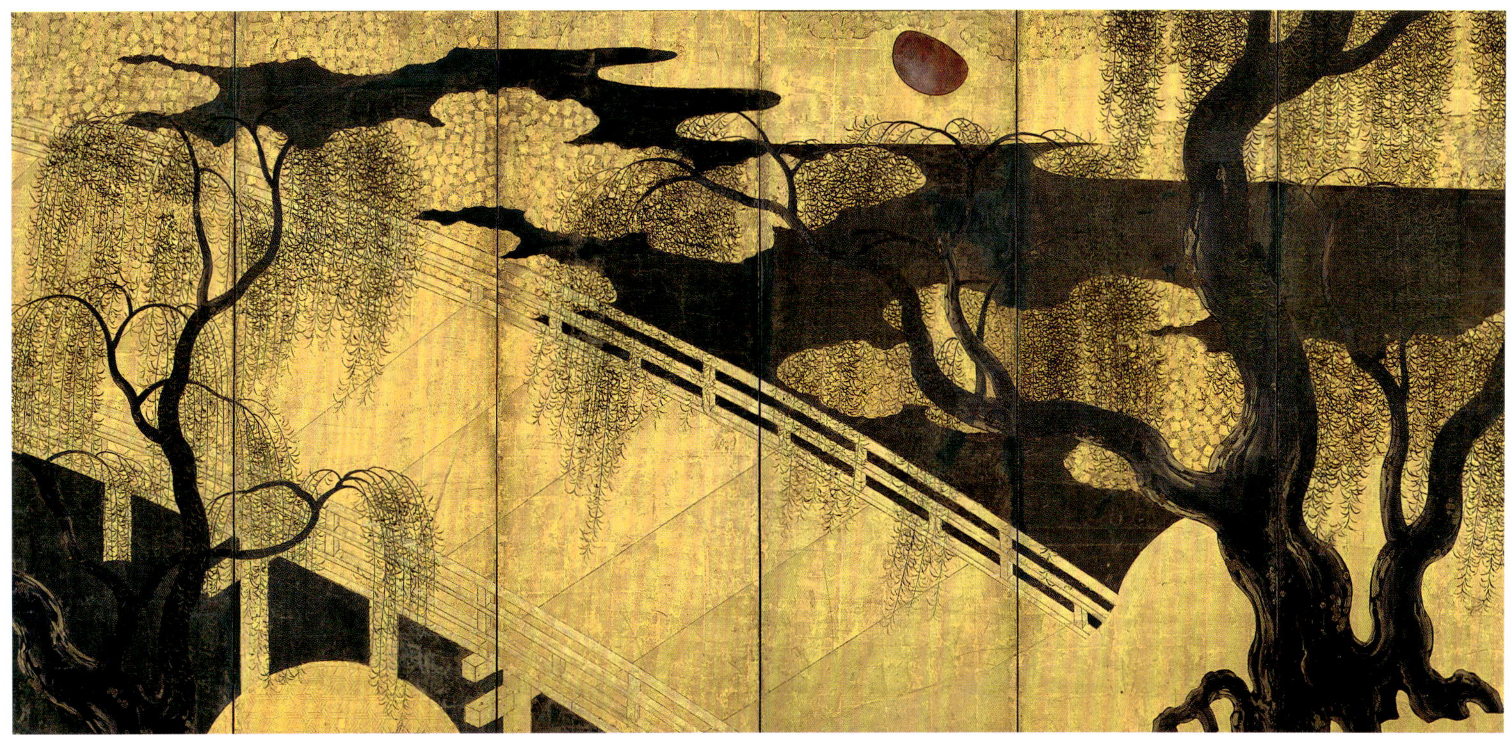

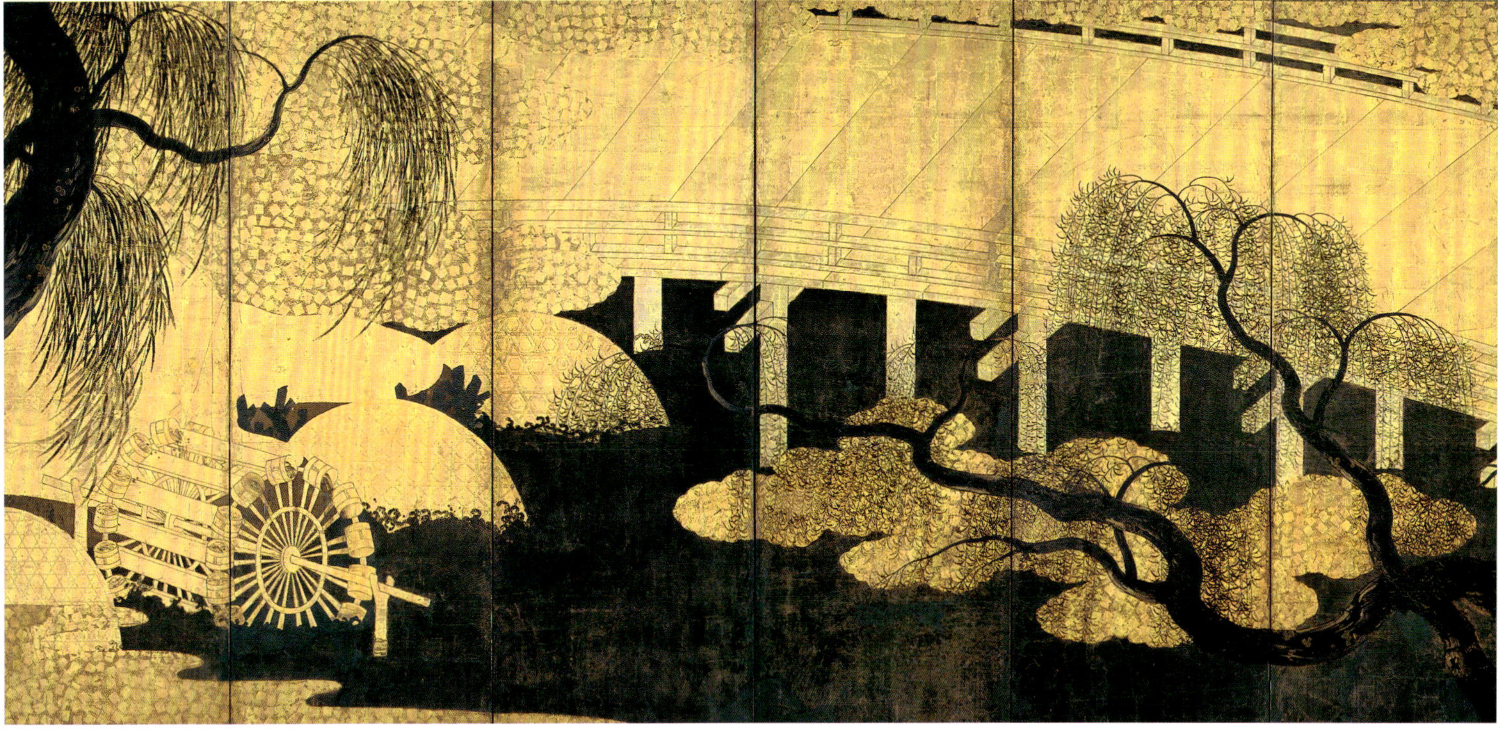

210. Willows and Bridge

Momoyama period, 17th century
Pair of six-panel folding screens; ink, color, gold, and copper on gilded paper
Each screen 170.1 x 345.3 cm (67 in. x 11 ft. 4 in.)

Ex coll.: Marquis Maeda, Tokyo

Literature: Murase 1971, no. 18; Murase 1975, no. 46; L. Cunningham 1984, no. 1; Tokyo National Museum 1985a, no. 27; Avitabile 1990, no. 50; Murase 2000, no. 80; Tsuji Nobuo et al. 2005, no. 69; Sugimoto Hidetarō 2007, pp. 190–91.

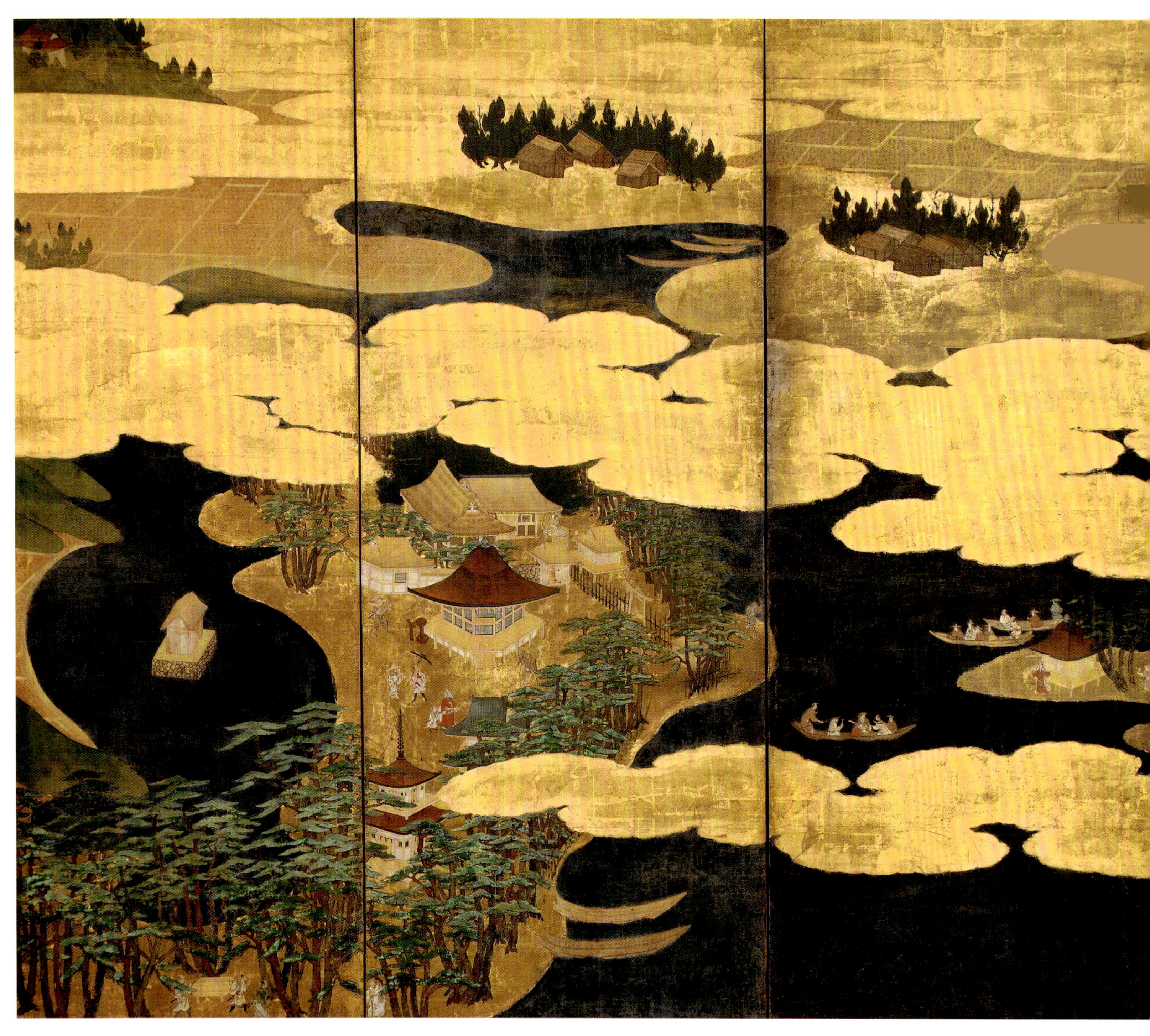

212. View of Ama no Hashidate
(天の橋立)

Edo period, early 17th century
Six-panel folding screen; ink, color, and gold on gilded paper
149.3 x 356 cm (58 3/4 in. x 11 ft. 8 1/8 in.)

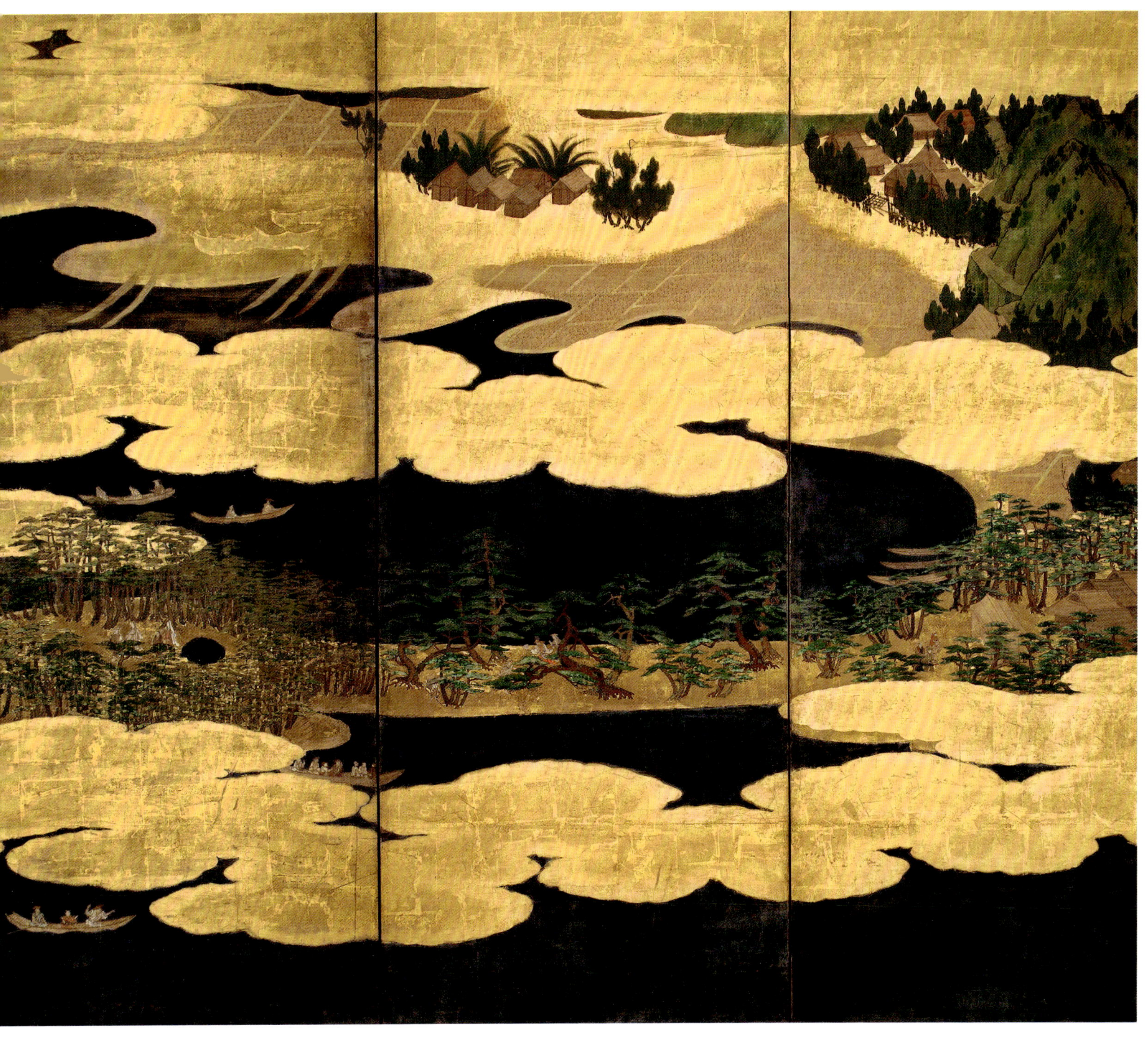

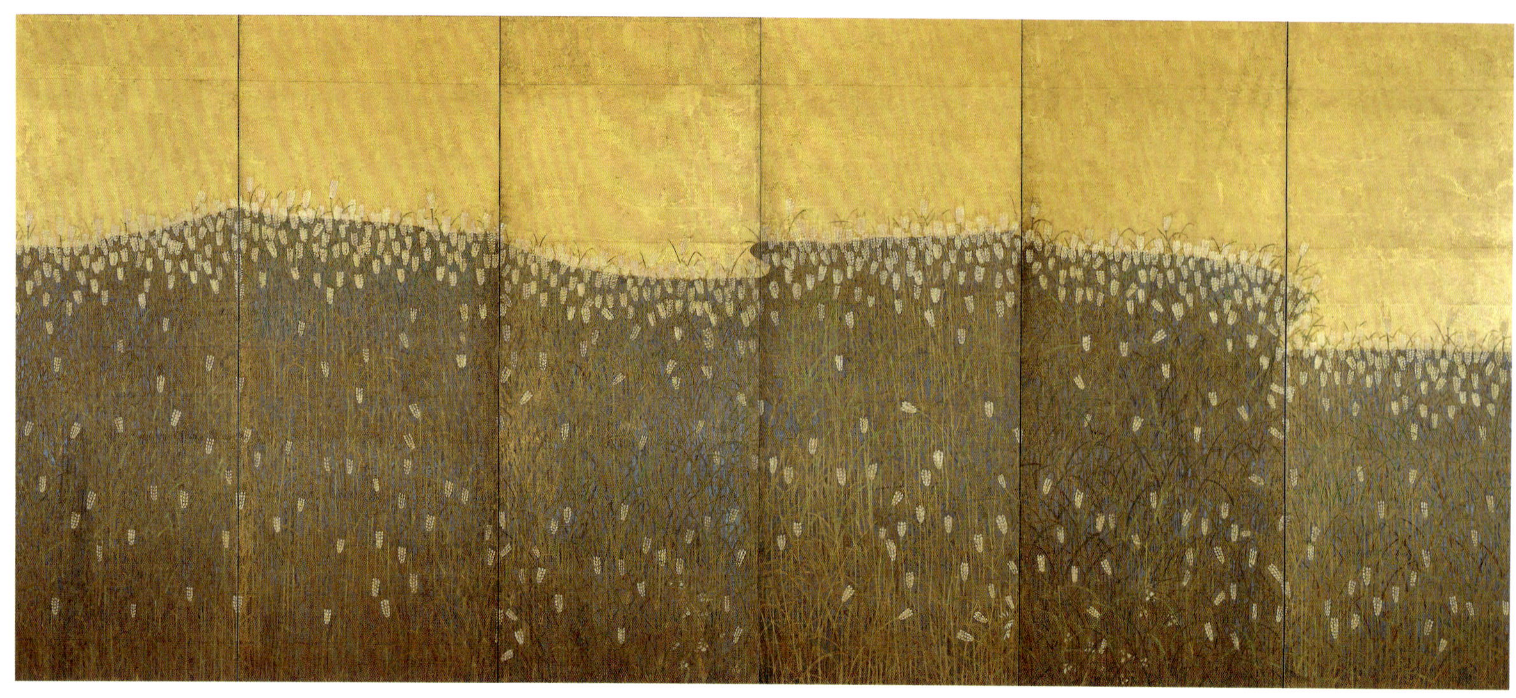

213. Barley Field

Edo period, early 17th century
Six-panel folding screen; ink, color, and silver on gilded paper
148.2 x 340.8 cm (4 ft. 10 in. x 11 ft. 2 1/8 in.)

LITERATURE: Murase 1993, no. 49; Tsuji Nobuo et al. 2005, no. 71.

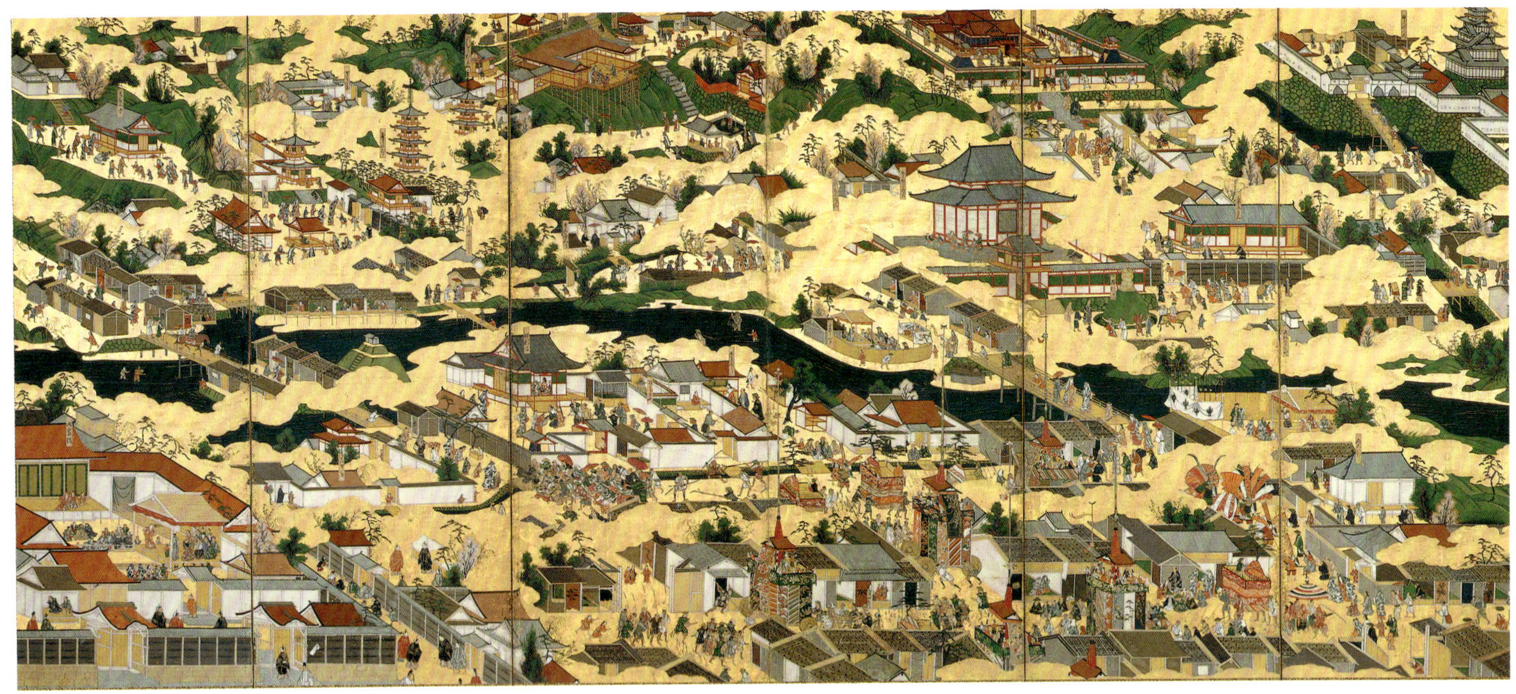

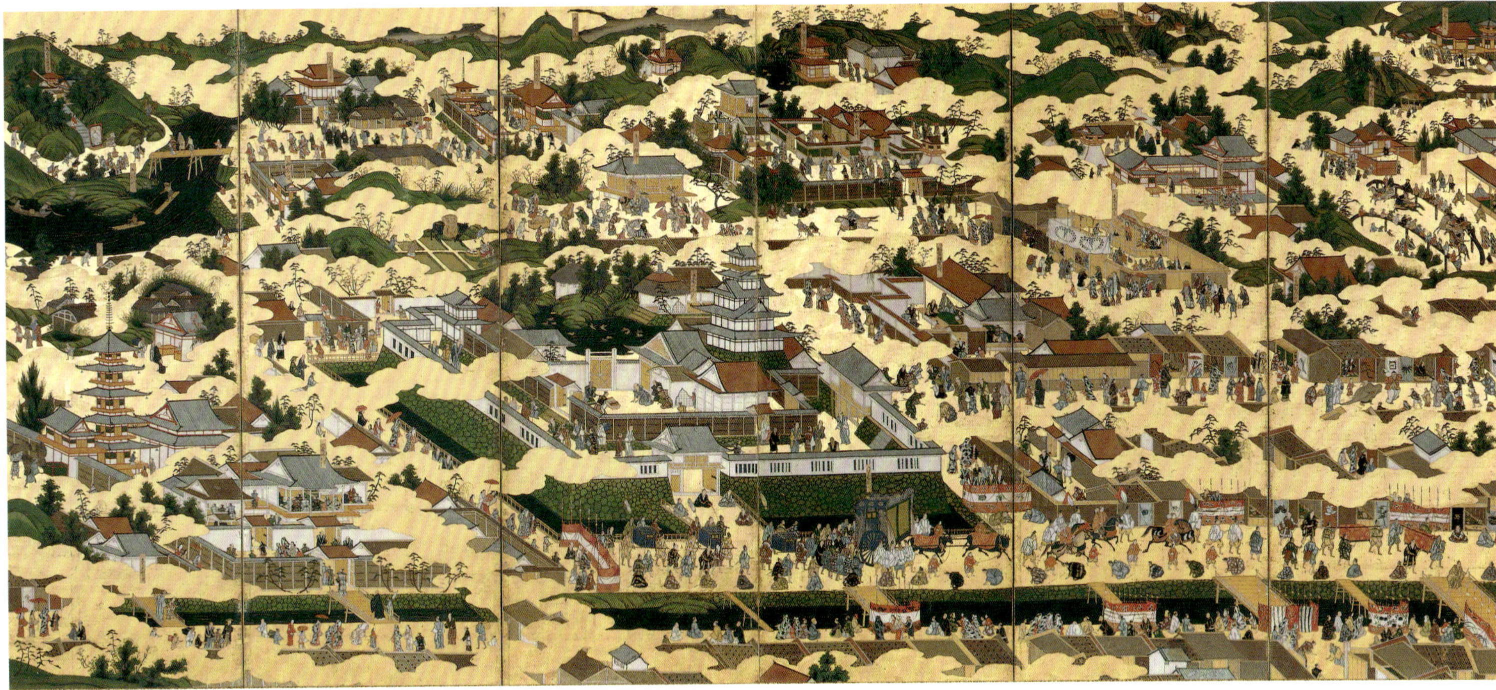

214. *Rakuchū-Rakugai* (Kyoto and Its Suburbs) (洛中洛外)

Edo period, first half of 17th century
Pair of six-panel folding screens; ink, color, and gold on gilded paper
Each screen 156.1 x 352.2 cm (61½ in. x 11 ft. 6⅝ in.)

LITERATURE: Narazaki Muneshige 1964, pp. 11–17; Shimada Shūjirō 1969, vol. 2, no. 22; Murase 1975, no. 45; Takeda Tsuneo 1978a, nos. 88, 89; L. Cunningham 1984, no. 4; Avitabile 1990, no. 49; Ruch 1991; McKelway 1997, pp. 48–57; Murase 2000, no. 139; Kimbrough 2001, p. 69 (detail); Murase 2003, no. 118; Tsuji Nobuo et al. 2005, no. 78; Ishikawa Tomohiko 2006, p. 9 (detail), pl. 2; Kimbrough 2008, p. 169, fig. 23.

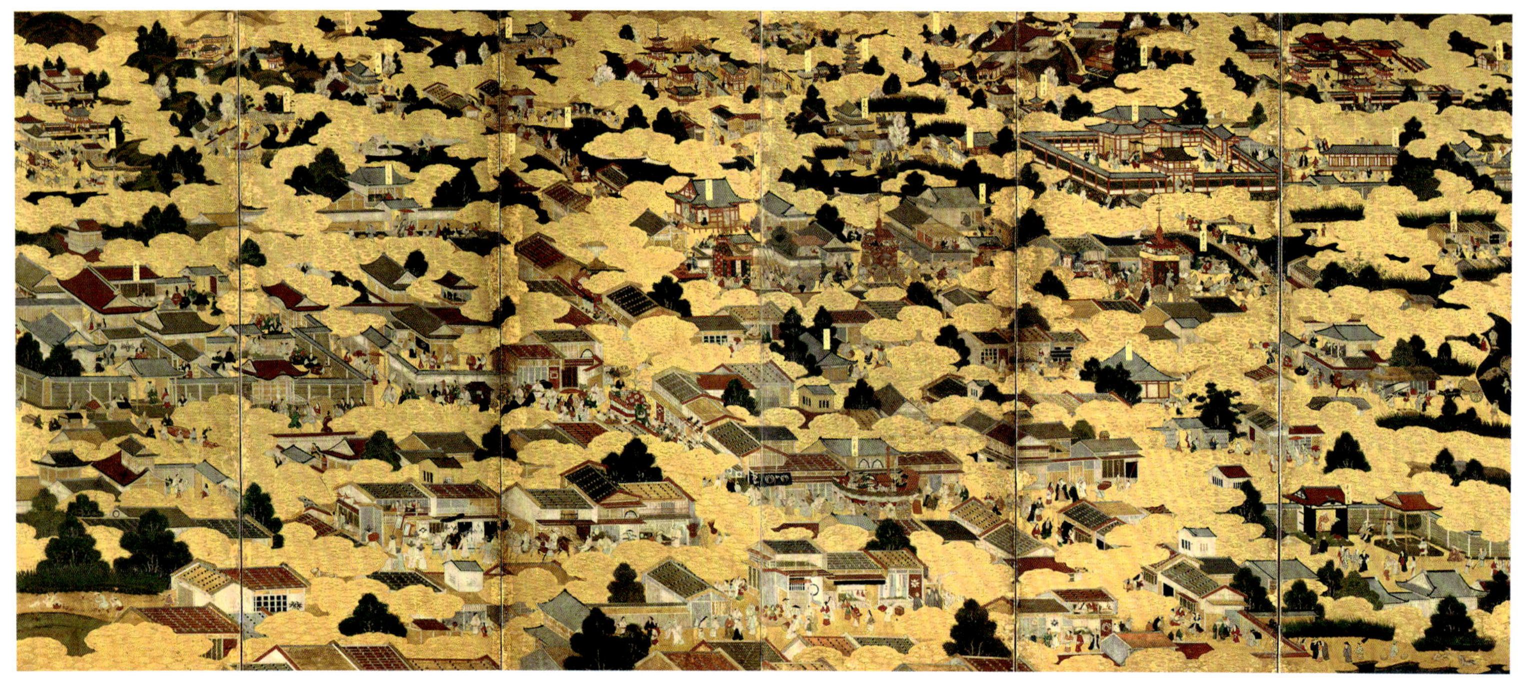

215. *Rakuchū-Rakugai* (Kyoto and Its Suburbs) (洛中洛外)

Edo period, early 17th century
Right screen of a pair of six-panel folding screens; ink, color, and gold on gilded paper
156 x 359.4 cm (61 3/8 in. x 11 ft. 9 1/2 in.)

Literature: Sin Ki-su and Nakao Hiroshi 1996, pp. 120–29, colorpls. 42–45; Toby 2008, pp. 204–5.

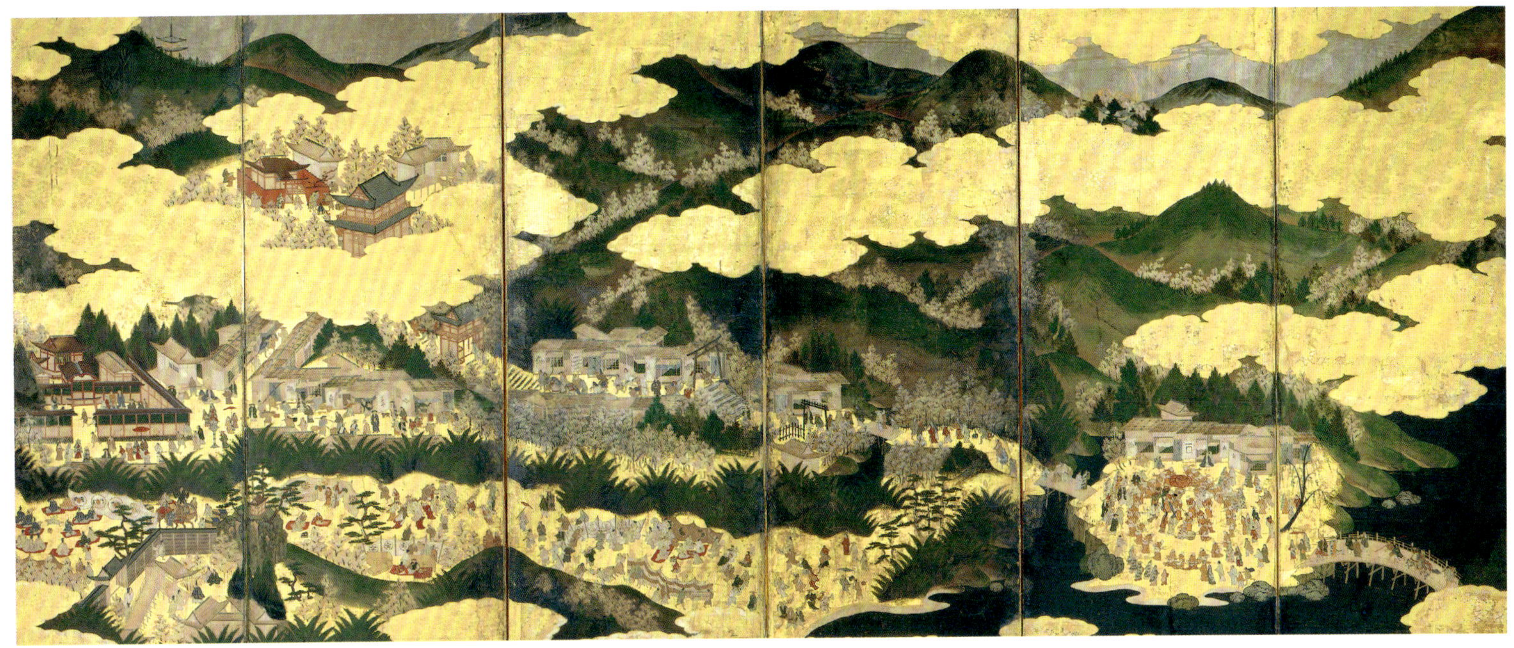

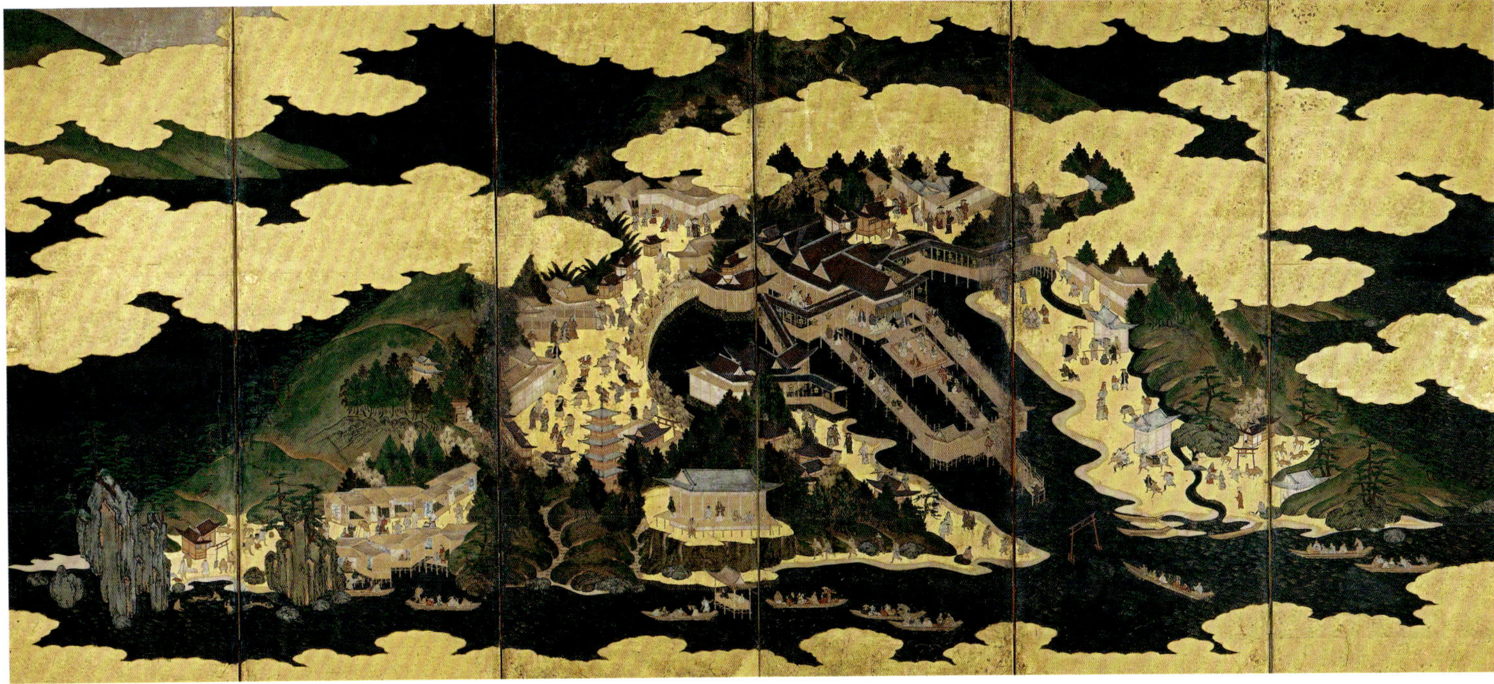

216. Viewing Cherry Blossoms at Yoshino (吉野) and Itsukushima (厳島)

Edo period, first half of 17th century
Pair of six-panel folding screens; ink and color on gilded paper
Each screen 153.6 x 348.6 cm (60½ in. x 11 ft. 5¼ in.)

LITERATURE: Murase 1990, no. 22; Murase 1993, no. 50; Murase 2000, no. 140; Buckland 2004, no. 9; Hiroshima Prefectural Museum of Art et al. 2005, no. 31; Miyake Hidekazu 2005, figs. 2, 6–8 (details), 11–13 (details), 15–16 (details); *Nihon sankei-ten* 2005, pp. 66–67, pl. 31; Suzuki Hiroyuki 2007, p. 68, fig. 72.

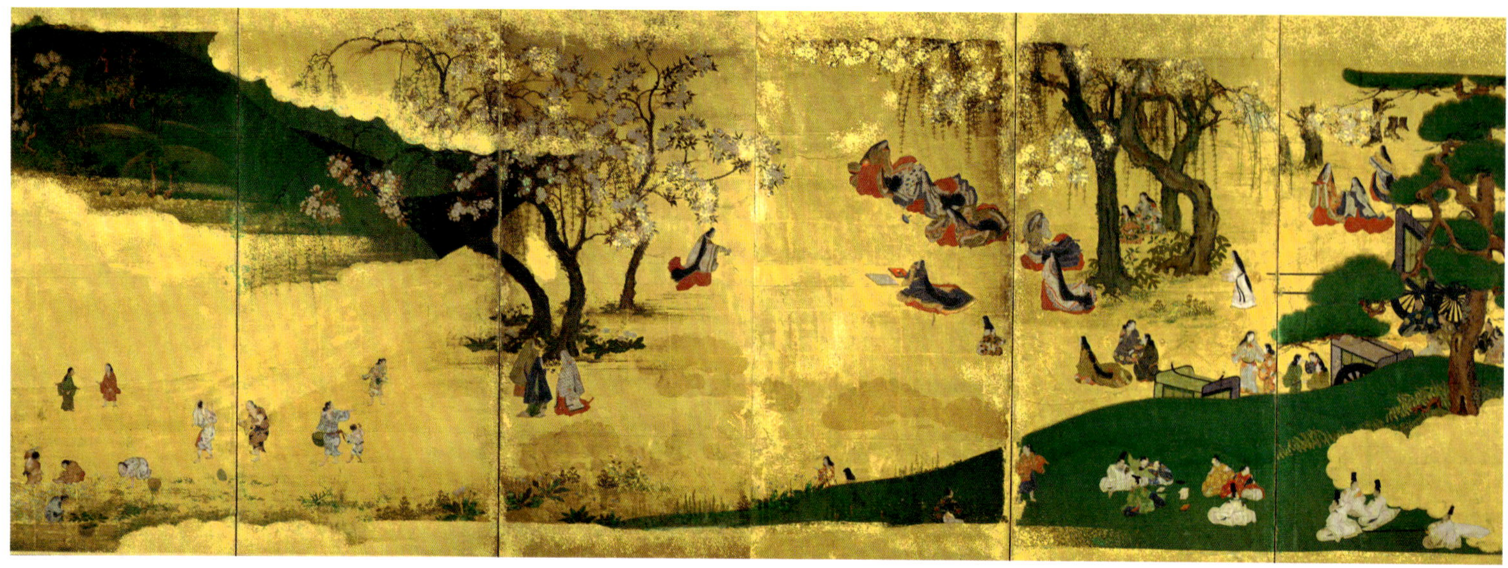

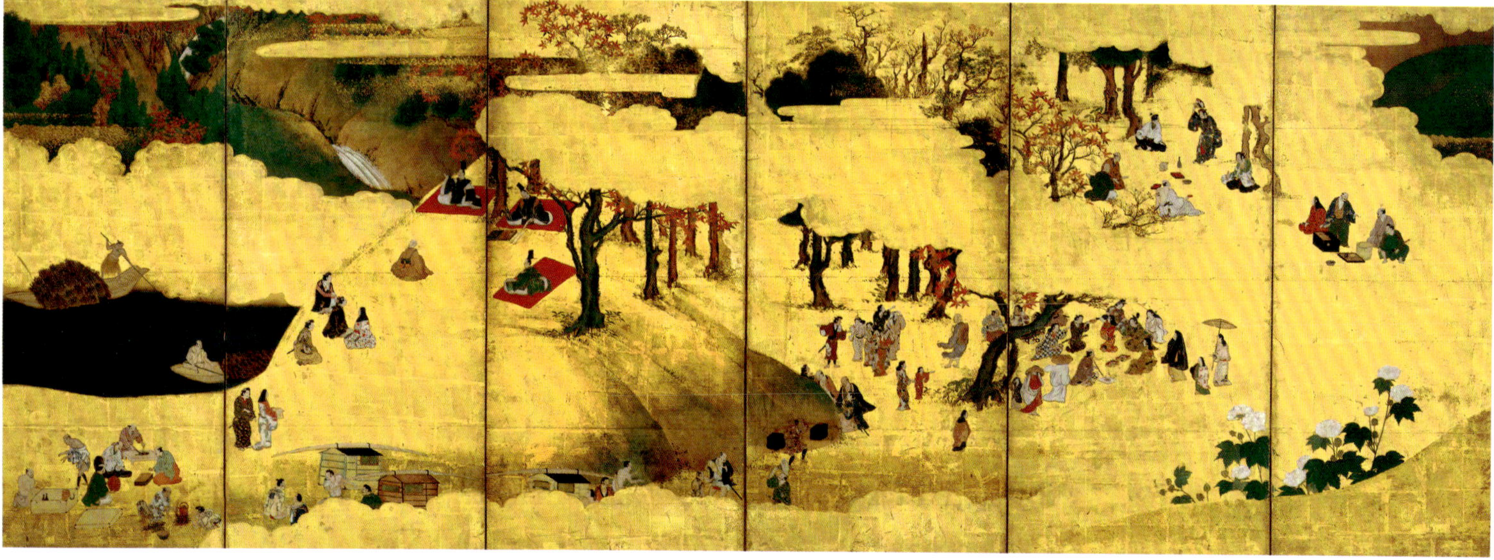

217

217. Cherry-Blossom and Maple-Leaf Viewing

Edo period, ca. 1630
Pair of six-panel folding screens; ink, color, and gold on gilded paper
Each screen 125.8 x 362.2 cm (49 1/2 in. x 11 ft. 11 in.)

Literature: Hayashiya Tatsusaburō et al. 1984, pp. 148–49, pls. 17, 18; Kobe Municipal Museum 1986, no. 34; Okudaira Shunroku 1987, pp. 105–10; Murase 2000, no. 141; Buckland 2004, no. 8; Tsuji Nobuo et al. 2005, no. 79.

218. Pleasurable Activities at Sumiyoshi (住吉)

Edo period, early 17th century
Six-panel folding screen; ink, color, and gold flecks on paper
47.2 x 165.2 cm (18 5/8 x 65 in.)

219. Arrival of the *Nanbans* (南蛮)

Edo period, ca. 1630
Pair of six-panel folding screens; ink, color, and gold on gilded paper
Each screen 105.1 x 260.7 cm (41 3/8 in. x 8 ft. 6 5/8 in.)

Ex coll.: Kyotaru & Co.; Kimbel Art Museum, Fort Worth; Tachibana Tarō, Takaoka, Toyama Prefecture

Literature: Tsuji Nobuo 1968b, pp. 101–4; Okamoto Yoshitomo and Takamizawa Tadao 1970, no. 5; Sakamoto Mitsuru 1977, figs. 13, 68 (detail), 114 (detail); *The Age of Navigation and Japan* 1978, pp. 67, 69 (detail); Murase 2003, no. 121; Tsuji Nobuo et al. 2005, no. 77; Sakamoto Mitsuru 2008, pp. 136–39, no. 37; Weston 2013, nos. 36a, b.

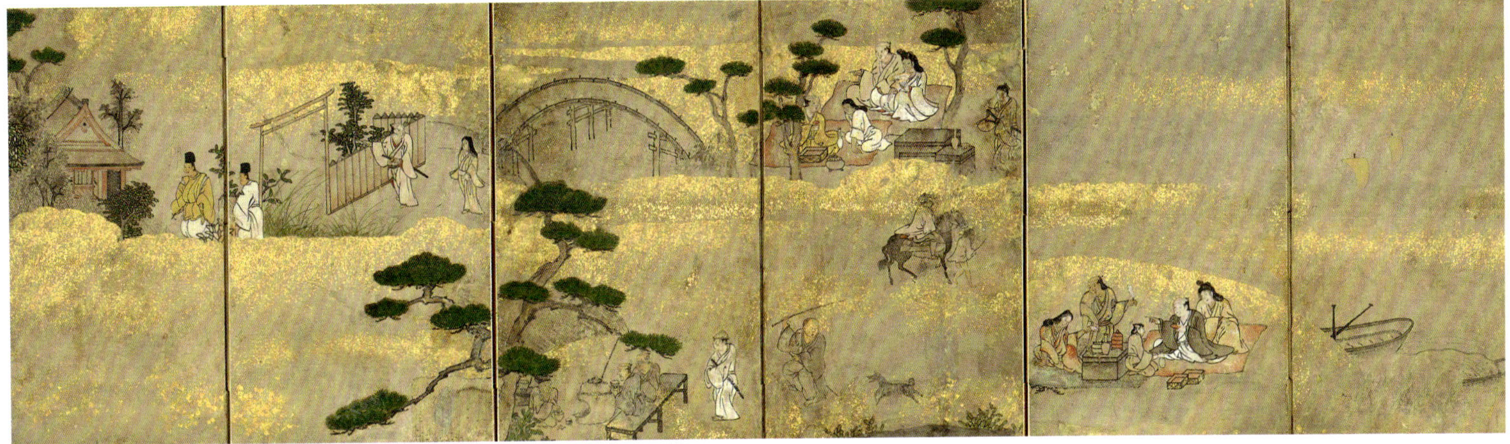

218

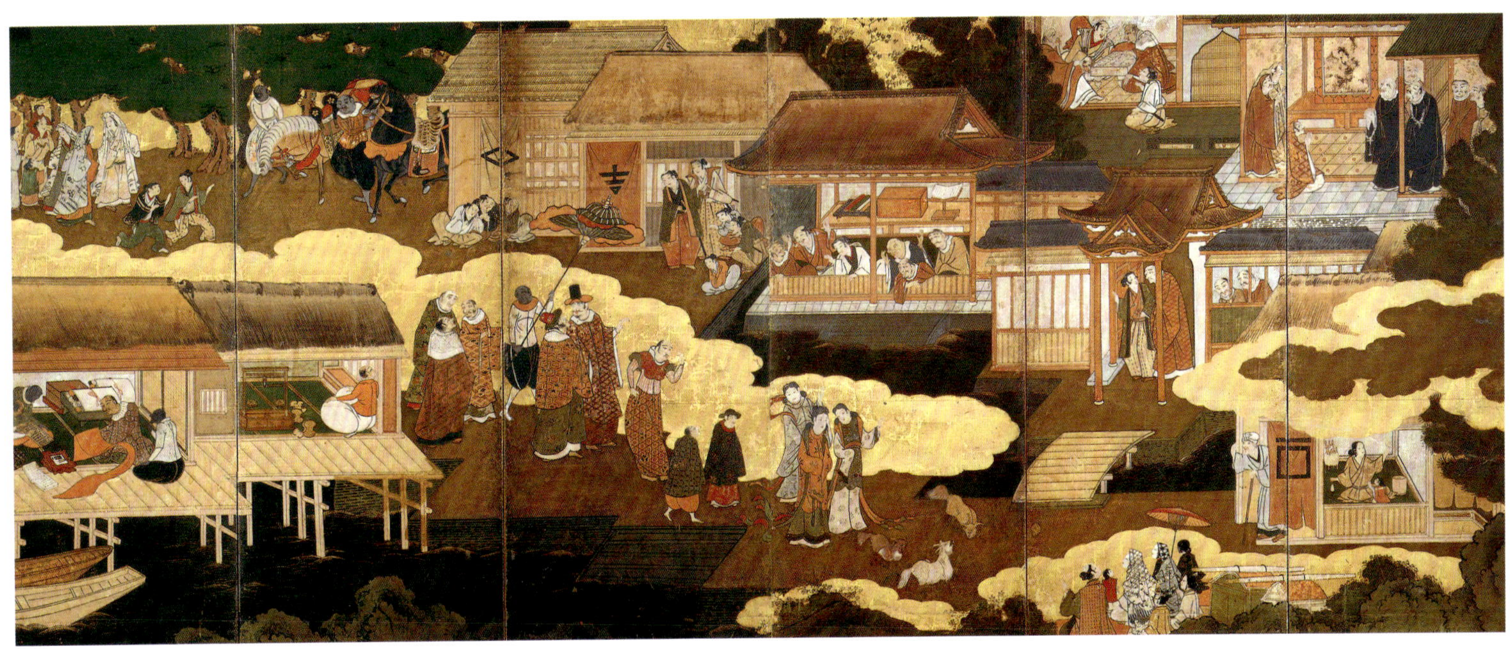

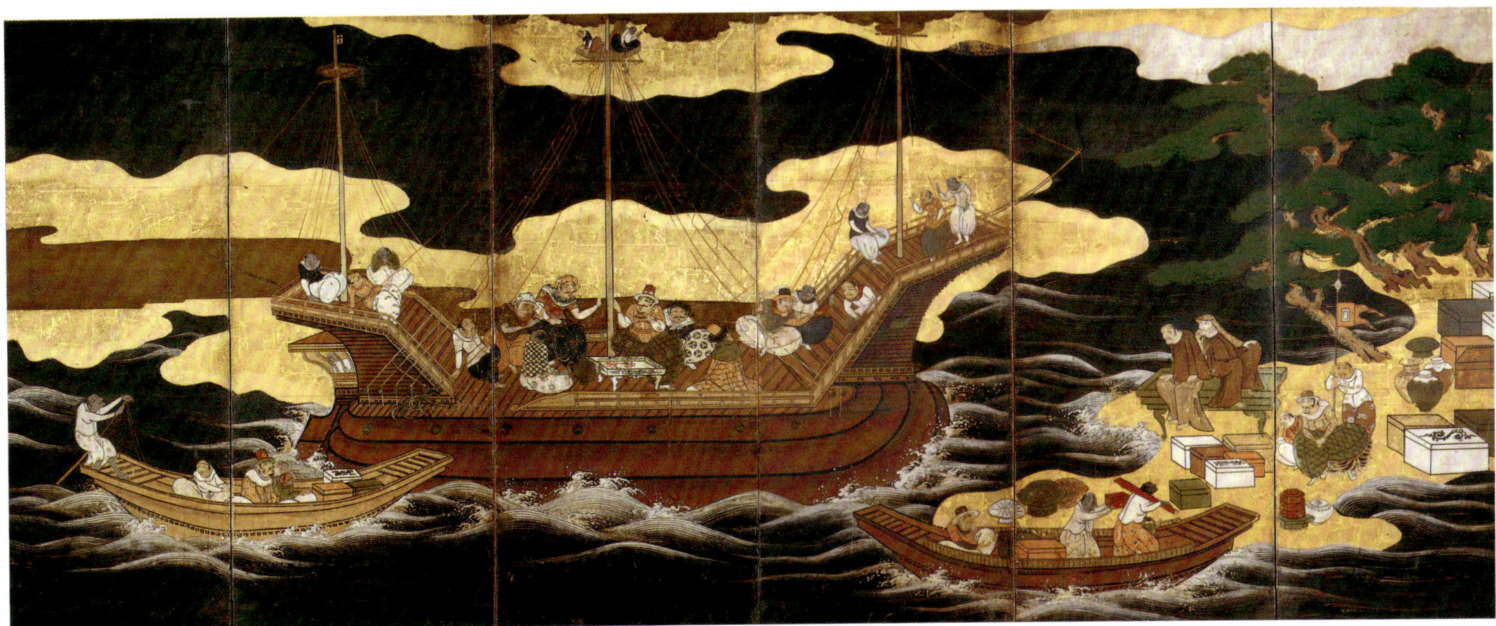

219

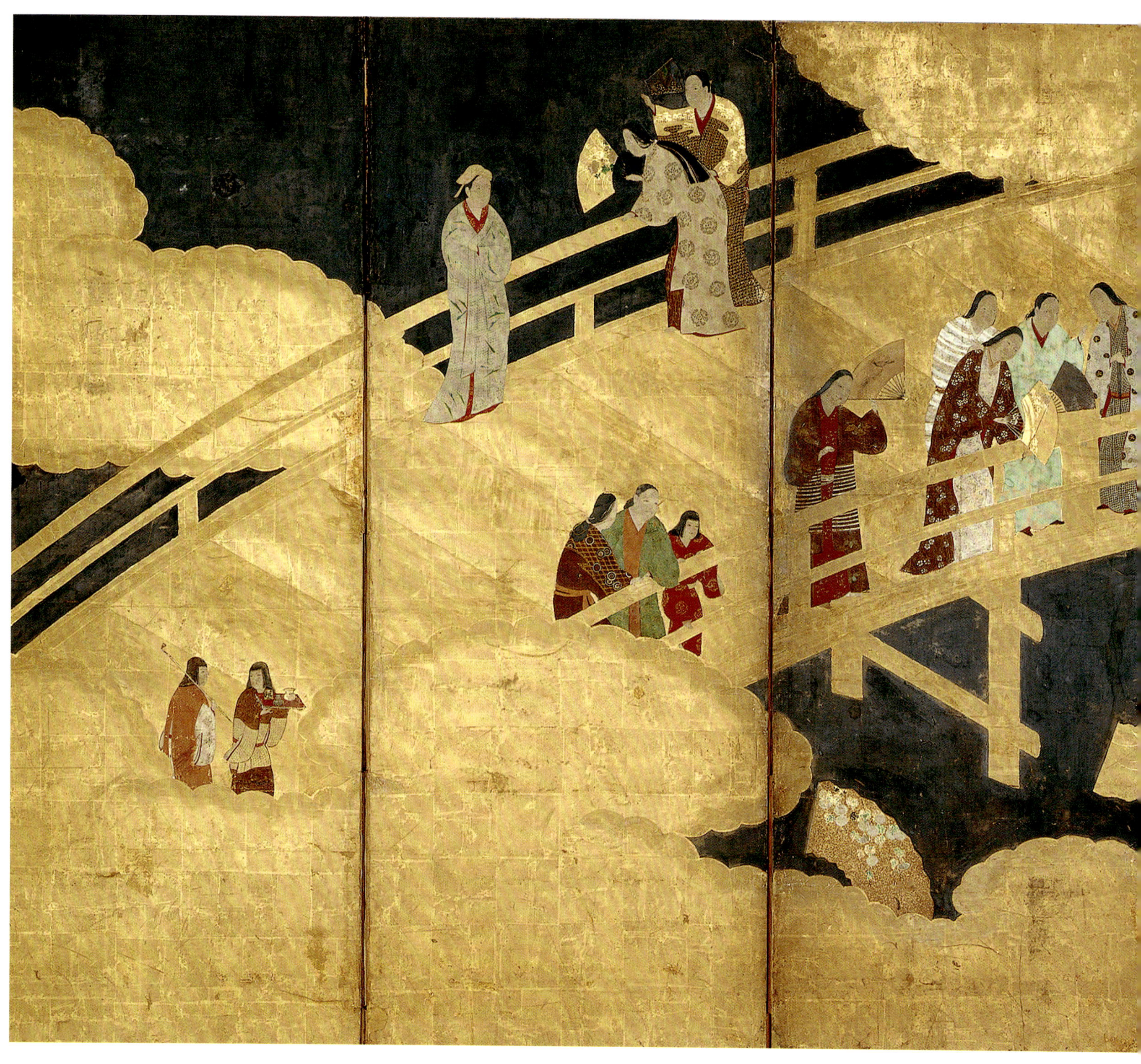

220. Women Contemplating Floating Fans

Edo period, early 17th century
Six-panel folding screen; ink, color, and gold on gilded paper
157 x 354.5 cm (61 7/8 in. x 11 ft. 7 1/2 in.)

LITERATURE: Murase 2000, no. 142; Tsuji Nobuo et al. 2005, no. 76; Suzuki Hiroyuki 2007, pl. 4.

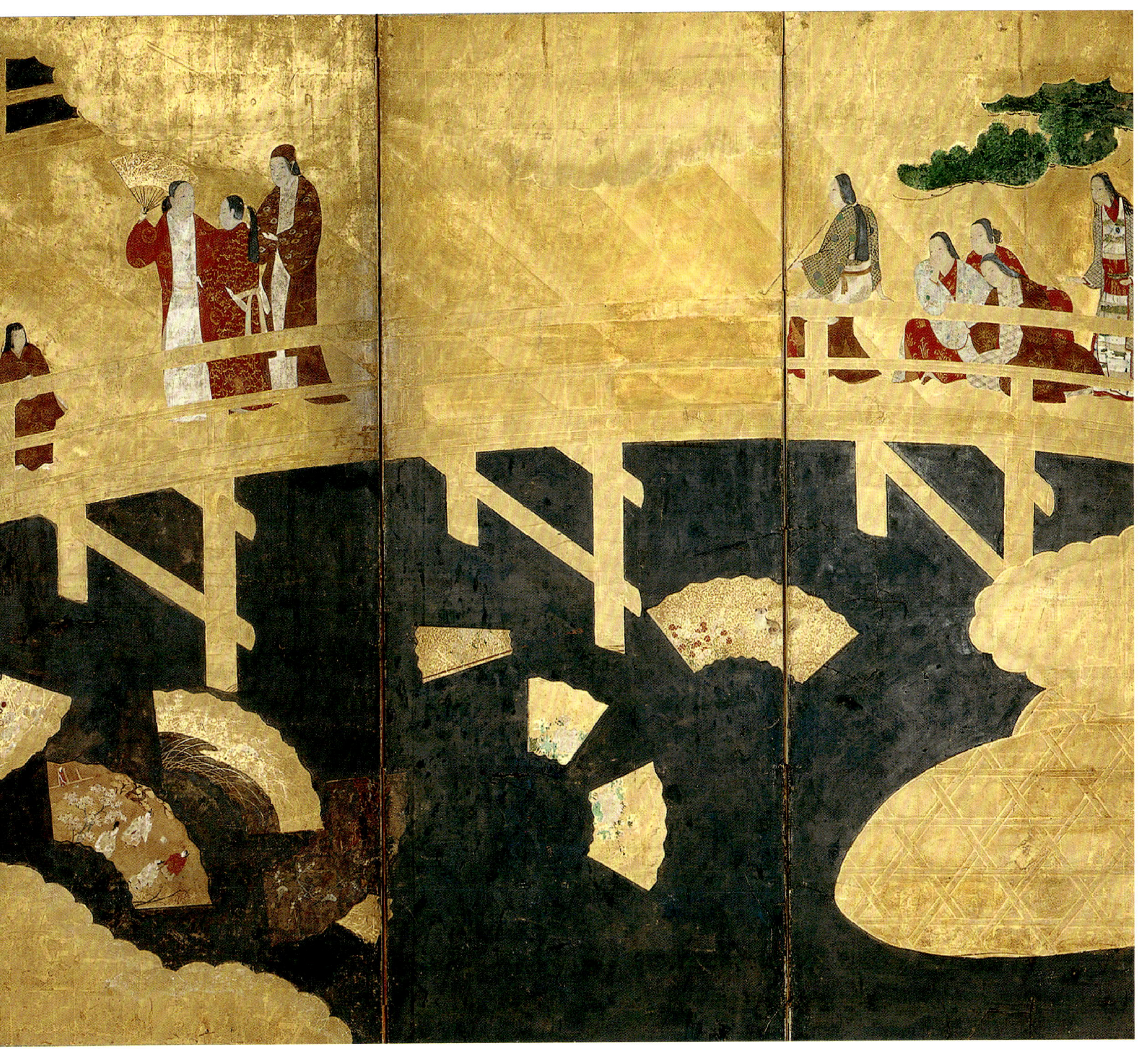

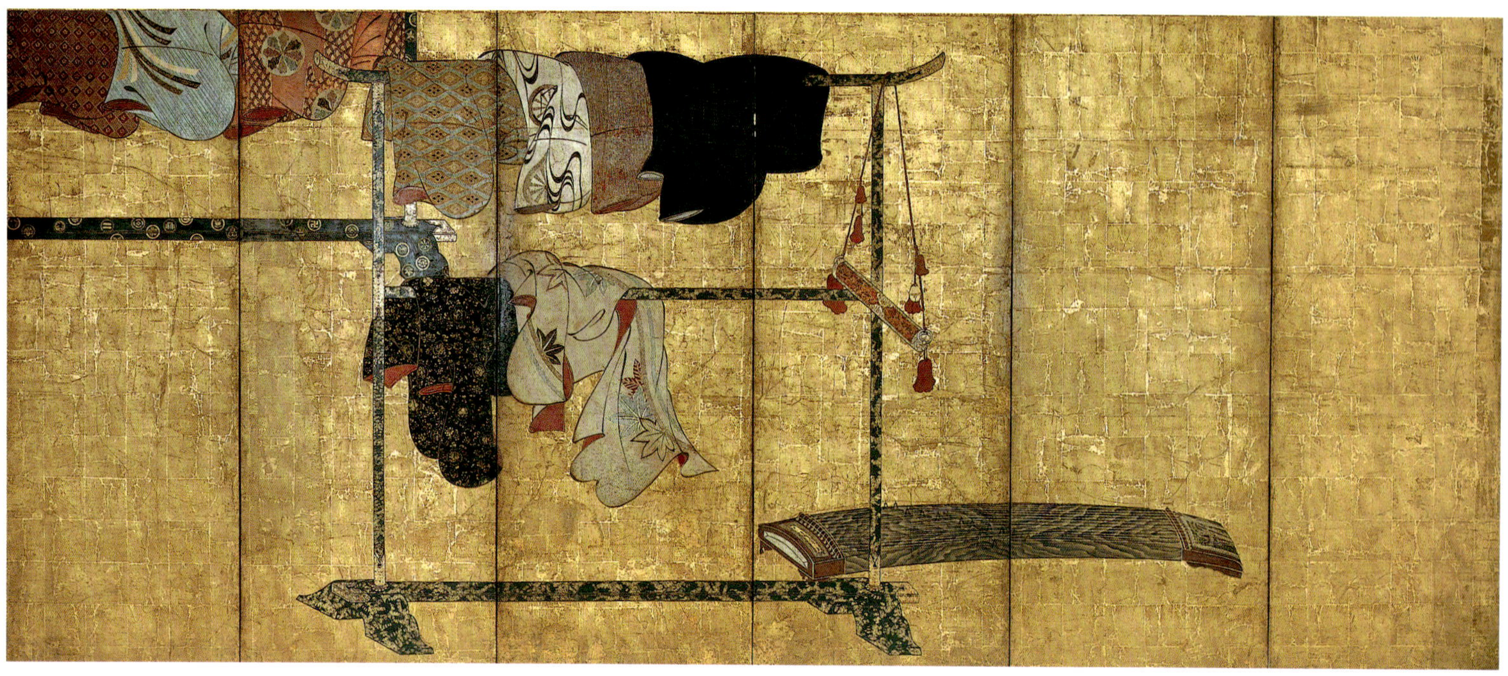

221. *Tagasode* (誰袖 / Whose Sleeves?)

Edo period, early 17th century
Six-panel folding screen; ink, color, and gold on gilded paper
170.7 x 380.8 cm (67¼ in. x 12 ft. 5⅞ in.)

Literature: Takeda Tsuneo 1967, pl. 13; Murase 1971, no. 19; Murase 1975, no. 47; Takeda Tsuneo et al. 1977, no. 104; Murase 1990, no. 21; Murase 1992, p. 184; Murase 2000, no. 143.

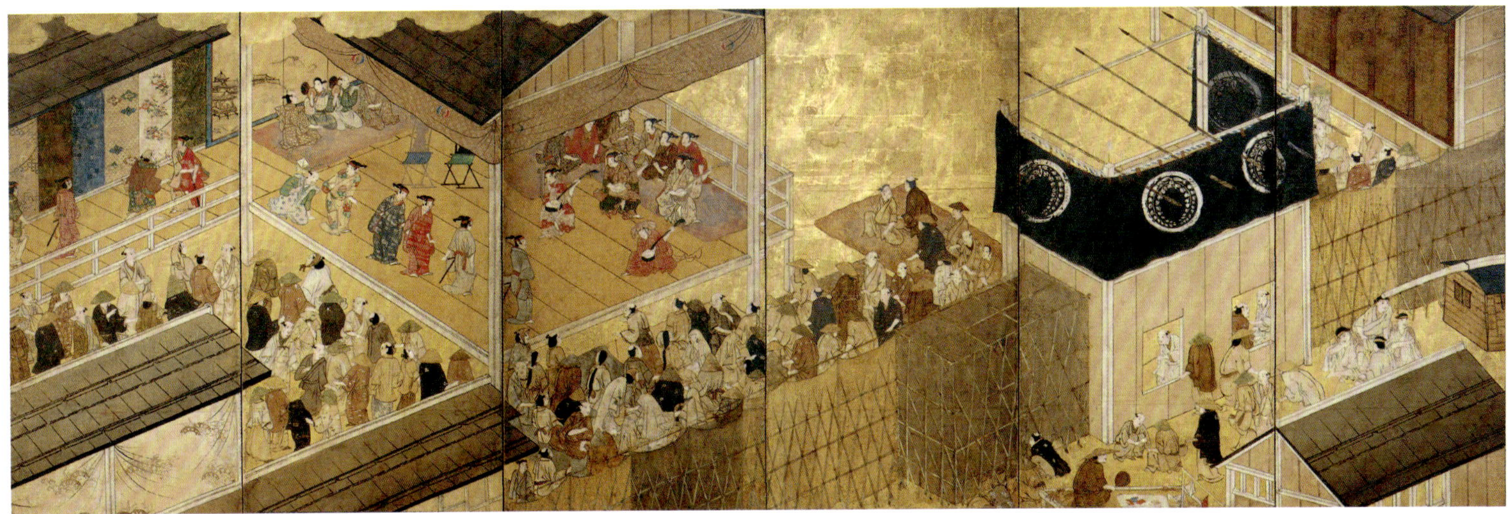

222. Okuni Kabuki (阿国歌舞伎)

Edo period, first quarter of 17th century
Six-panel folding screen; ink, color, and gold on gilded paper
81.4 x 247.2 cm (32 x 97 1/8 in.)

LITERATURE: Tsuji Nobuo et al. 2005, no. 80.

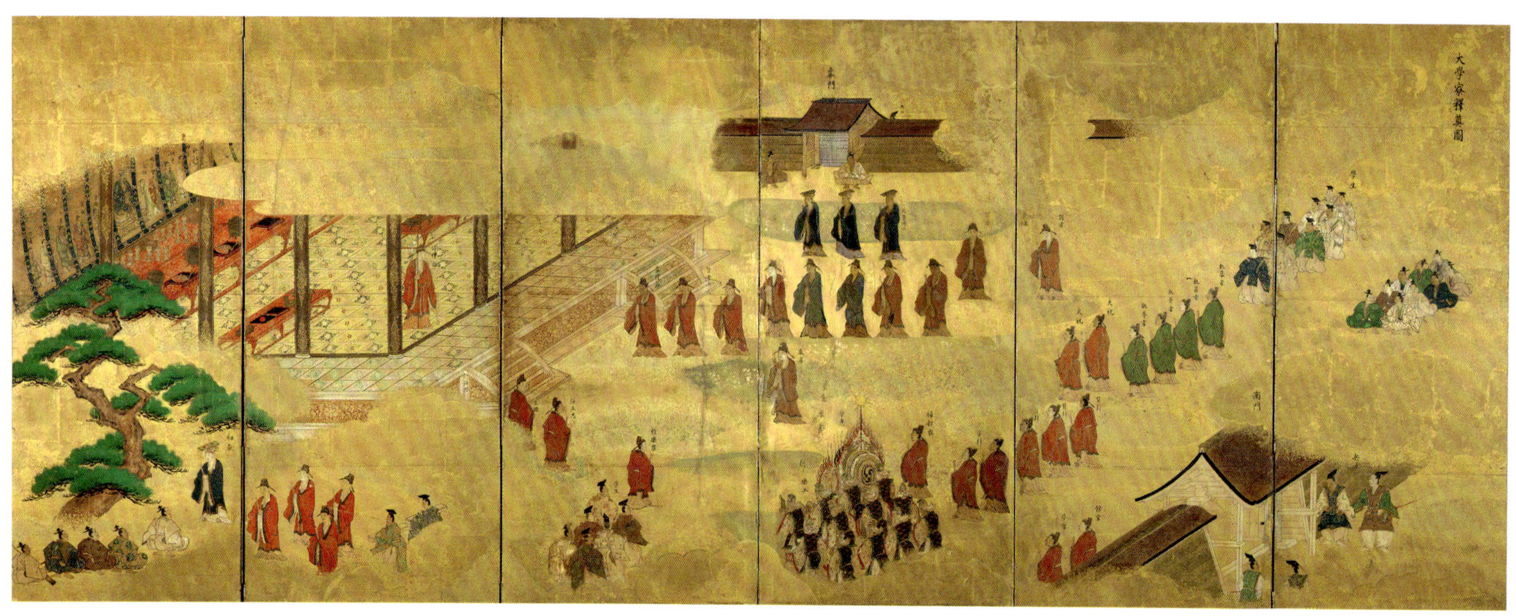

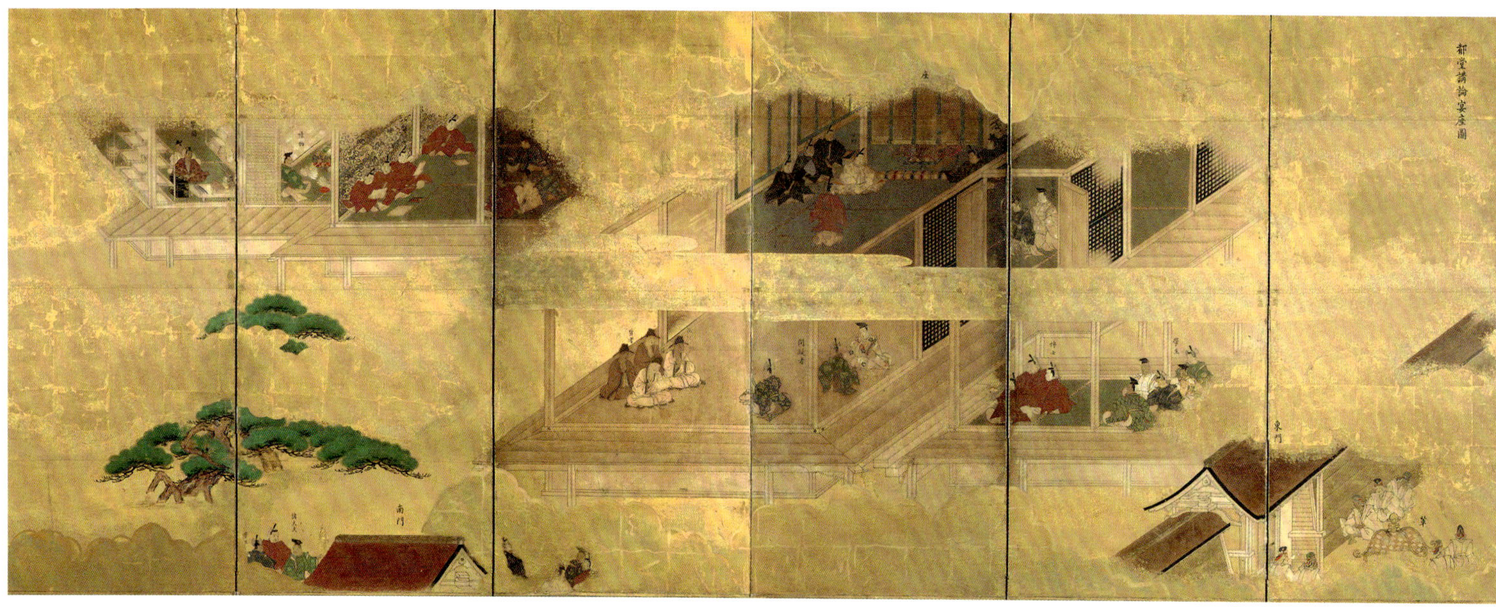

223. Scenes at the University with Images of the Ancient Sages (大学寮釈尊図); Debate and Banquet at the Administration Offices (都堂講論宴座図)

Edo period, 17th century
Pair of six-panel folding screens; ink, color, and gold on gilded paper
Each screen 120.3 x 312.6 cm (47 3/8 in. x 10 ft. 3 1/8 in.)
Text

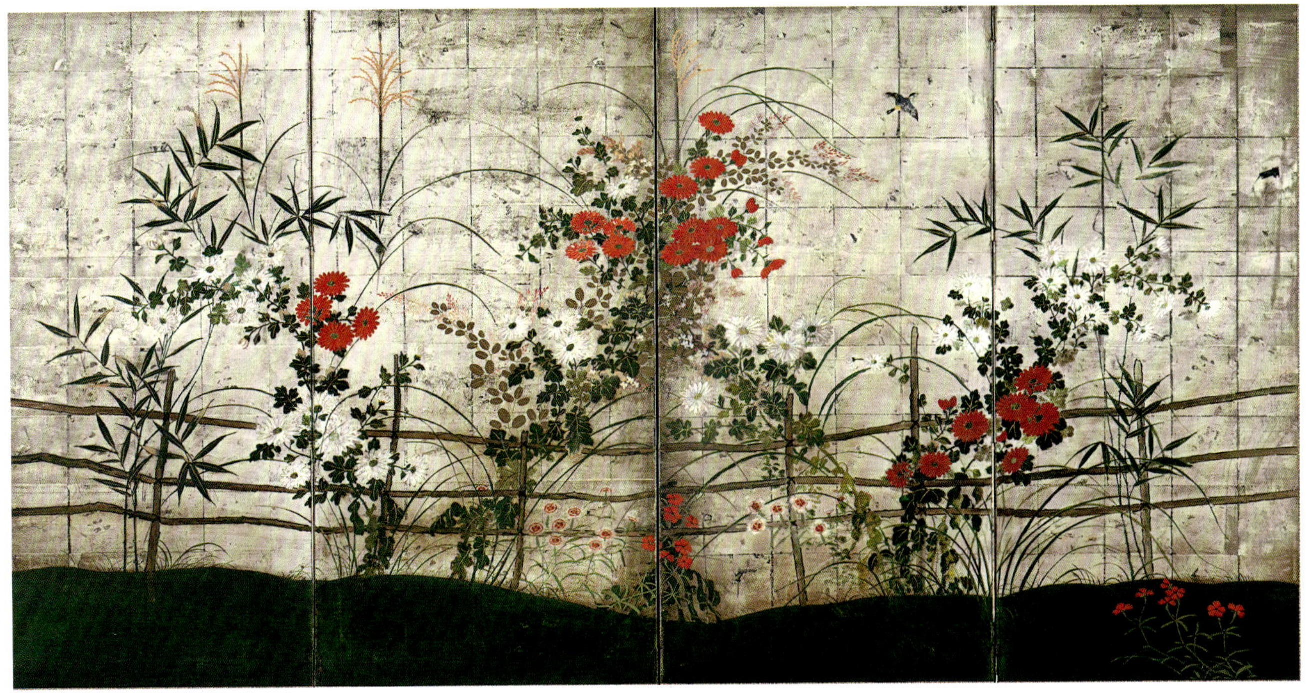

224. Autumn Grasses

Edo period, early 19th century
Four-panel screen; ink and color on paper with silver foil
106.5 x 205.4 cm (41 7/8 x 80 7/8 in.)

Chapter 6 Details

† *denotes illustrated items*

208. Seventeen scenes and poems from *Ise monogatari*

Text

[from panel 1 of the right screen, reading from right to left, top to bottom]

[Episode 4] *Is not the moon the same? / The spring / the spring of the old? / Only this body of mine / is the same body . . .*

[Episode 1] *Like random patterns of this robe, / dyed with the young purple / from Kasuga Plain— / even thus is the wild disorder / of my yearning heart.*

[Episode 27] *You will see me / in that pool, / for even frogs / cry in pairs / under the water.*

[Episode 17] *People call them evanescent, / these cherry blossoms— / yet they have waited / for someone whose visits / are months apart.*

[Episode 9] *Beside Mount Utsu / in Suruga / I can see you / neither waking / nor, alas, even in my dreams.*

[Episode 3] *If you love me, / let us sleep together, / though it be in a weed-choked house / with our sleeves / for a mattress.*

[Episode 53] *Why does the cock / herald the dawn / when the night is yet / deep as this love of mine, / unknown to others?*

[Episode 9] *Fuji is a mountain / that knows no seasons. / What time does it take this for, / that it should be dappled / with fallen snow?*

[Episode 101] *Longer than ever before / is the wisteria's shadow— / how many are those / who shelter beneath / its blossoms?*

[Left screen]

[Episode 9] *I have a beloved wife, / familiar as the skirt / of a well-worn robe. / And so this distant journeying / fills my heart with grief.*

[Episode 100] *Though the fields may seem / o'ergrown with forgetting grass, / this is the herb of remembrance— / and remembering, / I look to the future.*

[Episode 51] *If it has been well planted, / it will fail to bloom / only if autumn should fail to come. / And though the petals scatter / its roots will never die.*

[Episode 23] *My height that we measured / at the well curb / has, it seems, / passed the old mark / since last I saw you.*

[Episode 14] *When daylight comes / I shall toss him in the cistern— / that miserable rooster / who crows too soon / and drives my lover away.*

[Episode 41] *When the murasaki's hue / is strong and deep, / one can distinguish / no other plant / on the vast plain.*

[Episode 96]: *"In autumn . . . ," I said, / but it was not to be— / Our relationship has proved no deeper / than a shallow creek / strewn with fallen leaves.*

[Episode 23] *If wind blows, / white waves will rise at Tatsutayama— / Shall you be crossing / quite alone by night?*

† 223. Scenes at the University with the Images of the Ancient Sages; Debate and Banquet at the Administration Offices

Text

[right screen] *Scenes at the University with the Images of the Ancient Sages*

[left screen] *Debate and Banquet at the Administration Offices*

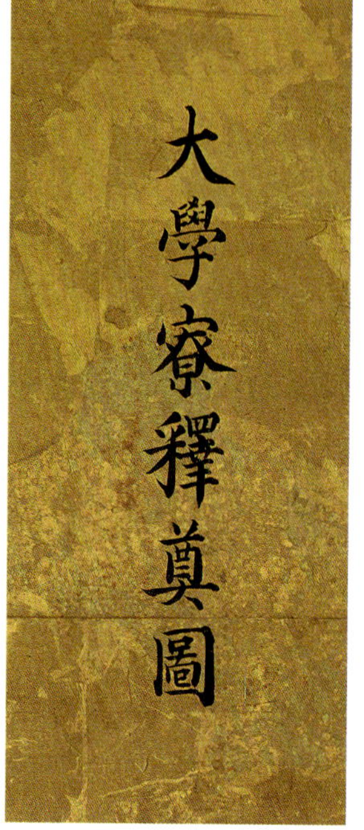

223

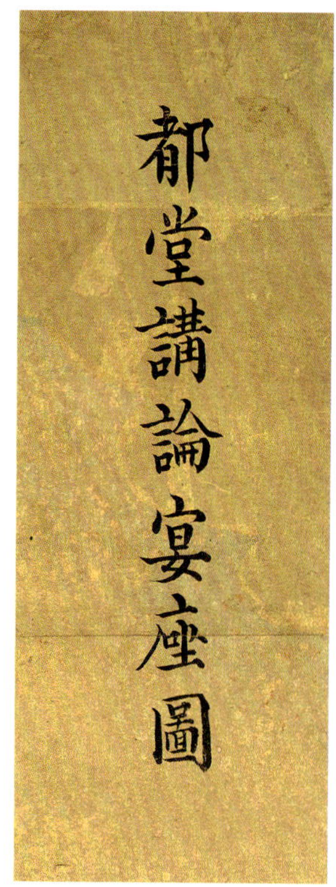

223

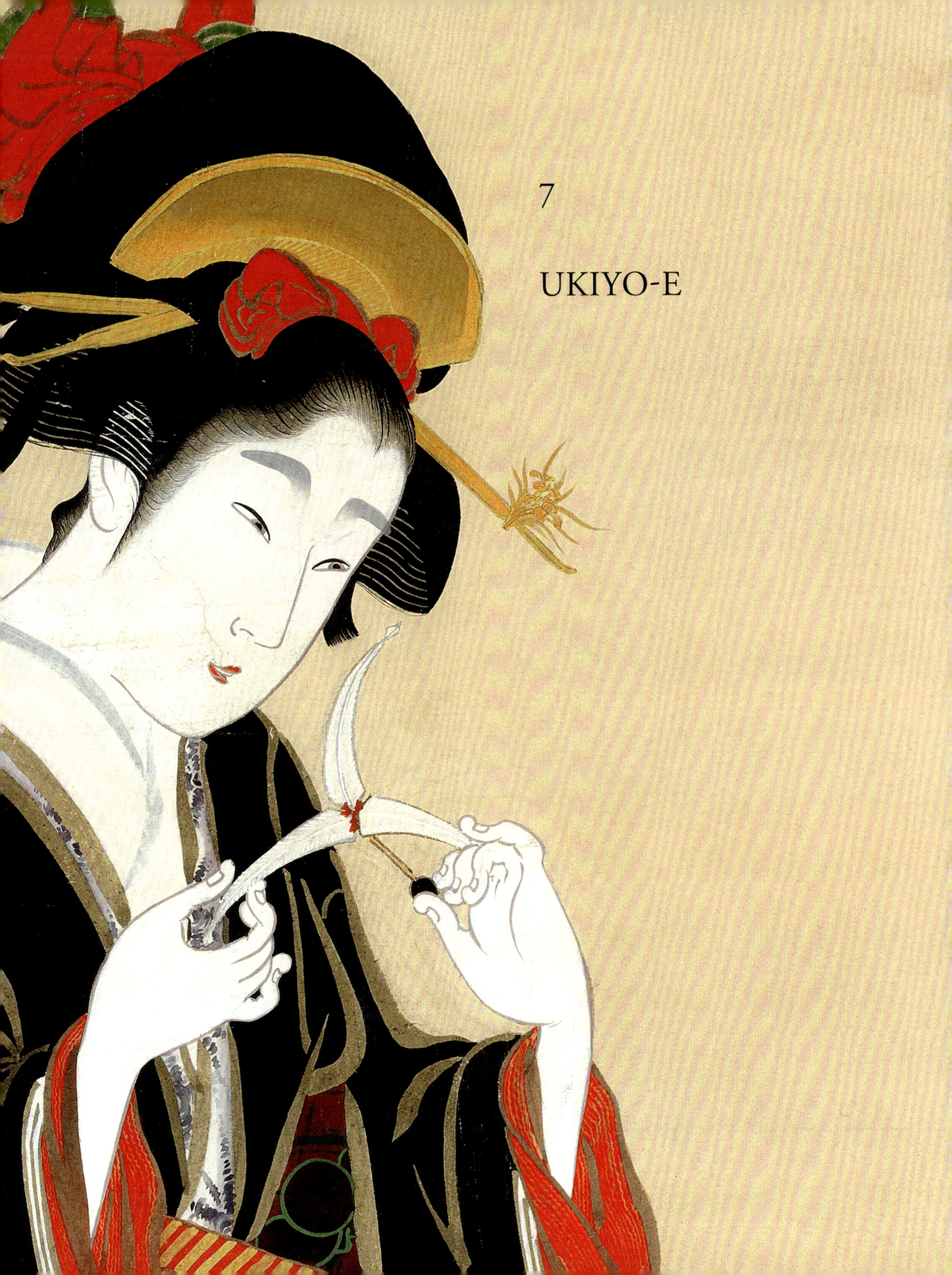

7

UKIYO-E

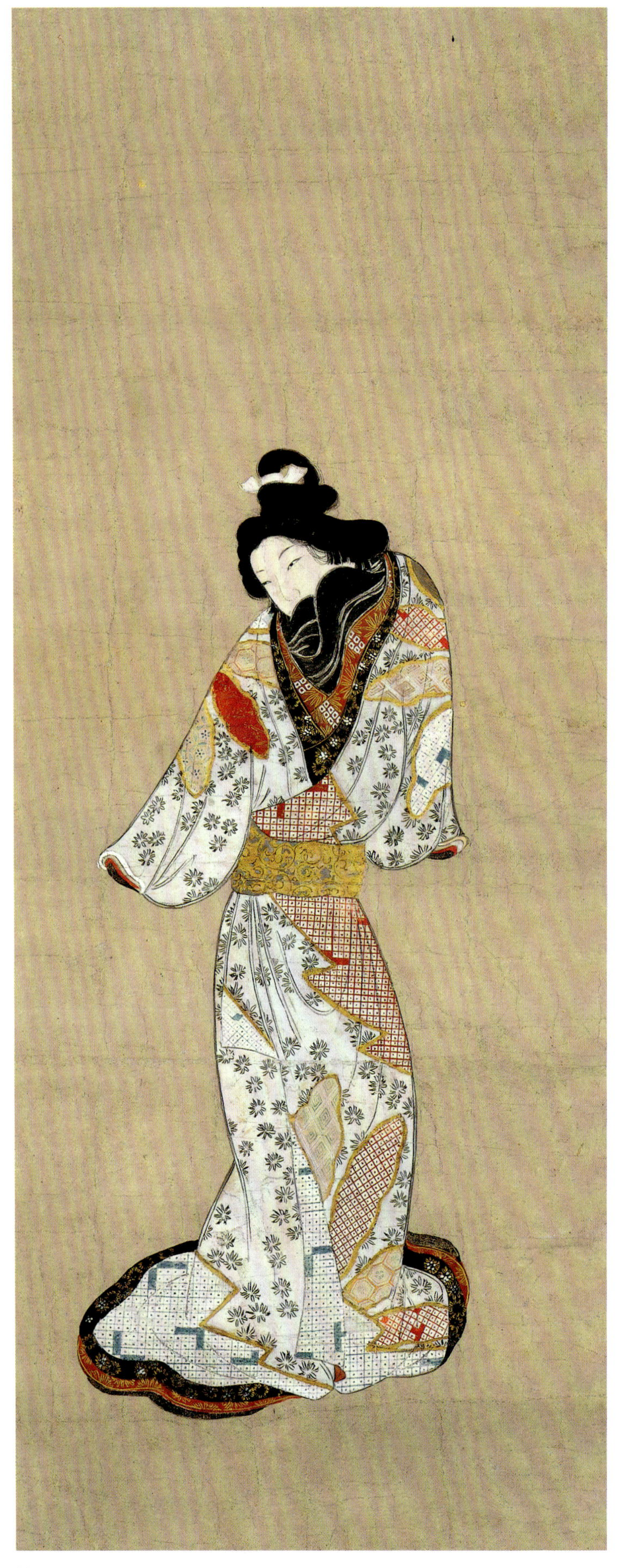

225

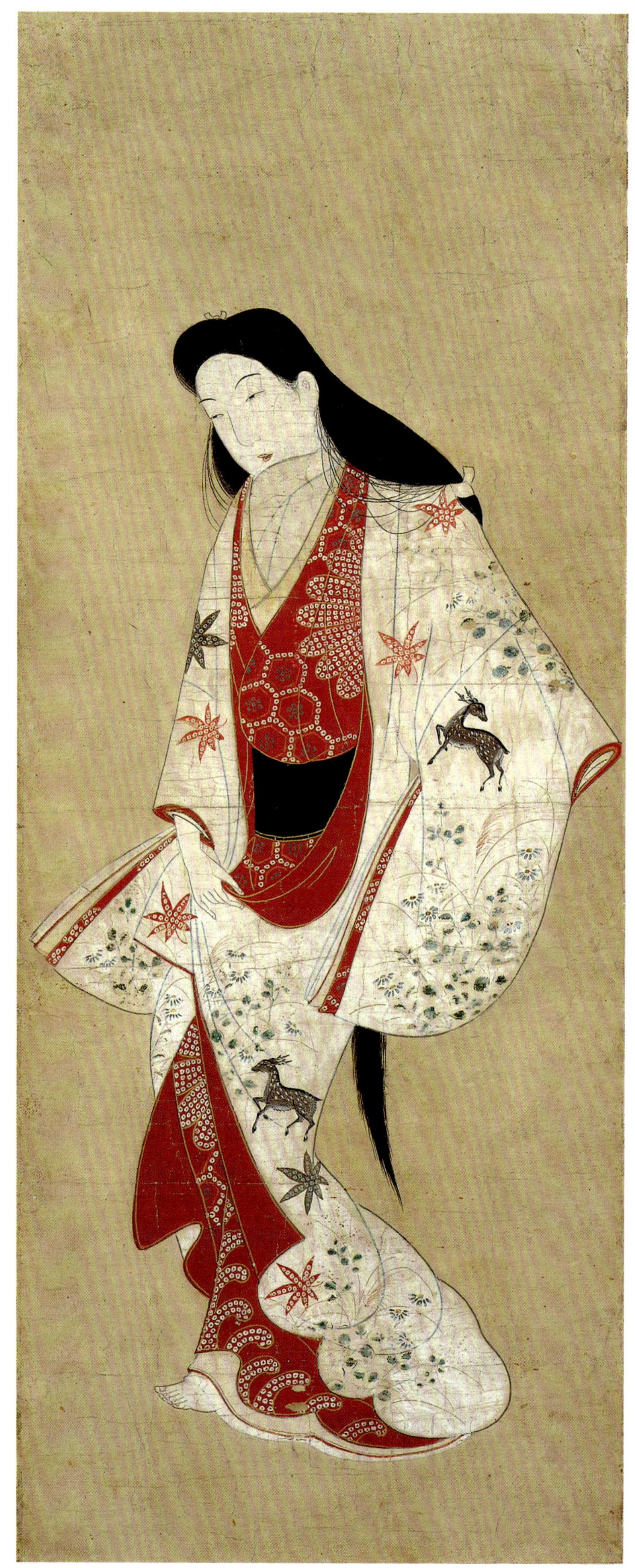

226

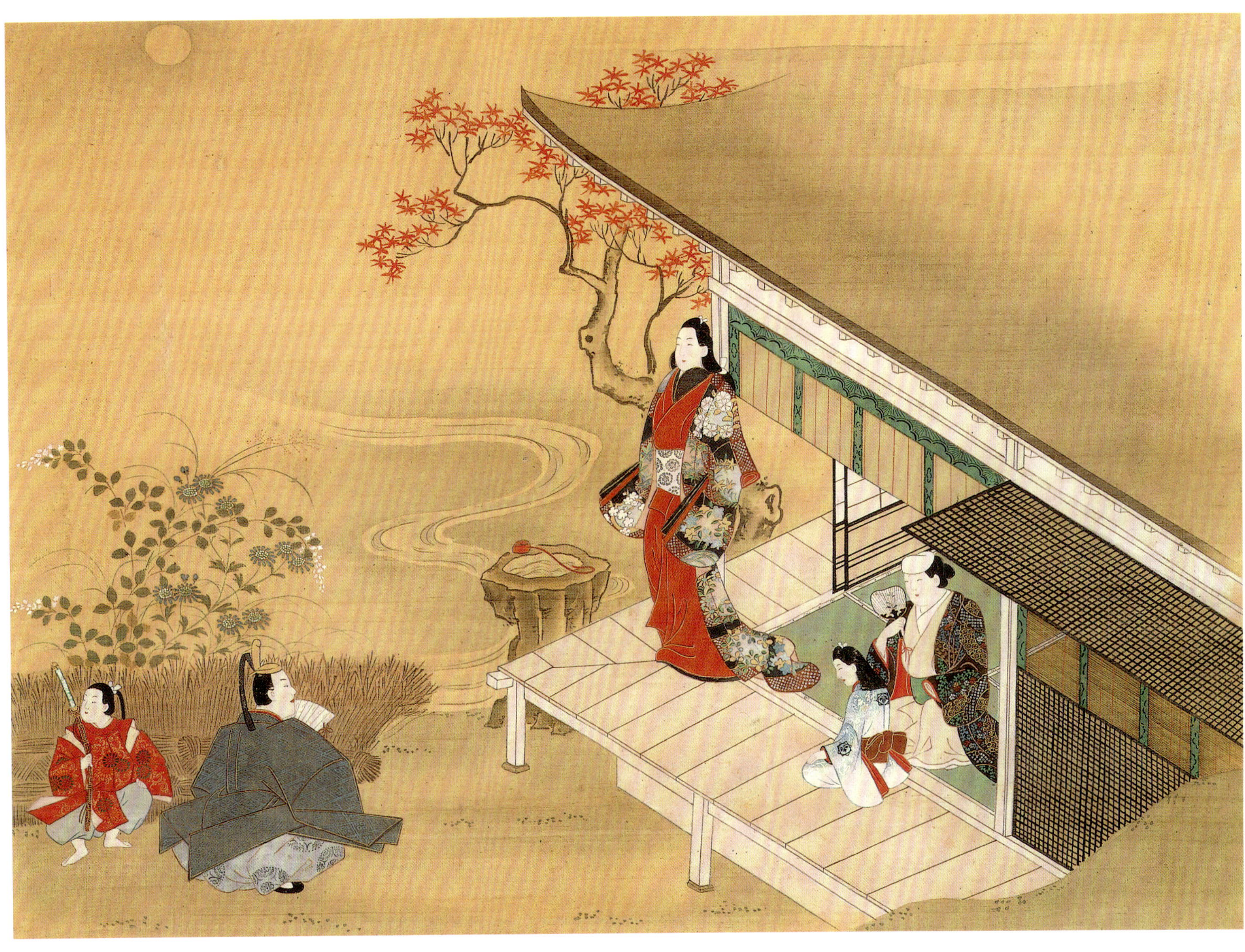

225. Kanbun Beauty (寛文美人)

Edo period, late 17th century
Hanging scroll; ink, color, and gold on paper
61.2 x 24.4 cm (24 1/8 x 9 5/8 in.)

LITERATURE: *Ukiyo-e meisaku senshū* 1967, illus.; Narazaki Muneshige 1969, pl. 18; Jenkins 1971, no. 1; Murase 1975, no. 87; Kobayashi Tadashi and Kitamura Tetsurō 1982, pl. 90; Tokyo National Museum 1985a, no. 63; Avitabile 1990, no. 81; Murase 1992, p. 168; Murase 2000, no. 144; Murase 2003, no. 129; Tsuji Nobuo et al. 2005, no. 81.

226. Lady from "Kawachigoe" (河内越), episode 23 of *Ise monogatari* (伊勢物語)

Edo period, second half of 17th century
Hanging scroll; ink and color on paper
63.6 x 25.6 cm (25 x 10 1/8 in.)

LITERATURE: Jenkins 1971, no. 2; Okudaira Shunroku 1989; Murase 1993, no. 44; Murase 2000, no. 145; Bayou 2004, no 29; Ōkubo Jun'ichi 2006, p. 34, fig. 46.

227. "Kawachigoe" (河内越), from episode 23 of *Ise monogatari* (伊勢物語)

Edo period, 18th century
Hanging scroll; ink, color, and gold on silk
50.4 x 69.4 cm (19 7/8 x 27 3/8 in.)

LITERATURE: Murase 2000, fig. 54.

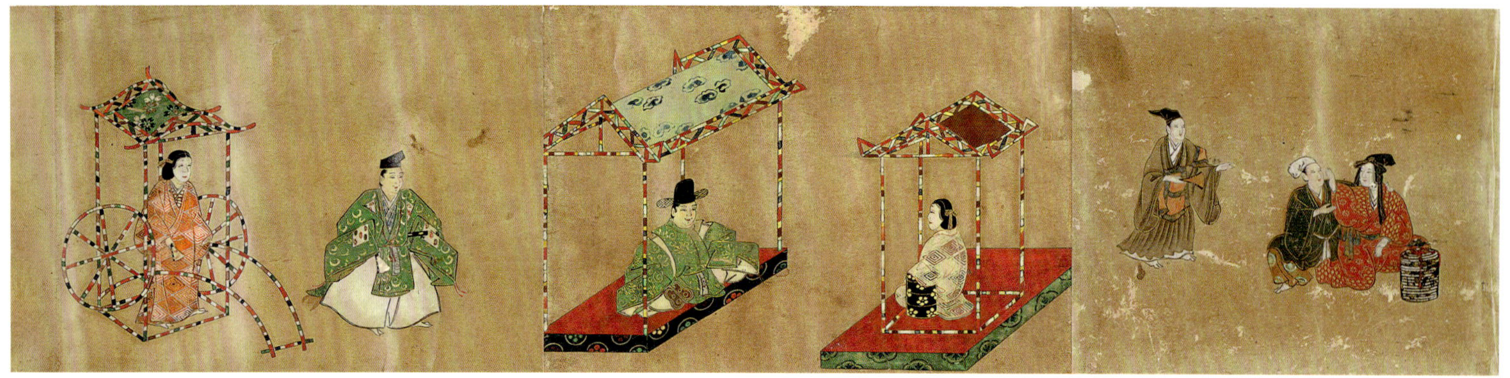

228. Six Noh and Kyōgen Pieces
(能狂言六種)

Edo period, 17th century
Handscroll; ink, color, and gold on paper
21.2 x 164.8 cm (8 3/8 x 64 7/8 in.)

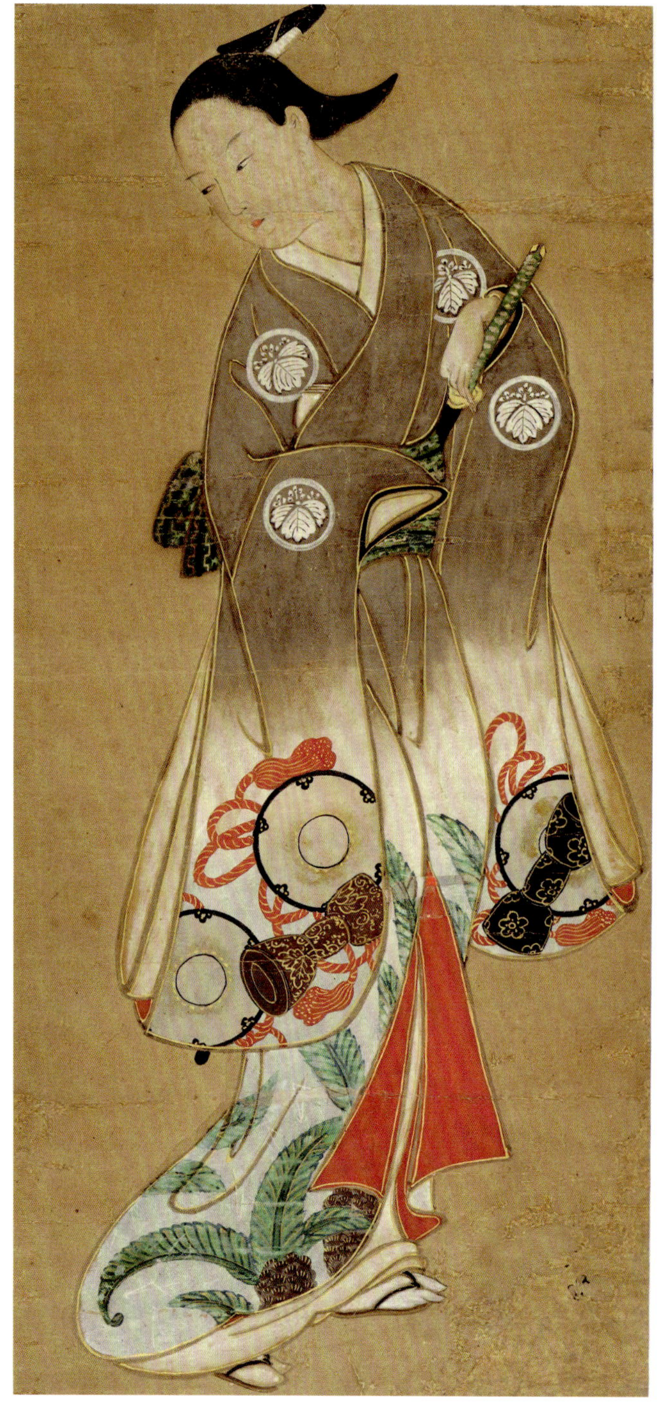

229. Young Man (若衆)

Edo period, 17th century
Unmounted painting; ink, color, and gold on paper
53.5 x 25 cm (21 x 9 7/8 in.)

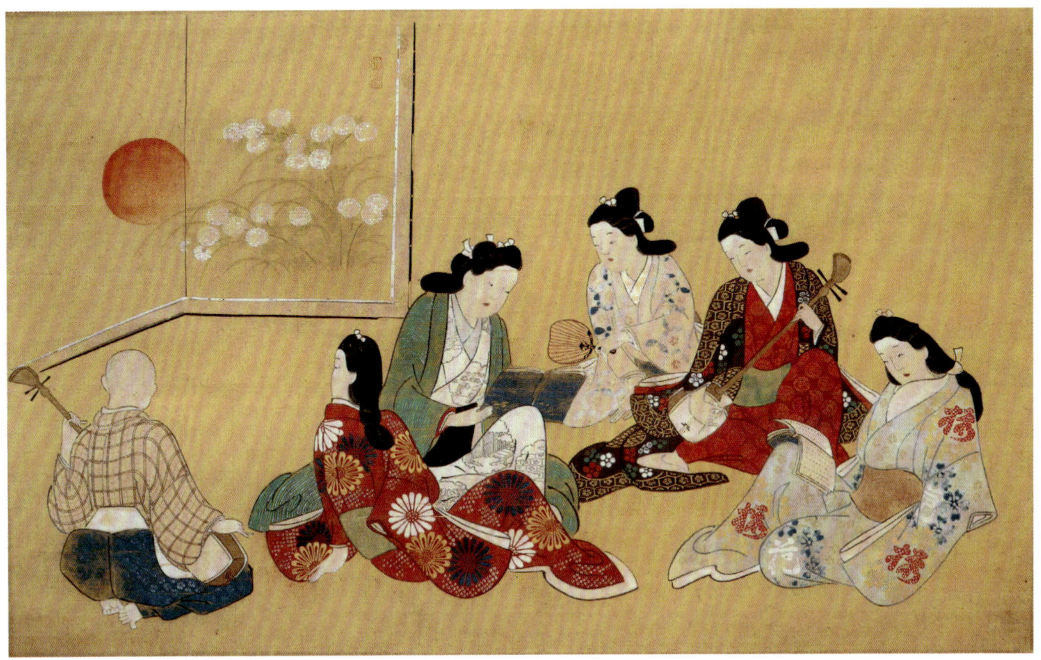

Hishikawa Moronobu
(菱川師宣; d. 1694)

230. Scene from the Pleasure Quarters

Edo period, ca. 1690
Hanging scroll; ink and color on silk
29.4 x 48 cm (11⅝ x 18⅞ in.)
Seals

Literature: Jenkins 1971, no. 4; Wheelwright 1986, p. 22, fig. 3; Swinton et al. 1995, pp. 122, 166–67, no. 64.

Hishikawa Moronobu
(菱川師宣; d. 1694)

231. Woman in a Palanquin

Edo period
Hanging scroll; ink and color on silk
37 x 61 cm (14⅝ x 24 in.)
Signature, seals

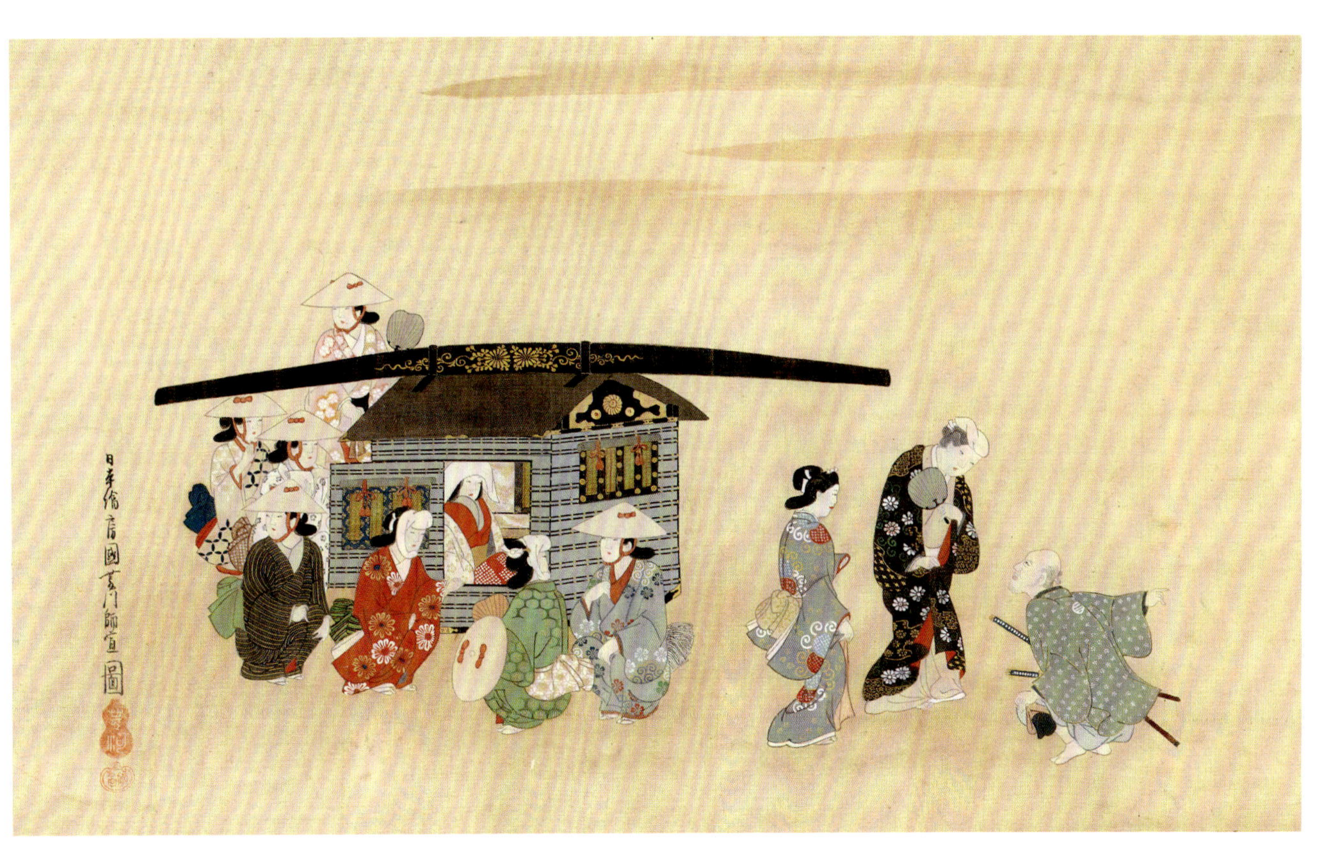

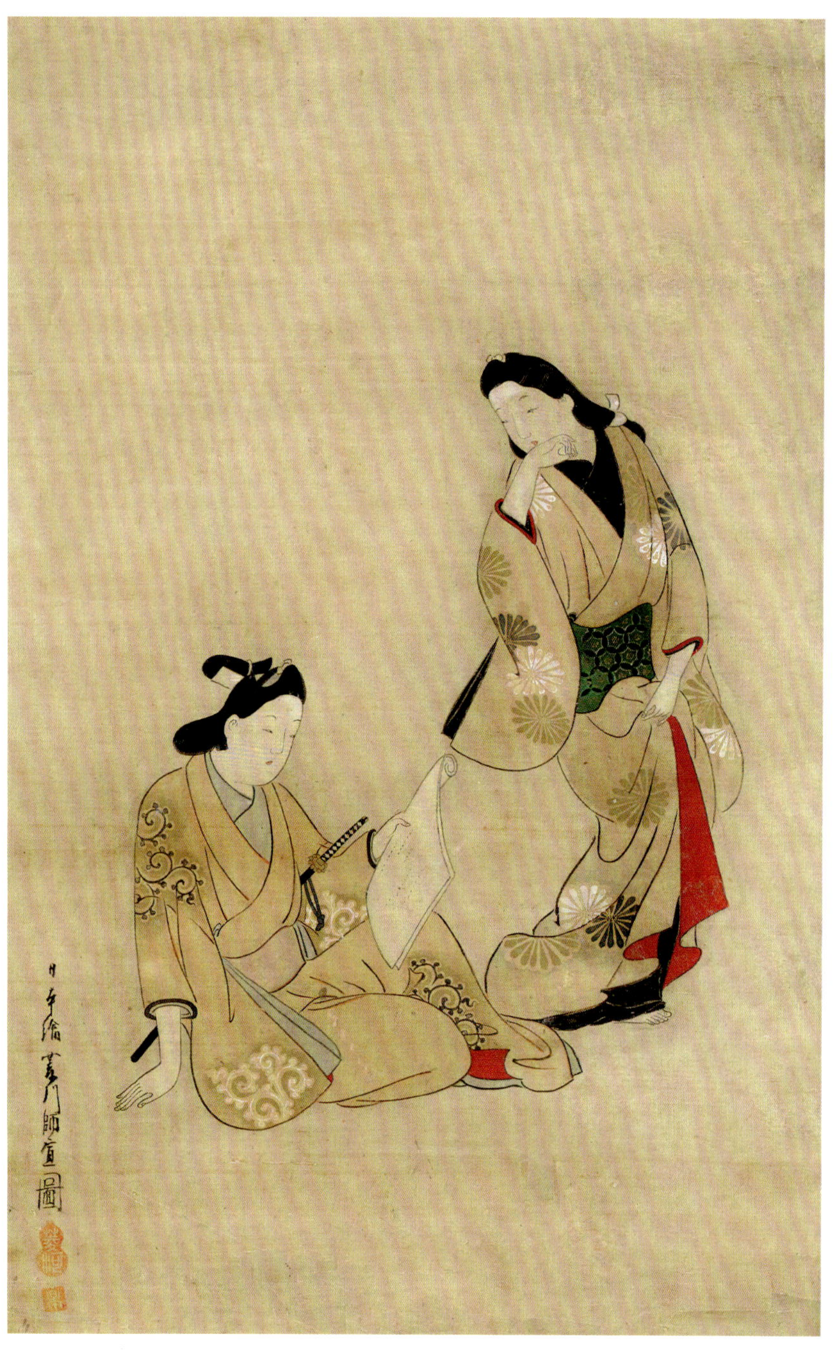

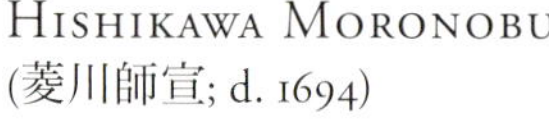

Hishikawa Moronobu
(菱川師宣; d. 1694)

232. Young Couple

Edo period
Hanging scroll; ink and color on silk
63.2 x 40.4 cm (24 7/8 x 15 7/8 in.)
Signature, seals

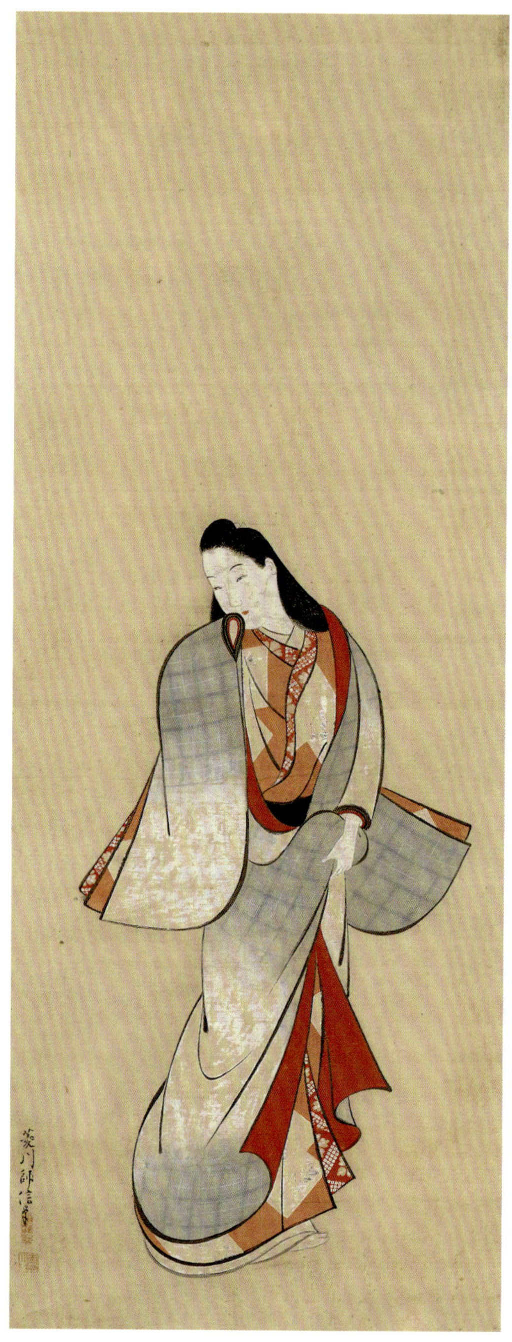

attributed to Hishikawa Moronobu
(菱川師宣; d. 1694)

233. Standing Beauty

Edo period
Hanging scroll; ink and color on silk
87 x 33.8 cm (34 1/4 x 13 1/4 in.)
Signature, seals

Ex coll.: Frank E. Hart

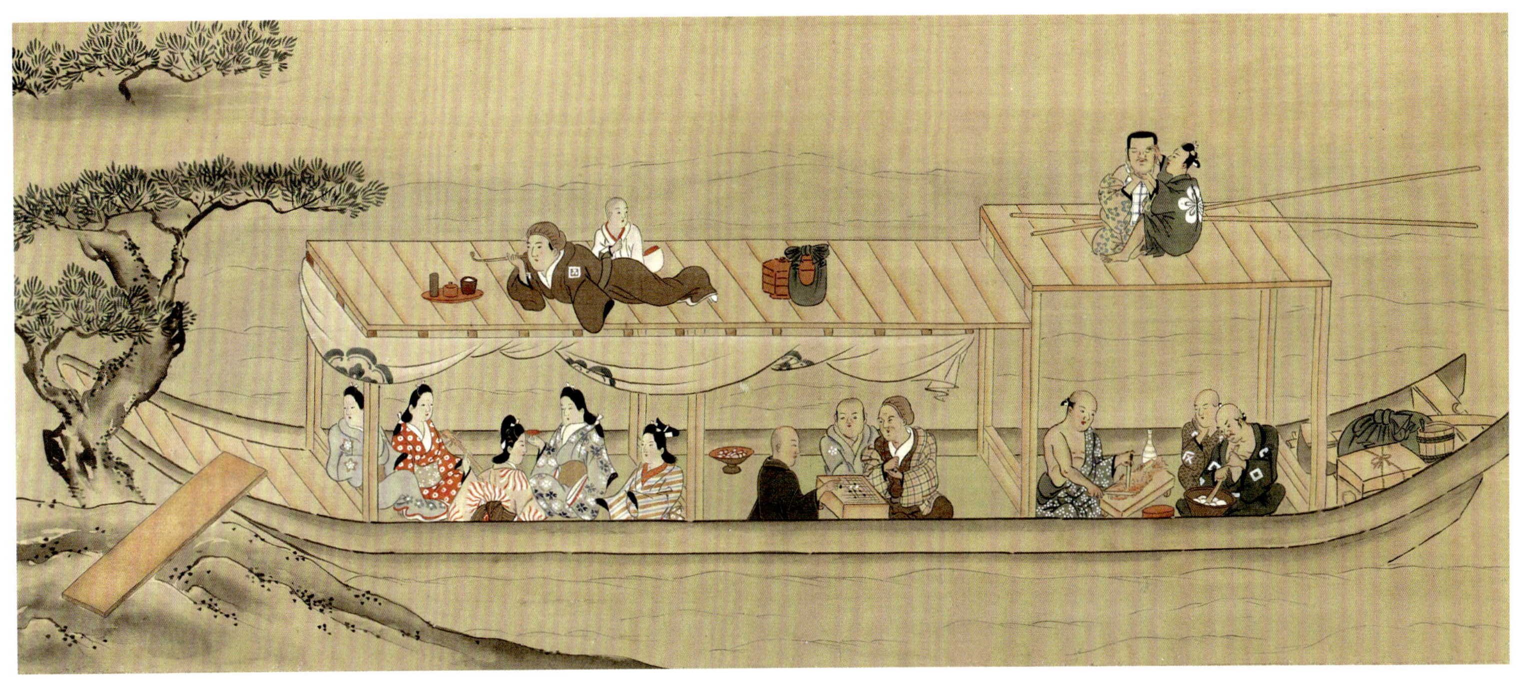

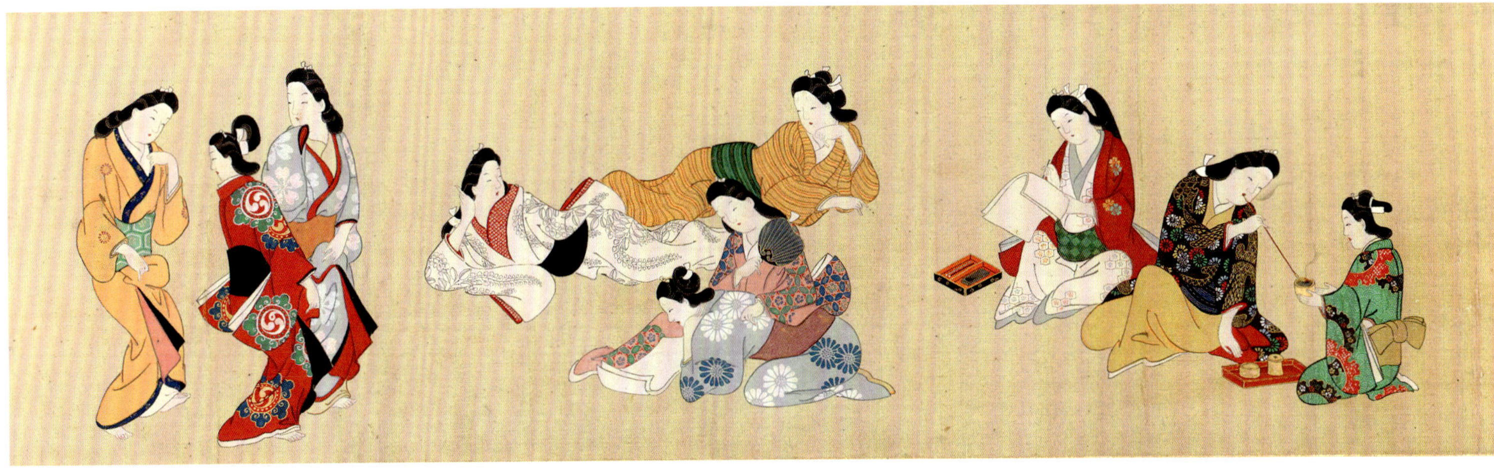

234. Pleasure Boat

Edo period, 18th century
Hanging scroll; ink and color on silk
36.7 x 82.8 cm (14 1/2 x 32 5/8 in.)

Ex coll.: Frank E. Hart

235. Pleasurable Activities

Edo period, late 17th century
Handscroll; ink, color, and gold on silk
24.5 x 324 cm (9 5/8 in. x 10 ft. 7 1/2 in.)

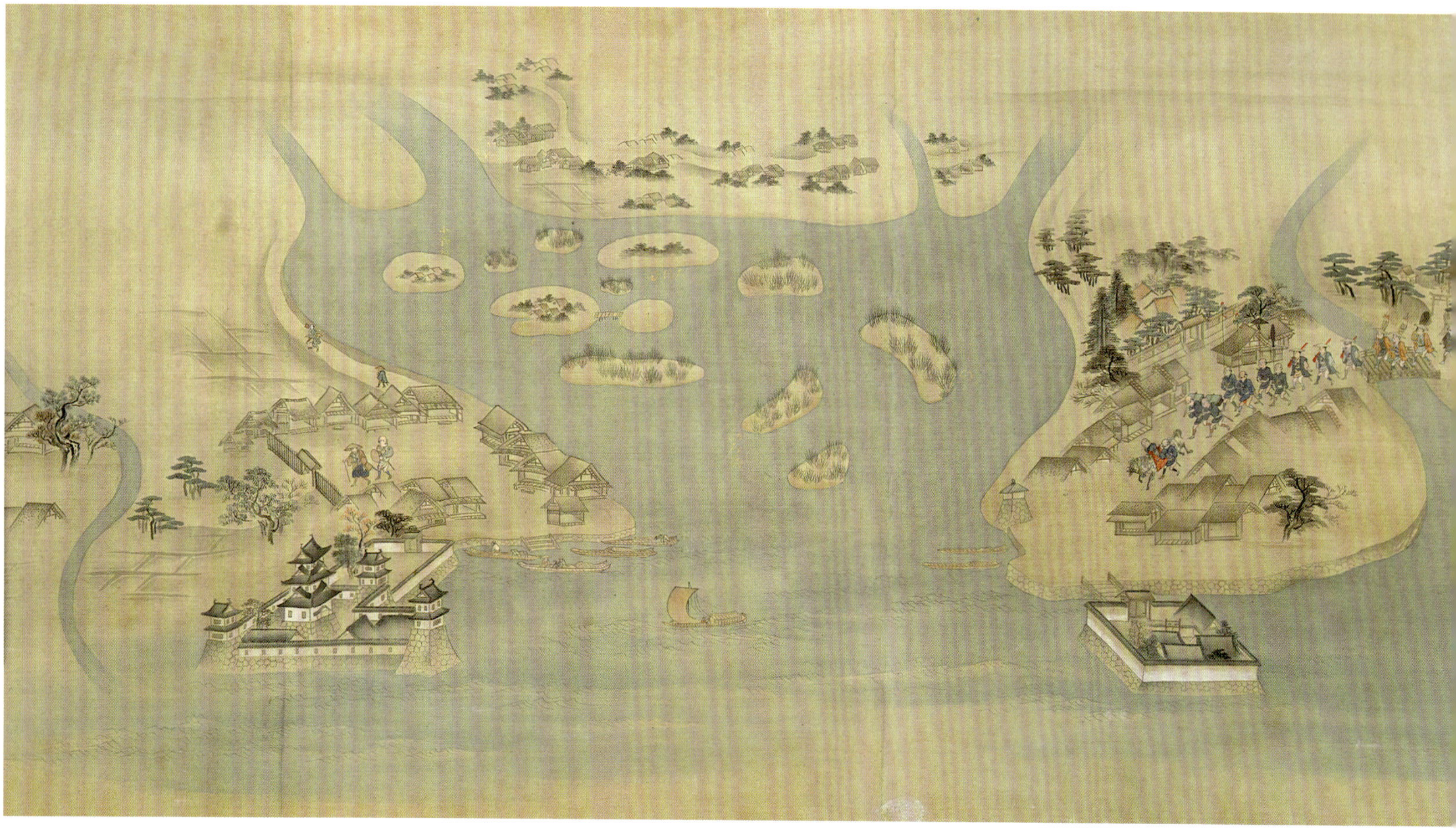

ATTRIBUTED TO HISHIKAWA MORONOBU
(菱川師宣; d. 1694)

236. Tōkaidō Zukan (東海道図巻)

Edo period, 17th century
Handscroll; ink, color, and gold on silk
47.2 x 1560 cm (18⅝ in. x 51 ft. 2⅛ in.)
Seals

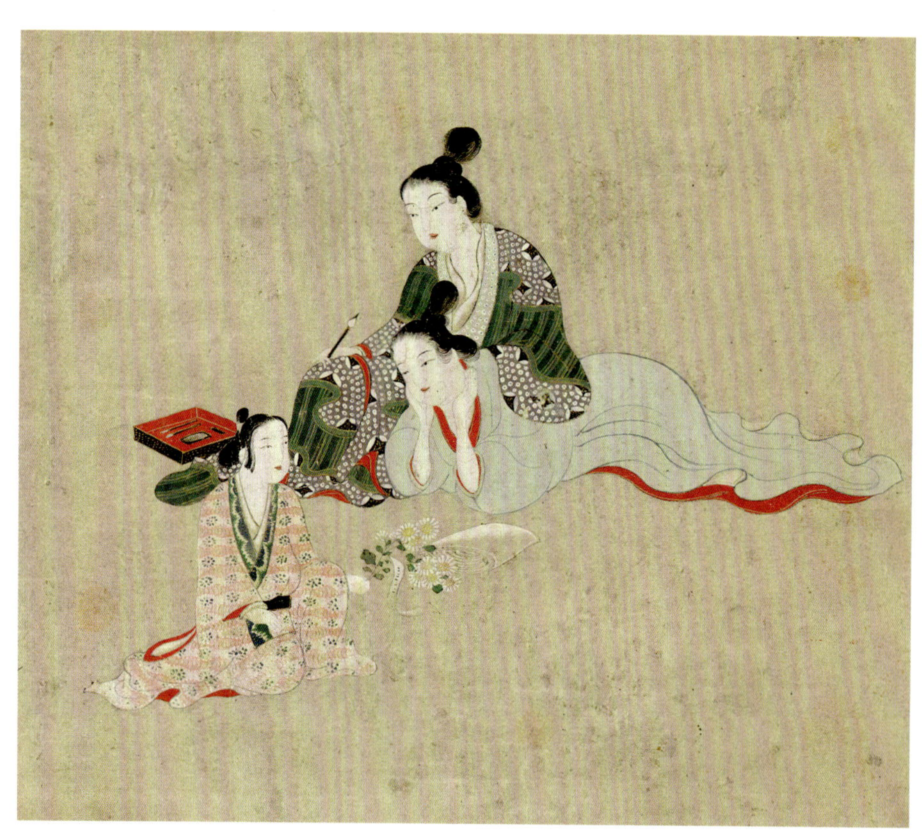

237. Two Beauties and Attendant

Edo period, 17th century
Hanging scroll; ink, color, and gold on paper
24.8 x 29.1 cm (9¾ x 11½ in.)

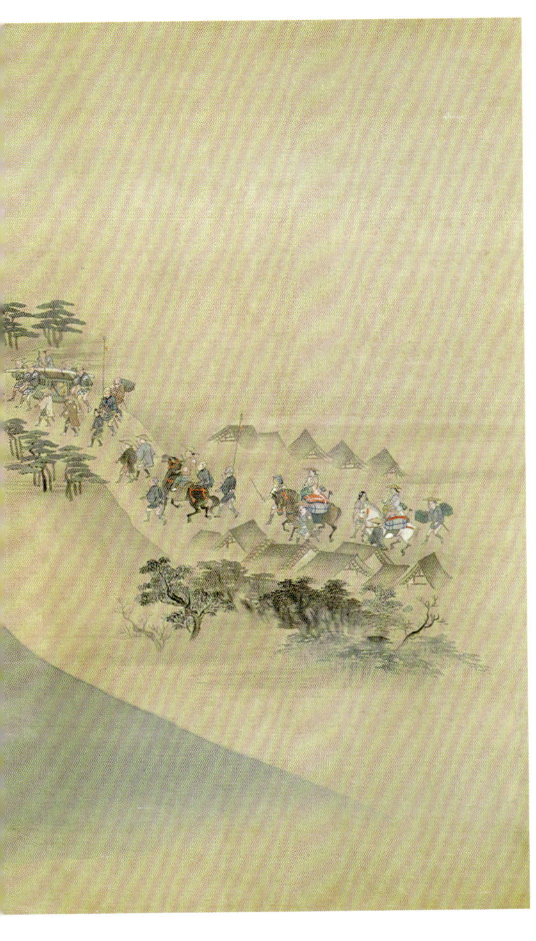

Furuyama Moroshige
(古山師重; fl. second half of 17th century)

238. Young Woman on a Veranda

Edo period
Hanging scroll; ink and color on silk
29.4 x 46.4 cm (11 5/8 x 18 1/4 in.)
Signature, seal

Ex coll.: Frank E. Hart

Literature: Jenkins 1971, no. 36.

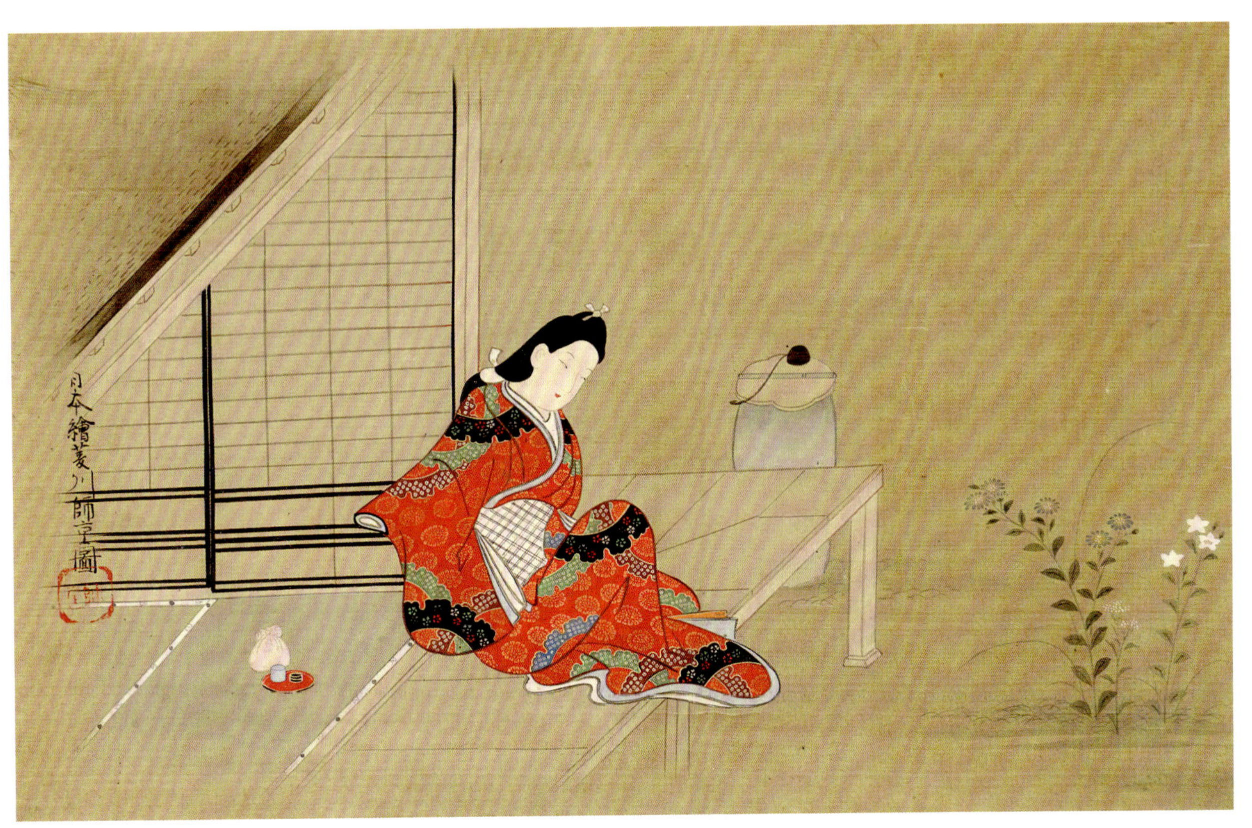

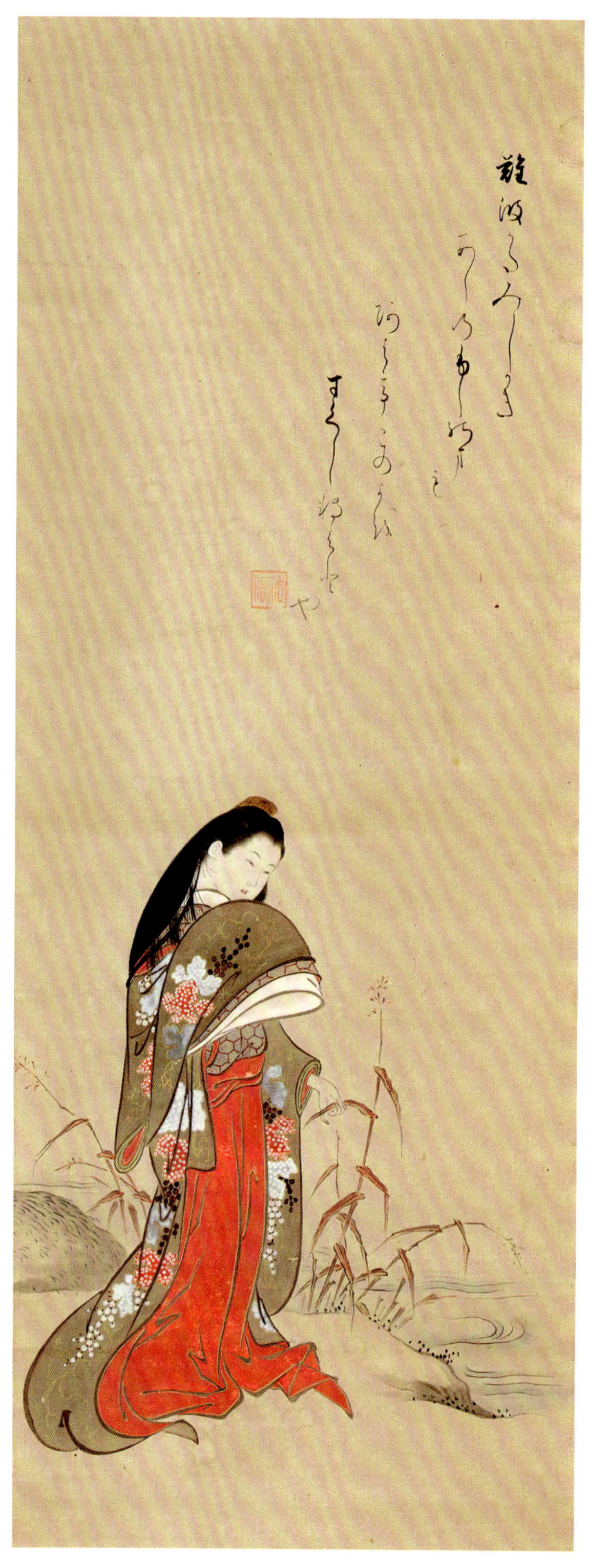

Nishikawa Sukenobu
(西川祐信; 1671–1751)

239. Lady Ise (伊勢) by the River Bank

Edo period
Hanging scroll; ink and color on paper
85.7 x 33 cm (33 3/4 x 13 in.)
Text, seal

Ex coll.: Frank E. Hart

Literature: Jenkins 1971, no. 169.

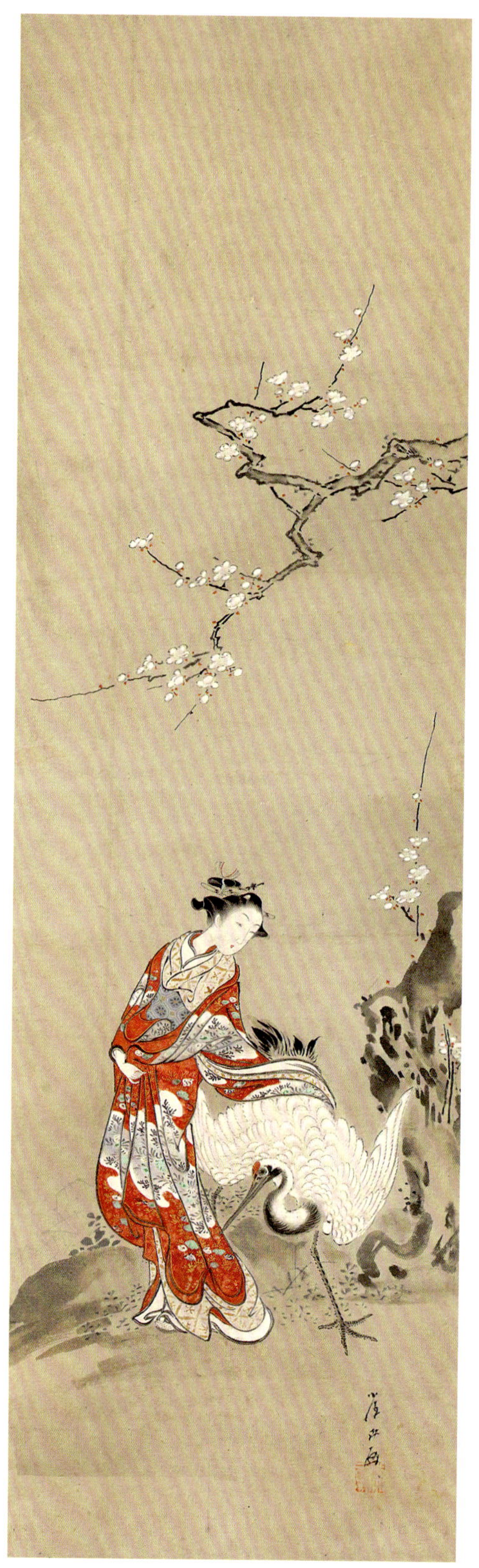

Kawamata Tsunemasa
(川又常正; fl. mid-18th century)

240. Rinnasei (Ch. Lin Hejing, 林和靖)

Edo period
Hanging scroll; ink, color, and gold on paper
89 x 27.2 cm (35 x 10 3/4 in.)
Signature, seal

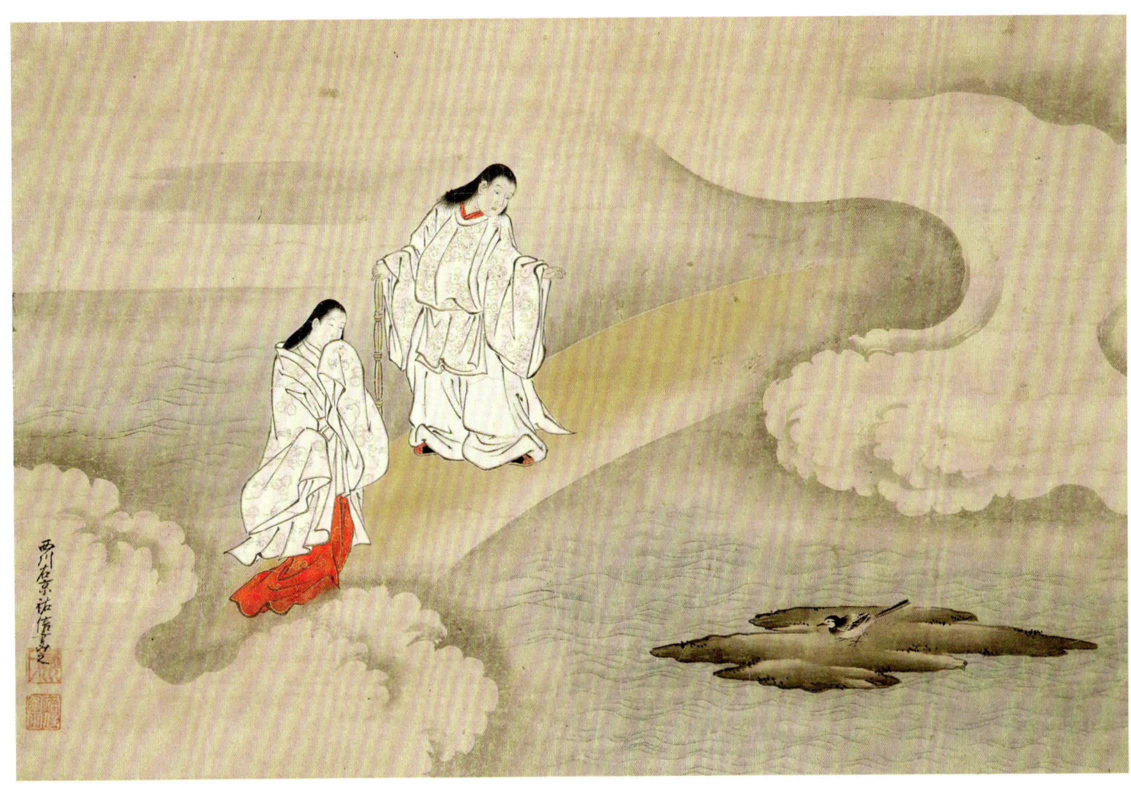

Nishikawa Sukenobu
(西川祐信; 1671–1751)

241. God Izanagi (伊弉諾尊) and Goddess Izanami (伊弉冉尊)

Edo period
Hanging scroll; ink and color on paper
38.1 x 57 cm (15 x 22½ in.)
Signature, seals

Ex coll.: Frank E. Hart

Literature: Edwards 1997, p. 32; Ronnberg and Martin 2010, p. 72, fig. 2; Yamamoto Yukari 2010, p. 2, pl. 1.

Ōoka Michinobu
(大岡道信; fl. 1720–1740)

242. Scenes from the Pleasure Quarters

Edo period
Handscroll; ink, color, and gold on paper
29.2 x 660 cm (11½ in. x 21 ft. 7⅞ in.)
Seal

Literature: Burke 1993, pl. 9, no. 23.

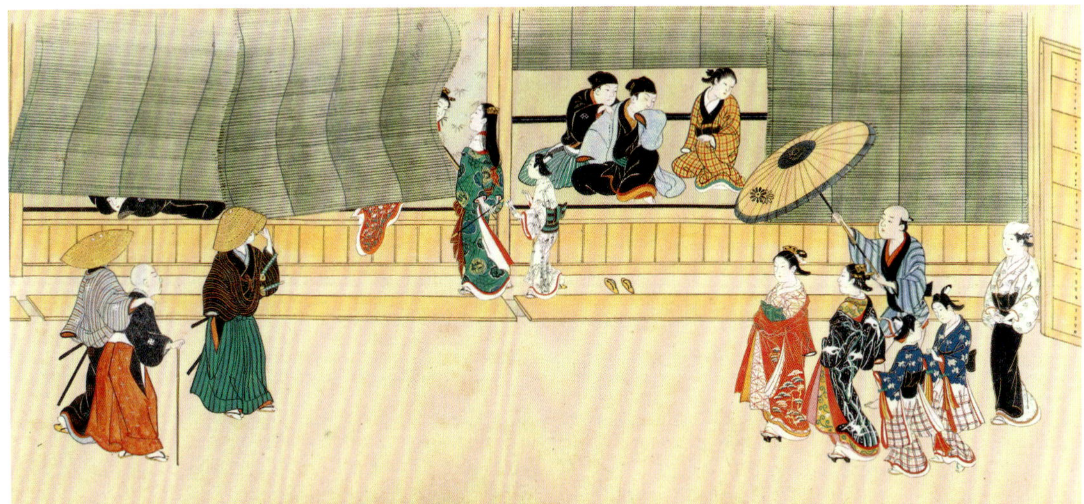

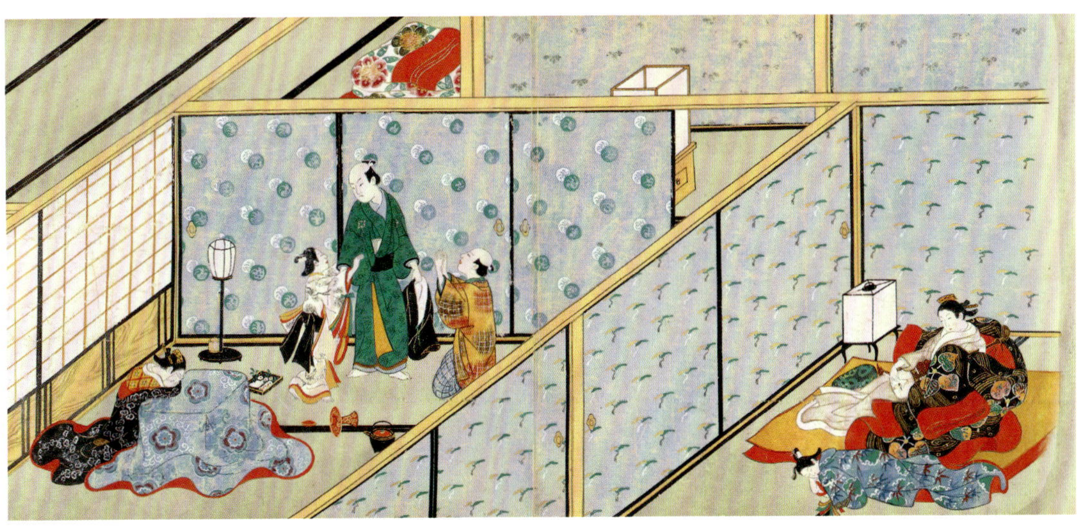

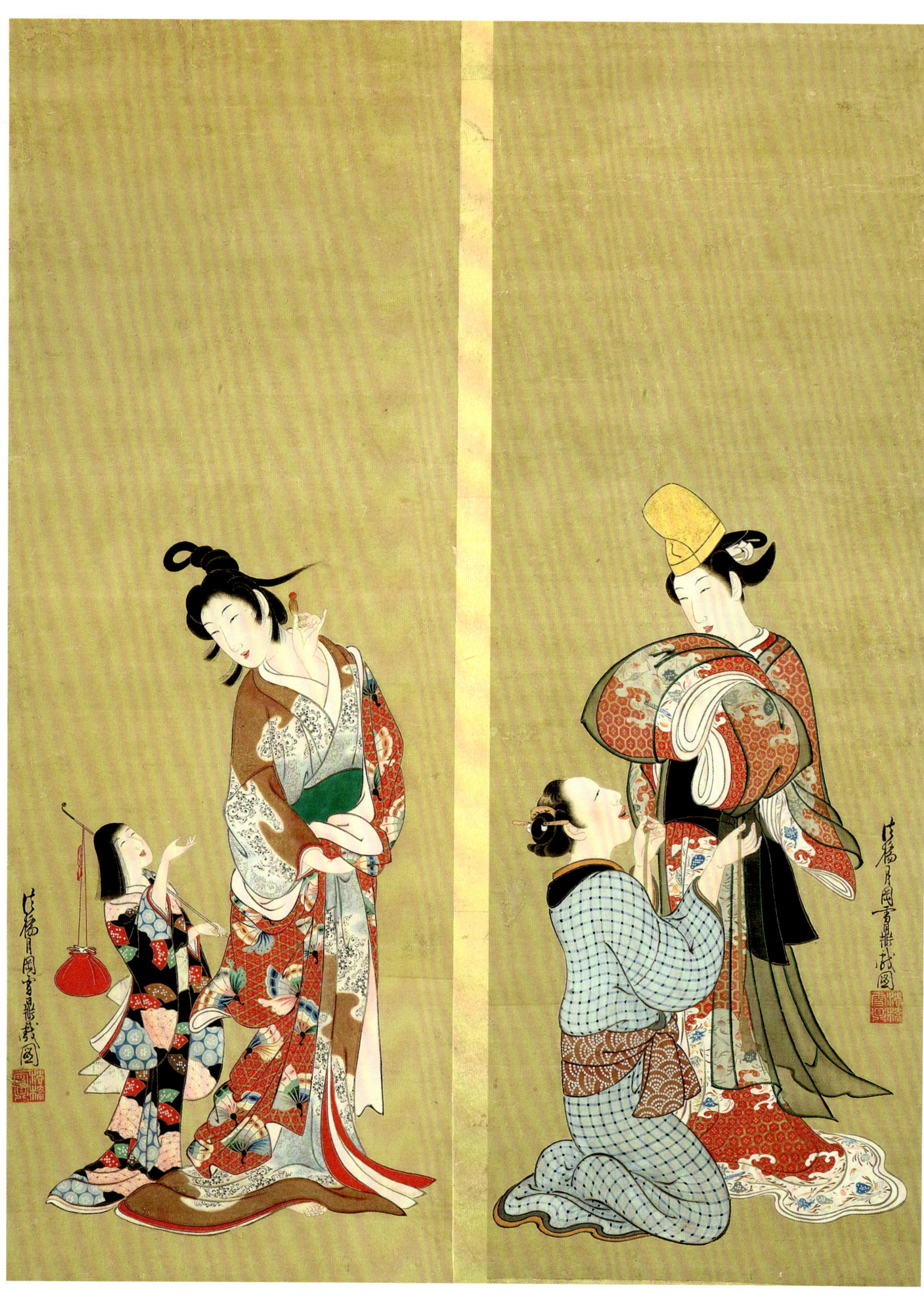

Tsukioka Settei
(月岡雪鼎; 1710–1786)

243. Courtesans and Their Attendants

Edo period
Paintings pasted on a two-panel screen; ink, color, and gold on silk
Each panel 114.3 x 41.9 cm (45 x 16 1/2 in.)
Signatures, seals

Ex coll.: Frank E. Hart

Literature: Burke 1993, pl. 8, no. 27.

Gion Seitoku
(祇園井特; 1781–ca. 1829)

244. Beauty

Edo period
Hanging scroll; ink, color, and gold on silk
83.8 x 33.3 cm (33 x 13 1/8 in.)
Signature, seals

Ex coll.: Manno Museum

Literature: Narazaki Muneshige 1969, p. 87.

Tsukioka Sessai
(月岡雪斎; d. 1839)

245. Kiku Jidō (菊慈童)

Edo period
Hanging scroll; ink on silk
81.4 x 30.6 cm (32 x 12 in.)
Signature, seals

Ex coll.: Frank E. Hart

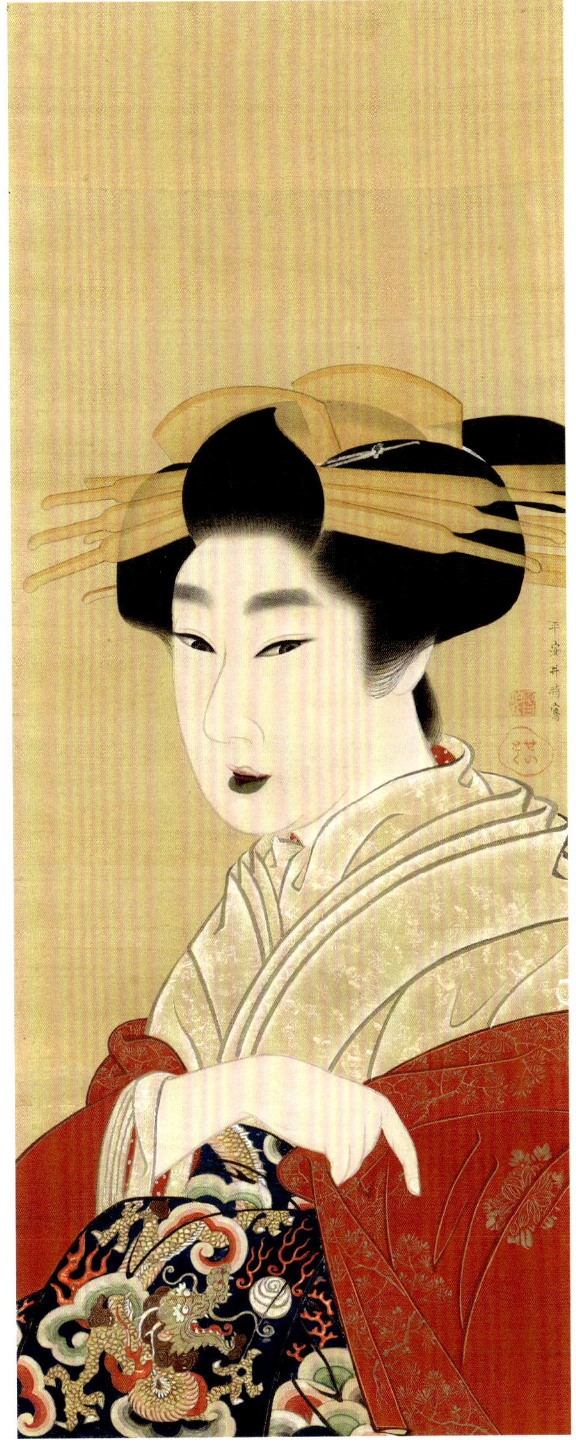

244

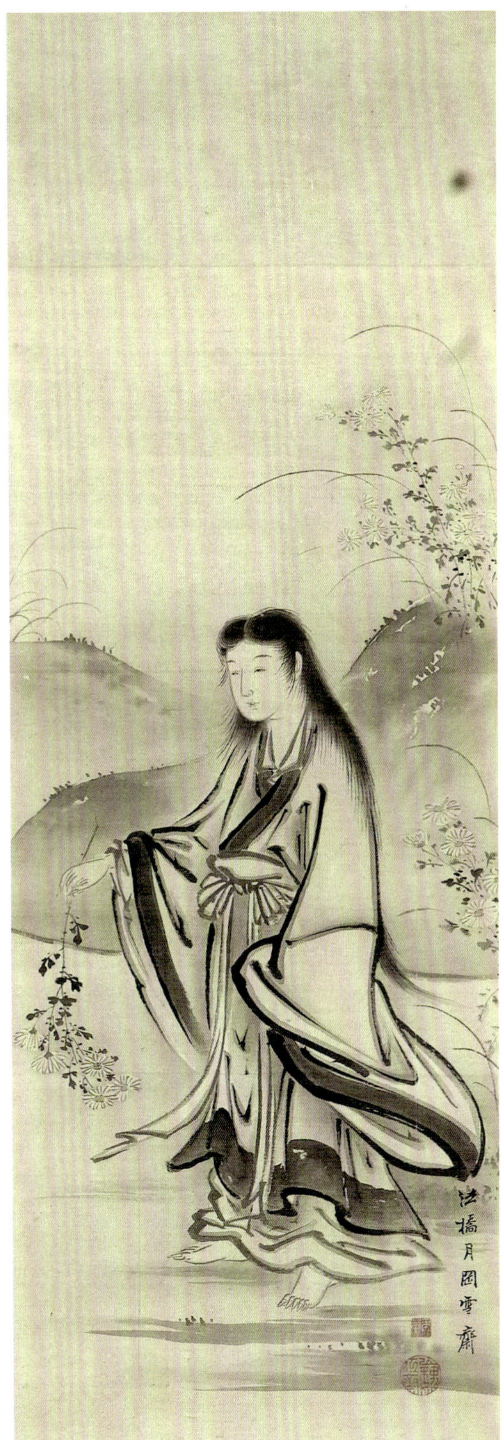

245

HISHIKAWA MITSUKUNI
(菱川光国; fl. 18th century)

246. Scenes from the Four Seasons

Edo period
Handscroll; ink and color on paper
34.5 x 672 cm (13 5/8 in. x 22 ft. 5/8 in.)
Signature, seal

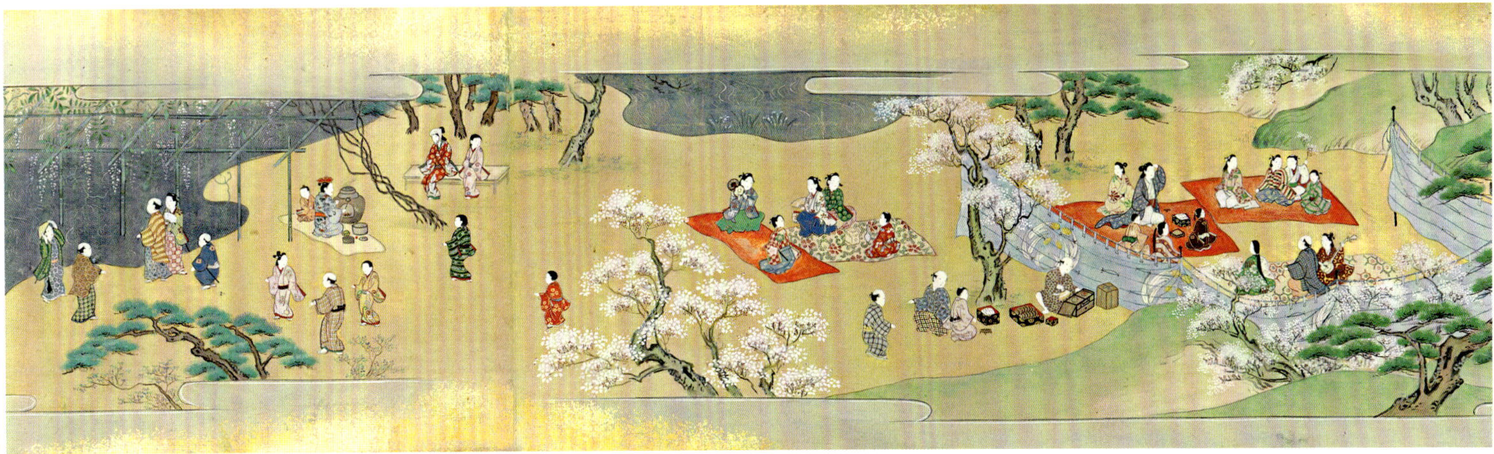

246. Spring scene

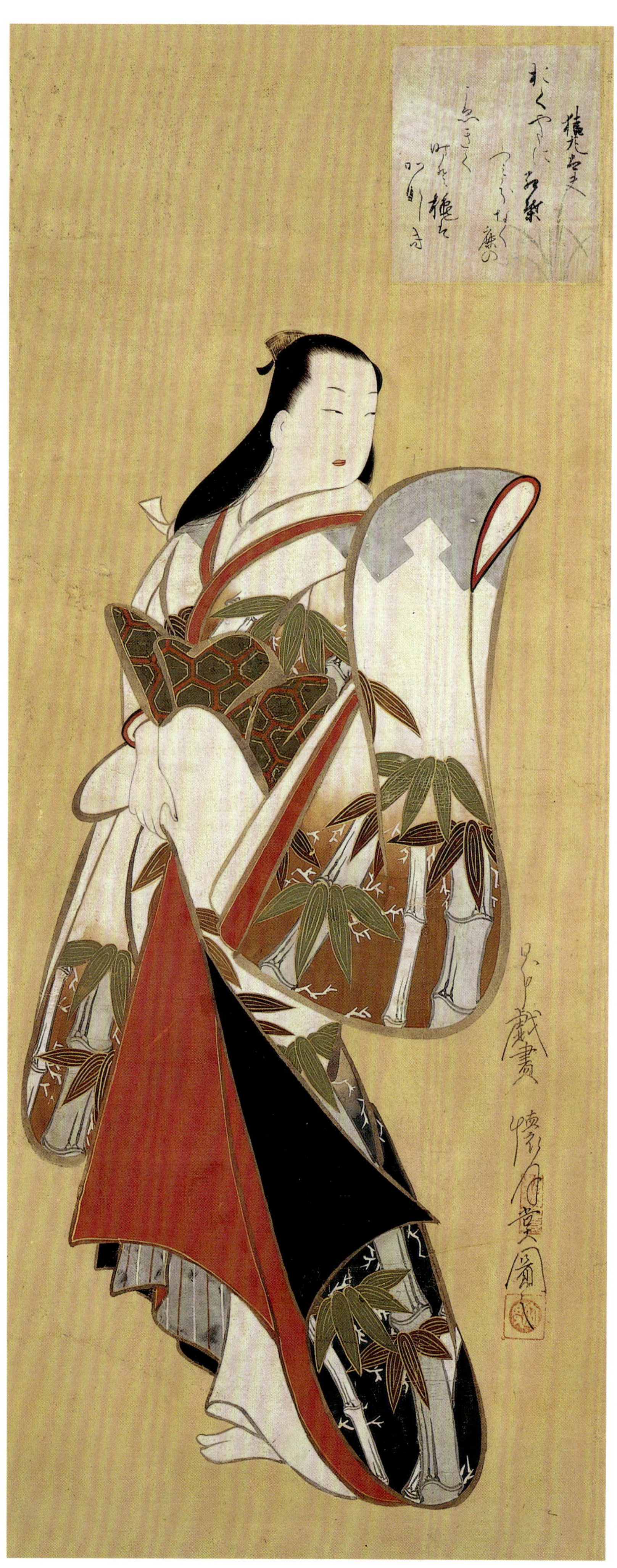

Kaigetsudō Ando
(懐月堂安度; fl. late 17th–early 18th century)

247. Standing Courtesan

Edo period
Framed painting, formerly a hanging scroll; ink, color, and gold on paper
100.4 x 42.3 cm (39½ x 16⅝ in.)
Text, signature, seals

Ex coll.: Frank E. Hart

Literature: Murase 1975, no. 88; Tokyo National Museum 1985a, no. 64; Avitabile 1990, no. 82; Murase 2000, no. 146; Tsuji Nobuo et al. 2005, no. 82.

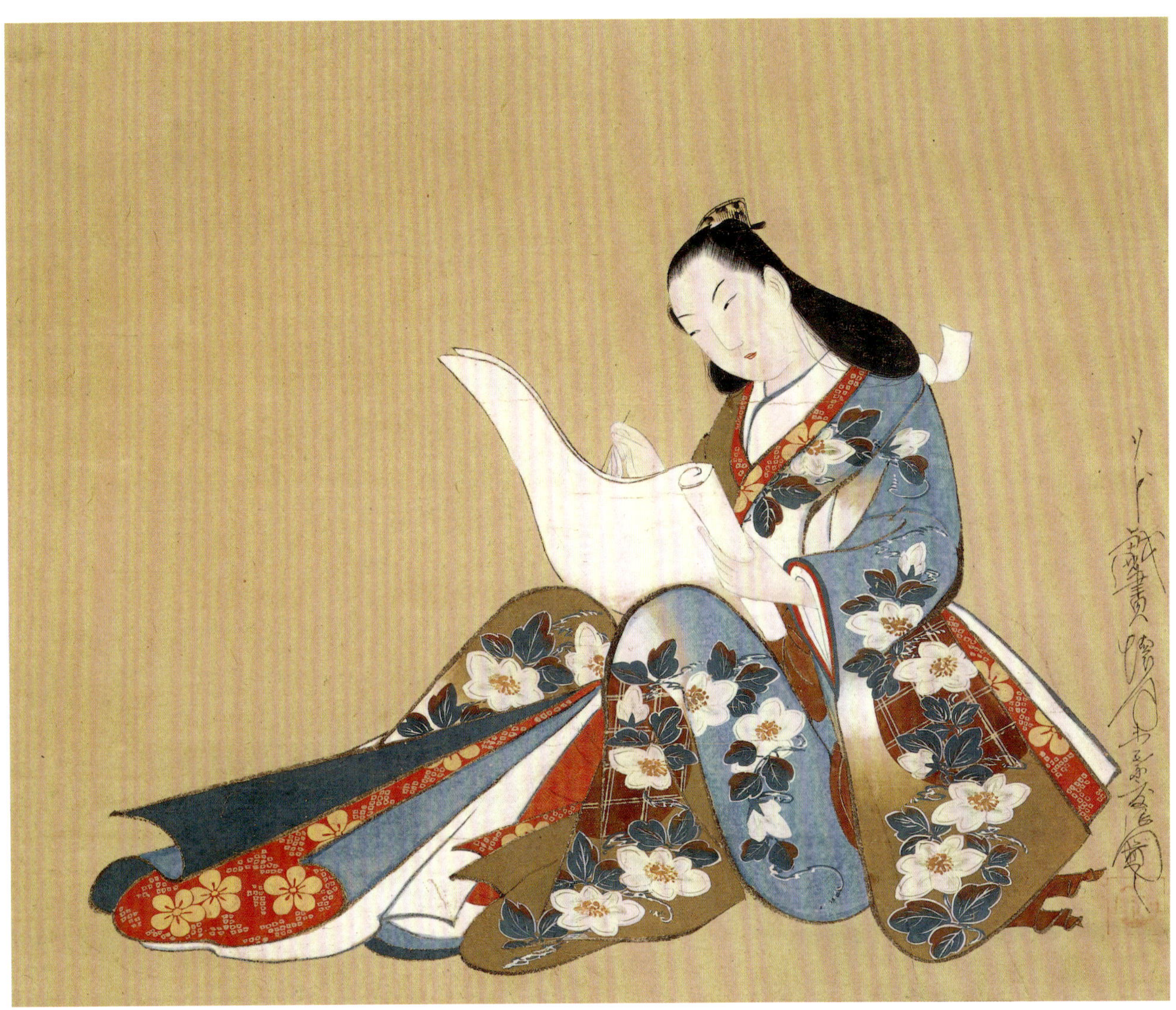

Kaigetsudō Doshin
(懐月堂度辰; fl. early 18th century)

248. Woman Writing a Letter

Edo period, ca. 1715
Hanging scroll; ink and color on paper
49.4 x 60 cm (19 1/2 x 23 5/8 in.)
Signature, seal

Ex coll.: Frank E. Hart

Literature: Jenkins 1971, no. 108; Murase 1993, no. 45; Murase 2000, no. 147; Bayou 2004, no. 52.

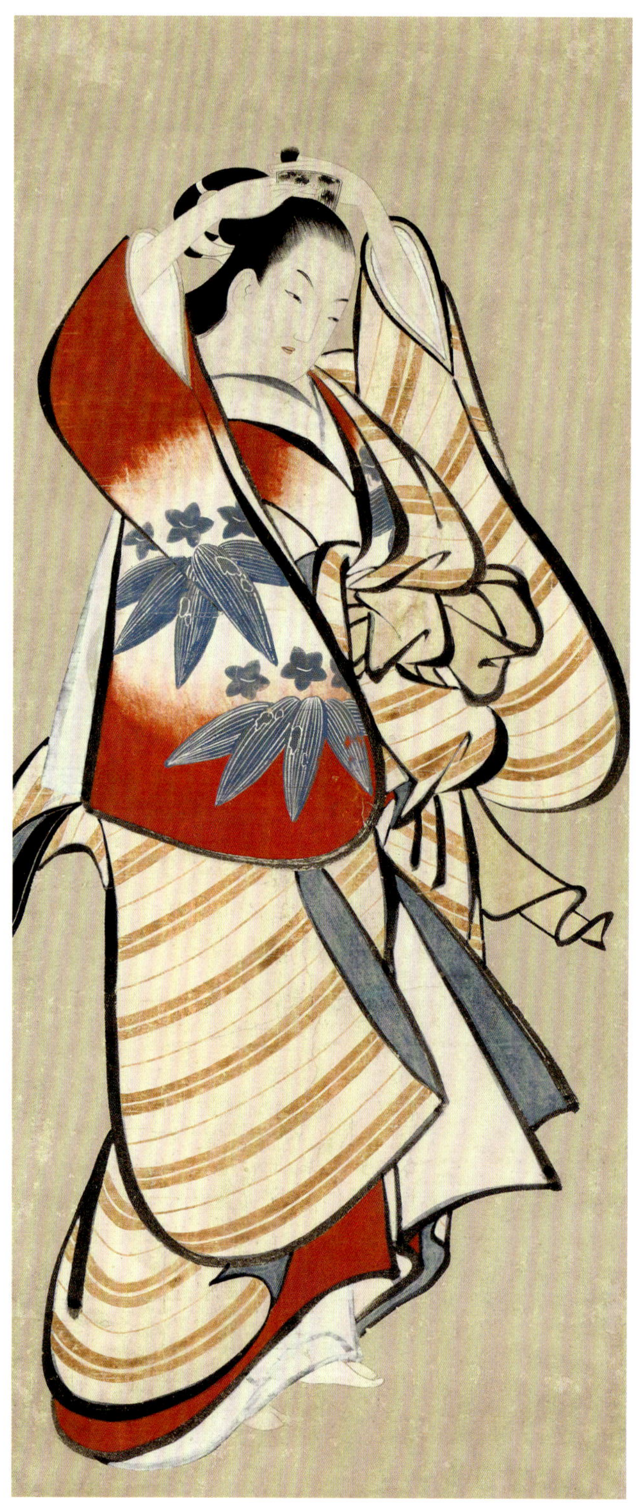

FOLLOWER OF KAIGETSUDŌ ANDO
(懐月堂安度)

249. Standing Beauty

Edo period, early 18th century
Hanging scroll; ink and color on paper
87.1 x 37.4 cm (34¼ x 14¾ in.)

EX COLL.: Frank E. Hart

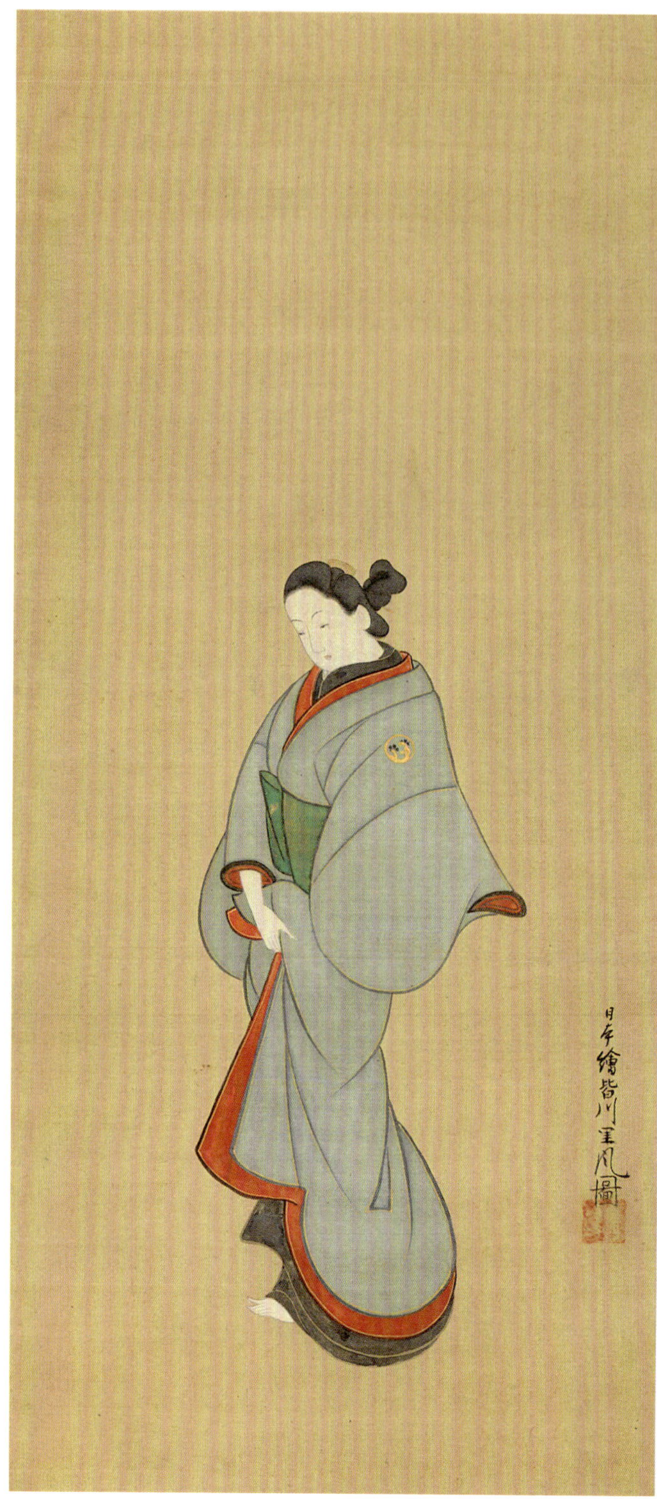

TŌSENDŌ RIFŪ
(東川堂里風; fl. ca. 1730)

250. Standing Woman

Edo period
Hanging scroll; ink and color on silk
68.4 x 30.9 cm (26⅞ x 12⅛ in.)
Signature, seal

EX COLL.: Frank E. Hart

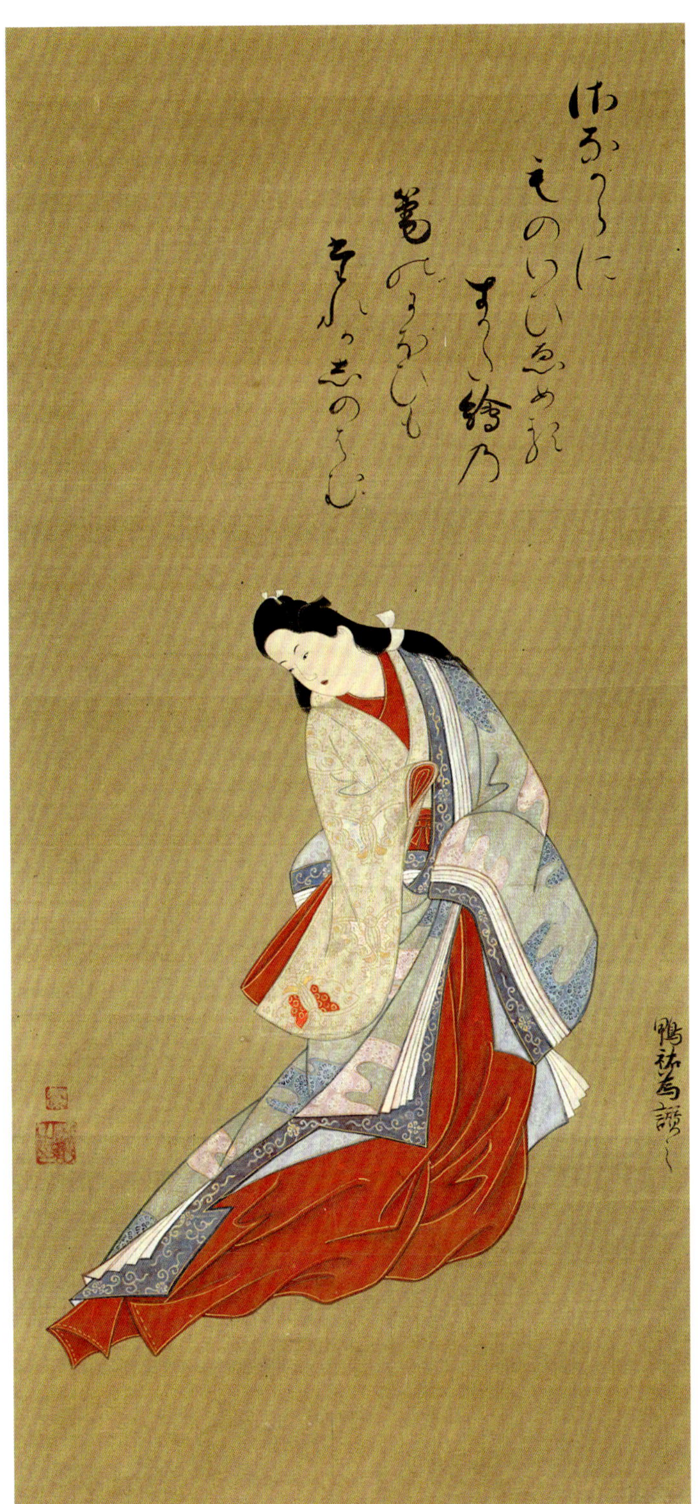

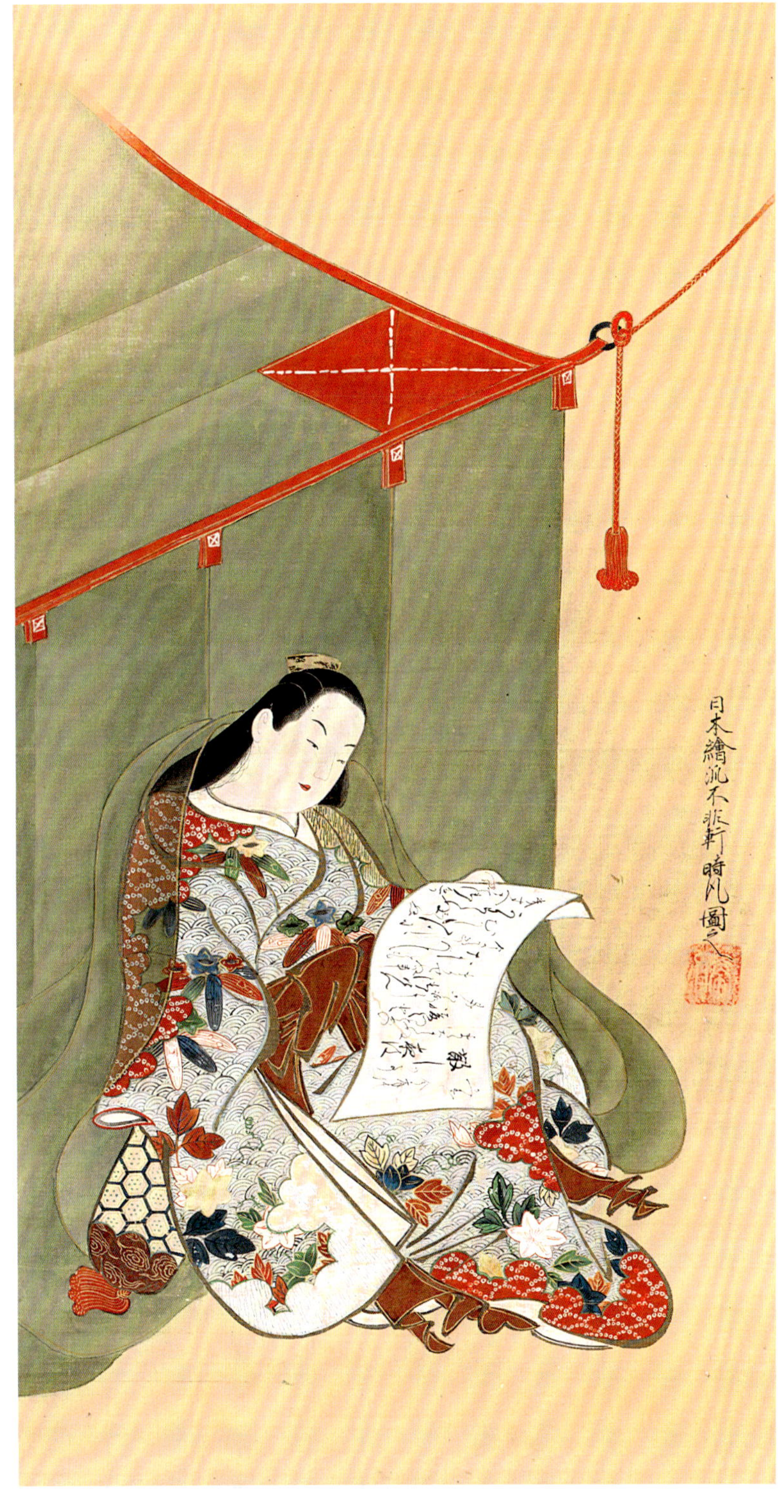

Tōsendō Rifū
(東川堂里風; fl. ca. 1730)

251. Standing Court Lady

Edo period, ca. 1720
Hanging scroll; ink and color on silk
71.1 x 33.5 cm (28 x $13^{1}/_{4}$ in.)
Text, signature, seals

Ex coll.: Frank E. Hart

Literature: Jenkins 1971, no. 125.

Fuhiken Tokikaze
(不非軒時風; fl. first half of 18th century)

252. Woman Reading by a Mosquito Net

Edo period, ca. 1720
Hanging scroll; ink and color on silk
69.8 x 37.1 cm ($27^{1}/_{2}$ x $14^{5}/_{8}$ in.)
Signature, seal

Ex coll.: Frank E. Hart

Literature: Jenkins 1971, no. 92.

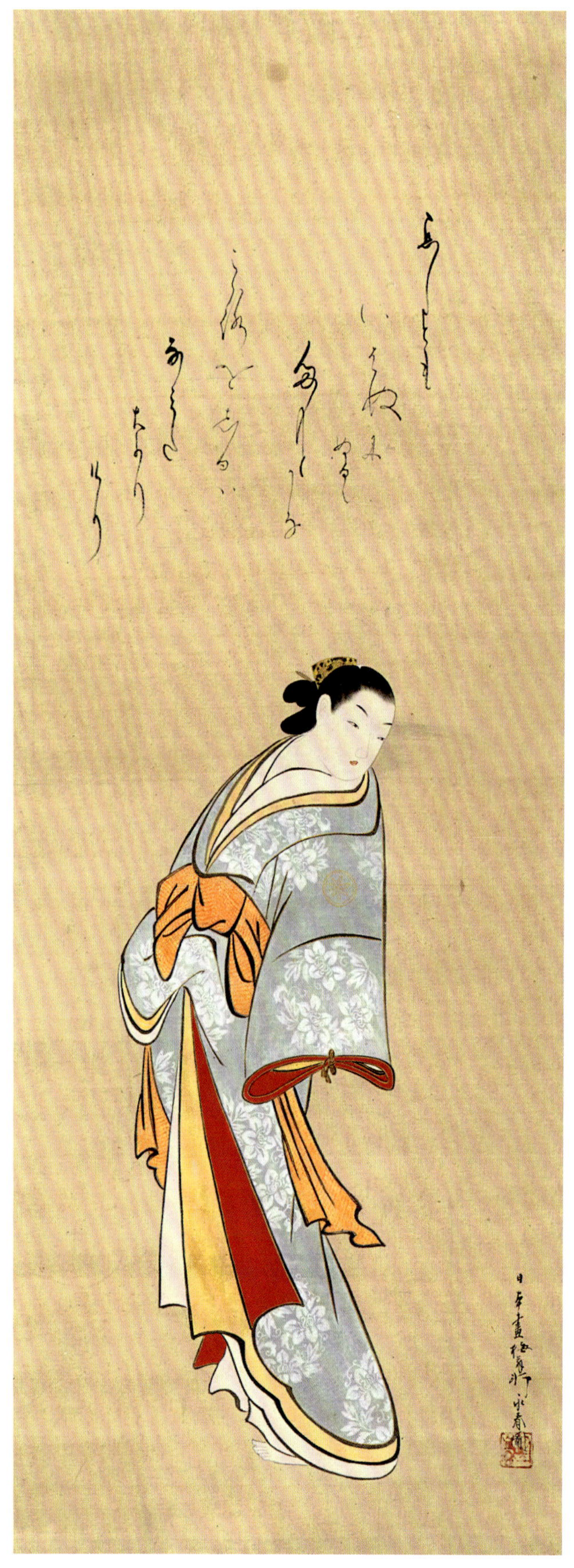

253

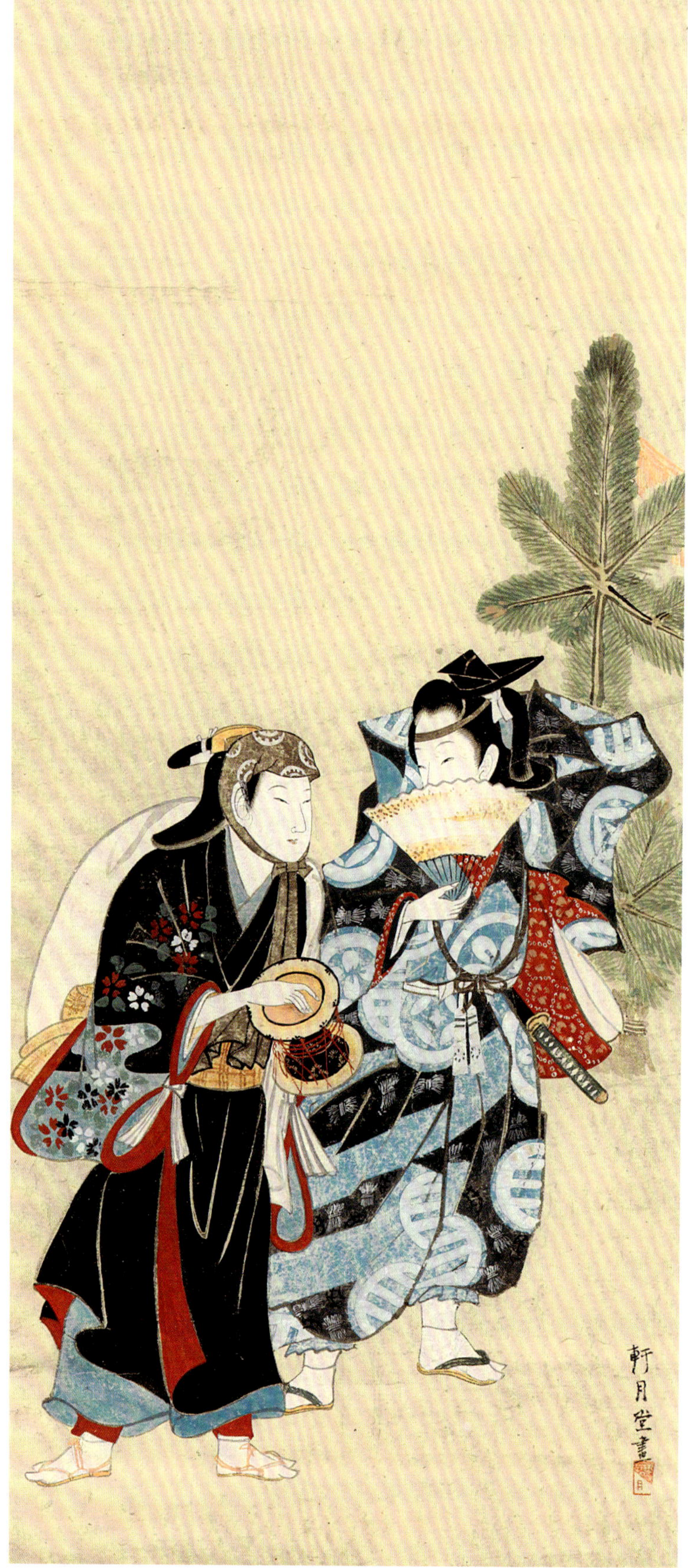

254

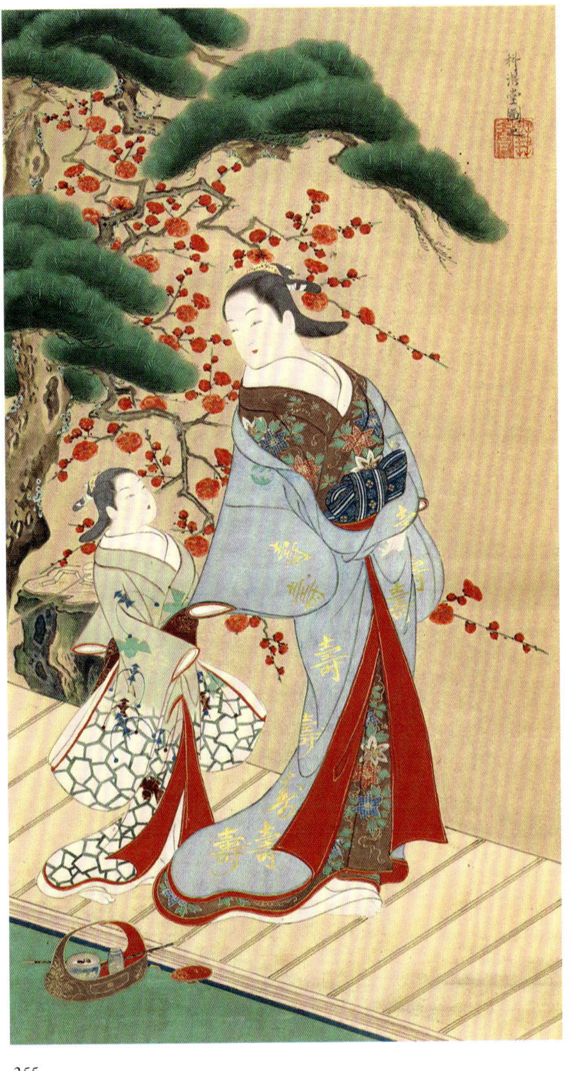

255

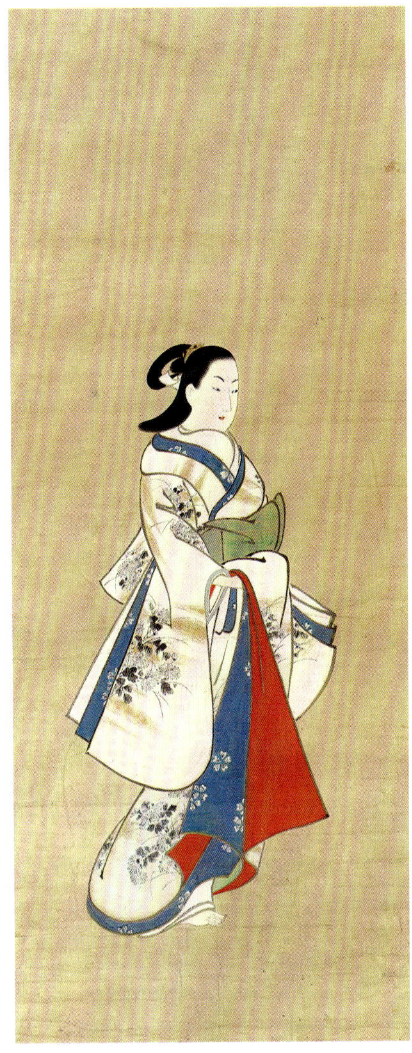

256

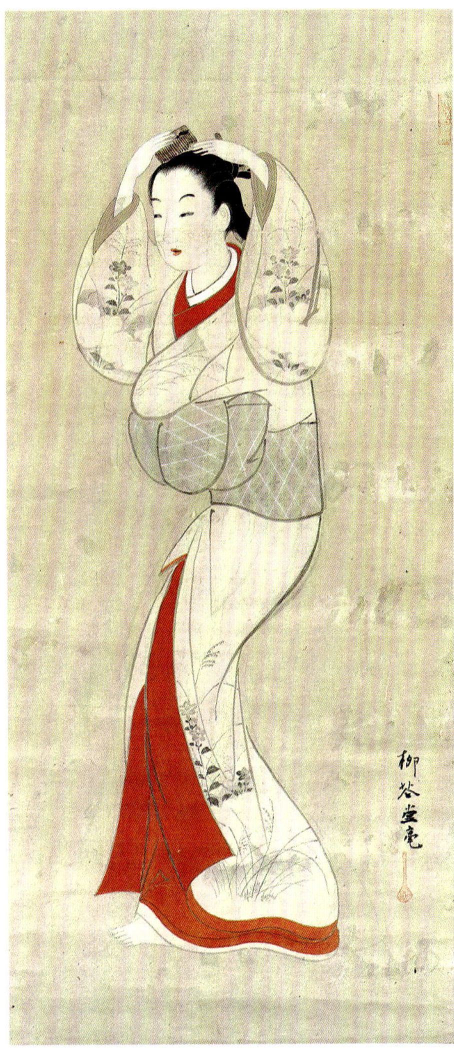

257

Baiōken Eishun
(梅翁軒永春; fl. ca. 1720)

253. Standing Courtesan

Edo period
Hanging scroll; ink and color on silk
102.6 x 41.3 cm (40 3/8 x 16 1/4 in.)
Text, signature, seal

Ex coll.: Frank E. Hart

Literature: Narazaki Muneshige 1969, no. 34; Jenkins 1971, no. 123.

Kengetsudō
(軒月堂; fl. 18th century)

254. Itinerant Actors

Edo period
Hanging scroll; ink and color on paper
106.7 x 46.8 cm (42 x 18 3/8 in.)
Signature, seal

Ex coll.: Frank E. Hart

Kakondō
(科混堂; fl. 18th century)

255. Courtesan and Attendant in Early Spring

Edo period
Hanging scroll; ink, color, and gold on paper
128 x 49.3 cm (50 3/8 x 19 3/8 in.)
Signature, seal

Ex coll.: Frank E. Hart

256. Standing Beauty

Edo period, 18th century
Hanging scroll; ink, color, and gold on paper
86.9 x 34.6 cm (34 1/4 x 13 5/8 in.)

Ex coll.: Frank E. Hart

Ryūkadō
(柳花堂; fl. 1740s)

257. Standing Woman

Edo period
Hanging scroll; ink and color on paper
72.8 x 33.2 cm (28 5/8 x 13 1/8 in.)
Signature, seals

Ex coll.: Frank E. Hart

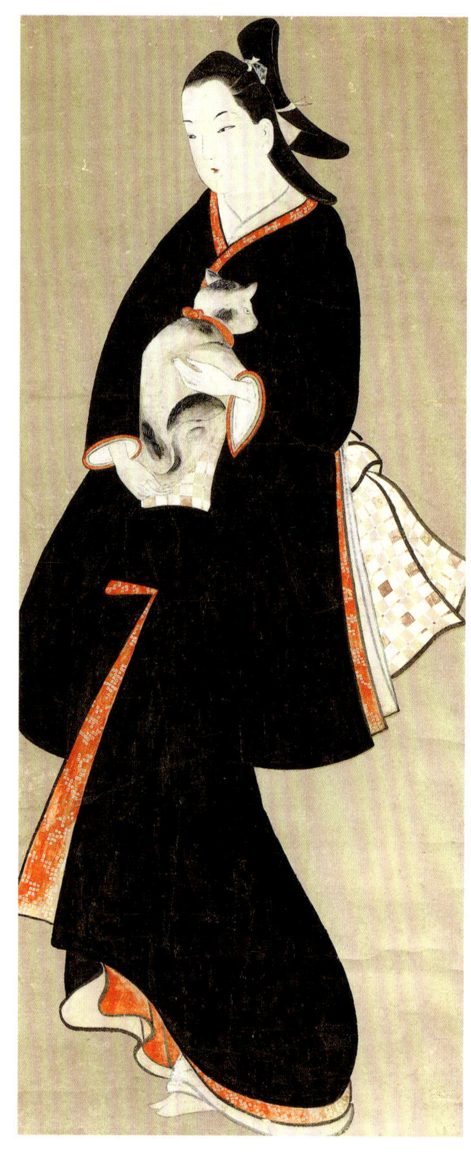

258. Woman with a Cat

Edo period, 18th century
Hanging scroll; ink and color on paper
92 x 38.7 cm (36¼ x 15¼ in.)

Ex coll.: Frank E. Hart

Takizawa Shigenobu
(滝沢重信; fl. 18th century)

259. Woman on a Veranda

Edo period
Hanging scroll; ink and color on silk
101.5 x 46.7 cm (40 x 18⅜ in.)
Signature, seal

Ex coll.: Frank E. Hart

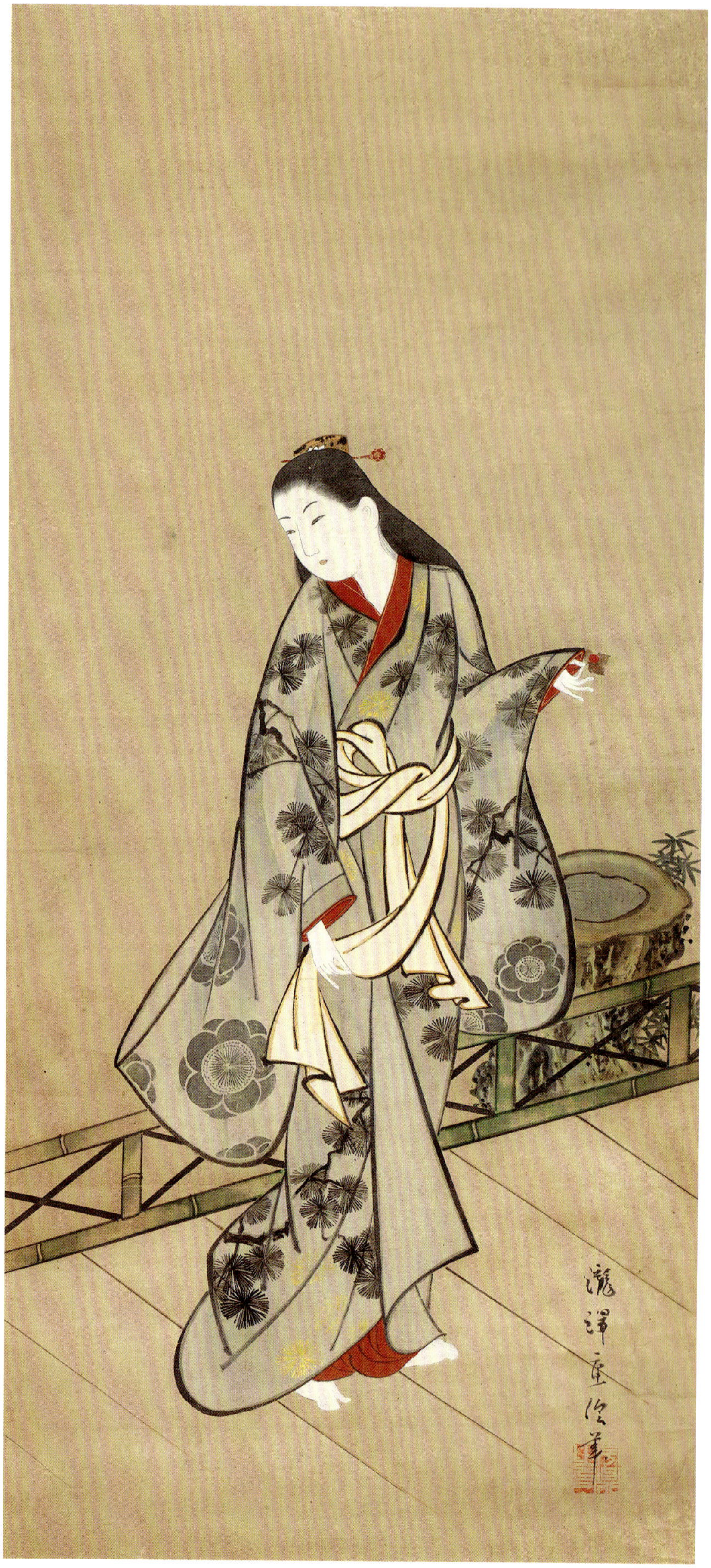

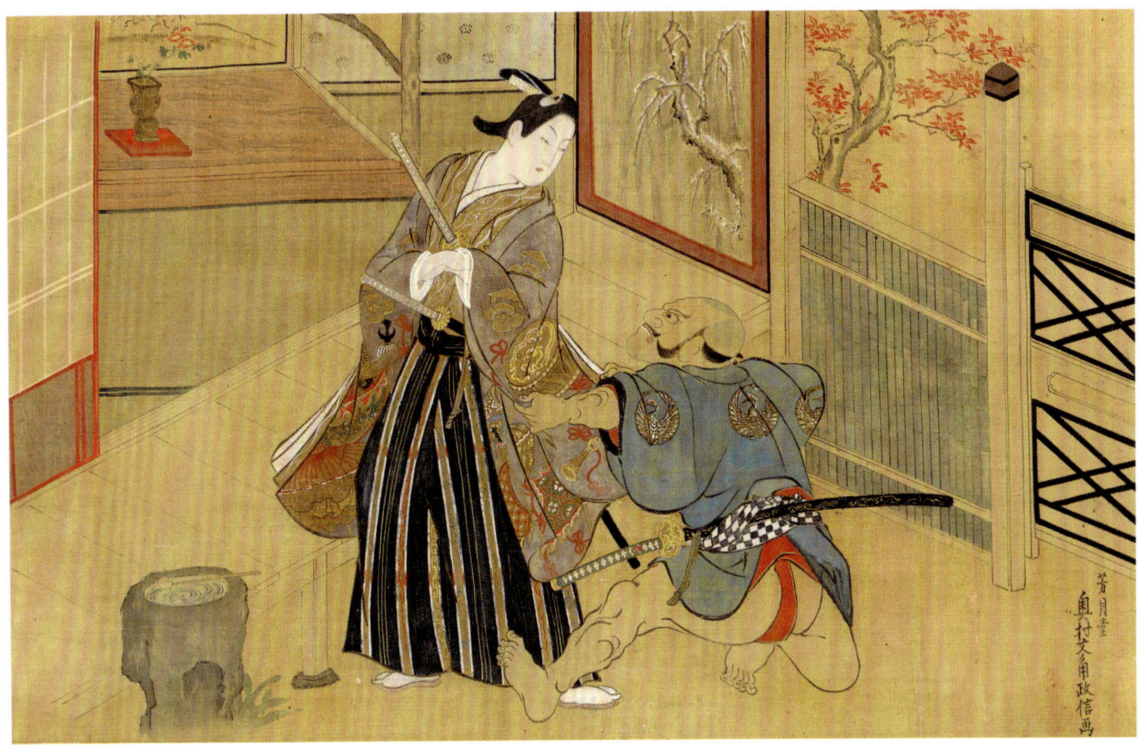

Okumura Masanobu
(奥村政信; 1686–1764)

260. The Kabuki Play *Kusazuribiki* (草摺引) from *Soga monogatari* (曽我物語)

Edo period, 18th century
Hanging scroll; ink and color on silk
31.6 x 50.2 cm ($12\frac{1}{2}$ x $19\frac{3}{4}$ in.)
Signature, seal

Ex coll.: Frank E. Hart

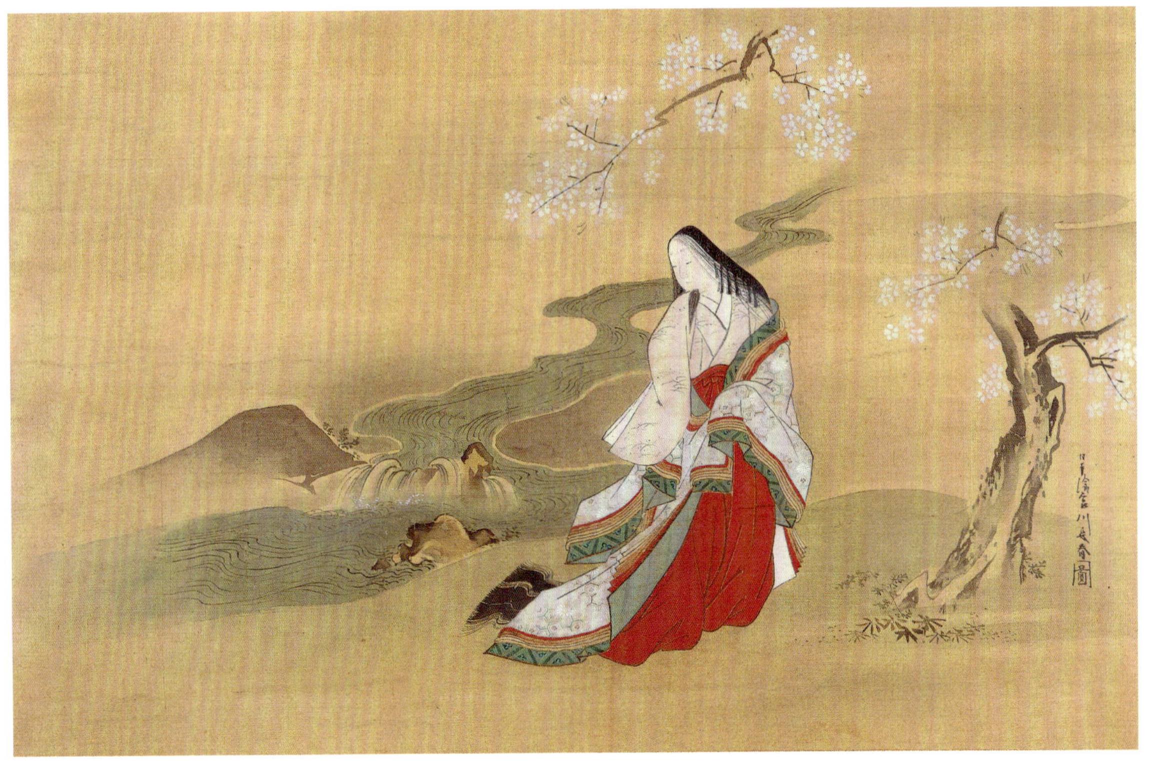

Miyagawa Chōshun
(宮川長春; 1683–1753)

261. Lady Ise (伊勢)

Edo period, 18th century
Hanging scroll; ink and color on silk
37.2 x 60.7 cm ($14\frac{5}{8}$ x $23\frac{7}{8}$ in.)
Signature

Ex coll.: Frank E. Hart

Literature: Jenkins 1971, no. 176; Tokyo National Museum 1985a, no. 65; Avitabile 1990, no. 83.

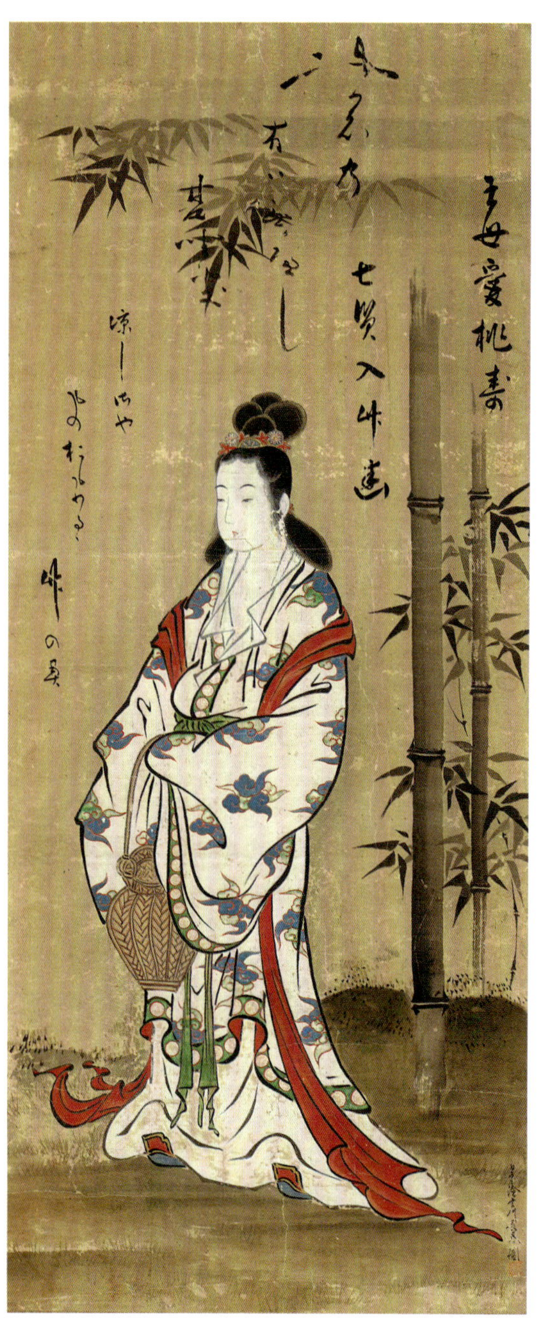

Miyagawa Chōshun
(宮川長春; 1683–1753)

262. Gyoran Kannon (魚籃観音)

Edo period
Hanging scroll; ink and color on paper
126.4 x 53.4 cm (49 3/4 x 21 in.)
Text, signature, seal

Ex coll.: Frank E. Hart

attributed to Miyagawa Chōshun (宮川長春; 1683–1753)

263. *Usugumo monogatari* (薄雲物語)

Edo period, 18th century
Handscroll; ink, color, and gold on silk
31.3 x 738.1 cm (12 3/8 in. x 24 ft. 2 5/8 in)

Ex coll.: Baba Zuiō; Kuki Ryūichi; Kuki Saburō

Literature: Yasuhara Makoto 2010, no. 105.

Torii Kiyotomo
(鳥居清友; fl. 18th century)

264. Woman with Battledore and Shuttlecock

Edo period
Hanging scroll; ink, color, and gold on paper
114.8 x 52.5 cm (45 1/4 x 20 5/8 in.)
Signature, seal

Ex coll.: Frank E. Hart

Torii Kiyoshige
(鳥居清重; fl. 1720–1760)

265. The Warrior Asahina Yoshihide (朝比奈義秀) with Courtesans

Edo period
Hanging scroll; ink, color, and gold on paper
76.2 x 20.1 cm (30 x 7 7/8 in.)
Signature, seal

Ex coll.: Frank E. Hart

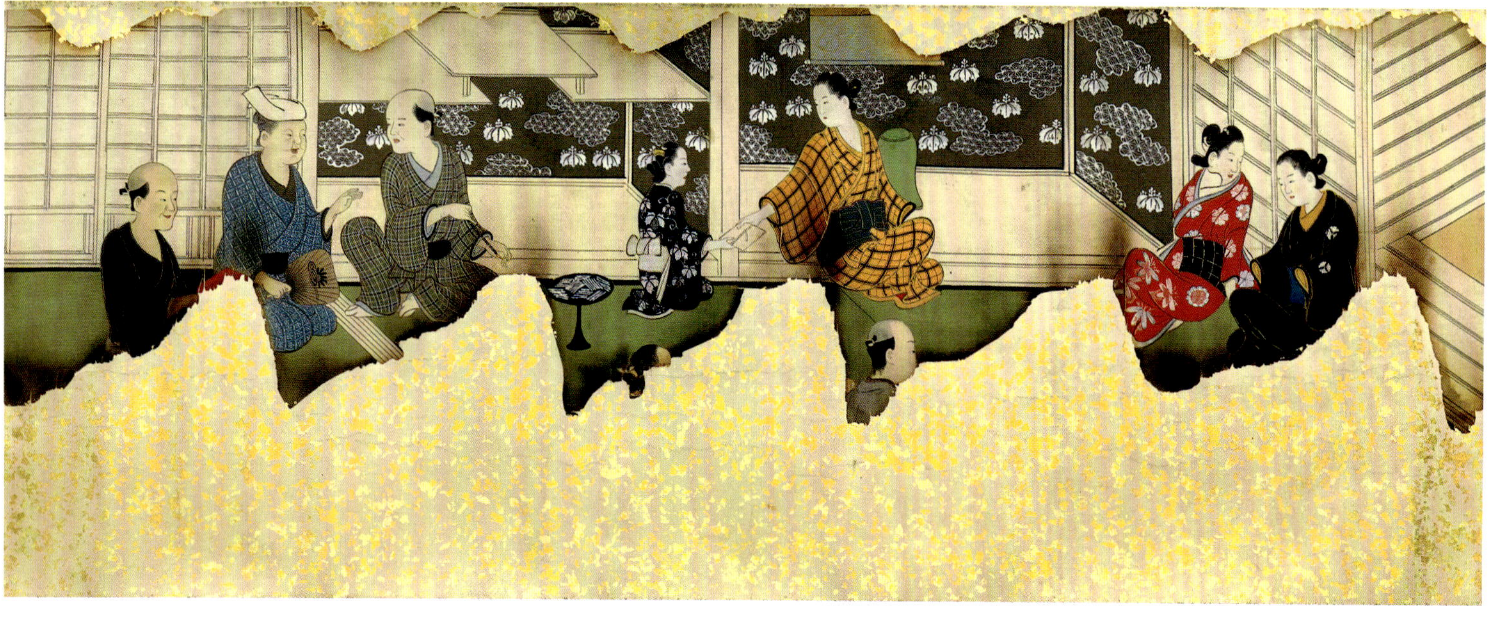

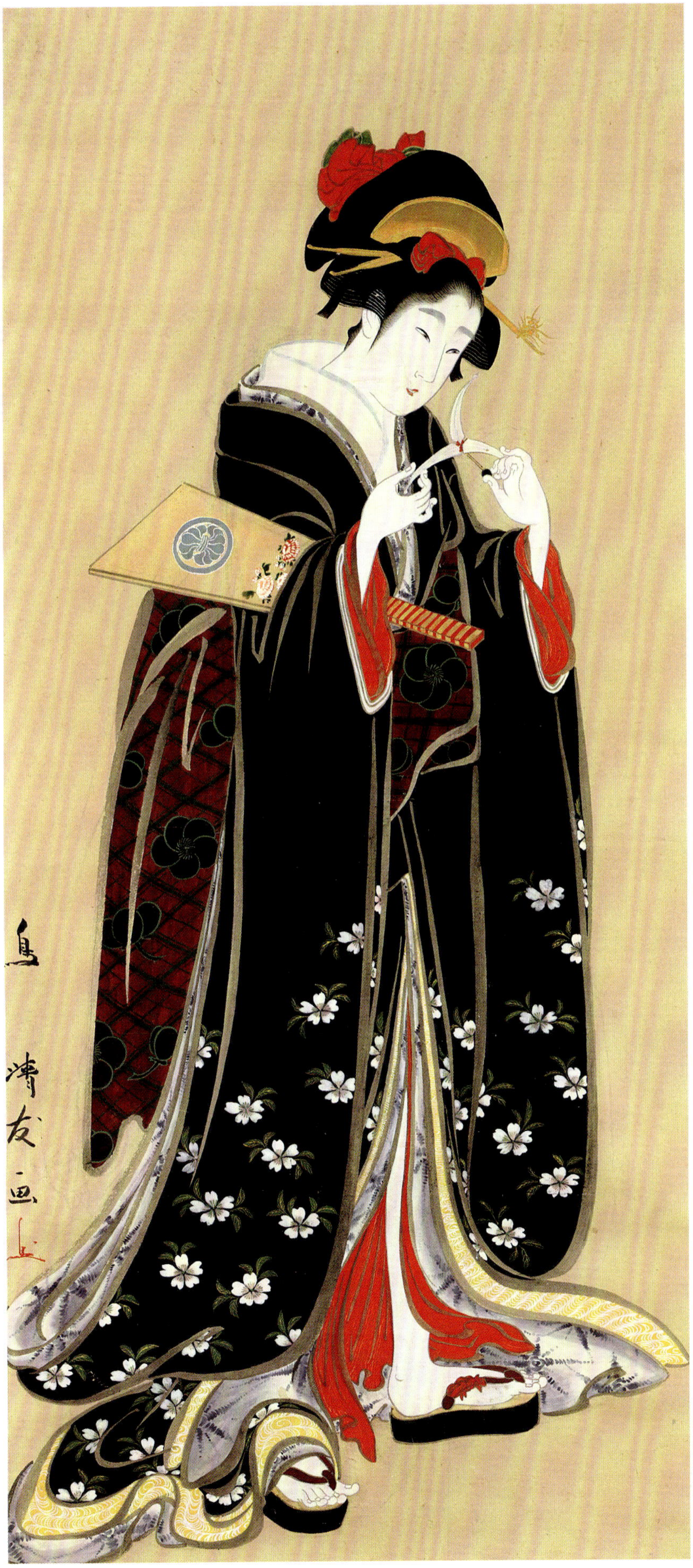

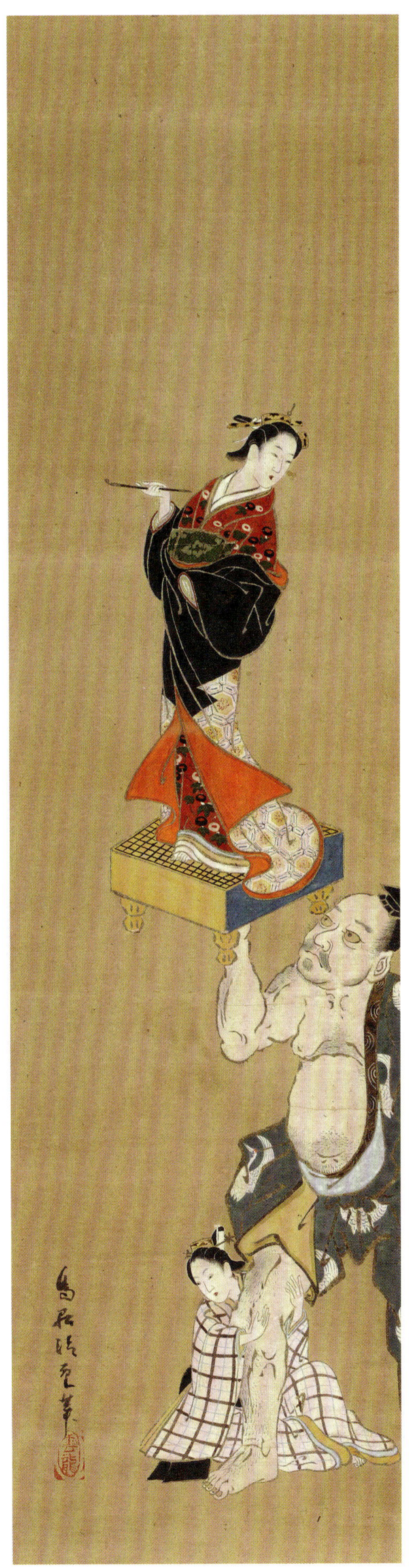

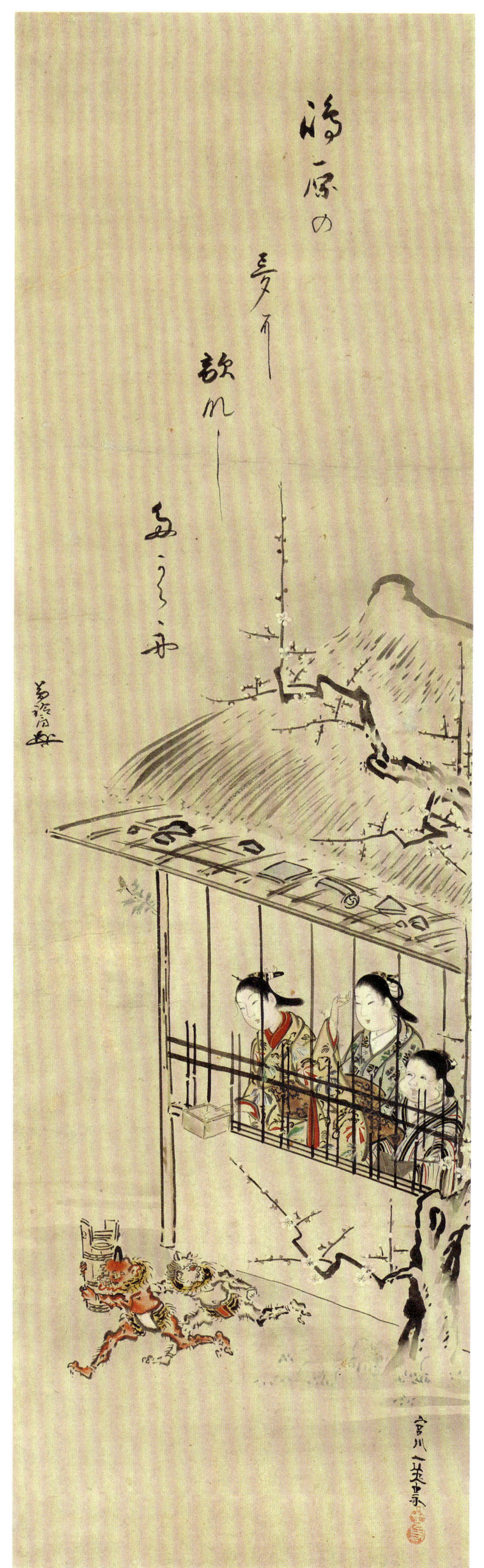

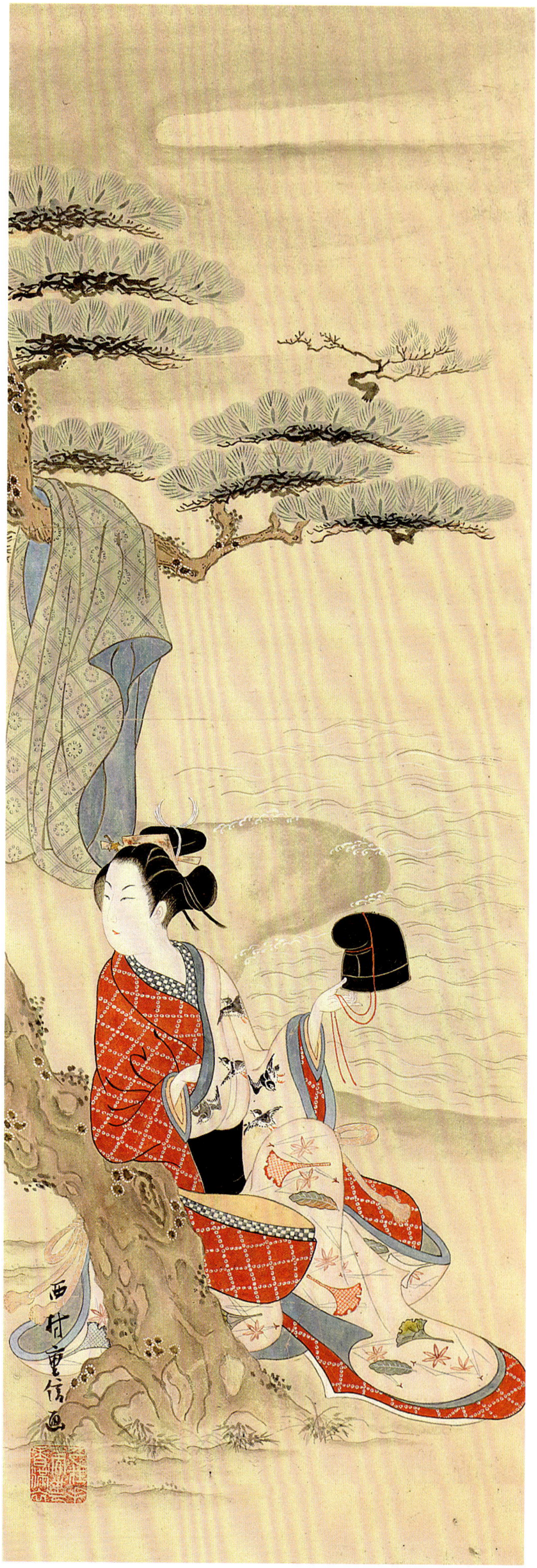

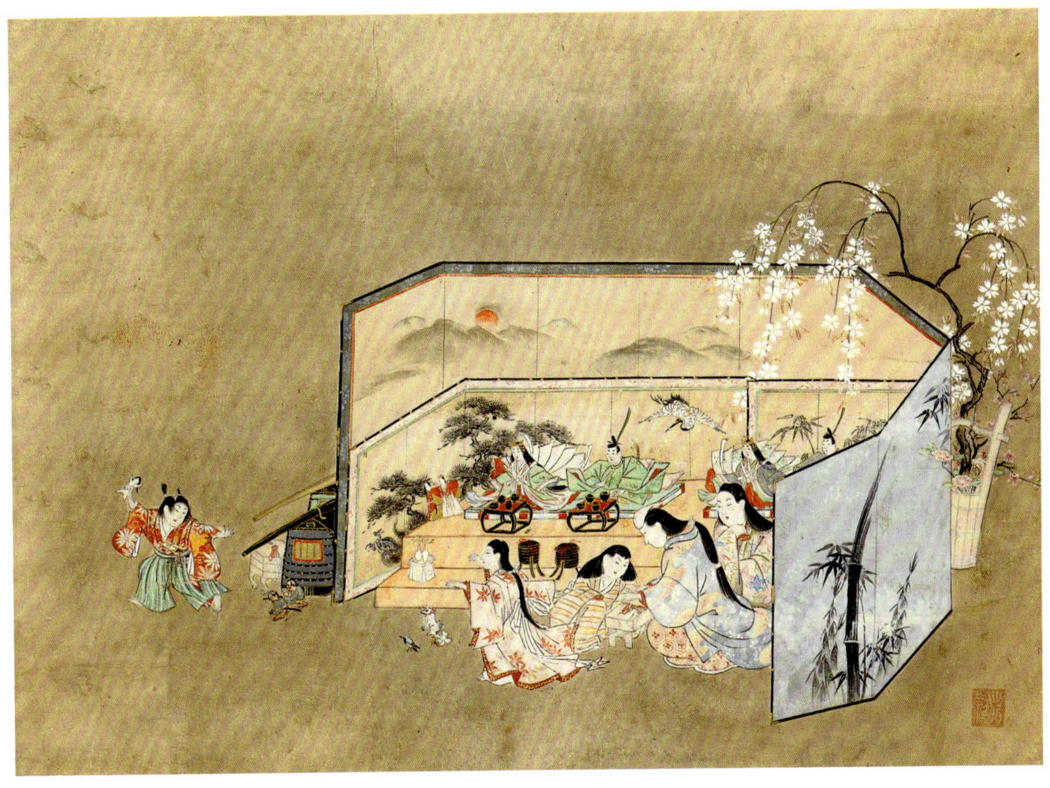

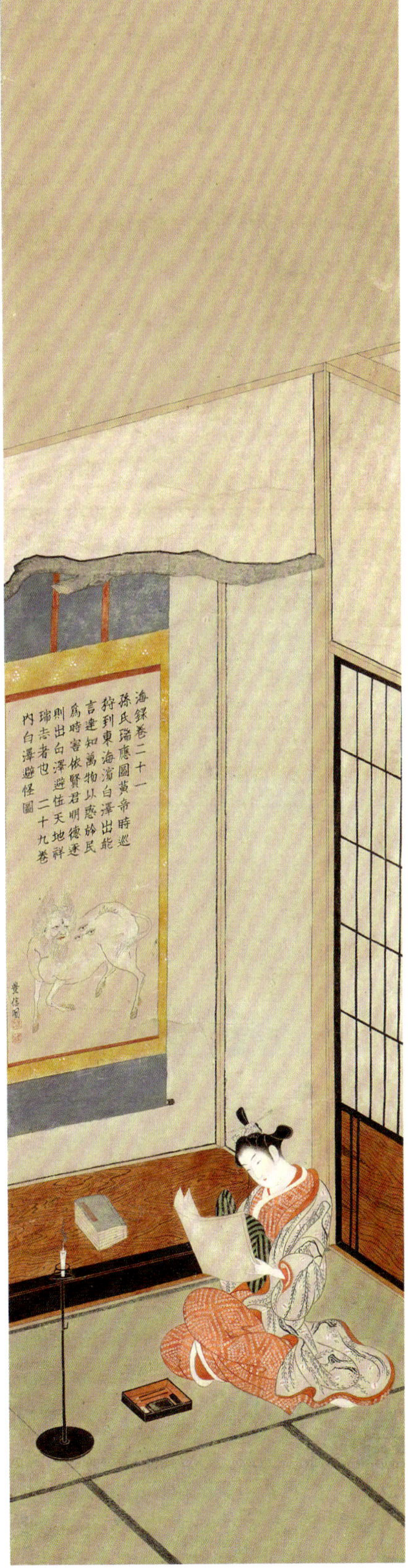

Miyagawa Isshō
(宮川一笑; fl. 1751–1763)

266. Setsubun (節分)

Edo period
Hanging scroll; ink and light color on paper
87.2 x 26.9 cm (34 3/8 x 10 5/8 in.)
Text, signatures, seals

Ex coll.: Frank E. Hart

Nishimura Shigenobu
(西村重信; fl. mid-18th century)

267. The Brine Maiden Matsukaze (松風)

Edo period
Hanging scroll; ink and color on paper
80.2 x 28.4 cm (31 5/8 x 11 1/8 in.)
Signature, seal

Ex coll.: Frank E. Hart

Literature: Murase 1993, no. 46.

268. Doll Festival (雛祭)

Edo period, 18th century
Hanging scroll; ink, color, and gold on paper
42.8 x 59.7 cm (16 7/8 x 23 1/2 in.)
Seal

Ex coll.: Frank E. Hart

Ishikawa Toyonobu
(石川豊信; 1711–1785)

269. Young Woman with a Book

Edo period
Hanging scroll; ink and light color on paper
83.2 x 21.7 cm (32 3/4 x 8 1/2 in.)
Text, signature, seals

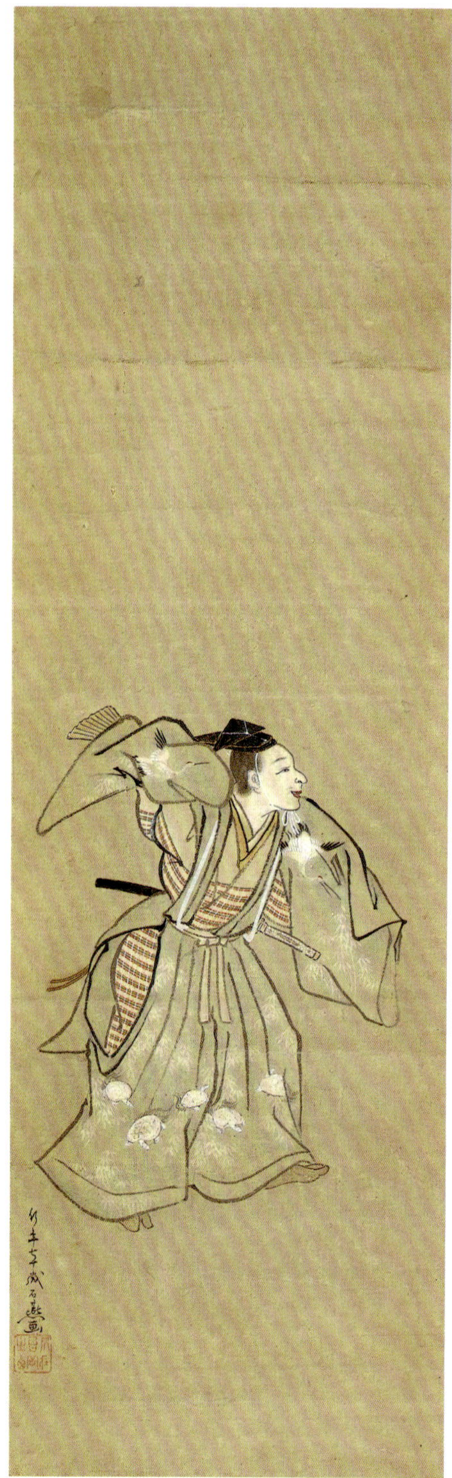

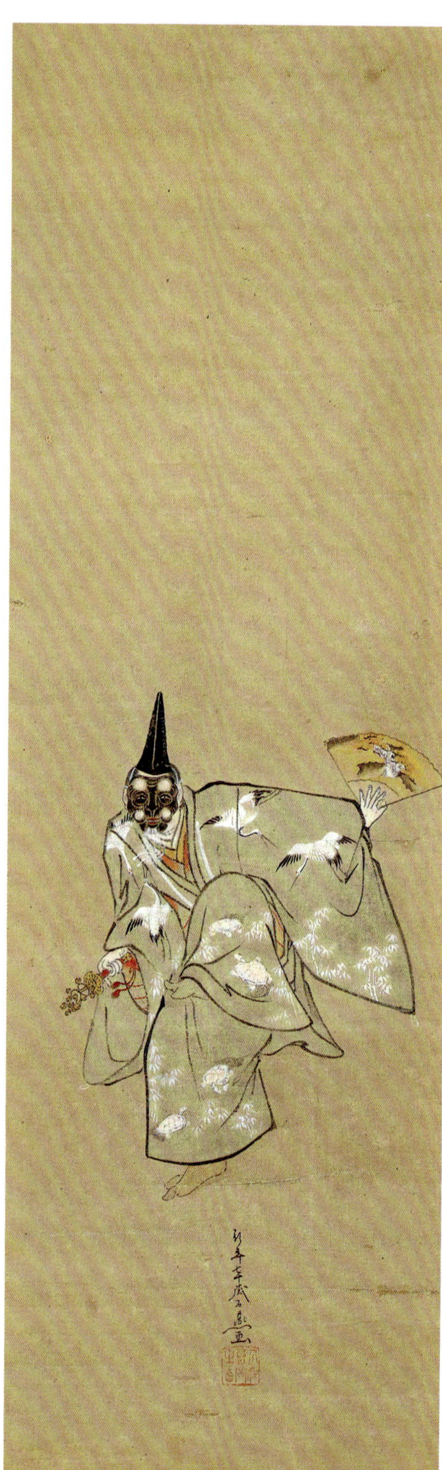

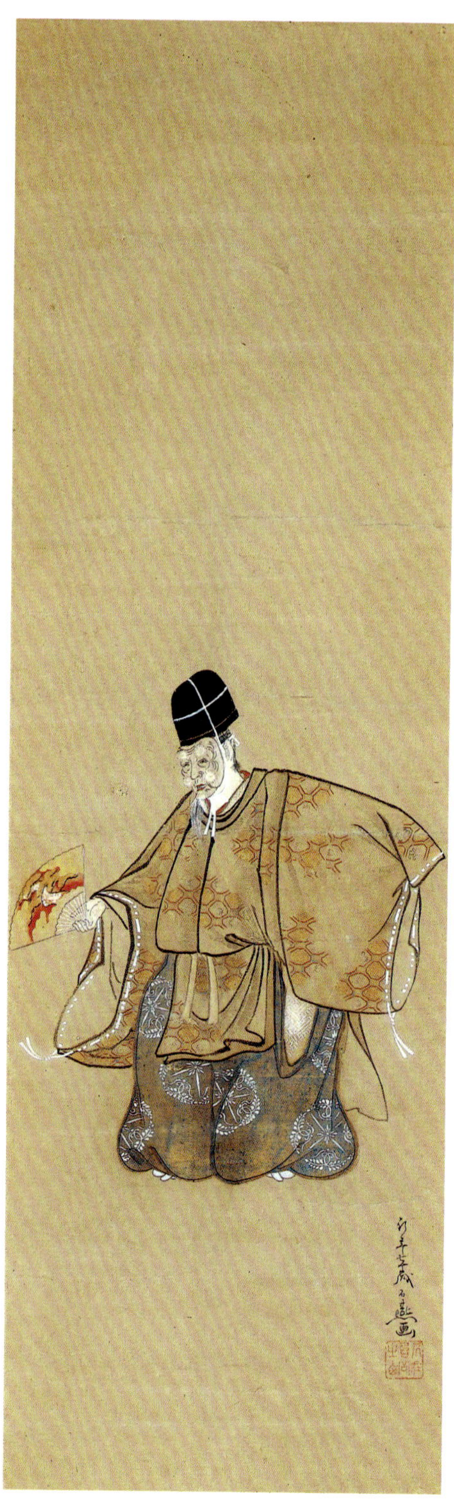

Toriyama Sekien
(鳥山石燕; 1712–1788)

270a–c. The Noh Dance *Okina* (翁)

Edo period, 1781
Triptych of hanging scrolls; ink, color, and gold on paper
Each scroll 87.3 x 27.2 cm (34 3/8 x 10 3/4 in.)
Signatures, seals

Ex coll.: Frank E. Hart

Literature: Young and Smith 1966, no. 46; Narazaki Muneshige 1969, pls. 50–52; Murase 1975, no. 91; Murase 2000, no. 148.

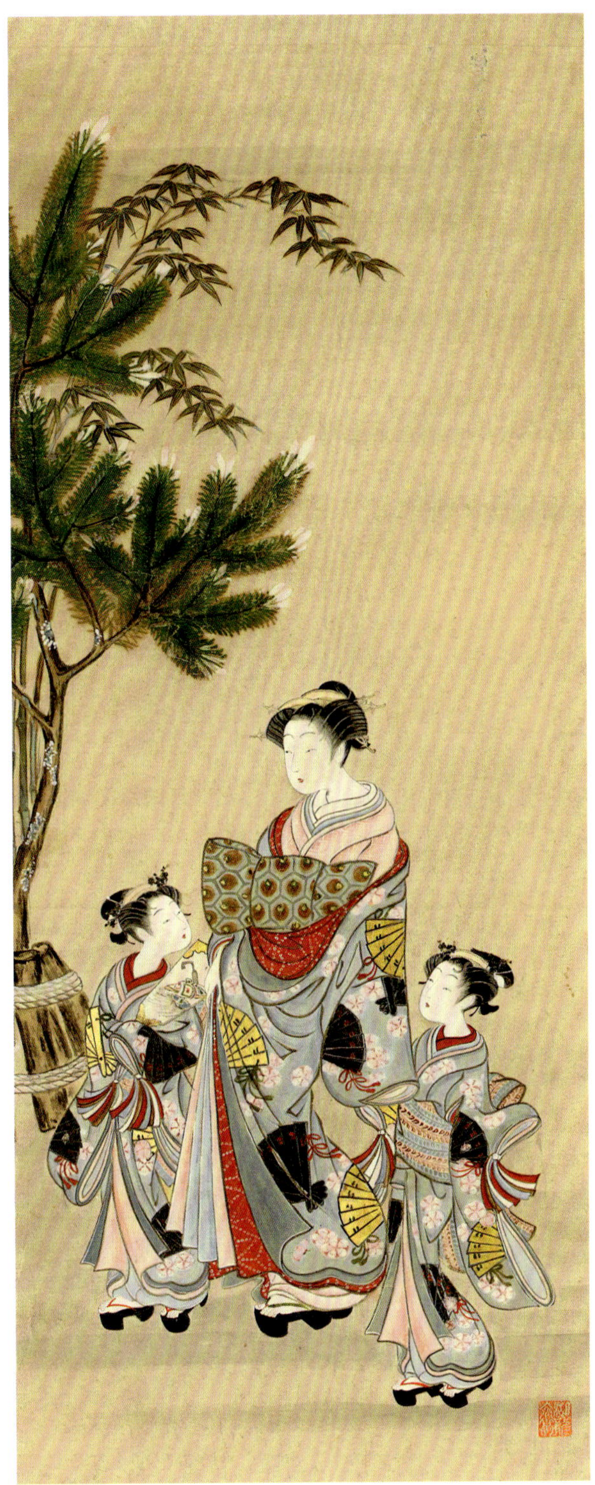

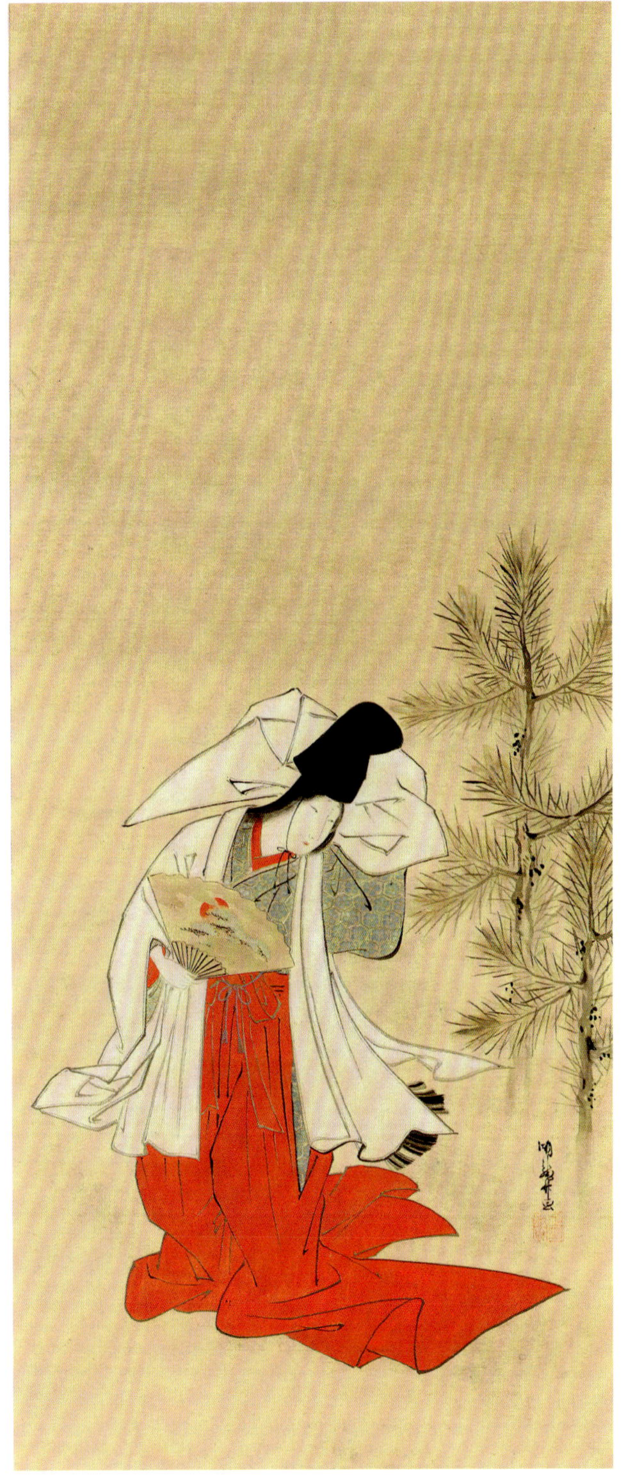

Isoda Koryūsai
(磯田湖竜斎; fl. ca. 1764–1788)

271. Courtesan and Two Attendants on New Year's Day

Edo period
Hanging scroll; ink, color, and gold on paper
85.6 x 34.7 cm (33 3/4 x 13 5/8 in.)
Seal

Ex coll.: Frank E. Hart

Literature: Young and Smith 1966, no. 41.

Isoda Koryūsai
(磯田湖竜斎; fl. ca. 1764–1788)

272. Courtesan-Dancer (*Shirabyōshi,* 白拍子) for the New Year

Edo period
Hanging scroll; ink and color on silk
81.5 x 34.6 cm (32 1/8 x 13 5/8 in.)
Signature, seal

Ex coll.: Frank E. Hart

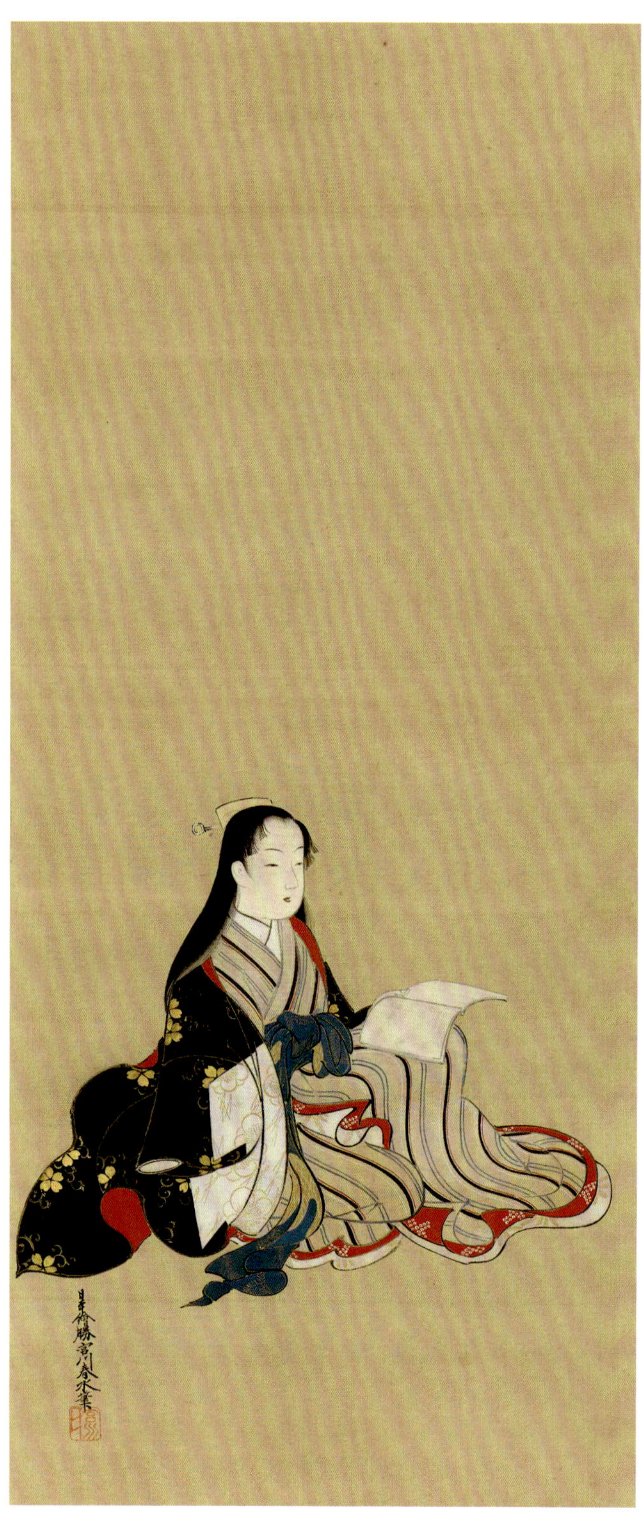

Katsukawa Shunsui
(勝川春水; fl. mid-18th century)

273. Young Woman with a Book

Edo period
Hanging scroll; ink, color, and gold on silk
78.5 x 35.2 cm (30 7/8 x 13 7/8 in.)
Signature, seal

Ex coll.: Frank E. Hart

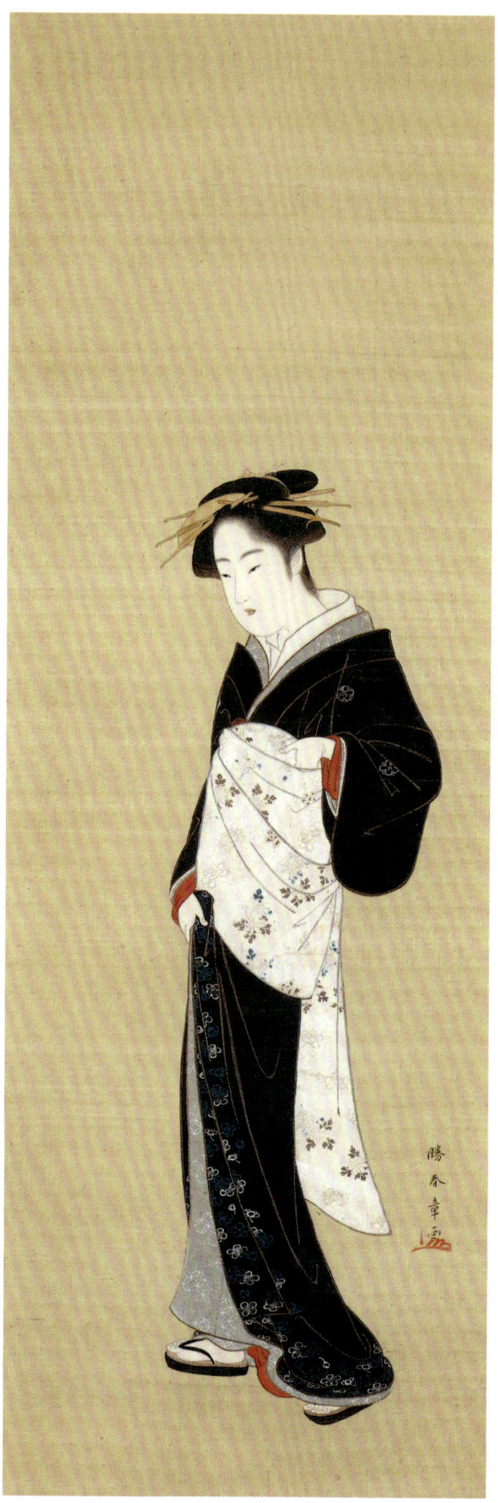

Katsukawa Shunshō
(勝川春章; 1726–1792)

274. Woman in a Black Kimono

Edo period, 1783–89
Hanging scroll; ink, color, and gold on silk
85.1 x 28.5 cm (33 1/2 x 11 1/4 in.)
Signature, seal

Literature: Murase 1993, no. 47; Murase 2000, no. 149; Meech and Oliver 2008, p. 21, fig. 7.

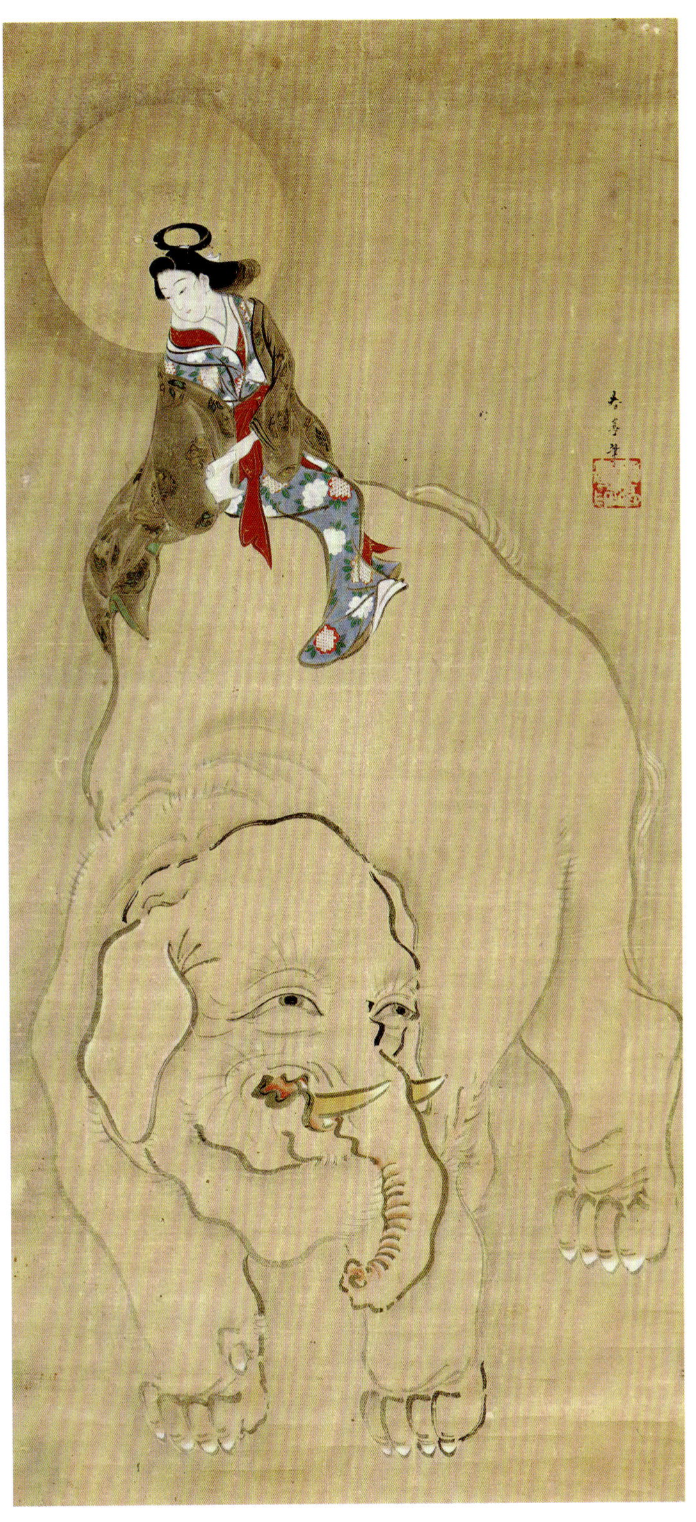

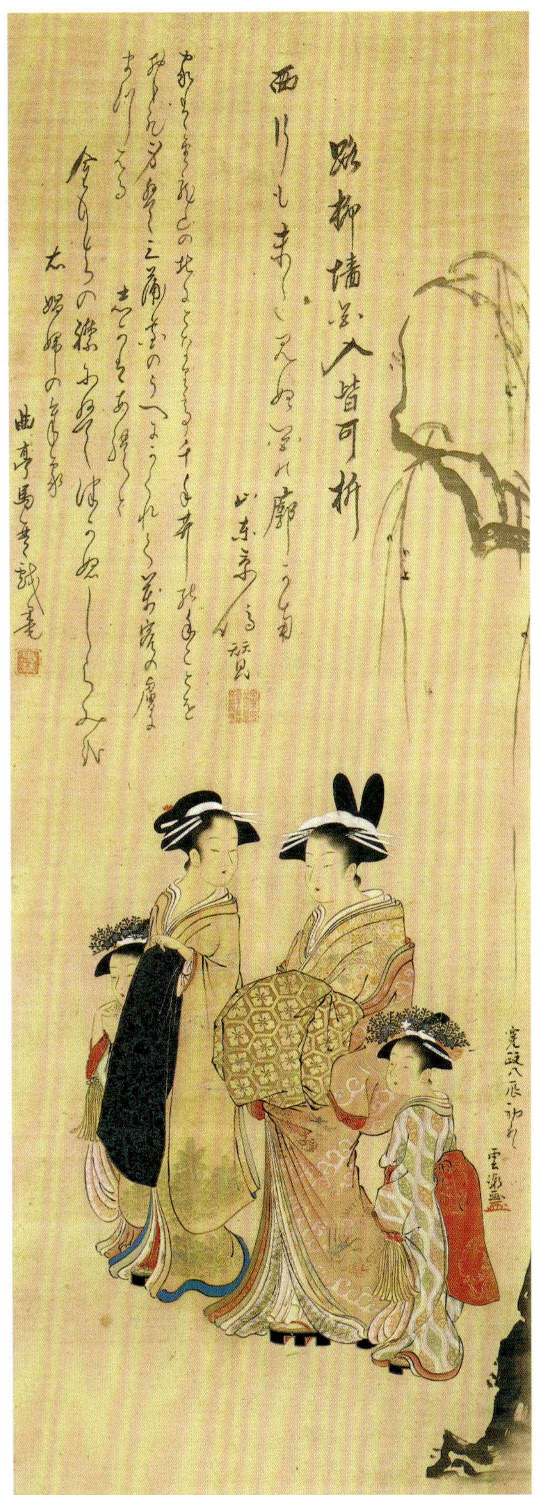

Katsukawa Shuntei
(勝川春亭; 1770–1820)

275. Eguchi no Kimi (江口の君)

Edo period
Hanging scroll; ink, color, and gold on paper
128.2 x 69.7 cm (50½ x 27½ in.)
Signature, seal

Ex coll.: Frank E. Hart

Unchō
(雲潮; fl. late 18th century)

276. Courtesan and Her Attendants under a Willow Tree

Edo period, 1796
Hanging scroll; ink, color, and gold on silk
92.7 x 34 cm (36½ x 13⅜ in.)
Text, signatures, seals

Literature: Narazaki Muneshige 1966, p. 34; Narazaki Muneshige 1969, pl. 64; Murase 1975, no. 93; Jenkins 1993, pp. 170–71, no. III-3; Murase 2000, no. 150.

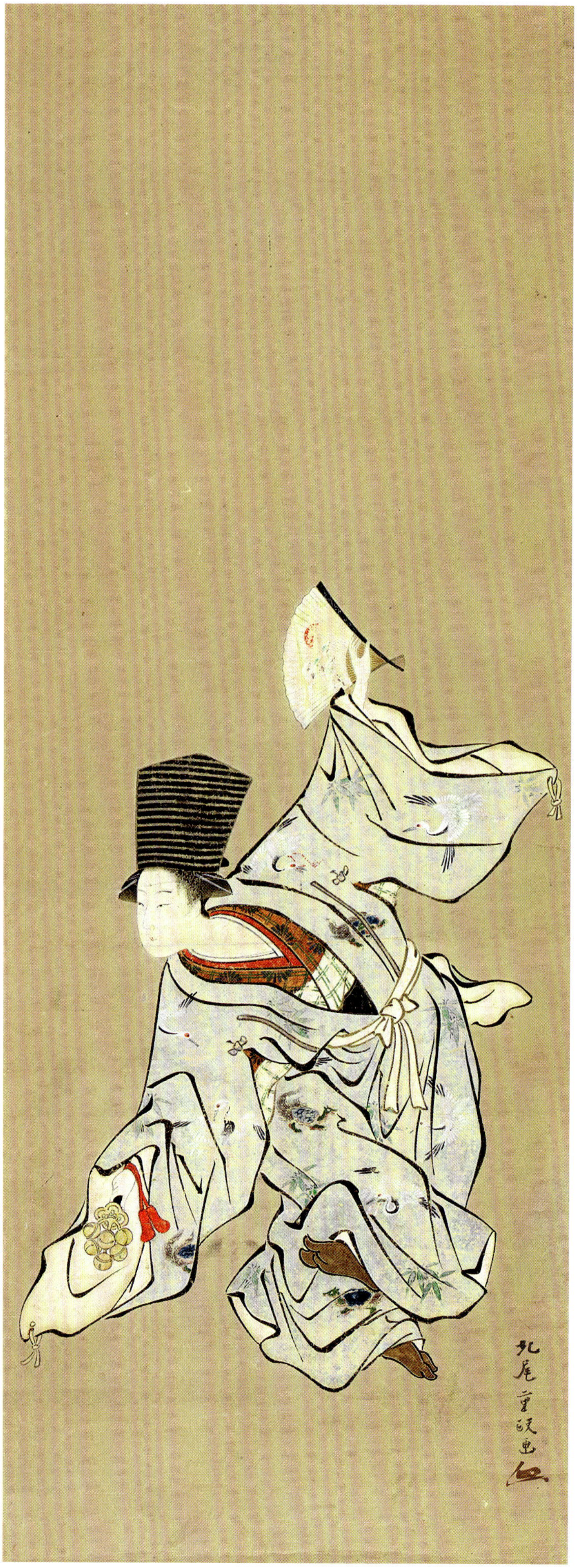

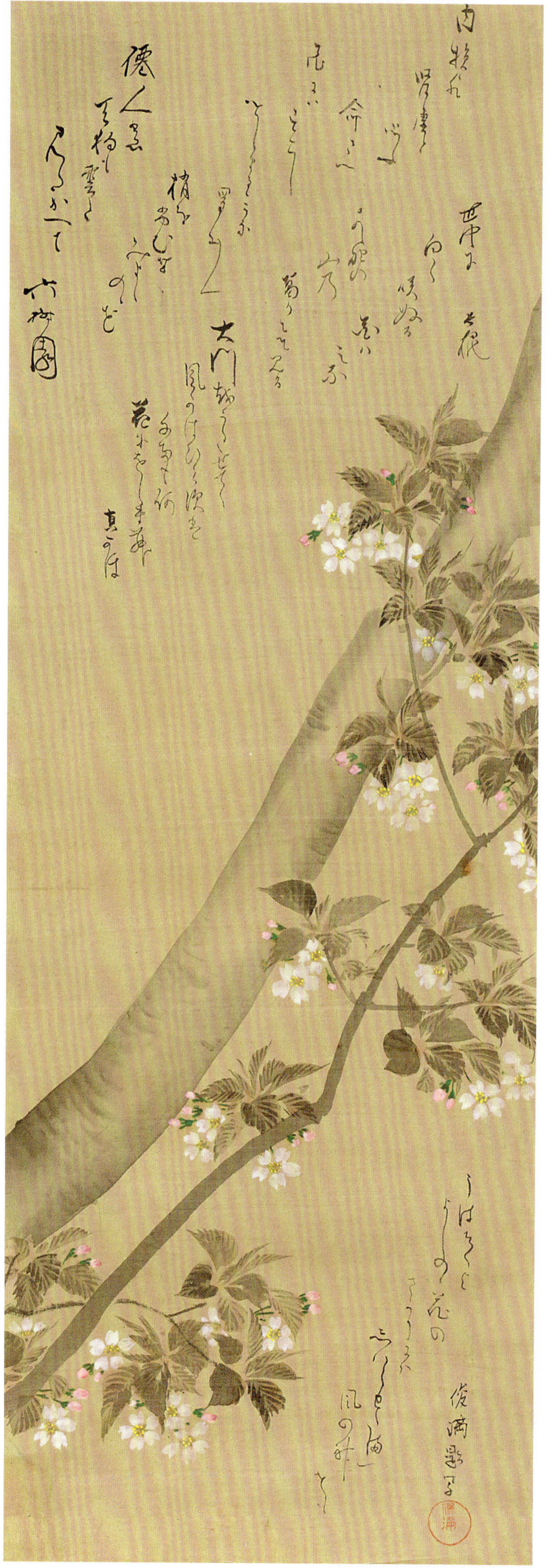

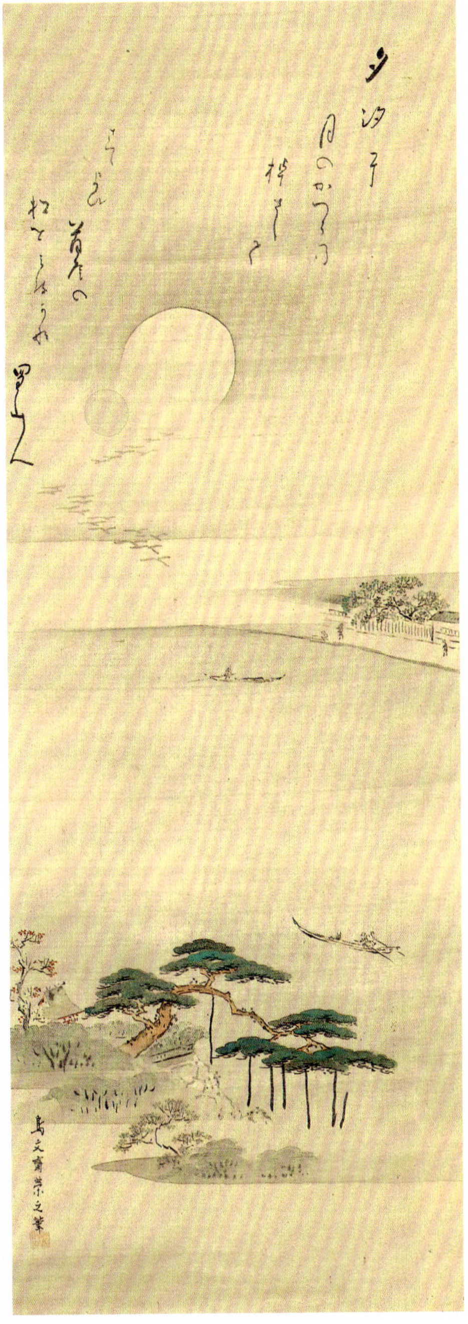

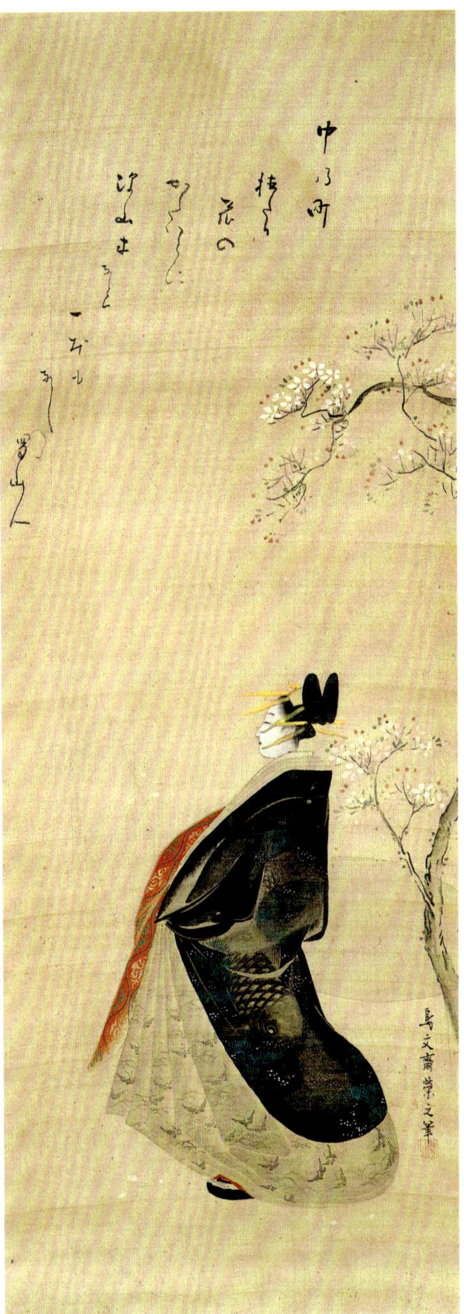

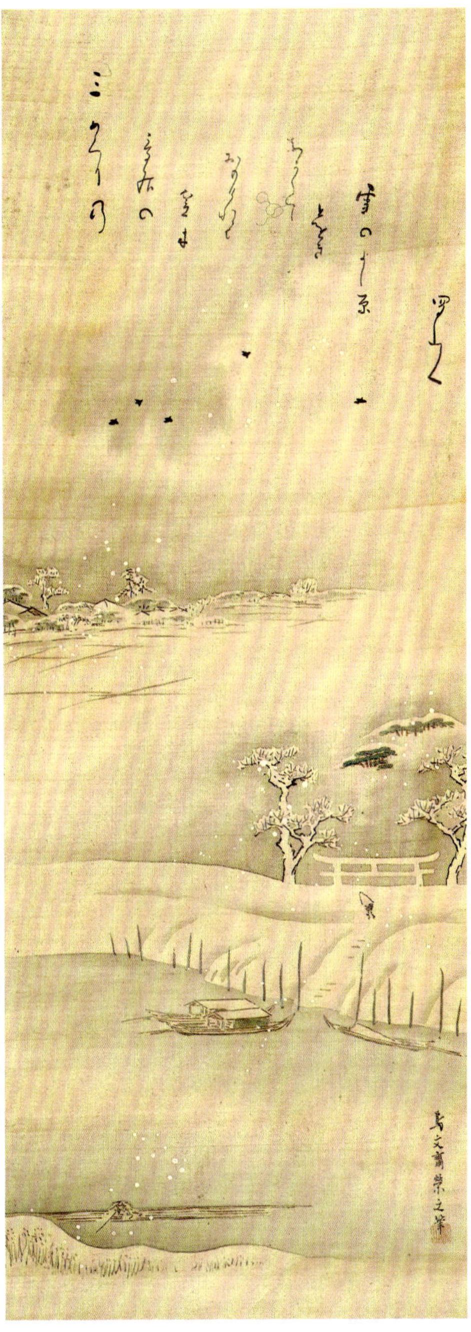

Kitao Shigemasa
(北尾重政; 1739–1820)

277. Sanbasō (三番叟)

Edo period
Hanging scroll; ink and color on paper
85.5 x 32.5 cm (33 5/8 x 12 3/4 in.)
Signature, seal

Ex coll.: Frank E. Hart

Kubo Shunman
(窪春満; 1757–1820)

278. Cherry Blossoms with Poems

Edo period
Hanging scroll; ink and color on silk
91 x 32.2 cm (35 7/8 x 12 5/8 in.)
Text, signatures, seal

Ex coll.: Frank E. Hart

Chōbunsai Eishi
(鳥文斎栄之; 1756–1829)

279a–c. Snow, Cherry Blossoms, and Moon (Yoshiwara in Three Seasons)

Edo period, 1804–15
Triptych of hanging scrolls; ink, color, and gold on silk
Each scroll 82.4 x 30.2 cm (32 1/2 x 11 7/8 in.)
Text, signatures, seals

Ex coll.: Frank E. Hart

Literature: Murase 1975, no. 92; Jenkins 1993, pp. 192–95, no. IV-2; Murase 2000, no. 151; Tsuji Nobuo et al. 2005, no. 85.

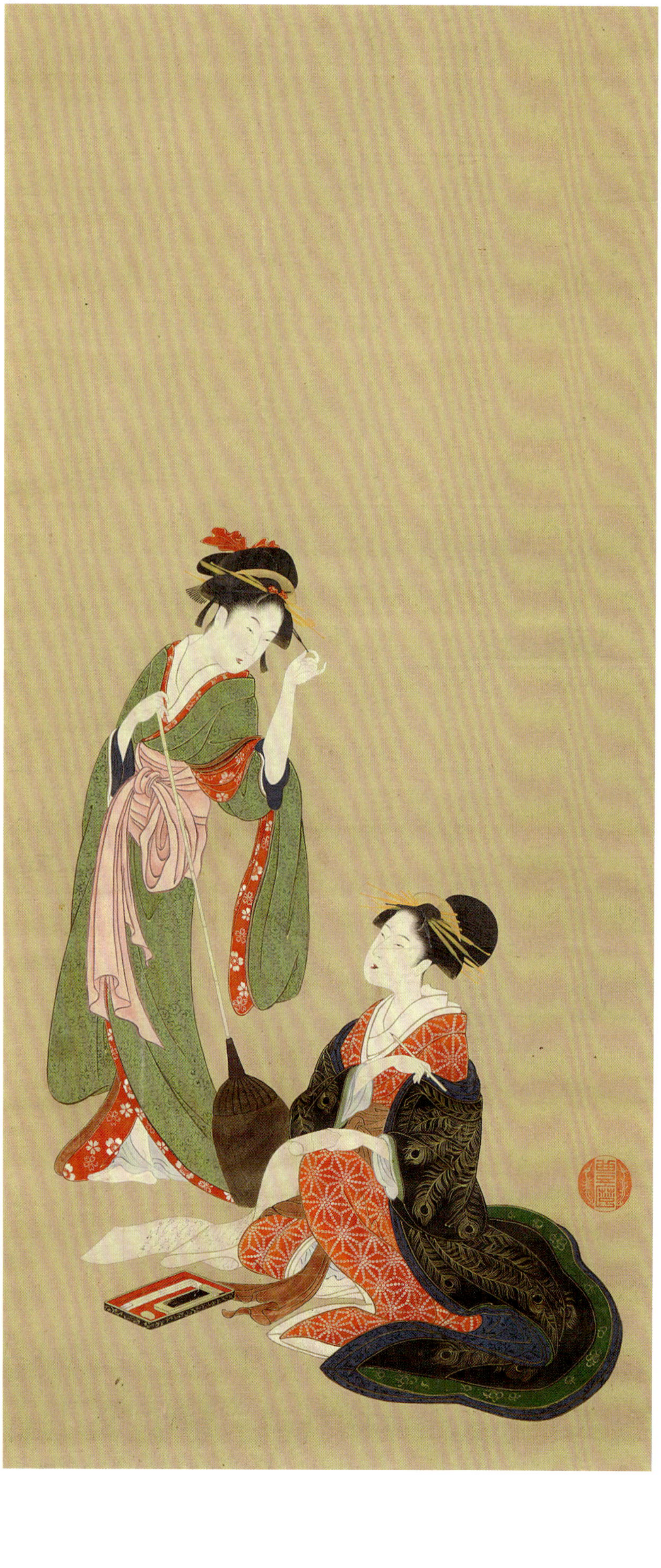

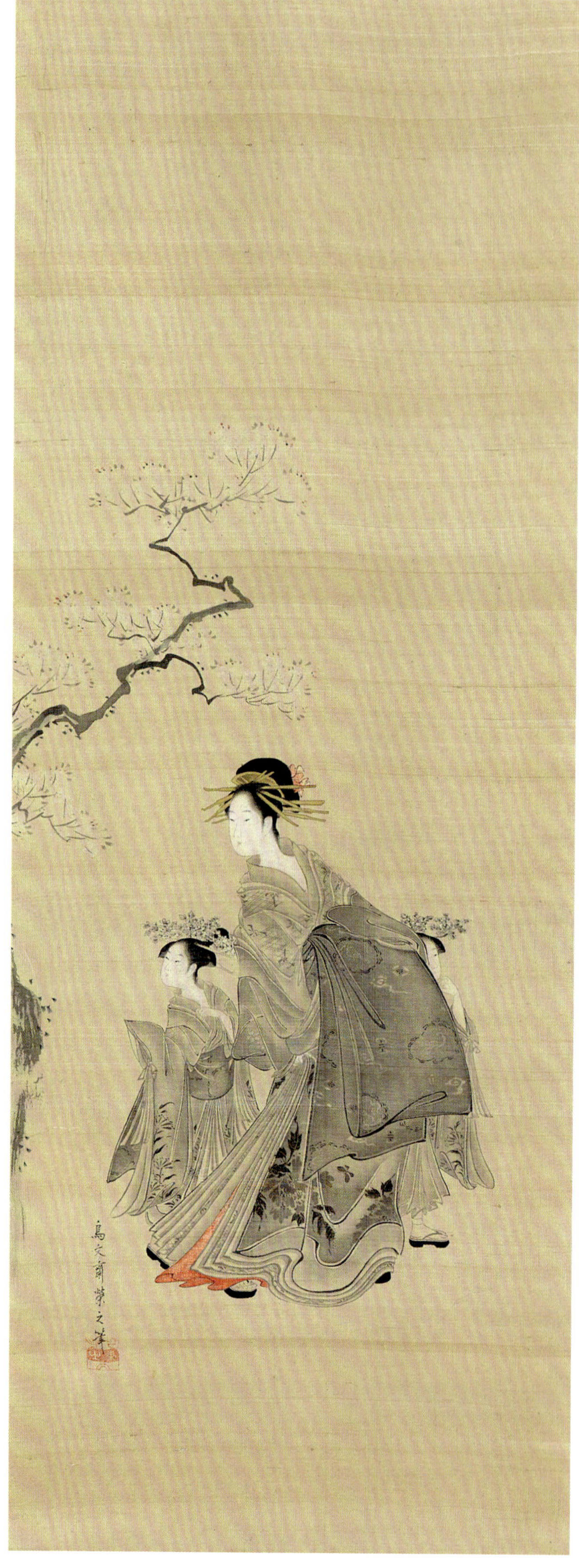

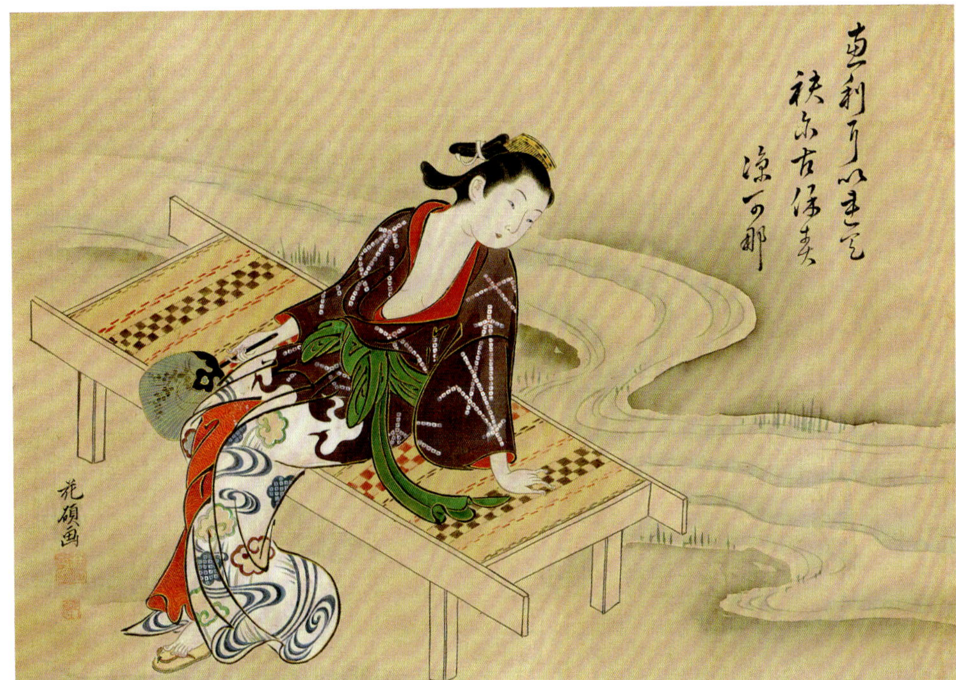

Kaseki
(花碩; fl. 18th century)

282. Young Woman Enjoying a Cool Evening

Edo period
Hanging scroll; ink and color on silk
36.8 x 53.3 cm (14½ x 21 in.)
Text, signature, seals

Ex coll.: Frank E. Hart

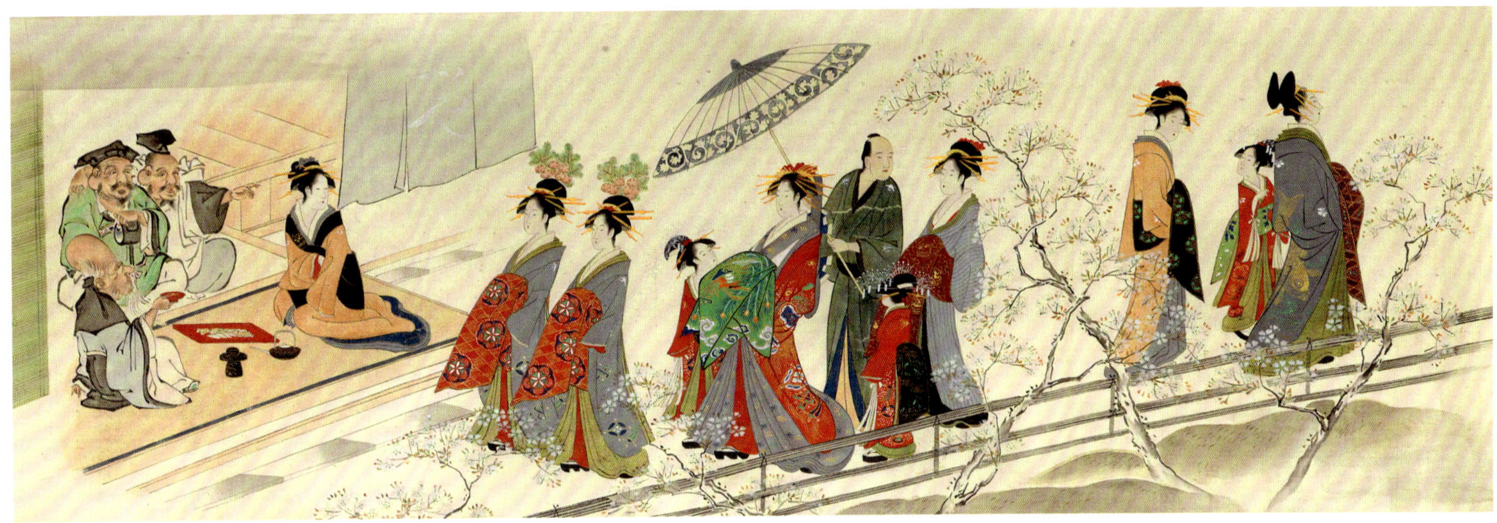

Kinpūsha Toyomaro
(琴風舎豊麿; fl. early 19th century)

280. Kanzan (寒山) and Jittoku (拾得)

Edo period
Hanging scroll; ink, color, and gold on paper
122.7 x 56.5 cm (48¼ x 22¼ in.)
Seal

Ex coll.: Frank E. Hart

Literature: Young and Smith 1966, no. 52; Narazaki Muneshige 1969, pl. 81; Murase 1975, no. 95.

Chōbunsai Eishi
(鳥文斎栄之; 1756–1829)

281. Courtesan and Her Attendants under a Cherry Tree

Edo period
Hanging scroll; ink, color, and gold on silk
83.2 x 30.6 cm (32¾ x 12 in.)
Signature, seal

Literature: Murase 1993, no. 48.

Chōbunsai Eishi
(鳥文斎栄之; 1756–1829)

283. Scenes of Pleasures at the Height of Spring (全盛季春遊戯)

Edo period
Handscroll; ink and color on silk
30.8 x 860 cm (12⅛ in. x 28 ft. 2⅝ in.)
Signature, seal

Literature: Swinton et al. 1995, p. 143, no. 9.

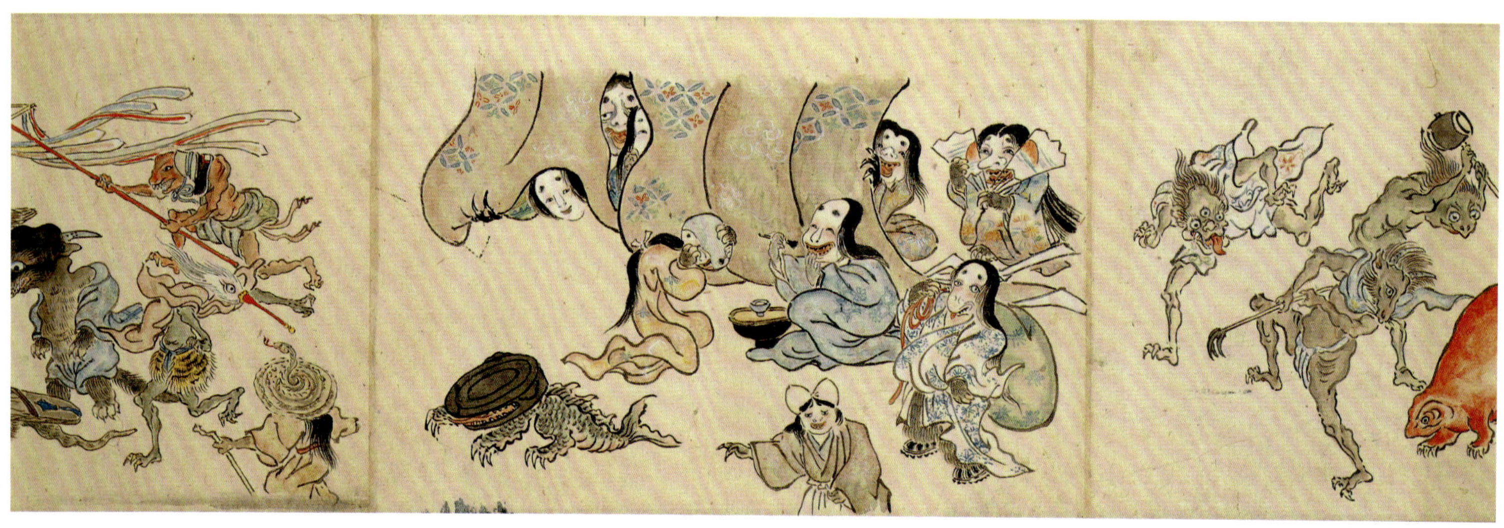

284. Night Parade of One Hundred Demons (百鬼夜行)

Edo period, 19th century
Handscroll; ink and color on paper
23.2 x 488.4 cm (9 1/8 in. x 16 ft. 1/4 in.)

Literature: Tsuji Nobuo et al. 2005, no. 87.

Utagawa Toyoharu
(歌川豊春; 1735–1814)

285. Courtesan and Her Attendant under a Cherry Tree

Edo period
Hanging scroll; ink and color on silk
90.4 x 35.8 cm (35 5/8 x 14 1/8 in.)
Signature, seal

Ex coll.: Frank E. Hart

Utagawa Toyokuni I
(歌川豊国; 1769–1825)

286. Bandō Mitsugorō II (二世坂東三津五郎; 1741–1828) as Shinbei (新兵衛) in the Kabuki play *Sukeroku* (助六)

Edo period
Hanging scroll; ink and color on paper
59.8 x 26.4 cm (23 1/2 x 10 3/8 in.)
Text, signatures, seals

Literature: Narazaki Muneshige 1969, p. 79.

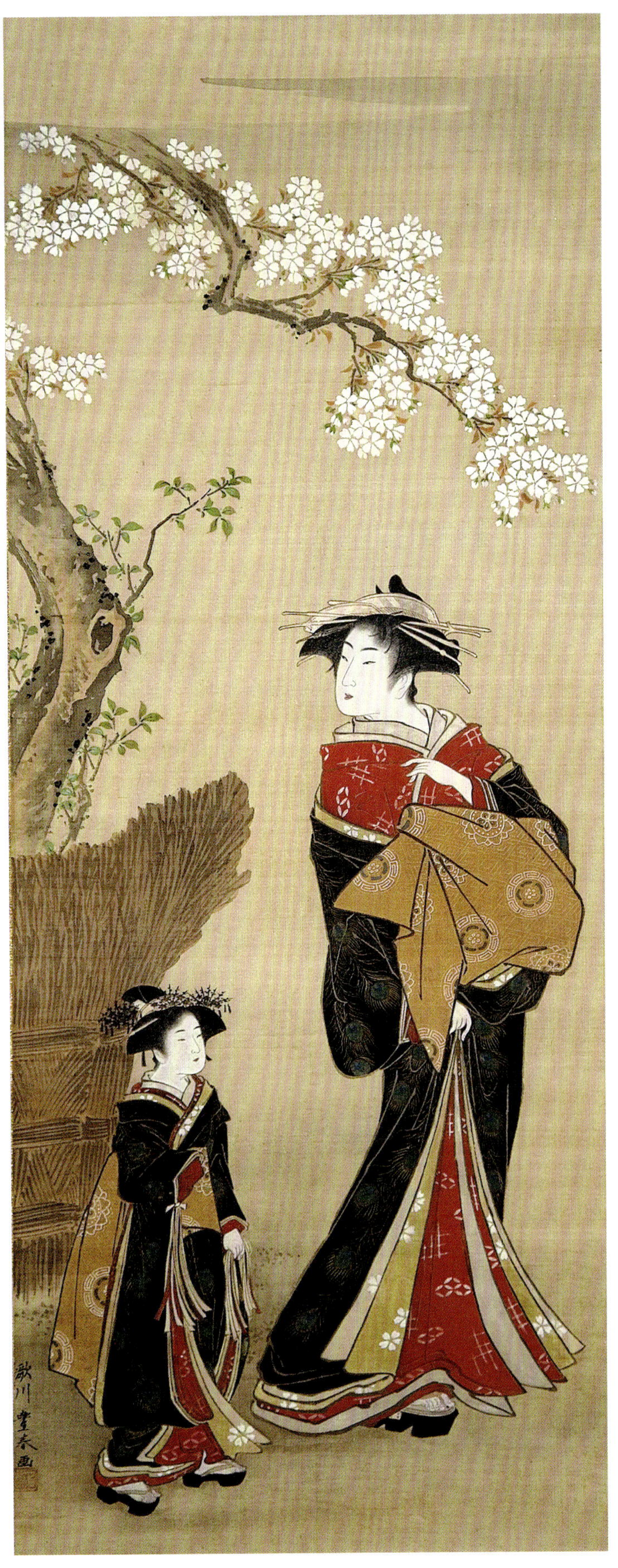

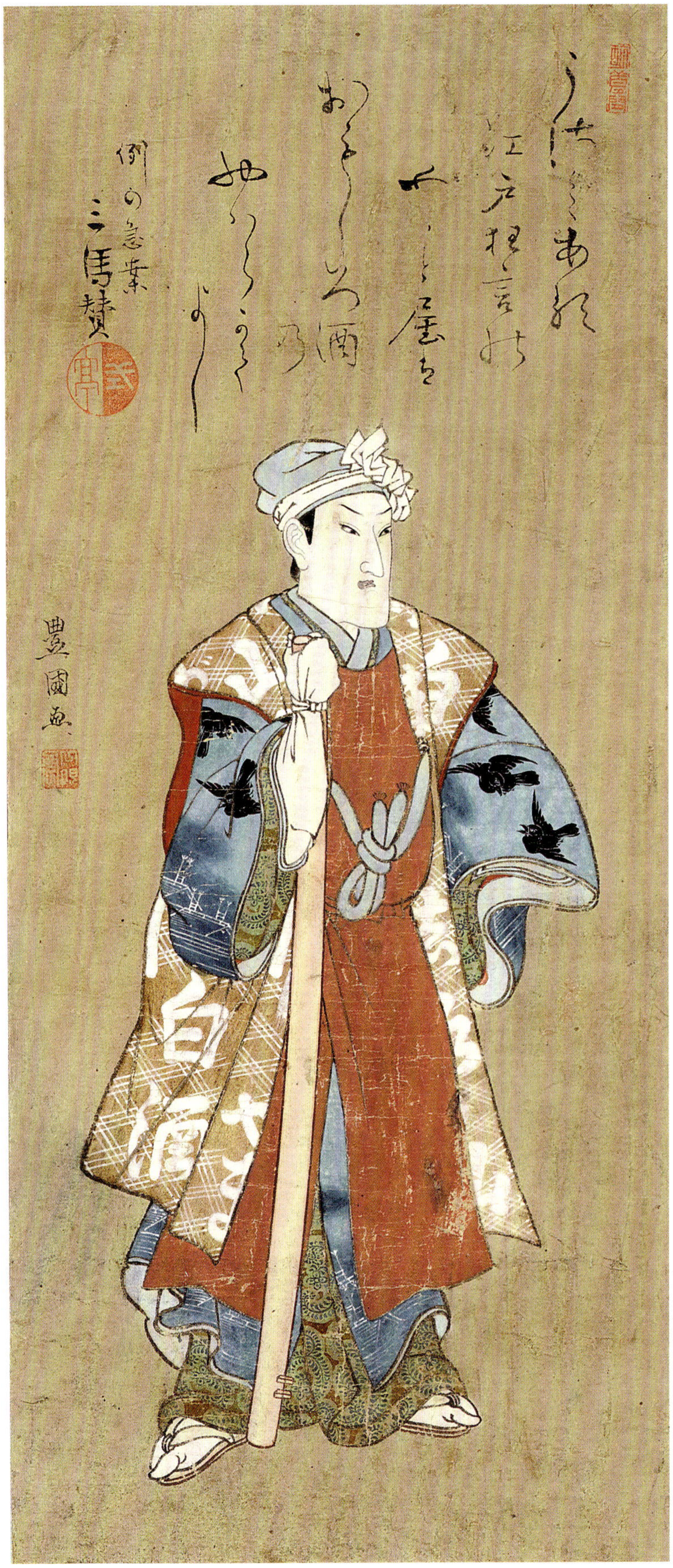

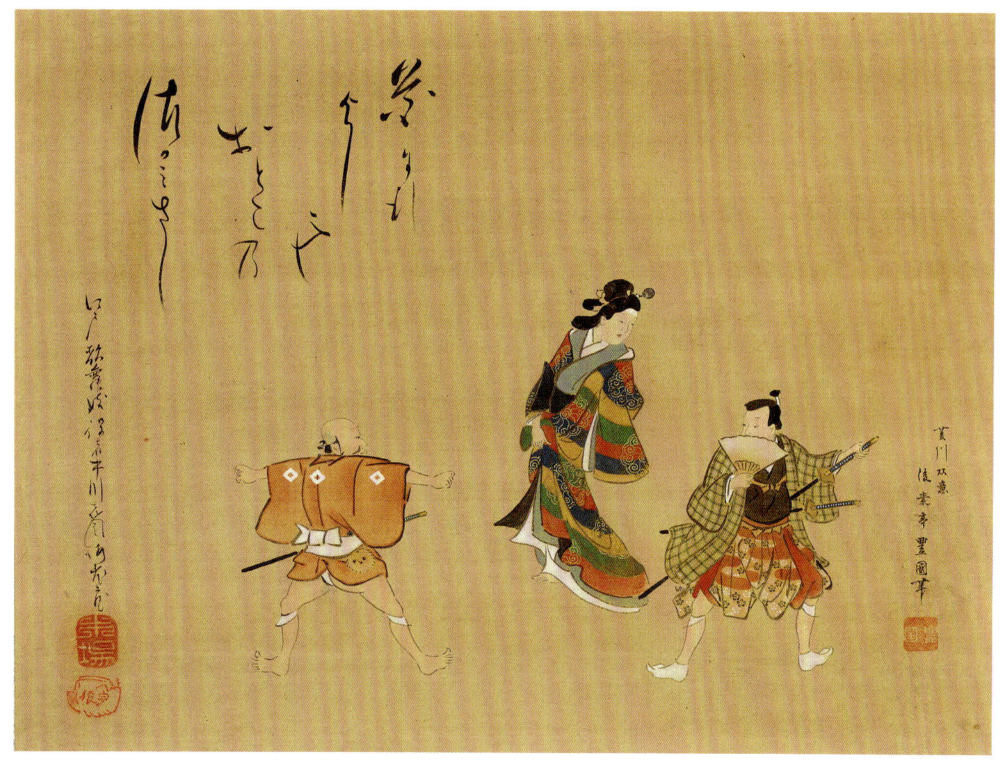

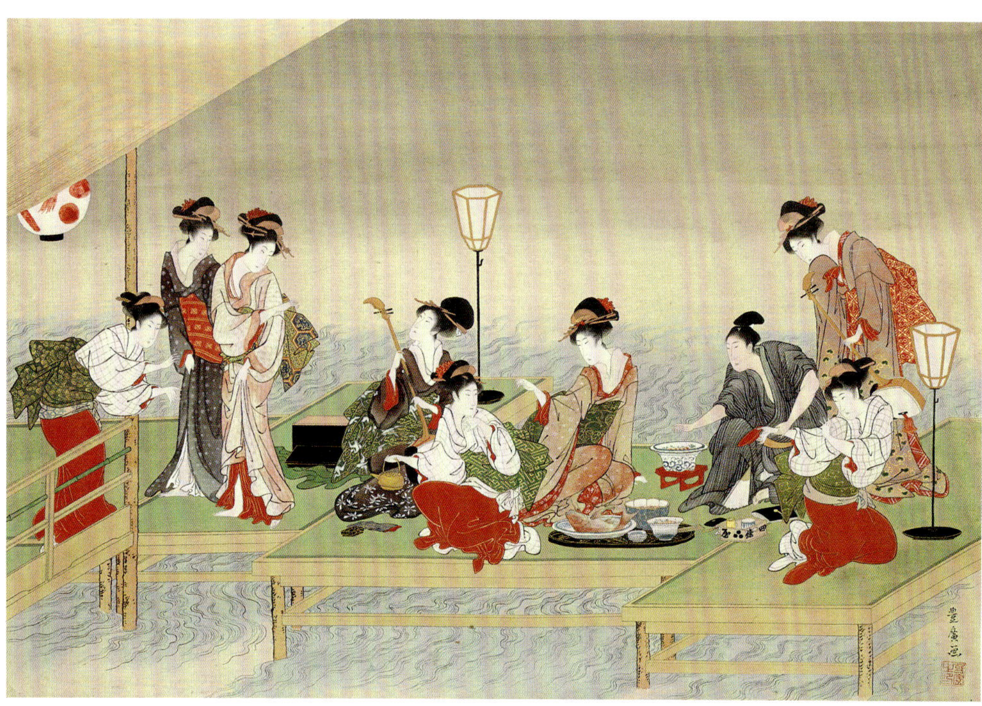

Utagawa Toyokuni II
(歌川豊国二代; 1777–1835)

287. Fuwa Banzaemon (不破伴左衛門)

Edo period, 19th century
Hanging scroll; ink and color on silk
40.6 x 54.6 cm (16 x 21 1/2 in.)
Text, signatures, seals

Ex coll.: Frank E. Hart

Literature: Narazaki Muneshige 1969, no. 77.

Utagawa Toyohiro
(歌川豊広; 1773–1828)

288. Summer Party on the Bank of the Kamo River (鴨川)

Edo period, early 19th century
Hanging scroll; ink and color on silk
50 x 73.9 cm (19 5/8 x 29 1/8 in.)
Signature, seal

Literature: Young and Smith 1966, no. 62; Murase 1975, no. 94.

Utagawa Toyohiro
(歌川豊広; 1773–1828)

289. Woman and Child under a Cherry Tree

Edo period
Hanging scroll; ink and color on silk
88.5 x 28.3 cm (34 7/8 x 11 1/8 in.)
Signature, seal

Ex coll.: Frank E. Hart

Utagawa Hiroshige
(歌川広重; 1797–1858)

290. Wealthy Merchant

Edo period
Hanging scroll; ink, color, and gold on silk
78.5 x 28.8 cm (30 7/8 x 11 3/8 in.)
Text, signature, seal

Ex coll.: Frank E. Hart

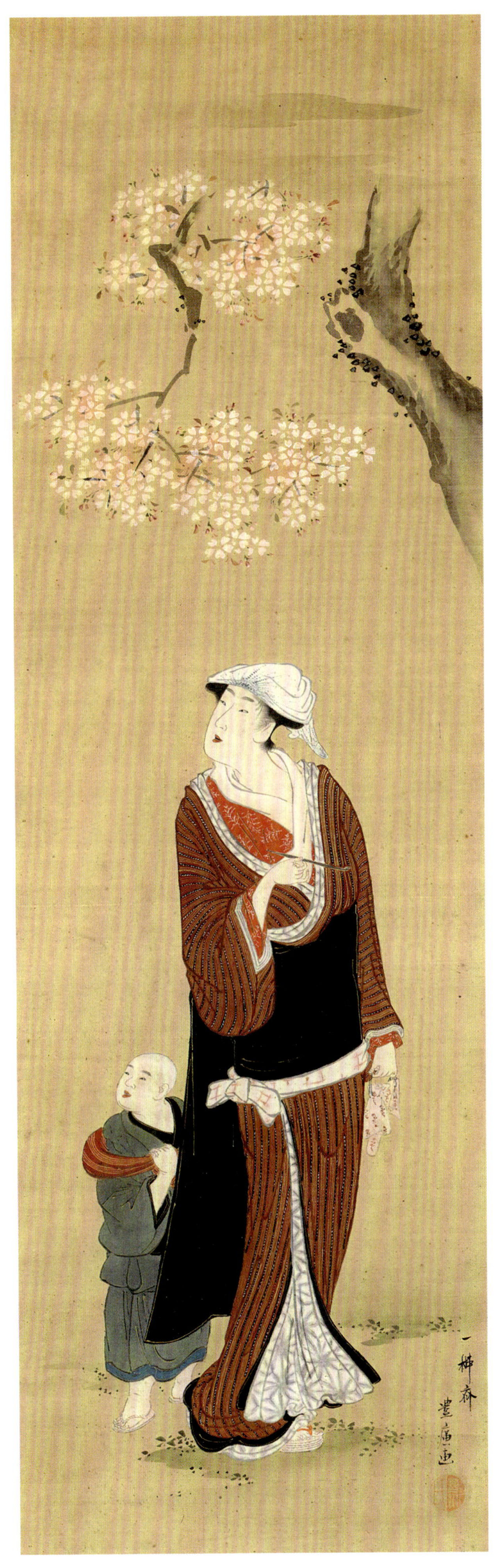

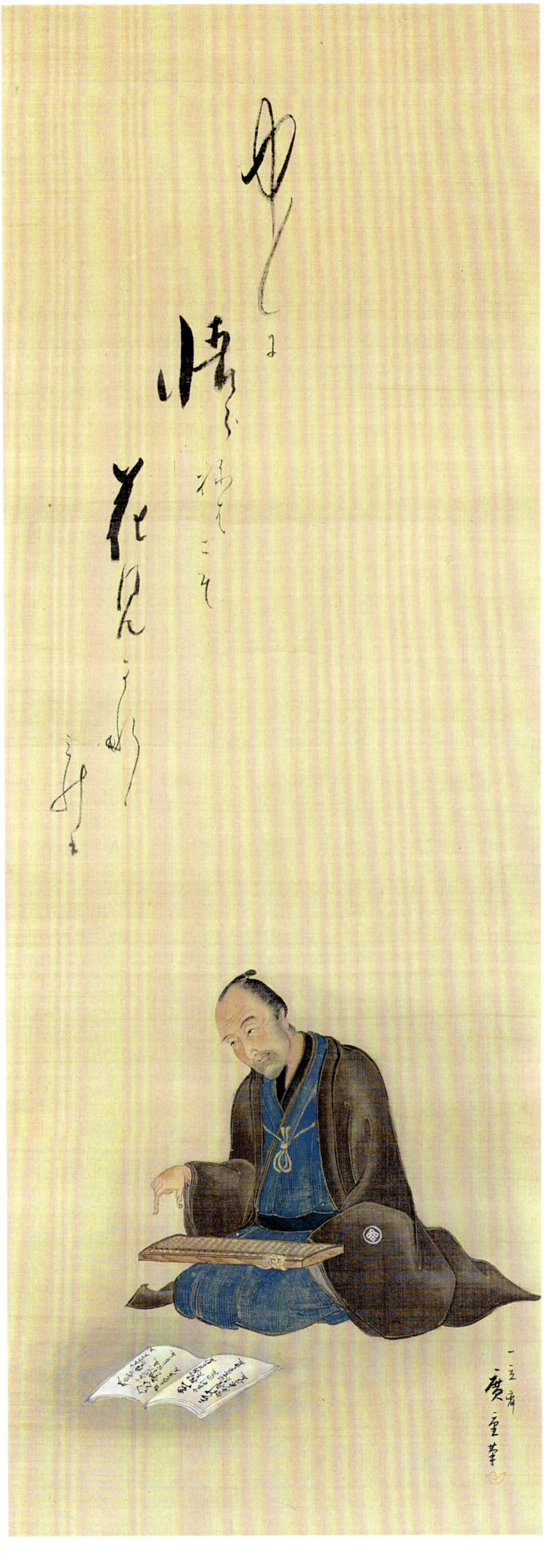

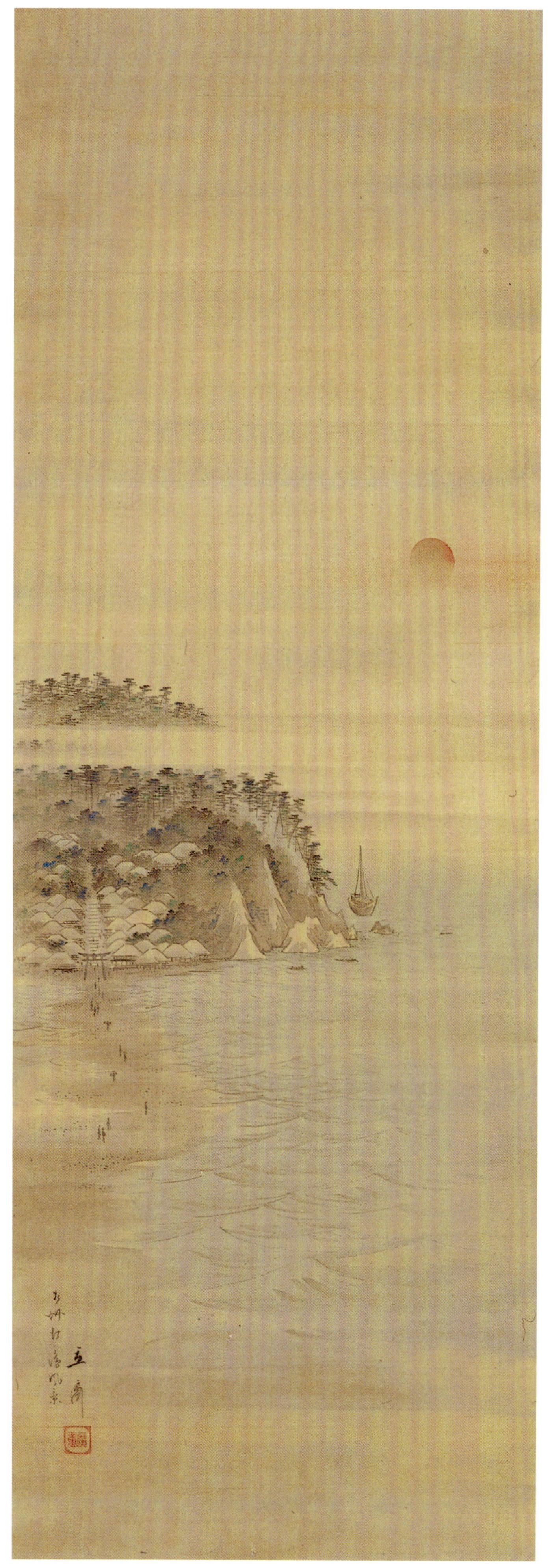

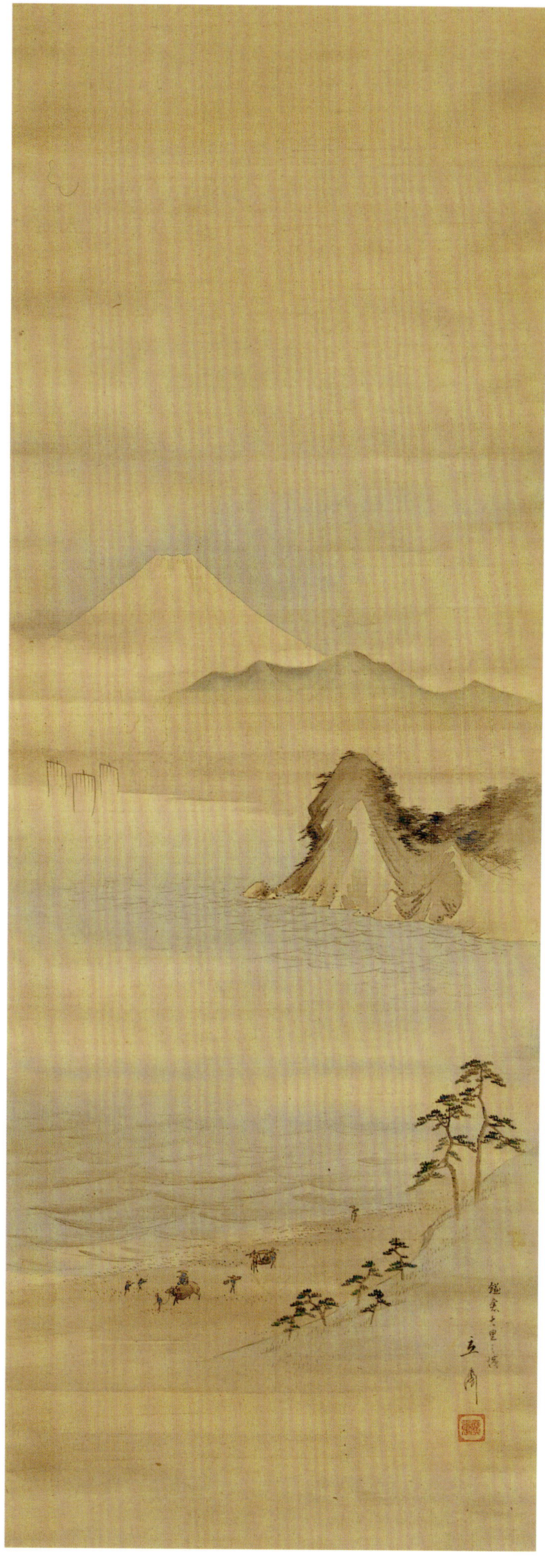

Utagawa Hiroshige
(歌川広重; 1797–1858)

291. Scenes of Shichirigahama (七里ケ浜) and Enoshima (江ノ島)

Edo period, ca. 1848–54
Diptych of hanging scrolls; ink and color on silk
Each scroll 92.8 x 31.1 cm (36½ x 12¼ in.)
Signatures, seals

Ex coll.: Frank E. Hart

Literature: L. Cunningham 1984, p. 44, figs. 12a, 12b, p. 45, no. 12; Tokyo National Museum 1985a, no. 66; Avitabile 1990, no. 84; Tsuji Nobuo et al. 2005, no. 86.

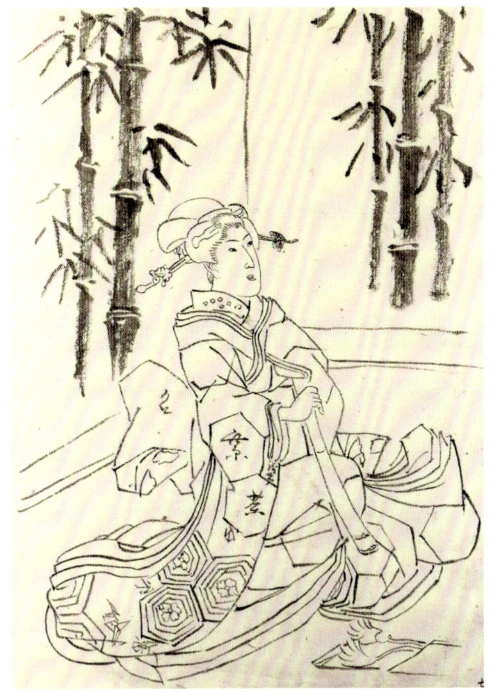

292

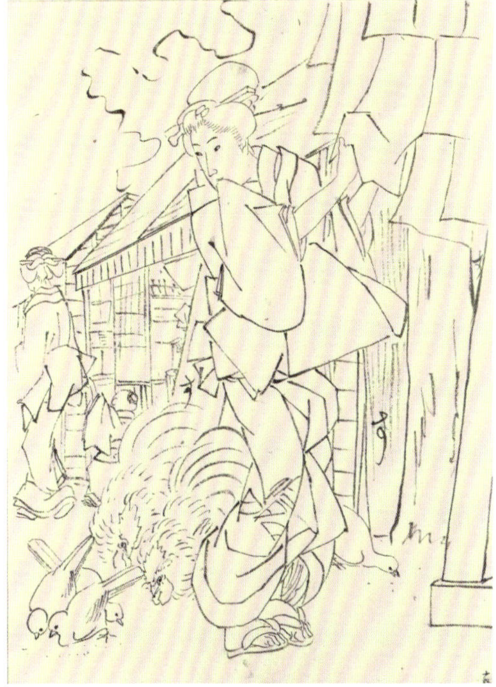

294

attributed to Utagawa Hiroshige
(歌川広重; 1797–1858)

292. Preparatory drawing for the print of a seated woman

Edo period, 19th century
Unmounted paper; ink on paper
33.8 x 24.2 cm (13¼ x 9½ in.)
Text

attributed to Utagawa Hiroshige
(歌川広重; 1797–1858)

293. Preparatory drawing for the print *Eight Views of the Sumida River* (隅田川八景)

Edo period, 19th century
Unmounted paper; ink on paper
33.1 x 24.4 cm (13 x 9⅝ in.)
Text

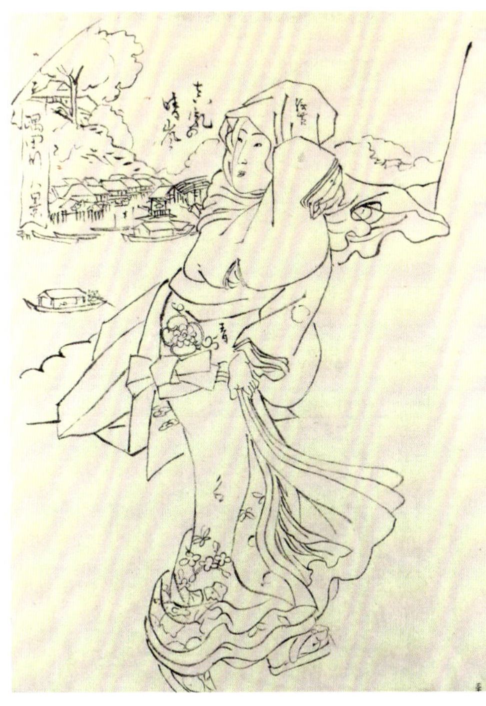

293

295

attributed to Utagawa Hiroshige
(歌川広重; 1797–1858)

294. Preparatory drawing for the print of a street scene

Edo period, 19th century
Unmounted paper; ink on paper
33.5 x 24.8 cm (13⅛ x 9¾ in.)
Text

attributed to Utagawa Hiroshige
(歌川広重; 1797–1858)

295. Preparatory drawing for the print of a woman arranging flowers

Edo period, 19th century
Unmounted paper; ink on paper
32.8 x 24.5 cm (12⅞ x 9⅝ in.)
Text

attributed to Katsushika Hokusai
(葛飾北斎; 1760–1849)

296. Dragon

Edo period, 19th century
Unmounted paper; ink on paper
40.6 x 66 cm (16 x 26 in.)

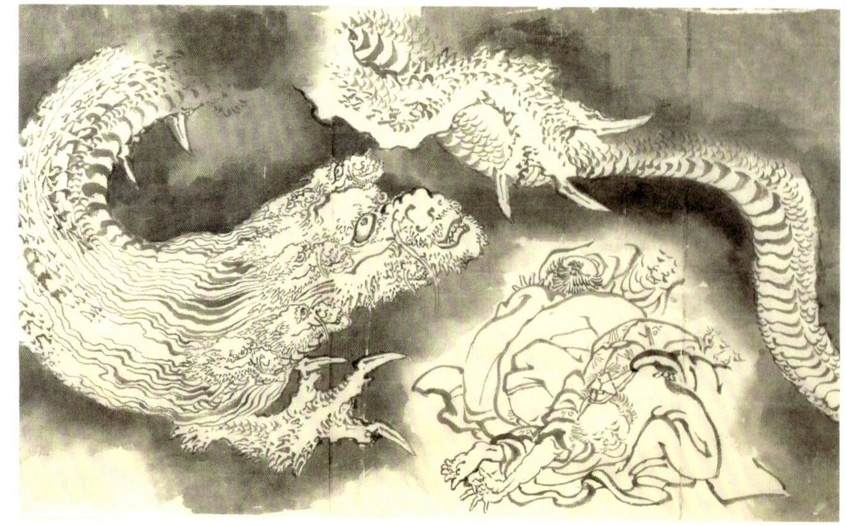

attributed to Katsushika Hokusai
(葛飾北斎; 1760–1849)

297. Tengu (天狗)

Edo period, 19th century
Unmounted paper; ink and color on paper
11.4 x 12.7 cm (4½ x 5 in.)

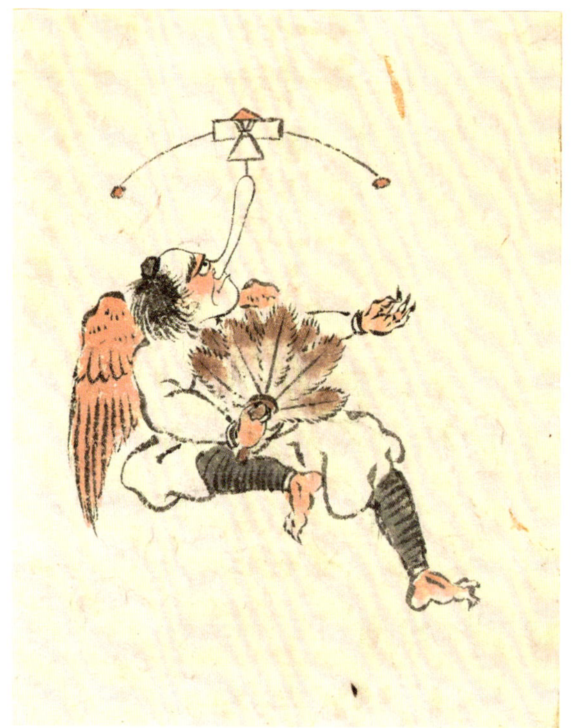

attributed to Katsushika Hokusai
(葛飾北斎; 1760–1849)

298. Three Men with a Tray

Edo period, 19th century
Unmounted paper; ink on paper
10.2 x 14 cm (4 x 5½ in.)
Text

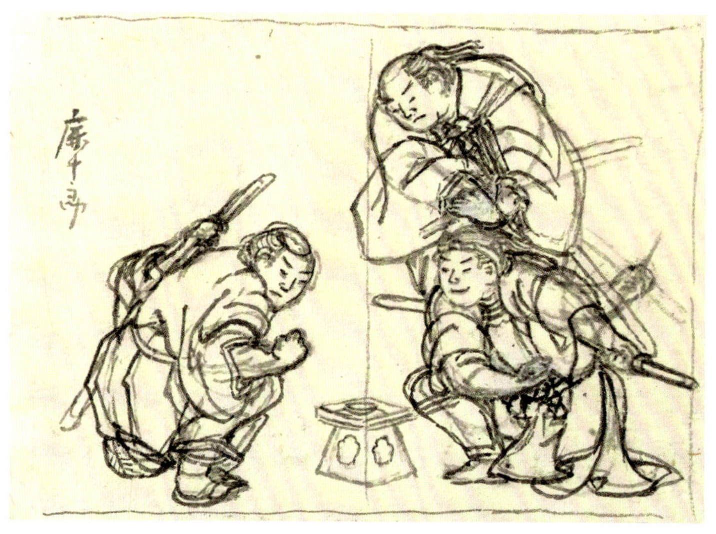

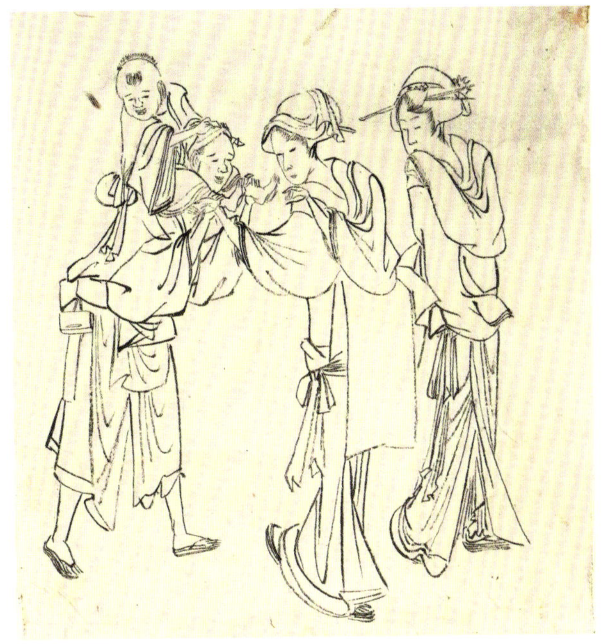

299

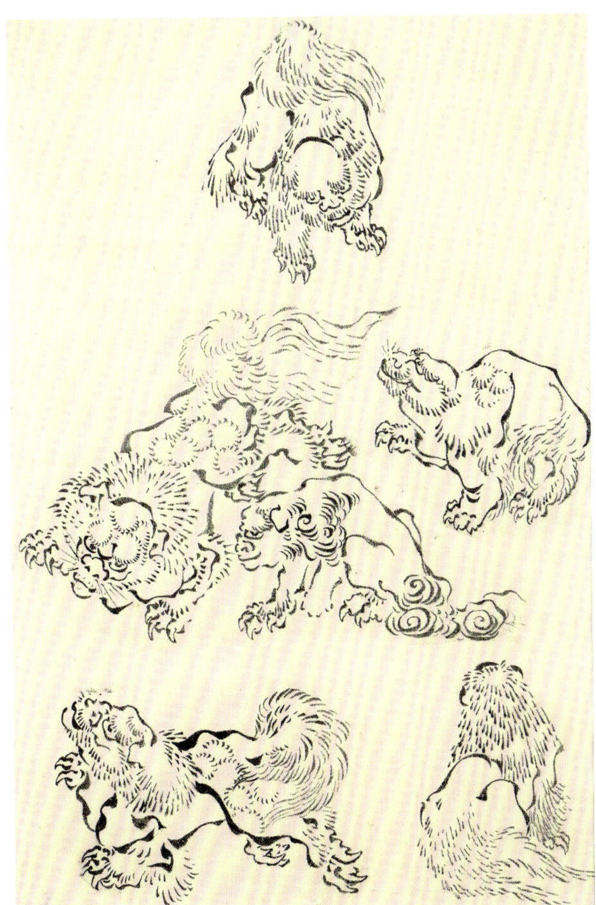

300

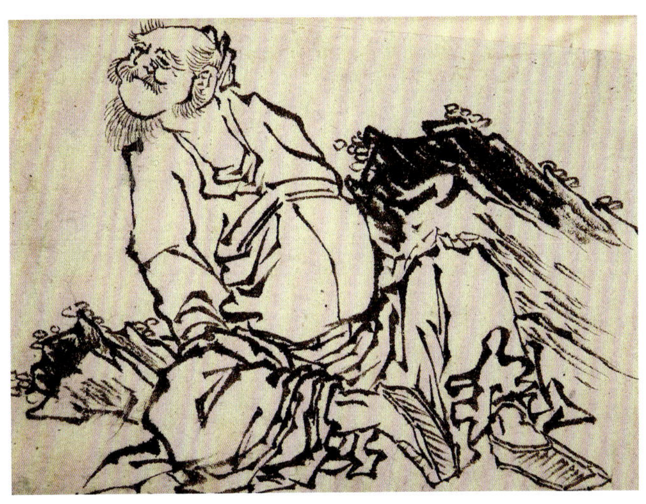

301

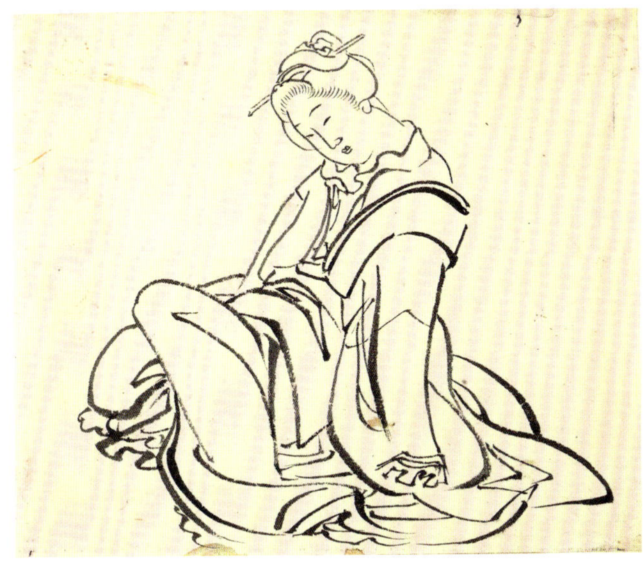

302

ATTRIBUTED TO
KATSUSHIKA HOKUSAI
(葛飾北斎; 1760–1849)

299. Man, Two Women, and Child

Edo period, 19th century
Unmounted paper; ink on paper
12.7 x 10.2 cm (5 x 4 in.)

ATTRIBUTED TO
KATSUSHIKA HOKUSAI
(葛飾北斎; 1760–1849)

300. Six Lions

Edo period, 19th century
Unmounted paper; ink on paper
29.2 x 44.5 cm (11½ x 17½ in.)

ATTRIBUTED TO
KATSUSHIKA HOKUSAI
(葛飾北斎; 1760–1849)

301. Chinese Warrior

Edo period, 19th century
Unmounted paper; ink on paper
12.7 x 17.2 cm (5 x 6¾ in.)

ATTRIBUTED TO
KATSUSHIKA HOKUSAI
(葛飾北斎; 1760–1849)

302. Seated Woman

Edo period, 19th century
Unmounted paper; ink on paper
15.2 x 17.8 cm (6 x 7 in.)

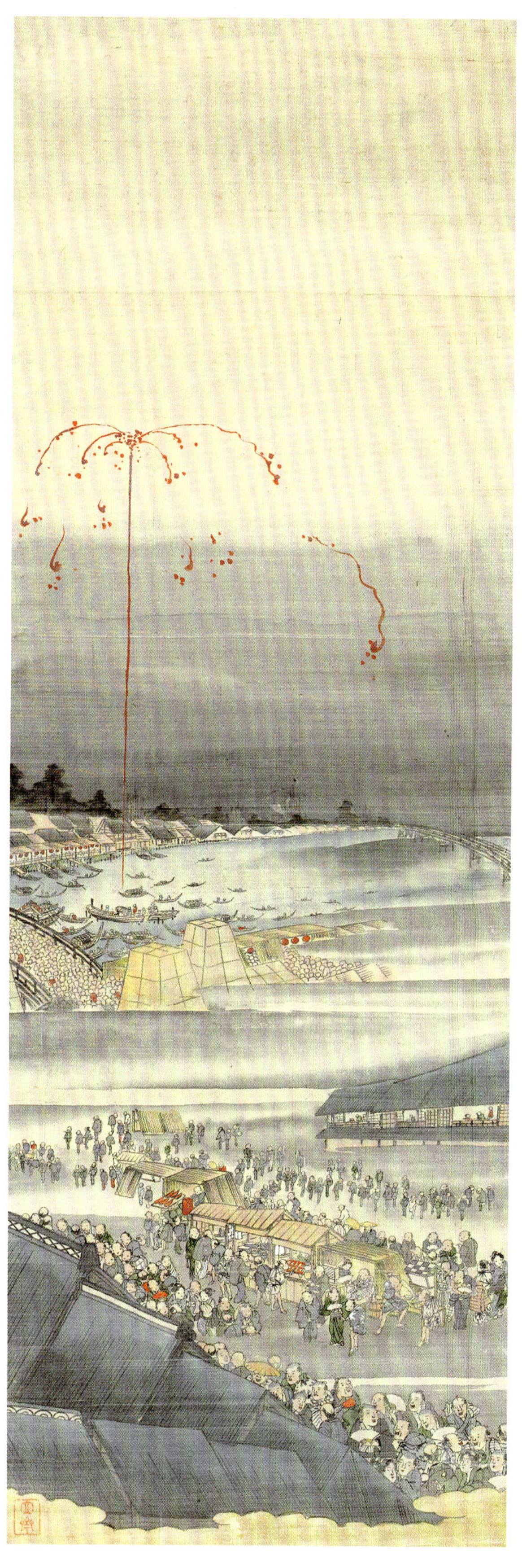

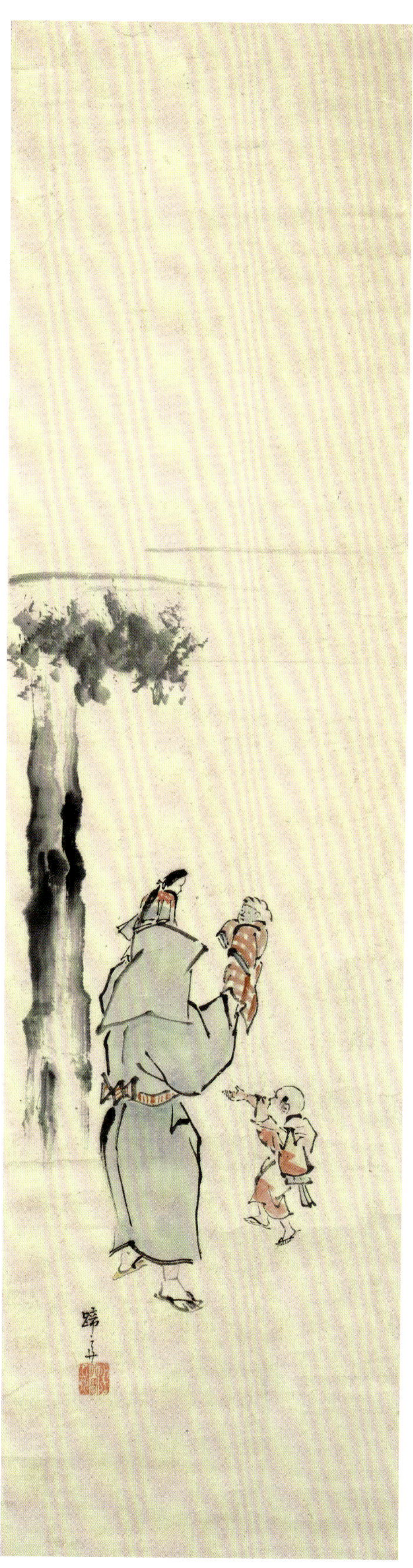

Utagawa Hiroshige II
(歌川広重二代; 1826–1869)

303. Fireworks at Ryōgoku (両国)

Edo period
Hanging scroll; ink and color on silk
98.4 x 33.8 cm (38 3/4 x 13 1/4 in.)
Seal

Teisai Hokuba
(蹄斎北馬; 1771–1844)

304. Puppeteer

Edo period, 19th century
Hanging scroll; ink and light color on paper
104.8 x 28.2 cm (41 1/4 x 11 1/8 in.)
Signature, seal

Ex coll.: Frank E. Hart

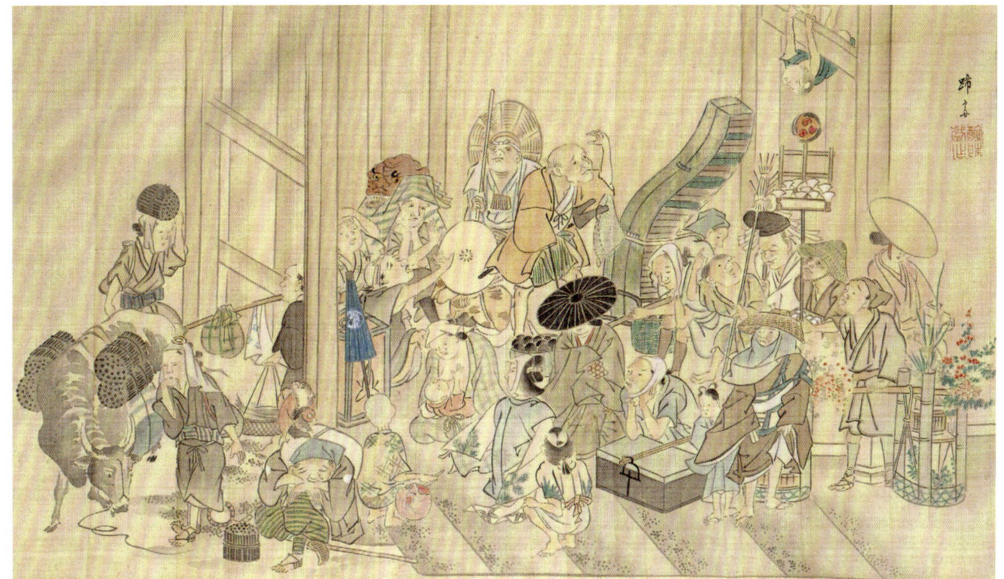

Teisai Hokuba
(蹄斎北馬; 1771–1844)

305. Taking Shelter from the Rain (雨宿り)

Edo period
Hanging scroll; ink and color on silk
39.4 x 69.3 cm (15 1/2 x 27 1/4 in.)
Signature, seal

Ex coll.: Frank E. Hart

306. Festivals of the Twelve Months

Edo period, early 18th century
Handscrolls; ink, color, and gold on paper
Scroll I (*detail, top*) 33.3 x 1129.5 cm
(13 1/8 in. x 37 ft. 5/8 in.)
Scroll II (*detail, bottom*) 33.3 x 1124.9 cm
(13 1/8 in. x 36 ft. 10 7/8 in.)

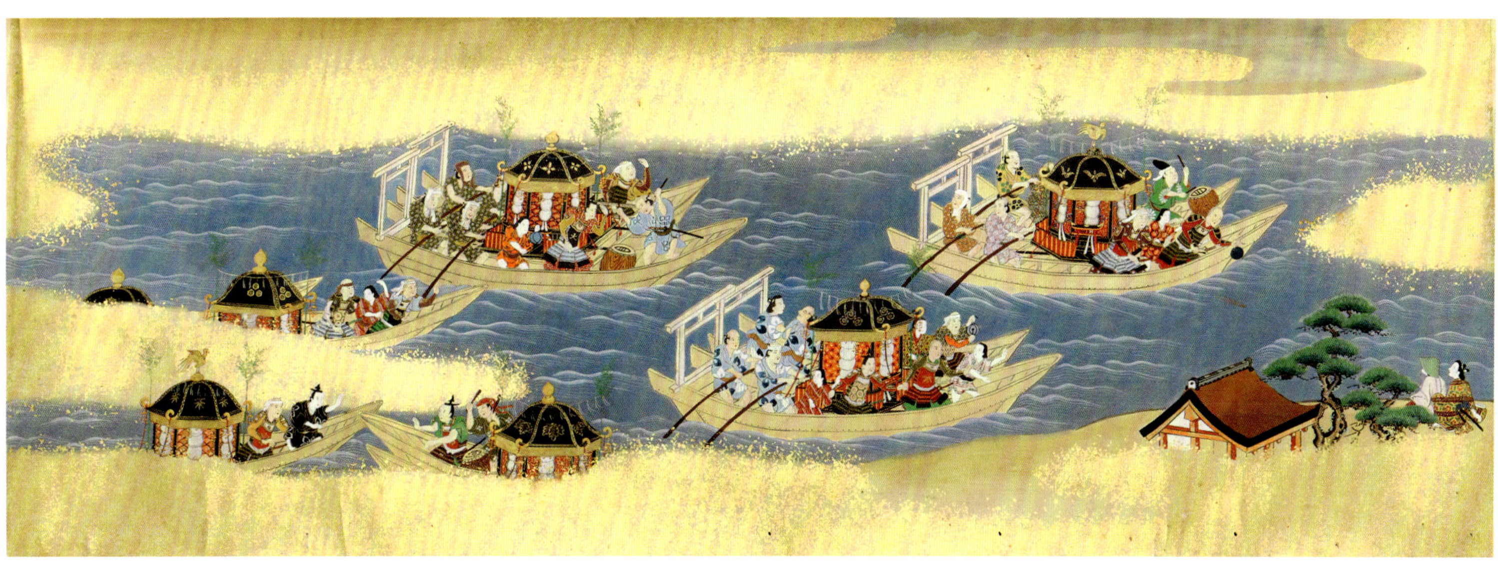

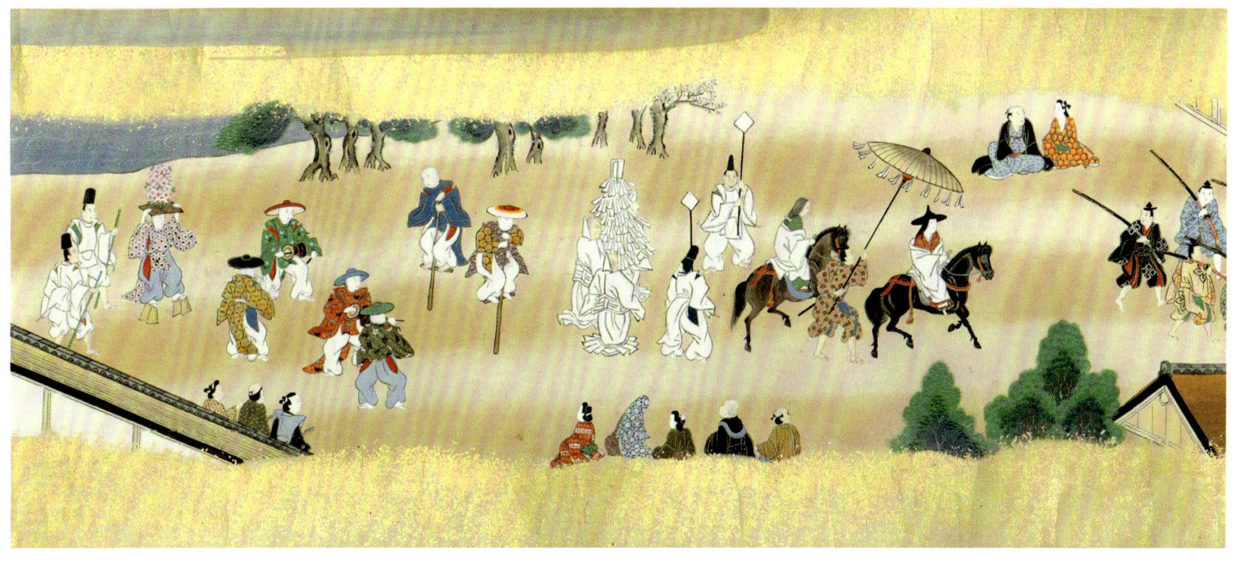

Chapter 7 Details

† *denotes illustrated items*

† 230. Scene from the Pleasure Quarters

Seals

Moro; *Nobu*

† 231. Woman in a Palanquin

Signature

Painted by the Yamato-e painter Hishikawa Moronobu from Fusa Province

Seals

Hishikawa; *Moronobu*

† 232. Young Couple

Signature

Painted by the Yamato-e painter Hishikawa Moronobu

Seals

Hishikawa; *Yamato*

† 233. Standing Beauty

Signature

Painted by Hishikawa Moronobu

Seals

Illegible; *Unsei*

† 236. Tōkaidō Zukan

Seals

[at end of scroll] *Hishikawa*; *Moronobu*

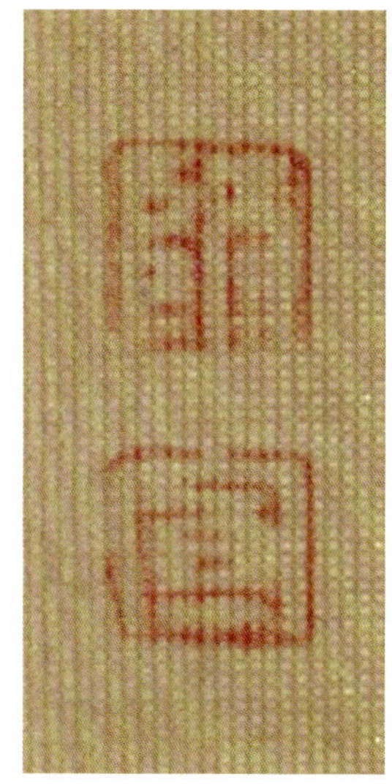

230

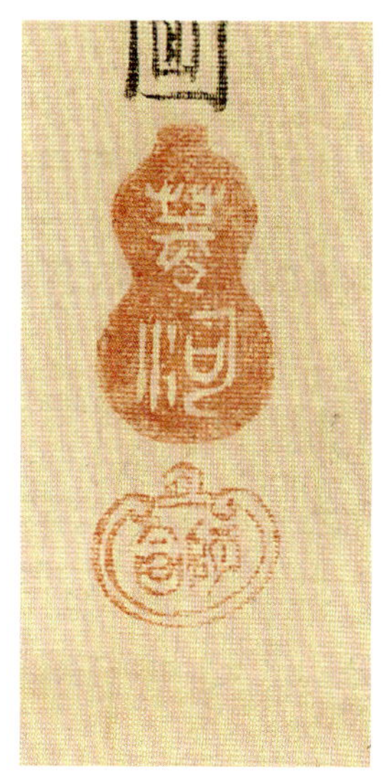

231

232

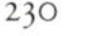

233

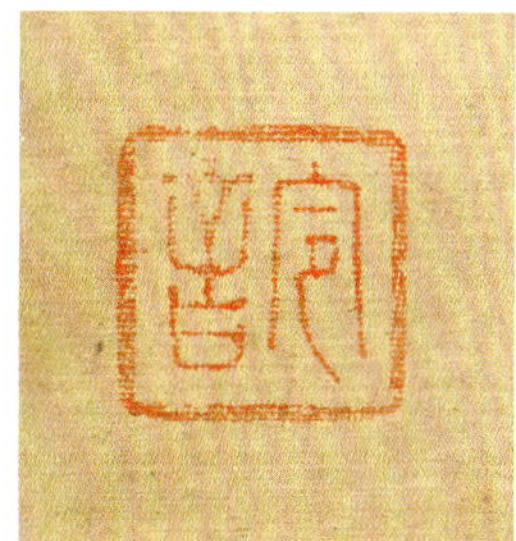

236

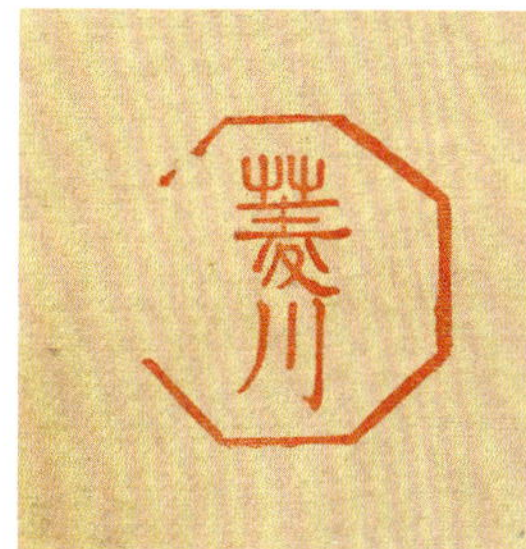

236

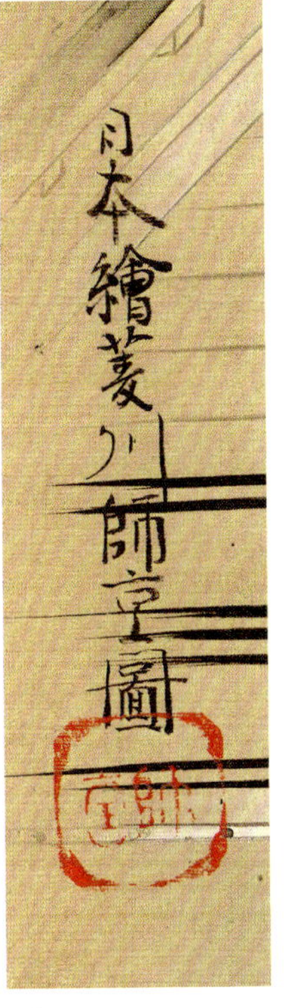

238

239

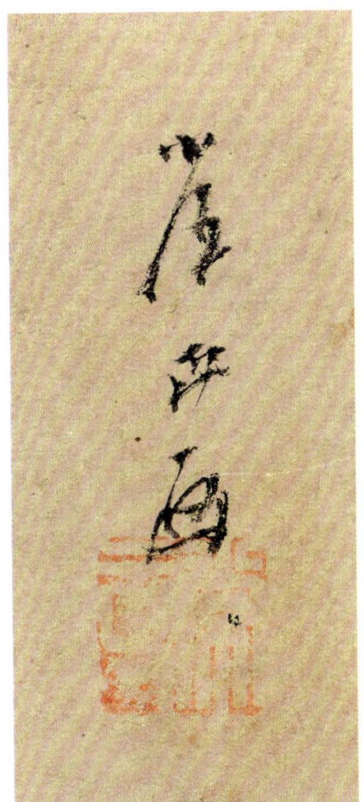
240

241

242

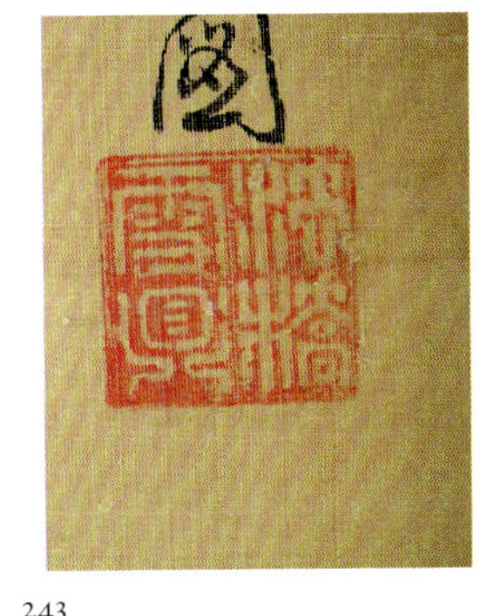
243

† 238. Young Woman on a Veranda

Signature

Painted by the Yamato-e painter Hishikawa Moroshige

Seal

Moroshige

† 239. Lady Ise by the River Bank

Text

Poem by Lady Ise from *Shin kokin wakashū*

[Poem 1049] *Must we pass through the world / without meeting even for a time / as short as the interval between / the nodes of the reeds at Naniwa Bay?*

Seal

Sukenobu

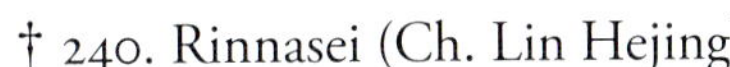

† 240. Rinnasei (Ch. Lin Hejing)

Signature

Painted by Tsunemasa

Seal

Tsunemasa

† 241. God Izanagi and Goddess Izanami

Signature

Painted by Nishikawa Ukyō Sukenobu

Seals

Nishikawashi; Sukenobu painted this

† 242. Scenes from the Pleasure Quarters

Seal

[at end of scroll] *Michinobu*

† 243. Courtesans and Their Attendants

Signatures

[on each panel] *Playfully painted by Hokkyō Tsukioka Settei*

Seals

[on each panel] *Hokkyō Settei*

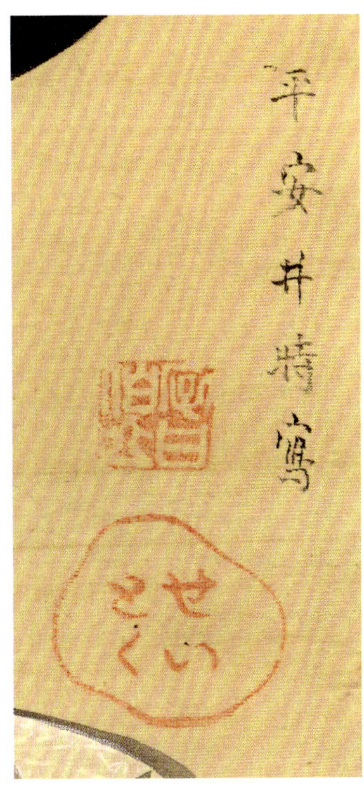

244

245

† 244. Beauty

Signature

Painted by Heian Seitoku

Seals

Aza iwaku Hakuritsu; Seitoku

† 245. Kiku Jidō

Signature

Hokkyō Tsukioka Sessai

Seals

Shūei; Gikōsai

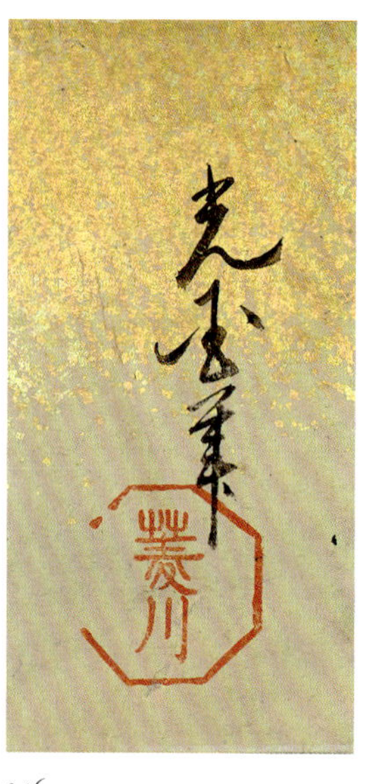

246

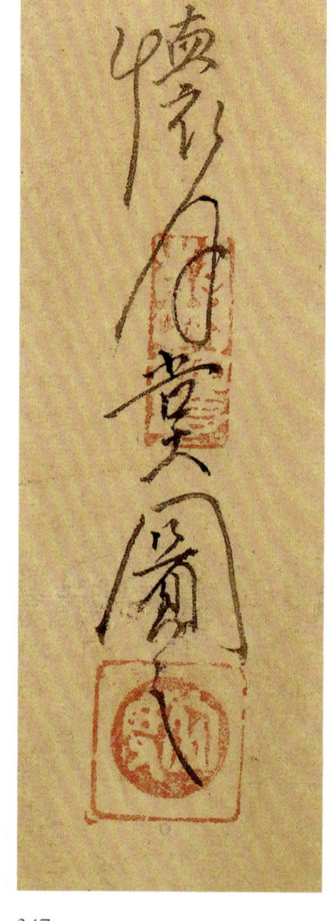

247

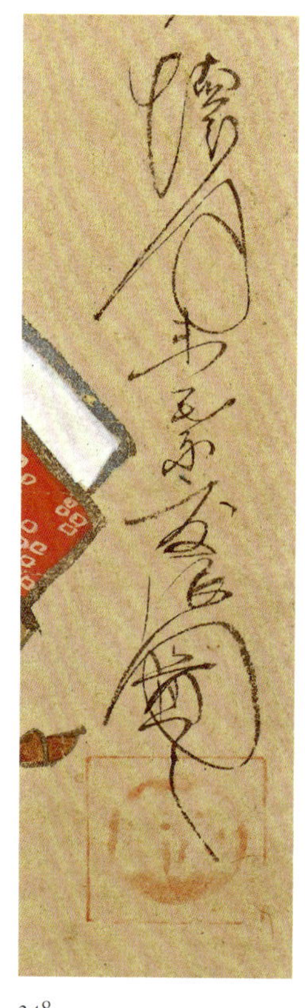

248

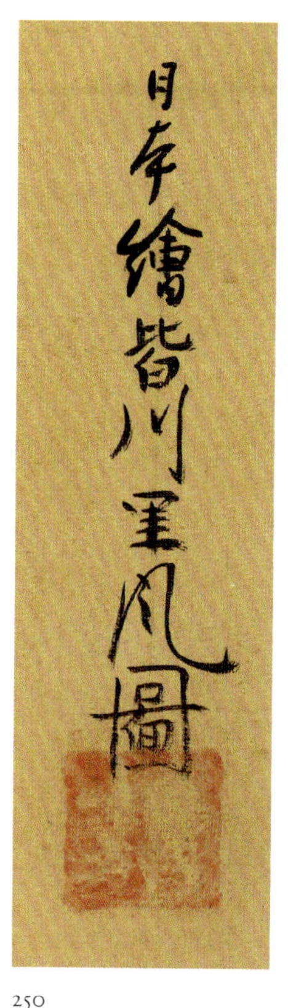

250

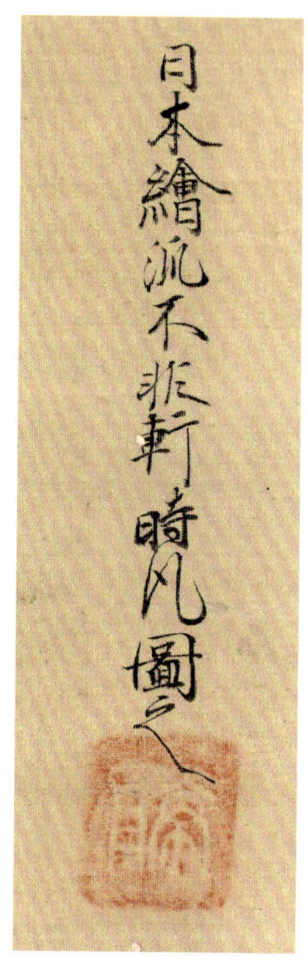

252

† 246. Scenes from the Four Seasons

Signature

[at end of scroll] *Painted by Mitsukuni*

Seal

[at end of scroll] *Hishikawa*

† 247. Standing Courtesan

Text

Poem by Sarumaru Dayū from *Kokin wakashū*

[Poem 215] *Treading through the autumn leaves in the deepest mountains, / I hear the belling of the lonely deer— / then it is that autumn is sad.*

Signature

Painted by Japan's playful painter Kaigetsudō

Seals

Kan'unshi [?]; *Ando*

† 248. Woman Writing a Letter

Signature

Painted by Doshin, descendant of Japan's playful painter Kaigetsudō

Seal

Ando

† 250. Standing Woman

Signature

Painted by the Yamato-e painter Minagawa Rifū

Seal

Illegible

† 251. Standing Court Lady

Text

As though this painted figure could speak, / its colors remind me of her fragrance.

Signature

Inscribed by Kamo Suketame [d. 1801]

Seals

Two illegible seals

† 252. Woman Reading by a Mosquito Net

Signature

Painted by the Yamato-e painter Fuhiken Tokikaze

Seal

Illegible

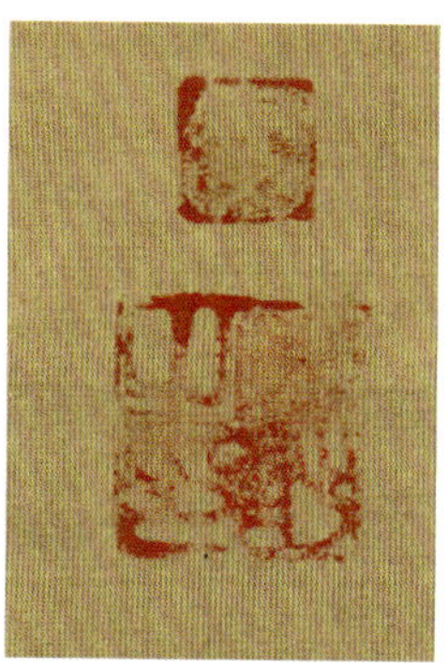

251

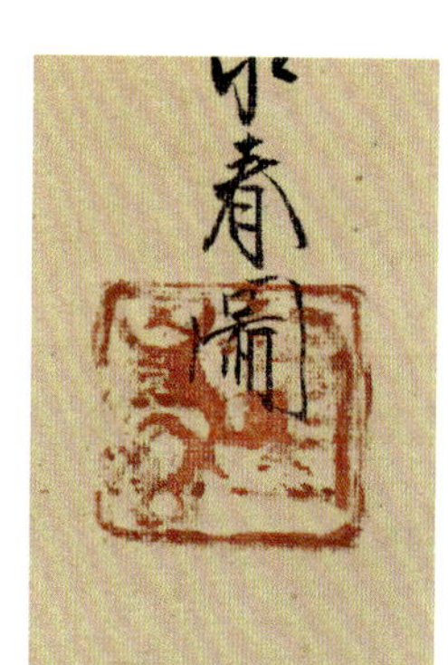

253

† 253. Standing Courtesan

Text

I did not say I retired for the night, / yet she loosens her sleeves. / The way she reads my mind / brings out my tears.

Signature

Painted by the Yamato-e painter Baiōken Eishun

Seal

Illegible

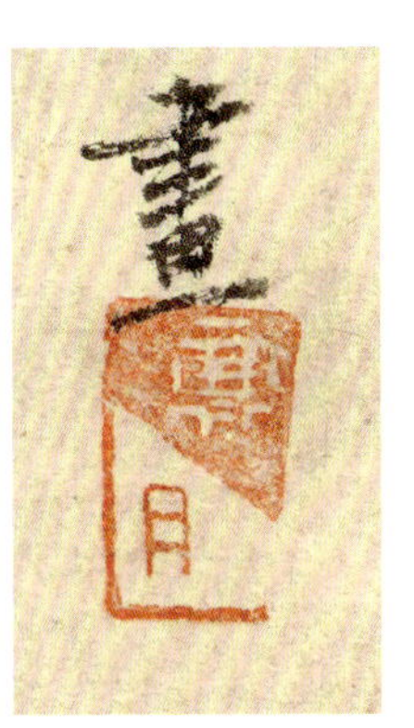
254

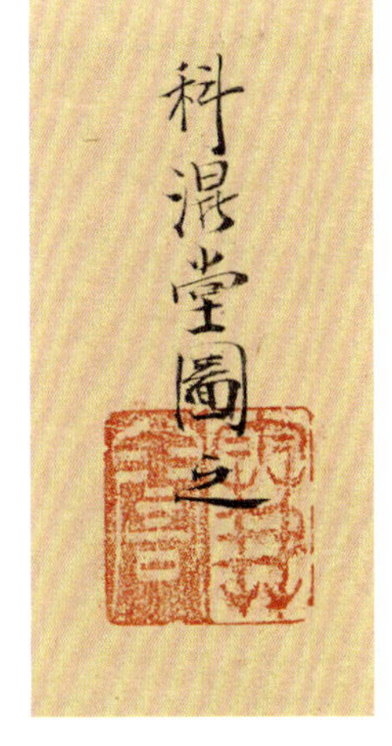
255

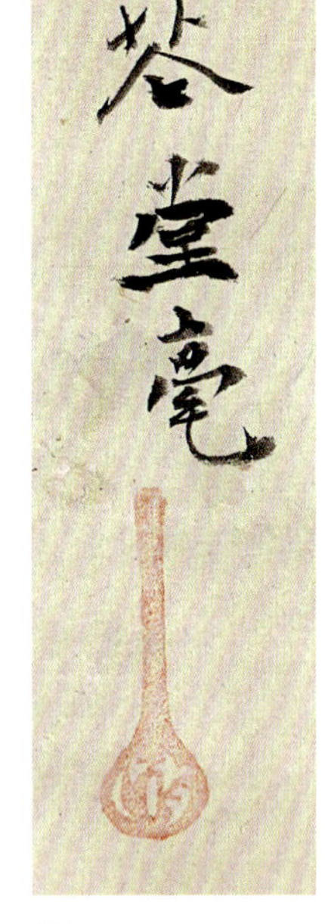
257

257

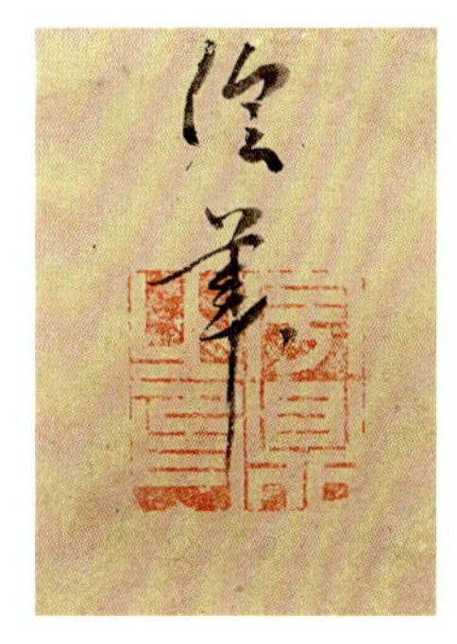
259

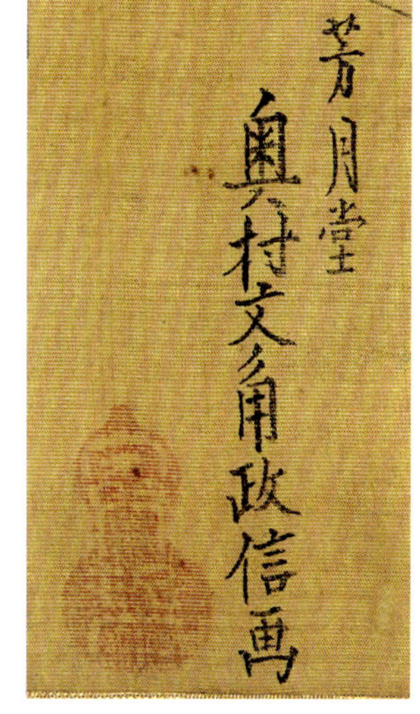
260

† 254. Itinerant Actors

Signature

Painted by Kengetsudō

Seal

Kengetsu

† 255. Courtesan and Attendant in Early Spring

Signature

Painted by Kakondō

Seal

Setsuan [?]

† 257. Standing Woman

Signature

Painted by Ryūkadō

Seals

Two illegible seals

† 259. Woman on a Veranda

Signature

Painted by Takizawa Shigenobu

Seal

Utei no in

† 260. The Kabuki Play *Kusazuribiki* from *Soga monogatari*

Signature

Painted by Hōgetsudō Okumura Bunkaku Masanobu

Seal

Illegible

† 261. Lady Ise

Signature

Painted by the Yamato-e painter Miyagawa Chōshun

† 262. Gyoran Kannon

Text

by Chōshun

Queen Mother of the West Loves Peaches of Longevity; / Seven Sages Enter the Bamboo Grove. // Deep in the bamboo grove / the coolness invites contemplation.

Signature

Painted by the Yamato-e painter Miyagawa Chōshun

Seal

Illegible

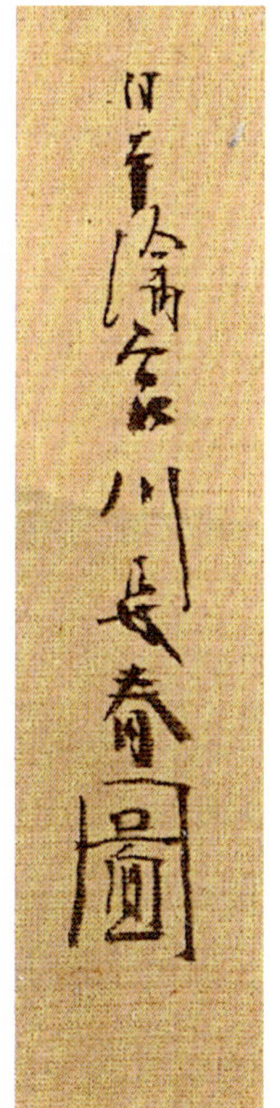
261

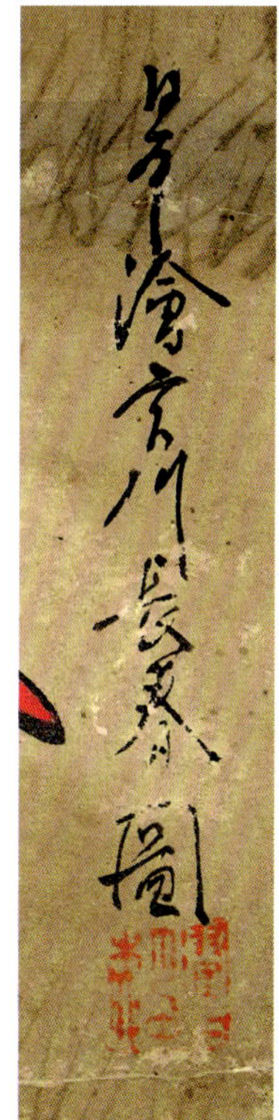
262

264. Woman with Battledore and Shuttlecock

Signature

Painted by Tori Kiyotomo

Seal

kaō

† 265. The Warrior Asahina Yoshihide with Courtesans

Signature

Painted by Torii Kiyoshige

Seal

Unryū

† 266. Setsubun

Signature

Miyagawa Isshōsai

Seal

Illegible

Text

by Kikusai

Dreams at Shimabara are songless, / like those riding the Ship of Treasures.

Signature

Miyagawa Isshōsai

Seal

Kikusai; kaō

† 267. The Brine Maiden Matsukaze

Signature

Painted by Nishimura Shigenobu

Seal

Gessōshu Shūka Kōmansai

† 268. Doll Festival

Seal

Illegible

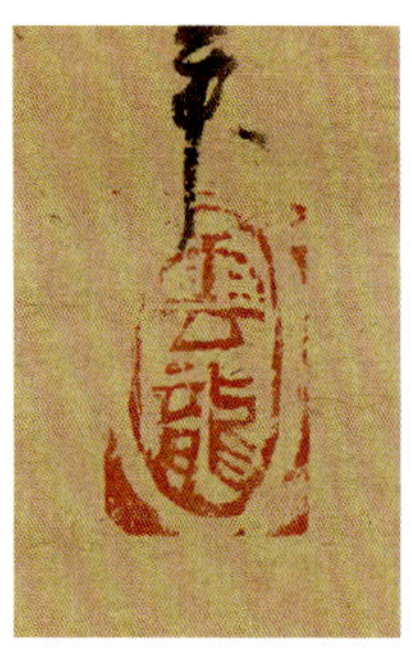

265

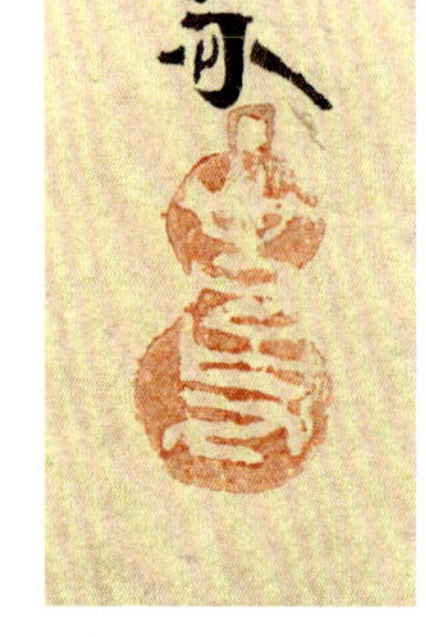

266

267

268

† 269. Young Woman with a Book

Text

by Toyonobu

Chapter 21 of Kairoku [Ch. Hailu] / *In Auspicious Signs by the author Sun, it says, "When the Yellow Emperor arrived at the shore of the Eastern Sea during his inspections and hunting tour, the White Beast appeared. It could take and commune with myriad creatures in the world. It bewildered people, which made it a pest at the time. It appeared with the rise of virtuous sage-kings. The White Beast, which fends off evil spirits, is an auspicious sign between heaven and earth." / In Chapter 29 is a picture of the White Beast fending off evil spirits.*

Signature

Painted by Toyonobu

Seals

Ishikawashi; Toyonobu

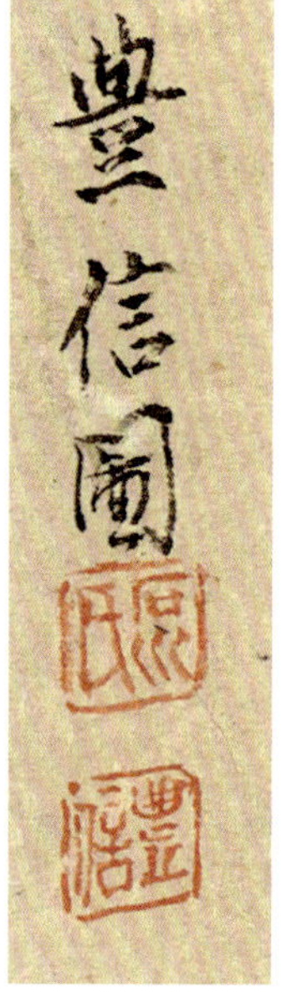

269

270

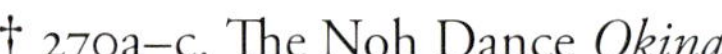

† 270a–c. The Noh Dance *Okina*

Signatures

[on each scroll] *Painted by Sekien at age 70*

Seals

[on each scroll] *Sekiso Tsukioka no in*

† 271. Courtesan and Two Attendants on New Year's Day

Seal

Koryūsai

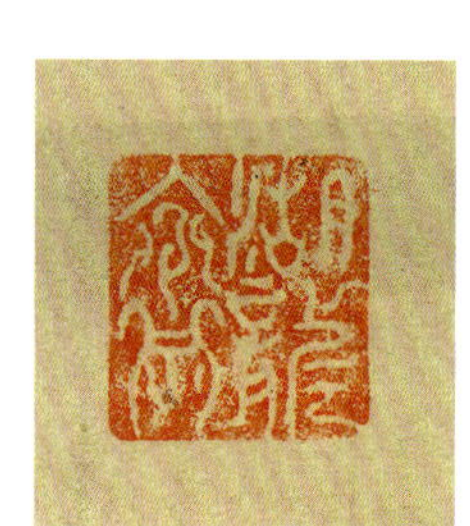

271

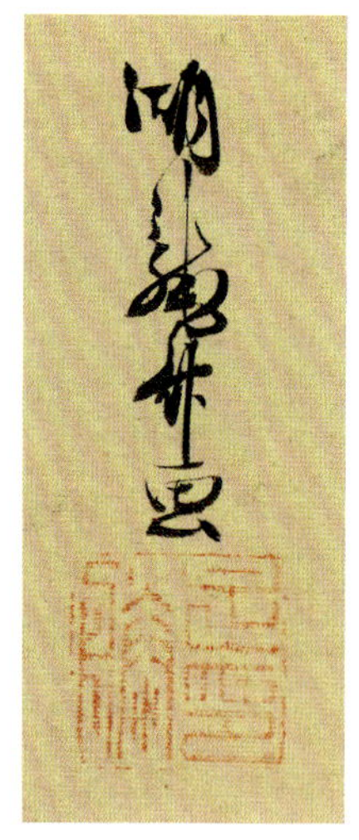

272

† 272. Courtesan-Dancer for the New Year

Signature

Painted by Koryūsai

Seal

Masakatsu in

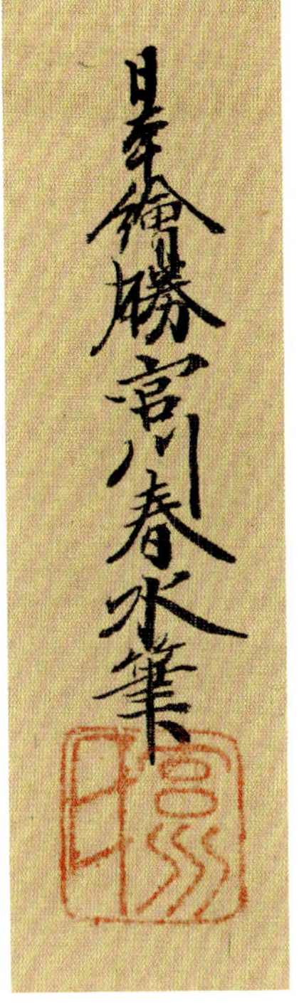

273

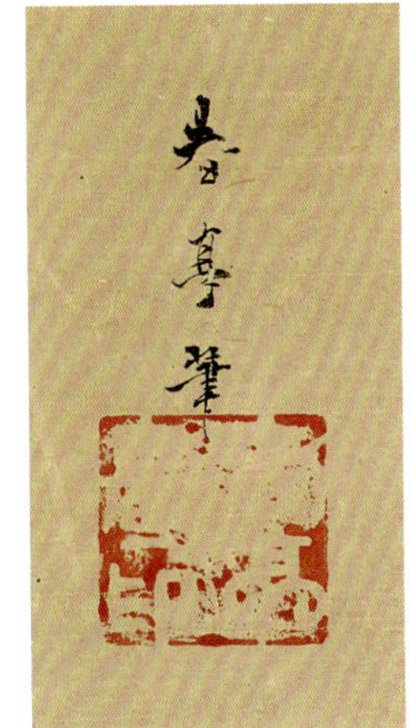

275

276

276

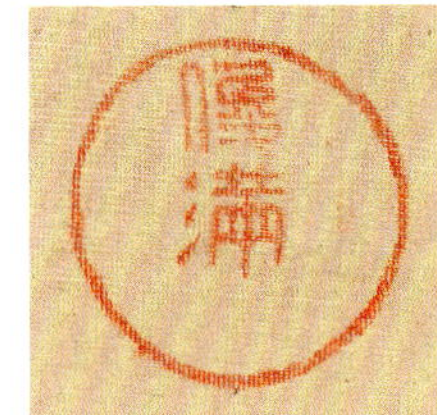

278

† 273. Young Woman with a Book

Signature

Painted by the Yamato-e painter Katsu Miyagawa Shunsui

Seal

Miyagawashi

274. Woman in a Black Kimono

Signature

Painted by Katsu Shunshō

Seal

kaō

† 275. Eguchi no Kimi

Signature

Painted by Shuntei

Seal

Shuntei gain [?]

† 276. Courtesan and Her Attendants under a Willow Tree

Signature

Painted by Unchō in the eleventh month of 1796

Seal

kaō

Text

by Santō Kyōden (1761–1816)

Anyone can break off the branch of a willow by the roadside or pick a flower from a fence. / Even Saigyō has not yet seen Yoshiwara in the season of flowers.

Signature

Inscribed by Santō Kyōden

Seal

[Not translated]

Text

by Takizawa Bakin (1767–1848)

The house of Yoshiwara is north of Kinryūzan; / the courtesan thinks often of Thousand-Armed Kannon. / She lies on three layers of quilts and touches the bodies of ten thousand men. / Yet lice never cling to the collars of her wealthy customers; / such is the disposition of the women of Yoshiwara.

Signature

Playfully inscribed by Kyokutei Bakin

Seal

Bakin

277. Sanbasō

Signature

Painted by Kitao Shigemasa

Seal

kaō

† 278. Cherry Blossoms with Poems

Text

by Ōta Nanpo (1749–1823)

Even a life that may be threatened by naison [intestinal damage] *or* jinkyo [venereal disease] *wishes to be saved, / at the time of cherry blossoms.*

Signature

Shokusanjin

Text

by Ishikawa Masamochi (1753–1830)

Immortals or goblins mistake / the branches of cherries at Yoshino / for banks of clouds.

Signature

Chikujuen

Text

by Sugawara Nagane (1768–1845)

All white flowers of the world / look like kuzu at Mount Yoshino.

Signature

Nagane

Text

by Kitagawa Kihei (1753–1829)

If the Ōmon of Yoshiwara could keep the wind from entering, / one thousand ryō *would not be spared / to pay for a flower there.*

Signature

Magao

Text

by Shunman

Please, lay monk, tie up the wind god / when the cherries at Yoshino are at their height.

Signature

Inscribed and painted by Shunman

Seal

Shunman

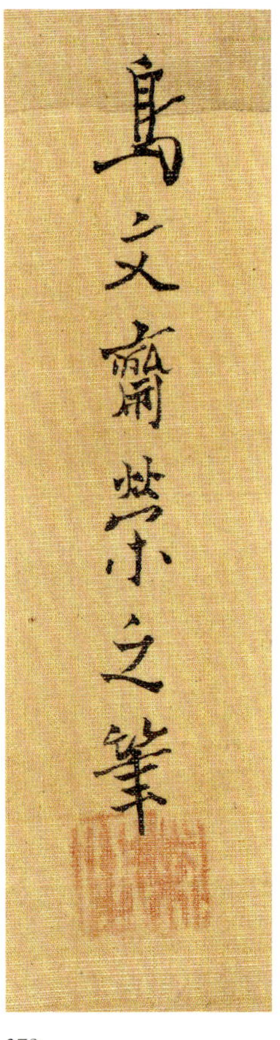

279

280

281

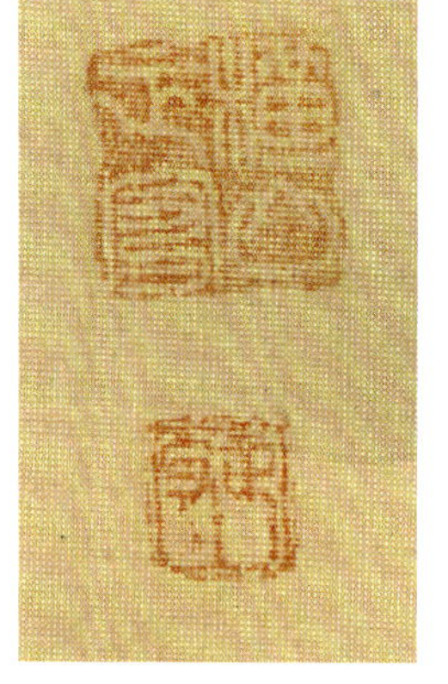
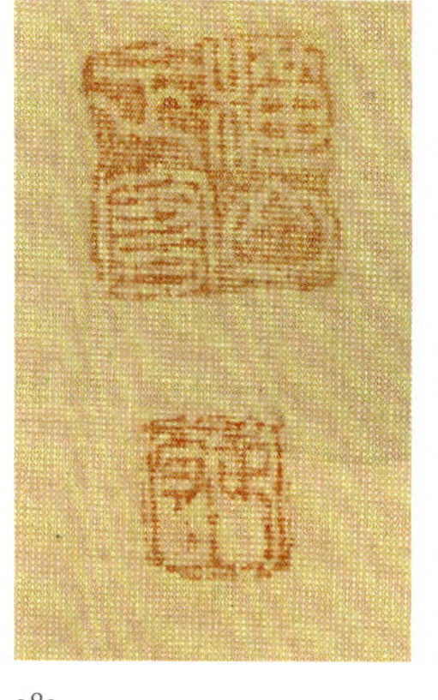

282

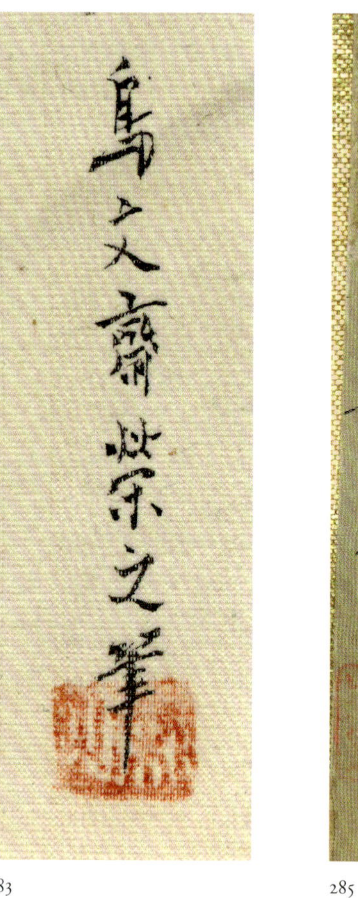

283

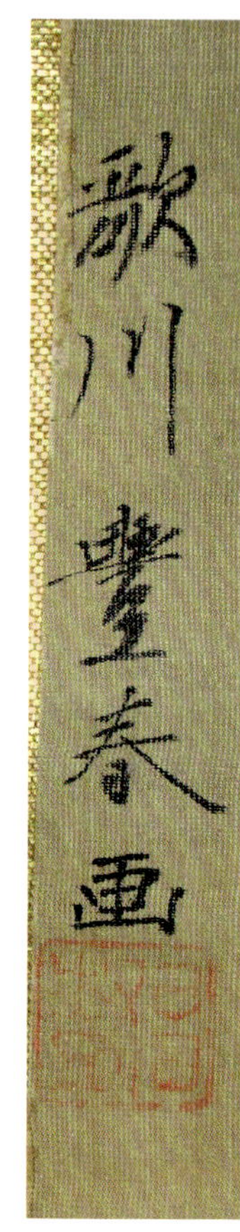

285

† 279a–c. Snow, Cherry Blossoms, and Moon (Yoshiwara in Three Seasons)

Signatures

[on each scroll] *Painted by Chōbunsai Eishi*

Seals

[on each scroll] *Eishi*

Text

by Ōta Nanpo (1749–1823)

[on right scroll] *Heavy snow is piled / on the lintel of the gate to the Mimeguri Shrine. / Yoshiwara is near, / but it seems distant in this snow.*

[on center scroll] *Beside the flowering cherries of Nakanochō, / not a single tree from the deep mountain valleys.*

[on left scroll] *On the evening tide, rowing the boat / with oars made of the katsura branch growing on the moon, / now I look at the Pine of Fate, / wishing for the best luck.*

Signatures

[on each scroll] *Shokusanjin*

† 280. Kanzan and Jittoku

Seal

Toyomaro

† 281. Courtesan and Her Attendants under a Cherry Tree

Signature

Painted by Chōbunsai Eishi

Seal

Eishi

† 282. Young Woman Enjoying the Cool Evening

Text

by Kaseki

The cool breeze comes in / through the collar of my dress / and it goes out from the sleeves.

Signature

Painted by Kaseki

Seals

Yokoyama Masahiro [?]; *Masahiro* [?]

† 283. Scenes of Pleasures at the Height of Spring

Signature

[at end of scroll] *Painted by Chōbunsai Eishi*

Seal

[at end of scroll] *Eishi*

† 285. Courtesan and Her Attendant under a Cherry Tree

Signature

Painted by Utagawa Toyoharu

Seal

Masaki (?)

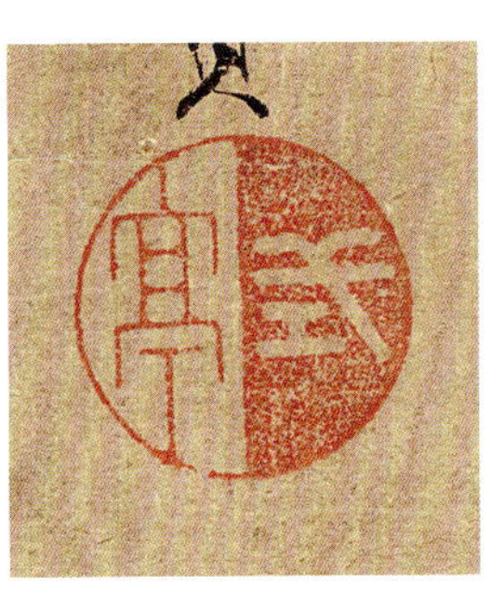

286

286

286

287

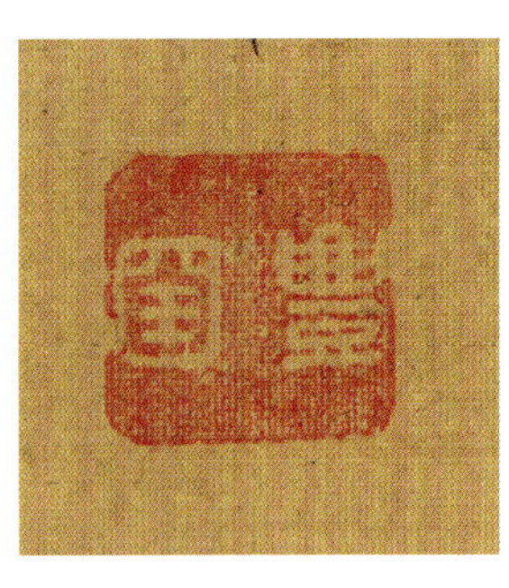

287

† 286. Bandō Mitsugorō II, as Shinbei in the Kabuki play *Sukeroku*

Signature

Painted by Toyokuni

Seal

Ichiyōsai

Text

by Shikitei Sanba (1776–1822)

The accomplished Yamatoya [Mitsugorō] of Edo theater / performs like a gentle and savory white wine.

Signature

Composed and inscribed as usual in haste by Sanba

Seals

Suimuken; Shikitei

† 287. Fuwa Banzaemon

Signature

Painted in the Hishikawa style by Kōsotei Toyokuni

Seal

Toyokuni

Text

by Ichikawa Ebizō (1791–1859)

The young dude parades through the streets [of Yoshiwara], / while grabbing hold of a long sword.

Signature

Actor of Edo Kabuki Ichikawa Ebizō VII

Seals

Kiba; Byakuen

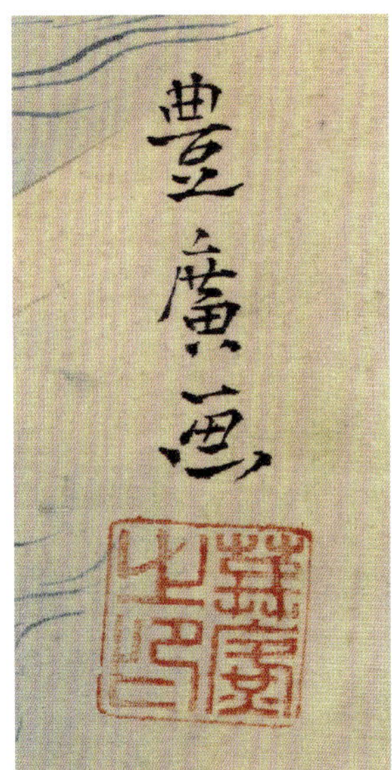

288

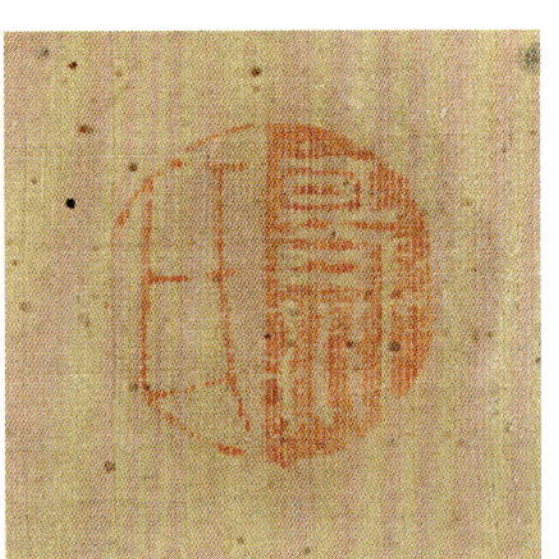

289

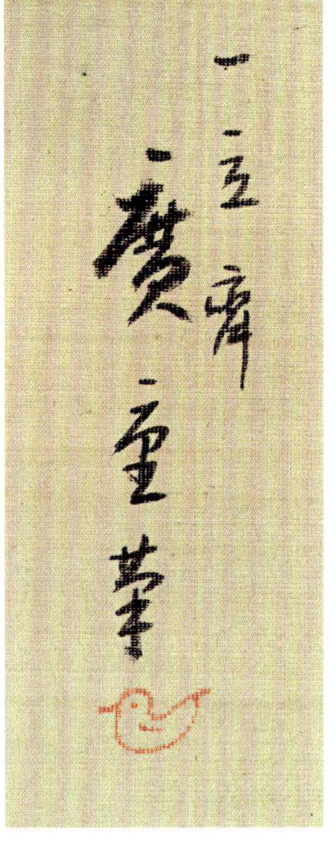

290

† 288. Summer Party on the Bank of the Kamo River

Signature

Painted by Toyohiro

Seal

Toyohiro no in

† 289. Woman and Child under a Cherry Tree

Signature

Painted by Ichiryūsai Toyohiro

Seal

Utagawashi

† 290. Wealthy Merchant

Text

by Sanshō (Ichikawa Danjūrō VII [?]; 1791–1859)

We go on visiting cherries / because enlightenment is / hard to come by.

Signature

Painted by Ichiryūsai Hiroshige

Seal

In the shape of a bird

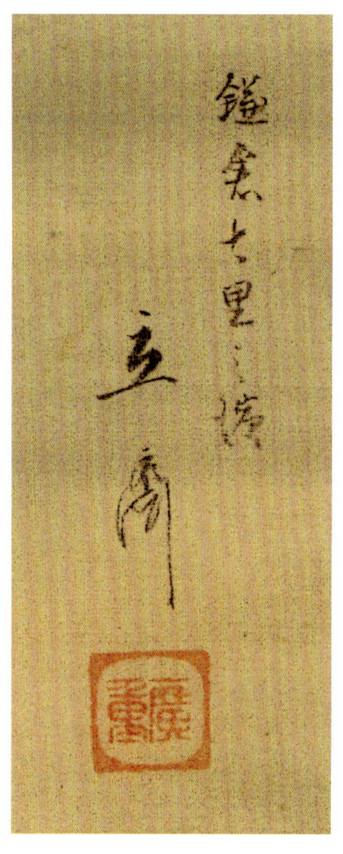

291

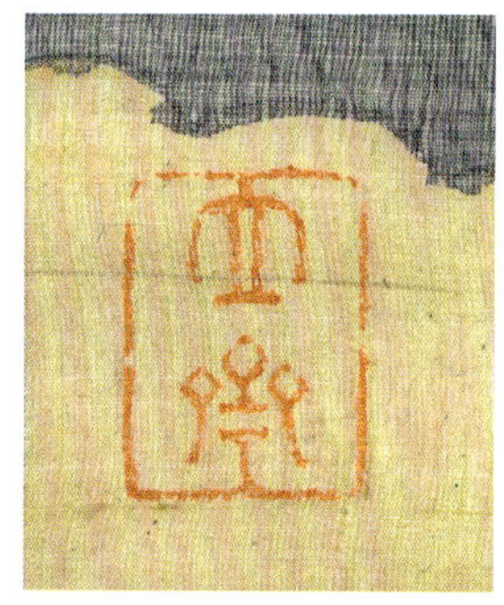

303

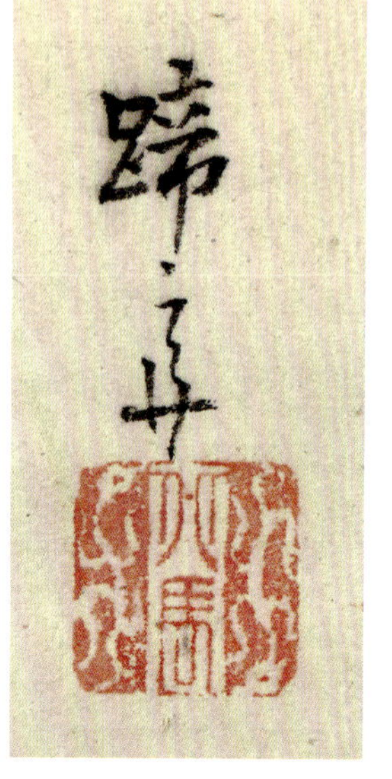

304

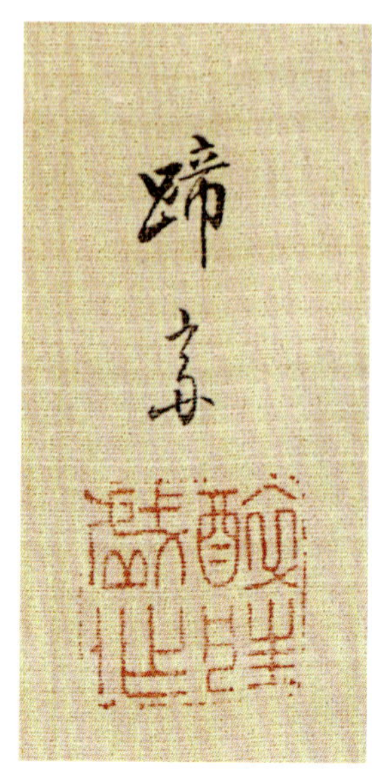

305

† 291. Scenes of Shichirigahama and Enoshima

Signatures

[on right scroll] *Kamakura Shichirigahama, Ryūsai*
[on left scroll] *Sōshū Enoshima fūkei, Ryūsai*

Seals

[on each scroll] *Hiroshige*

292. Preparatory drawing for the print of a seated woman

Text

[Color notations] *black, purple, brown*

293. Preparatory drawing for the print *Eight Views of the Sumida River*

Text

Eight Views of the Sumida River; *Spring Mist on a Clear Day at Matsuchi*; [color notations] *light yellow, blue, black*

294. Preparatory drawing for the print of a street scene

Text

[notations for objects] *Su* [blind], *Su*

295. Preparatory drawing for the print of a woman arranging flowers

Text

[color notations] *black, black, purple, blue*; *Kinoe*

298. Three Men with a Tray

Text

Renjū [?]

† 303. Fireworks at Ryōgoku

Seal

Ryūsai

† 304. Puppeteer

Signature

Teisai

Seal

Hokuba

† 305. Taking Shelter from the Rain

Signature

Teisai

Seal

Suikyō gisaku

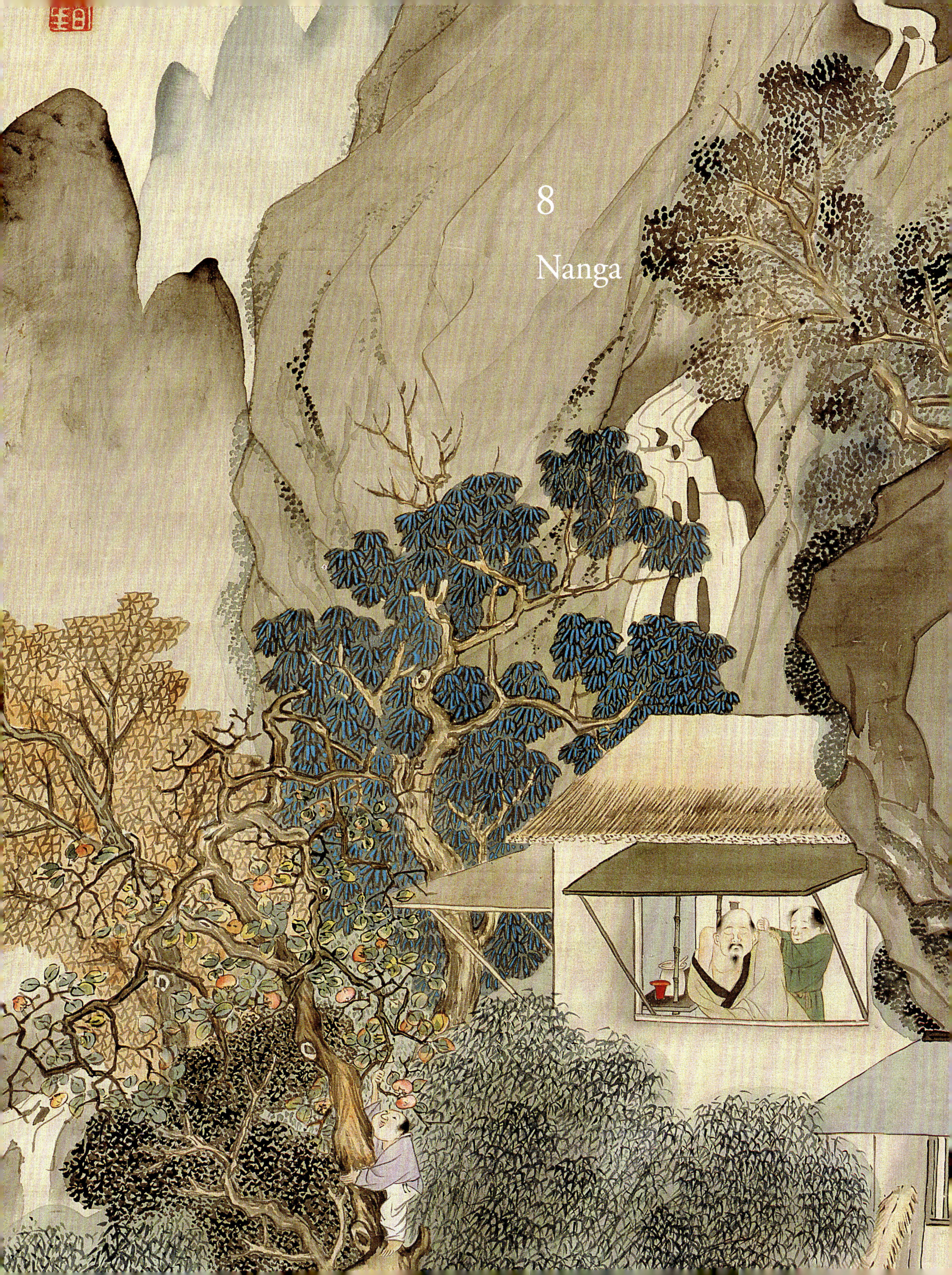

8

Nanga

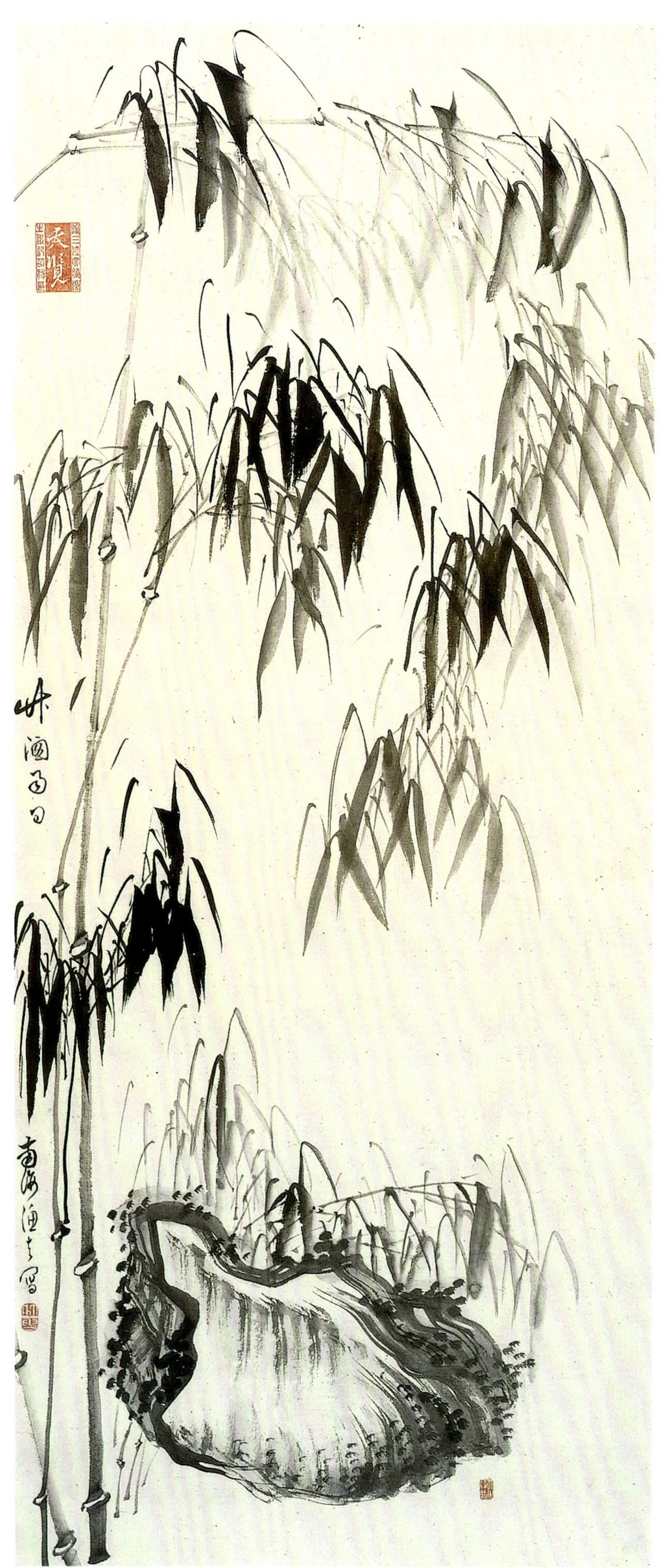

Gion Nankai
(祇園南海; 1677–1751)

307. Bamboo Window on a Rainy Day

Edo period, 18th century
Hanging scroll; ink on paper
131.8 x 58 cm ($51\frac{7}{8}$ x $22\frac{7}{8}$ in.)
Text, signature, seals
Literature: Murase 1975, no. 64; Murase 2000, no. 153.

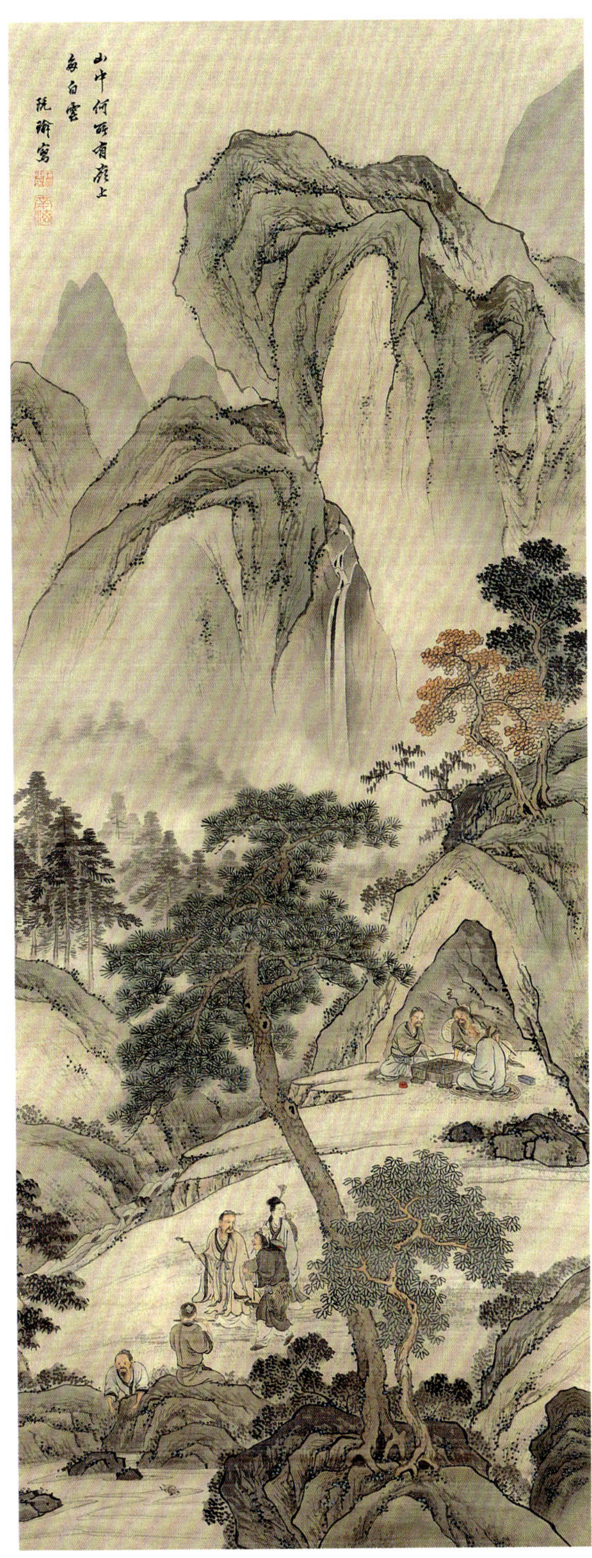

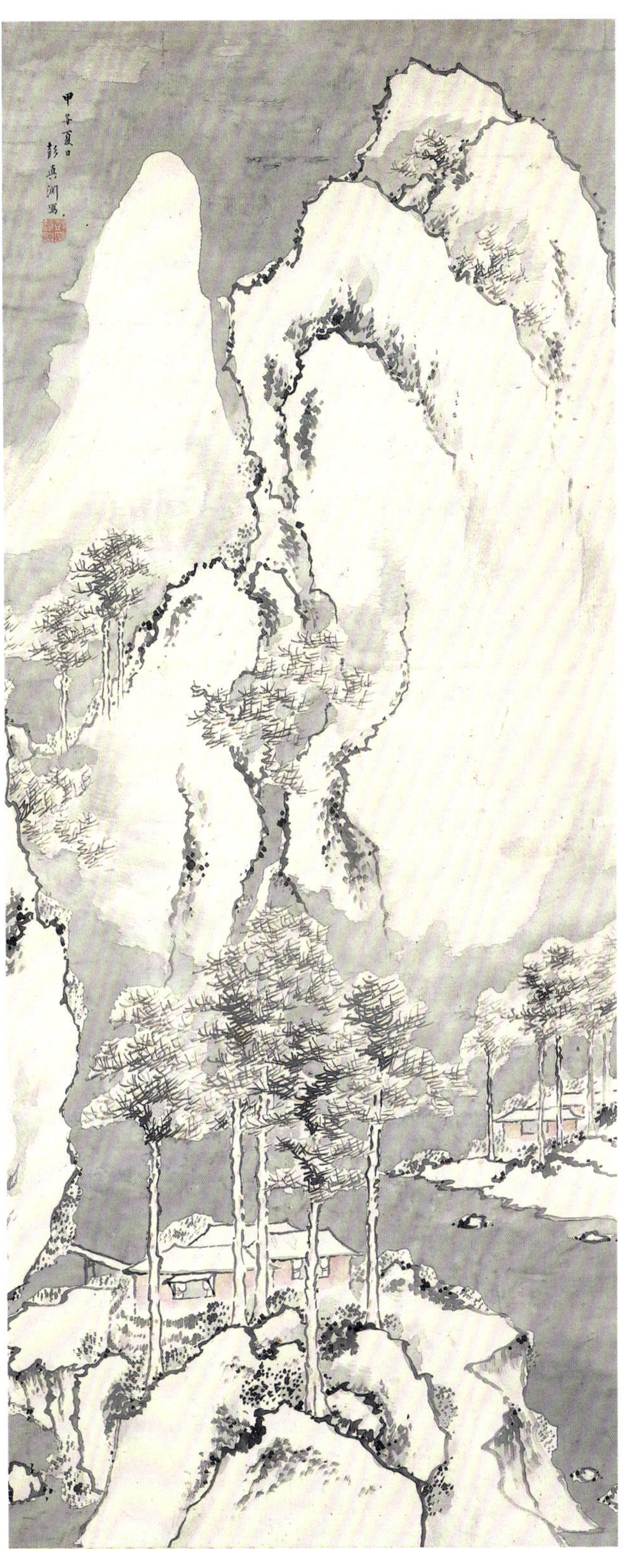

Gion Nankai
(祇園南海; 1677–1751)

308. Eight Daoist Immortals of China (八仙人)

Edo period, 18th century
Hanging scroll; ink and light color on silk
107.9 x 41.4 cm ($42\frac{1}{2}$ x $16\frac{1}{4}$ in.)
Text, signature, seals

Sakaki Hyakusen
(彭城百川; 1697–1752)

309. Snowy Landscape

Edo period, 1744
Hanging scroll; ink and light color on paper
121.4 x 50.3 cm ($47\frac{3}{4}$ x $19\frac{3}{4}$ in.)
Signature, seal

Literature: Murase 2000, no. 154.

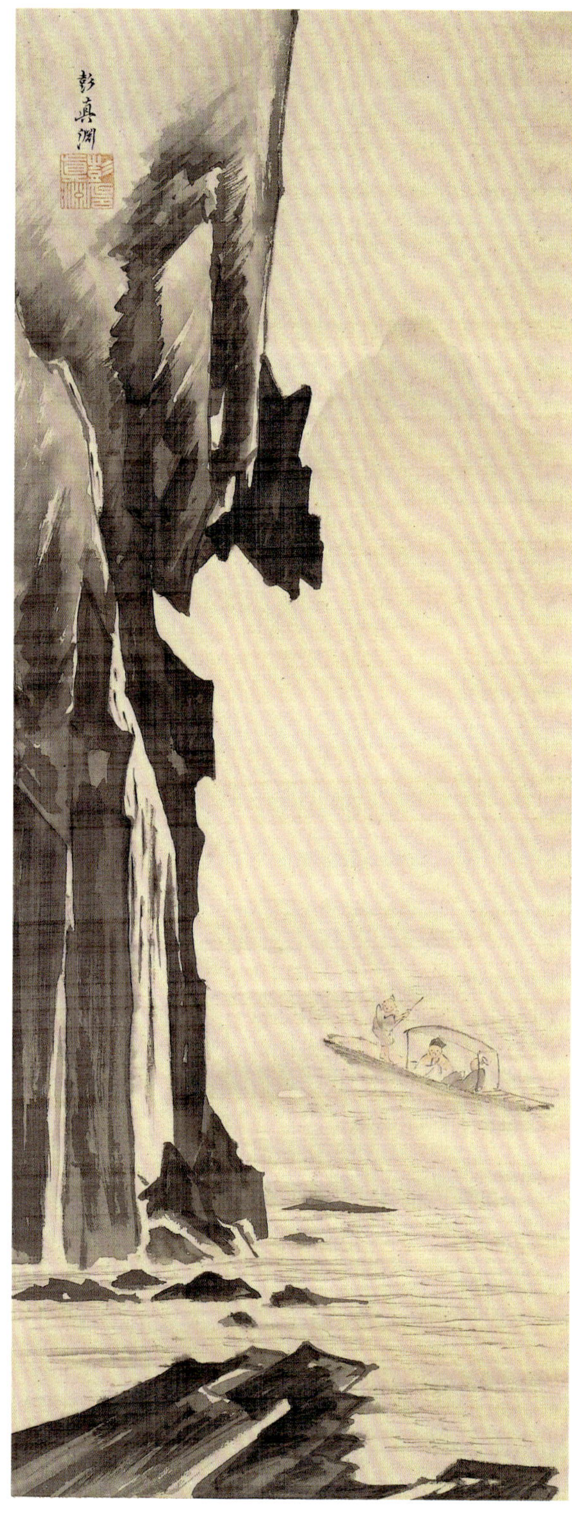

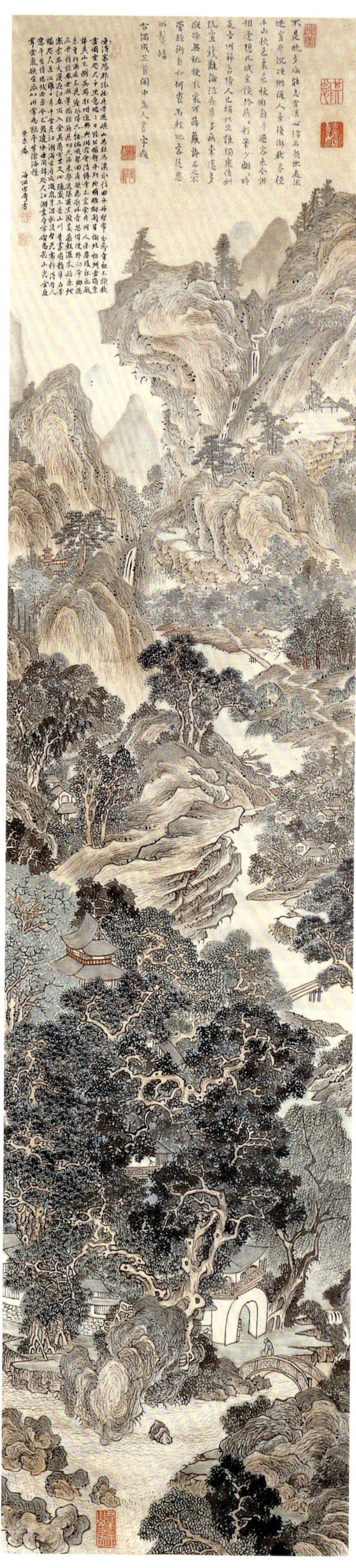

Sakaki Hyakusen
(彭城百川; 1697–1752)

310. So Shoku's (Ch. Su Shi, 蘇軾) Second Visit to the Red Cliff (後赤壁)

Edo period
Hanging scroll; ink and light color on silk
98 x 38.1 cm (38⅝ x 15 in.)
Signature, seal

Literature: Murase 1975, no. 65; Tsuji Nobuo et al. 2005, no. 107.

Yanagisawa Kien
(柳沢淇園; 1704–1758)

311. Landscape in Blue and Green

Edo period
Hanging scroll; ink and color on paper
137 x 31.9 cm (53⅞ x 12½ in.)
Text, signature, seals

Ex coll.: Itō Hirokuni

Literature: Tokyo National Museum 1917, pl. 43; Tokyo National Museum 1918, pl. 43; Kiyomi Mutsurō 1936, p. 26; Murase 1975, no. 66; Avitabile 1990, no. 88.

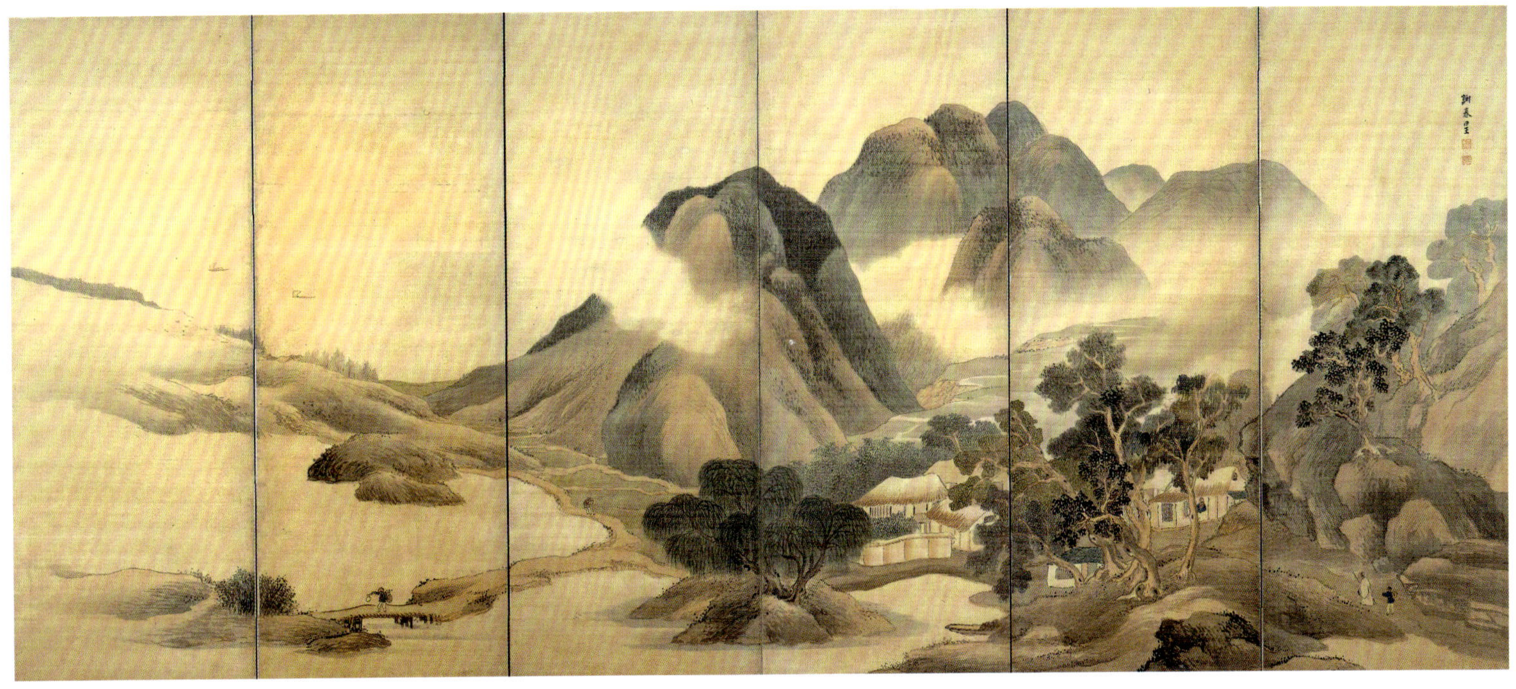

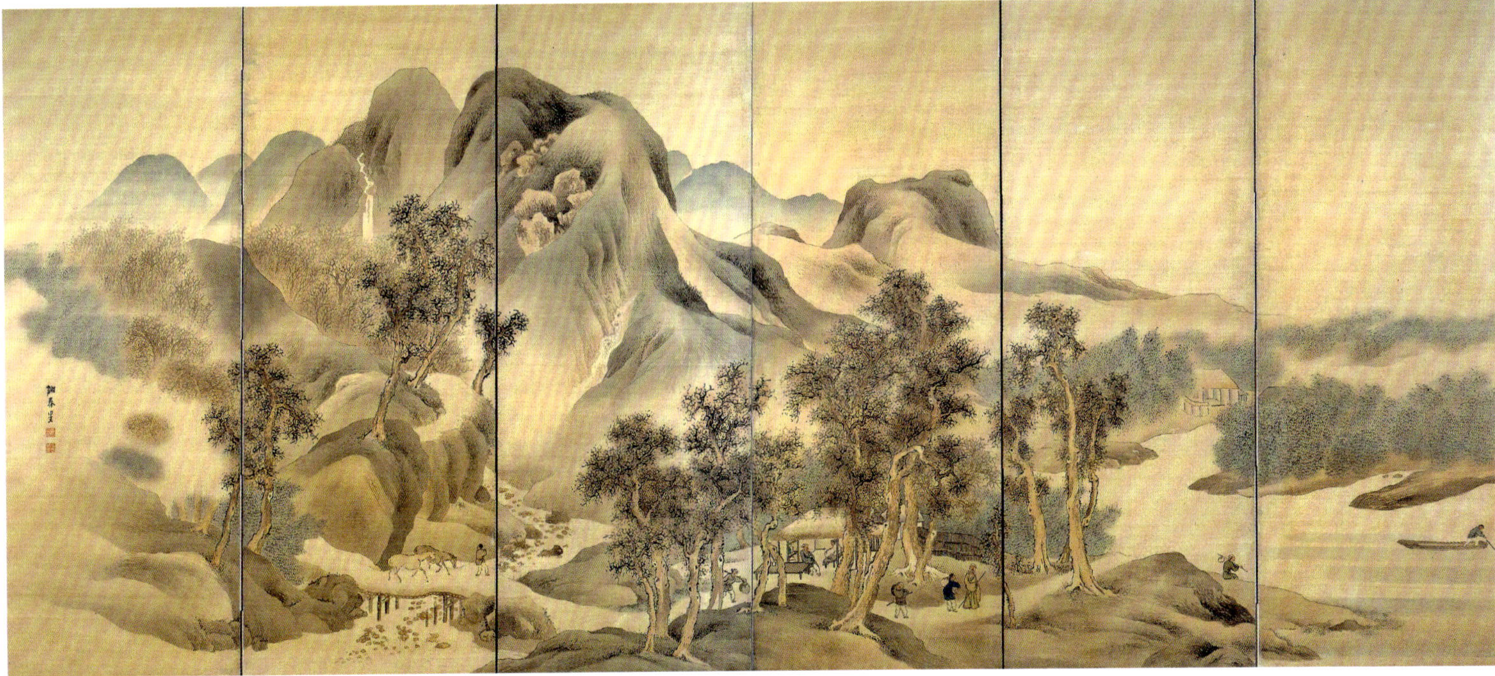

Yosa Buson
(与謝蕪村; 1716–1783)

312. Travels through Mountains and Fields

Edo period, ca. 1765
Pair of six-panel screens; ink and color on silk
Each screen 157.2 x 359.8 cm (61 7/8 in. x 11 ft. 9 5/8 in.)
Signatures, seals

Literature: Tokyo National Museum 1985a, no. 49; Avitabile 1990, no. 92; Tsuji Nobuo et al. 2005, no. 111.

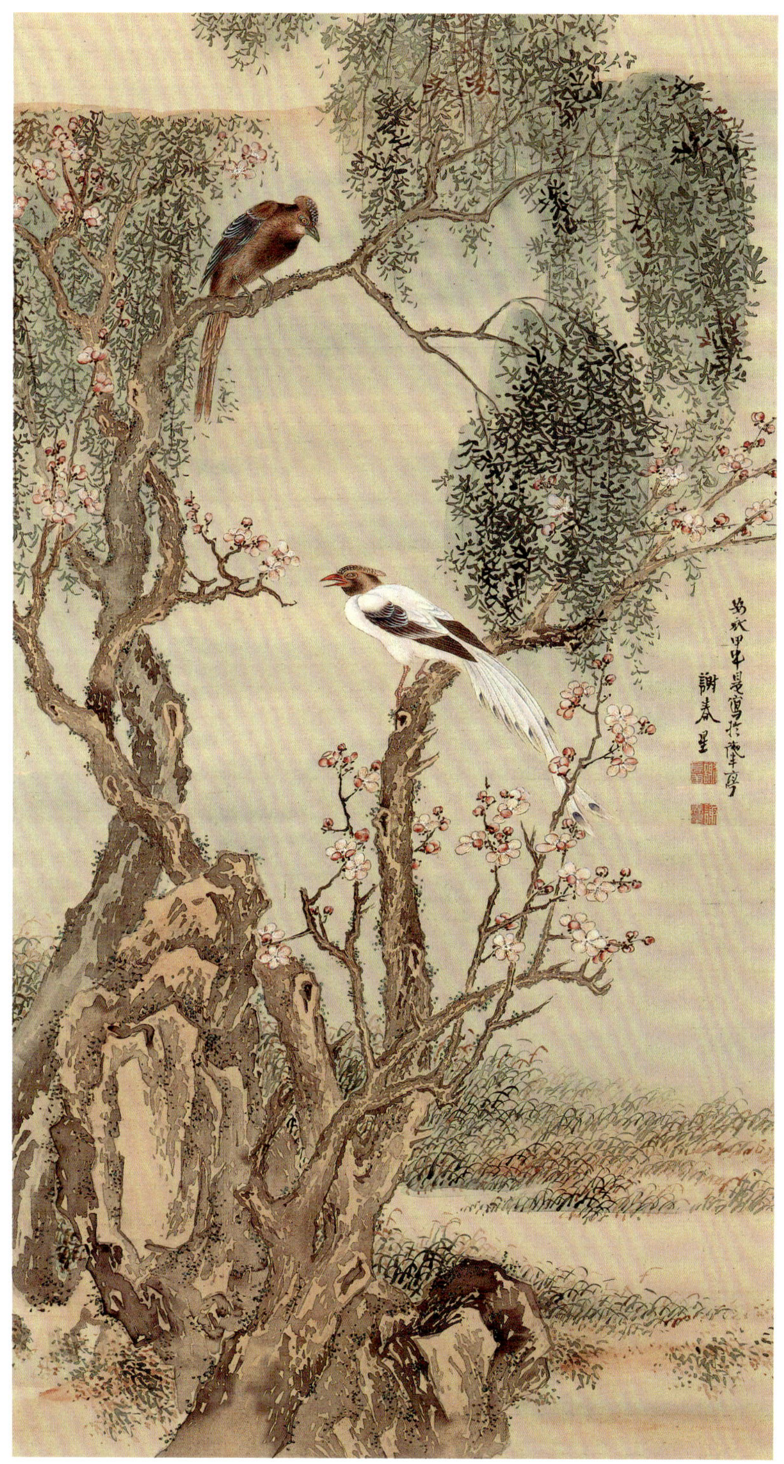

Yosa Buson
(与謝蕪村; 1716–1783)

313. Two Birds on Willow and Peach Trees

Edo period, 1774
Hanging scroll; ink and color on silk
128.9 x 70.5 cm (50 3/4 x 27 3/4 in.)
Signature, seals

Literature: "Yosa Buson hitsu Kachō zu kai" 1930, pl. III; Tsuji Nobuo 1980, no. 27; Murase 1993, no. 24; Haga Tōru and Hayakawa Monta 1994, pls. 50, 71; Murase 2000, no. 155; Tsuji Nobuo et al. 2005, no. 112.

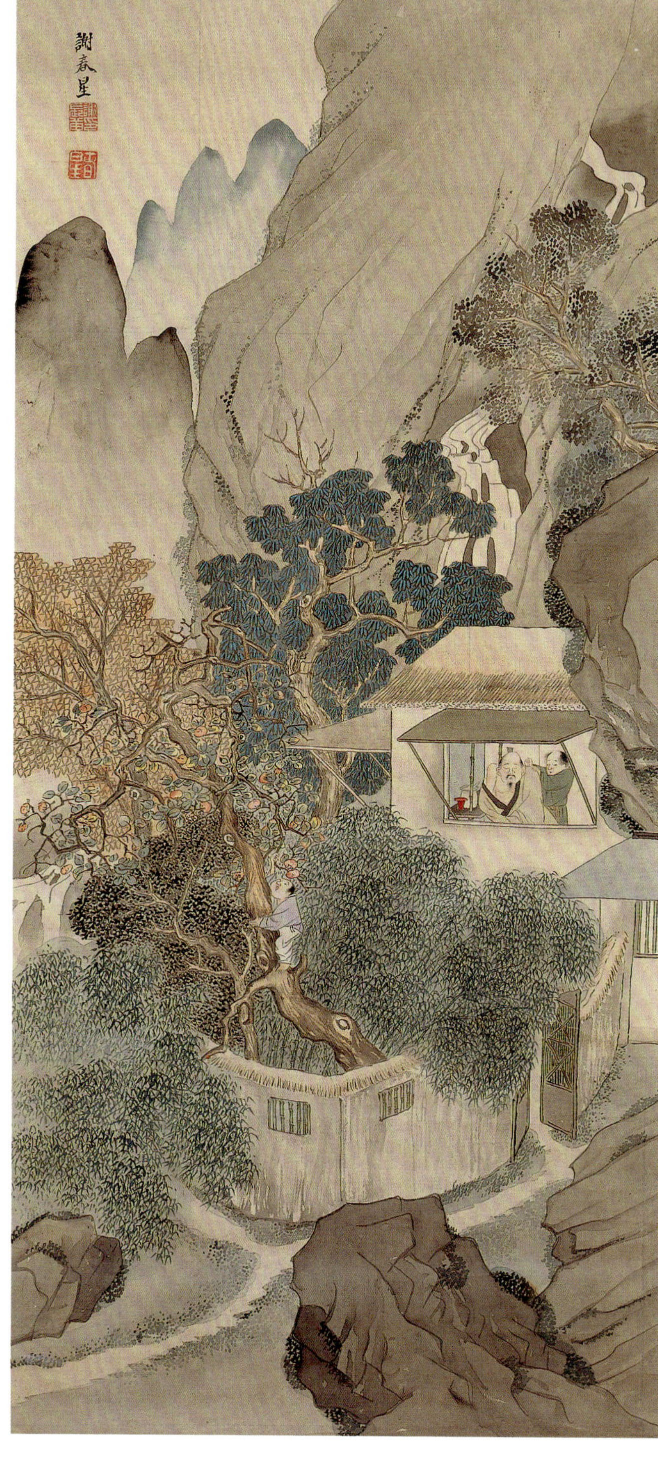

Yosa Buson
(与謝蕪村; 1716–1783)

314. Scholar's Mountain Retreat in Autumn

Edo period
Hanging scroll; ink and color on silk
109 x 50 cm (42 7/8 x 19 5/8 in.)
Signature, seals

Literature: Kōno Motoaki 2002; Tsuji Nobuo et al. 2005, no. 113.

Yosa Buson
(与謝蕪村; 1716–1783)

315. Landscape with Solitary Hut

Edo period
Hanging scroll; ink and light color on paper
116.2 x 33.5 cm ($45\frac{3}{4}$ x $13\frac{1}{4}$ in.)
Signature, seals

Literature: Murase 1975, no. 73.

Yosa Buson
(与謝蕪村; 1716–1783)

316. Crows

Edo period
Hanging scroll; ink and light color on silk
108.2 x 41.4 cm ($42\frac{5}{8}$ x $16\frac{1}{4}$ in.)
Signature, seals

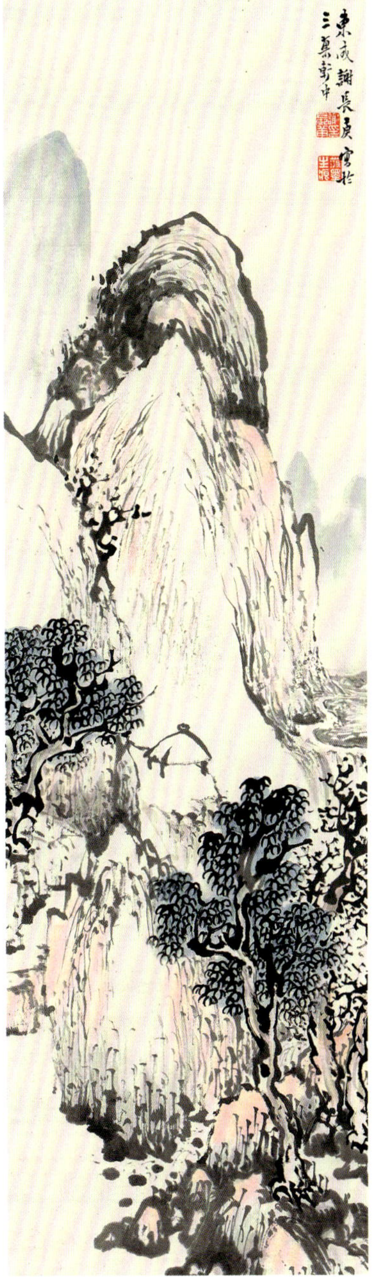

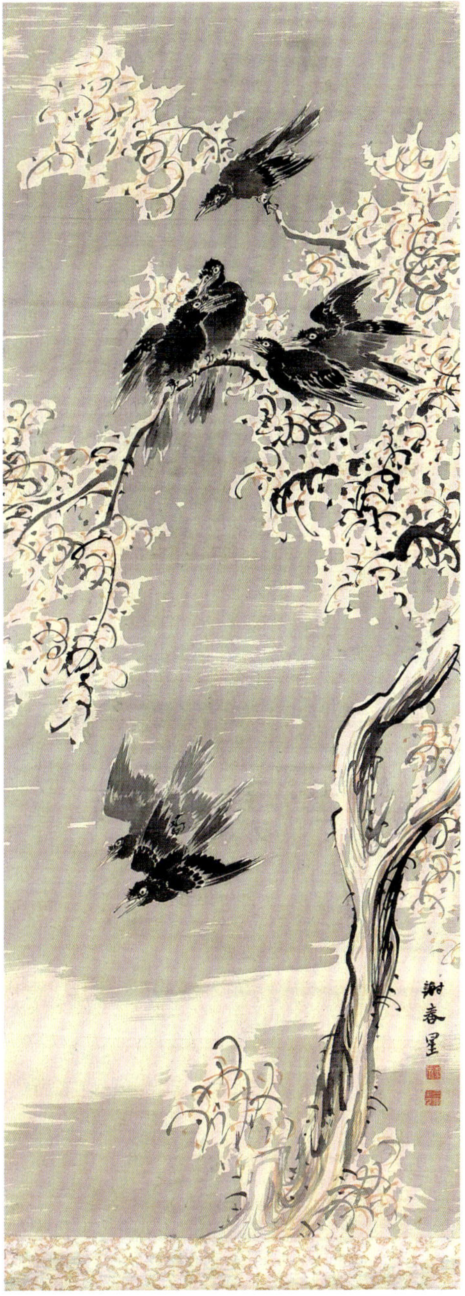

Yosa Buson
(与謝蕪村; 1716–1783)

317. Rocks

Edo period
Hanging scroll; ink and light color on paper
31.1 x 47.1 cm ($12\frac{1}{4}$ x $18\frac{1}{2}$ in.)
Text, signatures, seals

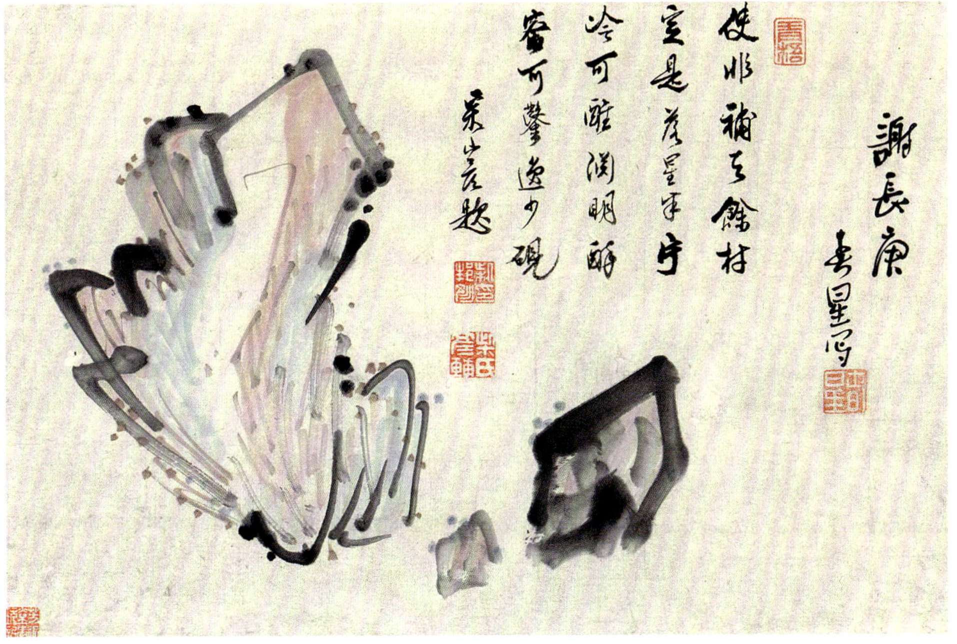

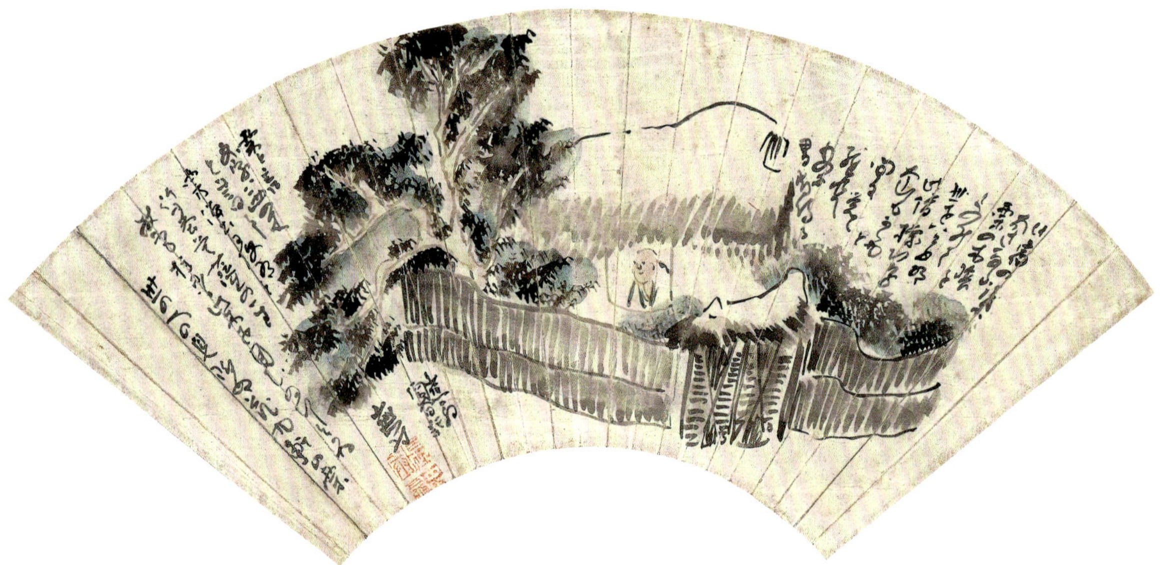

Yosa Buson
(与謝蕪村; 1716–1783)

318. Scene from *Oku no hosomichi* (奥の細道)

Edo period, ca. 1780
Folding fan, mounted as a hanging scroll; ink and color on paper
18 x 48.4 cm (7⅛ x 19 in.)
Text, signature, seals

Literature: Murase 1975, no. 74; L. Cunningham 1984, pp. 58–59, no. 18; Gitter and Fister 1985, no. 17; Avitabile 1990, no. 93; Murase 2000, no. 156.

Yosa Buson
(与謝蕪村; 1716–1783)

319. Sea in Spring (春の海)

Edo period
Hanging scroll; ink and light color on paper
27.3 x 23.6 cm (10¾ x 9¼ in.)
Text, signatures

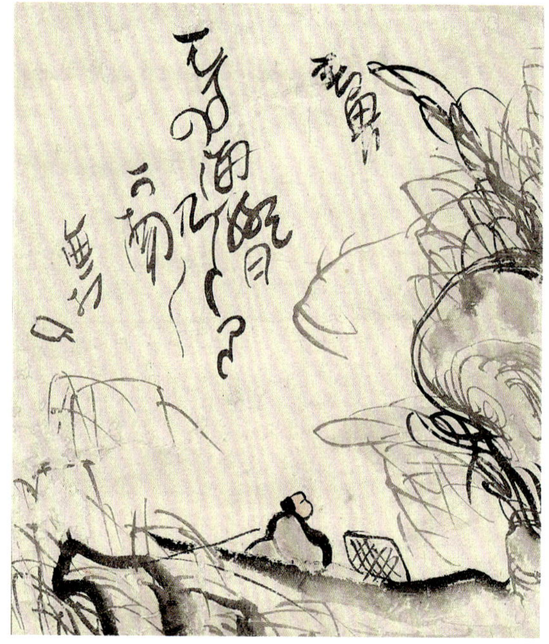

Yokoi Kinkoku
(横井金谷; 1761–1832)

320. Mount Fuji

Edo period, 19th century
Hanging scroll; ink and light color on paper
80.1 x 150.1 cm (31½ x 59⅛ in.)
Text, signature, seals

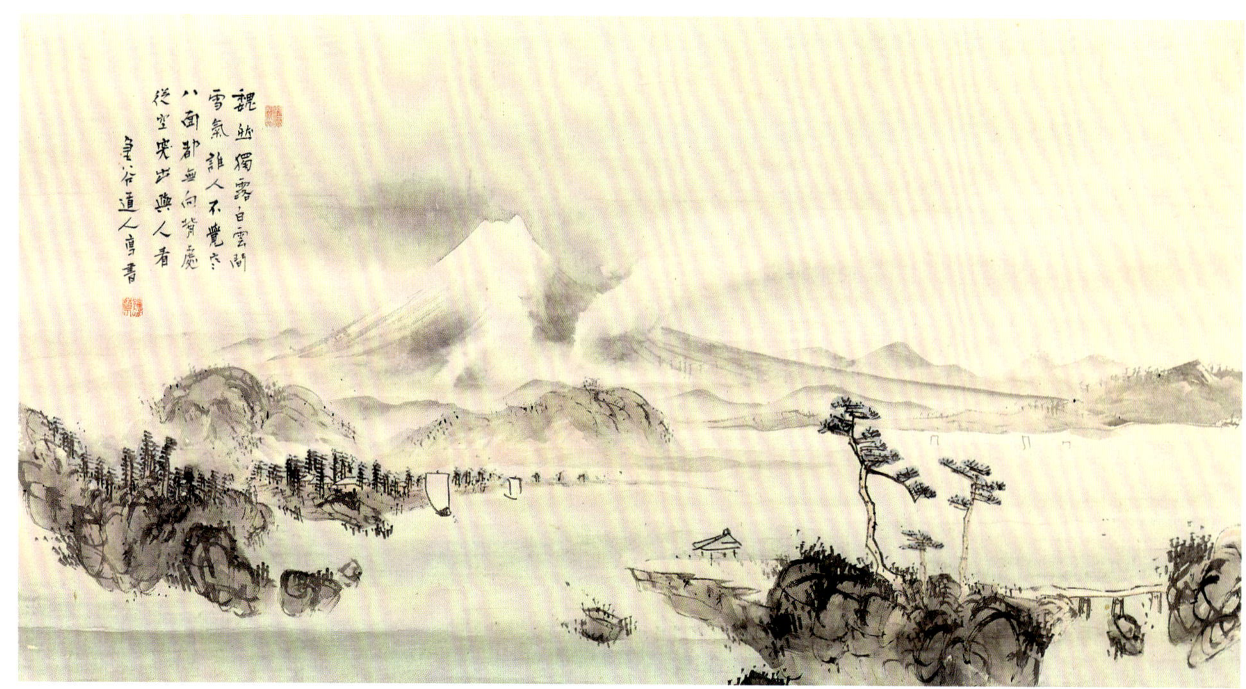

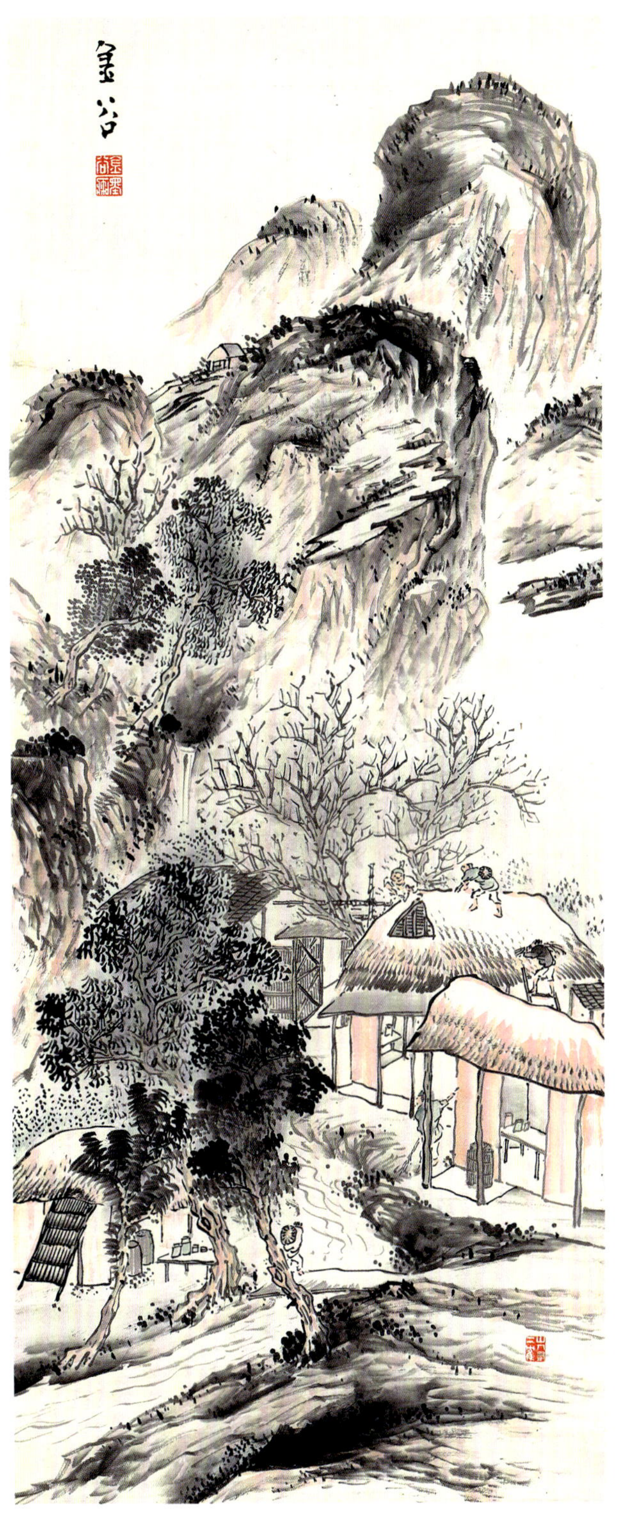

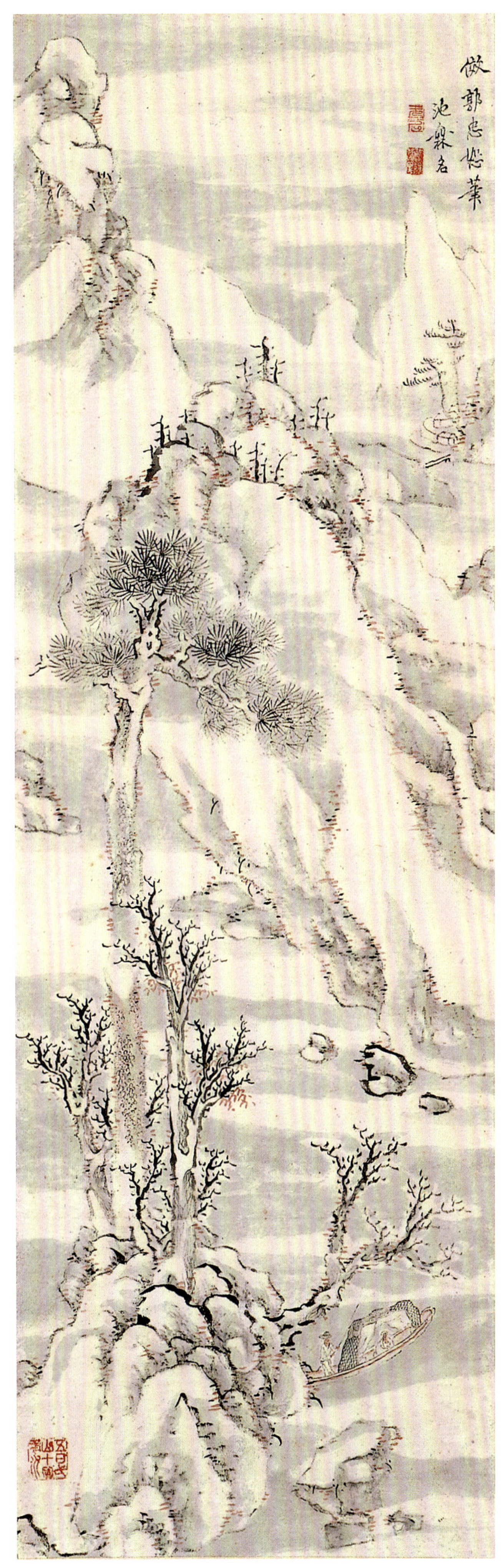

Yokoi Kinkoku
(横井金谷; 1761–1832)

321. Spring Cleaning

Edo period, 19th century
Hanging scroll; ink and light color on paper
108.5 x 44.9 cm (42 3/4 x 17 5/8 in.)
Signature, seals

Literature: Murase 1975, no. 75.

Ike Taiga
(池大雅; 1723–1776)

322. Wintry Landscape after Kaku Chūjo (Ch. Guo Zhongshu, 郭忠恕; fl. mid-10th century)

Edo period
Hanging scroll; ink and light color on paper
98.8 x 31.8 cm (38 7/8 x 12 1/2 in.)
Text, signature, seals

Literature: Murase 1993, no. 25; Fischer 2007, p. 434, no. 132.

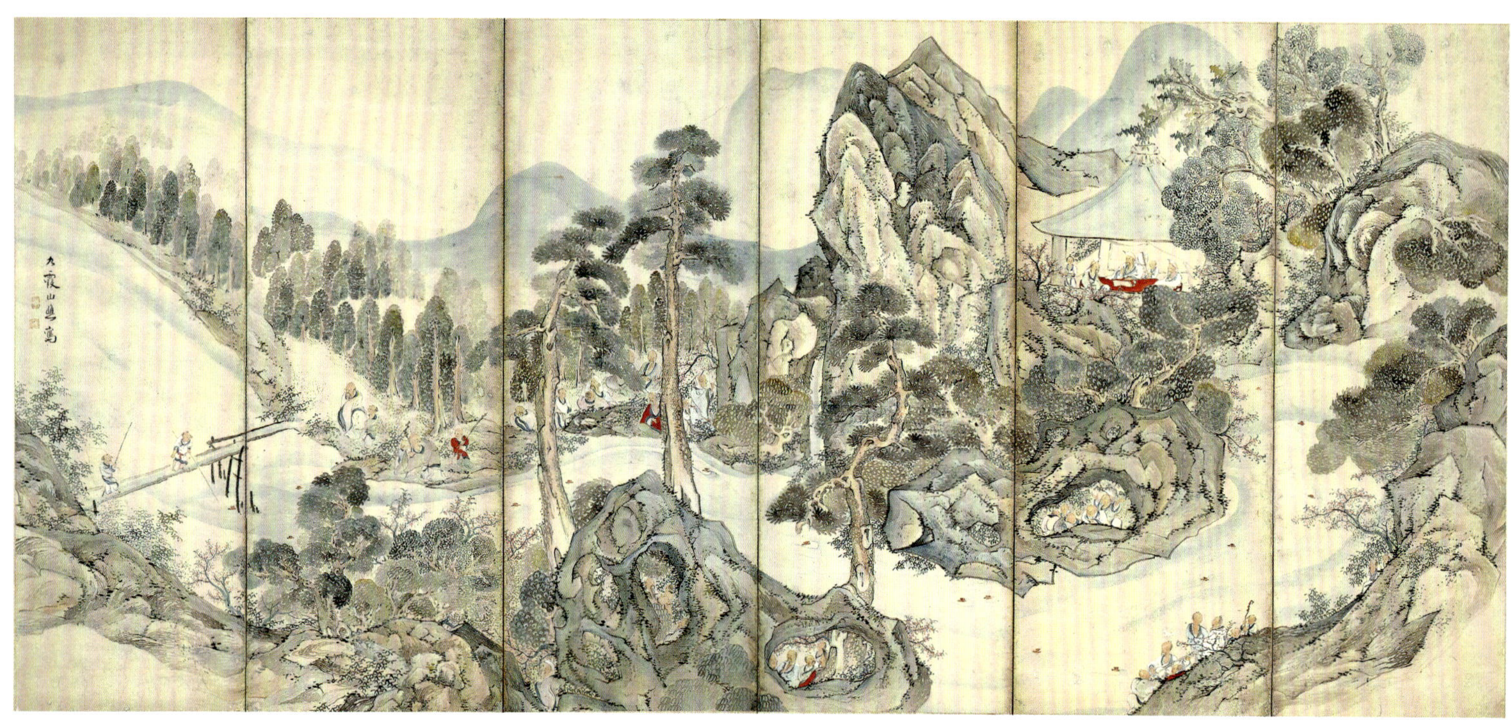

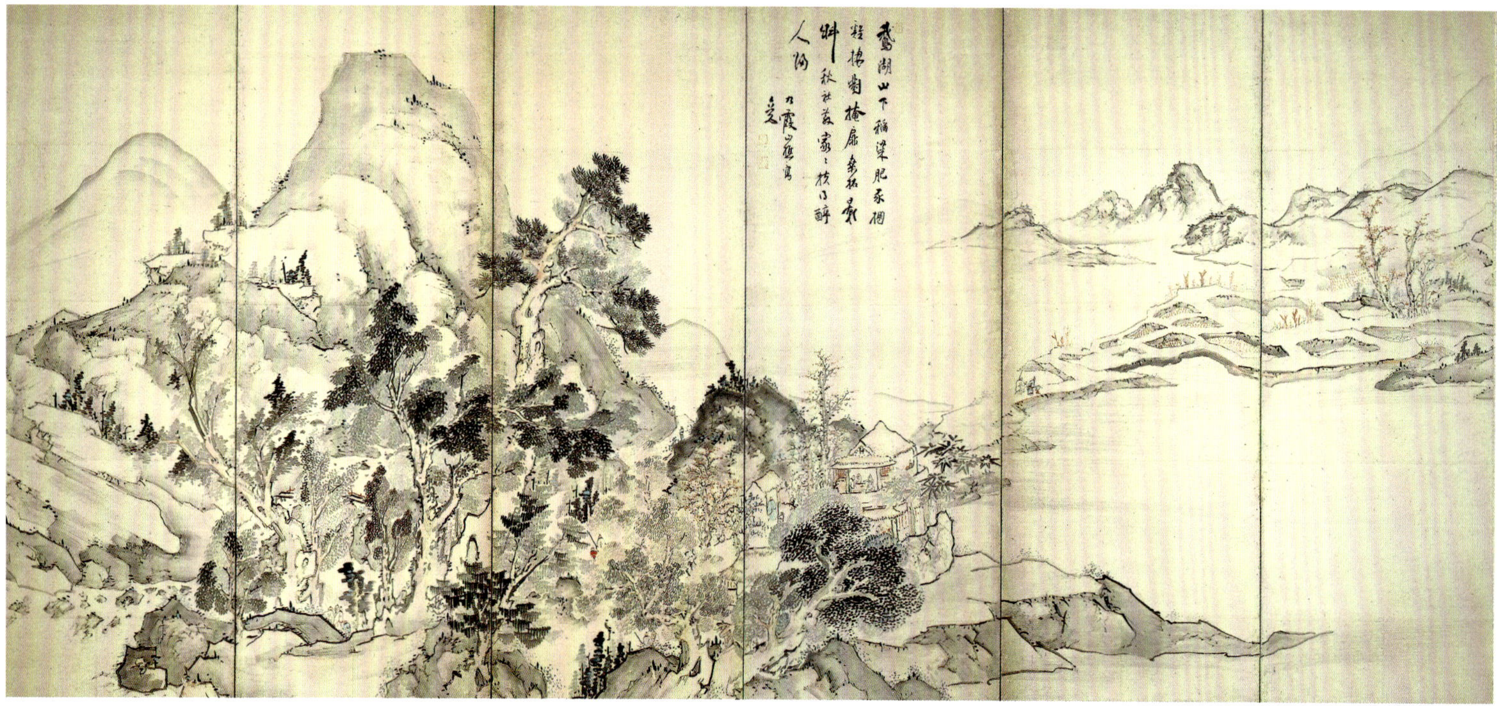

Ike Taiga
(池大雅; 1723–1776)

323. Gathering at the Orchid Pavilion (蘭亭曲水); Autumn Festival (秋祭)

Edo period, ca. 1763
Pair of six-panel folding screens; ink and light color on paper
Each screen 159.5 x 354.6 cm (62¾ in. x 11 ft. 7⅝ in.)
Text, signatures, seals

Ex coll.: Kuribayashi Shigeru, Tokyo

Literature: Tanaka Ichimatsu 1957, pp. 91–96; Tanaka Ichimatsu et al. 1957–59, nos. 241-1, 241-2; Cahill 1972, no. 10 (Gathering); Murase 1975, no. 70; Suzuki Susumu 1975, no. 10; Tokyo National Museum 1985a, no. 50 (Gathering); Yoshizawa Chū 1986, nos. 29, 30; Murase 1990, no. 15; Avitabile 1990, no. 89 (Gathering); Guth 1996, figs. 43, 44 (Gathering); Murase 2000, no. 159; Tsuji Nobuo et al. 2005, no. 109; Fischer 2007, p. 446, no. 156; Volk 2010, p. 183, fig. 80 (Gathering).

Ike Taiga
(池大雅; 1723–1776)

324. Landscape with River View

Edo period
Hanging scroll; ink and light color on paper
143.1 x 80.6 cm (56⅜ x 31¾ in.)
Signature, seals

Ex coll.: Nakamura

Literature: *Tōshi (Karihan) Nakamura-shi kyūzōhin mokuroku* 1915, unnumbered; Murase 1975, no. 72.

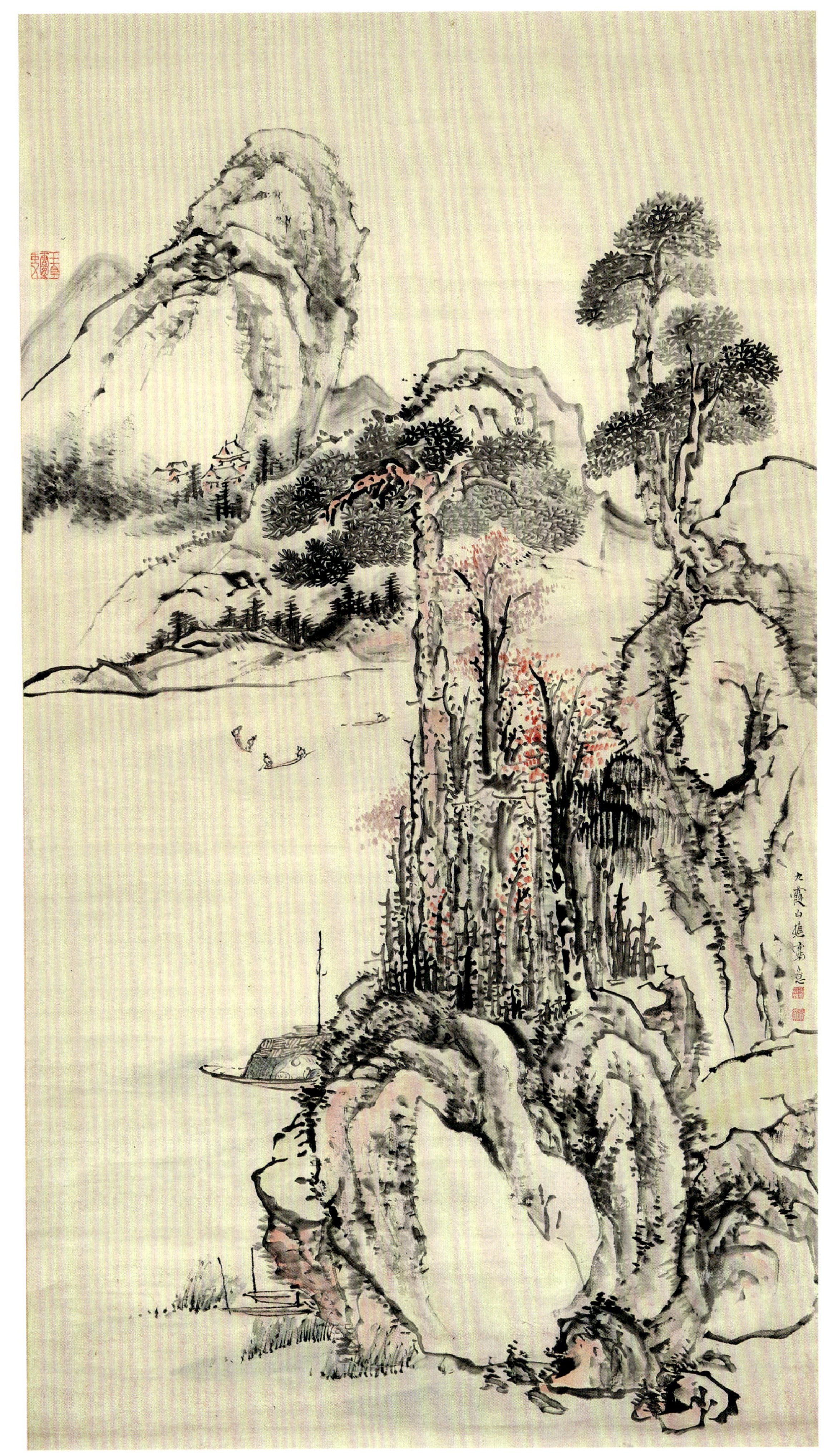

324

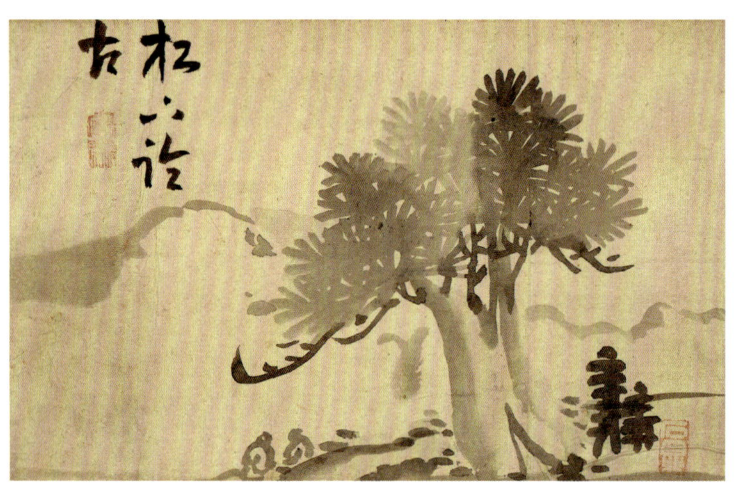

325

325

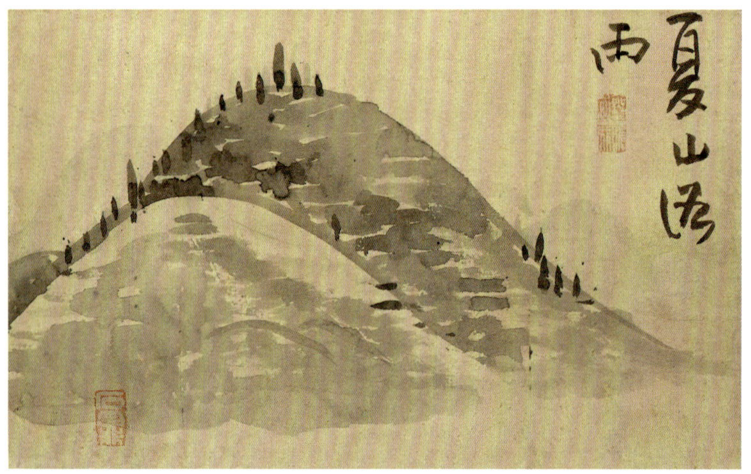

326

326

Ike Taiga
(池大雅; 1723–1776)

325–328. Discussion under Pine Tree about the Vicissitudes of Time (松下論古); Summer Mountains in the Rain (夏山浴雨); Fishing Boat at Reed-Covered Bank (葭汀釣舟); Evening Glow in Mountain Village (郊村返照)

Edo period
Four paintings and five calligraphies from an album, each mounted as a hanging scroll; ink on paper
Each scroll 23 x 37 cm (9 x $14\frac{5}{8}$ in.)
Text, signatures, seals

Ex coll.: Nozoe Heibei, Kyoto, and Wakamura Genzaemon, Shiga Prefecture (calligraphy)

Literature: Tanaka Ichimatsu et al. 1957–59, no. 197 (paintings only); Murase 1975, no. 69; Suzuki Susumu and Sasaki Jōhei 1979, pl. 61; Tsuji Nobuo 1980, nos. 13–16; Tokyo National Museum 1985a, no. 51; Avitabile 1990, no. 90; Murase 2000, no. 158; Tsuji Nobuo et al. 2005, no. 108.

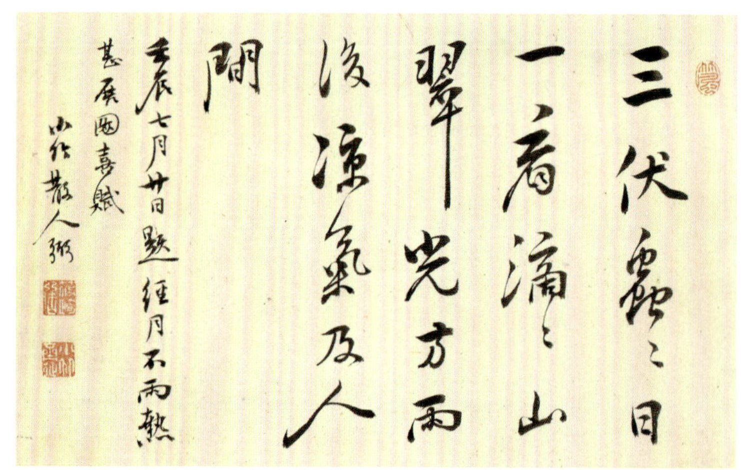

326

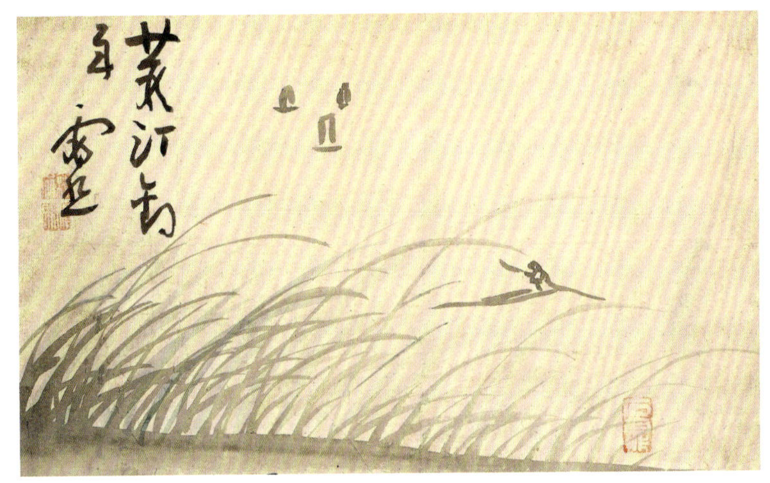

327

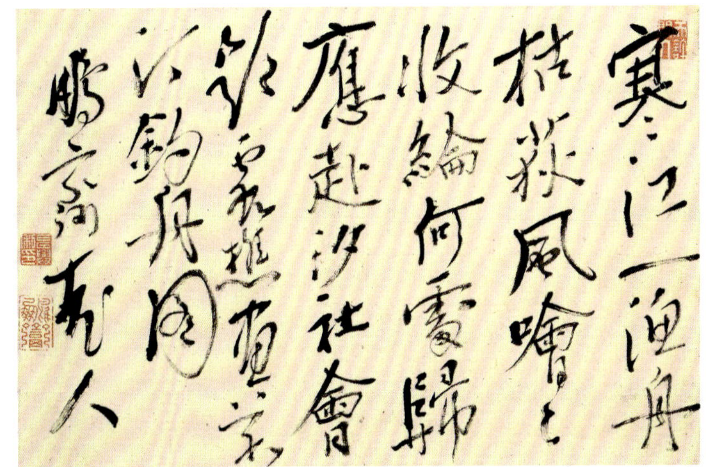

327

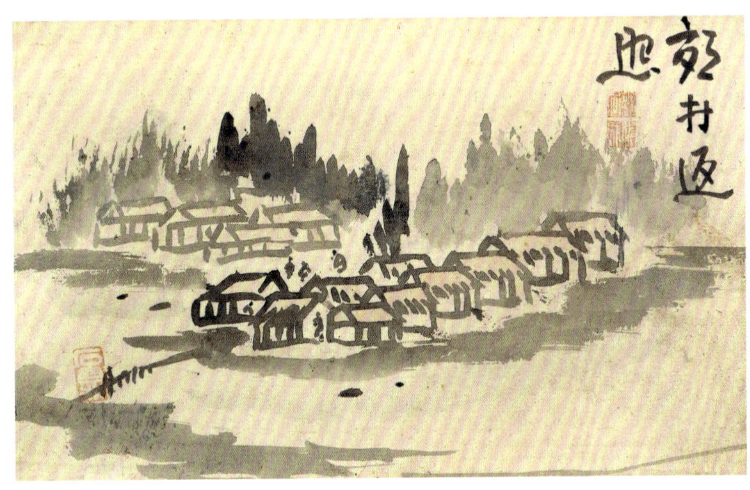

328

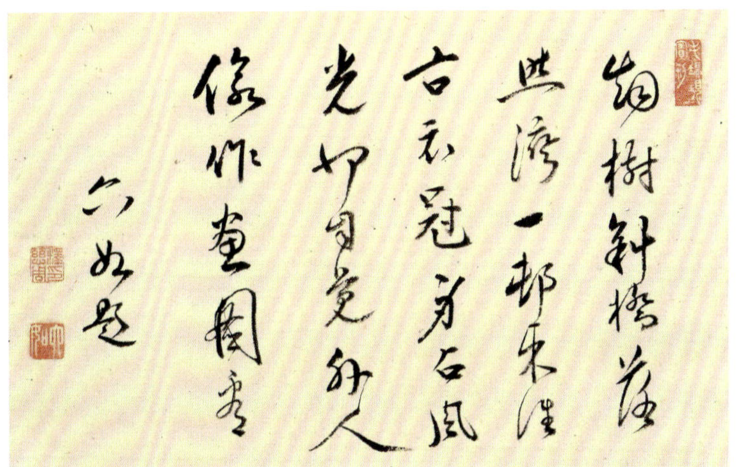

328

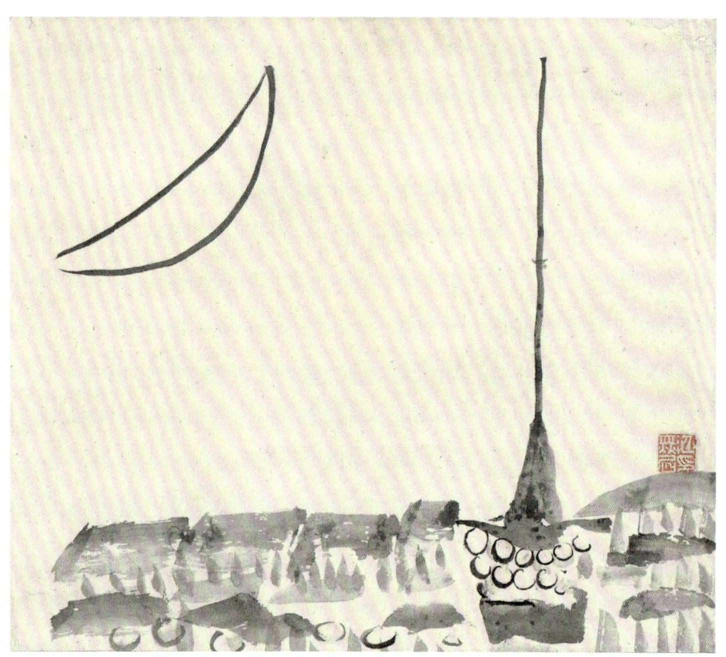

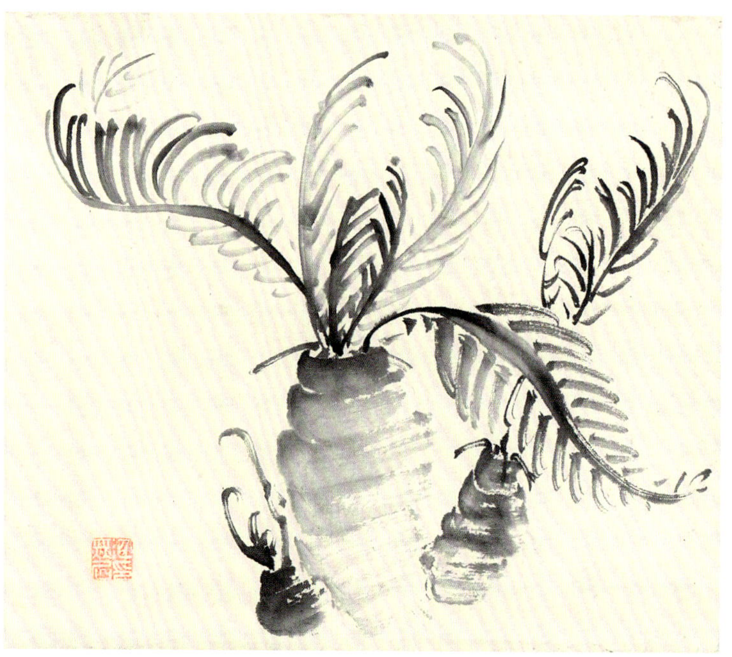

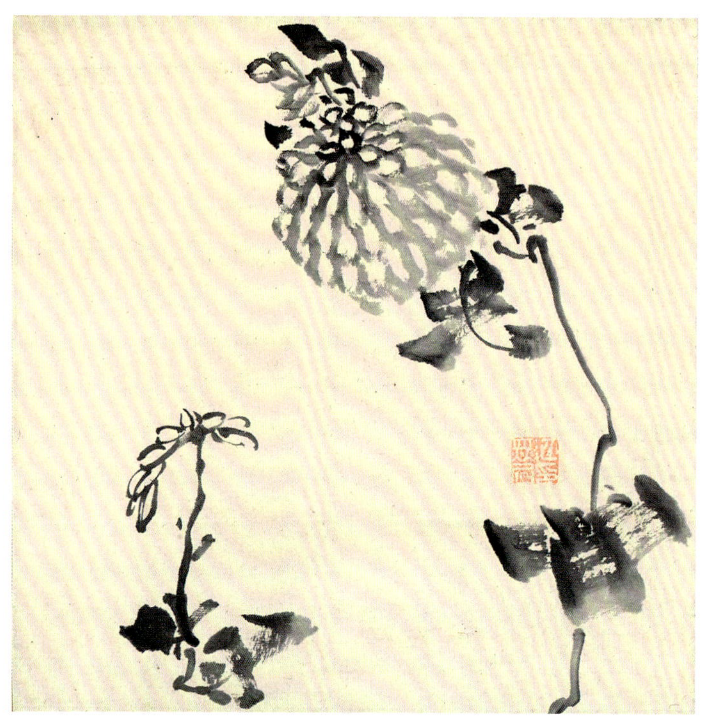

Ike Taiga
(池大雅; 1723–1776)

329. Gion Festival (祇園祭) Float under Moon

Edo period
Hanging scroll; ink and light color on paper
30.5 x 35.1 cm (12 x 13⅞ in.)
Seal

Ex coll.: Okamoto Kōhei, Kanagawa Prefecture

Literature: Tanaka Ichimatsu et al. 1957–59, no. 155; Murase 1993, no. 26; Fischer 2007, p. 415, no. 86.

Ike Taiga
(池大雅; 1723–1776)

330. Cycad

Edo period
Hanging scroll; ink on paper
28 x 32.1 cm (11 x 12⅝ in.)
Seal

Ex coll.: Okamoto Kōhei, Kanagawa Prefecture

Literature: Tanaka Ichimatsu et al. 1957–59, no. 159; Murase 1993, no. 27.

Ike Taiga
(池大雅; 1723–1776)

331. Chrysanthemum

Edo period
Hanging scroll; ink on paper
27.4 x 27.9 cm (10¾ x 11 in.)
Seal

Literature: Tanaka Ichimatsu et al. 1957–59, no. 157.

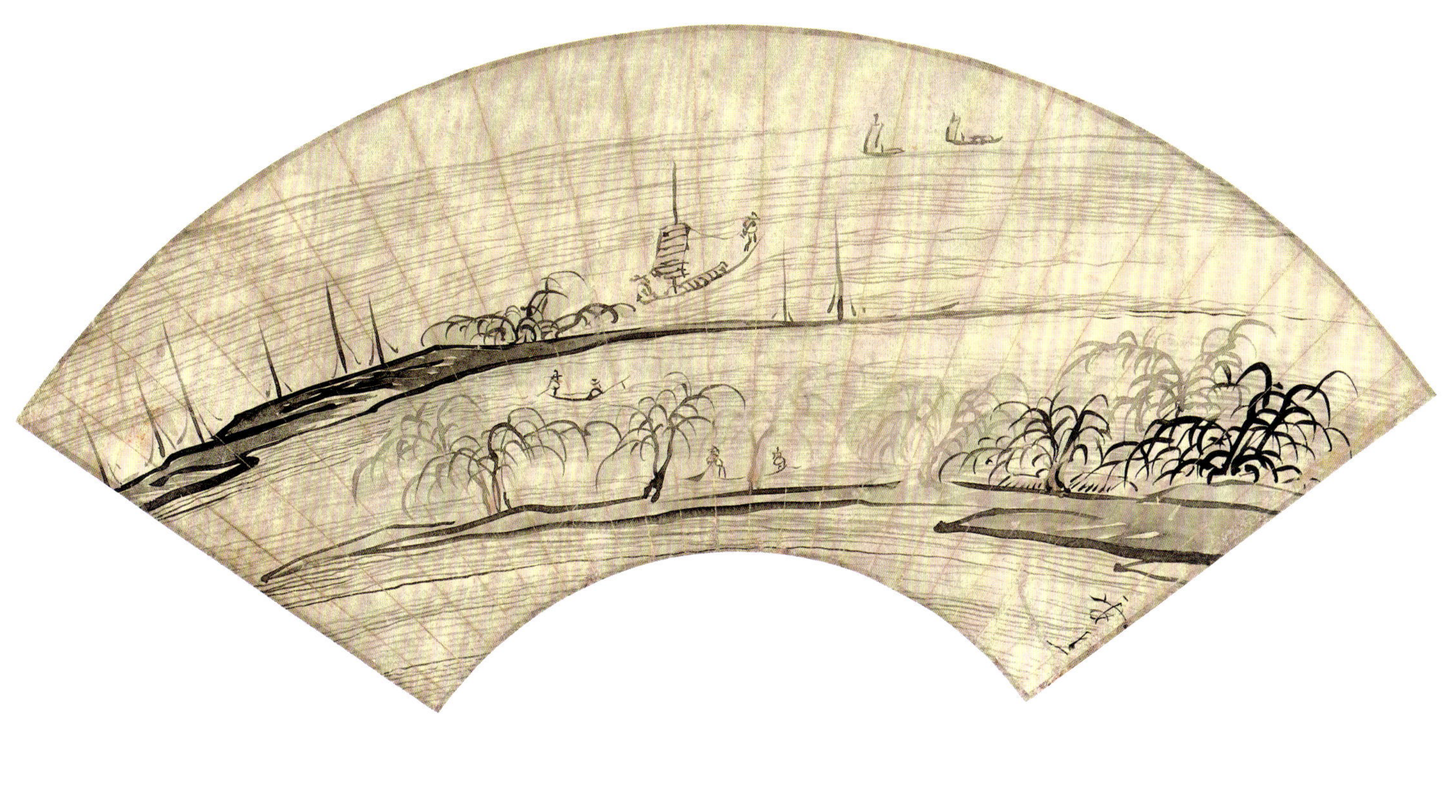

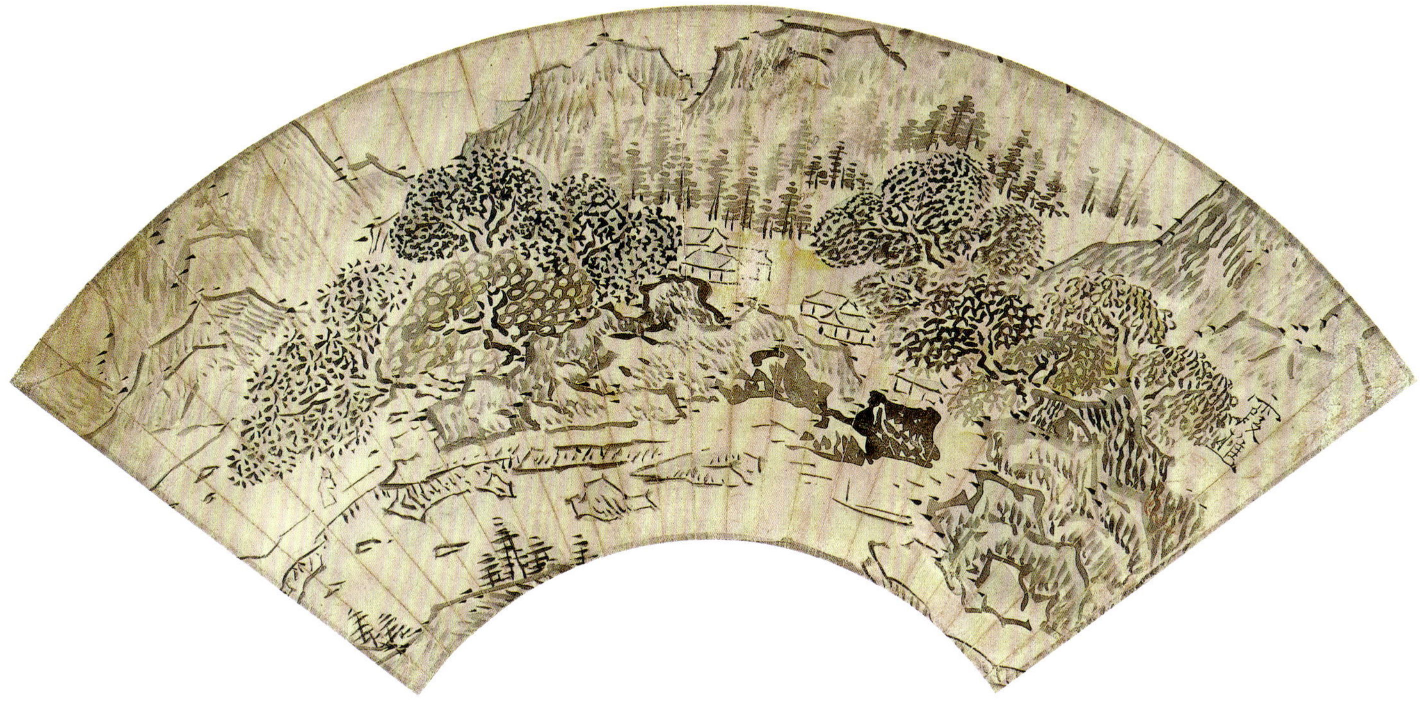

Ike Taiga
(池大雅; 1723–1776)

332. Homeward-Bound Fishing Boats

Edo period
Folding fan, mounted as a hanging scroll; ink and light color on paper
18.2 x 50 cm (7 1/8 x 19 5/8 in.)
Signature

Ex coll.: Okamoto Kōhei, Kanagawa Prefecture

Literature: Murase 1975, no. 71.

Ike Taiga
(池大雅; 1723–1776)

333. Country Retreat in Early Summer

Edo period
Folding fan, mounted as a hanging scroll; ink and light color on paper
18.2 x 50 cm (7 1/8 x 19 5/8 in.)
Signature, seals

Ex coll.: Okamoto Kōhei, Kanagawa Prefecture

Literature: Murase 1975, no. 71.

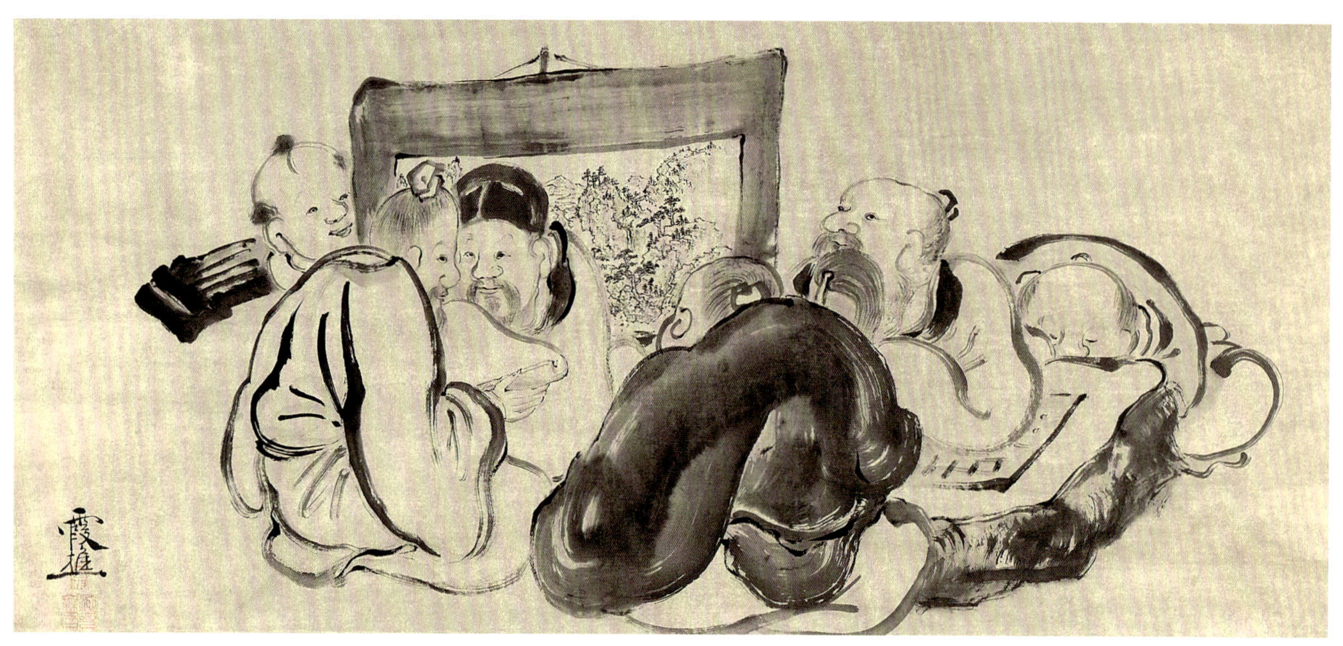

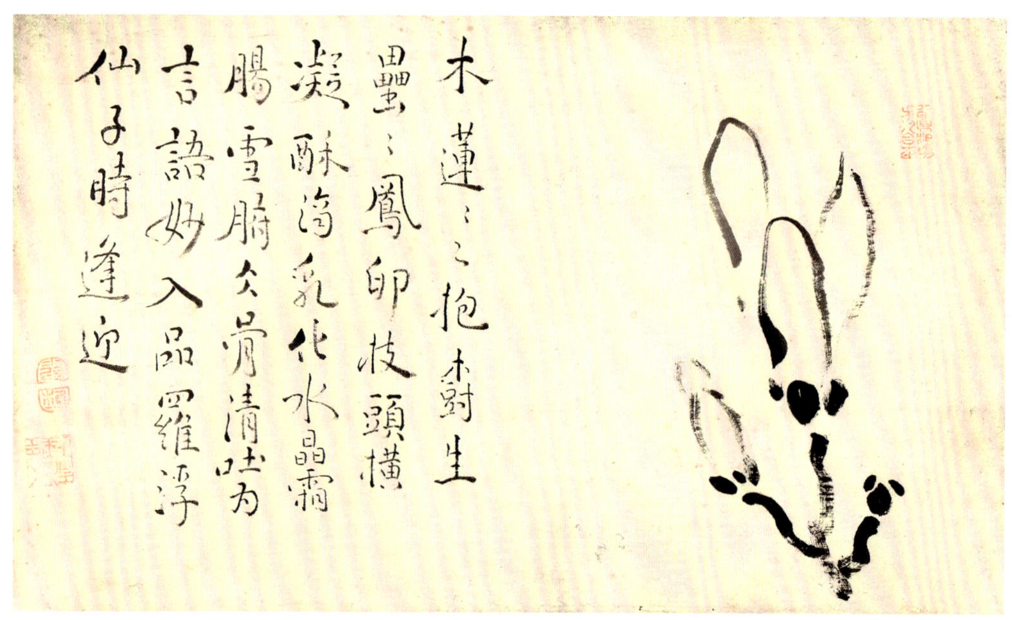

Ike Taiga
(池大雅; 1723–1776)

334. The Four Accomplishments
(琴棋書画)

Edo period
Hanging scroll; ink on paper
56.6 x 124.3 cm ($22\frac{1}{4}$ x $48\frac{7}{8}$ in.)
Signature, seals

Literature: Mason 1977, p. 11, no. 1; Burke 1993, pp. 50–51, fig. 12/no. 8.

Ike Taiga
(池大雅; 1723–1776)

335. Magnolia

Edo period
Hanging scroll; ink on paper
31.5 x 54.1 cm ($12\frac{3}{8}$ x $21\frac{1}{4}$ in.)
Text, seals

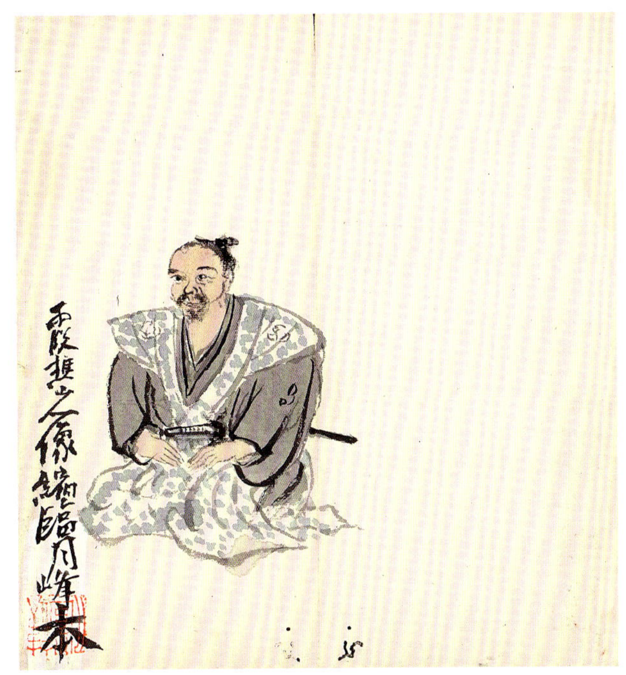

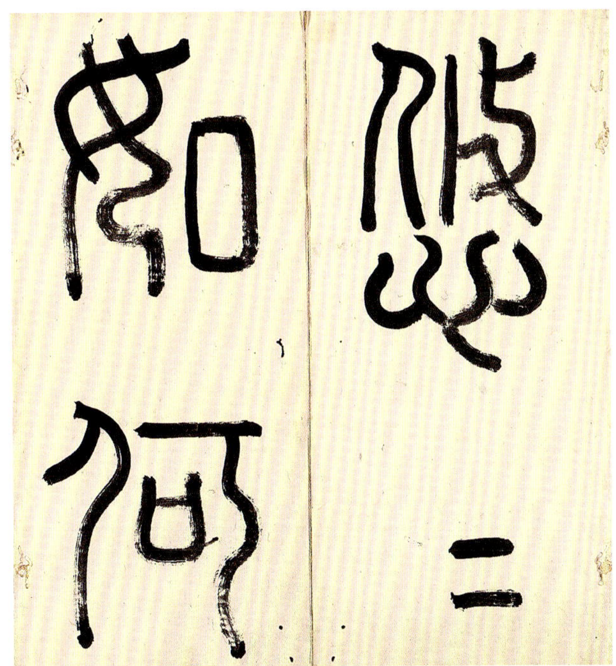

Tomioka Tessai
(富岡鉄斎; 1836–1924)

336. Portrait of Taiga (大雅) and His Calligraphies in Seal and Grass Styles copied by Tomioka Tessai

Edo period–Taishō era, 19th–20th century
Book; ink and color on paper
28 x 26.2 cm (11 x 10 3/8 in.)
Text, signature, seal

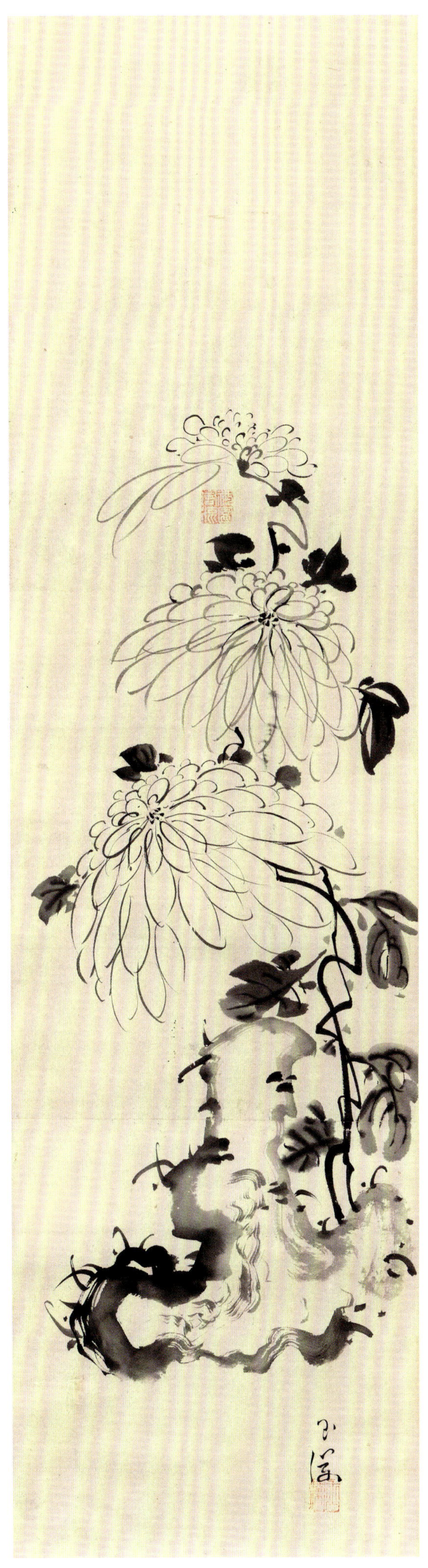

Tokuyama Gyokuran
(徳山玉瀾; ca. 1728–1784)

337. Chrysanthemums

Edo period
Hanging scroll; ink on paper
103.9 x 28.6 cm (40 7/8 x 11 1/4 in.)
Signature, seals

Literature: Fister 1988, p. 90, no. 32.

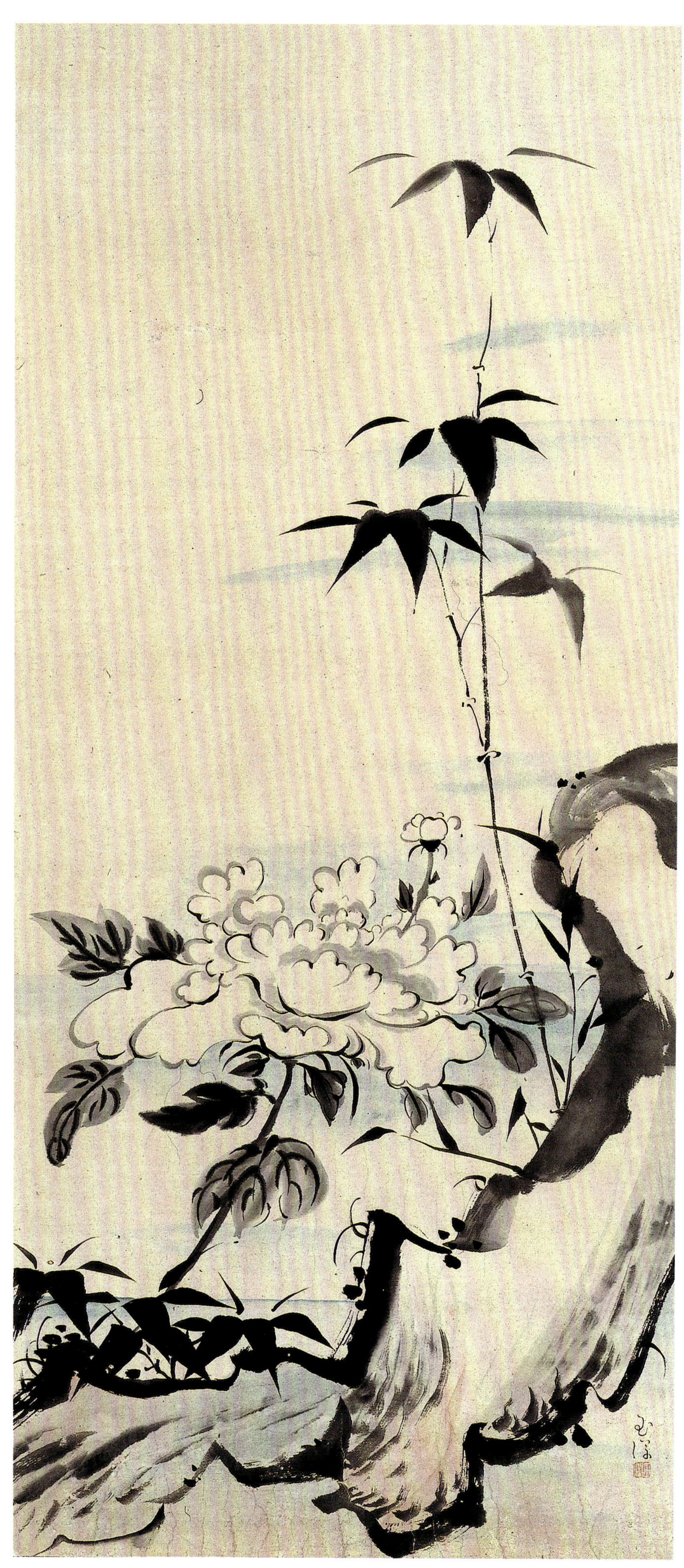

Tokuyama Gyokuran
(徳山玉瀾; ca. 1728–1784)

338. Peony and Bamboo by a Rock

Edo period, ca. 1768
Hanging scroll; ink and light color on paper
92.8 x 41.7 cm (36½ x 16⅜ in.)
Signature, seal

Literature: Fister 1988, p. 89, no. 31; Murase 1993, no. 28; Murase 2000, no. 160; Tsuji Nobuo et al. 2005, no. 110; Fischer 2007, p. 400, no. 54.

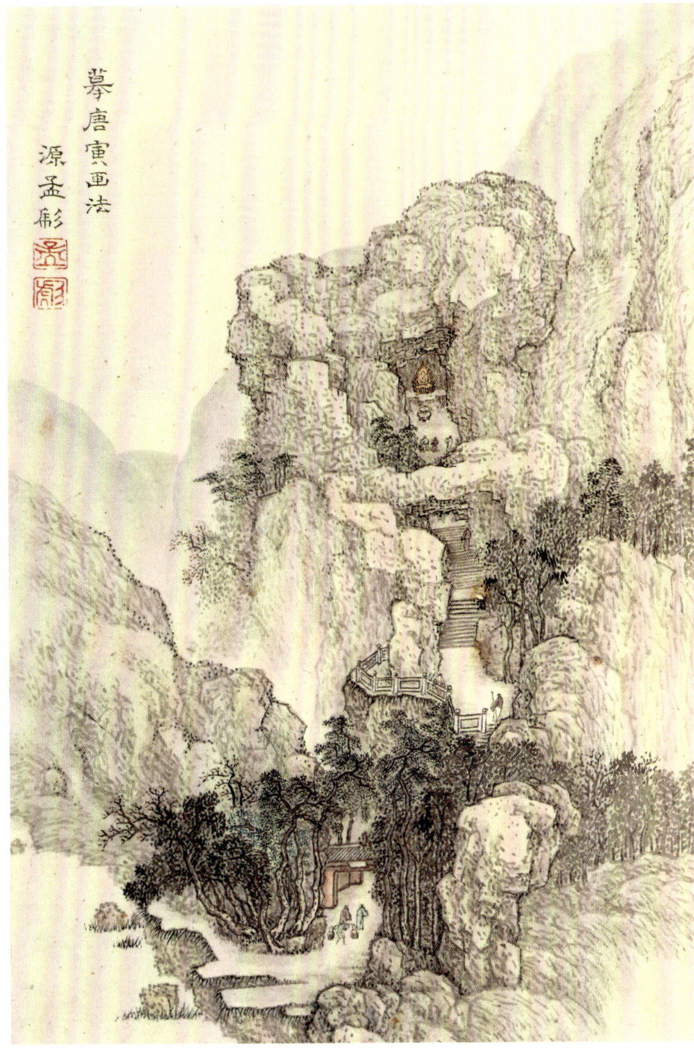

"Painting in the Manner of Tō In [Ch. Tang Yin, 唐寅]"

Kō Fuyō
(高芙蓉; 1722–1784)

339. Album of Landscapes

Edo period
Eight album leaves; ink and light color on paper
Each leaf 23.3 x 15.8 cm (9 1/8 x 6 1/4 in.)
Text, signatures, seals

Literature: Yoshizawa Chū 1967, pp. 21–26; Murase 1975, no. 67; Tokyo National Museum 1985a, no. 52; Avitabile 1990, no. 91.

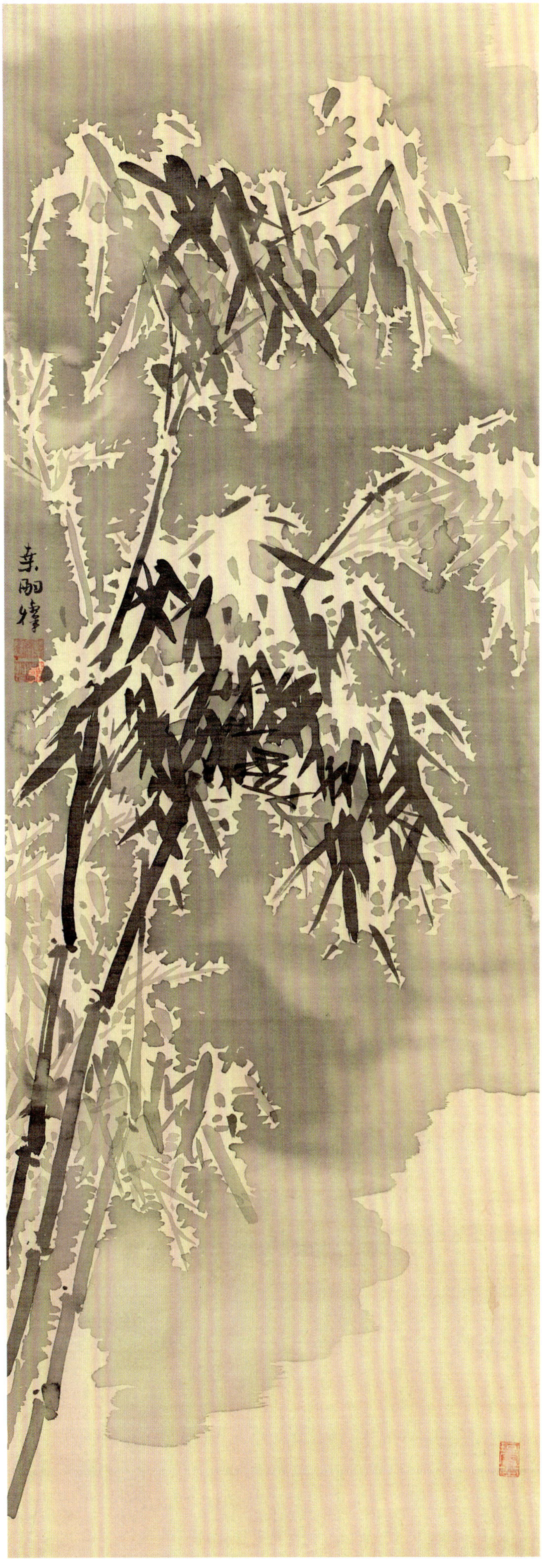

Kuwayama Gyokushū
(桑山玉州; 1746–1799)

340. Bamboo in Snow

Edo period
Hanging scroll; ink on silk
100.8 x 37 cm (39 5/8 x 14 5/8 in.)
Signature, seals

Ex coll.: Nomura Yasumasa

Literature: Matsushita Hidemaro 1959, fig. 41; Murase 1975, no. 79; Addiss and Wong 1978, no. 38.

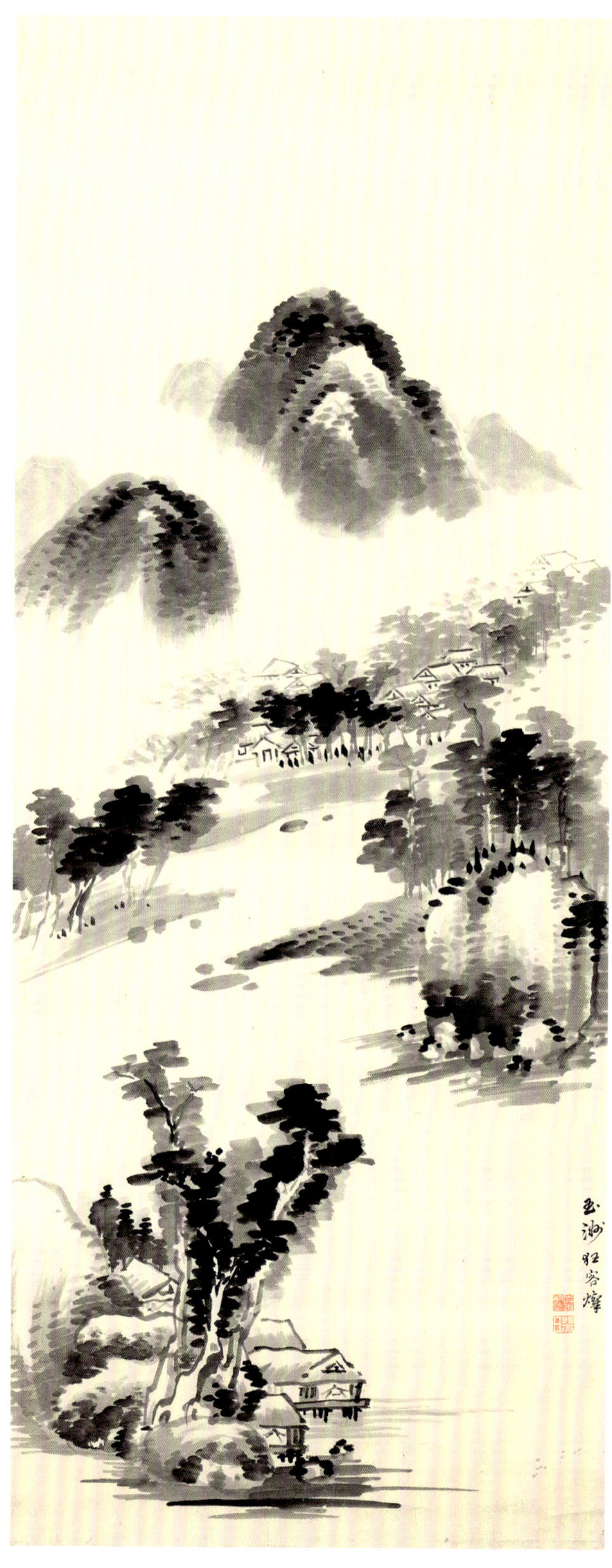

Kuwayama Gyokushū
(桑山玉州; 1746–1799)

341. Landscape

Edo period
Hanging scroll; ink on paper
121.5 x 49.5 cm ($47\frac{7}{8}$ x $19\frac{1}{2}$ in.)
Signature, seals

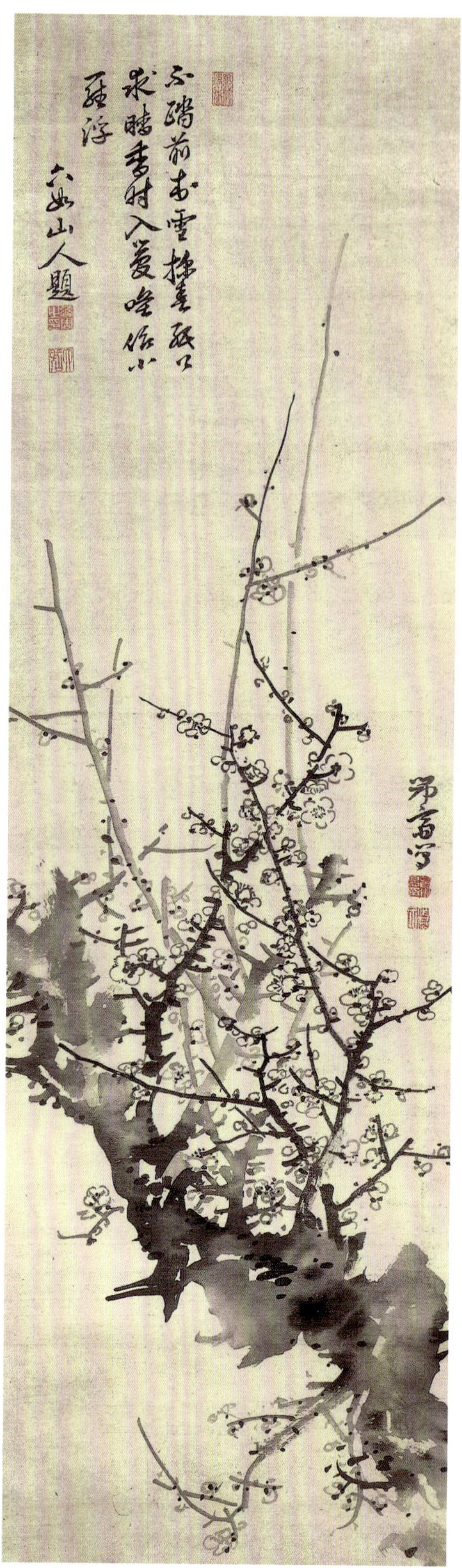

Minagawa Kien
(皆川淇園; 1734–1807)

342. Plum Blossoms

Edo period
Hanging scroll; ink on paper
105.2 x 32 cm ($41\frac{3}{8}$ x $12\frac{5}{8}$ in.)
Text, signatures, seals

Literature: Tokyo National Museum 1985a, no. 53; Avitabile 1990, no. 94.

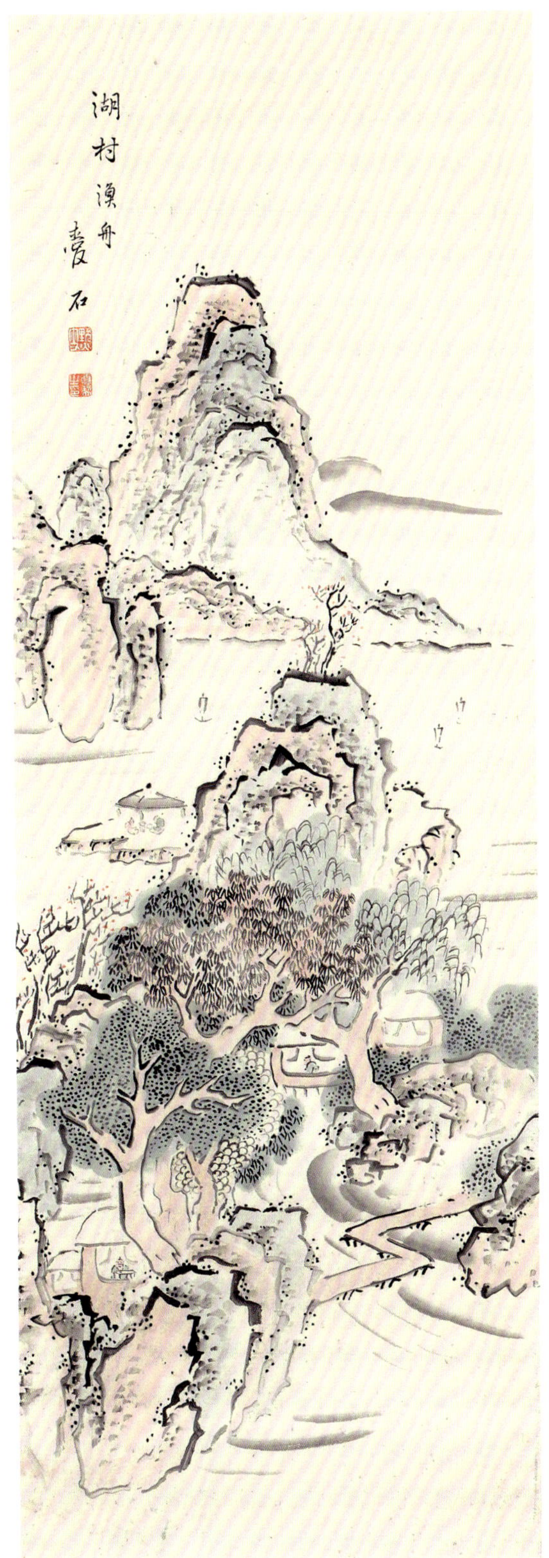

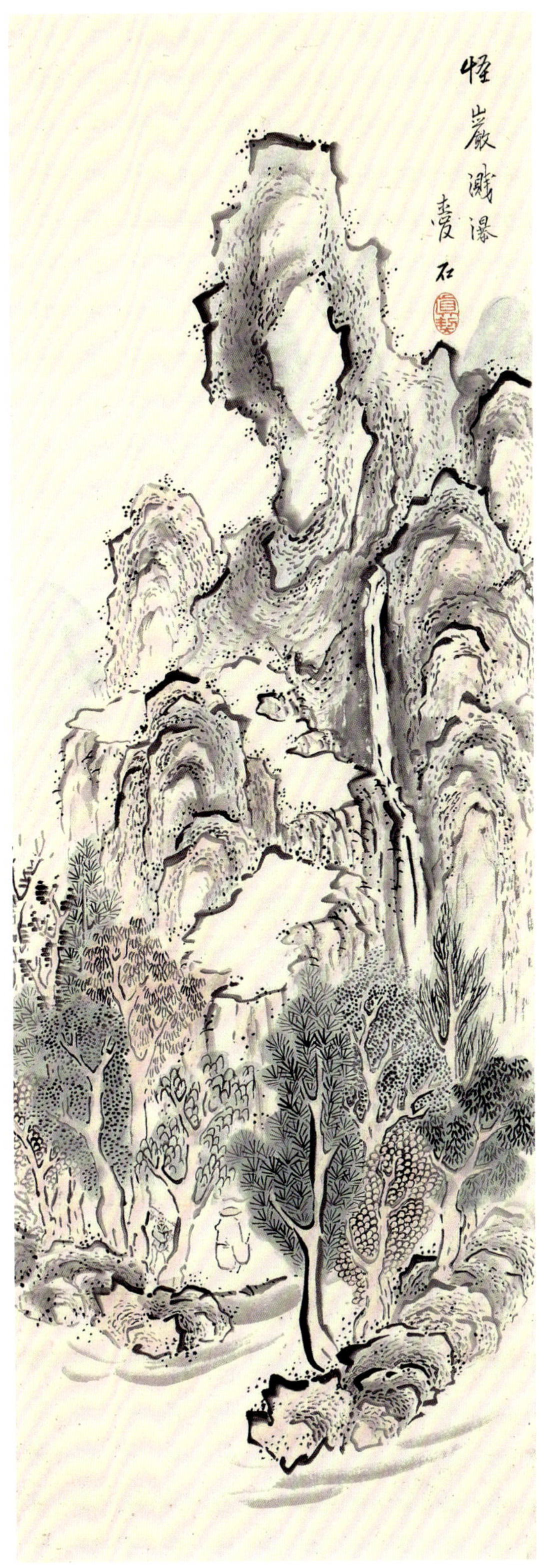

Aiseki
(愛石; first half of 19th century)

343. Fantastic Rocks with Cascading Waterfall; Fishing Boats by a Lake Hamlet

Edo period
Pair of hanging scrolls; ink and light color on paper
Each scroll 131.4 x 45.3 cm ($51^{3}/_{4}$ x $17^{7}/_{8}$ in.)
Text, signatures, seals

Literature: Mason 1977, pp. 12–13, nos. 2, 3.

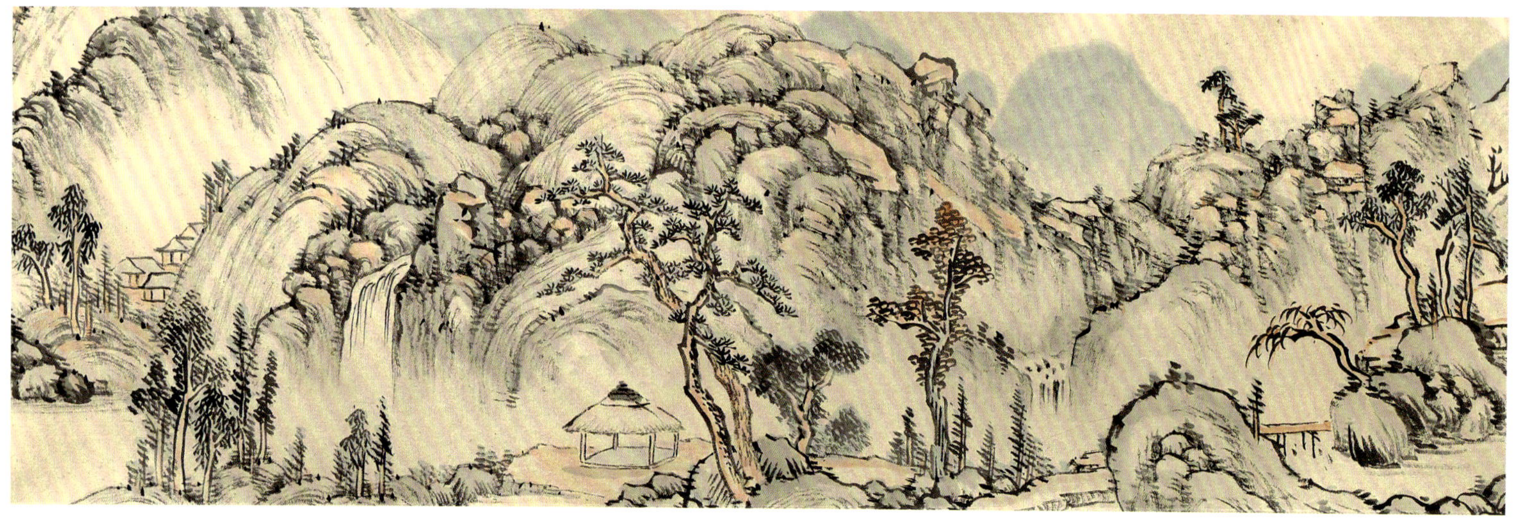

344

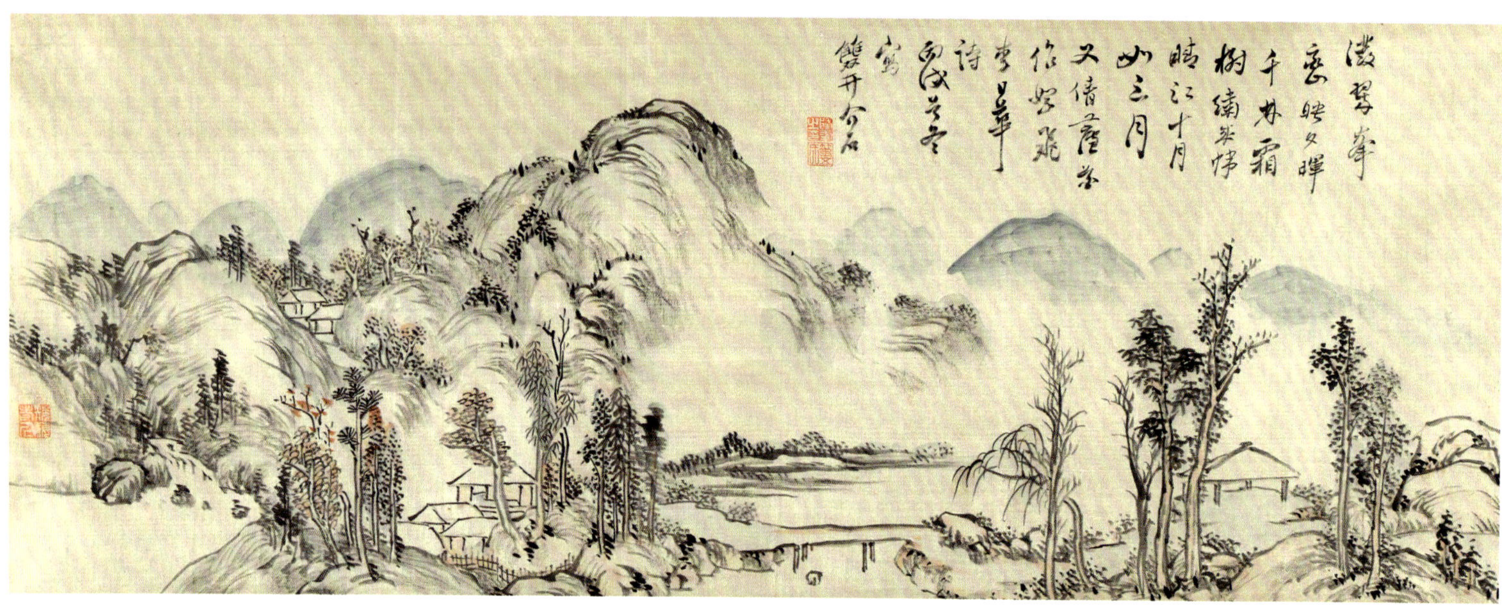

345

Noro Kaiseki
(野呂介石; 1747–1828)

344. Waters and Woods, Pure and Splendent

Edo period, 1822
Handscroll; ink and light color on paper
26.8 x 264.8 cm (10½ in. x 8 ft. 8¼ in.)
Text, signature, seals

Noro Kaiseki
(野呂介石; 1747–1828)

345. Green Peaks

Edo period, 1826
Hanging scroll; ink and light color on silk
35.5 x 92.8 cm (14 x 36½ in.)
Text, signature, seals

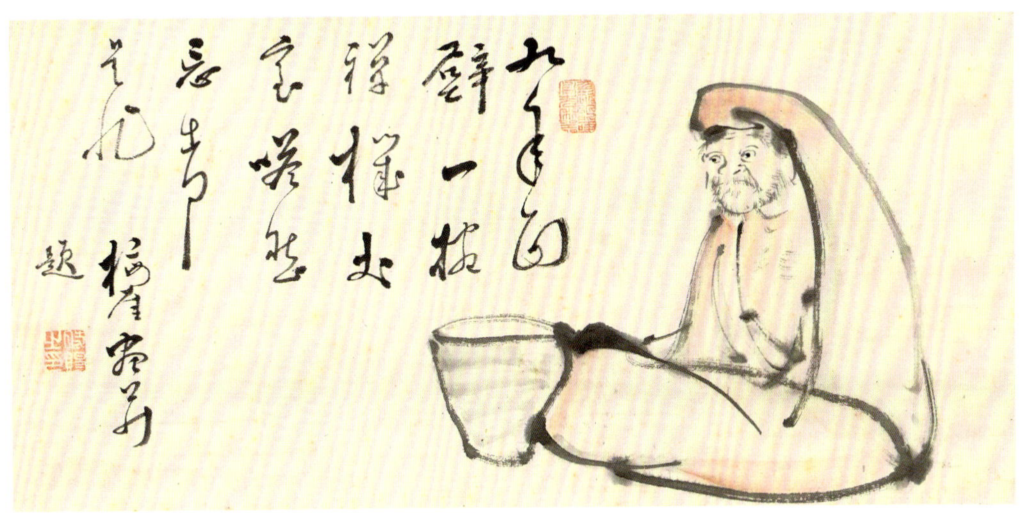

Totoki Baigai
(十時梅厓; 1749–1804)

346. Daruma (達磨)

Edo period, 18th century
Hanging scroll; ink and light color on paper
27.1 x 56.7 cm (10⁵/₈ x 22³/₈ in.)
Text, signature, seals

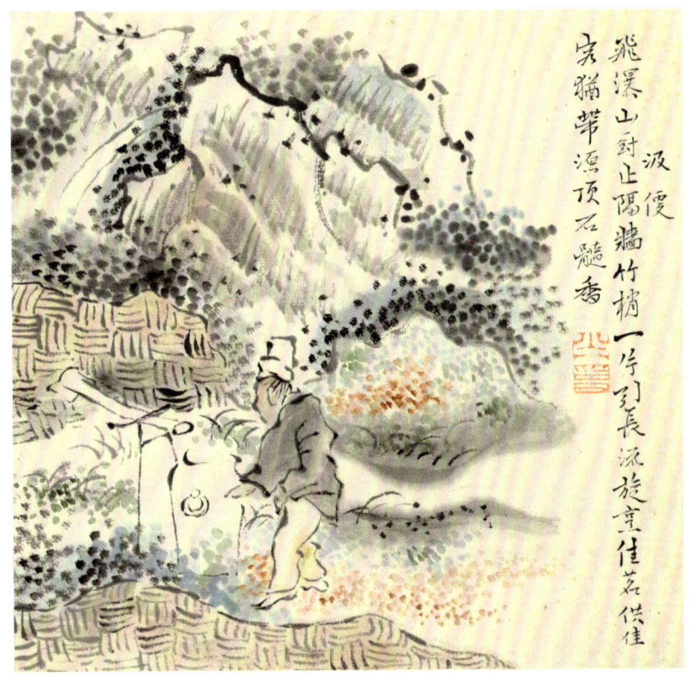

Totoki Baigai
(十時梅厓; 1749–1804)

347. "Convenience in Drawing Water" from *Jūben* (Ten Conveniences, 十便); "Pleasure of Dawn" from *Jūgi* (Ten Pleasures, 十宜)

Edo period, 1800
Two albums, each with ten leaves; ink and light color on paper
Each leaf 18.8 x 19.4 cm (7³/₈ x 7⁵/₈ in.)
Text, signatures, seals

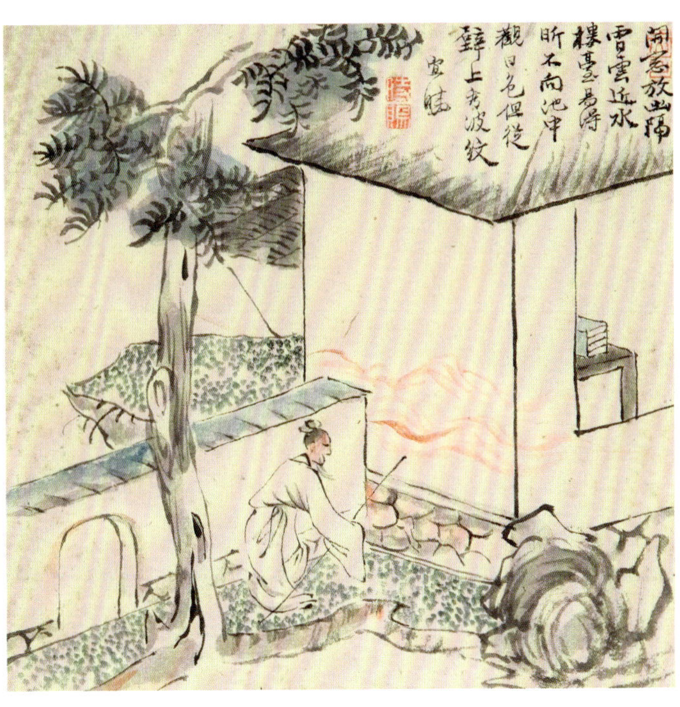

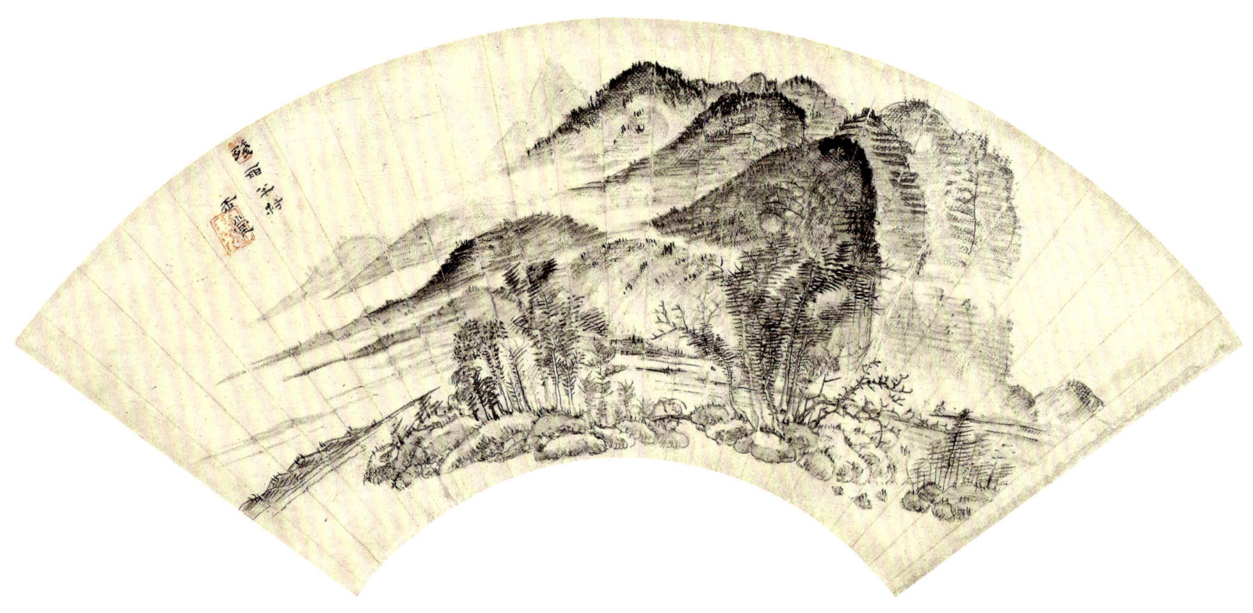

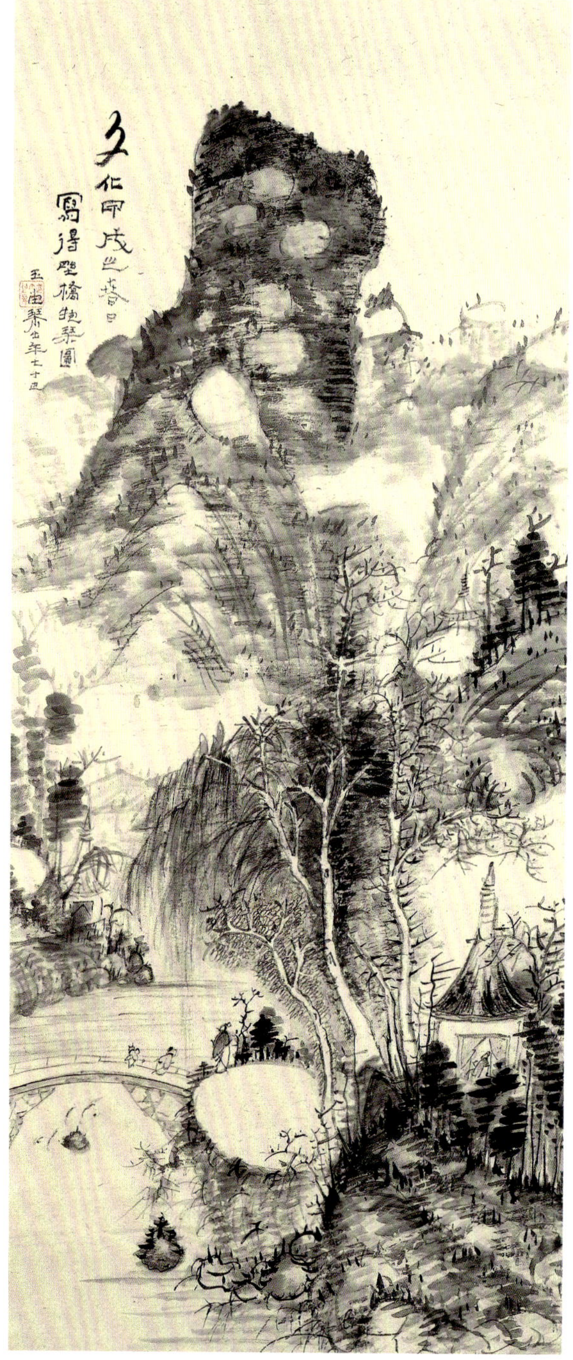

Uragami Gyokudō
(浦上玉堂; 1745–1820)

348. Lingering Rain over a Mountain Hamlet

Edo period, ca. 1815–20
Folding fan, mounted as a hanging scroll; ink on paper
16.6 x 47.9 cm (6½ x 18⅞ in.)
Text, signature, seals

Literature: Miyake Kyūnosuke 1955, pl. 28; Tokyo National Museum 1965, no. 200; Okayama Art Museum 1970, ill.; Suzuki Susumu 1970, p. 127; Murase 1975, no. 77; Suzuki Susumu 1978, fig. 141; Gitter and Fister 1985, no. 30; Tokyo National Museum 1985a, no. 54; Addiss 1987, fig. 5.22; Avitabile 1990, no. 95; Murase 2000, no. 162.

Uragami Gyokudō
(浦上玉堂; 1745–1820)

349. Crossing a Mountain Bridge with a Zither

Edo period, 1814
Hanging scroll; ink on paper
127.4 x 54.4 cm (50⅛ x 21⅜ in.)
Text, signature, seal

Ex coll.: Idegawa Shigeru, Kumamoto

Literature: Miyake Kyūnosuke 1955, pl. 25; Narazaki Muneshige 1955, p. 85; Tokyo National Museum 1965, no. 181; Murase 1975, no. 76; Suzuki Susumu 1978, fig. 26; Addiss 1987, p. 124, fig. 5.22; Guth 1996, fig. 45; Murase 2000, no. 161; Volk 2010, p. 157, fig. 72.

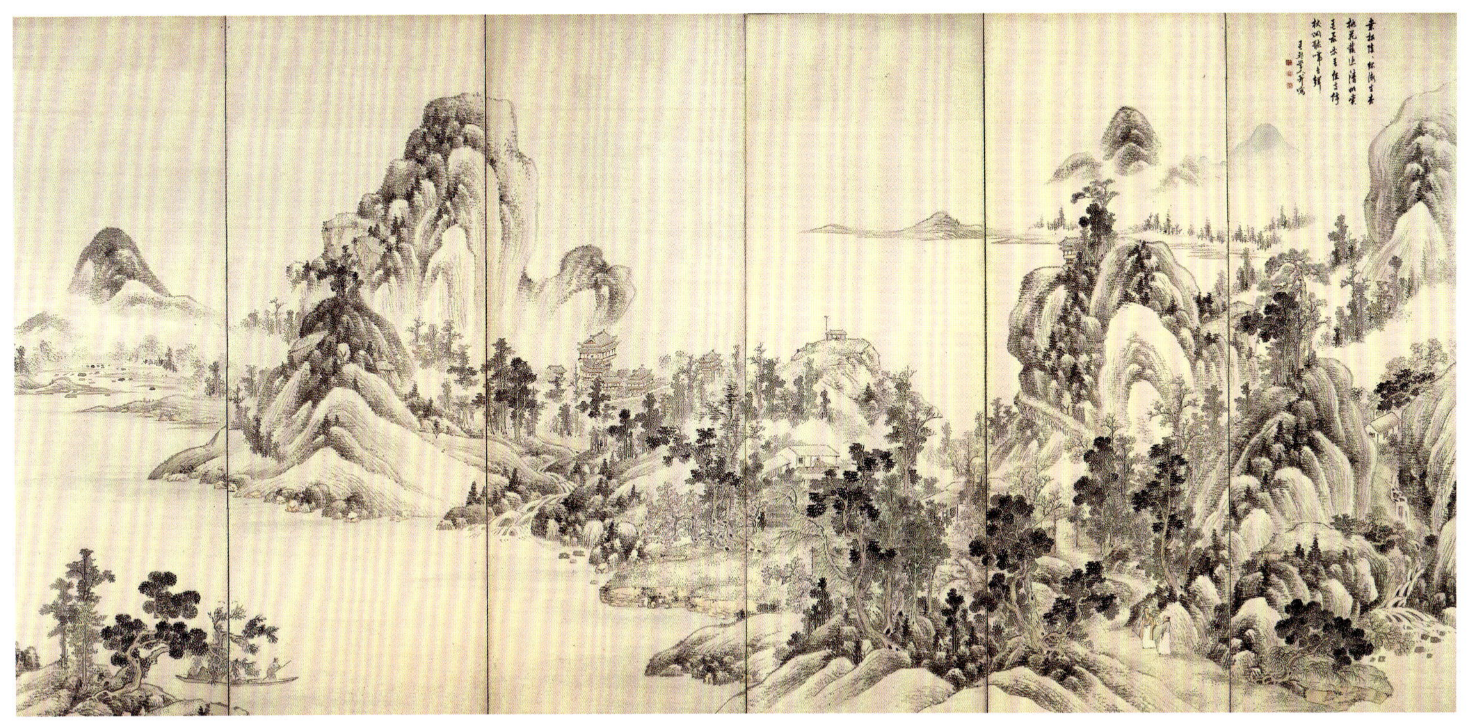

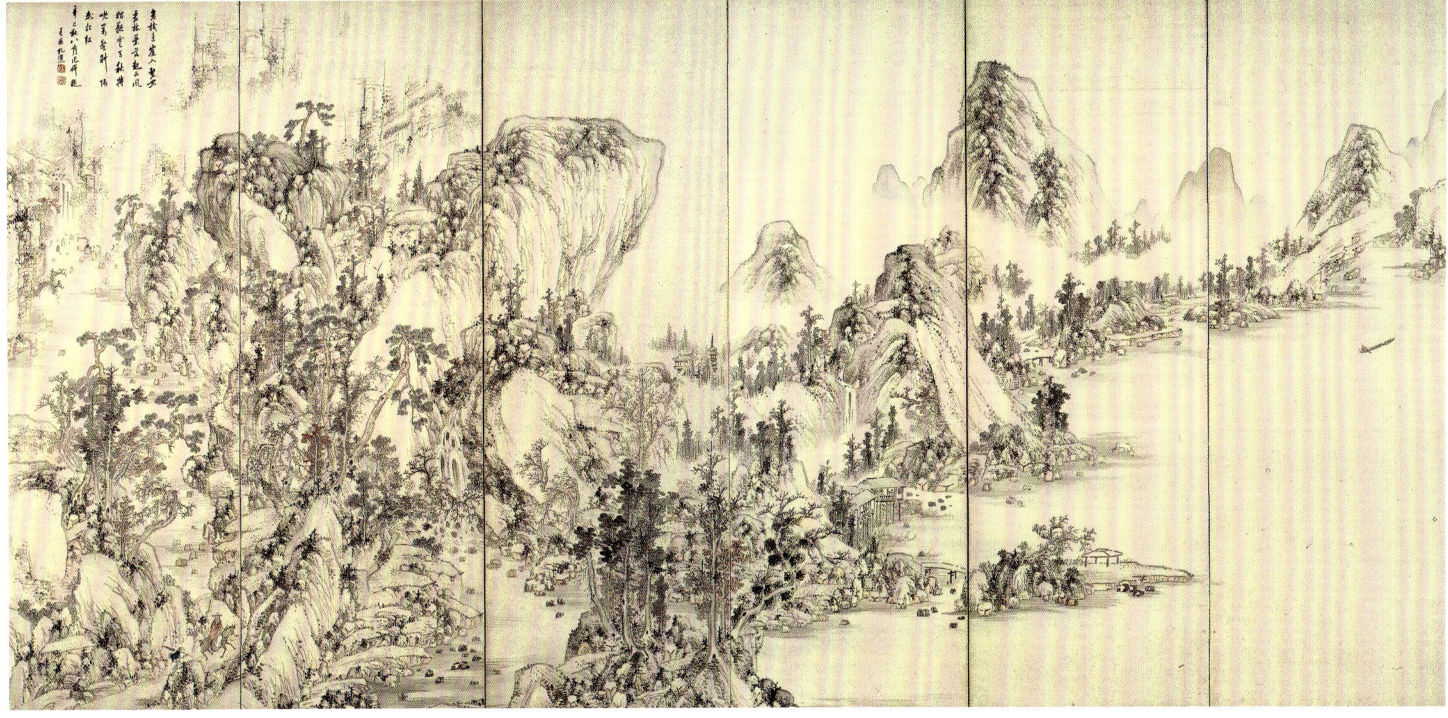

Uragami Shunkin
(浦上春琴; 1779–1846)

350. Landscapes of Spring and Autumn

Edo period, 1821
Pair of six-panel folding screens; ink and light color on silk
Each screen 178.7 x 370.8 cm (70 3/8 in. x 12 ft. 2 in.)
Text, signatures, seals

Literature: Murase 1975, no. 78; Avitabile 1990, no. 97; Tsuji Nobuo et al. 2005, no. 115.

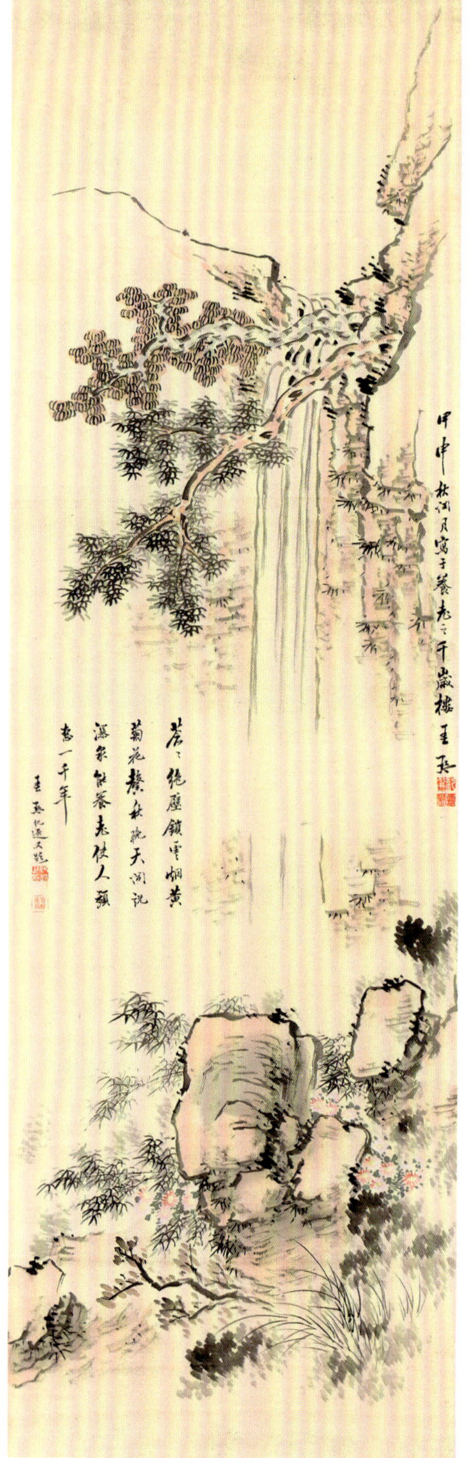

351

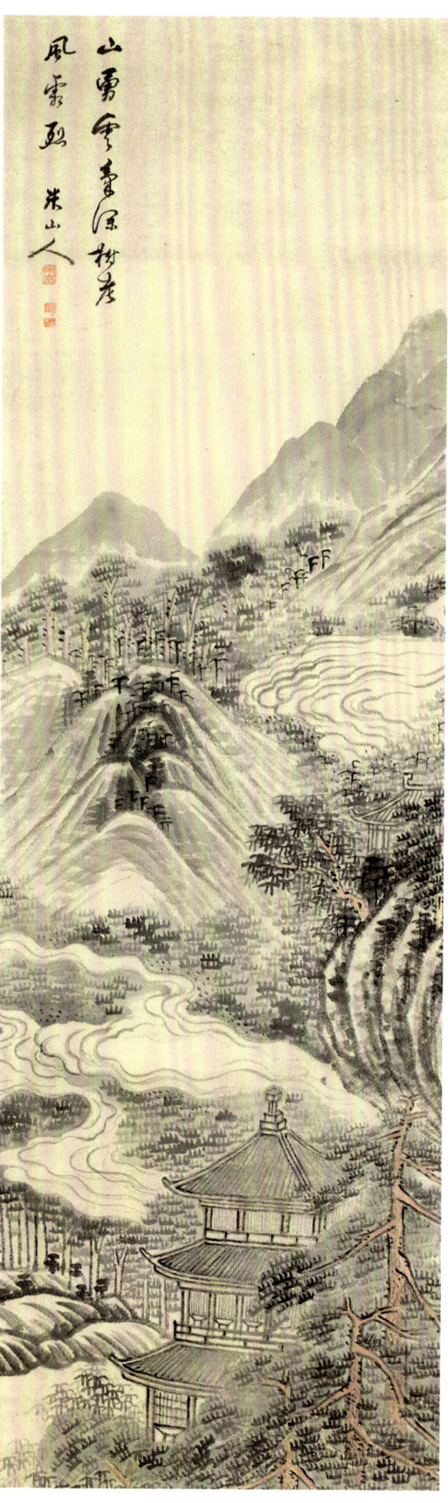

352

Uragami Shunkin
(浦上春琴; 1779–1846)

351. Yōrō Waterfall (養老の滝)

Edo period, 1824
Hanging scroll; ink and light color on silk
129.2 x 41.2 cm (50 7/8 x 16 1/4 in.)
Text, signatures, seals

Okada Beisanjin
(岡田米山人; 1744–1820)

352. Landscape with Pavilion

Edo period
Hanging scroll; ink and light color on paper
127.3 x 40.3 cm (50 1/8 x 15 7/8 in.)
Text, signature, seals

Literature: Murase 1975, no. 82.

Okada Hankō
(岡田半江; 1782–1846)

353. Bamboo and Plums in Early Spring

Edo period, 1843
Hanging scroll; ink and light color on paper
127.7 x 59.1 cm (50 1/4 x 23 1/4 in.)
Text, signatures, seals

Literature: Murase 1975, no. 83.

Okada Hankō
(岡田半江; 1782–1846)

354. Landscape after a Qing Chinese Work

Edo period, 19th century
Hanging scroll; ink and light color on paper
118.5 x 35.5 cm (46 5/8 x 14 in.)
Text, signature, seals

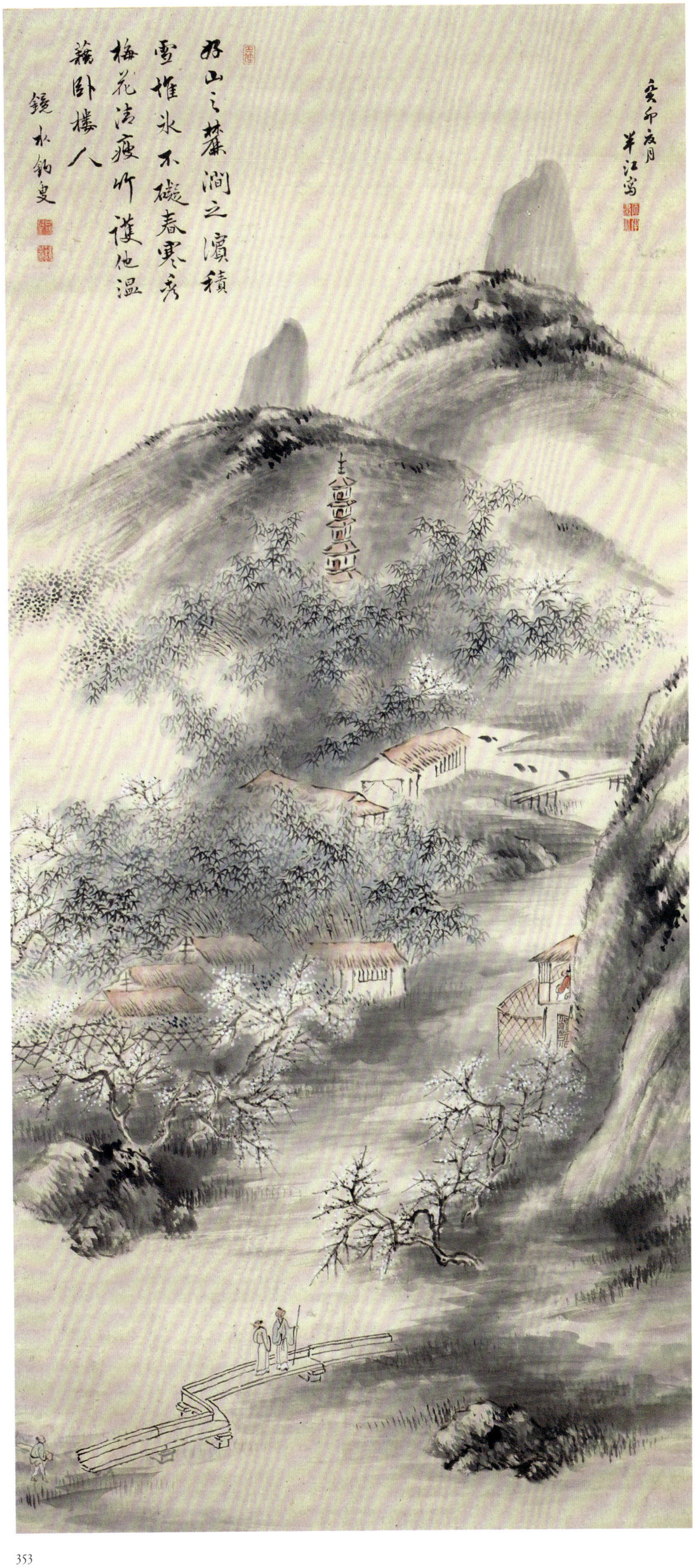

353

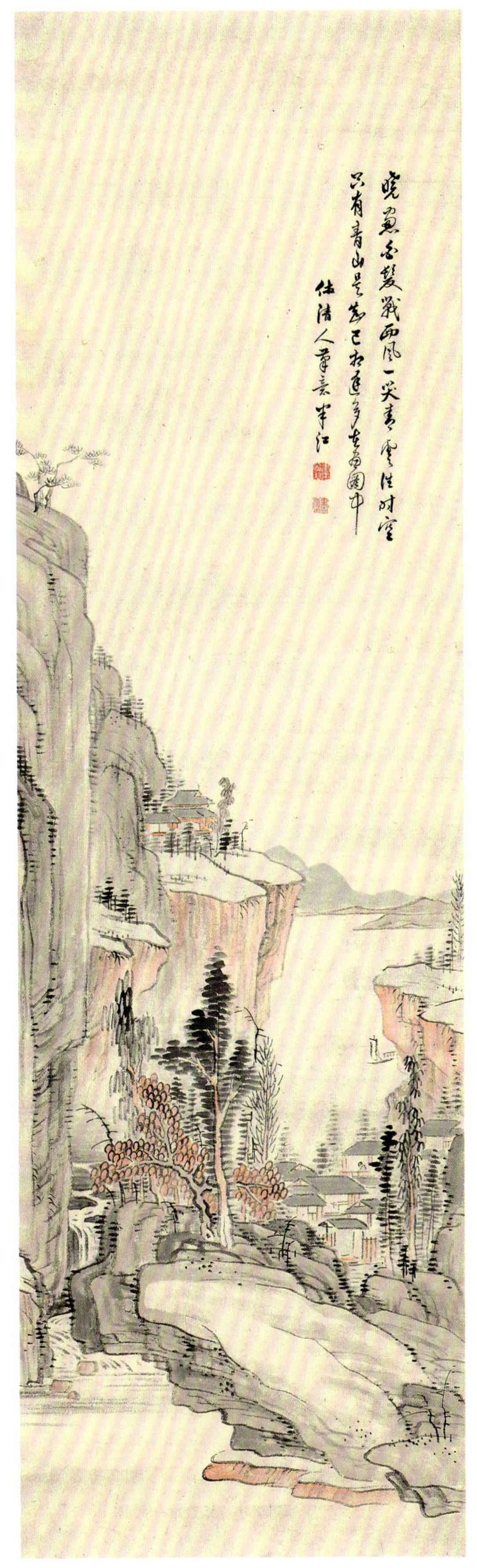

354

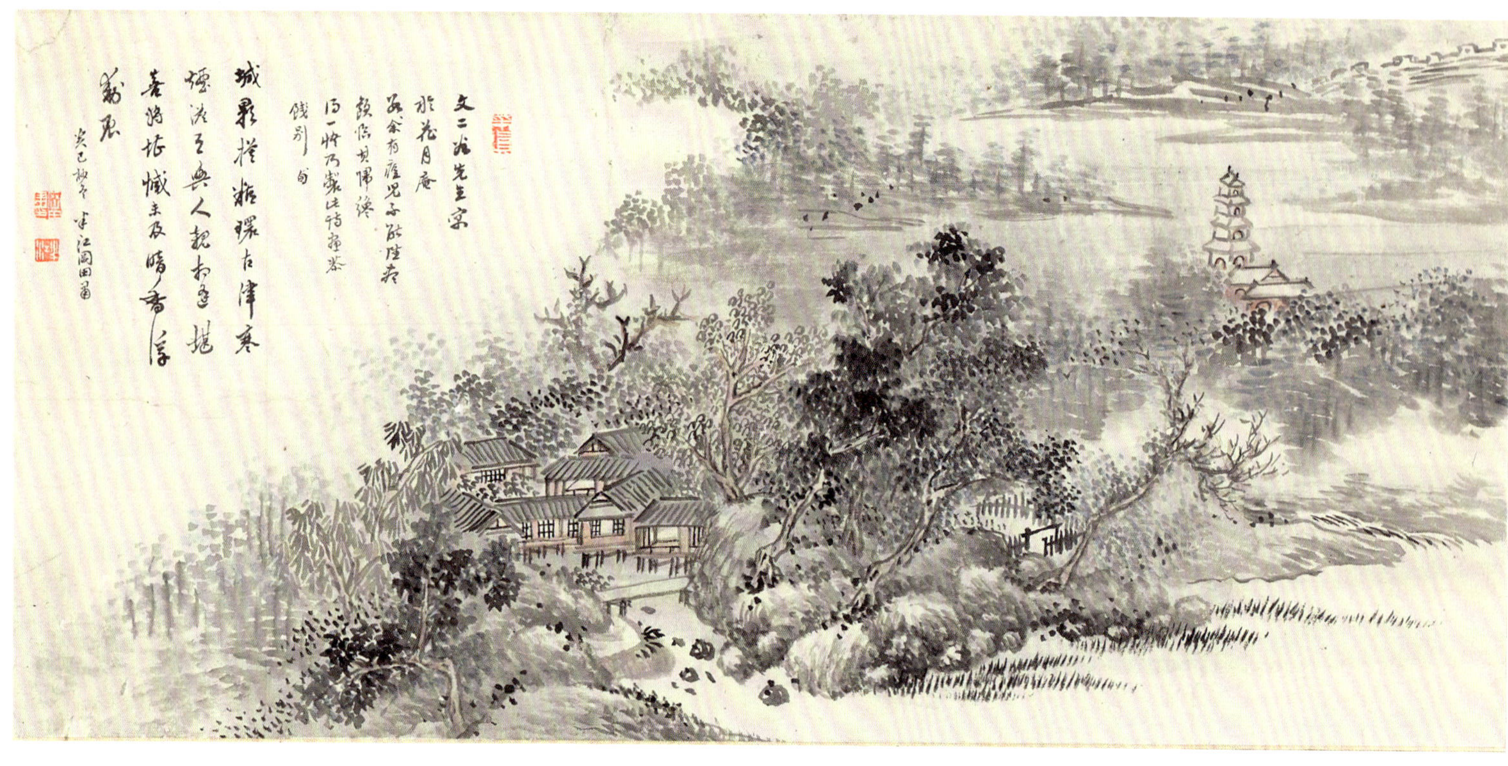

Okada Hankō
(岡田半江; 1782–1846)

355. Farewell Gift to Tani Bunji (谷文二)

Edo period, 1833
Hanging scroll; ink and light color on paper
30 x 63.7 cm (11¾ x 25⅛ in.)
Text, signature, seals

Aoki Mokubei
(青木木米; 1767–1833)

356. Preparing Tea by a Mountain Gorge

Edo period, 1825
Folding fan, mounted as a hanging scroll; ink and light color on paper
14.8 x 49.4 cm (5⅞ x 19½ in.)
Signature, seals

Ex coll.: Kuraishi

Literature: Murase 1975, no. 80; Tokyo National Museum 1985a, no. 55; Avitabile 1990, no. 96; Murase 2000, no. 163.

Tanomura Chikuden
(田能村竹田; 1777–1835)

357. Rainstorm over a River Village

Edo period
Hanging scroll; ink and light color on paper
132.3 x 42.2 cm (52⅛ x 16⅝ in.)
Text, signature, seals

Literature: Suzuki Susumu 1963, fig. 136; Murase 1975, no. 84; Murase 2000, no. 164.

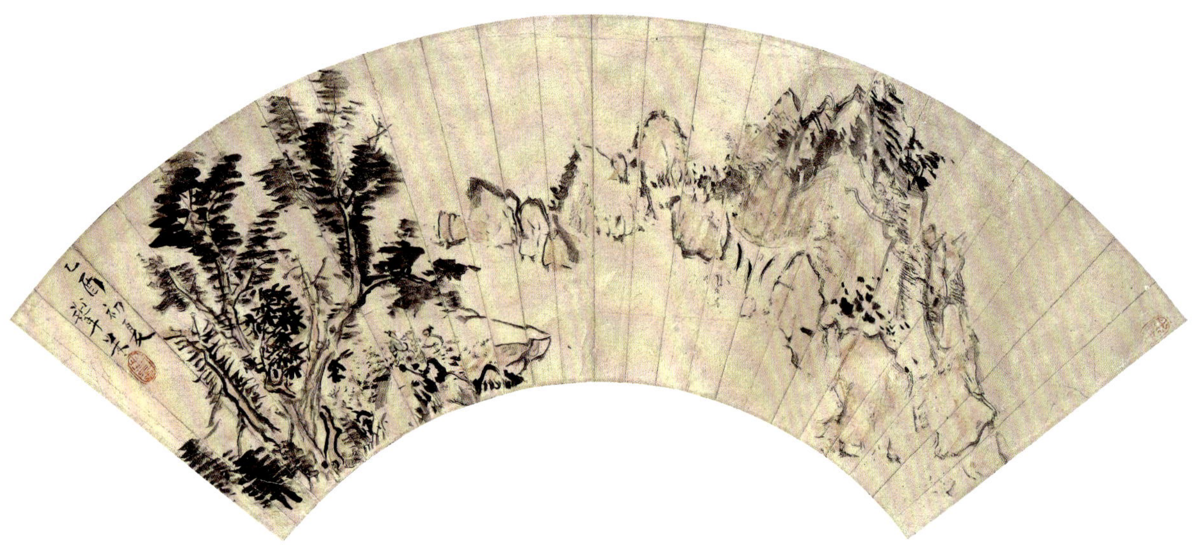

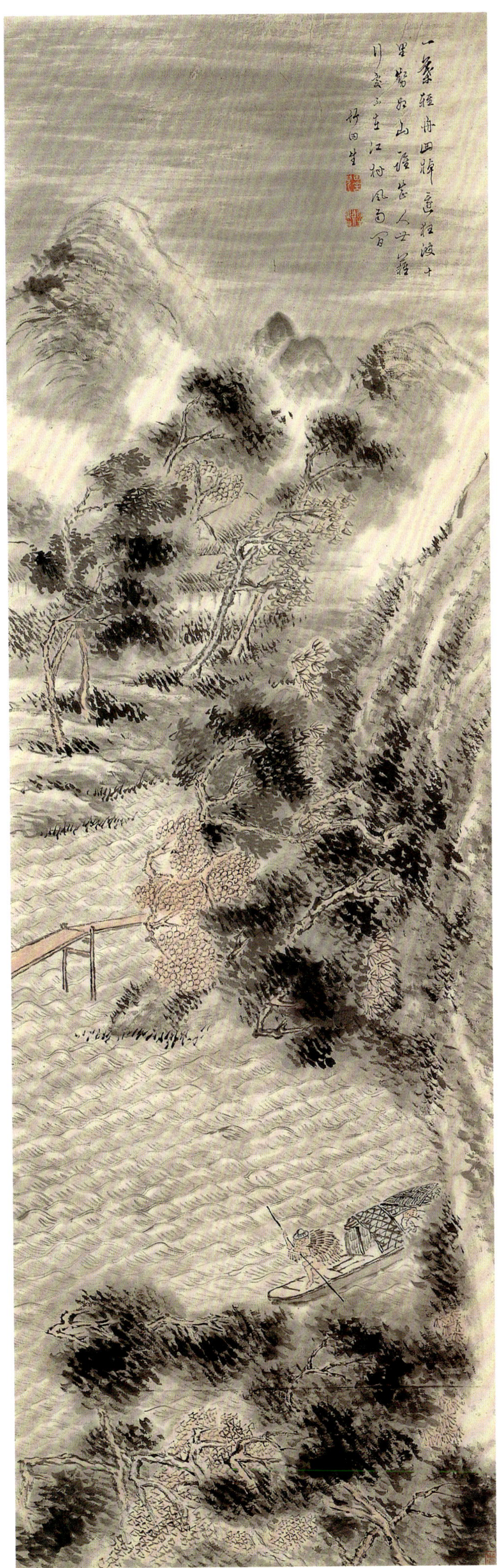

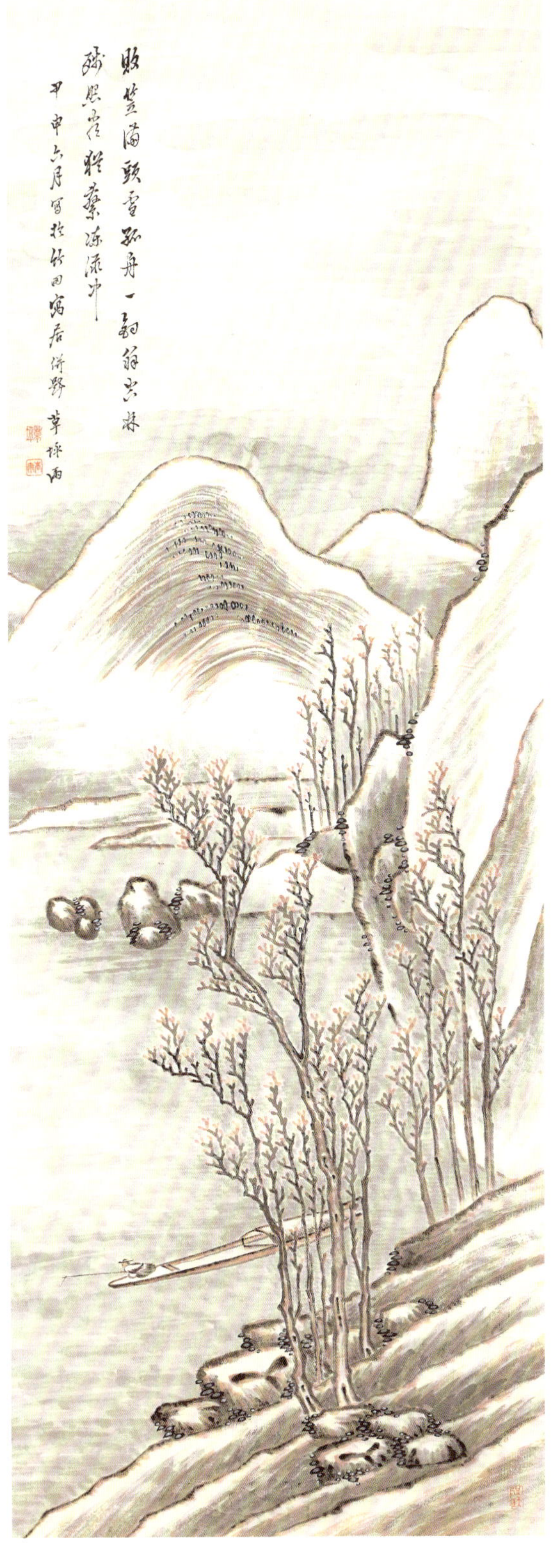

Takahashi Sōhei
(高橋草坪; 1802–1833)

358. Snowy Landscape

Edo period, 1824
Hanging scroll; ink and light color on paper
137.3 x 49.1 cm (54 x 19 3/8 in.)
Text, signature, seals

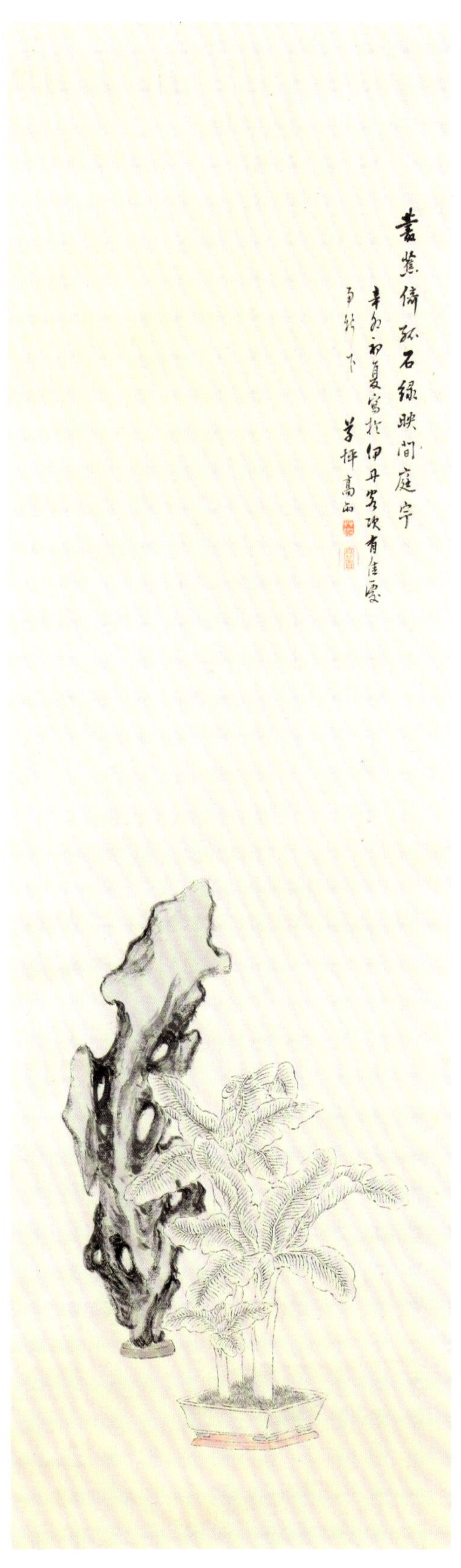

Takahashi Sōhei
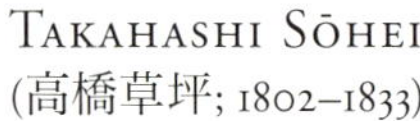
(高橋草坪; 1802–1833)

359. Taihu Rock and Banana Plant

Edo period, 1831
Hanging scroll; ink and light color on paper
100.3 x 50.1 cm (39 1/2 x 19 3/4 in.)
Text, signature, seals

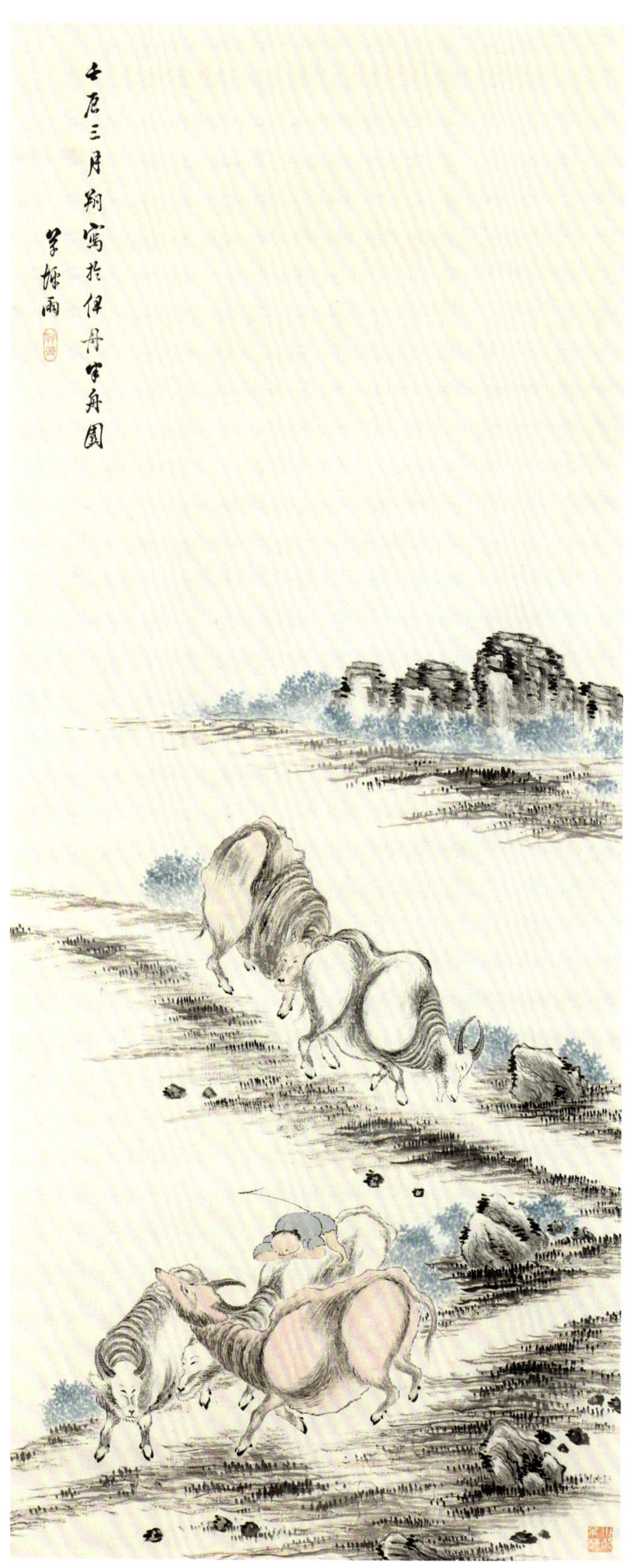

Takahashi Sōhei
(高橋草坪; 1802–1833)

360. Oxen and Herd Boy

Edo period, 1832
Hanging scroll; ink and light color on paper
101.8 x 41.8 cm (40 1/8 x 16 1/2 in.)
Signature, seals

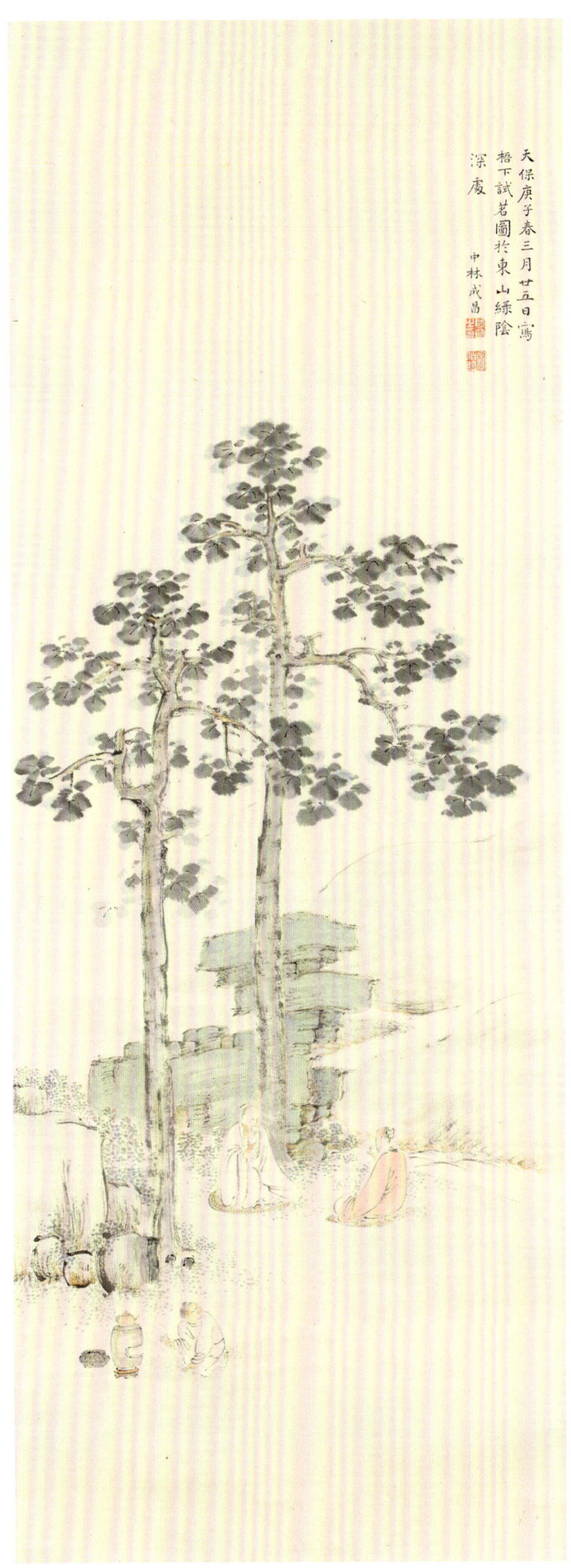

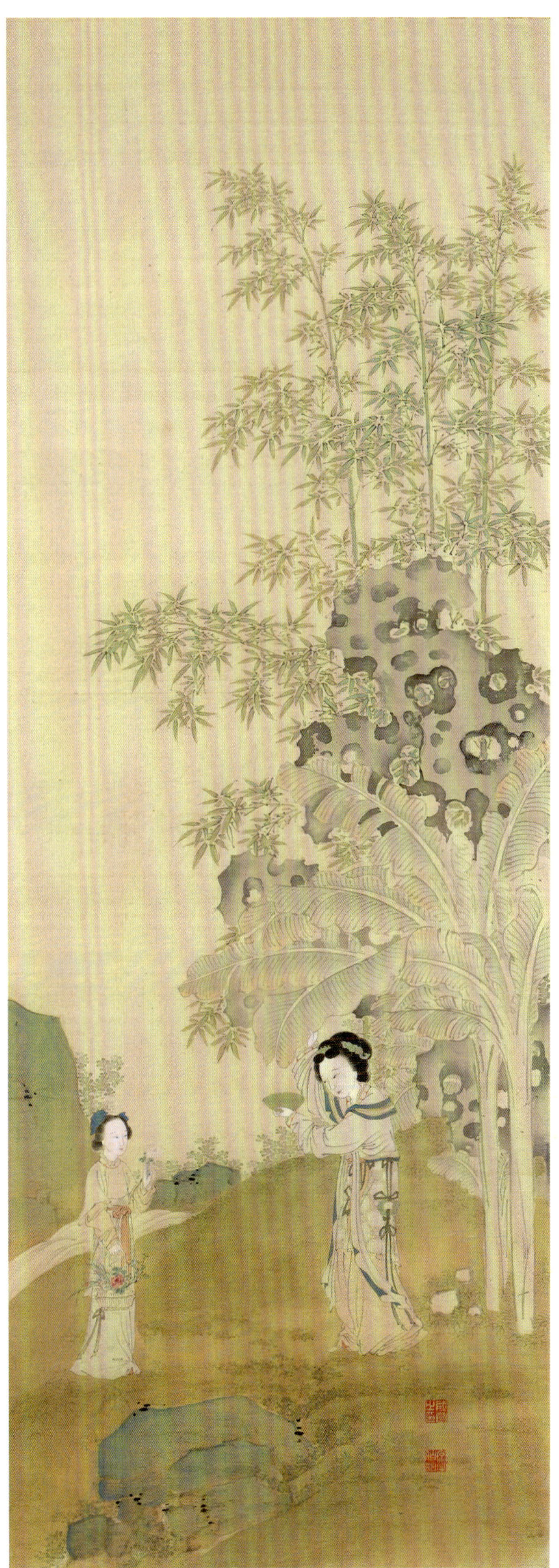

NAKABAYASHI CHIKUTŌ
(中林竹洞; 1776–1853)

361. Sampling Tea beneath Wu Trees (梧下試茗図)

Edo period, 1840
Hanging scroll; ink and light color on paper
119.2 x 54.1 cm ($46\frac{7}{8}$ x $21\frac{1}{4}$ in.)
Signature, seals

NAKABAYASHI CHIKUTŌ
(中林竹洞; 1776–1853)

362. Chinese Lady with Attendant

Edo period, 19th century
Hanging scroll; ink and color on silk
104.3 x 37.2 cm ($41\frac{1}{8}$ x $14\frac{5}{8}$ in.)
Seals

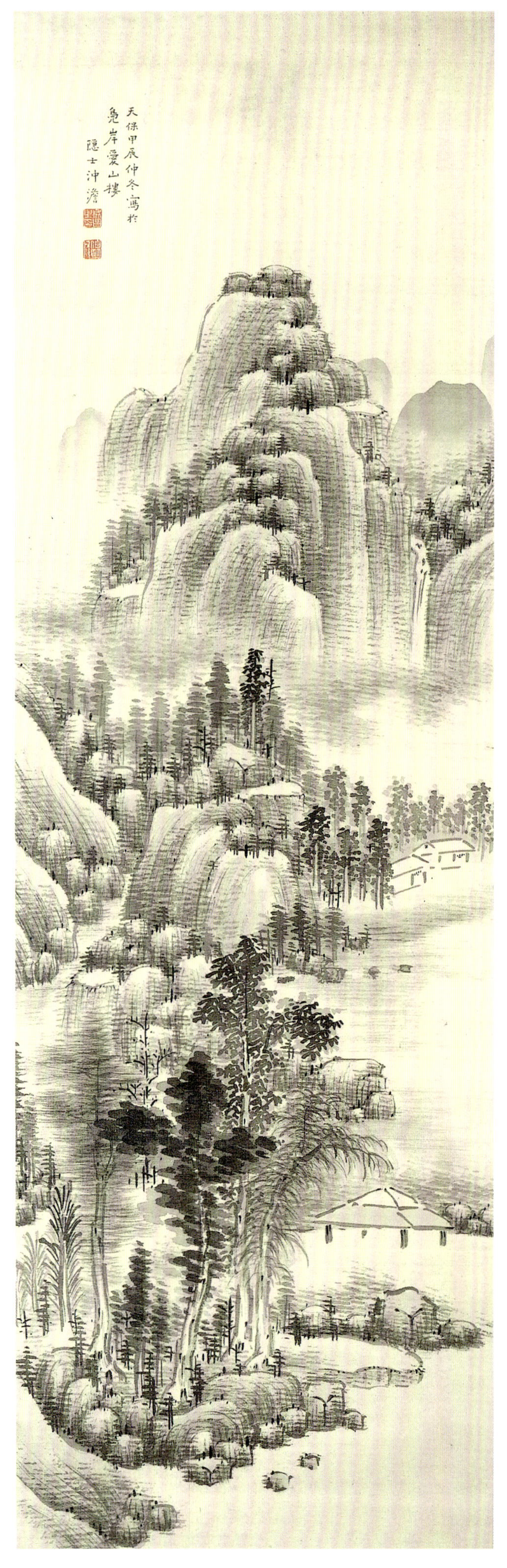

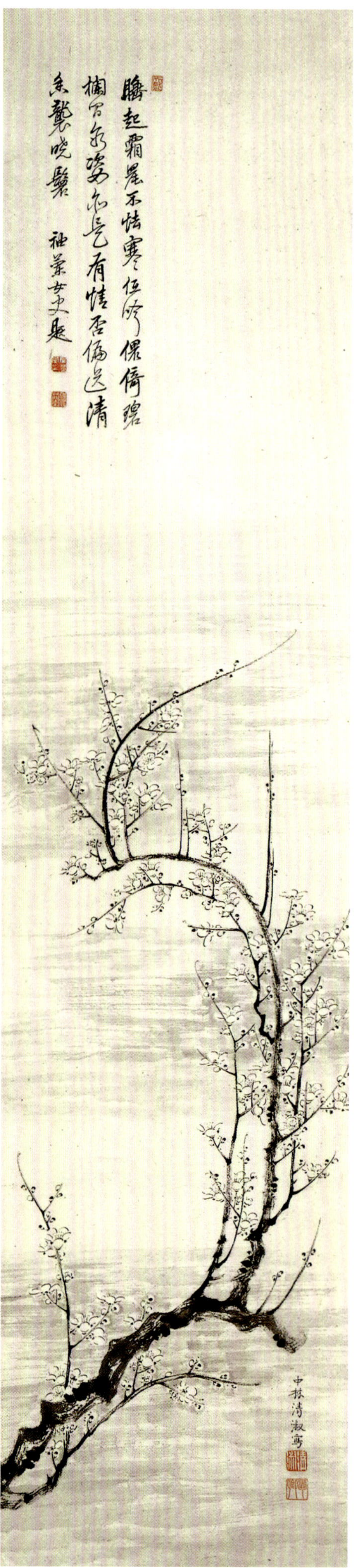

Nakabayashi Chikutō
(中林竹洞; 1776–1853)

363. Landscape

Edo period, 1844
Hanging scroll; ink on silk
126 x 41.3 cm (49⅝ x 16¼ in.)
Signature, seals

Literature: Mason 1977, no. 12; Tokyo National Museum 1985a, no. 59; Avitabile 1990, no. 101.

Nakabayashi Seishuku
(中林清淑; 1831–?)

364. Plum Tree

Edo period
Hanging scroll; ink on paper
129.2 x 29.9 cm (50⅞ x 11¾ in.)
Text, signatures, seals

Nukina Kaioku
(貫名海屋; 1778–1863)

365. Autumn Landscape at Eigenji (永源寺)

Edo period, 1833
Hanging scroll; ink and color on silk
30.1 x 17.9 cm (11⅞ x 7 in.)
Signature, seals

Literature: Yoshizawa Chū 1968, pp. 25–27; Murase 1975, no. 85; Tokyo National Museum 1985a, no. 57; Avitabile 1990, no. 99.

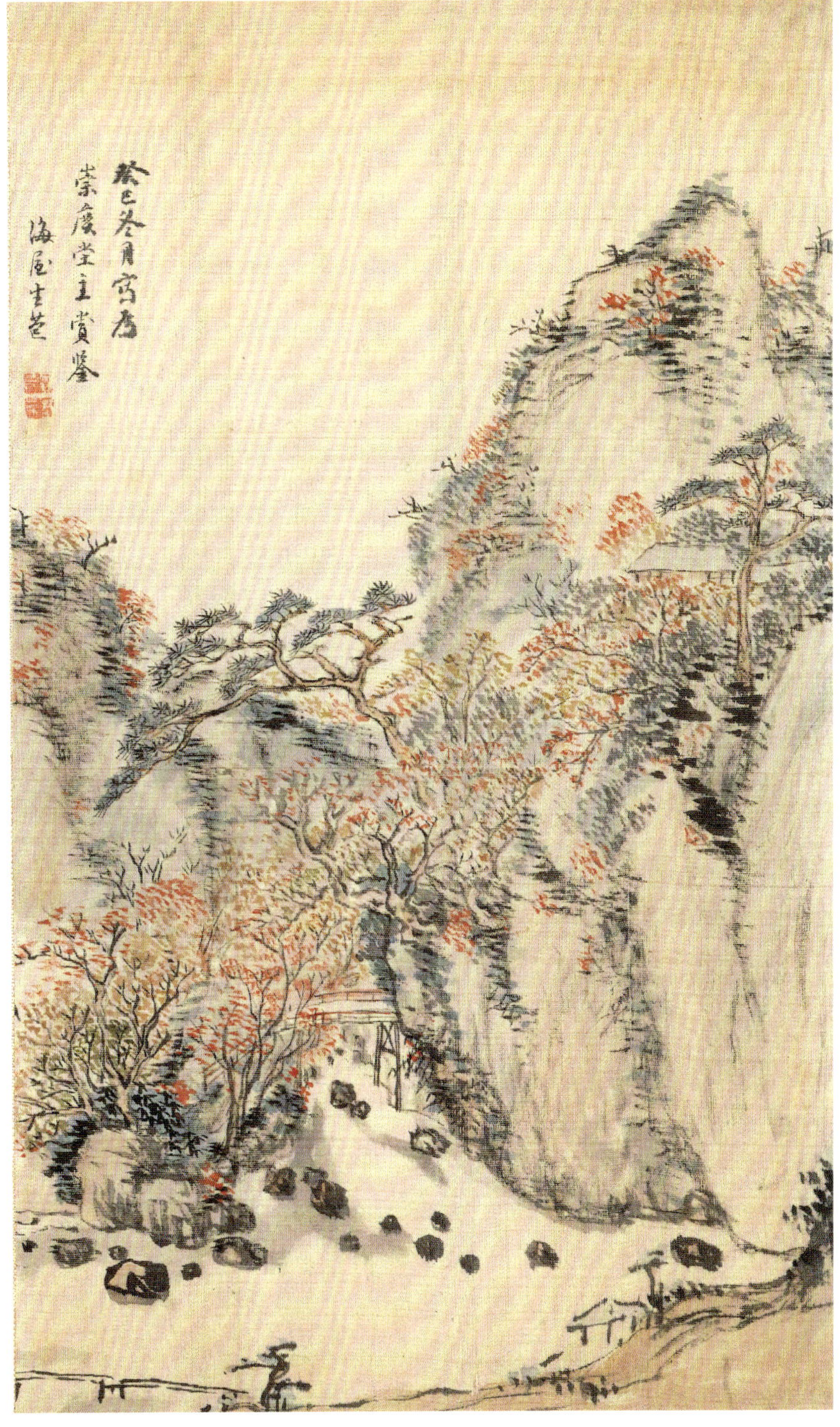

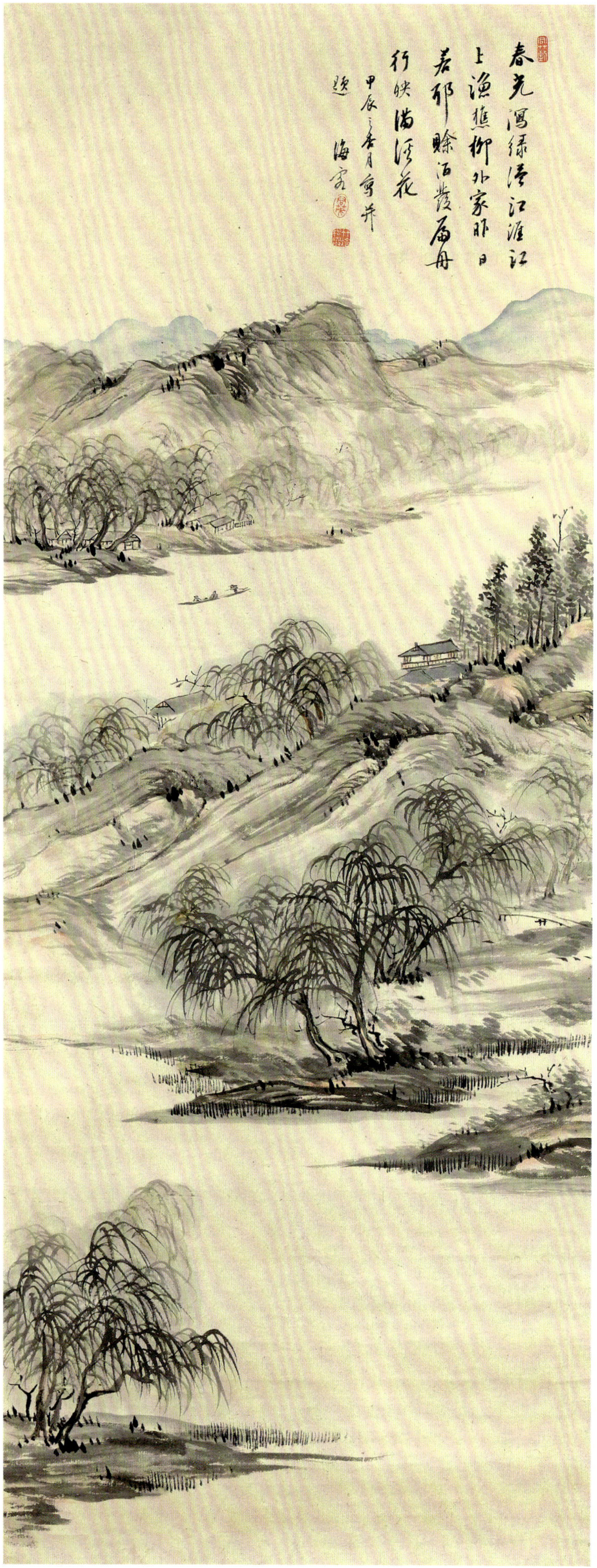

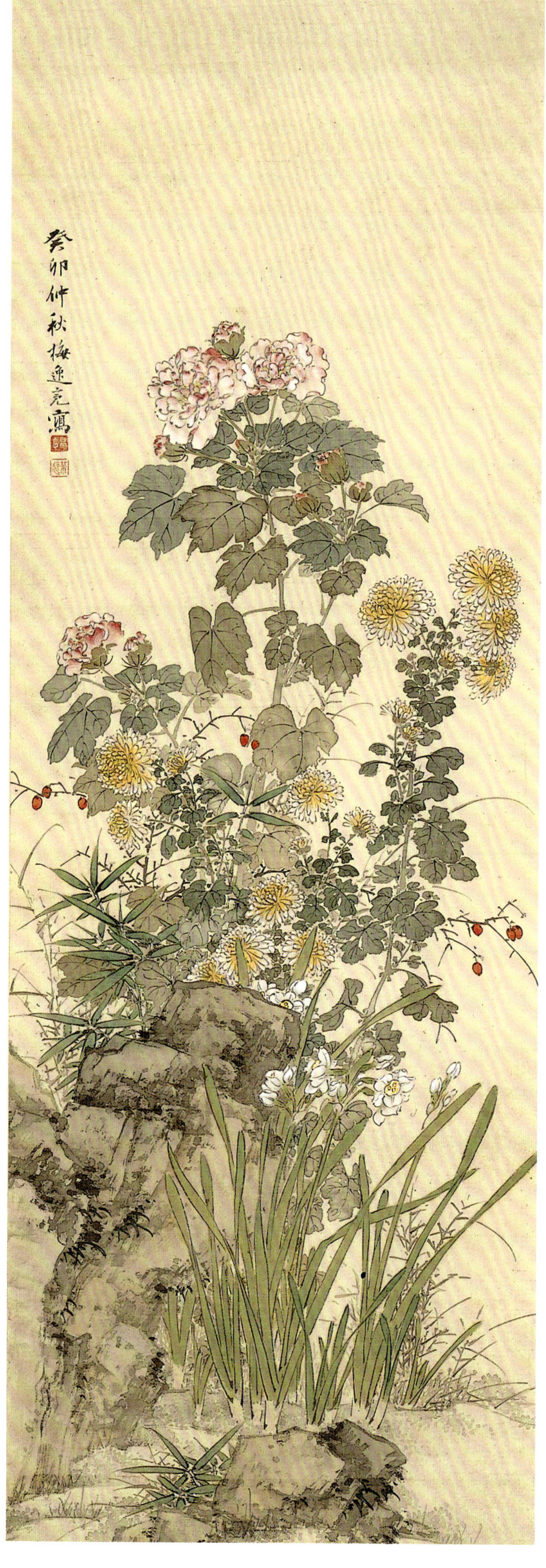

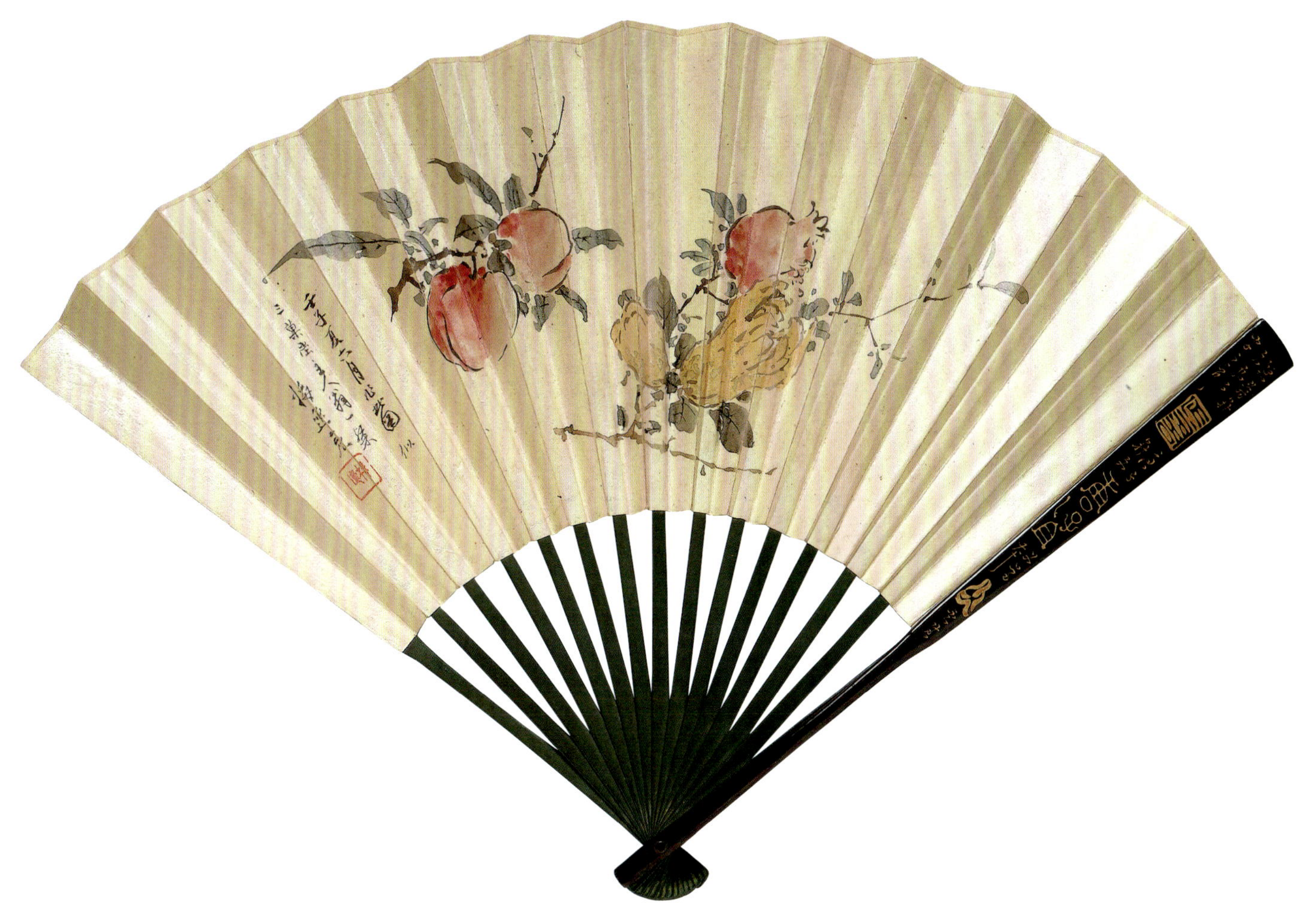

Nukina Kaioku
(貫名海屋; 1778–1863)

366. Spring Landscape

Edo period, 1844
Hanging scroll; ink and light color on paper
134.7 x 52.4 cm (53 x 20⅝ in.)
Text, signature, seals

Literature: Mason 1977, no. 18.

Yamamoto Baiitsu
(山本梅逸; 1783–1856)

367. Autumn Flowers

Edo period, 1843
Hanging scroll; ink and color on silk
115.8 x 40.9 cm (45⅝ x 16⅛ in.)
Signature, seals

Literature: Murase 1975, no. 86; Tokyo National Museum 1985a, no. 58; Avitabile 1990, no. 100.

Yamamoto Baiitsu
(山本梅逸; 1783–1856)

368. Peaches, Pomegranate, and Fingered Citron

Edo period, 1832
Folding fan; ink and color on paper
17 x 47.5 cm (6¾ x 18¾ in.)
Signature, seal

Overleaf:

Yamamoto Baiitsu
(山本梅逸; 1783–1856)

369. Landscapes of the Four Seasons

Edo period, 1848
Four hanging scrolls; ink and light color on silk
Each scroll (average) 102.6 x 35.2 cm (40⅜ x 13⅞ in.)
Signatures, seals

Literature: Iizuka Beiu 1932b, pls. 68–71; Suzuki Susumu 1973, pp. 75–82; Mason 1977, pp. 25–27, no. 15; Graham 1986, fig. 18 ("Summer"); Murase 1993, no. 30; Murase 2000, no. 165.

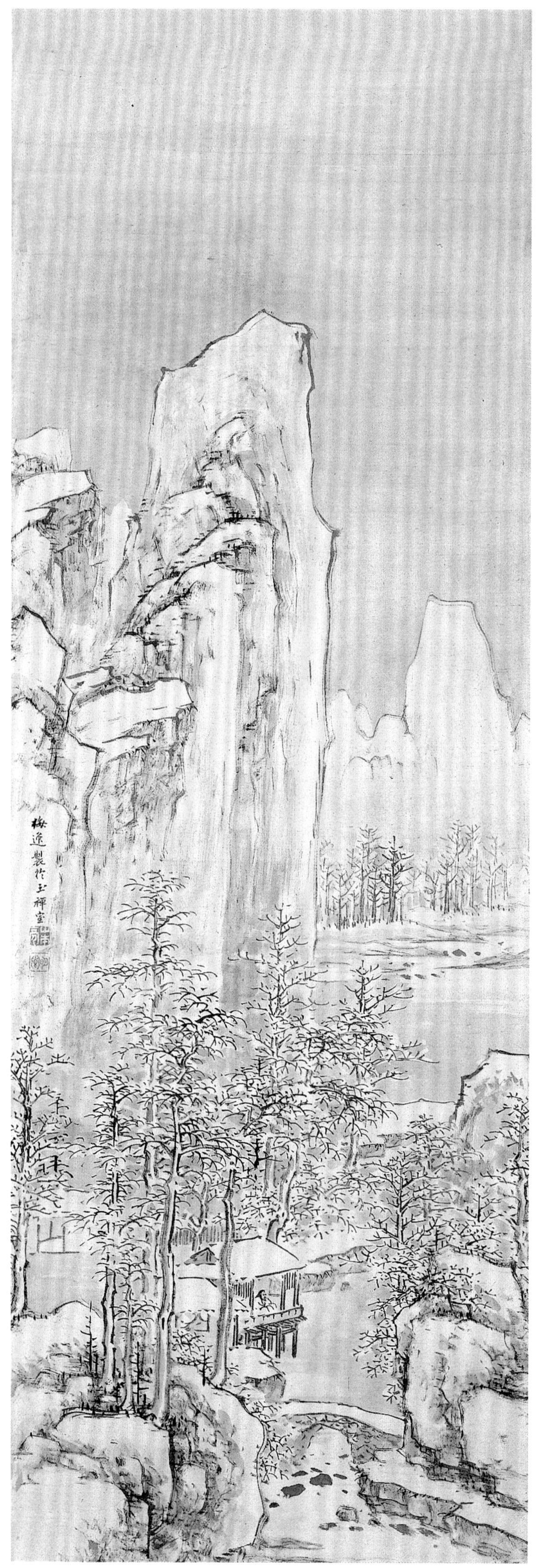

"Winter"

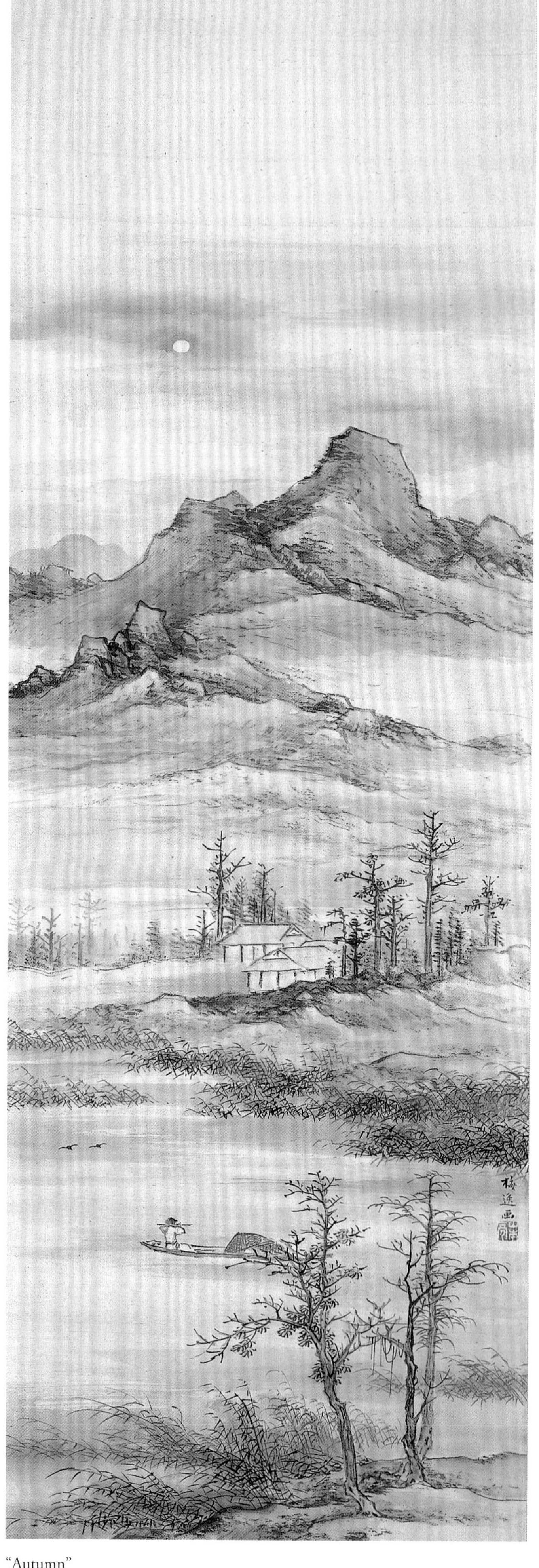

"Autumn"

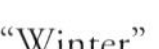

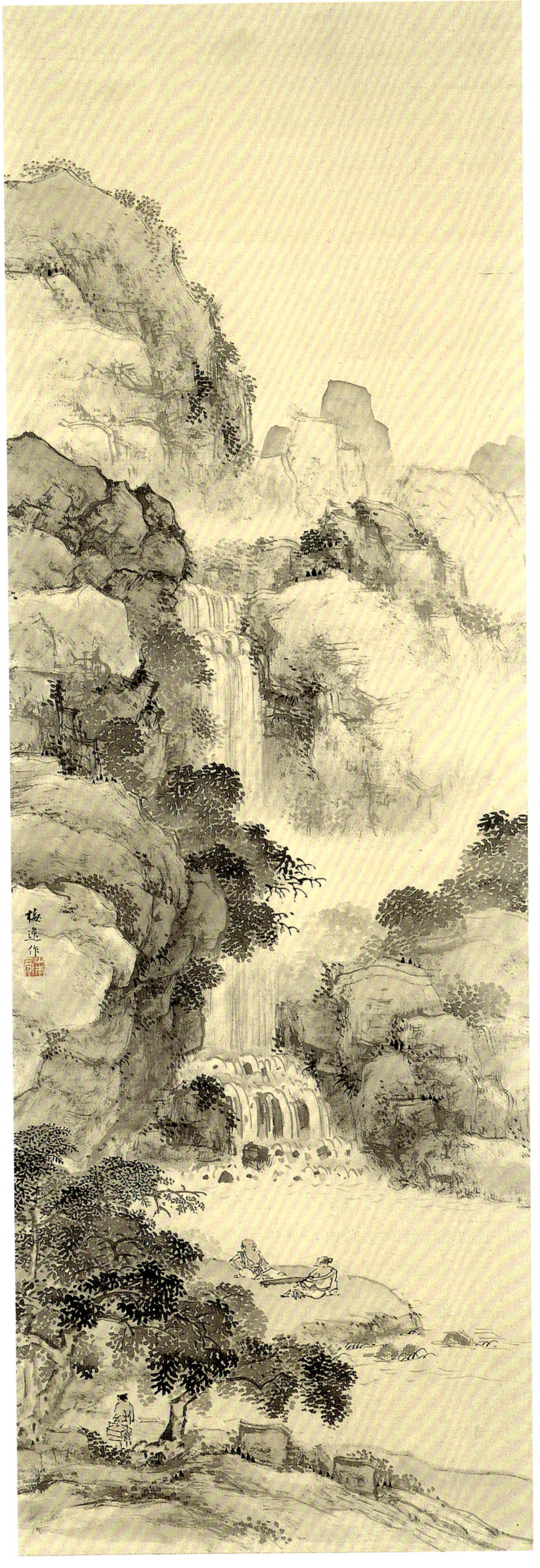

"Summer"

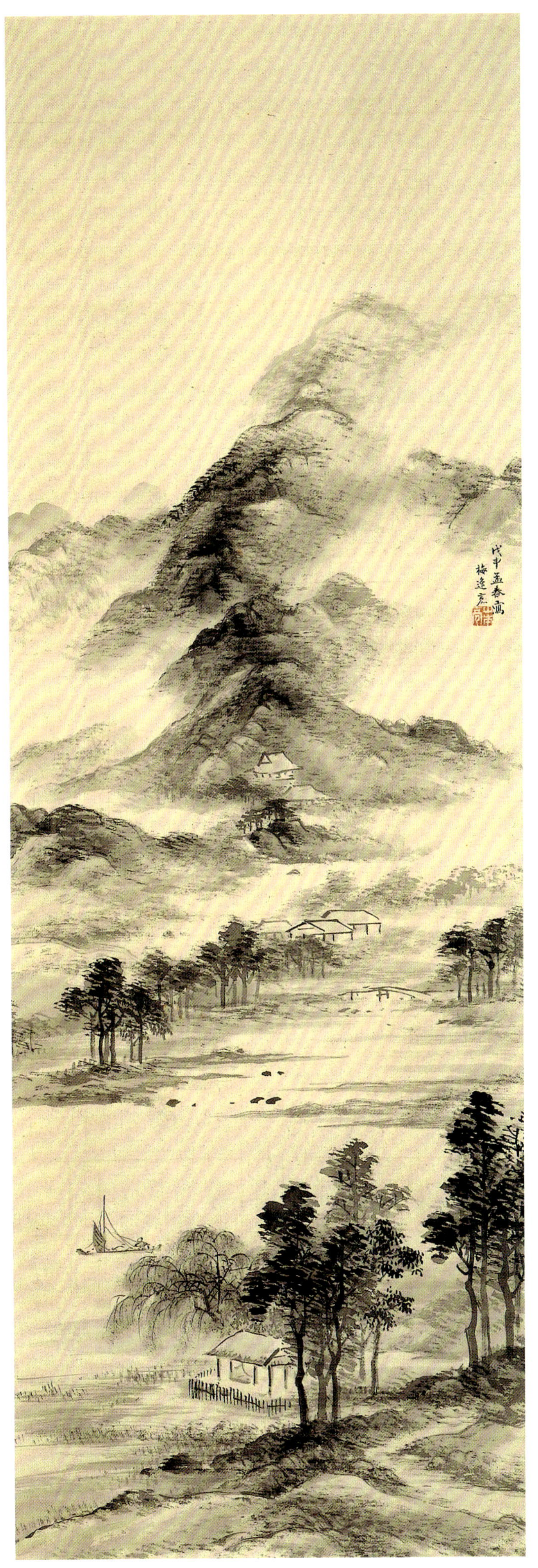

"Spring"

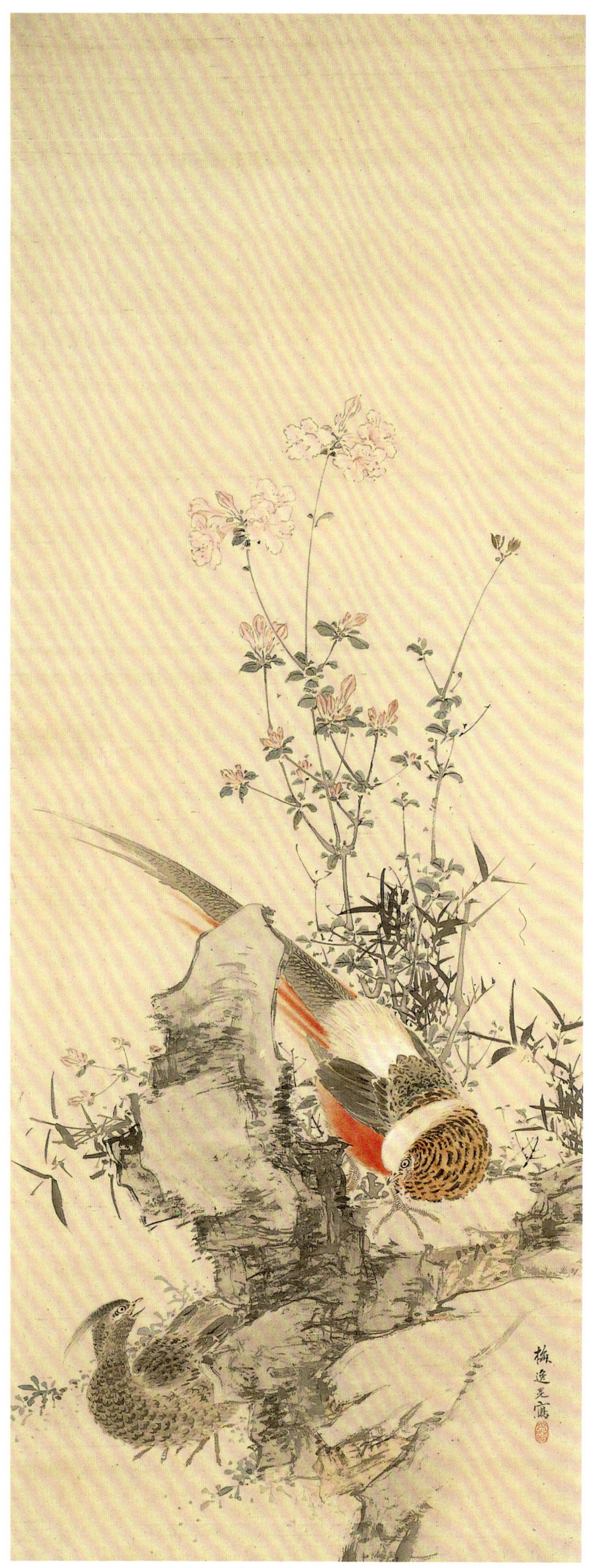

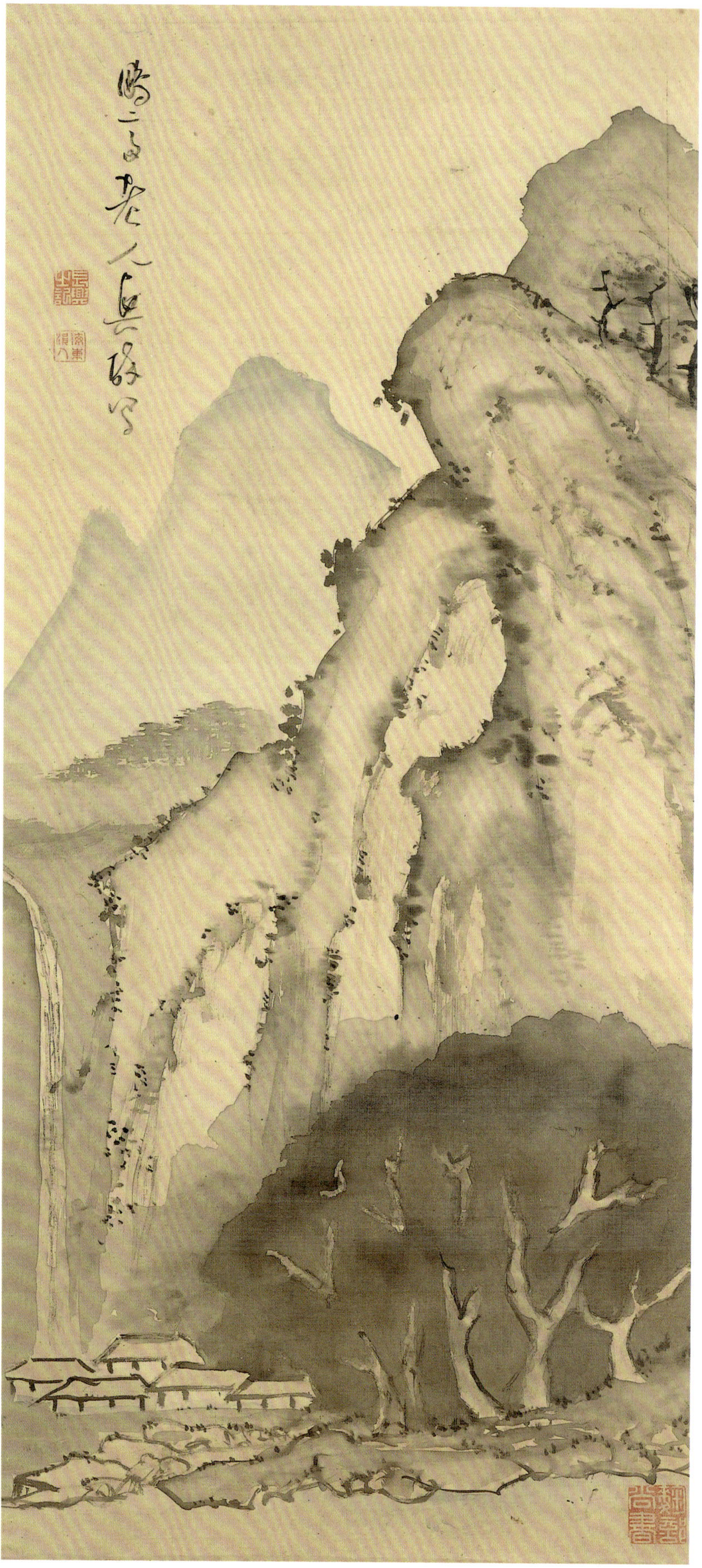

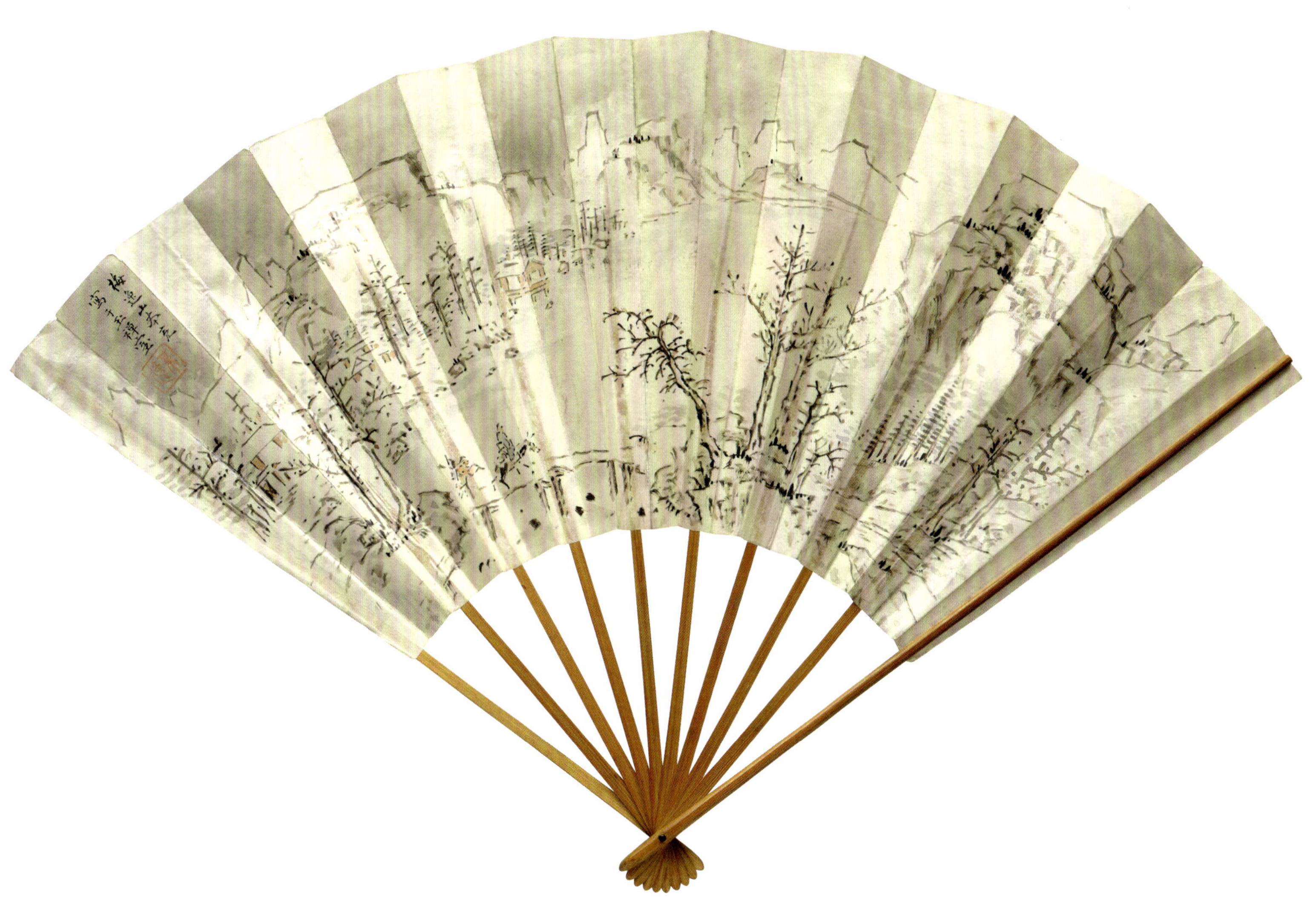

Yamamoto Baiitsu
(山本梅逸; 1783–1856)

370. Golden Pheasants among Rhododendrons

Edo period
Hanging scroll; ink and color on silk
108 x 41.8 cm (42 1/2 x 16 1/2 in.)
Signature, seal

Literature: Murase 1993, no 29.

Kameda Bōsai
(亀田鵬斎; 1752–1826)

371. Landscape with Waterfall

Edo period, ca. 1817
Hanging scroll; ink and light color on silk
107.2 x 48.6 cm (42 1/4 x 19 1/8 in.)
Signature, seals

Literature: Addiss 1984, no. 22; Murase 1993, no. 31; Murase 2000, no. 167.

Yamamoto Baiitsu
(山本梅逸; 1783–1856)

372. Snowy Landscape

Edo period
Folding fan; ink and light color on paper
18.1 x 48 cm (7 1/8 x 18 7/8 in.)
Signature, seal

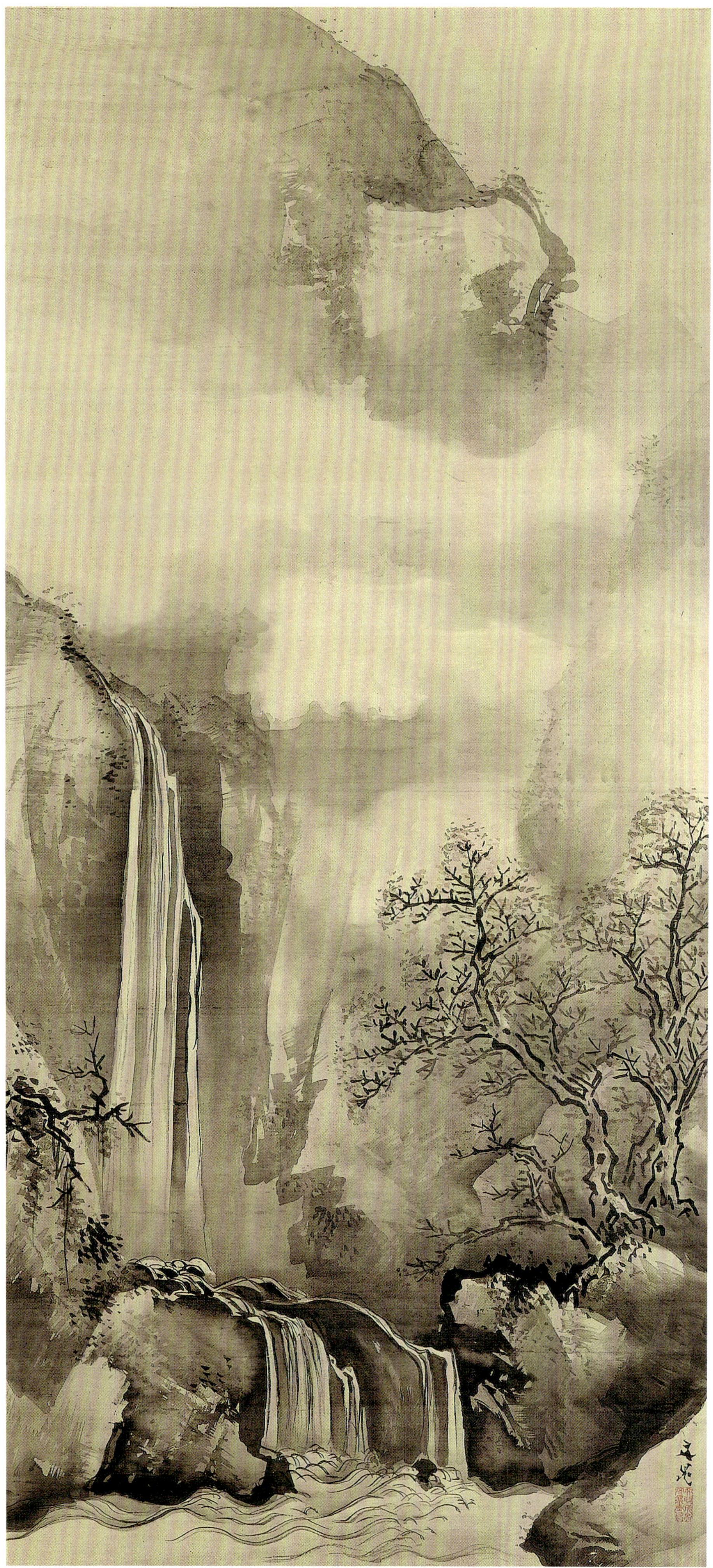

Tani Bunchō
(谷文晁; 1763–1840)

373. Landscape with Waterfall

Edo period, 1828
Hanging scroll; ink on silk
126.2 x 59.2 cm (49 5/8 x 23 1/4 in.)
Signature, seal

Literature: Kōno Motoaki 1971, p. 35; Murase 1975, no. 81; Ueno Kenji 1976, p. 43; Nakajima Ryōichi 1982, fig. 11-a; Tokyo National Museum 1985a, no. 56; Avitabile 1990, no. 98; Murase 2000, no. 168; Trinh 2003, pl. 90; Tsuji Nobuo et al. 2005, no. 116.

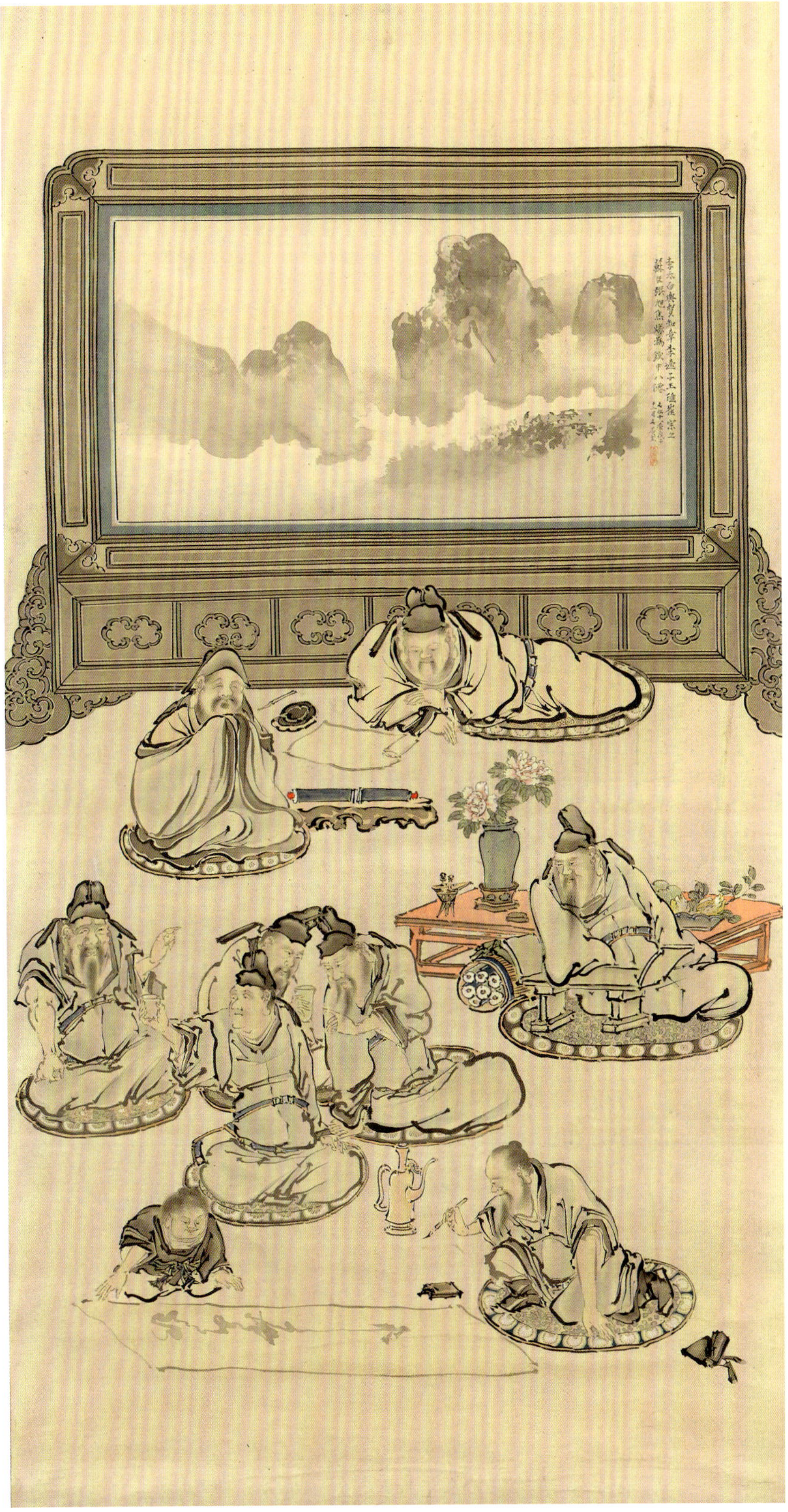

TANI BUNCHŌ
(谷文晁; 1763–1840)

374. The Eight Immortals of the Wine Cup (飲中八仙)

Edo period, 1828
Hanging scroll; ink and light color on silk
133 x 70.9 cm (52 3/8 x 27 7/8 in.)
Text, signature, seal

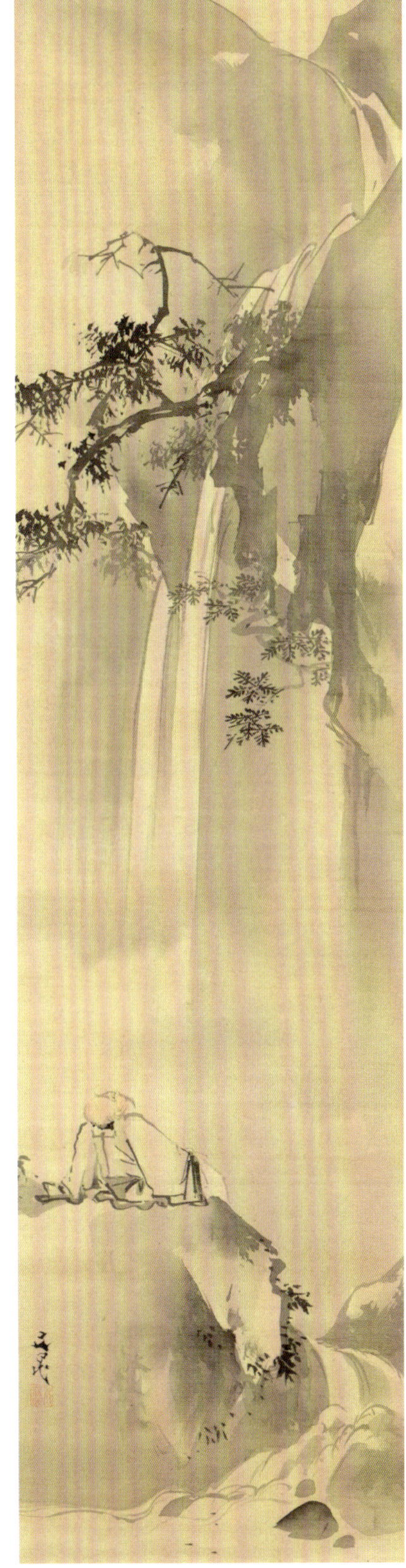

TANI BUNCHŌ
(谷文晁; 1763–1840)

375. Ri Haku (Ch. Li Bo, 李白) Viewing a Waterfall (李白観瀑図)

Edo period, 19th century
Hanging scroll; ink and light color on silk
105.4 x 27.1 cm (41 1/2 x 10 5/8 in.)
Signature, seal

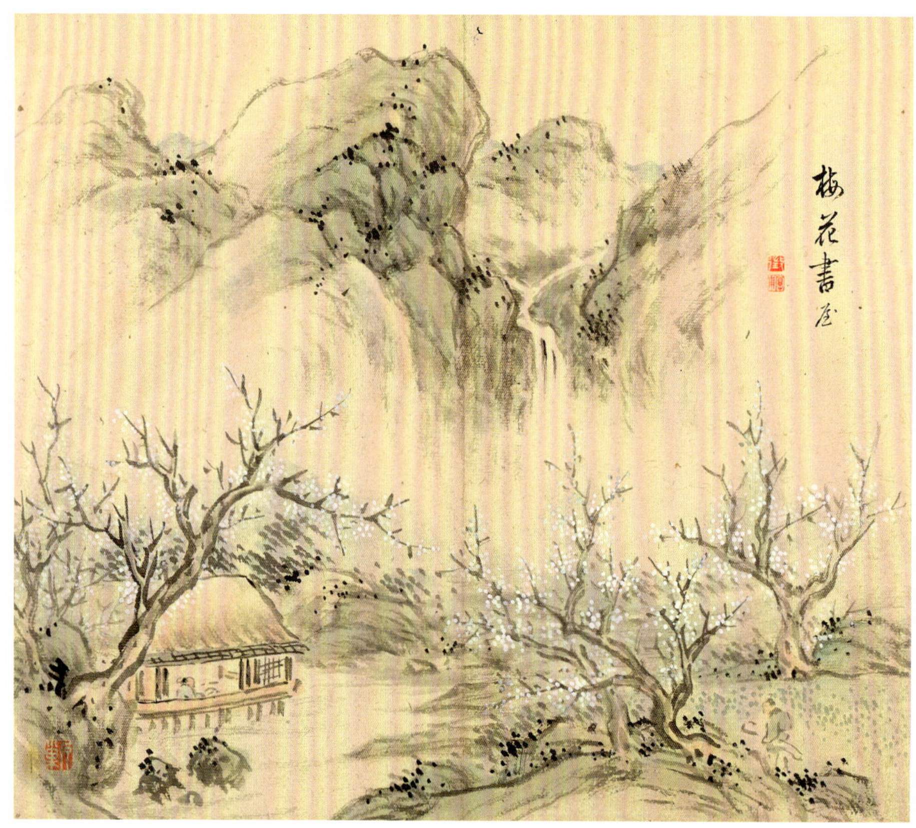

Takaku Aigai
(高久靄崖; 1796–1843)

376. Study among Plum Flowers (梅花書屋), from *Landscapes of the Four Seasons*

Edo period, 1833
Album with twelve leaves; ink and light color on paper
Each leaf 28.7 x 33.1 cm (11¼ x 13 in.)
Text, signature, seals

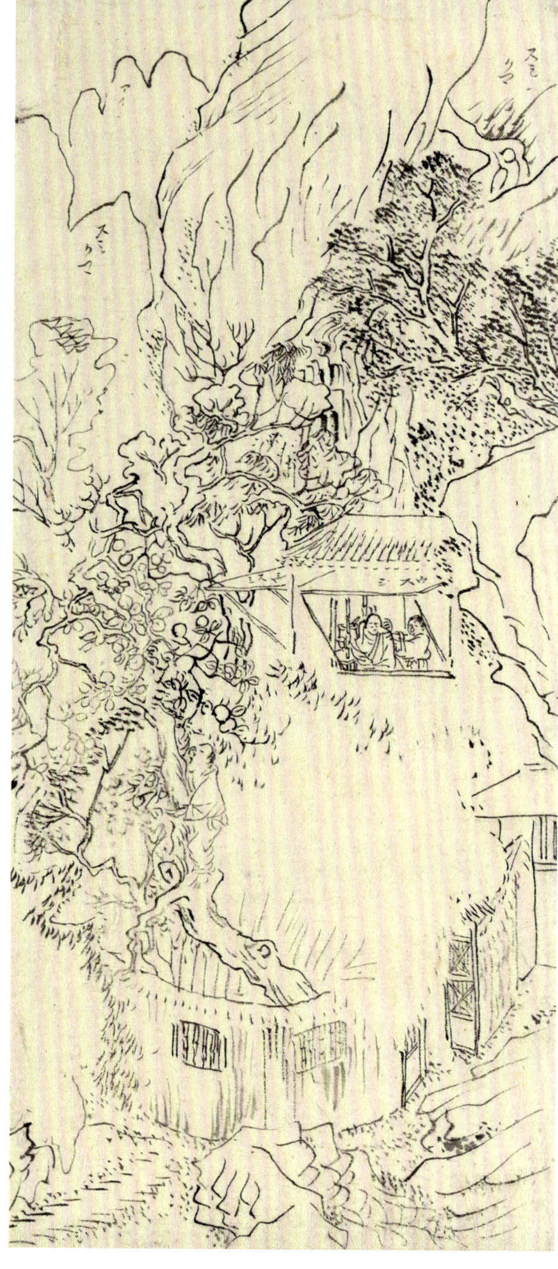

Watanabe Kazan
(渡辺崋山; 1793–1844)

377. Sketch after *Scholar's Mountain Retreat in Autumn* by Yosa Buson (与謝蕪村; 1716–1783)

Edo period–Meiji era, 19th century
From a book of 54 sketches by Watanabe Kazan, Tsubaki Chinzan (椿椿山; 1801–1854), and Takagi Goan (高木梧庵; fl. 19th century); ink and light color on paper
Each page 28.7 x 31.2 cm (11¼ x 12¼ in.)

Watanabe Shōka
(渡辺小華; 1835–1887)

378. Family of Cranes

Edo period
Hanging scroll; ink and color on silk
89.6 x 34.5 cm (35 1/4 x 13 5/8 in.)
Signature, seals

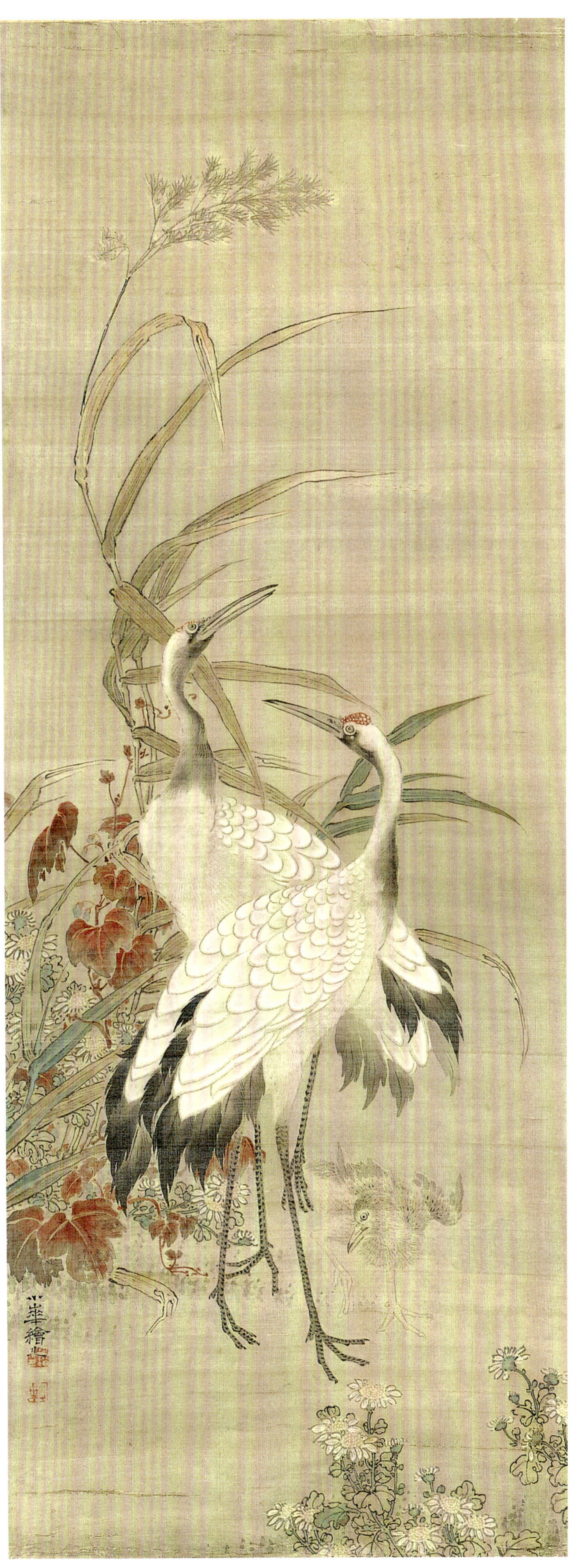

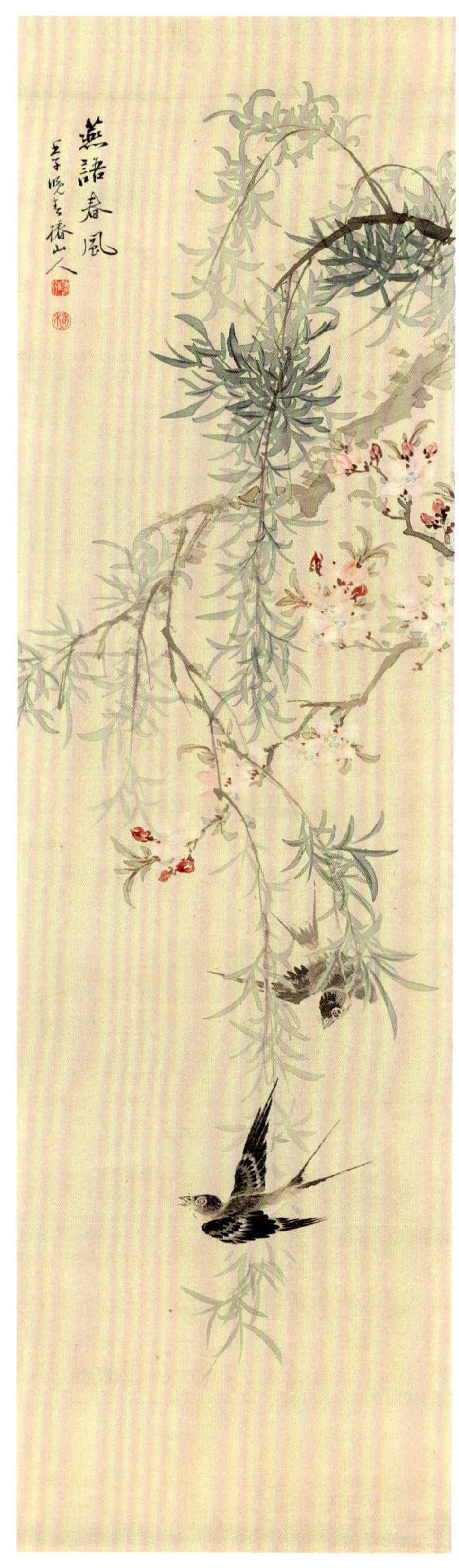

Tsubaki Chinzan
(椿椿山; 1801–1854)

379. Swallow's Song in Spring Breeze

Edo period, 1852
Hanging scroll; ink and color on silk
97.8 x 29 cm ($38\frac{1}{2}$ x $11\frac{3}{8}$ in.)
Text, signature, seals

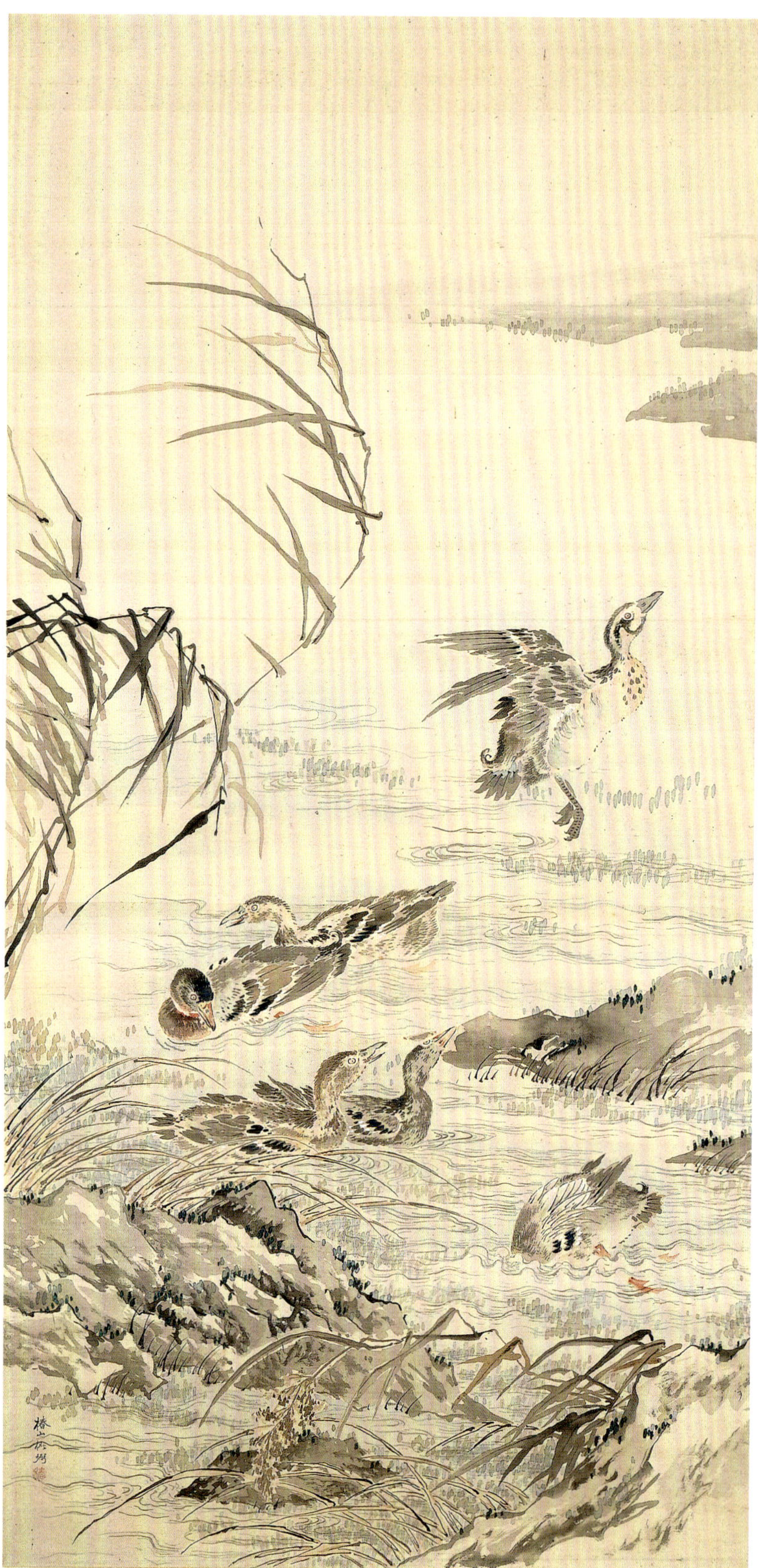

Tsubaki Chinzan
(椿椿山; 1801–1854)

380. Geese in Autumn Stream

Edo period
Hanging scroll; ink and light color on silk
144 x 71.5 cm ($56\frac{3}{4}$ x $28\frac{1}{8}$ in.)
Signature, seal

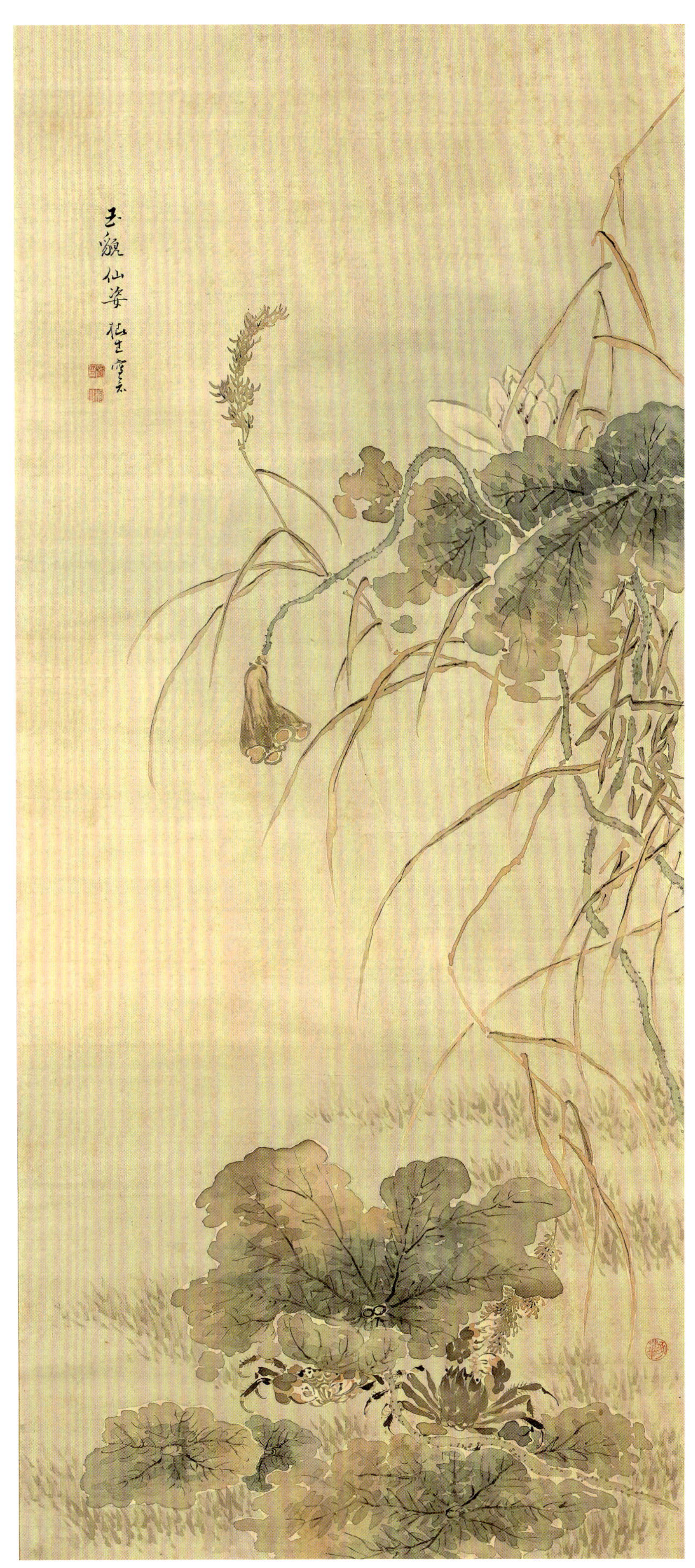

Tsubaki Chinzan
(椿椿山; 1801–1854)

381. Jewel-like Countenance, Gaze of a Recluse (玉貎仙姿)

Edo period
Hanging scroll; ink and light color on silk
123 x 55 cm ($48\frac{3}{8}$ x $21\frac{5}{8}$ in.)
Text, signature, seals

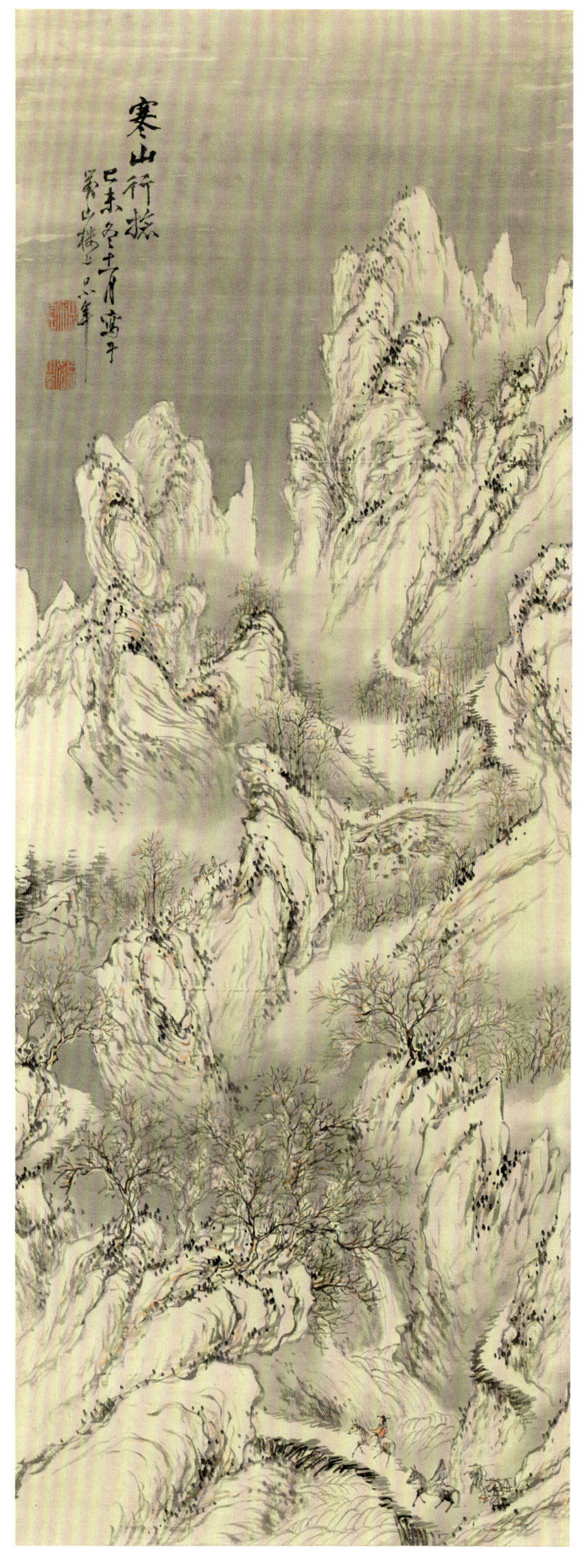

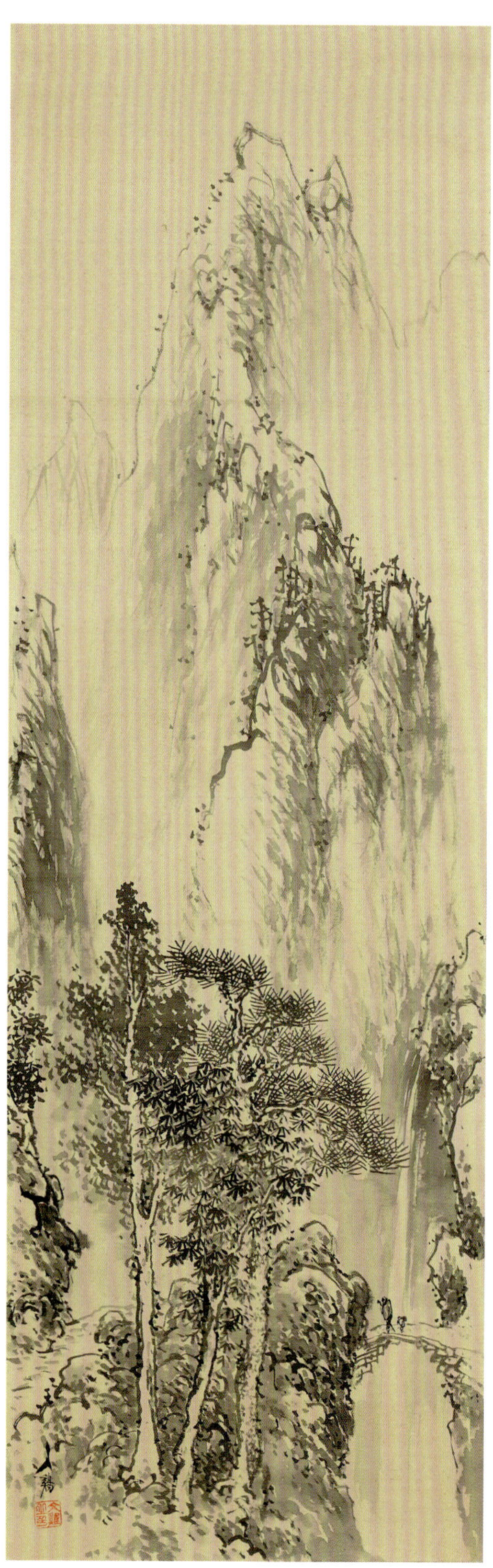

Hine (or Hineno) Taizan

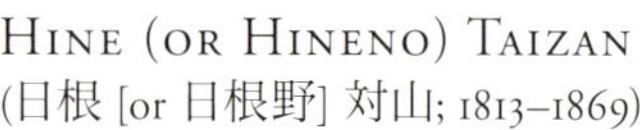

(日根 [or 日根野] 対山; 1813–1869)

382. Travelers in Cold Mountains

Edo period, 1859
Hanging scroll; ink and light color on silk
137.2 x 51.5 cm (54 x 20¼ in.)
Text, signature, seals

Bunkei
(文雞; fl. 19th century)

383. Landscape

Meiji era, 19th century
Hanging scroll; ink on silk
129.2 x 41.3 cm (50⅞ x 16¼ in.)
Signature, seal

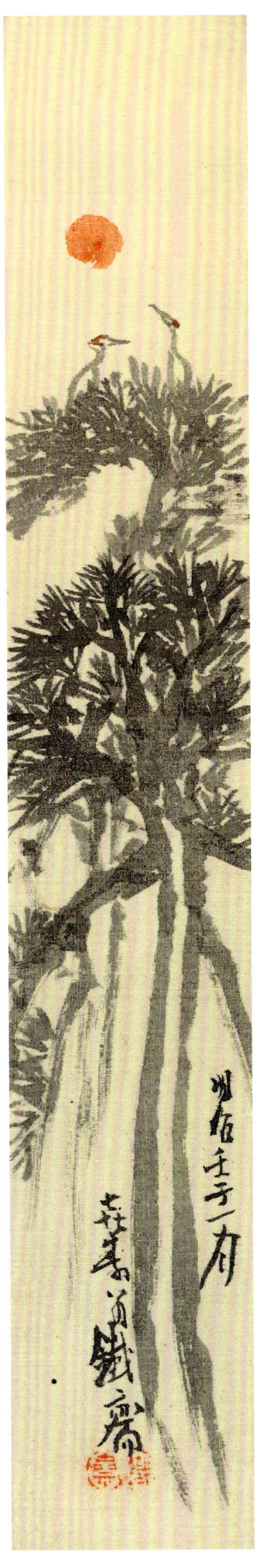

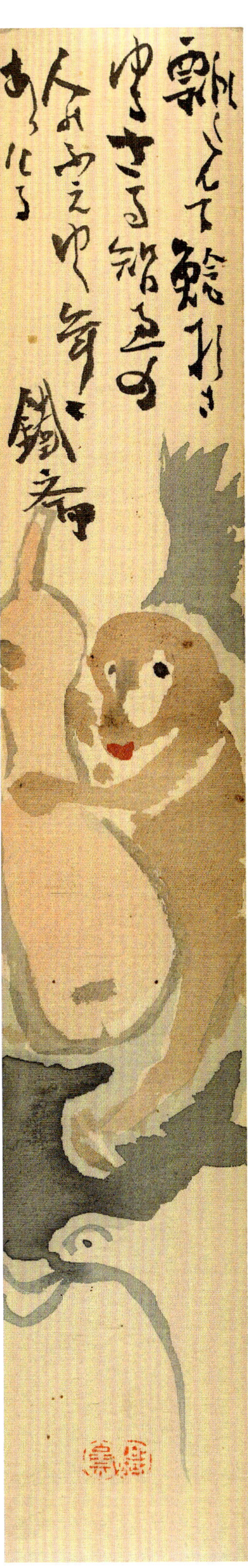

Tomioka Tessai
(富岡鉄斎; 1836–1924)

384. Monkey with Catfish in Gourd; Pine and Cranes

Meiji era, 1912
Pair of *tanzaku*; ink and light color on paper
Each *tanzaku* 36.2 x 6 cm (14¼ x 2⅜ in.)
Text, signatures, seals

Gift from Gordon Washburn, 1980

Shōzan
(晶山; fl. 20th century)

385. Peony in Basket

Taishō–Shōwa period, 20th century
Hanging scroll; ink and color on silk
49.2 x 56.4 cm (19⅜ x 22¼ in.)
Signature, seal

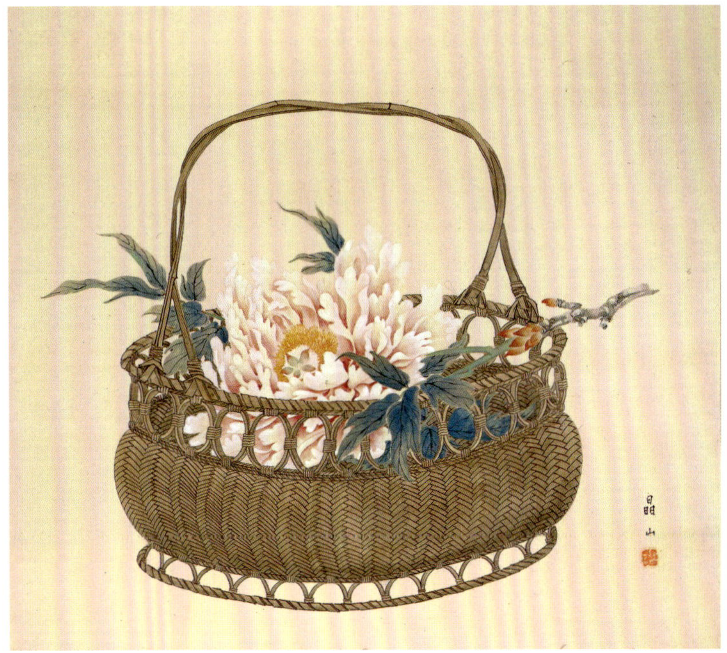

Chapter 8 Details

† *denotes illustrated items*

† 307. Bamboo Window on a Rainy Day

Text

by Nankai

Bamboo Window on a Rainy Day

Signature

Painted by Nankai Gyofu

Seals

[upper left] *Royal Viewing: Copy of Sanmi Ōkurakyō's identification mark for a seal*; [lower left] *Chikusō*; [lower right] *Kokko Danga*

307

307

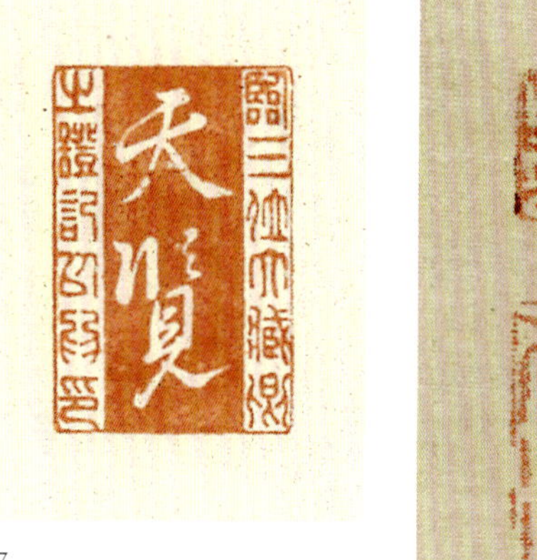

307

308

† 308. Eight Daoist Immortals of China

Text

Colophon by Nankai, quoted from a poem by Tō Kōkei [Ch. Tao Hongjing, 陶弘景; 456–536]

What's there in the mountains? / Plenty of white clouds over the peaks.

Signature

Painted by Gen'yu

Seals

Gen'yu no in; *Nankai*

309

310

† 309. Snowy Landscape

Signature

Painted by Bō Shin'en, summer of 1744

Seal

Bō Shin'en in

† 310. So Shoku's (Ch. Su Shi) Second Visit to the Red Cliff

Signature

Bō Shin'en

Seal

Bō Shin'en in

† 311. Landscape in Blue and Green

Seals

[upper right] *Kien*; *Ku Yo iwaku Kōmi*
[lower left] *Gungyoku Sanbō*

Text

Three poems by Uno Shishin (宇野士新; 1698–1745)

[Poem 1] *If not for frequent inflictions of illness, / how can I let go my high ambitions? / My undeserved fame stays whether in office or retirement. / Drifting about, how can I rise or fall in status? / Being lazy, I do not mind people who ignore me. / Roaming at will, I loathe intrusions from guests. / Myriad mountains in autumn colors. / Leaning on a walking cane, they are naturally hard to reach.*

[Poem 2] *When visitors come, I excuse myself from them all. / Upon encounters, I recline on my tea table for a nap. / Metaphysical discussions are ultimately plain chitchat. / Literary creativity has lost its former brilliance. / Time and again I puzzle over the cause. / People's love of antiquity is gone. / Who would sit alone in the present world? / The only thing left of Ruan Xuanzi is mere money.*

[Poem 3] *It is hard to judge the things of the world. / Frequently ill, I am nonetheless very fortunate. / Utterly free, I am no one's puppet. / Creeping figs and wild vines can be my attire. / Unconcerned with my fame as a poet, / I let my scholarship run its own course too. / Those who wear light furs and ride fat horses / regret in vain at hair turning gray. / To the right are three of my casually composed poems, transcribed for someone at my leisure.*

Signature

Utei

Seals

[right poem, upper right] *Meika*
[upper middle] *Utei no in*; *Shishin*

Text

Six poems by Miyazaki Kinpo (宮崎鈞圃; 1717–1774)

[Poem 1] *Having depicted Xiangyang County in painting, / I vividly recall past visits there. / On Mount Xian I once halted my horse. / Up and down the Han River I used to go boating. / The reddish valleys always feel like under a clearing sky. / The pines do not change*

311 (upper middle)

311 (right poem, upper right)

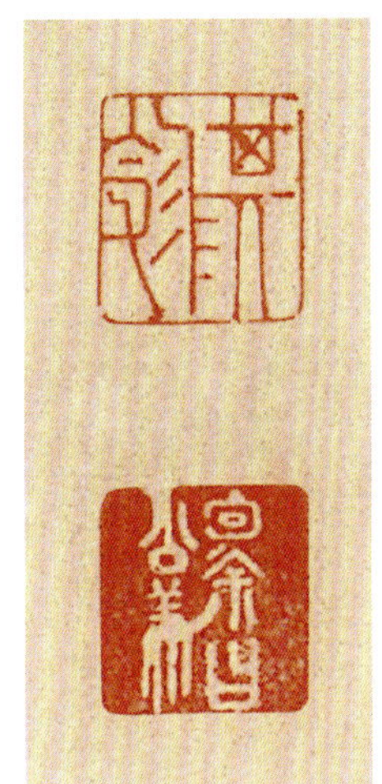
311 (upper right)

311 (lower left)

311 (upper left)

311 (left poem, upper right)

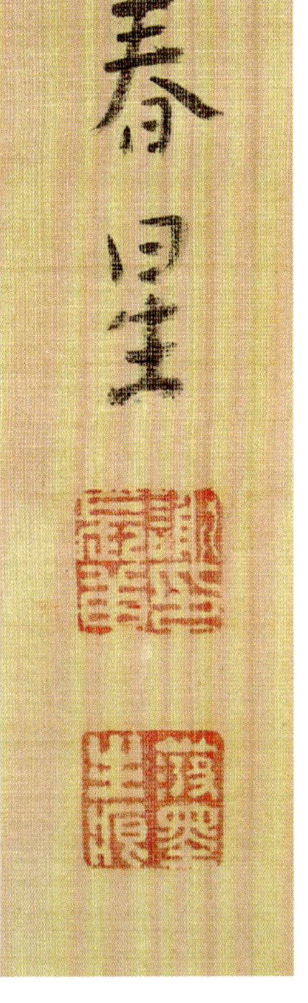

312

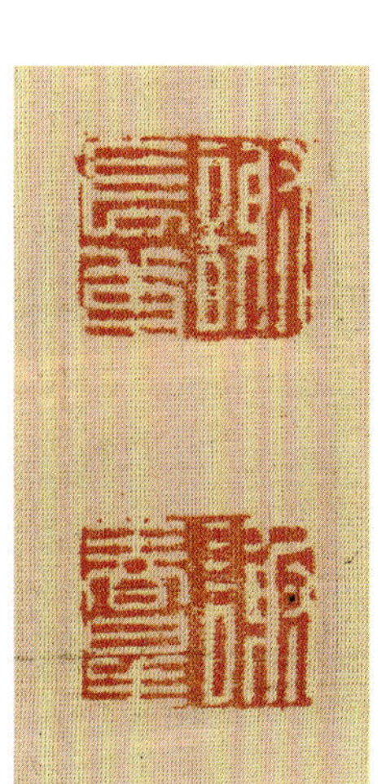
313

their green in autumn. / The painting is merely a few feet long, / but my thoughts travel thousands of miles afar.

[Poem 2] *The official residence is quiet by day. / The painting shows off the grandness of the landscape. / The Sword Gate Pass stands to the north of the Star Ridge. / To the east of Pine County lies the Snow Ridge. / Mountains extend from the Chinese realm all the way to aborigines' land. / The Wu is linked to the Shu by waterways. / Inspired by the beautiful clouds that meet our eyes, / we exult over the goblets filled with pure wine!*

[Poem 3] *Who painted these wisps of clouds? / Under dust, their powdered pigments have faded. / They did not leave to make rain, / nor follow the wind to return home. / Helplessly stuck frozen on the wall, / they seem yearning to float toward my clothes as I look back. / Through the art of painting, / they may ascend to heaven in flight.*

[Poem 4] *Artistic excellence through three generations of a family is unique in the world. / The lively brushwork here and there witnesses their superb skill. / Dark cliffs are endowed with free-flowing momentum; / dry bushes are lightly rendered in splashed ink. / Chilly clouds descend and devour the vast desert. / Spring rain crosses the river to spread over the entire Wu region. / Sitting long in this elegant hall, I grow increasingly confused, / realizing it is a painting rather than mountains and streams.*

[Poem 5] *The most essential is brushwork. / The limited picture space tests a painter's skill. / The sun and the moon appear in the main hall. / Rivers and lakes come into the view of seated guests. / The night haze turns moist and dewy; / the autumn cliffs glow in chilly air. / I empathize with the man of the past, / whose lifelong poetic sensibility lingers here.*

[Poem 6] *Youcheng* [Wang Wei, 701–761] *has passed away; / few of his paintings have survived. / The limited picture space covers an expanse of rivers and lakes, / where common waterfowls and birds fly. / The beauty of the mountains is entirely within his mastery; / The cloud vapor seems about to touch my clothes. / Taking delight in this every now and then, / I feel like withdrawing from the world for life. / Written by Kaisei Miyazaki in the spring of 1763*

Seals

[left poem, upper right] *Koike*
[upper left] *Miyazaki*; *Shijō*

† 312. Travels through Mountains and Fields

Signatures

[on each screen] *Sha Shunsei*

Seals

[on each screen] *Sha Chōkō in*; *Hatsuboku Seikon*

† 313. Two Birds on Willow and Peach Trees

Signature

Painted at Yahantei in the summer of 1774. Sha Shunsei

Seals

Sha Chōkō; *Sha Shunsei*

† 314. Scholar's Mountain Retreat in Autumn

Signature

Sha Shunsei

Seals

Sha Chōkō in; *Shunsei*

† 315. Landscape with Solitary Hut

Signature

Painted by Tōsei Sha Chōkō at Sankaken

Seals

Sha Chōkō in; *Hatsuboku Seikon*

† 316. Crows

Signature

Sha Shunsei

Seals

Tōsei; *Sanka shujin*

† 317. Rocks

Signature

Painted by Sha Chōkō Shunsei

Seal

Shunsei

Text

by Shibano Ritsuzan (1736–1807)

If it is not the leftover material from patching up the firmament, / it must be the fragment of a fallen star. / Cool enough to sober up the drunken Tō Enmei [Ch. Tao Yuanming], */ so dense as to be chiseled into Ō Gishi's* [Ch. Wang Xizhi's] *inkstone.*

Signature

Inscribed by Shiba Sangen

Seals

Seigo; *Shiba Kunihiko in*; *Shibashi Hikosuke*; *Hōdō aiganki* [collector]

† 318. Scene from *Oku no hosomichi*

Text

Shōō Oku nikki // There was a huge chestnut tree on the outskirts of this post town, and a priest was living in seclusion under its shade. When I stood there in front of the tree, I felt as if I were in the midst of the deep mountains where this priest [Saigyō] had picked horse chestnuts. I took a piece of paper and wrote as follows: The chestnut is a holy tree, for the Chinese ideograph for chestnut is Tree placed directly below West, the direction of the holy land. The priest Gyōki is said to have used it for his walking stick and chief support of his house. // The chestnut by the eaves / in magnificent bloom / passes unnoticed / by men of this world.

Signature

Buson

Seals

Chōkō; *Shunsei*

314

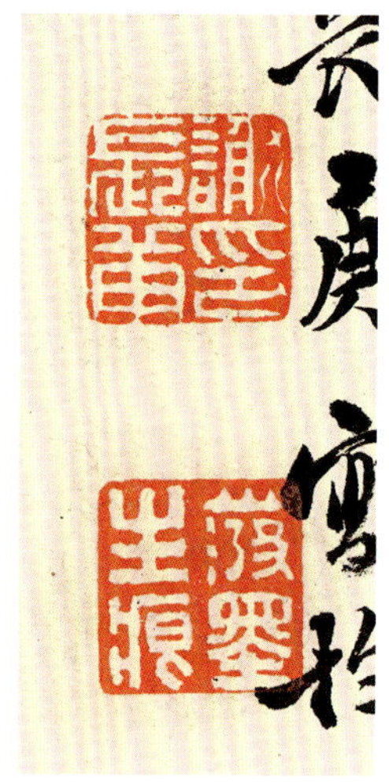

315

316

317

317

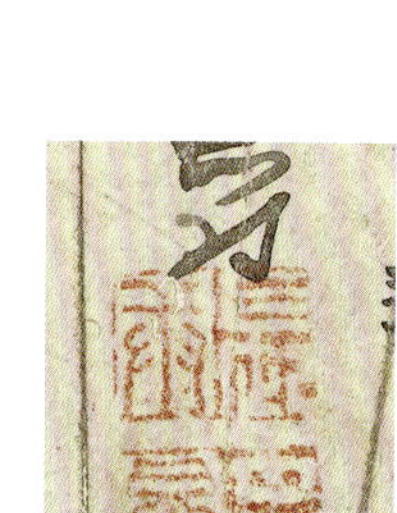

318

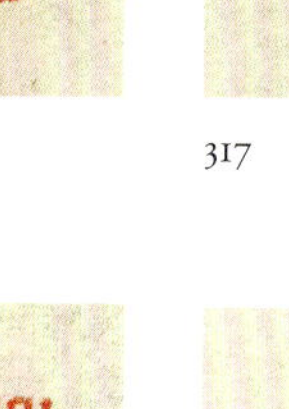

317

317

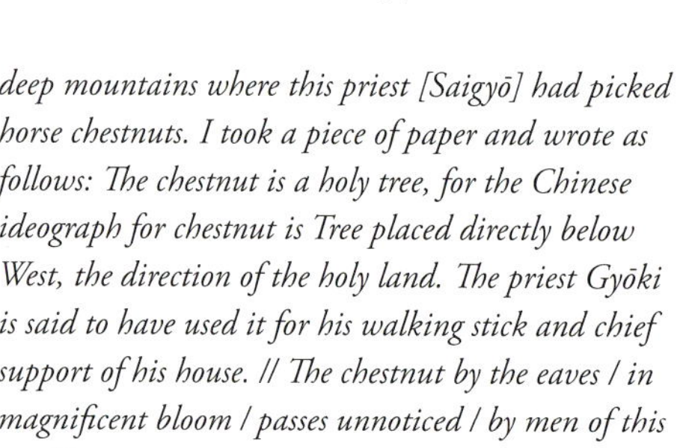

320

320

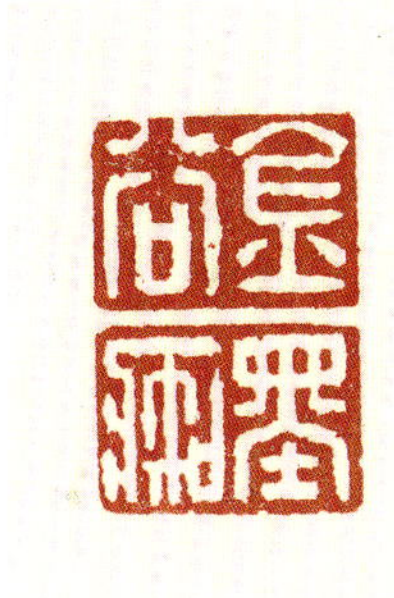
321

321

322

322

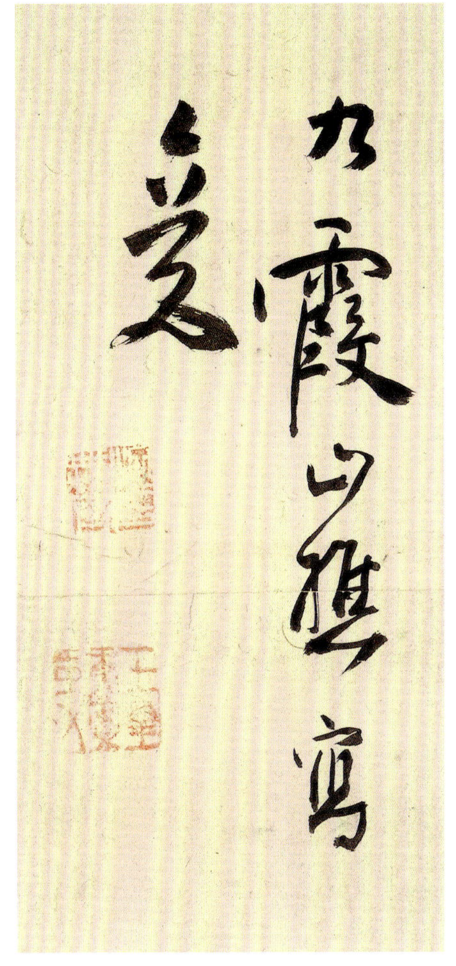

323

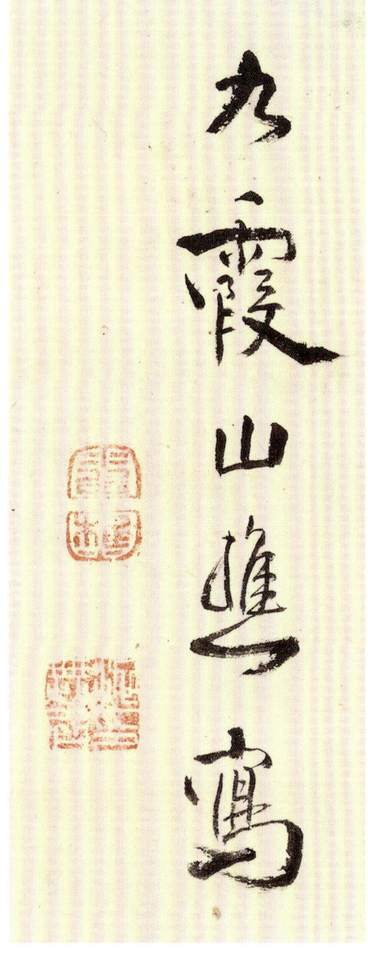

323

319. Sea in Spring

Text

Spring sea / all day, waves rise and fall, / rise and fall.

Signatures

Shunkō; Buson

† 320. Mount Fuji

Text

by Kinkoku

Alone it towers above the white clouds. / Who can help feeling the chill of the snow vapor? / Viewed from any angle, it has no front or back, / just erupts from midair to catch people's eyes.

Signature

Kinkoku Dōjin painted and inscribed

Seals

At age fifty-five I set my mind on learning; Kōmori Dōjin

† 321. Spring Cleaning

Signature

Kinkoku

Seals

Sanjin Yū Nijaku; Kinkoku; Bokuchi

† 322. Wintry Landscape after Kaku Chūjo (Ch. Guo Zhongshu)

Text

After the brush of Kaku Chūjo

Signature

Ike Mumei

Seals

Mumei; Hekigo Suichiku Sanbō; Itsuka Issan Tōka Issui

† 323. Gathering at the Orchid Pavilion; Autumn Festival

Text

[on left screen] *At the foot of Mount Ohu, the rice and millet grow fat; / pigs are in their pens, and chickens in their coops. / The door to the house has been left ajar. / The Autumn Festival is over, and in the evening / mulberry leaves cast long shadows. / To every household, tipsy men return, holding each other up.*

Signatures

[on right screen] *Kyūka Sanshō painted*
[on left screen] *Kyūka Sanshō painted the spirit*

Seals

[on right screen] *Kashō; Ike Mumei in*
[on left screen] *Ike Mumei in; A Clerk Tending the Jade Emperor's Incense Table*

† 324. Landscape with River View

Signature

Kyūka Sanshō painted the spirit

Seals

Ike Mumei in; Taisei; A Clerk Tending the Jade Emperor's Incense Table

324

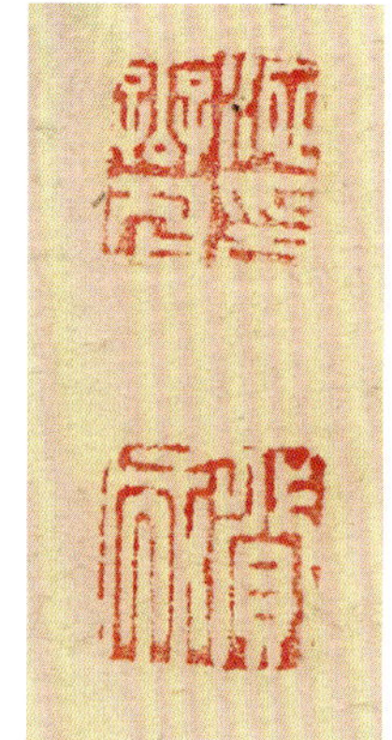

324

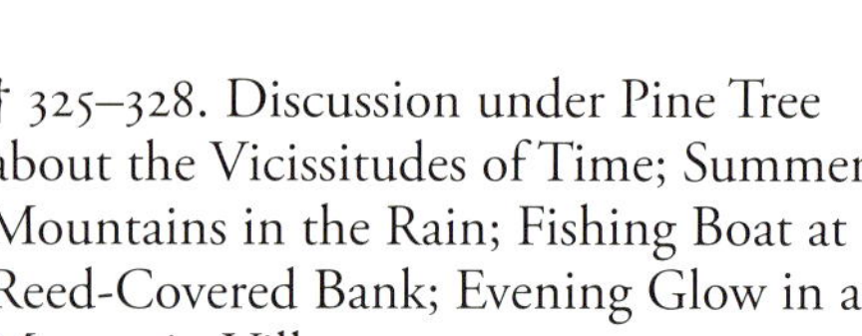

† 325–328. Discussion under Pine Tree about the Vicissitudes of Time; Summer Mountains in the Rain; Fishing Boat at Reed-Covered Bank; Evening Glow in a Mountain Village

[325]

Text

Discussion under Pine Tree about the Vicissitudes of Time

Seals

Sekisen; Mumei; Taisei

Text

by Minagawa Kien (1734–1807)

As we discuss history through thousands of years, / cast shadows in the mountains shift across. / Rights and wrongs are nothing constant, / which the towering pines alone understand. / An inscription for Ike Mumei's Discussion under Pine Tree about the Vicissitudes of Time.

Signature

Written by Minagawa Gen

Seals

Kien; Minagawa Gen in; Hakkyōshi

325–328

325–328

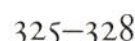

325

325

325

[326]

Text

Summer Mountains in the Rain

Seals

Mumei; Taisei; Sekisen

Text

by Ōkubo Shibutsu (1766–1837)

In free-flowing ink, moist with rich fragrance, / a scene of mountains after rain is painted in the Mi style. / Who knows that the magical hand of the Creator / is contained in the inch-long brush tip! / An inscription for Kashō Sanjin's Summer Mountains in the Rain.

Signature

Shibutsu Gyō

Seals

Shisei Sōdō; Shibutsu

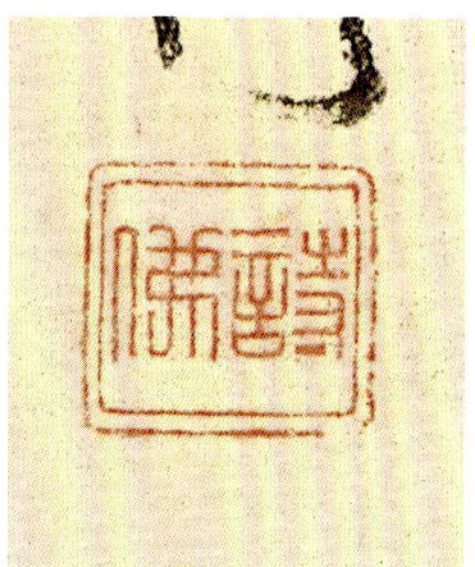

326

326

326

326

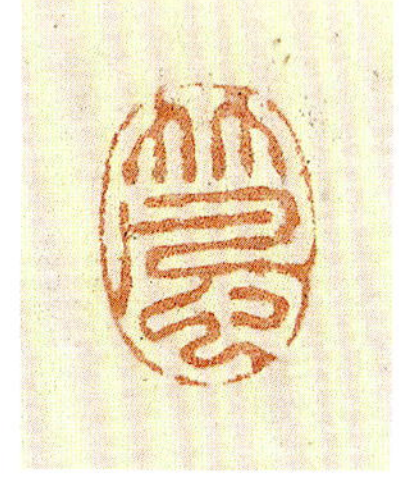

326

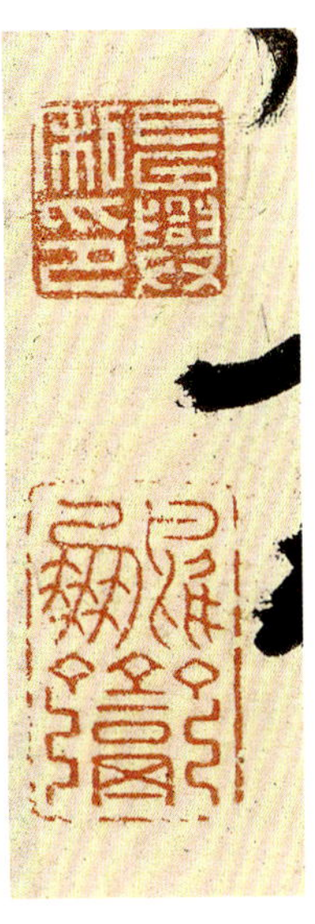

327

327

328

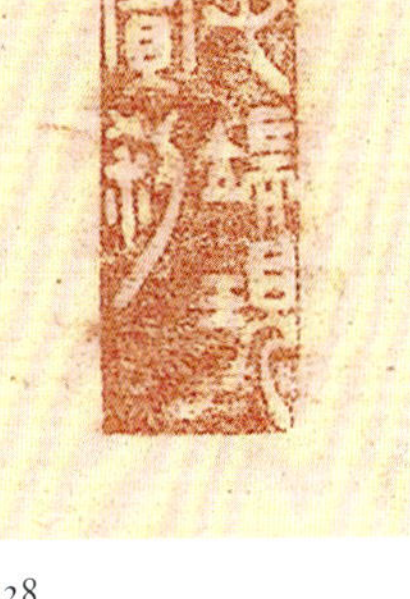

328

Text

by Shinozaki Shōchiku (1781–1851)

A dog day swarming with bugs, / a view of mountains humid with waterdrops. / Emerald luster fresh from the rain, / cool air reaching the world of man. / Inscribed on the twentieth day of the seventh lunar month of 1832. It was extremely hot after a whole month without rain. I spread the painting and composed the poem with joy.

Signature

Written by Shōchiku Sanjin

Seals

Chikufū; Shinozaki Hitsu; Shōchikusai

[327]

Text

Fishing Boat at Reed-Covered Bank

Seals

Sekisen; Mumei; Taisei

Text

by Kameda Bōsai (1752–1826)

A fishing boat on a chilly stream, / wilted reeds in the gasping wind. / Where shall I return after winding up the fish line? / Perhaps to the gathering of a literary society. / An inscription for Kashō's Fishing Boat at Reed-Covered Bank.

Signature

Bōsai Rōjin

Seals

Tenkyo Kanjin; Chōkō Shi in; Bōsai

[328]

Text

Evening Glow in a Mountain Village

Seals

Mumei; Taisei; Sekisen

Text

by Rokunyo (1737–1801)

Misty trees, beveled bridge, sunset over the bay, / a village of people fond of ancient accoutrements. / Unaware of being the subject of a spectacle, / they have been secretly turned into paintings by outsiders.

Signature

Inscribed by Rokunyo

Seals

Sacred temples appear at the tip of the brush; Shaku Jishū in; Rokunyo

---

† 329. Gion Festival Float under Moon

Seal

Ike Mumei in

---

† 330. Cycad

Seal

Ike Mumei in

---

† 331. Chrysanthemum

Seal

Ike Mumei in

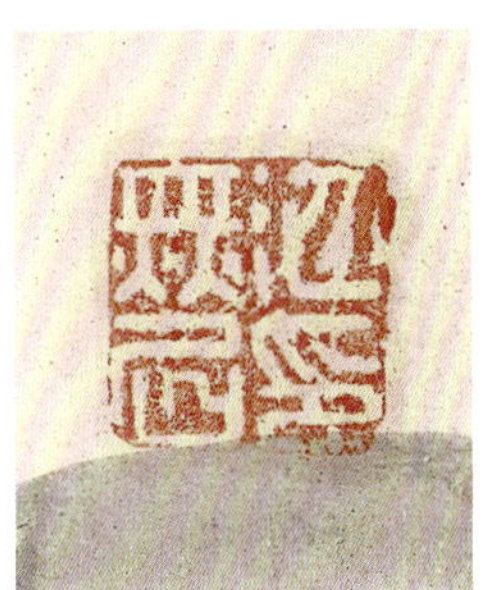

329

330

331

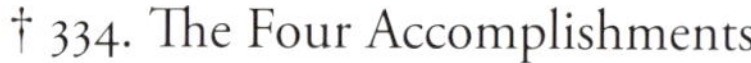

† 332. Homeward-Bound Fishing Boats

Signature

Kashō

† 333. Country Retreat in Early Summer

Signature

Kashō

Seals

Ka; *Shō*

† 334. The Four Accomplishments

Signature

Kashō

Seals

Sekisen; *Ike Mumei in*

† 335. Magnolia

Text

by Taiga

An abundance of magnolia blossoms enwrap the tree; / lumps of fruits like phoenix's eggs hang on the branches. / Crisp curds and dripping stalactites turn into crystals; / frost and snow are her substance, while ice makes her pure bone. / Her spoken words sound exquisitely marvelous. / The fairy of Mount Luofu greets her with joy all the time.

Seals

In my former life, I was the horse judge Fang Jiu-Gao; *Ka*; *Shō*; *A Clerk Tending the Jade Emperor's Incense Table*

† 336. Portrait of Taiga and His Calligraphies in Seal and Grass Styles copied by Tomioka Tessai

Text

Leisurely; *How?*

Signature

Portrait of Kashō copied from the work of Geppō [1760–1839]

Seal

Illegible

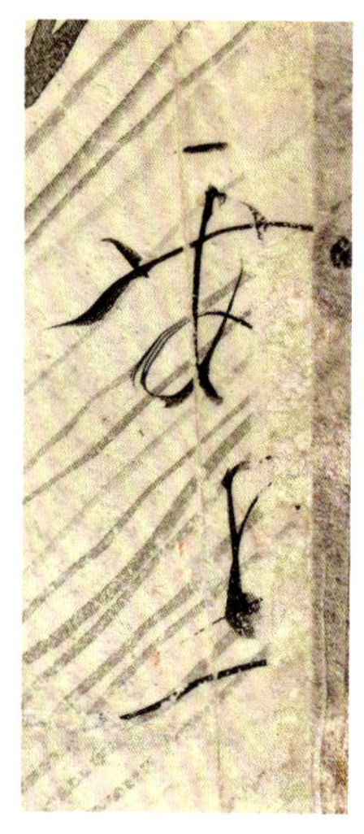

332

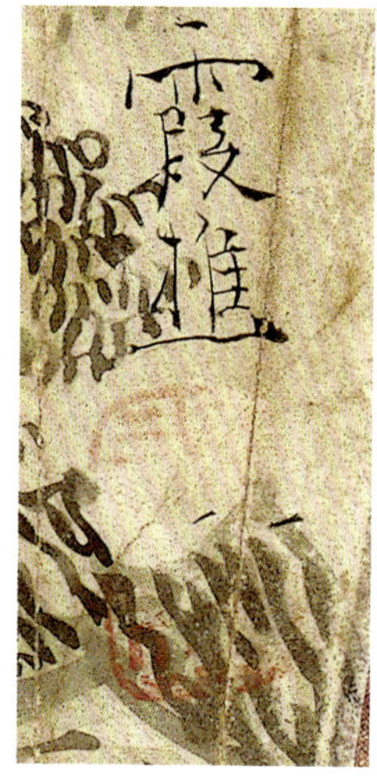

333

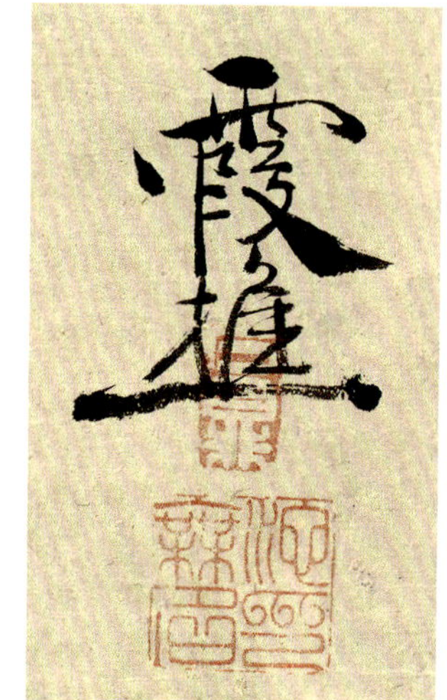

334

335

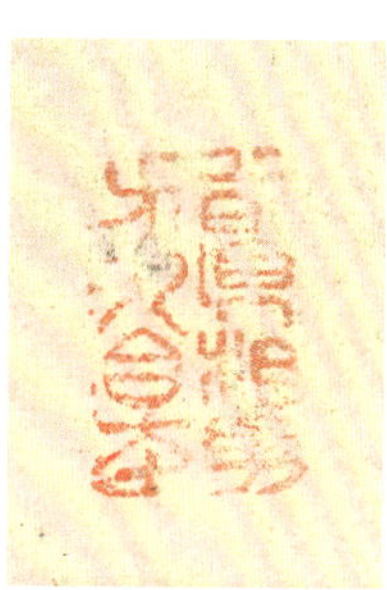

335

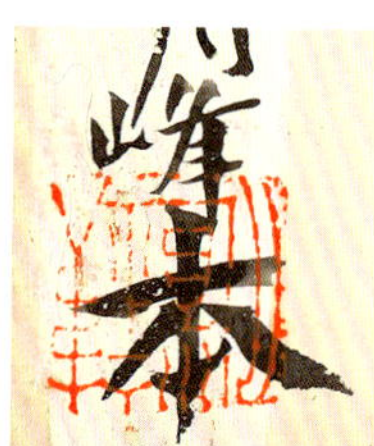

336

337

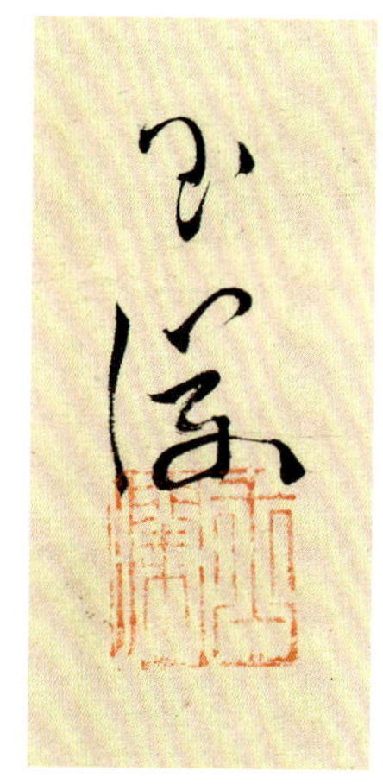

337

† 337. Chrysanthemums

Signature

Gyokuran

Seals

Gyokuran; *Gion Fūryū*

† 338. Peony and Bamboo by a Rock

Signature

Gyokuran

Seal

Gyokuran

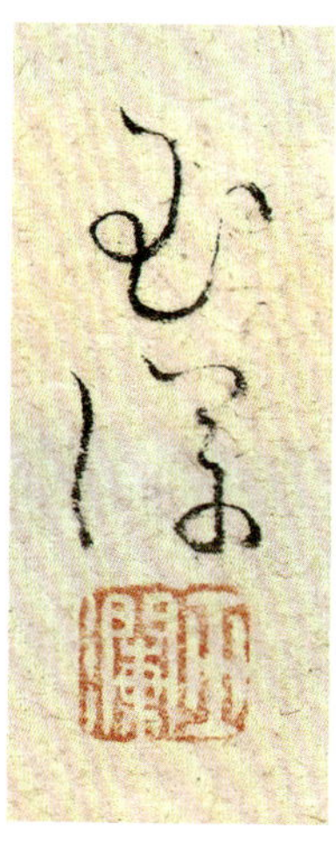

338

† 339. Album of Landscapes

Text

Painting in the Manner of Tō In [Ch. Tang Yin; 1470–1523]

Signatures

[on leaves 2, 5] *Mōhyō*; [no signature on leaf 3]; [on other leaves] *Minamoto Mōhyō*

Seals

[on each leaf] *Mō*; *hyō*

339

340

340

† 340. Bamboo in Snow

Signature

Sōshisan

Seals

[lower right] *Kasetsudō*; [middle left] *Sōshisan*; *Wakanourajin*

† 341. Landscape

Signature

Gyokushū Kyōyōsan

Seals

Sō Shisan; *Meifushi*

† 342. Plum Blossoms

Signature

Painted by Kyōsai

Seals

Minagawa Gen in; *Hakkyōshi*

Text

by Monk Rokunyo (1736–1801)

Rather than tread the snow through the village ahead, / I search for the spring on paper. / The faint fragrance enters my brush every now and then, / just to create dainty plum blossoms.

Signature

Inscribed by Rokunyo Sanjin

Seals

Unri Ginkō; *Jishū no in*; *Rokunyo*

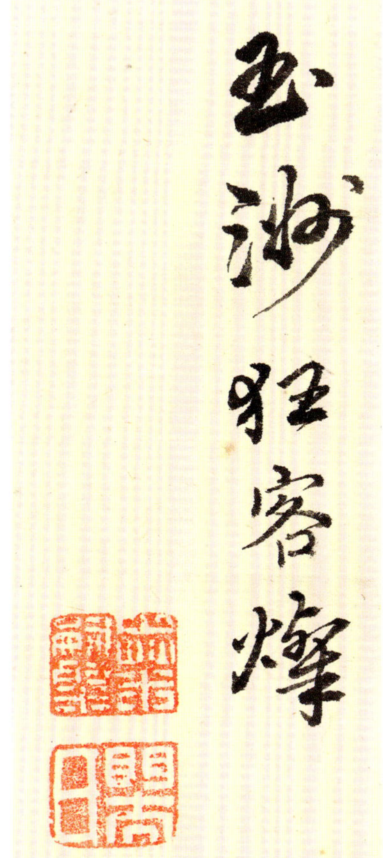

341

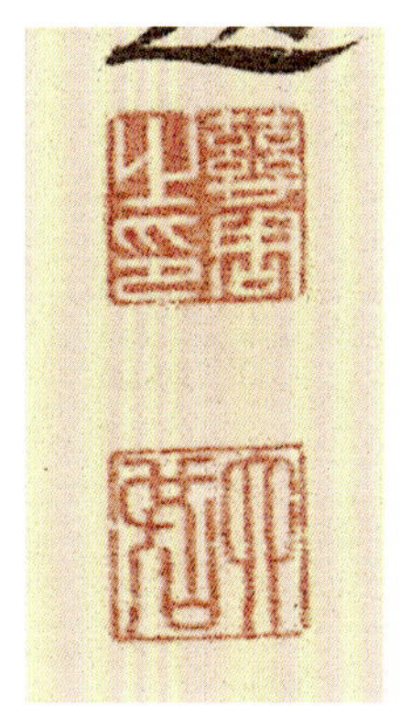

342

342

342

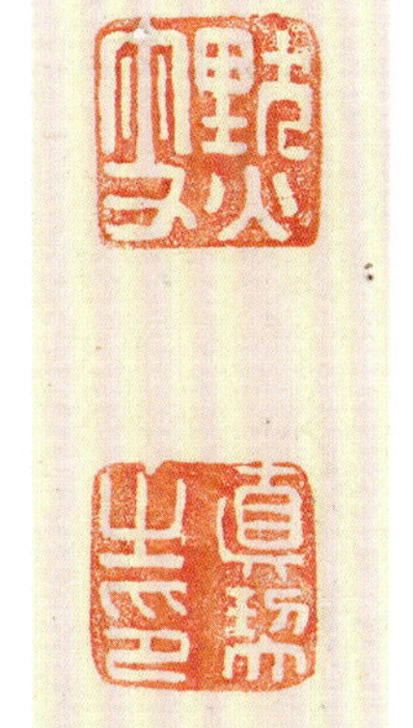

343

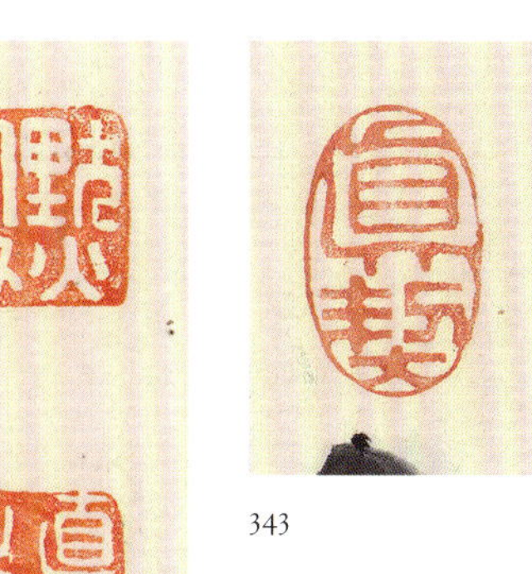

343

† 343. Fantastic Rocks with Cascading Waterfall; Fishing Boats by a Lake Hamlet

Text

by Aiseki

[on right scroll] *Fantastic / Rocks with Cascading Waterfall*
[on left scroll] *Fishing Boats by a Lake Hamlet*

Signatures

[on each scroll] *Aiseki*

Seals

[on right scroll] *Shinkei*
[on left scroll] *Tensetsu*; *Shinkei no in*

† 344. Waters and Woods, Pure and Splendent

Text

[at end of scroll] *In the summer, the fifth month of 1822, it rains continuously. So much so that it causes contagious diseases. In the deep shade of the verdant trees, I play with my brush to humor, a little, my longing for the wilderness.*

Signature

[at end of scroll] *An old man at seventy-six, Kaiseki Ryū*

Seals

[at beginning of scroll] *Shihekisai*; [at end of scroll] *Ryūnen*; *Daigo*

† 345. Green Peaks

Text

by Kaiseki

Peaks and hills splashed in green reflect / the sunset glow; / frosty trees in vast woods conjure up an embroidered drape. / The tenth month on a sunny river feels like the third month; / reed flowers can fly like willow catkins.

Signature

Poem by Ri Nikka [Ch. Li Rihua; 1565–1635], *transcribed in the first winter month of 1826. Futai Kaiseki*

Seals

Ryūnen no in; *Daigo shi*; *Waibai rōjin*

† 346. Daruma

Text

Facing the wall for nine years, / grasping the key of Zen in an instant. / Empty-minded in a dirt chamber, / oblivious to right and wrong.

Signature

Painted and inscribed by Baigai

Seals

To accomplish a task satisfactorily, one has first to sharpen one's tools; *Jishi no in*

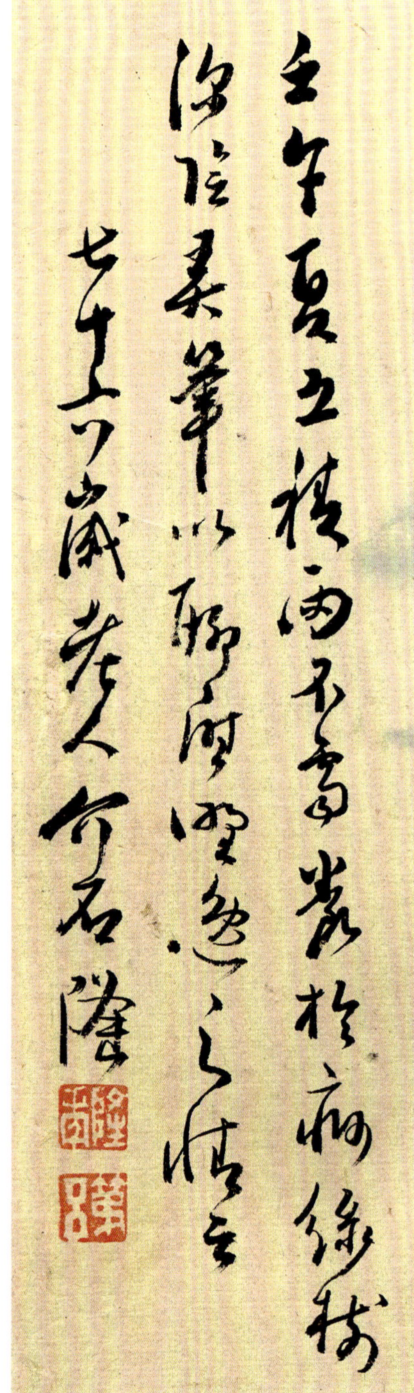

344

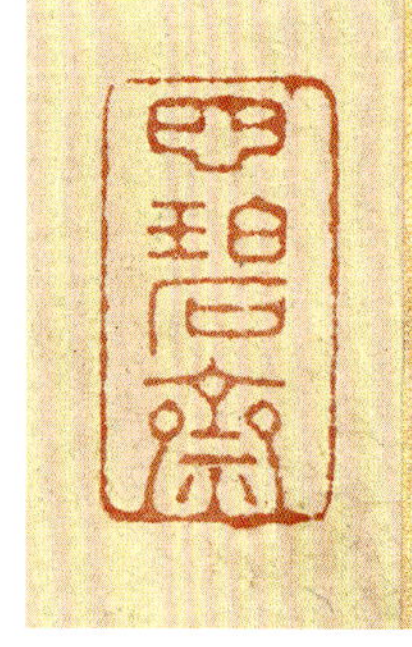

344

345

345

346

346

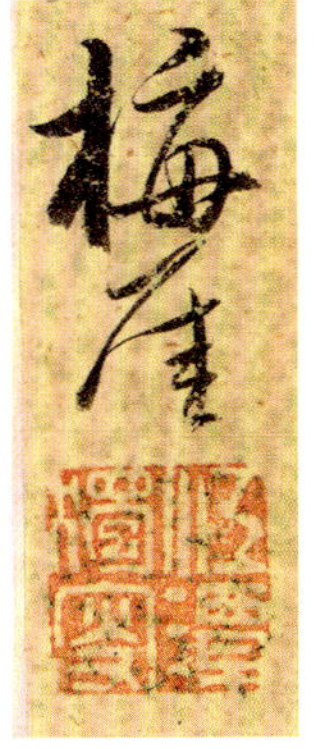
347

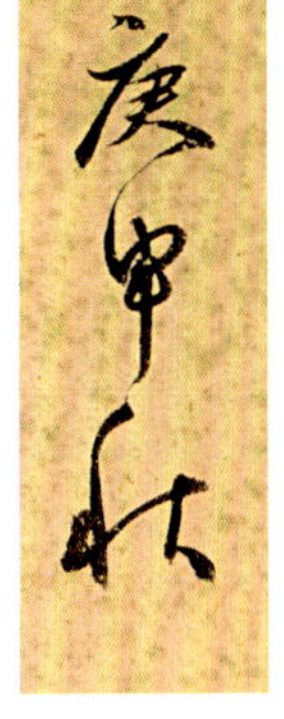
347

347

347

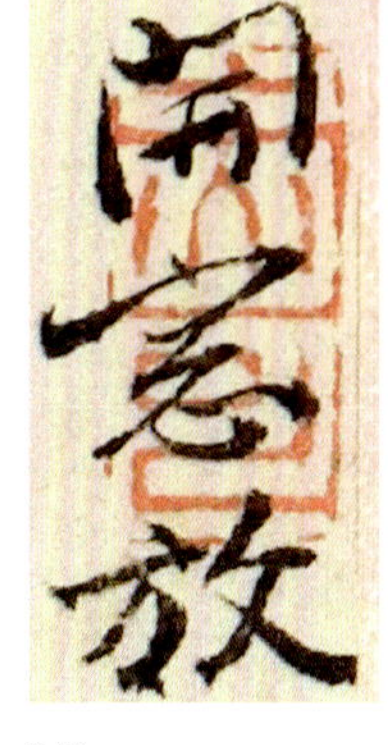
347

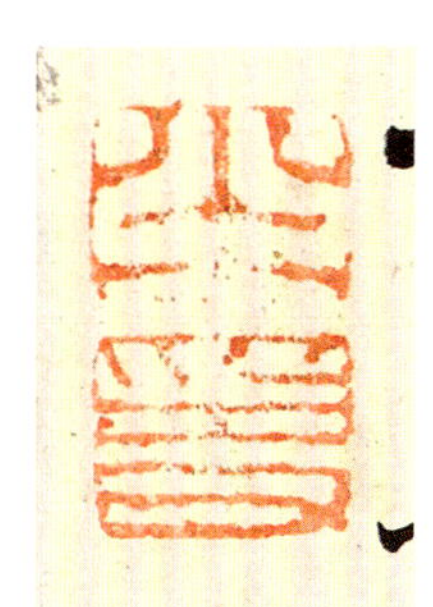
347

† 347. "Convenience in Drawing Water" from *Jūben* (Ten Conveniences); "Pleasure of Dawn" from *Jūgi* (Ten Pleasures)

["Convenience in Drawing Water"]

Text

Convenience in Drawing Water // A waterfall cascades right outside the kitchen of my mountain retreat. / A piece of bamboo sprout makes a conduit for a lasting flow. / Wonderful tea is soon brewed to serve wonderful guests, / with lingering fragrance of the pristine stones at the fountain-head.

Seal

Han'in

["Pleasure of Dawn"]

Text

Pleasure of Dawn // Opening the window, I let out the clouds that block the sky. / A pavilion near water is congenial to the enjoyment of dawn. / Rather than gaze into the pond for daybreak's splendor, / one can simply watch the waves reflected on the wall.

Seals

Sekka; *Ji*; *Shi*

Signature

[at end of *Jūgi* album] *In the autumn of 1800, Baigai*

Seal

[at end of *Jūgi* album] illegible; *Kōtaku dokusō*

† 348. Lingering Rain over a Mountain Hamlet

Text

by Gyokudō

Lingering Rain over a Mountain Hamlet

Signature

Gyokudō

Seals

Hakuzen Kinshi; *Kinsen*

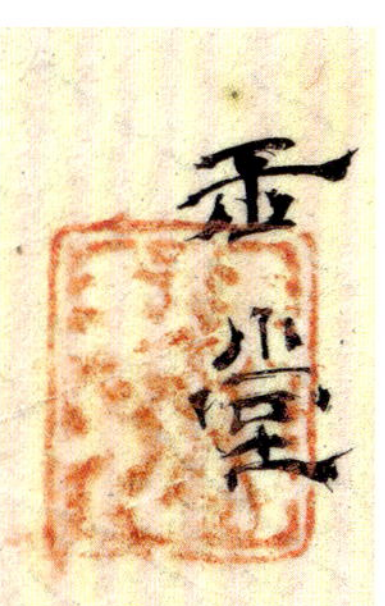
348

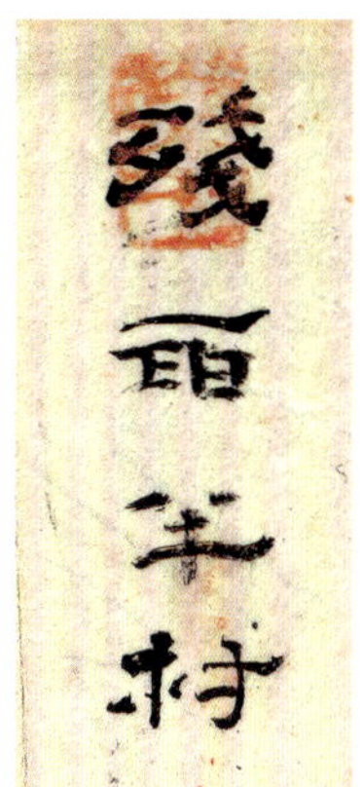
348

† 349. Crossing a Mountain Bridge with a Zither

Text

by Gyokudō

Painted the picture Crossing a Mountain Bridge with a Zither *on a spring day in 1814*

Signature

Gyokudō Kinshi is 70 years old

Seal

Takeuchi Daijin no mago

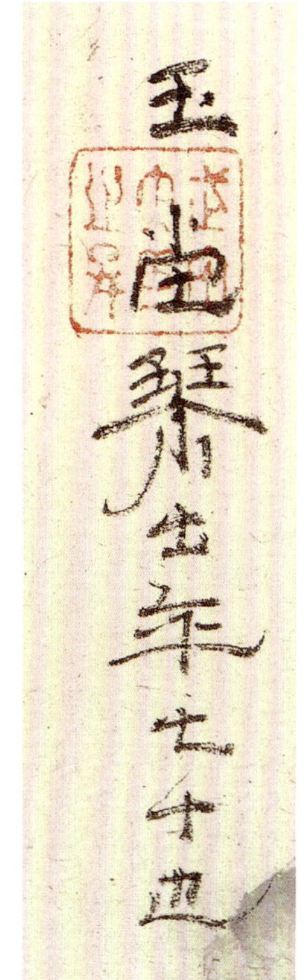
349

350

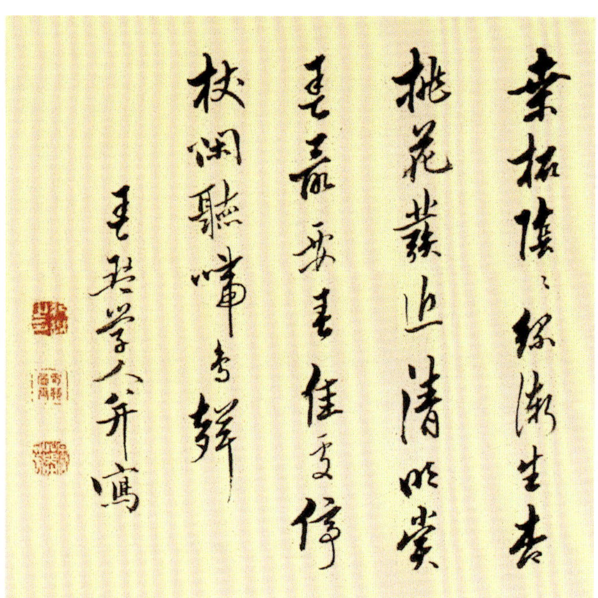

350

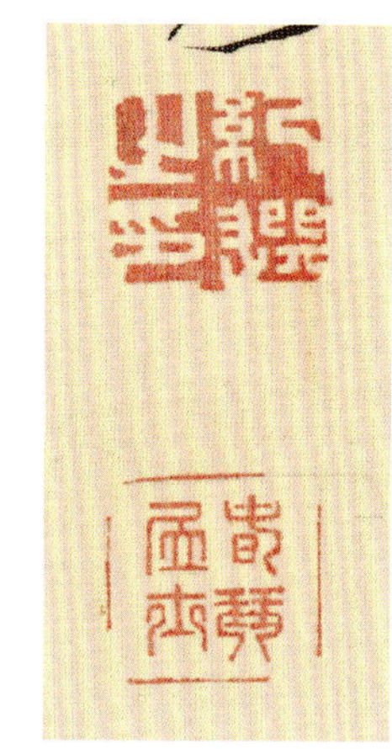

351

351

350

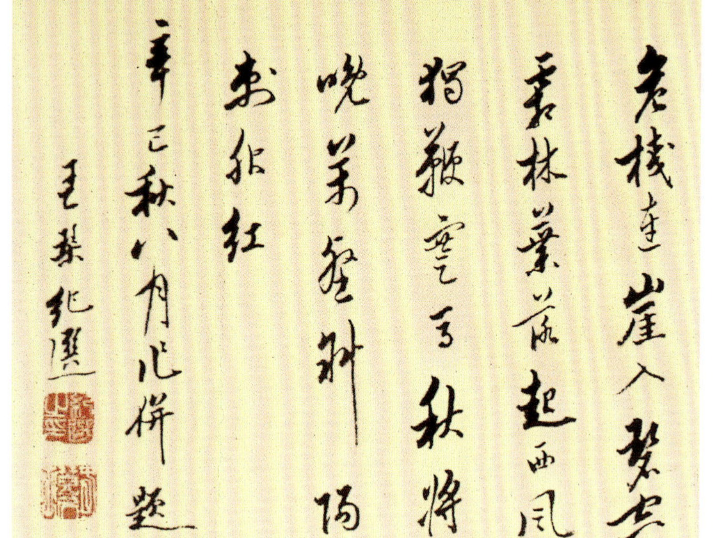

350

352

352

† 350. Landscapes of Spring and Autumn

[right screen]

Text

From the dark roots of the leaves' stems new greens gradually sprout. / Apricot and peach trees start blooming as Qingming approaches. / To enjoy spring it is most crucial to be where spring is lovely. / Halting my walking staff, I idly listen to the chirping birds.

Signature

Painted and inscribed by Shunkin Gakujin

Seals

Shinsen no in; Shunkin Koji; Ganha Tohō

[left screen]

Text

A perilous plank path runs across the crags toward the blue sky. / Leaves fall in frosty woods as the west wind arises. / A loner whips his crippled horse forward in the autumn dusk. / Over myriad valleys the setting sun glows glaringly red.

Signature

Painted and inscribed in the autumn, the eighth month of 1821. Shunkin Kisen

Seals

Kisen no in; Shunkin Koji

† 351. Yōrō Waterfall

Signature

Painted by Shunkin at the Senzairō at the Yōrō Falls in the leap month, autumn, 1824

Seals

Kisen; Shunkin

Text

Dark sheer cliffs in the grip of misty clouds; / fragrant yellow chrysanthemums under the / late autumn sky. / I heard that waterfalls could nourish a man in old age. / It makes me long for it for a thousand years.

Signature

Inscribed again by Shunkin Kisen

Seals

Kisen no in; Shunkin Koji

† 352. Landscape with Pavilion

Text

by Beisanjin

Expansive waves of clouds surge among the mountains, / old trees withstand severe wind and frost.

Signature

Beisanjin

Seals

Beisanjin; Den'en; Shigen

† 353. Bamboo and Plums in Early Spring

Signature

Painted by Hankō in the summer of 1843

Seals

Denshuku; Hankō

Text

by Hineno Kyōsui (1786–1854)

At the feet of lovely mountains and by the brooks, / piles of snow and ice cannot thwart the arrival of spring. / Cool, delicate plum blossoms and pure slender bamboo / shelter the tender-hearted one reclining in the pavilion.

Signature

Kyōsui Kinsō

Seals

Sekika; Hine Kōkyō; Kyōsui

353

353

353

† 354. Landscape after a Qing Chinese Work

Text

by Hankō

By the window at dawn, my white hair battles the west wind. / As I smile, the blue clouds are gone like the past. / Only the blue mountains are my bosom friends, / which I meet most often in paintings.

Signature

Emulating the brushwork of Qing Chinese painters, Hankō

Seals

Shuku Shiu in; Shuku in

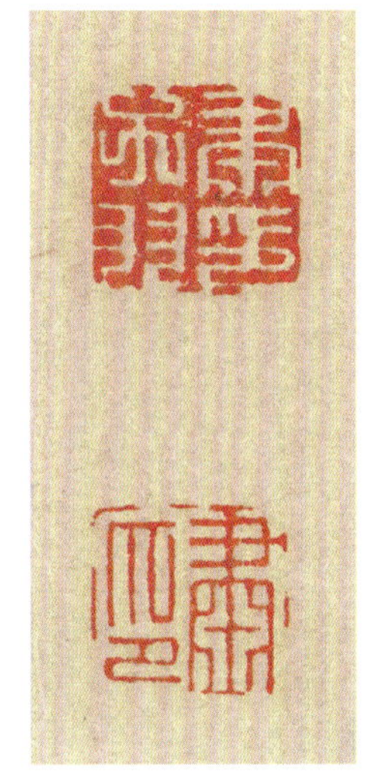

354

† 355. Farewell Gift to Tani Bunji

Text

by Hankō

Master Tani Bunji had lodged in the Kagetsuan for several days. / I was unable to go visit him, because my son caught smallpox. / It was not until his imminent return that we managed to meet. / I thereupon made this painting and poem to bid him farewell with respect. // Blurry silhouettes of the town encircle the ancient ford; / the chilly mist and pale moon are intimate to the feel. / Our meeting is worth cheering, / but not without regret; / it is not yet time for the plum trees to blossom.

Signature

In the late winter of 1833. Hankō Okada Shuku

Seals

Saishin; Okada Shuku in; Hankō

355

355

† 356. Preparing Tea by a Mountain Gorge

Signature

Fourth month, 1825. Rōbei

Seals

Mokubei; Aoki [seal impressed upside down]

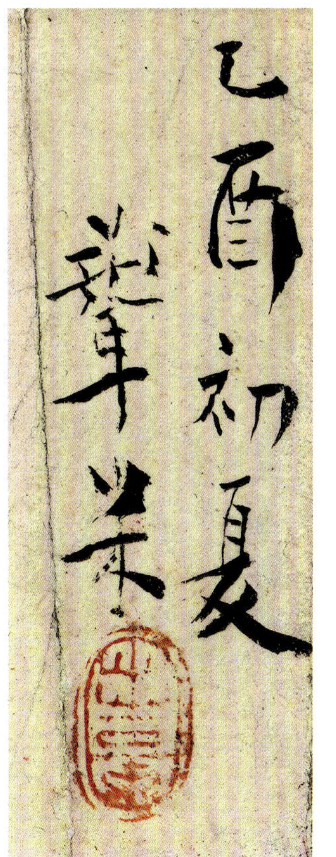

356

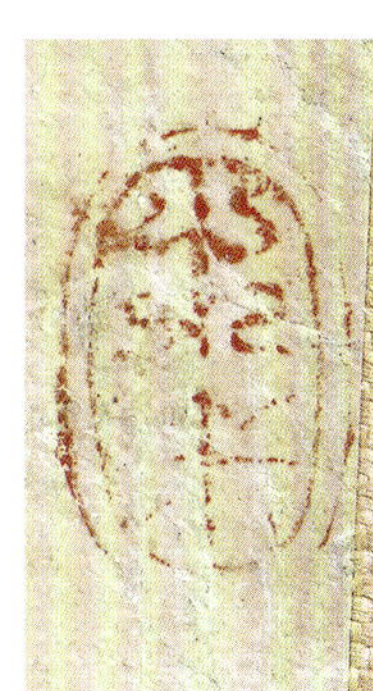

356

† 357. Rainstorm over a River Village

Text

by Chikuden

Rowing back home on a leaf-like boat, / ten miles of turbulent waves as overwhelming as the mountains. / Who knows that the difficult path in the world / is not the one in a stormy river village.

Signature

Chikudensei

Seals

Denshaji; Life is meant for the pursuit of happiness; [lower right] illegible

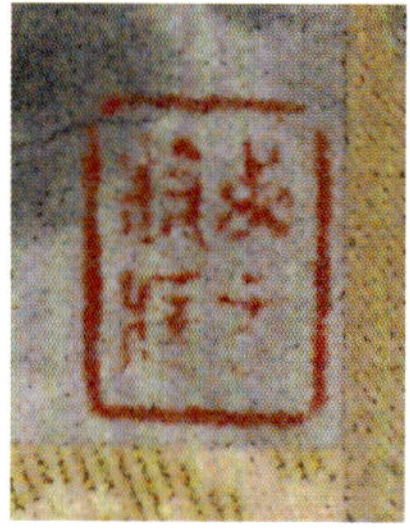

357

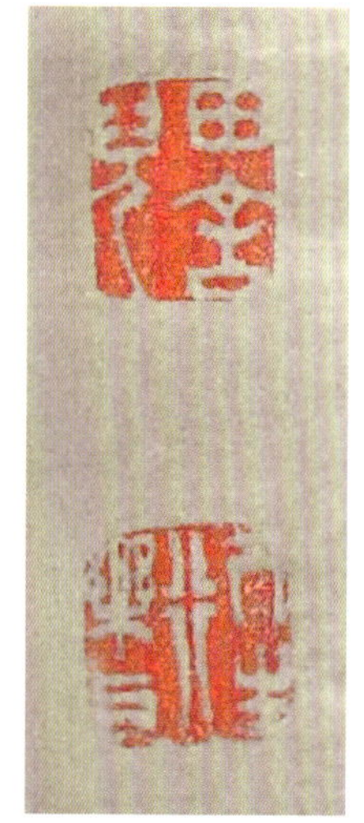

357

† 358. Snowy Landscape

Text

by Sōhei

The tattered bamboo hat is all covered with snow; / in a lone boat is an old fisherman. / Gazing at the empty woods in sunset, / he seems tied down in the frozen stream.

Signature

Painted at Chikuden's residence in the sixth month of 1824. Sōhei U

Seals

Shiseki Tengai; Sōhei; Kōu

358

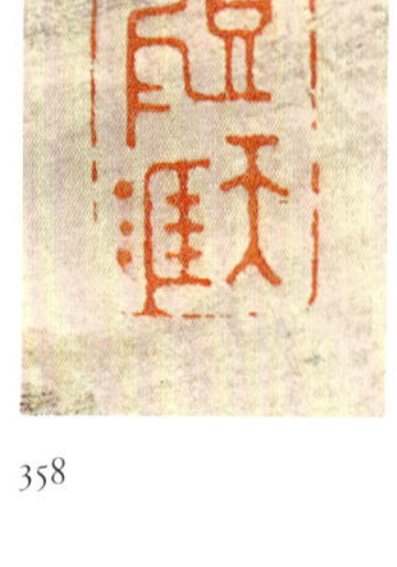

358

† 359. Taihu Rock and Banana Plant

Text

by Sōhei

Banana plants lean against a lone rock, / glimmering green in the courtyard

Signature

Painted while staying at Itami in the early summer of 1831. There is a lovely spot under the southern window. Sōhei Kōu

Seals

Sōhei; Kōu

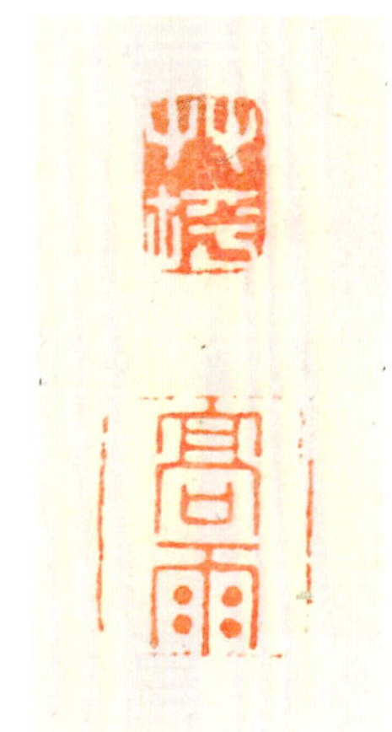

359

† 360. Oxen and Herd Boy

Signature

Painted this at Itami Hanshūen on the first day of the third month of 1832. Sōhei U

Seals

Shōshuku Hankun; Sōhei

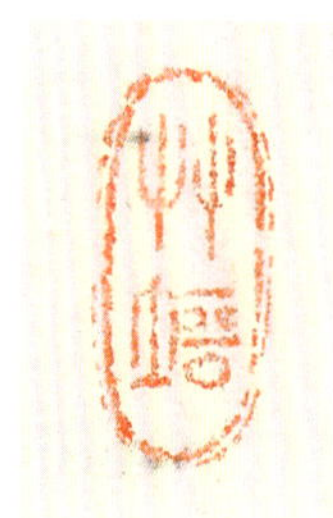

360

360

† 361. Sampling Tea beneath Wu Trees

Signature

Sampling Tea beneath Wu Trees *painted on the twenty-fifth day of the third month in spring 1840, in the deep green shade at Higashiyama. Nakabayashi Narimasa*

Seals

Narimasa no in; Aza Hakumei

361

† 362. Chinese Lady with Attendant

Seals

Narimasa no in; Aza Hakumei

362

† 363. Landscape

Signature

Painted at Fugan Aizanrō in the eleventh month of 1844. Inshi Chūtan

Seals

Narimasa no in; Hakumei shi

363

† 364. Plum Tree

Signature

Painted by Nakabayashi Seishuku

Seals

Seishuku; Chūkyō

Text

by Yoshida Shūran (1797–1866)

Getting up on a frosty morning, / I don't mind the chill, but chant poetry softly, / leaning on the green balustrade. / Does the icy beauty have romantic longing too? / She emanates pure fragance onto my morning coiffure.

Signature

Composed by Shūran Joshi

Seals

Tennen; Satō no in; Shūran

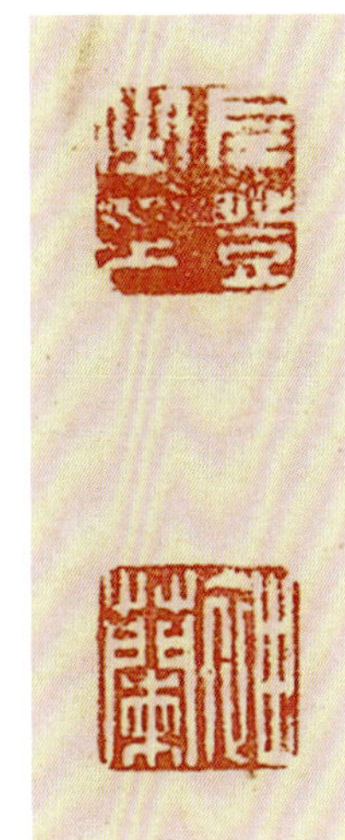

364

364

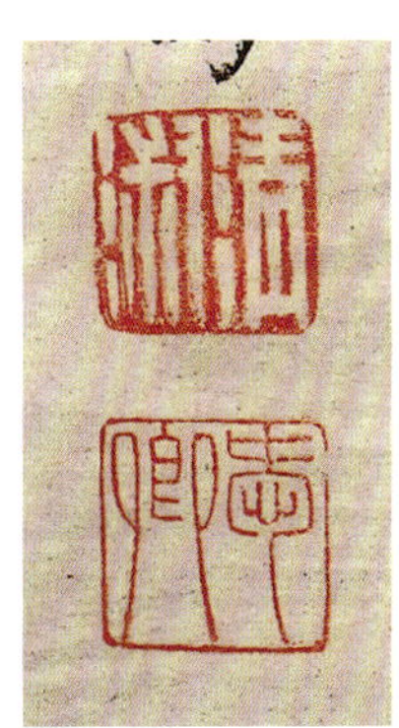

364

† 365. Autumn Landscape at Eigenji

Signature

Painted for the enjoyment of the master of the Sūkeidō on a winter day in 1833. Kaioku Seihō

Seals

Kanhō; Kunmo

365

† 366. Spring Landscape

Text

by Kaioku

Radiant spring decants such lush green as to brim over the riverbank; / fishermen and woodcutters on the river, / dwelling beyond the willows. / Yesterday I got some wine with credit / and boated down the Jakuya [Ch. Ruoye] *Stream; / my gliding skiff reflects upon the waterway teeming with flowers.*

Signature

Painted and inscribed by Kaikyaku in the second month of 1844

Seals

Kōtō; Kunmo; Chikurei Shōkan

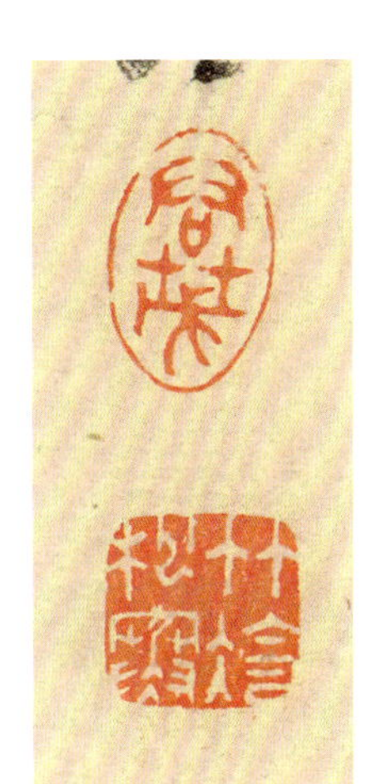

366

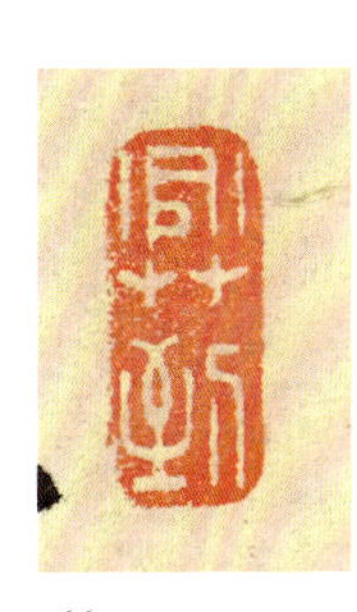

366

† 367. Autumn Flowers

Signature

Painted by Baiitsu Ryō in the eighth month of 1843

Seals

Ryō in; Baiitsu

367

† 368. Peaches, Pomegranate, and Fingered Citron

Signature

I painted this picture in summer, the sixth month of 1832, for the enjoyment of the Master of Sankadō / Issan. Baiitsu Ryō

Seal

Baiitsu

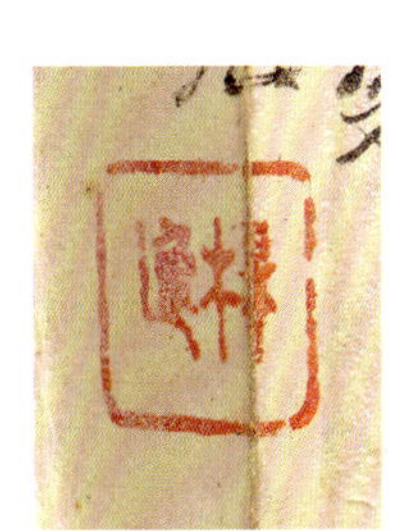

368

† 369. Landscapes of the Four Seasons

Signatures

[Spring scroll] *Painted in the first month of 1848. Baiitsu Ryō*
[Summer scroll] *By Baiitsu*
[Autumn scroll] *Painted by Baiitsu*
[Winter scroll] *By Baiitsu, at Gyokuzenshitsu*

Seals

[on Spring, Summer, and Autumn scrolls] *Yamamoto Ryō*
[on Winter scroll] *Yamamoto Ryō; Meikyō*

† 370. Golden Pheasants among Rhododendrons

Signature

Painted by Baiitsu Ryō

Seal

Ryō in

† 371. Landscape with Waterfall

Signature

Painted by Bōsai rōjin kōsui

Seals

Kikubu shōsho; Chōkō no ki; Kaitō rōnin

† 372. Snowy Landscape

Signature

Painted by Baiitsu Yamamoto Ryō at Gyokuzenshitsu

Seal

Baiitsu

† 373. Landscape with Waterfall

Signature

Bunchō

Seal

Bunsei boshi Bunchō ga in

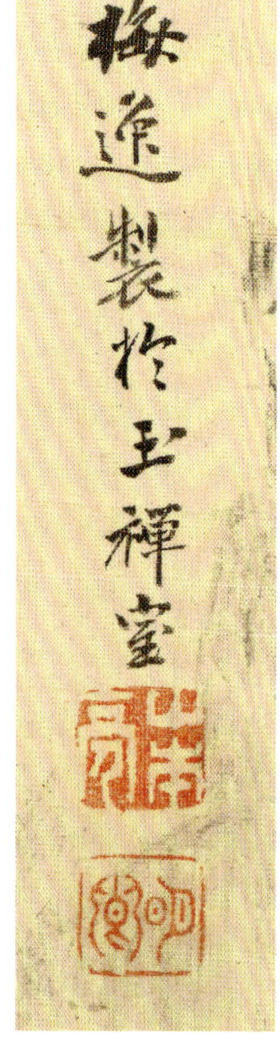

369. Winter

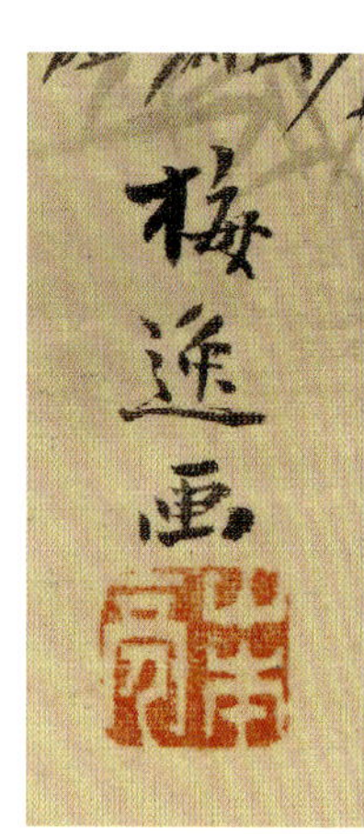

369. Autumn

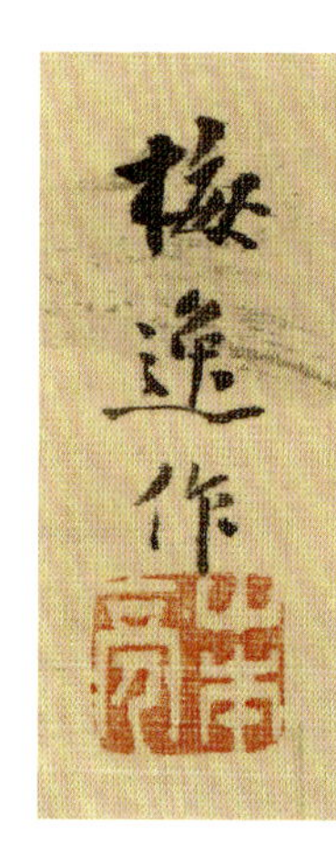

369. Summer

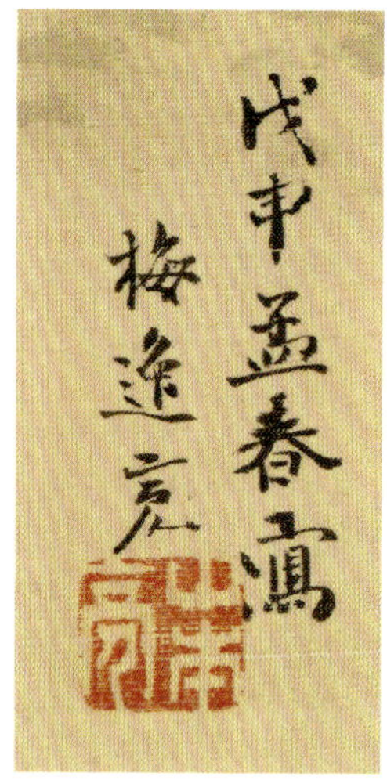

369. Spring

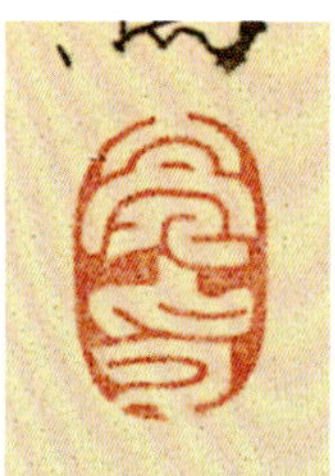

370

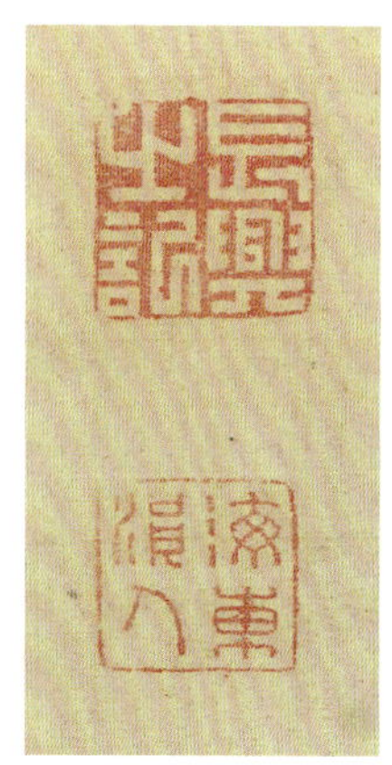

371

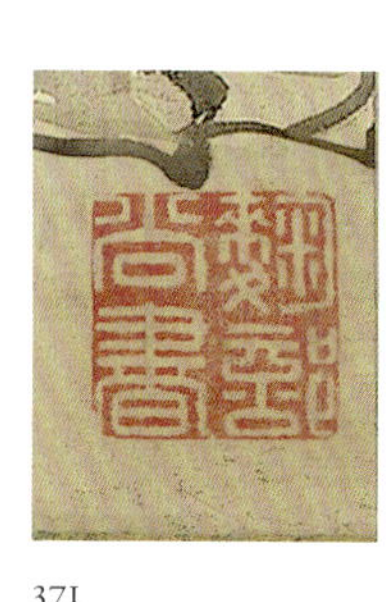

371

372

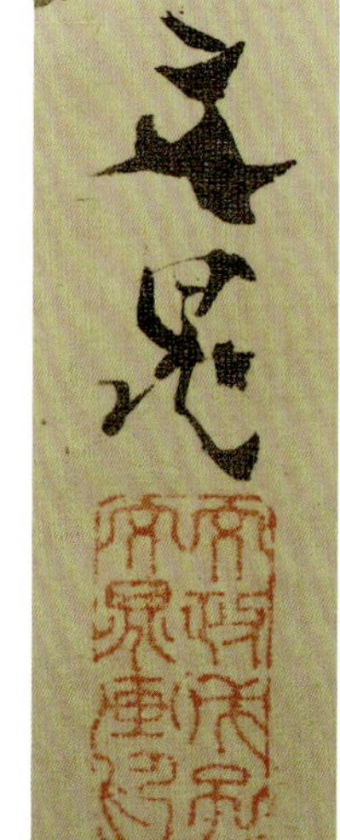

373

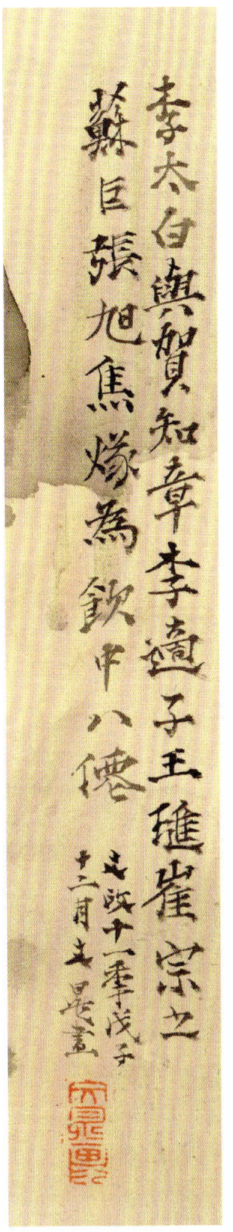

374

374

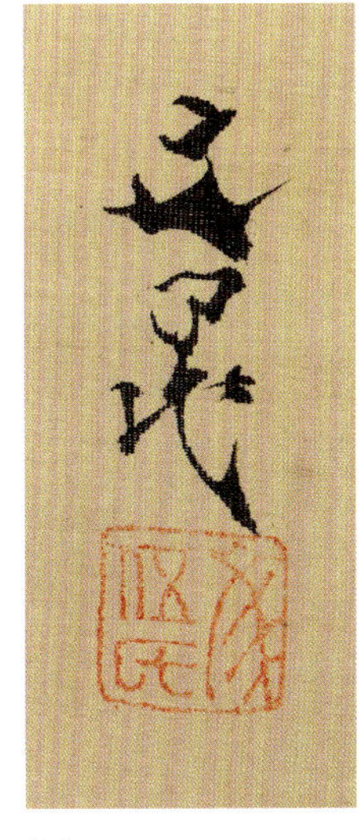

375

376

376

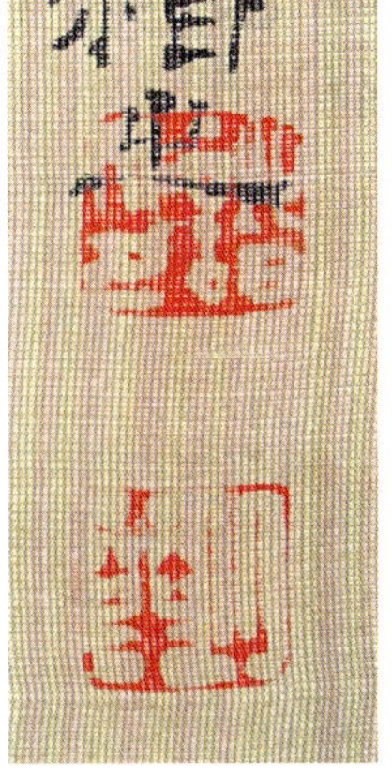

378

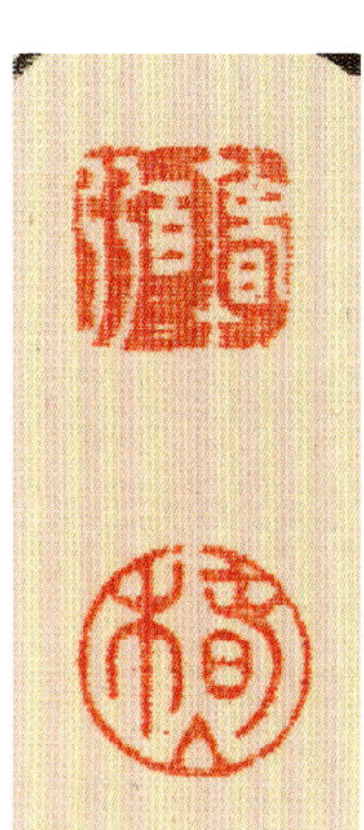

379

---

† 374. The Eight Immortals of the Wine Cup

Text

by Bunchō

Ri Taihaku [Ch. Li Taibai] *with Ga Chishō* [Ch. He Zhizhangh], *Ri Tekishi* [Ch. Li Shizi], *Ō Shin* [Ch. Wang Jin], *Sai Sōshi* [Ch. Cui Zongzhi], *So Kyo* [Ch. Su Ju], *Chō Kyoku* [Ch. Zhang Xu], *and Shō Sui* [Ch. Jiao Sui] *are collectively known as the Eight Immortals in the World of Wine.*

Signature

Painted by Bunchō in December 1828

Seal

Bunchō ga in

---

† 375. Ri Haku (Ch. Li Bo) Viewing a Waterfall

Signature

Bunchō

Seal

Bungo shi

---

† 376. Study among Plum Flowers from *Landscapes of the Four Seasons*

Text

by Aigai

Study among Plum Flowers

Signature

[on last leaf] *In the late summer of the fourth month of 1833. Aigai*

Seals

[on each leaf] *Chō*; *Kōho*; *Sekisō*

---

† 378. Family of Cranes

Signature

Painted by Shōka

Seals

Kai in; *Shōka*

---

† 379. Swallow's Song in Spring Breeze

Text

by Chinzan

Swallow's Song in Spring Breeze

Signature

Third month of 1852. Tsubaki Sanjin

Seals

Chinhitsu; *Chinzan*

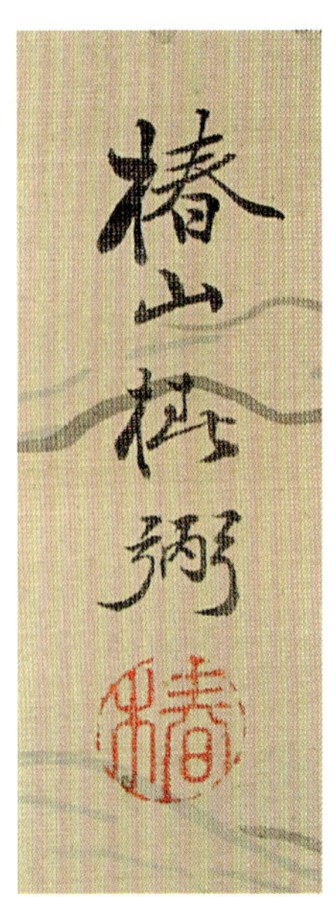

380

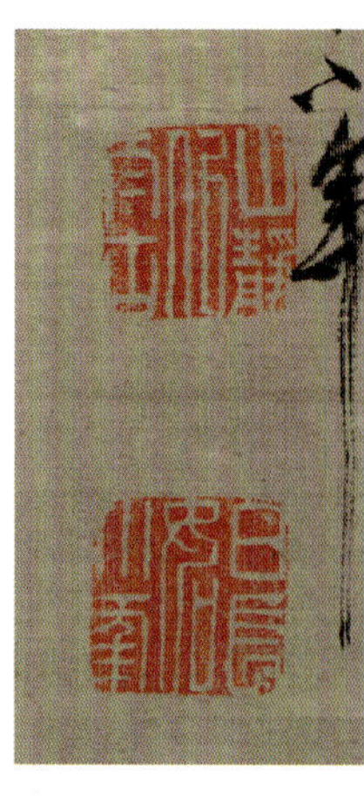

382

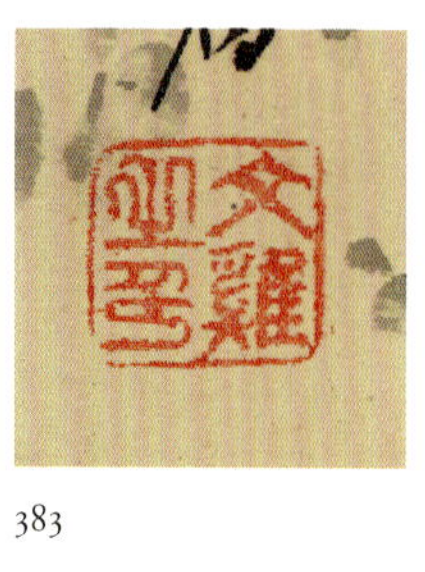

383

384

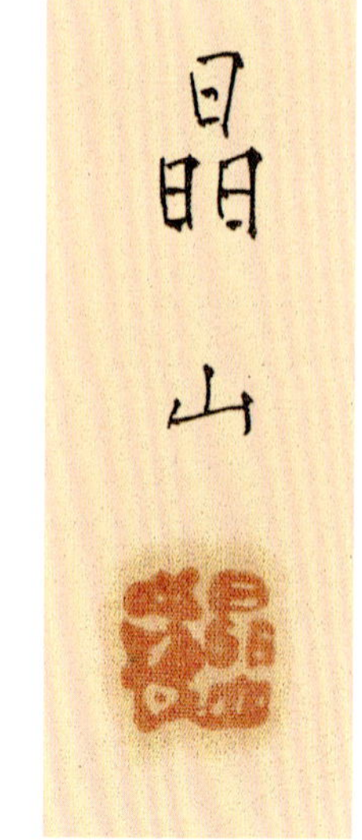

385

381

381

† 380. Geese in Autumn Stream

Signature

Chinzan Chinhitsu

Seal

Tsubaki

† 381. Jewel-like Countenance, Gaze of a Recluse

Text

by Chinzan

Jewel-like Countenance, Gaze of a Recluse

Signature

Tsubakisei painted the spirit

Seals

Takuka; Hitsu in; Chinzan

† 382. Travelers in Cold Mountains

Text

by Taizan

Travelers in Cold Mountains

Signature

Painted at Renzanrō in the winter, eleventh month of 1859. Hi Shōnen

Seals

The mountain is as quiet as primordial times; the day is as long as a slow year

† 383. Landscape

Signature

Kei

Seal

Bunkei no in

† 384. Monkey with Catfish in Gourd; Pine and Cranes

[Monkey with Catfish in Gourd]

Text

by Tessai

Lately there are many more men who have a monkey's guile to stick a catfish into a gourd

Signature

Tessai

Seal

Tessai

[Pine and Cranes]

Signature

January 1912. 77-year-old Tessai

Seal

Tessai

† 385. Peony in Basket

Signature

Shōzan

Seal

Illegible

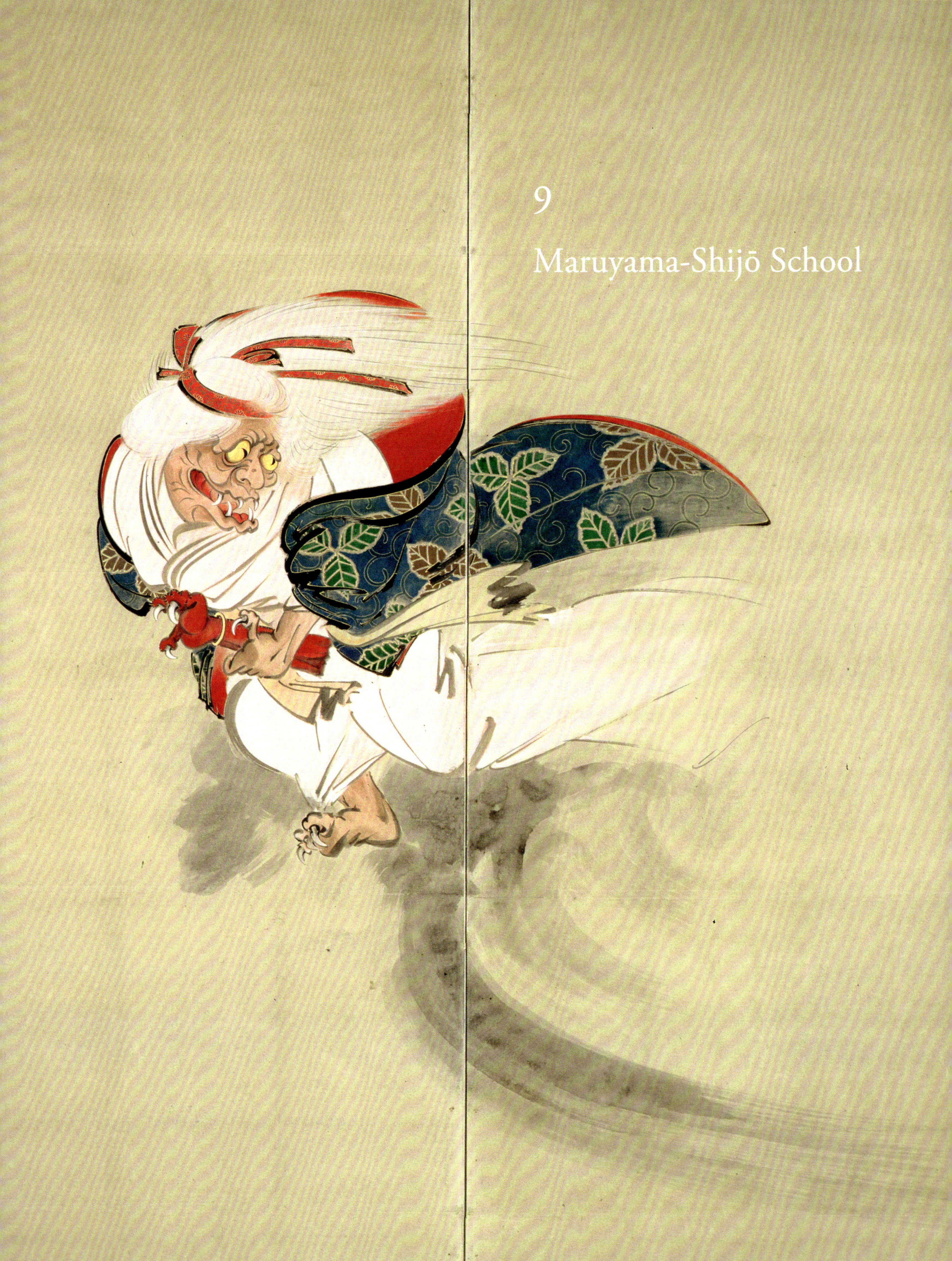

9

Maruyama-Shijō School

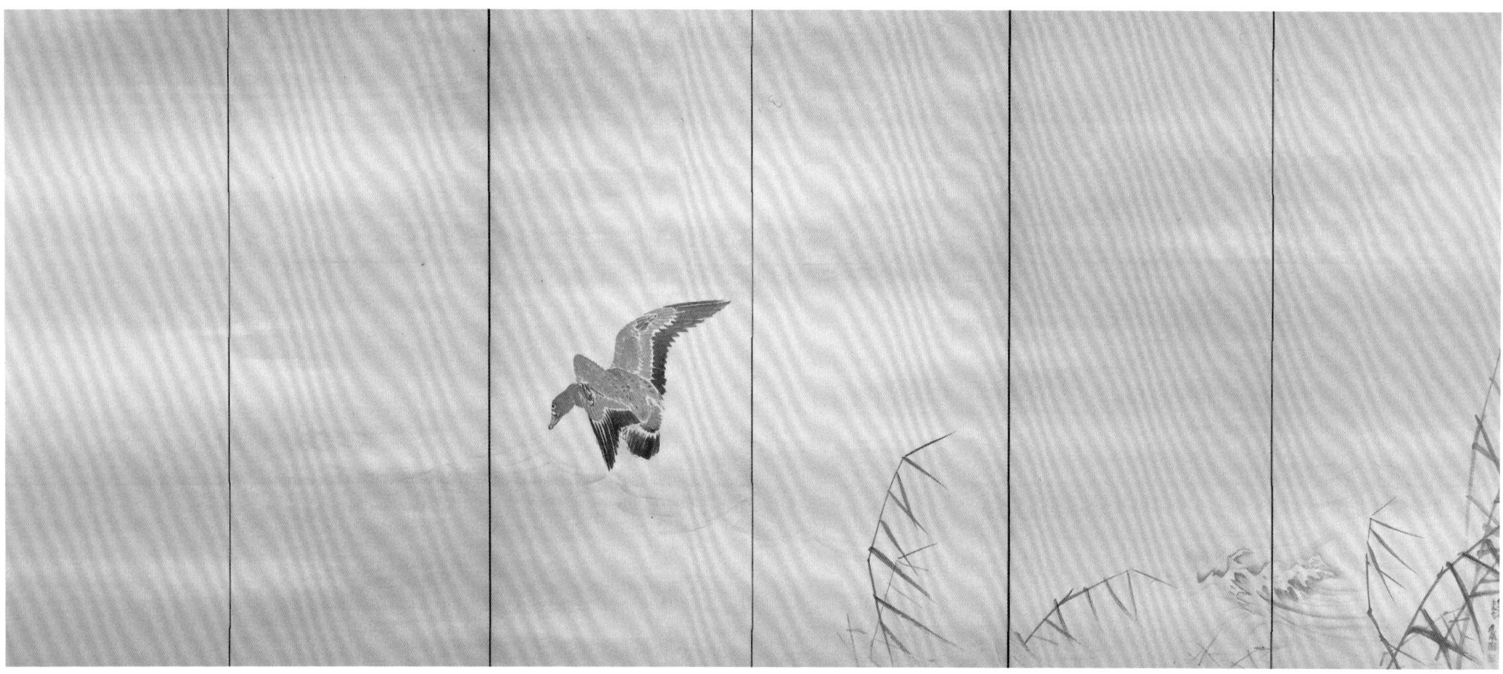

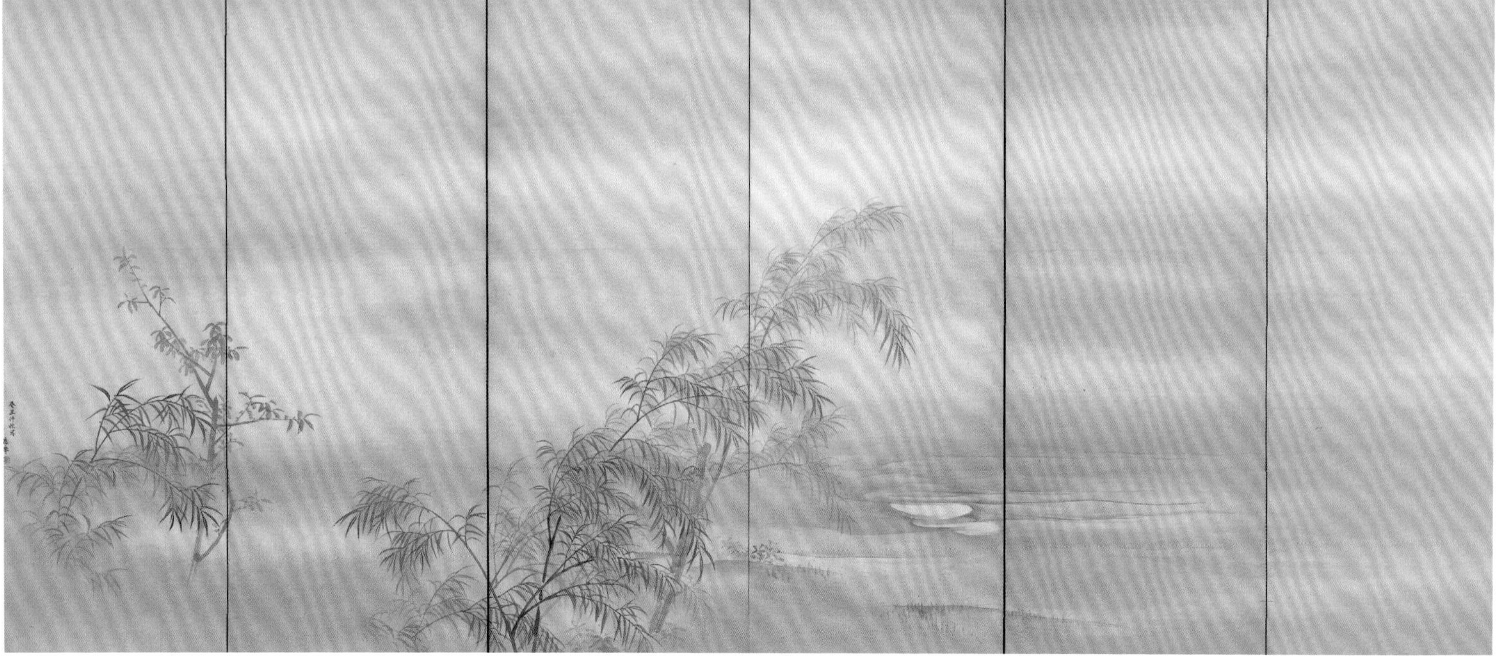

Maruyama Ōkyo
(円山応挙; 1733–1795)

386. Goose and Reeds; Moon and Willows

Edo period, 1774 (*right screen*), 1793 (*left screen*)
Pair of six-panel folding screens; ink, light color, and gold on paper
Each screen 153.9 x 354.4 cm (60⅝ in. x 11 ft. 7½ in.)
Signatures, seals

Literature: Burke 1993, fig. 14/no. 28; Tsuji Nobuo et al. 2005, no. 97

Maruyama Ōkyo
(円山応挙; 1733–1795)

387. Sweetfish in Summer and Autumn

Edo period, 1785
Pair of hanging scrolls; ink, color, and gold on silk
Each scroll 104.3 x 37 cm (41⅛ x 14⅝ in.)
Signatures, seals

Literature: Yamakawa Takeshi 1977a, pp. 17, 19; Tokyo National Museum 1985a, no. 60; Avitabile 1990, no. 103; Murase 2000, no. 115.

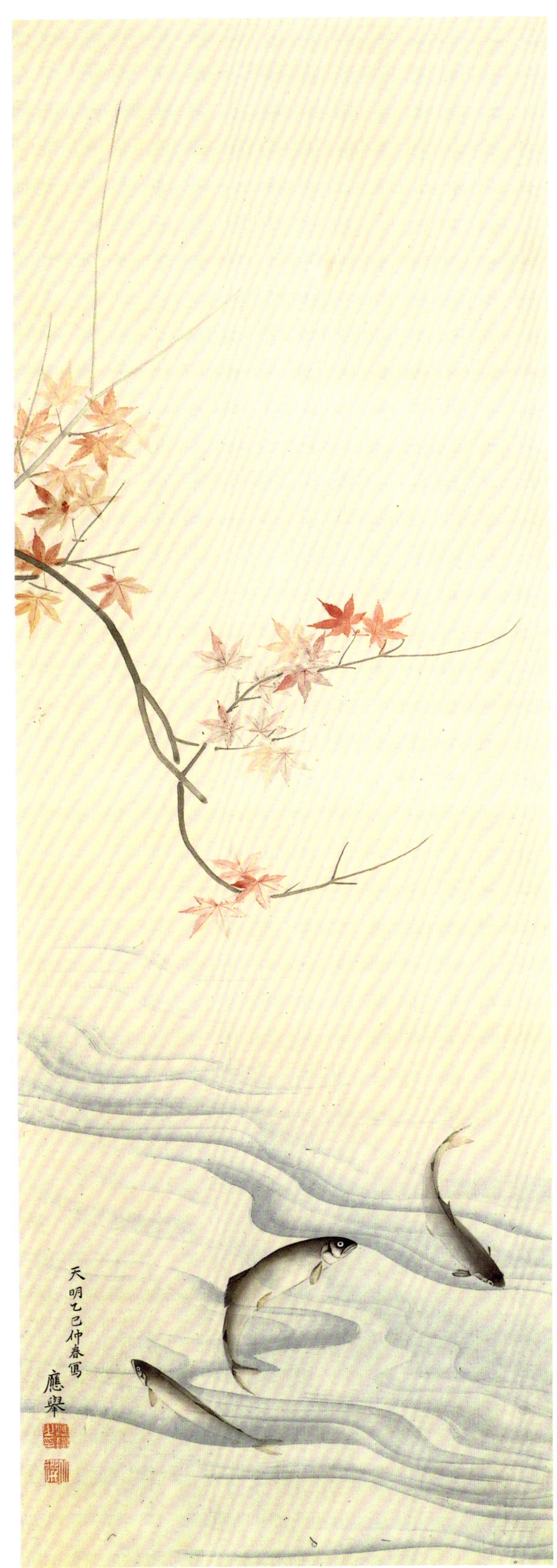
天明乙巳仲春寫
應擧

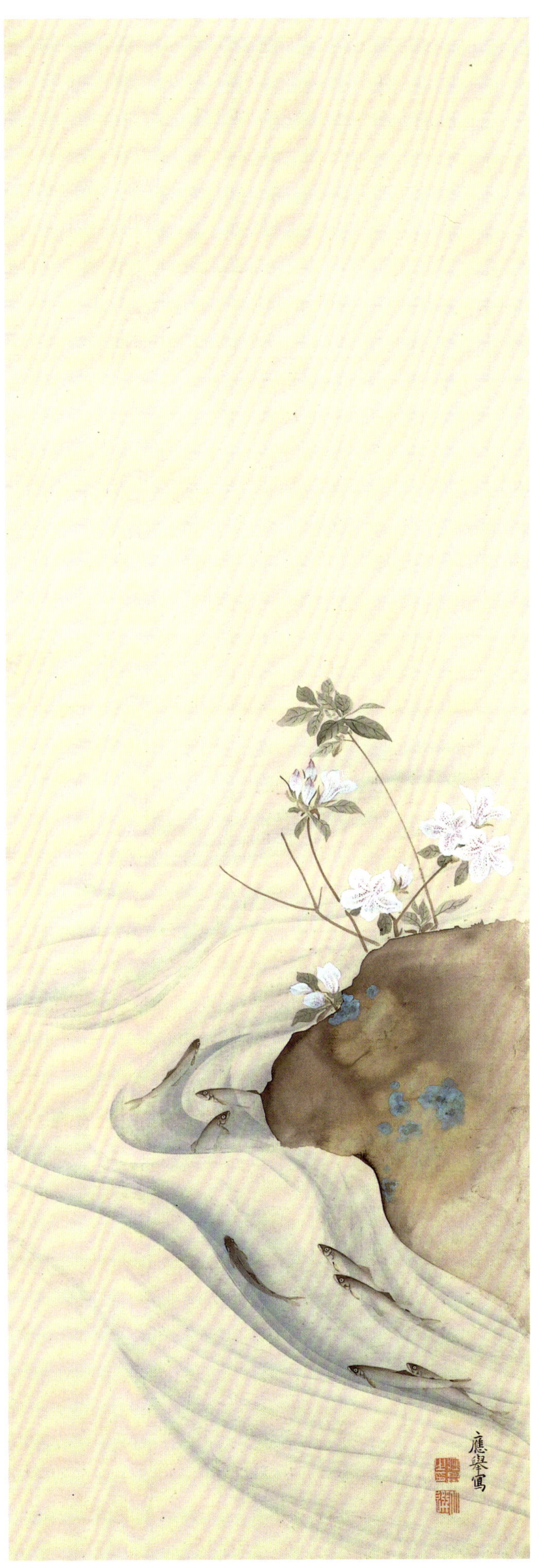
應擧寫

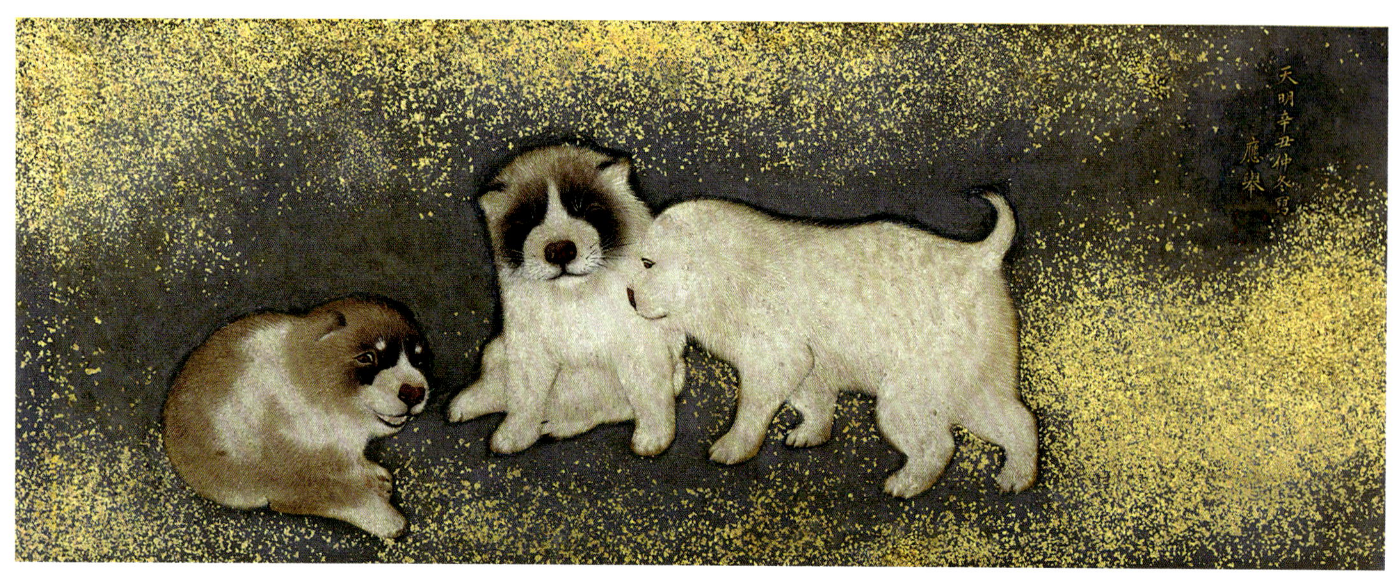

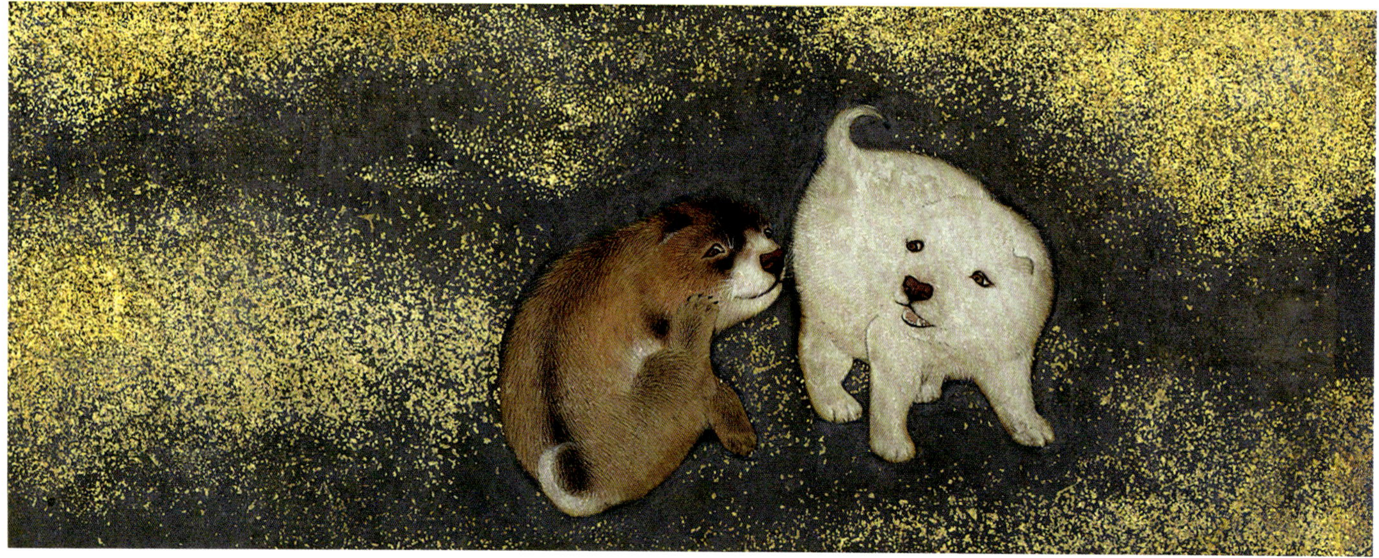

Maruyama Ōkyo
(円山応挙; 1733–1795)

388. Puppies

Edo period, 1781
Two-panel screen; ink, color, and gold on paper
24.6 x 63.2 cm ($9^{5}/_{8}$ x $24^{7}/_{8}$ in.)
Signature, seal

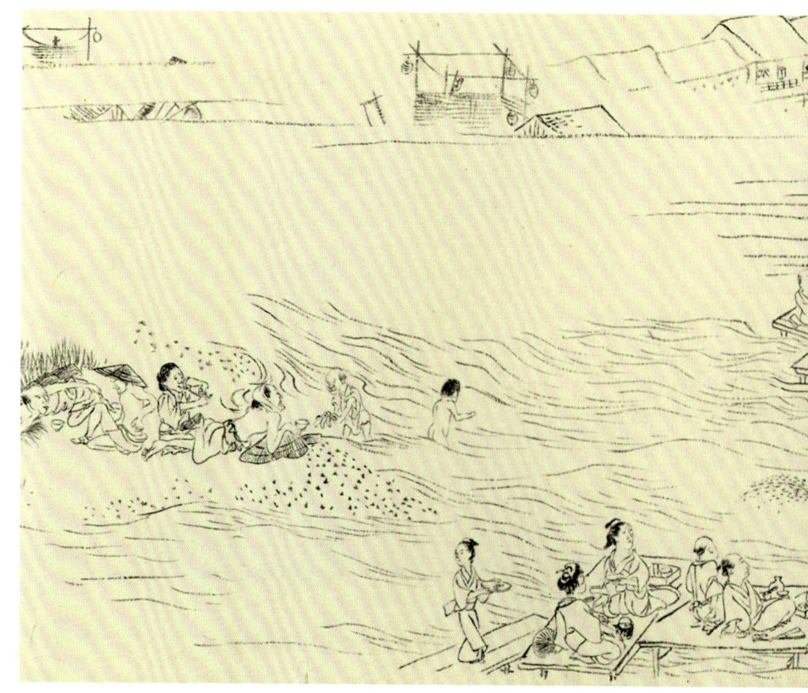

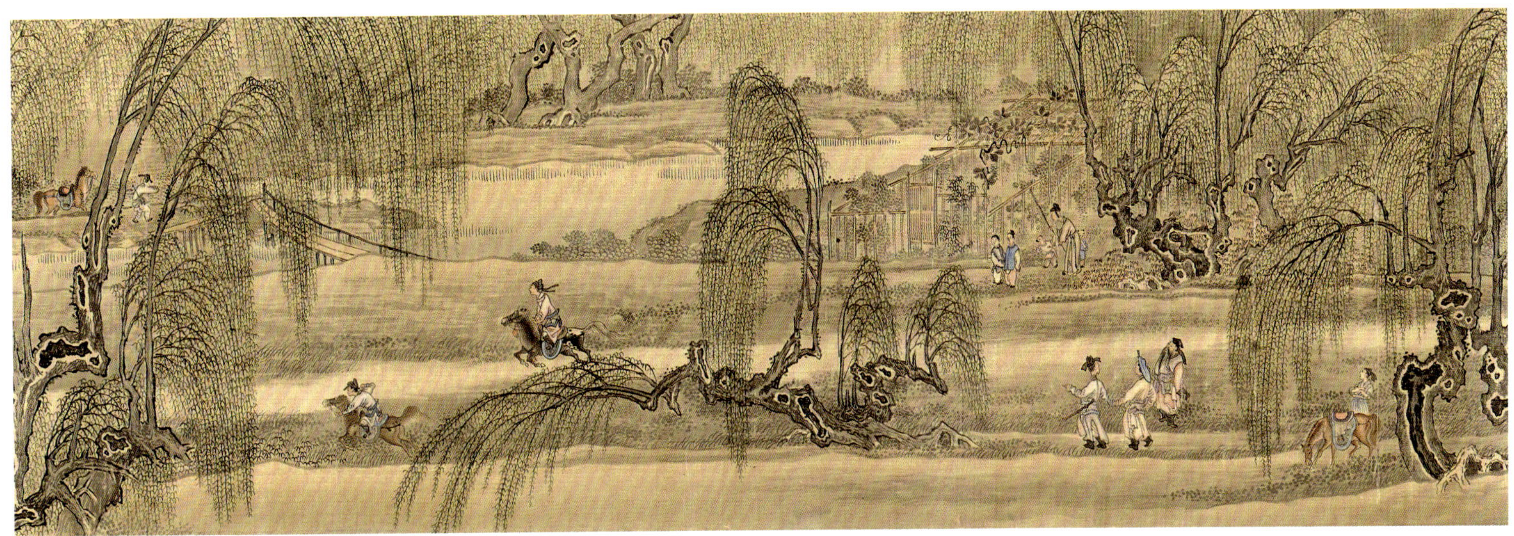

Maruyama Ōkyo
(円山応挙; 1733–1795)

389. Horseback Riding at West Lake
(西湖戯馬図)

Edo period, 1793
Handscroll; ink and light color on silk
30.8 x 438 cm (12 1/8 in. x 14 ft. 4 3/8 in.)
Signature, seals

Maruyama Ōkyo
(円山応挙; 1733–1795)

390. Preparatory drawing for scroll of the Four Seasons in Kyoto

Edo period
Handscroll; ink on paper
39.5 x 554.8 cm (15 1/2 in. x 18 ft. 2 3/8 in.)

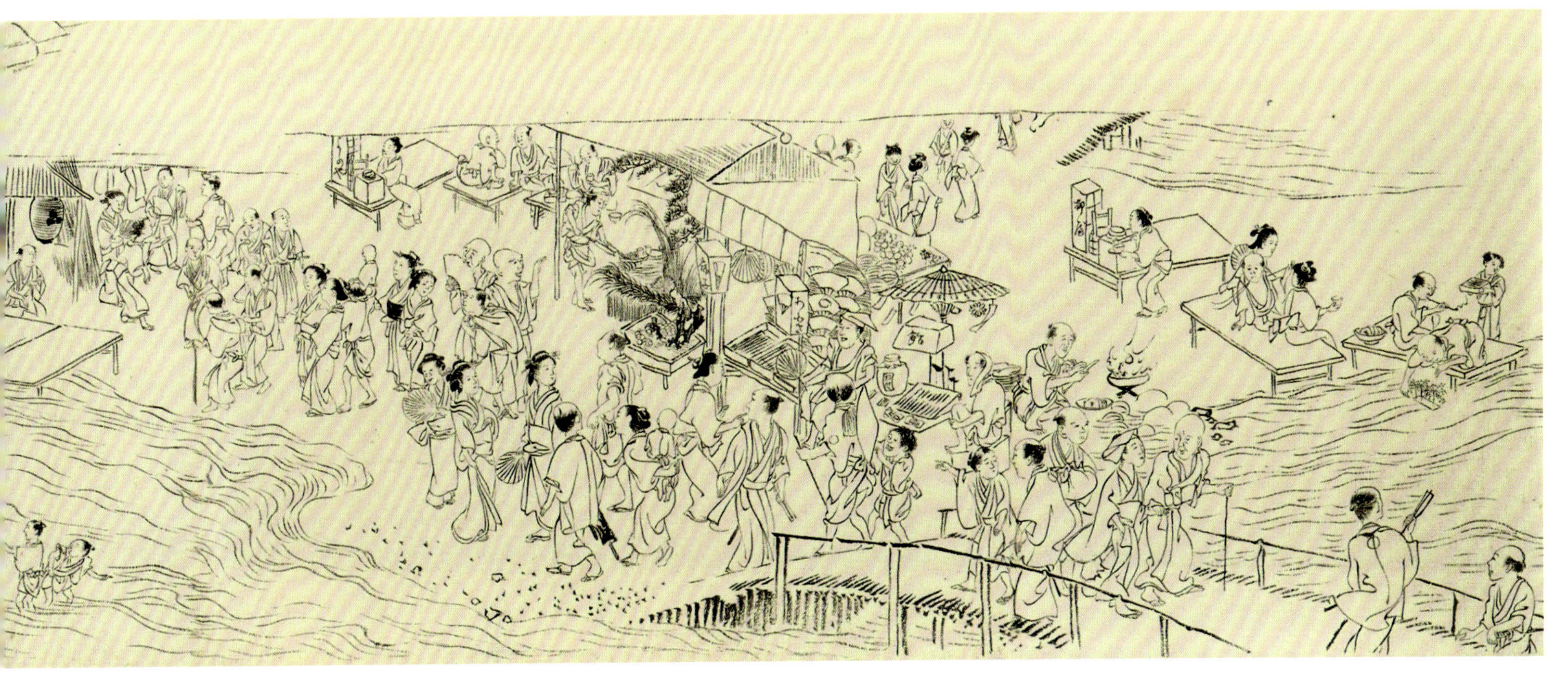

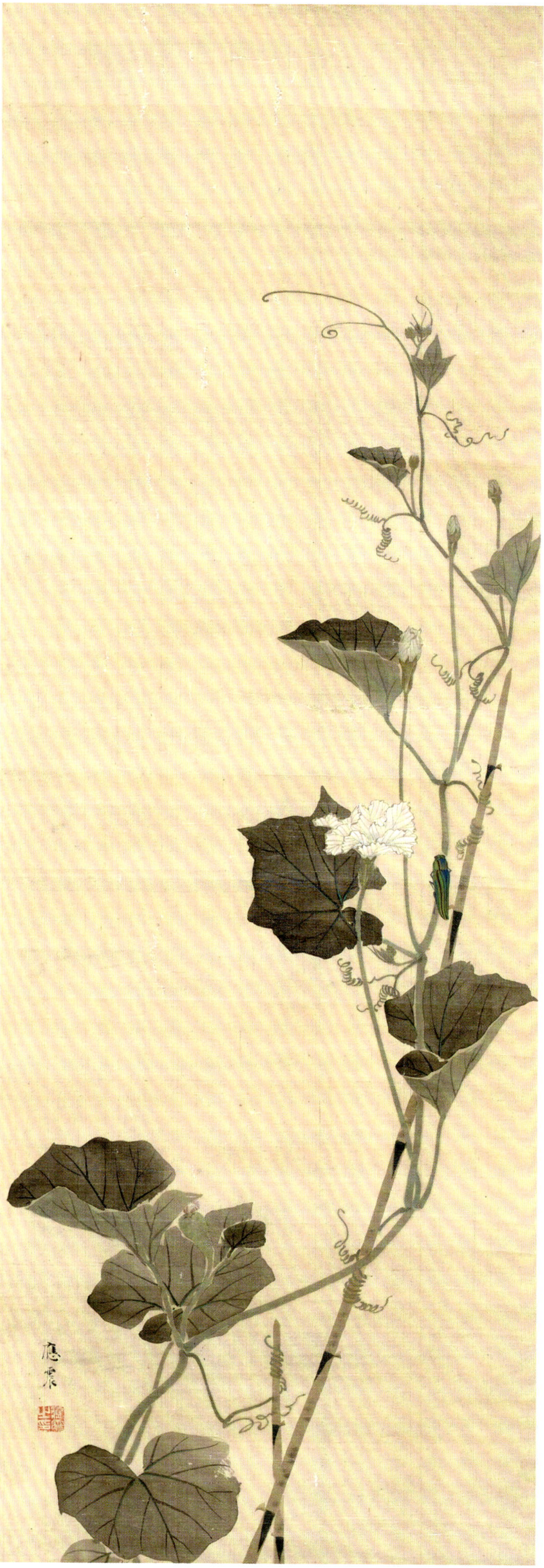

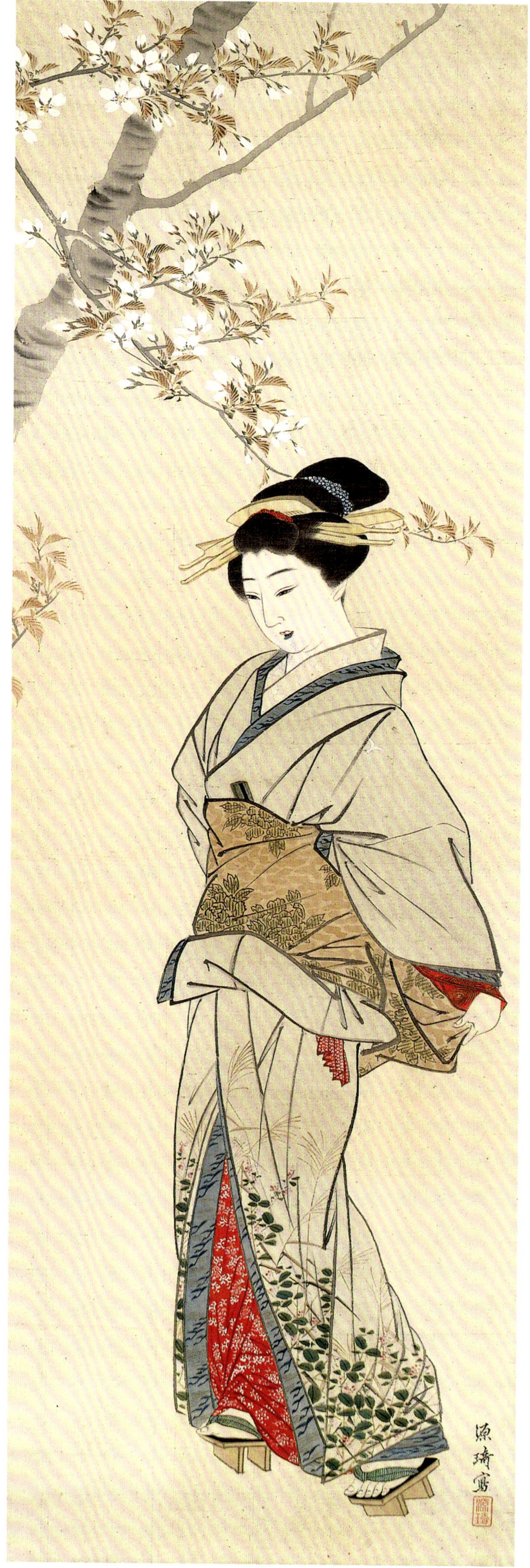
源琦寫

Maruyama Ōshin
(円山応震; 1790–1838)

391. Calabash Flowers and Beetle

Edo period
Hanging scroll; ink and color on silk
99.8 x 36.4 cm (39¼ x 14⅜ in.)
Signature, seal

Genki
(源琦, also known as Komai Ki [駒井 琦];
1747–1797)

392. Beauty under Cherry Tree

Edo period
Hanging scroll, ink, color, and gold on silk
91.4 x 30.8 cm (36 x 12⅛ in.)
Signature, seal

Ex coll.: C. D. Carter

Literature: Narazaki Muneshige 1969, no. 83; Moes 1975, no. 20; Murase 1993, no. 42.

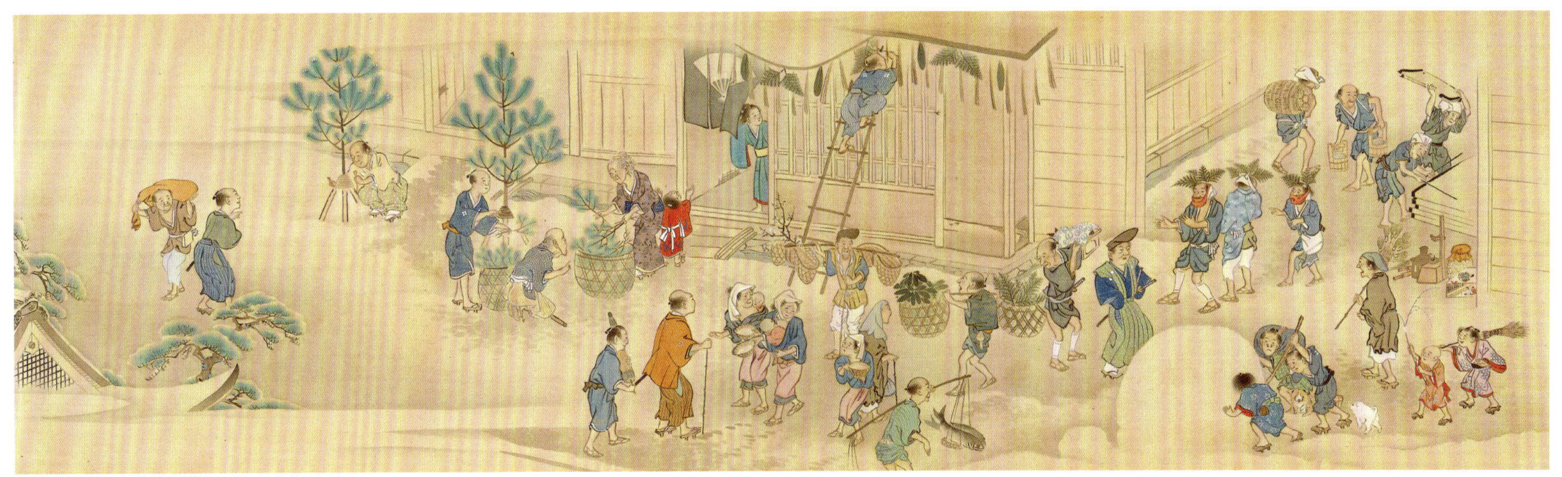

Genki
(源琦, also known as Komai Ki [駒井 琦];
1747–1797)

393. Winter scene from the Four Seasons in Kyoto

Edo period
Handscroll; ink and color on silk
32.5 x 507.8 cm (12¾ in. x 16 ft. 7⅞ in.)
Signatures, seals

Literature: Murase 1975, no. 63; L. Cunningham 1984, no. 8; Chiba Municipal Museum 1996b, no. 80.

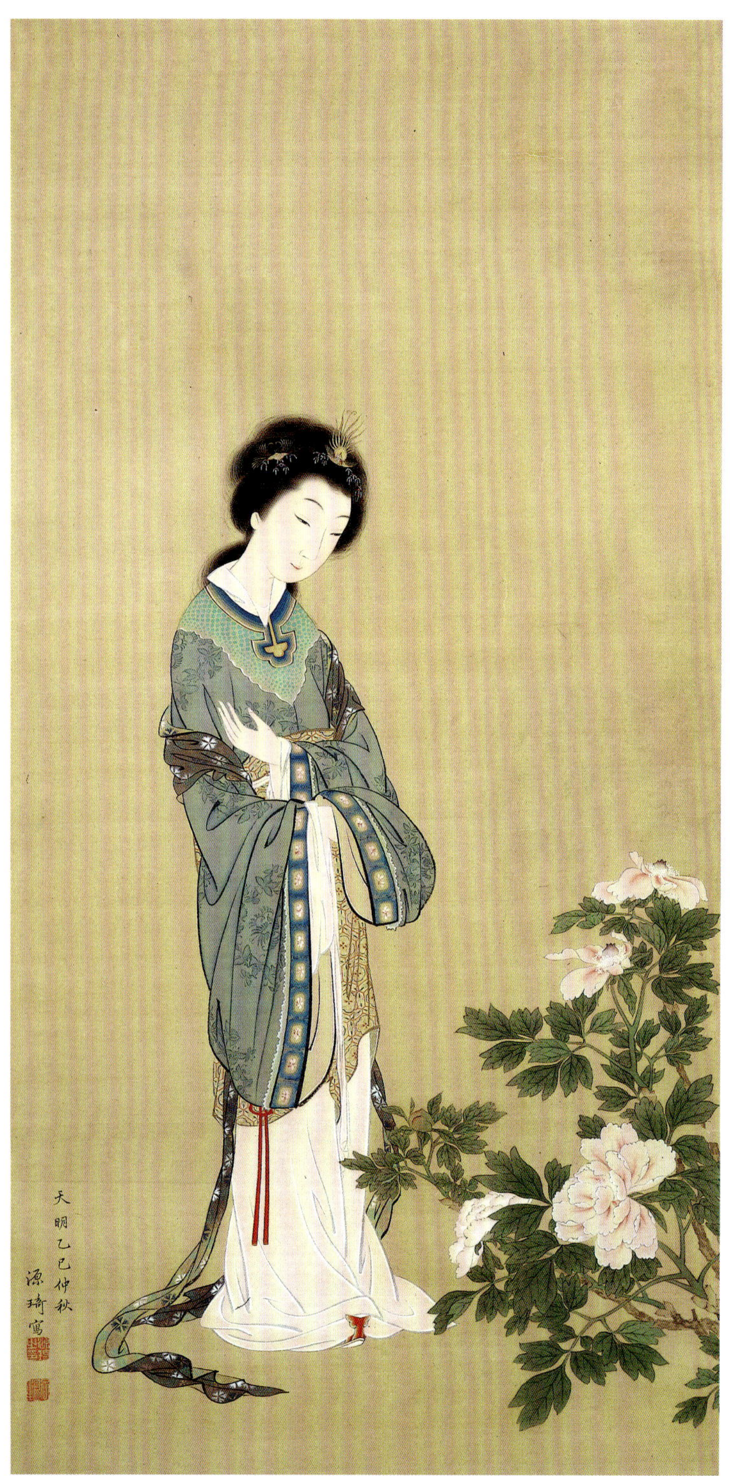

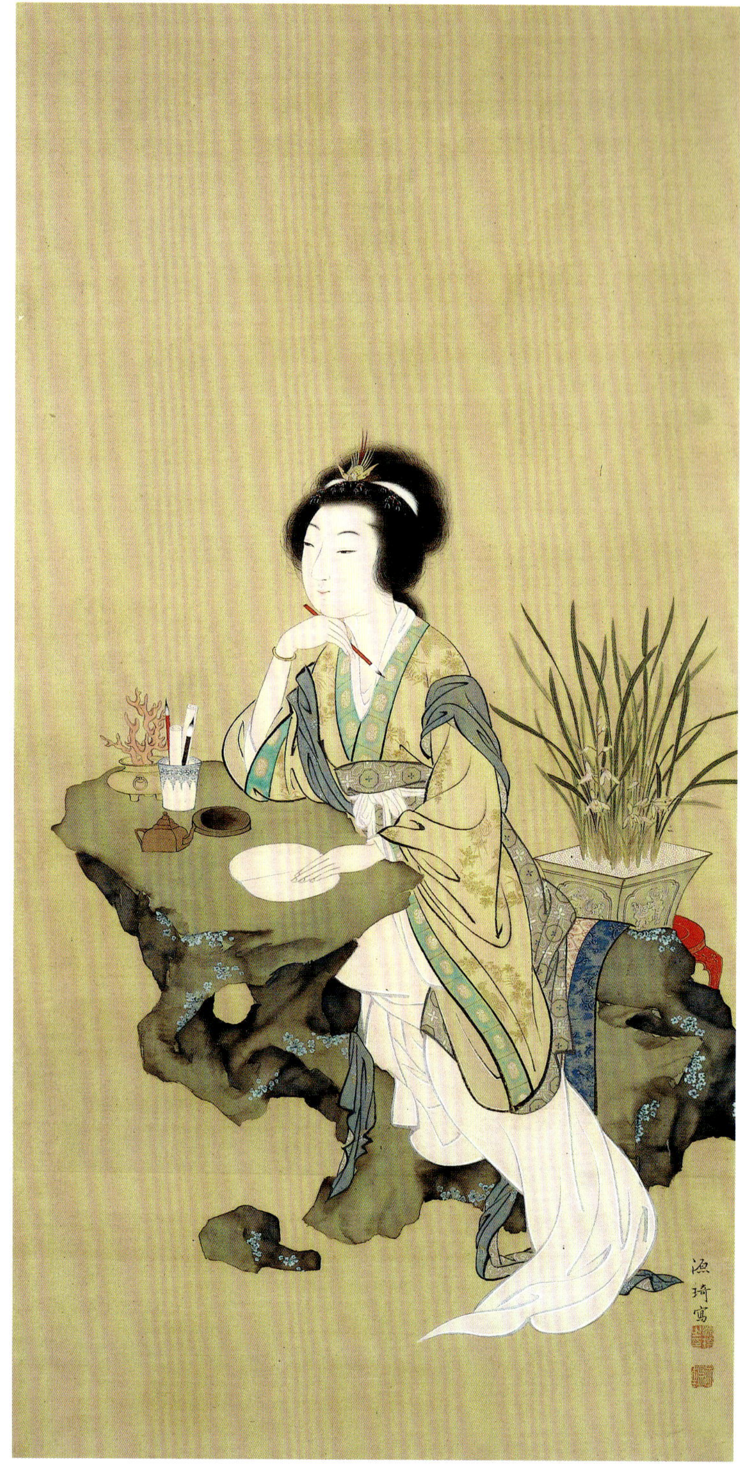

Genki
(源琦, also known as Komai Ki [駒井 琦];
1747–1797)

394. Enkitsu (Ch. Yanjie, 燕姞) with Orchids; Yō Kihi (Ch. Yang Guifei, 楊貴妃) with Peonies

Edo period, 1785
Pair of hanging scrolls; ink and color on silk
Each scroll 109.8 x 55.8 cm ($43^{1}/_{4}$ x 22 in.)
Signatures, seals

Literature: Nakamachi Keiko 1998, fig. 14; Murase 2000, no. 116; Tsuji Nobuo et al. 2005, no. 98.

Nagasawa Rosetsu
(長沢蘆雪; 1754–1799)

395. Family of Cranes

Edo period, ca. 1787
Pair of two-panel folding screens; ink and light color on paper
Each screen 156.5 x 172.4 cm (61 5/8 x 67 7/8 in.)
Signature, seal

Literature: Murase 2000, no. 118.

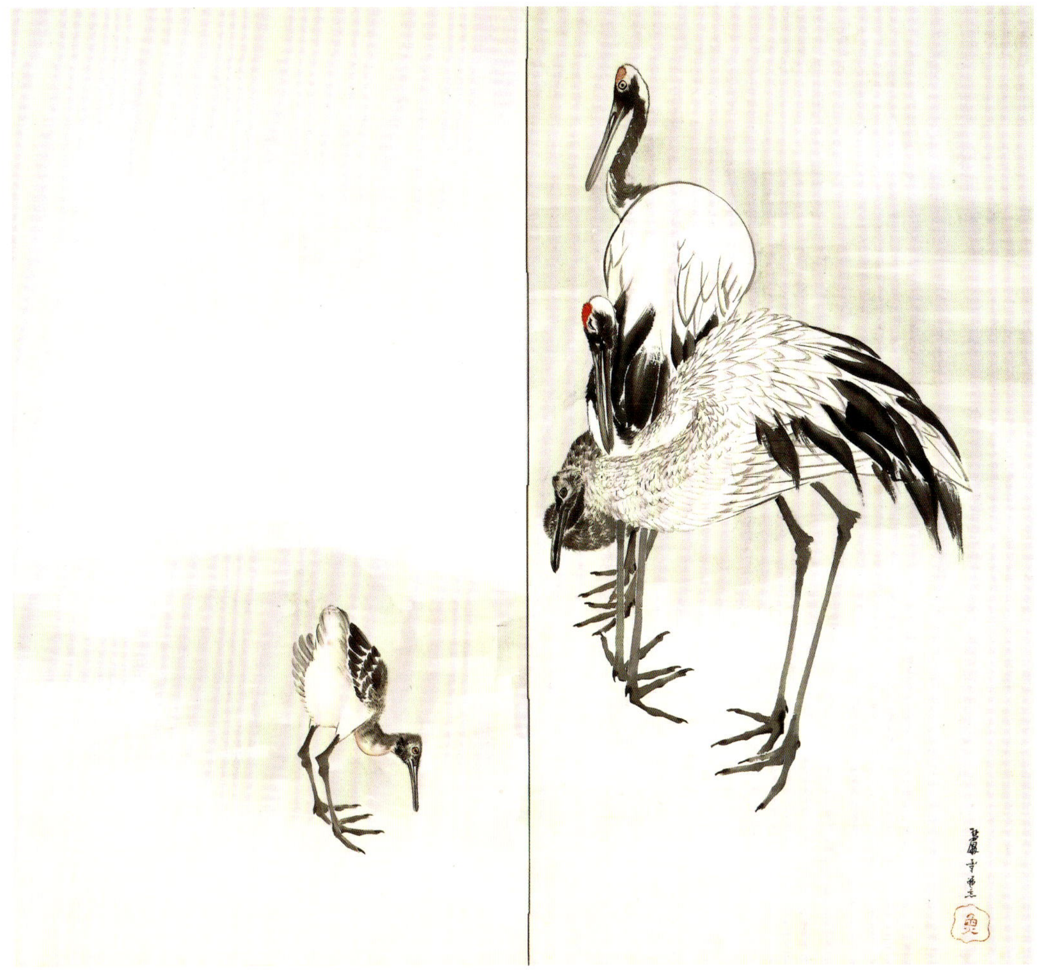

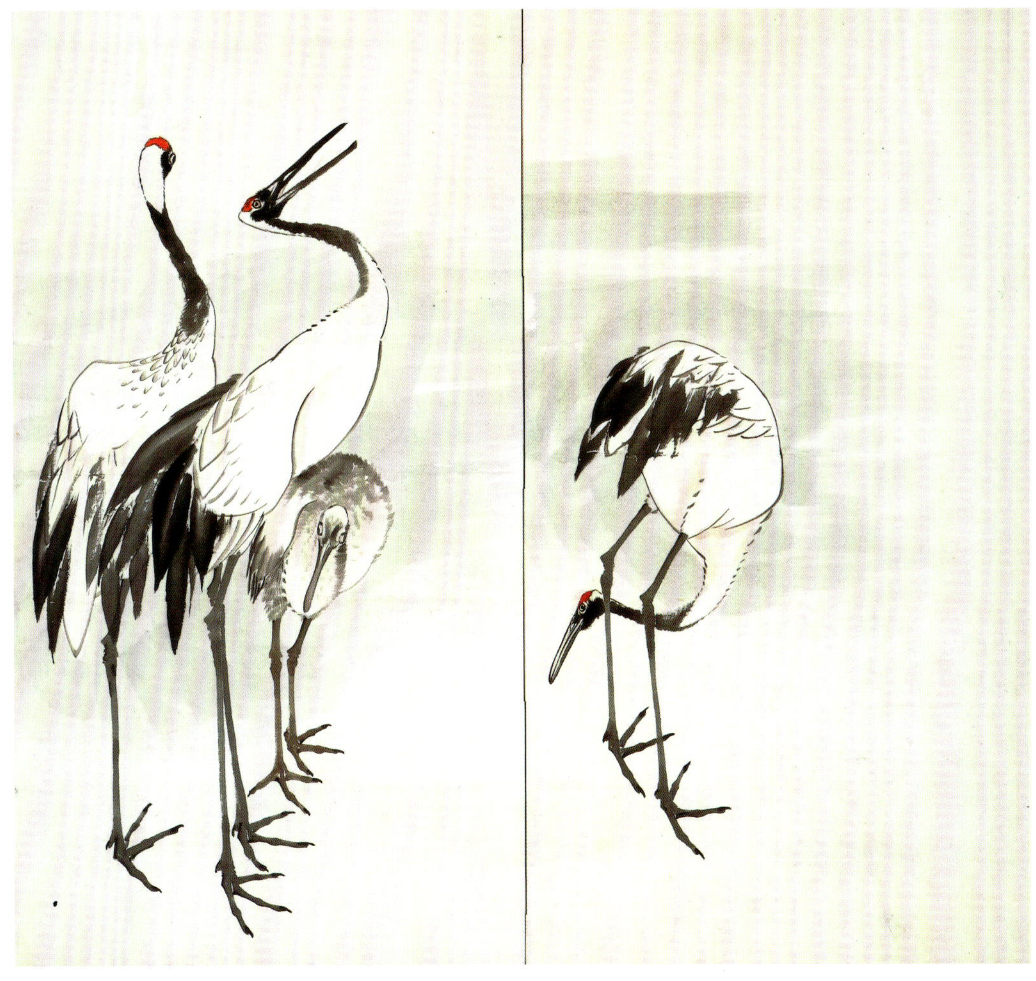

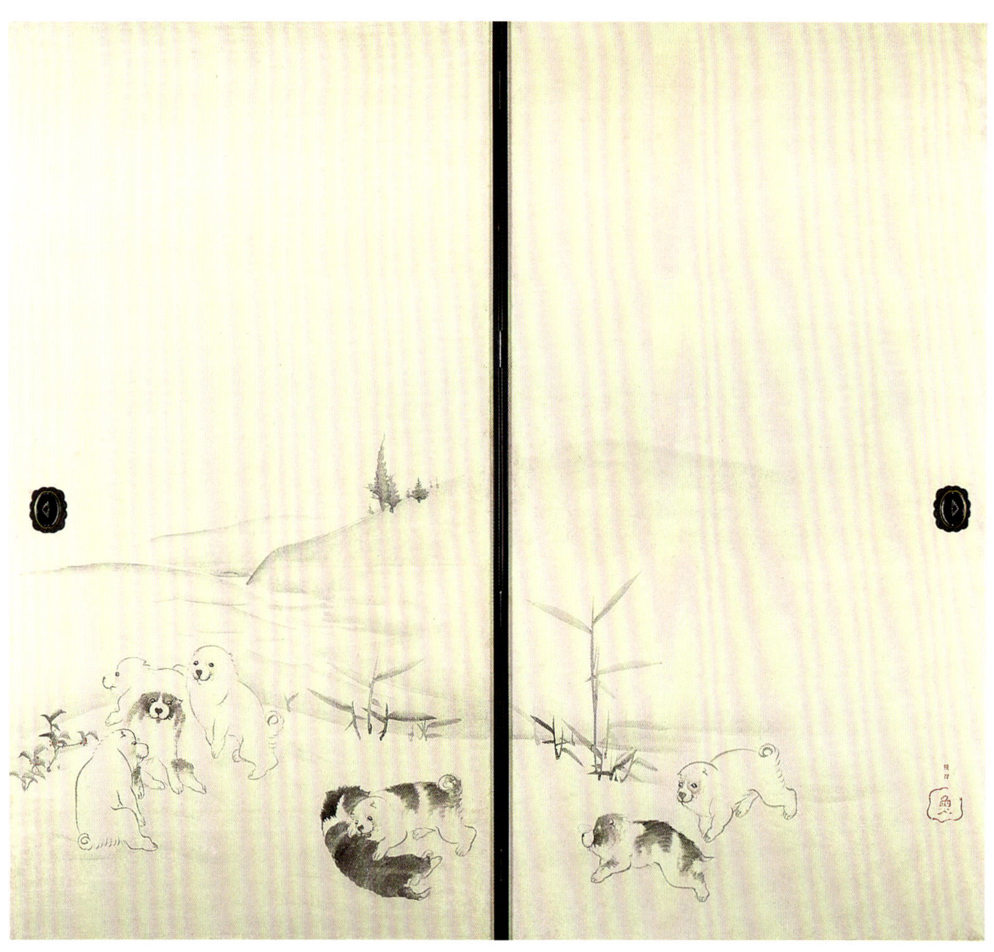

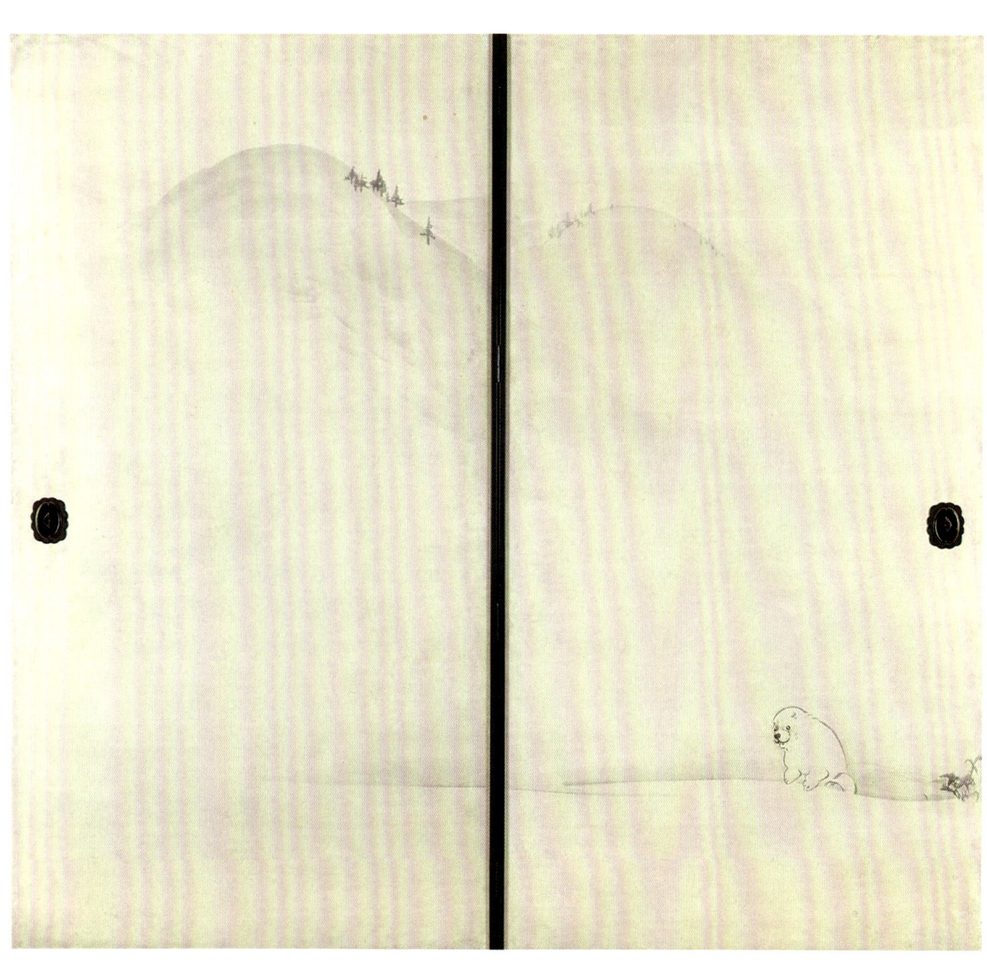

Nagasawa Rosetsu
(長沢蘆雪; 1754–1799)

396. Puppies in Snow

Edo period
Set of four sliding panels, now hinged together as a pair of two-panel screens; ink and light color on paper
Each screen 93 x 170.5 cm (36⅝ x 67⅛ in.)
Seals

Ex coll.: C. D. Carter

Literature: Nakamura Tanio 1967b, p. 91; Moes 1973, p. 142; Moes 1975, no. 21; Murase 1993, no. 53.

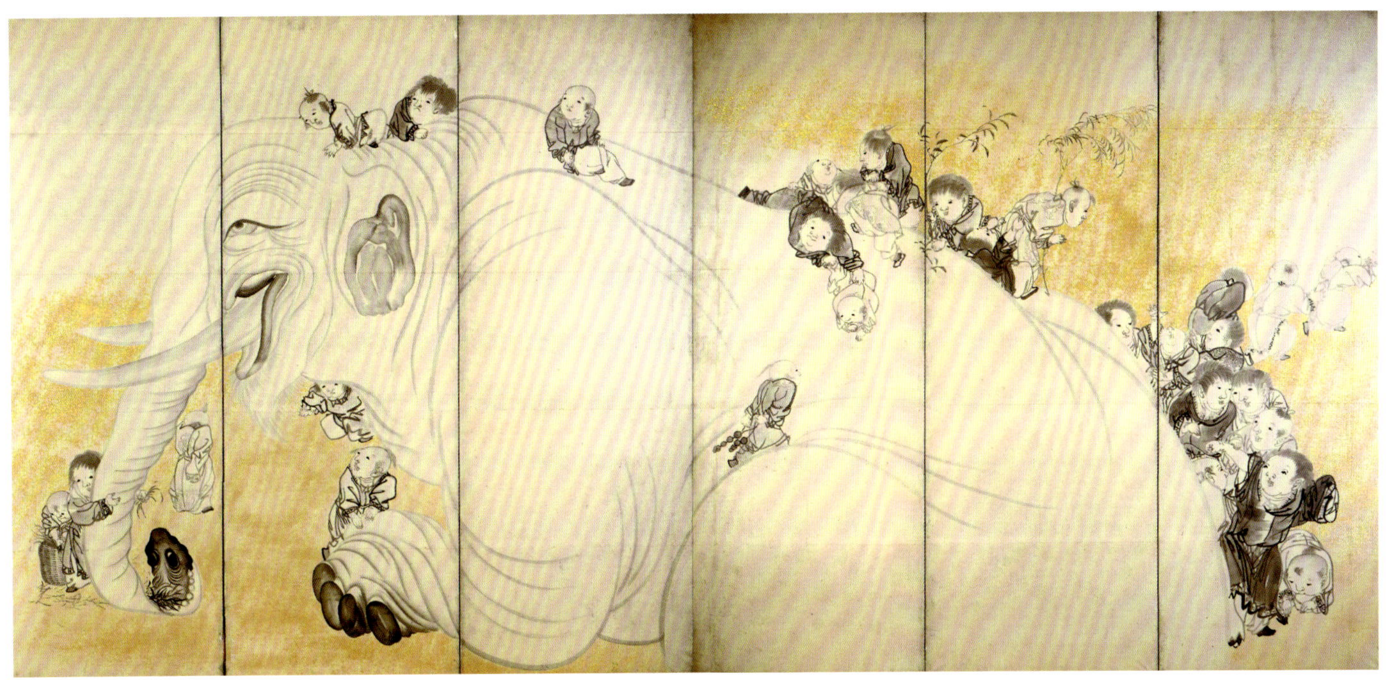

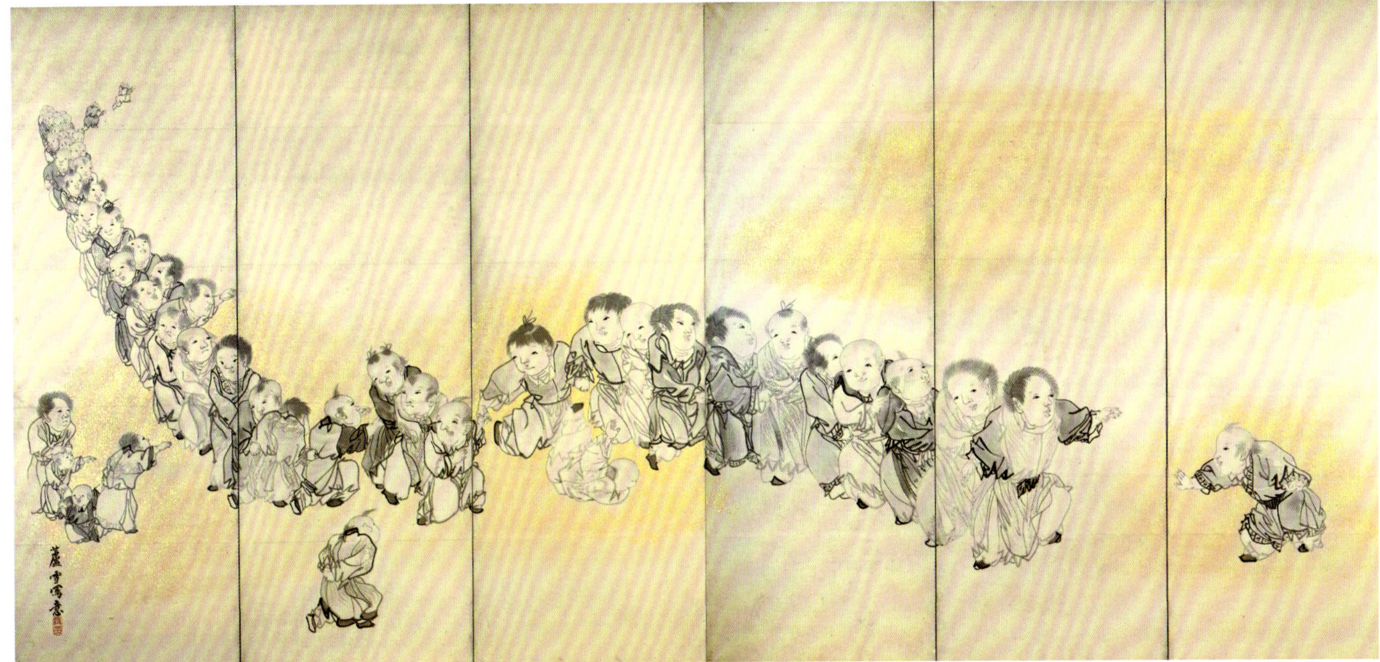

Nagasawa Rosetsu
(長沢蘆雪; 1754–1799)

397. Chinese Children at Play

Edo period
Pair of six-panel folding screens; ink and gold on paper
Each screen 168.7 x 360 cm (66 3/8 in. x 11 ft. 9 3/4 in.)
Signature, seals

Literature: Murase 1975, no. 62; Avitabile 1990, no. 87; Amino Yoshihiko et al. 1991, pp. 332–33; Guth 1992, color pls. 9a, b; Murase 1992, pp. 254–55 (details).

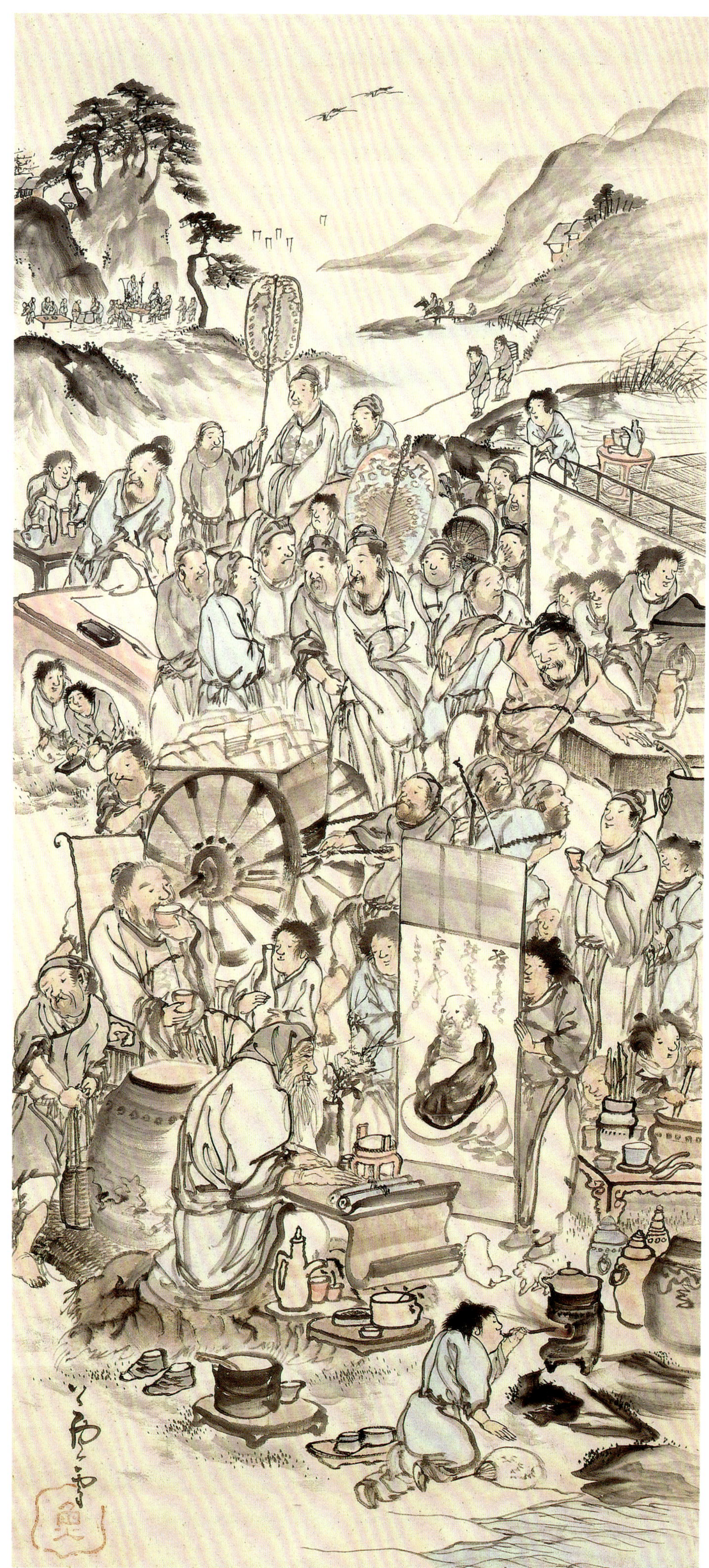

Nagasawa Rosetsu
(長沢蘆雪; 1754–1799)

398. Drinking Festival of the Eight Immortals (飲中八仙)

Edo period
Hanging scroll; ink and light color on paper
131.1 x 60.1 cm (51 5/8 x 23 5/8 in.)
Signature, seal

Literature: Burke 1993, pp. 56–58, 82, fig. 15/no. 10; Tsuji Nobuo et al. 2005, p. 103.

Nagasawa Rosetsu
(長沢蘆雪; 1754–1799)

399. Mice on Rice-Cake Flowers

Edo period
Hanging scroll; ink and color on silk
32.1 x 95.6 cm (12 5/8 x 37 5/8 in.)
Signature, seals

Nagasawa Rosetsu
(長沢蘆雪; 1754–1799)

400. Dragon and Moon in Rain

Edo period
Hanging scroll; ink on silk
100.6 x 36.1 cm (40 x 14 1/4 in.)
Signature, seals

Literature: Tsuji Nobuo et al. 2005, no. 104.

Nagasawa Rosetsu
(長沢蘆雪; 1754–1799)

401. Bird on Wisteria Branch

Edo period
Hanging scroll; ink and light color on paper
126.6 x 45.8 cm (49 7/8 x 18 in.)
Signature, seal

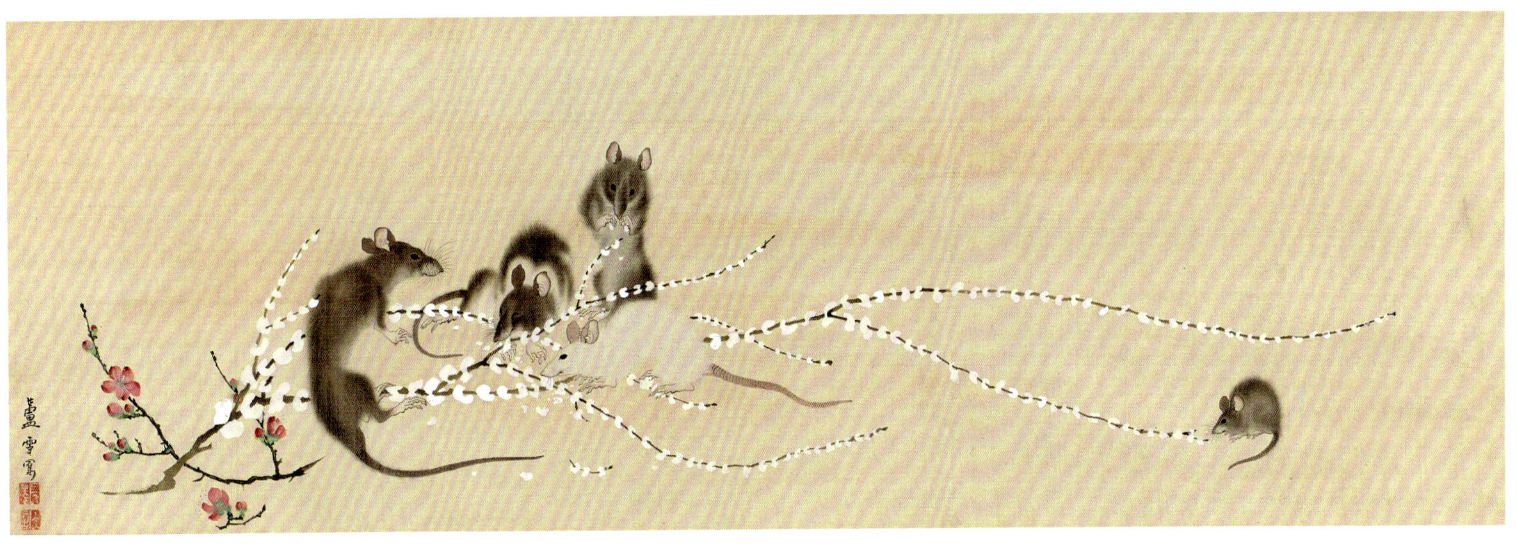

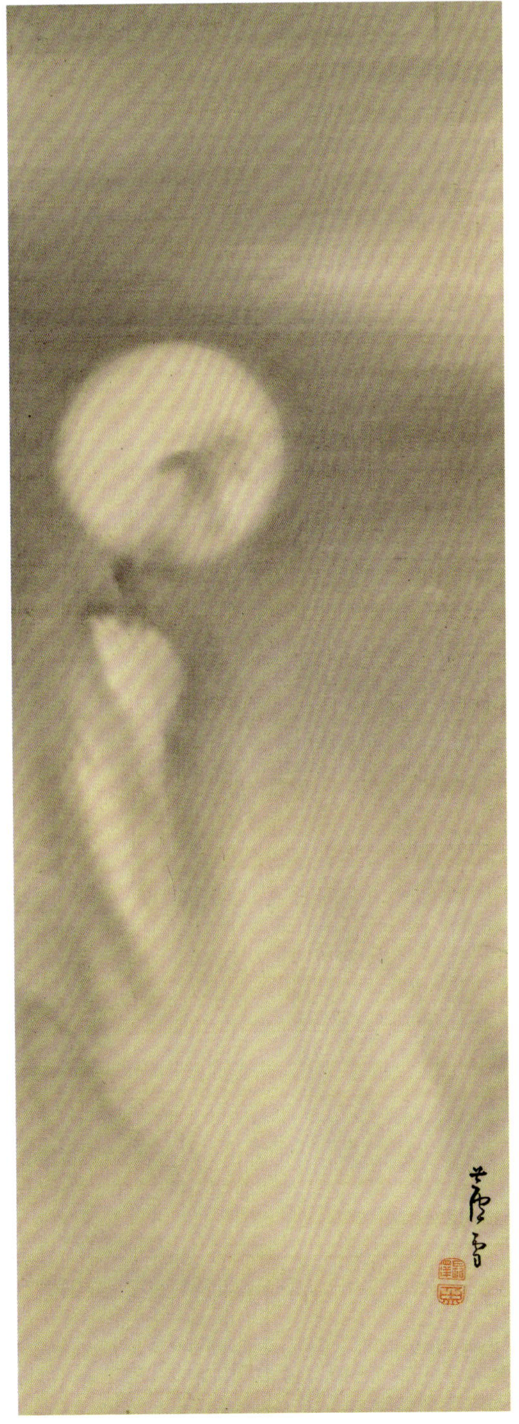

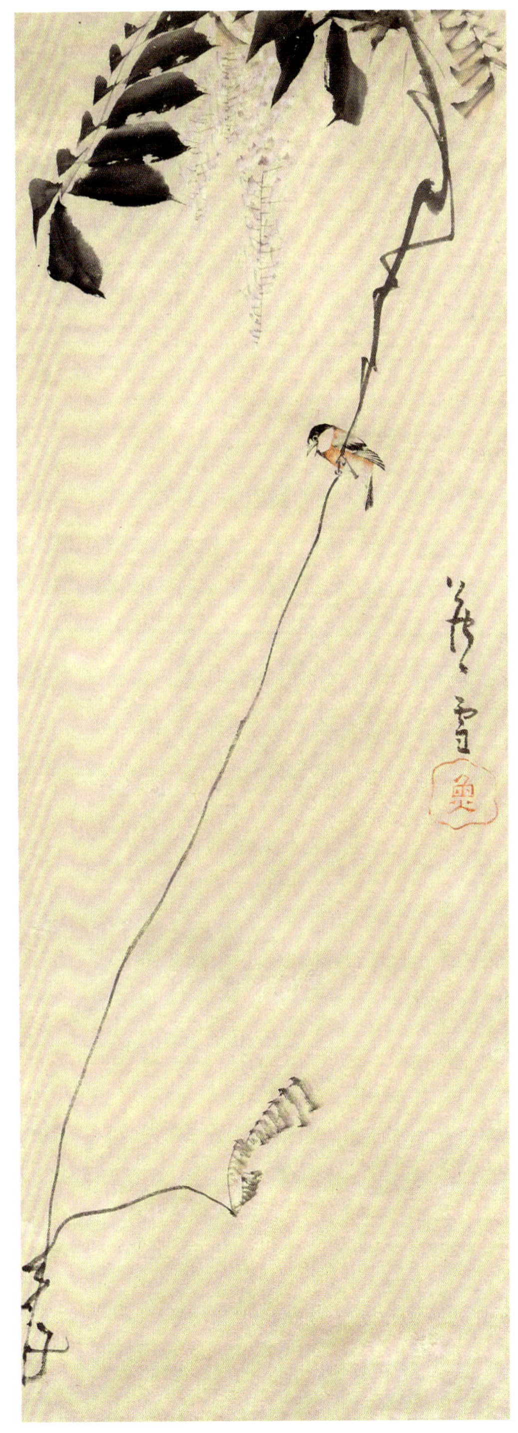

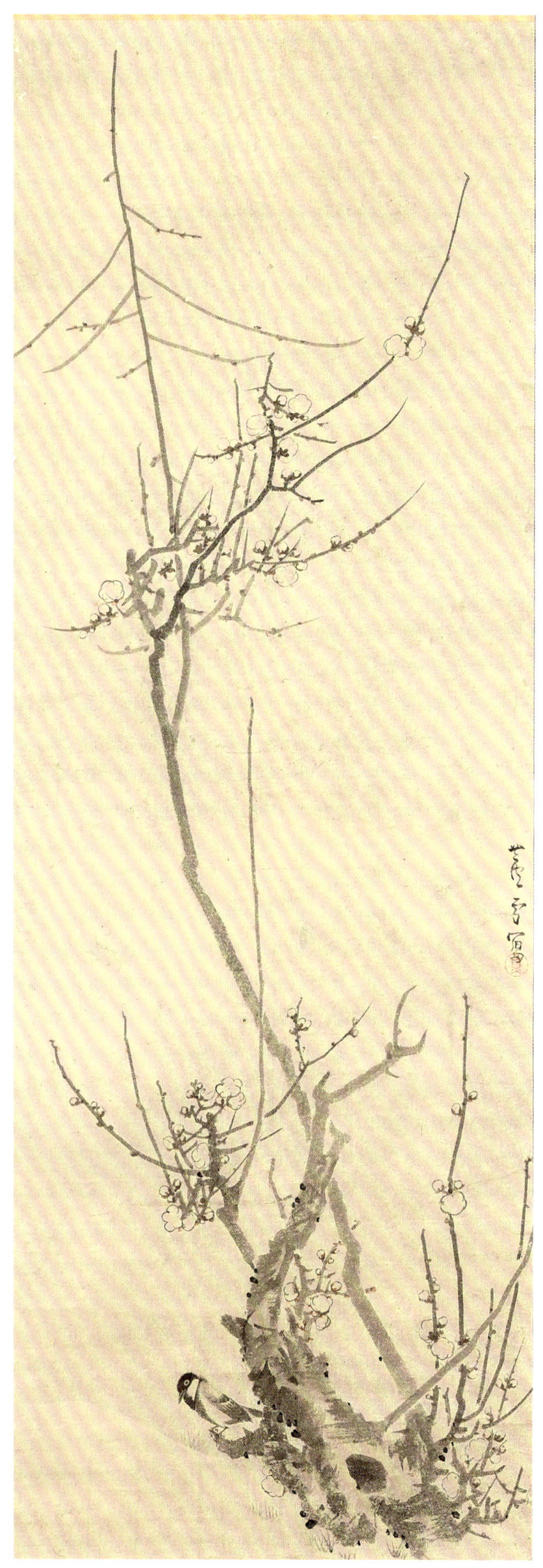

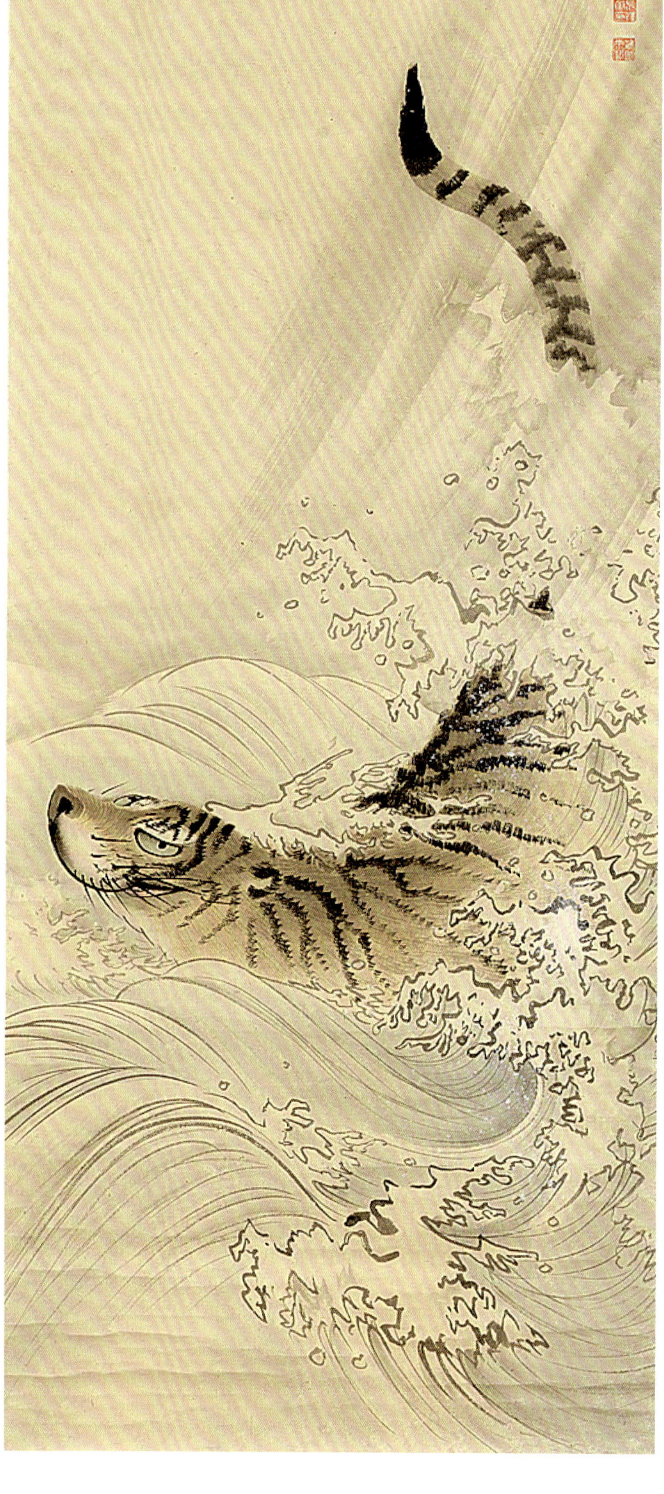

Nagasawa Rosetsu
(長沢蘆雪; 1754–1799)

402. Bird on Plum Tree

Edo period
Hanging scroll; ink and light color on paper
122.5 x 42.8 cm (48¼ x 16⅞ in.)
Signature, seal

Nagasawa Rosetsu
(長沢蘆雪; 1754–1799)

403. Swimming Tiger

Edo period
Hanging scroll; ink and light color on paper
129 x 53.2 cm (50¾ x 21 in.)
Seals

Gift from Jack Hillier, 1969

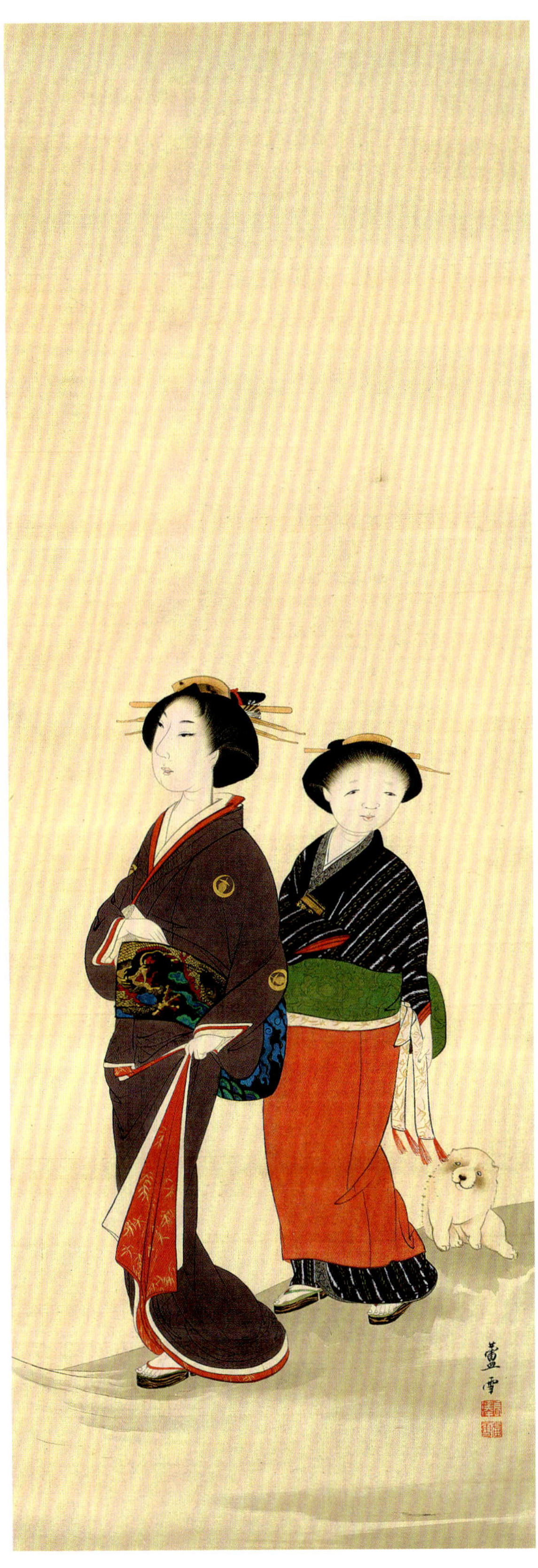

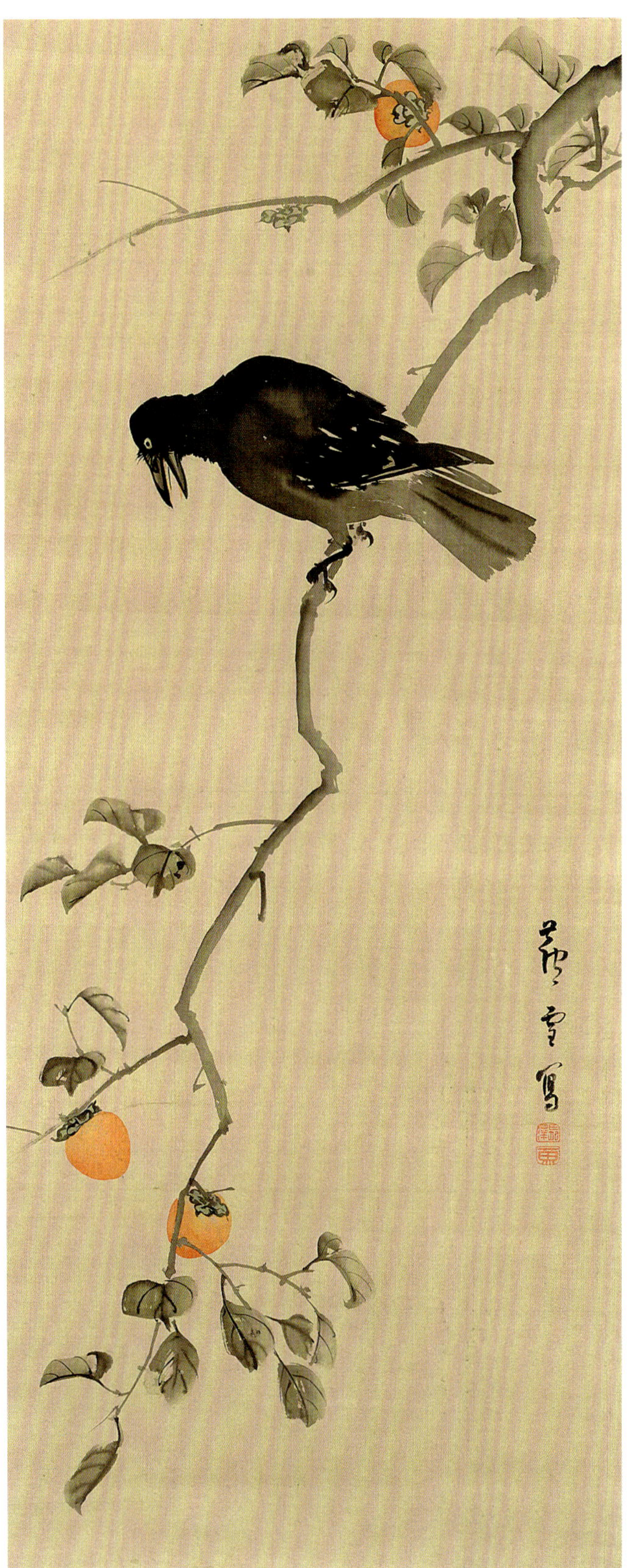

Nagasawa Rosetsu

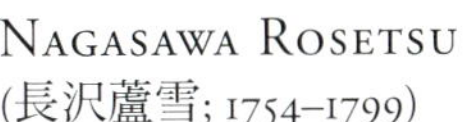

(長沢蘆雪; 1754–1799)

404. Two Women and a Puppy

Edo period
Hanging scroll; ink and color on silk
119.8 x 49.9 cm ($47\frac{1}{8}$ x $19\frac{5}{8}$ in.)
Signature, seals

Literature: Miyajima Shin'ichi 1984, no. 219, fig. 39.

Nagasawa Rosetsu
(長沢蘆雪; 1754–1799)

405. Crow on Persimmon Tree

Edo period
Hanging scroll; ink and color on silk
119.8 x 49.9 cm ($47\frac{1}{8}$ x $19\frac{5}{8}$ in.)
Signature, seals

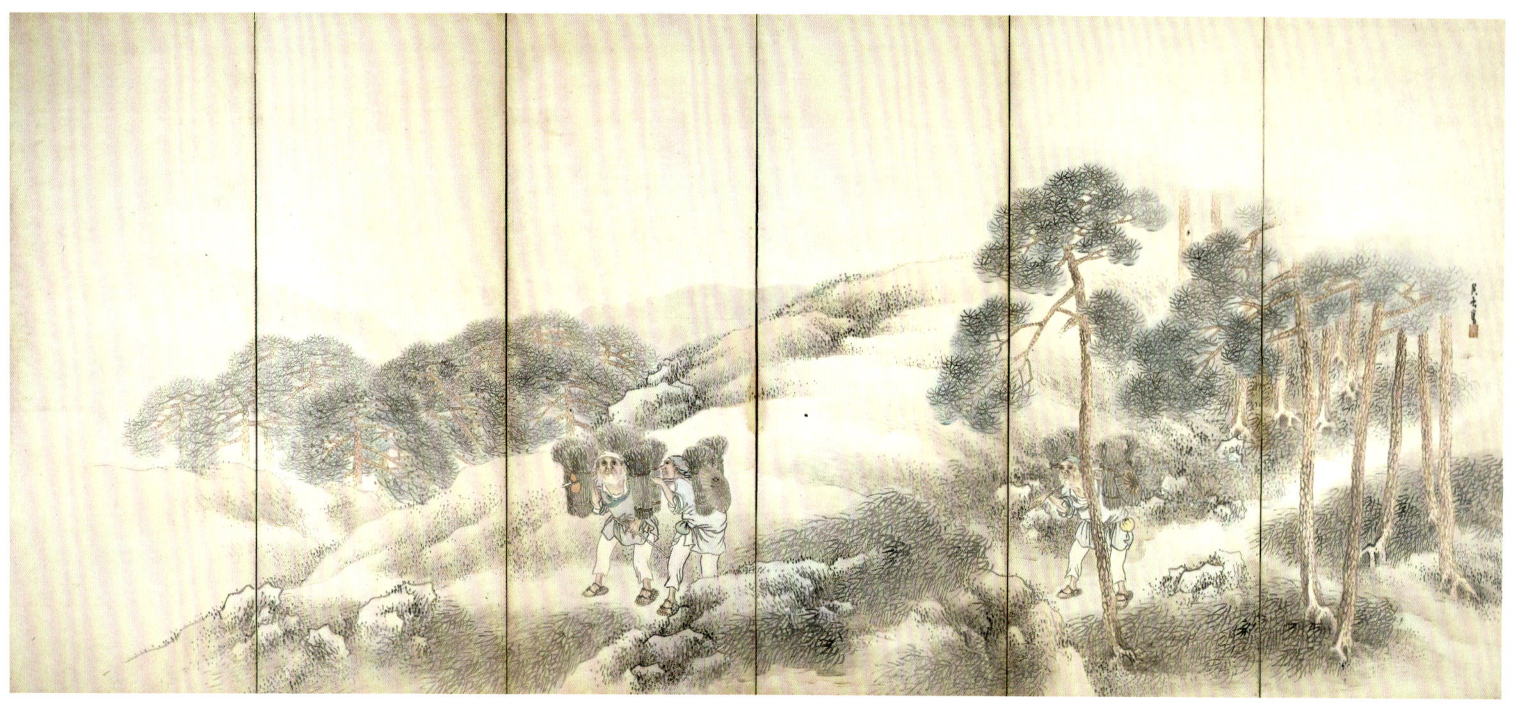

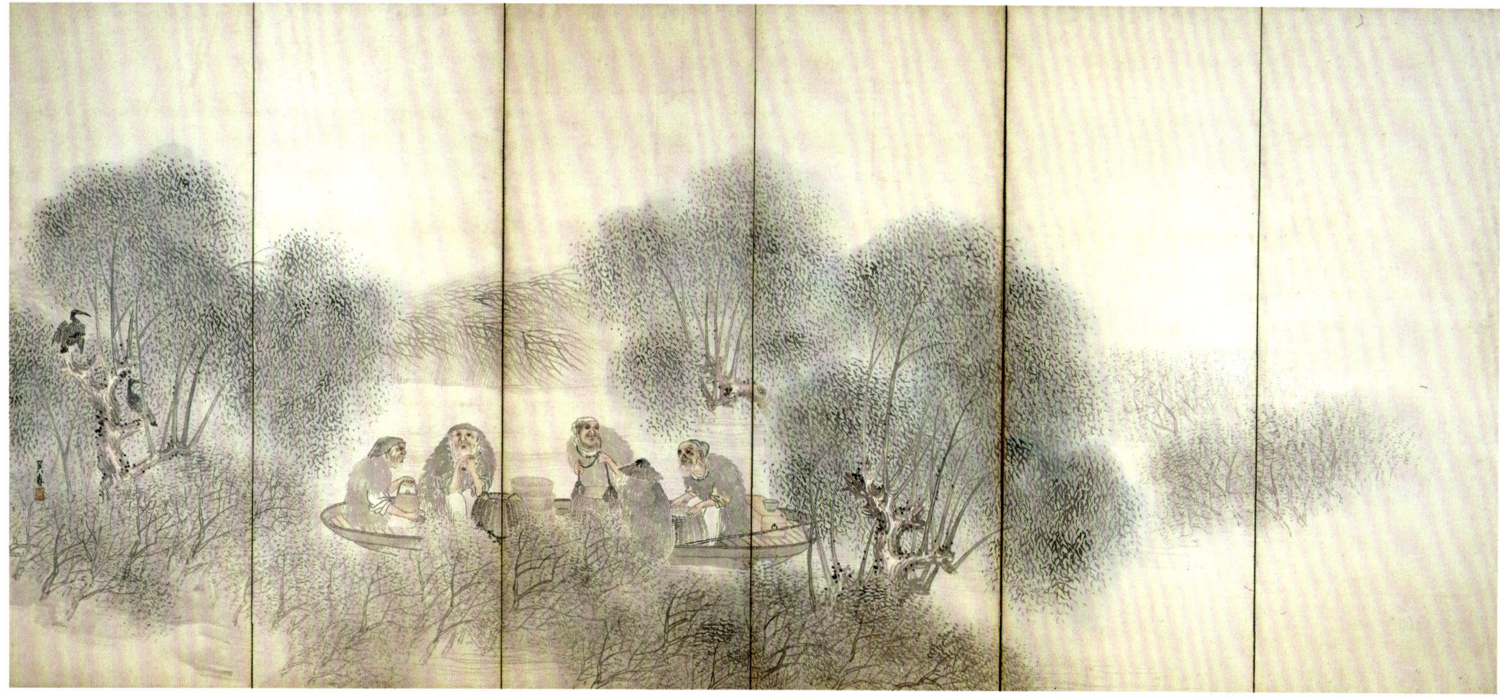

Matsumura Goshun
(松村呉春; 1752–1811)

406. Woodcutters; Fishermen

Edo period, ca. 1790–95
Pair of six-panel folding screens; ink and light color on paper
Each screen 170.8 x 347.6 cm (67¼ in. x 11 ft. 4⅞ in.)
Signatures, seals

Literature: Shimada Shūjirō 1969, vol. 2, no. 89; Murase 1971, no. 13; Hillier 1974, pl. 19 (*Fishermen*); Takeda Tsuneo et al. 1982, pp. 83, 171; Murase 1993, no. 32; Murase 2000, no. 117; Tsuji Nobuo et al. 2005, no. 114.

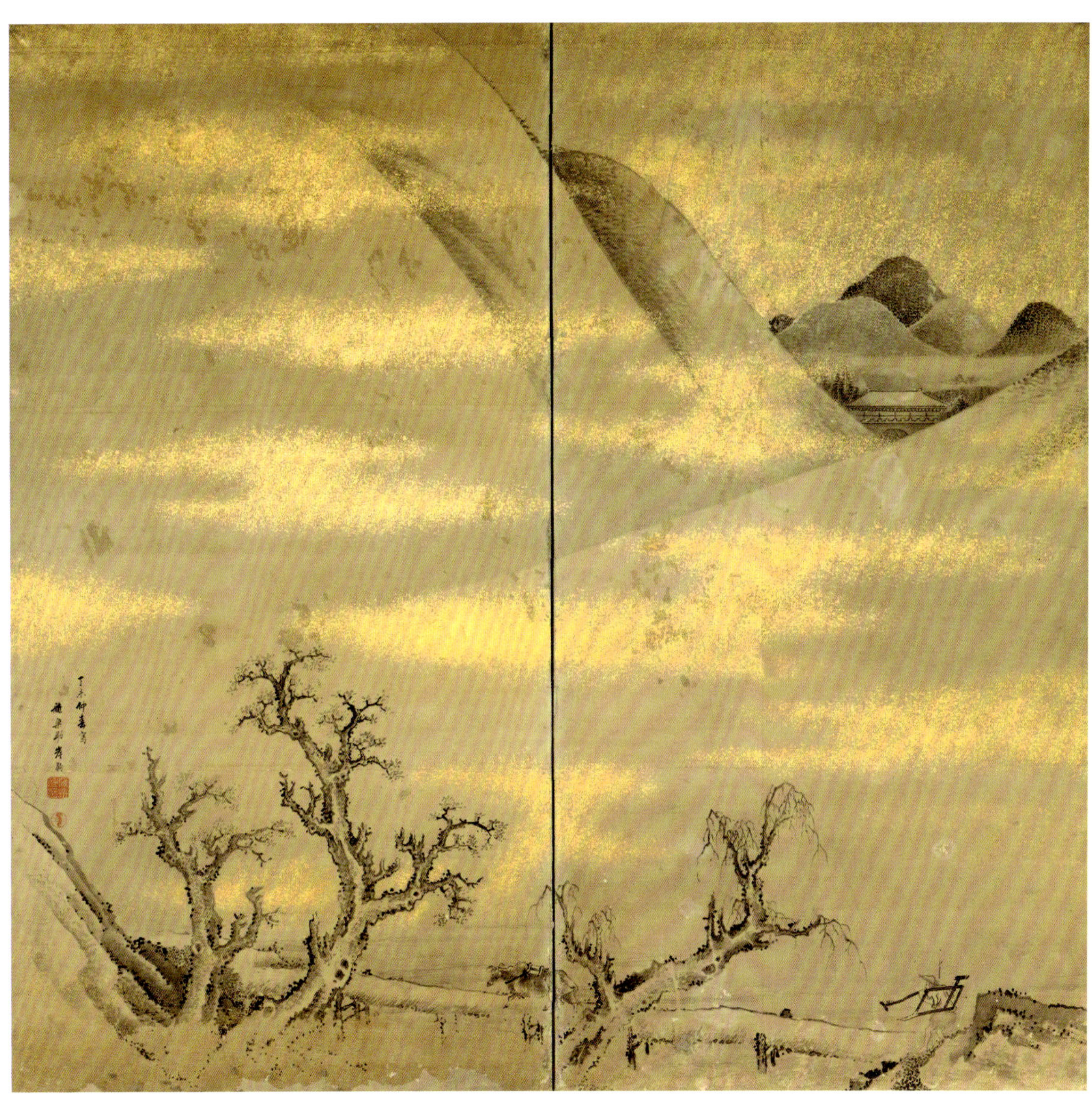

Ganku
(岸駒; 1749/56–1838)

407. Spring Landscape

Edo period, 1787
Two-panel folding screen; ink, light color, and gold on paper
169.8 x 175 cm (66⅞ x 68⅞ in.)
Signature, seals

Ex coll.: Frank E. Hart

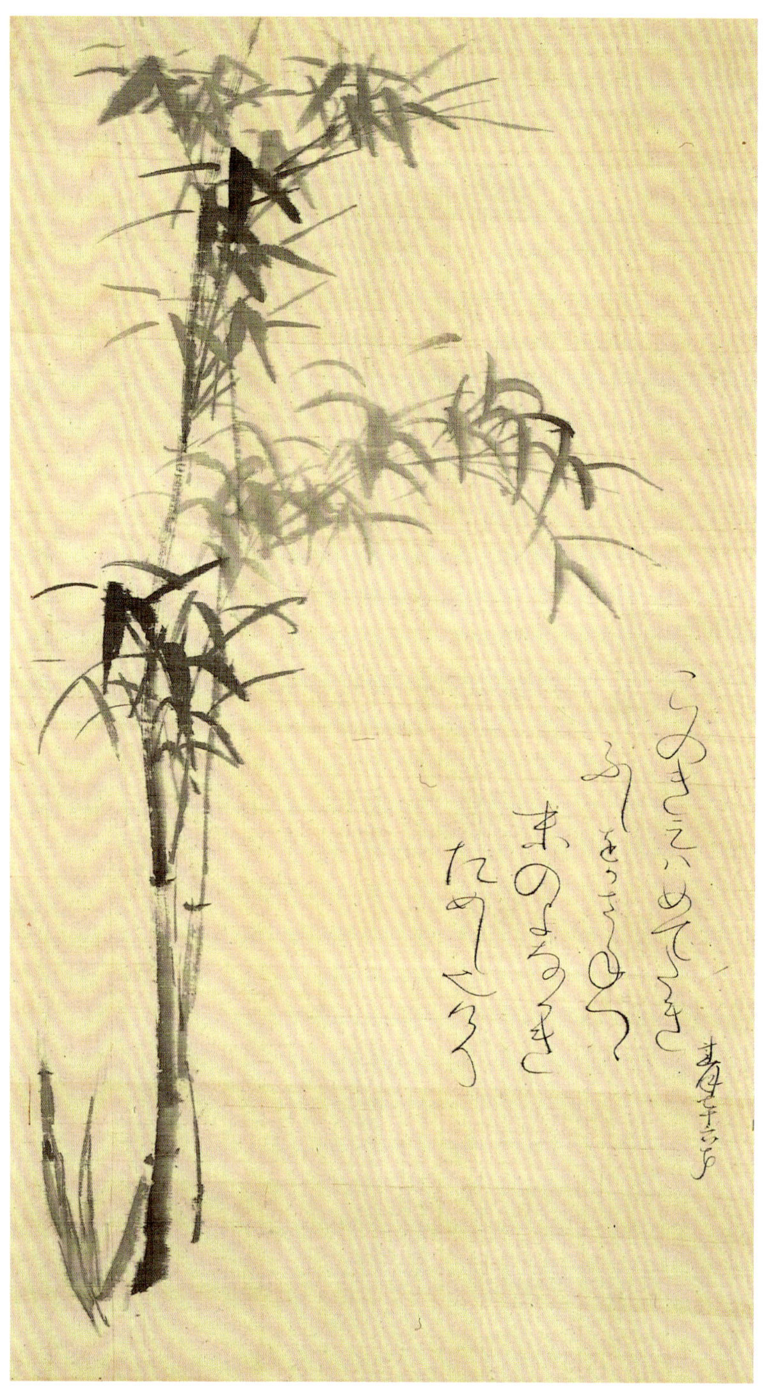

Matsumura Keibun
(松村景文; 1779–1843)

408. Sparrow and Spider

Edo period, 19th century
Hanging scroll; ink and light color on paper
89.2 x 15.2 cm (35 1/8 x 6 in.)
Signature, seals

Ōtagaki Rengetsu
(大田垣蓮月; 1791–1875)

409. Bamboo

Edo period, 1866
Hanging scroll; ink on silk
88.8 x 49.8 cm (35 x 19 5/8 in.)
Text, signature

Literature: Tokyo National Museum 1985a, no. 79; Fister 1988, no. 70; Avitabile 1990, no. 102.

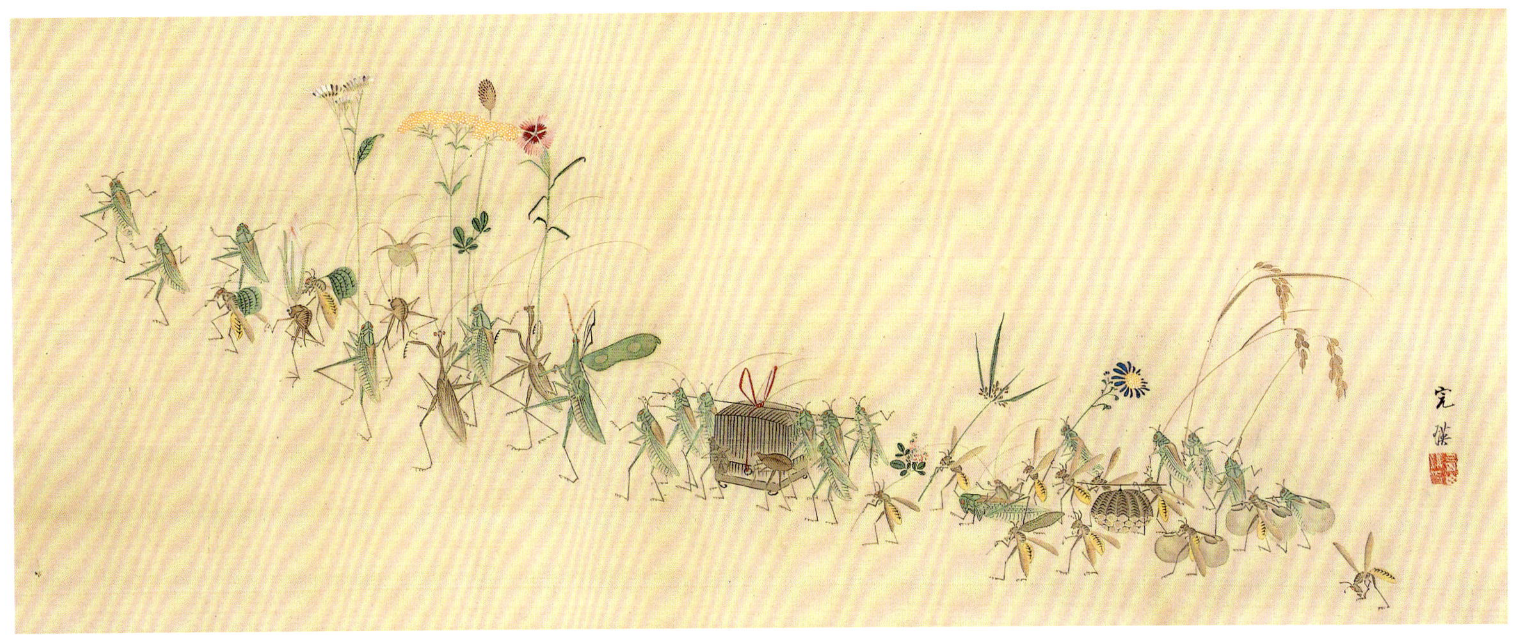

Nishiyama Hōen
(西山芳園; 1808–1867)

410. Procession of Insects

Edo period
Hanging scroll; ink and color on silk
33.5 x 81.8 cm (13 1/4 x 32 1/4 in.)
Signature, seal

Literature: Guth 1992, pl. 17.

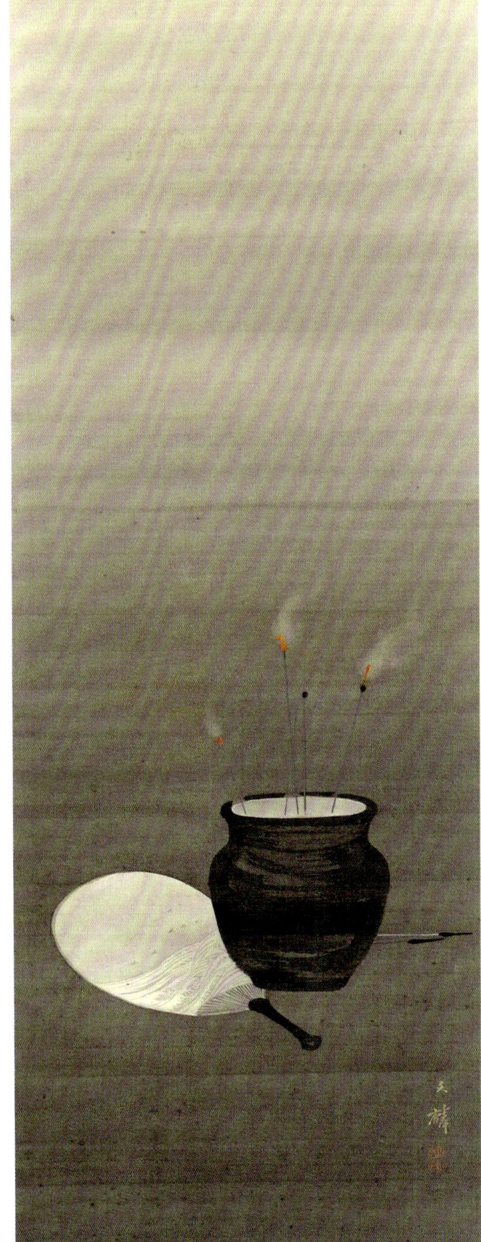

Shiokawa Bunrin
(塩川文麟; 1808–1877)

411. Sparklers on a Summer Evening

Edo period
Hanging scroll; ink, light color, and gold on silk
94.4 x 34.8 cm (37 1/8 x 13 3/4 in.)
Signature, seals

Literature: Murase 1993, no. 43.

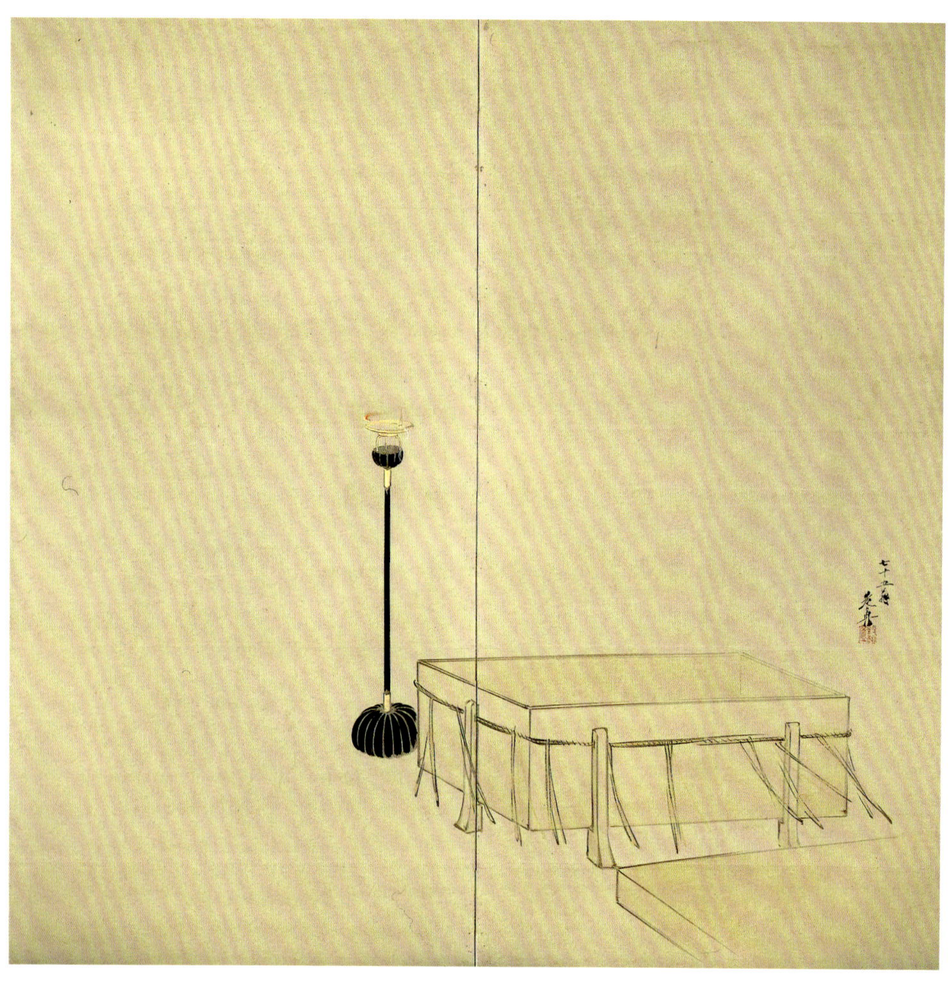

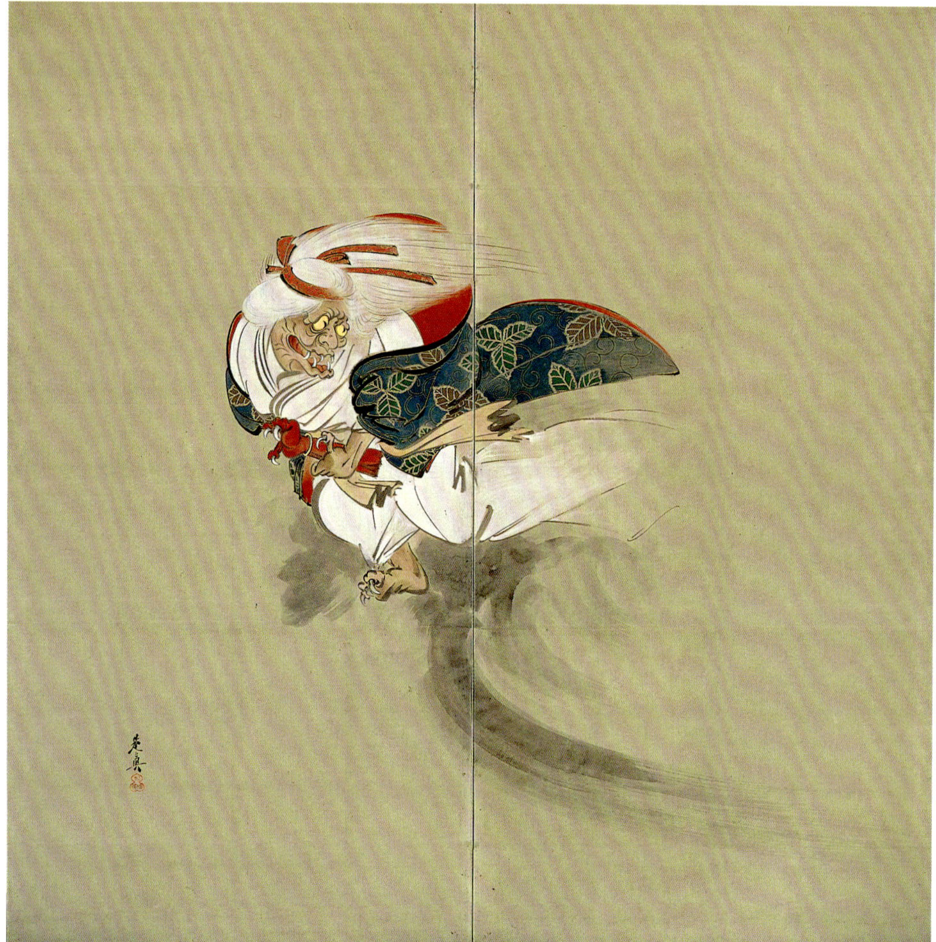

Shibata Zeshin
(柴田是真; 1807–1891)

412. Ibaraki (茨木)

Meiji era, 1882
Pair of two-panel folding screens; ink, color, and gold on paper
Each screen 168.6 x 166 cm (66 3/8 x 65 3/8 in.)
Signatures, seals

Ex coll.: Roger and Kathleen Weston, Chicago

Literature: Gōke Tadaomi 1974, fig. 78; Gōke Tadaomi 1981, vol. 1, nos. 209, 210; Murase 1990, no. 33; Murase 1993, no. 54; Murase 2000, no. 122; Tsuji Nobuo et al. 2005, no. 88.

Shibata Zeshin
(柴田是真; 1807–1891)

413. Plum Branch and Teapot

Meiji era
Folding fan; lacquer on paper
17.9 x 48.9 cm (7 x 19 1/4 in.)
Signature, seal

Shibata Zeshin
(柴田是真; 1807–1891)

414. Devil's Invocation

Meiji era
Folding fan mounted on hanging scroll; ink and light color on paper
14.8 x 48.7 cm (5 7/8 x 19 1/8 in.)
Signature, seal

Gift from Setsu Iwao, 1975

Shibata Zeshin
(柴田是真; 1807–1891)

415. Turnip

Meiji era
Folding fan mounted as framed picture; ink and color on paper
16.2 x 48.6 cm (6 3/8 x 19 1/8 in.)
Signature, seal

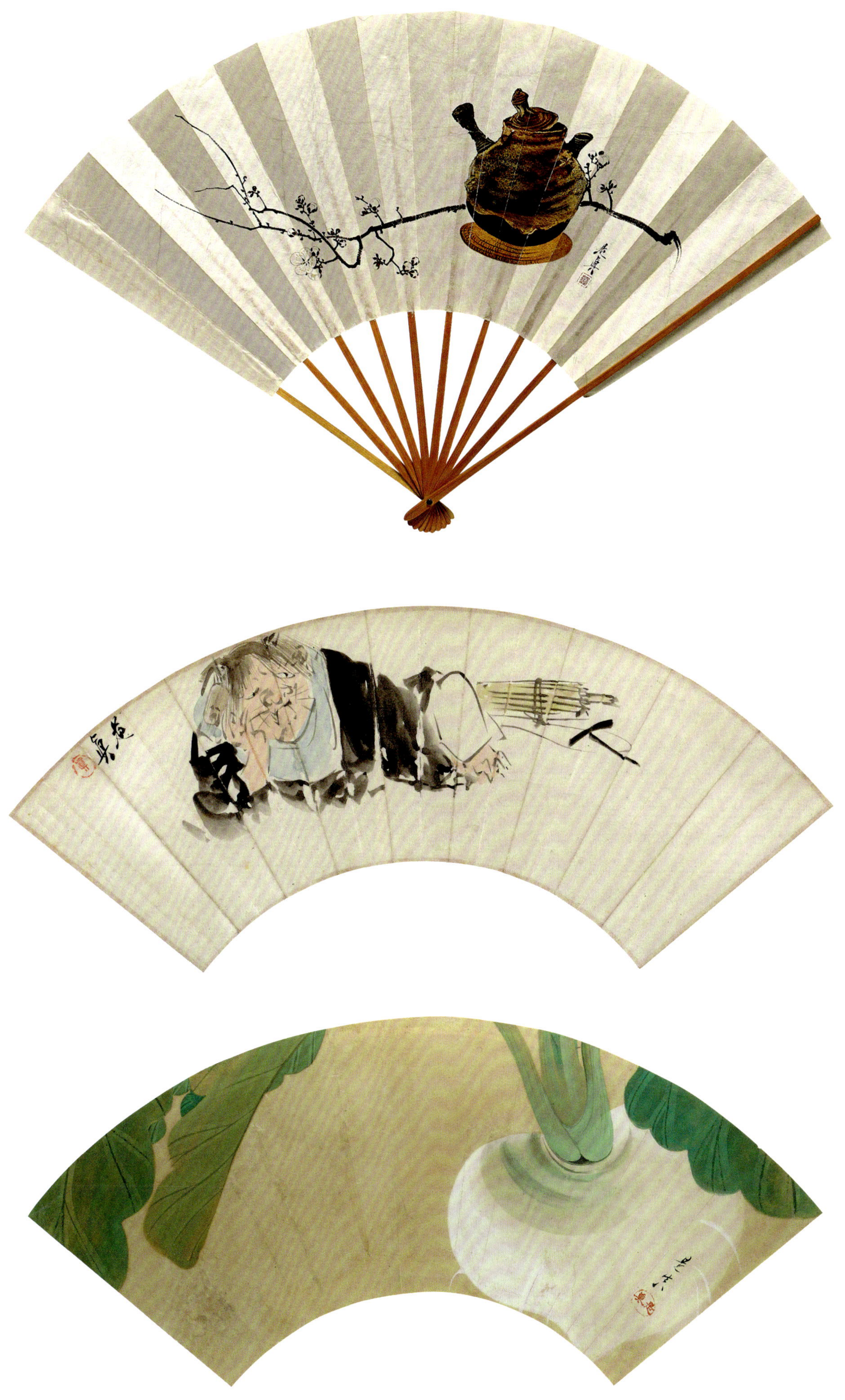

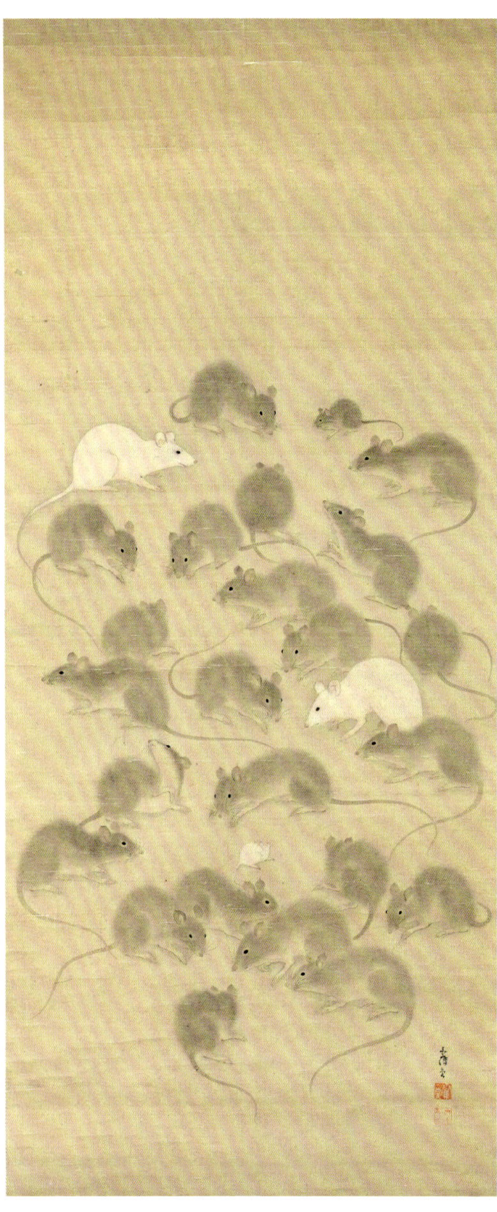

Kakudō
(霍堂; fl. early 19th century)

416. Mice

Edo period
Hanging scroll; ink and light color on silk
117.6 x 50.9 cm (46¼ x 20 in.)
Signature, seals

Mori Kansai
(森寛斎; 1814–1894)

417. Procession of Insects

Edo period–Meiji era
Hanging scroll; ink and gold on silk
110 x 35.4 cm (43¼ x 13⅞ in.)
Signature, seals

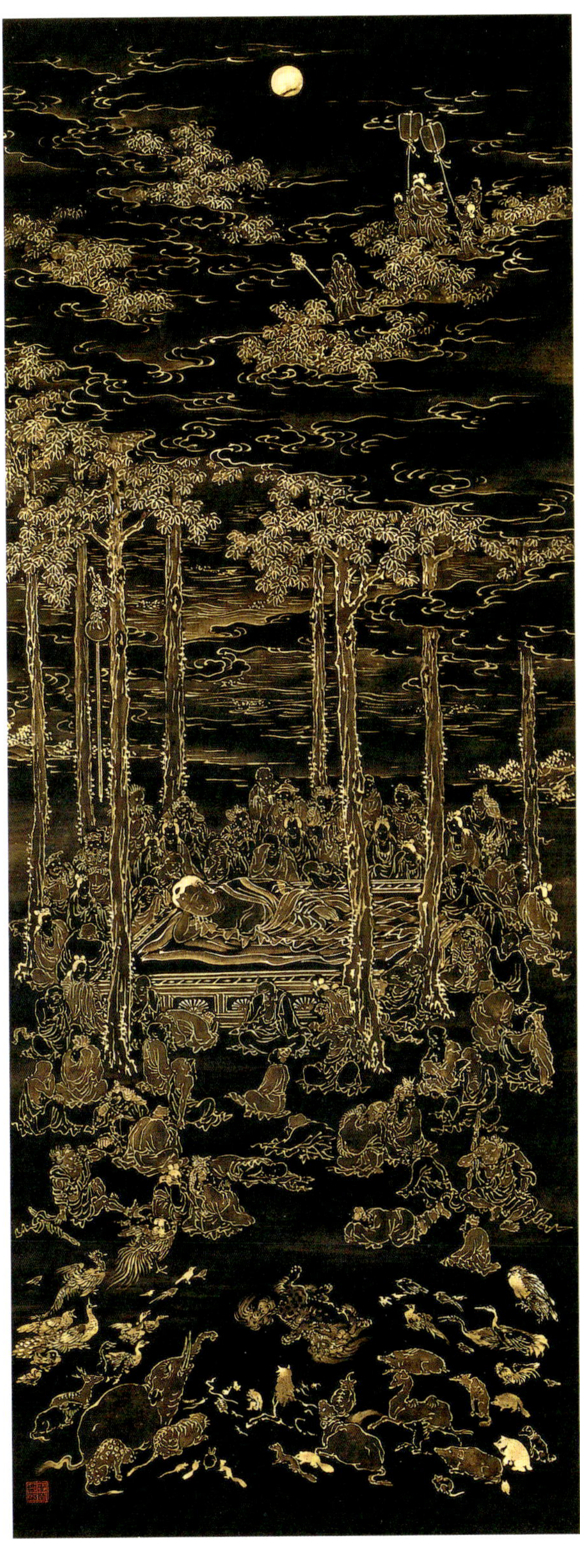

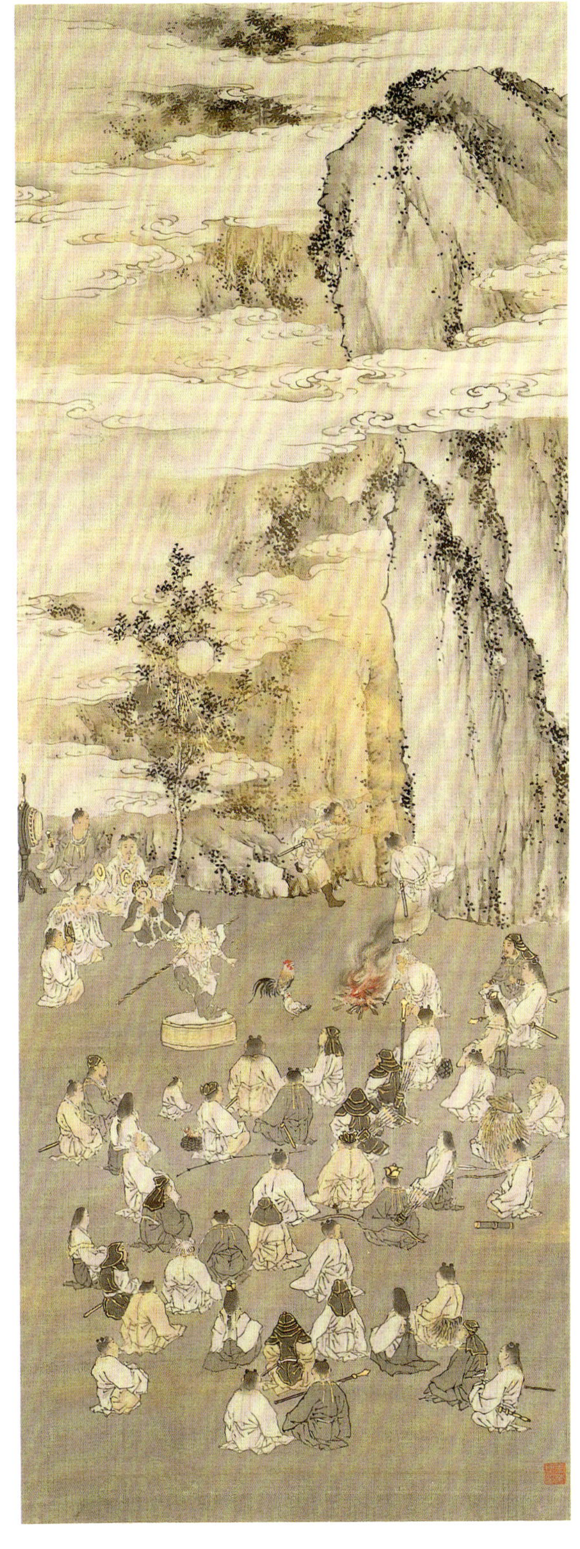

Kōno Bairei
(幸野楳嶺; 1844–1895)

418. The Legend of Amaterasu (天照), Who Locks Herself Inside the Rock-Cave of Heaven (天の岩戸); Nehan (仏涅槃)

Meiji era
Diptych of hanging scrolls; (Amaterasu) ink, color, and gold on silk; (Nehan) ink and gold on silk
Each scroll 70.5 x 27 cm (27 3/4 x 10 5/8 in.)
Seals

Literature: Burke 1993, pl. 12, 13/no. 18; Conant et al. 1995, no. 16.

Chapter 9 Details

† *denotes illustrated items*

---

† 386. Goose and Reeds; Moon and Willows

Signatures

[on each screen] *Ōkyo*; [on right screen] *Painted in the twelfth month of 1774*; [on left screen] *Painted in the eighth month of 1793*

Seals

[on right screen] *Ōkyo no in*; *Chūsen*
[on left screen] *Ōkyo no in*

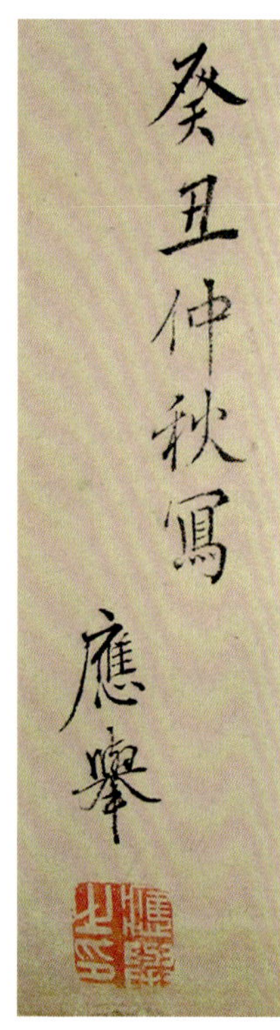

386

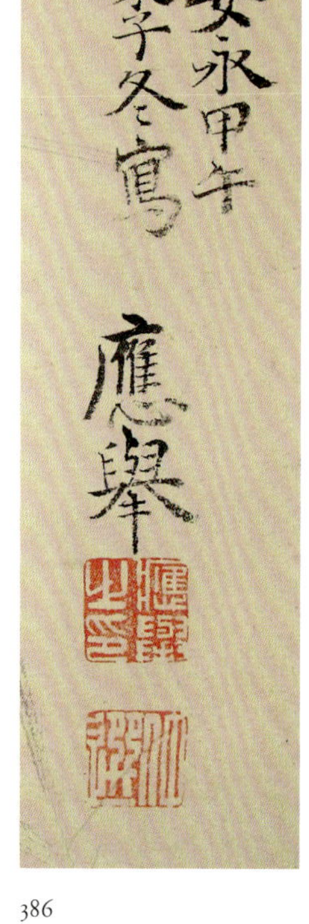

386

---

387. Sweetfish in Summer and Autumn

Signatures

[on right scroll] *Painted by Ōkyo*
[on left scroll] *Painted by Ōkyo, second month of 1785*

Seals

[on each screen] *Ōkyo no in*; *Chūsen*

---

†388. Puppies

Signature

Painted by Ōkyo, eleventh month of 1781

Seal

Illegible

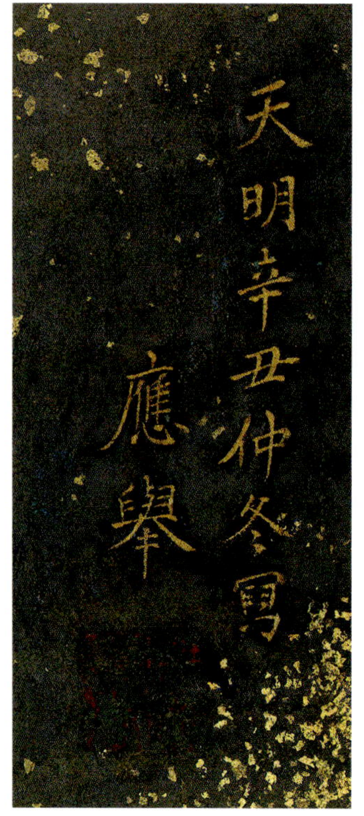

388

---

† 389. Horseback Riding at West Lake

Signature

[at end of scroll] *[I] copied a work by the Ming dynasty's Kyūei* [Ch. Qiu Ying, early 16th century] *in the spring, the first month of 1793. Minamoto Ōkyo*

Seals

Ōkyo no in; *Chūsen*

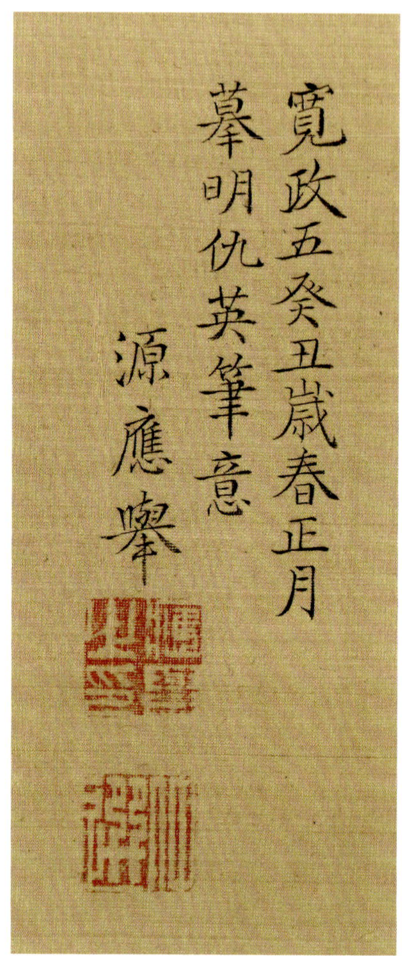

389

---

† 391. Calabash Flowers and Beetle

Signature

Ōshin

Seal

Ōshin no in

391

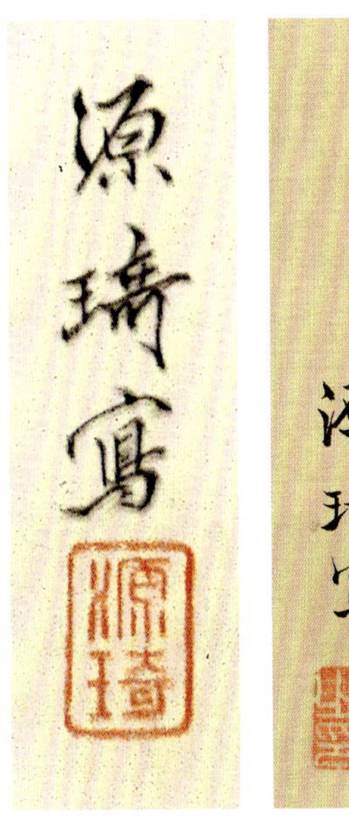

392

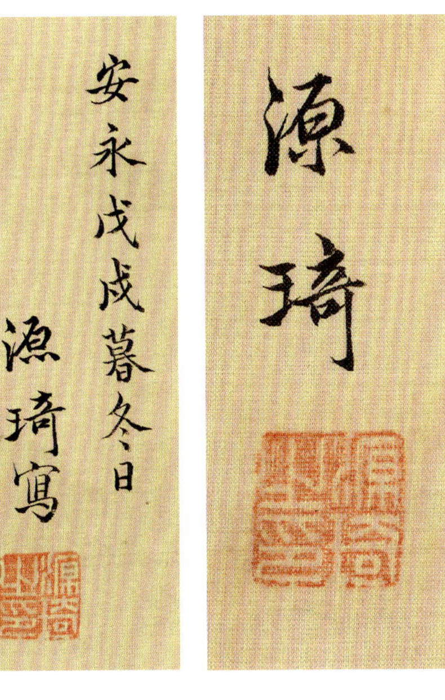

393 393

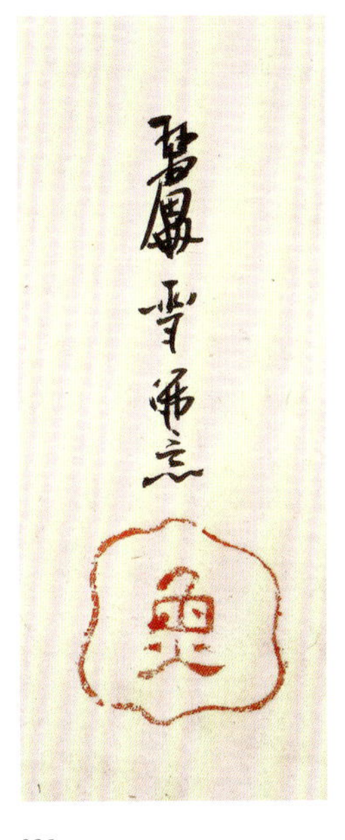

395

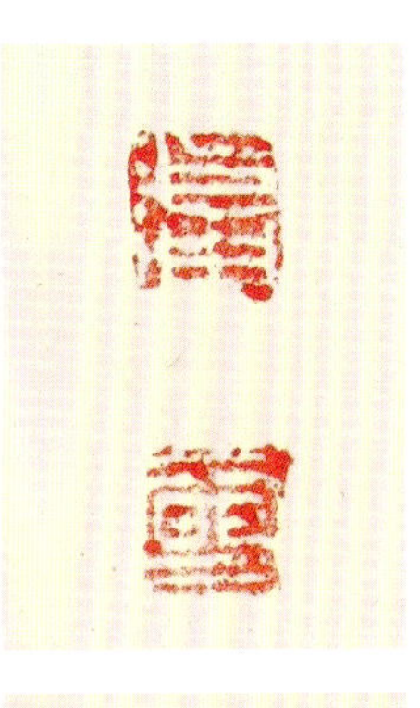

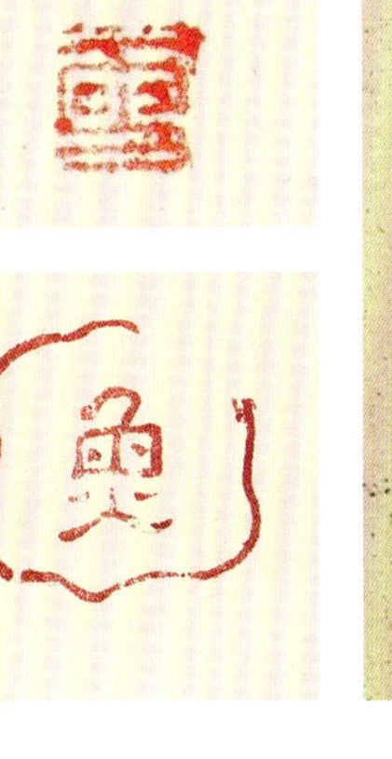

396

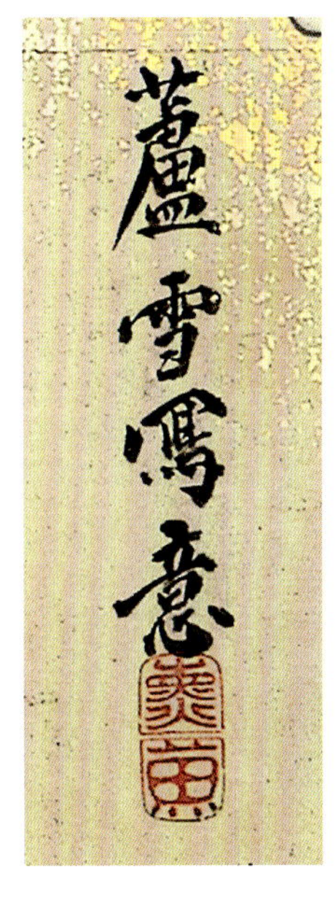

397

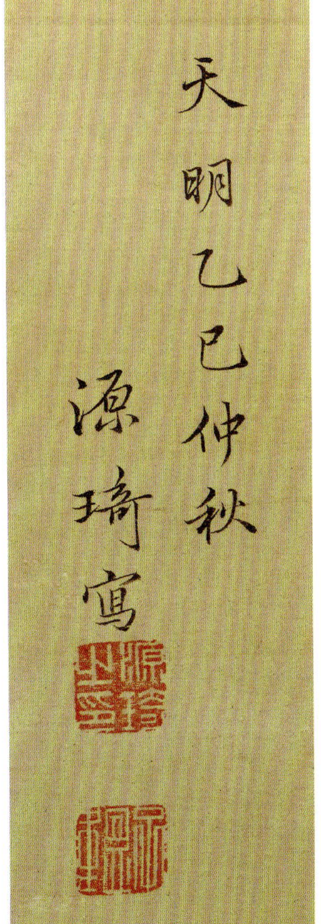

394

† 392. Beauty under Cherry Tree

Signature

Painted by Genki

Seal

Genki

† 393. Winter scene from the Four Seasons in Kyoto

Signatures

["Summer"] *Genki*
["Winter"] *Painted by Genki, late winter of 1778*

Seals

[on each scene] *Genki no in*

† 394. Enkitsu (Ch. Yanjie) with Orchids; Yō Kihi (Ch. Yang Guifei) with Peonies

Signatures

[on right scroll] *Painted by Genki*
[on left scroll] *Painted by Genki, eighth month of 1785*

Seals

[on each scroll] *Genki no in*; *Shion*

† 395. Family of Cranes

Signature

[on right screen] *Rosetsu painted the spirit*

Seal

[on right screen] *Gyo*

† 396. Puppies in Snow

Seals

[on right panel (as shown, upper right)] *Ro*; *Setsu*; *Gyo*

† 397. Chinese Children at Play

Signature

[on left screen] *Rosetsu painted the spirit*

Seals

[on left screen] *Kun*; *Gyo*

398. Drinking Festival of the Eight Immortals

Signature

Rosetsu

Seal

Gyo

† 399. Mice on Rice-Cake Flowers

Signature

Painted by Rosetsu

Seals

Nagasawa; Kazue

† 400. Dragon and Moon in Rain

Signature

Rosetsu

Seals

Nagasawa; Gyo

401. Bird on Wisteria Branch

Signature

Rosetsu

Seal

Gyo

† 402. Bird on Plum Tree

Signature

Painted by Rosetsu

Seal

Gyo

† 403. Swimming Tiger

Seals

Nagasawa Gyo in; Rosetsu

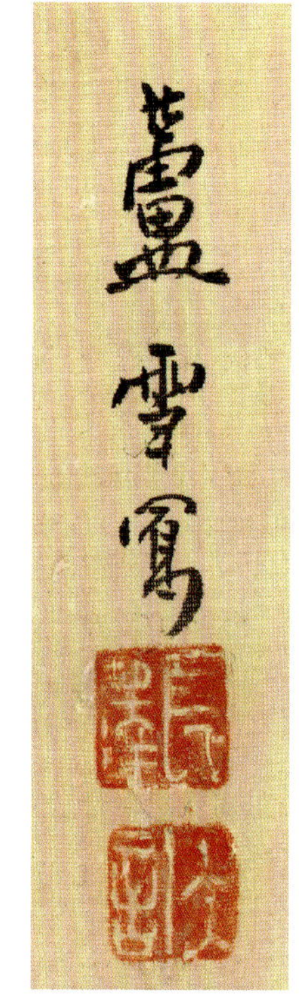

399

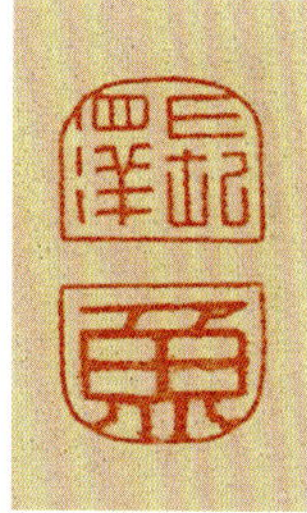

400

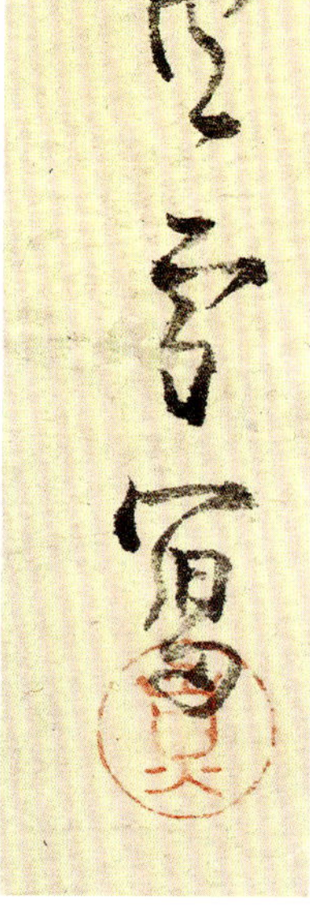

402

403

404

405

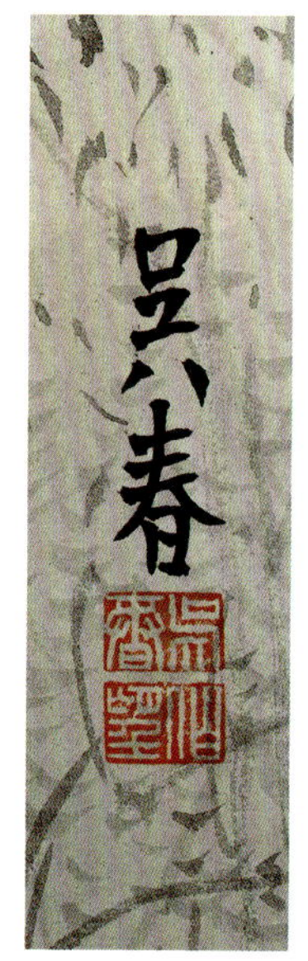

406

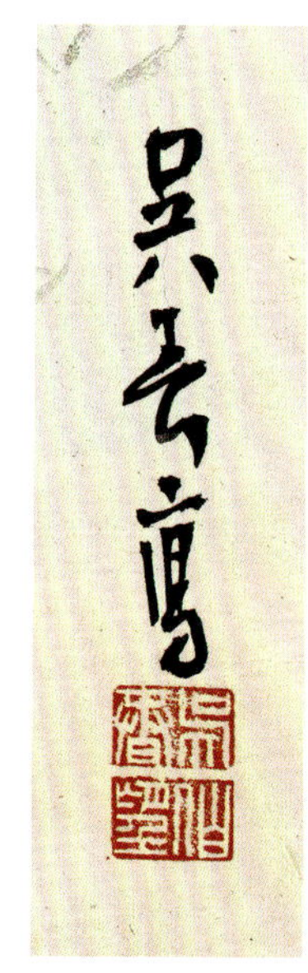

406

† 404. Two Women and a Puppy

Signature

Rosetsu

Seals

Nagasawa; Rosetsu

† 405. Crow on Persimmon Tree

Signature

Painted by Rosetsu

Seals

Nagasawa; Gyo

† 406. Woodcutters; Fishermen

Signatures

[on right screen] *Painted by Goshun*
[on left screen] *Goshun*

Seals

[on each screen] *Goshun; Hakubō*

† 407. Spring Landscape

Signature

Painted by Utanosuke Ganku in the second month of 1787

Seals

Utanosuke in; Uma

† 408. Sparrow and Spider

Signature

Keibun

Seals

Kei; Bun

409. Bamboo

Inscription

by Rengetsu
My lord accumulates splendid years / one after another, like nodes of a bamboo. / He is a paragon whose reign will be long.

Signature

Rengetsu at age 76

† 410. Procession of Insects

Signature

Kan'ei

Seal

Nishiyama Ei in

† 411. Sparklers on a Summer Evening

Signature

Bunrin

Seals

Sekken; Shion

† 412. Ibaraki

Signatures

[on right screen] *Old Zeshin at age 75*
[on left screen] *Zeshin*

Seals

[on each screen] *Tairyūkyo*

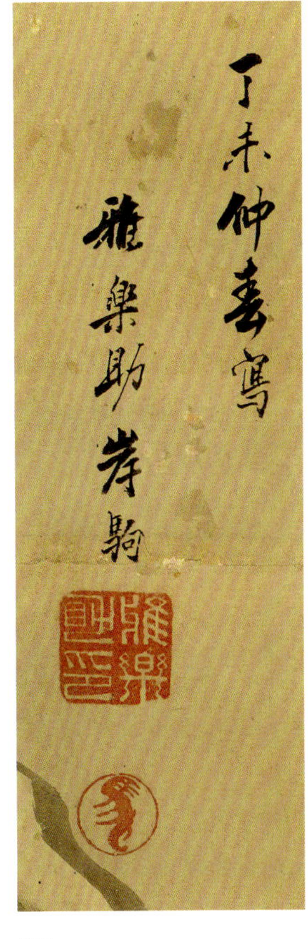

407

408

410

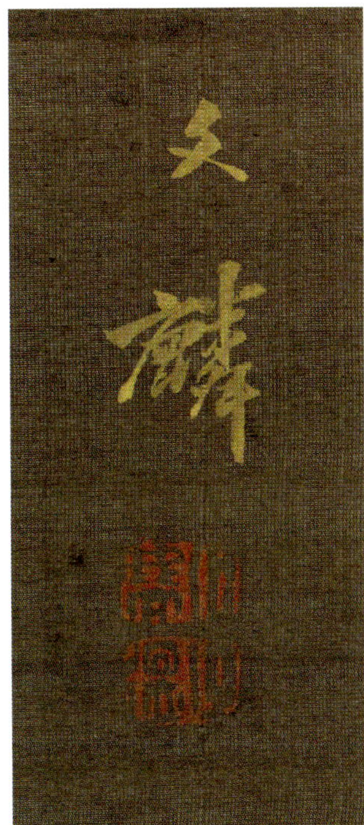

411

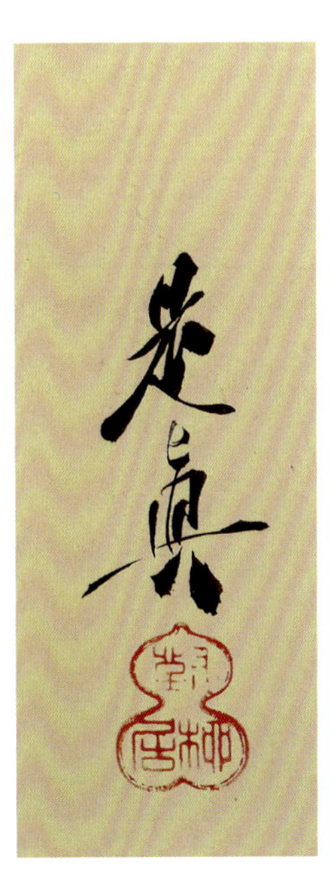

412

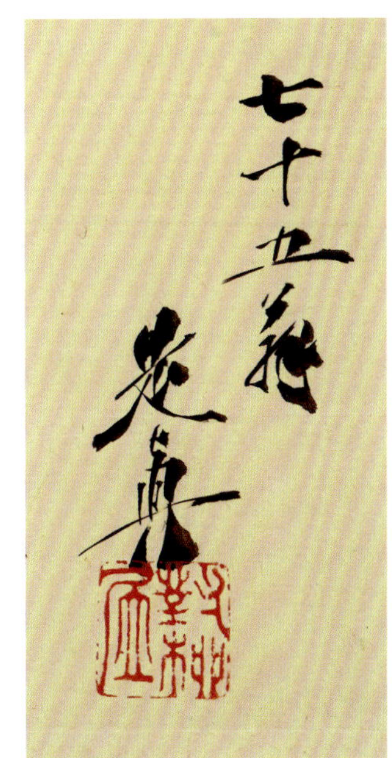

412

† 413. Plum Branch and Teapot

Signature

Zeshin

Seal

Zeshin

† 414. Devil's Invocation

Signature

Zeshin

Seal

Shin

† 415. Turnip

Signature

Zeshin

Seal

Zeshin

† 416. Mice

Signature

Kakudō

Seals

Kakudō; Gudon Chūjin

† 417. Procession of Insects

Signature

Kansai Mori Kōshuku

Seals

Tachibana Kōshuku in; Tachibana Shiyō

† 418. The Legend of Amaterasu, Who Locks Herself Inside the Rock-Cave of Heaven; Nehan

Seals

[on each scroll] *Kōno Hō in*

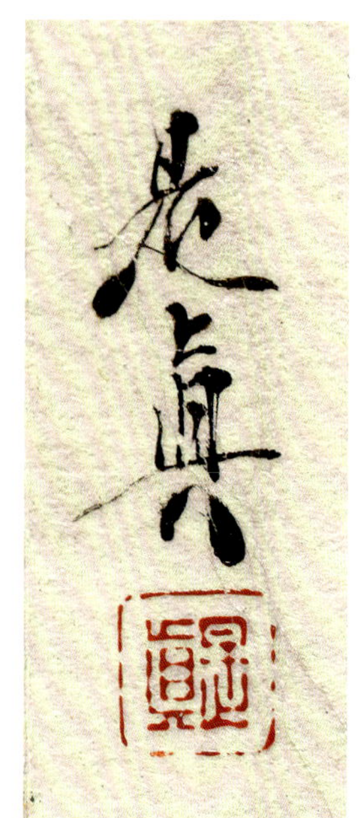

413

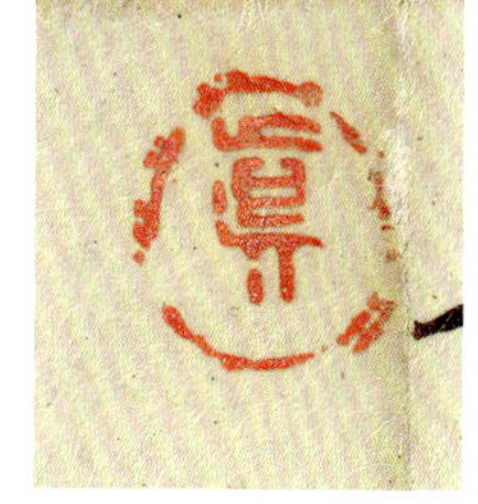

414

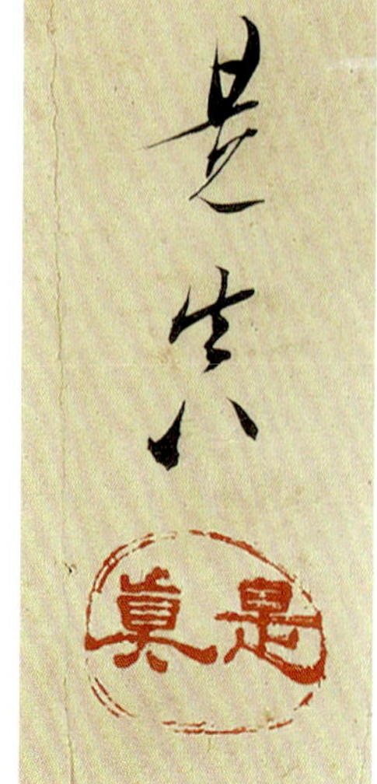

415

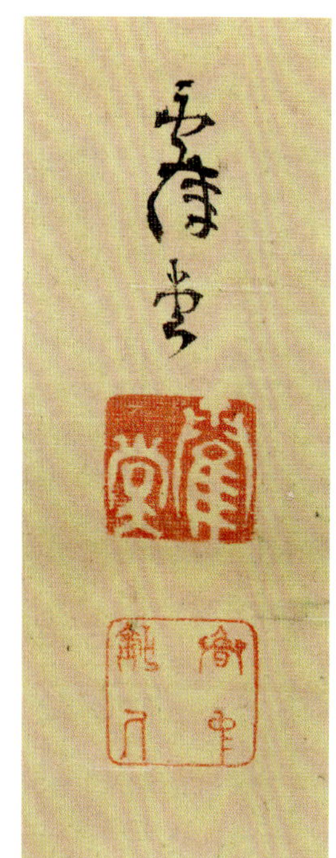

416

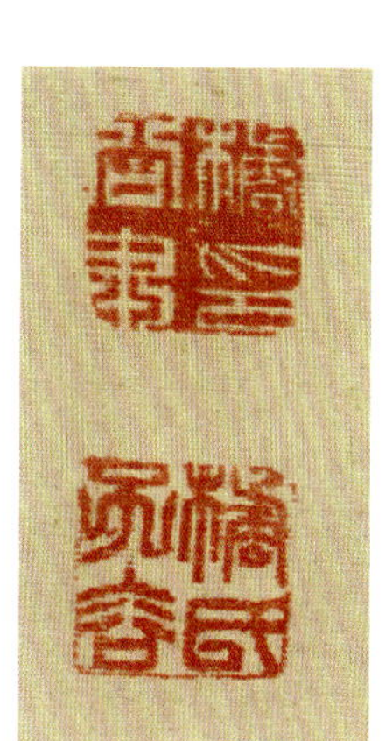

417

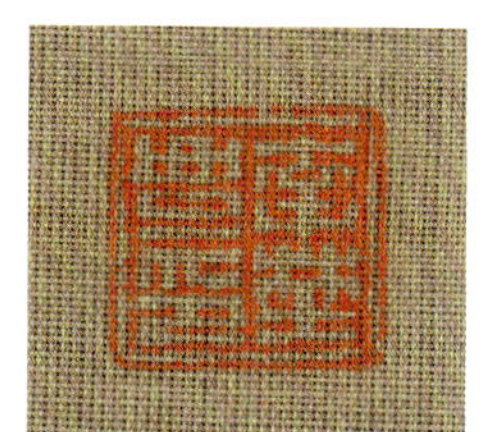

418

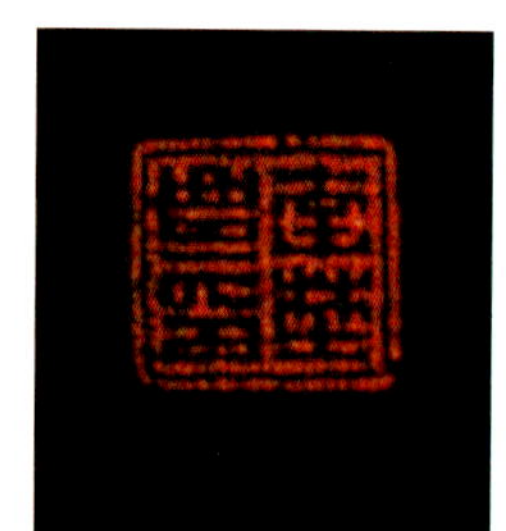

418

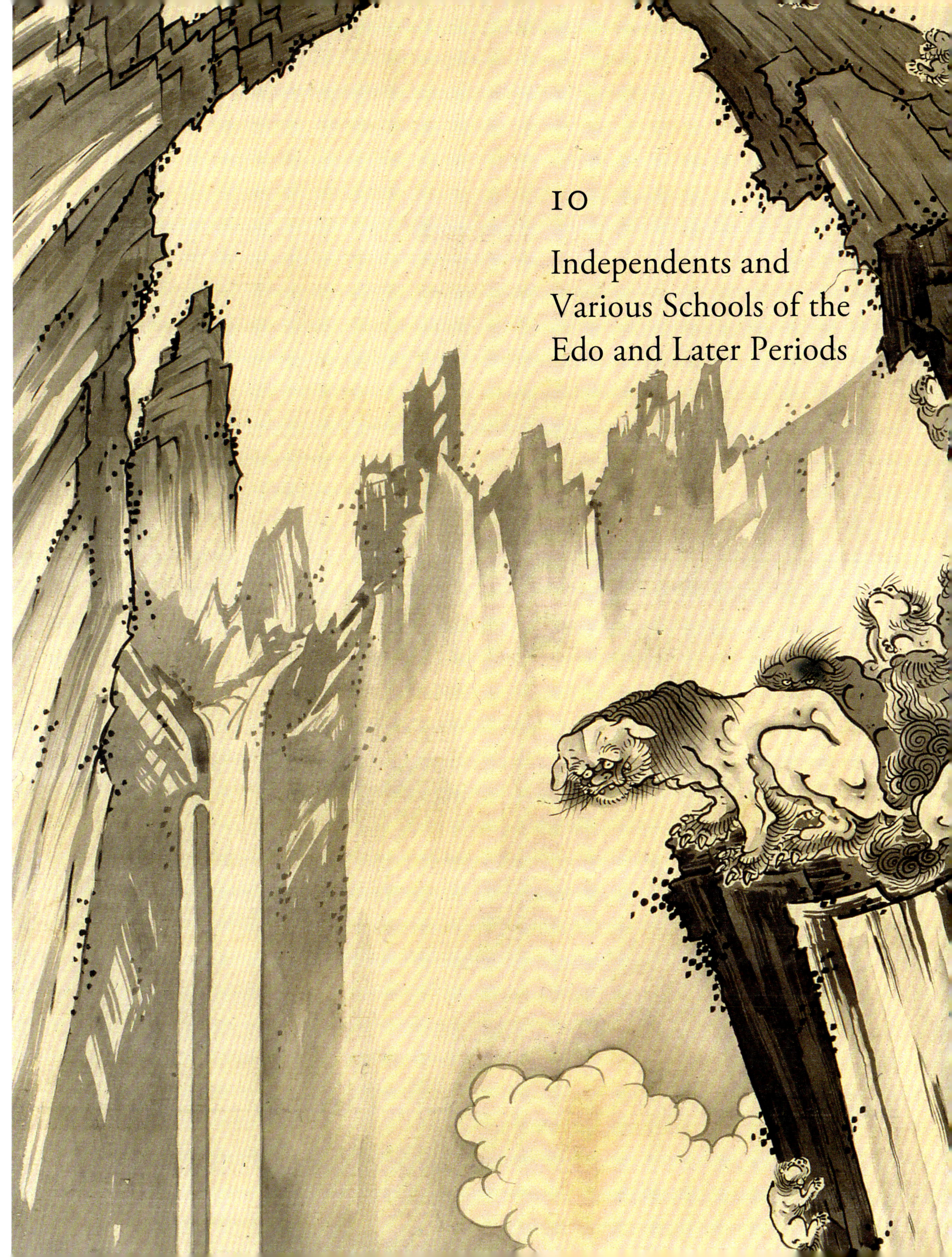

10

Independents and Various Schools of the Edo and Later Periods

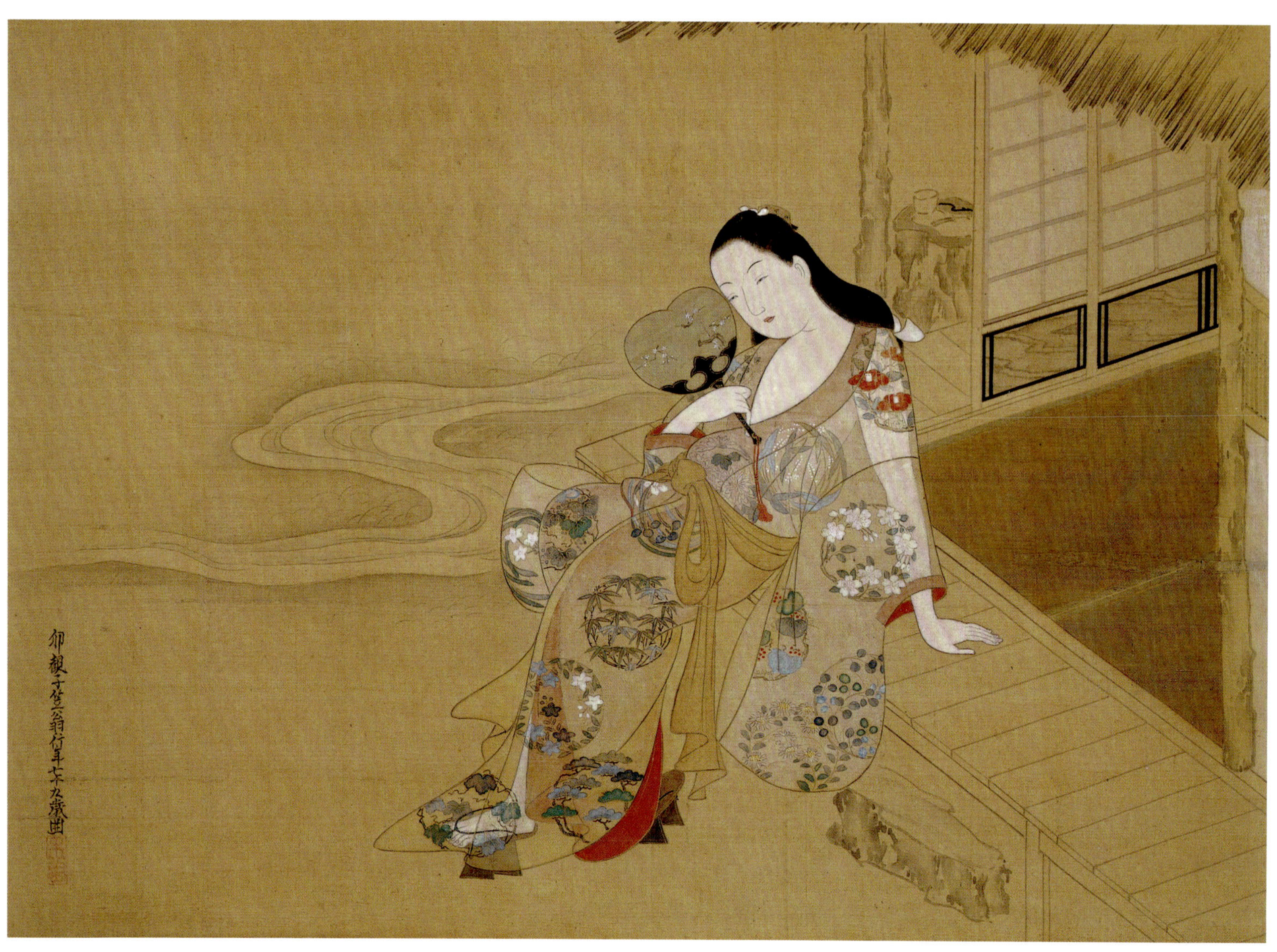

Ogawa Haritsu
(小川破笠; 1663–1747)

423. Courtesan Enjoying a Cool Summer Evening

Edo period, 1741
Hanging scroll; ink and color on silk
39 x 54.4 cm (15 3/8 x 21 3/8 in.)
Signature, seal

Ex coll.: Frank E. Hart

Literature: Murase 1975, no. 90; Tsuji Nobuo et al. 2005, no. 84.

Hakuin Ekaku
(白隠慧鶴; 1685–1768)

425. Tenjin on His Way to China
(渡唐天神)

Edo period, 18th century
Hanging scroll; ink on paper
109.4 x 26.3 cm (43 1/8 x 10 3/8 in.)
Text, seals

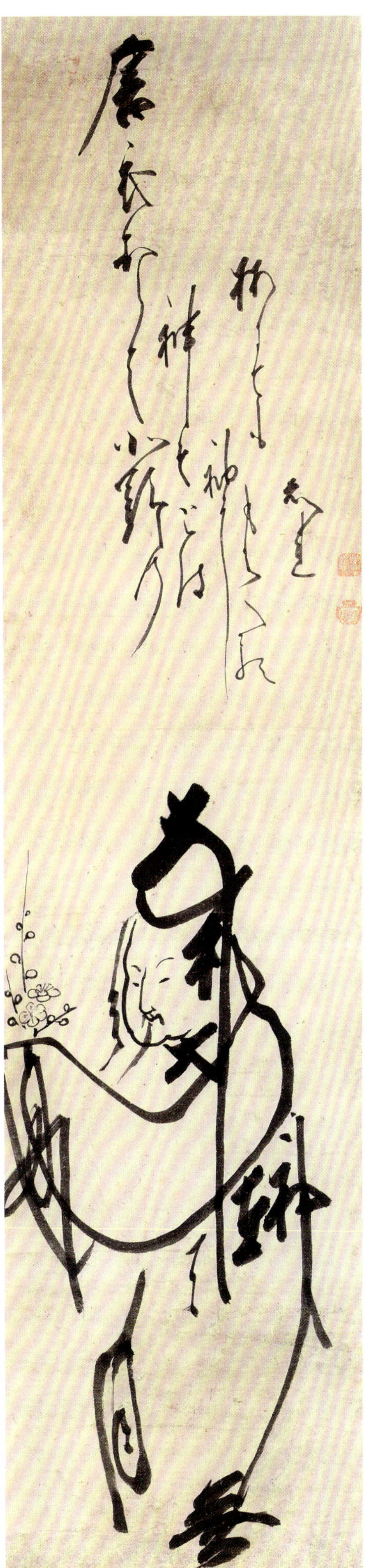

Hakuin Ekaku
(白隠慧鶴; 1685–1768)

424. First Dream of the New Year
(初夢)

Edo period, 18th century
Hanging scroll; ink on paper
52 x 64.6 cm (20 1/2 x 25 3/8 in.)
Text, seals

Literature: Burke 1993, fig. 8/no. 7.

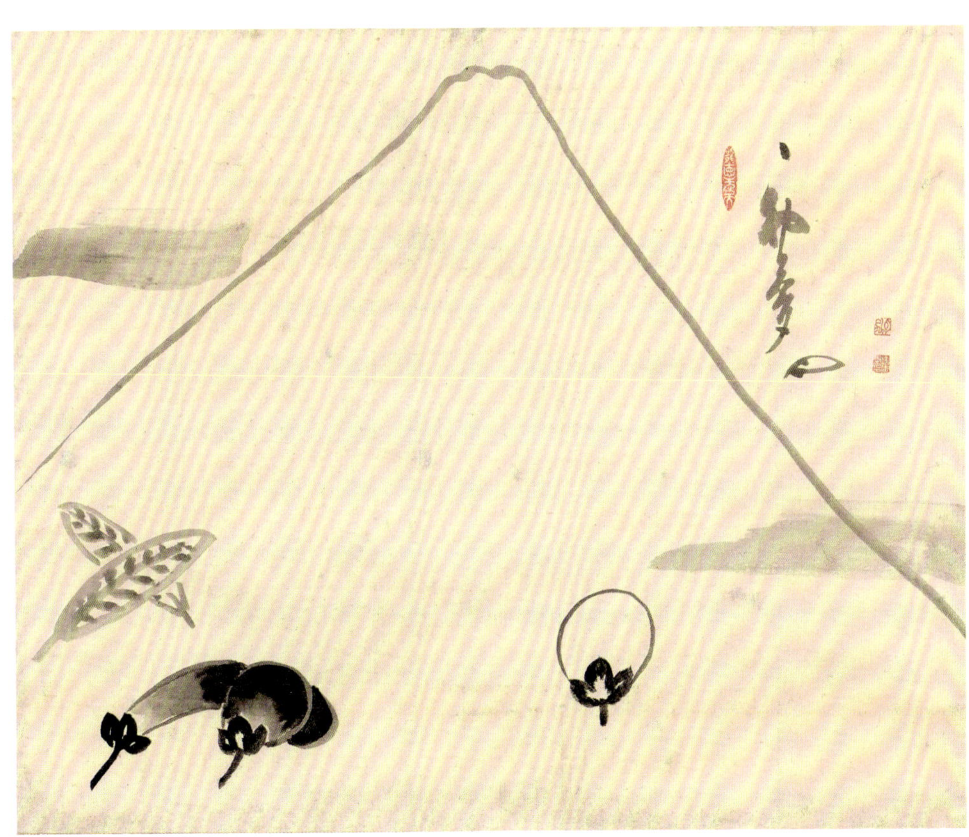

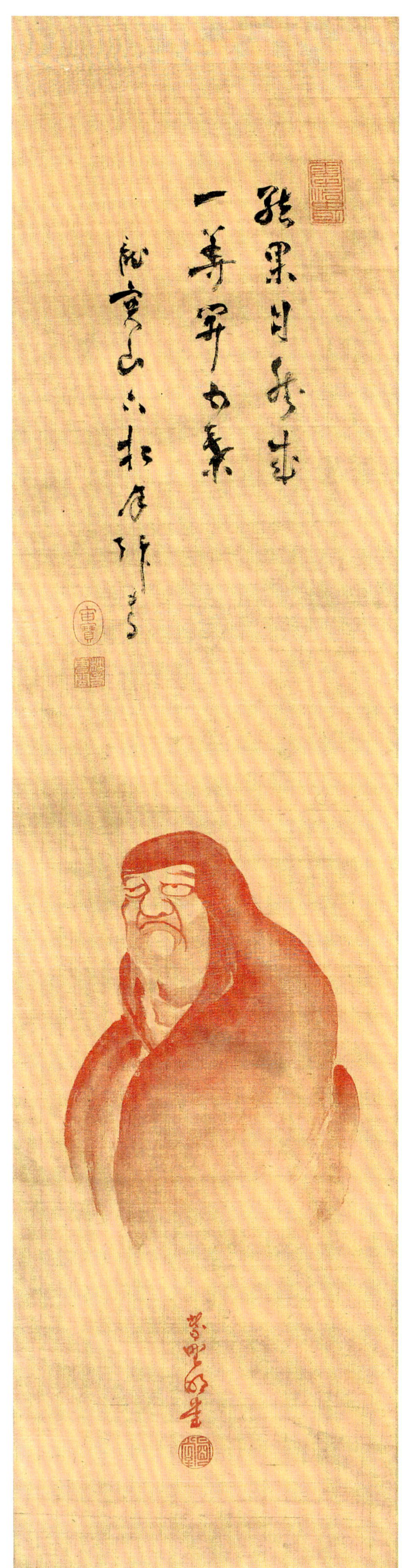

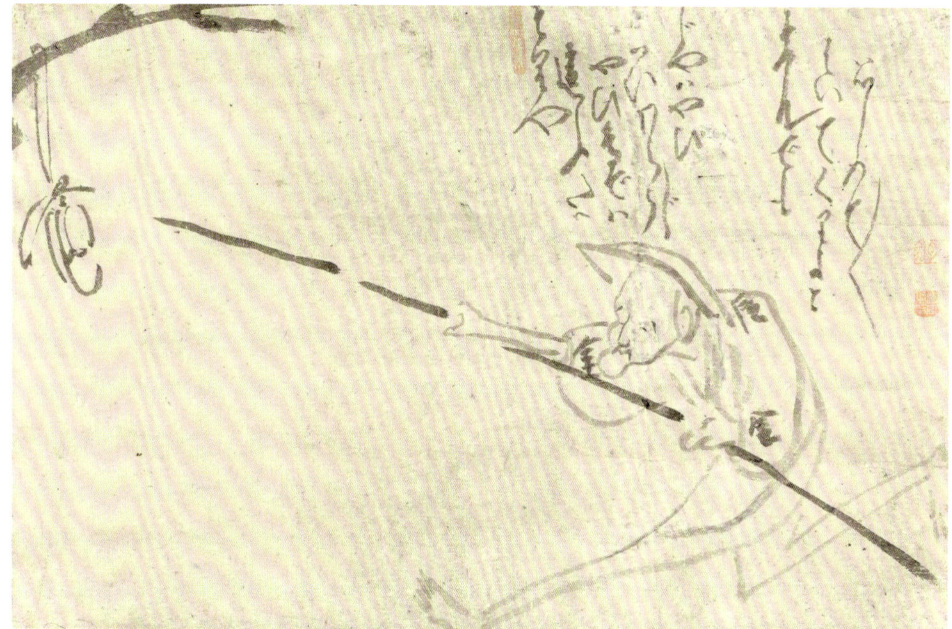

Hakuin Ekaku
(白隠慧鶴; 1685–1768)

427. Bird Catcher

Edo period, 18th century
Hanging scroll; ink on paper
30.5 x 46.6 cm (12 x 18 3/8 in.)
Text, seals

Mindō Sōsen
(明堂宗宣; fl. 18th century)

426. Daruma (達磨)

Edo period
Hanging scroll; red ink on silk
83 x 21 cm (32 5/8 x 8 1/4 in.)
Text, signatures, seals

Itō Jakuchū
(伊藤若冲; 1716–1800)

428. White Plum Blossoms and Moon

Edo period, 1755
Hanging scroll; ink and color on silk
140.8 x 79.4 cm (55 3/8 x 31 1/4 in.)
Text, signature, seals

Literature: Mizuo Hiroshi 1968, p. 35; Tsuji Nobuo 1974, pl. 63; Murase 1975, no. 60; Tsuji Nobuo et al. 1981, pl. 25; Tokyo National Museum 1985a, no. 61; Satō Yasuhiro 1987, fig. 36; Hickman and Satō 1989, fig. 26; Avitabile 1990, no. 85; Kano Hiroyuki 1993, pl. 40; Burke 1996a, p. 54, fig. 1; Kyoto National Museum 2000, pl. 35, pp. 156, 336; Murase 2000, no. 119; Tsuji Nobuo et al. 2005, no. 99.

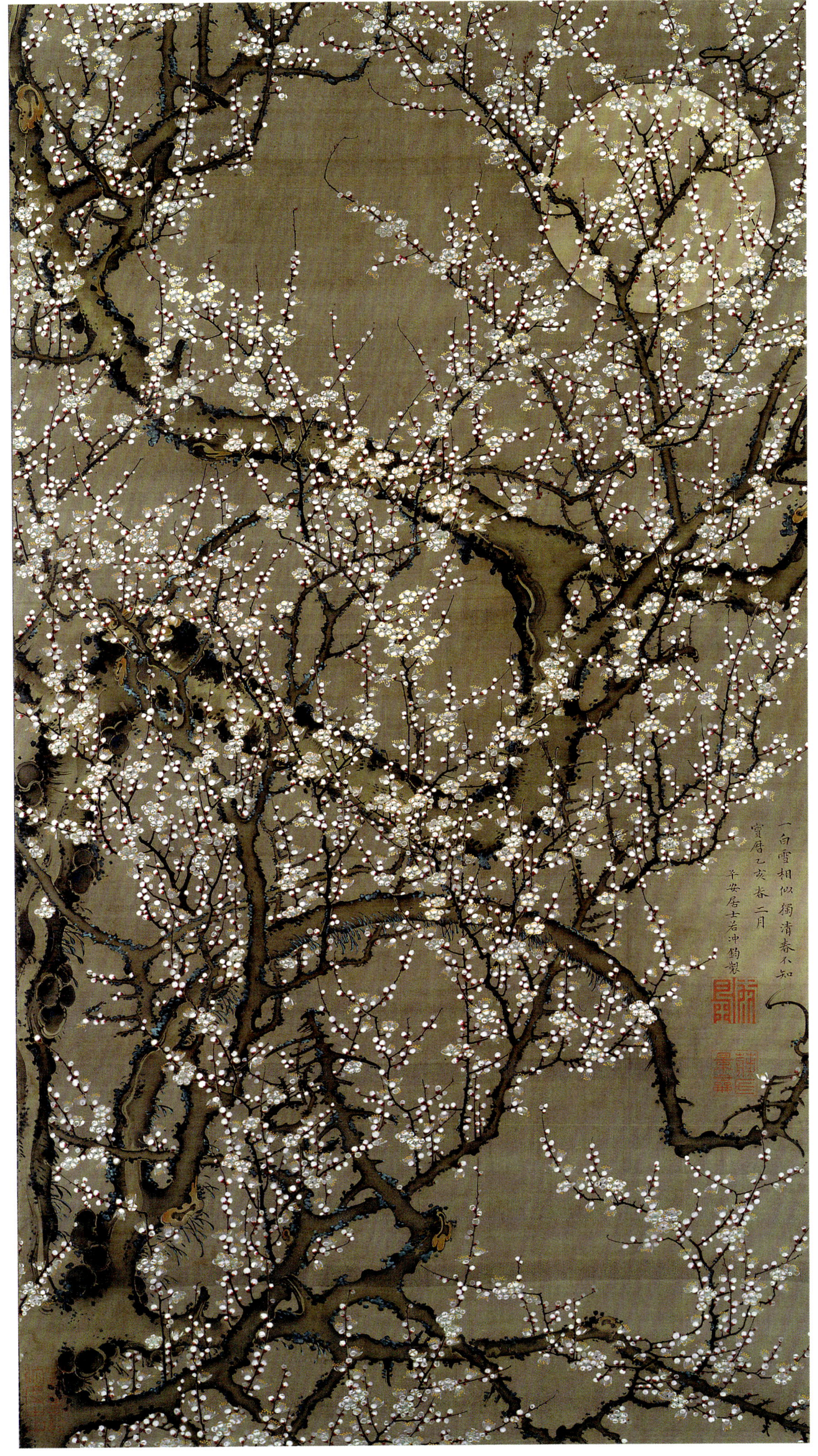
一白雪相似獨清春不知
寶暦乙亥春二月
平安居士若冲鈞製

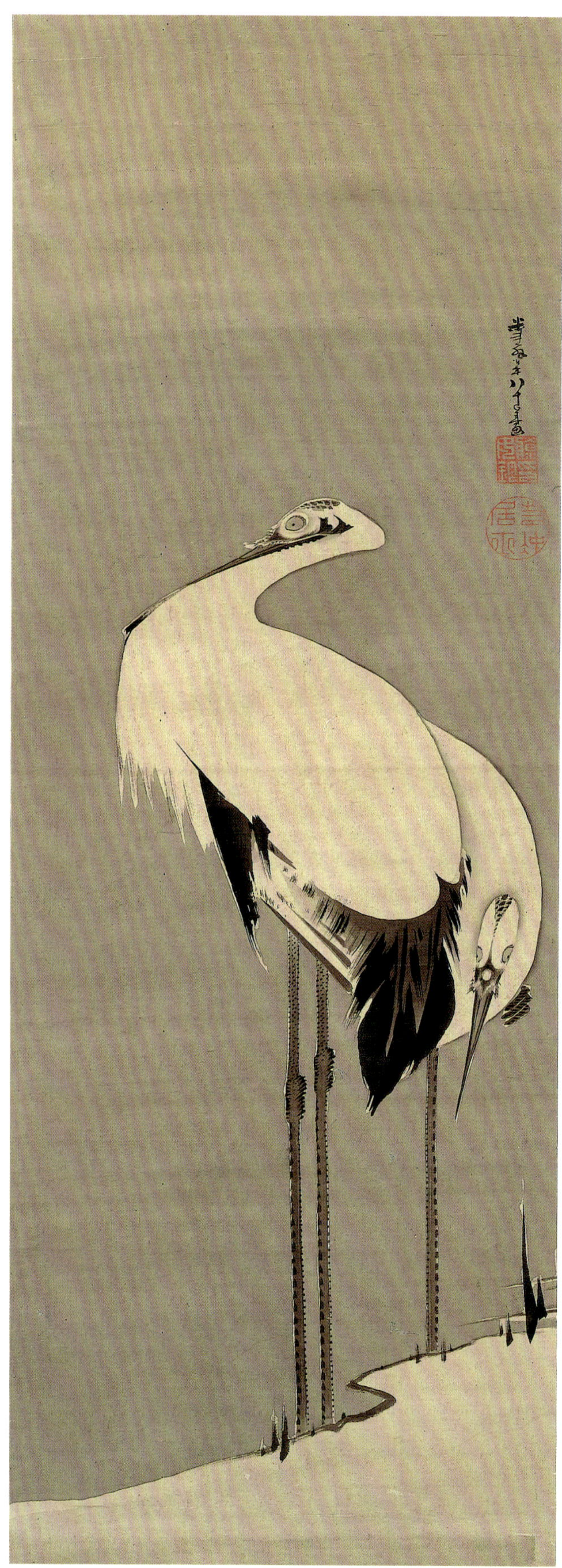

Itō Jakuchū
(伊藤若冲; 1716–1800)

429. Two Cranes

Edo period, 1795
Hanging scroll; ink on silk
140.8 x 79.4 cm (55 3/8 x 31 1/4 in.)
Signature, seals

Literature: Kyoto National Museum 2000; Murase 2000, no. 120; Tsuji Nobuo et al. 2005, no. 100.

Itō Jakuchū
(伊藤若冲; 1716–1800)

430. Nightingales on a Plum Tree

Edo period, 1795
Hanging scroll; ink on paper
26.5 x 30 cm (10 3/8 x 11 3/4 in.)
Signature, seals

Gift from Leighton R. Longhi to the Mary and Jackson Burke Foundation, 2003

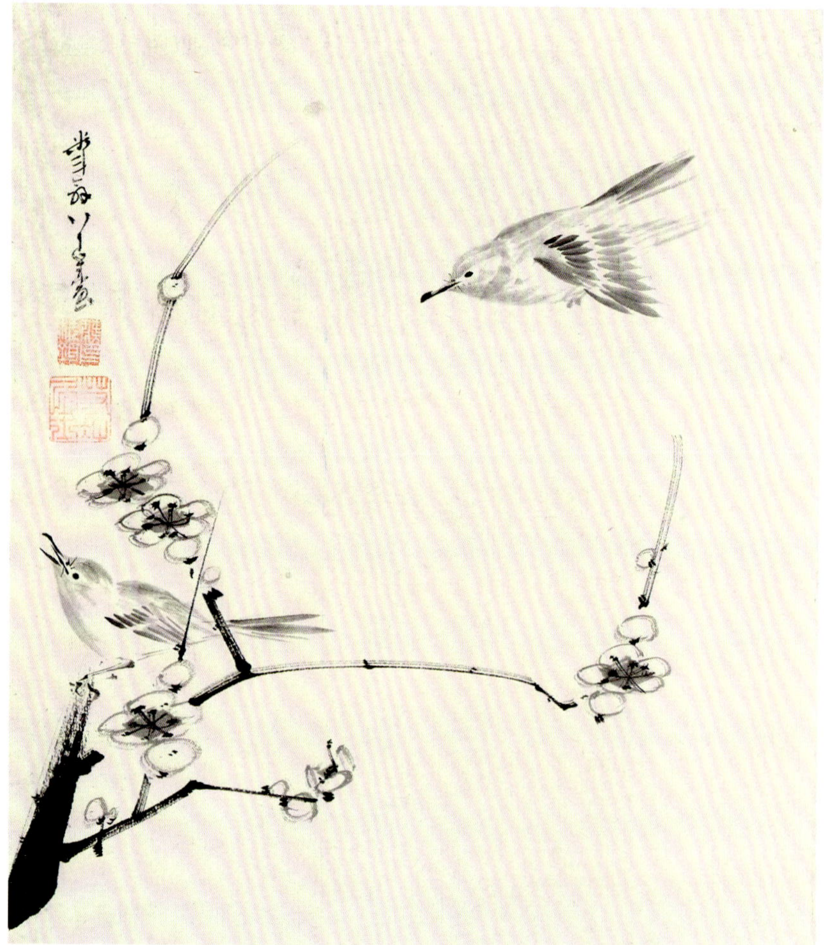

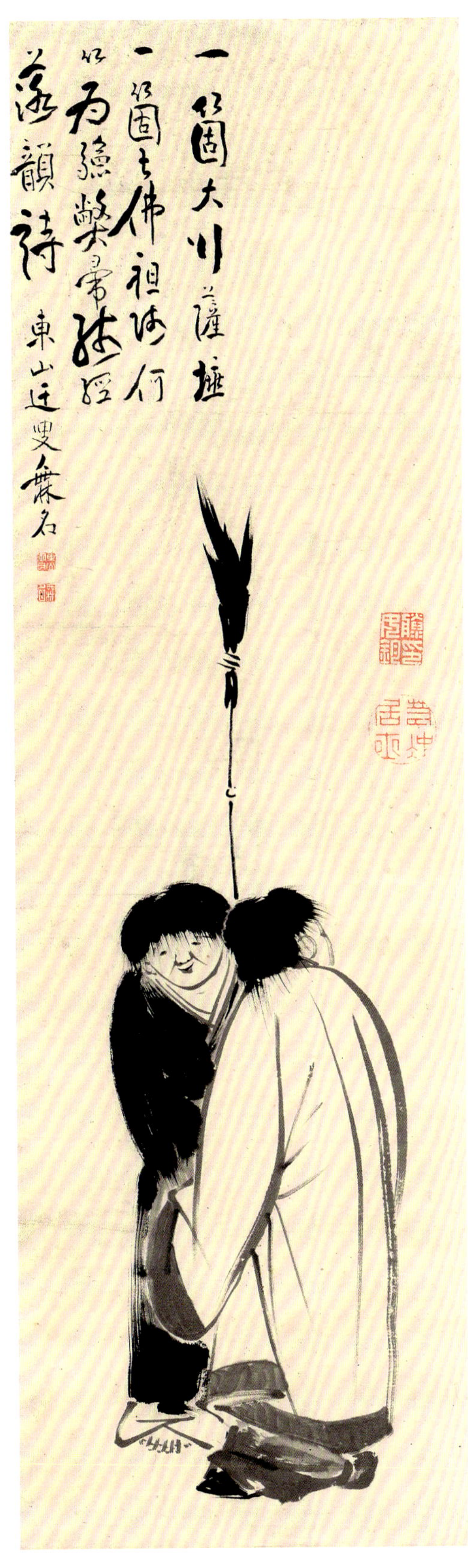

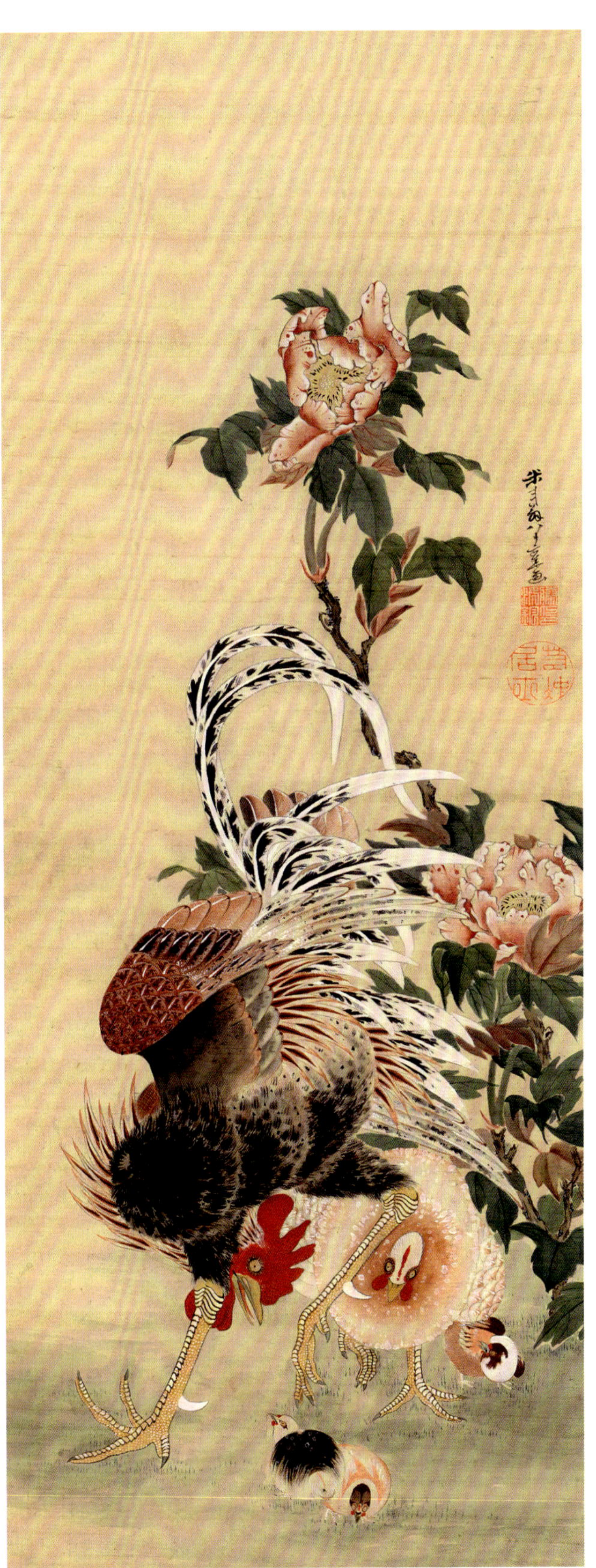

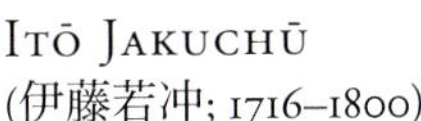

Itō Jakuchū
(伊藤若冲; 1716–1800)

431. Kanzan (Ch. Hanshan, 寒山) and Jittoku (Ch. Shide, 拾得)

Edo period
Hanging scroll; ink on paper
104 x 30.4 cm (41 x 12 in.)
Text, signature, seals

Itō Jakuchū
(伊藤若冲; 1716–1800)

432. Rooster and Family

Edo period, 1797
Hanging scroll; ink and color on silk
102.8 x 40.3 cm (40½ x 15⅞ in.)
Signature, seals

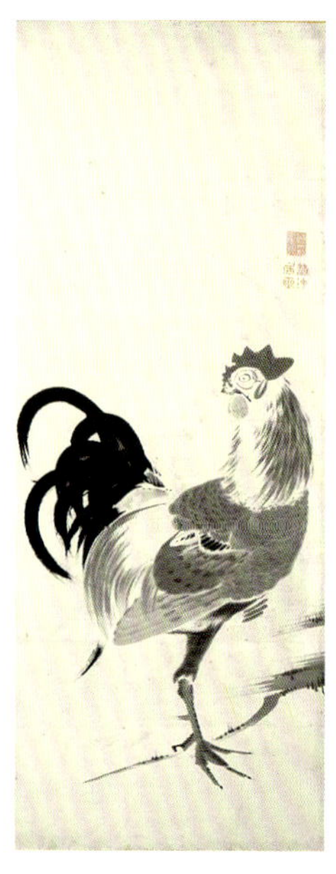
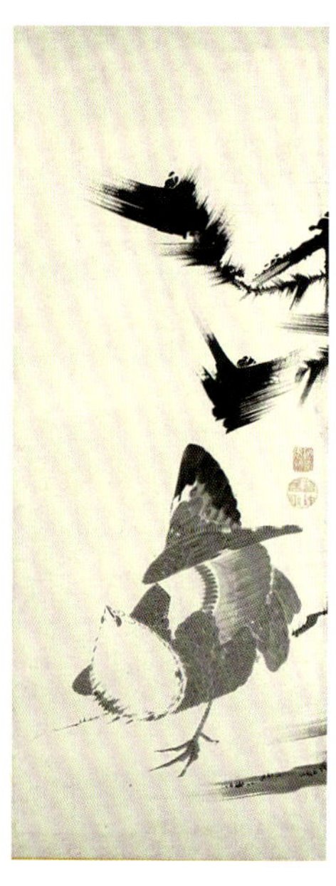
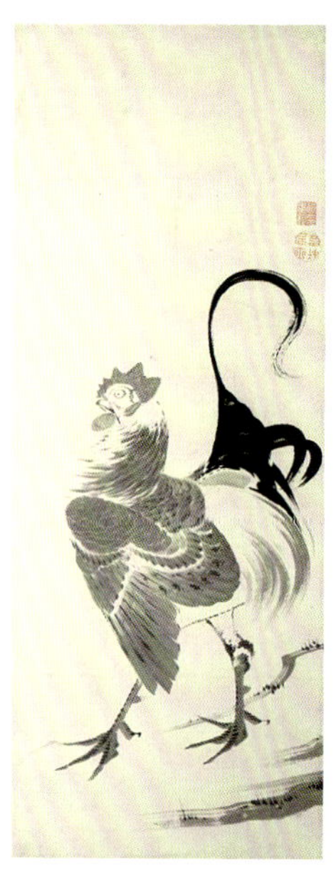
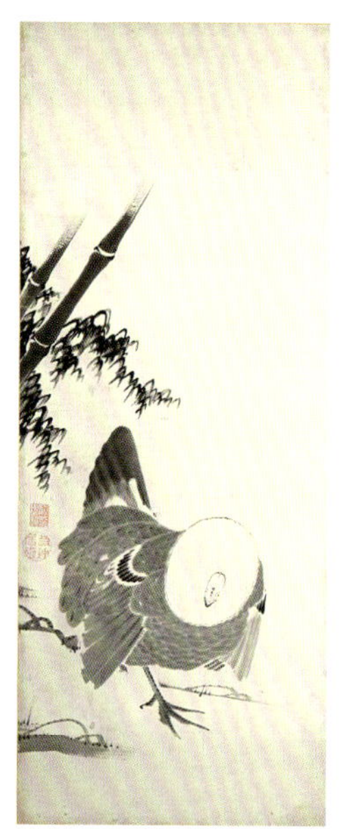
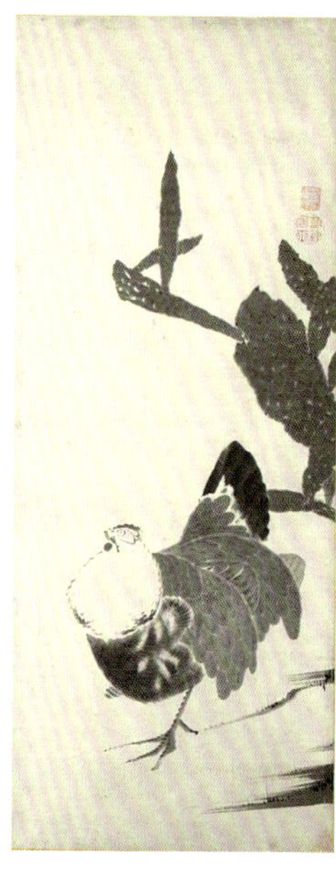
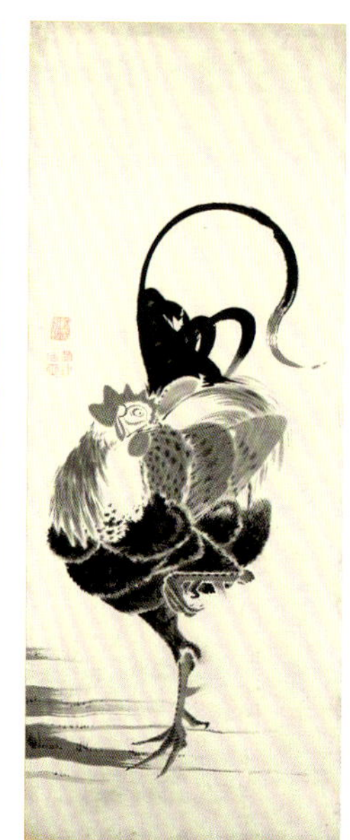
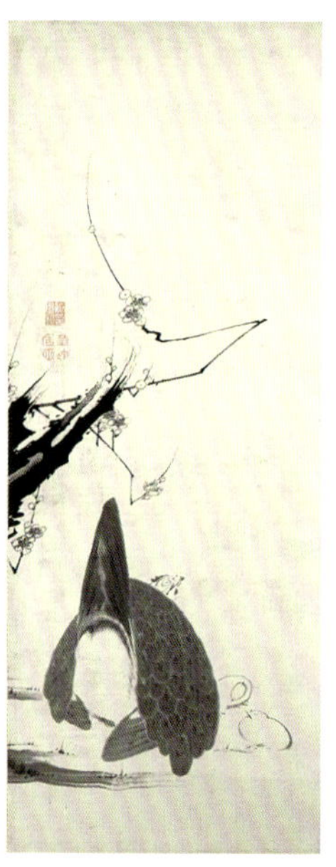
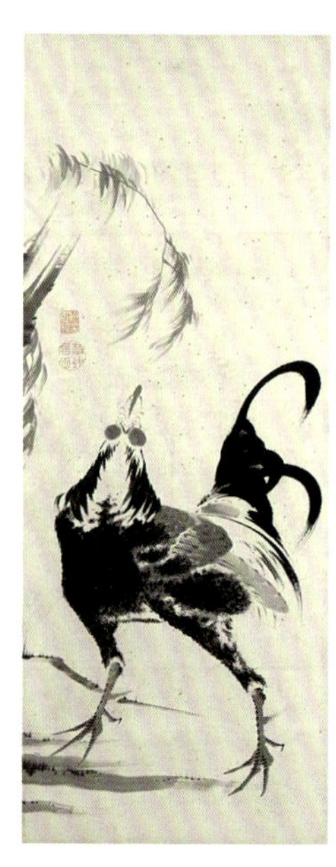
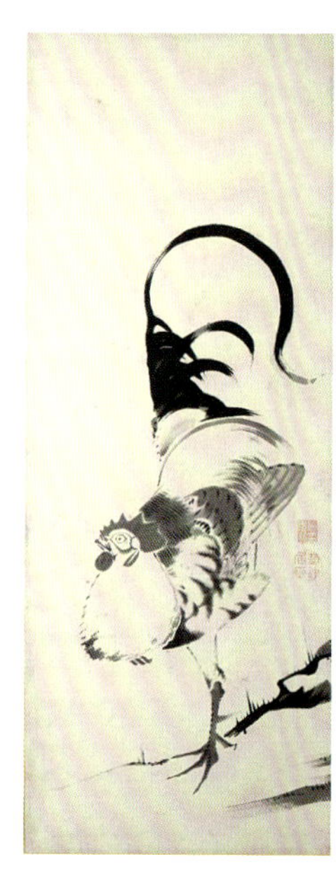
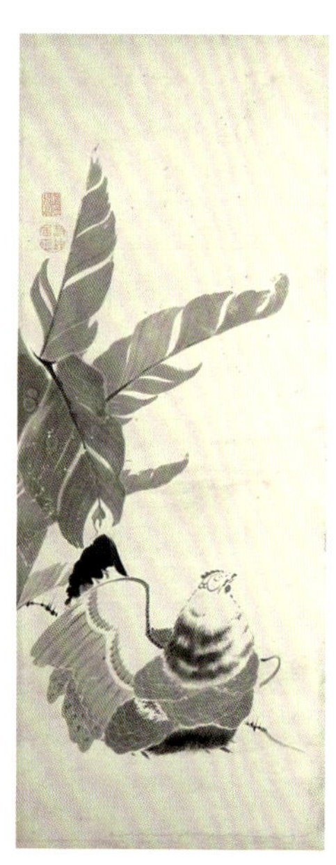
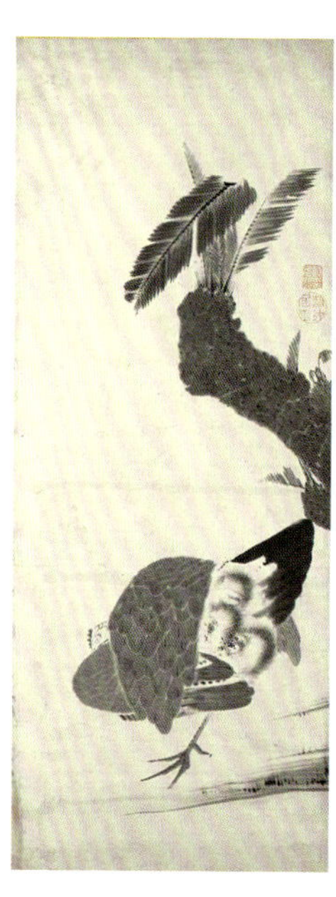
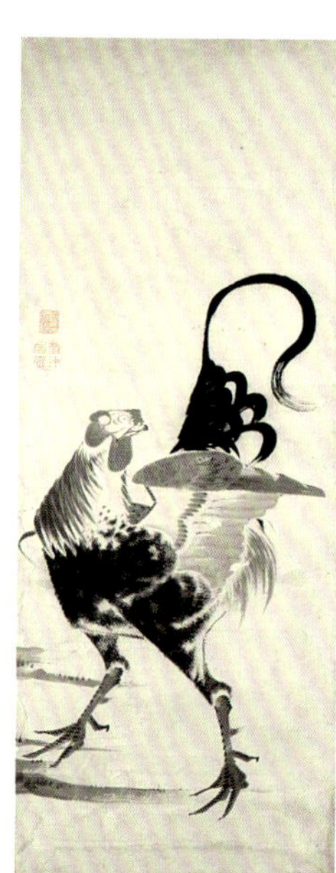

Itō Jakuchū
(伊藤若冲; 1716–1800)

433. Roosters and Hens

Edo period
Twelve panels pasted on a pair of six-panel folding screens; ink on paper
Each panel 49.7 x 126.4 cm (19 5/8 x 49 3/4 in.)
Seals

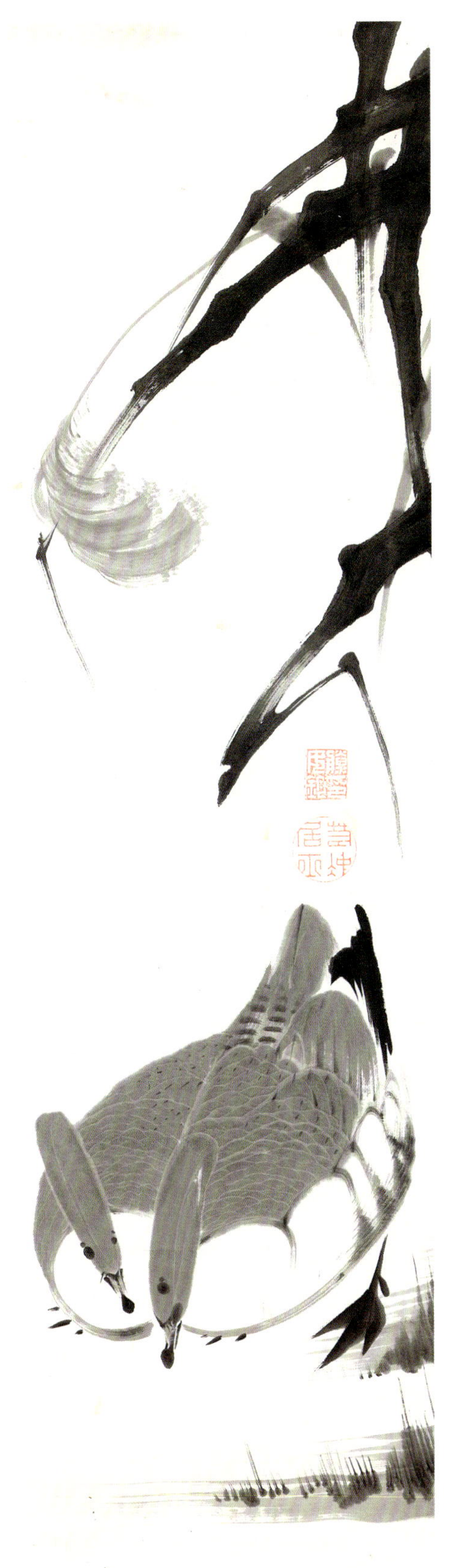

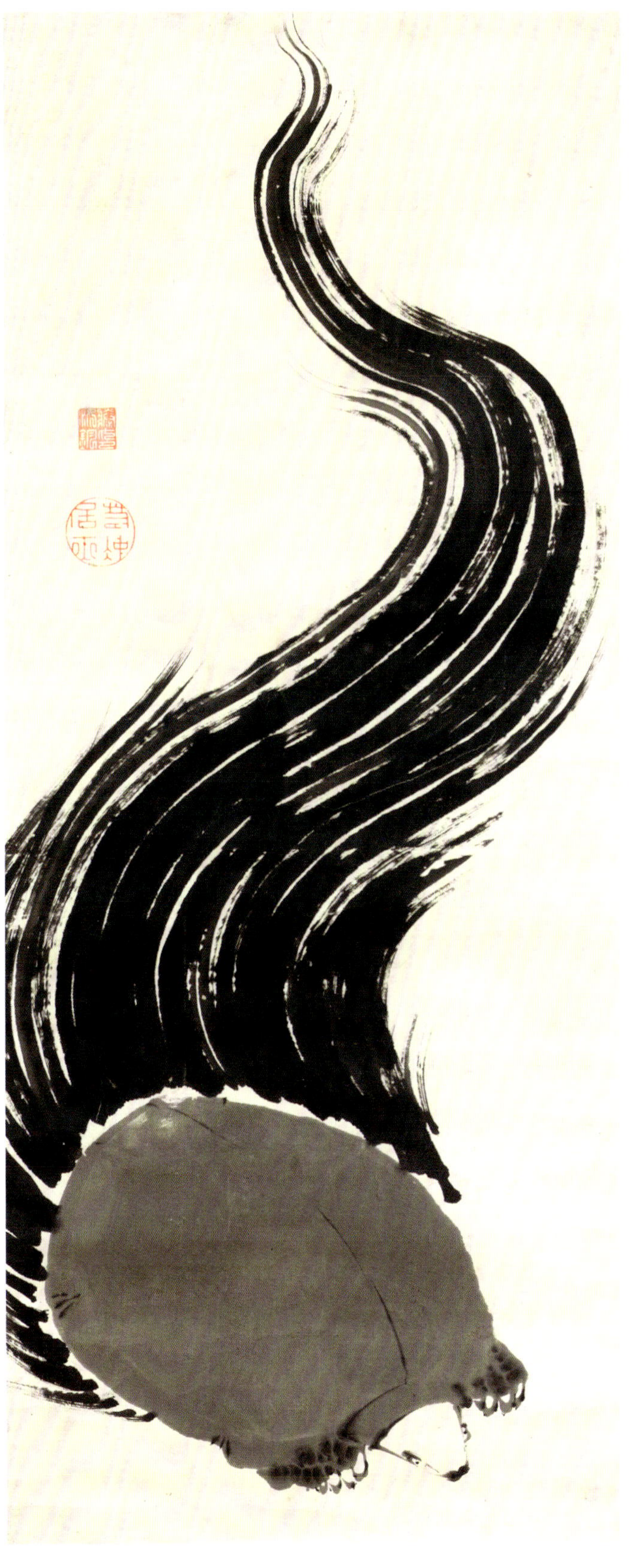

Itō Jakuchū
(伊藤若冲; 1716–1800)

434. Geese and Reeds

Edo period
Hanging scroll; ink on paper
109.2 x 30.4 cm (43 x 12 in.)
Seals

Itō Jakuchū
(伊藤若冲; 1716–1800)

435. Turtle

Edo period
Hanging scroll; ink on paper
97.4 x 40.5 cm (38 3/8 x 16 in.)
Seals

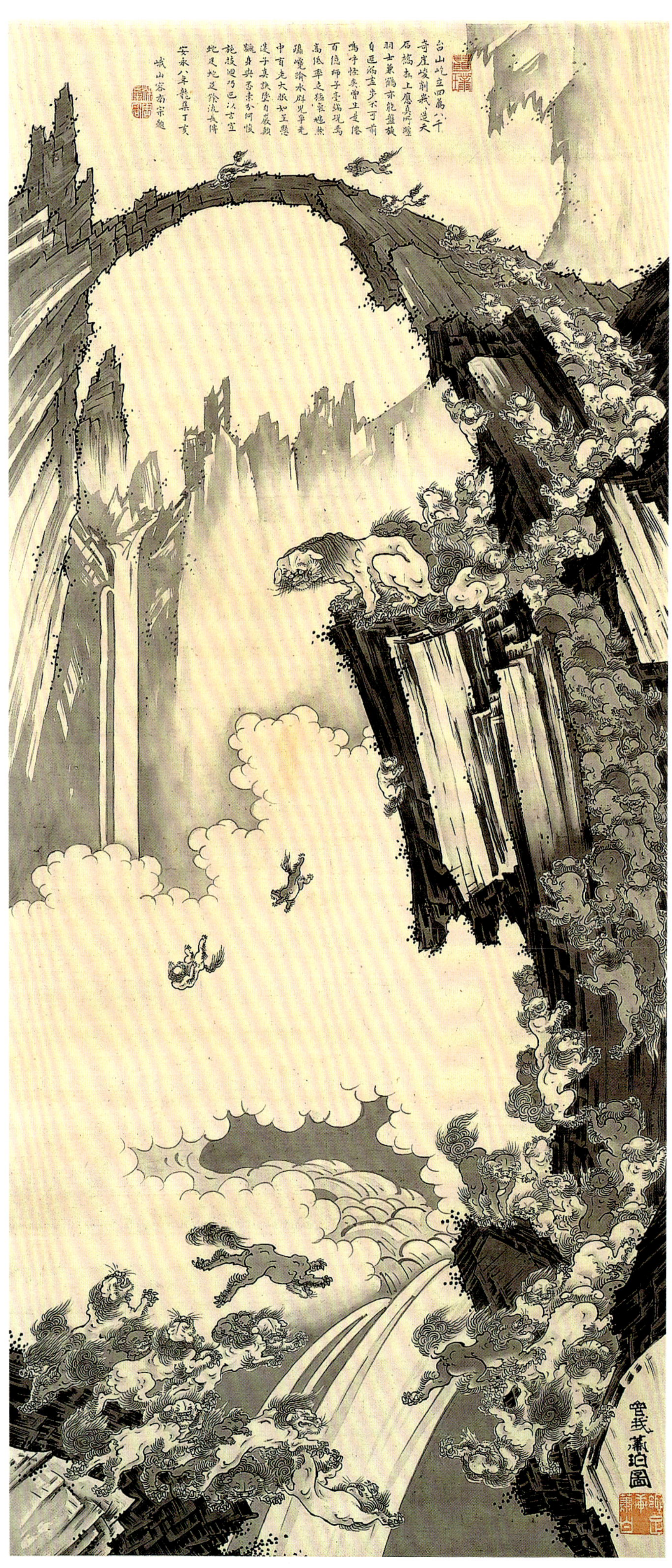

Soga Shōhaku
(曽我蕭白; 1730–1781)

436. Lions at the Stone Bridge of Tendaisan (Ch. Tiantaishan, 天台山石橋)

Edo period, 1779
Hanging scroll; ink on silk
113.9 x 50.8 cm (44 7/8 x 20 in.)
Text, signatures, seals

Literature: "Shōhaku hitsu Shakkyō zu" 1899, p. 193; Iizuka Beiu 1932c, pl. 57; Tsuji Nobuo 1970, fig. 25; Kobayashi Tadashi et al. 1973, pl. 84; Murase 1975, no. 61; Tsuji Nobuo et al. 1981, pl. 71; Tokyo National Museum 1985a, no. 62; Kano Hiroyuki 1987, fig. 56; Avitabile 1990, no. 86; Satō Yasuhiro 1991, pl. 66; Kōno Motoaki 1993, no. 60; Tanaka Yūko 1998, fig. 1; Tsuji Nobuo and Itō Shiori 1998, no. 35; Murase 2000, no. 121; Takashina Shūji 2000, pp. 197–200; Tanaka Yūko 2000, pp. 58–59; Tsuji Nobuo et al. 2005, no. 102.

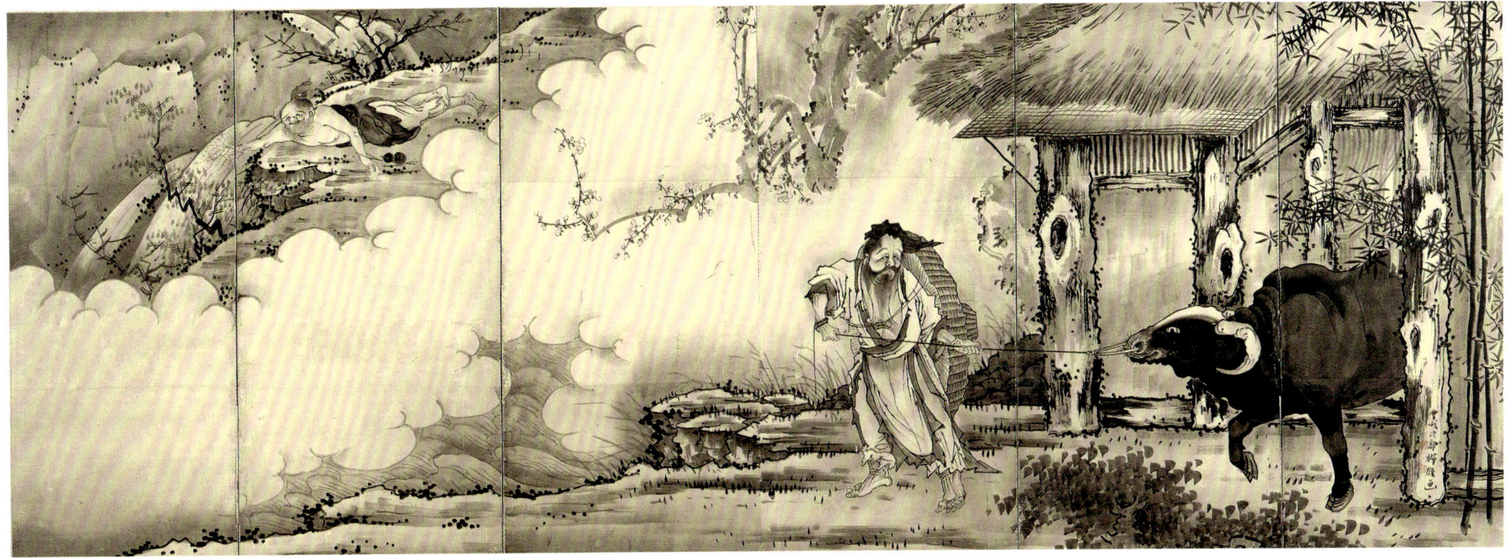

Legends of Kyoyū and Sōho

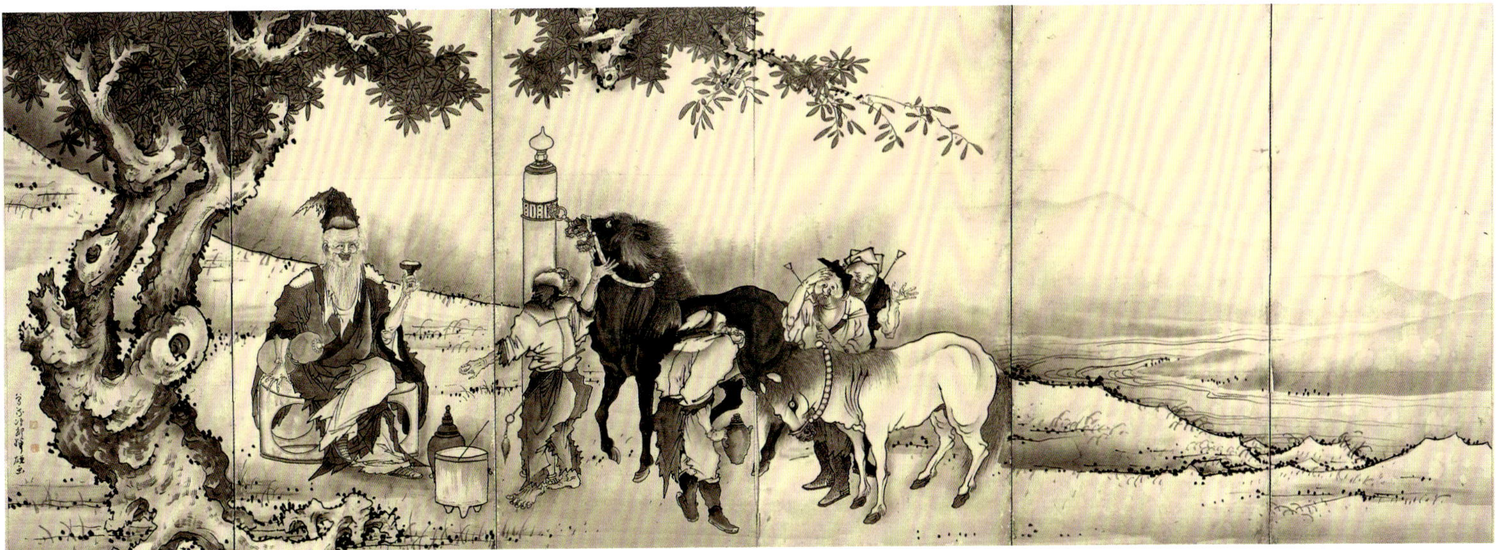

Hakuraku

Soga Shōhaku
(曽我蕭白; 1730–1781)

437. Legends of Kyoyū (Ch. Xuyou, 許由) and Sōho (Ch. Chaofu, 巣父); Hakuraku (Ch. Bole, 伯樂)

Edo period, early 1760s
Pair of six-panel folding screens; ink on paper
Each screen 93.1 x 261.4 cm (36 5/8 in. x 8 ft. 6 7/8 in.)
Signatures, seals

Literature: Tsuji Nobuo and Itō Shiori 1998, no. 66; Tsuji Nobuo et al. 2005, no. 101.

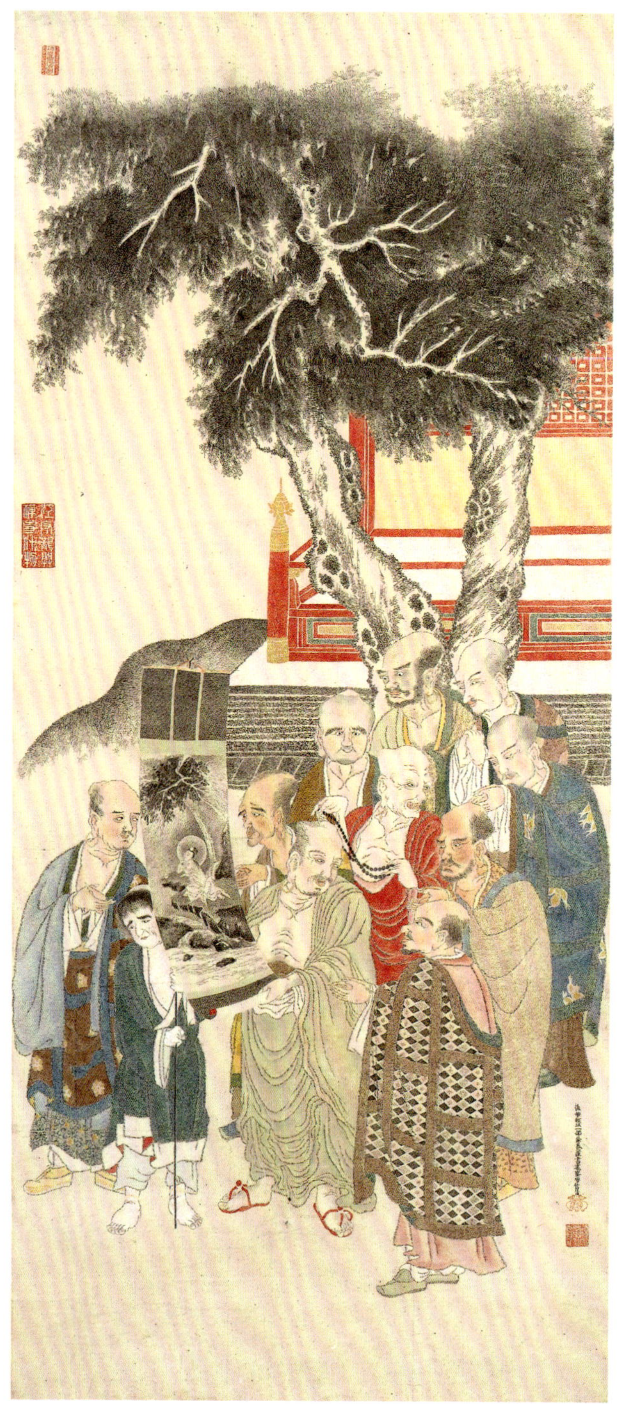

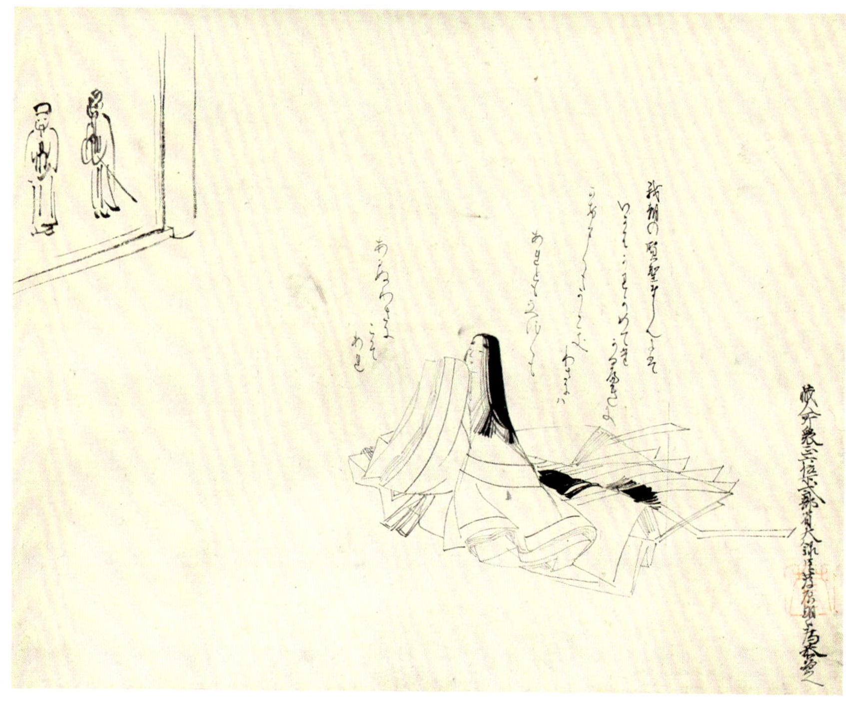

Katō Nobukiyo
(加藤信清; 1734–1810)

438. Ten Rakan (羅漢) Examining a Painting of White-Robed Kannon

Edo period, 1792
Hanging scroll; ink, color, and gold on paper
130.3 x 57.7 cm (51¼ x 22¾ in.)
Signature, seals

Ex coll.: Ryūkōji, Edo

Literature: Kaufman 1985, figs. 13, 14; Pal and Meech-Pekarik 1988, figs. 130, 131; Avitabile 1990, no. 104; Murase 1993, no. 7; Morse and Morse 1995, no. 50; Murase 2000, no. 113; Graham 2007, fig. 6e (detail), pl. 20.

Okada (or Reizei) Tametaka (or Tamechika) (岡田「冷泉」為恭; 1823–1864)

439. Court Lady with Painting of Japanese Sages

Edo period
Hanging scroll; ink on paper
32.7 x 26.2 cm (12⅞ x 10¼ in.)
Text, signature, seal

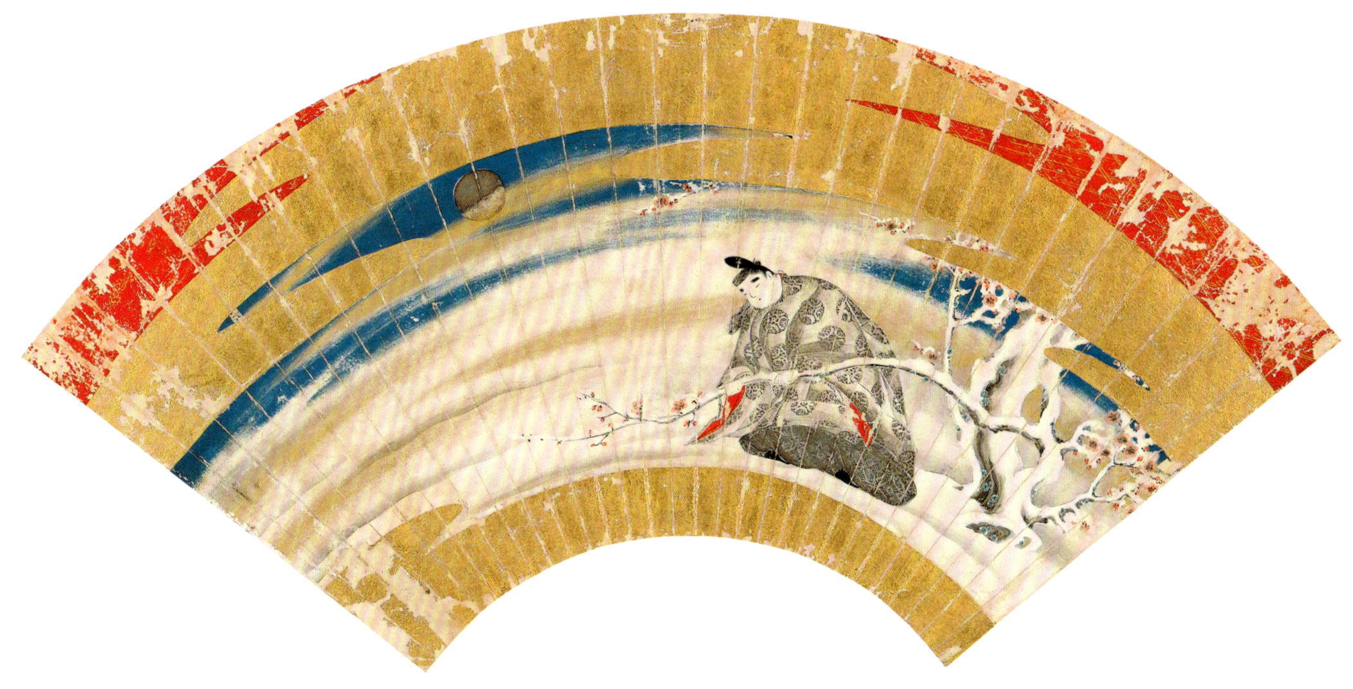

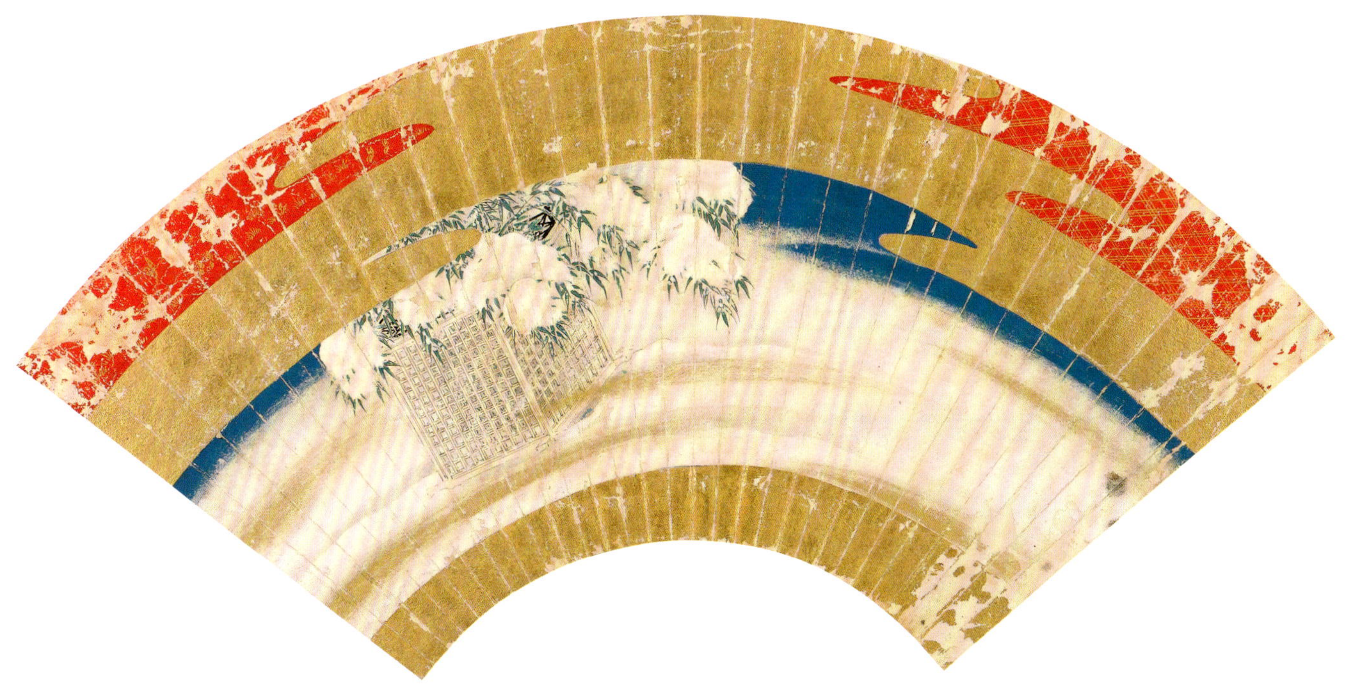

ATTRIBUTED TO OKADA (OR REIZEI) TAMETAKA (OR TAMECHIKA)
(岡田「冷泉」為恭; 1823–1864)

440. Breaking a Plum Branch on a Snowy Night; Bamboo in Snow

Edo period
Pair of painted fans, mounted on panels; ink, color, and gold on paper
Each fan 18.8 x 48.7 cm ($7^{3}/_{8}$ x $19^{1}/_{8}$ in.)

LITERATURE: Murase 1993, no. 40.

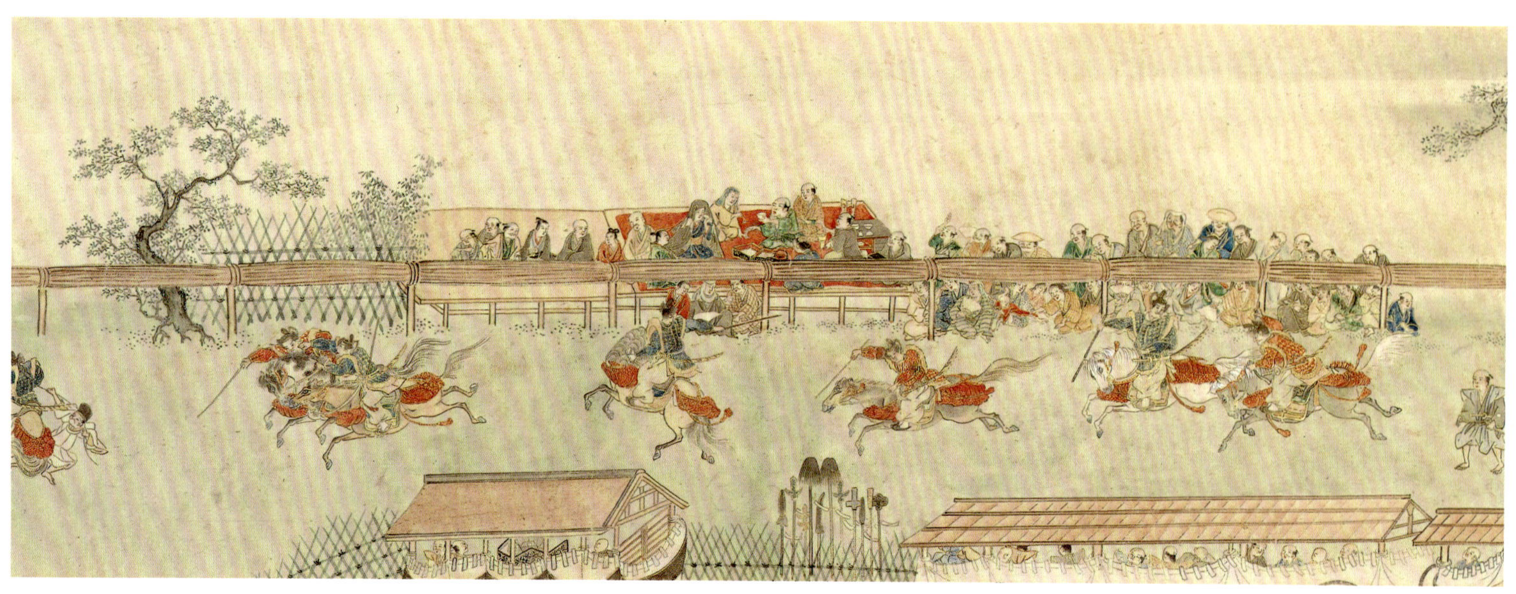

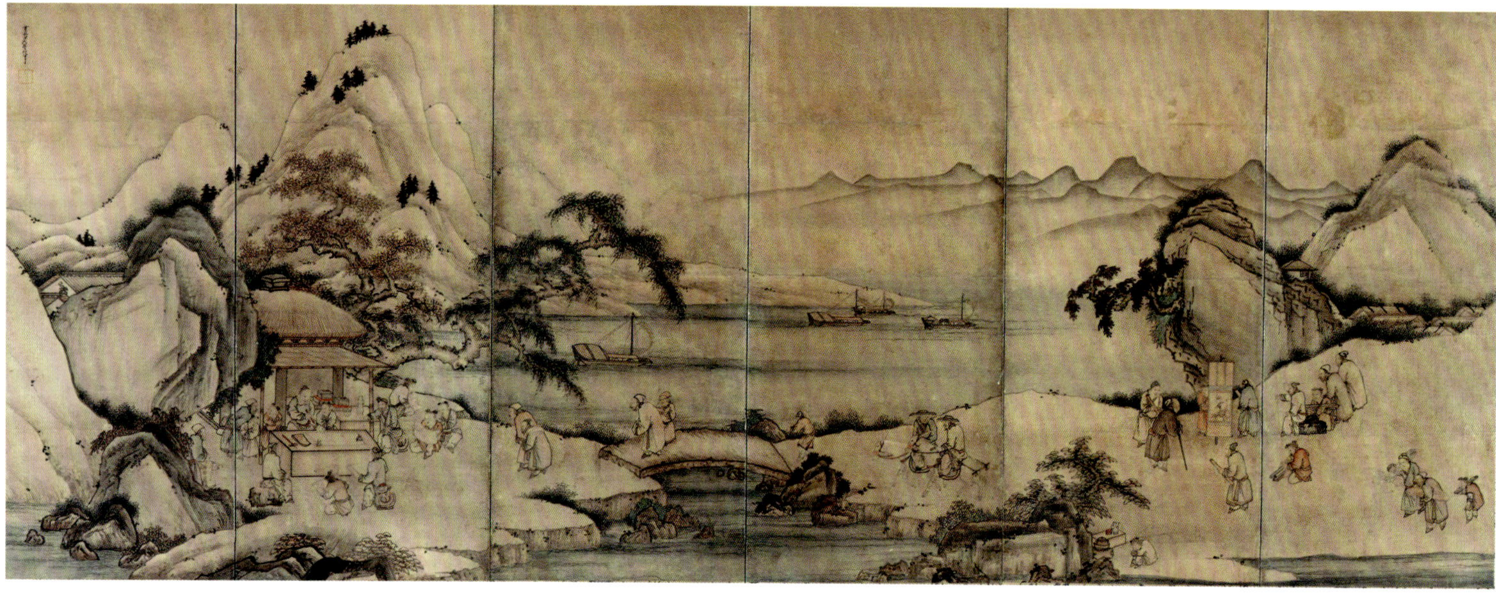

Various Schools

Sumiyoshi Hiromori
(住吉廣守; 1705–1777)

441. Horse Race at Kamo (賀茂競馬)

Edo period
Handscroll; ink, color and gold on paper
33.9 x 359.3 cm (13 3/8 in. x 11 ft. 9 1/2 in.)
Signature, seal

Literature: L. Cunningham 1984, no. 7; Guth 1992, pl. 1.

Untaku Tōetsu
(雲沢等悦; fl. ca. 1675)

442. Painting and Calligraphy from the Four Gentlemanly Accomplishments (琴棋書画の中、書画)

Edo period
Left screen from a pair of six-panel screens; ink and light color on paper
137.2 x 364 cm (54 in. x 11 ft. 11 1/4 in.)
Signature, seals

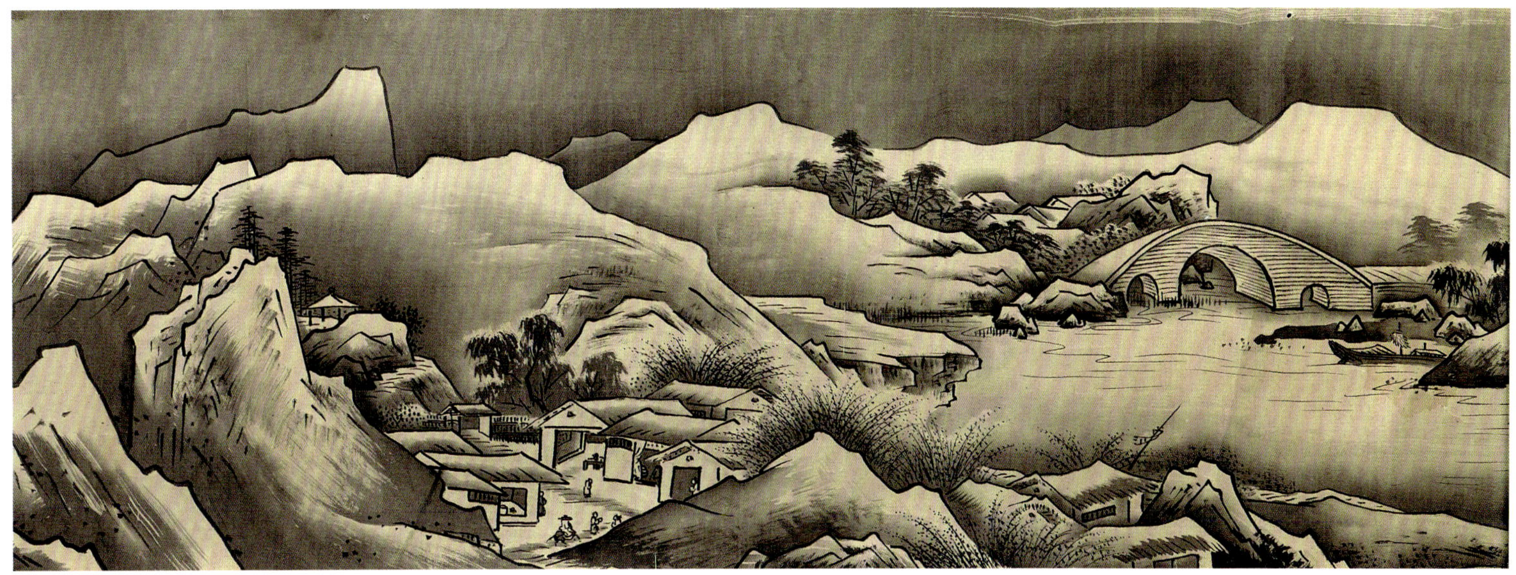

Unkoku Tōban
(雲谷等幡; 1635–1724)

443. Landscape

Edo period, 17th century
Handscroll; ink on silk
41.2 x 930 cm (16 1/4 in. x 30 ft. 6 1/8 in.)
Signature, seals

Kaihō Yūsetsu
(海北友雪; 1598–1677)

444. Shū Moshuku (Ch. Zhou Maoshu) Contemplating a Lotus Blossom (周茂叔愛蓮)

Edo period
Hanging scroll; ink on silk
32.4 x 49.8 cm (12 3/4 x 19 5/8 in.)
Signature, seals

Literature: Murase 1993, no. 22.

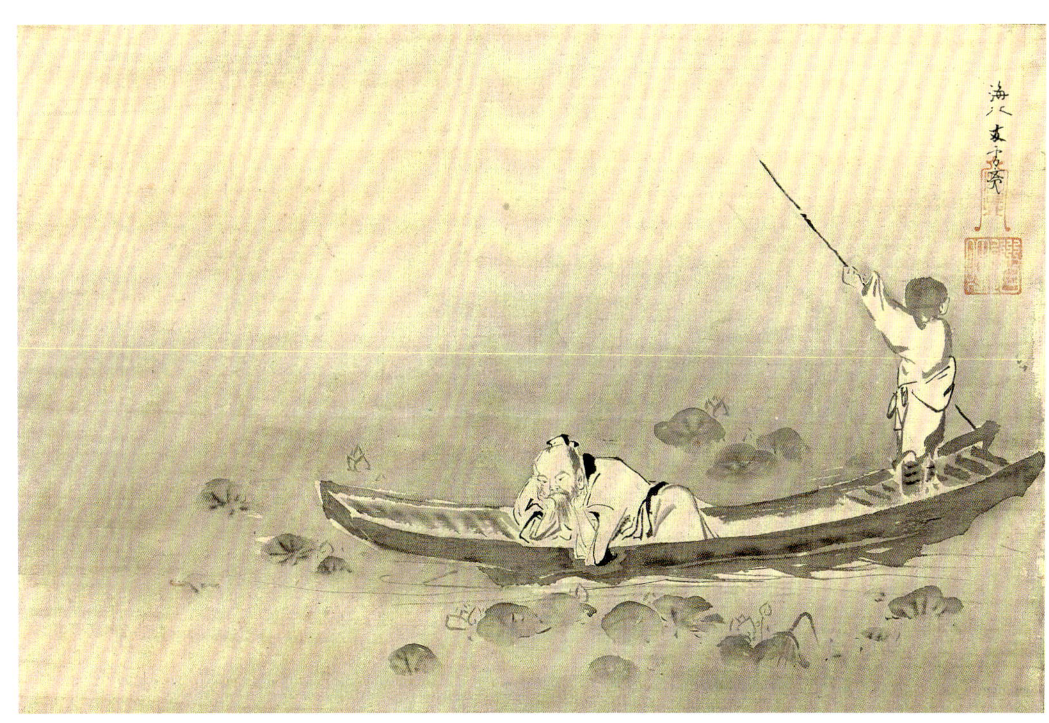

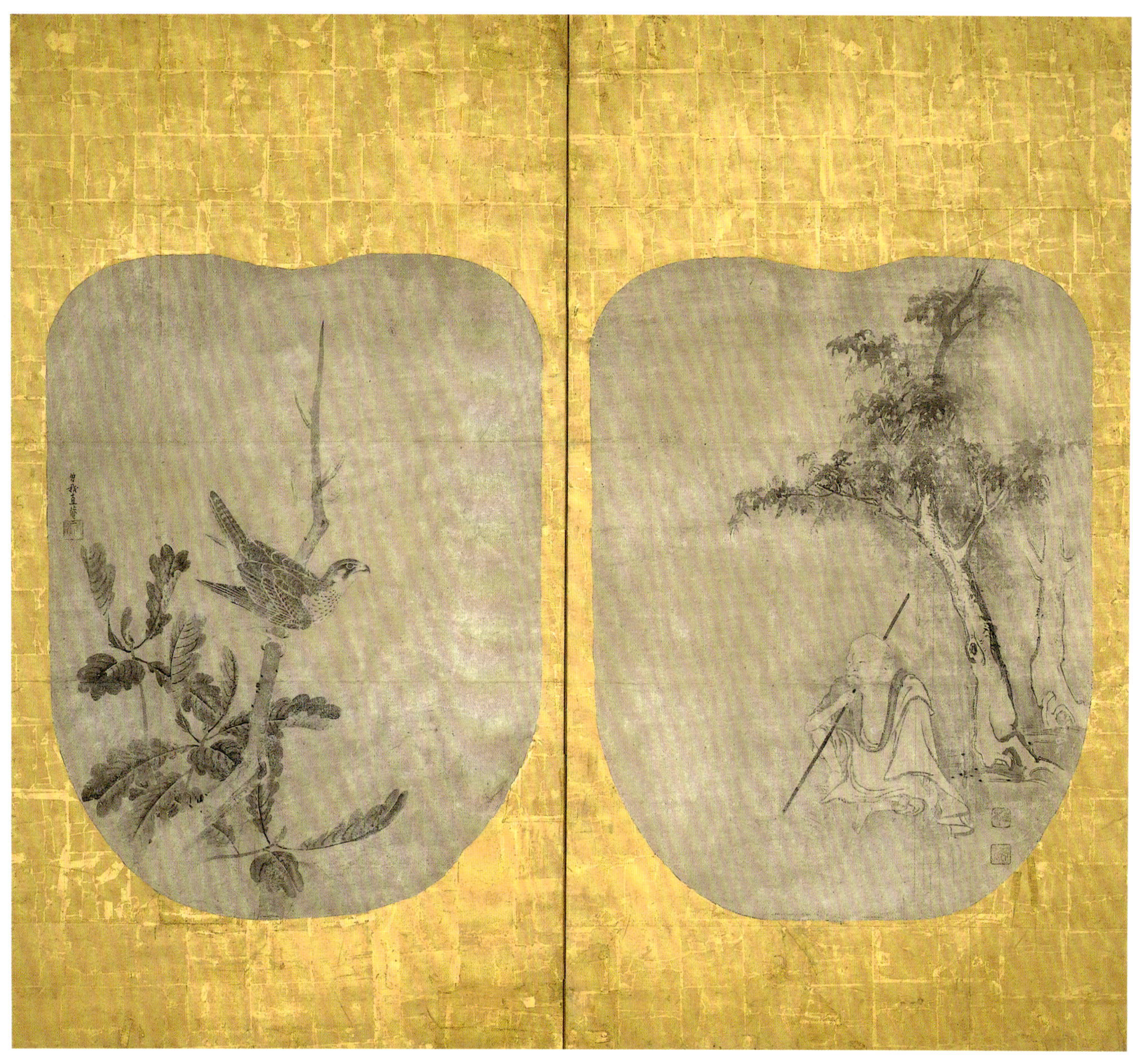

Soga Nichokuan
(曾我二直庵; fl. mid-17th century)

445. Daoist Immortal and Hawk on an Oak Tree

Edo period
Pair of fan-shaped paintings, mounted on a two-panel folding screen, ink on paper
Each painting 98.9 x 76 cm (39 x 29 7/8 in.), overall screen 155.1 x 171.2 cm (61 x 67 3/8 in.)
Signature, seals

Literature: Hayashi Susumu 1980, p. 51, no. 50 (right panel only); Tokyo National Museum 1985a, no. 35; Lillehoj 1989, fig. 5; Avitabile 1990, no. 79; Murase 2000, no. 106.

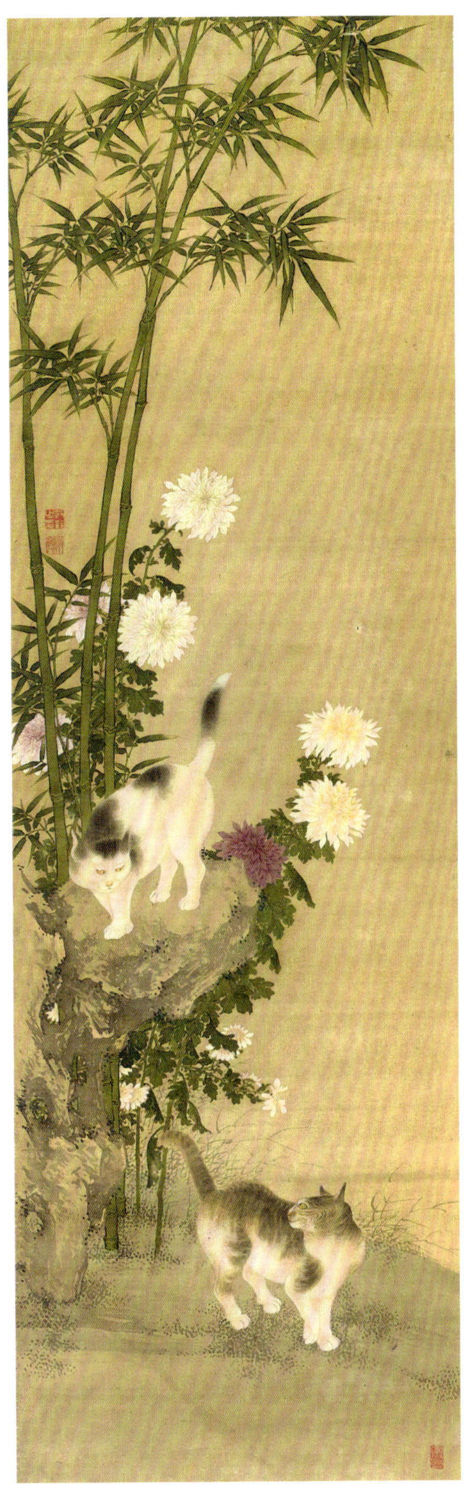

Nagasaki School

Chin Sen
(Ch. Shen Quan, 沈銓, also known as Chin Nanpin [沈南蘋]; 1682–after 1758)

446. Cats by Bamboo and Chrysanthemums

Edo period, ca. 1732
Hanging scroll; ink and color on silk
146.5 x 45.9 cm (57⅝ x 18⅛ in.)
Seals

Chin Sen
(Ch. Shen Quan, 沈銓, also known as Chin Nanpin [沈南蘋]; 1682–after 1758)

447. Cat and Butterfly among Peonies

Edo period, ca. 1732
Hanging scroll; ink and color on silk
38.1 x 51.3 cm (15 x 20¼ in.)
Signature, seals

448. Rakan (羅漢)

Edo period
Handscroll; ink and color on paper
28.3 x 548.2 cm (11⅛ x 17 ft. 11⅞ in.)
Seals

Ex coll.: Hekiko Sōdō

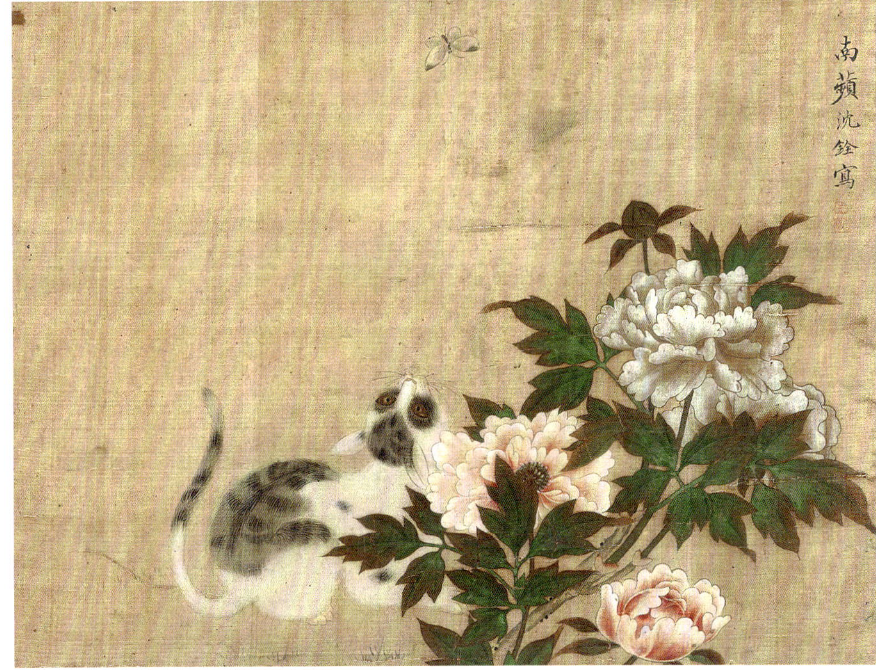

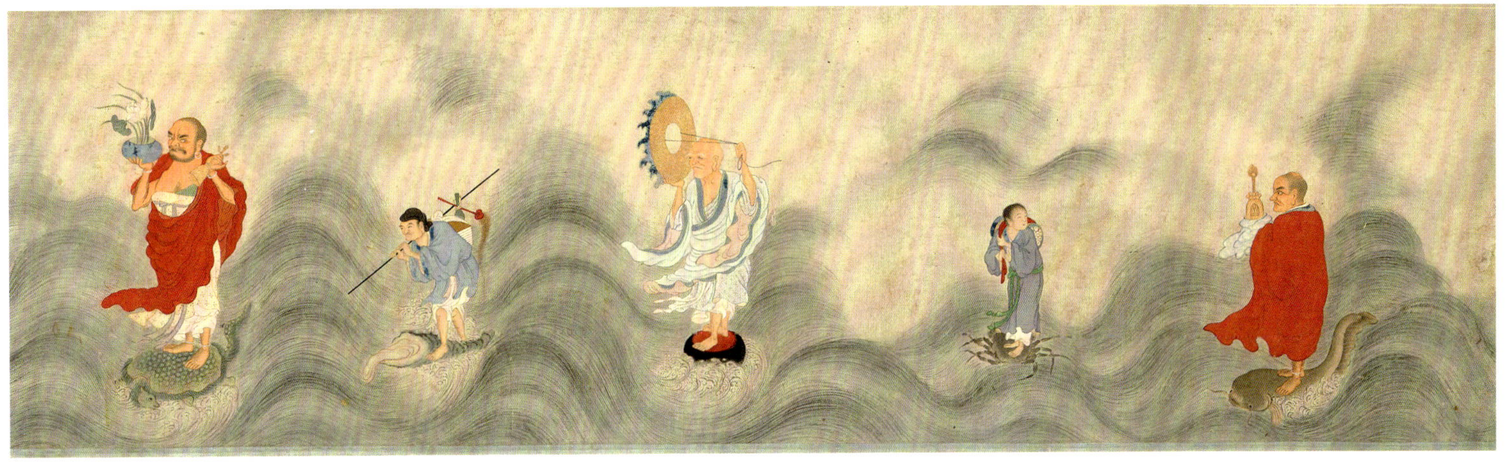

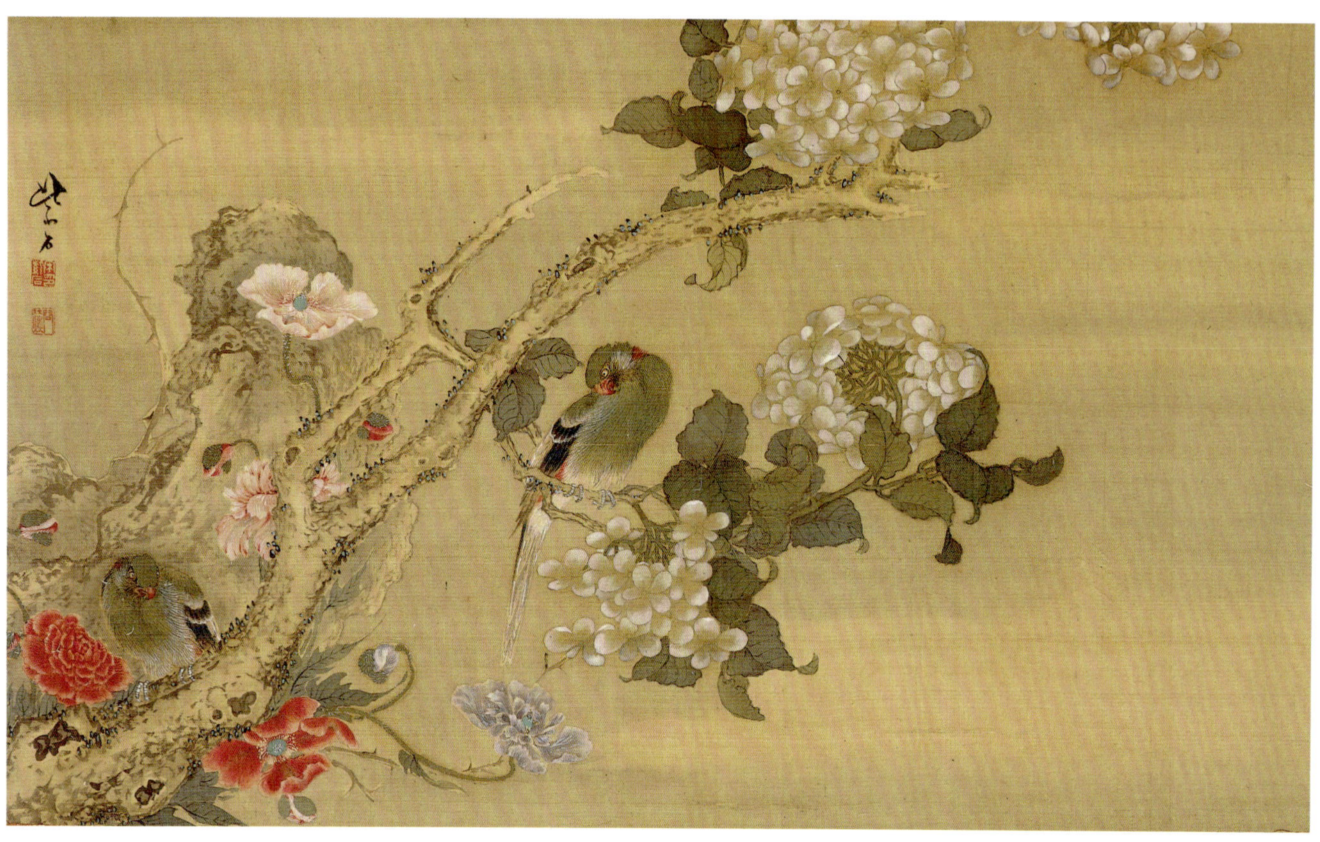

Sō Shiseki
(宋紫石; 1715–1786)

449. Parakeets among Flowers

Edo period, after 1770
Hanging scroll; ink and color on silk
34.8 x 57.8 cm (13 3/4 x 22 3/4 in.)
Signature, seals

Literature: Murase 1993, no. 23; Tsuji Nobuo et al. 2005, no. 105.

Kakuō
(鶴翁; fl. early 19th century)

450. Bird on a Plum Tree

Edo period
Hanging scroll; ink and color on paper
115 x 28.3 cm (45 1/4 x 11 1/8 in.)
Signature, seals

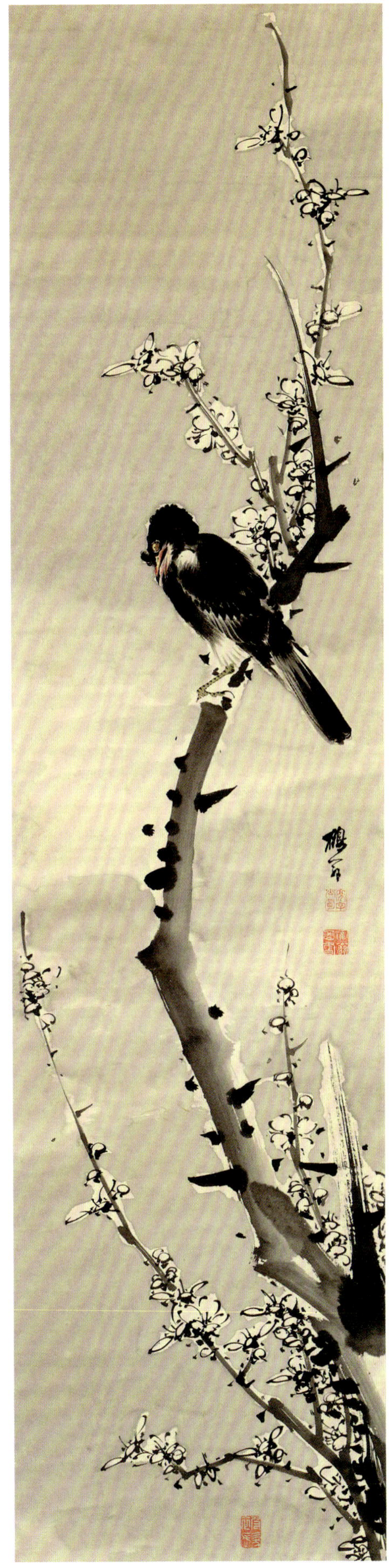

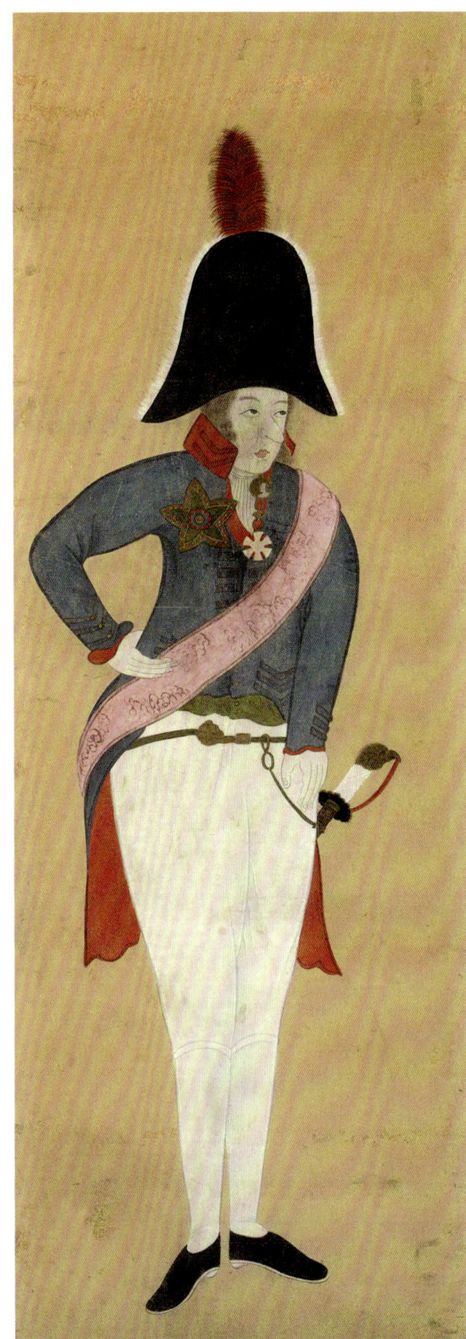

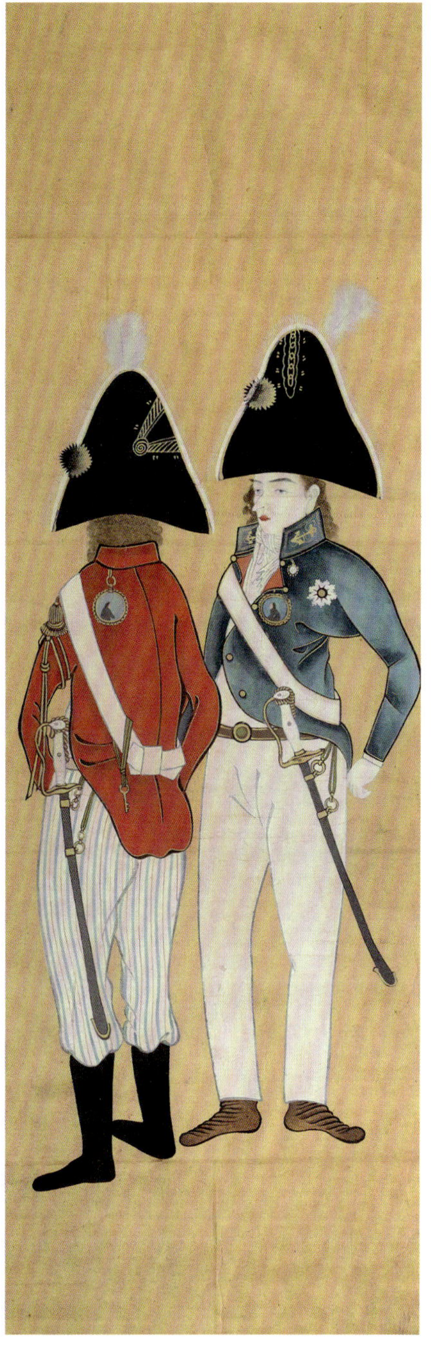

451. Russian Admiral

Edo period, 19th century
Framed painting; ink and color on paper
92.8 x 32.7 cm (36½ x 12⅞ in.)

452. Two Russian Soldiers

Edo period, 19th century
Framed painting; ink, color, and gold on paper
43.2 x 119.4 cm (17 x 47 in.)

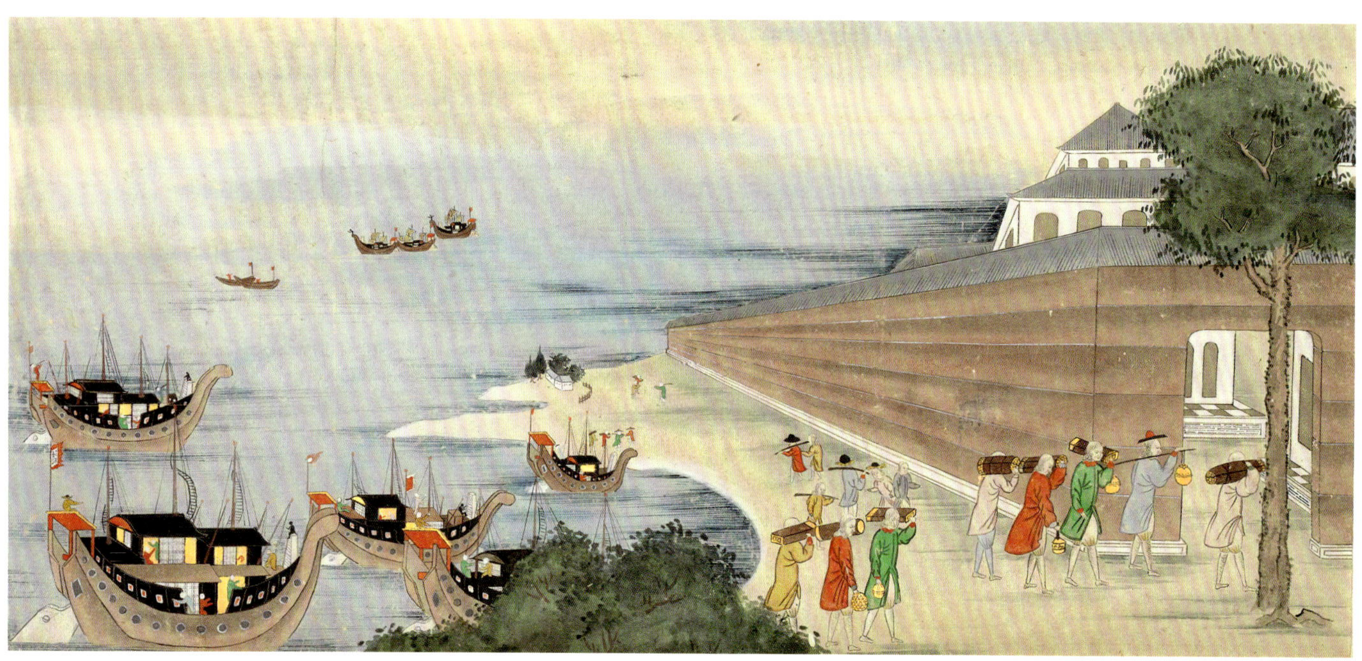

453. Scene at Dejima (出島)

Edo period, 19th century
Framed painting; ink, color, and gold on paper
32 x 68.8 cm (12 5/8 x 27 1/8 in.)

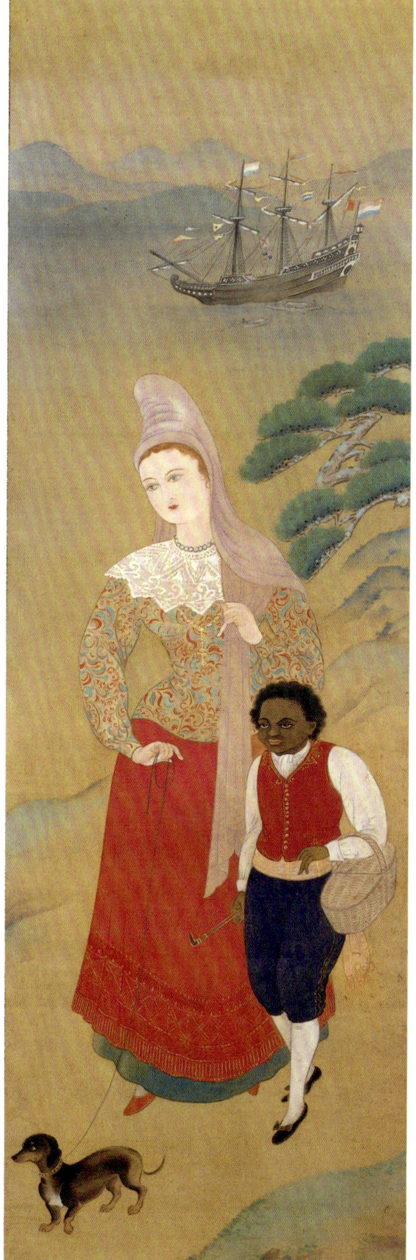

454. Dutch Lady with a Servant

Edo period, 18th century
Hanging scroll; ink and color on silk
106.5 x 34.5 cm (41 7/8 x 13 5/8 in.)

Literature: Burke 1993, pl. 11/no. 11; Tsuji Nobuo et al. 2005, no. 106.

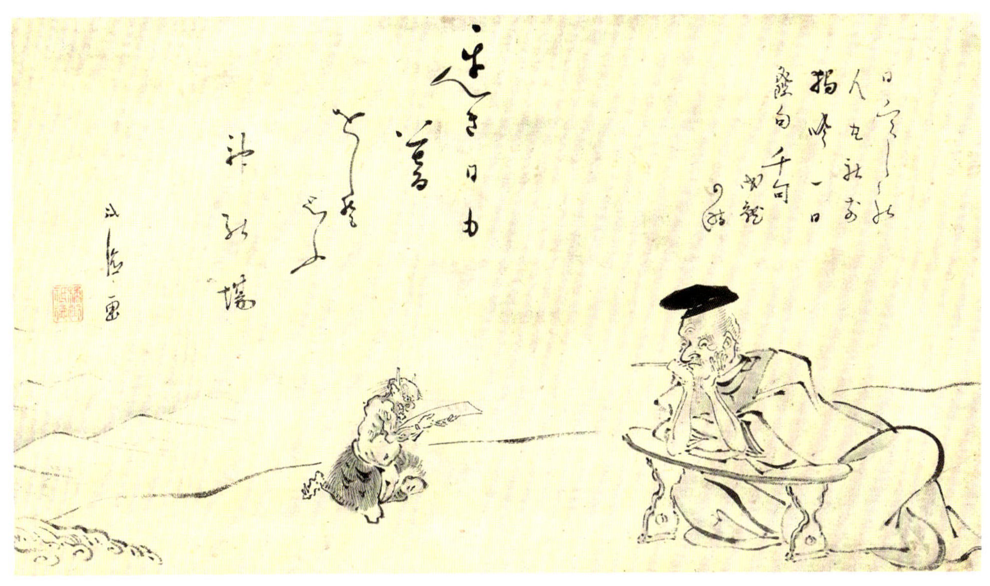

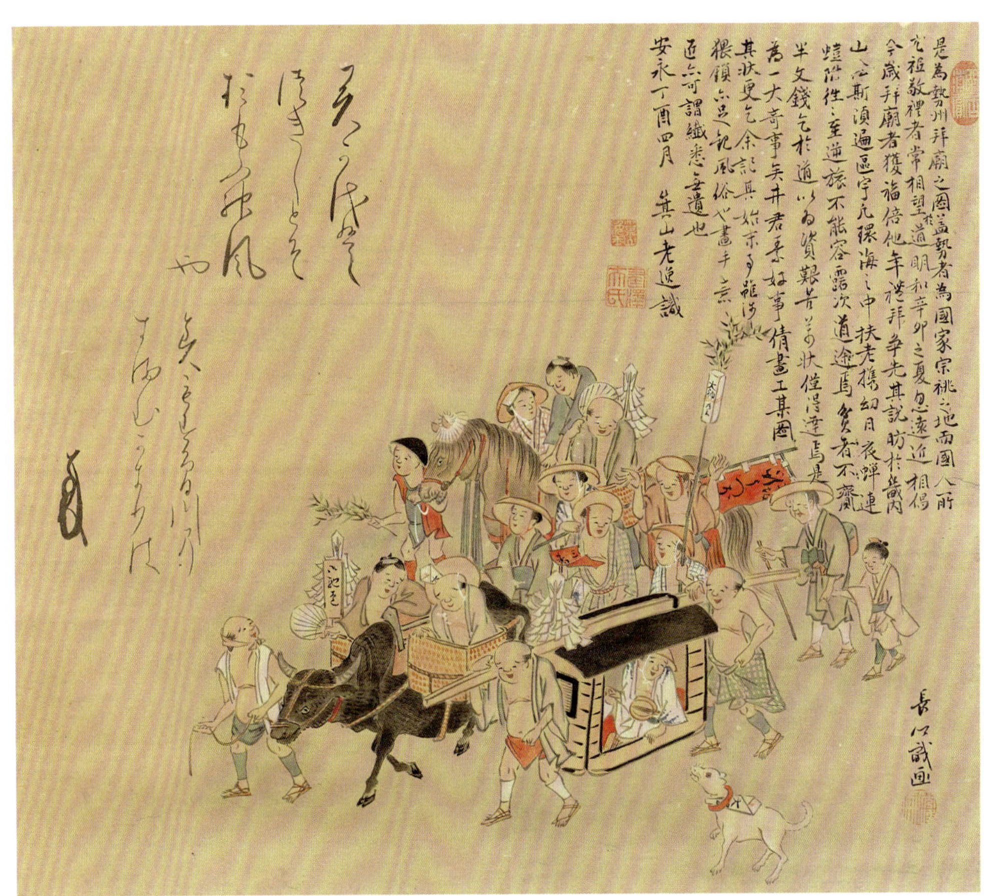

Others

Jochiku
(如竹; fl. mid-17th century?)

455. Eggplants

Edo period
Hanging scroll; ink on paper
111.3 x 17.6 cm (43⅞ x 6⅞ in.)
Signature, seal

Gift from the Ōkura family, 1977

Tachibana Gitoku
(橘祇徳; d. 1767)

456. Composing One Thousand Poems in a Day

Edo period
Hanging scroll; ink on paper
26.5 x 47.2 cm (10⅜ x 18⅝ in.)
Text, signature, seal

Chōgō
(長郷; fl. 18th century)

457. Pilgrimage to Ise (伊勢)

Edo period, 1777
Hanging scroll; ink and light color on paper
48.3 x 55.5 cm (19 x 21⅞ in.)
Text, signatures, seals

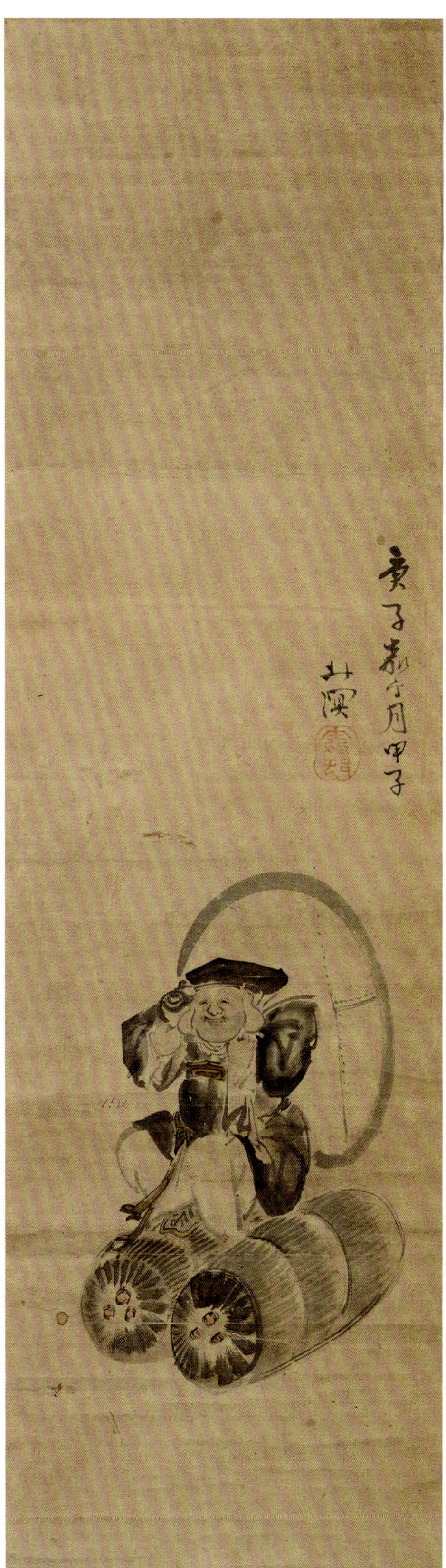

Ikuta Hokumei
(生田北溟; mid-19th century)

458. Daikokuten (大黒天)

Edo period
Hanging scroll; ink and light color on paper
99.5 x 28.3 cm ($39\frac{1}{8}$ x $11\frac{1}{8}$ in.)
Signature, seal

Ex coll.: Frank E. Hart

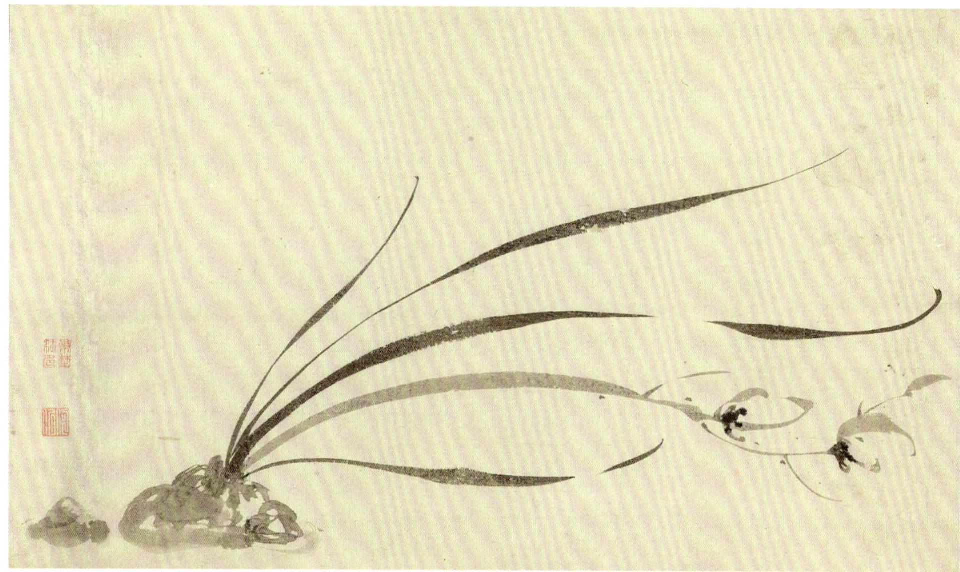

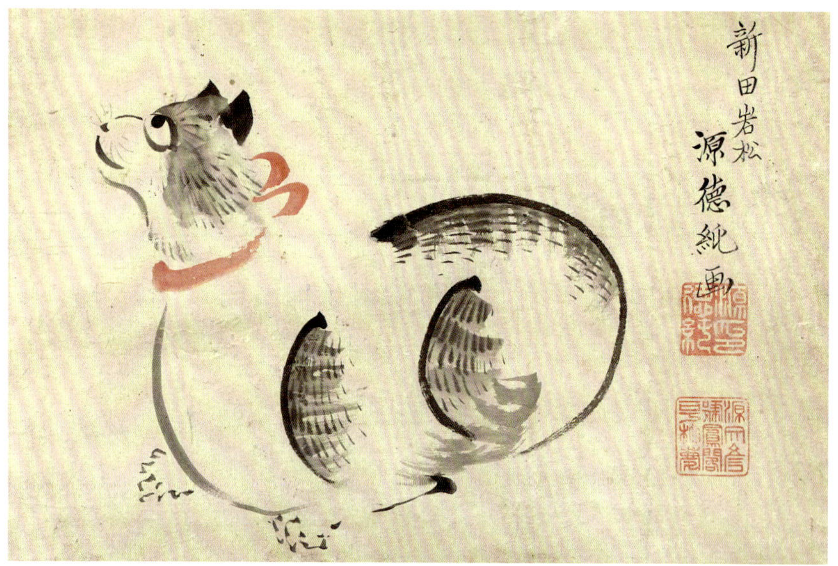

Tōno Sōkai
(東埜; 19th century)

459. Orchid

Edo period
Hanging scroll; ink on paper
30.3 x 52.7 cm (12 x $20\frac{3}{4}$ in.)
Seals

Iwamatsu Tokujun
(岩松徳純; 18th–19th century)

460. Cat

Edo period
Hanging scroll; ink and light color on paper
29.8 x 45.5 cm ($11\frac{3}{4}$ x $17\frac{7}{8}$ in.)
Signature, seals

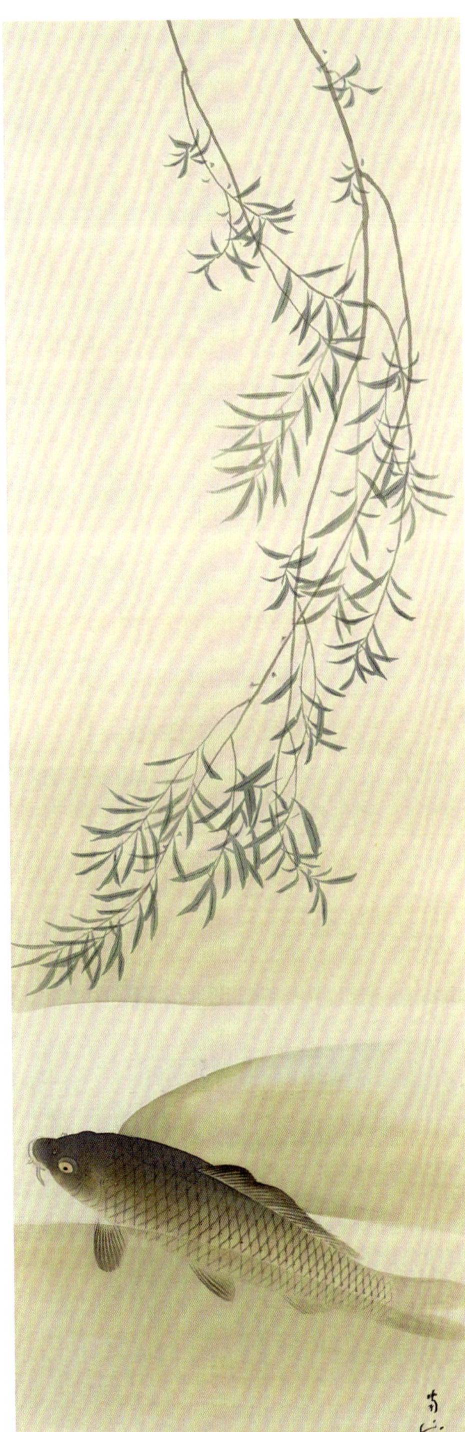

Nanzan Jusei
(南山寿星; Meiji era)

461. Carp

Meiji era
Hanging scroll; ink and color on silk
116.2 x 35.5 cm (45 3/4 x 14 in.)
Signature, seal

Gift from the Ōkura family, 1977

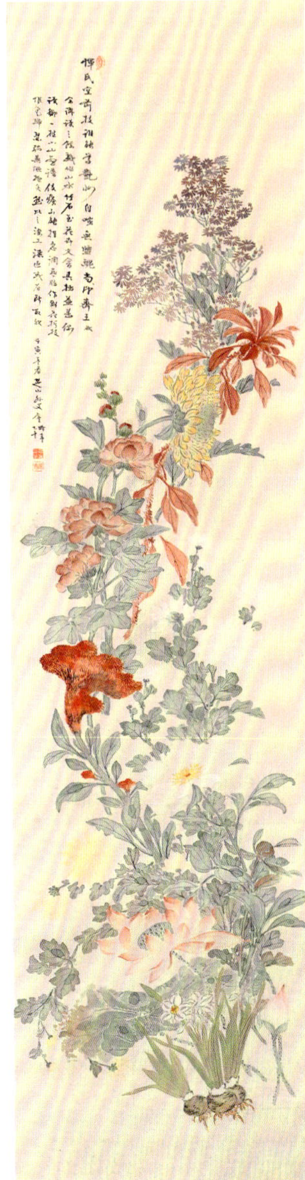

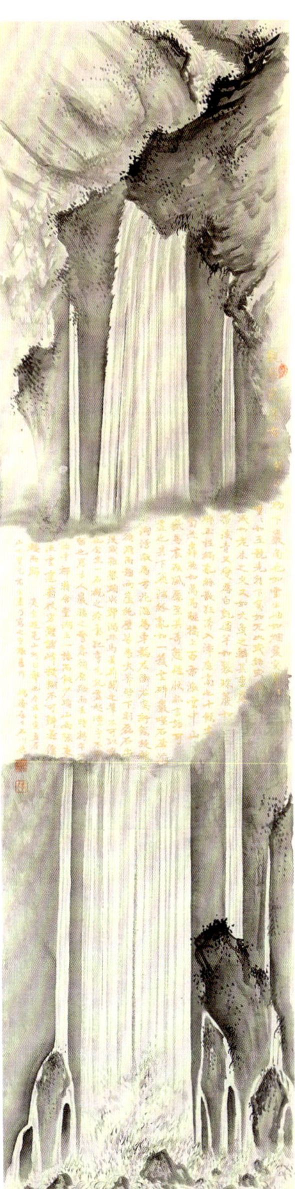

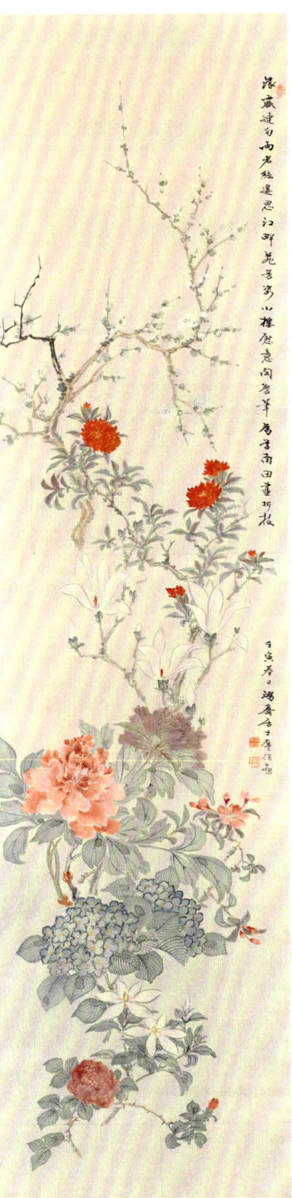

Ishikawa Kōsai
(石川鴻斎; late 19th–early 20th century)

462. Kegon Falls and Flowers

Meiji era, 1902
Triptych of hanging scrolls: two panels of flowers flanking central panel depicting *Viewing Kegon Falls* (観華厳滝); ink, color, and gold on silk
Each panel 111.8 x 29 cm (44 x 11 3/8 in.)
Text, signatures, seals

Gift from Leighton R. Longhi to the Mary and Jackson Burke Foundation, 1986

Shūtō (秋濤; fl. 20th century)
and six others

463. Buddhist Jewels (宝珠)

Taishō–Shōwa era
Hanging scroll; ink on silk
121.7 x 35.5 cm ($47\frac{7}{8}$ x 14 in.)
Signatures

Shinoda Tōkō
(篠田桃紅; b. 1913)

464. Boat

Shōwa era
Two-panel screen; silver on blue paper
33.4 x 176 cm ($13\frac{1}{8}$ x $69\frac{1}{4}$ in.)
Seal

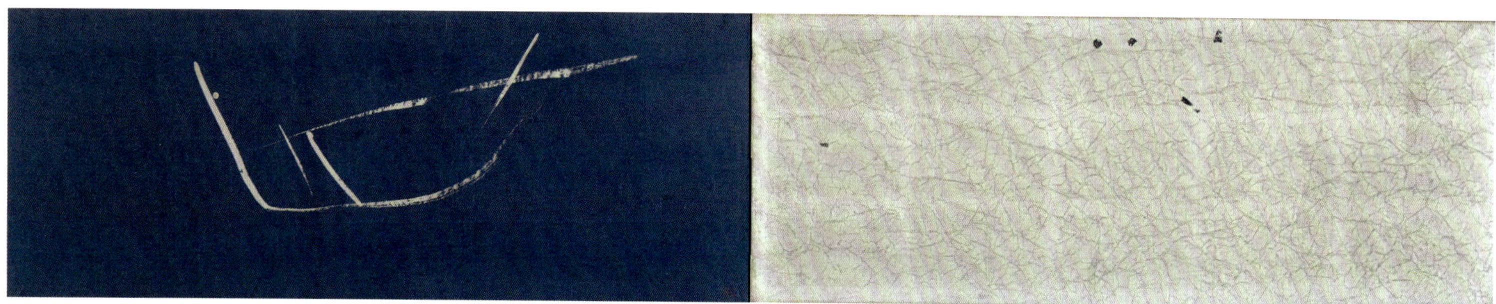

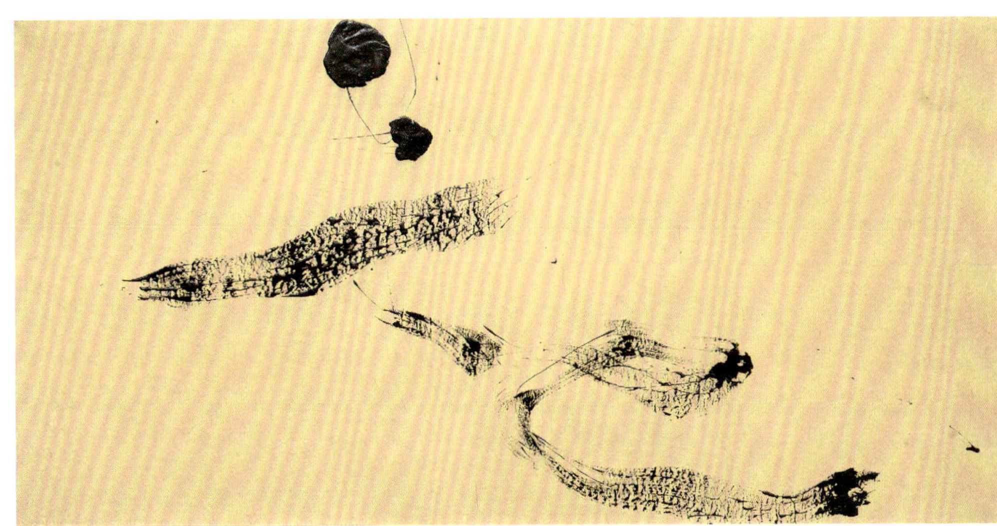

Morita Shiryū
(森田子龍; b. 1912)

465. Untitled

Shōwa era
Ink on paper
180.3 x 136.5 cm (71 x 53 3/4 in.)
Signature, seal

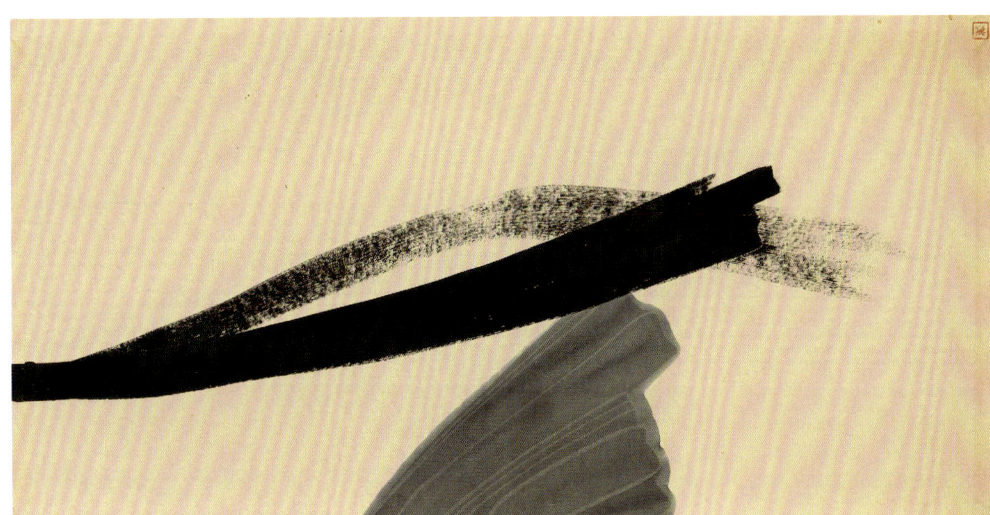

Shinoda Tōkō
(篠田桃紅; b. 1913)

466. Movement and Stillness

Shōwa era, 1964
Ink on paper
91.4 x 182.8 cm (36 x 72 in.)
Seal

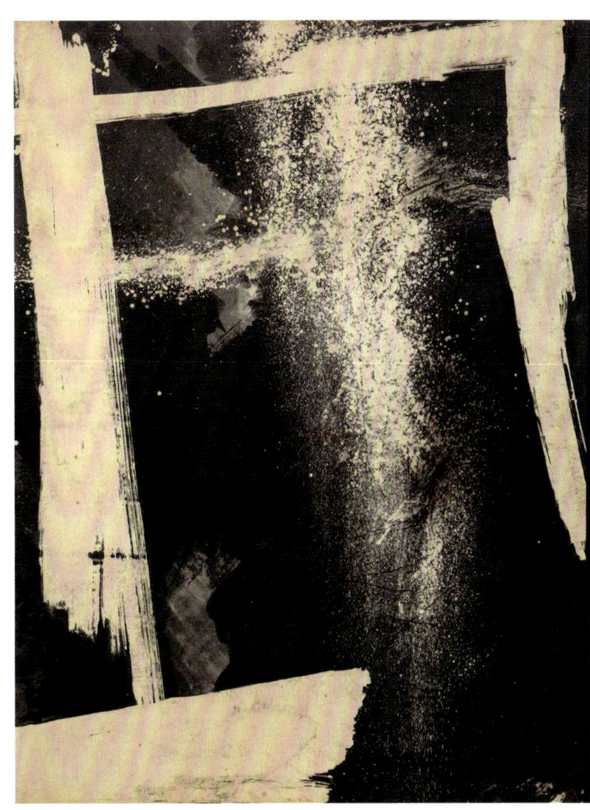

Shinoda Tōkō
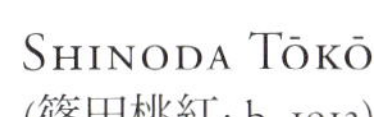
(篠田桃紅; b. 1913)

467. Untitled

Shōwa era
Ink and paint on paper
180.3 x 136.5 cm (71 x 53 3/4 in.)
Signature, seal

Chapter 10 Details

† *denotes illustrated items*

419. Pictures with Letters

Text

[recto]
Fukurokuju; [for the figure] *Fukurokuju*

[verso]
Saigyō hōshi; [for the figure] *Saigyō hōshi // Does the moon say "Grieve!" / Does it force / these thoughts on me? / And yet the tears come / to my reproving eyes.*

Signature

[on page inscribed "*Toshi no hajime*"] *Inscribed by Iwasa Matabei*

† 420. Hotei

Seal

[at lower right] *Shōjō*

Text

by Kozan Dōjin
A floating skiff, / pavilions and grand halls in the other realm, / soundless wind and waves, / a serene face turning upward.

Signature

Kozan Dōjin mansan

Seals

Kōko; *Shōkō*

421. Mt. Fuji

Text

by Mitsuhiro
White clouds, appearing like a cloth in the sky, / compete with the festive feeling in my mind.

Signature

Inscribed by Mitsuhiro

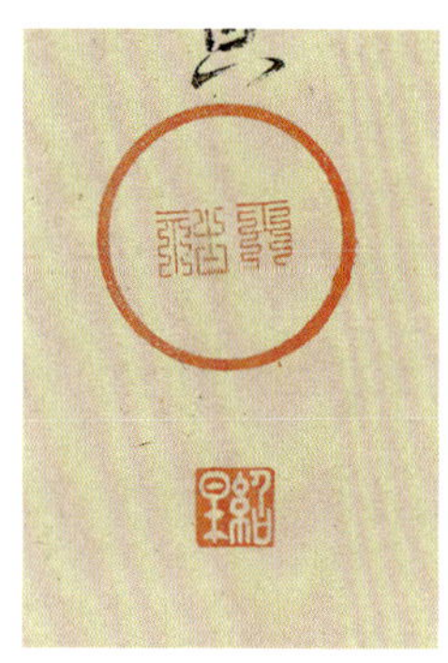

420

420

† 422. Hotei

Text

by Seigan Sōi
Moving through past and present / is this Hotei? / In myriad incarnations / in fish markets and wine shops.

Signature

Ryūfu Seigan, so-called Mansō Tokugō

Seals

Seigan; *Koroan*

† 423. Courtesan Enjoying a Cool Summer Evening

Signature

Crafted by Ukanshi Ritsuō at age 79

Seal

Ichiboku Hachion

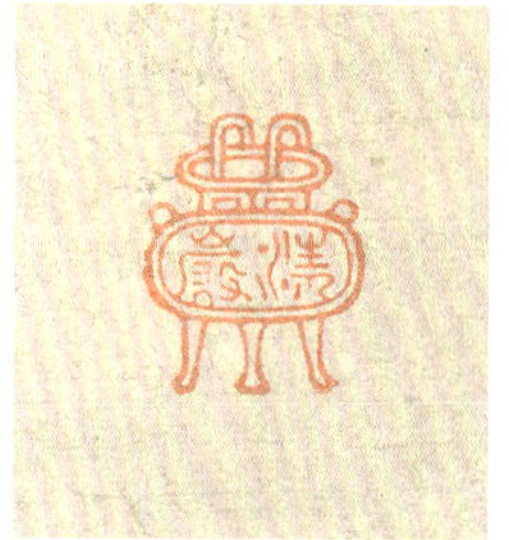

422

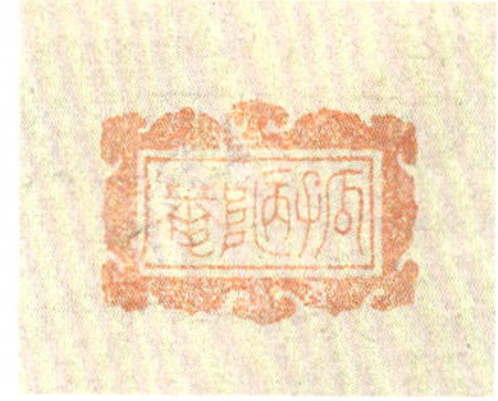

422

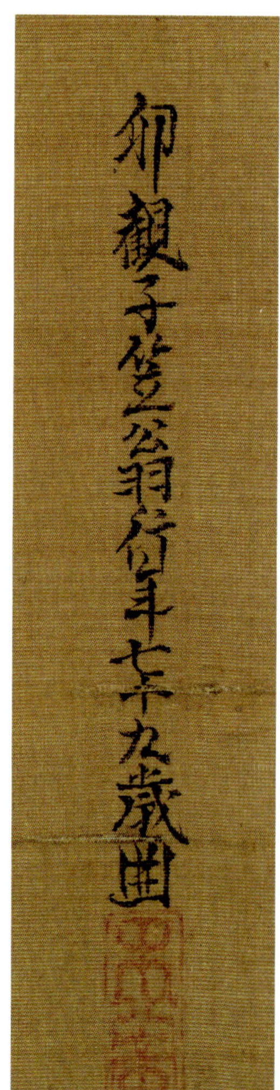

423

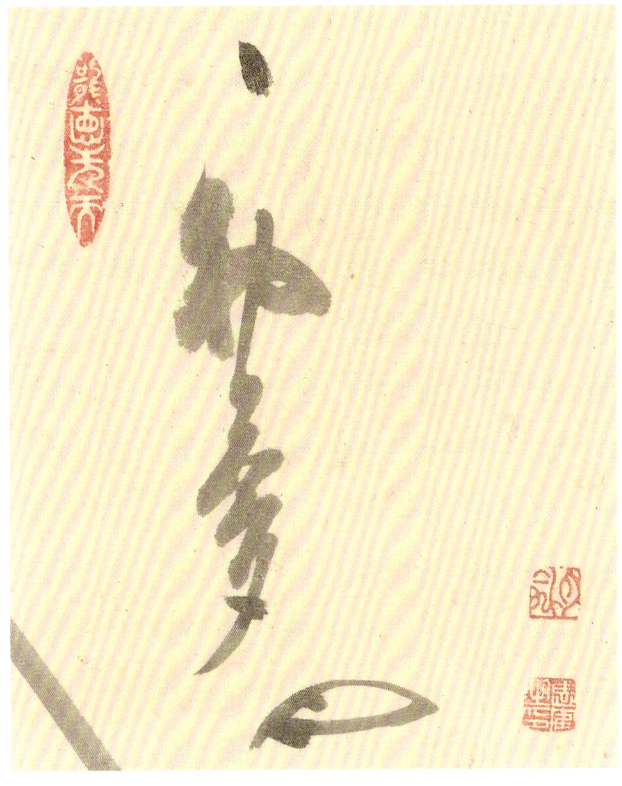

424

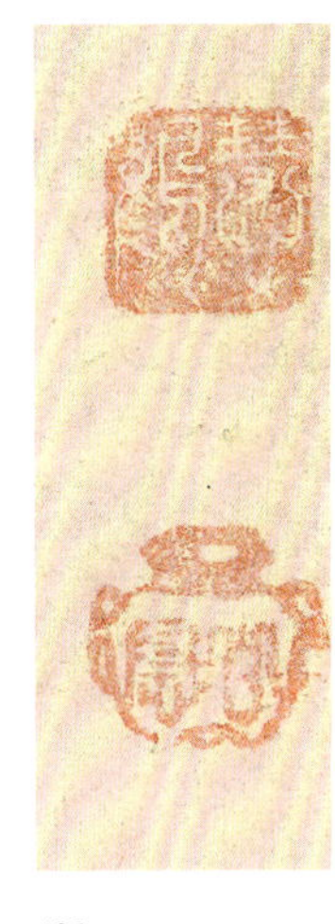

425

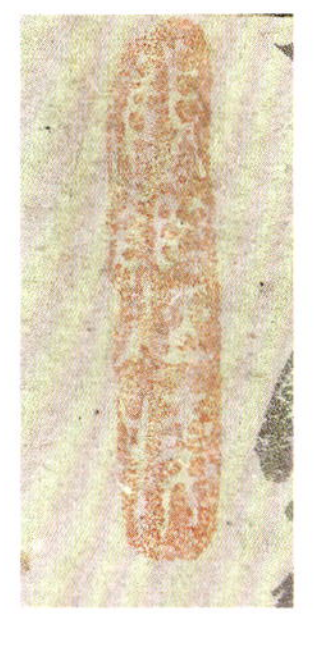

427

427

† 424. First Dream of the New Year

Text

by Hakuin
Hatsuyume

Seals

Hakuin; *Ekaku no in*; *kaō*; *Ryūtoku senten*

† 425. Tenjin on His Way to China

Text

by Hakuin
Without a Chinese robe, / yet known as the god of Kitano, / because of a branch of plum tree / held in a sleeve. / Figure made of characters for Namu Tenman Daijizai Tenjin.

Seals

Ekaku; *Shin'in*

426. Daruma

Signature

[at bottom, under subject, in red pigment] *Murasakino Mindō*

Seal

[at bottom] *Mindō*

Text

by Shōgetsuken
The fruit comes into being naturally; / one flower brings forth five leaves.

Signature

[above figure] *Inscribed by Shōgetsuken at the foot of Ryūhōzan*

Seals

[above figure] *Unshutsu Dōsanmei*; *Chūhō*; *Shōrō Sekkan*

† 427. Bird Catcher

Text

by Hakuin
Don't be a fool. / It's not a bird. It's only a straw sandal / that is looking for a wearer.

Seals

Hakuin; *Ekaku no in*; [illegible]

† 428. White Plum Blossoms and Moon

Text

by Jakuchū
[The white blossoms] resemble white snowflakes. / They are pure all alone, / oblivious of spring.

428

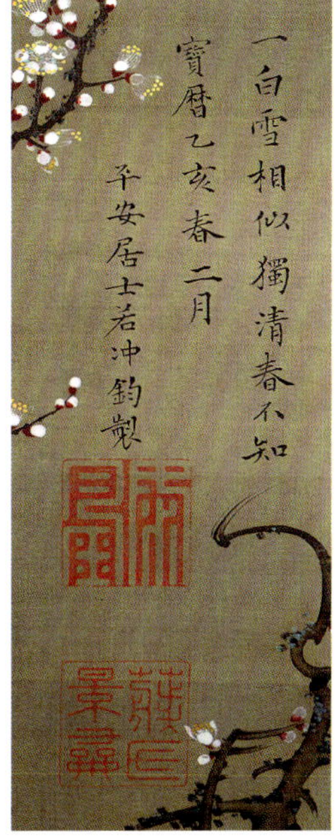

428

Signature

Spring, second month, year of the boar, fifth year of the Hōreki era [1755] */ Respectfully painted by Jakuchū, Heian koji*

Seals

Jokin; *Tōshi Keiwa*; [lower left] *Expressing new ideas within the framework of rules*

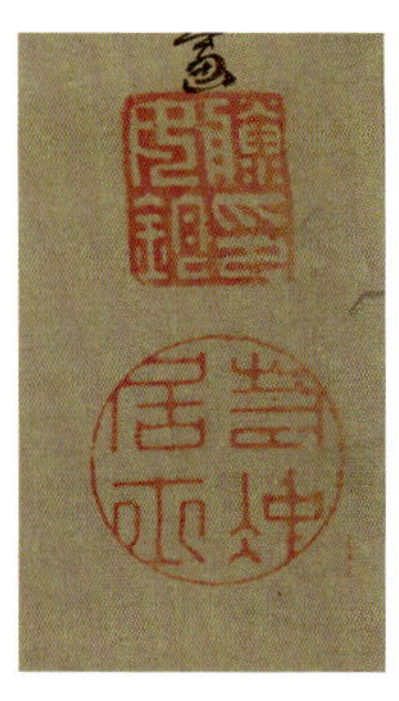

429

430

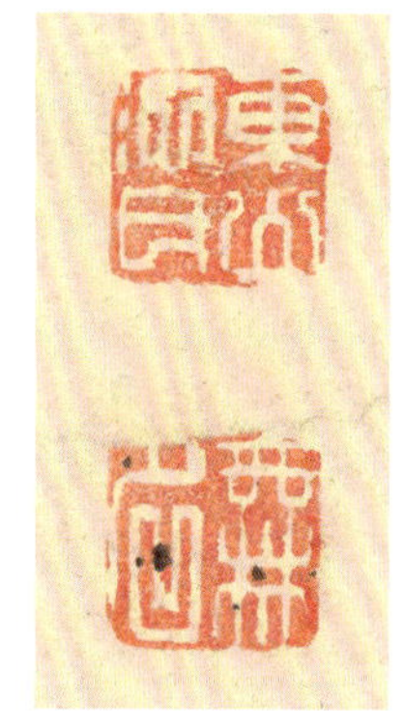

431

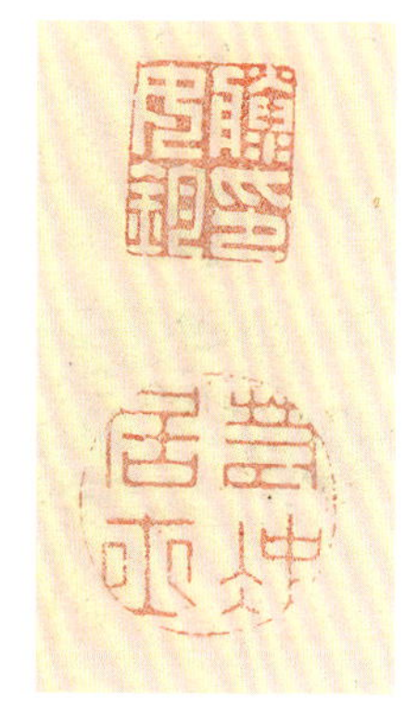

431

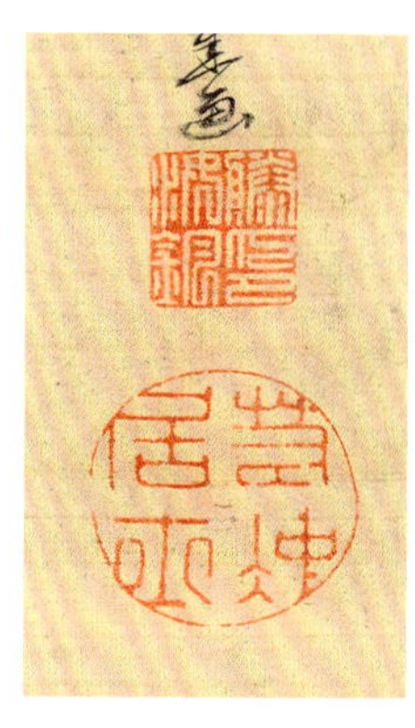

432

† 429. Two Cranes

Signature

Painted by Beito-ō at age 83

Seals

Tō Jokin in; *Jakuchū koji*

† 430. Nightingale on a Plum Tree

Signature

Painted by Beito-ō at age 80

Seals

Tō Jokin in; *Jakuchū koji*

† 431. Kanzan and Jittoku

Seals

[middle right edge] *Tō Jokin in*; *Jakuchū koji*

Text

by Ike Taiga (1723–1776)
One is the bodhisattva Fugen / and the other a grand Buddhist master. / How can one tell? / By the worn brooms, tattered sutras, and poems that follow no rhyme schemes.

Signature

[upper left] *Higashiyama Usō Mumei*

Seals

[upper left] *Higashiyama Ikeshi*; *Mumei*

† 432. Rooster and Family

Signature

Painted by Beito-ō at age 82

Seals

Tō Jokin in; *Jakuchū koji*

† 433. Roosters and Hens

Seals

[on each panel] *Tō Jokin in*; *Jakuchū koji*

434. Geese and Reeds

Seals

Tō Jokin in; *Jakuchū koji*

435. Turtle

Seals

Tō Jokin in; *Jakuchū koji*

† 436. Lions at the Stone Bridge of Tendaisan (Ch. Tiantaishan)

Signature

Painted by Soga Shōhaku

Seal

Jasokuken Shōhaku

Text

by Gazan Nansō (1727–1797)
Tendaisan [Mount Tiantai] *rises 48,000 feet high. / Fantastic crags, steep and sheer, lofty scarps reach for the sky. / At the top of a stone bridge there are arhats' footsteps. / Daoist mystics can circle about on their*

433

cranes too. / Without ridding all disturbances, one must not tread forward. / Oh, how extraordinary! He must have once been an immortal. / Innumerable lions and cubs appear at the tip of his brush. / Leading one another, they walk up and down, ferociously growling and snarling. / Scaling peaks, fording streams, the cubs strive for first place. / Among them is a big principal with eyes like stars in the sky. / Unenlightened cubs seeking the secret to truth would fall from the precipice. / Whether they can reverse their fate depends on how they reform their nature. / The marvel of the painter's superb skill cannot be expressed in words. / Though as superfluous as adding feet to a snake, may it last through endless generations.

Signature

Written in 1779 by Gazan Yōnansō

Seals

Soboku; *Yokuma Shūyō*

436

436

436

† 437. Legends of Kyoyū (Ch. Xuyou) and Sōho (Ch. Chaofu); Hakuraku (Ch. Bole)

Signatures

[on each screen] *Painted by Soga Jirō Teruo*

Seals

Soga Teruo; *Shōhaku*

† 438. Ten Rakan Examining a Painting of White-Robed Kannon

Signature

A part of the Hokekyō was respectfully copied by Enjinsai Nobukiyo

Seals

Nobukiyo; *Nobukiyo in*; *Kudoku muhen*; *A Treasure of the Edo Zen Temple Ryūkōji*

† 439. Court Lady with Painting of Japanese Sages

Text

by Tametaka

In our country's history of the wise and the learned, / how worthy they are . . . [illegible]

Signature

Painted by Kurōdodokoroshū Shōrokuinoge Shikibushō Tairokushin Sugawara Ason Tametaka

Seal

Suga

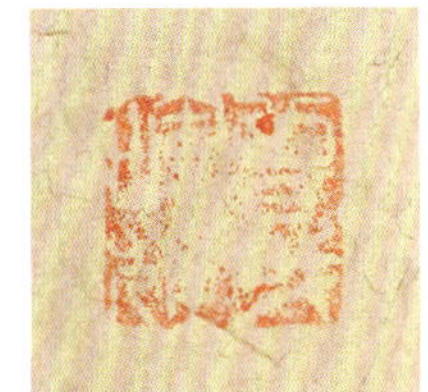

437

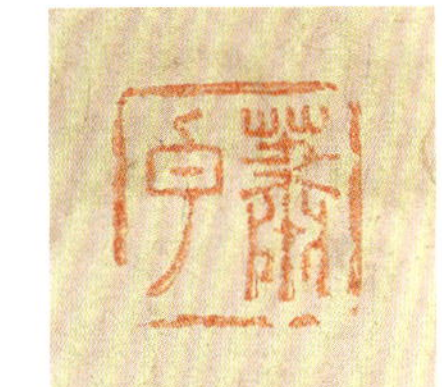

437

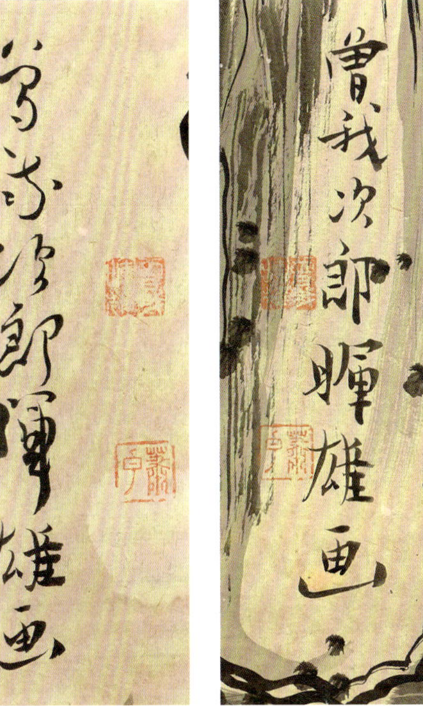

437 437

438

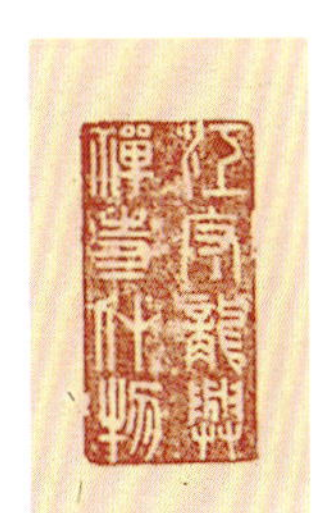

438

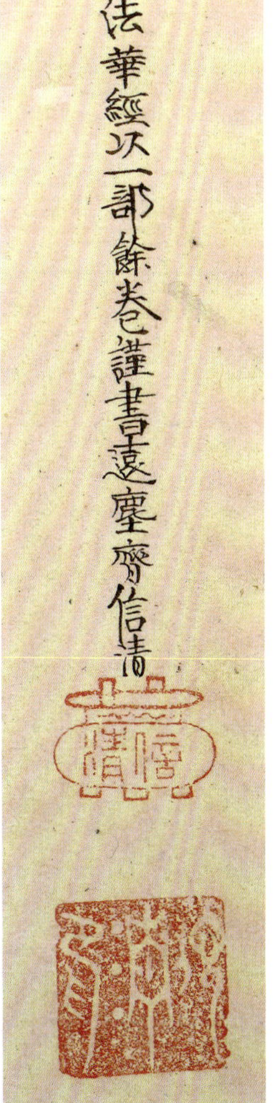

438

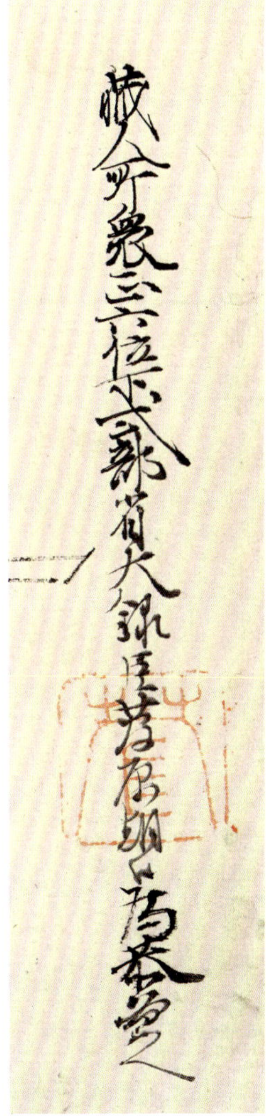

439

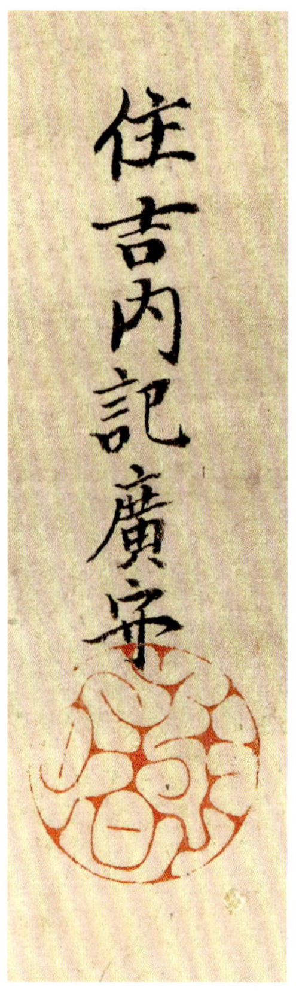

441

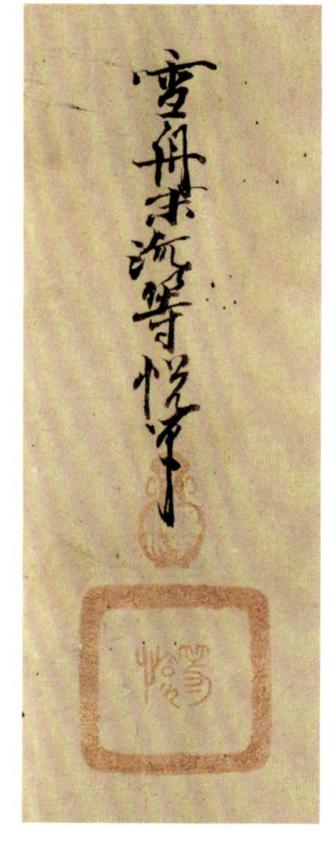

442

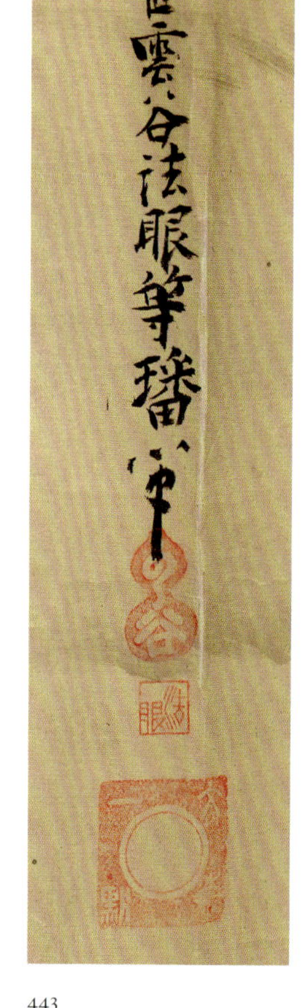

443

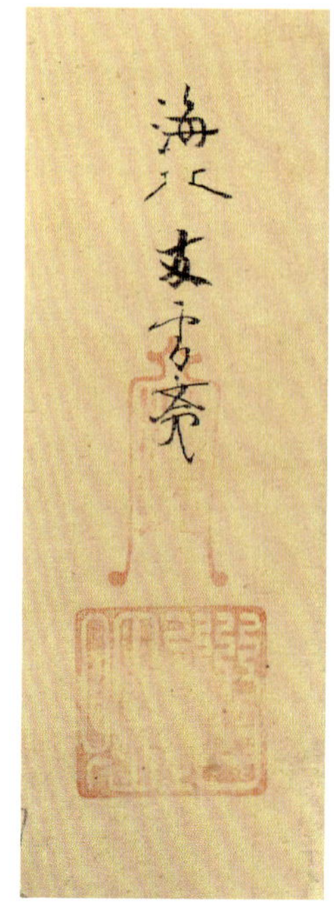

444

† 441. Horse Race at Kamo

Signature

[at end of scroll] *Sumiyoshi Naiki Hiromori*

Seal

[at end of scroll] Illegible

† 442. Painting and Calligraphy from the Four Gentlemanly Accomplishments

Signature

Painted by Sesshū matsuryū Tōetsu

Seals

Untaku; *Tōetsu*

† 443. Landscape

Signature

[at end of scroll] *Painted by the sixth descendant of Sesshū, Unkoku hōgen Tōban*

Seals

[at end of scroll] *Unkoku*; *Hōgen*; *Bun*[?] *Itten*

† 444. Shū Moshuku (Ch. Zhou Maoshu) Contemplating a Lotus Blossom

Signature

Kaihō Yūsetsusai

Seals

Kaiho; *Dōki*

† 445. Daoist Immortal and Hawk on an Oak Tree

Signature

[on left painting] *Soga Chokuan Ni*

Seals

[on right painting] *Nichokuan*; *Hōin*
[on left painting] *Hōin*

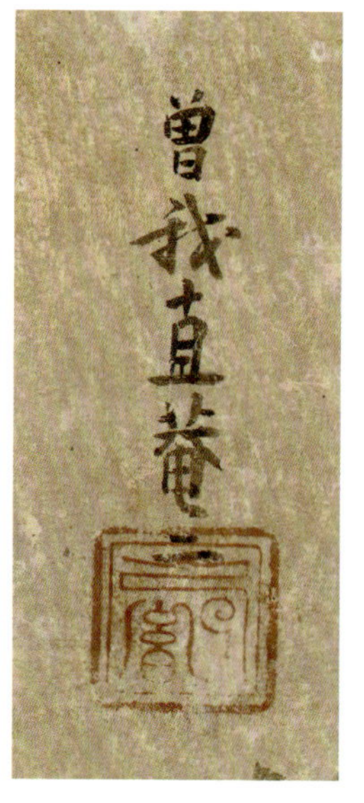

445

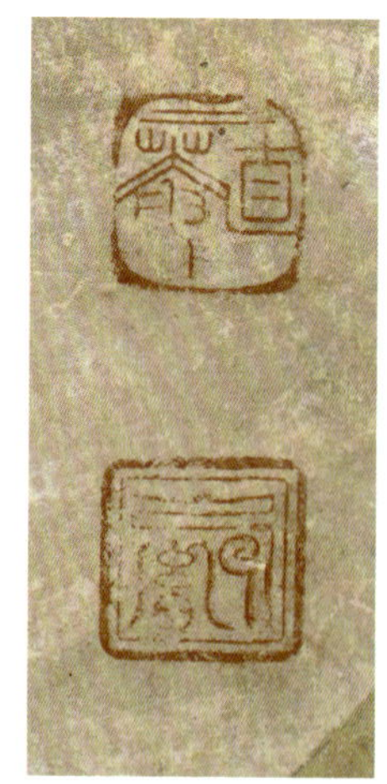

445

446

446

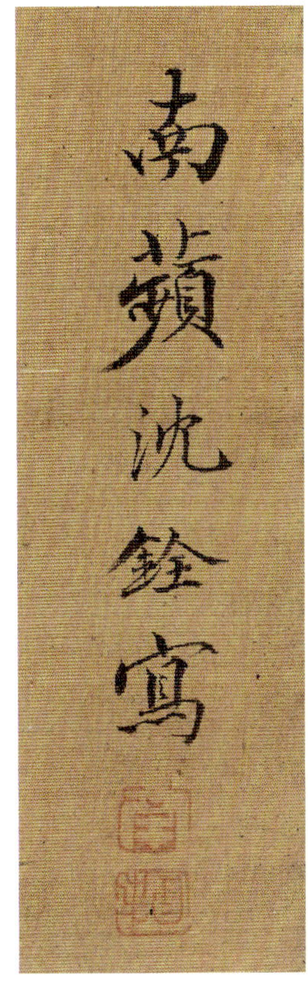

447

448

448

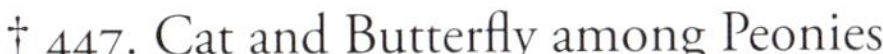

† 446. Cats by Bamboo and Chrysanthemums

Seals

Eisai; *Chin Sen no in*; *Nanpin shi*

† 447. Cat and Butterfly among Peonies

Signature

Painted by Nanpin Chinsen

Seals

Illegible

† 448. Rakan

Seals

[at beginning of scroll] *Go Shin no in*; *Wukyūsai* [?]
[at end of scroll] *Hekiko Sōdō chingan*

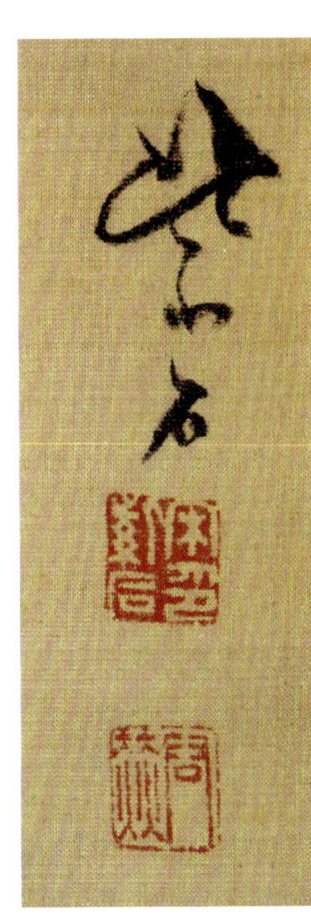

449

† 449. Parakeets among Flowers

Signature

Shiseki

Seals

Sō Shiseki in; *Kunkaku*

† 450. Bird on a Plum Tree

Signature

Kakuō

Seals

Ryō aza Shōmei; *Kakuō Tosho*; *Hibatsu*

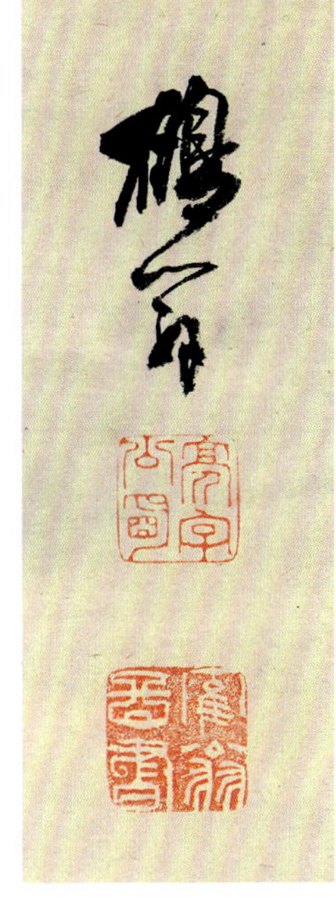

450

450

† 455. Eggplants

Signature

Jochiku

Seal

Jochiku

† 456. Composing One Thousand Poems in a Day

Text

by Gitoku
In front of Hitomaro Shrine / composed poems all day all alone / to fulfill the vow to compose one thousand poems in a day. // Late in the day / that is drawing to a close / at the God's domicile.

Signature

Painted by Gitoku

Seal

Tachibana gai Gitoku

† 457. Pilgrimage to Ise

Signature

Playfully painted by Chōgō

Seal

Shūhōken

Text

by Minoyama
This painting depicts the pilgrims on their way to the shrine in Ise. Since Ise is the site of the imperial ancestral shrine, people going there to pay homage to the deities often crowd the roads. In the summer of 1771 a rumor suddenly spread near and far, alleging that good fortune for the pilgrims would multiply this year from previous years and they should hurry to act upon their devotion. It began circulating in the Kyoto-Nara area and San'in regions, and soon reached the entire region. From everywhere on the island, people came with their seniors and children in continual streams night and day. As there were not enough accommodations for them all, many were left exposed to the elements on the roadside. The penniless poor had to beg along the way to sustain themselves and only barely made the trip after extreme hardship. It was quite a phenomenon. A certain Mr. I, an art aficionado as ever, commissioned a painter to depict the scene and asked me to record the entire incident. Though a trivial fad, it reflected the social mores nonetheless. It is fair to say that the thoughtful painter did not leave out the smallest details.

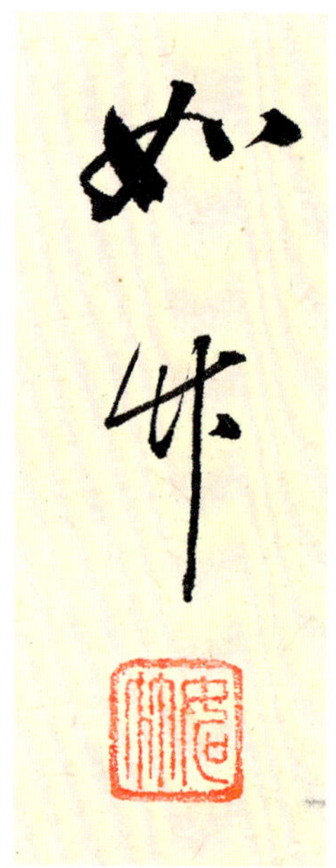

455

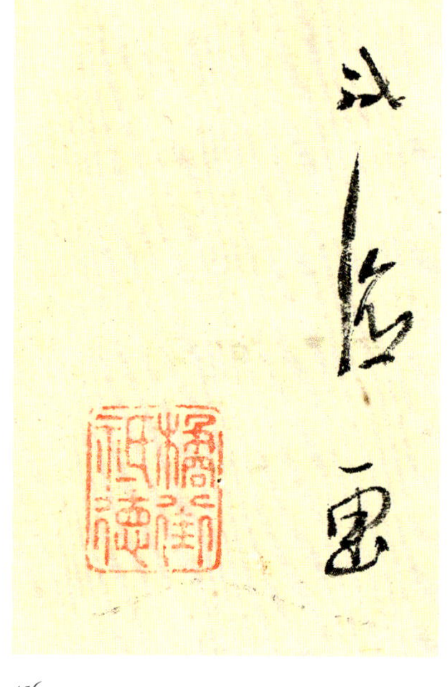

456

457

457

457

Signature

The old Mr. Minoyama inscribed this in the fourth month of 1777

Seals

Kankyo seishō; Minoyama Isshi; Tatesawa Daishi

Text

by Chōgō
The divine wind assures / the royal reign remains infinite / as long as the Mimosuso River remains clean and unsoiled.

Seal

kaō

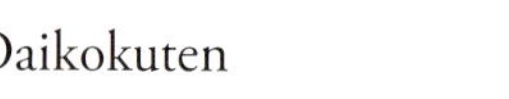

† 458. Daikokuten

Signature

On the first day of the twelfth month of the year 1840, Hokumei

Seal

Kason

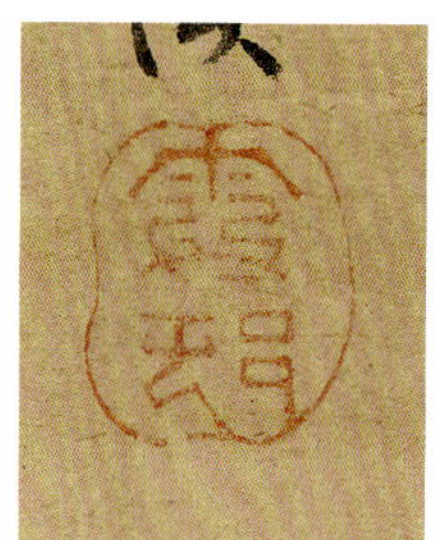

458

459

† 459. Orchid

Seals

Tōno To in; Kaji

460. Cat

Signature

Painted by Nitta Iwamatsu Minamoto Tokujun

Seals

Minamoto Tokujun in; Minamoto Ji Gen gō Hōkakuryō Ryūsei

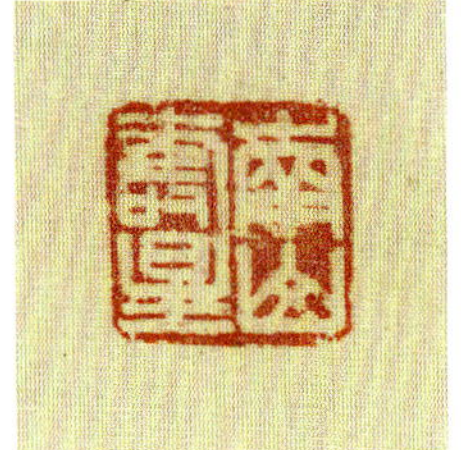

461

† 461. Carp

Signature

Nanzan

Seal

Nanzan Jusei

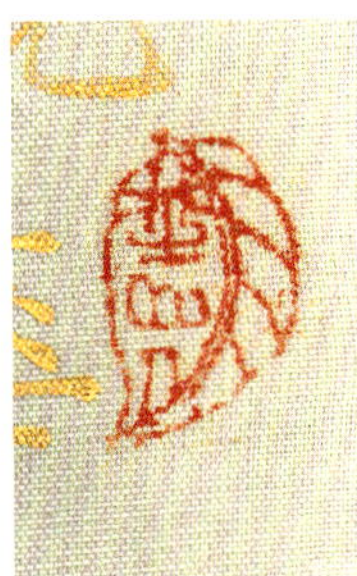

462

462

462

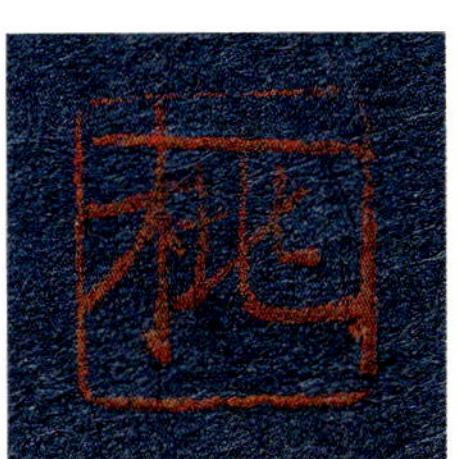

464

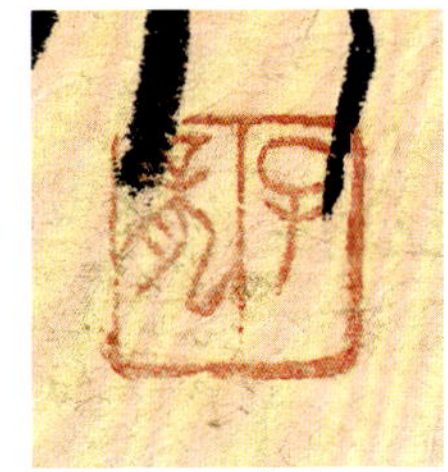

465

† 462. Kegon Falls and Flowers

[on center scroll]

Text

Recorded at viewing the Kegon Waterfall, in early . . . [illegible].

Signature

Kōsai Koji Ishikawa Ten

Seals

Shiba Sanjin; Sekikeiei in; Kunka

[on right scroll]

After drizzling for scores of days, even the rain gets old. / I envision the flowers in disarray by the river far away. / To soothe my mind, in a small pavilion, I leisurely pick up a brush / and paint some cut branches in the manner of Nanden [Un Juhei (Ch. Yun Shouping, 1633–1690)].

Signature

Painted by Kōsai Koji Sekiei in the spring of 1902

Seals

Shiba Sanjin; Sekikeiei in; Kunka

[on left scroll]

Text

The skill of Master Un Juhei [Ch. Yun Shouping] *has no precedent; / who can emulate his painting of gorgeous flowers? // Self-mocking as the ugly one from Wuyan* [modern Shandong] *Province, she still expects appreciation from the King of Sai* [Ch. Qi]. *// In my spare time after lecturing and reading, I paint landscapes and bamboo with rocks for fun. When it comes to flowers and birds with patterned plumage, my awkwardness becomes even worse. A chance reading of 'Shōzan gafu'* [Ch. Xiaoshan huapu] *by Sū Ikkei* [Ch. Zou Yigui, 1686–1772] *made me eager to try my hand. I rushed to gather some rosy pigments and painted a variety of flowers and cut branches. It is deplorable that my brush has turned rusty and the painting appears extremely crude. Compared with professional dyers and paint-workers, however, I may boast certain merits.*

Signature

In the late spring of 1902, Shibayama Gaishi Sekiei [1833–?] *at the age of seventy*

Seals

Shiba Sanjin; Sekiei Kunka; Kōsai

463. Buddhist Jewels

Signatures

Suitō; Kakurei; Tōkan; [illegible]*hō; Shūtō; Kahō; Shōu*

† 464. Boat

Seal

[on right screen] *Tō*

† 465. Untitled

Signature

[on the back] *Morita Shiryū*

Seal

[on the back] *Shiryū*

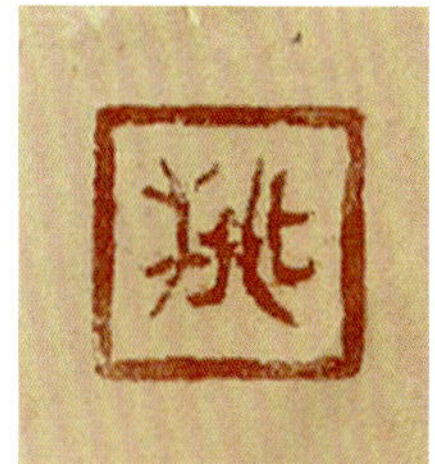

466

† 466. Movement and Stillness

Seal

Tō

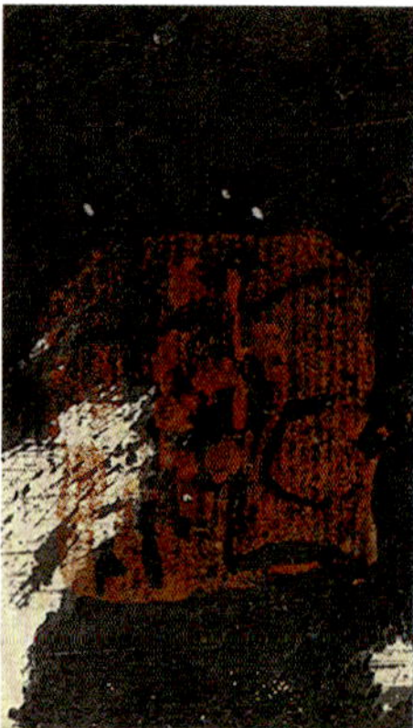

467

† 467. Untitled

Signature

Shinoda

Seal

Illegible

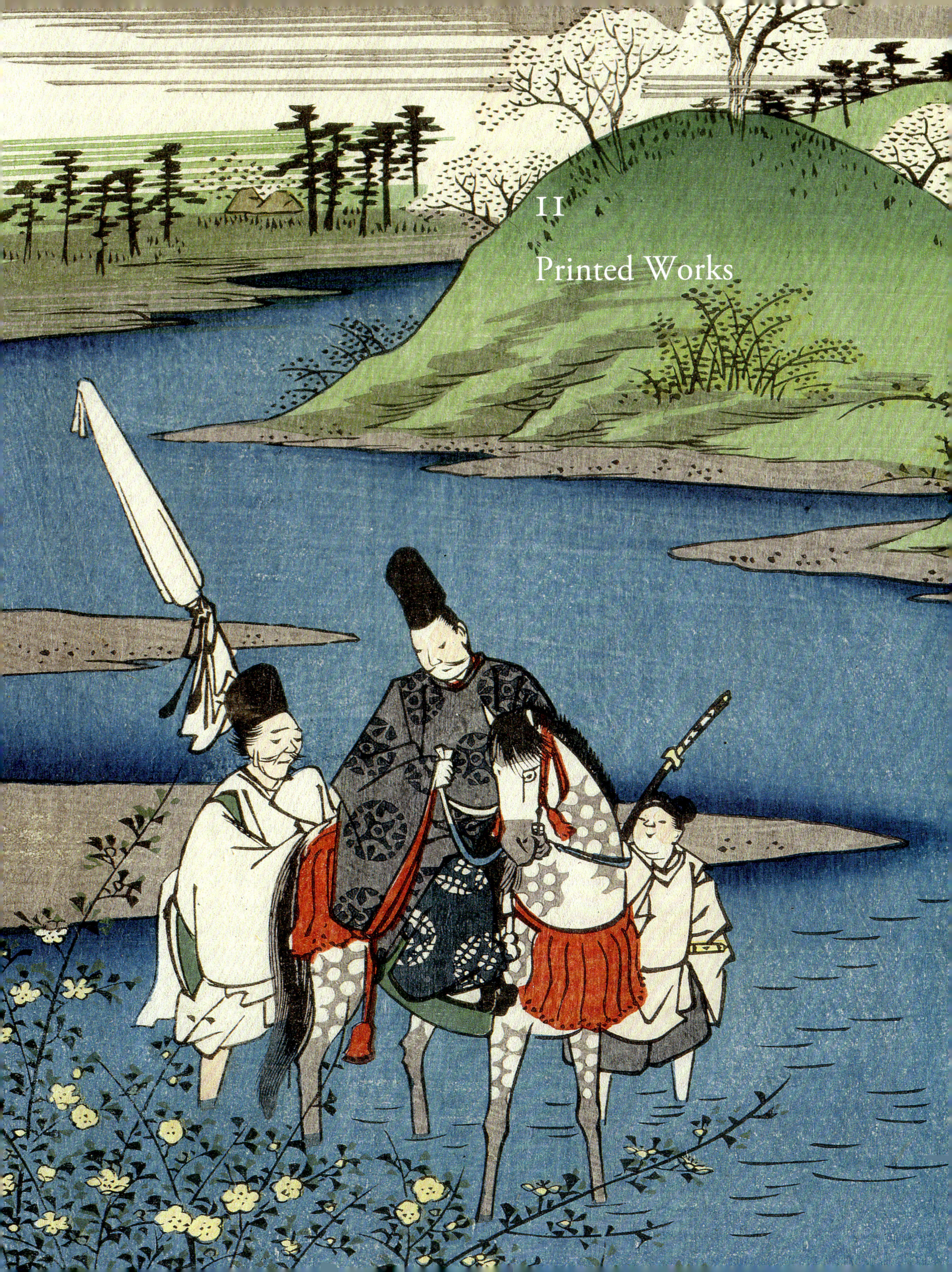

11

Printed Works

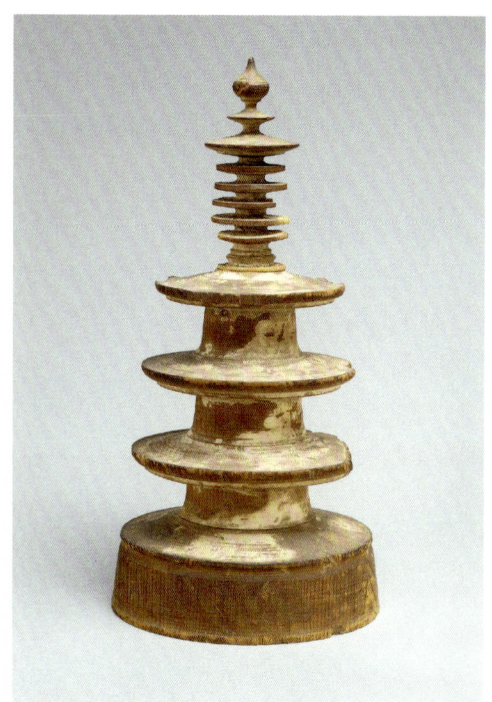

468. Darani sutra (陀羅尼経); pagoda from a set of *Hyakumantō* (百万塔 / One Million Pagodas)

Nara period, ca. 767
Sutra; ink printed on paper
5.8 x 46.4 cm (2¼ x 18¼ in.)
Pagoda; Japanese cypress (*hinoki*) and *Cleyera ochnacea japonica* (*sakaki*)
H. 22 cm (8⅝ in.)

LITERATURE: Kaufman 1985, fig. 6; Murase 1993, no. 2; Murase 2000, no. 7.

469. Chapter 579 of *Daihannya haramitakyō* (大般若波羅密多経五百七十九)

Kamakura period, 14th century
Handscroll; ink printed on paper
26.4 x 952.5 cm (10⅜ in. x 31 ft. 3 in.)
Signature

470. One Hundred Fudō Myōō (不動明王)

Kamakura period
Framed picture of one hundred stamped images; ink on paper
46.1 x 30.8 cm ($18\frac{1}{8}$ x $12\frac{1}{8}$ in.)

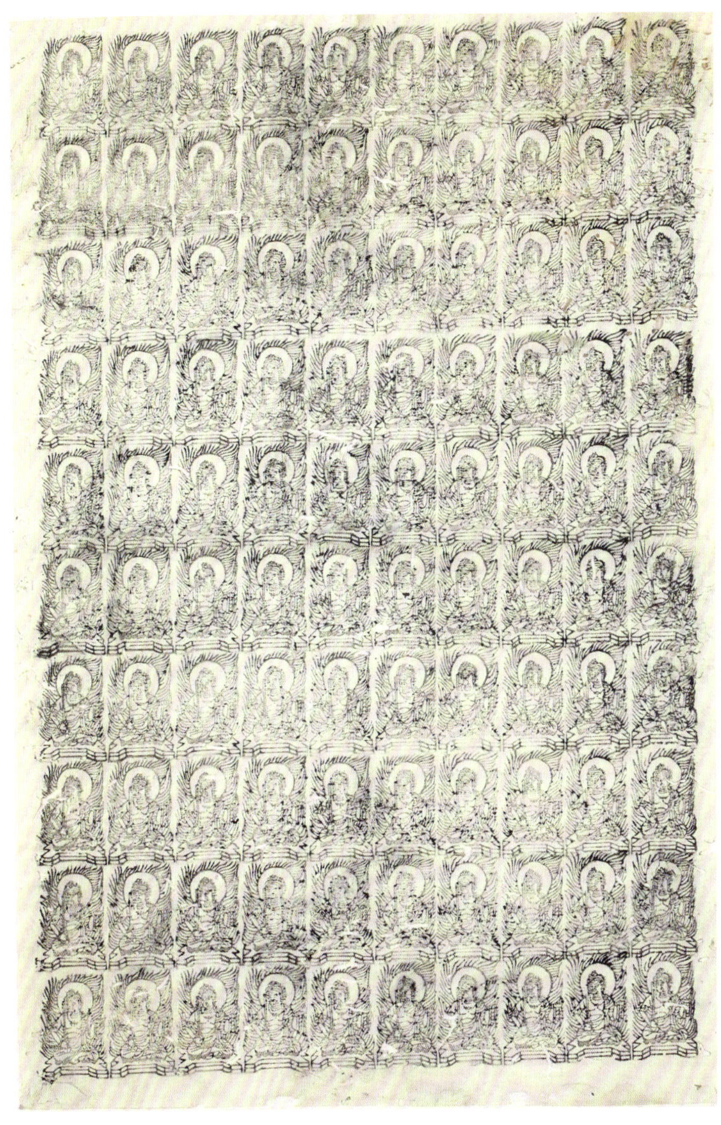

471. Raigō of Amida and Twenty-five Bodhisattvas (阿弥陀二十五菩薩来迎)

Muromachi period, 16th century
Framed picture; ink outlines printed with hand-applied color and gold on paper
24.3 x 37.3 cm ($9\frac{5}{8}$ x $14\frac{5}{8}$ in.)

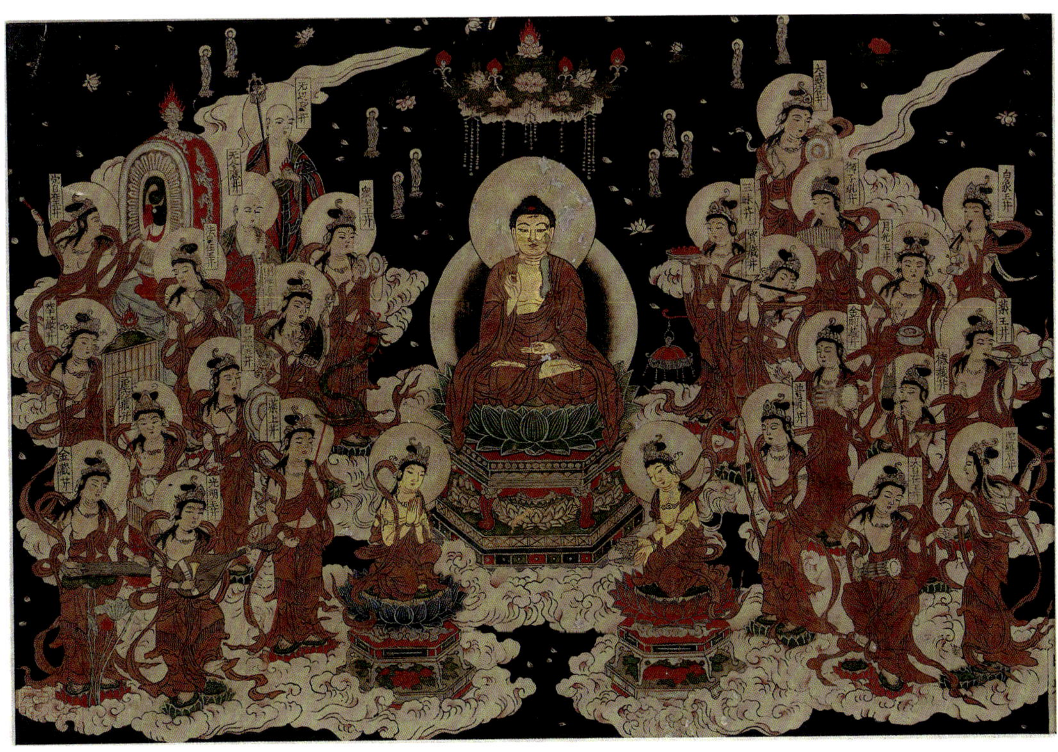

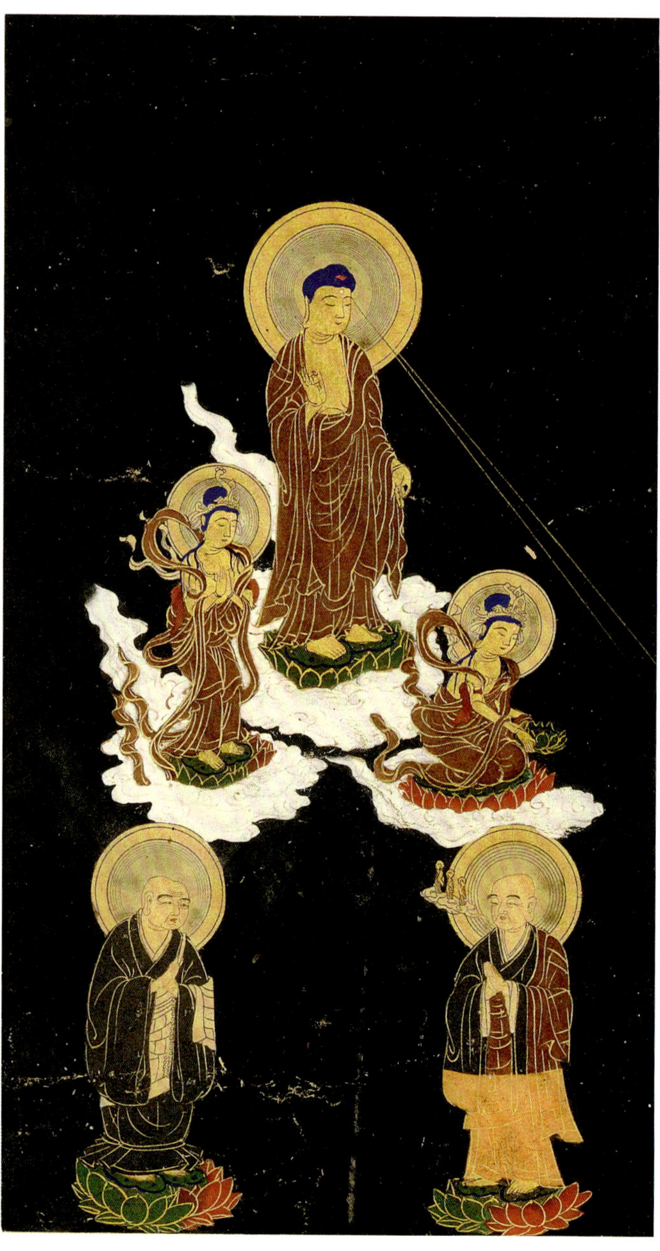

472. Raigō of Amida Triad
(阿弥陀三尊来迎)

Edo period, 17th century
Framed painting; ink outlines printed with color and gold on paper
24.5 x 13.5 cm ($9\frac{5}{8}$ x $5\frac{1}{4}$ in.)

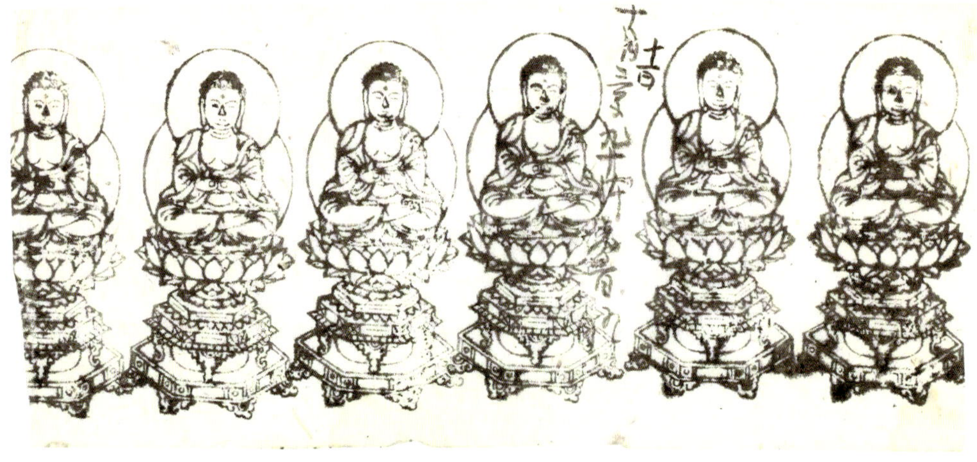

473. Six Amida Buddhas

Muromachi period, 15th century
Framed picture; ink printed on paper
11.8 x 26.5 cm ($4\frac{5}{8}$ x $10\frac{3}{8}$ in.)
Text

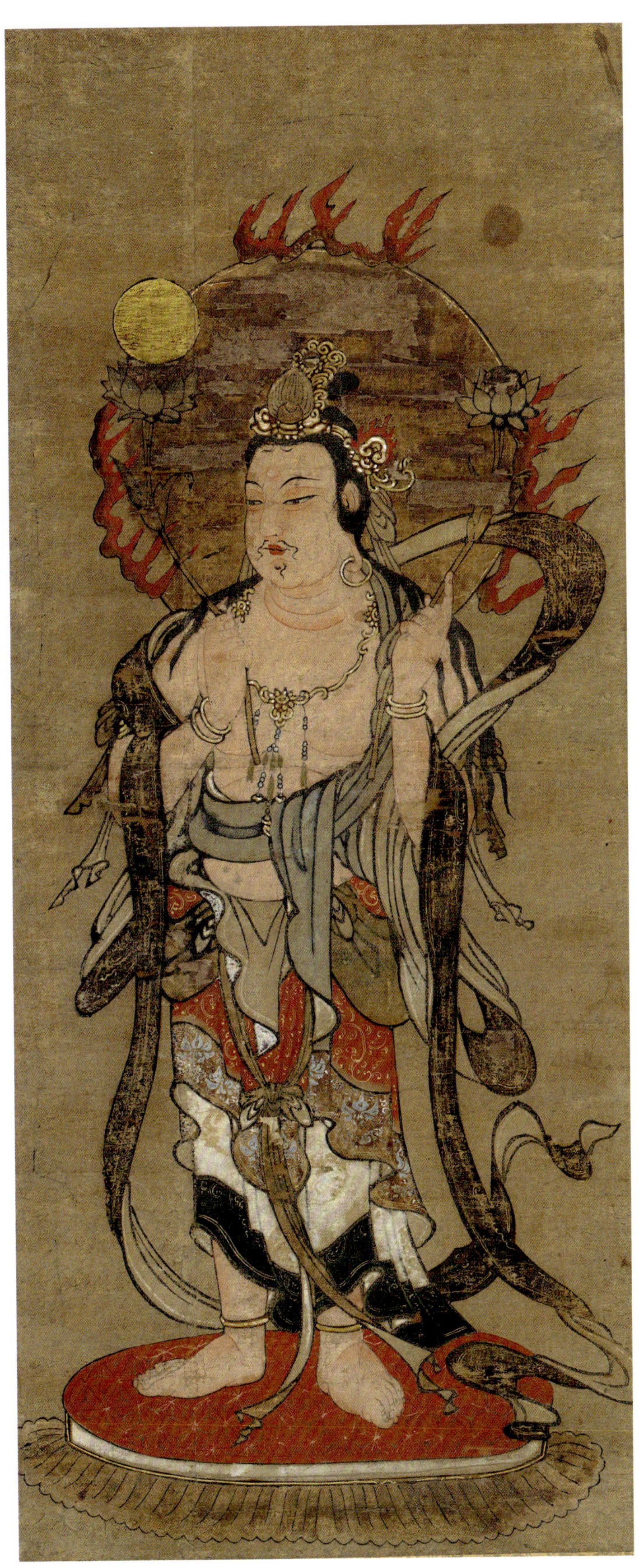

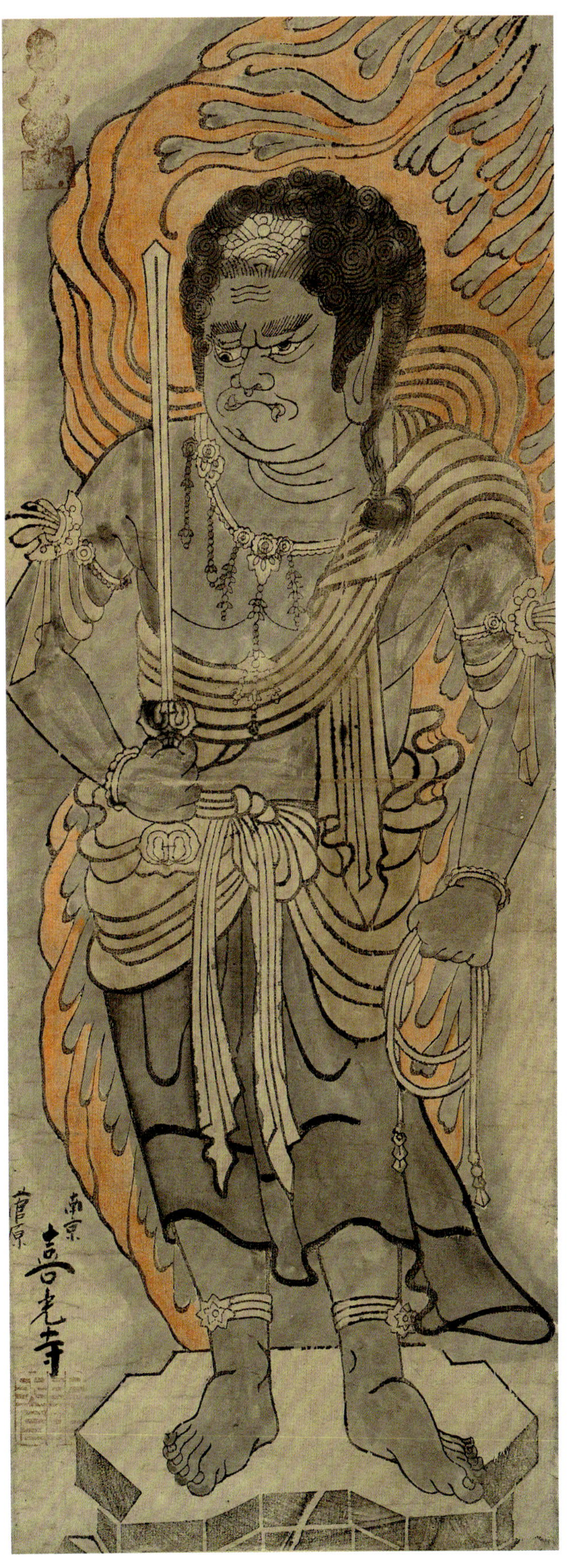

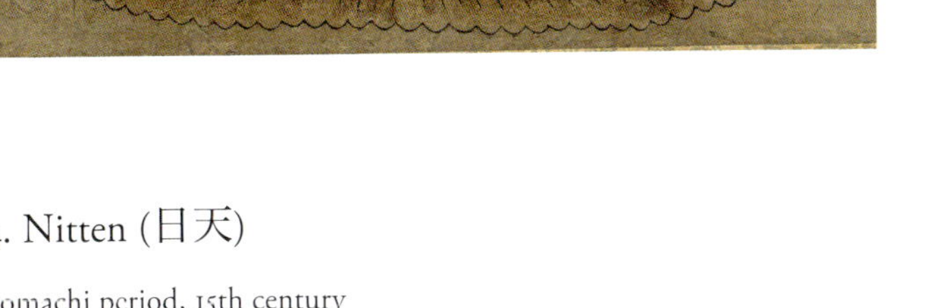

474. Nitten (日天)

Muromachi period, 15th century
Hanging scroll; ink outlines printed with color and gold on paper
86.1 x 36 cm (33 7/8 x 14 1/8 in.)

475. Fudō Myōō (不動明王)

Edo period, 18th century
Hanging scroll; ink outlines printed with hand-applied color (?) on paper
93.5 x 34.7 cm (36 3/4 x 13 5/8 in.)
Text, seals

476. *Bussetsu jūōkyō* (仏説十王経)

Momoyama period, 1594
Two volumes; illustrations in ink on paper
(a) 25.8 x 18 cm (10 1/8 x 7 1/8 in.); (b) 26.3 x 19 cm (10 3/8 x 7 1/2 in.)
Postscript, in vol. 2: "Illustrations made in July / 1594 by monk Senka"

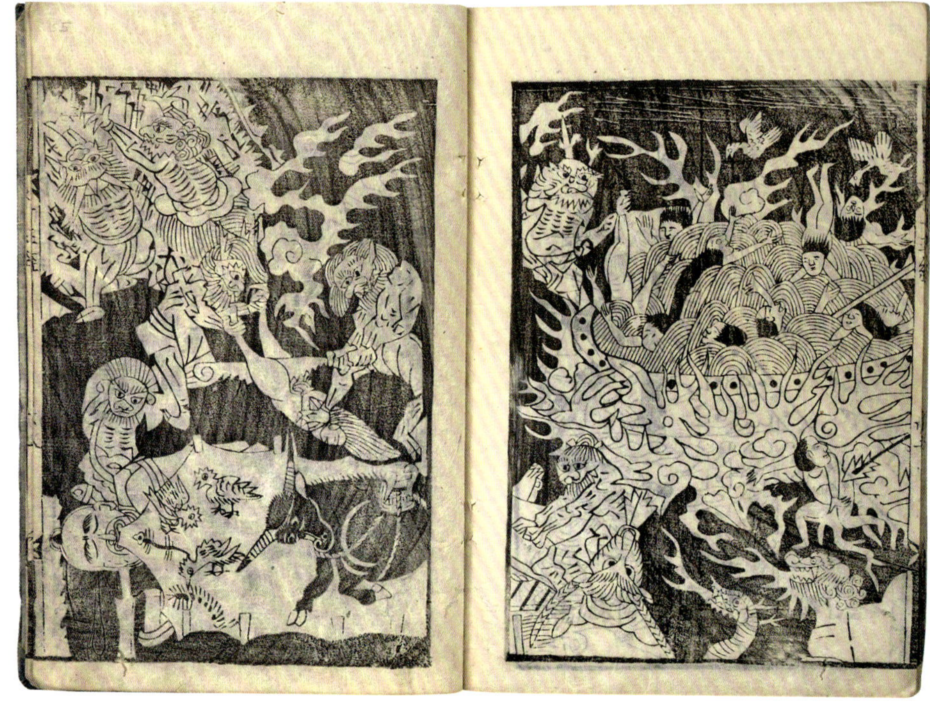

477. Life of Kōbō Daishi (弘法大師行状図画)

Edo period, 17th century
Ten handscrolls; ink printed with hand-applied color on paper
scroll I (*detail, below*) 29.2 x 794.2 cm (11 1/2 in. x 26 ft. 5/8 in.)
scroll II: 29.2 x 728.3 cm (11 1/2 in. x 23 ft. 10 3/4 in.)
scroll III: 29.2 x 842.9 cm (11 1/2 in. x 27 ft. 7 7/8 in.)
scroll IV: 29.3 x 507 cm (11 1/2 in. x 16 ft. 7 5/8 in.)
scroll V: 29.1 x 588.2 cm (11 1/2 in. x 19 ft. 3 5/8 in.)
scroll VI: 29.2 x 480 cm (11 1/2 in. x 15 ft. 9 in.)
scroll VII: 29.1 x 701.7 cm (11 1/2 in. x 23 ft. 1/4 in.)
scroll VIII: 29 x 575.2 cm (11 3/8 in. x 18 ft. 10 1/2 in.)
scroll IX: 29 x 574 cm (11 3/8 in. x 18 ft. 10 in.)
scroll X: 29 x 726.8 cm (11 3/8 in. x 23 ft. 10 1/8 in.)

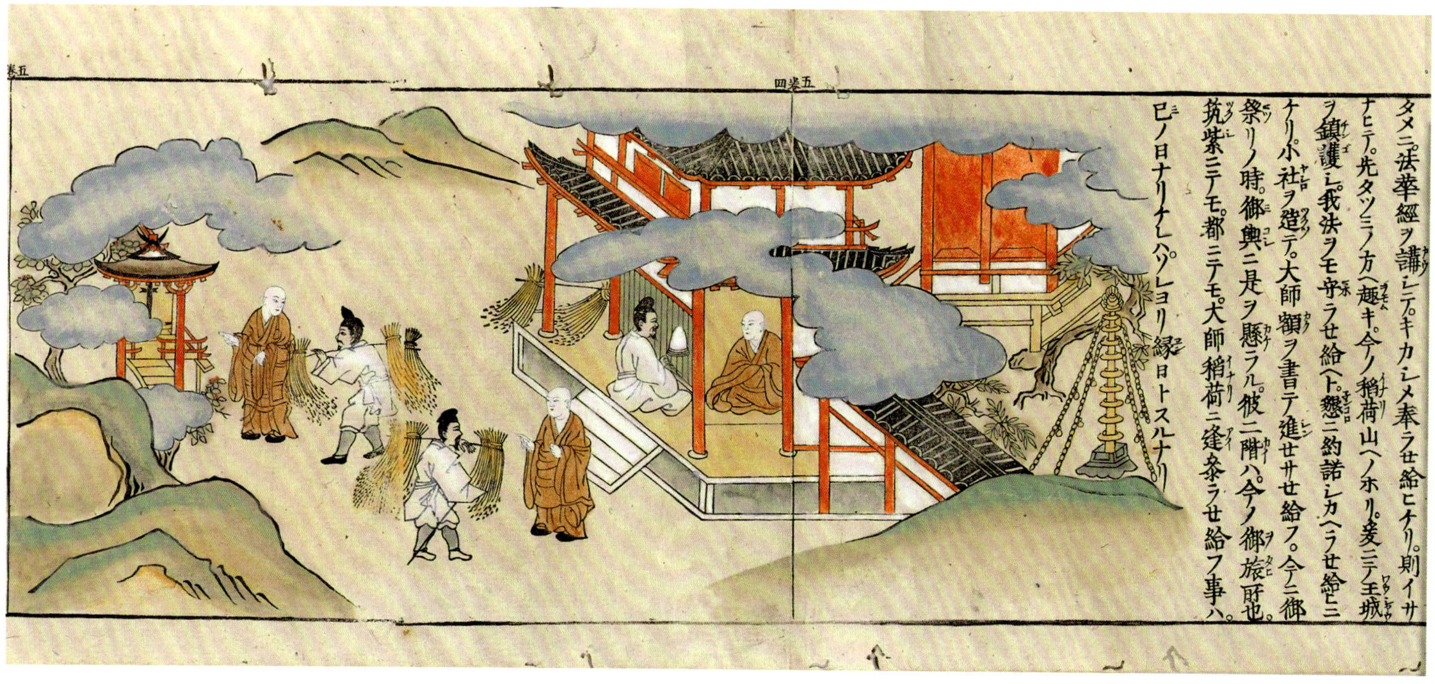

Endō Motomori
(遠藤元閑; 17th century)

478. *Nishiki no mizuguki* (錦の水茎 / Traces of Japanese Calligraphy)

Edo period, 1651
Book; ink on paper
39 x 29 cm (15 3/8 x 11 3/8 in.)
Signature

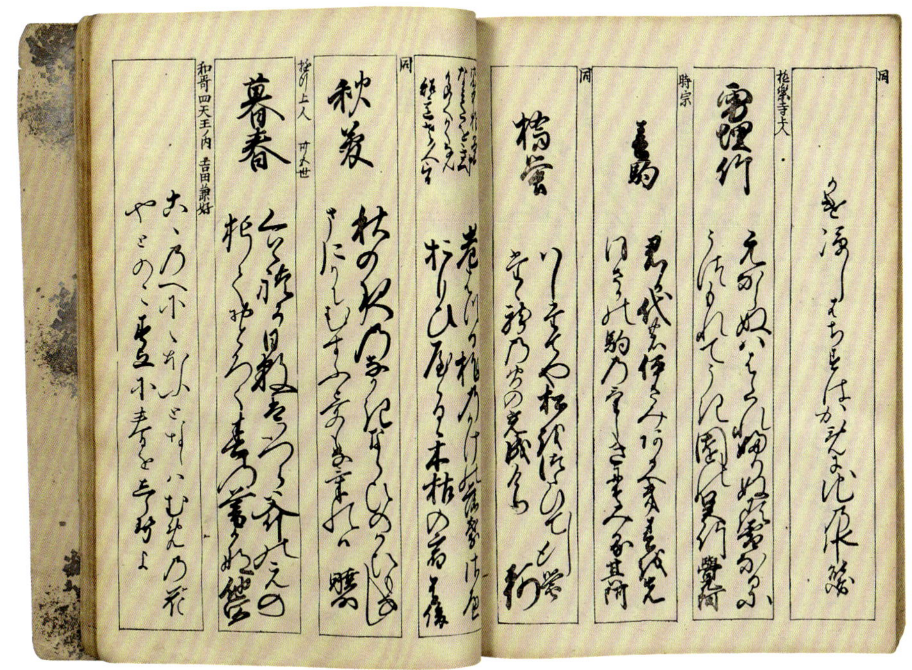

Endō Motomori
(遠藤元閑; 17th century)

479. *Tōryū chanoyu rudenshū* (当流茶之湯流伝集 / For the Dissemination of the Contemporary Tea Ceremony)

Edo period, 1694
Six books, bound into five volumes; illustrations in ink on paper
Each volume approx. 22.3 x 16.1 cm (8 3/4 x 6 3/8 in.)
Postscript, in vol. 6: "The eighteenth day of the sixth month [1694]" / Endō Motomori"

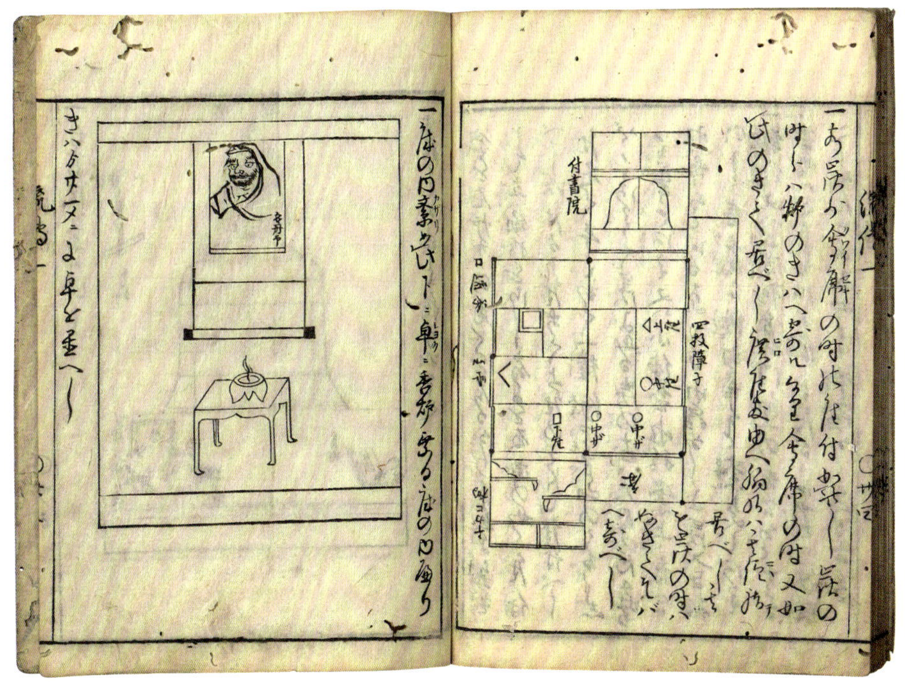

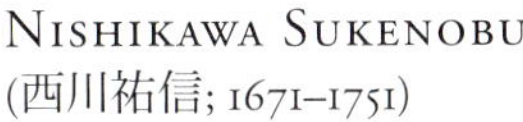

Nishikawa Sukenobu
(西川祐信; 1671–1751)

480. Women's Work and Manners

Edo period, 1729
Handscroll; illustrations printed in ink, with occasional hand-applied ink, on paper
23.2 x 838.7 cm (9 1/8 in. x 27 ft. 6 1/4 in.)
Text

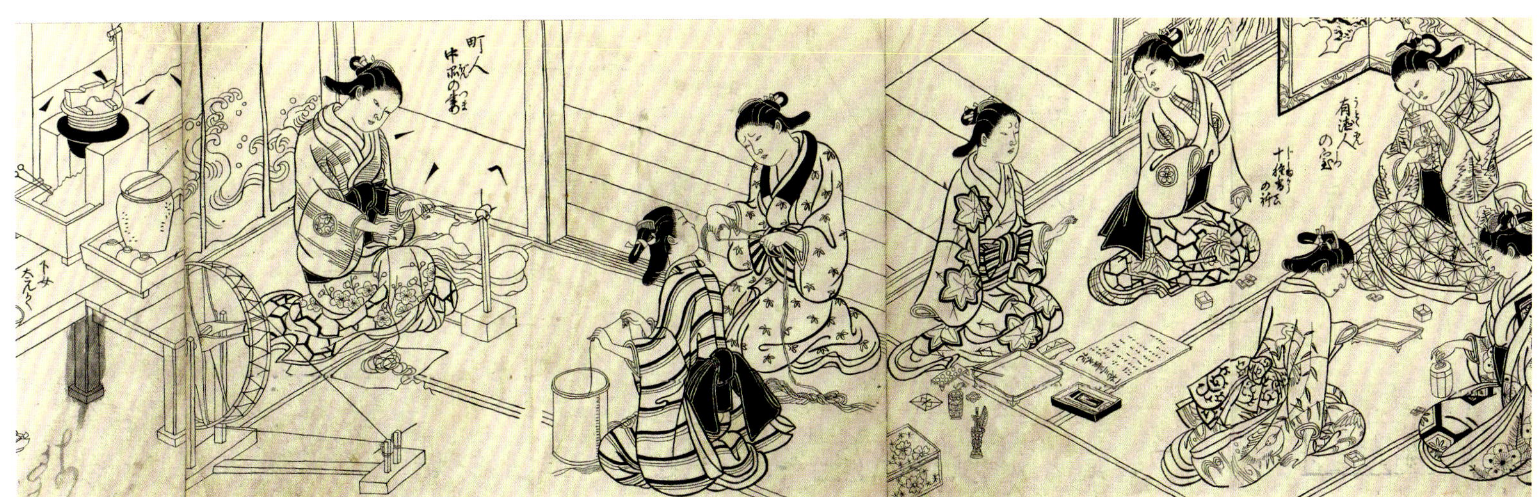

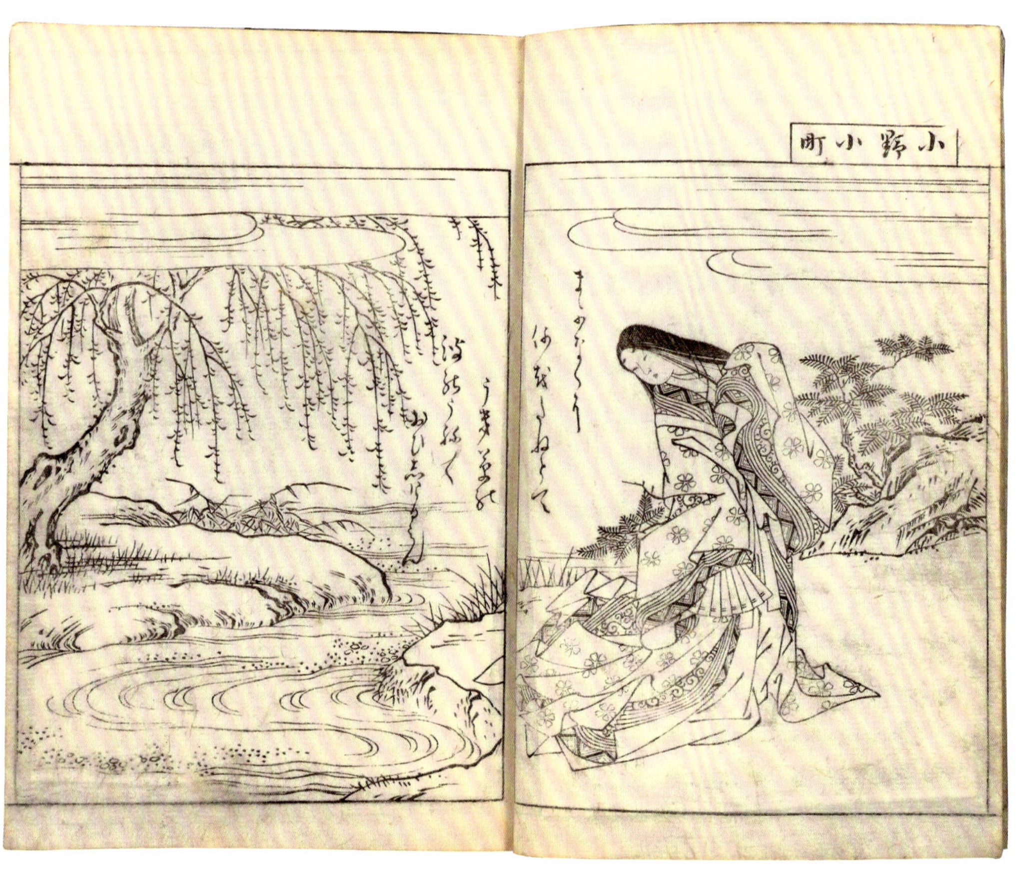

Nishikawa Sukenobu
(西川祐信; 1671–1751)

481. *Ehon tokiwagusa* (絵本常磐草 / Illustrated Lives of Famous and Not-So-Famous Women)

Edo period, March 1731
Three-volume book; illustrations in ink on paper
Each volume approx. 27.1 x 18.6 cm
(10 5/8 x 7 3/8 in.)
Text
Preface: "By the Kyoto painter Bunkadō Nishikawa Sukenobu, the third month of 1731"

"Taking Shelter from the Rain (雨宿り)," from volume 1.

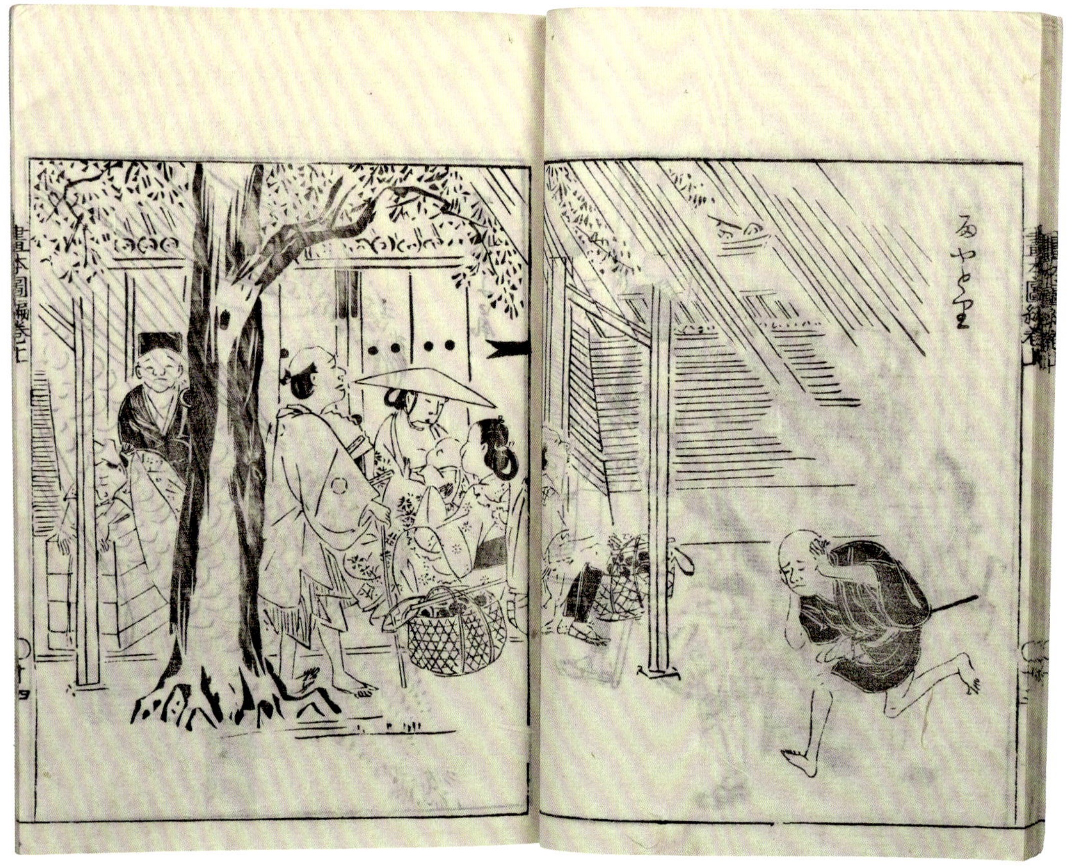

Hanabusa Ippō
(英一峰; 1691–1760)

482. *Gahon zuhen* (画本図編 / Collected Manual of Paintings)

Edo period, May 1751
Three-volume book; illustrations in ink on paper
Each volume approx. 25.7 x 18.5 cm
(10 1/8 x 7 1/4 in.)

Sō Shiseki
(宋紫石; 1712–1786)

483. *Sō Shiseki gafu* (宋紫石画譜 / Paintings by Sō Shiseki)

Edo period, August 1765
Three-volume book; illustrations in ink and color on paper
Each volume approx. 27 x 16.7 cm (10 5/8 x 6 5/8 in.)

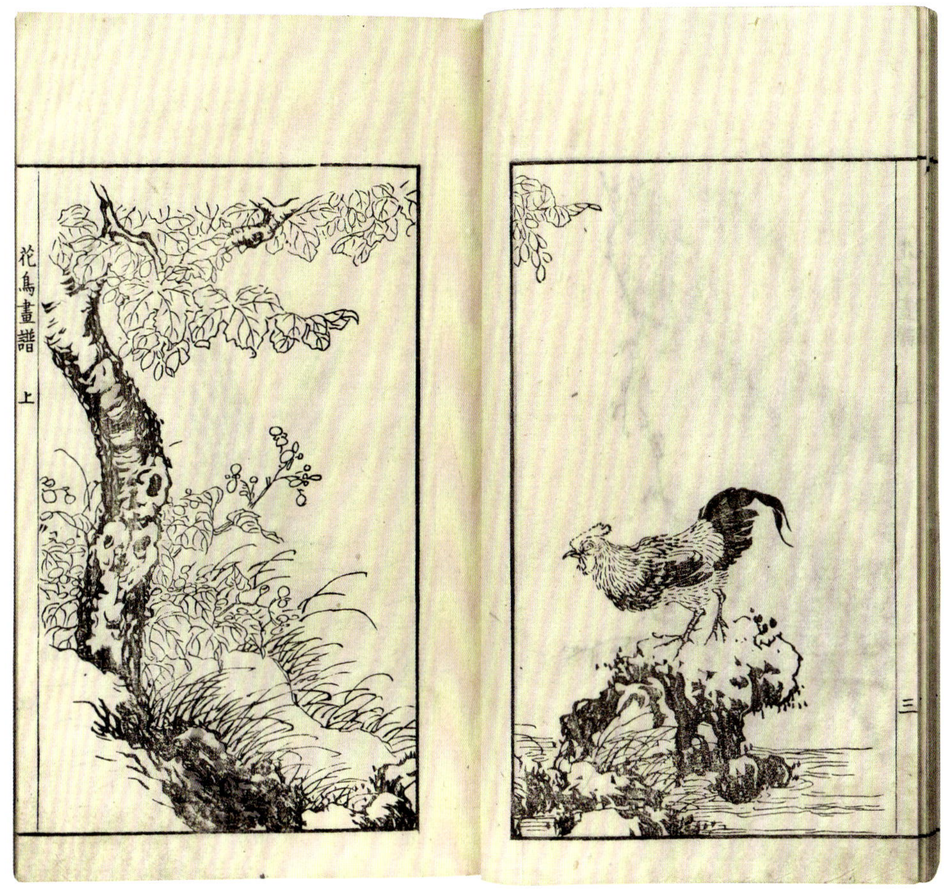

484. *Kōyō seika hyakuhei zu* (甲陽生花百瓶図 / One Hundred Examples of Kai-Style Flower Arrangements)

Edo period, May 1774
Three-volume book; illustrations in ink on paper
Each volume approx. 27.2 x 17.3 cm (10 3/4 x 6 3/4 in.)
Preface by Shōmeian Rochū (松鳴菴露中), May 1774
Postscript by Shisentei Kanwa (志川亭関和), May 1774

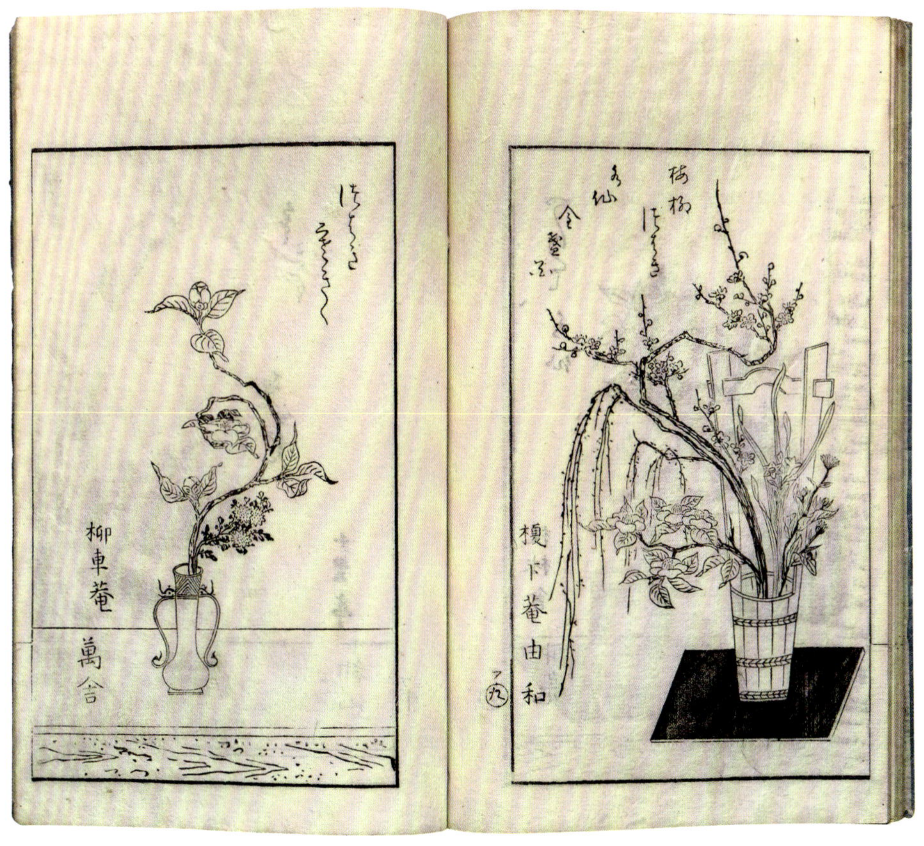

485. *Rantei ki* (蘭亭記 / Orchid Pavilion)

Edo period, mid-summer 1787
Book, no illustrations; ink on paper
27.3 x 17.6 cm (10 3/4 x 6 7/8 in.)

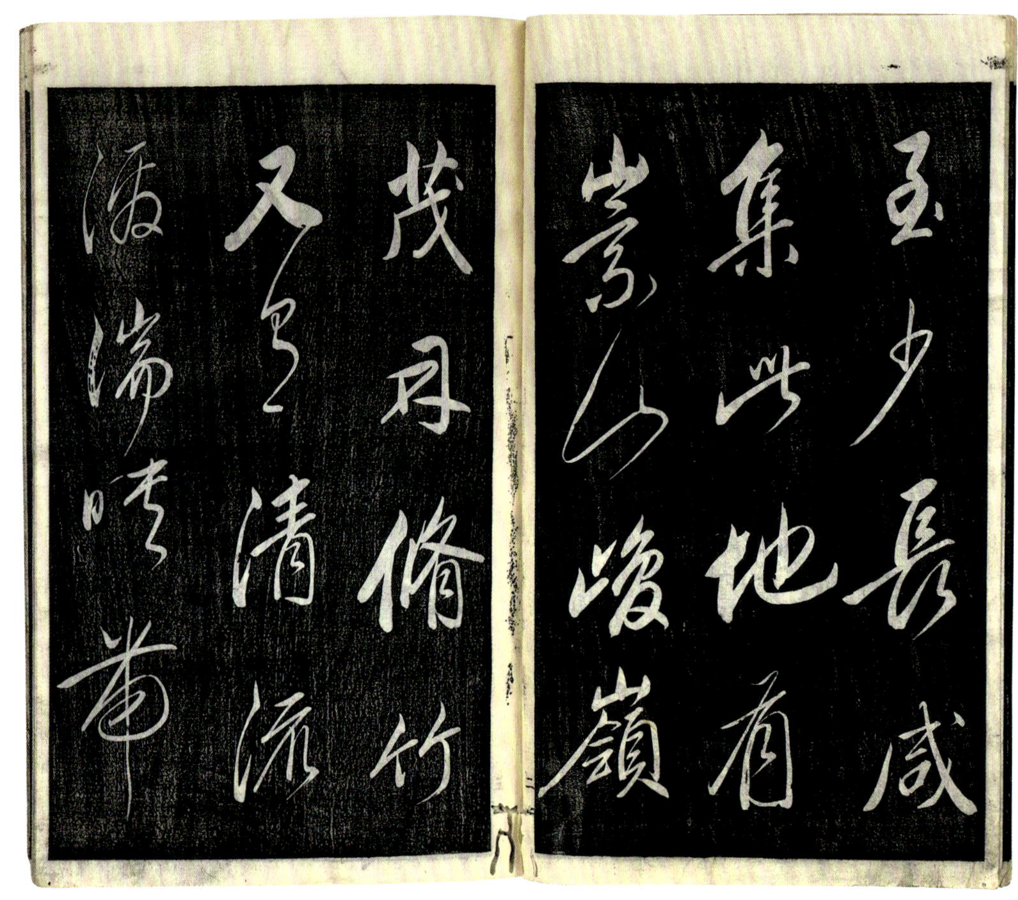

TSURUOKA ROSUI
(鶴岡蘆水; fl. late 18th–early 19th century)

486. Both Banks of the Sumida River (両岸一覧)

Edo period, 1781
Two handscrolls; ink and color printed on paper
Scroll I: 26 x 840 cm (10 1/4 in. x 27 ft. 6 3/4 in.)
Scroll II (*detail, below*): 26 x 1386.6 cm (10 1/4 in. x 45 ft. 5 7/8 in.)
Text, signature, seals

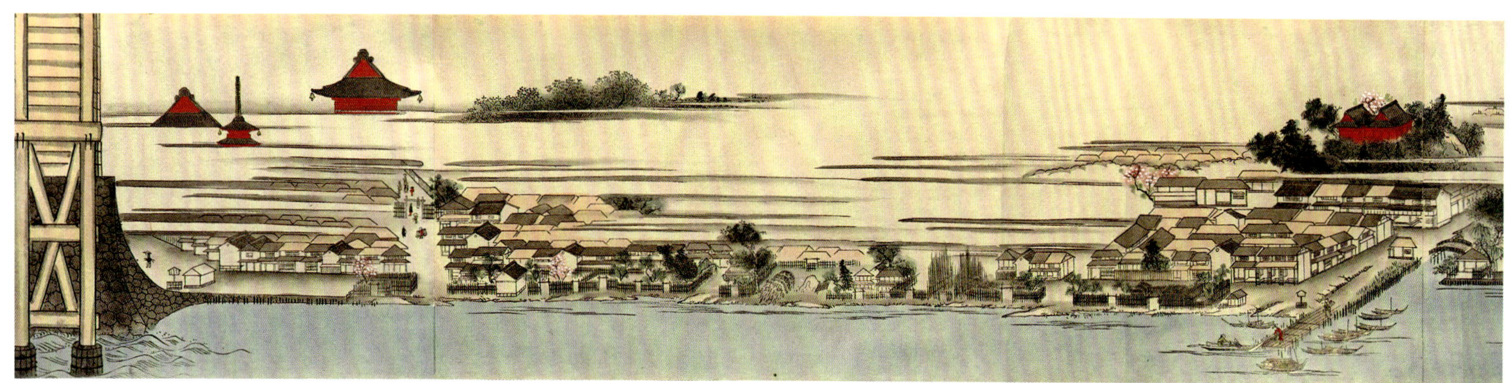

Tani Bunchō
(谷文晁; 1763–1840)

487. *Honchō gasan* (本朝画簒 / Collection of Japanese Paintings)

Edo period, 1809
Eight-volume book; illustrations printed in ink and light color on paper
5 books 23.5 x 16 cm (9¼ x 6¼ in.);
1 book 23.7 x 15.8 cm (9¼ x 6¼ in.);
1 book 22.8 x 15.8 cm (9 x 6¼ in.);
1 book 22.7 x 16.1 cm (8⅞ x 6⅜ in.)
Signature, seals
Postscript, in vol. 8: "Bunchō, the first month of 1809"

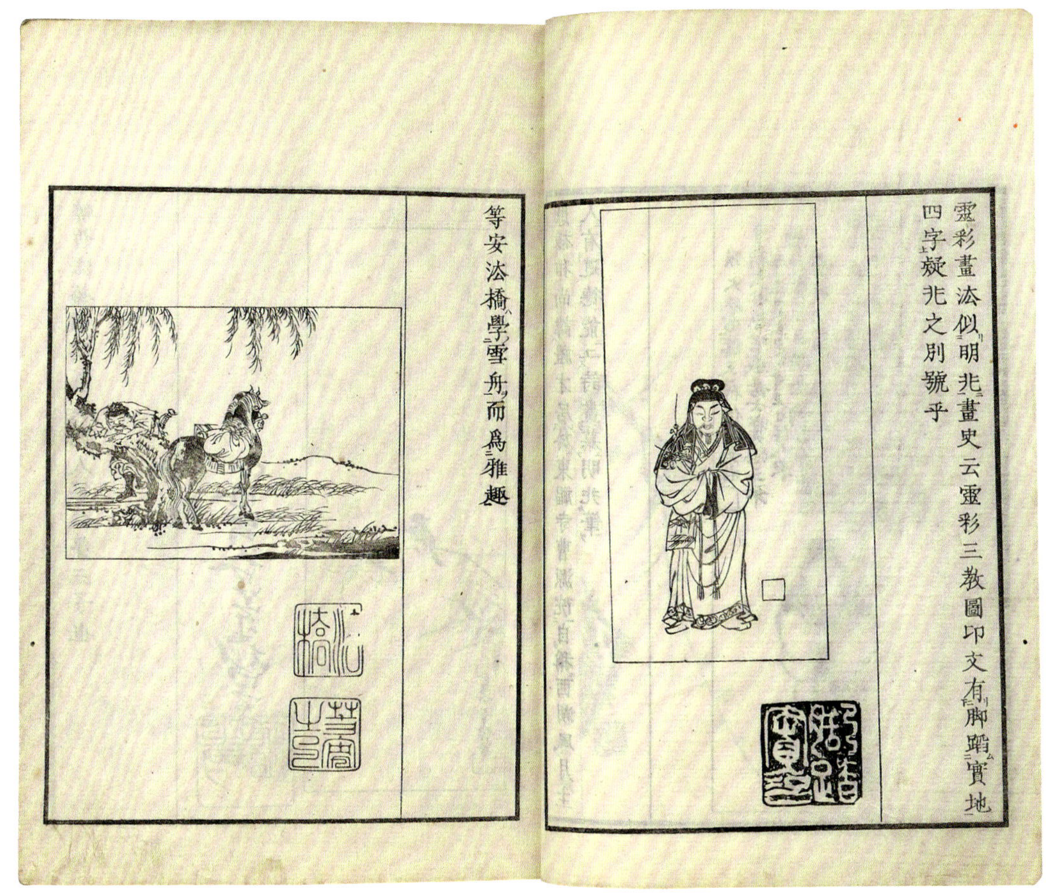

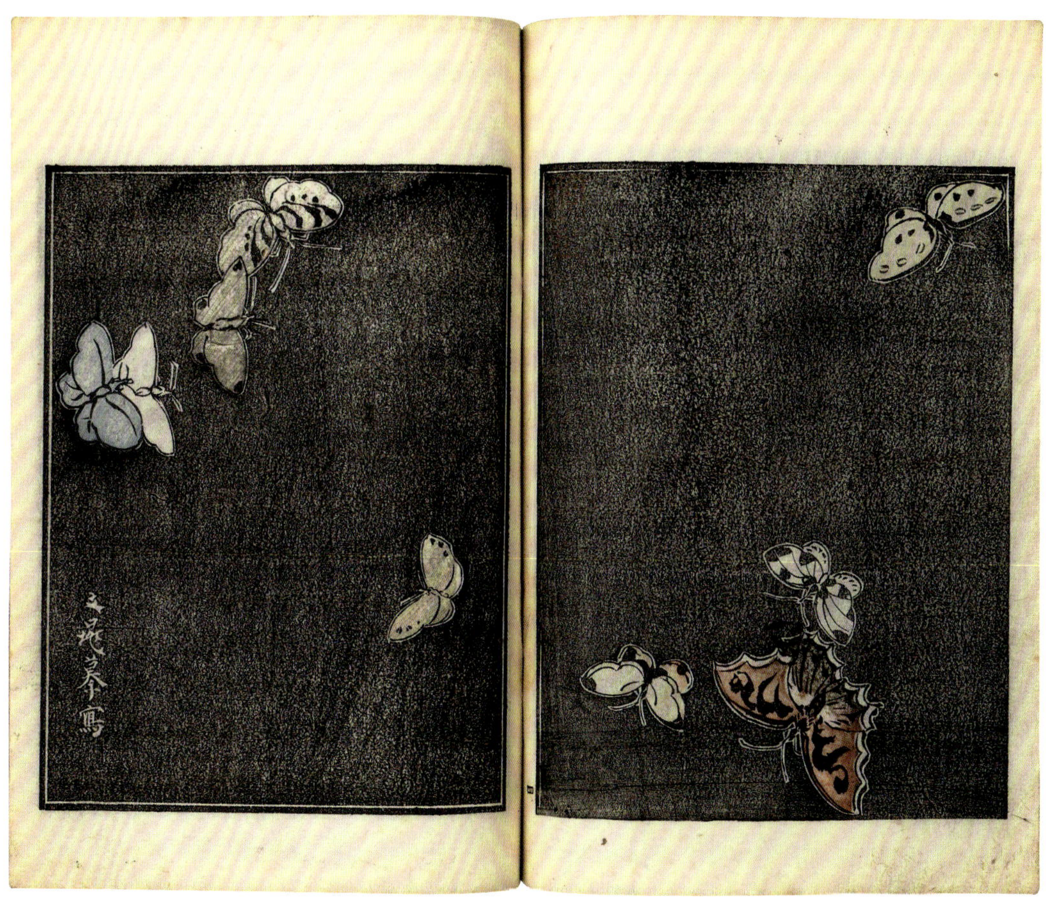

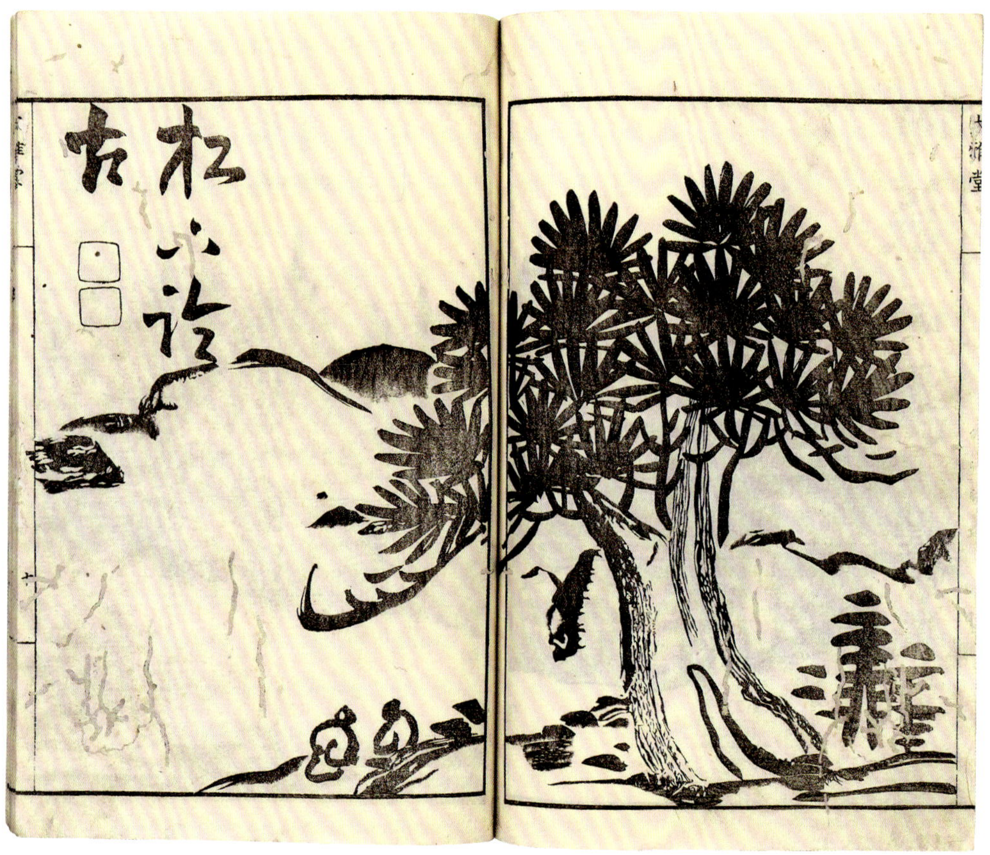

"After Taiga's Discussion under a Pine Tree about the Vicissitudes of Time," from *Ike Taiga gafu*

Nakagawa Tenju
(中川天寿; d. 1795)

488. *Ike Taiga gafu* (Paintings of Ike Taiga / 池大雅画譜); *I Fukyū gafu* (Paintings of Yi Fujiu / 伊孚九画譜)

Edo period, 1803
Two books; illustrations in ink on paper
Each book approx. 26.7 x 18.3 cm (10½ x 7¼ in.)
Postscript, in *I Fukyū gafu*: "Kan Tenju's reproductions in reduced scale; Spring 1803"

Gift from James Cahill, 1968

Tani Bunchō
(谷文晁; 1763–1840)

489. *Shazanrō ehon* (写山楼画本 / Book of Pictures by Shazanrō)

Edo period, 1811
Book; ink and light color on paper
26.7 x 18.4 cm (10½ x 7¼ in.)
Seals

Gift from James Cahill, 1972

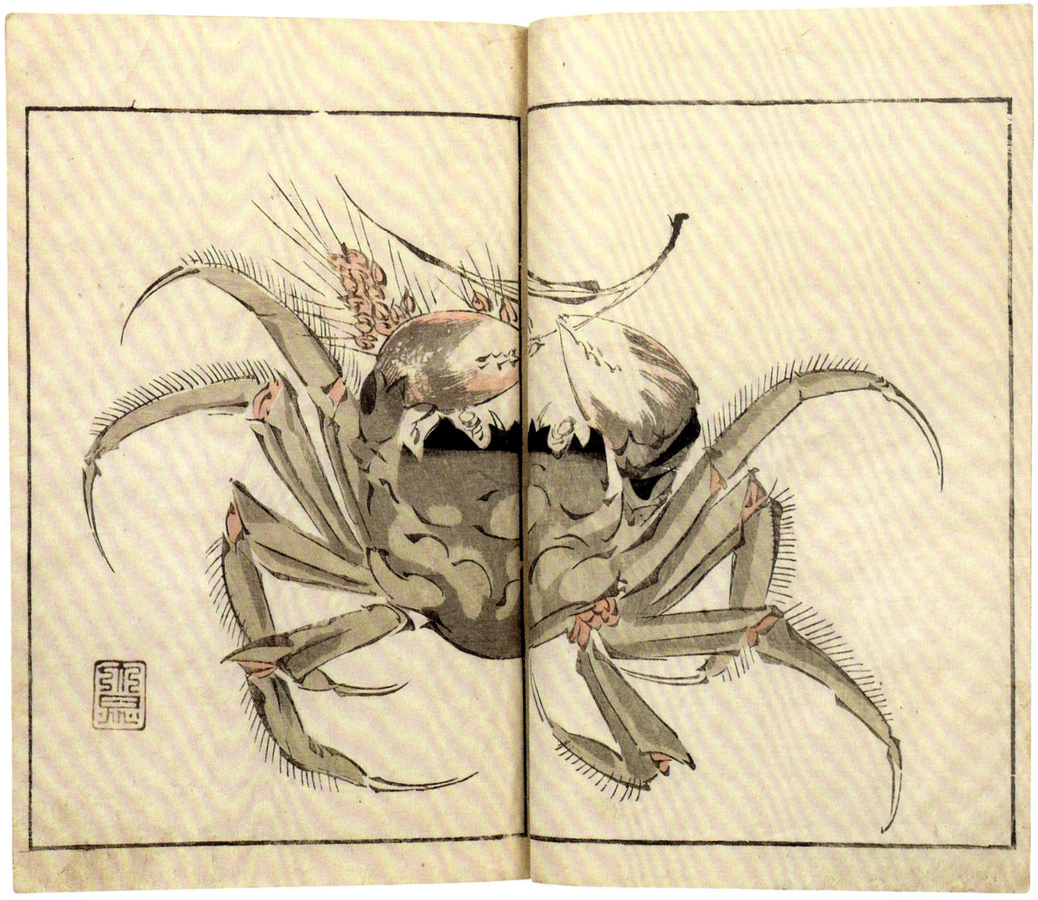

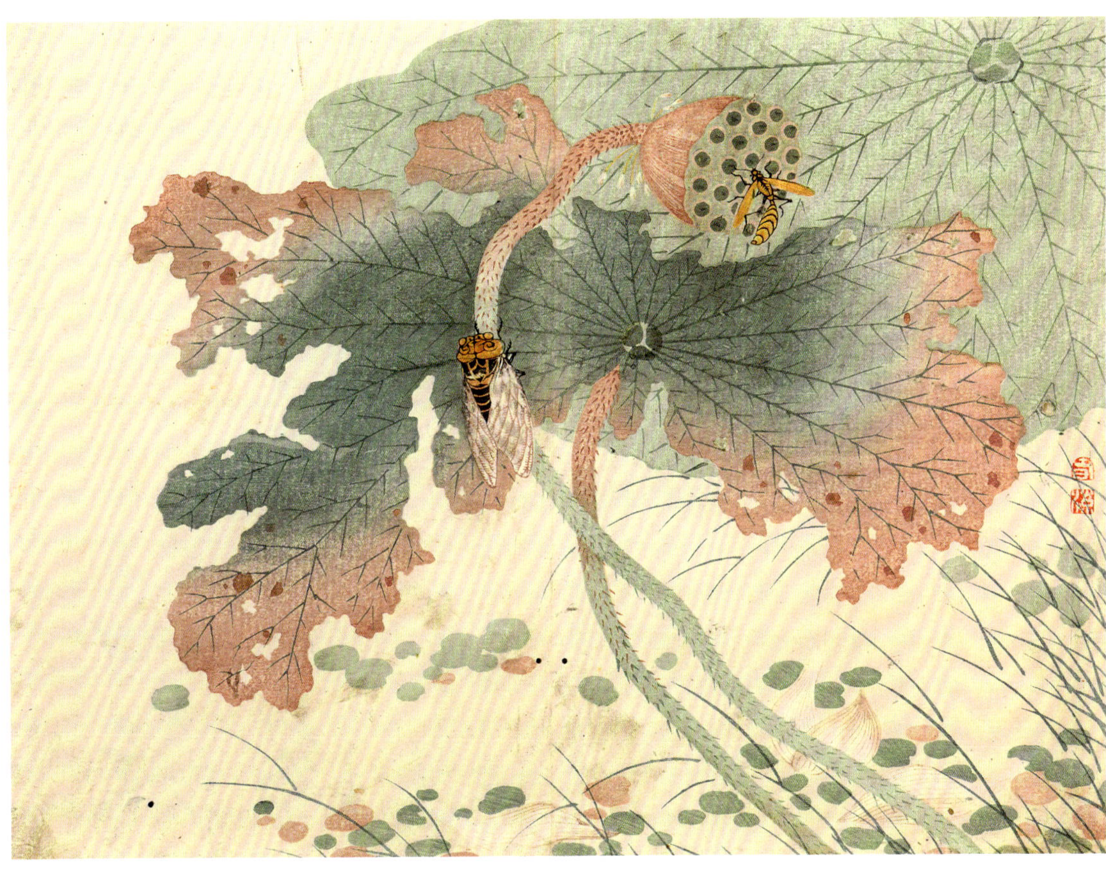

Mori Shunkei
(森春溪; fl. 1800–1820)

490. *Chūka senzen* (肘下選蠕 / Selected Insects from Close at Hand)

Edo period, July 1820
Book; ten illustrations in ink and color on paper
21 x 14.1 cm ($8^{1}/_{4}$ x $5^{1}/_{2}$ in.)
Preface by Shinozaki Shōchiku (篠崎小竹; 1781–1851), July 1820

491. *Kinsei jufu* (金生樹譜 / Manual on Arboriculture) by Chōseisha Aruji (長生舍主人)

Edo period, June 1833
Three-volume book; illustrations in ink on paper
Each volume approx. 22.4 x 15.5 cm ($8^{7}/_{8}$ x $6^{1}/_{8}$ in.)

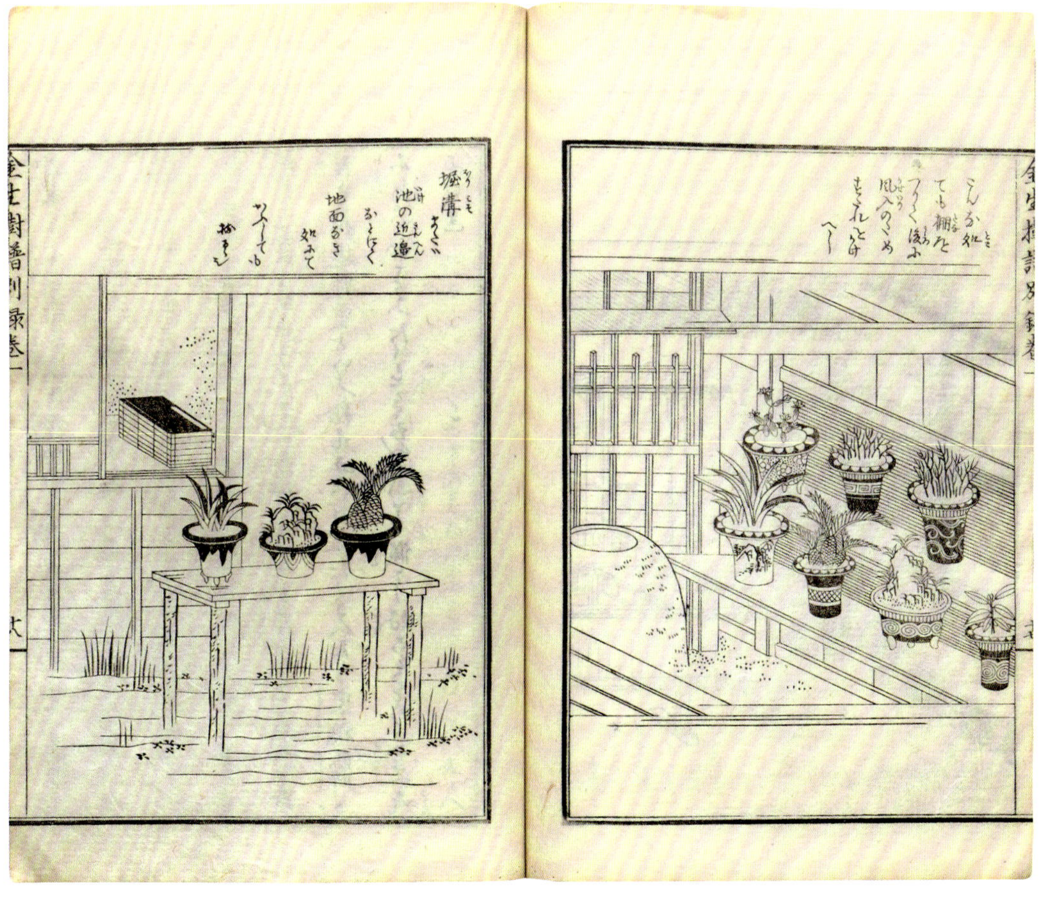

Katsushika Hokusai
(葛飾北斎; 1760–1849)

492. *Banshoku zukō* (万職図考 / Pictorial Designs for All Artisans)

Edo period, mid-January 1850
Five-volume book; ink and color on paper
Each volume approx. 22.1 x 15.1 cm (8 3/4 x 6 in.)
Postscript: "mid-January, 1850"

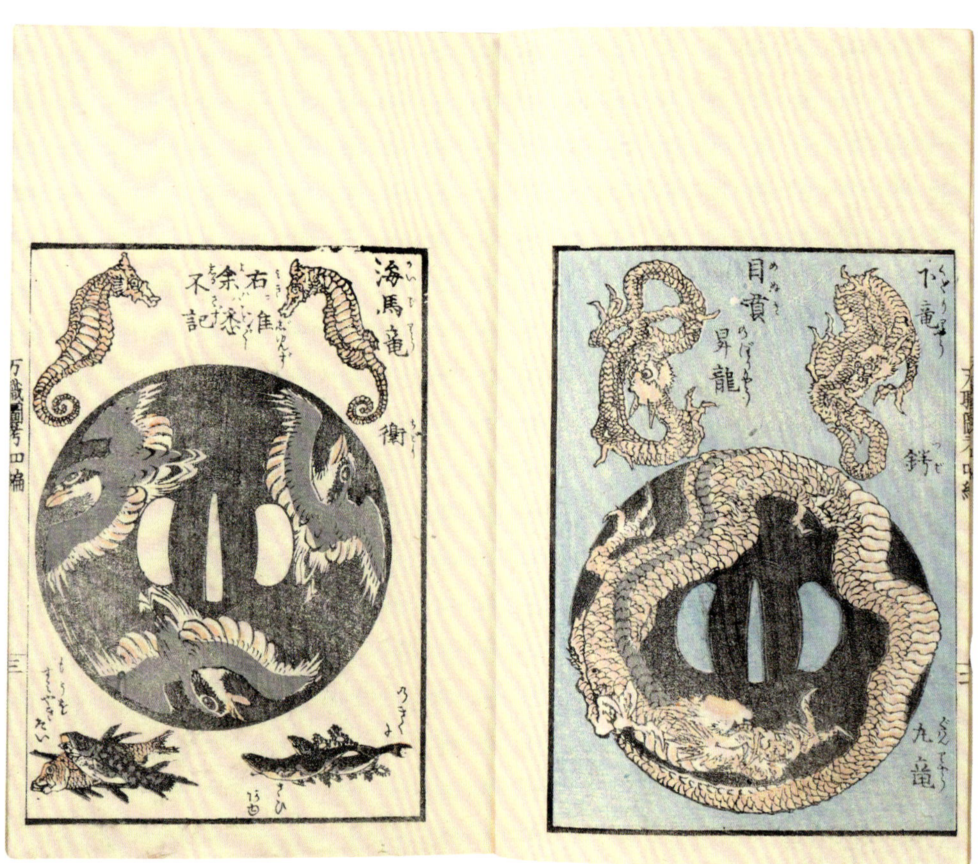

Detail, vol. 4

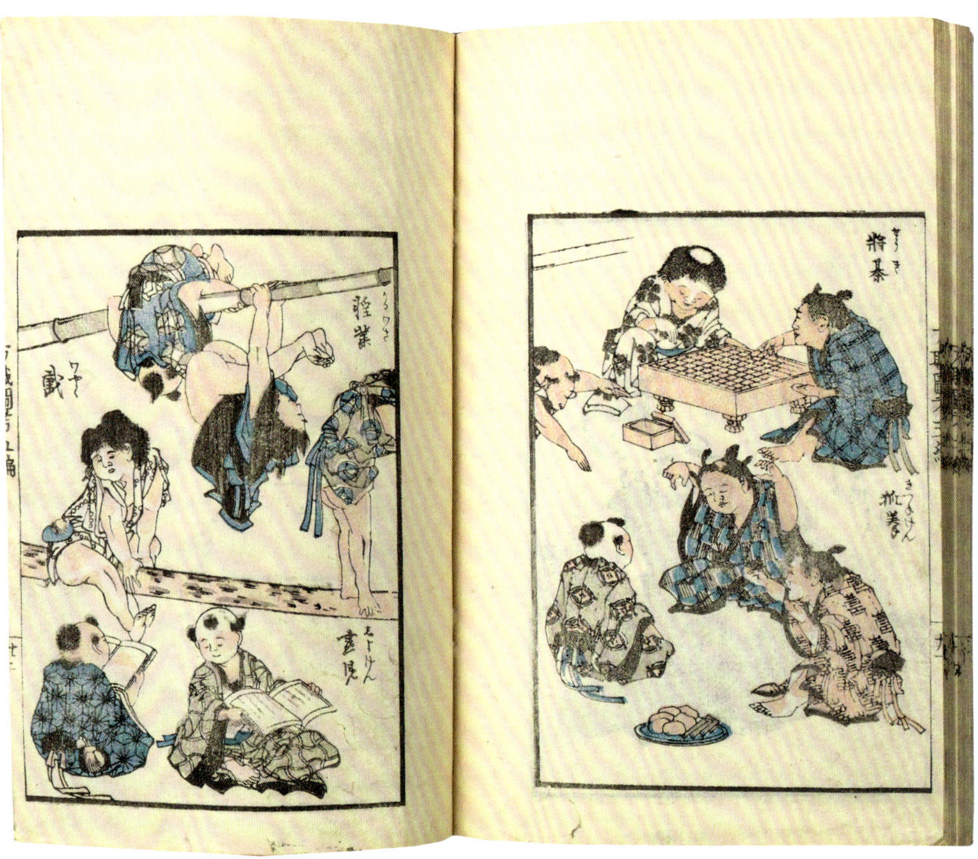

Detail, vol. 5

Utagawa Hiroshige
(歌川広重; 1797–1858)

493. "Tōto Meguro Yūhigaoka" (Twilight Hill at Meguro in the eastern capital), from *Thirty-six Views of Mt. Fuji*

Edo period, ca. 1858
Woodblock print; ink and color on paper; *oban tate-e*, no. 10 in series of 36
33.4 x 22.1 cm ($13\frac{1}{8}$ x $8\frac{3}{4}$ in.)
Signature, seals

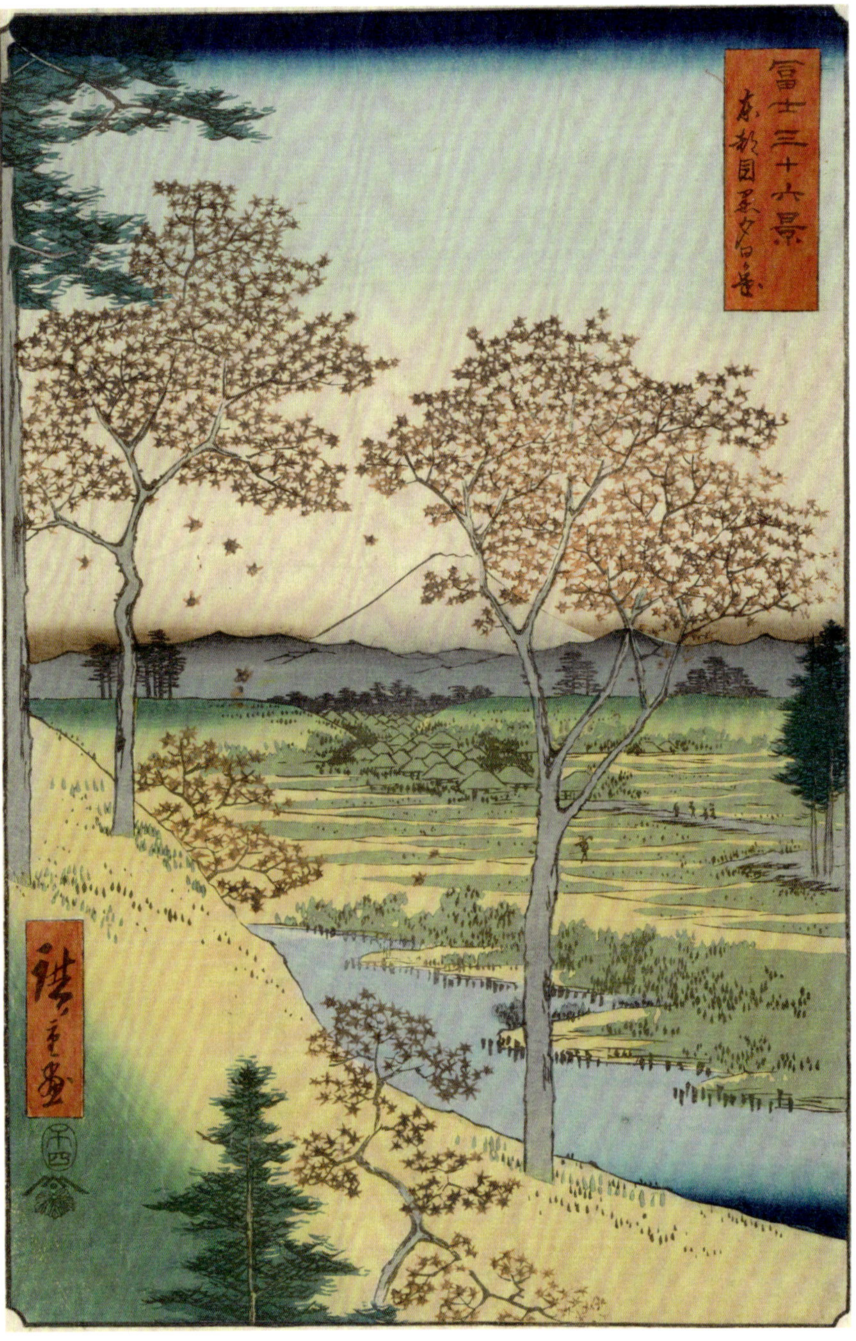

Utagawa Hiroshige
(歌川広重; 1797–1858)

494. *Shokoku Mu Tamagawa* (諸國六玉川 / Six Tamagawa Rivers from Different Regions)

Edo period, 1857
Six woodblock prints; ink and color on paper
Each print 36.2 x 24.5 cm ($14^{1}/_{4}$ x $9^{5}/_{8}$ in.)
Text, signatures, seals

Literature: Murase 2000, no. 152.

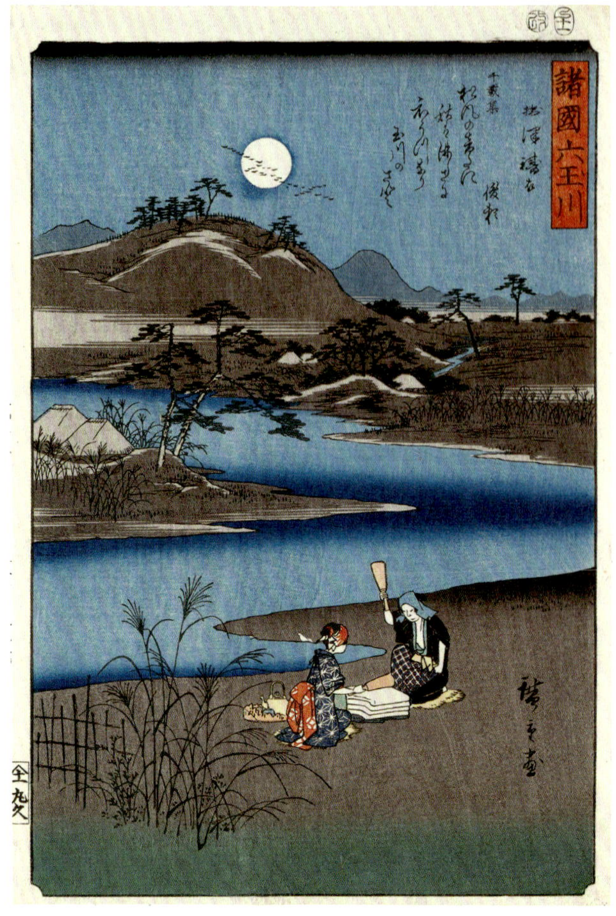

Kinuta no Tamagawa

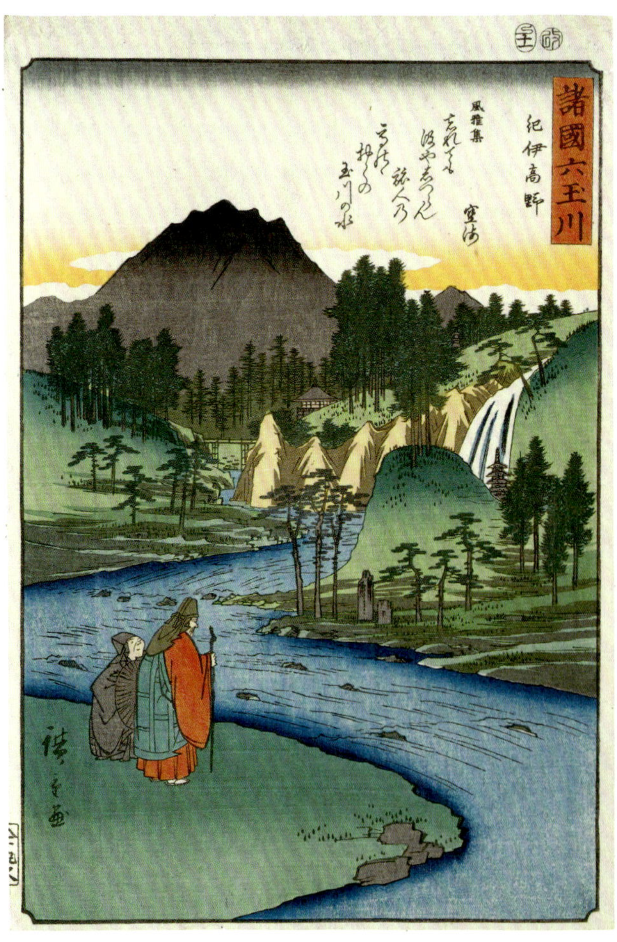

Kōya no Tamagawa

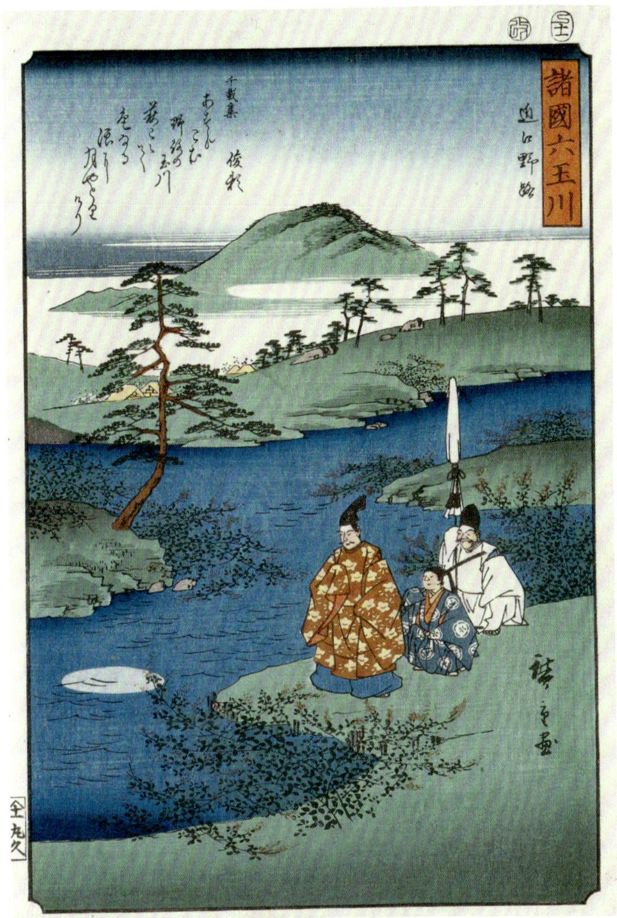

Noji no Tamagawa

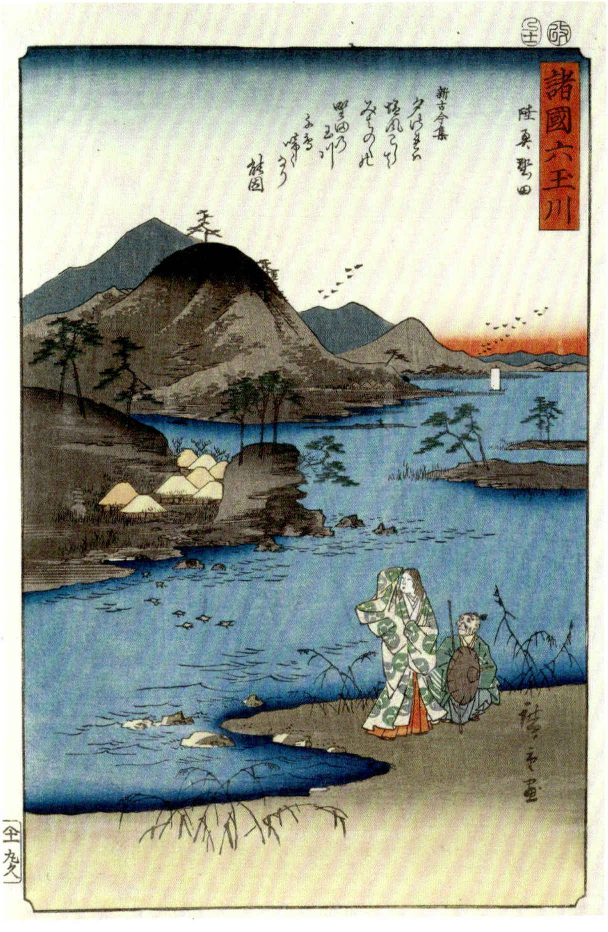

Noda no Tamagawa

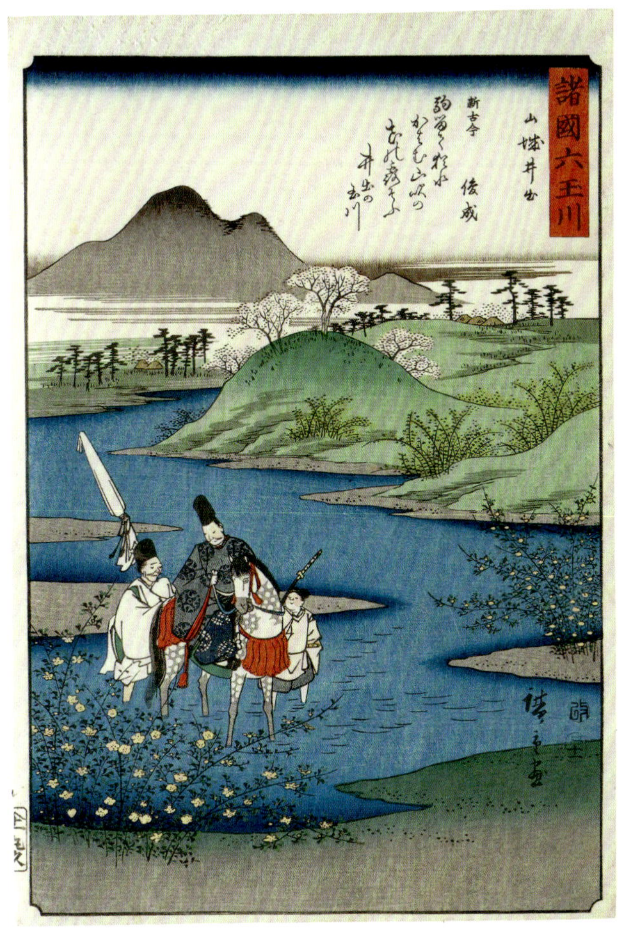

Ide no Tamagawa

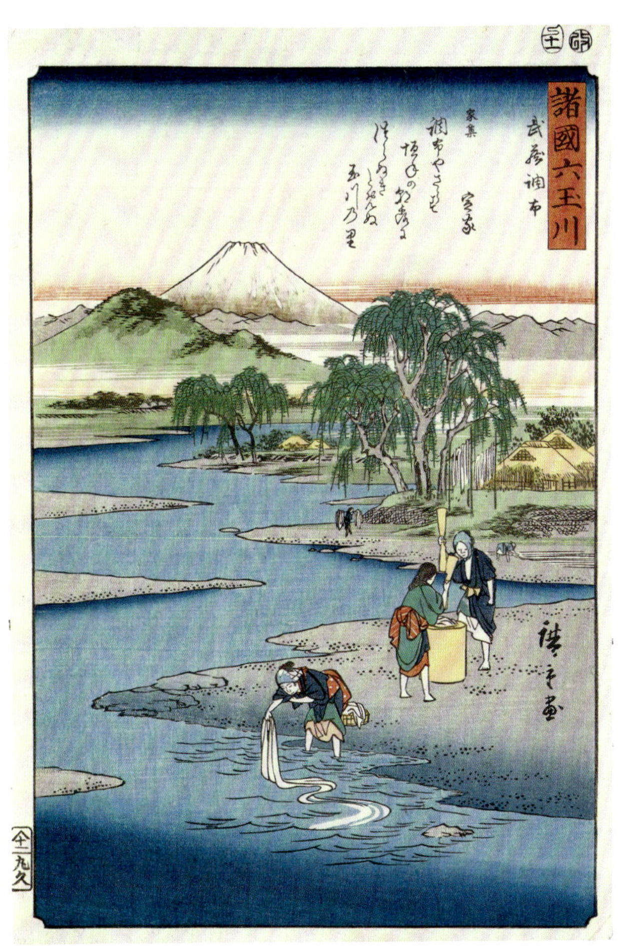

Tetsukuri no Tamagawa

Utagawa Hiroshige
(歌川広重; 1797–1858)

495. *Hiroshige sōhitsu gafu* (広重草筆画譜 / Collection of Hiroshige's Sketches)

Edo period
Two-volume book; illustrations in ink and color on paper
Each book approx. 17.6 x 11.6 cm (6⅞ x 4⅝ in.)

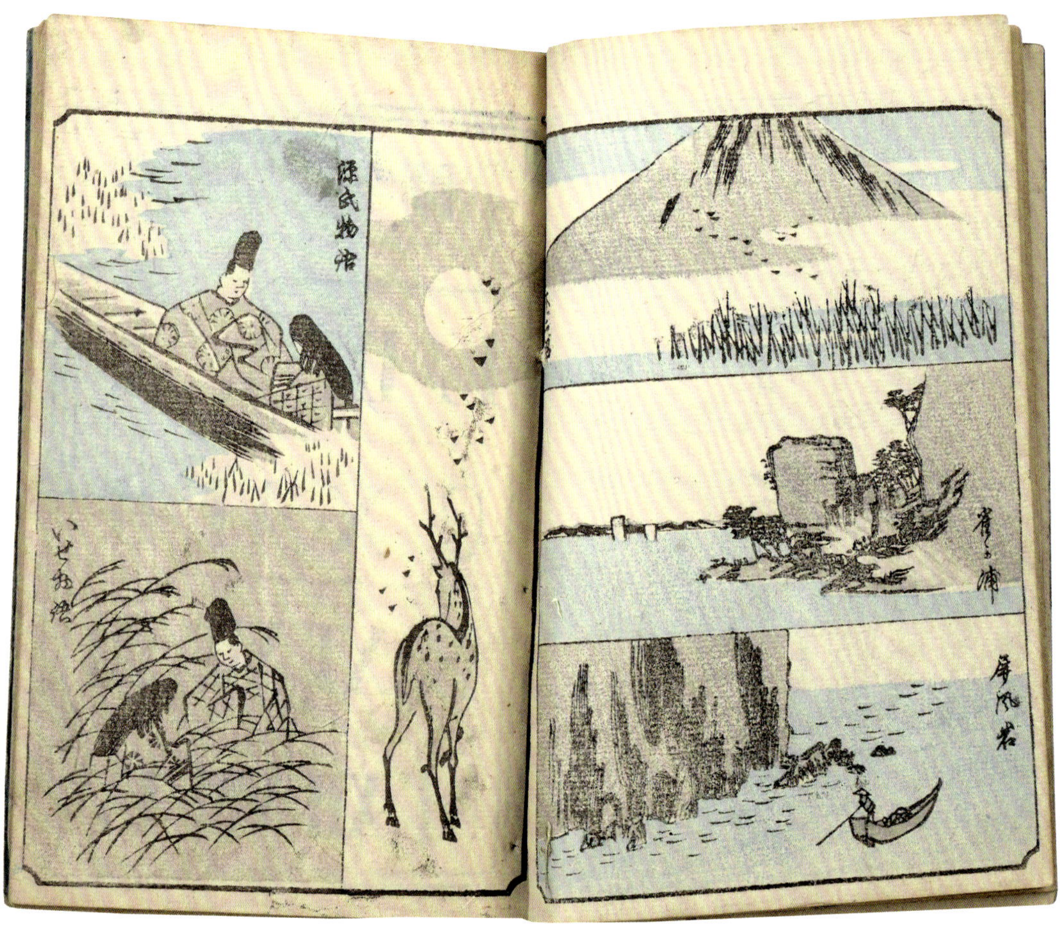

496. *Renpō shiryaku* (聯邦志略 / Brief History of the United States)

Edo period, 1861
Two-volume book; illustrations in ink and color on paper
Each volume approx. 26.9 x 18.3 cm (10⅝ x 7¼ in.)

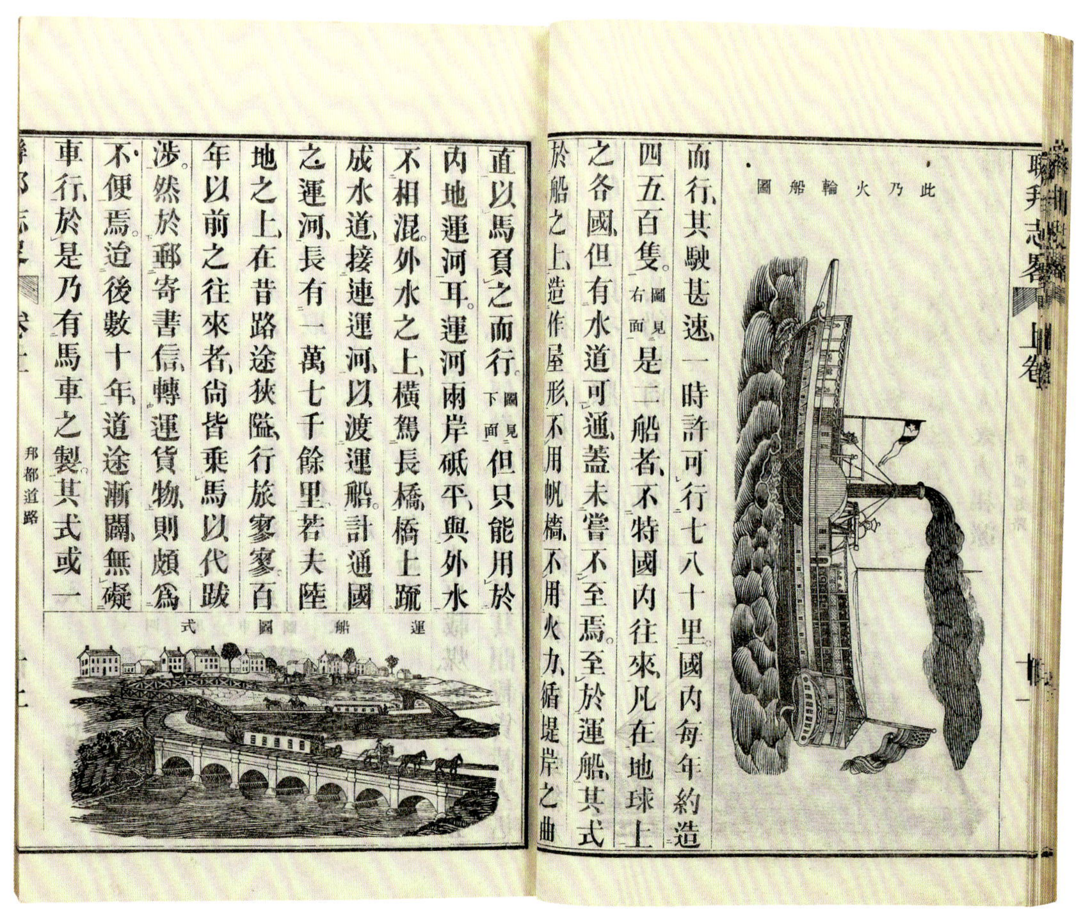

聯邦志畧 上巻

此乃火輪船圖

而行其駛甚速一時許可行七八十里國內每年約造四五百隻(圖見右面)是二船者不特國內往來凡在地球上之各國但有水道可通蓋未嘗不至焉至於運船其式於船之上造作屋形不用帆檣不用火力循堤岸之曲直以馬負之而行(圖見下面)但只能用於內地運河耳運河兩岸砥平與外水不相混外水之上橫駕長橋橋上疏成水道接連運河以渡運船計通國之運河長有一萬七千餘里若夫陸地之上在昔路途狹隘行旅寥寥百年以前之往來者尚皆乘馬以代跋涉然於郵寄書信轉運貨物則頗爲不便焉迨後數十年道途漸闢無礙車行於是乃有馬車之製其式或一

運船圖式

聯邦志畧 巻上 邦都道路

497. *Tsūzoku nichijō Seiyō shohō shinsho sōkō* (通俗日常西洋諸法新書草稿 / New Guide to the Ways of the West: Draft)

Meiji era, ca. 1870s
Book; illustrations in ink on paper
27.9 x 19.6 cm (11 x 7¾ in.)

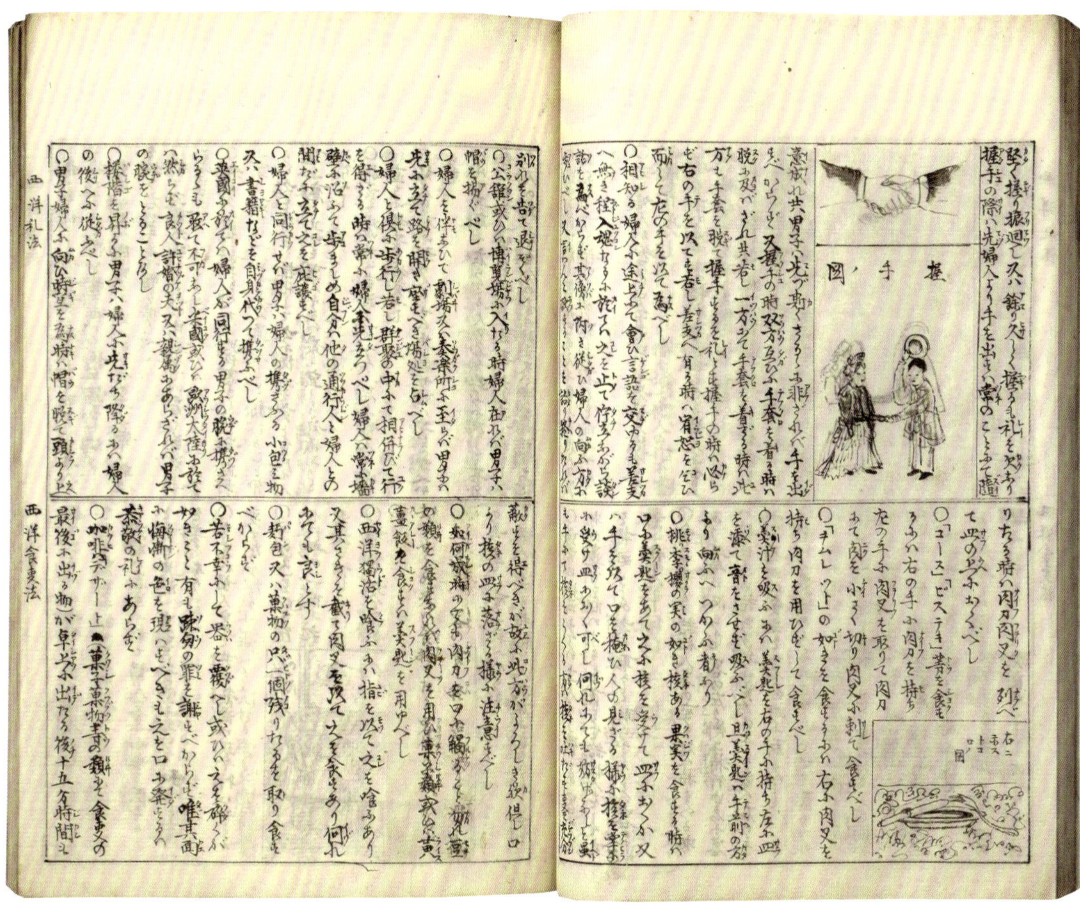

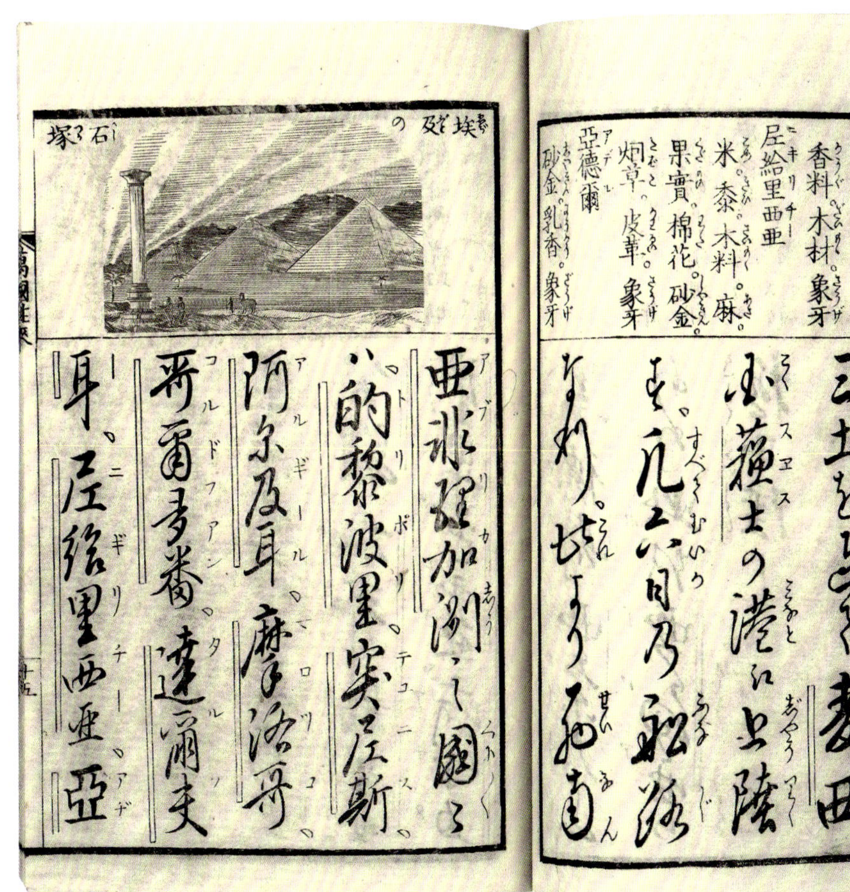

Yomo Shunsui
(四方春翠)
Kitamura Yūzan
(北村友山)

498. *Bankoku ōrai* (万国往来 / Views of the World)

Meiji era, 1871
Book of engravings; illustrations in ink and light color on paper
22.4 x 15.4 cm (8⅞ x 6 in.)
Postscript: "Printed in winter 1871 by Yomo Shunsui with the help of protégé Kitamura Yūzan."

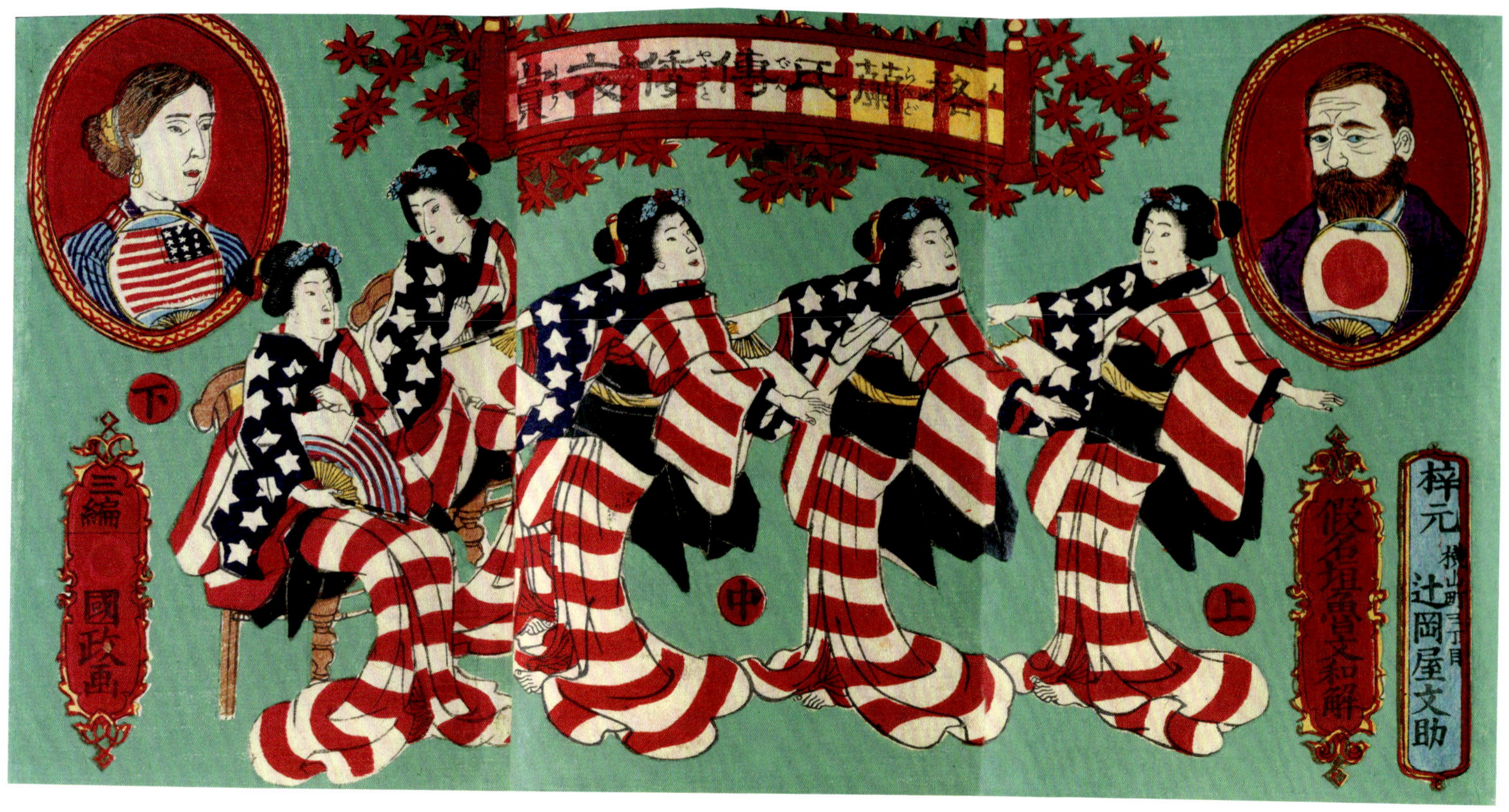

Utagawa Kunimasa V
(歌川国政 V; fl. late 19th–early 20th century)

499. *Gurando-shi den wabunshō* (格蘭氏伝倭文賞 / The Life of President Grant in Japanese)

Meiji era, 1879
Book; illustrations in ink and color on paper
20.8 x 14.1 cm (8⅛ x 5½ in.)
Postscripts: "Translation into Japanese by Kanagaki Robun [假名垣魯文; 1829–1894]"; "Published by Tsujiokaya Bunsuke [辻岡屋文助]"

Literature: Meech-Pekarik 1986, pl. 19; Guth 2004, p. 27, no. 1.14.

Kanagaki Robun (editor)
(仮名垣魯文; 1829–1894)
Kawanabe Kyōsai (Gyōsai)
(河鍋暁斎; 1831–1889) and
Utagawa Yoshiiku (歌川芳幾; fl. 1870s)
(illustrators)

500. *Kokkei zansai bukuro* (滑稽残菜嚢 / Collection of Humorous Leftovers), including *Aguranabe* (安愚楽鍋 / Kettle of Peaceful and Simple Pleasures)

Meiji era, mid-February 1882
Five volumes of eleven-volume book; illustrations in ink and color on paper
Each volume approx. 18.2 x 12.3 cm (7⅛ x 4⅞ in.)

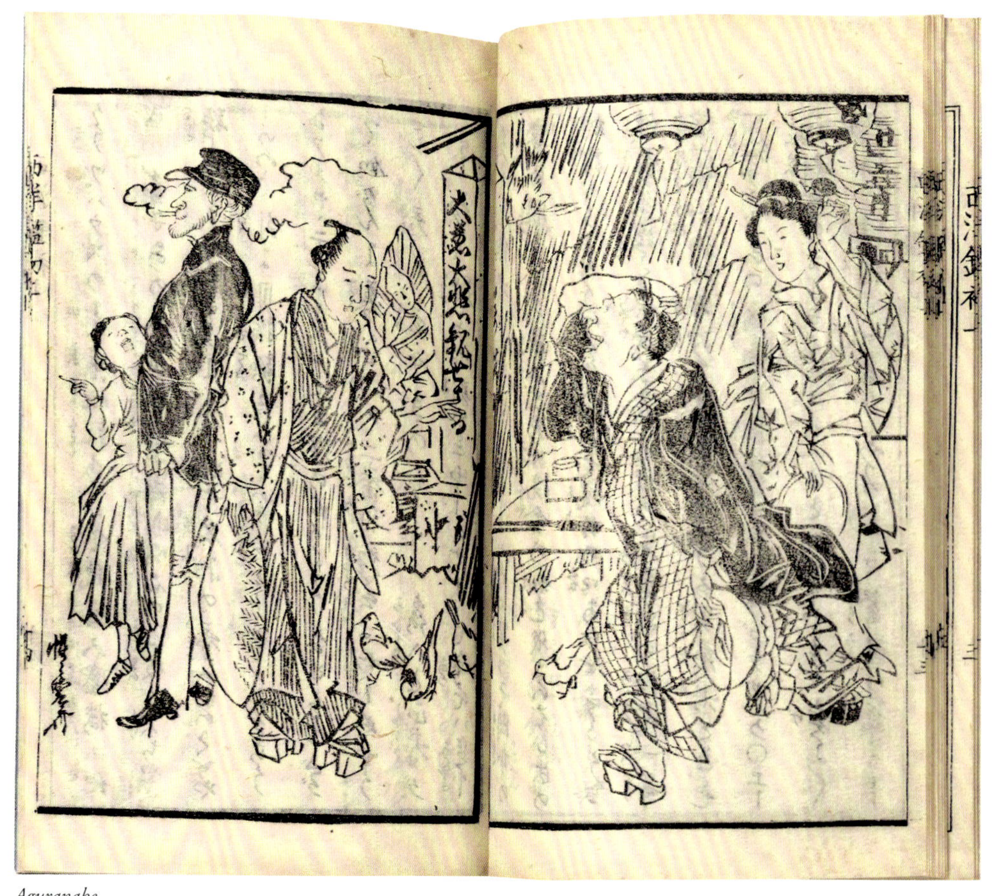

Aguranabe

Saitō Gesshin (editor)
(斉藤月岑; 1804–1878)
Hasegawa Settei (illustrator)
(長谷川雪堤; 1819–1882)

501. *Seikyoku ruisan* (声曲類纂 / Encyclopedia of Musical Theater Performances)

Meiji era, 1889
Six-volume book; illustrations in ink on paper
Each volume approx. 26 x 17.6 cm (10¼ x 6⅞ in.)
First published in 1839; second edition, 1847; third edition, 1889
Text, seal

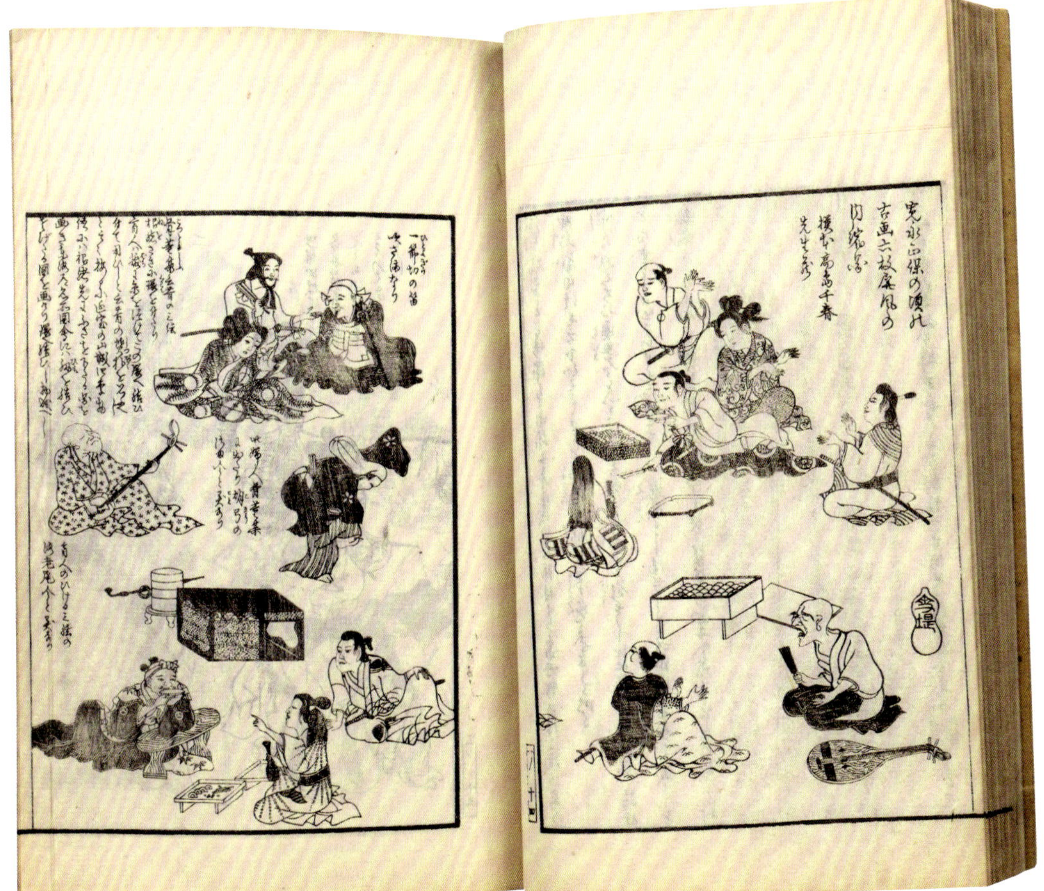

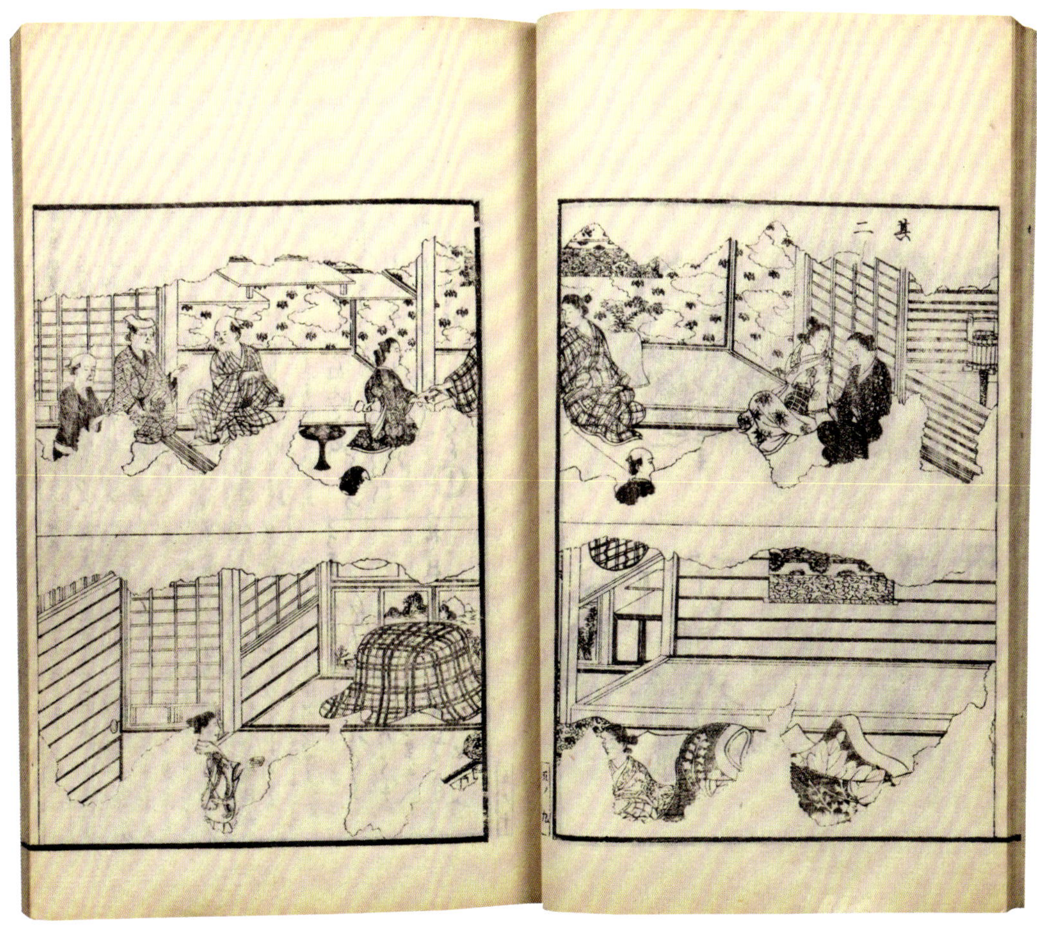

502. *Senden Ishigumi Ensei Yaegaki den* (鮮伝石組園生八重垣伝 / Instructions for Garden Design)

Meiji era, 1890
Two-volume book; ink on paper
22.5 x 15.6 cm ($8\frac{7}{8}$ x $6\frac{1}{8}$ in.)

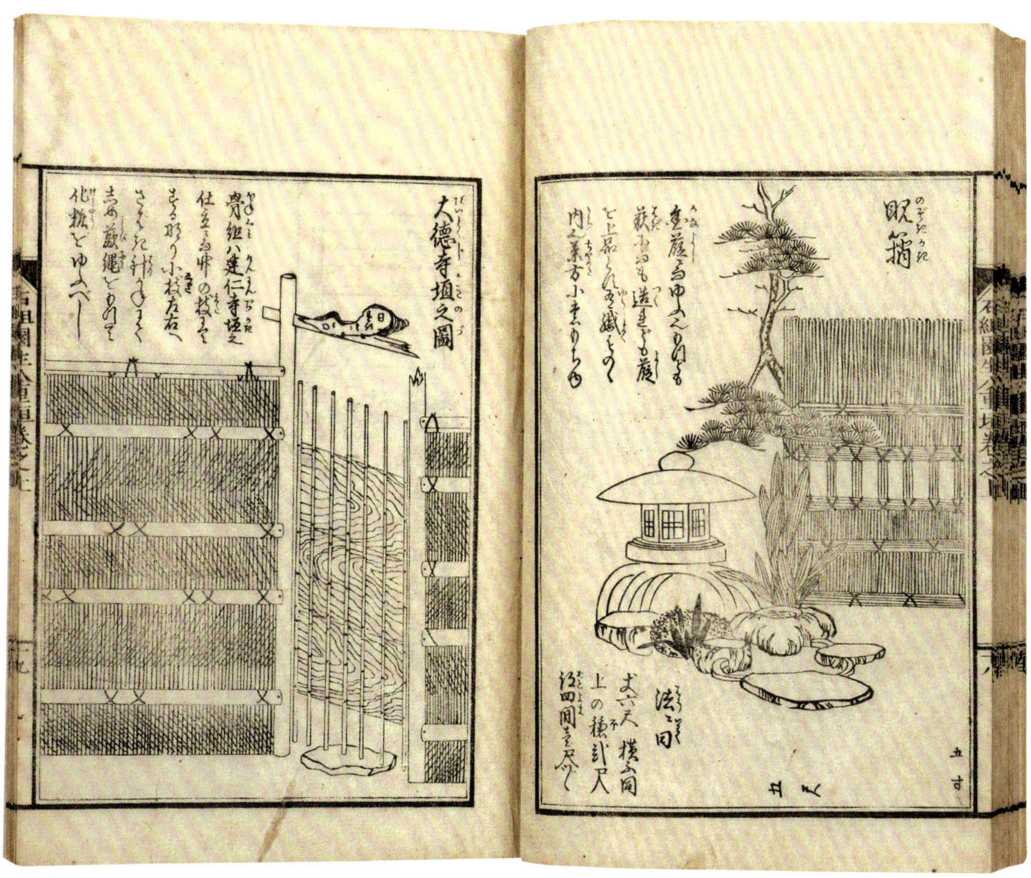

503. *Kenzan iboku* (乾山遺墨 / Collected Works of Ogata Kenzan)

Meiji era, 1912
Book; illustrations in ink on paper
26.4 x 18.2 cm ($10\frac{3}{8}$ x $7\frac{1}{8}$ in.)
Signatures
Postscript: "June 2, 1912, Kokka-sha"

Literature: McKelway 2012, pp. 82–83, no. 15.

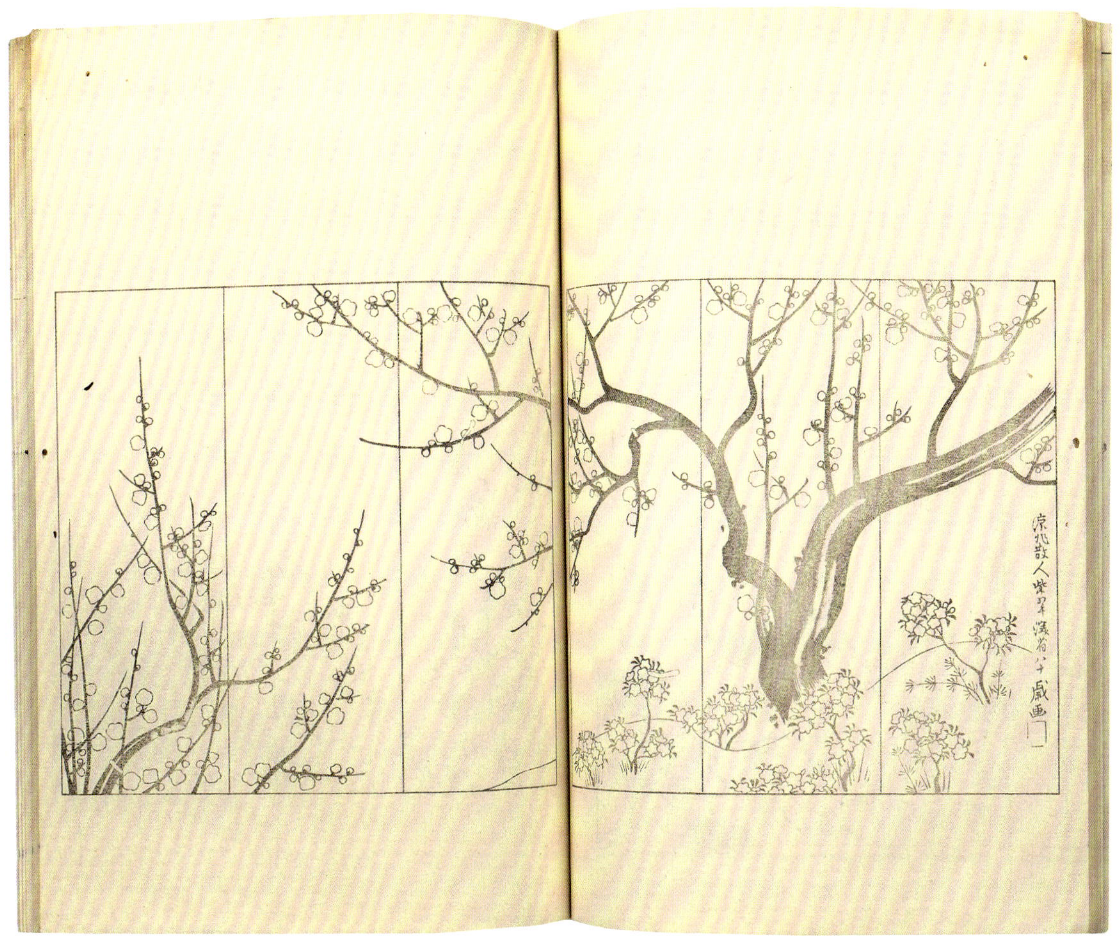

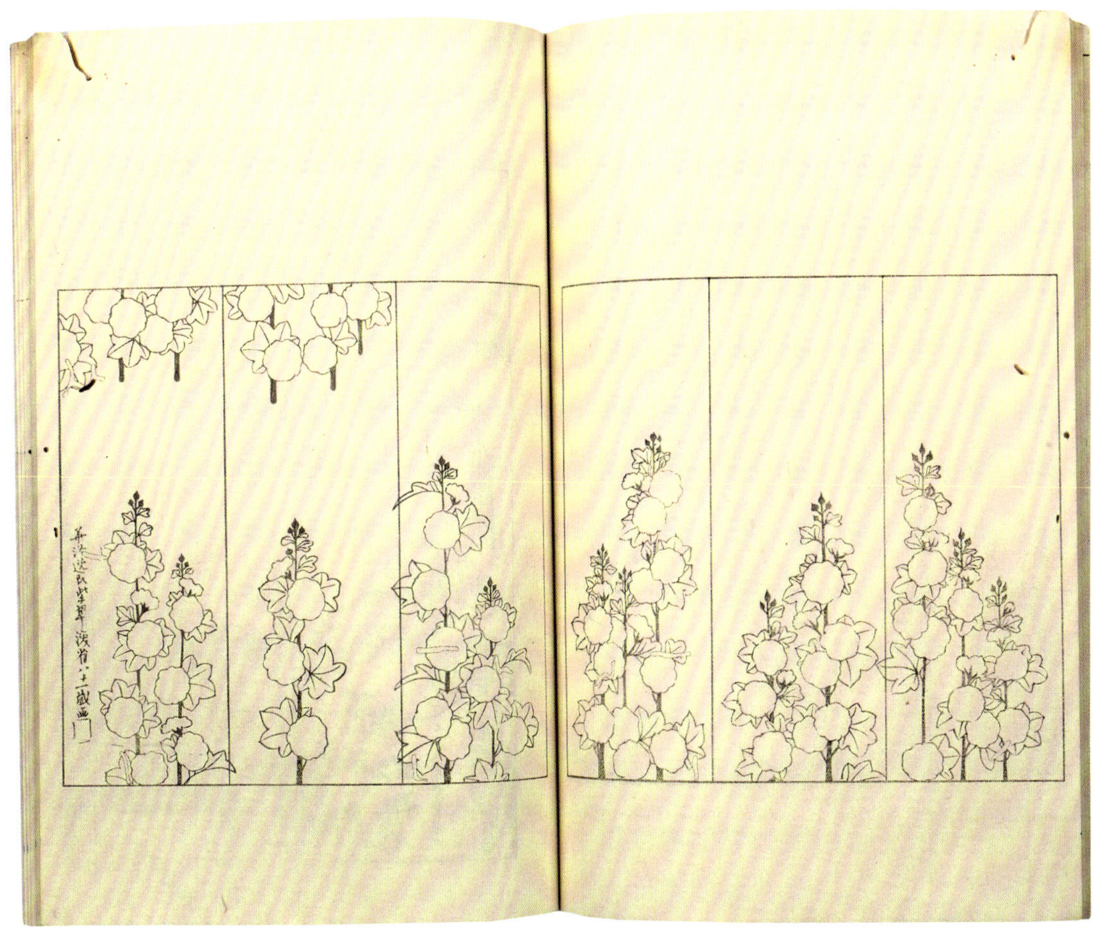

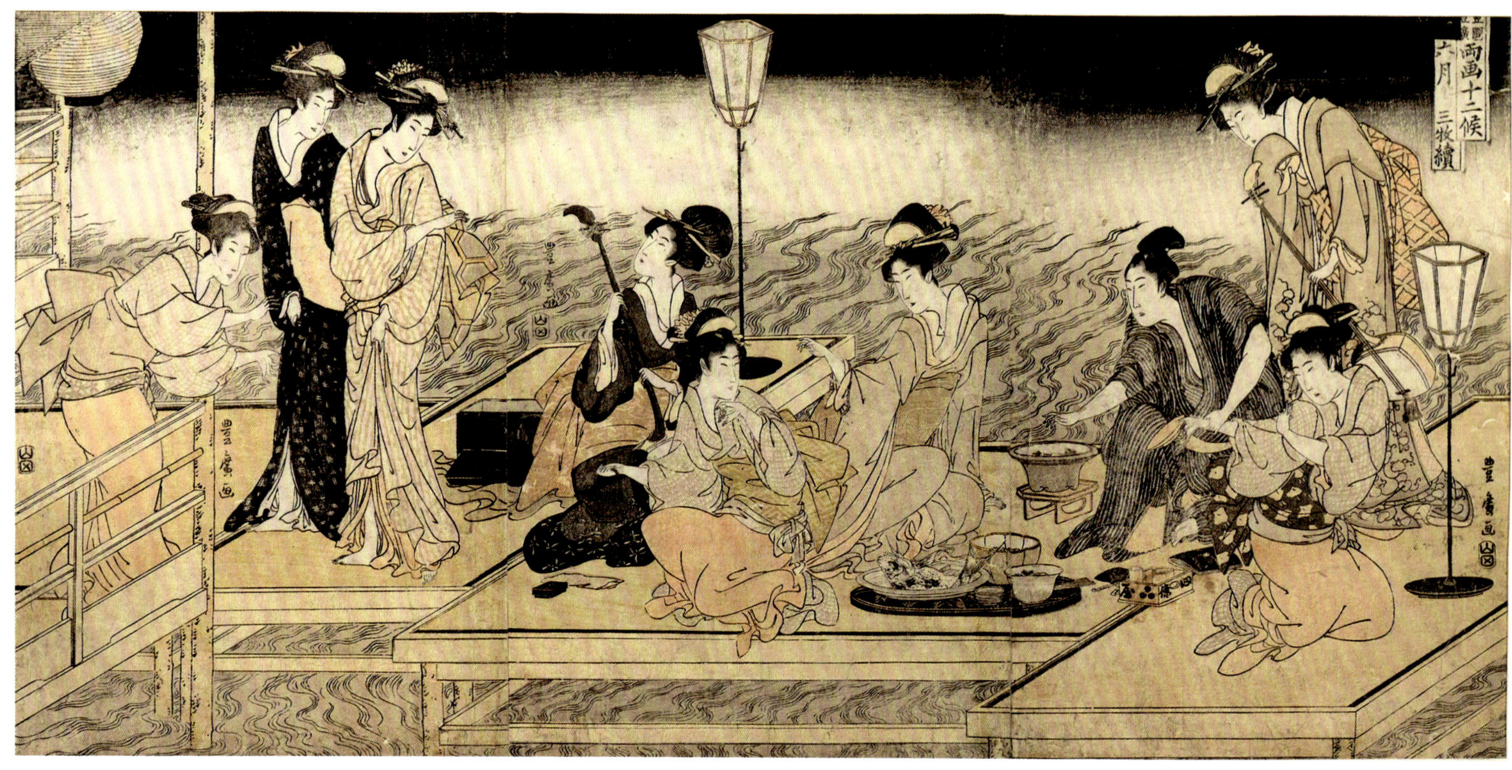

Utagawa Toyokuni
(歌川豊国; 1769–1825)
Utagawa Toyohiro
(歌川豊広; 1773–1828)

504. *Sixth Month*, from *Pictures of the Twelve Months*

Edo period, 19th century
Triptych of prints; ink and color on paper
36 x 74.5 cm (14⅛ x 29⅜ in.)
Signatures, seals

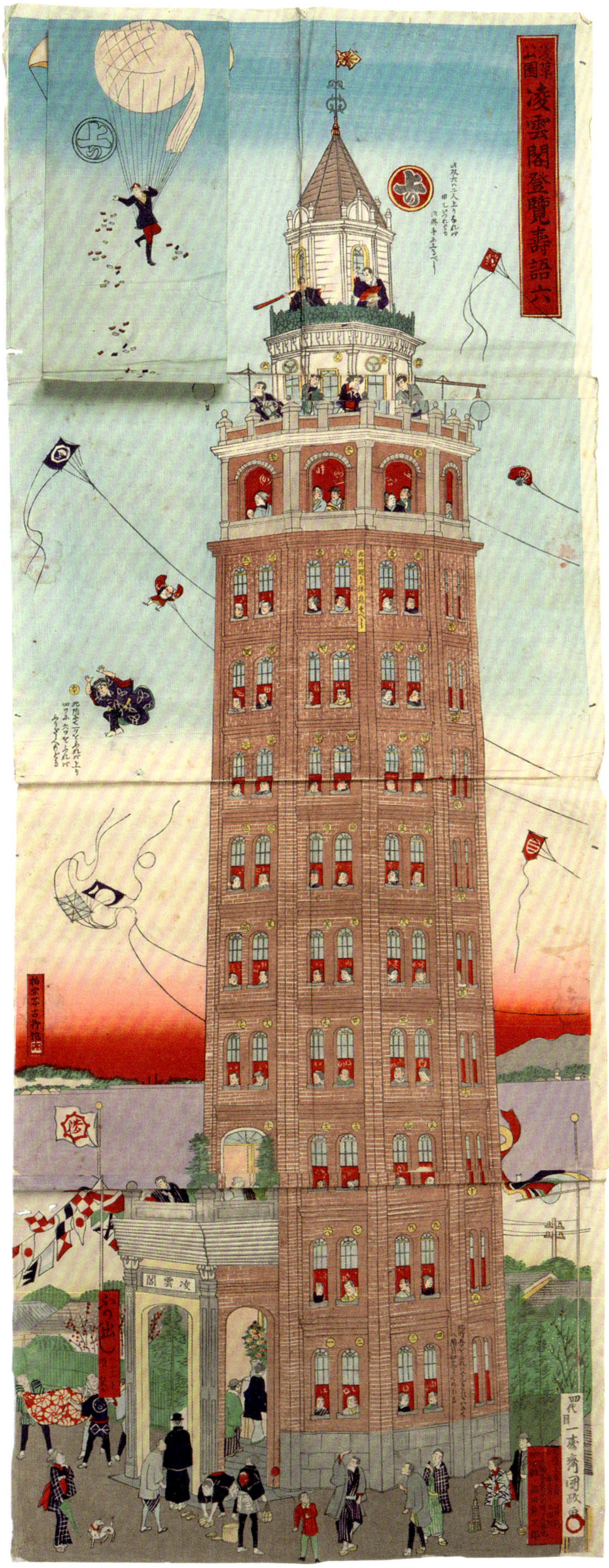

Utagawa Kunimasa IV
(歌川国政 IV; 1848–1920)

505. Parcheesi of Ryōunkaku (凌雲閣双六)

Meiji era, November 1890
Unmounted woodblock prints on four sheets of paper with paper flap; ink and color
95.5 x 37.2 cm ($37\frac{5}{8}$ x $14\frac{5}{8}$ in.)
Text, signature
Printed and published by Fukuda Kumajirō at No. 19, Hasegawa-chō, Nihonbashi

Utagawa Sadakage
(歌川貞景; fl. first half of 19th century)

506. The Hermit Sōho (Ch. Chaofu, 巣父)

Edo period
Framed *surimono*; ink and color on paper
19.2 x 17.7 cm ($7\frac{1}{2}$ x 7 in.)
Signature

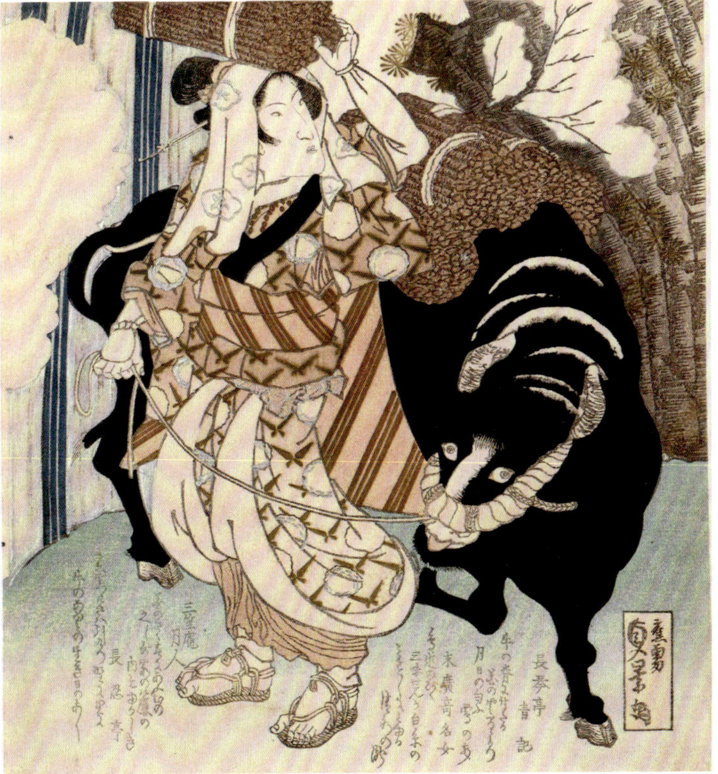

Chapter 11 Details

† denotes illustrated items

† 469. Chapter 579 of *Daihannya haramitakyō*

Signature

[at end of scroll] *Daihannya haramitakyō, chapter 579, Buddhist monk Senshin*

473. Six Amida Buddhas

Text

Eleventh day; copied on the third day of the tenth month; ninety Buddhas . . . [illegible]

† 475. Fudō Myōō

Text

Nankyō; Sugahara; Kikōji

Seals

Stone pagoda shape; *Gankō*

478. *Nishiki no mizuguki* (Traces of Japanese Calligraphy)

Signature

[at end of book] *Carved in mid-spring, 1651, by Tōrian*

480. Women's Work and Manners

Text

Wife of rich and virtuous; essence of Jusshukō incense; wife of a mid-level merchant; female servant Dai [illegible]

481. *Ehon tokiwagusa* (Illustrated Lives of Famous and Not-So-Famous Women)

Text

[Poem] *No seeds were sown, / yet floating weeds thrive / on the ripples of the water.*

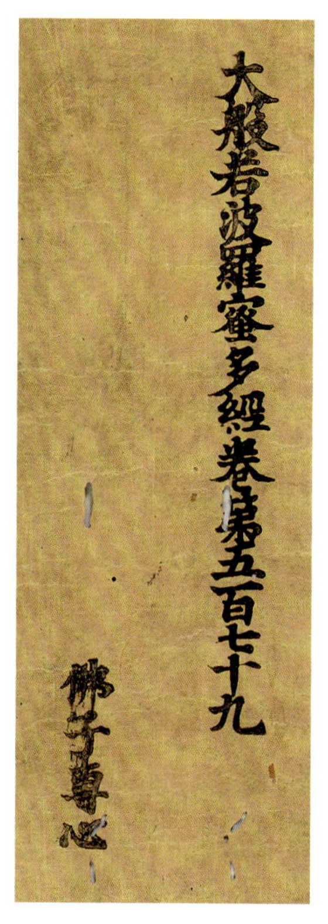

469

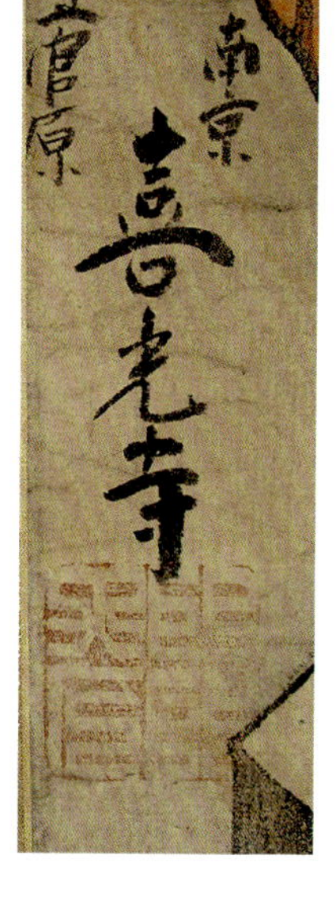

475

486

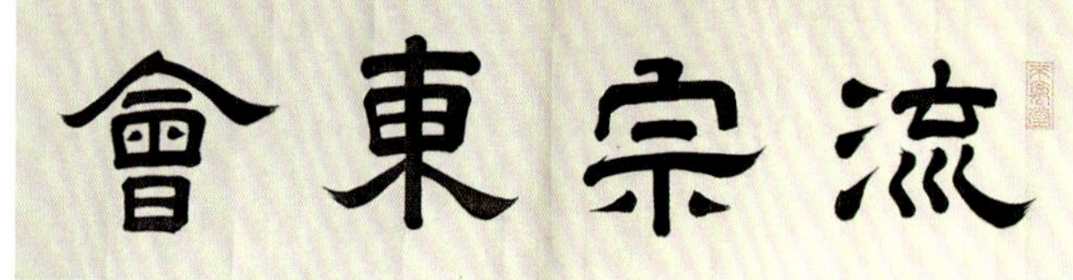

486

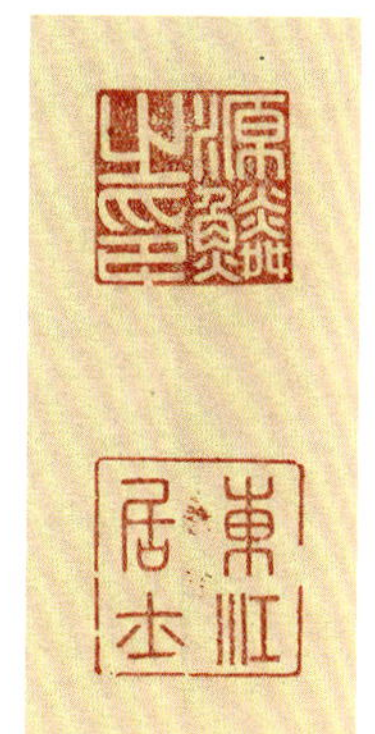

486

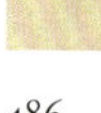

486

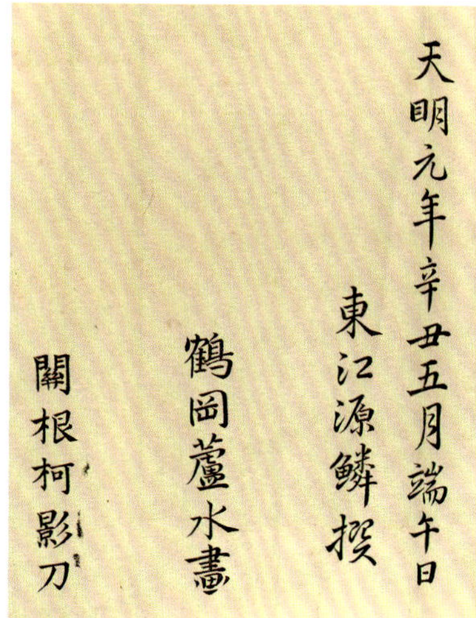

486

† 486. Both Banks of the Sumida River

Text

Ryūsō Tōkai

Signature

[at beginning of scroll I] *Inscribed by Tōkō Genrin* [1732–1796] */ summer 1781*
[at end of scroll II] *Selected by Tōkō Genrin, painted by Tsuruoka Rosui, and engraved by Sekine Kaei in the fifth day of the fifth month of 1781.*

Seals

[at beginning of scroll I] *Raikindō; Genrin no in; Tōkō koji*

487. *Honchō gasan* (Collection of Japanese Paintings)

Signature

Painted by Tani Bunchō

Seals

Kyakutō Jicchi; Hokkyō; Tōan

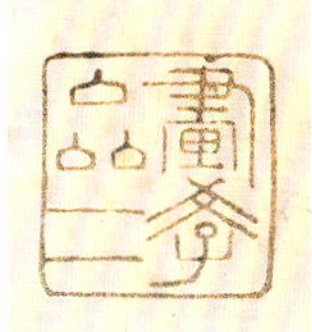

489

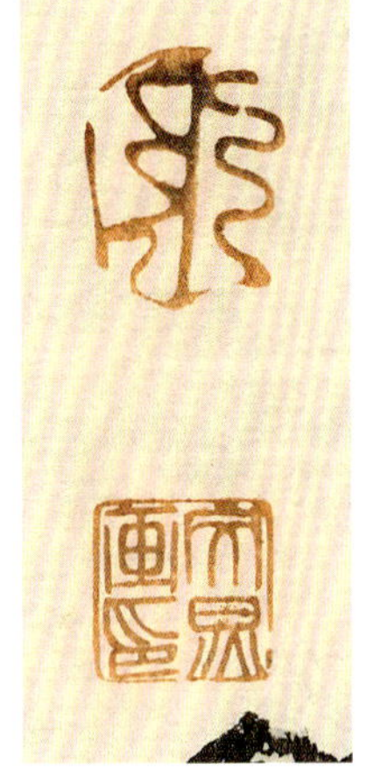

489

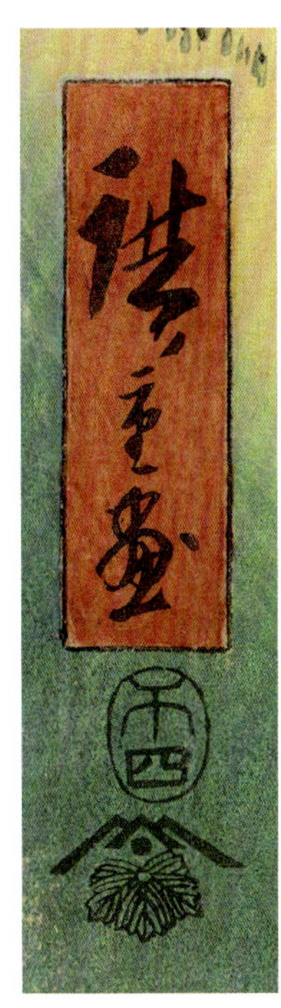

493

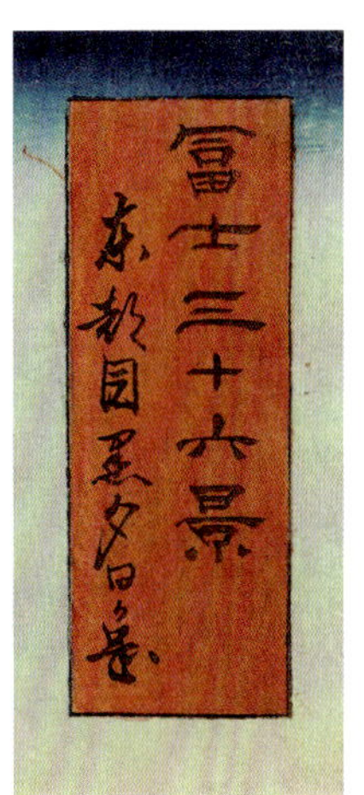

493

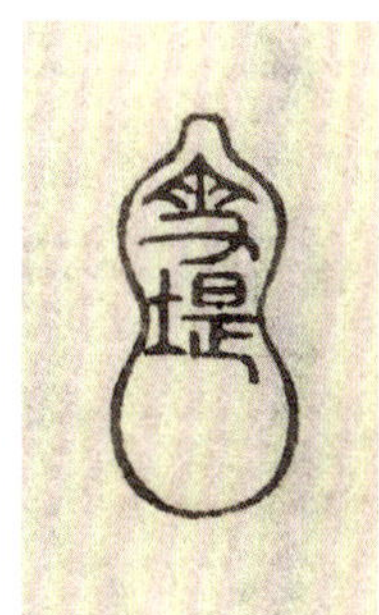

501

† 489. *Shazanrō ehon* (Book of Pictures by Shazanrō)

Seals

Bunchō; *Bunchō ga in*; [at end of book] *Gagaku muni*

† 493. "Tōto Meguro Yūhigaoka" (Twilight Hill at Meguro in the eastern capital), from *Thirty-six Views of Mt. Fuji*

Signature

Painted by Hiroshige

Seals

[of publisher] *Fourth month, Maruya Kyūshirō*

494. Shokoku Mu Tamagawa (Six Tamagawa Rivers from Different Regions)

Text

Six Tamagawa Rivers in Many Regions

[upper right] *Noda no Tamagawa*, poem 643 by Nōin Hōshi (b. 988) from *Shin kokin wakashū*

When evening approaches, / plovers cry in the briny air / over Tamagawa's stream at Noda in Michinoku.

[lower right] *Tetsukuri no Tamagawa*, poem 1292 by Fujiwara Teika (1162–1241) from *Shūi gusō*

The cloth that is hung over the fence for bleaching / catches the morning dew at the village of Tamagawa.

[upper middle] *Noji no Tamagawa*, poem 280 by Minamoto Toshiyori from *Senzaishū*

I shall come back again tomorrow / to the Tamagawa at Noji. / The moon shines over the bush clover / and rests upon the river's colored waves.

[lower middle] *Ide no Tamagawa*, poem 159 by Fujiwara Shunzei (1114–1204) from *Shin kokin wakashū*

As I stop my horse to give him water, / dew drops from yamabuki *flowers are lost / in the stream of the Tamagawa at Ide.*

[upper left] *Kinuta no Tamagawa*, poem 339 by Minamoto Toshiyori (ca. 1055–ca. 1129) from *Senzaishū*

The autumn wind over the pines sounds forlorn. / In the loneliness, / the sound of fulling cloth at Tamagawa.

[lower left] *Kōya no Tamagawa*, poem 1788 by Kōbō Daishi (774–835) from *Fūgashū*

Forgetting the warning / not to do so, / a traveler at the Tamagawa in Kōya / dips his hand in the water.

Signatures

[on each print] *Painted by Hiroshige*

Seals

[in margin, top right] *eleventh month*; *Aratame* [of publisher; in margin, lower left] *Maruya Kyūshirō*

† 501. *Seikyoku ruisan* (Encyclopedia of Musical Theater Performances)

Text

[at end of sixth volume] *Copy of old six-panel screen painting from around the Kan'ei* [1624–43] *or Shoho* [1644–47] *era*

Seal

Settei

† 503. *Kenzan iboku* (Collected Works of Ogata Kenzan)

Signatures

[upper right] *Playfully painted by the recluse from the capital, Kyoto, Shisui Shinsei at age 80*
[lower left] *Painted by the eremite from the flowering capital, Shisui Shinsei at age 81*

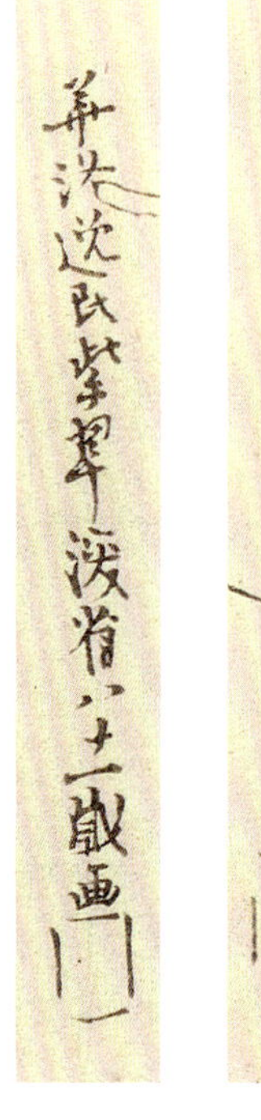

503 503

504. *Sixth Month,* from *Pictures of the Twelve Months*

Signatures

[on each print] *Painted by Toyohiro*

Seals

[of publisher, on each print] *Yamada*

505. Parcheesi of Ryōunkaku

Text

Parcheesi board entitled "Looking Out from Ryōunkaku, Asakusa Park"

Signature

Painted by Ichijusai Kunimasa IV / November 1890

† 506. The Hermit Sōho (Ch. Chaofu)

Signature

Sadakage on request, Kaō

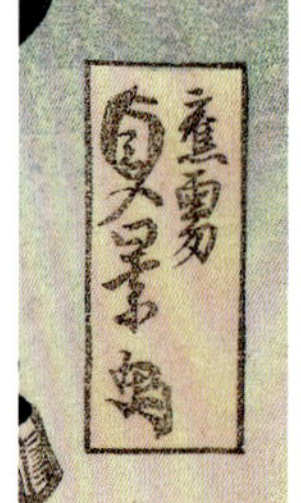

506

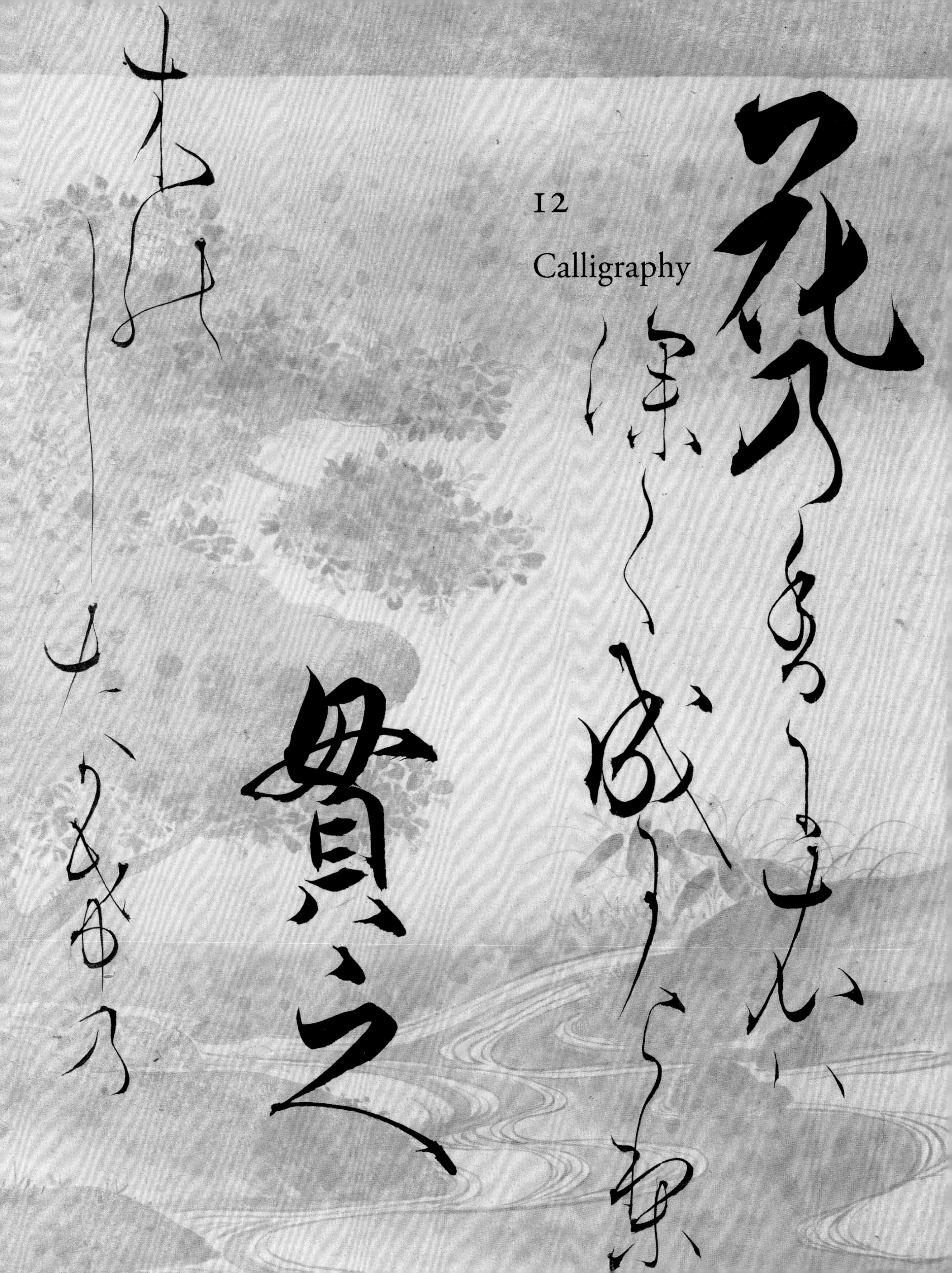

12

Calligraphy

Kojima Sōshin
(小島宗真; 1580–ca. 1656)

507. Poem from *Tsurayukishū I* (貫之集上), in album entitled *Mokagami* (藻鏡)

Edo period, 17th century
Album containing 298 calligraphies from Nara–Edo periods; ink, color, and gold on paper
40 x 34.4 cm (15 3/4 x 13 1/2 in.)
Text

Literature: Murase 1993, no. 33.

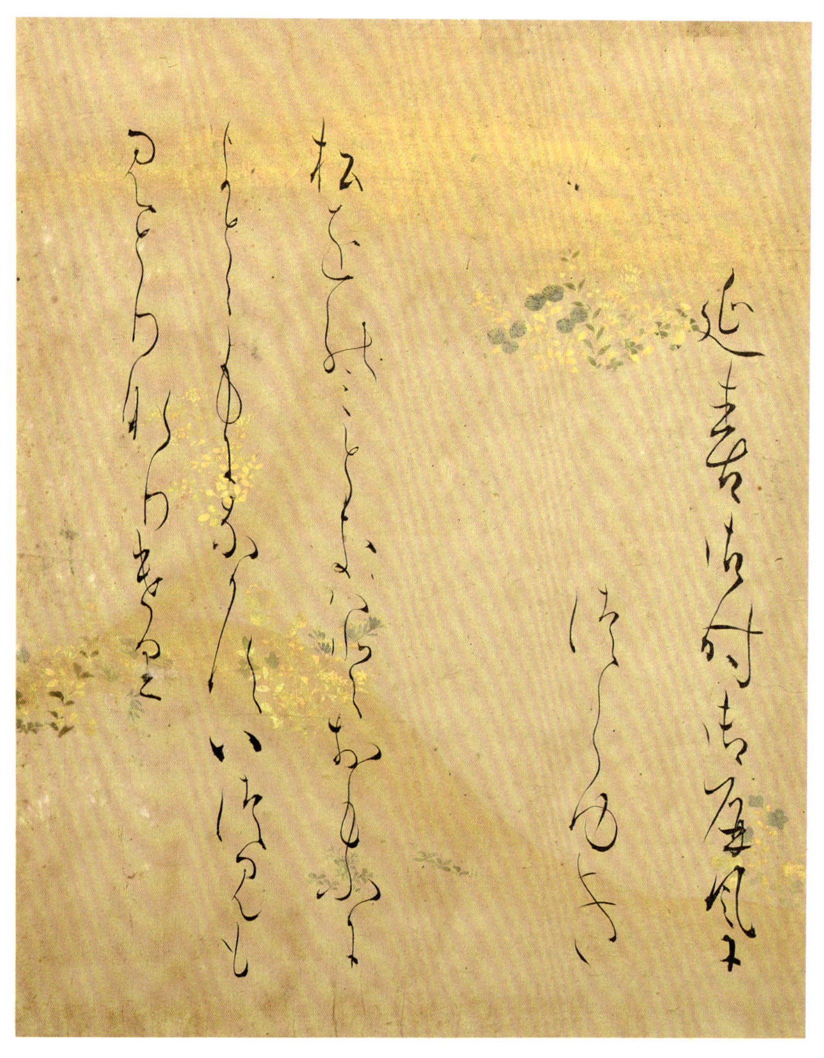

508. *Daihōkōbutsu kegonkyō*

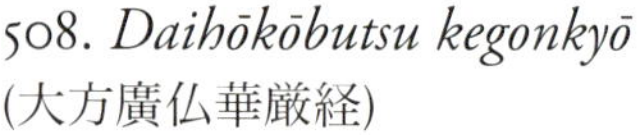

(大方廣仏華厳経)

Commonly known as *Yakekyō* (焼経)
Nara period, ca. 744
Fragment of a handscroll, mounted as hanging scroll; silver ink on indigo paper
24 x 55.6 cm (9 1/2 x 21 7/8 in.)

Ex coll.: Nigatsudō, Tōdaiji, Nara

Literature: Kaufman 1985, fig. 9; Tokyo National Museum 1985a, no. 67; Avitabile 1990, no. 14; Murase 2000, no. 6.

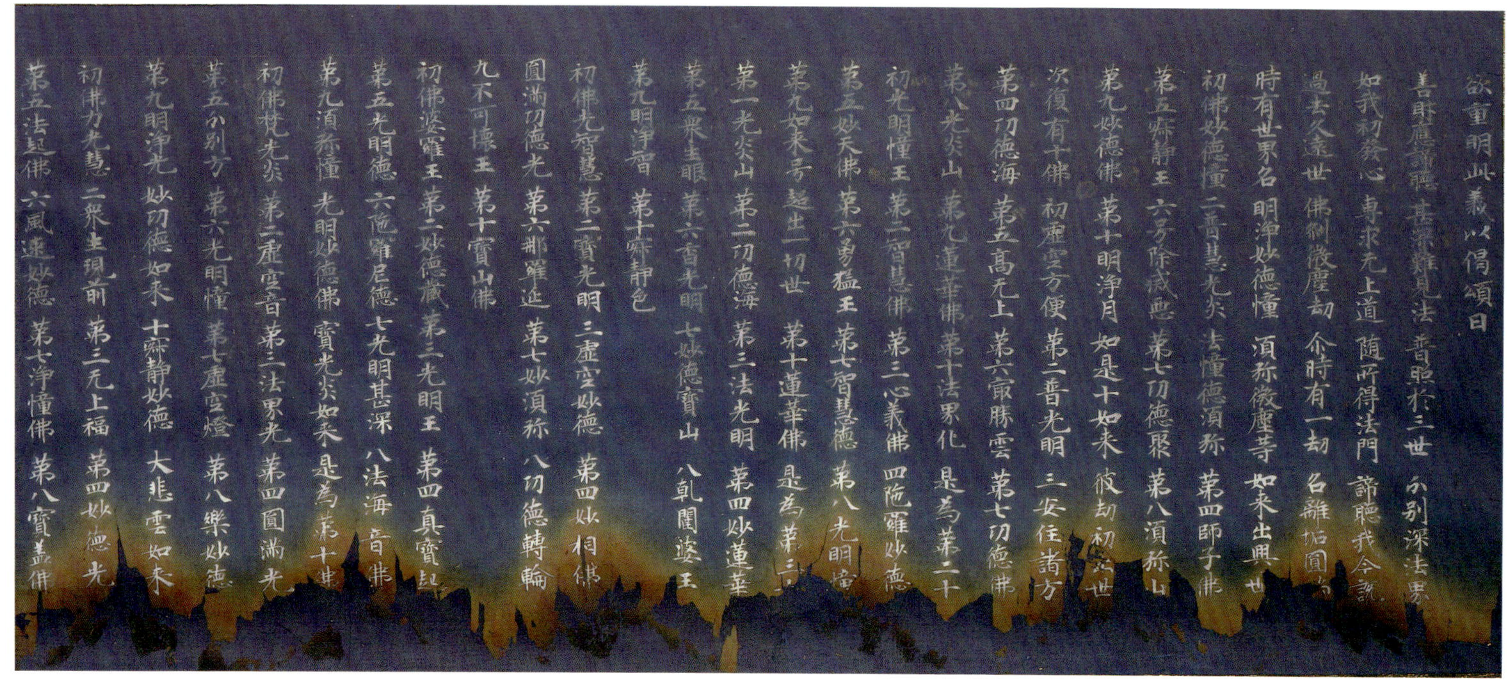

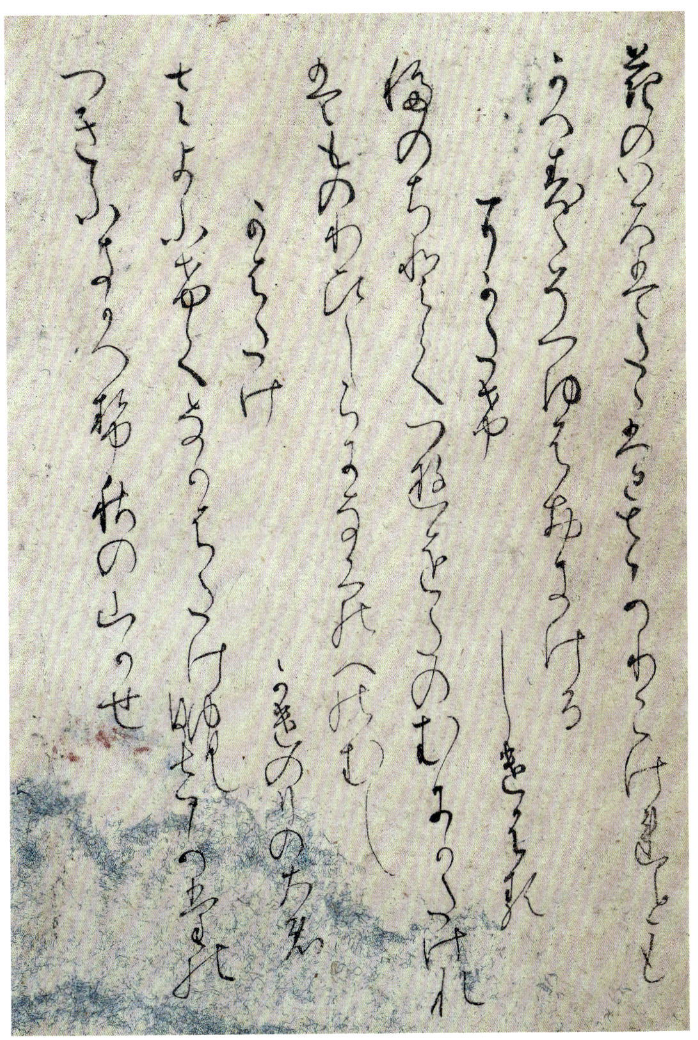

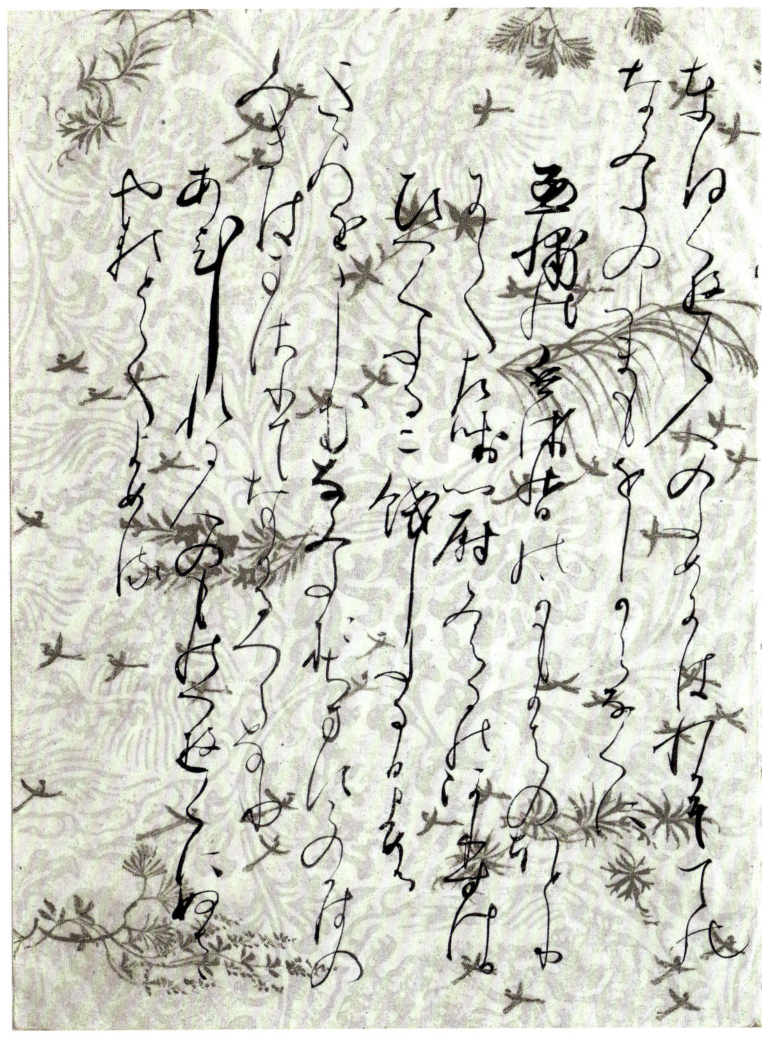

509. Three poems from *Kokin wakashū* (古今和歌集)

Commonly known as *Araki-gire* (荒木切)
Late Heian period, second half of 11th century
Page from book, mounted as hanging scroll; ink on decorated paper
20.3 x 13.8 cm (8 x 5 3/8 in.)
Text

Ex coll.: Araki Sōhaku

Literature: Komatsu Shigemi 1985b, vol. 1, p. 55; Tokyo National Museum 1985a, no. 71; Avitabile 1990, no. 26; Murase 2000, no. 18.

Fujiwara Sadanobu
(藤原定信; 1088–1156)

510. Page from *Tsurayukishū II* (貫之集下)

Commonly known as *Ishiyama-gire* (石山切)
Late Heian period, ca. 1112
Page from book, mounted as hanging scroll; ink on decorated paper
20.2 x 16 cm (8 x 6 1/4 in.)
Text

Ex coll.: Nishi Honganji, Kyoto

Literature: Meech-Pekarik 1985, fig. 3; Tokyo National Museum 1985a, no. 70; Wheelwright 1989, no. 35; Avitabile 1990, no. 25; Murase 2000, no. 19; Tsuji Nobuo et al. 2005, no. 12.

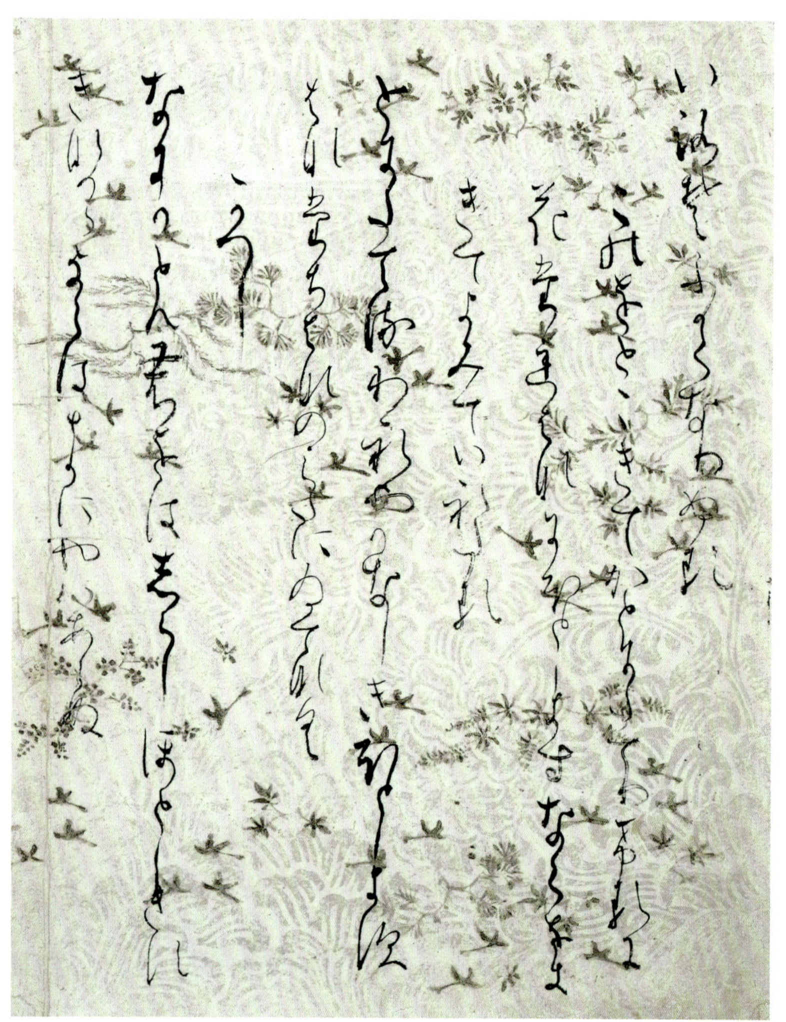

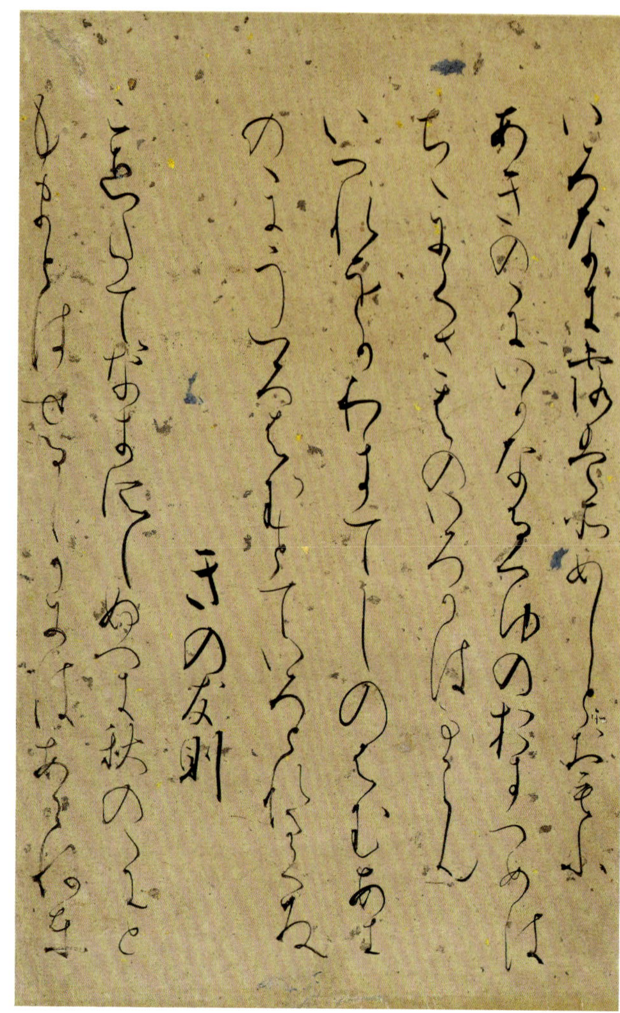

511. Page from *Iseshū* (伊勢集)

Commonly known as *Ishiyama-gire* (石山切)
Late Heian period, 12th century
Page from book, mounted as hanging scroll; ink on decorated paper
20.1 x 15.8 cm (7 7/8 x 6 1/4 in.)
Text

Ex coll.: Osaragi Jirō; Nishi Honganji, Kyoto

Literature: Rosenfield 1967, no. 37d; Murase 1975, no. 19; Tokyo National Museum 1978, no. 114; Kita Haruchiyo 1985, p. 85; Meech-Pekarik 1985, fig. 2; Tokyo National Museum 1985a, no. 69; Avitabile 1990, no. 24; Murase 2000, no. 20; Tsuji Nobuo et al. 2005, no. 13.

512. Three poems from *Gosen wakashū* (後選和歌集)

Commonly known as *Karasumaru-gire* (烏丸切)
Late Heian period, 12th century
Page from book, mounted as hanging scroll; ink on paper
20.5 x 12.8 cm (8 1/8 x 5 in.)
Text

Literature: Tokyo National Museum 1985a, no. 72; Avitabile 1990, no. 28.

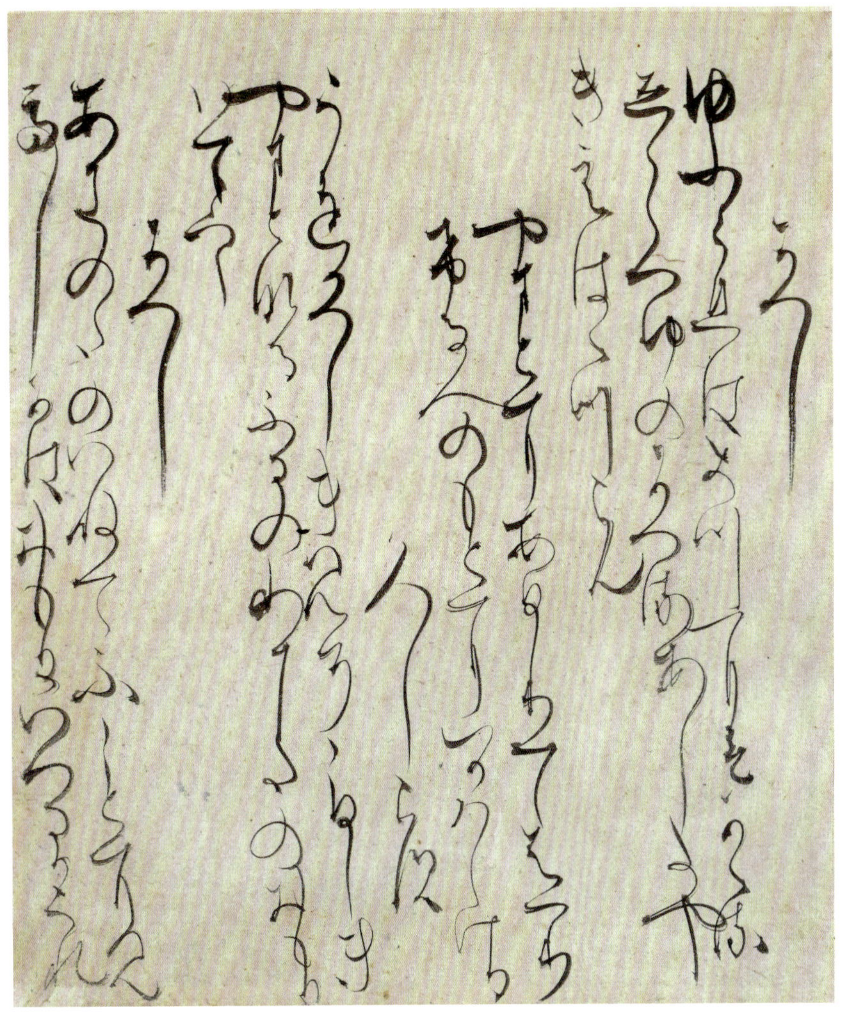

513. Three poems from *Gosen wakashū* (後選和歌集)

Commonly known as *Shirakawa-gire* (白河切)
Late Heian period, 12th century
Page from book, mounted as hanging scroll; ink on paper
17.6 x 14.9 cm (6⁷/₈ x 5⁷/₈ in.)
Text

LITERATURE: Tokyo National Museum 1985a, no. 73; Avitabile 1990, no. 29.

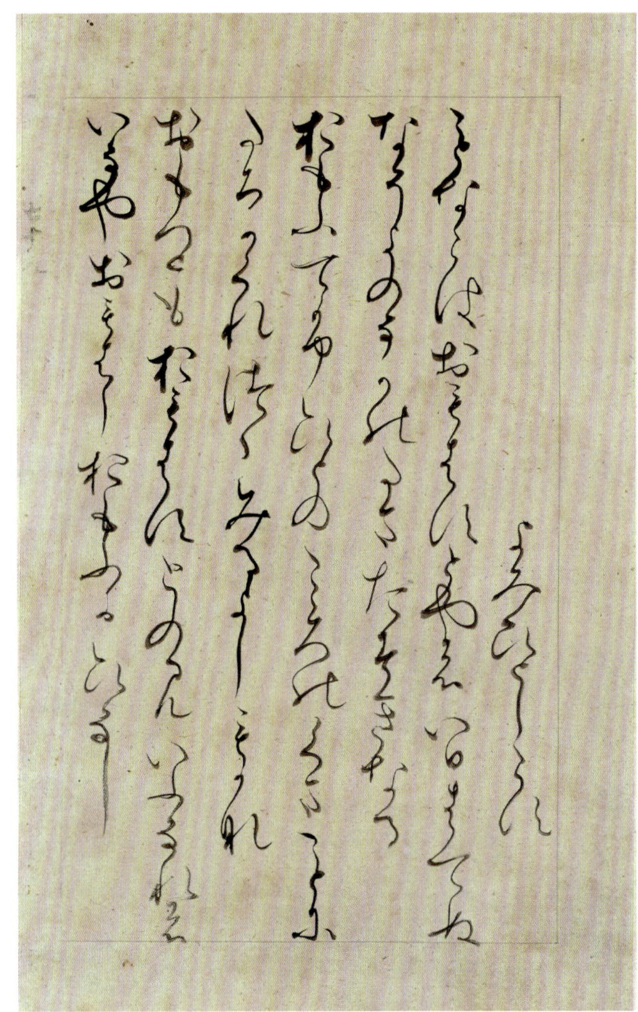

514. Three poems from *Kokin wakashū* (古今和歌集)

Commonly known as *Imaki-gire* (今城切)
Late Heian period, 12th century
Page from book, mounted as hanging scroll; ink on paper
25.3 x 15.9 cm (10 x 6¹/₄ in.)
Text

LITERATURE: Tokyo National Museum 1985a, no. 74; Avitabile 1990, no. 27.

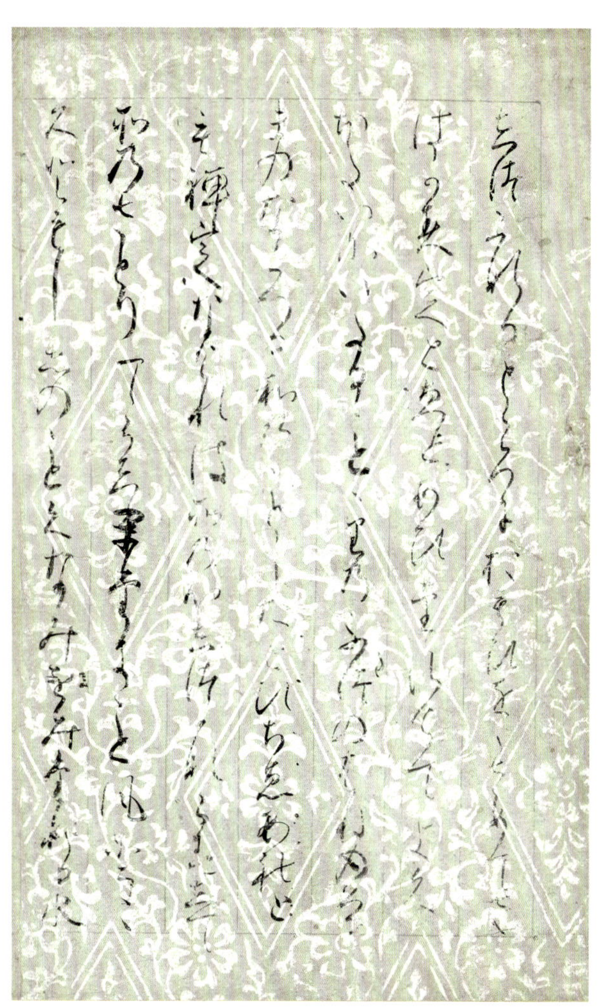

515. *Sanbō ekotoba* (三宝絵詞)

Commonly known as *Tōdaiji-gire* (東大寺切)
Heian period, 12th century
Page from book, mounted as hanging scroll; ink on decorated paper
23.7 x 15 cm (9 3/8 x 5 7/8 in.)
Text

516. Two poems from *Zoku kokin wakashū* (続古今和歌集)

Kamakura period, 13th century
Hanging scroll; ink on paper
23.4 x 9.8 cm (9 1/4 x 3 7/8 in.)
Text

517. Three poems from *Kokin wakashū* (古今和歌集)

Kamakura period, 13th century
Hanging scroll; ink on paper
23.4 x 14.1 cm (9 1/4 x 5 1/2 in.)
Text

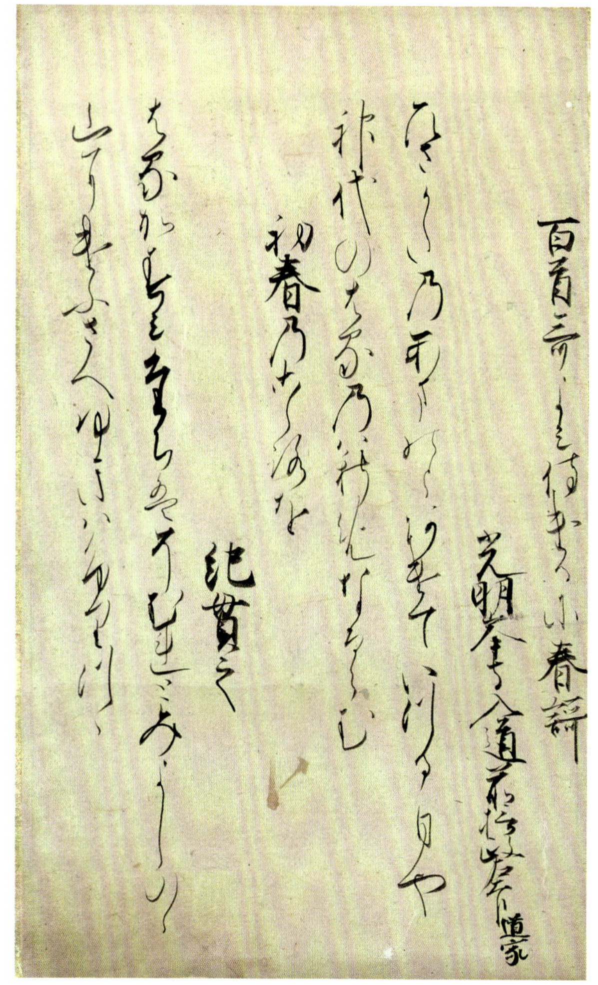

516

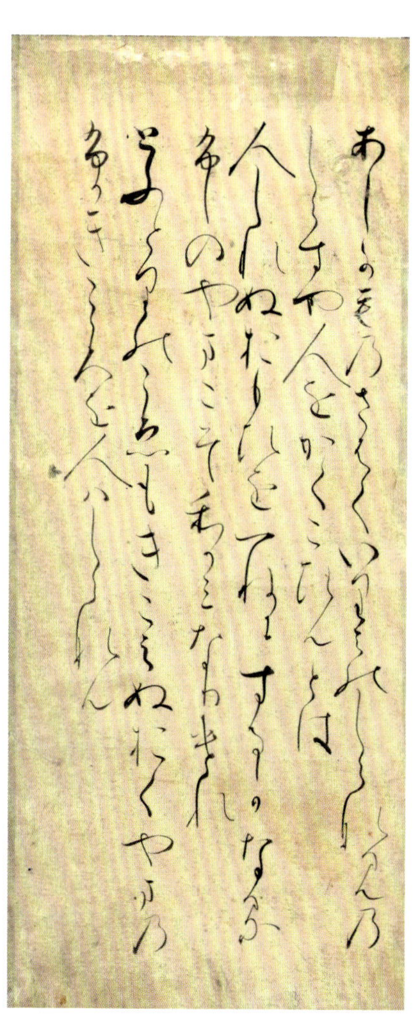

517

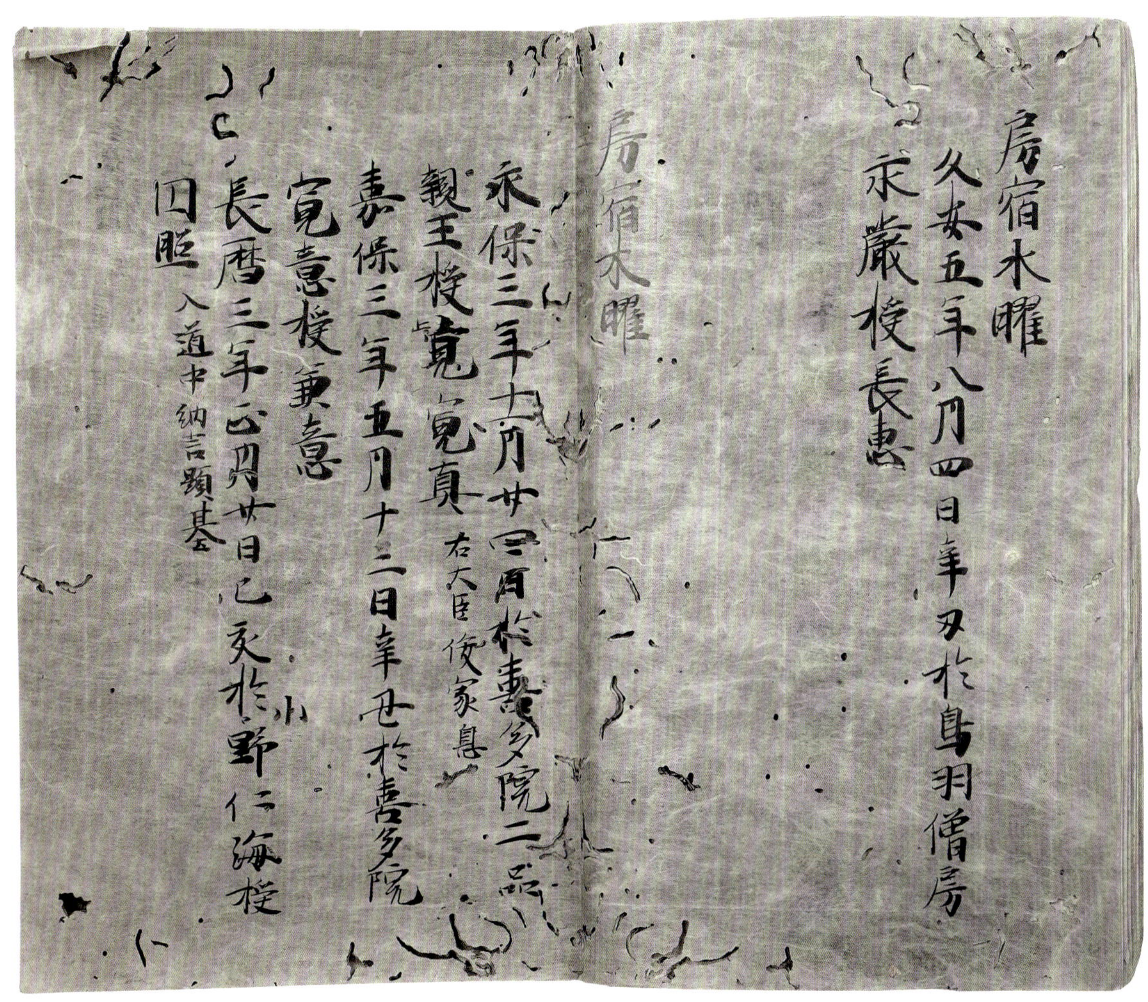

518. *Kanjō yōshukuji* (灌頂曜宿事 / Ordination and Star Signs)

Kamakura period, 13th century
Book; ink on paper
25 x 15.3 cm (9 7/8 x 6 in.)

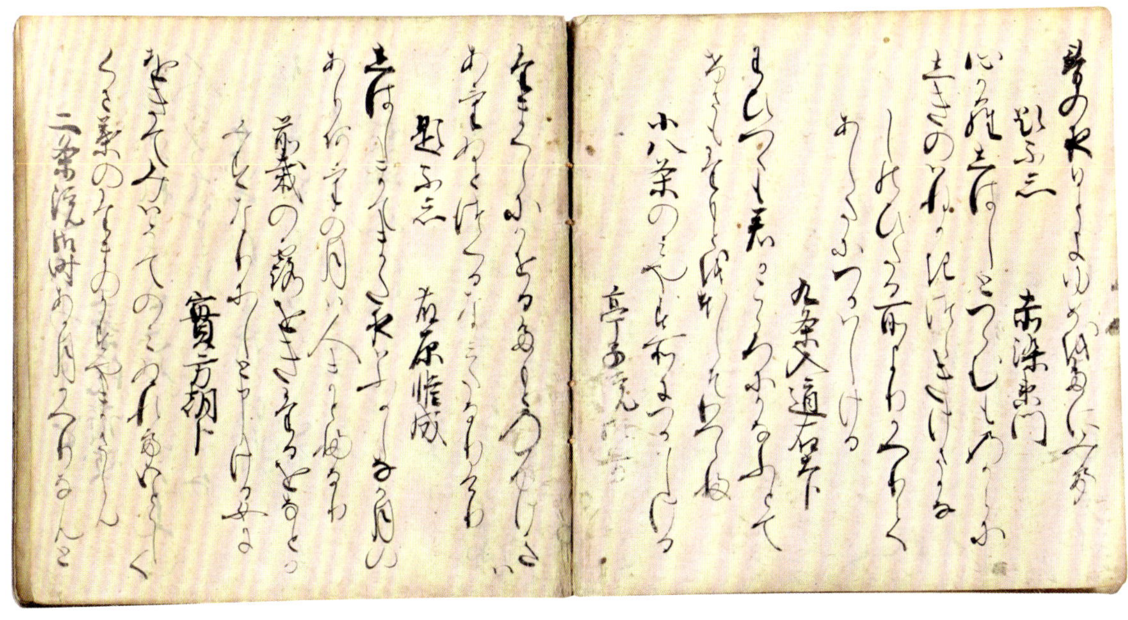

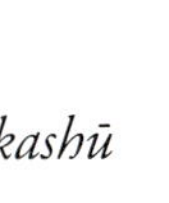

519. *Shin kokin wakashū* (新古今和歌集)

Nanbokuchō period, mid 14th century
Book; ink on paper
9.8 x 9.5 cm (3 7/8 x 3 3/4 in.)

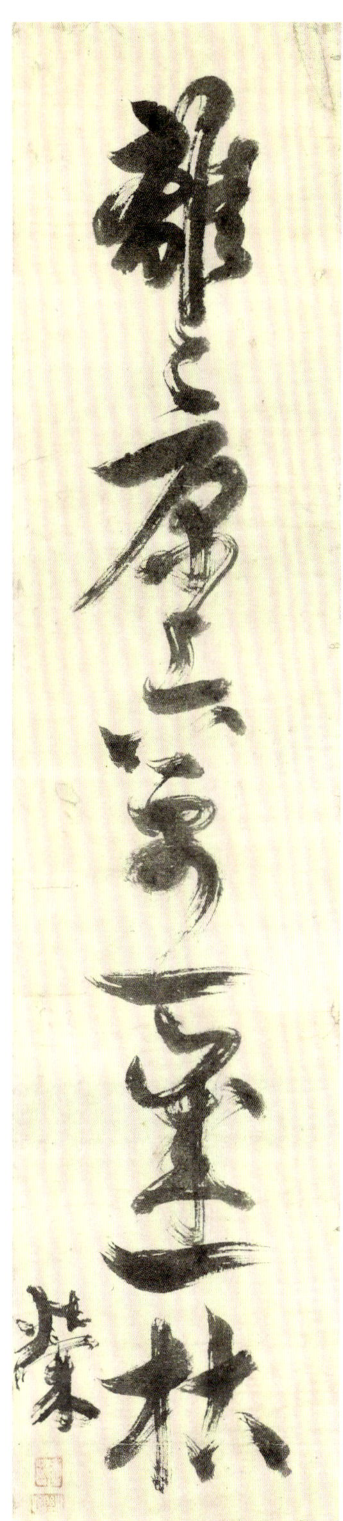

Motsurin (or Botsurin) Jōtō
(没倫紹等; also known as Bokusai, 墨斎; d. 1491)

520. Couplet from the poem "Grass" by Haku Kyoi (Ch. Bai Juyi, 白居易; 772–846)

Muromachi period
Hanging scroll; ink on paper
118.8 x 26.4 cm (46 3/4 x 10 3/8 in.)
Text, seals

Literature: Murase 1993, no. 10.

Konoe Taneie
(近衛稙家; fl. 16th century)

521. *Eikataigai* (詠歌大概)

Muromachi period, 1531
Book of 102 *waka* by various poets; ink on paper
25.8 x 17.7 cm (10 1/8 x 7 in.)

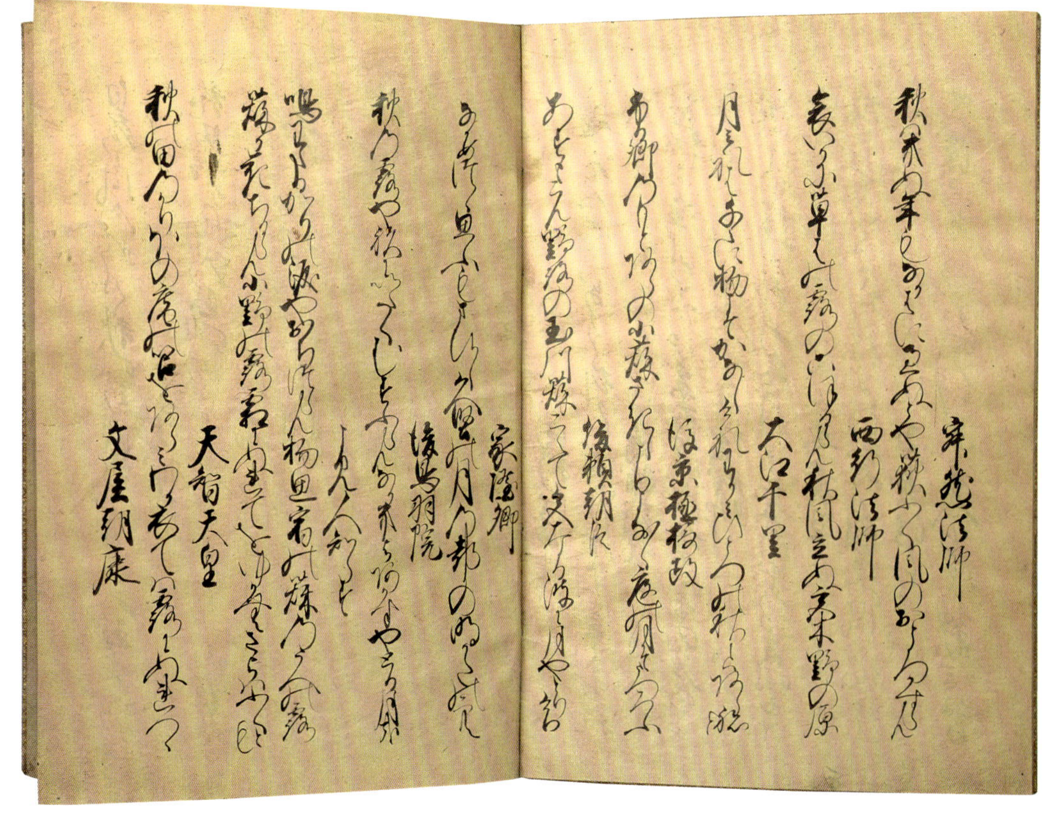

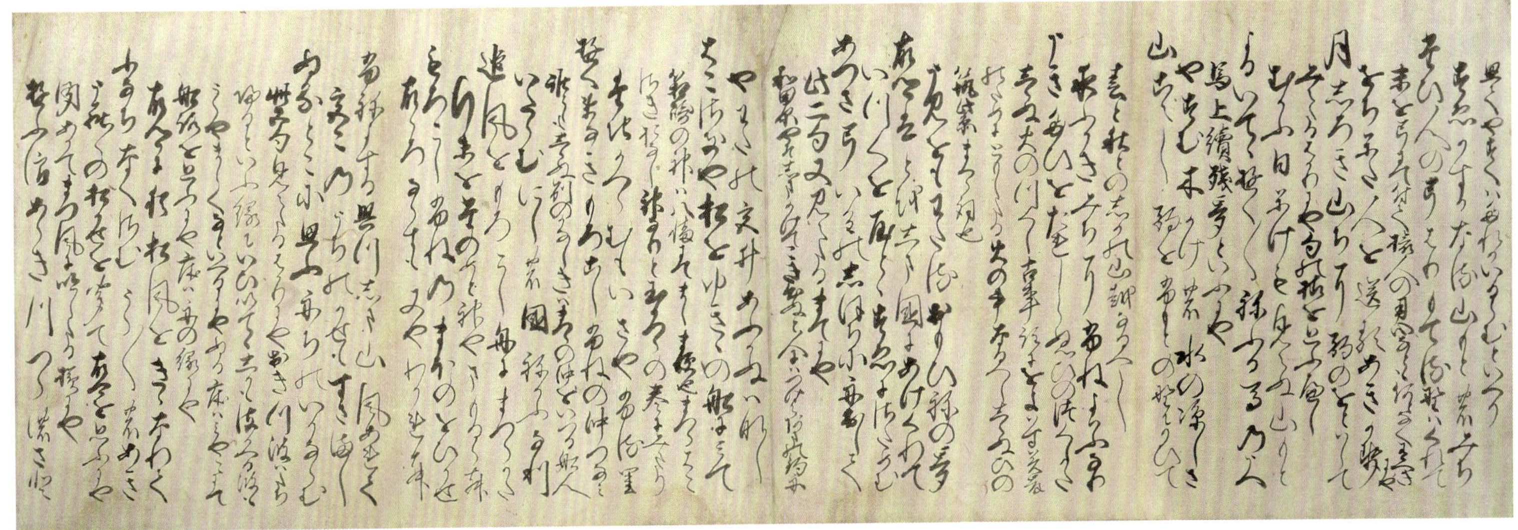

Mizoga Ryūkō
(溝我 柳江; fl. 16th century)

522. *Wakuraba* (老葉)

Muromachi period, 1533
Book mounted as handscroll; ink on paper
23 x 307.2 cm (9 in. x 10 ft. 1 in.)
Signature

Prince Sonchō
(尊朝法親王; 1552–1597)

523. Page from *Teikin Ōrai* (庭訓往来)

Momoyama period
Book; ink on paper
31 x 25 cm (12 1/4 x 9 7/8 in.)

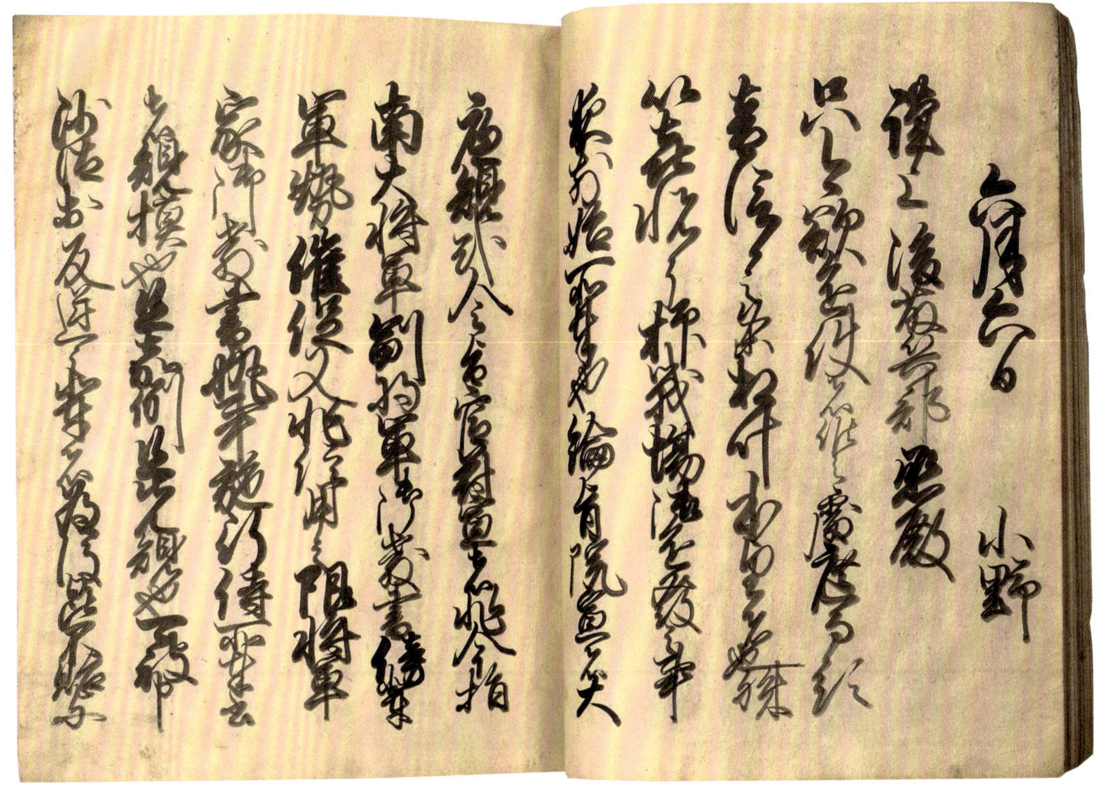

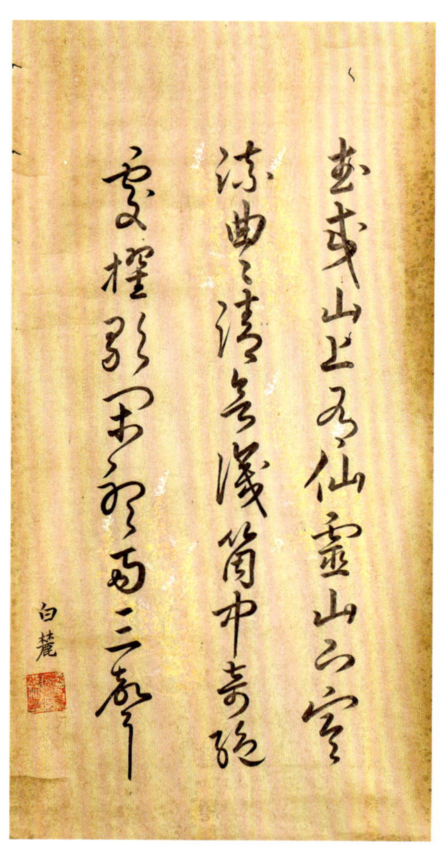

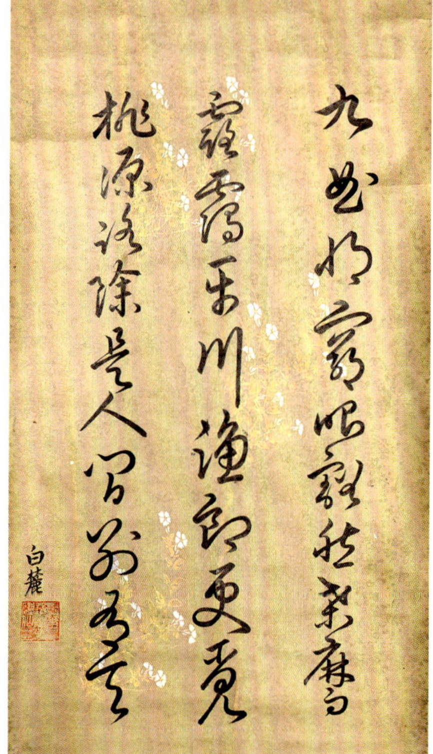

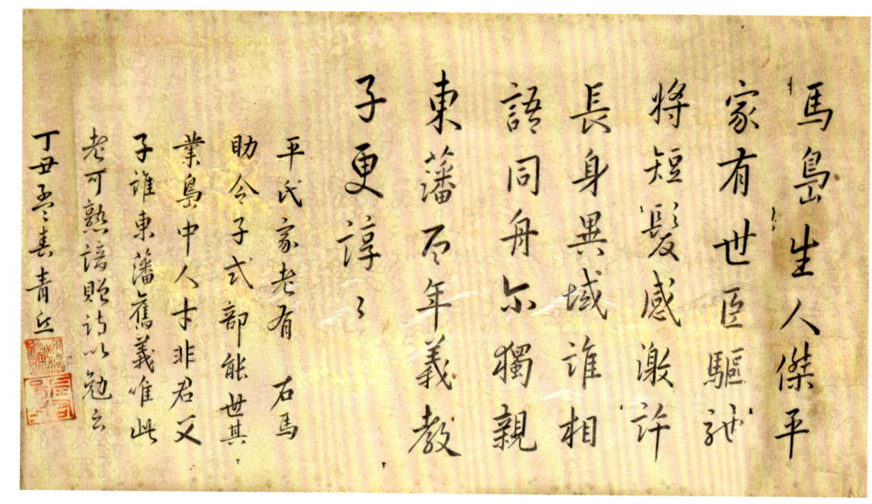

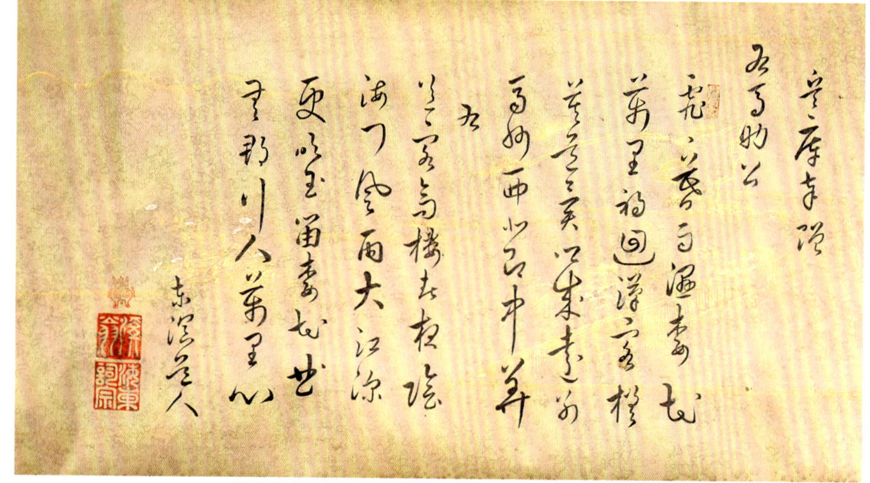

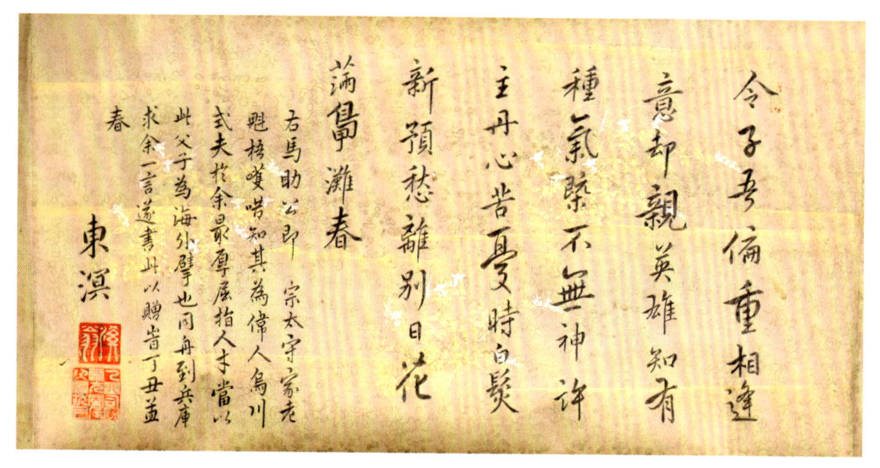

530. Five poems dedicated to Umanosuke (右馬助), written by Seikyū (青丘), Tōmei (東溟), and Hakuroku (白麓)

Edo period, 1697
One handscroll; ink on decorated paper
35.7 x 333.7 cm (14 in. x 10 ft. 11 3/8 in.)
Signatures, seals

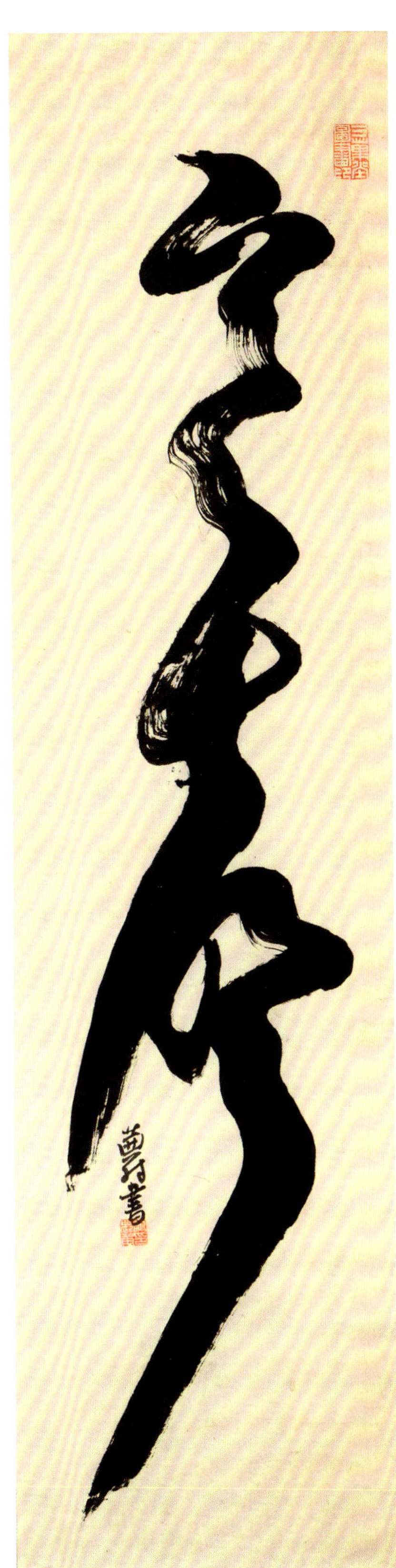

Yosa Buson
(与謝蕪村; 1716–1783)

531. *Kansei* (寒声 / Sound of Cold Air)

Edo period
Hanging scroll; ink on paper
126.2 x 32.4 cm (49 5/8 x 12 3/4 in.)
Text, signature, seals

Ike Taiga
(池大雅; 1723–1776)

532. Two poems from *Kokin wakashū* (古今和歌集)

Edo period, 1733
Hanging scroll; ink on paper
26.8 x 33.3 cm (10 1/2 x 13 1/8 in.)
Text, signature, seal

Ex coll.: Okamoto Kōhei, Kanagawa Prefecture; Mizuta Chikuho

Literature: Kyoto National Museum 1933, pl. 79; Hitomi Shōka 1940, p. 3; Tanaka Ichimatsu et al. 1957–59, no. 1; Matsushita Hidemaro 1970, fig. 8; Murase 1975, no. 68; Shimizu and Rosenfield 1984, no. 116; Fischer 2007, no. 1.

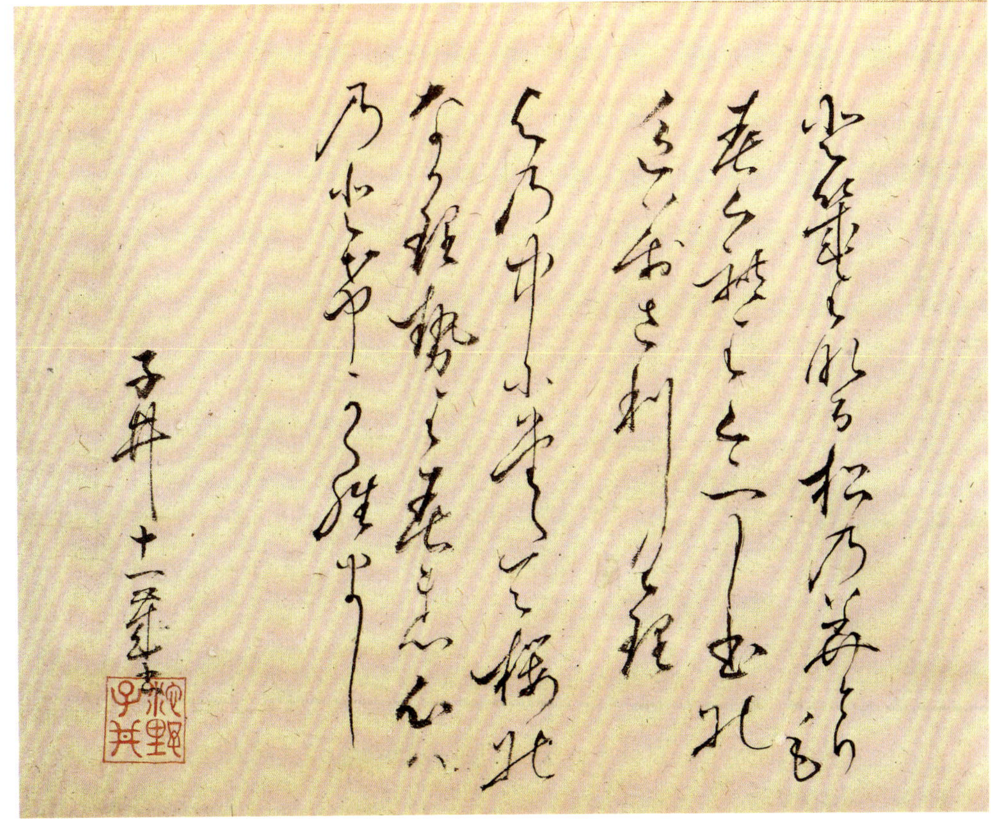

Ike Taiga
(池大雅; 1723–1776)

537. Letter addressed to Itō Kakō (伊藤華岡; 1709–1776)

Edo period, 1759
Hanging scroll; ink on paper
23.7 x 34.1 cm (9 3/8 x 13 3/8 in.)
Text

Ex coll.: Okamoto Kōhei, Kanagawa Prefecture

Literature: Tanaka Ichimatsu et al. 1960, no. 798; Shimizu and Rosenfeld 1984, no. 117; Fischer 2007, no. 76.

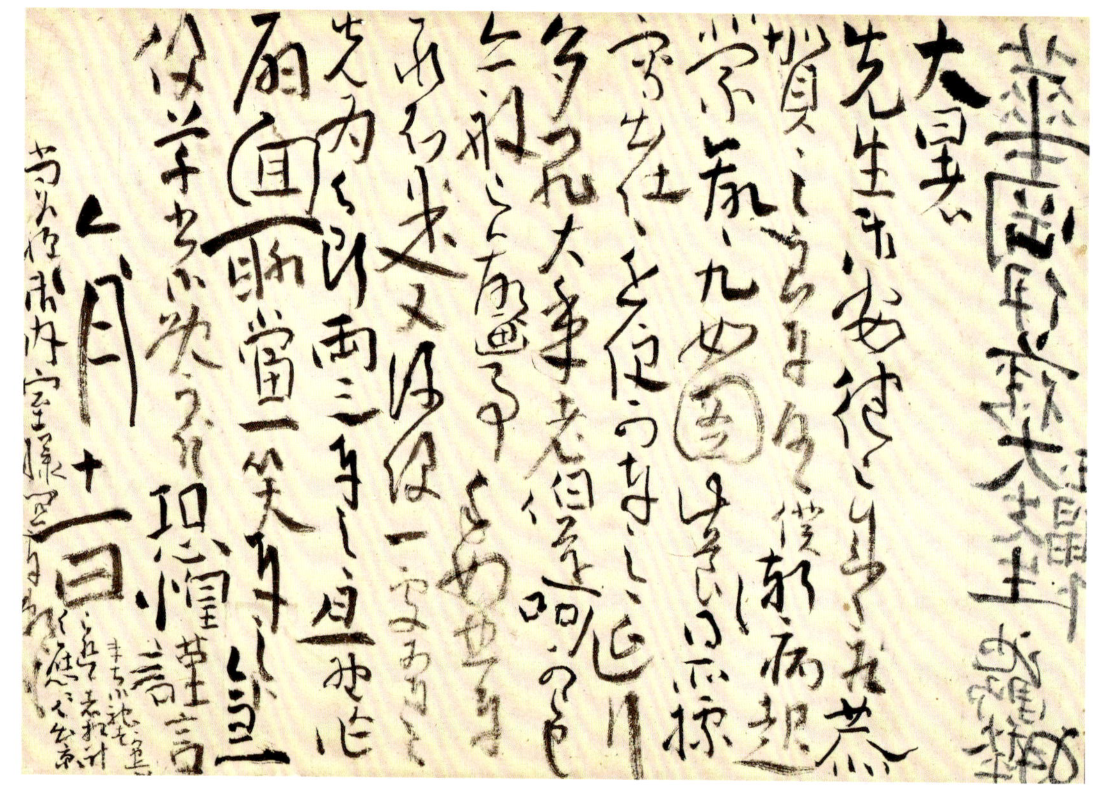

538. Paintings by Ike Taiga (池大雅; 1723–1776) and Colophons by Eight Calligraphers

Edo period, 18th–19th century
Album of paintings and calligraphies; ink on paper
30.2 x 41.2 cm (11 7/8 x 16 1/4 in.)

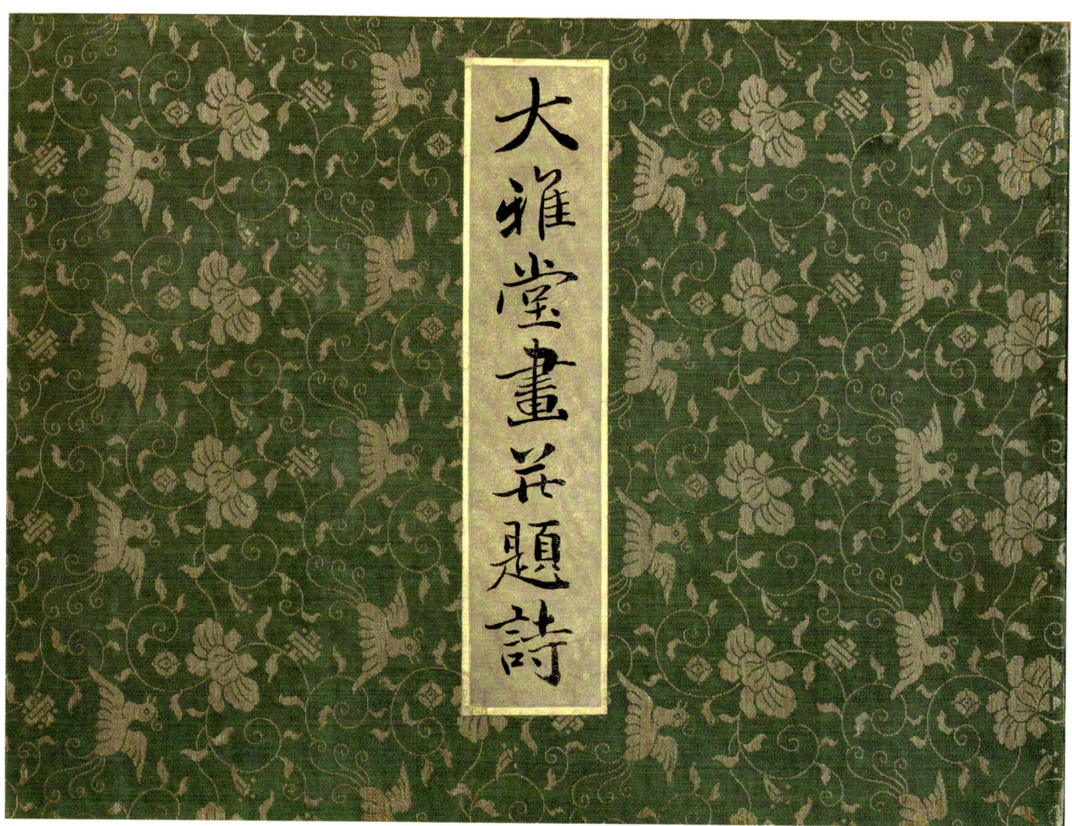

Ike Taiga
(池大雅; 1723–1776)

539. Two Calligraphies

One handscroll; ink on paper
33.7 x 172.3 cm (13¼ x 67⅞ in.)
Text, signatures, seals

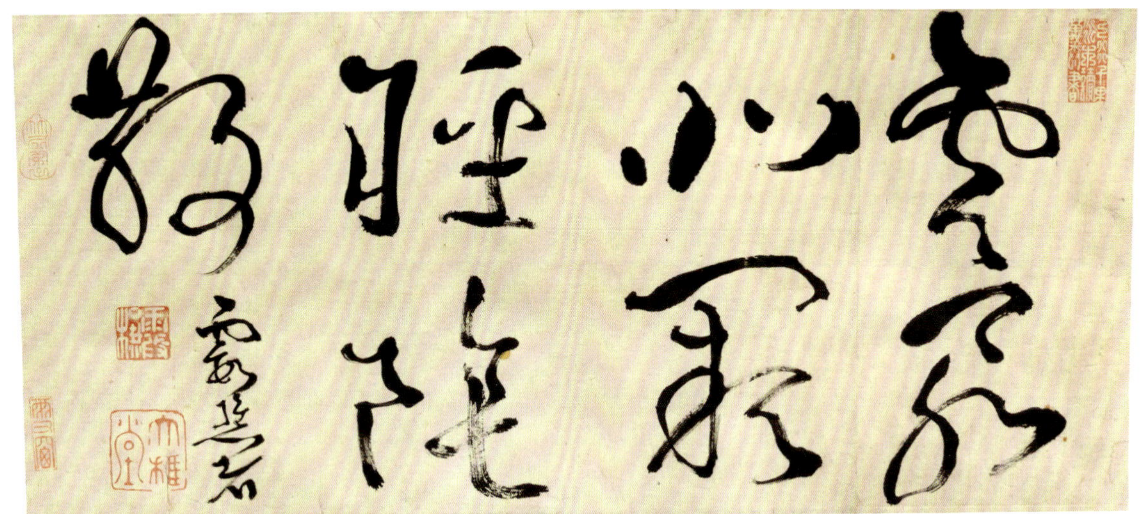

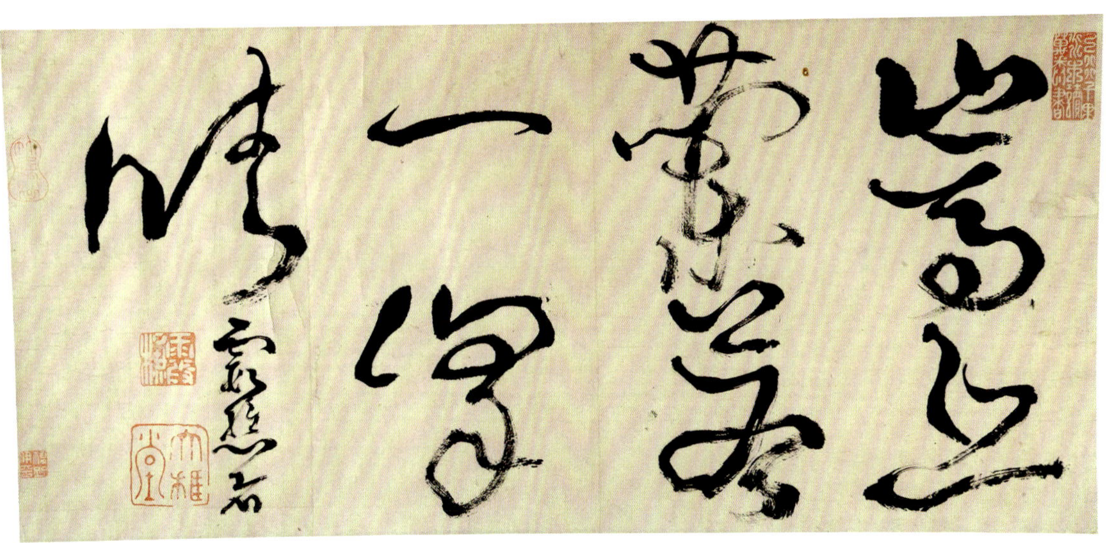

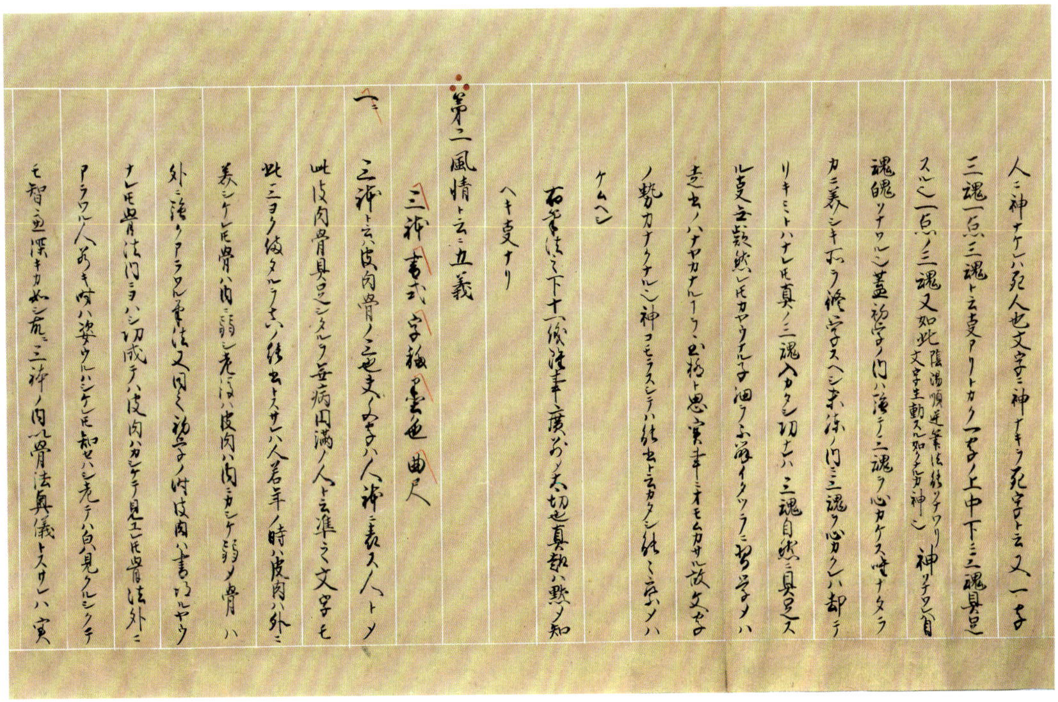

540. *Hippō Rikugishō* (筆法六義抄 / Commentary on Six Rules of Calligraphy)

Edo period, 18th century
Unmounted handscroll; ink on paper
32.4 x 529.6 cm (12¾ in. x 17 ft. 4½ in.)

Kaimon
(海門; fl. 18th century)

541. *Mu* (無 / Nothingness)

Edo period
Hanging scroll; ink on paper
54.6 cm x 121.9 cm (21 1/2 x 48 in.)
Text, signature, seals

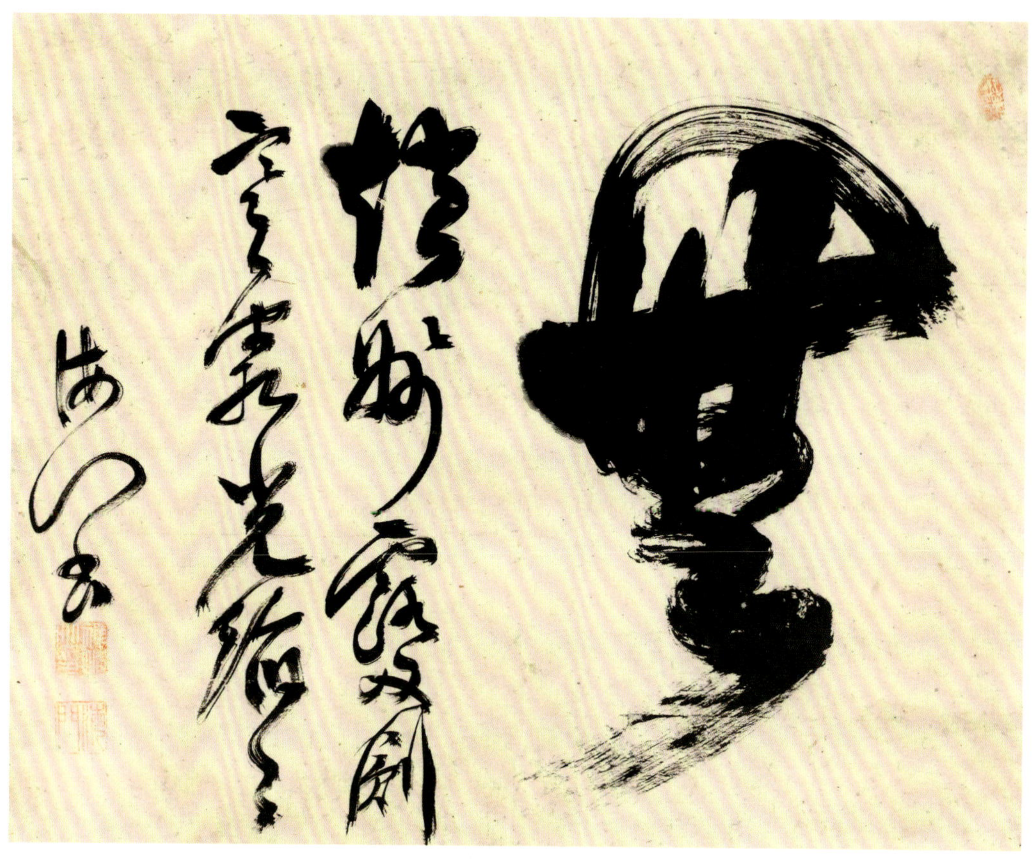

542. Letter from Courtesan Sono
(その)

Edo period, 19th century
Hanging scroll; ink on paper
29.9 x 56.6 cm (11 3/4 x 22 1/4 in.)
Text, signature

Literature: Guth 1992, fig. 9.

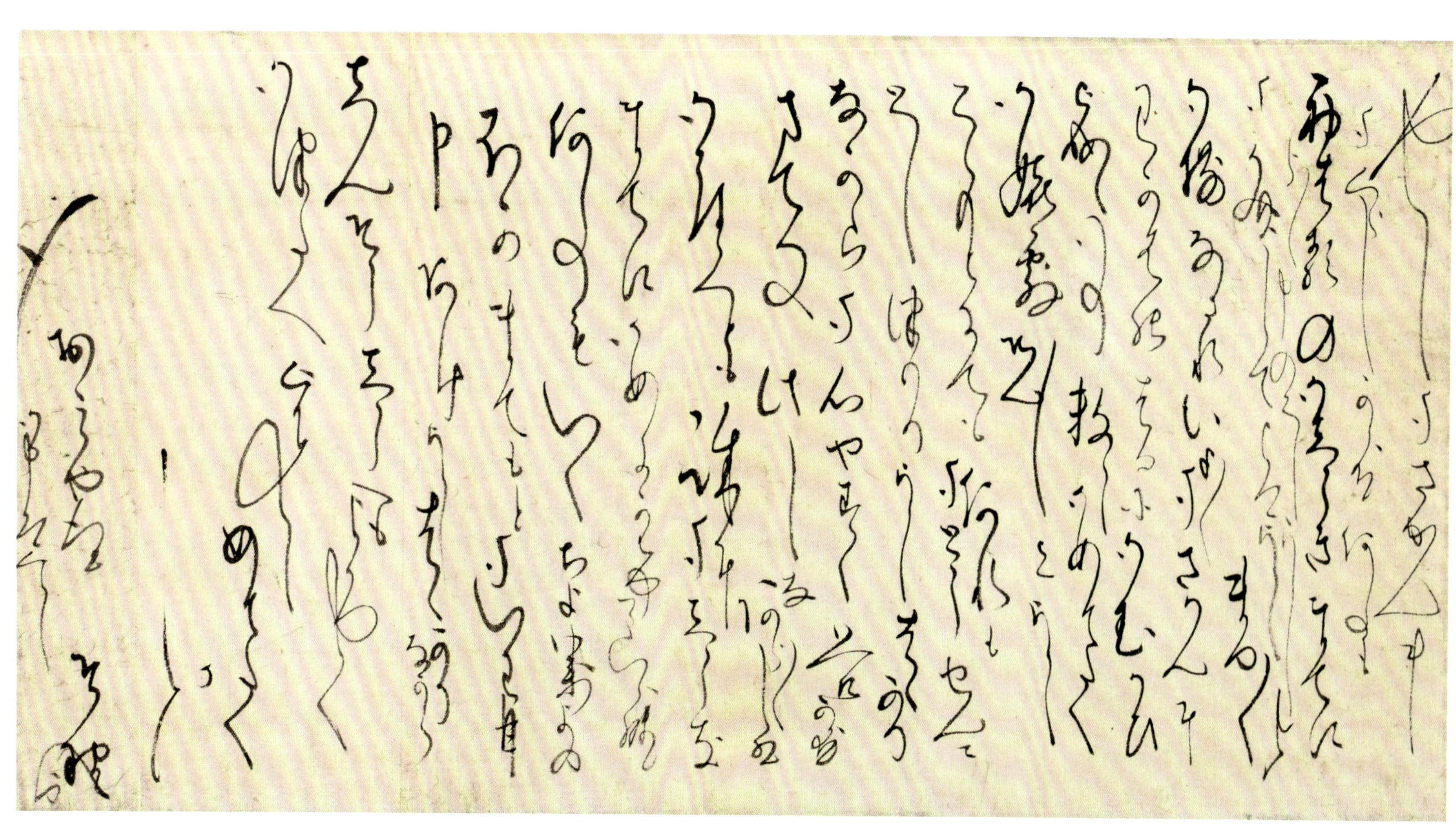

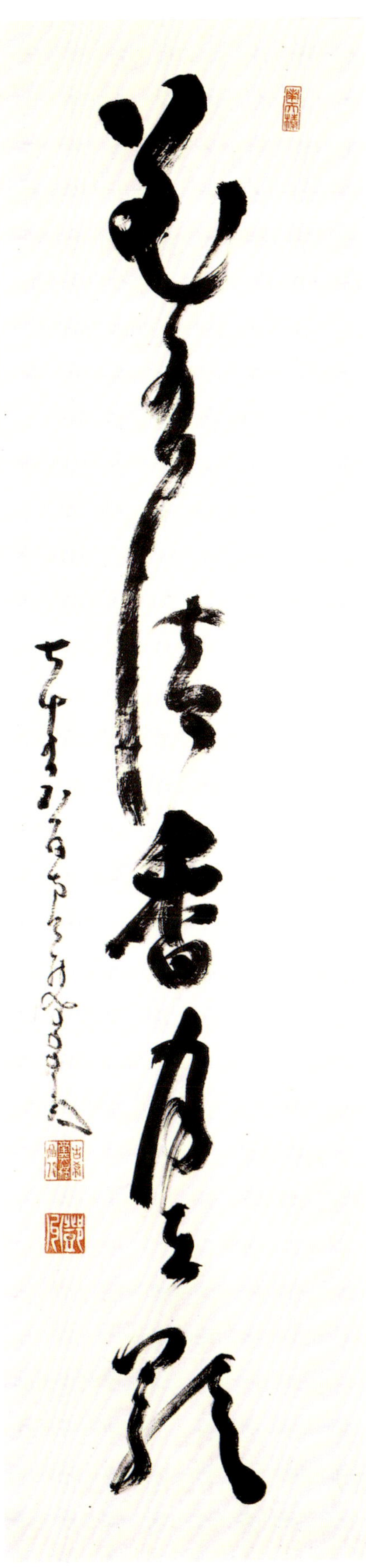

Nakahara Nantenbō
(中原南天棒; 1839–1925)

543. Flower's Fragrance

Taishō era, 1915
Hanging scroll; ink on paper
135.4 x 33.4 cm (53¼ x 13⅛ in.)
Text, signature, seals

Kamata Ukei
(鎌田雨溪; b. 1948)

544. Folding Fans with Calligraphy

Ca. 1998
Silk hanging with folding fans; ink on paper
215 x 98.8 cm (84⅝ x 38⅞ in.)
Text, signatures, seals

Gift from the artist to the Mary and Jackson Burke Foundation, 2006

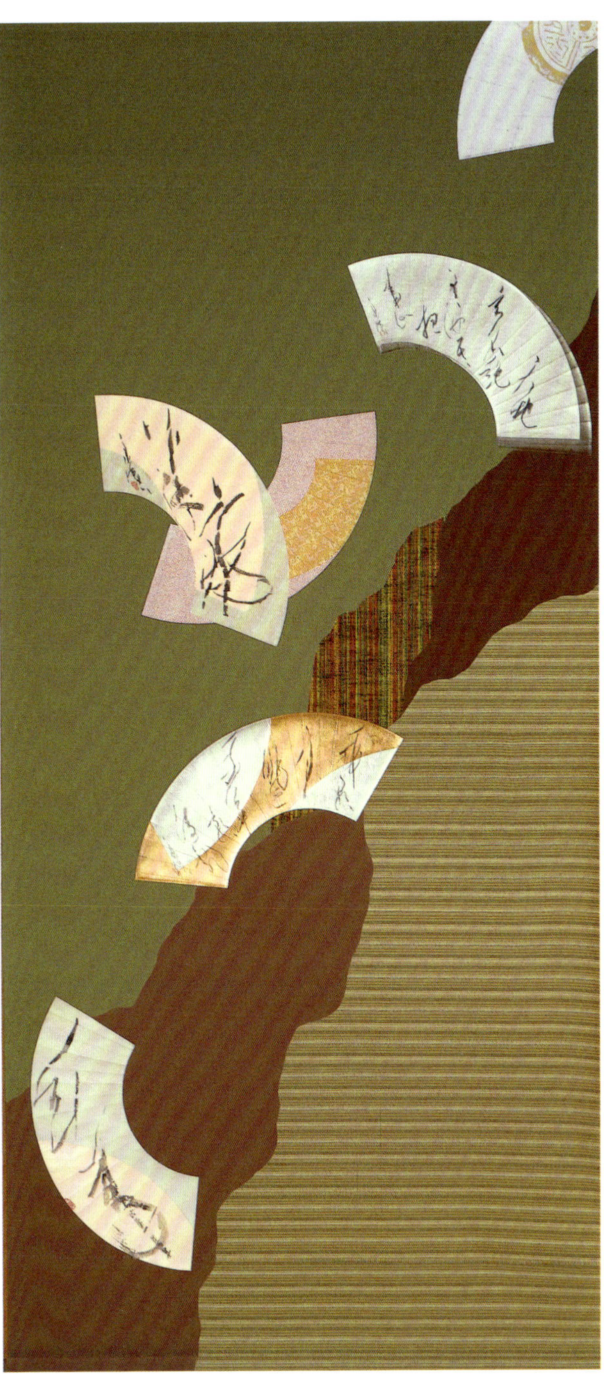

Chapter 12 Details

† *denotes illustrated items*

507. Poem from *Tsurayukishū I,* in album entitled *Mokagami*

Text

Ki no Tsurayuki [ca. 872–945] *composed for a folding screen during the Engi era* [901–23] *// I thought only pines are evergreens, / but the spring water that flows constantly / also shines in green.*

509. Three poems from *Kokin wakashū*

Text

[Poem 450] *Only briefly do the autumn grasses display their beauties, / yet each night the dew has come to dye the petals deeper colors.*

[Poem 451 by Ariwara no Shigeharu (d. ca. 905)] *Nigatake* [Long-Jointed Bamboo] *// Shigeharu // Difficult it is to depend on sips of dew / to sustain one's life— / so anxiously they pipe long, lonely hours, / insects of the fields.*

[Poem 452 by Kagenori no Ōkimi (fl. late 9th c)] *Kawatake* [Mushroom] *// Kagenori no Ōkimi // Already the moon has half climbed the celestial dome / as night grows old— / oh autumn wind from the peaks / blow it backward on its course!*

510. Page from *Tsurayukishū II*

Text

Seeing someone off to a faraway place, / no regrets to wet my sleeves with so many teardrops. // Hyōe no suke Kanesuke bids farewell to his friend Miharu no Arisuke, an officer of the Left Guard, on the banks of the Kamo River // My tears, which mourn your departure, / make the river swell. / It overflows its banks. // Composed while seeing someone off who is departing with a gift to see a mutual friend.

511. Page from *Iseshū*

Text

. . . the color has deepened. // The man came and stood at her gate; hearing a cuckoo singing in a flowering orange tree, he composed the following verse and sent it to the lady: / Standing at your gate / forlorn am I as the mournful / cuckoo that sings / my sadness from his perch / among the branches of your blossoming orange tree. // To this she replied: / Hardly can he know / what errand brings you here, / the cuckoo in my tree— / Is it not his tuneful nature / thus to come and sing?

512. Three poems from *Gosen wakashū*

Text

. . . but I believe no white dew taints leaves or grasses. // What sort of dews / turned leaves and grasses / into thousands of different colors / in the autumn field? // Which grasses should I choose / to remind me of the autumn field / where all of them change colors? // Ki no Tomonori [fl. ca. 890] */ Although I am not a deer / who lost its mate, / still I want to moan in the autumn field.*

513. Three poems from *Gosen wakashū*

Text

Response: / White dews that descend / on pine branches in the evening / disappear in the morning. // Unknown poet sent this poem to an acquaintance who is in the service in Yamato: / In return / I yearn for you, / while I remember a young friend in Yamato from the past. // Response: / I was only reminded / of the rice plants in autumn fields. / My memories of them / do not excite me.

514. Three poems from *Kokin wakashū*

Text

By unknown poet

[Poem 1037] *If things have come to this / why not simply say that you no longer love [me] / that our union has broken / like bright jeweled suspenders.*

[Poem 1038] *Ah for a way to hide myself and peer into each secret recess / within the mysterious heart of one who claims he loves [me].*

[Poem 1039] *Although I love him / he only says he does not love me / ah no, I must not go on loving / for my love is unavailing.*

515. *Sanbō ekotoba*

Text

So he went to a quiet place, put his thoughts in order, calmed his heart, and was never disturbed. As a result, his meditations and his wisdom joined to help him achieve enlightenment. They acted like the two wings of a bird, the two wheels of a cart. If you have wisdom but you do not meditate, your mind will not come to rest. The radiance of enlightenment will not be able to shine but will merely flicker as a lamp flickers in the wind, and you will be like a sea tossed by waves.

516. Two poems from *Zoku kokin wakashū*

Text

[Poem 8] *A spring poem among one hundred poems composed. // Kōmyōbuji nyūdō Former Regent Minister of the Left Michiie // The sun rises, opening up the heaven's door. / The spring of the divine age must have arrived.*

[Poem 9] *Kino Tsurayuki* [ca. 872–945] *// Spring mist has risen, yet at Yoshino mountains / snow is falling even today.*

517. Three poems from *Kokin wakashū*

Text

[Poem 533] *No more than the white waves dancing across the inlet / where reed ducks cry out noisily / does my love know of my yearning.*

[Poem 534] *Like fiery Mount Fuji in Suruga / my yearning burns within—as eternally smoldering / passion my love can never know.*

[Poem 535] *Would that my love could know my yearning / deep as these lonely mountains / where not even the songs of soaring wild birds can be heard.*

520

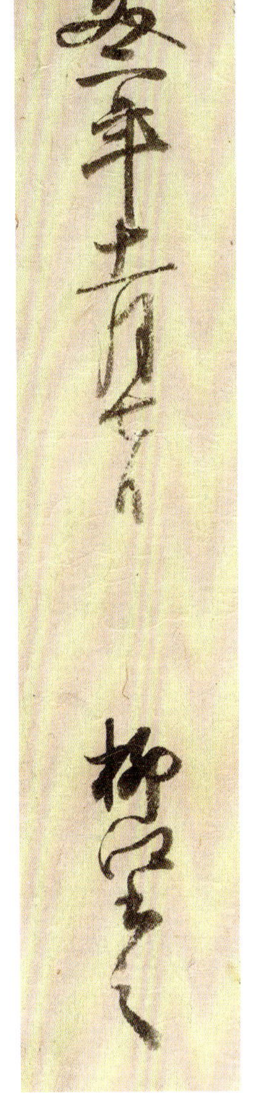

522

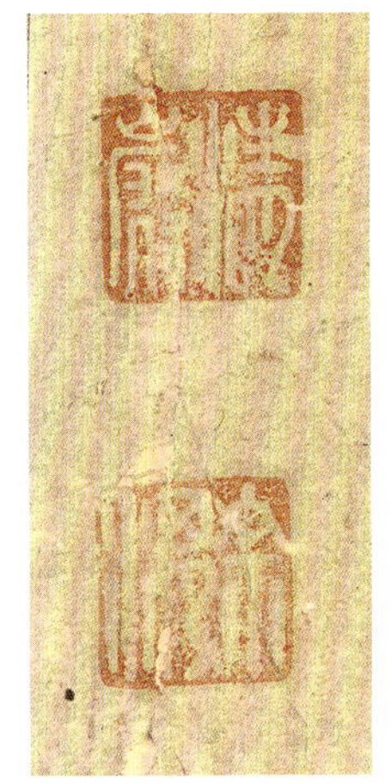

524

524

529

529

† 520. Couplet from the poem "Grass" by Haku Kyoi (Ch. Bai Juyi)

Text

Taller, taller, wild grasses grow in the field, / only to wither at the end of the season.

Seals

Jōtō; Shiran

---

† 522. *Wakuraba*

Signature

[at end of scroll] *Ryūkō inscribed this, on the seventh day of the eleventh month, 1533.*

---

† 524. Sophisticated Eloquence

Seals

Monji Seisei; Seigan; Sōi

---

525. *Renga kaishi*

Text

[at end] *Dedicated in the twenty-eighth day in the third month of 1661, in commemoration of Lord Yorinobu's sixtieth birthday*

---

527. Poem by Saigyō from *Shin kokin wakashū*

Text

[Poem 362] *Monk Saigyō // Even a person free of passion / would be moved / to sadness: / autumn evening / in a marsh where snipes fly up.*

---

528. Two poems from *Shin kokin wakashū*

Text

[Poem 111] *Tsurayuki* [Ki no Tsurayuki (ca. 872–945)] // *With blossom-scent / the fragrance of these garments / takes on new depth / in every gust of wind that blows / beneath the shadow of the trees.*

[Poem 969] *Travel poem / submitted with a 100-poem sequence / Lord Fujiwara Ietaka* [1158–1237] // *Although no promise / kept me here, the night has passed— / Kiyomi Strand / where now the waves are left behind / by the brightening sky of dawn.*

---

† 529. Triptych of calligraphies

[center scroll]

Text

Eternal blessing on the sagacious ruler

Signature

Written in 1690 by Bukkoku Kōsen

Seals

Rinzai Seishū; Bukkoku Shujin; Seidon

[right scroll]

Text

Religious spirit spreads across the four seas

Signature

Donge Dōjin

Seals

Rinzai Seishū; Bukkoku Shujin; Seidon

[left scroll]

Text

Beneficent graces permeate the world

Signature

Donge Dōjin

Seals

Rinzai Seishū; Bukkoku Shujin; Seidon

530. Five poems dedicated to Umanosuke, written by Seikyū, Tōmei, and Hakuroku

Signatures

Seikyū; *Tōmei Dōjin*; *Tōmei*; *Hakuroku; Hakuroku*

Seals

Illegible; illegible; *Dōsen*; *Keiō*; *Kaitō Shisō*; *Keiō*; illegible; illegible; illegible

† 531. *Kansei* (Sound of Cold Air)

Text

Kansei

Signature

Written by Buson

Seals

Sankadō tosho in; *Sha Chōkō in*

532. Two poems from *Kokin wakashū*

Text

by Shisei
[Poem 24, by Minamoto Muneyuki (d. 939)] *Now that spring has come / even the unchanging pine is dressed / in fresh new foliage that is / dyed a brighter shade of green.*

[Poem 53, by Ariwara Narihira (825–880)] *If this world had never / known the ephemeral charms of cherry blossoms / then our hearts in spring might match / nature's deep tranquility.*

Signature

Written by Shisei at age 11

Seal

Ikeno Shisei

† 533. "Senjimon" (Thousand-Character Classic)

Signature

Written by Ikeshi Kashōsha Mumei at Gion Sōan in Kyoto

Seals

Higashiyama; *Ike*; *Mumei*

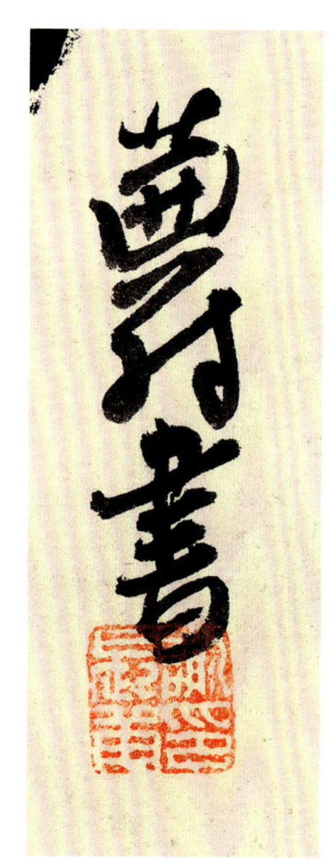

531

531

533

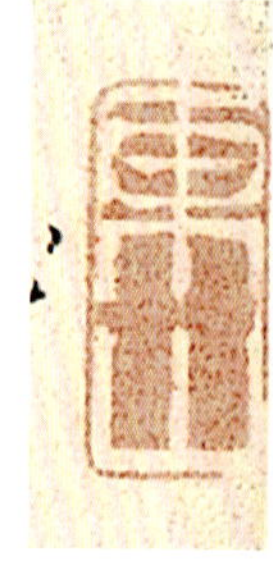

533

† 534. Poem from *Man'yōshū*

Text

For my love I want a jewel. / Foaming waves, / bring me the pearls / of the open sea!

[on back] *Ike Mumei* [illegible]

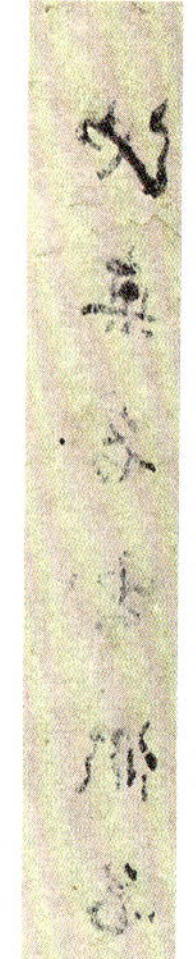

534, on back

535. Letter addressed to Shōemon

Text

[My message is] as follows: Dear Old Yo Shōemon Sensei: / I respectfully reviewed your letter. I will send you the painting that you have asked for in a day or two. I am relieved to learn you were able to obtain the rare mirror. I waited for your visit the day before yesterday. / Yours truly, Mumei

† 536. Letter addressed to Aoki Shukuya

Text

Dear Mr. Shukuya: / I am presenting that scroll to you as a gift. As to your request, I asked one or two people I thought helpful. Yet the decision has not been made. I will bring it to you in a few days so that you will be able to work on it. This is a hasty reply. / Twenty-third day of the ninth month.

Signature

Respectfully, Shūhei

Seal

Ike Mumei in

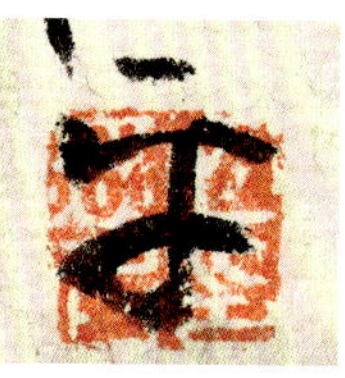

536

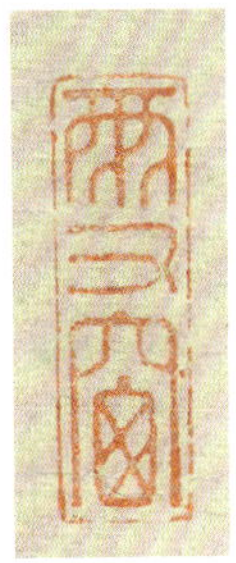

539

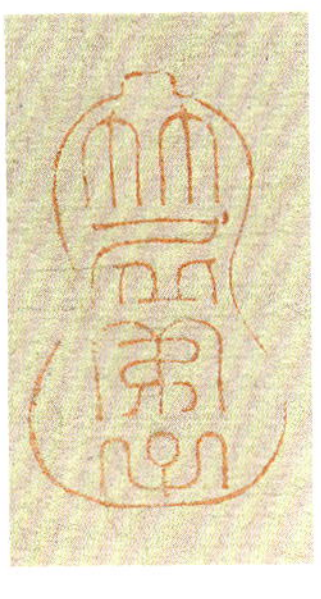

539

539

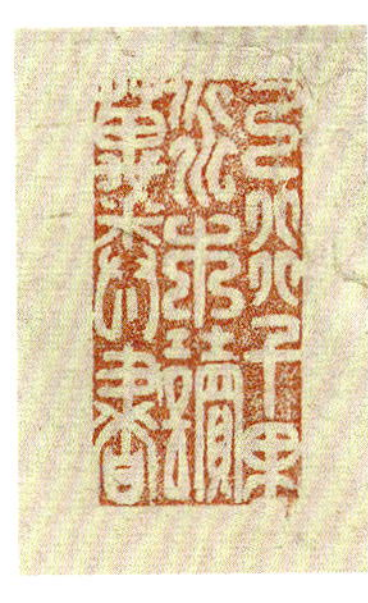

539

537. Letter addressed to Itō Kakō

Text

Congratulations Master Kakō on your continued health. I have been ill recently. The painting entitled "Kyūjo" [Nine Similarities] *has been completed and I deeply apologize for taking so long. Dainen* [Kan Tenju] *has returned. Now that I finished this painting, I can begin a fan painting. Will be able to make one more fan painting as you request. Hope it makes you happy. / Sincerely yours, / On the eleventh day of the sixth month. / [P.S.] To Mrs. Itō Kakō, I will arrange Master Kakō's trip to Kyoto.*

[on verso] *To Itō Kakō, great teacher, from Ikeno Shūhei, sincerely bowing before the jade bench.*

† 539. Two calligraphies

[top]

Text

Darkness over the imperial palace by the Gusui [Ch. Yu River] *dissolves by itself.*

Signature

Kashōsha

Seals

[upper right] *Having traveled one thousand miles, I have not yet read ten thousand books*; *Kashō*; *Taigadō*; [upper left] *Chikkyo deshi*; [lower left] *Sessō*

[bottom]

Text

The peak near the monastery on Sūgaku [Ch. Mount Song] *clears up.*

Signature

Kashōsha

Seals

[upper right] *Having traveled one thousand miles, I have not yet read ten thousand books*; *Kashō*; *Taigadō*; [upper left] *Chikkyo deshi*; [lower left] illegible

† 541. *Mu* (Nothingness)

Text

Monk Zhaozhou's drawn sword / glistens like chilly frost blazing bright.

Signature

Written by Kaimon

Seals

[upper right] illegible; [lower left] *Zenkaku no in*; *Kaimon*

542. Letter from Courtesan Sono

Text

Dear Omiya, / I am writing this to you to celebrate the New Year. I am very happy that all of you are well and flourishing to welcome the new spring. On my side, all of us are getting older like everyone else, so please be reassured. The thing I am sending you is not very refined, but I want you to see it as a gift from me for the celebration. I just want to celebrate for years to come. Please give my best to the new courtesans. / Sincerely, / Sono / [P.S.] I hope your life will be prosperous. I have touched only on a few things and left many others [unmentioned].

Signature

Sono

† 543. Flower's Fragrance

Text

Flowers exude fragrance / in the moonlight.

Signature

An old man at age seventy-eight, Nantenbō

Seals

[upper right] *Nantenbō*; [lower left] *kaō*; *Seventy plus eight, Nantenbō*; *Tōjū*

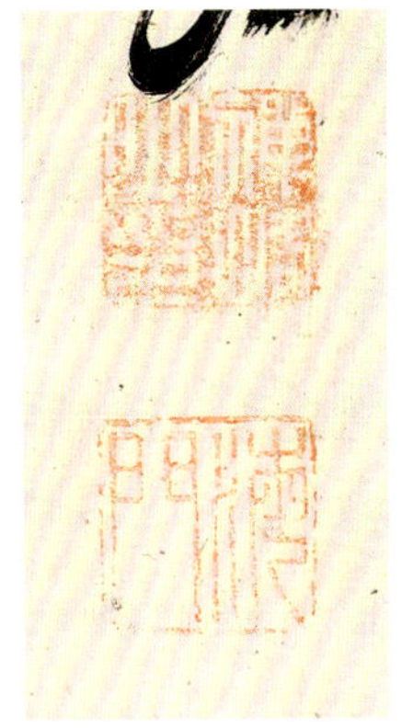

541

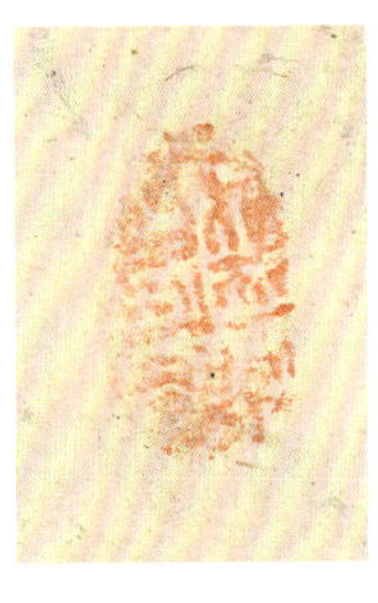

541

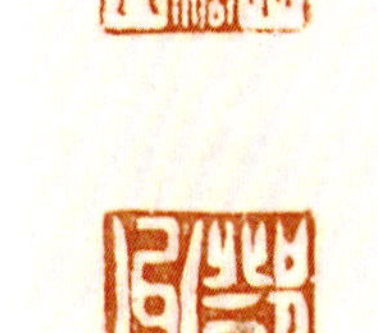

543

543

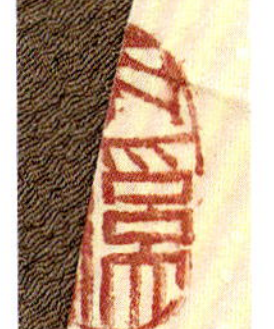

544

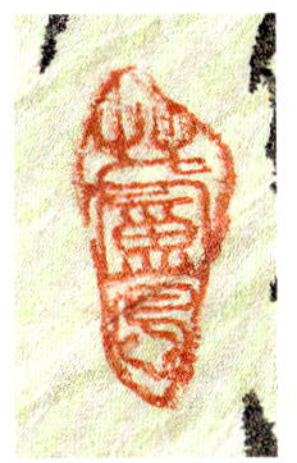

544

544

† 544. Folding Fans with Calligraphy

Text

[from top to bottom] [fan 1] *If Heaven and Earth should cease to be, / we would stop meeting. / However, this will never happen.*

[fan 2] *halfway drunk*

[fan 3] *When I sing, the moon drifts. / When I dance, my shadow wavers.*

[fan 4] *peacefulness*

Signatures

[on fans 1–3] *Ukei sho*

Seals

[on fans 1, 2] *Rofūan*; [on fan 4] *Ukei*

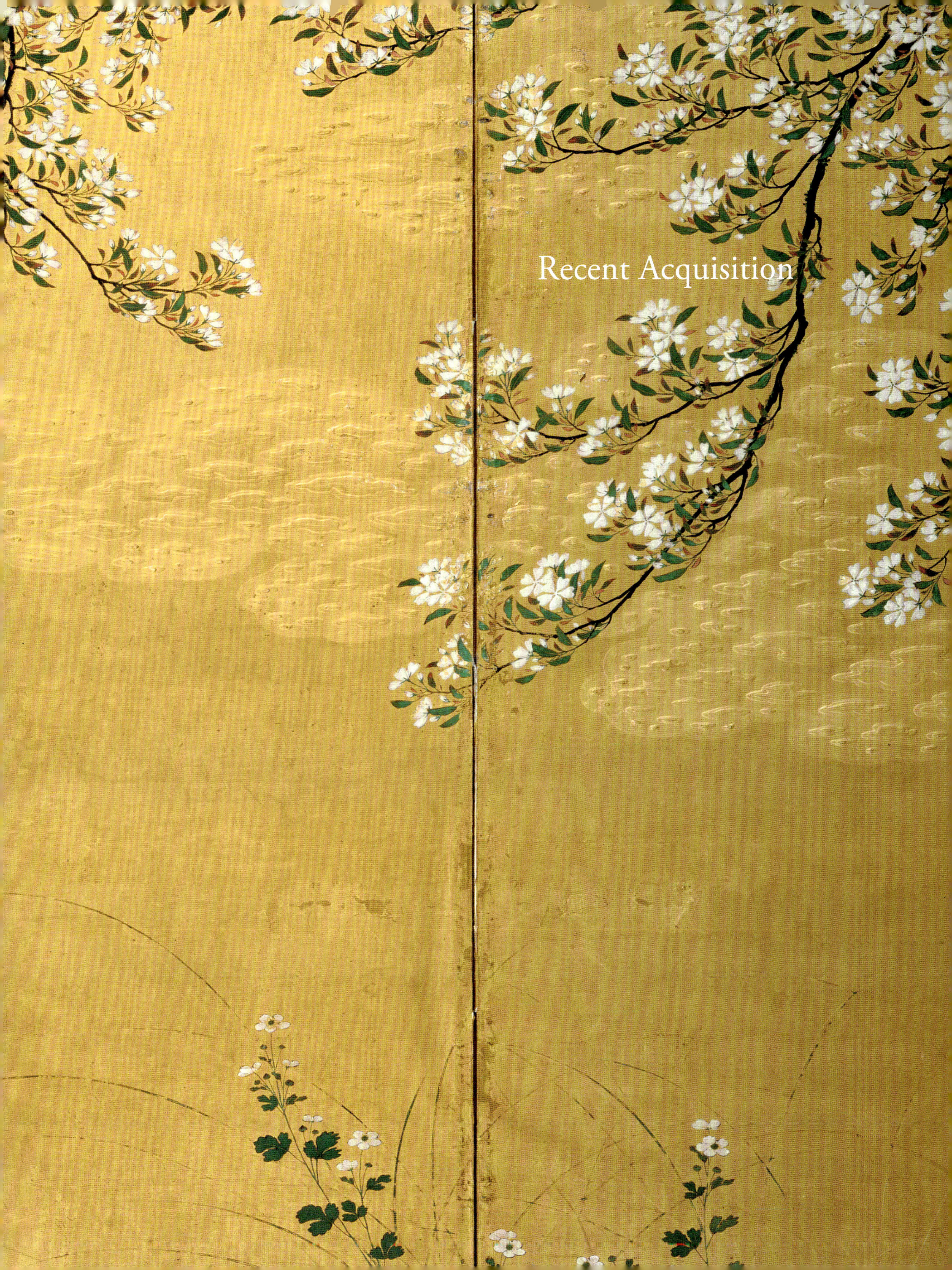

Recent Acquisition

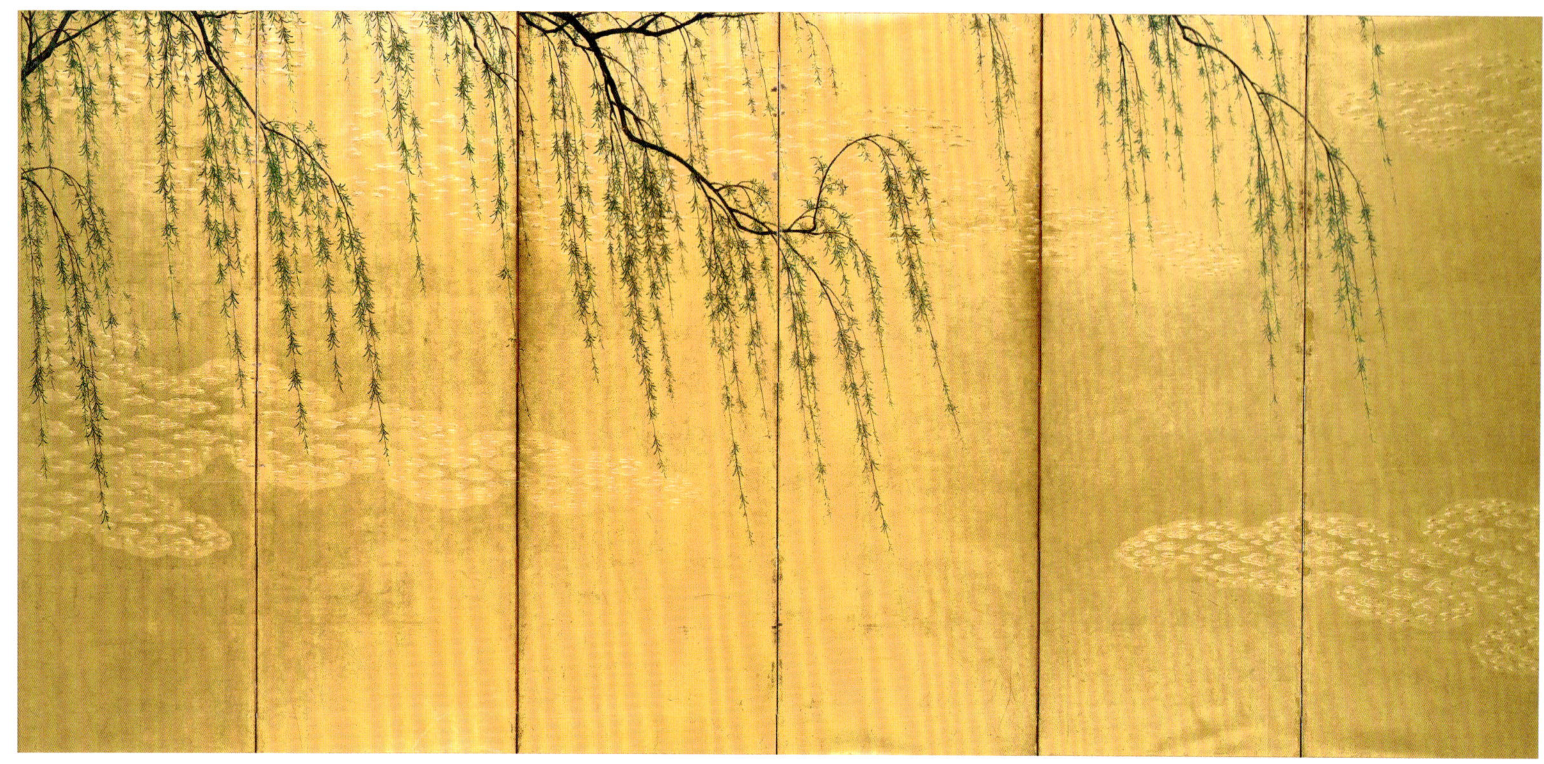

545. Cherry and Willow

Edo period, 17th century

Pair of six-panel folding screens; ink and color on gilded paper

159.5 x 359.4 cm (62¾ in. x 11 ft. 9½ in.)

Ex coll.: George Gund III

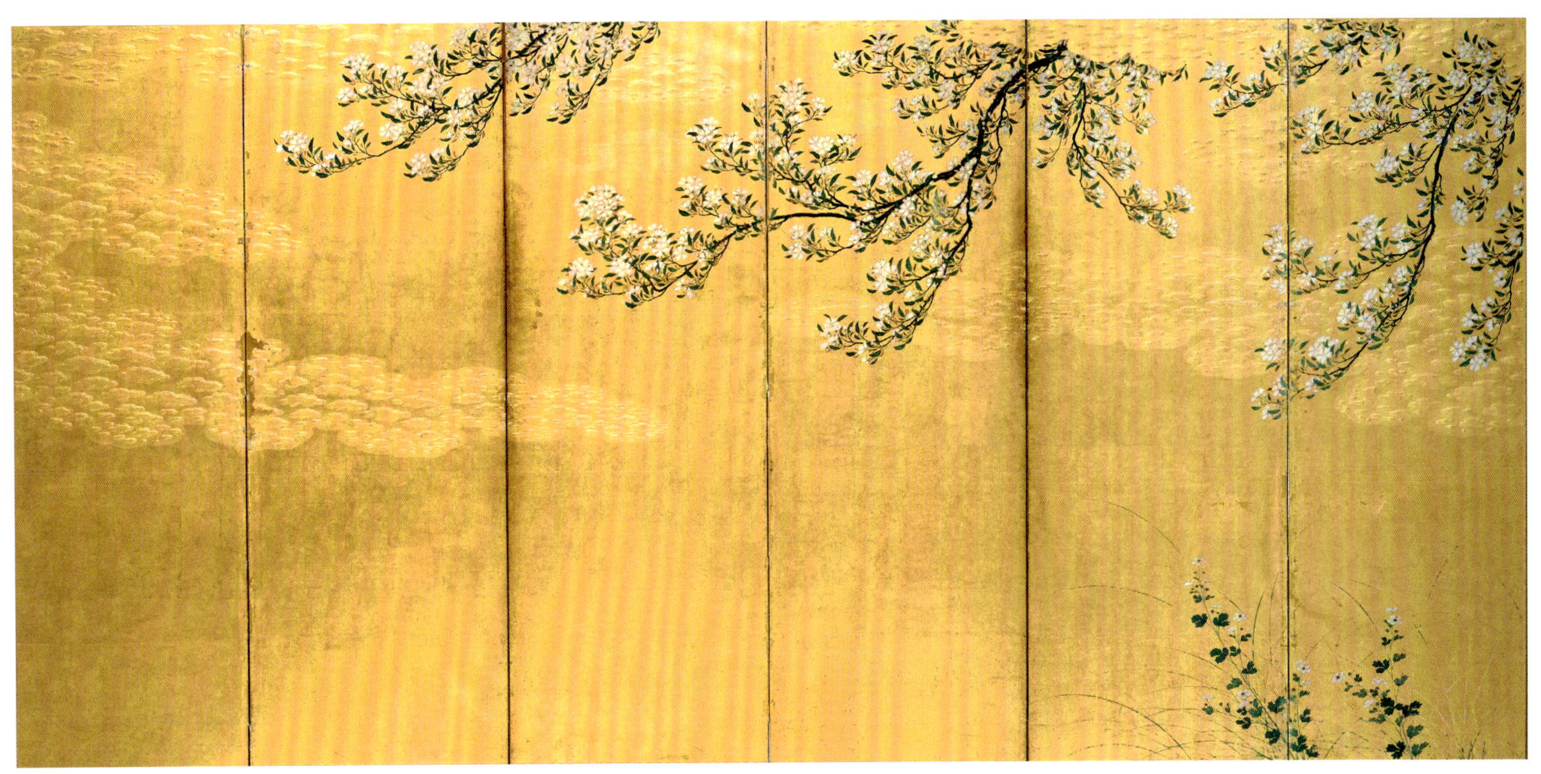

Record of Ownership

These objects, listed by catalogue number, include only those in the Estate of Mary Griggs Burke and those in the collection of the Mary and Jackson Burke Foundation. If a work is now in the collection of another institution, a credit line appears in the entry itself.

Estate of Mary Griggs Burke

7, 10, 12, 20, 22–24, 26, 42–44, 52, 56, 60, 61, 71, 74, 76, 77, 79–81, 83, 84, 91, 95, 99, 103–110, 113, 114, 116, 120–126, 133, 141, 148, 150, 167, 175–179, 184, 185, 188, 189, 191, 195, 197, 199, 204, 206, 207, 210, 215, 216, 218, 221, 224, 226, 229, 239, 243, 276, 280, 307, 308, 312, 316, 321, 323, 324, 330–335, 340, 341, 343–345, 352, 355, 359, 360, 366, 376–378, 381, 382, 384–386, 396, 397, 401, 403, 405, 410, 413–415, 417, 433, 434, 436, 437, 440, 442–444, 446–448, 451–453, 455, 461, 464–467, 469, 476, 478, 479, 481–485, 487, 488, 490–493, 495–504, 506, 511, 518, 521–523, 525–528, 530, 533, 535, 536, 538–540, 543

Mary and Jackson Burke Foundation

2, 3, 5, 6, 8, 9, 11, 13–15, 17, 18, 21, 25, 27–41, 45–51, 53–55, 57–59, 62–70, 72, 73, 75, 78, 82, 85–90, 92–94, 96–98, 100–102, 111, 112, 115, 117–119, 127–132, 134–140, 142, 144–147, 149, 151–166, 168, 169, 172–174, 180–183, 186, 187, 190, 192–194, 196, 198, 200–203, 205, 208, 209, 211–214, 217, 219, 220, 222, 223, 225, 227, 228, 230–238, 240–242, 244–275, 277–279, 281–306, 309–311, 313–315, 317–320, 322, 325–329, 336–339, 342, 346–351, 353, 354, 356–358, 361–365, 367–375, 379, 380, 383, 387–395, 398–400, 402, 404, 406–409, 411, 412, 416, 418–432, 435, 438, 439, 441, 445, 449, 450, 454, 456–460, 462, 463, 468, 470–475, 477, 480, 486, 489, 494, 505, 507–510, 512–517, 519, 520, 524, 529, 531, 532, 534, 537, 541, 542, 544, 545

Translation Sources

All translations are by Miyeko Murase and Shi-yee Liu unless otherwise noted below.

No. 31: *The Zen Ox-Herder*. Translation by Gen P. Sakomoto. Illustrated by Stephanie Wada. Copyright © 2002 by George Braziller. New York, NY: George Braziller, Inc. Used by permission of George Braziller, Inc. All rights reserved.

Nos. 47, 192, 509, 514, 516, 532: *Kokinshū: A Collection of Poems Ancient and Modern*, translated and annotated by Laurel Rasplica Rodd with Mary Catherine Henkenius, copyright © 1996 by Cheng & Tsui Company, Inc. Used by permission of Cheng & Tsui Company, Inc.

No. 48: From *Japanese Court Poetry* by Robert H. Brower and Earl Roy Miner. Copyright © 1961 by the Board of Trustees of the Leland Stanford Jr. University, renewed 1989. All rights reserved. Used with the permission of Stanford University Press, www.sup.org.

Nos. 56, 419, 527: From *Saigyō: Poems of a Mountain Home*, translations by Burton Watson. Copyright © 1991 Columbia University Press. Reprinted with permission of the publisher.

Nos. 57, 528: Carolyn Wheelwright, ed., *Word in Flower: The Visualization of Classical Literature in Seventeenth-Century Japan*, exh. cat. (New Haven, Conn.: Yale University Art Gallery, 1989). Used with the permission of the publisher. All rights reserved.

Nos. 70, 72: Excerpt from *The Tale of Genji* by Shikibu Murasaki, translation copyright © 1976, copyright renewed 2004 by Edward G. Seidensticker. Used by permission of Alfred A. Knopf, an imprint of the Knopf Doubleday Publishing Group, a division of Random House LLC. All rights reserved.

No. 319: Cheryl Crowley, *Haikai Poet Yosa Buson and the Bashō Revival*, translation by Cheryl Crowley. Copyright © 2007 Koninklijke Brill NV. Used with the permission of the publisher.

Nos. 157, 208: From *Tales of Ise: Lyrical Episodes from Tenth-Century Japan*, translated by Helen Craig McCullough. Copyright © 1968 by the Board of Trustees of the Leland Stanford Jr. University. All rights reserved. Used with the permission of the Stanford University Press, www.sup.org.

No. 172: Translation by Ronald C. Egan in *Word, Image, and Deed in the Life of Su Shi*, trans. Ronald C. Egan. Harvard-Yenching Institute Monograph Series, 39. Copyright © 1994 by the President and Fellows of Harvard University. Used with the permission of the publisher. All rights reserved.

Nos. 174, 192: From *One Hundred Poets, One Poem Each: A Translation of the Ogura Hyakunin Isshu*, by Peter McMillan. Copyright © 2008 Columbia University Press. Reprinted with permission of the publisher and the author.

No. 318: From *The Narrow Road to the Deep North and Other Travel Sketches* by Matsuo Bashō, translated with an introduction by Nobuyuki Yuasa (Penguin Classics, 1966). Copyright © Nobuyuki Yuasa, 1966.

No. 511: From *Japanese Arts of the Heian Period, 794–1185*, by John M. Rosenfield, trans. Edwin A. Cranston and Fumiko Cranston, no. 37d. Copyright © 1967 The Asia Society. Used with the permission of the Asia Society. All rights reserved.

No. 515: Edward Kamens, *The Three Jewels: A Study and Translation of Minamoto Tamenori's Sanbōe*, Michigan Monograph Series in Japanese Studies, Number 2 (Ann Arbor: Center for Japanese Studies, The University of Michigan, 1988), p. 123. Copyright © 1988 Center for Japanese Studies, The University of Michigan. All rights reserved. Used with the permission of the publisher.

Nos. 534, 537: Translation by Felice Fischer. From Felice Fischer et al., *Ike Taiga and Tokuyama Gyokuran: Japanese Masters of the Brush* (Philadelphia: Philadelphia Museum of Art, 2007), p. 418, cat. 91 [No. 534], p. 410, cat. 76 [No. 537]. © 2007 Philadelphia Museum of Art. Used by permission of the Philadelphia Museum of Art.

Photography Credits

Many of the photographers also shot separate images of inscriptions, signatures, or seals if those details were not visible in the overall image or were too small to be readable.

Christopher Burke

3, 6, 9, 18, 83, 84, 91, 153, 169, 204, 364, 469, 471, 472, 476, 478, 479, 481–485, 487–492, 495–498, 500–505, 518, 521–523, 526, 540, plus details

Sheldan C. Collins

38, 89, 229, 230, 385, plus details

Courtesy of Kōichi Yanagi

68 (seal), 212

Courtesy of Leighton Longhi

545

Courtesy of The Metropolitan Museum of Art

16, 19, 143

Courtesy of the Minneapolis Institute of Arts

1, 4, 170, 171

Gratia Williams Nakahashi

Details

Carl Nardiello

34, 78, 159, 179, 194, 200, 213, 242, 284, 370, 378, 392, 418, 438, 440, 454

Otto E. Nelson

120, 499

Bruce Schwarz

2, 17, 20, 22, 23, 26, 28, 30–33, 35, 39, 40, 42–46, 50, 65, 66, 69–71, 73, 81, 90, 92, 93, 97, 99–111, 113–117, 122, 123, 127, 129, 130, 132, 135–137, 141, 142, 145–147, 161, 163, 174–178, 181–183, 191, 193, 196, 198, 201, 202, 206–210, 214, 216, 217, 220–222, 225, 226, 241, 243–245, 247, 248, 270, 271, 274, 276, 279, 285, 307, 309, 313, 314, 318, 323 (right), 325–329, 338, 348–350, 357, 369, 371, 373, 386, 387, 394, 395, 400, 406, 412, 428, 429, 436, 437, 449, 463, 468, 494, 508–511, 532, 539 (bottom), plus details

John Bigelow Taylor, courtesy of George Braziller, Inc.

74

Malcolm Varon

77

Bruce White

5, 7, 8, 10–15, 21, 24, 25, 27, 29, 36, 37, 41, 47–49, 51–64, 67, 68, 72, 75, 76, 79, 80, 82, 85–88, 94–96, 98, 112, 118, 119, 121, 124–126, 128, 131, 133, 134, 138–140, 144, 148–152, 154–158, 160a–c, 162, 164–168, 172, 173a–f, 180, 184–190, 192, 195, 197, 199, 203, 205, 211, 215, 218, 219, 223, 224, 227, 228, 231–240, 246, 249–269, 272, 273, 275, 277, 278, 280–283, 286–306, 308, 310–312, 315–317, 319–322, 323 (left), 324, 330–337, 339–347, 351–356, 358–363, 365–368, 372, 374–377, 379–384, 388–391, 393, 396–399, 401–405, 407–411, 413–417, 419–427, 430–435, 439, 441–448, 450–453, 455–462, 464–467, 470, 473–475, 477, 480, 486, 493, 506, 507, 512–517, 519, 520, 524, 525, 527–531, 533–538, 539 (top), 541–544, plus details